MySQL Cookbook

Paul DuBois

O'REILLY®

Beijing · Cambridge · Farnham · Köln · Paris · Sebastopol · Taipei · Tokyo

MySQL Cookbook
by Paul DuBois

Published by O'Reilly & Associates, Inc., 1005 Gravenstein Highway North, Sebastopol, CA 95472.

O'Reilly & Associates books may be purchased for educational, business, or sales promotional use. Online editions are also available for most titles (*safari.oreilly.com*). For more information, contact our corporate/institutional sales department: (800) 998-9938 or *corporate@oreilly.com*.

Editor:	Laurie Petrycki
Production Editor:	Linley Dolby
Cover Designer:	Ellie Volckhausen
Interior Designer:	David Futato

Printing History:

October 2002:	First Edition.

ISBN: 0-596-00145-2

[M]

Table of Contents

Preface xv

1. Using the mysql Client Program 1

   1.1 Setting Up a MySQL User Account   2
   1.2 Creating a Database and a Sample Table   4
   1.3 Starting and Terminating mysql   5
   1.4 Specifying Connection Parameters by Using Option Files   7
   1.5 Protecting Option Files   9
   1.6 Mixing Command-Line and Option File Parameters   10
   1.7 What to Do if mysql Cannot Be Found   10
   1.8 Setting Environment Variables   12
   1.9 Issuing Queries   14
  1.10 Selecting a Database   15
  1.11 Canceling a Partially Entered Query   17
  1.12 Repeating and Editing Queries   18
  1.13 Using Auto-Completion for Database and Table Names   19
  1.14 Using SQL Variables in Queries   20
  1.15 Telling mysql to Read Queries from a File   23
  1.16 Telling mysql to Read Queries from Other Programs   25
  1.17 Specifying Queries on the Command Line   26
  1.18 Using Copy and Paste as a mysql Input Source   27
  1.19 Preventing Query Output from Scrolling off the Screen   28
  1.20 Sending Query Output to a File or to a Program   29
  1.21 Selecting Tabular or Tab-Delimited Query Output Format   31
  1.22 Specifying Arbitrary Output Column Delimiters   31
  1.23 Producing HTML Output   33
  1.24 Producing XML Output   34

1.25	Suppressing Column Headings in Query Output	35
1.26	Numbering Query Output Lines	36
1.27	Making Long Output Lines More Readable	37
1.28	Controlling mysql's Verbosity Level	38
1.29	Logging Interactive mysql Sessions	39
1.30	Creating mysql Scripts from Previously Executed Queries	40
1.31	Using mysql as a Calculator	41
1.32	Using mysql in Shell Scripts	42

2. Writing MySQL-Based Programs **48**

2.1	Connecting to the MySQL Server, Selecting a Database, and Disconnecting	53
2.2	Checking for Errors	65
2.3	Writing Library Files	73
2.4	Issuing Queries and Retrieving Results	85
2.5	Moving Around Within a Result Set	100
2.6	Using Prepared Statements and Placeholders in Queries	101
2.7	Including Special Characters and NULL Values in Queries	106
2.8	Handling NULL Values in Result Sets	114
2.9	Writing an Object-Oriented MySQL Interface for PHP	118
2.10	Ways of Obtaining Connection Parameters	132
2.11	Conclusion and Words of Advice	147

3. Record Selection Techniques **149**

3.1	Specifying Which Columns to Display	151
3.2	Avoiding Output Column Order Problems When Writing Programs	152
3.3	Giving Names to Output Columns	153
3.4	Using Column Aliases to Make Programs Easier to Write	156
3.5	Combining Columns to Construct Composite Values	157
3.6	Specifying Which Rows to Select	158
3.7	WHERE Clauses and Column Aliases	161
3.8	Displaying Comparisons to Find Out How Something Works	162
3.9	Reversing or Negating Query Conditions	163
3.10	Removing Duplicate Rows	165
3.11	Working with NULL Values	166
3.12	Negating a Condition on a Column That Contains NULL Values	168
3.13	Writing Comparisons Involving NULL in Programs	169
3.14	Mapping NULL Values to Other Values for Display	170
3.15	Sorting a Result Set	171

3.16 Selecting Records from the Beginning or End of a Result Set   172

3.17 Pulling a Section from the Middle of a Result Set   175

3.18 Choosing Appropriate LIMIT Values   177

3.19 Calculating LIMIT Values from Expressions   179

3.20 What to Do When LIMIT Requires the "Wrong" Sort Order   180

3.21 Selecting a Result Set into an Existing Table   182

3.22 Creating a Destination Table on the Fly from a Result Set   183

3.23 Moving Records Between Tables Safely   185

3.24 Creating Temporary Tables   187

3.25 Cloning a Table Exactly   188

3.26 Generating Unique Table Names   190

4. Working with Strings **192**

4.1 Writing Strings That Include Quotes or Special Characters   193

4.2 Preserving Trailing Spaces in String Columns   195

4.3 Testing String Equality or Relative Ordering   196

4.4 Decomposing or Combining Strings   197

4.5 Checking Whether a String Contains a Substring   201

4.6 Pattern Matching with SQL Patterns   201

4.7 Pattern Matching with Regular Expressions   203

4.8 Matching Pattern Metacharacters Literally   208

4.9 Controlling Case Sensitivity in String Comparisons   211

4.10 Controlling Case Sensitivity in Pattern Matching   215

4.11 Using FULLTEXT Searches   218

4.12 Using a FULLTEXT Search with Short Words   222

4.13 Requiring or Excluding FULLTEXT Search Words   224

4.14 Performing Phrase Searches with a FULLTEXT Index   226

5. Working with Dates and Times **228**

5.1 Changing MySQL's Date Format   231

5.2 Telling MySQL How to Display Dates or Times   232

5.3 Determining the Current Date or Time   234

5.4 Decomposing Dates and Times Using Formatting Functions   235

5.5 Decomposing Dates or Times Using Component-Extraction
Functions   236

5.6 Decomposing Dates or Times Using String Functions   239

5.7 Synthesizing Dates or Times Using Formatting Functions   241

5.8 Synthesizing Dates or Times Using Component-Extraction Functions   242

5.9 Combining a Date and a Time into a Date-and-Time Value   243

5.10 Converting Between Times and Seconds 244
5.11 Converting Between Dates and Days 246
5.12 Converting Between Date-and-Time Values and Seconds 247
5.13 Adding a Temporal Interval to a Time 248
5.14 Calculating Intervals Between Times 250
5.15 Breaking Down Time Intervals into Components 251
5.16 Adding a Temporal Interval to a Date 252
5.17 Calculating Intervals Between Dates 255
5.18 Canonizing Not-Quite-ISO Date Strings 258
5.19 Calculating Ages 259
5.20 Shifting Dates by a Known Amount 263
5.21 Finding First and Last Days of Months 265
5.22 Finding the Length of a Month 267
5.23 Calculating One Date from Another by Substring Replacement 268
5.24 Finding the Day of the Week for a Date 270
5.25 Finding Dates for Days of the Current Week 271
5.26 Finding Dates for Weekdays of Other Weeks 272
5.27 Performing Leap Year Calculations 274
5.28 Treating Dates or Times as Numbers 277
5.29 Forcing MySQL to Treat Strings as Temporal Values 279
5.30 Selecting Records Based on Their Temporal Characteristics 280
5.31 Using TIMESTAMP Values 283
5.32 Recording a Row's Last Modification Time 284
5.33 Recording a Row's Creation Time 286
5.34 Performing Calculations with TIMESTAMP Values 287
5.35 Displaying TIMESTAMP Values in Readable Form 288

6. **Sorting Query Results** **290**
6.1   Using ORDER BY to Sort Query Results 291
6.2   Sorting Subsets of a Table 296
6.3   Sorting Expression Results 297
6.4   Displaying One Set of Values While Sorting by Another 299
6.5   Sorting and NULL Values 304
6.6   Controlling Case Sensitivity of String Sorts 306
6.7   Date-Based Sorting 308
6.8   Sorting by Calendar Day 310
6.9   Sorting by Day of Week 312
6.10 Sorting by Time of Day 314
6.11 Sorting Using Substrings of Column Values 315

6.12	Sorting by Fixed-Length Substrings	315
6.13	Sorting by Variable-Length Substrings	318
6.14	Sorting Hostnames in Domain Order	323
6.15	Sorting Dotted-Quad IP Values in Numeric Order	325
6.16	Floating Specific Values to the Head or Tail of the Sort Order	327
6.17	Sorting in User-Defined Orders	330
6.18	Sorting ENUM Values	331

7. Generating Summaries **335**

7.1	Summarizing with COUNT()	337
7.2	Summarizing with MIN() and MAX()	339
7.3	Summarizing with SUM() and AVG()	341
7.4	Using DISTINCT to Eliminate Duplicates	342
7.5	Finding Values Associated with Minimum and Maximum Values	345
7.6	Controlling String Case Sensitivity for MIN() and MAX()	348
7.7	Dividing a Summary into Subgroups	350
7.8	Summaries and NULL Values	354
7.9	Selecting Only Groups with Certain Characteristics	357
7.10	Determining Whether Values are Unique	358
7.11	Grouping by Expression Results	359
7.12	Categorizing Non-Categorical Data	361
7.13	Controlling Summary Display Order	365
7.14	Finding Smallest or Largest Summary Values	367
7.15	Date-Based Summaries	368
7.16	Working with Per-Group and Overall Summary Values Simultaneously	372
7.17	Generating a Report That Includes a Summary and a List	374

8. Modifying Tables with ALTER TABLE **378**

8.1	Dropping, Adding, or Repositioning a Column	379
8.2	Changing a Column Definition or Name	380
8.3	The Effect of ALTER TABLE on Null and Default Value Attributes	383
8.4	Changing a Column's Default Value	384
8.5	Changing a Table Type	385
8.6	Renaming a Table	387
8.7	Adding or Dropping Indexes	388
8.8	Eliminating Duplicates by Adding an Index	391
8.9	Using ALTER TABLE to Normalize a Table	392

9. Obtaining and Using Metadata **398**

9.1   Obtaining the Number of Rows Affected by a Query   399
9.2   Obtaining Result Set Metadata   401
9.3   Determining Presence or Absence of a Result Set   409
9.4   Formatting Query Results for Display   410
9.5   Getting Table Structure Information   414
9.6   Getting ENUM and SET Column Information   422
9.7   Database-Independent Methods of Obtaining Table Information 424
9.8   Applying Table Structure Information   426
9.9   Listing Tables and Databases   433
9.10 Testing Whether a Table Exists   434
9.11 Testing Whether a Database Exists   435
9.12 Getting Server Metadata   436
9.13 Writing Applications That Adapt to the MySQL Server Version 437
9.14 Determining the Current Database   438
9.15 Determining the Current MySQL User   439
9.16 Monitoring the MySQL Server   440
9.17 Determining Which Table Types the Server Supports   441

10. Importing and Exporting Data **444**

10.1   Importing Data with LOAD DATA and mysqlimport   448
10.2   Specifying the Datafile Location   450
10.3   Specifying the Datafile Format   452
10.4   Dealing with Quotes and Special Characters   453
10.5   Importing CSV Files   454
10.6   Reading Files from Different Operating Systems   455
10.7   Handling Duplicate Index Values   456
10.8   Getting LOAD DATA to Cough Up More Information   456
10.9   Don't Assume LOAD DATA Knows More than It Does   457
10.10 Skipping Datafile Lines   459
10.11 Specifying Input Column Order   459
10.12 Skipping Datafile Columns   460
10.13 Exporting Query Results from MySQL   461
10.14 Exporting Tables as Raw Data   464
10.15 Exporting Table Contents or Definitions in SQL Format   465
10.16 Copying Tables or Databases to Another Server   467
10.17 Writing Your Own Export Programs   468
10.18 Converting Datafiles from One Format to Another   473
10.19 Extracting and Rearranging Datafile Columns   474

10.20 Validating and Transforming Data   478

10.21 Validation by Direct Comparison   481

10.22 Validation by Pattern Matching   481

10.23 Using Patterns to Match Broad Content Types   484

10.24 Using Patterns to Match Numeric Values   485

10.25 Using Patterns to Match Dates or Times   487

10.26 Using Patterns to Match Email Addresses and URLs   491

10.27 Validation Using Table Metadata   492

10.28 Validation Using a Lookup Table   495

10.29 Converting Two-Digit Year Values to Four-Digit Form   498

10.30 Performing Validity Checking on Date or Time Subparts   499

10.31 Writing Date-Processing Utilities   502

10.32 Using Dates with Missing Components   507

10.33 Performing Date Conversion Using SQL   508

10.34 Using Temporary Tables for Data Transformation   511

10.35 Dealing with NULL Values   513

10.36 Guessing Table Structure from a Datafile   516

10.37 A LOAD DATA Diagnostic Utility   520

10.38 Exchanging Data Between MySQL and Microsoft Access   526

10.39 Exchanging Data Between MySQL and Microsoft Excel   527

10.40 Exchanging Data Between MySQL and FileMaker Pro   530

10.41 Exporting Query Results as XML   532

10.42 Importing XML into MySQL   535

10.43 Epilog   537

11. **Generating and Using Sequences** **539**

11.1 Using AUTO_INCREMENT To Set Up a Sequence Column   540

11.2 Generating Sequence Values   542

11.3 Choosing the Type for a Sequence Column   544

11.4 The Effect of Record Deletions on Sequence Generation   546

11.5 Retrieving Sequence Values   549

11.6 Determining Whether to Resequence a Column   553

11.7 Extending the Range of a Sequence Column   555

11.8 Renumbering an Existing Sequence   556

11.9 Reusing Values at the Top of a Sequence   557

11.10 Ensuring That Rows Are Renumbered in a Particular Order   558

11.11 Starting a Sequence at a Particular Value   559

11.12 Sequencing an Unsequenced Table   561

11.13 Using an AUTO_INCREMENT Column to Create Multiple
      Sequences   562
11.14 Managing Multiple Simultaneous AUTO_INCREMENT Values   567
11.15 Using AUTO_INCREMENT Values to Relate Tables   569
11.16 Using Single-Row Sequence Generators   572
11.17 Generating Repeating Sequences   575
11.18 Numbering Query Output Rows Sequentially   577

12. Using Multiple Tables **578**
12.1 Combining Rows in One Table with Rows in Another   578
12.2 Performing a Join Between Tables in Different Databases   582
12.3 Referring to Join Output Column Names in Programs   583
12.4 Finding Rows in One Table That Match Rows in Another   586
12.5 Finding Rows with No Match in Another Table   591
12.6 Finding Rows Containing Per-Group Minimum or Maximum
      Values   596
12.7 Computing Team Standings   599
12.8 Producing Master-Detail Lists and Summaries   605
12.9 Using a Join to Fill in Holes in a List   609
12.10 Enumerating a Many-to-Many Relationship   614
12.11 Comparing a Table to Itself   619
12.12 Calculating Differences Between Successive Rows   626
12.13 Finding Cumulative Sums and Running Averages   628
12.14 Using a Join to Control Query Output Order   633
12.15 Converting Subselects to Join Operations   634
12.16 Selecting Records in Parallel from Multiple Tables   639
12.17 Inserting Records in One Table That Include Values from Another   644
12.18 Updating One Table Based on Values in Another   645
12.19 Using a Join to Create a Lookup Table from Descriptive Labels   650
12.20 Deleting Related Rows in Multiple Tables   655
12.21 Identifying and Removing Unattached Records   665
12.22 Using Different MySQL Servers Simultaneously   671

13. Statistical Techniques **674**
13.1 Calculating Descriptive Statistics   675
13.2 Per-Group Descriptive Statistics   679
13.3 Generating Frequency Distributions   681
13.4 Counting Missing Values   684
13.5 Calculating Linear Regressions or Correlation Coefficients   686

13.6 Generating Random Numbers   688
13.7 Randomizing a Set of Rows   689
13.8 Selecting Random Items from a Set of Rows   694
13.9 Assigning Ranks   695

14. Handling Duplicates **699**
14.1 Preventing Duplicates from Occurring in a Table   701
14.2 Dealing with Duplicates at Record-Creation Time   703
14.3 Counting and Identifying Duplicates   705
14.4 Eliminating Duplicates from a Query Result   709
14.5 Eliminating Duplicates from a Self-Join Result   711
14.6 Eliminating Duplicates from a Table   713

15. Performing Transactions **720**
15.1 Verifying Transaction Support Requirements   721
15.2 Performing Transactions Using SQL   724
15.3 Performing Transactions from Within Programs   725
15.4 Using Transactions in Perl Programs   728
15.5 Using Transactions in PHP Programs   730
15.6 Using Transactions in Python Programs   732
15.7 Using Transactions in Java Programs   732
15.8 Using Alternatives to Transactions   733

16. Introduction to MySQL on the Web **737**
16.1 Basic Web Page Generation   739
16.2 Using Apache to Run Web Scripts   743
16.3 Using Tomcat to Run Web Scripts   752
16.4 Encoding Special Characters in Web Output   762

17. Incorporating Query Results into Web Pages **770**
17.1 Displaying Query Results as Paragraph Text   771
17.2 Displaying Query Results as Lists   773
17.3 Displaying Query Results as Tables   784
17.4 Displaying Query Results as Hyperlinks   790
17.5 Creating a Navigation Index from Database Content   793
17.6 Storing Images or Other Binary Data   799
17.7 Retrieving Images or Other Binary Data   806
17.8 Serving Banner Ads   808
17.9 Serving Query Results for Download   811

18. Processing Web Input with MySQL **814**

18.1 Creating Forms in Scripts   817
18.2 Creating Single-Pick Form Elements from Database Content   820
18.3 Creating Multiple-Pick Form Elements from Database Content   836
18.4 Loading a Database Record into a Form   841
18.5 Collecting Web Input   845
18.6 Validating Web Input   855
18.7 Using Web Input to Construct Queries   857
18.8 Processing File Uploads   859
18.9 Performing Searches and Presenting the Results   867
18.10 Generating Previous-Page and Next-Page Links   869
18.11 Generating "Click to Sort" Table Headings   874
18.12 Web Page Access Counting   878
18.13 Web Page Access Logging   883
18.14 Using MySQL for Apache Logging   885

19. Using MySQL-Based Web Session Management **893**

19.1 Using MySQL-Based Sessions in Perl Applications   896
19.2 Using MySQL-Based Storage with the PHP Session Manager   902
19.3 Using MySQL for Session Backing Store with Tomcat   915

A. Obtaining MySQL Software **925**

B. JSP and Tomcat Primer **930**

C. References **958**

Index **961**

Preface

The MySQL database management system has become quite popular in recent years. This has been true especially in the Linux and open source communities, but MySQL's presence in the commercial sector now is increasing as well. It is well liked for several reasons: MySQL is fast, and it's easy to set up, use, and administrate. MySQL runs under many varieties of Unix and Windows, and MySQL-based programs can be written in many languages. MySQL is especially heavily used in combination with a web server for constructing database-backed web sites that involve dynamic content generation.

With MySQL's rise in popularity comes the need to address the questions posed by its users about how to solve specific problems. That is the purpose of *MySQL Cookbook*. It's designed to serve as a handy resource to which you can turn when you need quick solutions or techniques for attacking particular types of questions that come up when you use MySQL. Naturally, because it's a cookbook, it contains recipes: straightforward instructions you can follow rather than develop your own code from scratch. It's written using a problem-and-solution format designed to be extremely practical and to make the contents easy to read and assimilate. It contains many short sections, each describing how to write a query, apply a technique, or develop a script to solve a problem of limited and specific scope. This book doesn't attempt to develop full-fledged applications. Instead, it's intended to assist you in developing such applications yourself by helping you get past problems that have you stumped.

For example, a common question is, "How can I deal with quotes and special characters in data values when I'm writing queries?" That's not difficult, but figuring out how to do it is frustrating when you're not sure where to start. This book demonstrates what to do; it shows you where to begin and how to proceed from there. This knowledge will serve you repeatedly, because after you see what's involved, you'll be able to apply the technique to any kind of data, such as text, images, sound or video clips, news articles, compressed files, PDF files, or word processing documents. Another common question is, "Can I access tables from two databases at the same time?" The answer is "Yes," and it's easy to do because it's just a matter of knowing the proper SQL syntax. But it's hard to do until you see how; this book will show you. Other things that you'll learn from this book include:

- How to use SQL to select, sort, and summarize records.
- How to find matches or mismatches between records in two tables.
- How to perform a transaction.
- How to determine intervals between dates or times, including age calculations.
- How to remove duplicate records.
- How to store images into MySQL and retrieve them for display in web pages.
- How to convert the legal values of an ENUM column into radio buttons in a web page, or the values of a SET column into checkboxes.
- How to get LOAD DATA to read your datafiles properly, or find out which values in the file are bad.
- How to use pattern matching techniques to cope with mismatches between the CCYY-MM-DD date format that MySQL uses and dates in your datafiles.
- How to copy a table or a database to another server.
- How to resequence a sequence number column, and why you really don't want to.

One part of knowing how to use MySQL is understanding how to communicate with the server—that is, how to use SQL, the language through which queries are formulated. Therefore, one major emphasis of this book is on using SQL to formulate queries that answer particular kinds of questions. One helpful tool for learning and using SQL is the mysql client program that is included in MySQL distributions. By using this client interactively, you can send SQL statements to the server and see the results. This is extremely useful because it provides a direct interface to SQL. The mysql client is so useful, in fact, that the entire first chapter is devoted to it.

But the ability to issue SQL queries alone is not enough. Information extracted from a database often needs to be processed further or presented in a particular way to be useful. What if you have queries with complex interrelationships, such as when you need to use the results of one query as the basis for others? SQL by itself has little facility for making these kinds of choices, which makes it difficult to use decision-based logic to determine which queries to execute. Or what if you need to generate a specialized report with very specific formatting requirements? This too is difficult to achieve using just SQL. These problems bring us to the other major emphasis of the book—how to write programs that interact with the MySQL server through an application programming interface (API). When you know how to use MySQL from within the context of a programming language, you gain the ability to exploit MySQL's capabilities in the following ways:

- You can remember the result from a query and use it at a later time.
- You can make decisions based on success or failure of a query, or on the content of the rows that are returned. Difficulties in implementing control flow disappear

when using an API because the host language provides facilities for expressing decision-based logic: if-then-else constructs, while loops, subroutines, and so forth.

- You can format and display query results however you like. If you're writing a command-line script, you can generate plain text. If it's a web-based script, you can generate an HTML table. If it's an application that extracts information for transfer to some other system, you might write a datafile expressed in XML.

When you combine SQL with a general purpose programming language and a MySQL client API, you have an extremely flexible framework for issuing queries and processing their results. Programming languages increase your expressive capabilities by giving you a great deal of additional power to perform complex database operations. This doesn't mean this book is complicated, though. It keeps things simple, showing how to construct small building blocks by using techniques that are easy to understand and easily mastered.

I'll leave it to you to combine these techniques within your own programs, which you can do to produce arbitrarily complex applications. After all, the genetic code is based on only four nucleic acids, but these basic elements have been combined to produce the astonishing array of biological life we see all around us. Similarly, there are only 12 notes in the scale, but in the hands of skilled composers, they can be interwoven to produce a rich and endless variety of music. In the same way, when you take a set of simple recipes, add your imagination, and apply them to the database programming problems you want to solve, you can produce that are perhaps not works of art, but certainly applications that are useful and that will help you and others be more productive.

MySQL APIs Used in This Book

MySQL programming interfaces exist for many languages, including (in alphabetical order) C, C++, Eiffel, Java, Pascal, Perl, PHP, Python, Ruby, Smalltalk, and Tcl.* Given this fact, writing a MySQL cookbook presents an author with something of a challenge. Clearly the book should provide recipes for doing many interesting and useful things with MySQL, but which API or APIs should the book use? Showing an implementation of every recipe in every language would result either in covering very few recipes or in a very, very large book! It would also result in a lot of redundancy when implementations in different languages bear a strong resemblance to each other. On the other hand, it's worthwhile taking advantage of multiple languages, because one language often will be more suitable than another for solving a particular type of problem.

---

* To see what APIs are currently available, visit the development portal at the MySQL web site, located at *http://www.mysql.com/portal/development/html/*.

To resolve this dilemma, I've picked a small number of APIs from among those that are available and used them to write the recipes in this book. This limits its scope to a manageable number of APIs while allowing some latitude to choose from among them. The primary APIs covered here are:

Perl

Using the DBI module and its MySQL-specific driver

PHP

Using its set of built-in MySQL support functions

Python

Using the DB-API module and its MySQL-specific driver

Java™

Using a MySQL-specific driver for the Java Database Connectivity (JDBC) interface

Why these languages? Perl and PHP were easy to pick. Perl is arguably the most widely used language on the Web, and it became so based on certain strengths such as its text-processing capabilities. In particular, it's very popular for writing MySQL programs. PHP also is widely deployed, and its use is increasing steadily. One of PHP's strengths is the ease with which you can use it to access databases, making it a natural choice for MySQL scripting. Python and Java are not as popular as Perl or PHP for MySQL programming, but each has significant numbers of followers. In the Java community in particular, MySQL seems to be making strong inroads among developers who use JavaServer Pages (JSP) technology to build database-backed web applications. (An anecdotal observation: After I wrote *MySQL* (New Riders), Python and Java were the two languages not covered in that book that readers most often said they would have liked to have seen addressed. So here they are!)

I believe these languages taken together reflect pretty well the majority of the existing user base of MySQL programmers. If you prefer some language not shown here, you can still use this book, but be sure to pay careful attention to Chapter 2, to familiarize yourself with the book's primary API languages. Knowing how database operations are performed with the APIs used here will help you understand the recipes in later chapters so that you can translate them into languages not discussed.

Who This Book Is For

This book should be useful for anybody who uses MySQL, ranging from novices who want to use a database for personal reasons, to professional database and web developers. The book should also appeal to people who do not now use MySQL, but would like to. For example, it should be useful to beginners who want to learn about databases but realize that Oracle isn't the best choice for that.

If you're relatively new to MySQL, you'll probably find lots of ways to use it here that you hadn't thought of. If you're more experienced, you'll probably be familiar with many of the problems addressed here, but you may not have had to solve them before and should find the book a great timesaver; take advantage of the recipes given in the book and use them in your own programs rather than figuring out how to write the code from scratch.

The book also can be useful for people who aren't even using MySQL. You might suppose that because this is a MySQL cookbook and not a PostgreSQL cookbook or an InterBase cookbook that it won't apply to databases other than MySQL. To some extent that's true, because some of the SQL constructs are MySQL-specific. On the other hand, many of the queries are standard SQL that is portable to many other database engines, so you should be able to use them with little or no modification. And several of our programming language interfaces provide database-independent access methods; you use them the same way regardless of which database you're connecting to.

The material ranges from introductory to advanced, so if a recipe describes techniques that seem obvious to you, skip it. Or if you find that you don't understand a recipe, it may be best to set it aside for a while and come back to it later, perhaps after reading some of the preceding recipes.

More advanced readers may wonder on occasion why in a book on MySQL I sometimes provide explanatory material on certain basic topics that are not directly MySQL-related, such as how to set environment variables. I decided to do this based on my experience in helping novice MySQL users. One thing that makes MySQL attractive is that it is easy to use, which makes it a popular choice for people without extensive background in databases. However, many of these same people also tend to be thwarted by simple barriers to more effective use of MySQL, as evidenced by the common question, "How can I avoid having to type the full pathname of mysql each time I invoke it?" Experienced readers will recognize immediately that this is simply a matter of appropriately setting the PATH environment variable to include the directory where mysql is installed. But other readers will not, particularly Windows users who are used to dealing only with a graphical interface and, more recently, Mac OS X users who find their familiar user interface now augmented by the powerful but sometimes mysterious command line provided by the Terminal application. If you are in this situation, you'll find these more elementary sections helpful in knocking down barriers that keep you from using MySQL more easily. If you're a more advanced user, just skip over such sections.

What's in This Book

It's very likely when you use this book that you'll have an application in mind you're trying to develop but are not sure how to implement certain pieces of it. In this case, you'll already know what type of problem you want to solve, so you should search the table of contents or the index looking for a recipe that shows how to do what you want. Ideally, the recipe will be just what you had in mind. Failing that, you should be able to find a recipe for a similar problem that you can adapt to suit the issue at hand. (I try to explain the principles involved in developing each technique so that you'll be able to modify it to fit the particular requirements of your own applications.)

Another way to approach this book is to just read through it with no specific problem in mind. This can help you because it will give you a broader understanding of the things MySQL can do, so I recommend that you page through the book occasionally. It's a more effective tool if you have a general familiarity with it and know the kinds of problems it addresses. The following paragraphs summarize each chapter, to help give you an overview of the book's contents.

Chapter 1, *Using the mysql Client Program*, describes how to use the standard MySQL command-line client. mysql is often the first interface to MySQL that people use, and it's important to know how to exploit its capabilities. This program allows you to issue queries and see the results interactively, so it's good for quick experimentation. You can also use it in batch mode to execute canned SQL scripts or send its output into other programs. In addition, the chapter discusses other ways to use mysql, such as how to number output lines or make long lines more readable, how to generate various output formats, and how to log mysql sessions.

Chapter 2, *Writing MySQL-Based Programs*, demonstrates the basic elements of MySQL programming in each API language: how to connect to the server, issue queries, retrieve the results, and handle errors. It also discusses how to handle special characters and NULL values in queries, how to write library files to encapsulate code for commonly used operations, and various ways to gather the parameters needed for making connections to the server.

Chapter 3, *Record Selection Techniques*, covers several aspects of the SELECT statement, which is the primary vehicle for retrieving data from the MySQL server: specifying which columns and rows you want to retrieve, performing comparisons, dealing with NULL values, selecting one section of a query result, using temporary tables, and copying results into other tables. Later chapters cover some of these topics in more detail, but this chapter provides an overview of the concepts on which they depend. You should read it if you need some introductory background on record selection, for example, if you don't yet know a lot about SQL.

Chapter 4, *Working with Strings*, describes how to deal with string data. It addresses string comparisons, pattern matching, breaking apart and combining strings, dealing with case-sensitivity issues, and performing FULLTEXT searches.

Chapter 5, *Working with Dates and Times*, shows how to work with temporal data. It describes MySQL's date format and how to display date values in other formats. It also covers conversion between different temporal units, how to perform date arithmetic to compute intervals or generate one date from another, leap-year calculations, and how to use MySQL's special TIMESTAMP column type.

Chapter 6, *Sorting Query Results*, describes how to put the rows of a query result in the order you want. This includes specifying the sort direction, dealing with NULL values, accounting for string case sensitivity, and sorting by dates or partial column values. It also provides examples that show how to sort special kinds of values, such as domain names, IP numbers, and ENUM values.

Chapter 7, *Generating Summaries*, shows techniques that are useful for assessing the general characteristics of a set of data, such as how many values it contains or what the minimum, maximum, or average values are.

Chapter 8, *Modifying Tables with ALTER TABLE*, describes how to alter the structure of tables by adding, dropping, or modifying columns, and how to set up indexes.

Chapter 9, *Obtaining and Using Metadata*, discusses how to get information about the data a query returns, such as the number of rows or columns in the result, or the name and type of each column. It also shows how to ask MySQL what databases and tables are available or about the structure of a table and its columns.

Chapter 10, *Importing and Exporting Data*, describes how to transfer information between MySQL and other programs. This includes how to convert files from one format to another, extract or rearrange columns in datafiles, check and validate data, rewrite values such as dates that often come in a variety of formats, and how to figure out which data values cause problems when you load them into MySQL with LOAD DATA.

Chapter 11, *Generating and Using Sequences*, discusses AUTO_INCREMENT columns, MySQL's mechanism for producing sequence numbers. It shows how to generate new sequence values or determine the most recent value, how to resequence a column, how to begin a sequence at a given value, and how to set up a table so that it can maintain multiple sequences at once. It also shows how to use AUTO_INCREMENT values to maintain a master-detail relationship between tables, including some of the pitfalls to avoid.

Chapter 12, *Using Multiple Tables*, shows how to perform joins, which are operations that combine rows in one table with those from another. It demonstrates how to compare tables to find matches or mismatches, produce master-detail lists and summaries, enumerate many-to-many relationships, and update or delete records in one table based on the contents of another.

Chapter 13, *Statistical Techniques*, illustrates how to produce descriptive statistics, frequency distributions, regressions, and correlations. It also covers how to randomize a set of rows or pick a row at random from the set.

Chapter 14, *Handling Duplicates*, discusses how to identify, count, and remove duplicate records—and how to prevent them from occurring in the first place.

Chapter 15, *Performing Transactions*, shows how to handle multiple SQL statements that must execute together as a unit. It discusses how to control MySQL's auto-commit mode, how to commit or roll back transactions, and demonstrates some workarounds you can use if transactional capabilities are unavailable in your version of MySQL.

Chapter 16, *Introduction to MySQL on the Web*, gets you set up to write web-based MySQL scripts. Web programming allows you to generate dynamic pages or collect information for storage in your database. The chapter discusses how to configure Apache to run Perl, PHP, and Python scripts, and how to configure Tomcat to run Java scripts written using JSP notation. It also provides an overview of the Java Standard Tag Library (JSTL) that is used heavily in JSP pages in the following chapters.

Chapter 17, *Incorporating Query Results into Web Pages*, shows how to use the results of queries to produce various types of HTML structures, such as paragraphs, lists, tables, hyperlinks, and navigation indexes. It also describes how to store images into MySQL, retrieve and display them later, and how to send a downloadable result set to a browser.

Chapter 18, *Processing Web Input with MySQL*, discusses ways to obtain input from users over the Web and use it to create new database records or as the basis for performing searches. It deals heavily with form processing, including how to construct form elements, such as radio buttons, pop-up menus, or checkboxes, based on information contained in your database.

Chapter 19, *Using MySQL-Based Web Session Management*, describes how to write web applications that remember information across multiple requests, using MySQL for backing store. This is useful when you want to collect information in stages, or when you need to make decisions based on what the user has done earlier.

Appendix A, *Obtaining MySQL Software*, indicates where to get the source code for the examples shown in this book, and where to get the software you need to use MySQL and write your own database programs.

Appendix B, *JSP and Tomcat Primer*, provides a general overview of JSP and installation instructions for the Tomcat web server. Read this if you need to install Tomcat or are not familiar with it, or if you're never written JSP pages.

Appendix C, *References*, lists sources of information that provide additional information about topics covered in this book. It also lists some books that provide introductory background for the programming languages used here.

As you get into later chapters, you'll sometimes find recipes that assume a knowledge of topics covered in earlier chapters. This also applies within a chapter, where later sections often use techniques discussed earlier in the chapter. If you jump into a chapter and find a recipe that uses a technique with which you're not familiar, check the table of contents or the index to find out where the technique is covered. You should find that it's been explained earlier. For example, if you find that a recipe sorts a query result using an ORDER BY clause that you don't understand, turn to Chapter 6, which discusses various sorting methods and explains how they work.

Platform Notes

Development of the code in this book took place under MySQL 3.23 and 4.0. Because new features are added to MySQL on a regular basis, some examples will not work under older versions. I've tried to point out version dependencies when introducing such features for the first time.

The MySQL language API modules that I used include DBI 1.20 and up, *DBD::mysql* 2.0901 and up, MySQLdb 0.9 and up, MM.MySQL 2.0.5 and up, and MySQL Connector/J 2.0.14. DBI requires Perl 5.004_05 or higher up through DBI 1.20, after which it requires Perl 5.005_03 or higher. MySQLdb requires Python 1.5.6 or higher. MM.MySQL and MySQL Connector/J require Java SDK 1.1 or higher.

Language processors include Perl 5.6 and 5.6.1; PHP 3 and 4; Python 1.5.6, 2.2; and 2.3, and Java SDK 1.3.1. Most PHP scripts shown here will run under either PHP 3 or PHP 4 (although I strongly recommend PHP 4 over PHP 3). Scripts that require PHP 4 are so noted.

I do not assume that you are using Unix, although that is my own preferred development platform. Most of the material here should be applicable both to Unix and Windows. The operating systems I used most for development of the recipes in this book were Mac OS X; RedHat Linux 6.2, 7.0, and 7.3; and various versions of Windows (Me, 98, NT, and 2000).

I do assume that MySQL is installed already and available for you to use. I also assume that if you plan to write your own MySQL-based programs, you're reasonably familiar with the language you'll use. If you need to install software, see Appendix A. If you require background material on the programming languages used here, see Appendix C.

Conventions Used in This Book

The following font conventions have been used throughout the book:

Constant width
> Used for program listings, as well as within paragraphs to refer to program elements such as variable or function names.

Constant width bold
> Used to indicate text that you type when running commands.

Constant width italic

Used to indicate variable input; you should substitute a value of your own choosing.

Italic

Used for URLs, hostnames, names of directories and files, Unix commands and options, and occasionally for emphasis.

Commands often are shown with a prompt to illustrate the context in which they are used. Commands that you issue from the command line are shown with a % prompt:

```
% chmod 600 my.cnf
```

That prompt is one that Unix users are used to seeing, but it doesn't necessarily signify that a command will work only under Unix. Unless indicated otherwise, commands shown with a % prompt generally should work under Windows, too.

If you should run a command under Unix as the root user, the prompt is # instead:

```
# chkconfig --add tomcat4
```

For commands that are specific only to Windows, the C:\> prompt is used:

```
C:\> copy C:\mysql\lib\cygwinb19.dll C:\Windows\System
```

SQL statements that are issued from within the mysql client program are shown with a mysql> prompt and terminated with a semicolon:

```
mysql> SELECT * FROM my_table;
```

For examples that show a query result as you would see it when using mysql, I sometimes truncate the output, using an ellipsis (...) to indicate that the result consists of more rows than are shown. The following query produces many rows of output, of which those in the middle have been omitted:

```
mysql> SELECT name, abbrev FROM states ORDER BY name;
+----------------+--------+
| name           | abbrev |
+----------------+--------+
| Alabama        | AL     |
| Alaska         | AK     |
| Arizona        | AZ     |
...
| West Virginia  | WV     |
| Wisconsin      | WI     |
| Wyoming        | WY     |
+----------------+--------+
```

Examples that just show the syntax for SQL statements do not include the mysql> prompt, but they do include semicolons as necessary to make it clear where statements end. For example, this is a single statement:

```
CREATE TABLE t1 (i INT)
SELECT * FROM t2;
```

But this example represents two statements:

```
CREATE TABLE t1 (i INT);
SELECT * FROM t2;
```

The semicolon is a notational convenience used within mysql as a statement terminator. But it is not part of SQL itself, so when you issue SQL statements from within programs that you write (for example, using Perl or Java), you should not include terminating semicolons.

 This icon indicates a tip, suggestion, or general note.

The Companion Web Site

MySQL Cookbook has a companion web site that you can visit to obtain the source code and sample data for examples developed throughout this book:

> *http://www.kitebird.com/mysql-cookbook/*

The main software distribution is named recipes and you'll find many references to it throughout the book. You can use it to save a lot of typing. For example, when you see a CREATE TABLE statement in the book that describes what a database table looks like, you'll find a SQL batch file in the *tables* directory of the recipes distribution that you can use to create the table instead of typing out the definition. Change location into the *tables* directory, then execute the following command, where *filename* is the name of the containing the CREATE TABLE statement:

```
% mysql cookbook < filename
```

If you need to specify MySQL username or password options, put them before the database name.

For more information about the distributions, see Appendix A.

The Kitebird site also makes some of the examples from the book available online so that you can try them out from your browser.

Comments and Questions

Please address comments and questions concerning this book to the publisher:

> O'Reilly & Associates, Inc.
> 1005 Gravenstein Highway North
> Sebastopol, CA 95472
> (800) 998-9938 (in the United States or Canada)
> (707) 829-0515 (international/local)
> (707) 829-0104 (fax)

O'Reilly keeps a web page for this book that you can access at:

http://www.oreilly.com/catalog/mysqlckbk/

To comment or ask technical questions about this book, send email to:

bookquestions@oreilly.com

For more information about books, conferences, Resource Centers, and the O'Reilly Network, see the O'Reilly web site at:

http://www.oreilly.com

Additional Resources

Any language that attracts a following tends to benefit from the efforts of its user community, because people who use the language produce code that they make available to others. Perl in particular is served by an extensive support network designed to provide external modules that are not distributed with Perl itself. This is called the Comprehensive Perl Archive Network (CPAN), a mechanism for organizing and distributing Perl code and documentation. CPAN contains modules that allow database access, web programming, and XML processing, to name a few of direct relevance to this cookbook. External support exists for the other languages as well, though none of them currently enjoys the same level of organization as CPAN. PHP has the PEAR archive, and Python has a module archive called the Vaults of Parnassus. For Java, a good starting point is Sun's Java site. Sites that you can visit to find more information are shown in the following table.

API language	Where to find external support
Perl	*http://cpan.perl.org/*
PHP	*http://pear.php.net/*
Python	*http://www.python.org/*
Java	*http://java.sun.com/*

Acknowledgments

I'd like to thank my technical reviewers, Tim Allwine, David Lane, Hugh Williams, and Justin Zobel. They made several helpful suggestions and corrections with regard to both organizational structure and technical accuracy. Several members of MySQL AB were gracious enough to add their comments: In particular, principal MySQL developer Monty Widenius combed the text and spotted many problems. Arjen Lentz, Jani Tolonen, Sergei Golubchik, and Zak Greant reviewed sections of the manuscript as well. Andy Dustman, author of the Python MySQLdb module, and Mark Matthews, author of MM.MySQL and MySQL Connector/J, also provided feedback. My thanks to all for improving the manuscript; any errors remaining are my own.

Laurie Petrycki, executive editor, conceived the idea for the book and provided valuable overall editorial guidance and cattle-prodding. Lenny Muellner, tools expert, assisted in the conversion of the manuscript from my original format into something printable. David Chu acted as editorial assistant. Ellie Volckhausen designed the cover, which I am happy to see is reptilian in nature. Linley Dolby served as the production editor and proofreader, and Colleen Gorman, Darren Kelly, Jeffrey Holcomb, Brian Sawyer, and Claire Cloutier provided quality control.

Thanks to Todd Greanier and Sean Lahman of The Baseball Archive for all their hard work in putting together the baseball database that is used for several of the examples in this book.

Some authors are able to compose text productively while sitting at a keyboard, but I write better while sitting far from a computer—preferably with a cup of coffee. That being so, I'd like to acknowledge my debt to the Sow's Ear coffee shop in Verona for providing pleasant surroundings in which to spend many hours scribbling on paper.

My wife Karen provided considerable support and understanding in what turned out to be a much longer endeavor than anticipated. Her encouragement is much appreciated, and her patience something to marvel at.

## CHAPTER 1

Using the mysql Client Program

1.0 Introduction

The MySQL database system uses a client-server architecture that centers around the server, *mysqld*. The server is the program that actually manipulates databases. Client programs don't do that directly; rather, they communicate your intent to the server by means of queries written in Structured Query Language (SQL). The client program or programs are installed locally on the machine from which you wish to access MySQL, but the server can be installed anywhere, as long as clients can connect to it. MySQL is an inherently networked database system, so clients can communicate with a server that is running locally on your machine or one that is running somewhere else, perhaps on a machine on the other side of the planet. Clients can be written for many different purposes, but each interacts with the server by connecting to it, sending SQL queries to it to have database operations performed, and receiving the query results from it.

One such client is the *mysql* program that is included in MySQL distributions. When used interactively, *mysql* prompts for a query, sends it to the MySQL server for execution, and displays the results. This capability makes *mysql* useful in its own right, but it's also a valuable tool to help you with your MySQL programming activities. It's often convenient to be able to quickly review the structure of a table that you're accessing from within a script, to try a query before using it in a program to make sure it produces the right kind of output, and so forth. *mysql* is just right for these jobs. *mysql* also can be used non-interactively, for example, to read queries from a file or from other programs. This allows you to use it from within scripts or *cron* jobs or in conjunction with other applications.

This chapter describes *mysql*'s capabilities so that you can use it more effectively. Of course, to try out for yourself the recipes and examples shown in this book, you'll need a MySQL user account and a database to work with. The first two sections of the chapter describe how to use *mysql* to set these up. For demonstration purposes, the examples assume that you'll use MySQL as follows:

- The MySQL server is running on the local host.
- Your MySQL username and password are cbuser and cbpass.
- Your database is named cookbook.

For your own experimentation, you can violate any of these assumptions. Your server need not be running locally, and you need not use the username, password, or database name that are used in this book. Naturally, if you don't use MySQL in the manner just described, you'll need to change the examples to use values that are appropriate for your system. Even if you do use different names, I recommend that you at least create a database specifically for trying the recipes shown here, rather than one you're using currently for other purposes. Otherwise, the names of your existing tables may conflict with those used in the examples, and you'll have to make modifications to the examples that are unnecessary when you use a separate database.

1.1 Setting Up a MySQL User Account

Problem

You need to create an account to use for connecting to the MySQL server running on a given host.

Solution

Use the GRANT statement to set up the MySQL user account. Then use that account's name and password to make connections to the server.

Discussion

Connecting to a MySQL server requires a username and password. You can also specify the name of the host where the server is running. If you don't specify connection parameters explicitly, *mysql* assumes default values. For example, if you specify no hostname, *mysql* typically assumes the server is running on the local host.

The following example shows how to use the *mysql* program to connect to the server and issue a GRANT statement that sets up a user account with privileges for accessing a database named cookbook. The arguments to *mysql* include -*h localhost* to connect to the MySQL server running on the local host, -*p* to tell *mysql* to prompt for a password, and -*u root* to connect as the MySQL root user. Text that you type is shown in bold; non-bold text is program output:

```
% mysql -h localhost -p -u root
Enter password: ******
```

```
mysql> GRANT ALL ON cookbook.* TO 'cbuser'@'localhost' IDENTIFIED BY 'cbpass';
Query OK, 0 rows affected (0.09 sec)
mysql> QUIT
Bye
```

After you enter the *mysql* command shown on the first line, if you get a message indicating that the program cannot be found or that it is a bad command, see Recipe 1.7. Otherwise, when *mysql* prints the password prompt, enter the MySQL root password where you see the ******. (If the MySQL root user has no password, just press Return at the password prompt.) Then issue a GRANT statement like the one shown.

To use a database name other than cookbook, substitute its name where you see cookbook in the GRANT statement. Note that you need to grant privileges for the database even if the user account already exists. However, in that case, you'll likely want to omit the IDENTIFIED BY 'cbpass' part of the statement, because otherwise you'll change that account's current password.

The hostname part of 'cbuser'@'localhost' indicates the host *from which* you'll be connecting to the MySQL server to access the cookbook database. To set up an account that will connect to a server running on the local host, use localhost, as shown. If you plan to make connections to the server from another host, substitute that host in the GRANT statement. For example, if you'll be connecting to the server as cbuser from a host named *xyz.com*, the GRANT statement should look like this:

```
mysql> GRANT ALL ON cookbook.* TO 'cbuser'@'xyz.com' IDENTIFIED BY 'cbpass';
```

It may have occurred to you that there's a bit of a paradox involved in the procedure just described. That is, to set up a user account that can make connections to the MySQL server, you must connect to the server first so that you can issue the GRANT statement. I'm assuming that you can already connect as the MySQL root user, because GRANT can be used only by a user such as root that has the administrative privileges needed to set up other user accounts. If you can't connect to the server as root, ask your MySQL administrator to issue the GRANT statement for you. Once that has been done, you should be able to use the new MySQL account to connect to the server, create your own database, and proceed from there on your own.

MySQL Accounts and Login Accounts

MySQL accounts and login accounts for your operating system are different. For example, the MySQL root user and the Unix root user are separate and have nothing to do with each other, even though the username is the same in each case. This means they are very likely to have different passwords. It also means you cannot create new MySQL accounts by creating login accounts for your operating system; use the GRANT statement instead.

1.2 Creating a Database and a Sample Table

Problem

You want to create a database and to set up tables within it.

Solution

Use a CREATE DATABASE statement to create a database, a CREATE TABLE statement for each table you want to use, and INSERT to add records to the tables.

Discussion

The GRANT statement used in the previous section defines privileges for the cookbook database, but does not create it. You need to create the database explicitly before you can use it. This section shows how to do that, and also how to create a table and load it with some sample data that can be used for examples in the following sections.

After the cbuser account has been set up, verify that you can use it to connect to the MySQL server. Once you've connected successfully, create the database. From the host that was named in the GRANT statement, run the following commands to do this (the host named after -h should be the host where the MySQL server is running):

```
% mysql -h localhost -p -u cbuser
Enter password: cbpass
mysql> CREATE DATABASE cookbook;
Query OK, 1 row affected (0.08 sec)
```

Now you have a database, so you can create tables in it. Issue the following statements to select cookbook as the default database, create a simple table, and populate it with a few records:*

```
mysql> USE cookbook;
mysql> CREATE TABLE limbs (thing VARCHAR(20), legs INT, arms INT);
mysql> INSERT INTO limbs (thing,legs,arms) VALUES('human',2,2);
mysql> INSERT INTO limbs (thing,legs,arms) VALUES('insect',6,0);
mysql> INSERT INTO limbs (thing,legs,arms) VALUES('squid',0,10);
mysql> INSERT INTO limbs (thing,legs,arms) VALUES('octopus',0,8);
mysql> INSERT INTO limbs (thing,legs,arms) VALUES('fish',0,0);
mysql> INSERT INTO limbs (thing,legs,arms) VALUES('centipede',100,0);
mysql> INSERT INTO limbs (thing,legs,arms) VALUES('table',4,0);
mysql> INSERT INTO limbs (thing,legs,arms) VALUES('armchair',4,2);
mysql> INSERT INTO limbs (thing,legs,arms) VALUES('phonograph',0,1);
mysql> INSERT INTO limbs (thing,legs,arms) VALUES('tripod',3,0);
mysql> INSERT INTO limbs (thing,legs,arms) VALUES('Peg Leg Pete',1,2);
mysql> INSERT INTO limbs (thing,legs,arms) VALUES('space alien',NULL,NULL);
```

---

* If you don't want to enter the complete text of the INSERT statements (and I don't blame you), skip ahead to Recipe 1.12 for a shortcut. And if you don't want to type in *any* of the statements, skip ahead to Recipe 1.15.

The table is named `limbs` and contains three columns to records the number of legs and arms possessed by various life forms and objects. (The physiology of the alien in the last row is such that the proper values for the `arms` and `legs` column cannot be determined; NULL indicates "unknown value.")

Verify that the table contains what you expect by issuing a SELECT statement:

```
mysql> SELECT * FROM limbs;
+--------------+------+------+
| thing        | legs | arms |
+--------------+------+------+
| human        |    2 |    2 |
| insect       |    6 |    0 |
| squid        |    0 |   10 |
| octopus      |    0 |    8 |
| fish         |    0 |    0 |
| centipede    |  100 |    0 |
| table        |    4 |    0 |
| armchair     |    4 |    2 |
| phonograph   |    0 |    1 |
| tripod       |    3 |    0 |
| Peg Leg Pete |    1 |    2 |
| space alien  | NULL | NULL |
+--------------+------+------+
12 rows in set (0.00 sec)
```

At this point, you're all set up with a database and a table that can be used to run some example queries.

1.3 Starting and Terminating mysql

Problem

You want to start and stop the *mysql* program.

Solution

Invoke *mysql* from your command prompt to start it, specifying any connection parameters that may be necessary. To leave *mysql*, use a QUIT statement.

Discussion

To start the *mysql* program, try just typing its name at your command-line prompt. If *mysql* starts up correctly, you'll see a short message, followed by a mysql> prompt that indicates the program is ready to accept queries. To illustrate, here's what the welcome message looks like (to save space, I won't show it in any further examples):

```
% mysql
Welcome to the MySQL monitor.  Commands end with ; or \g.
Your MySQL connection id is 18427 to server version: 3.23.51-log
```

```
Type 'help;' or '\h' for help. Type '\c' to clear the buffer.

mysql>
```

If *mysql* tries to start but exits immediately with an "access denied" message, you'll need to specify connection parameters. The most commonly needed parameters are the host to connect to (the host where the MySQL server runs), your MySQL username, and a password. For example:

```
% mysql -h localhost -p -u cbuser
Enter password: cbpass
```

In general, I'll show *mysql* commands in examples with no connection parameter options. I assume that you'll supply any parameters that you need, either on the command line, or in an option file (Recipe 1.4) so that you don't have to type them each time you invoke *mysql*.

If you don't have a MySQL username and password, you need to obtain permission to use the MySQL server, as described earlier in Recipe 1.1.

The syntax and default values for the connection parameter options are shown in the following table. These options have both a single-dash short form and a double-dash long form.

Parameter type	Option syntax forms	Default value
Hostname	*-h hostname* *--host=hostname*	localhost
Username	*-u username* *--user=username*	Your login name
Password	*-p* *--password*	None

As the table indicates, there is no default password. To supply one, use *--password* or *-p*, then enter your password when *mysql* prompts you for it:

```
% mysql -p
Enter password:                    ← enter your password here
```

If you like, you can specify the password directly on the command line by using either *-ppassword* (note that there is no space after the *-p*) or *--password=password*. I don't recommend doing this on a multiple-user machine, because the password may be visible momentarily to other users who are running tools such as *ps* that report process information.

If you get an error message that *mysql* cannot be found or is an invalid command when you try to invoke it, that means your command interpreter doesn't know where *mysql* is installed. See Recipe 1.7.

To terminate a *mysql* session, issue a QUIT statement:

```
mysql> QUIT
```

You can also terminate the session by issuing an EXIT statement or (under Unix) by typing Ctrl-D.

The way you specify connection parameters for *mysql* also applies to other MySQL programs such as *mysqldump* and *mysqladmin*. For example, some of the actions that *mysqladmin* can perform are available only to the MySQL root account, so you need to specify name and password options for that user:

```
% mysqladmin -p -u root shutdown
Enter password:
```

1.4   Specifying Connection Parameters by Using Option Files

Problem

You don't want to type connection parameters on the command line every time you invoke *mysql*.

Solution

Put the parameters in an option file.

Discussion

To avoid entering connection parameters manually, put them in an option file for *mysql* to read automatically. Under Unix, your personal option file is named *.my.cnf* in your home directory. There are also site-wide option files that administrators can use to specify parameters that apply globally to all users. You can use */etc/my.cnf* or the *my.cnf* file in the MySQL server's data directory. Under Windows, the option files you can use are *C:\my.cnf*, the *my.ini* file in your Windows system directory, or *my.cnf* in the server's data directory.

 Windows may hide filename extensions when displaying files, so a file named *my.cnf* may appear to be named just *my*. Your version of Windows may allow you to disable extension-hiding. Alternatively, issue a DIR command in a DOS window to see full names.

The following example illustrates the format used to write MySQL option files:

```
# general client program connection options
[client]
host=localhost
user=cbuser
password=cbpass
```

```
# options specific to the mysql program
[mysql]
no-auto-rehash
# specify pager for interactive mode
pager=/usr/bin/less
```

This format has the following general characteristics:

- Lines are written in groups. The first line of the group specifies the group name inside of square brackets, and the remaining lines specify options associated with the group. The example file just shown has a [client] group and a [mysql] group. Within a group, option lines are written in *name=value* format, where *name* corresponds to an option name (without leading dashes) and *value* is the option's value. If an option doesn't take any value (such as for the no-auto-rehash option), the name is listed by itself with no trailing *=value* part.

- If you don't need some particular parameter, just leave out the corresponding line. For example, if you normally connect to the default host (localhost), you don't need any host line. If your MySQL username is the same as your operating system login name, you can omit the user line.

- In option files, only the long form of an option is allowed. This is in contrast to command lines, where options often can be specified using a short form or a long form. For example, the hostname can be given using either *-h hostname* or *--host=hostname* on the command line; in an option file, only host=*hostname* is allowed.

- Options often are used for connection parameters (such as host, user, and password). However, the file can specify options that have other purposes. The pager option shown for the [mysql] group specifies the paging program that *mysql* should use for displaying output in interactive mode. It has nothing to do with how the program connects to the server.

- The usual group for specifying client connection parameters is [client]. This group actually is used by all the standard MySQL clients, so by creating an option file to use with *mysql*, you make it easier to invoke other programs such as *mysqldump* and *mysqladmin* as well.

- You can define multiple groups in an option file. A common convention is for a program to look for parameters in the [client] group and in the group named after the program itself. This provides a convenient way to list general client parameters that you want all client programs to use, but still be able to specify options that apply only to a particular program. The preceding sample option file illustrates this convention for the *mysql* program, which gets general connection parameters from the [client] group and also picks up the no-auto-rehash and pager options from the [mysql] group. (If you put the *mysql*-specific options in the [client] group, that will result in "unknown option" errors for all other programs that use the [client] group and they won't run properly.)

- If a parameter is specified multiple times in an option file, the last value found takes precedence. This means that normally you should list any program-specific groups after the [client] group so that if there is any overlap in the options set by the two groups, the more general options will be overridden by the program-specific values.
- Lines beginning with # or ; characters are ignored as comments. Blank lines are ignored, too.
- Option files must be plain text files. If you create an option file with a word processor that uses some non-text format by default, be sure to save the file explicitly as text. Windows users especially should take note of this.
- Options that specify file or directory pathnames should be written using / as the pathname separator character, even under Windows.

If you want to find out which options will be taken from option files by *mysql*, use this command:

```
% mysql --print-defaults
```

You can also use the *my_print_defaults* utility, which takes as arguments the names of the option file groups that it should read. For example, *mysql* looks in both the [client] and [mysql] groups for options, so you can check which values it will take from option files like this:

```
% my_print_defaults client mysql
```

1.5   Protecting Option Files

Problem

Your MySQL username and password are stored in your option file, and you don't want other users reading it.

Solution

Change the file's mode to make it accessible only by you.

Discussion

If you use a multiple-user operating system such as Unix, you should protect your option file to prevent other users from finding out how to connect to MySQL using your account. Use *chmod* to make the file private by setting its mode to allow access only by yourself:

```
% chmod 600 .my.cnf
```

1.6 Mixing Command-Line and Option File Parameters

Problem

You'd rather not store your MySQL password in an option file, but you don't want to enter your username and server host manually.

Solution

Put the username and host in the option file, and specify the password interactively when you invoke *mysql*; it looks both in the option file and on the command line for connection parameters. If an option is specified in both places, the one on the command line takes precedence.

Discussion

mysql first reads your option file to see what connection parameters are listed there, then checks the command line for additional parameters. This means you can specify some options one way, and some the other way.

Command-line parameters take precedence over parameters found in your option file, so if for some reason you need to override an option file parameter, just specify it on the command line. For example, you might list your regular MySQL username and password in the option file for general purpose use. If you need to connect on occasion as the MySQL root user, specify the user and password options on the command line to override the option file values:

```
% mysql -p -u root
```

To explicitly specify "no password" when there is a non-empty password in the option file, use *-p* on the command line, and then just press Return when *mysql* prompts you for the password:

```
% mysql -p
Enter password:        ← press Return here
```

1.7 What to Do if mysql Cannot Be Found

Problem

When you invoke *mysql* from the command line, your command interpreter can't find it.

Solution

Add the directory where *mysql* is installed to your PATH setting. Then you'll be able to run *mysql* from any directory easily.

Discussion

If your shell or command interpreter can't find *mysql* when you invoke it, you'll see some sort of error message. It may look like this under Unix:

```
% mysql
mysql: Command not found.
```

Or like this under Windows:

```
C:\> mysql
Bad command or invalid filename
```

One way to tell your shell where to find *mysql* is to type its full pathname each time you run it. The command might look like this under Unix:

```
% /usr/local/mysql/bin/mysql
```

Or like this under Windows:

```
C:\> C:\mysql\bin\mysql
```

Typing long pathnames gets tiresome pretty quickly, though. You can avoid doing so by changing into the directory where *mysql* is installed before you run it. However, I recommend that you *not* do that. If you do, the inevitable result is that you'll end up putting all your datafiles and query batch files in the same directory as *mysql*, thus unnecessarily cluttering up what should be a location intended only for programs.

A better solution is to make sure that the directory where *mysql* is installed is included in the PATH environment variable that lists pathnames of directories where the shell looks for commands. (See Recipe 1.8.) Then you can invoke *mysql* from any directory by entering just its name, and your shell will be able to find it. This eliminates a lot of unnecessary pathname typing. An additional benefit is that because you can easily run *mysql* from anywhere, you will have no need to put your datafiles in the same directory where *mysql* is located. When you're not operating under the burden of running *mysql* from a particular location, you'll be free to organize your files in a way that makes sense to you, not in a way imposed by some artificial necessity. For example, you can create a directory under your home directory for each database you have and put the files associated with each database in the appropriate directory.

I've pointed out the importance of the search path here because I receive many questions from people who aren't aware of the existence of such a thing, and who consequently try to do all their MySQL-related work in the *bin* directory where *mysql* is installed. This seems particularly common among Windows users. Perhaps the reason is that, except for Windows NT and its derivatives, the Windows Help application seems to be silent on the subject of the command interpreter search path or how to set it. (Apparently, Windows Help considers it dangerous for people to know how to do something useful for themselves.)

Another way for Windows users to avoid typing the pathname or changing into the *mysql* directory is to create a shortcut and place it in a more convenient location. That has the advantage of making it easy to start up *mysql* just by opening the shortcut. To specify command-line options or the startup directory, edit the shortcut's properties. If you don't always invoke *mysql* with the same options, it might be useful to create a shortcut corresponding to each set of options you need—for example, one shortcut to connect as an ordinary user for general work and another to connect as the MySQL root user for administrative purposes.

1.8   Setting Environment Variables

Problem

You need to modify your operating environment, for example, to change your shell's PATH setting.

Solution

Edit the appropriate shell startup file. Under Windows NT–based systems, another alternative is to use the System control panel.

Discussion

The shell or command interpreter you use to run programs from the command-line prompt includes an environment in which you can store variable values. Some of these variables are used by the shell itself. For example, it uses PATH to determine which directories to look in for programs such as *mysql*. Other variables are used by other programs (such as PERL5LIB, which tells Perl where to look for library files used by Perl scripts).

Your shell determines the syntax used to set environment variables, as well as the startup file in which to place the settings. Typical startup files for various shells are shown in the following table. If you've never looked through your shell's startup files, it's a good idea to do so to familiarize yourself with their contents.

Shell	Possible startup files
csh, tcsh	.login, .cshrc, .tcshrc
sh, bash, ksh	.profile .bash_profile, .bash_login, .bashrc
DOS prompt	C:\AUTOEXEC.BAT

The following examples show how to set the PATH variable so that it includes the directory where the *mysql* program is installed. The examples assume there is an existing PATH setting in one of your startup files. If you have no PATH setting currently, simply add the appropriate line or lines to one of the files.

 If you're reading this section because you've been referred here from another chapter, you'll probably be more interested in changing some variable other than PATH. The instructions are similar because you use the same syntax.

The PATH variable lists the pathnames for one or more directories. If an environment variable's value consists of multiple pathnames, it's conventional under Unix to separate them using the colon character (:). Under Windows, pathnames may contain colons, so the separator is the semicolon character (;).

To set the value of PATH, use the instructions that pertain to your shell:

- For *csh* or *tcsh*, look for a setenv PATH command in your startup files, then add the appropriate directory to the line. Suppose your search path is set by a line like this in your *.login* file:

    ```
    setenv PATH /bin:/usr/bin:/usr/local/bin
    ```

  If *mysql* is installed in */usr/local/mysql/bin*, add that directory to the search path by changing the setenv line to look like this:

    ```
    setenv PATH /usr/local/mysql/bin:/bin:/usr/bin:/usr/local/bin
    ```

  It's also possible that your path will be set with set path, which uses different syntax:

    ```
    set path = (/usr/local/mysql/bin /bin /usr/bin /usr/local/bin)
    ```

- For a shell in the Bourne shell family such as *sh*, *bash*, or *ksh*, look in your startup files for a line that sets up and exports the PATH variable:

    ```
    export PATH=/bin:/usr/bin:/usr/local/bin
    ```

  The assignment and the export might be on separate lines:

    ```
    PATH=/bin:/usr/bin:/usr/local/bin
    export PATH
    ```

  Change the setting to this:

    ```
    export PATH=/usr/local/mysql/bin:/bin:/usr/bin:/usr/local/bin
    ```

  Or:

    ```
    PATH=/usr/local/mysql/bin:/bin:/usr/bin:/usr/local/bin
    export PATH
    ```

- Under Windows, check for a line that sets the PATH variable in your *AUTOEXEC.BAT* file. It might look like this:

    ```
    PATH=C:\WINDOWS;C:\WINDOWS\COMMAND
    ```

Or like this:

```
SET PATH=C:\WINDOWS;C:\WINDOWS\COMMAND
```

Change the PATH value to include the directory where *mysql* is installed. If this is *C:\mysql\bin*, the resulting PATH setting looks like this:

```
PATH=C:\mysql\bin;C:\WINDOWS;C:\WINDOWS\COMMAND
```

Or:

```
SET PATH=C:\mysql\bin;C:\WINDOWS;C:\WINDOWS\COMMAND
```

- Under Windows NT–based systems, another way to change the PATH value is to use the System control panel (use its Environment or Advanced tab, whichever is present). In other versions of Windows, you can use the Registry Editor application. Unfortunately, the name of the Registry Editor key that contains the path value seems to vary among versions of Windows. For example, on the Windows machines that I use, the key has one name under Windows Me and a different name under Windows 98; under Windows 95, I couldn't find the key at all. It's probably simpler just to edit *AUTOEXEC.BAT*.

After setting an environment variable, you'll need to cause the modification to take effect. Under Unix, you can log out and log in again. Under Windows, if you set PATH using the System control panel, you can simply open a new DOS window. If you edited *AUTOEXEC.BAT* instead, restart the machine.

1.9   Issuing Queries

Problem

You've started *mysql* and now you want to send queries to the MySQL server.

Solution

Just type them in, but be sure to let *mysql* know where each one ends.

Discussion

To issue a query at the mysql> prompt, type it in, add a semicolon (;) at the end to signify the end of the statement, and press Return. An explicit statement terminator is necessary; *mysql* doesn't interpret Return as a terminator because it's allowable to enter a statement using multiple input lines. The semicolon is the most common terminator, but you can also use \g ("go") as a synonym for the semicolon. Thus, the following examples are equivalent ways of issuing the same query, even though they are entered differently and terminated differently:[*]

---

[*] Example queries in this book are shown with SQL keywords like SELECT in uppercase for distinctiveness, but that's simply a typographical convention. You can enter keywords in any lettercase.

```
mysql> SELECT NOW();
+---------------------+
| NOW()               |
+---------------------+
| 2001-07-04 10:27:23 |
+---------------------+
mysql> SELECT
    -> NOW()\g
+---------------------+
| NOW()               |
+---------------------+
| 2001-07-04 10:27:28 |
+---------------------+
```

Notice for the second query that the prompt changes from mysql> to -> on the second input line. *mysql* changes the prompt this way to let you know that it's still waiting to see the query terminator.

Be sure to understand that neither the ; character nor the \g sequence that serve as query terminators are part of the query itself. They're conventions used by the *mysql* program, which recognizes these terminators and strips them from the input before sending the query to the MySQL server. It's important to remember this when you write your own programs that send queries to the server (as we'll begin to do in the next chapter). In that context, you don't include any terminator characters; the end of the query string itself signifies the end of the query. In fact, adding a terminator may well cause the query to fail with an error.

1.10   Selecting a Database

Problem

You want to tell *mysql* which database to use.

Solution

Name the database on the *mysql* command line or issue a USE statement from within *mysql*.

Discussion

When you issue a query that refers to a table (as most queries do), you need to indicate which database the table is part of. One way to do so is to use a fully qualified table reference that begins with the database name. (For example, cookbook.limbs refers to the limbs table in the cookbook database.) As a convenience, MySQL also allows you to select a default (current) database so that you can refer to its tables without explicitly specifying the database name each time. You can specify the database on the command line when you start *mysql*:

```
% mysql cookbook
```

If you provide options on the command line such as connection parameters when you run *mysql*, they should precede the database name:

```
% mysql -h host -p -u user cookbook
```

If you've already started a *mysql* session, you can select a database (or switch to a different one) by issuing a USE statement:

```
mysql> USE cookbook;
Database changed
```

If you've forgotten or are not sure which database is the current one (which can happen easily if you're using multiple databases and switching between them several times during the course of a *mysql* session), use the following statement:

```
mysql> SELECT DATABASE();
+------------+
| DATABASE() |
+------------+
| cookbook   |
+------------+
```

DATABASE() is a function that returns the name of the current database. If no database has been selected yet, the function returns an empty string:

```
mysql> SELECT DATABASE();
+------------+
| DATABASE() |
+------------+
|            |
+------------+
```

The STATUS command (and its synonym, \s) also display the current database name, in additional to several other pieces of information:

```
mysql> \s
--------------
Connection id:      5589
Current database:   cookbook
Current user:       cbuser@localhost
Current pager:      stdout
Using outfile:      ''
Server version:     3.23.51-log
Protocol version:   10
Connection:      Localhost via UNIX socket
Client characterset:    latin1
Server characterset:    latin1
UNIX socket:        /tmp/mysql.sock
Uptime:         9 days 39 min 43 sec
```

```
Threads: 4  Questions: 42265  Slow queries: 0  Opens: 82  Flush tables: 1
Open tables: 52 Queries per second avg: 0.054
--------------
```

Temporarily Using a Table from Another Database

To use a table from another database temporarily, you can switch to that database and then switch back when you're done using the table. However, you can also use the table without switching databases by referring to the table using its fully qualified name. For example, to use the table other_tbl in another database other_db, you can refer to it as other_db.other_tbl.

1.11 Canceling a Partially Entered Query

Problem

You start to enter a query, then decide not to issue it after all.

Solution

Cancel the query using your line kill character or the \c sequence.

Discussion

If you change your mind about issuing a query that you're entering, cancel it. If the query is on a single line, use your line kill character to erase the entire line. (The particular character to use depends on your terminal setup; for me, the character is Ctrl-U.) If you've entered a statement over multiple lines, the line kill character will erase only the last line. To cancel the statement completely, enter \c and type Return. This will return you to the mysql> prompt:

```
mysql> SELECT *
    -> FROM limbs
    -> ORDER BY\c
mysql>
```

Sometimes \c appears to do nothing (that is, the mysql> prompt does not reappear), which leads to the sense that you're "trapped" in a query and can't escape. If \c is ineffective, the cause usually is that you began typing a quoted string and haven't yet entered the matching end quote that terminates the string. Let *mysql*'s prompt help you figure out what to do here. If the prompt has changed from mysql> to ">, That means *mysql* is looking for a terminating double quote. If the prompt is '> instead, *mysql* is looking for a terminating single quote. Type the appropriate matching quote to end the string, then enter \c followed by Return and you should be okay.

1.12   Repeating and Editing Queries

Problem

The query you just entered contained an error, and you want to fix it without typing the whole thing again. Or you want to repeat an earlier statement without retyping it.

Solution

Use *mysql*'s built-in query editor.

Discussion

If you issue a long query only to find that it contains a syntax error, what should you do? Type in the entire corrected query from scratch? No need. *mysql* maintains a statement history and supports input-line editing. This allows you to recall queries so that you can modify and reissue them easily. There are many, many editing functions, but most people tend to use a small set of commands for the majority of their editing.* A basic set of useful commands is shown in the following table. Typically, you use Up Arrow to recall the previous line, Left Arrow and Right Arrow to move around within the line, and Backspace or Delete to erase characters. To add new characters to the line, just move the cursor to the appropriate spot and type them in. When you're done editing, press Return to issue the query (the cursor need not be at the end of the line when you do this).

Editing Key	Effect of Key
Up Arrow	Scroll up through statement history
Down Arrow	Scroll down through statement history
Left Arrow	Move left within line
Right Arrow	Move right within line
Ctrl-A	Move to beginning of line
Ctrl-E	Move to end of line
Backspace	Delete previous character
Ctrl-D	Delete character under cursor

Input-line editing is useful for more than just fixing mistakes. You can use it to try out variant forms of a query without retyping the entire thing each time. It's also handy for entering a series of similar statements. For example, if you wanted to use the query history to issue the series of INSERT statements shown earlier in Recipe 1.2

---

* The input-line editing capabilities in *mysql* are based on the GNU Readline library. You can read the documentation for this library to find out more about the many editing functions that are available. For more information, check the Bash manual, available online at *http://www.gnu.org/manual/*.

to create the limbs table, first enter the initial INSERT statement. Then, to issue each successive statement, press the Up Arrow key to recall the previous statement with the cursor at the end, backspace back through the column values to erase them, enter the new values, and press Return.

To recall a statement that was entered on multiple lines, the editing procedure is a little trickier than for single-line statements. In this case, you must recall and reenter each successive line of the query in order. For example, if you've entered a two-line query that contains a mistake, press Up Arrow twice to recall the first line. Make any modifications necessary and press Return. Then press Up Arrow twice more to recall the second line. Modify it, press Return, and the query will execute.

Under Windows, *mysql* allows statement recall only for NT-based systems. For versions such as Windows 98 or Me, you can use the special *mysqlc* client program instead. However, *mysqlc* requires an additional library file, *cygwinb19.dll*. If you find a copy of this library in the same directory where *mysqlc* is installed (the *bin* dir under the MySQL installation directory), you should be all set. If the library is located in the MySQL *lib* directory, copy it into your Windows system directory. The command looks something like this; you should modify it to reflect the actual locations of the two directories on your system:

```
C:\> copy C:\mysql\lib\cygwinb19.dll C:\Windows\System
```

After you make sure the library is in a location where *mysqlc* can find it, invoke *mysqlc* and it should be capable of input-line editing.

One unfortunate consequence of using *mysqlc* is that it's actually a fairly old program. (For example, even in MySQL 4.x distributions, *mysqlc* dates back to 3.22.7.) This means it doesn't understand newer statements such as SOURCE.

1.13 Using Auto-Completion for Database and Table Names

Problem

You wish there was a way to type database and table names more quickly.

Solution

There is; use *mysql*'s name auto-completion facility.

Discussion

Normally when you use *mysql* interactively, it reads the list of database names and the names of the tables and columns in your current database when it starts up.

mysql remembers this information to provide name completion capabilities that are useful for entering statements with fewer keystrokes:

- Type in a partial database, table, or column name and then hit the Tab key.
- If the partial name is unique, *mysql* completes it for you. Otherwise, you can hit Tab again to see the possible matches.
- Enter additional characters and hit Tab again once to complete it or twice to see the new set of matches.

mysql's name auto-completion capability is based on the table names in the current database, and thus is unavailable within a *mysql* session until a database has been selected, either on the command line or by means of a USE statement.

Auto-completion allows you to cut down the amount of typing you do. However, if you don't use this feature, reading name-completion information from the MySQL server may be counterproductive because it can cause *mysql* to start up more slowly when you have a lot of tables in your database. To tell *mysql* not to read this information so that it starts up more quickly, specify the *-A* (or *--no-auto-rehash*) option on the *mysql* command line. Alternatively, put a no-auto-rehash line in the [mysql] group of your MySQL option file:

```
[mysql]
no-auto-rehash
```

To force *mysql* to read name completion information even if it was invoked in no-completion mode, issue a REHASH or \# command at the mysql> prompt.

1.14 Using SQL Variables in Queries

Problem

You want to save a value from a query so you can refer to it in a subsequent query.

Solution

Use a SQL variable to store the value for later use.

Discussion

As of MySQL 3.23.6, you can assign a value returned by a SELECT statement to a variable, then refer to the variable later in your *mysql* session. This provides a way to save a result returned from one query, then refer to it later in other queries. The syntax for assigning a value to a SQL variable within a SELECT query is @*var_name* := *value*, where *var_name* is the variable name and *value* is a value that you're retrieving. The variable may be used in subsequent queries wherever an expression is allowed, such as in a WHERE clause or in an INSERT statement.

A common situation in which SQL variables come in handy is when you need to issue successive queries on multiple tables that are related by a common key value. Suppose you have a customers table with a cust_id column that identifies each customer, and an orders table that also has a cust_id column to indicate which customer each order is associated with. If you have a customer name and you want to delete the customer record as well as all the customer's orders, you need to determine the proper cust_id value for that customer, then delete records from both the customers and orders tables that match the ID. One way to do this is to first save the ID value in a variable, then refer to the variable in the DELETE statements:*

```
mysql> SELECT @id := cust_id FROM customers WHERE cust_id='customer name';
mysql> DELETE FROM customers WHERE cust_id = @id;
mysql> DELETE FROM orders WHERE cust_id = @id;
```

The preceding SELECT statement assigns a column value to a variable, but variables also can be assigned values from arbitrary expressions. The following statement determines the highest sum of the arms and legs columns in the limbs table and assigns it to the @max_limbs variable:

```
mysql> SELECT @max_limbs := MAX(arms+legs) FROM limbs;
```

Another use for a variable is to save the result from LAST_INSERT_ID() after creating a new record in a table that has an AUTO_INCREMENT column:

```
mysql> SELECT @last_id := LAST_INSERT_ID();
```

LAST_INSERT_ID() returns the value of the new AUTO_INCREMENT value. By saving it in a variable, you can refer to the value several times in subsequent statements, even if you issue other statements that create their own AUTO_INCREMENT values and thus change the value returned by LAST_INSERT_ID(). This is discussed further in Chapter 11.

SQL variables hold single values. If you assign a value to a variable using a statement that returns multiple rows, the value from the last row is used:

```
mysql> SELECT @name := thing FROM limbs WHERE legs = 0;
+----------------+
| @name := thing |
+----------------+
| squid          |
| octopus        |
| fish           |
| phonograph     |
+----------------+
mysql> SELECT @name;
+------------+
| @name      |
+------------+
| phonograph |
+------------+
```

---

* In MySQL 4, you can use multiple-table DELETE statements to accomplish tasks like this with a single query. See Chapter 12 for examples.

If the statement returns no rows, no assignment takes place and the variable retains its previous value. If the variable has not been used previously, that value is NULL:

```
mysql> SELECT @name2 := thing FROM limbs WHERE legs < 0;
Empty set (0.00 sec)
mysql> SELECT @name2;
+--------+
| @name2 |
+--------+
| NULL   |
+--------+
```

To set a variable explicitly to a particular value, use a SET statement. SET syntax uses = rather than := to assign the value:

```
mysql> SET @sum = 4 + 7;
mysql> SELECT @sum;
+------+
| @sum |
+------+
|   11 |
+------+
```

A given variable's value persists until you assign it another value or until the end of your *mysql* session, whichever comes first.

Variable names are case sensitive:

```
mysql> SET @x = 1; SELECT @x, @X;
+------+------+
| @x   | @X   |
+------+------+
|    1 | NULL |
+------+------+
```

SQL variables can be used only where expressions are allowed, not where constants or literal identifiers must be provided. Although it's tempting to attempt to use variables for such things as table names, it doesn't work. For example, you might try to generate a temporary table name using a variable as follows, but the result is only an error message:

```
mysql> SET @tbl_name = CONCAT('tbl_',FLOOR(RAND()*1000000));
mysql> CREATE TABLE @tbl_name (int_col INT);
ERROR 1064 at line 2: You have an error in your SQL syntax near '@tbl_name
(int_col INT)' at line 1
```

SQL variables are a MySQL-specific extension, so they will not work with other database engines.

1.15   Telling mysql to Read Queries from a File

Problem

You want *mysql* to read queries stored in a file so you don't have to enter them manually.

Solution

Redirect *mysql*'s input or use the SOURCE command.

Discussion

By default, the *mysql* program reads input interactively from the terminal, but you can feed it queries in batch mode using other input sources such as a file, another program, or the command arguments. You can also use copy and paste as a source of query input. This section discusses how to read queries from a file. The next few sections discuss how to take input from other sources.

To create a SQL script for *mysql* to execute in batch mode, put your statements in a text file, then invoke *mysql* and redirect its input to read from that file:

```
% mysql cookbook < filename
```

Statements that are read from an input file substitute for what you'd normally type in by hand, so they must be terminated with semicolons (or \g), just as if you were entering them manually. One difference between interactive and batch modes is the default output style. For interactive mode, the default is tabular (boxed) format. For batch mode, the default is to delimit column values with tabs. However, you can select whichever output style you want using the appropriate command-line options. See the section on selecting tabular or tab-delimited format later in the chapter (Recipe 1.21).

Batch mode is convenient when you need to issue a given set of statements on multiple occasions, because then you need not enter them manually each time. For example, batch mode makes it easy to set up *cron* jobs that run with no user intervention. SQL scripts are also useful for distributing queries to other people. Many of the examples shown in this book can be run using script files that are available as part of the accompanying recipes source distribution (see Appendix A). You can feed these files to *mysql* in batch mode to avoid typing queries yourself. A common instance of this is that when an example shows a CREATE TABLE statement that describes what a particular table looks like, you'll find a SQL batch file in the distribution that can be used to create (and perhaps load data into) the table. For example, earlier in the chapter, statements for creating and populating the limbs table were shown. The recipes distribution includes a file *limbs.sql* that contains statements to do the same thing. The file looks like this:

```
DROP TABLE IF EXISTS limbs;
CREATE TABLE limbs
(
    thing   VARCHAR(20),    # what the thing is
    legs    INT,            # number of legs it has
    arms    INT             # number of arms it has
);

INSERT INTO limbs (thing,legs,arms) VALUES('human',2,2);
INSERT INTO limbs (thing,legs,arms) VALUES('insect',6,0);
INSERT INTO limbs (thing,legs,arms) VALUES('squid',0,10);
INSERT INTO limbs (thing,legs,arms) VALUES('octopus',0,8);
INSERT INTO limbs (thing,legs,arms) VALUES('fish',0,0);
INSERT INTO limbs (thing,legs,arms) VALUES('centipede',100,0);
INSERT INTO limbs (thing,legs,arms) VALUES('table',4,0);
INSERT INTO limbs (thing,legs,arms) VALUES('armchair',4,2);
INSERT INTO limbs (thing,legs,arms) VALUES('phonograph',0,1);
INSERT INTO limbs (thing,legs,arms) VALUES('tripod',3,0);
INSERT INTO limbs (thing,legs,arms) VALUES('Peg Leg Pete',1,2);
INSERT INTO limbs (thing,legs,arms) VALUES('space alien',NULL,NULL);
```

To execute the statements in this SQL script file in batch mode, change directory into the *tables* directory of the recipes distribution where the table-creation scripts are located, then run this command:

```
% mysql cookbook < limbs.sql
```

You'll note that the script contains a statement to drop the table if it exists before creating it anew and loading it with data. That allows you to experiment with the table without worrying about changing its contents, because you can restore the table to its baseline state any time by running the script again.

The command just shown illustrates how to specify an input file for *mysql* on the command line. As of MySQL 3.23.9, you can read a file of SQL statements from within a *mysql* session by using a SOURCE *filename* command (or \. *filename*, which is synonymous). Suppose the SQL script file *test.sql* contains the following statements:

```
SELECT NOW();
SELECT COUNT(*) FROM limbs;
```

You can execute that file from within *mysql* as follows:

```
mysql> SOURCE test.sql;
+---------------------+
| NOW()               |
+---------------------+
| 2001-07-04 10:35:08 |
+---------------------+
1 row in set (0.00 sec)
```

```
+----------+
| COUNT(*) |
+----------+
|       12 |
+----------+
1 row in set (0.01 sec)
```

SQL scripts can themselves include SOURCE or \. commands to include other scripts. The danger of this is that it's possible to create a source loop. Normally you should take care to avoid such loops, but if you're feeling mischievous and want to create one deliberately to find out how deep *mysql* can nest input files, here's how to do it. First, issue the following two statements manually to create a counter table to keep track of the source file depth and initialize the nesting level to zero:

```
mysql> CREATE TABLE counter (depth INT);
mysql> INSERT INTO counter SET depth = 0;
```

Then create a script file *loop.sql* that contains the following lines (be sure each line ends with a semicolon):

```
UPDATE counter SET depth = depth + 1;
SELECT depth FROM counter;
SOURCE loop.sql;
```

Finally, invoke *mysql* and issue a SOURCE command to read the script file:

```
% mysql cookbook
mysql> SOURCE loop.sql;
```

The first two statements in *loop.sql* increment the nesting counter and display the current depth value. In the third statement, *loop.sql* sources itself, thus creating an input loop. You'll see the output whiz by, with the counter display incrementing each time through the loop. Eventually *mysql* will run out of file descriptors and stop with an error:

```
ERROR:
Failed to open file 'loop.sql', error: 24
```

What is error 24? Find out by using MySQL's *perror* (print error) utility:

```
% perror 24
Error code 24:  Too many open files
```

1.16   Telling mysql to Read Queries from Other Programs

Problem

You want to shove the output from another program into *mysql*.

Solution

Use a pipe.

Discussion

An earlier section used the following command to show how *mysql* can read SQL statements from a file:

```
% mysql cookbook < limbs.sql
```

mysql can also read a pipe, to receive output from other programs as its input. As a trivial example, the preceding command is equivalent to this one:

```
% cat limbs.sql | mysql cookbook
```

Before you tell me that I've qualified for this week's "useless use of *cat* award,"* allow me to observe that you can substitute other commands for *cat*. The point is that *any* command that produces output consisting of semicolon-terminated SQL statements can be used as an input source for *mysql*. This can be useful in many ways. For example, the *mysqldump* utility is used to generate database backups. It writes a backup as a set of SQL statements that recreate the database, so to process *mysqldump* output, you feed it to *mysql*. This means you can use the combination of *mysqldump* and *mysql* to copy a database over the network to another MySQL server:

```
% mysqldump cookbook | mysql -h some.other.host.com cookbook
```

Program-generated SQL also can be useful when you need to populate a table with test data but don't want to write the INSERT statements by hand. Instead, write a short program that generates the statements and send its output to *mysql* using a pipe:

```
% generate-test-data | mysql cookbook
```

See Also

mysqldump is discussed further in Chapter 10.

1.17 Specifying Queries on the Command Line

Problem

You want to specify a query directly on the command line for *mysql* to execute.

---

* Under Windows, the equivalent would be the "useless use of *type* award":

```
C:\> type limbs.sql | mysql cookbook
```

Solution

mysql can read a query from its argument list. Use the *-e* (or *--execute*) option to specify a query on the command line.

Discussion

For example, to find out how many records are in the limbs table, run this command:

```
% mysql -e "SELECT COUNT(*) FROM limbs" cookbook
+----------+
| COUNT(*) |
+----------+
|       12 |
+----------+
```

To run multiple queries with the *-e* option, separate them with semicolons:

```
% mysql -e "SELECT COUNT(*) FROM limbs;SELECT NOW()" cookbook
+----------+
| COUNT(*) |
+----------+
|       12 |
+----------+
+---------------------+
| NOW()               |
+---------------------+
| 2001-07-04 10:42:22 |
+---------------------+
```

See Also

By default, results generated by queries that are specified with *-e* are displayed in tabular format if output goes to the terminal, and in tab-delimited format otherwise. To produce a different output style, see Recipe 1.21.

1.18   Using Copy and Paste as a mysql Input Source

Problem

You want to take advantage of your graphical user interface (GUI) to make *mysql* easier to use.

Solution

Use copy and paste to supply *mysql* with queries to execute. In this way, you can take advantage of your GUI's capabilities to augment the terminal interface presented by *mysql*.

Discussion

Copy and paste is useful in a windowing environment that allows you to run multiple programs at once and transfer information between them. If you have a document containing queries open in a window, you can just copy the queries from there and paste them into the window in which you're running *mysql*. This is equivalent to typing the queries yourself, but often quicker. For queries that you issue frequently, keeping them visible in a separate window can be a good way to make sure they're always at your fingertips and easily accessible.

1.19 Preventing Query Output from Scrolling off the Screen

Problem

Query output zooms off the top of your screen before you can see it.

Solution

Tell *mysql* to display output a page at a time, or run *mysql* in a window that allows scrollback.

Discussion

If a query produces many lines of output, normally they just scroll right off the top of the screen. To prevent this, tell *mysql* to present output a page at a time by specifying the *--pager* option.* *--pager=program* tells *mysql* to use a specific program as your pager:

```
% mysql --pager=/usr/bin/less
```

--pager by itself tells *mysql* to use your default pager, as specified in your PAGER environment variable:

```
% mysql --pager
```

If your PAGER variable isn't set, you must either define it or use the first form of the command to specify a pager program explicitly. To define PAGER, use the instructions in Recipe 1.8 for setting environment variables.

---

* The *--pager* option is not available under Windows.

Within a *mysql* session, you can turn paging on and off using \P and \n. \P without an argument enables paging using the program specified in your PAGER variable. \P with an argument enables paging using the argument as the name of the paging program:

```
mysql> \P
PAGER set to /bin/more
mysql> \P /usr/bin/less
PAGER set to /usr/bin/less
mysql> \n
PAGER set to stdout
```

Output paging was introduced in MySQL 3.23.28.

Another way to deal with long result sets is to use a terminal program that allows you to scroll back through previous output. Programs such as *xterm* for the X Window System, Terminal for Mac OS X, MacSSH or BetterTelnet for Mac OS, or Telnet for Windows allow you to set the number of output lines saved in the scrollback buffer. Under Windows NT, 2000, or XP, you can set up a DOS window that allows scrollback using the following procedure:

1. Open the Control Panel.
2. Create a shortcut to the MS-DOS prompt by right clicking on the Console item and dragging the mouse to where you want to place the shortcut (on the desktop, for example).
3. Right click on the shortcut and select the Properties item from the menu that appears.
4. Select the Layout tab in the resulting Properties window.
5. Set the screen buffer height to the number of lines you want to save and click the OK button.

Now you should be able to launch the shortcut to get a scrollable DOS window that allows output produced by commands in that window to be retrieved by using the scrollbar.

1.20   Sending Query Output to a File or to a Program

Problem

You want to send *mysql* output somewhere other than to your screen.

Solution

Redirect *mysql*'s output or use a pipe.

Discussion

mysql chooses its default output format according to whether you run it interactively or non-interactively. Under interactive use, *mysql* normally sends its output to the terminal and writes query results using tabular format:

```
mysql> SELECT * FROM limbs;
+--------------+------+------+
| thing        | legs | arms |
+--------------+------+------+
| human        |    2 |    2 |
| insect       |    6 |    0 |
| squid        |    0 |   10 |
| octopus      |    0 |    8 |
| fish         |    0 |    0 |
| centipede    |  100 |    0 |
| table        |    4 |    0 |
| armchair     |    4 |    2 |
| phonograph   |    0 |    1 |
| tripod       |    3 |    0 |
| Peg Leg Pete |    1 |    2 |
| space alien  | NULL | NULL |
+--------------+------+------+
12 rows in set (0.00 sec)
```

In non-interactive mode (that is, when either the input or output is redirected), *mysql* writes output in tab-delimited format:

```
% echo "SELECT * FROM limbs" | mysql cookbook
thing   legs    arms
human   2       2
insect  6       0
squid   0       10
octopus 0       8
fish    0       0
centipede       100     0
table   4       0
armchair        4       2
phonograph      0       1
tripod  3       0
Peg Leg Pete    1       2
space alien     NULL    NULL
```

However, in either context, you can select any of *mysql*'s output formats by using the appropriate command-line options. This section describes how to send *mysql* output somewhere other than the terminal. The next several sections discuss the various *mysql* output formats and how to select them explicitly according to your needs when the default format isn't what you want.

To save output from *mysql* in a file, use your shell's standard redirection capability:

```
% mysql cookbook > outputfile
```

However, if you try to run *mysql* interactively with the output redirected, you won't be able to see what you're typing, so generally in this case you'll also take query input from a file (or another program):

```
% mysql cookbook < inputfile > outputfile
```

You can also send query output to another program. For example, if you want to mail query output to someone, you might do so like this:

```
% mysql cookbook < inputfile | mail paul
```

Note that because *mysql* runs non-interactively in that context, it produces tab-delimited output, which the mail recipient may find more difficult to read than tabular output. Recipe 1.21 shows how to fix this problem.

1.21 Selecting Tabular or Tab-Delimited Query Output Format

Problem

mysql produces tabular output when you want tab-delimited output, or vice versa.

Solution

Select the desired format explicitly with the appropriate command-line option.

Discussion

When you use *mysql* non-interactively (such as to read queries from a file or to send results into a pipe), it writes output in tab-delimited format by default. Sometimes it's desirable to produce tabular output instead. For example, if you want to print or mail query results, tab-delimited output doesn't look very nice. Use the *-t* (or *--table*) option to produce tabular output that is more readable:

```
% mysql -t cookbook < inputfile | lpr
% mysql -t cookbook < inputfile | mail paul
```

The inverse operation is to produce batch (tab-delimited) output in interactive mode. To do this, use *-B* or *--batch*.

1.22 Specifying Arbitrary Output Column Delimiters

Problem

You want *mysql* to produce query output using a delimiter other than tab.

Solution

Postprocess *mysql*'s output.

Discussion

In non-interactive mode, *mysql* separates output columns with tabs and there is no option for specifying the output delimiter. Under some circumstances, it may be desirable to produce output that uses a different delimiter. Suppose you want to create an output file for use by a program that expects values to be separated by colon characters (:) rather than tabs. Under Unix, you can convert tabs to arbitrary delimiters by using utilities such as *tr* and *sed*. For example, to change tabs to colons, any of the following commands would work (*TAB* indicates where you type a tab character):*

```
% mysql cookbook < inputfile   | sed -e "s/TAB/:/g" > outputfile
% mysql cookbook < inputfile   | tr "TAB" ":" > outputfile
% mysql cookbook < inputfile   | tr "\011" ":" > outputfile
```

sed is more powerful than *tr* because it understands regular expressions and allows multiple substitutions. This is useful when you want to produce output in something like comma-separated values (CSV) format, which requires three substitutions:

- Escape any quote characters that appear in the data by doubling them so that when you use the resulting CSV file, they won't be taken as column delimiters.

- Change the tabs to commas.

- Surround column values with quotes.

sed allows all three substitutions to be performed in a single command:

```
% mysql cookbook < inputfile \
    | sed -e 's/"/""/g' -e 's/TAB/","/g' -e 's/^/"/' -e 's/$/"/' > outputfile
```

That's fairly cryptic, to say the least. You can achieve the same result with other languages that may be easier to read. Here's a short Perl script that does the same thing as the *sed* command (it converts tab-delimited input to CSV output), and includes comments to document how it works:

```perl
#! /usr/bin/perl -w
while (<>)             # read next input line
{
    s/"/""/g;         # double any quotes within column values
    s/\t/","/g;       # put `","' between column values
    s/^/"/;           # add `"' before the first value
    s/$/"/;           # add `"' after the last value
    print;            # print the result
}
exit (0);
```

---

* The syntax for some versions of *tr* may be different; consult your local documentation. Also, some shells use the tab character for special purposes such as filename completion. For such shells, type a literal tab into the command by preceding it with Ctrl-V.

If you name the script *csv.pl*, you can use it like this:

```
% mysql cookbook < inputfile | csv.pl > outputfile
```

If you run the command under a version of Windows that doesn't know how to associate .pl files with Perl, it may be necessary to invoke Perl explicitly:

```
C:\> mysql cookbook < inputfile | perl csv.pl > outputfile
```

Perl may be more suitable if you need a cross-platform solution, because it runs under both Unix and Windows. *tr* and *sed* normally are unavailable under Windows.

See Also

An even better way to produce CSV output is to use the Perl *Text::CSV_XS* module, which was designed for that purpose. This module is discussed in Chapter 10, where it's used to construct a more general-purpose file reformatter.

1.23 Producing HTML Output

Problem

You'd like to turn a query result into HTML.

Solution

mysql can do that for you.

Discussion

mysql generates result set output as HTML tables if you use *-H* (or *--html*) option. This gives you a quick way to produce sample output for inclusion into a web page that shows what the result of a query looks like.[*] Here's an example that shows the difference between tabular format and HTML table output (a few line breaks have been added to the HTML output to make it easier to read):

```
% mysql -e "SELECT * FROM limbs WHERE legs=0" cookbook
+------------+------+------+
| thing      | legs | arms |
+------------+------+------+
| squid      |    0 |   10 |
| octopus    |    0 |    8 |
| fish       |    0 |    0 |
| phonograph |    0 |    1 |
+------------+------+------+
```

---

[*] I'm referring to writing static HTML pages here. If you're writing a script that produces web pages on the fly, there are better ways to generate HTML output from a query. For more information on writing web scripts, see Chapter 16.

```
% mysql -H -e "SELECT * FROM limbs WHERE legs=0" cookbook
<TABLE BORDER=1>
<TR><TH>thing</TH><TH>legs</TH><TH>arms</TH></TR>
<TR><TD>squid</TD><TD>0</TD><TD>10</TD></TR>
<TR><TD>octopus</TD><TD>0</TD><TD>8</TD></TR>
<TR><TD>fish</TD><TD>0</TD><TD>0</TD></TR>
<TR><TD>phonograph</TD><TD>0</TD><TD>1</TD></TR>
</TABLE>
```

The first line of the table contains column headings. If you don't want a header row, see Recipe 1.25.

The -H and --html options produce output only for queries that generate a result set. No output is written for queries such as INSERT or UPDATE statements.

-H and --html may be used as of MySQL 3.22.26. (They actually were introduced in an earlier version, but the output was not quite correct.)

1.24 Producing XML Output

Problem

You'd like to turn a query result into XML.

Solution

mysql can do that for you.

Discussion

mysql creates an XML document from the result of a query if you use the -X (or --xml) option. Here's an example that shows the difference between tabular format and the XML created from the same query:

```
% mysql -e "SELECT * FROM limbs WHERE legs=0" cookbook
+------------+------+------+
| thing      | legs | arms |
+------------+------+------+
| squid      |    0 |   10 |
| octopus    |    0 |    8 |
| fish       |    0 |    0 |
| phonograph |    0 |    1 |
+------------+------+------+
% mysql -X -e "SELECT * FROM limbs WHERE legs=0" cookbook
<?xml version="1.0"?>

<resultset statement="SELECT * FROM limbs WHERE legs=0">
  <row>
    <thing>squid</thing>
    <legs>0</legs>
```

```
      <arms>10</arms>
    </row>

    <row>
      <thing>octopus</thing>
      <legs>0</legs>
      <arms>8</arms>
    </row>

    <row>
      <thing>fish</thing>
      <legs>0</legs>
      <arms>0</arms>
    </row>

    <row>
      <thing>phonograph</thing>
      <legs>0</legs>
      <arms>1</arms>
    </row>
  </resultset>
```

-X and *--xml* may be used as of MySQL 4.0. If your version of MySQL is older than that, you can write your own XML generator. See Recipe 10.41.

1.25   Suppressing Column Headings in Query Output

Problem

You don't want to include column headings in query output.

Solution

Turn column headings off with the appropriate command-line option. Normally this is *-N* or *--skip-column-names*, but you can use *-ss* instead.

Discussion

Tab-delimited format is convenient for generating datafiles that you can import into other programs. However, the first row of output for each query lists the column headings by default, which may not always be what you want. Suppose you have a program named *summarize* the produces various descriptive statistics for a column of numbers. If you're producing output from *mysql* to be used with this program, you wouldn't want the header row because it would throw off the results. That is, if you ran a command like this, the output would be inaccurate because *summarize* would count the column heading:

```
% mysql -e "SELECT arms FROM limbs" cookbook | summarize
```

To create output that contains only data values, suppress the column header row with the *-N* (or *--skip-column-names*) option:

```
% mysql -N -e "SELECT arms FROM limbs" cookbook | summarize
```

-N and *--skip-column-names* were introduced in MySQL 3.22.20. For older versions, you can achieve the same effect by specifying the "silent" option (*-s* or *--silent*) twice:

```
% mysql -ss -e "SELECT arms FROM limbs" cookbook | summarize
```

Under Unix, another alternative is to use *tail* to skip the first line:

```
% mysql -e "SELECT arms FROM limbs" cookbook | tail +2 | summarize
```

1.26 Numbering Query Output Lines

Problem

You'd like the lines of a query result nicely numbered.

Solution

Postprocess the output from *mysql*, or use a SQL variable.

Discussion

The *-N* option can be useful in combination with *cat -n* when you want to number the output rows from a query under Unix:

```
% mysql -N -e "SELECT thing, arms FROM limbs" cookbook | cat -n
     1  human      2
     2  insect     0
     3  squid      10
     4  octopus    8
     5  fish       0
     6  centipede         0
     7  table             0
     8  armchair          2
     9  phonograph        1
    10  tripod  0
    11  Peg Leg Pete      2
    12  NULL
```

Another option is to use a SQL variable. Expressions involving variables are evaluated for each row of a query result, a property that you can use to provide a column of row numbers in the output:

```
mysql> SET @n = 0;
mysql> SELECT @n := @n+1 AS rownum, thing, arms, legs FROM limbs;
+--------+---------------+------+------+
| rownum | thing         | arms | legs |
+--------+---------------+------+------+
|      1 | human         |    2 |    2 |
```

```
|     2 | insect       |    0 |    6 |
|     3 | squid        |   10 |    0 |
|     4 | octopus      |    8 |    0 |
|     5 | fish         |    0 |    0 |
|     6 | centipede    |    0 |  100 |
|     7 | table        |    0 |    4 |
|     8 | armchair     |    2 |    4 |
|     9 | phonograph   |    1 |    0 |
|    10 | tripod       |    0 |    3 |
|    11 | Peg Leg Pete |    2 |    1 |
|    12 | space alien  | NULL | NULL |
+-------+--------------+------+------+
```

1.27 Making Long Output Lines More Readable

Problem

The output lines from a query are too long. They wrap around and make a mess of your screen.

Solution

Use vertical output format.

Discussion

Some queries generate output lines that are so long they take up more than one line on your terminal, which can make query results difficult to read. Here is an example that shows what excessively long query output lines might look like on your screen:[*]

```
mysql> SHOW FULL COLUMNS FROM limbs;
+-------+-------------+------+-----+---------+-------+------------------------
--------+
| Field | Type        | Null | Key | Default | Extra | Privileges
       |
+-------+-------------+------+-----+---------+-------+------------------------
--------+
| thing | varchar(20) | YES  |     | NULL    |       | select,insert,update,ref
erences |
| legs  | int(11)     | YES  |     | NULL    |       | select,insert,update,ref
erences |
| arms  | int(11)     | YES  |     | NULL    |       | select,insert,update,ref
erences |
+-------+-------------+------+-----+---------+-------+------------------------
--------+
```

An alternative is to generate "vertical" output with each column value on a separate line. This is done by terminating a query with \G rather than with a ; character or

---

[*] Prior to MySQL 3.23.32, omit the FULL keyword from the SHOW COLUMNS statement.

with \g. Here's what the result from the preceding query looks like when displayed using vertical format:

```
mysql> SHOW FULL COLUMNS FROM limbs\G
*************************** 1. row ***************************
    Field: thing
     Type: varchar(20)
     Null: YES
      Key:
  Default: NULL
    Extra:
Privileges: select,insert,update,references
*************************** 2. row ***************************
    Field: legs
     Type: int(11)
     Null: YES
      Key:
  Default: NULL
    Extra:
Privileges: select,insert,update,references
*************************** 3. row ***************************
    Field: arms
     Type: int(11)
     Null: YES
      Key:
  Default: NULL
    Extra:
Privileges: select,insert,update,references
```

To specify vertical output from the command line, use the -E (or --vertical) option when you invoke mysql. This affects all queries issued during the session, something that can be useful when using mysql to execute a script. (If you write the statements in the SQL script file using the usual semicolon terminator, you can select normal or vertical output from the command line by selective use of -E.)

1.28 Controlling mysql's Verbosity Level

Problem

You want mysql to produce more output. Or less.

Solution

Use the -v or -s options for more or less verbosity.

Discussion

When you run mysql non-interactively, not only does the default output format change, it becomes more terse. For example, mysql doesn't print row counts or indicate how long queries took to execute. To tell *mysql* to be more verbose, use -*v* or --*verbose*. These options can be specified multiple times for increasing verbosity. Try the following commands to see how the output differs:

```
% echo "SELECT NOW()" | mysql
% echo "SELECT NOW()" | mysql -v
% echo "SELECT NOW()" | mysql -vv
% echo "SELECT NOW()" | mysql -vvv
```

The counterparts of -*v* and --*verbose* are -*s* and --*silent*. These options too may be used multiple times for increased effect.

1.29 Logging Interactive mysql Sessions

Problem

You want to keep a record of what you did in a *mysql* session.

Solution

Create a tee file.

Discussion

If you maintain a log of an interactive MySQL session, you can refer back to it later to see what you did and how. Under Unix, you can use the *script* program to save a log of a terminal session. This works for arbitrary commands, so it works for interactive *mysql* sessions, too. However, *script* also adds a carriage return to every line of the transcript, and it includes any backspacing and corrections you make as you're typing. A method of logging an interactive *mysql* session that doesn't add extra messy junk to the log file (and that works under both Unix and Windows) is to start *mysql* with a --*tee* option that specifies the name of the file in which to record the session:*

```
% mysql --tee=tmp.out cookbook
```

To control session logging from within *mysql*, use \T and \t to turn tee output on and off. This is useful if you want to record only parts of a session:

```
mysql> \T tmp.out
Logging to file 'tmp.out'
mysql> \t
Outfile disabled.
```

A tee file contains the queries you enter as well as the output from those queries, so it's a convenient way to keep a complete record of them. It's useful, for example, when you want to print or mail a session or parts of it, or for capturing query output

---

* It's called a "tee" because it's similar to the Unix *tee* utility. For more background, try this command:

```
% man tee
```

to include as an example in a document. It's also a good way to try out queries to make sure you have the syntax correct before putting them in a script file; you can create the script from the tee file later by editing it to remove everything except those queries you want to keep.

mysql appends session output to the end of the tee file rather than overwriting it. If you want an existing file to contain only the contents of a single session, remove it first before invoking *mysql*.

The ability to create tee files was introduced in MySQL 3.23.28.

1.30 Creating mysql Scripts from Previously Executed Queries

Problem

You want to reuse queries that were issued during an earlier *mysql* session.

Solution

Use a tee file from the earlier session, or look in *mysql*'s statement history file.

Discussion

One way to create a batch file is to enter your queries into the file from scratch with a text editor and hope that you don't make any mistakes while typing them. But it's often easier to use queries that you've already verified as correct. How? First, try out the queries "by hand" using *mysql* in interactive mode to make sure they work properly. Then, extract the queries from a record of your session to create the batch file. Two sources of information are particularly useful for creating SQL scripts:

- You can record all or parts of a *mysql* session by using the --*tee* command-line option or the \T command from within *mysql*. (See Recipe 1.29 for more information.)

- Under Unix, a second option is to use your history file. *mysql* maintains a record of your queries, which it stores in the file .*mysql_history* in your home directory.

A tee file session log has more context because it contains both query input and output, not just the text of the queries. This additional information can make it easier to locate the parts of the session you want. (Of course, you must also remove the extra stuff to create a batch file from the tee file.) Conversely, the history file is more concise. It contains only of the queries you issue, so there are fewer extraneous lines to delete to obtain the queries you want. Choose whichever source of information best suits your needs.

1.31   Using mysql as a Calculator

Problem

You need a quick way to evaluate an expression.

Solution

Use *mysql* as a calculator. MySQL doesn't require every SELECT statement to refer to a table, so you can select the results of arbitrary expressions.

Discussion

SELECT statements typically refer to some table or tables from which you're retrieving rows. However, in MySQL, SELECT need not reference any table at all, which means that you can use the *mysql* program as a calculator for evaluating an expression:

```
mysql> SELECT (17 + 23) / SQRT(64);
+----------------------+
| (17 + 23) / SQRT(64) |
+----------------------+
|           5.00000000 |
+----------------------+
```

This is also useful for checking how a comparison works. For example, to determine whether or not string comparisons are case sensitive, try the following query:

```
mysql> SELECT 'ABC' = 'abc';
+---------------+
| 'ABC' = 'abc' |
+---------------+
|             1 |
+---------------+
```

The result of this comparison is 1 (meaning "true"; in general, nonzero values are true). This tells you that string comparisons are not case sensitive by default. Expressions that evaluate to false return zero:

```
mysql> SELECT 'ABC' = 'abcd';
+----------------+
| 'ABC' = 'abcd' |
+----------------+
|              0 |
+----------------+
```

If the value of an expression cannot be determined, the result is NULL:

```
mysql> SELECT 1/0;
+------+
| 1/0  |
+------+
| NULL |
+------+
```

SQL variables may be used to store the results of intermediate calculations. The following statements use variables this way to compute the total cost of a hotel bill:

```
mysql> SET @daily_room_charge = 100.00;
mysql> SET @num_of_nights = 3;
mysql> SET @tax_percent = 8;
mysql> SET @total_room_charge = @daily_room_charge * @num_of_nights;
mysql> SET @tax = (@total_room_charge * @tax_percent) / 100;
mysql> SET @total = @total_room_charge + @tax;
mysql> SELECT @total;
+--------+
| @total |
+--------+
|    324 |
+--------+
```

1.32   Using mysql in Shell Scripts

Problem

You want to invoke *mysql* from within a shell script rather than using it interactively.

Solution

There's no rule against that. Just be sure to supply the appropriate arguments to the command.

Discussion

If you need to process query results within a program, you'll typically use a MySQL programming interface designed specifically for the language you're using (for example, in a Perl script you'd use the DBI interface). But for simple, short, or quick-and-dirty tasks, it may be easier just to invoke *mysql* directly from within a shell script, possibly postprocessing the results with other commands. For example, an easy way to write a MySQL server status tester is to use a shell script that invokes *mysql*, as is demonstrated later in this section. Shell scripts are also useful for prototyping programs that you intend to convert for use with a standard API later.

For Unix shell scripting, I recommend that you stick to shells in the Bourne shell family, such as *sh*, *bash*, or *ksh*. (The *csh* and *tcsh* shells are more suited to interactive use than to scripting.) This section provides some examples showing how to write Unix scripts for */bin/sh*. It also comments briefly on DOS scripting. The sidebar "Using Executable Programs" describes how to make scripts executable and run them.

Using Executable Programs

When you write a program, you'll generally need to make it executable before you can run it. In Unix, you do this by setting the "execute" file access modes using the *chmod* command:

```
% chmod +x myprog
```

To run the program, name it on the command line:

```
% myprog
```

However, if the program is in your current directory, your shell might not find it. The shell searches for programs in the directories named in your PATH environment variable, but for security reasons, the search path for Unix shells often is deliberately set not to include the current directory (.). In that case, you need to include a leading path of ./ to explicitly indicate the program's location:

```
% ./myprog
```

Some of the programs developed in this book are intended only to demonstrate a particular concept and probably never will be run outside your current directory, so examples that use them generally show how to invoke them using the leading ./ path. For programs that are intended for repeated use, it's more likely that you'll install them in a directory named in your PATH setting. In that case, no leading path will be necessary to invoke them. This also holds for common Unix utilities (such as *chmod*), which are installed in standard system directories.

Under Windows, programs are interpreted as executable based on their filename extensions (such as *.exe* or *.bat*), so *chmod* is unnecessary. Also, the command interpreter includes the current directory in its search path by default, so you should be able to invoke programs that are located there without specifying any leading path. (Thus, if you're using Windows and you want to run an example command that is shown in this book using ./, you should omit the ./ from the command.)

Writing Shell Scripts Under Unix

Here is a shell script that reports the current uptime of the MySQL server. It runs a SHOW STATUS query to get the value of the Uptime status variable that contains the server uptime in seconds:

```
#! /bin/sh
# mysql_uptime.sh - report server uptime in seconds

mysql -B -N -e "SHOW STATUS LIKE 'Uptime'"
```

The first line of the script that begins with #! is special. It indicates the pathname of the program that should be invoked to execute the rest of the script, */bin/sh* in this case. To use the script, create a file named *mysql_uptime.sh* that contains the preceding lines and make it executable with *chmod +x*. The *mysql_uptime.sh* script runs *mysql* using *-e* to indicate the query string, *-B* to generate batch (tab-delimited) output, and *-N* to suppress the column header line. The resulting output looks like this:

```
% ./mysql_uptime.sh
Uptime  1260142
```

The command shown here begins with *./*, indicating that the script is located in your current directory. If you move the script to a directory named in your PATH setting, you can invoke it from anywhere, but then you should omit the *./* from the command. Note that moving the script make cause *csh* or *tcsh* not to know where the script is located until your next login. To remedy this without logging in again, use *rehash* after moving the script. The following example illustrates this process:

```
% ./mysql_uptime.sh
Uptime  1260348
% mv mysql_uptime.sh /usr/local/bin
% mysql_uptime.sh
mysql_uptime.sh: Command not found.
% rehash
% mysql_uptime.sh
Uptime  1260397
```

If you prefer a report that lists the time in days, hours, minutes, and seconds rather than just seconds, you can use the output from the *mysql* STATUS statement, which provides the following information:

```
mysql> STATUS;
Connection id:          12347
Current database:       cookbook
Current user:           cbuser@localhost
Current pager:          stdout
Using outfile:          ''
Server version:         3.23.47-log
Protocol version:       10
Connection:             Localhost via UNIX socket
Client characterset:    latin1
Server characterset:    latin1
UNIX socket:            /tmp/mysql.sock
Uptime:                 14 days 14 hours 2 min 46 sec
```

For uptime reporting, the only relevant part of that information is the line that begins with Uptime. It's a simple matter to write a script that sends a STATUS command to the server and filters the output with *grep* to extract the desired line:

```
#! /bin/sh
# mysql_uptime2.sh - report server uptime

mysql -e STATUS | grep "^Uptime"
```

The result looks like this:

```
% ./mysql_uptime2.sh
Uptime:                 14 days 14 hours 2 min 46 sec
```

The preceding two scripts specify the statement to be executed by means of the *-e* command-line option, but you can use other *mysql* input sources described earlier in the chapter, such as files and pipes. For example, the following *mysql_uptime3.sh* script is like *mysql_uptime2.sh* but provides input to *mysql* using a pipe:

```
#! /bin/sh
# mysql_uptime3.sh - report server uptime

echo STATUS | mysql | grep "^Uptime"
```

Some shells support the concept of a "here-document," which serves essentially the same purpose as file input to a command, except that no explicit filename is involved. (In other words, the document is located "right here" in the script, not stored in an external file.) To provide input to a command using a here-document, use the following syntax:

```
command <<MARKER
input line 1
input line 2
input line 3
...
MARKER
```

<<*MARKER* signals the beginning of the input and indicates the marker symbol to look for at the end of the input. The symbol that you use for *MARKER* is relatively arbitrary, but should be some distinctive identifier that does not occur in the input given to the command.

Here-documents are a useful alternative to the *-e* option when you need to specify lengthy query input. In such cases, when *-e* becomes awkward to use, a here-document is more convenient and easier to write. Suppose you have a log table `log_tbl` that contains a column `date_added` to indicate when each row was added. A query to report the number of records that were added yesterday looks like this:

```
SELECT COUNT(*) As 'New log entries:'
FROM log_tbl
WHERE date_added = DATE_SUB(CURDATE(),INTERVAL 1 DAY);
```

That query could be specified in a script using *-e*, but the command line would be difficult to read because the query is so long. A here-document is a more suitable choice in this case because you can write the query in more readable form:

```
#! /bin/sh
# new_log_entries.sh - count yesterday's log entries

mysql cookbook <<MYSQL_INPUT
SELECT COUNT(*) As 'New log entries:'
FROM log_tbl
WHERE date_added = DATE_SUB(CURDATE(),INTERVAL 1 DAY);
MYSQL_INPUT
```

When you use *-e* or here-documents, you can refer to shell variables within the query input—although the following example demonstrates that it might be best to avoid the practice. Suppose you have a simple script *count_rows.sh* for counting the rows of any table in the cookbook database:

```
#! /bin/sh
# count_rows.sh - count rows in cookbook database table

# require one argument on the command line·
if [ $# -ne 1 ]; then
    echo "Usage: count_rows.sh tbl_name";
    exit 1;
fi

# use argument ($1) in the query string
mysql cookbook <<MYSQL_INPUT
SELECT COUNT(*) AS 'Rows in table:' FROM $1;
MYSQL_INPUT
```

The script uses the $# shell variable, which holds the command-line argument count, and $1, which holds the first argument after the script name. *count_rows.sh* makes sure that exactly one argument was provided, then uses it as a table name in a row-counting query. To run the script, invoke it with a table name argument:

```
% ./count_rows.sh limbs
Rows in table:
12
```

Variable substitution can be helpful for constructing queries, but you should use this capability with caution. A malicious user could invoke the script as follows:

```
% ./count_rows.sh "limbs;DROP TABLE limbs"
```

In that case, the resulting query input to *mysql* becomes:

```
SELECT COUNT(*) AS 'Rows in table:' FROM limbs;DROP TABLE limbs;
```

This input counts the table rows, then destroys the table! For this reason, it may be prudent to limit use of variable substitution to your own private scripts. Alternatively, rewrite the script using an API that allows special characters such as ; to be dealt with and rendered harmless (see Recipe 2.7).

Writing Shell Scripts Under Windows

Under Windows, you can run *mysql* from within a batch file (a file with a *.bat* extension). Here is a Windows batch file, *mysql_uptime.bat*, that is similar to the *mysql_uptime.sh* Unix shell script shown earlier:

```
@ECHO OFF
REM mysql_uptime.bat - report server uptime in seconds

mysql -B -N -e "SHOW STATUS LIKE 'Uptime'"
```

Batch files may be invoked without the *.bat* extension:

```
C:\> mysql_uptime
Uptime  9609
```

DOS scripting has some serious limitations, however. For example, here-documents are not supported, and command argument quoting capabilities are more limited. One way around these problems is to install a more reasonable working environment; see the sidebar "Finding the DOS Prompt Restrictive?"

Finding the DOS Prompt Restrictive?

If you're a Unix user who is comfortable with the shells and utilities that are part of the Unix command-line interface, you probably take for granted some of the commands used in this chapter, such as *grep*, *sed*, *tr*, and *tail*. These tools are so commonly available on Unix systems that it can be a rude and painful shock to realize that they are nowhere to be found if at some point you find it necessary to work at the DOS prompt under Windows.

One way to make the DOS command-line environment more palatable is to install Cygnus tools for Windows (Cygwin) or Unix for Windows (UWIN). These packages include some of the more popular Unix shells as well as many of the utilities that Unix users have come to expect. Programming tools such as compilers are available with each package as well. The package distributions may be obtained at the following locations:

http://www.cygwin.com/
http://www.research.att.com/sw/tools/uwin/

These distributions can change the way you use this book under Windows, because they eliminate some of the exceptions where I qualify commands as available under Unix but not Windows. By installing Cygwin or UWIN, many of those distinctions become irrelevant.

CHAPTER 2
Writing MySQL-Based Programs

2.0   Introduction

This chapter discusses how to write programs that use MySQL. It covers basic API operations that are fundamental to your understanding of the recipes in later chapters, such as connecting to the MySQL server, issuing queries, and retrieving the results.

MySQL Client Application Programming Interfaces

This book shows how to write MySQL-based programs using Perl, PHP, Python, and Java, and it's possible to use several other languages as well. But one thing all MySQL clients have in common, no matter which language you use, is that they connect to the server using some kind of application programming interface (API) that implements a communications protocol. This is true regardless of the program's purpose, whether it's a command-line utility, a job that runs automatically on a predetermined schedule, or a script that's used from a web server to make database content available over the Web. MySQL APIs provide a standard way for you, the application developer, to express database operations. Each API translates your instructions into something the MySQL server can understand.

The server itself speaks a low-level protocol that I call the raw protocol. This is the level at which direct communication takes place over the network between the server and its clients. A client establishes a connection to the port on which the server is listening and communicates with it by speaking the client-server protocol in its most basic terms. (Basically, the client fills in data structures and shoves them over the network.) It's not productive to attempt to communicate directly with the server at this level (see the sidebar "Want to Telnet to the MySQL Server?"), nor to write programs that do so. The raw protocol is a binary communication stream that is efficient, but not particularly easy to use, a fact that usually deters developers from attempting to write programs that talk to the server this way. More convenient access to the MySQL server is provided through a programming interface that is written at a level above that of the raw protocol level. The interface handles the details of the raw protocol on behalf of your programs. It provides calls for operations such as connecting to the server, sending queries, retrieving the results of queries, and obtaining query status information.

Java drivers implement this low-level protocol directly. They plug into the Java Database Connectivity (JDBC) interface, so you write your programs using standard JDBC calls. JDBC passes your requests for database operations to the MySQL driver, which maps them into operations that communicate with the MySQL server using the raw protocol.

The MySQL drivers for Perl, PHP, and Python adopt a different approach. They do not implement the raw protocol directly. Instead, they rely on the MySQL client library that is included with MySQL distributions. This client library is written in C and thus provides the basis of an application programming interface for communicating with the server from within C programs. Most of the standard clients in the MySQL distribution are written in C and use this API. You can use it in your own programs, too, and should consider doing so if you want the most efficient programs possible. However, most third-party application development is not done in C. Instead, the C API is most often used indirectly as an embedded library within other languages. This is how MySQL communication is implemented for Perl, PHP, Python, and several other languages. The API for these higher-level languages is written as a "wrapper" around the C routines, which are linked into the language processor.

The benefit of this approach is that it allows a language processor to talk to the MySQL server on your behalf using the C routines while providing to you an interface in which you express database operations more conveniently. For example, scripting languages such as Perl typically make it easy to manipulate text without having to allocate string buffers or dispose of them when you're done with them the way you do in C. Higher-level languages let you concentrate more on what you're trying to do and less on the details that you must think about when you're writing directly in C.

This book doesn't cover the C API in any detail, because we never use it directly; the programs developed in this book use higher-level interfaces that are built on top of the C API. However, if you'd like to try writing MySQL client programs in C, the following sources of information may be helpful:

- The MySQL Reference Manual contains a chapter that provides a reference for the C API functions. You should also have a look at the source for the standard MySQL clients provided with the MySQL source distribution that are written in C. Source distributions and the manual both are available at the MySQL web site, *http://www.mysql.com/*, and you can obtain the manual in printed form from O'Reilly & Associates.

- The book *MySQL* (New Riders) contains reference material for the C API, and also includes a chapter that provides detailed tutorial instructions for writing MySQL programs in C. In fact, you needn't even buy the book to get this particular chapter; it's available in PDF form at *http://www.kitebird.com/mysql-book/*.

The source code for the sample programs discussed in the chapter is available from the same site for you to study and use. These programs were deliberately written for instructional purposes, so you may find them easier to understand than the standard clients in the MySQL source distribution.

Want to Telnet to the MySQL Server?

Some networking protocols such as SMTP and POP are ASCII based. This makes it possible to talk directly to a server for those protocols by using Telnet to connect to the port on which the server is listening and typing in commands from the keyboard. Because of this, people sometimes assume that it should also be possible to communicate with the MySQL server the same way: by opening a Telnet connection to it and entering commands. That doesn't work, due to the binary nature of the raw protocol that the server uses. You can verify this for yourself. Suppose the MySQL server is running on the local host and listening on the default port (3306). Connect to it using the following command:

```
% telnet localhost 3306
```

You'll see something that looks like a version number, probably accompanied by a bunch of gibberish characters. What you're seeing is the raw protocol. You can't get very far by communicating with the server in this fashion, which is why the answer to the common question, "How can I Telnet to the MySQL server?" is, "Don't bother." The only thing you can find out this way is whether or not the server is up and listening for connections on the port.

MySQL client APIs provide the following capabilities, each of which is covered in this chapter:

Connecting to the MySQL server; selecting a database; disconnecting from the server. Every program that uses MySQL must first establish a connection to the server, and most programs also will specify which database to use. Some APIs expect the database name to be supplied at connect time (which is why connecting and selecting are covered in the same section). Others provide an explicit call for selecting the database. In addition, well-behaved MySQL programs close the connection to the server when they're done with it.

Checking for errors. Many people write MySQL programs that perform no error checking at all, which makes them difficult to debug when things go wrong. Any database operation can fail and you should know how to find out when that occurs and why. This is necessary so that you can take appropriate action such as terminating the program or informing the user of the problem.

Issuing queries and retrieving results. The whole point of connecting to a database server is to run queries. Each API provides at least one way to issue queries, as well as several functions for processing the results of queries. Because of the many options available to you, this section is easily the most extensive of the chapter.

Using prepared statements and placeholders in queries. One way to write a query that refers to specific data values is to embed the values directly in the query string. Most APIs provide another mechanism that allows you to prepare a query in advance that refers to the data values symbolically. When you execute the statement, you supply the data values separately and the API places them into the query string for you.

Including special characters and NULL values in queries. Some characters such as quotes and backslashes have special meaning in queries, and you must take certain precautions when constructing queries containing them. The same is true for NULL values. If you do not handle these properly, your programs may generate SQL statements that are erroneous or that yield unexpected results. This section discusses how to avoid these problems.

Handling NULL values in result sets. NULL values are special not only when you construct queries, but in results returned from queries. Each API provides a convention for dealing with them.

To write your own programs, it's necessary to know how to perform each of the fundamental database API operations no matter which language you use, so each one is shown in each of our languages (PHP, Perl, Python, and Java). Seeing how each API handles a given operation should help you see the correspondences between APIs more easily and facilitate understanding of recipes shown in the following chapters, even if they're written in a language you don't use very much. (Later chapters usually illustrate recipe implementations using just one or two languages.)

I recognize that it may seem overwhelming to see each recipe in four different languages if you're interested only in one particular API. In that case, I advise you to approach the recipes as follows: read just the introductory part that provides the general background, then go directly to the section for the language in which you're interested. Skip the other languages. Should you develop an interest in writing programs in other languages later, you can always come back and read the other sections then.

This chapter also discusses the following topics, which are not directly part of MySQL APIs but can help you use them more easily:

Writing library files. As you write program after program, you may find that there are certain operations you carry out repeatedly. Library files provide a way to encapsulate the code for these operations so that you can perform them from multiple scripts without including all the code in each script. This reduces code duplication and makes your programs more portable. This section shows how to write a library file for each API that includes a function for connecting to the server—one operation that every program that uses MySQL must perform. (Later chapters develop additional library routines for other operations.)

Writing an object-oriented MySQL interface for PHP. The APIs for Perl, Python, and Java each are class-based and provide an object-oriented programming model based on a database-independent architecture. PHP's built-in interface is based on MySQL-specific function calls. The section describes how to write a PHP class that can be used to take an object-oriented approach to developing MySQL scripts.

Ways of obtaining connection parameters. The earlier section on establishing connections to the MySQL server relies on connection parameters hardwired into the code. However, there are several other ways to obtain parameters, ranging from storing them in a separate file to allowing the user to specify them at runtime.

To avoid typing in the example programs, you should obtain the recipes source distribution (see Appendix A). Then when an example says something like "create a file named *xyz* that contains the following information..." you can just use the corresponding file from the recipes distribution. The scripts for this chapter are located under the *api* directory, with the exception of the library files, which can be found in the *lib* directory.

The primary table used for examples in this chapter is named profile. It's created in Recipe 2.4, which you should know in case you skip around in the chapter and wonder where it came from. See also the note at the very end of the chapter about resetting the profile table to a known state for use in other chapters.

Assumptions

Several assumptions should be satisfied for the material in this chapter to be used most effectively:

- You should have MySQL support installed for any language processors you plan to use. If you need to install any of the APIs, see Appendix A.

- You should already have set up a MySQL user account for accessing the server and a database to use for trying out queries. As described in Chapter 1, the examples use a MySQL account with a name and password of cbuser and cbpass, and we'll connect to a MySQL server running on the local host to access a database named cookbook. If you need to create the account or the database, see the instructions in that chapter.

- The recipes assume a certain basic understanding of the API languages. If a recipe uses constructs with which you're not familiar, consult a good general text for the language in which you're interested. Appendix C lists some sources that may be helpful.

- Proper execution of some of the programs may require that you set environment variables that control their behavior. See Recipe 1.8 for details about how to do this.

2.1 Connecting to the MySQL Server, Selecting a Database, and Disconnecting

Problem

You need to establish a connection to the server to access a database, and to shut down the connection when you're done.

Solution

Each API provides functions for connecting and disconnecting. The connection routines require that you provide parameters specifying the MySQL user account you want to use. You can also specify a database to use. Some APIs allow this at connection time; others require a separate call after connecting.

Discussion

The programs in this section show how to perform three fundamental operations that are common to the vast majority of MySQL programs:

Establishing a connection to the MySQL server. Every program that uses MySQL does this, no matter which API you use. The details on specifying connection parameters vary between APIs, and some APIs provide more flexibility than others. However, there are many common elements. For example, you must specify the host where the server is running, as well as the name and password for the MySQL account that you're using to access the server.

Selecting a database. Most MySQL programs select a database, either when they connect to the server or immediately thereafter.

Disconnecting from the server. Each API provides a means of shutting down an open connection. It's best to close the connection as soon as you're done with the server so that it can free up any resources that are allocated to servicing the connection. Otherwise, if your program performs additional computations after accessing the server, the connection will be held open longer than necessary. It's also preferable to close the connection explicitly. If a program simply terminates without closing the connection, the MySQL server eventually notices, but shutting down the connection explicitly allows the server to perform an orderly close on its end immediately.

Our example programs for each API in this section show how to connect to the server, select the cookbook database, and disconnect. However, on occasion you might want to write a MySQL program that doesn't select a database. This would be the case if you plan to issue a query that doesn't require a default database, such as SHOW VARIABLES or SHOW DATABASES. Or perhaps you're writing an interactive program that connects to the server and allows the user to specify the database after the connection has been made. To cover such situations, the discussion for each API also indicates how to connect without selecting any database.

The Meaning of localhost in MySQL

One of the parameters you specify when connecting to a MySQL server is the host where the server is running. Most programs treat the hostname *localhost* and the IP address 127.0.0.1 as synonymous. Under Unix, MySQL programs behave differently; by convention, they treat the hostname *localhost* specially and attempt to connect to the server using a Unix domain socket file. To force a TCP/IP connection to the local host, use the IP address 127.0.0.1 rather than the hostname *localhost*. (Under Windows, *localhost* and 127.0.0.1 are treated the same, because Windows doesn't have Unix domain sockets.)

The default port is 3306 for TCP/IP connections. The pathname for the Unix domain socket varies, although it's often */tmp/mysql.sock*. The recipes indicate how to specify the socket file pathname or TCP/IP port number explicitly if you don't want to use the default.

Perl

To write MySQL scripts in Perl, you should have the DBI module installed, as well as the MySQL-specific DBI driver module, *DBD::mysql*. Appendix A contains information on getting these if they're not already installed. There is an older interface for Perl named MysqlPerl, but it's obsolete and is not covered here.

Here is a simple Perl script that connects to the cookbook database, then disconnects:

```
#! /usr/bin/perl -w
# connect.pl - connect to the MySQL server

use strict;
use DBI;
my $dsn = "DBI:mysql:host=localhost;database=cookbook";
my $dbh = DBI->connect ($dsn, "cbuser", "cbpass")
                or die "Cannot connect to server\n";
print "Connected\n";
$dbh->disconnect ();
print "Disconnected\n";
exit (0);
```

To try the script, create a file named *connect.pl* that contains the preceding code. To run *connect.pl* under Unix, you may need to change the pathname on the first line if your Perl program is located somewhere other than */usr/bin/perl*. Then make the script executable with *chmod +x*, and invoke it as follows:

```
% chmod +x connect.pl
% ./connect.pl
```

```
Connected
Disconnected
```

Under Windows, *chmod* will not be necessary; you run *connect.pl* like this:

```
C:\> perl connect.pl
Connected
Disconnected
```

If you have a filename association set up that allows *.pl* files to be executed directly from the command line, you need not invoke Perl explicitly:

```
C:\> connect.pl
Connected
Disconnected
```

For more information on running programs that you've written yourself, see the sidebar "Using Executable Programs" in Recipe 1.32.

The *-w* option turns on warning mode so that Perl produces warnings for any questionable constructs. Our example script has no such constructs, but it's a good idea to get in the habit of using *-w*; as you modify your scripts during the development process, you'll often find that Perl has useful comments to make about them.

The use strict line turns on strict variable checking and causes Perl to complain about any variables that are used without having been declared first. This is a sensible precaution because it helps find errors that might otherwise go undetected. The use DBI statement tells Perl that the program needs to use the DBI module. It's unnecessary to load the MySQL driver module (*DBD::mysql*) explicitly, because DBI will do that itself when the script connects to the database server.

The next two lines establish the connection to MySQL by setting up a data source name (DSN) and calling the DBI connect() method. The arguments to connect() are the DSN, the MySQL username, the password, and any connection attributes you want to specify. The DSN is required. The other arguments are optional, although usually it's necessary to supply a name and password to get very far.

The DSN specifies which database driver to use and other options indicating where to connect. For MySQL programs, the DSN has the format DBI:mysql:*options*. The three components of which have the following meanings:

- The first component is always DBI. It's not case sensitive; dbi or Dbi would do just as well.
- The second component tells DBI which database driver to use. For MySQL, the name must be mysql and it *is* case sensitive. You can't use MySQL, MYSQL, or any other variation.
- The third component, if present, is a semicolon-separated list of *name=value* pairs specifying additional connection options. The order of any options you provide doesn't matter. For our purposes here, the two most relevant options are host and database. They specify the hostname where the MySQL server is running

and the database you want to use. Note that the second colon in the DSN is *not* optional, even if you don't specify any options.

Given this information, the DSN for connecting to the cookbook database on the local host *localhost* looks like this:

```
DBI:mysql:host=localhost;database=cookbook
```

If you leave out the host option, its default value is localhost. Thus, these two DSNs are equivalent:

```
DBI:mysql:host=localhost;database=cookbook
DBI:mysql:database=cookbook
```

If you omit the database option, no database is selected when you connect.

The second and third arguments of the connect() call are your MySQL username and password. You can also provide a fourth argument following the password to specify attributes that control DBI's behavior when errors occur. By default, DBI prints error messages when errors occur but does not terminate your script. That's why *connect.pl* checks whether connect() returns undef to indicate failure:

```
my $dbh = DBI->connect ($dsn, "cbuser", "cbpass")
                or die "Cannot connect to server\n";
```

Other error-handling strategies are possible. For example, you can tell DBI to terminate the script automatically when an error occurs in a DBI call by disabling the PrintError attribute and enabling RaiseError instead. Then you don't have to check for errors yourself:

```
my $dbh = DBI->connect ($dsn, $user_name, $password,
                {PrintError => 0, RaiseError => 1});
```

Error handling is discussed further in Recipe 2.2.

Assuming that connect() succeeds, it returns a database handle that contains information about the state of the connection. (In DBI parlance, references to objects are called "handles.") Later we'll see other handles, such as statement handles that are associated with particular queries. DBI scripts in this book conventionally use $dbh and $sth to signify database and statement handles.

Additional connection parameters

For connections to *localhost*, you can provide a mysql_socket option in the DSN to specify the path to the Unix domain socket:

```
my $dsn = "DBI:mysql:host=localhost;mysql_socket=/var/tmp/mysql.sock"
                . ";database=cookbook";
```

The mysql_socket option is available as of MySQL 3.21.15.

For non-*localhost* connections, you can provide a port option to specify the port number:

```
my $dsn = "DBI:mysql:host=mysql.snake.net;port=3307;database=cookbook";
```

PHP

To write PHP scripts that use MySQL, your PHP interpreter must have MySQL support compiled in. If it doesn't, your scripts will terminate with an error message like this:

```
Fatal error: Call to undefined function: mysql_connect()
```

Should that occur, check the instructions included with your PHP distribution to see how to enable MySQL support.

PHP scripts usually are written for use with a web server. I'll assume that if you're going to use PHP that way here, you can simply drop PHP scripts into your server's document tree, request them from your browser, and they will execute. For example, if you run Apache as the web server on the host *http://apache.snake.net/* and you install a PHP script *myscript.php* at the top level of the Apache document tree, you should be able to access the script by requesting this URL:

http://apache.snake.net/myscript.php

This book uses the *.php* extension (suffix) for PHP script filenames. If you use a different extension, such as *.php3* or *.phtml*, you'll need to change the script names or else reconfigure your web server to recognize the *.php* extension. Otherwise, when you request a PHP script from your browser, the literal text of the script will appear in your browser window. You don't want this to happen, particularly if the script contains the username and password you use for connecting to MySQL. (For additional information about configuring Apache for use with PHP, see Recipe 16.2.)

PHP scripts often are written as a mixture of HTML and PHP code, with the PHP code embedded between the special <?php and ?> tags. Here is a simple example:

```
<html>
<head><title>A simple page</title></head>
<body>
<p>
<?php
    print ("I am PHP code, hear me roar!\n");
?>
</p>
</body>
</html>
```

For brevity, when I show PHP examples consisting entirely of code, typically I'll omit the enclosing <?php and ?> tags. Examples that switch between HTML and PHP code include the tags.

To use MySQL in a PHP script, you connect to the MySQL server and select a database in two steps, by calling the mysql_connect() and mysql_select_db() functions. Our first PHP script, *connect.php*, shows how this works:

```
# connect.php - connect to the MySQL server
if (!($conn_id = @mysql_connect ("localhost", "cbuser", "cbpass")))
    die ("Cannot connect to server\n");
```

```
    print ("Connected\n");
    if (!@mysql_select_db ("cookbook", $conn_id))
        die ("Cannot select database\n");
    mysql_close ($conn_id);
    print ("Disconnected\n");
```

mysql_connect( ) takes three arguments: the host where the MySQL server is running, and the name and password of the MySQL account you want to use. If the connection attempt succeeds, mysql_connect( ) returns a connection identifier that can be passed to other MySQL-related functions later. PHP scripts in this book conventionally use $conn_id to signify connection identifiers.

If the connection attempt fails, mysql_connect( ) prints a warning and returns FALSE. (The script prevents any such warning by putting @ (the warning-suppression operator) in front of the function name so it can print its own message instead.)

mysql_select_db( ) takes the database name and an optional connection identifier as arguments. If you omit the second argument, the function assumes it should use the current connection (that is, the one most recently opened). The script just shown calls mysql_select_db( ) immediately after it connects, so the following calls are equivalent:

```
    if (!@mysql_select_db ("cookbook", $conn_id))
        die ("Cannot select database\n");

    if (!@mysql_select_db ("cookbook"))
        die ("Cannot select database\n");
```

If mysql_select_db( ) selects the database successfully, it returns TRUE. Otherwise, it prints a warning and returns FALSE. (Again, as with the mysql_connect( ) call, the script uses the @ operator to suppress the warning.) If you don't want to select any database, just omit the call to mysql_select_db( ).

To try the *connect.php* script, copy it to your web server's document tree and request it from your browser. Alternatively, if you have a standalone version of the PHP interpreter that can be run from the command line, you can try the script without a web server or browser:

```
% php -q connect.php
Connected
Disconnected
```

PHP actually provides two functions for connecting to the MySQL server. The script *connect.php* uses mysql_connect( ), but you can use mysql_pconnect( ) instead if you want to establish a persistent connection that doesn't close when the script terminates. This allows the connection to be reused by subsequent PHP scripts run by the web server, thus avoiding the overhead of setting up a new connection. However, MySQL is so efficient at opening connections that you might not notice much difference between the two functions. Also, you should consider that use of mysql_pconnect( ) sometimes results in too many connections being left open. A symptom of this is that the MySQL server stops accepting new connections because so many persistent connections have been opened by web server processes. Using `mysql_connect()` rather than `mysql_pconnect()` may help to avoid this problem.

Additional connection parameters

For connections to *localhost*, you can specify a pathname for the Unix domain socket by adding *:/path/to/socket* to the hostname in the connect call:

```
$hostname = "localhost:/var/tmp/mysql.sock";
if (!($conn_id = @mysql_connect ($hostname, "cbuser", "cbpass")))
    die ("Cannot connect to server\n");
```

For non-*localhost*, connections, you can specify a port number by adding *:port_num* to the hostname:

```
$hostname = "mysql.snake.net:3307";
if (!($conn_id = @mysql_connect ($hostname, "cbuser", "cbpass")))
    die ("Cannot connect to server\n");
```

The socket pathname option is available as of PHP 3.0.B4. The port number option is available as of PHP 3.0.10.

In PHP 4, you can use the PHP initialization file to specify a default hostname, username, password, socket path, or port number by setting the values of the `mysql.default_host`, `mysql.default_user`, `mysql.default_password`, `mysql.default_socket`, or `mysql.default_port` configuration directives.

Python

To write MySQL programs in Python, you need the MySQLdb module that provides MySQL connectivity for Python's DB-API interface. If you don't have this module, see Appendix A for instructions. DB-API, like Perl's DBI module, provides a relatively database-independent way to access database servers, and supplants earlier Python DBMS-access modules that each had their own interfaces and calling conventions. This book doesn't cover the older, obsolete MySQL Python interface.

Python avoids the use of functions that return a special value to indicate the occurrence of an error. In other words, you typically don't write code like this:

```
if (func1 () == some_bad_value or func2 () == another_bad_value):
    print "An error occurred"
else:
    print "No error occurred"
```

Instead, put the statements you want to execute in a `try` block. Errors cause exceptions to be raised that you can catch with an except block containing the error handling code:

```
try:
    func1 ()
    func2 ()
except:
    print "An error occurred"
```

Exceptions that occur at the top level of a script (that is, outside of any try block) are caught by the default exception handler, which prints a stack trace and exits.

To use the DB-API interface, import the database driver module you want to use (which is MySQLdb for MySQL programs). Then create a database connection object by calling the driver's connect() method. This object provides access to other DB-API methods, such as the close() method that severs the connection to the database server. Here is a short Python program, *connect.py*, that illustrates these operations:

```
#! /usr/bin/python
# connect.py - connect to the MySQL server

import sys
import MySQLdb

try:
    conn = MySQLdb.connect (db = "cookbook",
                            host = "localhost",
                            user = "cbuser",
                            passwd = "cbpass")
    print "Connected"
except:
    print "Cannot connect to server"
    sys.exit (1)

conn.close ()
print "Disconnected"
sys.exit (0)
```

The import lines give the script access to the sys module (needed for the sys.exit() function) and to the MySQLdb module. Then the script attempts to establish a connection to the MySQL server by calling connect() to obtain a connection object, conn. Python scripts in this book conventionally use conn to signify connection objects.

If the connection cannot be established, an exception occurs and the script prints an error message. Otherwise, it closes the connection by using the close() method.

Because the arguments to connect() are named, their order does not matter. If you omit the host argument from the connect() call, its default value is localhost. If you leave out the db argument or pass a db value of "" (the empty string), no database is selected. If you pass a value of None, however, the call will fail.

To try the script, create a file called *connect.py* containing the code just shown. Under Unix, you may need to change the path to Python on the first line of the script if your Python interpreter is located somewhere other than */usr/bin/python*. Then make the script executable with *chmod +x* and run it:

```
% chmod +x connect.py
% ./connect.py
Connected
Disconnected
```

Under Windows, run the script like this:

```
C:\> python connect.py
Connected
Disconnected
```

If you have a filename association set up that allows *.py* files to be executed directly from the command line, you need not invoke Python explicitly:

```
C:\> connect.py
Connected
Disconnected
```

Additional connection parameters

For connections to *localhost*, you can provide a unix_socket parameter to specify the path to the Unix domain socket:

```
conn = MySQLdb.connect (db = "cookbook",
                        host = "localhost",
                        unix_sock = "/var/tmp/mysql.sock",
                        user = "cbuser",
                        passwd = "cbpass")
```

For non-*localhost* connections, you can provide a port parameter to specify the port number:

```
conn = MySQLdb.connect (db = "cookbook",
                        host = "mysql.snake.net",
                        port = 3307,
                        user = "cbuser",
                        passwd = "cbpass")
```

Java

Database programs in Java are written using the JDBC interface, in conjunction with a driver for the particular database engine you wish to access. This makes the JDBC architecture similar to that used by the Perl DBI and Python DB-API modules: a generic interface used in conjunction with database-specific drivers. Java itself is similar to Python in that you don't test specific function calls for return values that indicate an error. Instead, you provide handlers that are called when exceptions are thrown.

Java programming requires a software development kit (SDK). See the sidebar, "Installing a Java SDK" for instructions on installing one if you need it. To write MySQL-based Java programs, you'll also need a MySQL-specific JDBC driver. Several are listed in Appendix A. I use the MySQL Connector/J driver because it is free and is actively maintained; use one of the other drivers if you prefer. (MySQL Connector/J is the successor to MM.MySQL, and if you already have MM.MySQL installed, you can use it instead by making a simple change: whenever you see org.gjt.mm.mysql in Java code, replace it with com.mysql.jdbc.)

The following Java program, *Connect.java*, illustrates how to connect to and disconnect from the MySQL server:

```java
// Connect.java - connect to the MySQL server

import java.sql.*;

public class Connect
{
    public static void main (String[] args)
    {
        Connection conn = null;
        String url = "jdbc:mysql://localhost/cookbook";
        String userName = "cbuser";
        String password = "cbpass";

        try
        {
            Class.forName ("com.mysql.jdbc.Driver").newInstance ();
            conn = DriverManager.getConnection (url, userName, password);
            System.out.println ("Connected");
        }
        catch (Exception e)
        {
            System.err.println ("Cannot connect to server");
        }
        finally
        {
            if (conn != null)
            {
```

```
                try
                {
                    conn.close ();
                    System.out.println ("Disconnected");
                }
                catch (Exception e) { /* ignore close errors */ }
            }
        }
    }
}
```

The `import java.sql.*` statement references the classes and interfaces that provide access to the data types you use to manage different aspects of your interaction with the database server. These are required for all JDBC programs.

Connecting to the server is a two-step process. First, register the database driver with JDBC by calling `Class.forName()`. Then call `DriverManager.getConnection()` to initiate the connection and obtain a `Connection` object that maintains information about the state of the connection. Java programs in this book conventionally use `conn` to signify connection objects.

Use `com.mysql.jdbc.Driver` for the name of the MySQL Connector/J JDBC driver. If you use a different driver, check its documentation and use the name specified there. `DriverManager.getConnection()` takes three arguments: a URL describing where to connect and the database to use, the MySQL username, and the password. The format of the URL string is as follows:

    jdbc:driver://host_name/db_name

This format follows the usual Java convention that the URL for connecting to a network resource begins with a protocol designator. For JDBC programs, the protocol is jdbc, and you'll also need a subprotocol designator that specifies the driver name (mysql, for MySQL programs). Many parts of the connection URL are optional, but the leading protocol and subprotocol designators are not. If you omit *host_name*, the default host value is localhost. If you omit the database name, no database is selected when you connect. However, you should not omit any of the slashes in any case. For example, to connect to the local host without selecting a database name, the URL is:

    jdbc:mysql:///

To try out the program, you should compile it and execute it. The class statement indicates the program's name, which in this case is Connect. The name of the file containing the program should match this name and include a *.java* extension, so the filename for the example program is *Connect.java.** Compile the program using *javac*:

    % javac Connect.java

---

* If you make a copy of *Connect.java* to use as the basis for a new program, you'll need to change the class name in the class statement to match the name of your new file.

If you prefer a different Java compiler, just substitute its name in compilation commands. For example, if you'd rather use Jikes, compile the file like this instead:

```
% jikes Connect.java
```

javac (or *jikes*, or whatever) generates compiled byte code to produce a class file named *Connect.class*. Use the *java* program to run the class file (note that you specify the name of the class file without the *.class* extension):

```
% java Connect
Connected
Disconnected
```

You may need to set your CLASSPATH environment variable before the example program will compile and run. The value of CLASSPATH should include at least your current directory (.) and the path to the MySQL Connector/J JDBC driver. On my system, that driver is located in */usr/local/lib/java/lib/mysql-connector-java-bin.jar*, so for *tcsh* or *csh*, I'd set CLASSPATH like this:

```
setenv CLASSPATH .:/usr/local/lib/java/lib/mysql-connector-java-bin.jar
```

For shells such as *sh*, *bash*, and *ksh*, I'd set it like this:

```
export CLASSPATH=.:/usr/local/lib/java/lib/mysql-connector-java-bin.jar
```

Under Windows, I'd set CLASSPATH as follows if the driver is in the *D:\Java\lib* directory:

```
CLASSPATH=.;D:\Java\lib\mysql-connector-java-bin.jar
```

You may also need to add other class directories or libraries to your CLASSPATH setting; the specifics depend on how your system is set up.

Beware of Class.forName()!

The example program *Connect.java* registers the JDBC driver like this:

```
Class.forName ("com.mysql.jdbc.Driver").newInstance ();
```

You're supposed to be able to register drivers without invoking newInstance(), like so:

```
Class.forName ("com.mysql.jdbc.Driver");
```

However, that call doesn't work for some Java implementations, so be sure not to omit newInstance(), or you may find yourself enacting the Java motto, "write once, debug everywhere."

Some JDBC drivers (MySQL Connector/J among them) allow you to specify the username and password as parameters at the end of the URL. In this case, you omit the second and third arguments of the getConnection() call. Using that URL style, the code that establishes the connection in the example program could have been written like this:

```
// connect using username and password included in URL
Connection conn = null;
```

```
String url = "jdbc:mysql://localhost/cookbook?user=cbuser&password=cbpass";

try
{
    Class.forName ("com.mysql.jdbc.Driver").newInstance ();
    conn = DriverManager.getConnection (url);
    System.out.println ("Connected");
}
```

The character that separates the user and password parameters should be &, not ;.

Additional connection parameters

For non-*localhost* connections, specify an explicit port number by adding *:port_num* to the hostname in the connection URL:

```
String url = "jdbc:mysql://mysql.snake.net:3307/cookbook";
```

For connections to *localhost*, there is no option for specifying the Unix domain socket pathname, at least not for MySQL Connector/J. Other MySQL JDBC drivers may allow for this; check their documentation.

2.2   Checking for Errors

Problem

Something went wrong with your program and you don't know what.

Solution

Everybody has problems getting programs to work correctly. But if you don't antici-pate difficulties by checking for errors, you make the job a lot harder. Add some error-checking code so your programs can help you figure out what went wrong.

Discussion

You now know how to connect to the MySQL server. It's also a good idea to know how to check for errors and how to retrieve MySQL-related error information from the API, so that's what we'll cover next. When errors occur, MySQL provides a numeric error code and a corresponding descriptive text error message. The recipes in this section show how to access this information. You're probably anxious to see how to do more interesting things (such as issue queries and get back the results), but error checking is fundamentally important. Programs sometimes fail, especially during development, and if you don't know how to determine why failures occur, you'll be flying blind.

The example programs in this section show how to check for errors, but will in fact execute without any problems if your MySQL account is set up properly. Thus, you may have to modify the examples slightly to force errors to occur so that the error-handling statements are triggered. For example, you can change a connection-establishment call to supply a bad password. This will give you a feel for how the code acts when errors do occur.

A general debugging aid that is not specific to any API is to check the MySQL query log to see what queries the server actually is receiving. (This requires that you have query logging turned on and that you have access to the log on the MySQL server host.) The log often will show you that a query is malformed in a particular way and give you a clue about why your program is not constructing the proper query string. If you're running a script under a web server and it fails, check the server's error log.

Perl

The DBI module provides two attributes that control what happens when DBI method invocations fail:

- PrintError, if enabled, causes DBI to print an error message using warn( ).
- RaiseError, if enabled, causes DBI to print an error message using die( ); this terminates your script.

By default, PrintError is enabled and RaiseError is disabled, so a script continues executing after printing a message if errors occur. Either or both attributes can be specified in the connect( ) call. Setting an attribute to 1 or 0 enables or disables it, respectively. To specify either or both attributes, pass them in a hash reference as the fourth argument to the connect( ) call. (The syntax is demonstrated shortly.)

The following code uses the default settings for the error-handling attributes. This results in a warning message if the connect( ) call fails, but the script will continue executing:

```
my $dbh = DBI->connect ($dsn, "cbuser", "cbpass");
```

However, because you really can't do much if the connection attempt fails, it's often prudent to exit instead after DBI prints a message:

```
my $dbh = DBI->connect ($dsn, "cbuser", "cbpass") or exit;
```

To print your own error messages, leave RaiseError disabled and disable PrintError as well. Then test the results of DBI method calls yourself. When a method fails, the $DBI::err and $DBI::errstr variables will contain the MySQL numeric error code and descriptive error string, respectively:

```
my $dbh = DBI->connect ($dsn, "cbuser", "cbpass", {PrintError => 0})
            or die "Connection error: $DBI::errstr ($DBI::err)\n";
```

If no error occurs, $DBI::err will be 0 or undef, and $DBI::errstr will be the empty string or undef.

When checking for errors, you should access these variables immediately after invoking the DBI method that sets them. If you invoke another method before using them, their values will be reset.

The default settings (PrintError enabled, RaiseError disabled) are not so useful if you're printing your own messages. In this case, DBI prints a message automatically, then your script prints its own message. This is at best redundant, and at worst confusing to the person using the script.

If you enable RaiseError, you can call DBI methods without checking for return values that indicate errors. If a method fails, DBI prints an error and terminates your script. If the method returns, you can assume it succeeded. This is the easiest approach for script writers: let DBI do all the error checking! However, if PrintError and RaiseError both are enabled, DBI may call warn() and die() in succession, resulting in error messages being printed twice. To avoid this problem, it's best to disable PrintError whenever you enable RaiseError. That's the approach generally used in this book, as illustrated here:

```
my $dbh = DBI->connect ($dsn, "cbuser", "cbpass",
                        {PrintError => 0, RaiseError => 1});
```

If you don't want the all-or-nothing behavior of enabling RaiseError for automatic error checking versus having to do all your own checking, you can adopt a mixed approach. Individual handles have PrintError and RaiseError attributes that can be enabled or disabled selectively. For example, you can enable RaiseError globally by turning it on when you call connect(), then disable it selectively on a per-handle basis. Suppose you have a script that reads the username and password from the command-line arguments, then loops while the user enters queries to be executed. In this case you'd probably want DBI to die and print the error message automatically if the connection fails (there's not much you can do if the user doesn't provide a valid name and password). After connecting, on the other hand, you wouldn't want the script to exit just because the user enters a syntactically invalid query. It would be better for the script to trap the error, print a message, then loop to get the next query. The following code shows how this can be done (the do() method used in the example executes a query and returns undef to indicate an error):

```
my $user_name = shift (@ARGV);
my $password = shift (@ARGV);
my $dbh = DBI->connect ($dsn, $user_name, $password,
                        {PrintError => 0, RaiseError => 1});
$dbh->{RaiseError} = 0; # disable automatic termination on error
print "Enter queries to be executed, one per line; terminate with Control-D\n";
while (<>)              # read and execute queries
{
    $dbh->do ($_) or warn "Query failed: $DBI::errstr ($DBI::err)\en";
}
$dbh->{RaiseError} = 1; # re-enable automatic termination on error
```

If RaiseError is enabled, you can trap errors without terminating your program by executing code within an eval block. If an error occurs within the block, eval fails and returns a message in the $@ variable. Typically, eval is used something like this:

```
eval
{
    # statements that might fail go here...
};
if ($@)
{
    print "An error occurred: $@\n";
}
```

This technique is commonly used, for example, to implement transactions. (See Chapter 15.) Using RaiseError in combination with eval differs from using RaiseError alone in the following ways:

- Errors terminate only the eval block, not the entire script.
- Any error terminates the eval block, whereas RaiseError applies only to DBI-related errors.

When you use eval with RaiseError enabled, be sure to disable PrintError. Otherwise, in some versions of DBI, an error may simply cause warn() to be called without terminating the eval block as you expect.

In addition to using the error-handling attributes PrintError and RaiseError, you can get lots of useful information about your script's execution by turning on DBI's tracing mechanism. Invoke the trace() method with an argument indicating the trace level. Levels 1 to 9 enable tracing with increasingly more verbose output, and level 0 disables tracing:

```
DBI->trace (1);     # enable tracing, minimal output
DBI->trace (3);     # elevate trace level
DBI->trace (0);     # disable tracing
```

Individual database and statement handles have trace() methods, too. That means you can localize tracing to a single handle if you want.

Trace output normally goes to your terminal (or, in the case of a web script, to the web server's error log). You can write trace output to a specific file by providing a second argument indicating a filename:

```
DBI->trace (1, "/tmp/trace.out");
```

If the trace file already exists, trace output is appended to the end; the file's contents are not cleared first. Beware of turning on a file trace while developing a script, then forgetting to disable the trace when you put the script into production. You'll eventually find to your chagrin that the trace file has become quite large. (Or worse, a filesystem will fill up and you'll have no idea why!)

PHP

In PHP, most functions that can succeed or fail indicate what happened by means of their return value. You can check that value and take action accordingly. Some functions also print a warning message when they fail. (`mysql_connect()` and `mysql_select_db()` both do this, for example.) Automatic printing of warnings can be useful sometimes, but if the purpose of your script is to produce a web page (which is likely), you may not want PHP to splatter these messages into the middle of the page. You can suppress such warnings two ways. First, to prevent an individual function call from producing an error message, put the @ warning-suppression operator in front of its name. Then test the return value and deal with errors yourself. That was the approach used for the previous section on connecting to the MySQL server, where *connect.php* printed its own messages:

```
if (!($conn_id = @mysql_connect ("localhost", "cbuser", "cbpass")))
    die ("Cannot connect to server\n");
print ("Connected\n");
if (!@mysql_select_db ("cookbook", $conn_id))
    die ("Cannot select database\n");
```

Second, you can disable these warnings globally by using the `error_reporting()` function to set the PHP error level to zero:

```
error_reporting (0);
```

However, be aware that by turning off warnings this way, you won't get any notification for things that are wrong with your script that you really should know about, such as parse errors caused by malformed syntax.

To obtain specific error information about failed MySQL-related operations, use `mysql_errno()` and `mysql_error()`, which return a numeric error code and descriptive error string. Each function takes an optional connection identifier argument. if you omit the identifier, both functions assume you want error information for the most recently opened connection. However, prior to PHP 4.0.6, both functions require that there *is* a connection. For older versions of PHP, this requirement makes the error functions useless for reporting problems with the connection-establishment routines. (If `mysql_connect()` or `mysql_pconnect()` fail, `mysql_errno()` and `mysql_error()` return 0 and the empty string, just as if no error had occurred.) To work around this, you can use the PHP global variable $php_errormsg instead, as shown in the following example. The code shows how to print error messages, both for failed connection attempts and for errors that occur subsequent to a successful connection. For problems connecting, it attempts to use `mysql_errno()` and `mysql_error()` if they return useful information. Otherwise, it falls back to using $php_errormsg:

```
if (!($conn_id = @mysql_connect ("localhost", "cbuser", "cbpass")))
{
    # If mysql_errno()/mysql_error() work for failed connections, use
    # them (invoke with no argument). Otherwise, use $php_errormsg.
    if (mysql_errno ())
```

```
    {
        die (sprintf ("Cannot connect to server: %s (%d)\n",
                htmlspecialchars (mysql_error ()),
                mysql_errno ()));
    }
    else
    {
        die ("Cannot connect to server: "
                . htmlspecialchars ($php_errormsg) . "\n");
    }
}
print ("Connected\n");
if (!@mysql_select_db ("cookbook", $conn_id))
{
    die (sprintf ("Cannot select database: %s (%d)\n",
            htmlspecialchars (mysql_error ($conn_id)),
            mysql_errno ($conn_id)));
}
```

The htmlspecialchars() function escapes the <, >, and & characters so they display properly in web pages. It's useful here when displaying error messages because we don't know what particular characters a message contains.

Use of $php_errormsg requires the track_errors variable to be enabled in your PHP initialization file. On my system, that file is */usr/local/lib/php.ini*. Locate the file on your system, then make sure the track_errors line looks like this:

```
track_errors = On;
```

If you change the track_errors setting and you're using PHP as an Apache module, you'll need to restart Apache to make the change take effect.

Python

Python programs signal errors by raising exceptions, and handle errors by catching exceptions in an except block. To obtain MySQL-specific error information, name an exception class and provide a variable to receive the information. Here's an example:

```
try:
    conn = MySQLdb.connect (db = "cookbook",
                            host = "localhost",
                            user = "cbuser",
                            passwd = "cbpass")
    print "Connected"
except MySQLdb.Error, e:
    print "Cannot connect to server"
    print "Error code:", e.args[0]
    print "Error message:", e.args[1]
    sys.exit (1)
```

If an exception occurs, the first and second elements of e.args will be set to the numeric error code and descriptive error message, respectively. (Note that the Error class is accessed through the MySQLdb driver module name.)

Java

Java programs handle errors by catching exceptions. If you simply want to do the minimum amount of work, print a stack trace to inform the user where the problem lies:

```
catch (Exception e)
{
    e.printStackTrace ();
}
```

The stack trace shows the location of the problem, but not necessarily what the problem is. It may not be all that meaningful except to you, the program's developer. To be more specific, you can print the error message and code associated with an exception:

- All `Exception` objects support the `getMessage()` method. JDBC methods may throw exceptions using `SQLException` objects; these are like `Exception` objects but also support `getErrorCode()` and `getSQLState()` methods.
- For MySQL errors, `getErrorCode()` and `getMessage()` return the numeric error code and descriptive error string.
- `getSQLState()` returns a string that provides error values defined according to the XOPEN SQL specification (which you may or may not find useful).
- You can also get information about non-fatal warnings, which some methods generate using `SQLWarning` objects. `SQLWarning` is a subclass of `SQLException`, but warnings are accumulated in a list rather than thrown immediately, so they don't interrupt your program and you can print them at your leisure.

The following example program, *Error.java*, demonstrates how to access error messages by printing all the error information it can get its hands on. It attempts to connect to the MySQL server and prints exception information if the attempt fails. Then it issues a query and prints exception and warning information if the query fails:

```java
// Error.java - demonstrate MySQL error-handling

import java.sql.*;

public class Error
{
    public static void main (String[] args)
    {
        Connection conn = null;
        String url = "jdbc:mysql://localhost/cookbook";
        String userName = "cbuser";
        String password = "cbpass";

        try
        {
            Class.forName ("com.mysql.jdbc.Driver").newInstance ();
            conn = DriverManager.getConnection (url, userName, password);
```

```
            System.out.println ("Connected");
            tryQuery (conn);        // issue a query
        }
        catch (Exception e)
        {
            System.err.println ("Cannot connect to server");
            System.err.println (e);
            if (e instanceof SQLException)  // JDBC-specific exception?
            {
                // print general message plus any database-specific message
                // (note how e is cast from Exception to SQLException to
                // access the SQLException-specific methods)
                System.err.println ("SQLException: " + e.getMessage ());
                System.err.println ("SQLState: "
                                    + ((SQLException) e).getSQLState ());
                System.err.println ("VendorCode: "
                                    + ((SQLException) e).getErrorCode ());
            }
        }
        finally
        {
            if (conn != null)
            {
                try
                {
                    conn.close ();
                    System.out.println ("Disconnected");
                }
                catch (SQLException e)
                {
                    // print general message plus any
                    // database-specific message
                    System.err.println ("SQLException: " + e.getMessage ());
                    System.err.println ("SQLState: " + e.getSQLState ());
                    System.err.println ("VendorCode: " + e.getErrorCode ());
                }
            }
        }
    }

    public static void tryQuery (Connection conn)
    {
        Statement s = null;

        try
        {
            // issue a simple query
            s = conn.createStatement ();
            s.execute ("USE cookbook");
            s.close ();

            // print any accumulated warnings
            SQLWarning w = conn.getWarnings ();
            while (w != null)
```

```
        {
            System.err.println ("SQLWarning: " + w.getMessage ());
            System.err.println ("SQLState: " + w.getSQLState ());
            System.err.println ("VendorCode: " + w.getErrorCode ());
            w = w.getNextWarning ();
        }
    }
    catch (SQLException e)
    {
        // print general message plus any database-specific message
        System.err.println ("SQLException: " + e.getMessage ());
        System.err.println ("SQLState: " + e.getSQLState ());
        System.err.println ("VendorCode: " + e.getErrorCode ());
    }
    }
}
```

2.3   Writing Library Files

Problem

You notice that you're writing similar code for common operations in several programs.

Solution

Put functions to perform those operations in a library file. Then you write the code only once.

Discussion

This section describes how to put code for common operations in library files. Encapsulation (or modularization) isn't really a "recipe" so much as a programming technique. Its principal benefit is that you don't have to repeat code in each program you write; instead, you just call a function that's in the library. For example, by putting the code for connecting to the cookbook database into a library function, you need not write out all the parameters associated with making that connection. Simply invoke the function from your program and you're connected.

Connection establishment isn't the only operation you can encapsulate, of course. Later on in the book, other utility functions are developed and placed in library files. All such files, including those shown in this section, can be found under the *lib* directory of the recipes distribution. As you write your own programs, you'll probably identify several operations that you perform often and that are good candidates for inclusion in a library. The techniques demonstrated in this section will help you write your own library files.

Library files have other benefits besides making it easier to write programs. They can help portability. For example, if you write connection parameters into each program that connects to the MySQL server, you have to change each program if you move them to another machine where you use different parameters. If instead you write your programs to connect to the database by calling a library function, you localize the changes that need to be made: it's necessary to modify only the affected library function, not all the programs that use it.

Code encapsulation also can improve security in some ways. If you make a private library file readable only to yourself, only scripts run by you can execute routines in the file. Or suppose you have some scripts located in your web server's document tree. A properly configured server will execute the scripts and send their output to remote clients. But if the server becomes misconfigured somehow, the result can be that your scripts get sent to clients as plain text, thus displaying your MySQL username and password. (And you'll probably realize it too late. Oops.) If the code for establishing a connection to the MySQL server is placed in a library file that's located outside the document tree, those parameters won't be exposed to clients. (Be aware, though, that if you install a library file to be readable by your web server, you don't have much security should you share the web server with other developers. Any of those developers can write a web script to read and display your library file, because by default the script will run with the permissions of the web server and thus will have access to the library.)

The recipes that follow demonstrate how to write, for each API, a library file that contains a routine for connecting to the cookbook database on the MySQL server. The Perl, PHP, and Python routines are written to return the appropriate type of value (a database handle, a connection identifier, or connection object), or to exit with an error message if the connection cannot be established. (The error-checking techniques used by these routines are those discussed in Recipe 2.2.) The Java connection routine demonstrates a different approach. It returns a connection object if it succeeds and otherwise throws an exception that the caller can deal with. To assist in handling such exceptions, the library also includes utility functions that return or print an error message that includes the error information returned by MySQL.

Libraries are of no use by themselves; the way that each one is used is illustrated by a short "test harness" program. You can use any of these harness programs as the basis for creating new programs of your own: Make a copy of the file and add your own code between the connect and disconnect calls.

Library file writing involves not only the question of what to put in the file, but also subsidiary issues such as where to install the file so it can be accessed by your programs and (on multiuser systems such as Unix) how to set its access privileges so its contents aren't exposed to people who shouldn't see it. Writing the library file and setting up your language processor to be able to find it are API-specific issues; they're dealt with in the language-specific sections to follow. By contrast, questions about file ownership and access mode are more general issues about which you'll need to make some decisions no matter which language you use (at least if you're using Unix):

- If a library file is private and contains code to be used only by you, the file can be placed under your own account and made accessible only to you. Assuming a library file *mylib* is already owned by you, you can make it private like this:

  ```
  % chmod 600 mylib
  ```

- If the library file is to be used only by your web server, you can install it in a server library directory and make the file owned by and accessible only to the server user ID. You may need to be root to do this. For example, if the web server runs as wwwusr, these commands make the file private to that user:

  ```
  # chown wwwusr mylib
  # chmod 600 mylib
  ```

- If the library file is public, you can place it in a location that your programming language searches automatically when it looks for libraries. (Most language processors search for libraries in some default set of directories.) You may need to be root to install files in one of these directories. Then you can make the file world readable:

  ```
  # chmod 444 mylib
  ```

The example programs in this section assume that you'll install library files somewhere other than the directories the language processors search by default, as an excuse to demonstrate how to modify each language's search algorithm to look in a directory of your choosing. Many of the programs written in this book execute in a web context, so the library file installation directories used for the examples are the *perl*, *php*, *python*, and *java* directories under */usr/local/apache/lib*. If you want to put the files somewhere else, just adjust the pathnames in the programs appropriately, or else take advantage of the facility that many programming languages provide for specifying where to look for library files by means of an environment or configuration variable. For our API languages, these variables are listed in the following table:

Language	Variable name	Variable type
Perl	PERL5LIB	Environment variable
PHP	include_path	Configuration variable
Python	PYTHONPATH	Environment variable
Java	CLASSPATH	Environment variable

In each case, the variable value is a directory or set of directories. For example, if under Unix I put Perl library files in the */u/paul/lib/perl* directory, I can set the PERL5LIB environment variable for *tcsh* like this in my *.login* file:

```
setenv PERL5LIB /u/paul/lib/perl
```

Under Windows, if I put Perl library files in *D:\lib\perl*, I can set PERL5LIB as follows in *AUTOEXEC.BAT*:

```
SET PERL5LIB=D:\lib\perl
```

In each case, the variable setting tells Perl to look in the specified directory for library files, in addition to whatever other directories it would search by default. The other environment variables (PYTHONPATH and CLASSPATH) are specified using the same syntax. For more information on setting environment variables, see Recipe 1.8.

For PHP, the search path is defined by the value of the include_path variable in the PHP initialization file (typically named *php.ini* or *php3.ini*). On my system, the file's pathname is */usr/local/lib/php.ini*; under Windows, the file is likely to be found in the Windows system directory or under the main PHP installation directory. The value of include_path is defined with a line like this:

```
include_path = "value"
```

The value is specified using the same syntax as for environment variables that name directories. That is, it's a list of directory names, with the names separated by colons under Unix and semicolons under Windows. For example, if you want PHP to look for include files in the current directory and in the *lib/php* directory under the web server root directory */usr/local/apache*, include_path should be set like this under Unix:

```
include_path = ".:/usr/local/apache/lib/php"
```

If you modify the initialization file and PHP is running as an Apache module, you'll need to restart Apache to make the change take effect.

Now let's construct a library for each API. Each section here demonstrates how to write the library file itself, then discusses how to use the library from within programs.

Perl

In Perl, library files are called modules, and typically have an extension of *.pm* ("Perl module"). Here's a sample module file, *Cookbook.pm*, that implements a module named Cookbook. (It's conventional for the basename of a Perl module file to be the same as the identifier on the package line in the file.)

```
package Cookbook;
# Cookbook.pm - library file with utility routine for connecting to MySQL

use strict;
use DBI;

# Establish a connection to the cookbook database, returning a database
# handle.  Dies with a message if the connection cannot be established.

sub connect
{
my $db_name = "cookbook";
my $host_name = "localhost";
```

```
    my $user_name = "cbuser";
    my $password = "cbpass";
    my $dsn = "DBI:mysql:host=$host_name;database=$db_name";

        return (DBI->connect ($dsn, $user_name, $password,
                             { PrintError => 0, RaiseError => 1}));
    }

    1;  # return true
```

The module encapsulates the code for establishing a connection to the MySQL server into a function connect(), and the package identifier establishes a Cookbook namespace for the module, so you invoke the connect() function using the module name:

```
    $dbh = Cookbook::connect ();
```

The final line of the module file is a statement that trivially evaluates to true. This is needed because Perl assumes something is wrong with a module and exits after reading it if the module doesn't return a true value.

Perl locates module files by searching through the directories named in its @INC array. This array contains a default list of directories. To find out what they are on your system, invoke Perl as follows at the command line:

```
    % perl -V
```

The last part of the output from the command shows the directories listed in the @INC array. If you install a module file in one of those directories, your scripts will find it automatically. If you install the module somewhere else, you'll need to tell your scripts where to find it by including a use lib statement. For example, if you install the *Cookbook.pm* module file in */usr/local/apache/lib/perl*, you can write a test harness script *harness.pl* that uses the module as follows:

```
    #! /usr/bin/perl -w
    # harness.pl - test harness for Cookbook.pm library

    use strict;
    use lib qw(/usr/local/apache/lib/perl);
    use Cookbook;

    my $dbh = Cookbook::connect ();
    print "Connected\n";
    $dbh->disconnect ();
    print "Disconnected\n";

    exit (0);
```

Note that *harness.pl* does not have a use DBI statement. It's not necessary, because the Cookbook module itself imports the DBI module, so any script that uses Cookbook also gets DBI.

Another way to specify where Perl should look for module files (in addition to the directories that it searches by default) is to set the PERL5LIB environment variable. If you do that, the advantage is that your scripts won't need the use lib statement. (The corresponding disadvantage is that every user who runs scripts that use the Cookbook module will have to set PERL5LIB.)

PHP

PHP provides an include statement that allows the contents of a file to be read into and included as part of the current script. This provides a natural mechanism for creating libraries: put the library code into an include file, install it in one of the directories in PHP's search path, and include it into scripts that need it. For example, if you create an include file named *Cookbook.php*, any script that needs it can use a statement like this:

```
include "Cookbook.php";
```

The contents of PHP include files are written like regular scripts. We can write such a file, *Cookbook.php*, to contain a function, cookbook_connect( ), as follows:

```
<?php
# Cookbook.php - library file with utility routine for connecting to MySQL

# Establish a connection to the cookbook database, returning a connection
# identifier.  Dies with a message if the connection cannot be established.

function cookbook_connect ()
{
    $db_name = "cookbook";
    $host_name = "localhost";
    $user_name = "cbuser";
    $password = "cbpass";

    $conn_id = @mysql_connect ($host_name, $user_name, $password);
    if (!$conn_id)
    {
        # If mysql_errno()/mysql_error() work for failed connections, use
        # them (invoke with no argument). Otherwise, use $php_errormsg.
        if (mysql_errno ())
        {
            die (sprintf ("Cannot connect to server: %s (%d)\n",
                    htmlspecialchars (mysql_error ()),
                    mysql_errno ()));
        }
        else
        {
            die ("Cannot connect to server: "
                    . htmlspecialchars ($php_errormsg) . "\n");
        }
    }
    if (!@mysql_select_db ($db_name))
```

```
    {
        die (sprintf ("Cannot select database: %s (%d)\n",
                htmlspecialchars (mysql_error ($conn_id)),
                mysql_errno ($conn_id)));
    }
    return ($conn_id);
}

?>
```

Although most PHP examples throughout this book don't show the <?php and ?> tags, I've shown them as part of *Cookbook.php* here to emphasize that include files must enclose all PHP code within those tags. The PHP interpreter doesn't make any assumptions about the contents of an include file when it begins parsing it, because you might include a file that contains nothing but HTML. Therefore, you must use <?php and ?> to specify explicitly which parts of the include file should be considered as PHP code rather than as HTML, just as you do in the main script.

Assuming that *Cookbook.php* is installed in a directory that's named in PHP's search path (as defined by the include_path variable in the PHP initialization file), it can be used from a test harness script, *harness.php*. The entire script looks like this:

```
<?php
# harness.php - test harness for Cookbook.php library

include "Cookbook.php";
$conn_id = cookbook_connect ();
print ("Connected\n");
mysql_close ($conn_id);
print ("Disconnected\n");

?>
```

If you don't have permission to modify the PHP initialization file, you can access an include file by specifying its full pathname. For example:

```
include "/usr/local/apache/lib/php/Cookbook.php";
```

PHP also provides a require statement that is like include except that PHP reads the file even if the require occurs inside a control structure that never executes (such as an if block for which the condition is never true). PHP 4 adds include_once and require_once statements. These are like include and require except that if the file has already been read, its contents are not processed again. This is useful for avoiding multiple-declaration problems that can easily occur in situations where library files include other library files.

A way to simulate single-inclusion behavior under PHP 3 is to associate a unique symbol with a library and process its contents only if the symbol is not already defined. For example, a library file, *MyLibrary.php*, might be structured like this:

```
<?php
# MyLibrary.php - illustrate how to simulate single-inclusion behavior in PHP 3
```

```
# Check whether or not the symbol associated with the file is defined.
# If not, define the symbol and process the file's contents.  Otherwise,
# the file has already been read; skip the remainder of its contents.

if (!defined ("_MYLIBRARY_PHP_"))
{
    define ("_MYLIBRARY_PHP_", 1);

    # ... put rest of library here ...

}   # end _MYLIBRARY_PHP_

?>
```

Where Should PHP Include Files Be Installed?

PHP scripts often are placed in the document tree of your web server, and clients can request them directly. For PHP library files, I recommend that you place them somewhere outside the document tree, especially if (like *Cookbook.php*) they contain names and passwords. This is particularly true if you use a different extension such as *.inc* for the names of include files. If you do that and install include files in the document tree, they might be requested directly by clients and will be displayed as plain text, exposing their contents. To prevent that from happening, reconfigure Apache so that it treats files with the *.inc* extension as PHP code to be processed by the PHP interpreter rather than being displayed literally.

Python

Python libraries are written as modules and referenced from scripts using `import` or `from` statements. To put the code for connecting to MySQL into a function, we can write a module file *Cookbook.py*:

```python
# Cookbook.py - library file with utility routine for connecting to MySQL

import sys
import MySQLdb

# Establish a connection to the cookbook database, returning a connection
# object.  Dies with a message if the connection cannot be established.

def connect ():
    host_name = "localhost"
    db_name = "cookbook"
    user_name = "cbuser"
    password = "cbpass"

    try:
        conn = MySQLdb.connect (db = db_name,
```

```
                        host = host_name,
                        user = user_name,
                        passwd = password)
        return conn
    except MySQLdb.Error, e:
        print "Cannot connect to server"
        print "Error code:", e.args[0]
        print "Error message:", e.args[1]
        sys.exit (1)
```

The filename basename determines the module name, so the module is called Cookbook. Module methods are accessed through the module name, thus you would invoke the connect() method of the Cookbook module like this:

```
conn = Cookbook.connect ();
```

The Python interpreter searches for modules in directories named in the sys.path variable. Just as with Perl's @INC array, sys.path is initialized to a default set of directories. You can find out what those directories are on your system by running Python interactively and entering a couple of commands:

```
% python
>>> import sys
>>> sys.path
```

If you put *Cookbook.py* in one of the default directories, you can reference it from a script using an import statement and Python will find it automatically:

```
import Cookbook
```

If you install *Cookbook.py* somewhere else, you can add the directory where it's installed to the value of sys.path. Do this by importing the sys module and invoking sys.path.insert(). The following test harness script, *harness.py*, shows how to do this, assuming the Cookbook module is installed in the */usr/local/apache/lib/python* directory:

```
#! /usr/bin/python
# harness.py - test harness for Cookbook.py library

# Import sys module and add directory to search path
import sys
sys.path.insert (0, "/usr/local/apache/lib/python")
import MySQLdb
import Cookbook

conn = Cookbook.connect ()
print "Connected"
conn.close ()
print "Disconnected"
sys.exit (0)
```

Another way to tell Python where to find module files is to set the PYTHONPATH environment variable. If you set that variable to include your module directory, scripts that you run need not modify sys.path.

It's also possible to import individual symbols from a module using a `from` statement:

```
from Cookbook import connect
```

This makes the `connect()` routine available to the script without the need for the module name, so you'd use it like this:

```
conn = connect ()
```

Java

Java library files are similar to Java programs in most ways:

- The `class` line in the source file indicates a class name.
- The file should have the same name as the class (with a *.java* extension).
- You compile the *.java* file to produce a *.class* file.

However, unlike regular program files, Java library files have no `main()` function. In addition, the file should begin with a `package` identifier that specifies the location of the class within the Java namespace. A common convention is to begin package identifiers with the reverse domain of the code author; this helps make identifiers unique and avoid conflict with classes written by other authors.[*] In my case, the domain is *kitebird.com*, so if I want to write a library file and place it under `mcb` within my domain's namespace, the library should begin with a `package` statement like this:

```
package com.kitebird.mcb;
```

Java packages developed for this book will be placed within the `com.kitebird.mcb` namespace to ensure their naming uniqueness.

The following library file, *Cookbook.java*, defines a `Cookbook` class that implements a `connect()` method for connecting to the cookbook database. `connect()` returns a `Connection` object if it succeeds, and throws an exception otherwise. To help the caller deal with failures, the `Cookbook` class also defines `getErrorMessage()` and `printErrorMessage()`, utility routines that return the error message as a string or print it to `System.err`.

```
// Cookbook.java - library file with utility routine for connecting to MySQL

package com.kitebird.mcb;

import java.sql.*;

public class Cookbook
{
    // Establish a connection to the cookbook database, returning
    // a connection object.  Throws an exception if the connection
```

---

[*] Domain names proceed right to left from more general to more specific within the domain namespace, whereas the Java class namespace proceeds left to right from general to specific. Thus, to use a domain as the prefix for a package name within the Java class namespace, it's necessary to reverse it.

```
    // cannot be established.

    public static Connection connect () throws Exception
    {
        String url = "jdbc:mysql://localhost/cookbook";
        String user = "cbuser";
        String password = "cbpass";

        Class.forName ("com.mysql.jdbc.Driver").newInstance ();
        return (DriverManager.getConnection (url, user, password));
    }

    // Return an error message as a string

    public static String getErrorMessage (Exception e)
    {
        StringBuffer s = new StringBuffer ();
        if (e instanceof SQLException)  // JDBC-specific exception?
        {
            // print general message plus any database-specific message
            s.append ("Error message: " + e.getMessage () + "\n");
            s.append ("Error code: "
                        + ((SQLException) e).getErrorCode () + "\n");
        }
        else
        {
            s.append (e + "\n");
        }
        return (s.toString ());
    }

    // Get the error message and print it to System.err

    public static void printErrorMessage (Exception e)
    {
        System.err.println (Cookbook.getErrorMessage (e));
    }
}
```

The routines within the class are declared using the static keyword, which makes them class methods rather than instance methods. That's because the class is used directly rather than by creating an object from it and invoking the methods through the object.

To use the *Cookbook.java* file, compile it to produce *Cookbook.class*, then install the class file in a directory that corresponds to the package identifier. This means that *Cookbook.class* should be installed in a directory named *com/kitebird/mcb* (or *com\ kitebird\mcb* under Windows) that is located under some directory named in your CLASSPATH setting. For example, if CLASSPATH includes */usr/local/apache/lib/java* under Unix, you could install *Cookbook.class* in the */usr/local/apache/lib/java/com/kitebird/ mcb* directory. (See Recipe 2.1 for more information about the CLASSPATH variable.)

To use the Cookbook class from within a Java program, you must first import it, then invoke the Cookbook.connect() method. The following test harness program, *Harness.java*, shows how to do this:

```java
// Harness.java - test harness for Cookbook library class

import java.sql.*;
import com.kitebird.mcb.Cookbook;

public class Harness
{
    public static void main (String[] args)
    {
        Connection conn = null;
        try
        {
            conn = Cookbook.connect ();
            System.out.println ("Connected");
        }
        catch (Exception e)
        {
            Cookbook.printErrorMessage (e);
            System.exit (1);
        }
        finally
        {
            if (conn != null)
            {
                try
                {
                    conn.close ();
                    System.out.println ("Disconnected");
                }
                catch (Exception e)
                {
                    String err = Cookbook.getErrorMessage (e);
                    System.out.println (err);
                }
            }
        }
    }
}
```

Harness.java also shows how to use the error message routines from the Cookbook class when a MySQL-related exception occurs. printErrorMessage() takes the exception object and uses it to print an error message to System.err. getErrorMessage() returns the error message as a string. You can display the message yourself, write it to a log file, or whatever.

2.4   Issuing Queries and Retrieving Results

Problem

You want your program to send a query to the MySQL server and retrieve the result.

Solution

Some statements only return a status code, others return a result set (a set of rows). Most APIs provide different functions for each type of statement; if so, use the function that's appropriate for your query.

Discussion

This section is the longest of the chapter because there are two categories of queries you can execute. Some statements retrieve information from the database; others make changes to that information. These two types of queries are handled differently. In addition, some APIs provide several different functions for issuing queries, which complicates matters further. Before we get to the examples demonstrating how to issue queries from within each API, I'll show the table used for examples, then discuss the general statement categories and outline a strategy for processing them.

In Chapter 1, we created a table named `limbs` to use for some sample queries. In this chapter, we'll use a different table named `profile`. It's based on the idea of a "buddy list," that is, the set of people we like to keep in touch with while we're online. To maintain a profile about each person, we can use the following table:

```
CREATE TABLE profile
(
    id      INT UNSIGNED NOT NULL AUTO_INCREMENT,
    name    CHAR(20) NOT NULL,
    birth   DATE,
    color   ENUM('blue','red','green','brown','black','white'),
    foods   SET('lutefisk','burrito','curry','eggroll','fadge','pizza'),
    cats    INT,
    PRIMARY KEY (id)
);
```

The `profile` table reflects that the things that are important to us are each buddy's name, age, favorite color, favorite foods, and number of cats—obviously one of those goofy tables that are used only for examples in a book!* The table includes an `id` column containing unique values so that we can distinguish records from each other, even if two buddies have the same name. `id` and `name` are `NOT NULL` because they're

---

* Actually, it's not that goofy. The table uses several different data types for its columns, and these will come in handy later for illustrating how to solve particular kinds of problems that pertain to specific column types.

each required to have a value. The other columns are allowed to be NULL because we might not know the value to put into them for any given individual. (We'll use NULL to signify "unknown.") Notice that although we want to keep track of age, there is no age column in the table. Instead, there is a birth column of DATE type. That's because ages change, but birthdays don't. If we recorded age values, we'd have to keep updating them. Storing the birth date is better because it's stable, and we can use it to calculate age at any given moment. (Age calculations are discussed in Recipe 5.19.) color is an ENUM column; color values can be any one of the listed values. foods is a SET, which allows the value to be chosen as any combination of the individual set members. That way we can record multiple favorite foods for any buddy.

To create the table, use the *profile.sql* script in the *tables* directory of the recipes distribution. Change location into that directory, then run the following command:

```
% mysql cookbook < profile.sql
```

Another way to create the table is to issue the CREATE TABLE statement manually from within the *mysql* program, but I recommend that you use the script, because it also loads sample data into the table. That way you can experiment with the table, then restore it after changing it by running the script again.[*]

The initial contents of the profile table loaded by the *profile.sql* script look like this:

```
mysql> SELECT * FROM profile;
+----+---------+------------+-------+-----------------------+------+
| id | name    | birth      | color | foods                 | cats |
+----+---------+------------+-------+-----------------------+------+
|  1 | Fred    | 1970-04-13 | black | lutefisk,fadge,pizza  |    0 |
|  2 | Mort    | 1969-09-30 | white | burrito,curry,eggroll |    3 |
|  3 | Brit    | 1957-12-01 | red   | burrito,curry,pizza   |    1 |
|  4 | Carl    | 1973-11-02 | red   | eggroll,pizza         |    4 |
|  5 | Sean    | 1963-07-04 | blue  | burrito,curry         |    5 |
|  6 | Alan    | 1965-02-14 | red   | curry,fadge           |    1 |
|  7 | Mara    | 1968-09-17 | green | lutefisk,fadge        |    1 |
|  8 | Shepard | 1975-09-02 | black | curry,pizza           |    2 |
|  9 | Dick    | 1952-08-20 | green | lutefisk,fadge        |    0 |
| 10 | Tony    | 1960-05-01 | white | burrito,pizza         |    0 |
+----+---------+------------+-------+-----------------------+------+
```

Most of the columns in the profile table allow NULL values, but none of the rows in the sample dataset actually contain NULL yet. This is because NULL values complicate query processing a bit and I don't want to deal with those complications until we get to Recipes 2.7 and 2.8.

SQL Statement Categories

SQL statements can be divided into two broad categories:

---

[*] See the note at the very end of this chapter on the importance of restoring the profile table.

- Statements that do not return a result set (that is, a set of rows). This statement category includes INSERT, DELETE, and UPDATE. As a general rule, statements of this type generally change the database in some way. There are some exceptions, such as USE *db_name*, which changes the current (default) database for your session without making any changes to the database itself.

- Statements that return a result set, such as SELECT, SHOW, EXPLAIN, and DESCRIBE. I refer to such statements generically as SELECT statements, but you should understand that category to include any statement that returns rows.

The first step in processing a query is to send it to the MySQL server for execution. Some APIs (Perl and Java, for example) recognize a distinction between the two categories of statements and provide separate calls for executing them. Others (such as PHP and Python) do not and have a single call for issuing all statements. However, one thing all APIs have in common is that you don't use any special character to indicate the end of the query. No terminator is necessary because the end of the query string implicitly terminates the query. This differs from the way you issue queries in the *mysql* program, where you terminate statements using a semicolon (;) or \g. (It also differs from the way I normally show the syntax for SQL statements, because I include semicolons to make it clear where statements end.)

After sending the query to the server, the next step is to check whether or not it executed successfully. *Do not neglect this step.* You'll regret it if you do. If a query fails and you proceed on the basis that it succeeded, your program won't work. If the query did execute, your next step depends on the type of query you issued. If it's one that returns no result set, there's nothing else to do (unless you want to check how many rows were affected by the query). If the query does return a result set, you can fetch its rows, then close the result set.

Don't Shoot Yourself in the Foot: Check for Errors

Apparently, the principle that you should check for errors is not so obvious or widely appreciated as one might hope. Many messages posted on MySQL-related mailing lists are requests for help with programs that fail for reasons unknown to the people that wrote them. In a surprising number of cases, the reason these developers are mystified by their programs is that they put in *no* error checking, and thus gave themselves no way to know that there was a problem or to find out what it was! You cannot help yourself this way. Plan for failure by checking for errors so that you can take appropriate action if they occur.

Now we're ready to see how to issue queries in each API. Note that although the scripts check for errors as necessary, for brevity they just print a generic message that an error occurred. You can display more specific error messages using the techniques illustrated in Recipe 2.2.

Perl

The Perl DBI module provides two basic approaches to query execution, depending on whether or not you expect to get back a result set. To issue a query such as INSERT or UPDATE that returns no result set, use the do( ) method. It executes the query and returns the number of rows affected by the query, or undef if an error occurs. For example, if Fred gets a new kitty, the following query can be used to increment his cats count by one:

```perl
my $count = $dbh->do ("UPDATE profile SET cats = cats+1 WHERE name = 'Fred'");
if ($count)     # print row count if no error occurred
{
    $count += 0;
    print "$count rows were updated\n";
}
```

If the query executes successfully but affects no rows, do( ) returns a special value, the string "0E0" (that is, the value zero in scientific notation). "0E0" can be used for testing the execution status of a query because it is true in Boolean contexts (unlike undef). For successful queries, it can also be used when counting how many rows were affected, because it is treated as the number zero in numeric contexts. Of course, if you print that value as is, you'll print "0E0", which might look kind of weird to people who use your program. The preceding example shows one way to make sure this doesn't happen: adding zero to the value explicitly coerces it to numeric form so that it displays as 0. You can also use printf with a %d format specifier to cause an implicit numeric conversion:

```perl
my $count = $dbh->do ("UPDATE profile SET color = color WHERE name = 'Fred'");
if ($count)      # print row count if no error occurred
{
    printf "%d rows were updated\n", $count;
}
```

If RaiseError is enabled, your script will terminate automatically if a DBI-related error occurs and you don't need to bother checking $count to see if do( ) failed:

```perl
my $count = $dbh->do ("UPDATE profile SET color = color WHERE name = 'Fred'");
printf "%d rows were updated\n", $count;
```

To process queries such as SELECT that do return a result set, use a different approach that involves four steps:

- Specify the query by calling prepare( ) using the database handle. prepare( ) returns a statement handle to use with all subsequent operations on the query. (If an error occurs, the script terminates if RaiseError is enabled; otherwise, prepare( ) returns undef.)
- Call execute( ) to execute the query and generate the result set.
- Perform a loop to fetch the rows returned by the query. DBI provides several methods you can use in this loop, which we'll describe shortly.
- Release resources associated with the result set by calling finish( ).

The following example illustrates these steps, using `fetchrow_array()` as the row-fetching method and assuming `RaiseError` is enabled:

```
my $sth = $dbh->prepare ("SELECT id, name, cats FROM profile");
$sth->execute ();
my $count = 0;
while (my @val = $sth->fetchrow_array ())
{
    print "id: $val[0], name: $val[1], cats: $val[2]\n";
    ++$count;
}
$sth->finish ();
print "$count rows were returned\n";
```

The row-fetching loop just shown is followed by a call to `finish()`, which closes the result set and tells the server that it can free any resources associated with it. You don't actually need to call `finish()` if you fetch every row in the set, because DBI notices when you've reached the last row and releases the set for itself. Thus, the example could have omitted the `finish()` call without ill effect. It's more important to invoke `finish()` explicitly if you fetch only part of a result set.

The example illustrates that if you want to know how many rows a result set contains, you should count them yourself while you're fetching them. Do not use the DBI `rows()` method for this purpose; the DBI documentation discourages this practice. (The reason is that it is not necessarily reliable for `SELECT` statements—not because of some deficiency in DBI, but because of differences in the behavior of various database engines.)

DBI has several functions that can be used to obtain a row at a time in a row-fetching loop. The one used in the previous example, `fetchrow_array()`, returns an array containing the next row, or an empty list when there are no more rows. Elements of the array are accessed as `$val[0]`, `$val[1]`, ..., and are present in the array in the same order they are named in the `SELECT` statement. This function is most useful for queries that explicitly name columns to selected. (If you retrieve columns with `SELECT *`, there are no guarantees about the positions of columns within the array.)

`fetchrow_arrayref()` is like `fetchrow_array()`, except that it returns a reference to the array, or `undef` when there are no more rows. Elements of the array are accessed as `$ref->[0]`, `$ref->[1]`, and so forth. As with `fetchrow_array()`, the values are present in the order named in the query:

```
my $sth = $dbh->prepare ("SELECT id, name, cats FROM profile");
$sth->execute ();
my $count = 0;
while (my $ref = $sth->fetchrow_arrayref ())
{
    print "id: $ref->[0], name: $ref->[1], cats: $ref->[2]\n";
    ++$count;
}
print "$count rows were returned\n";
```

`fetchrow_hashref()` returns a reference to a hash structure, or `undef` when there are no more rows:

```
my $sth = $dbh->prepare ("SELECT id, name, cats FROM profile");
$sth->execute ();
my $count = 0;
while (my $ref = $sth->fetchrow_hashref ())
{
    print "id: $ref->{id}, name: $ref->{name}, cats: $ref->{cats}\n";
    ++$count;
}
print "$count rows were returned\n";
```

The elements of the hash are accessed using the names of the columns that are selected by the query (`$ref->{id}`, `$ref->{name}`, and so forth). `fetchrow_hashref()` is particularly useful for `SELECT *` queries, because you can access elements of rows without knowing anything about the order in which columns are returned. You just need to know their names. On the other hand, it's more expensive to set up a hash than an array, so `fetchrow_hashref()` is slower than `fetchrow_array()` or `fetchrow_arrayref()`. It's also possible to "lose" row elements if they have the same name, because column names must be unique. The following query selects two values, but `fetchrow_hashref()` would return a hash structure containing a single element named `id`:

```
SELECT id, id FROM profile
```

To avoid this problem, you can use column aliases to ensure that like-named columns have distinct names in the result set. The following query retrieves the same columns as the previous query, but gives them the distinct names `id` and `id2`:

```
SELECT id, id AS id2 FROM profile
```

Admittedly, this query is pretty silly, but if you're retrieving columns from multiple tables, you may very easily run into the problem of having columns in the result set that have the same name. An example where this occurs may be seen in Recipe 12.3.

In addition to the methods for performing the query execution process just described, DBI provides several high-level retrieval methods that issue a query and return the result set in a single operation. These all are database handle methods that take care of creating and disposing of the statement handle internally before returning the result set. Where the methods differ is the form in which they return the result. Some return the entire result set, others return a single row or column of the set, as summarized in the following table:[*]

---

[*] `selectrow_arrayref()` and `selectall_hashref()` require DBI 1.15 or newer. `selectrow_hashref()` requires DBI 1.20 or newer (it was present a few versions before that, but with a different behavior than it uses now).

Method	Return value
selectrow_array()	First row of result set as an array
selectrow_arrayref()	First row of result set as a reference to an array
selectrow_hashref()	First row of result set as a reference to a hash
selectcol_arrayref()	First column of result set as a reference to an array
selectall_arrayref()	Entire result set as a reference to an array of array references
selectall_hashref()	Entire result set as a reference to a hash of hash references

Most of these methods return a reference. The exception is selectrow_array(), which selects the first row of the result set and returns an array or a scalar, depending on how you call it. In array context, selectrow_array() returns the entire row as an array (or the empty list if no row was selected). This is useful for queries from which you expect to obtain only a single row:

```
my @val = $dbh->selectrow_array (
        "SELECT name, birth, foods FROM profile WHERE id = 3");
```

When selectrow_array() is called in array context, the return value can be used to determine the size of the result set. The column count is the number of elements in the array, and the row count is 1 or 0:

```
my $ncols = @val;
my $nrows = ($ncols ? 1 : 0);
```

You can also invoke selectrow_array() in scalar context, in which case it returns only the first column from the row. This is especially convenient for queries that return a single value:

```
my $buddy_count = $dbh->selectrow_array ("SELECT COUNT(*) FROM profile");
```

If a query returns no result, selectrow_array() returns an empty array or undef, depending on whether you call it in array or scalar context.

selectrow_arrayref() and selectrow_hashref() select the first row of the result set and return a reference to it, or undef if no row was selected. To access the column values, treat the reference the same way you treat the return value from fetchrow_arrayref() or fetchrow_hashref(). You can also use the reference to get the row and column counts:

```
my $ref = $dbh->selectrow_arrayref ($query);
my $ncols = (defined ($ref) ? @{$ref} : 0);
my $nrows = ($ncols ? 1 : 0);

my $ref = $dbh->selectrow_hashref ($query);
my $ncols = (defined ($ref) ? keys (%{$ref}) : 0);
my $nrows = ($ncols ? 1 : 0);
```

With selectcol_arrayref(), a reference to a single-column array is returned, representing the first column of the result set. Assuming a non-undef return value, elements of the array are accessed as $ref->[i] for the value from row i. The number of rows is the number of elements in the array, and the column count is 1 or 0:

```
my $ref = $dbh->selectcol_arrayref ($query);
my $nrows = (defined ($ref) ? @{$ref} : 0);
my $ncols = ($nrows ? 1 : 0);
```

selectall_arrayref() returns a reference to an array, where the array contains an element for each row of the result. Each of these elements is a reference to an array. To access row i of the result set, use $ref->[i] to get a reference to the row. Then treat the row reference the same way as a return value from fetchrow_arrayref() to access individual column values in the row. The result set row and column counts are available as follows:

```
my $ref = $dbh->selectall_arrayref ($query);
my $nrows = (defined ($ref) ? @{$ref} : 0);
my $ncols = ($nrows ? @{$ref->[0]} : 0);
```

selectall_hashref() is somewhat similar to selectall_arrayref(), but returns a reference to a hash, each element of which is a hash reference to a row of the result. To call it, specify an argument that indicates which column to use for hash keys. For example, if you're retrieving rows from the profile table, the PRIMARY KEY is the id column:

```
my $ref = $dbh->selectall_hashref ("SELECT * FROM profile", "id");
```

Then access rows using the keys of the hash. For example, if one of the rows has a key column value of 12, the hash reference for the row is accessed as $ref->{12}. That value is keyed on column names, which you can use to access individual column elements (for example, $ref->{12}->{name}). The result set row and column counts are available as follows:

```
my @keys = (defined ($ref) ? keys (%{$ref}) : ());
my $nrows = scalar (@keys);
my $ncols = ($nrows ? keys (%{$ref->{$keys[0]}}) : 0);
```

The selectall_XXX() methods are useful when you need to process a result set more than once, because DBI provides no way to "rewind" a result set. By assigning the entire result set to a variable, you can iterate through its elements as often as you please.

Take care when using the high-level methods if you have RaiseError disabled. In that case, a method's return value may not always allow you to distinguish an error from an empty result set. For example, if you call selectrow_array() in scalar context to retrieve a single value, an undef return value is particularly ambiguous because it may indicate any of three things: an error, an empty result set, or a result set consisting of a single NULL value. If you need to test for an error, you can check the value of $DBI::errstr or $DBI::err.

PHP

PHP doesn't have separate functions for issuing queries that return result sets and those that do not. Instead, there is a single function mysql_query() for all queries. mysql_query() takes a query string and an optional connection identifier as arguments, and returns a result identifier. If you leave out the connection identifier argument, mysql_query() uses the most recently opened connection by default. The first statement below uses an explicit identifier; the second uses the default connection:

```
$result_id = mysql_query ($query, $conn_id);
$result_id = mysql_query ($query);
```

If the query fails, $result_id will be FALSE. This means that an error occurred because your query was bad: it was syntactically invalid, you didn't have permission to access a table named in the query, or some other problem prevented the query from executing. A FALSE return value does *not* mean that the query affected 0 rows (for a DELETE, INSERT, or UPDATE) or returned 0 rows (for a SELECT).

If $result_id is not FALSE, the query executed properly. What you do at that point depends on the type of query. For queries that don't return rows, $result_id will be TRUE, and the query has completed. If you want, you can call mysql_affected_rows() to find out how many rows were changed:

```
$result_id = mysql_query ("DELETE FROM profile WHERE cats = 0", $conn_id);
if (!$result_id)
    die ("Oops, the query failed");
print (mysql_affected_rows ($conn_id) . " rows were deleted\n");
```

mysql_affected_rows() takes the connection identifier as its argument. If you omit the argument, the current connection is assumed.

For queries that return a result set, mysql_query() returns a nonzero result identifier. Generally, you use this identifier to call a row-fetching function in a loop, then call mysql_free_result() to release the result set. The result identifier is really nothing more than a number that tells PHP which result set you're using. This identifier is *not* a count of the number of rows selected, nor does it contain the contents of any of those rows. Many beginning PHP programmers make the mistake of thinking mysql_query() returns a row count or a result set, but it doesn't. Make sure you're clear on this point and you'll save yourself a lot of trouble.

Here's an example that shows how to run a SELECT query and use the result identifier to fetch the rows:

```
$result_id = mysql_query ("SELECT id, name, cats FROM profile", $conn_id);
if (!$result_id)
    die ("Oops, the query failed");
while ($row = mysql_fetch_row ($result_id))
    print ("id: $row[0], name: $row[1], cats: $row[2]\n");
print (mysql_num_rows ($result_id) . " rows were returned\n");
mysql_free_result ($result_id);
```

The example demonstrates that you obtain the rows in the result set by executing a loop in which you pass the result identifier to one of PHP's row-fetching functions. To obtain a count of the number of rows in a result set, pass the result identifier to mysql_num_rows(). When there are no more rows, pass the identifier to mysql_free_result() to close the result set. (After you call mysql_free_result(), don't try to fetch a row or get the row count, because at that point $result_id is no longer valid.)

Each PHP row-fetching function returns the next row of the result set indicated by $result_id, or FALSE when there are no more rows. Where they differ is in the data type of the return value. The function shown in the preceding example, mysql_fetch_row(), returns an array whose elements correspond to the columns selected by the query and are accessed using numeric subscripts. mysql_fetch_array() is like mysql_fetch_row(), but the array it returns also contains elements that can be accessed using the names of the selected columns. In other words, you can access each column using either its numeric position or its name:

```
$result_id = mysql_query ("SELECT id, name, cats FROM profile", $conn_id);
if (!$result_id)
    die ("Oops, the query failed");
while ($row = mysql_fetch_array ($result_id))
{
    print ("id: $row[0], name: $row[1], cats: $row[2]\n");
    print ("id: $row[id], name: $row[name], cats: $row[cats]\n");
}
print (mysql_num_rows ($result_id) . " rows were returned\n");
mysql_free_result ($result_id);
```

Despite what you might expect, mysql_fetch_array() is not appreciably slower than mysql_fetch_row(), even though the array it returns contains more information.

The previous example does not quote the non-numeric element names because they appear inside a quoted string. Should you refer to the elements outside of a string, the element names should be quoted:

```
printf ("id: %s, name: %s, cats: %s\n",
        $row["id"], $row["name"], $row["cats"]);
```

mysql_fetch_object() returns an object having members that correspond to the columns selected by the query and that are accessed using the column names:

```
$result_id = mysql_query ("SELECT id, name, cats FROM profile", $conn_id);
if (!$result_id)
    die ("Oops, the query failed");
while ($row = mysql_fetch_object ($result_id))
    print ("id: $row->id, name: $row->name, cats: $row->cats\n");
print (mysql_num_rows ($result_id) . " rows were returned\n");
mysql_free_result ($result_id);
```

PHP 4.0.3 adds a fourth row-fetching function, mysql_fetch_assoc(), that returns an array containing elements that are accessed by name. In other words, it is like mysql_fetch_array(), except that the row does not contain the values accessed by numeric index.

Don't Use count() to Get a Column Count in PHP 3

PHP programmers sometimes fetch a result set row and then use count($row) to determine how many values the row contains. It's preferable to use mysql_num_fields() instead, as you can see for yourself by executing the following fragment of PHP code:

```
if (!($result_id = mysql_query ("SELECT 1, 0, NULL", $conn_id)))
    die ("Cannot issue query\n");
$count = mysql_num_fields ($result_id);
print ("The row contains $count columns\n");
if (!($row = mysql_fetch_row ($result_id)))
    die ("Cannot fetch row\n");
$count = count ($row);
print ("The row contains $count columns\n");
```

If you run the code under PHP 3, you'll find that count() returns 2. With PHP 4, count() returns 3. These differing results occur because count() counts array values that correspond to NULL values in PHP 4, but not in PHP 3. By contrast, mysql_field_count() uniformly returns 3 for both versions of PHP. The moral is that count() won't necessarily give you an accurate value. Use mysql_field_count() if you want to know the true column count.

Python

The Python DB-API interface does not have distinct calls for queries that return a result set and those that do not. To process a query in Python, use your database connection object to get a cursor object.* Then use the cursor's execute() method to send the query to the server. If there is no result set, the query is completed, and you can use the cursor's rowcount attribute to determine how many records were changed:†

```
try:
    cursor = conn.cursor ()
    cursor.execute ("UPDATE profile SET cats = cats+1 WHERE name = 'Fred'")
    print "%d rows were updated" % cursor.rowcount
except MySQLdb.Error, e:
    print "Oops, the query failed"
    print e
```

If the query does return a result set, fetch its rows and close the set. DB-API provides a couple of methods for retrieving rows. fetchone() returns the next row as a sequence (or None when there are no more rows):

```
try:
    cursor = conn.cursor ()
```

---

* If you're familiar with the term "cursor" as provided on the server side in some databases, MySQL doesn't really provide cursors the same way. Instead, the MySQLdb module emulates cursors on the client side of query execution.

† Note that rowcount is an attribute, not a function. Refer to it as rowcount, not rowcount(), or an exception will be raised.

```
        cursor.execute ("SELECT id, name, cats FROM profile")
        while 1:
            row = cursor.fetchone ()
            if row == None:
                break
            print "id: %s, name: %s, cats: %s" % (row[0], row[1], row[2])
        print "%d rows were returned" % cursor.rowcount
        cursor.close ()
    except MySQLdb.Error, e:
        print "Oops, the query failed"
        print e
```

As you can see from the preceding example, the rowcount attribute is useful for SELECT queries, too; it indicates the number of rows in the result set.

Another row-fetching method, fetchall(), returns the entire result set as a sequence of sequences. You can iterate through the sequence to access the rows:

```
    try:
        cursor = conn.cursor ()
        cursor.execute ("SELECT id, name, cats FROM profile")
        rows = cursor.fetchall ()
        for row in rows:
            print "id: %s, name: %s, cats: %s" % (row[0], row[1], row[2])
        print "%d rows were returned" % cursor.rowcount
        cursor.close ()
    except MySQLdb.Error, e:
        print "Oops, the query failed"
        print e
```

Like DBI, DB-API doesn't provide any way to rewind a result set, so fetchall() can be convenient when you need to iterate through the rows of the result set more than once or access individual values directly. For example, if rows holds the result set, you can access the value of the third column in the second row as rows[1][2] (indexes begin at 0, not 1).

To access row values by column name, specify the DictCursor cursor type when you create the cursor object. This causes rows to be returned as Python dictionary objects with named elements:

```
    try:
        cursor = conn.cursor (MySQLdb.cursors.DictCursor)
        cursor.execute ("SELECT id, name, cats FROM profile")
        for row in cursor.fetchall ():
            print "id: %s, name: %s, cats: %s" \
                    % (row["id"], row["name"], row["cats"])
        print "%d rows were returned" % cursor.rowcount
        cursor.close ()
    except MySQLdb.Error, e:
        print "Oops, the query failed"
        print e
```

Java

The JDBC interface provides specific object types for the various phases of query processing. Queries are issued in JDBC by passing SQL strings to Java objects of one type. The results, if there are any, are returned as objects of another type. Problems that occur while accessing the database cause exceptions to be thrown.

To issue a query, the first step is to get a `Statement` object by calling the `createStatement()` method of your `Connection` object:

```
Statement s = conn.createStatement ();
```

Then use the `Statement` object to send the query to the server. JDBC provides several methods for doing this. Choose the one that's appropriate for the type of statement you want to issue: `executeUpdate()` for statements that don't return a result set, `executeQuery()` for statements that do, and `execute()` when you don't know.

The `executeUpdate()` method sends a query that generates no result set to the server and returns a count indicating the number of rows that were affected. When you're done with the statement object, close it. The following example illustrates this sequence of events:

```
try
{
    Statement s = conn.createStatement ();
    int count = s.executeUpdate ("DELETE FROM profile WHERE cats = 0");
    s.close ();      // close statement
    System.out.println (count + " rows were deleted");
}
catch (Exception e)
{
    Cookbook.printErrorMessage (e);
}
```

For statements that return a result set, use `executeQuery()`. Then get a result set object and use it to retrieve the row values. When you're done, close both the result set and statement objects:

```
try
{
    Statement s = conn.createStatement ();
    s.executeQuery ("SELECT id, name, cats FROM profile");
    ResultSet rs = s.getResultSet ();
    int count = 0;
    while (rs.next ())  // loop through rows of result set
    {
        int id = rs.getInt (1);      // extract columns 1, 2, and 3
        String name = rs.getString (2);
        int cats = rs.getInt (3);
        System.out.println ("id: " + id
                                + ", name: " + name
                                + ", cats: " + cats);
```

```
        ++count;
    }
    rs.close ();      // close result set
    s.close ();       // close statement
    System.out.println (count + " rows were returned");
}
catch (Exception e)
{
    Cookbook.printErrorMessage (e);
}
```

The ResultSet object returned by the getResultSet() method of your Statement object has a number of methods of its own, such as next() to fetch rows and various getXXX() methods that access columns of the current row. Initially the result set is positioned just before the first row of the set. Call next() to fetch each row in succession until it returns false, indicating that there are no more rows. To determine the number of rows in a result set, count them yourself, as shown in the preceding example.

Column values are accessed using methods such as getInt(), getString(), getFloat(), and getDate(). To obtain the column value as a generic object, use getObject(). The getXXX() calls can be invoked with an argument indicating either column position (beginning at 1, not 0) or column name. The previous example shows how to retrieve the id, name, and cats columns by position. To access columns by name instead, the row-fetching loop of that example can be rewritten as follows:

```
while (rs.next ())  // loop through rows of result set
{
    int id = rs.getInt ("id");
    String name = rs.getString ("name");
    int cats = rs.getInt ("cats");
    System.out.println ("id: " + id
                        + ", name: " + name
                        + ", cats: " + cats);
    ++count;
}
```

You can retrieve a given column value using any getXXX() call that makes sense for the column type. For example, you can use getString() to retrieve any column value as a string:

```
String id = rs.getString ("id");
String name = rs.getString ("name");
String cats = rs.getString ("cats");
System.out.println ("id: " + id
                    + ", name: " + name
                    + ", cats: " + cats);
```

Or you can use getObject() to retrieve values as generic objects and convert the values as necessary. The following code uses toString() to convert object values to printable form:

```
Object id = rs.getObject ("id");
Object name = rs.getObject ("name");
Object cats = rs.getObject ("cats");
System.out.println ("id: " + id.toString ()
                    + ", name: " + name.toString ()
                    + ", cats: " + cats.toString ());
```

To find out how many columns are in each row, access the result set's metadata. The following code uses the column count to print each row's columns as a comma-separated list of values:

```
try
{
    Statement s = conn.createStatement ();
    s.executeQuery ("SELECT * FROM profile");
    ResultSet rs = s.getResultSet ();
    ResultSetMetaData md = rs.getMetaData ();   // get result set metadata
    int ncols = md.getColumnCount ();           // get column count from metadata
    int count = 0;
    while (rs.next ())  // loop through rows of result set
    {
        for (int i = 0; i < ncols; i++) // loop through columns
        {
            String val = rs.getString (i+1);
            if (i > 0)
                System.out.print (", ");
            System.out.print (val);
        }
        System.out.println ();
        ++count;
    }
    rs.close ();     // close result set
    s.close ();      // close statement
    System.out.println (count + " rows were returned");
}
catch (Exception e)
{
    Cookbook.printErrorMessage (e);
}
```

The third JDBC query-executing method, execute(), works for either type of query. It's particularly useful when you receive a query string from an external source and don't know whether or not it generates a result set. The return value from execute() indicates the query type so that you can process it appropriately: if execute() returns true, there is a result set, otherwise not. Typically you'd use it something like this, where queryStr represents an arbitrary SQL statement:

```
try
{
    Statement s = conn.createStatement ();
```

```
if (s.execute (queryStr))
{
    // there is a result set
    ResultSet rs = s.getResultSet ();

    // ... process result set here ...

    rs.close ();     // close result set
}
else
{
    // there is no result set, just print the row count
    System.out.println (s.getUpdateCount ()
                        + " rows were affected");
}
    s.close ();     // close statement
}
catch (Exception e)
{
    Cookbook.printErrorMessage (e);
}
```

Closing JDBC Statement and Result Set Objects

The JDBC query-issuing examples in this section close the statement and result set objects explicitly when they are done with those objects. Some Java implementations close them automatically when you close the connection. However, buggy implementations may fail to do this properly, so it's best not to rely on that behavior. Close the objects yourself when you're done with them to avoid difficulties.

2.5   Moving Around Within a Result Set

Problem

You want to iterate through a result set multiple times, or to move to arbitrary rows within the result.

Solution

If your API has functions that provide these capabilities, use them. If not, fetch the result set into a data structure so that you can access the rows however you please.

Discussion

Some APIs allow you to "rewind" a result set so you can iterate through its rows again. Some also allow you to move to arbitrary rows within the set, which in effect gives you random access to the rows. Our APIs offer these capabilities as follows:

- Perl DBI and Python DB-API don't allow direct positioning within a result set.
- PHP allows row positioning with the mysql_data_seek() function. Pass it a result set identifier and a row number (in the range from 0 to mysql_num_rows()−1). Subsequent calls to row-fetching functions return rows sequentially beginning with the given row. PHP also provides a mysql_result() function that takes row and column indexes for random access to individual values within the result set. However, mysql_result() is slow and normally should not be used.
- JDBC 2 introduces the concept of a "scrollable" result set, along with methods for moving back and forth among rows. This is not present in earlier versions of JDBC, although the MySQL Connector/J driver does happen to support next() and previous() methods even for JDBC 1.12.

Whether or not a particular database-access API allows rewinding and positioning, your programs can achieve random access into a result set by fetching all rows from a result set and saving them into a data structure. For example, you can use a two-dimensional array that stores result rows and columns as elements of a matrix. Once you've done that, you can iterate through the result set multiple times or use its elements in random access fashion however you please. If your API provides a call that returns an entire result set in a single operation, it's relatively trivial to generate a matrix. (Perl and Python can do this.) Otherwise, you need to run a row-fetching loop and save the rows yourself.

2.6   Using Prepared Statements and Placeholders in Queries

Problem

You want to write queries that are more generic and don't refer to specific data values, so that you can reuse them.

Solution

Use your API's placeholder mechanism, if it has one.

Discussion

One way to construct SQL statements from within a program is to put data values literally into the query string, as in these examples:

```
SELECT * FROM profile WHERE age > 40 AND color = 'green'

INSERT INTO profile (name,color) VALUES('Gary','blue')
```

Some APIs provide an alternative that allows you to specify query strings that do not include literal data values. Using this approach, you write the statement using placeholders—special characters that indicate where the values go. One common placeholder character is ?, so the previous queries might be rewritten to use placeholders like this:

```
SELECT * FROM profile WHERE age > ? AND color = ?

INSERT INTO profile (name,color) VALUES(?,?)
```

For APIs that support this kind of thing, you pass the string to the database to allow it to prepare a query plan. Then you supply data values and bind them to the placeholders when you execute the query. You can reuse the prepared query by binding different values to it each time it's executed.

One of the benefits of prepared statements and placeholders is that parameter binding operations automatically handle escaping of characters such as quotes and backslashes that you have to worry about yourself if you put the data values into the query yourself. This can be especially useful if you're inserting binary data such as images into your database, or using data values with unknown content such as input submitted by a remote user through a form in a web page.

Another benefit of prepared statements is that they encourage statement reuse. Statements become more generic because they contain placeholders rather than specific data values. If you're executing an operation over and over, you may be able to reuse a prepared statement and simply bind different data values to it each time you execute it. If so, you gain a performance benefit, at least for databases that support query planning. For example, if a program issues a particular type of SELECT statement several times while it runs, such a database can construct a plan for the statement, then reuse it each time, rather than rebuilding the plan over and over. MySQL doesn't build query plans, so you don't get any performance boost from using prepared statements. However, if you port a program to a database that does use query plans, you'll gain the advantage of prepared statements automatically if you've written your program from the outset to use them. You won't have to convert from nonprepared statements to enjoy that benefit.

A third benefit is that code that uses placeholder-based queries can be easier to read, although that's somewhat subjective. As you read through this section, you might compare the queries used here with those from the previous section that did not use placeholders, to see which you prefer.

Perl

To use placeholders in DBI scripts, put a ? in your query string at each location where you want to insert a data value, then bind the values to the query. You can bind values by passing them to do( ) or execute( ), or by calling a DBI method specifically intended for placeholder substitution.

With do( ), pass the query string and the data values in the same call:

```perl
my $count = $dbh->do ("UPDATE profile SET color = ? WHERE name = ?",
                      undef,
                      "green", "Mara");
```

The arguments after the query string should be undef followed by the data values, one value for each placeholder. (The undef argument that follows the query string is a historical artifact, but must be present.)

With prepare( ) plus execute( ), pass the query string to prepare( ) to get a statement handle. Then use that handle to pass the data values via execute( ):

```perl
my $sth = $dbh->prepare ("UPDATE profile SET color = ? WHERE name = ?");
my $count = $sth->execute ("green", "Mara");
```

You can use placeholders for SELECT statements, too. The following query looks for records having a name value that begins with "M":

```perl
my $sth = $dbh->prepare ("SELECT * FROM profile WHERE name LIKE ?");
$sth->execute ("M%");
while (my $ref = $sth->fetchrow_hashref ())
{
    print "id: $ref->{id}, name: $ref->{name}, cats: $ref->{cats}\n";
}
$sth->finish ();
```

A third way of binding values to placeholders is to use the bind_param( ) call. It takes two arguments, a placeholder position and a value to be bound to the placeholder at that position. (Placeholder positions begin with 1, not 0.) The previous two examples can be rewritten to use bind_param( ) as follows:

```perl
my $sth = $dbh->prepare ("UPDATE profile SET color = ? WHERE name = ?");
$sth->bind_param (1, "green");
$sth->bind_param (2, "Mara");
my $count = $sth->execute ();

my $sth = $dbh->prepare ("SELECT * FROM profile WHERE name LIKE ?");
$sth->bind_param (1, "M%");
$sth->execute ();
while (my $ref = $sth->fetchrow_hashref ())
{
    print "id: $ref->{id}, name: $ref->{name}, cats: $ref->{cats}\n";
}
$sth->finish ();
```

No matter which method you use for placeholders, don't put any quotes around the ? characters, not even for placeholders that represent strings. DBI adds quotes as necessary on its own. In fact, if you do put quotes around the placeholder character, DBI will interpret it as the literal string constant "?", not as a placeholder.

The high-level retrieval methods such as selectrow_array() and selectall_arrayref() can be used with placeholders, too. Like the do() method, the arguments are the query string and undef, followed by the data values to be bound to the placeholders that occur in the query string. Here's an example:

```
my $ref = $dbh->selectall_arrayref (
                "SELECT name, birth, foods FROM profile
                 WHERE id > ? AND color = ?",
                undef, 3, "green");
```

Generating a List of Placeholders

When you want to use placeholders for a set of data values that may vary in size, you must construct a list of placeholder characters. For example, in Perl, the following statement creates a string consisting of *n* placeholder characters separated by commas:

```
$str = join (",", ("?") x n);
```

The x repetition operator, when applied to a list, produces *n* copies of the list, so the join() call joins these lists to produce a single string containing *n* comma-separated instances of the ? character. This is handy when you want to bind an array of data values to a list of placeholders in a query string, because the size of the array indicates how many placeholder characters are needed:

```
$str = join (",", ("?") x @values);
```

Another method of generating a list of placeholders that is perhaps less cryptic looks like this:

```
$str = "?" if @values;
$str .= ",?" for 1 .. @values-1;
```

Yet a third method is as follows:

```
$str = "?" if @values;
for (my $i = 1; $i < @values; $i++)
{
    $str .= ",?";
}
```

That method's syntax is less Perl-specific and therefore easier to translate into other languages. For example, the equivalent method in Python looks like this:

```
str = ""
if len (values) > 0:
    str = "?"
for i in range (1, len (values)):
    str = str + ",?"
```

PHP

PHP provides no support for placeholders. See Recipe 2.8 to find out how to construct queries that refer to data values that may contain special characters. Or see Recipe 2.9, which develops a class-based interface for PHP that emulates placeholders.

Python

Python's MySQLdb module implements the concept of placeholders by using format specifiers in the query string. To use placeholders, invoke the execute() method with two arguments: a query string containing format specifiers, and a sequence containing the values to be bound to the query string. The following query uses placeholders to search for records where the number of cats is less than 2 and the favorite color is green:

```
try:
    cursor = conn.cursor ()
    cursor.execute ("SELECT * FROM profile WHERE cats < %s AND color = %s", \
                                                       (2, "green"))

    for row in cursor.fetchall ():
        print row
    print "%d rows were returned" % cursor.rowcount
    cursor.close ()
except MySQLdb.Error, e:
    print "Oops, the query failed"
    print e
```

If you have only a single value *val* to bind to a placeholder, you can write it as a sequence using the syntax (*val*,). The following UPDATE statement demonstrates this:

```
try:
    cursor = conn.cursor ()
    cursor.execute ("UPDATE profile SET cats = cats+1 WHERE name = %s", \
                                                       ("Fred",))

    print "%d rows were updated" % cursor.rowcount
except MySQLdb.Error, e:
    print "Oops, the query failed"
    print e
```

Some of the Python DB-API driver modules support several format specifiers (such as %d for integers and %f for floating-point numbers). With MySQLdb, you should use a placeholder of %s to format all data values as strings. MySQL will perform type conversion as necessary. If you want to place a literal % character into the query, use %% in the query string.

Python's placeholder mechanism provides quotes around data values as necessary when they are bound to the query string, so you need not add them yourself.

Java

JDBC provides support for placeholders if you use prepared statements rather than regular statements. Recall that the process for issuing regular statements is to create a Statement object and then pass the query string to one of the query-issuing functions executeUpdate(), executeQuery(), or execute(). To use a prepared statement instead, create a PreparedStatement object by passing a query string containing ? placeholder characters to your connection object's prepareStatement() method. Then bind your data values to the statement using set*XXX*() methods. Finally, execute the statement by calling executeUpdate(), executeQuery(), or execute() with an empty argument list. Here is an example that uses executeUpdate() to issue a DELETE query:

```
PreparedStatement s;
int count;
s = conn.prepareStatement ("DELETE FROM profile WHERE cats = ?");
s.setInt (1, 2);    // bind a 2 to the first placeholder
count = s.executeUpdate ();
s.close ();       // close statement
System.out.println (count + " rows were deleted");
```

For a query that returns a result set, the process is similar, but you use executeQuery() instead:

```
PreparedStatement s;
s = conn.prepareStatement ("SELECT id, name, cats FROM profile"
                    + " WHERE cats < ? AND color = ?");
s.setInt (1, 2);    // bind 2 and "green" to first and second placeholders
s.setString (2, "green");
s.executeQuery ();
// ... process result set here ...
s.close ();       // close statement
```

The set*XXX*() methods that bind data values to queries take two arguments: a placeholder position (beginning with 1, not 0) and the value to be bound to the placeholder. The type of the value should match the type in the set*XXX*() method name. For example, you should pass an integer value to setInt(), not a string.

Placeholder characters need no surrounding quotes in the query string. JDBC supplies quotes as necessary when it binds values to the placeholders.

2.7   Including Special Characters and NULL Values in Queries

Problem

You've having trouble constructing queries that include data values containing special characters such as quotes or backslashes, or special values such as NULL.

Solution

Use your API's placeholder mechanism or quoting function.

Discussion

Up to this point, our queries have used "safe" data values requiring no special treatment. This section describes how to construct queries when you're using values that contain special characters such as quotes, backslashes, binary data, or values that are NULL. The difficulty with such values is as follows. Suppose you have the following INSERT query:

```
INSERT INTO profile (name,birth,color,foods,cats)
VALUES('Alison','1973-01-12','blue','eggroll',4);
```

There's nothing unusual about that. But if you change the name column value to something like De'Mont that contains a single quote, the query becomes syntactically invalid:

```
INSERT INTO profile (name,birth,color,foods,cats)
VALUES('De'Mont','1973-01-12','blue','eggroll',4);
```

The problem is that there is a single quote inside a single-quoted string. To make the query legal, the quote could be escaped by preceding it either with a single quote or with a backslash:

```
INSERT INTO profile (name,birth,color,foods,cats)
VALUES('De''Mont','1973-01-12','blue','eggroll',4);

INSERT INTO profile (name,birth,color,foods,cats)
VALUES('De\'Mont','1973-01-12','blue','eggroll',4);
```

Alternatively, you could quote the name value itself within double quotes rather than within single quotes:

```
INSERT INTO profile (name,birth,color,foods,cats)
VALUES("De'Mont",'1973-01-12','blue','eggroll',4);
```

Naturally, if you are writing a query literally in your program, you can escape or quote the name value by hand because you know what the value is. But if you're using a variable to provide the name value, you don't necessarily know what the variable's value is. Worse yet, single quote isn't the only character you must be prepared to deal with; double quotes and backslashes cause problems, too. And if you want to store binary data such as images or sound clips in your database, such values might contain anything—not just quotes or backslashes, but other characters such as nulls (zero-valued bytes). The need to handle special characters properly is particularly acute in a web environment where queries are constructed using form input (for example, if you're searching for records that match search terms entered by the remote user). You must be able to handle any kind of input in a general way, because you can't predict in advance what kind of information people will supply. In fact, it is not uncommon for malicious users to enter garbage values containing problematic characters in a deliberate attempt to break your scripts.

The SQL NULL value is not a special character, but it too requires special treatment. In SQL, NULL indicates "no value." This can have several meanings depending on context, such as "unknown," "missing," "out of range," and so forth. Our queries thus far have not used NULL values, to avoid dealing with the complications that they introduce, but now it's time to address these issues. For example, if you don't know De'Mont's favorite color, you can set the color column to NULL—but not by writing the query like this:

```
INSERT INTO profile (name,birth,color,foods,cats)
VALUES('De''Mont','1973-01-12','NULL','eggroll',4);
```

Instead, the NULL value shouldn't have any surrounding quotes at all:

```
INSERT INTO profile (name,birth,color,foods,cats)
VALUES('De''Mont','1973-01-12',NULL,'eggroll',4);
```

If you were writing the query literally in your program, you'd simply write the word "NULL" without surrounding quotes. But if the color value comes from a variable, the proper action is not so obvious. You must know something about the variable's value to be able to determine whether or not to surround it with quotes when you construct the query.

There are two general means at your disposal for dealing with special characters such as quotes and backslashes, and with special values such as NULL:

- Use placeholders if your API supports them. Generally, this is the preferred method, because the API itself will do all or most of the work for you of providing quotes around values as necessary, quoting or escaping special characters within the data value, and possibly interpreting a special value to map onto NULL without surrounding quotes. Recipe 2.6 provides general background on placeholder support; you should read that section if you haven't already.

- Use a quoting function if your API provides one for converting data values to a safe form that is suitable for use in query strings.

The remainder of this section shows how to handle special characters for each API. The examples demonstrate how to insert a profile table record that contains De'Mont for the name value and NULL for the color value. The techniques shown work generally to handle any special characters, including those found in binary data. (The techniques are not limited to INSERT queries. They work for other kinds of statements as well, such as SELECT queries.) Examples showing specifically how to work with a particular kind of binary data—images—are provided in Chapter 17.

A related issue not covered here is the inverse operation of transforming special characters in values returned from your database for display in various contexts. For example, if you're generating HTML pages that include values taken from your database, you have to convert < and > characters in those values to the HTML entities < and > to make sure they display properly. This topic is discussed in Chapter 16.

Perl

DBI supports a placeholder mechanism for binding data values to queries, as discussed in Recipe 2.6. Using this mechanism, we can add the profile record for De'Mont by using do( ):

```
my $count = $dbh->do ("INSERT INTO profile (name,birth,color,foods,cats)
                       VALUES(?,?,?,?,?)",
                  undef,
                  "De'Mont", "1973-01-12", undef, "eggroll", 4);
```

Alternatively, use prepare( ) plus execute( ):

```
my $sth = $dbh->prepare ("INSERT INTO profile (name,birth,color,foods,cats)
                          VALUES(?,?,?,?,?)");
my $count = $sth->execute ("De'Mont", "1973-01-12", undef, "eggroll", 4);
```

In either case, the resulting query generated by DBI is as follows:

```
INSERT INTO profile (name,birth,color,foods,cats)
VALUES('De\'Mont','1973-01-12',NULL,'eggroll','4')
```

Note how DBI adds quotes around data values, even though there were none around the ? placeholder characters in the original query string. (The placeholder mechanism adds quotes around numeric values, too, but that's okay, because the MySQL server performs type conversion as necessary to convert strings to numbers.) Also note the DBI convention that when you bind undef to a placeholder, DBI puts a NULL into the query and correctly refrains from adding surrounding quotes.

DBI also provides a quote( ) method as an alternative to using placeholders. quote( ) is a database handle method, so you must have a connection open to the server before you can use it. (This is because the proper quoting rules cannot be selected until the driver is known; some databases have different quoting rules than others.) Here's how to use quote( ) to create a query string for inserting a new record in the profile table:

```
my $stmt = sprintf (
             "INSERT INTO profile (name,birth,color,foods,cats)
             VALUES(%s,%s,%s,%s,%s)",
                  $dbh->quote ("De'Mont"),
                  $dbh->quote ("1973-01-12"),
                  $dbh->quote (undef),
                  $dbh->quote ("eggroll"),
                  $dbh->quote (4));
my $count = $dbh->do ($stmt);
```

The query string generated by this code is the same as when you use placeholders. The %s format specifiers are written without surrounding quotes because quote( )

provides them automatically as necessary: undef values are inserted as NULL without quotes, and non-undef values are inserted with quotes.

PHP

PHP has no placeholder capability, but does provide an addslashes() function that you can use to make values safe for insertion into query strings. addslashes() escapes special characters such as quotes and backslashes, but does not add surrounding quotes around values; you must add them yourself. We also need a convention for specifying NULL values; let's try using unset() to force a variable to have "no value" (somewhat like Perl's undef value). Here is some PHP code for adding De'Mont's profile table record:

```
unset ($null);  # create a "null" value
$stmt = sprintf ("
        INSERT INTO profile (name,birth,color,foods,cats)
        VALUES('%s','%s','%s','%s','%s')",
            addslashes ("De'Mont"),
            addslashes ("1973-01-12"),
            addslashes ($null),
            addslashes ("eggroll"),
            addslashes (4));
$result_id = mysql_query ($stmt, $conn_id);
```

In the example, the %s format specifiers in the query string are surrounded with quotes because addslashes() doesn't provide them. Unfortunately, the resulting query string looks like this, which isn't quite correct:

```
INSERT INTO profile (name,birth,color,foods,cats)
VALUES('De\'Mont','1973-01-12','','eggroll','4')
```

The quote in the name field has been escaped properly, but the "null" (unset) value we passed for the color column turned into an empty string, not NULL. Let's fix this by writing a helper function sql_quote() to use in place of addslashes(). sql_quote() is similar to addslashes(), but returns NULL (without surrounding quotes) for unset values and adds quotes around the value otherwise. Here's what it looks like:

```
function sql_quote ($str)
{
    return (isset ($str) ? "'" . addslashes ($str) . "'" : "NULL");
}
```

Because sql_quote() itself adds quote characters around the data value if they're needed, we can remove the quotes that surround the %s format specifiers in the query string and generate the INSERT statement like this:

```
unset ($null);  # create a "null" value
$stmt = sprintf ("
        INSERT INTO profile (name,birth,color,foods,cats)
        VALUES(%s,%s,%s,%s,%s)",
            sql_quote ("De'Mont"),
            sql_quote ("1973-01-12"),
```

```
                sql_quote ($null),
                sql_quote ("eggroll"),
                sql_quote (4));
    $result_id = mysql_query ($stmt, $conn_id);
```

After making the preceding changes, the value of $stmt includes a properly unquoted
NULL value:

```
INSERT INTO profile (name,birth,color,foods,cats)
VALUES('De\'Mont','1973-01-12',NULL,'eggroll','4')
```

If you're using PHP 4, you have some additional options for handling NULL values
and special characters. First, PHP 4 has a special value NULL that is like an unset
value, so you could use that in place of $null in the preceding code that generated
the INSERT statement. (However, to write code that works for both PHP 3 and PHP 4,
use an unset variable such as $null.) Second, as of PHP 4.0.3, an alternative to
addslashes() is to use mysql_escape_string(), which is based on the function of the
same name in the MySQL C API. For example, you could rewrite sql_quote() to use
mysql_escape_string() like this:

```
function sql_quote ($str)
{
    return (isset ($str) ? "'" . mysql_escape_string ($str) . "'" : "NULL");
}
```

If you want a version that uses mysql_escape_string() if it's present and falls back to
addslashes() otherwise, write sql_quote() like this:

```
function sql_quote ($str)
{
    if (!isset ($str))
        return ("NULL");
    $func = function_exists ("mysql_escape_string")
                ? "mysql_escape_string"
                : "addslashes";
    return ("'" . $func ($str) . "'");
}
```

Whichever version of sql_quote() you use, it's the kind of routine that is a good candidate for inclusion in a library file. I'll assume its availability for PHP scripts in the
rest of this book. You can find it as part of the *Cookbook_Utils.php* file in the *lib*
directory of the recipes distribution. To use the file, install it in the same location
where you put *Cookbook.php* and reference it from scripts like this:

```
include "Cookbook_Utils.php";
```

Python

Python provides a placeholder mechanism that you can use for handling special characters in data values, as described in Recipe 2.6. To add the profile table record for
De'Mont, the code looks like this:

```
try:
    cursor = conn.cursor ()
```

```
        cursor.execute ("""
                INSERT INTO profile (name,birth,color,foods,cats)
                VALUES(%s,%s,%s,%s,%s)
                """, ("De'Mont", "1973-01-12", None, "eggroll", 4))
        print "%d row was inserted" % cursor.rowcount
    except:
        print "Oops, the query failed"
```

The parameter binding mechanism adds quotes around data values where necessary. DB-API treats None as logically equivalent to the SQL NULL value, so you can bind None to a placeholder to produce a NULL in the query string. The query that is sent to the server by the preceding execute( ) call looks like this:

```
INSERT INTO profile (name,birth,color,foods,cats)
VALUES('De\'Mont','1973-01-12',NULL,'eggroll',4)
```

With MySQLdb 0.9.1 or newer, an alternative method of quoting data values is to use the literal( ) method. To produce the INSERT statement for De'Mont by using literal( ), do this:

```
    try:
        cursor = conn.cursor ()
        str = """
                INSERT INTO profile (name,birth,color,foods,cats)
                VALUES(%s,%s,%s,%s,%s)
                """ % \
                    (conn.literal ("De'Mont"), \
                    conn.literal ("1973-01-12"), \
                    conn.literal (None), \
                    conn.literal ("eggroll"), \
                    conn.literal (4))
        cursor.execute (str)
        print "%d row was inserted" % cursor.rowcount
    except:
        print "Oops, the query failed"
```

Java

Java provides a placeholder mechanism that you can use to handle special characters in data values, as described in Recipe 2.6. To add the profile table record for De'Mont, create a prepared statement, bind the data values to it, then execute the statement:

```
PreparedStatement s;
int count;
s = conn.prepareStatement (
        "INSERT INTO profile (name,birth,color,foods,cats)"
        + " VALUES(?,?,?,?,?)");
s.setString (1, "De'Mont");
s.setString (2, "1973-01-12");
s.setNull (3, java.sql.Types.CHAR);
s.setString (4, "eggroll");
s.setInt (5, 4);
count = s.executeUpdate ();
s.close ();      // close statement
```

Each value-binding call here is chosen to match the data type of the column to which the value is bound: setString() to bind a string to the name column, setInt() to bind an integer to the cats column, and so forth. (Actually, I cheated a bit by using setString() to treat the date value for birth as a string.) The set*XXX*() calls add quotes around data values if necessary, so no quotes are needed around the ? placeholder characters in the query string. One difference between JDBC and the other APIs is that you don't specify a special value to bind a NULL to a placeholder by specifying some special value (such as undef in Perl or None in Python). Instead, you invoke a special method setNull(), where the second argument indicates the type of the column (java.sql.Types.CHAR for a string, java.sql.Types.INTEGER for an integer, etc.).

To achieve some uniformity in the value-binding calls, a helper function bindParam() can be defined that takes a Statement object, a placeholder position, and a data value. This allows the same function to be used to bind any data value. We can even use the convention that passing the Java null value binds a SQL NULL to the query. After rewriting the previous example to use bindParam(), it looks like this:

```
PreparedStatement s;
int count;
s = conn.prepareStatement (
        "INSERT INTO profile (name,birth,color,foods,cats)"
        + " VALUES(?,?,?,?,?)");
bindParam (s, 1, "De'Mont");
bindParam (s, 2, "1973-01-12");
bindParam (s, 3, null);
bindParam (s, 4, "eggroll");
bindParam (s, 5, 4);
count = s.executeUpdate ();
s.close ();      // close statement
```

The implementation of bindParam() requires multiple functions, because the third argument can be of different types, so we need one function for each type. The following code shows versions that handle integer and string data values (the string version handles null and binds it to NULL):

```
public static void bindParam (PreparedStatement s, int pos, int val)
{
    try
    {
        s.setInt (pos, val);
    }
    catch (Exception e) { /* catch and ignore */ }
}

public static void bindParam (PreparedStatement s, int pos, String val)
{
    try
    {
        if (val == null)
            s.setNull (pos, java.sql.Types.CHAR);
        else
```

```
                    s.setString (pos, val);
        }
        catch (Exception e) { /* catch and ignore */ }
    }
```

To handle additional data types, you'd write other versions of `bindParam()` that accept arguments of the appropriate type.

Special Characters in Database, Table, and Column Names

In MySQL versions 3.23.6 and later, you can quote database, table, and column names by surrounding them with backquotes. This allows you to include characters in such names that normally would be illegal. For example, spaces in names are not allowed by default:

```
mysql> CREATE TABLE my table (i INT);
ERROR 1064 at line 1: You have an error in your SQL syntax
near 'table (i INT)' at line 1
```

To include the space, protect the name with backquotes:

```
mysql> CREATE TABLE `my table` (i INT);
Query OK, 0 rows affected (0.04 sec)
```

The backquote mechanism gives you wider latitude in choosing names, but makes it more difficult to write programs correctly. (When you actually use a backquoted name, you must remember to include the backquotes every time you refer to it.) Because of this additional bit of complexity, I prefer to avoid using such names, and I recommend that you don't use them, either. If you want to ignore that advice, a strategy you may find helpful in this situation is to define a variable that holds the name (including backquotes) and then use the variable whenever you need to refer to the name. For example, in Perl, you can do this:

```
$tbl_name = "`my table`";
$dbh->do ("DELETE FROM $tbl_name");
```

2.8   Handling NULL Values in Result Sets

Problem

A query result includes NULL values, but you're not sure how to tell where they are.

Solution

Your API probably has some value that represents NULL by convention. You just have to know what it is and how to test for it.

Discussion

Recipe 2.8 described how to refer to NULL values when you send queries *to* the database. In this section, we'll deal instead with the question of how to recognize and process NULL values that are returned *from* the database. In general, this is a matter of knowing what special value the API maps NULL values onto, or what function to call. These values are shown in the following table:

Language	NULL-detection value or function
Perl	undef
PHP	an unset value
Python	None
Java	wasNull()

The following sections show a very simple application of NULL value detection. The examples retrieve a result set and print all values in it, mapping NULL values onto the printable string "NULL".

To make sure the profile table has a row that contains some NULL values, use *mysql* to issue the following INSERT statement, then issue the SELECT query to verify that the resulting row has the expected values:

```
mysql> INSERT INTO profile (name) VALUES('Juan');
mysql> SELECT * FROM profile WHERE name = 'Juan';
+----+------+-------+-------+-------+------+
| id | name | birth | color | foods | cats |
+----+------+-------+-------+-------+------+
| 11 | Juan | NULL  | NULL  | NULL  | NULL |
+----+------+-------+-------+-------+------+
```

The id column might contain a different number, but the other columns should appear as shown.

Perl

In Perl DBI scripts, NULL is represented by undef. It's easy to detect such values using the defined() function, and it's particularly important to do so if you use the *-w* option on the #! line that begins your script. Otherwise, accessing undef values causes Perl to issue the following complaint:

```
Use of uninitialized value
```

To avoid this warning, test column values that might be undef with defined() before using them. The following code selects a few columns from the profile column and prints "NULL" for any undefined values in each row. This makes NULL values explicit in the output without activating any warning messages:

```
my $sth = $dbh->prepare ("SELECT name, birth, foods FROM profile");
$sth->execute ();
```

```
while (my $ref = $sth->fetchrow_hashref ())
{
    printf "name: %s, birth: %s, foods: %s\n",
                defined ($ref->{name}) ? $ref->{name} : "NULL",
                defined ($ref->{birth}) ? $ref->{birth} : "NULL",
                defined ($ref->{foods}) ? $ref->{foods} : "NULL";
}
```

Unfortunately, all that testing of column values is ponderous, and becomes worse the more columns there are. To avoid this, you can test and set undefined values in a loop prior to printing them. Then the amount of code to perform the tests is constant, not proportional to the number of columns to be tested. The loop also makes no reference to specific column names, so it can be copied and pasted to other programs more easily, or used as the basis for a utility routine:

```
my $sth = $dbh->prepare ("SELECT name, birth, foods FROM profile");
$sth->execute ();
while (my $ref = $sth->fetchrow_hashref ())
{
    foreach my $key (keys (%{$ref}))
    {
        $ref->{$key} = "NULL" unless defined ($ref->{$key});
    }
    printf "name: %s, birth: %s, foods: %s\n",
                $ref->{name}, $ref->{birth}, $ref->{foods};
}
```

If you fetch rows into an array rather than into a hash, you can use map() to convert any undef values:

```
my $sth = $dbh->prepare ("SELECT name, birth, foods FROM profile");
$sth->execute ();
while (my @val = $sth->fetchrow_array ())
{
    @val = map { defined ($_) ? $_ : "NULL" } @val;
    printf "name: %s, birth: %s, foods: %s\n",
                $val[0], $val[1], $val[2];
}
```

PHP

PHP represents NULL values in result sets as unset values, so you can use the isset() function to detect NULL values in query results. The following code shows how to do this:

```
$result_id = mysql_query ("SELECT name, birth, foods FROM profile", $conn_id);
if (!$result_id)
    die ("Oops, the query failed\n");
while ($row = mysql_fetch_row ($result_id))
{
    while (list ($key, $value) = each ($row))
    {
        if (!isset ($row[$key]))    # test for unset value
```

```
                    $row[$key] = "NULL";
        }
        print ("name: $row[0], birth: $row[1], foods: $row[2]\n");
    }
    mysql_free_result ($result_id);
```

PHP 4 has a special value NULL that is like an unset value. If you can assume your
scripts will run under PHP 4, you can test for NULL values like this:

```
    if ($row[$key] === NULL)    # test for PHP NULL value
        $row[$key] = "NULL";
```

Note the use of the === "triple-equal" operator, which in PHP 4 means "exactly equal
to." The usual == "equal to" comparison operator is not suitable here; with ==, the
PHP NULL value, the empty string, and 0 all compare equal to each other.

Python

Python DB-API programs represent NULL values in result sets using None. The following example shows how to detect NULL values:

```
    try:
        cursor = conn.cursor ()
        cursor.execute ("SELECT name, birth, foods FROM profile")
        for row in cursor.fetchall ():
            row = list (row)    # convert non-mutable tuple to mutable list
            for i in range (0, len (row)):
                if row[i] == None:  # is the column value NULL?
                    row[i] = "NULL"
            print "name: %s, birth: %s, foods: %s" % (row[0], row[1], row[2])
        cursor.close ()
    except:
        print "Oops, the query failed"
```

The inner loop checks for NULL column values by looking for None and converts them
to the string "NULL". Note how the example converts row to a mutable object prior to
the loop; that is done because fetchall() returns rows as sequence values, which are
non-mutable (read-only).

Java

For JDBC programs, if it's possible for a column in a result set to contain NULL values, it's best to check for them explicitly. The way to do this is to fetch the value and
then invoke wasNull(), which returns true if the column is NULL and false otherwise.
For example:

```
    Object obj = rs.getObject (index);
    if (rs.wasNull ())
    { /* the value's a NULL */ }
```

The preceding example uses getObject(), but the principle holds for other getXXX()
calls as well.

Here's an example that prints each row of a result set as a comma-separated list of values, with each NULL value printed as the string "NULL":

```
Statement s = conn.createStatement ();
s.executeQuery ("SELECT name, birth, foods FROM profile");
ResultSet rs = s.getResultSet ();
ResultSetMetaData md = rs.getMetaData ();
int ncols = md.getColumnCount ();
while (rs.next ())  // loop through rows of result set
{
    for (int i = 0; i < ncols; i++) // loop through columns
    {
        String val = rs.getString (i+1);
        if (i > 0)
            System.out.print (", ");
        if (rs.wasNull ())
            System.out.print ("NULL");
        else
            System.out.print (val);
    }
    System.out.println ();
}
rs.close ();    // close result set
s.close ();     // close statement
```

2.9   Writing an Object-Oriented MySQL Interface for PHP

Problem

You want an approach for writing PHP scripts that is less tied to PHP's native MySQL-specific functions.

Solution

Use one of the abstract interfaces that are available, or write your own.

Discussion

You may have noticed that the Perl, Python, and Java operations that connect to the MySQL server each return a value that allows you to process queries in an object-oriented manner. Perl has database and statement handles, Python has connection and cursor objects, and Java uses objects for everything in sight: connections, statements, result sets, and metadata. These object-oriented interfaces all are based on a two-level architecture.

The top level of this architecture provides database-independent methods that implement database access in a portable way that's the same no matter which database management system you're using, be it MySQL, PostgreSQL, Oracle, or whatever. The lower level consists of a set of drivers, each of which implements the details for a particular database system. The two-level architecture allows application programs to use an abstract interface that is not tied to the details involved with accessing any particular database server. This enhances portability of your programs, because you just select a different lower-level driver to use a different type of database. That's the theory, at least. In practice, perfect portability can be somewhat elusive:

- The interface methods provided by the top level of the architecture are consistent regardless of the driver you use, but it's still possible to issue SQL statements that contain constructs supported only by a particular server. For MySQL, a good example is the SHOW statement that provides information about database and table structure. If you use SHOW with a non-MySQL server, an error is the likely result.

- Lower-level drivers often extend the abstract interface to make it more convenient to get at database-specific features. For example, the MySQL driver for DBI makes the most recent AUTO_INCREMENT value available as an attribute of the database handle so that you can access it as $dbh->{mysql_insertid}. These features often make it easier to write a program initially, but at the same time make it less portable and require some rewriting should you port the program for use with another database system.

Despite these factors that compromise portability, the two-level architecture provides significant benefits for Perl, Python, and Java programmers. It would be nice to use this approach when writing PHP scripts, too, but PHP itself provides no such support. Its interface to MySQL consists of a set of functions, and these are inherently non-portable because their names all are of the form mysql_xxx(). To work around this, you can write your own database abstraction mechanism.

That is the purpose of this section. It shows how to write an object-oriented PHP interface that hides many MySQL-specific details and is relatively database independent—certainly more so than PHP's function-based MySQL interface. As discussed here, the interface is written specifically for MySQL, but if you want to adapt it for use with a different database, you should be able to do so by supplying a different set of underlying class methods.

If you want to write PHP scripts in a database-independent fashion, but prefer not to write your own interface, you can use a third-party abstraction interface. One such is the database-access class that is a part of the PHP Extension and Add-on Repository (PEAR). PEAR is included with current releases of PHP 4.

The following discussion shows how to write a MySQL_Access class that implements an object-oriented interface to MySQL, and a Cookbook_DB_Access class that is built on top of MySQL_Access but automatically supplies default values for connecting to the cookbook database. (If you're not familiar with PHP classes, you may want to consult the "Classes and Objects" chapter of the PHP manual for background information.)

The primary goal of this class interface is to make it easier to use MySQL by reducing the number of operations your scripts must perform explicitly:

- The interface automatically establishes a connection to the MySQL server if you issue a query without connecting first; you need never issue a connect call explicitly. The connection parameters must be specified somehow, of course, but as we'll see, that can be done automatically as well.

- The interface provides automatic error checking for MySQL calls. This is more convenient than checking for them yourself, and helps eliminate one of the most common problems with PHP scripts: failure to check for database errors on a consistent basis. The default behavior is to exit with an error message when a problem occurs, but you can override that if you want to handle errors yourself.

- When you reach the end of a result set while fetching rows, the class automatically releases the set.

The class-based interface also provides a method for quoting data values to make them safe for use in queries, and a placeholder mechanism so you don't need to do any quoting at all if you don't want to. These capabilities are not present in PHP's native function-based interface.

The following example illustrates how using an object-oriented interface changes the way you write PHP scripts to access MySQL, compared to writing function-based scripts. A script based on PHP's native function calls typically accesses MySQL something like this:

```
if (!($conn_id = mysql_connect ("localhost", "cbuser", "cbpass")))
    die ("Cannot connect to database\n");
if (!mysql_select_db ("cookbook", $conn_id))
    die ("Cannot select database\n");
$query = "UPDATE profile SET cats=cats+1 WHERE name = 'Fred'";
$result_id = mysql_query ($query, $conn_id);
if (!$result_id)
    die (mysql_error ($conn_id));
print (mysql_affected_rows ($conn_id) . " rows were updated\n");
$query = "SELECT id, name, cats FROM profile";
$result_id = mysql_query ($query, $conn_id);
if (!$result_id)
    die (mysql_error ($conn_id));
while ($row = mysql_fetch_row ($result_id))
    print ("id: $row[0], name: $row[1], cats: $row[2]\n");
mysql_free_result ($result_id);
```

A first step toward eliminating some of that code is to replace the first few lines by calling the cookbook_connect() function from the PHP library file, *Cookbook.php*, developed in Recipe 2.3. That function encapsulates the connection and database selection operations:

```
include "Cookbook.php";
$conn_id = cookbook_connect ();
$query = "UPDATE profile SET cats=cats+1 WHERE name = 'Fred'";
```

```
$result_id = mysql_query ($query, $conn_id);
if (!$result_id)
    die (mysql_error ($conn_id));
print (mysql_affected_rows ($conn_id) . " rows were updated\n");
$query = "SELECT id, name, cats FROM profile";
$result_id = mysql_query ($query, $conn_id);
if (!$result_id)
    die (mysql_error ($conn_id));
while ($row = mysql_fetch_row ($result_id))
    print ("id: $row[0], name: $row[1], cats: $row[2]\n");
mysql_free_result ($result_id);
```

A class-based interface can carry encapsulation further and shorten the script even more by eliminating the need to connect explicitly, to check for errors, or to close the result set. All of that can be handled automatically:

```
include "Cookbook_DB_Access.php";
$conn = new Cookbook_DB_Access;
$query = "UPDATE profile SET cats=cats+1 WHERE name = 'Fred'";
$conn->issue_query ($query);
print ($conn->num_rows . " rows were updated\n");
$query = "SELECT id, name, cats FROM profile";
$conn->issue_query ($query);
while ($row = $conn->fetch_row ())
    print ("id: $row[0], name: $row[1], cats: $row[2]\n");
```

A class interface can make MySQL easier to use by reducing the amount of code you need to write when creating new scripts, but it has other benefits as well. For example, it can also serve as a recipe translation aid. Suppose a program in a later chapter is shown in Perl, but you'd rather use in it PHP and there is no PHP version on the Cookbook web site. Perl DBI is object oriented, so you'll likely find it easier to translate a Perl script into a PHP script that is object oriented, rather than into one that is function based.

Class Overview

The class interface implementation uses the PHP recipes and techniques developed earlier in this chapter, so you should familiarize yourself with those. For example, the class interface needs to know how to make connections to the server and process queries, and we'll use include (library) files to encapsulate the interface so that it can be used easily from multiple PHP scripts.

The interface shown here works only with PHP 4. This is something that is not true of PHP's native MySQL routines, which work both with PHP 3 and PHP 4. The restriction is necessitated by the use of a few constructs that are not available or do not work properly in PHP 3. Specifically, the interface assumes the availability of the include_once statement and the PHP NULL value. It also assumes that count() correctly counts unset values in arrays, which is true only for PHP 4.

The implementation strategy involves two classes. The first is a generic base class MySQL_Access that provides the variables and methods needed for using MySQL. The second is a derived class Cookbook_DB_Access that has access to everything in the base class but automatically sets up connection parameters specifically for the cookbook database so we don't have to do that ourselves. An alternative implementation might use just a single class and hardwire the cookbook database parameters directly into it. However, writing the base class to be generic allows it to be used more easily for scripts that access a database other than cookbook. (For such scripts, you'd just write another derived class that uses the base class but provides a different set of connection parameters.)

A PHP class definition begins with a class line that specifies the class name, then defines the variables and methods associated with the class. An outline of the base class, MySQL_Access, looks like this:

```
class MySQL_Access
{
    var $host_name = "";
    var $user_name = "";
    var $password = "";
    var $db_name = "";
    var $conn_id = 0;
    var $errno = 0;
    var $errstr = "";
    var $halt_on_error = 1;
    var $query_pieces = array ();
    var $result_id = 0;
    var $num_rows = 0;
    var $row = array ();

    # ... method definitions ...

} # end MySQL_Access
```

The class definition begins with several variables that are used as follows:

- The first few variables hold the parameters for connecting to the MySQL server ($host_name, $user_name, $password, and $db_name). These are empty initially and must be set before attempting a connection.

- Once a connection is made, the connection identifier is stored in $conn_id. Its initial value, 0, means "no connection." This allows a class instance to determine whether or not it has connected to the database server yet.

- $errno and $errstr hold error information; the class sets them after each MySQL operation to indicate the success or failure of the operation. The initial values, 0 and the empty string, mean "no error." For errors that occur but not as a result of interacting with the server, $errno is set to −1, which is a nonzero error value never used by MySQL. This can happen, for example, if you use placeholder characters in a query string but don't provide the correct number of data values when you bind them to the placeholders. In that case, the class detects the error without sending anything to the server.

- $halt_on_error determines whether or not to terminate script execution when an error occurs. The default is to do so. Scripts that want to perform their own error-checking can set this to zero.

- $query_pieces is used to hold a query string for prepared statements and parameter binding. (I'll explain later why this variable is an array.)

- $result_id, $num_rows, and $row are used during result set processing to hold the result set identifier, the number of rows changed by or returned by the query, and the current row of the result set.

PHP Class Constructor Functions

In PHP, you can designate a constructor function in a class definition to be called automatically when new class instances are created. This is done by giving the function the same name as the class. You might do this, for example, if you need to initialize an object's variables to non-constant values. (In PHP 4, object variables can only take constant initializers.) The MySQL_Access class has no constructor because its variables all have constant initial values.

The "method definitions" line near the end of the class outline is where we'll put the functions that connect to the MySQL server, check for errors, issue queries, and so forth. We'll fill in that part shortly, but before doing so, let's get a sense of how the class can be used. We can put the code for the class in an include file, *MySQL_Access.php*, and install it in a directory that PHP searches when looking for include files (for example, */usr/local/apache/lib/php*, as described in Recipe 2.3.) Then we can use the file by referencing it with an include statement, creating an instance of the class to get a connection object $conn, and setting up the connection parameters for that object:

```
include "MySQL_Access.php";        # include the MySQL_Access class
$conn = new MySQL_Access;          # create new class object
$conn->host_name = "localhost";    # initialize connection parameters
$conn->db_name = "cookbook";
$conn->user_name = "cbuser";
$conn->password = "cbpass";
```

However, using the class this way wouldn't really make it very convenient to connect to the server, due to the need to write all those assignment statements that set the connection parameters. Here's where a derived class that uses the base class comes in handy, because the derived class can be written to set the parameters automatically. To that end, let's create a class, Cookbook_DB_Access, that extends MySQL_Access by supplying parameters for connecting to the cookbook database. Then you can write scripts that prepare to access the cookbook database with just two lines of code:

```
include "Cookbook_DB_Access.php";
$conn = new Cookbook_DB_Access;
```

The implementation of Cookbook_DB_Access is quite simple. Create a file, *Cookbook_DB_Access.php*, that looks like this:

```
include_once "MySQL_Access.php";

class Cookbook_DB_Access extends MySQL_Access
{
    # override default class variable values
    var $host_name = "localhost";
    var $user_name = "cbuser";
    var $password = "cbpass";
    var $db_name = "cookbook";
}
```

The class line names the class, Cookbook_DB_Access, and the extends clause indicates that it's based on the MySQL_Access class. Extending a class this way is called subclassing the base class, or creating a derived class from the base class. The new class definition is almost trivial, containing only variable assignments for connection parameters. These override the (empty) values that are supplied by the base class. The effect is that when you create an instance of the Cookbook_DB_Access class, you get an object that's just like a MySQL_Access object, except that the connection parameters are set automatically for connecting to the cookbook database.

Now you can see more clearly why we left the connection parameters in the MySQL_Access class empty rather than setting them for accessing the cookbook database. By leaving them blank, we create a more generic class that can be extended for any number of databases by creating different derived classes. Cookbook_DB_Access is one such class. If you're writing a set of scripts that use a different database, derive another extended class that supplies appropriate connection parameters for that database. Then have the scripts use the second extended class rather than *Cookbook_DB_Access.php*.

Incidentally, the reason that *Cookbook_DB_Access.php* includes *MySQL_Access.php* is so that you don't need to. When your scripts include *Cookbook_DB_Access.php*, they get *MySQL_Access.php* "for free." The include_once statement is used rather than include to prevent duplicate-definition problems from occurring if your scripts happen to include *MySQL_Access.php* anyway.

Connecting and Disconnecting

Now we need to write the methods of the base class, MySQL_Access, that interact with MySQL. These go in the *MySQL_Access.php* source file. First, we need a connect() method that sets up a connection to the MySQL server:

```
function connect ()
{
    $this->errno = 0;            # clear the error variables
    $this->errstr = "";
    if ($this->conn_id == 0)     # connect if not already connected
    {
        $this->conn_id = @mysql_connect ($this->host_name,
                                         $this->user_name,
                                         $this->password);
        # use mysql_errno()/mysql_error() if they work for
        # connection errors; use $php_errormsg otherwise
        if (!$this->conn_id)
        {
            # mysql_errno() returns nonzero if it's
            # functional for connection errors
            if (mysql_errno ())
            {
                $this->errno = mysql_errno ();
                $this->errstr = mysql_error ();
            }
            else
            {
                $this->errno = -1;   # use alternate values
                $this->errstr = $php_errormsg;
            }
            $this->error ("Cannot connect to server");
            return (FALSE);
        }
        # select database if one has been specified
        if (isset ($this->db_name) && $this->db_name != "")
        {
            if (!@mysql_select_db ($this->db_name, $this->conn_id))
            {
                $this->errno = mysql_errno ();
                $this->errstr = mysql_error ();
                $this->error ("Cannot select database");
                return (FALSE);
            }
        }
    }
    return ($this->conn_id);
}
```

The connect() method checks for an existing connection and attempts to establish one only if it hasn't already done so. connect() does this so other class methods that require a connection can call this method to make sure there is one. Specifically, we can write the query-issuing method to call connect() before sending a query. That way, all a script has to do is create a class object and start issuing queries; the class methods automatically take care of making the connection for us. By writing the class this way, it becomes unnecessary for scripts that use the class ever to establish a connection explicitly.

For a successful connection attempt, or if a connection is already in place, connect()
returns the connection identifier (a non-FALSE value). If an error occurs, connect()
calls error() and one of two things can happen:

- If $halt_on_error is set, error() prints a message and terminates the script.
- Otherwise, error() does nothing and returns to connect(), which returns FALSE.

Note that if a connection failure occurs, connect() tries to use mysql_errno() and
mysql_error() if they are the versions provided in PHP 4.0.6 and up that return
usable information for mysql_connect() errors (see Recipe 2.2). Otherwise, it sets
$errno to –1 and $errstr to $php_errormsg.

There is also a disconnect() method corresponding to connect() in case you want to
disconnect explicitly. (Otherwise, PHP closes the connection for you when your
script exits.) The method calls mysql_close() if a connection is open:

```
function disconnect ()
{
    if ($this->conn_id != 0)     # there's a connection open; close it
    {
        mysql_close ($this->conn_id);
        $this->conn_id = 0;
    }
    return (TRUE);
}
```

Error Handling

MySQL_Access methods handle errors by calling the error() method. The behavior of
this method depends on the value of the $halt_on_error variable. If $halt_on_error is
true (nonzero), error() prints an error message and exits. This is the default behavior, which means you never need to check for errors if you don't want to. If you disable $halt_on_error by setting it to zero, error() simply returns to its caller, which
then can pass back an error return status to its own caller. Thus, error-handling code
within MySQL_Access typically looks like this:

```
if (some error occurred)
{
    $this->error ("some error occurred");
    return (FALSE);
}
```

If $halt_on_error is enabled when an error occurs, error() is invoked and termi-
nates the script. Otherwise, it returns and the return() statement that follows it is
executed.

To write code that does its own error checking, disable $halt_on_error. In that case,
you may also want to access the $errno and $errstr variables, which hold the
MySQL numeric error code and descriptive text message. The following example
shows how to disable $halt_on_error for the duration of a single operation:

```
$conn->halt_on_error = 0;
print ("Test of error-trapping:\n");
if (!$conn->issue_query ($query_str))
    print ("Hey, error $conn->errno occurred: $conn->errstr\n");
$conn->halt_on_error = 1;
```

When error() prints a message, it also displays the values of the error variables if $errno is nonzero. error() converts the message to properly escaped HTML, on the assumption that the class will be used in a web environment:

```
function error ($msg)
{
    if (!$this->halt_on_error)  # return silently
        return;
    $msg .= "\n";
    if ($this->errno)   # if an error code is known, include error info
        $msg .= sprintf ("Error: %s (%d)\n", $this->errstr, $this->errno);
    die (nl2br (htmlspecialchars ($msg)));
}
```

Issuing Queries and Processing the Results

Now we get to the heart of the matter, issuing queries. To execute a statement, pass it to issue_query():

```
function issue_query ($query_str)
{
    if (!$this->connect ())      # establish connection to server if
        return (FALSE);          # necessary

    $this->num_rows = 0;
    $this->result_id = mysql_query ($query_str, $this->conn_id);
    $this->errno = mysql_errno ();
    $this->errstr = mysql_error ();
    if ($this->errno)
    {
        $this->error ("Cannot execute query: $query_str");
        return (FALSE);
    }
    # get number of affected rows for non-SELECT; this also returns
    # number of rows for a SELECT
    $this->num_rows = mysql_affected_rows ($this->conn_id);
    return ($this->result_id);
}
```

issue_query() first calls connect() to make sure that a connection has been established before it sends the query to the server. Then it executes the query, sets the error variables (which will be 0 and the empty string if no error occurs), and checks whether or not the query succeeded. If it failed, issue_query() takes the appropriate error-handling action. Otherwise, it sets $num_rows and the result set identifier becomes the return value. For a non-SELECT query, $num_rows indicates the number of rows changed by the query. For a SELECT query, it indicates the number of rows returned. (There's a little bit of cheating here. `mysql_affected_rows()` really is intended only for non-SELECT statements, but happens to return the number of rows in the result set for SELECT queries.)

If a query produces a result set, you'll want to fetch its rows. PHP provides several functions for this, which were discussed in Recipe 2.4: `mysql_fetch_row()`, `mysql_fetch_array()`, and `mysql_fetch_object()`. These functions can be used as the basis for corresponding MySQL_Access methods `fetch_row()`, `fetch_array()`, and `fetch_object()`. Each of these methods fetches the next row and returns it, or, if there are no more rows left, releases the result set and returns FALSE. They also set the error variables automatically on every call. The `fetch_row()` method is shown here; `fetch_array()` and `fetch_object()` are very similar:

```
# Fetch the next row as an array with numeric indexes

function fetch_row ()
{
    $this->row = mysql_fetch_row ($this->result_id);
    $this->errno = mysql_errno ();
    $this->errstr = mysql_error ();
    if ($this->errno)
    {
        $this->error ("fetch_row error");
        return (FALSE);
    }
    if (is_array ($this->row))
        return ($this->row);
    $this->free_result ();
    return (FALSE);
}
```

The `free_result()` method used by the row-fetching methods releases the result set, if there is one:

```
function free_result ()
{
    if ($this->result_id)
        mysql_free_result ($this->result_id);
    $this->result_id = 0;
    return (TRUE);
}
```

Freeing the result set automatically when the last record has been fetched is one way the class interface simplifies MySQL access, compared to the PHP function-based interface. However, any script that fetches only part of a result set should invoke `free_result()` itself to release the set explicitly.

To determine whether or not a value from a result set represents a NULL value, compare it to the PHP NULL value by using the triple-equals operator:

```
if ($val === NULL)
{
    # $val is a NULL value
}
```

Alternatively, use `isset( )`:

```
if (!isset ($val))
{
    # $val is a NULL value
}
```

At this point, enough machinery is present in the class interface that it is usable for writing scripts that issue queries and process the results:

```
# instantiate connection object
include "Cookbook_DB_Access.php";
$conn = new Cookbook_DB_Access;

# issue query that returns no result set
$query = "UPDATE profile SET cats=cats+1 WHERE name = 'Fred'";
$conn->issue_query ($query);
print ($conn->num_rows . " rows were updated\n");

# issue queries that fetch rows, using each row-fetching method
$query = "SELECT id, name, cats FROM profile";
$conn->issue_query ($query);
while ($row = $conn->fetch_row ())
    print ("id: $row[0], name: $row[1], cats: $row[2]\n");
$conn->issue_query ($query);
while ($row = $conn->fetch_array ())
{
    print ("id: $row[0], name: $row[1], cats: $row[2]\n");
    print ("id: $row[id], name: $row[name], cats: $row[cats]\n");
}
$conn->issue_query ($query);
while ($row = $conn->fetch_object ())
    print ("id: $row->id, name: $row->name, cats: $row->cats\n");
```

Quoting and Placeholder Support

In Recipe 2.8, we developed a PHP `sql_quote( )` function for PHP to handle quoting, escaping, and NULL (unset) values, so that any value can be inserted easily into a query:

```
function sql_quote ($str)
{
    if (!isset ($str))
        return ("NULL");
    $func = function_exists ("mysql_escape_string")
            ? "mysql_escape_string"
            : "addslashes";
    return ("'" . $func ($str) . "'");
}
```

If we add `sql_quote( )` to the MySQL_Access class, it becomes available automatically to any class instance as an object method and you can construct query strings that include properly quoted values like so:

```
$stmt = sprintf ("INSERT INTO profile (name,birth,color,foods,cats)
            VALUES(%s,%s,%s,%s,%s)",
```

```
                            $conn->sql_quote ("De'Mont"),
                            $conn->sql_quote ("1973-01-12"),
                            $conn->sql_quote (NULL),
                            $conn->sql_quote ("eggroll"),
                            $conn->sql_quote (4));
        $conn->issue_query ($stmt);
```

In fact, we can employ the sql_quote() method as the basis for a placeholder emulation mechanism, to be used as follows:

1. Begin by passing a query string to the prepare_query() method.

2. Indicate placeholders in the query string by using ? characters.

3. Execute the query and supply an array of values to be bound to the query, one value per placeholder. (To bind NULL to a placeholder, pass the PHP NULL value.)

One way to perform parameter binding is to do a lot of pattern matching and substitution in the query string wherever ? occurs as a placeholder character. An easier approach is simply to break the query string at the ? characters, then glue the pieces back together at query execution time with the properly quoted data values inserted between the pieces. Splitting the query also is an easy way to find out how many placeholders there are (it's the number of pieces, minus one). That's useful for determining whether or not the proper number of data values is present when it comes time to bind those values to the placeholders.

The prepare_query() method is quite simple. All it does is split up the query string at ? characters, placing the result into the $query_pieces array for later use at parameter-binding time:

```
function prepare_query ($query)
{
    $this->query_pieces = explode ("?", $query);
    return (TRUE);
}
```

We could invent new calls for binding data values to the query and for executing it, but it's also possible to modify issue_query() a little, to have it determine what to do by examining the type of its argument. If the argument is a string, it's interpreted as a query that should be executed directly (which is how issue_query() behaved before). If the argument is an array, it is assumed to contain data values to be bound to a previously prepared statement. With this change, issue_query() looks like this:

```
function issue_query ($arg = "")
{
    if ($arg == "")             # if no argument, assume prepared statement
        $arg = array ();        # with no values to be bound
    if (!$this->connect ())     # establish connection to server if
        return (FALSE);         # necessary

    if (is_string ($arg))       # $arg is a simple query
        $query_str = $arg;
    else if (is_array ($arg))   # $arg contains data values for placeholders
```

```
    {
        if (count ($arg) != count ($this->query_pieces) - 1)
        {
            $this->errno = -1;
            $this->errstr = "data value/placeholder count mismatch";
            $this->error ("Cannot execute query");
            return (FALSE);
        }
        # insert data values into query at placeholder
        # positions, quoting values as we go
        $query_str = $this->query_pieces[0];
        for ($i = 0; $i < count ($arg); $i++)
        {
            $query_str .= $this->sql_quote ($arg[$i])
                        . $this->query_pieces[$i+1];
        }
    }
    else                        # $arg is garbage
    {
        $this->errno = -1;
        $this->errstr = "unknown argument type to issue_query";
        $this->error ("Cannot execute query");
        return (FALSE);
    }

    $this->num_rows = 0;
    $this->result_id = mysql_query ($query_str, $this->conn_id);
    $this->errno = mysql_errno ();
    $this->errstr = mysql_error ();
    if ($this->errno)
    {
        $this->error ("Cannot execute query: $query_str");
        return (FALSE);
    }
    # get number of affected rows for non-SELECT; this also returns
    # number of rows for a SELECT
    $this->num_rows = mysql_affected_rows ($this->conn_id);
    return ($this->result_id);
}
```

Now that quoting and placeholder support is in place, the class provides three ways of issuing queries. First, you can write out the entire query string literally and perform quoting, escaping, and NULL handling yourself:

```
$conn->issue_query ("INSERT INTO profile (name,birth,color,foods,cats)
                    VALUES('De\'Mont','1973-01-12',NULL,'eggroll','4')");
```

Second, you can use the sql_quote() method to insert data values into the query string:

```
$stmt = sprintf ("INSERT INTO profile (name,birth,color,foods,cats)
                VALUES(%s,%s,%s,%s,%s)",
                    $conn->sql_quote ("De'Mont"),
                    $conn->sql_quote ("1973-01-12"),
```

```
                    $conn->sql_quote (NULL),
                    $conn->sql_quote ("eggroll"),
                    $conn->sql_quote (4));
    $conn->issue_query ($stmt);
```

Third, you can use placeholders and let the class interface handle all the work of binding values to the query:

```
    $conn->prepare_query ("INSERT INTO profile (name,birth,color,foods,cats)
                    VALUES(?,?,?,?,?)");
    $conn->issue_query (array ("De'Mont", "1973-01-12", NULL, "eggroll", 4));
```

The `MySQL_Access` and `Cookbook_DB_Access` classes now provide a reasonably convenient means of writing PHP scripts that is easier to use than the native MySQL PHP calls. The class interface also includes placeholder support, something that PHP does not provide at all.

The development of these classes illustrates how you can write your own interface that hides MySQL-specific details. The interface is not without its shortcomings, naturally. For example, it allows you to prepare only one statement at a time, unlike DBI and JDBC, which support multiple simultaneous prepared statements. Should you require such functionality, you might consider how to reimplement `MySQL_Access` to provide it.

2.10   Ways of Obtaining Connection Parameters

Problem

You need to obtain connection parameters for a script so that it can connect to a MySQL server.

Solution

There are lots of ways to do this. Take your pick.

Discussion

Any program that connects to MySQL needs to specify connection parameters such as the username, password, and hostname. The recipes shown so far have put connection parameters directly into the code that attempts to establish the connection, but that is not the only way for your programs to obtain the parameters. This section briefly surveys some methods you can use, then shows how to implement two of them.

Hardwire the parameters into the program.   The parameters can be given either in the main source file or in a library file that is used by the program. This is convenient because users need not enter the values themselves. The flip side, of course, is that it's not very flexible. To change the parameters, you must modify your program.

Ask for the parameters interactively. In a command-line environment, you can ask the user a series of questions. In a web or GUI environment, this might be done by presenting a form or dialog. Either way, this gets to be tedious for people who use the program frequently, due to the need to enter the parameters each time.

Get the parameters from the command line. This method can be used either for commands that you run interactively or that are run from within a script. Like the method of obtaining parameters interactively, this requires you to supply parameters each time you use MySQL, and can be similarly tiresome. (A factor that significantly mitigates this burden is that many shells allow you to recall commands from your history list for reexecution.)

Get the parameters from the execution environment. The most common way of using this method is to set the appropriate environment variables in one of your shell's startup files (such as *.cshrc* for *csh*; *.tcshrc* for *tcsh*; or *.profile* for *sh*, *bash*, and *ksh*). Programs that you run during your login session then can get parameter values by examining their environment.

Get the parameters from a separate file. With this method, you store information such as the username and password in a file that programs can read before connecting to the MySQL server. Reading parameters from a file that's separate from your program gives you the benefit of not having to enter them each time you use the program, while allowing you to avoid hardwiring the values into the program itself. This is especially convenient for interactive programs, because then you need not enter parameters each time you run the program. Also, storing the values in a file allows you to centralize parameters for use by multiple programs, and you can use the file access mode for security purposes. For example, you can keep other users from reading the file by setting its mode to allow access only to yourself.

The MySQL client library itself supports an option file mechanism, although not all APIs provide access to it. For those that don't, workarounds may exist. (As an example, Java supports the use of properties files and supplies utility routines for reading them.)

Use a combination of methods. It's often useful to combine some of the preceding methods, to afford users the option of providing parameters different ways. For example, MySQL clients such as *mysql* and *mysqladmin* look for option files in several locations and read any that are present. Then they check the command-line arguments for further parameters. This allows users to specify connection parameters in an option file or on the command line.

These methods of obtaining connection parameters do involve some security issues. Briefly summarized, these issues are:

- Any method that stores connection parameters in a file may result in compromise unless the file is protected against read access by unauthorized users. This is true whether parameters are stored in a source file, an option file, or a script that invokes a command and specifies the parameters on the command line. (Web scripts that can be read only by the web server don't qualify as secure if other users have administrative access to the server.)

- Parameters specified on the command line or in environment variables are not particularly secure. While a program is executing, its command-line arguments and environment may be visible to other users who run process status commands such as *ps -e*. In particular, storing the password in an environment variable perhaps is best limited to use in situations where you're the only user on the machine or you trust all other users.

The rest of this section shows how to process command-line arguments to get connection parameters, and how to read parameters from option files.

Getting Parameters from the Command Line

The usual MySQL convention for command-line arguments (that is, the convention followed by standard MySQL clients such as *mysql*) is to allow parameters to be specified using either a short option or a long option. For example, the username cbuser can be specified either as *-u* cbuser (or *-u*cbuser) or *--user*=cbuser. In addition, for the options that specify the password (*-p* or *--password*), the password value may be omitted after the option name to indicate that the program should prompt for the password interactively.

The next set of example programs shows how to process command arguments to obtain the hostname, username, and password. The standard flags for these are *-h* or *--host*, *-u* or *--user*, and *-p* or *--password*. You can write your own code to iterate through the argument list, but in general, it's much easier to use existing option-processing modules written for that purpose. The programs presented here are implemented using a getopt( )-style function for each API, with the exception of PHP. Insofar as possible, the examples mimic the behavior of the standard MySQL clients. (No example program is provided for PHP, because few PHP scripts are written for use from the command line.)

Perl

Perl passes command-line arguments to scripts in the @ARGV array, which can be processed using the GetOptions( ) function of the *Getopt::Long* module. The following program shows how to parse the command arguments for connection parameters. If a password option is specified with no following argument, the script prompts the user for the password value.

```
#! /usr/bin/perl -w
# cmdline.pl - demonstrate command-line option parsing in Perl

use strict;
use DBI;
```

```
use Getopt::Long;
$Getopt::Long::ignorecase = 0; # options are case sensitive
$Getopt::Long::bundling = 1;   # allow short options to be bundled

# connection parameters - all missing (undef) by default
my ($host_name, $password, $user_name);

GetOptions (
    # =s means a string argument is required after the option
    # :s means a string argument is optional after the option
    "host|h=s"      => \$host_name,
    "password|p:s"  => \$password,
    "user|u=s"      => \$user_name
) or exit (1);   # no error message needed; GetOptions() prints its own

# solicit password if option specified without option value
if (defined ($password) && $password eq "")
{
    # turn off echoing but don't interfere with STDIN
    open (TTY, "/dev/tty") or die "Cannot open terminal\n";
    system ("stty -echo < /dev/tty");
    print STDERR "Enter password: ";
    chomp ($password = <TTY>);
    system ("stty echo < /dev/tty");
    close (TTY);
    print STDERR "\n";
}

# construct data source name
my $dsn = "DBI:mysql:database=cookbook";
$dsn .= ";host=$host_name" if defined ($host_name);

# connect to server
my $dbh = DBI->connect ($dsn, $user_name, $password,
                        {PrintError => 0, RaiseError => 1});
print "Connected\n";

$dbh->disconnect ();
print "Disconnected\n";
exit (0);
```

The arguments to GetOptions() are pairs of option specifiers and references to the
script variables into which option values should be placed. An option specifier lists
both the long and short forms of the option (without leading dashes), followed by =s
if the option requires a following argument or :s if it may be followed by an argu-
ment. For example, "host|h=s" allows both *--host* and *-h* and indicates that a string
argument is required following the option. You need not pass the @ARGV array
because GetOptions() uses it implicitly. When GetOptions() returns, @ARGV contains
any remaining arguments following the last option.

The *Getopt::Long* module's $bundling variable affects the interpretation of arguments
that begin with a single dash, such as *-u*. Normally, we'd like to accept both *-u* cbuser

and *-uc*buser as the same thing, because that's how the standard MySQL clients act. However, if $bundling is zero (the default value), GetOptions( ) interprets *-uc*buser as a single option named "ucbuser". By setting $bundling to nonzero, GetOptions( ) understands both *-u* c*buser and *-uc*buser the same way. This happens because it interprets an option beginning with a single dash character by character, on the basis that several single-character options may be bundled together. For example, when it sees *-uc*buser, it looks at the *u*, then checks whether or not the option takes a following argument. If not, the next character is interpreted as another option letter. Otherwise, the rest of the string is taken as the option's value. For *-uc*buser, *u* does take an argument, so GetOptions( ) interprets cbuser as the option value.

One problem with GetOptions( ) is that it doesn't support *-p* without a password the same way as the standard MySQL client programs. If *-p* is followed by another option, GetOptions( ) correctly determines that there is no password value present. But if *-p* is followed by a non-option argument, it misinterprets that argument as the password. The result is that these two invocations of *cmdline.pl* are not quite equivalent:

```
% cmdline.pl -h localhost -p -u cbuser xyz
Enter password:
% cmdline.pl -h localhost -u cbuser -p xyz
DBI->connect(database=cookbook;host=localhost) failed: Access denied for
user: 'cbuser@localhost' (Using password: YES) at ./cmdline.pl line 40
```

For the first command, GetOptions( ) determines that no password is present and the script prompts for one. In the second command, GetOptions( ) has taken xyz as the password value.

A second problem with *cmdline.pl* is that the password-prompting code is Unix specific and doesn't work under Windows. You could try using *Term::ReadKey*, which is a standard Perl module, but it doesn't work under Windows, either. (If you have a good password prompter for Windows, you might consider sending it to me for inclusion in the recipes distribution.)

PHP

PHP provides little support for option processing from the command line because it is used predominantly in a web environment where command-line arguments are not widely used. Hence, I'm providing no getopt( )-style example for PHP. If you want to go ahead and write your own argument processing routine, use the $argv array containing the arguments and the $argc variable indicating the number of arguments. $argv[0] is the program name, and $argv[1] to $argv[$argc-1] are the following arguments. The following code illustrates how to access these variables:

```
print ("Number of arguments: $argc\n");
print ("Program name: $argv[0]\n");
print ("Arguments following program name:\n");
if ($argc == 1)
    print ("None\n");
else
```

```
{
    for ($i = 1; $i < $argc; $i++)
        print ("$i: $argv[$i]\n");
}
```

Python

Python passes command arguments to scripts as a list in the `sys.argv` variable. You can access this variable by importing the sys module, then process its contents with `getopt()` if you also import the getopt module. The following program illustrates how to get parameters from the command arguments and use them for establishing a connection to the server:

```python
#! /usr/bin/python
# cmdline.py - demonstrate command-line option parsing in Python

import sys
import getopt
import MySQLdb

try:
    opts, args = getopt.getopt (sys.argv[1:],
                                "h:p:u:",
                                [ "host=", "password=", "user=" ])
except getopt.error, e:
    # print program name and text of error message
    print "%s: %s" % (sys.argv[0], e)
    sys.exit (1)

# default connection parameter values
host_name = password = user_name = ""

# iterate through options, extracting whatever values are present
for opt, arg in opts:
    if opt in ("-h", "--host"):
        host_name = arg
    elif opt in ("-p", "--password"):
        password = arg
    elif opt in ("-u", "--user"):
        user_name = arg

try:
    conn = MySQLdb.connect (db = "cookbook",
                            host = host_name,
                            user = user_name,
                            passwd = password)
    print "Connected"
except MySQLdb.Error, e:
    print "Cannot connect to server"
    print "Error:", e.args[1]
    print "Code:", e.args[0]
    sys.exit (1)
```

```
conn.close ()
print "Disconnected"
sys.exit (0)
```

getopt( ) takes either two or three arguments:

- A list of command arguments. This should not include the program name, sys.argv[0]. You can use sys.argv[1:] to refer to the list of arguments that follow the program name.

- A string naming the short option letters. Any of these may be followed by a colon character (:) to indicate that the option requires a following argument that specifies the option's value.

- An optional list of long option names. Each name may be followed by = to indicate that the option requires a following argument.

getopt( ) returns two values. The first is a list of option/value pairs, and the second is a list of any remaining arguments following the last option. *cmdline.py* iterates through the option list to determine which options are present and what their values are. Note that although you do not specify leading dashes in the option names passed to getopt( ), the names returned from that function do include leading dashes.

cmdline.py doesn't prompt for a missing password, because the getopt( ) module doesn't provide any way to specify that an option's argument is optional. Unfortunately, this means the *-p* and *--password* arguments cannot be specified without a password value.

Java

Java passes command-line arguments to programs in the array that you name in the main( ) declaration. The following declaration uses args for that array:

```
public static void main (String[] args)
```

A Getopt class for parsing arguments in Java is available at *http://www.urbanophile. com/arenn/coding/download.html* Install this class somewhere and make sure its installation directory is named in the value of your CLASSPATH environment variable. Then you can use Getopt as shown in the following example program:

```
// Cmdline.java - demonstrate command-line option parsing in Java

import java.io.*;
import java.sql.*;
import gnu.getopt.*;    // need this for the Getopt class

public class Cmdline
{
    public static void main (String[] args)
    {
        Connection conn = null;
```

```
String url = null;
String hostName = null;
String password = null;
String userName = null;
boolean promptForPassword = false;
LongOpt[] longOpt = new LongOpt[3];
int c;

longOpt[0] =
    new LongOpt ("host", LongOpt.REQUIRED_ARGUMENT, null, 'h');
longOpt[1] =
    new LongOpt ("password", LongOpt.OPTIONAL_ARGUMENT, null, 'p');
longOpt[2] =
    new LongOpt ("user", LongOpt.REQUIRED_ARGUMENT, null, 'u');

// instantiate option-processing object, then
// loop until there are no more options
Getopt g = new Getopt ("Cmdline", args, "h:p::u:", longOpt);
while ((c = g.getopt ()) != -1)
{
    switch (c)
    {
    case 'h':
        hostName = g.getOptarg ();
        break;
    case 'p':
        // if password option was given with no following
        // value, need to prompt for the password
        password = g.getOptarg ();
        if (password == null)
            promptForPassword = true;
        break;
    case 'u':
        userName = g.getOptarg ();
        break;
    case ':':                 // a required argument is missing
    case '?':                 // some other error occurred
        // no error message needed; getopt() prints its own
        System.exit (1);
    }
}

if (password == null && promptForPassword)
{
    try
    {
        DataInputStream s = new DataInputStream (System.in);
        System.err.print ("Enter password: ");
        // really should turn off character echoing here...
        password = s.readLine ();
    }
    catch (Exception e)
    {
        System.err.println ("Error reading password");
```

```
                    System.exit (1);
            }
        }

        try
        {
            // construct URL, noting whether or not hostName
            // was given; if not, MySQL will assume localhost
            if (hostName == null)
                hostName = "";
            url = "jdbc:mysql://" + hostName + "/cookbook";
            Class.forName ("com.mysql.jdbc.Driver").newInstance ();
            conn = DriverManager.getConnection (url, userName, password);
            System.out.println ("Connected");
        }
        catch (Exception e)
        {
            System.err.println ("Cannot connect to server");
        }
        finally
        {
            if (conn != null)
            {
                try
                {
                    conn.close ();
                    System.out.println ("Disconnected");
                }
                catch (Exception e) { }
            }
        }
    }
}
```

As the example program demonstrates, you prepare to parse arguments by instantiating a new Getopt object to which you pass the program's arguments and information describing the options the program allows. Then you call getopt() in a loop until it returns −1 to indicate that no more options are present. Each time through the loop, getopt() returns a value indicating which option it's seen, and getOptarg() may be called to obtain the option's argument, if necessary. (getOptarg() returns null if no following argument was provided.)

When you create an instance of the Getopt() class, pass it either three or four arguments:

- The program name; this is used for error messages.
- The argument array named in your main() declaration.
- A string listing the short option letters (without leading dashes). Any of these may be followed by a colon (:) to indicate that the option requires a following argument, or by a double colon (::) to indicate that a following argument is optional.

- An optional array that contains long option information. To specify long options, you must set up an array of LongOpt objects. Each of these describes a single option, using four parameters:

  — The option name as a string (without leading dashes).

  — A value indicating whether the option takes a following argument. This value may be LongOpt.NO_ARGUMENT, LongOpt.REQUIRED_ARGUMENT, or LongOpt.OPTIONAL_ARGUMENT.

  — A StringBuffer object or null. getopt() determines how to use this value based on the fourth parameter of the LongOpt object.

  — A value to be used when the option is encountered. This value becomes the return value of getopt() if the StringBuffer object named in the third parameter is null. If the buffer is non-null, getopt() returns zero after placing a string representation of the fourth parameter into the buffer.

The example program uses null as the StringBuffer parameter for each long option object and the corresponding short option letter as the fourth parameter. This is an easy way to cause getopt() to return the short option letter for both the short and long options, so that you can handle them with the same case statement.

After getopt() returns −1 to indicate that no more options were found in the argument array, getOptind() returns the index of the first argument following the last option. The following code fragment shows one way to access the remaining arguments:

```
for (int i = g.getOptind (); i < args.length; i++)
    System.out.println (args[i]);
```

The Getopt class offers other option-processing behavior in addition to what I've described here. Read the documentation included with the class for more information.

One deficiency of *Cmdline.java* that you may want to address is that it doesn't disable character echoing while it's reading the password.

Getting Parameters from Option Files

If your API allows it, you can specify connection parameters in a MySQL option file and the API will read the parameters from the file for you. For APIs that do not support option files directly, you may be able to arrange to read other types of files in which parameters are stored, or to write your own functions that read option files.

The format of option files was described in Chapter 1. I'll assume that you've read the discussion there and concentrate here on how to use option files from within programs. Under Unix, user-specific options are specified by convention in *~/.my.cnf* (that is, in the *.my.cnf* file in your home directory). However, the MySQL option file mechanism can look in several different files. The standard search order is */etc/my.cnf*, the *my.cnf* file in the server's default data directory, and the *~/.my.cnf* file for the current user. Under Windows, the search order is the *my.ini* file in the Windows system directory, *C:\my.cnf*, and the *my.cnf* file in the server's default data directory. If multiple option files exist and a parameter is specified in several of them, the last value found takes precedence. However, it's not an error for any given option file not to exist.

MySQL option files will not be used by your own programs unless you tell them to do so. Perl and Python provide direct API support for reading option files; simply indicate that you want to use them at the time that you connect to the server. It's possible to specify that only a particular file should be read, or that the standard search order should be used to look for multiple option files. PHP and Java do not support option files. As a workaround for PHP, we'll write a simple option file parsing function. For Java, we'll adopt a different approach that uses properties files.

Although the conventional name under Unix for the user-specific option file is *.my.cnf* in the current user's home directory, there's no rule your programs must use this particular file. You can name an option file anything you like and put it wherever you want. For example, you might set up a file */usr/local/apache/lib/cb.cnf* for use by web scripts that access the cookbook database. Under some circumstances, you may even want to create multiple files. Then, from within any given script, you can select the file that's appropriate for the type of permissions the script needs. For example, you might have one option file, *cb.cnf*, that lists parameters for a full-access MySQL account, and another file, *cb-ro.cnf*, that lists connection parameters for an account that needs only read-only access to MySQL. Another possibility is to list multiple groups within the same option file and have your scripts select options from the appropriate group.

C API Support for Option Files

The Perl and Python APIs are built using the C API, and option file support was not added to the C client library until MySQL 3.22.10. This means that even for Perl and Python, you must have MySQL 3.22.10 or later to use option files from within your own programs.

Historically, the database name has not been a parameter you get from an option file. (Programs typically provide this value themselves or expect the user to specify it.) As of MySQL 3.23.6, support was added to the C client library to look for option file lines of the form database=*db_name*, but the examples in this section do not use this fact.

Perl

Perl DBI scripts can use option files if you have *DBD::mysql* 1.21.06 or later. To take advantage of this, place the appropriate option specifiers in the third component of the data source name string:

- To specify an option group, use `mysql_read_default_group=`*groupname*. This tells MySQL to search the standard option files for options in the named group and in the [client] group. The *groupname* value should be written without the square brackets that are part of the line that begins the group. For example, if a group in an option file begins with a [my_prog] line, specify my_prog as the *groupname* value. To search the standard files but look only in the [client] group, *groupname* should be client.

- To name a specific option file, use `mysql_read_default_file=`*filename* in the DSN. When you do this, MySQL looks only in that file, and only for options in the [client] group.

- If you specify both an option file and an option group, MySQL reads only the named file, but looks for options both in the named group and in the [client] group.

The following example tells MySQL to use the standard option file search order to look for options in both the [cookbook] and [client] groups:

```
# basic DSN
my $dsn = "DBI:mysql:database=cookbook";
# look in standard option files; use [cookbook] and [client] groups
$dsn .= ";mysql_read_default_group=cookbook";
my $dbh = DBI->connect ($dsn, undef, undef,
                        { PrintError => 0, RaiseError => 1 });
```

The next example explicitly names the option file located in $ENV{HOME}, the home directory of the user running the script. Thus, MySQL will look only in that file and will use options from the [client] group:

```
# basic DSN
my $dsn = "DBI:mysql:database=cookbook";
# look in user-specific option file owned by the current user
$dsn .= ";mysql_read_default_file=$ENV{HOME}/.my.cnf";
my $dbh = DBI->connect ($dsn, undef, undef,
                        { PrintError => 0, RaiseError => 1 });
```

If you pass an empty value (undef or the empty string) for the username or password arguments of the connect() call, connect() uses whatever values are found in the option file or files. A nonempty username or password in the connect() call overrides any option file value. Similarly, a host named in the DSN overrides any option file value. You can use this behavior to allow DBI scripts to obtain connection parameters both from option files as well as from the command line as follows:

1. Create $host_name, $user_name, and $password variables and initialize them to undef. Then parse the command-line arguments to set the variables to non-undef values if the corresponding options are present on the command line. (See the Perl script earlier in this section to see how this is done.)

2. After parsing the command arguments, construct the DSN string and call connect(). Use `mysql_read_default_group` and `mysql_read_default_file` in the

DSN to specify how you want option files to be used, and, if $host_name is not undef, add host=$host_name to the DSN. In addition, pass $user_name and $password as the username and password arguments to connect(). These will be undef by default; if they were set from the command-line arguments, they will have non-undef values that override any option file values.

If a script follows this procedure, parameters given by the user on the command line are passed to connect() and take precedence over the contents of option files.

PHP

PHP has no native support for using MySQL option files, at least at the moment. To work around that limitation, use a function that reads an option file, such as the read_mysql_option_file() function shown below. It takes as arguments the name of an option file and an option group name or an array containing group names. (Group names should be named without square brackets.) Then it reads any options present in the file for the named group or groups. If no option group argument is given, the function looks by default in the [client] group. The return value is an array of option name/value pairs, or FALSE if an error occurs. It is not an error for the file not to exist.

```php
function read_mysql_option_file ($filename, $group_list = "client")
{
    if (is_string ($group_list))            # convert string to array
        $group_list = array ($group_list);
    if (!is_array ($group_list))            # hmm ... garbage argument?
        return (FALSE);
    $opt = array ();                        # option name/value array
    if (!($fp = fopen ($filename, "r")))    # if file does not exist,
        return ($opt);                      # return an empty list
    $in_named_group = 0;    # set non-zero while processing a named group
    while ($s = fgets ($fp, 1024))
    {
        $s = trim ($s);
        if (ereg ("^[#;]", $s))                     # skip comments
            continue;
        if (ereg ("^\[([^]]+)]", $s, $arg))       # option group line?
        {
            # check whether we're in one of the desired groups
            $in_named_group = 0;
            reset ($group_list);
            while (list ($key, $group_name) = each ($group_list))
            {
                if ($arg[1] == $group_name)
                {
                    $in_named_group = 1;        # we are
                    break;
                }
            }
        }
```

```
                continue;
        }
        if (!$in_named_group)                    # we're not in a desired
            continue;                            # group, skip the line
        if (ereg ("^([^ \t=]+)[ \t]*=[ \t]*(.*)", $s, $arg))
            $opt[$arg[1]] = $arg[2];             # name=value
        else if (ereg ("^([^ \t]+)", $s, $arg))
            $opt[$arg[1]] = "";                  # name only
        # else line is malformed
    }
    return ($opt);
}
```

Here are a couple of examples showing how to use read_mysql_option_file(). The first reads a user's option file to get the [client] group parameters, then uses them to connect to the server. The second reads the system-wide option file and prints the server startup parameters that are found there (that is, the parameters in the [mysqld] and [server] groups):

```
$opt = read_mysql_option_file ("/u/paul/.my.cnf");
$link = @mysql_connect ($opt["host"], $opt["user"], $opt["password"]);

$opt = read_mysql_option_file ("/etc/my.cnf", array ("mysqld", "server"));
while (list ($name, $value) = each ($opt))
    print ("$name => $value\n");
```

If you're using the MySQL_Access interface that was developed in Recipe 2.9, you might think about how to extend the class by implementing a derived class that gets the username, password, and hostname from an option file. You could also give this derived class the ability to search multiple files, which is an aspect of the usual option file behavior that read_mysql_option_file() does not provide.

Python

The MySQLdb module for DB-API provides direct support for using MySQL option files. Specify an option file or option group using read_default_file or read_default_group arguments to the connect() method. These two arguments act the same way as the mysql_read_default_file and mysql_read_default_group options for the Perl DBI connect() method (see the Perl discussion earlier in this section). To use the standard option file search order to look for options in both the [cookbook] and [client] groups, do something like this:

```
try:
    conn = MySQLdb.connect (db = "cookbook", read_default_group = "cookbook")
    print "Connected"
except:
    print "Cannot connect to server"
    sys.exit (1)
```

The following example shows how to use the *.my.cnf* file in the current user's home directory to obtain parameters from the [client]group:[*]

```
try:
    option_file = os.environ["HOME"] + "/" + ".my.cnf"
    conn = MySQLdb.connect (db = "cookbook", read_default_file = option_file)
    print "Connected"
except:
    print "Cannot connect to server"
    sys.exit (1)
```

Java

The MySQL Connector/J JDBC driver doesn't support option files. However, the Java class library provides support for reading properties files that contain lines in *name=value* format. This is somewhat similar to MySQL option file format, although there are some differences (for example, properties files do not allow [*groupname*] lines). Here is a simple properties file:

```
# this file lists parameters for connecting to the MySQL server
user=cbuser
password=cbpass
host=localhost
```

The following program, *ReadPropsFile.java*, shows one way to read a properties file named *Cookbook.properties* to obtain connection parameters. The file must be in a directory named in your CLASSPATH variable, or else you must specify it using a full pathname (the example shown here assumes the file is in a CLASSPATH directory):

```
import java.sql.*;
import java.util.*;      // need this for properties file support

public class ReadPropsFile
{
    public static void main (String[] args)
    {
        Connection conn = null;
        String url = null;
        String propsFile = "Cookbook.properties";
        Properties props = new Properties ();

        try
        {
            props.load (ReadPropsFile.class.getResourceAsStream (propsFile));
        }
        catch (Exception e)
        {
            System.err.println ("Cannot read properties file");
            System.exit (1);
        }
```

[*] You must import the os module to access os.environ.

```
    try
    {
        // construct connection URL, encoding username
        // and password as parameters at the end
        url = "jdbc:mysql://"
                    + props.getProperty ("host")
                    + "/cookbook"
                    + "?user=" + props.getProperty ("user")
                    + "&password=" + props.getProperty ("password");
        Class.forName ("com.mysql.jdbc.Driver").newInstance ();
        conn = DriverManager.getConnection (url);
        System.out.println ("Connected");
    }
    catch (Exception e)
    {
        System.err.println ("Cannot connect to server");
    }
    finally
    {
        try
        {
            if (conn != null)
            {
                conn.close ();
                System.out.println ("Disconnected");
            }
        }
        catch (SQLException e) { /* ignore close errors */ }
    }
}
```

If you want getProperty() to return a particular default value when the named property is not found, pass that value as a second argument. For example, to use localhost as the default host value, call getProperty() like this:

```
String hostName = props.getProperty ("host", "localhost");
```

The *Cookbook.class* library file developed earlier in the chapter (Recipe 2.3) includes a propsConnect() routine that is based on the concepts discussed here. To use it, set up the contents of the properties file, *Cookbook.properties*, and copy the file to the same location where you installed *Cookbook.class*. Then you can establish a connection within a program by importing the Cookbook class and calling Cookbook.propsConnect() rather than by calling Cookbook.connect().

2.11   Conclusion and Words of Advice

This chapter discusses the basic operations provided by each of our APIs for handling various aspects of interacting with the MySQL server. These operations allow you to write programs that issue any kind of query and retrieve the results. Up to this point, we've used simple queries because the focus is on the APIs rather than on SQL. The next chapter focuses on SQL instead, to show how to ask the database server more complex questions.

Before you proceed, it would be a good idea to reset the profile table used in this chapter to a known state. Several queries in later chapters use this table; by reinitializing it, you'll get the same results displayed in those chapters when you run the queries shown there. To reset the table, change location into the *tables* directory of the recipes distribution and run the following commands:

```
% mysql cookbook < profile.sql
% mysql cookbook < profile2.sql
```

CHAPTER 3
Record Selection Techniques

3.0 Introduction

This chapter focuses on the SELECT statement that is used for retrieving information from a database. It provides some essential background that shows various ways you can use SELECT to tell MySQL what you want to see. You should find the chapter helpful if your SQL background is limited or if you want to find out about the MySQL-specific extensions to SELECT syntax. However, there are so many ways to write SELECT queries that we'll necessarily touch on just a few. You may wish to consult the MySQL Reference Manual or a MySQL text for more information about the syntax of SELECT, as well as the functions and operators that you can use for extracting and manipulating data.

SELECT gives you control over several aspects of record retrieval:

- Which table to use
- Which columns to display from the table
- What names to give the columns
- Which rows to retrieve from the table
- How to sort the rows

Many useful queries are quite simple and don't specify all those things. For example, some forms of SELECT don't even name a table—a fact used in Recipe 1.31, which discusses how to use *mysql* as a calculator. Other non–table-based queries are useful for purposes such as checking what version of the server you're running or the name of the current database:

```
mysql> SELECT VERSION(), DATABASE();
+-------------+------------+
| VERSION()   | DATABASE() |
+-------------+------------+
| 3.23.51-log | cookbook   |
+-------------+------------+
```

However, to answer more involved questions, normally you'll need to pull information from one or more tables. Many of the examples in this chapter use a table named mail, which contains columns used to maintain a log of mail message traffic between users on a set of hosts. Its definition looks like this:

```
CREATE TABLE mail
(
    t        DATETIME,      # when message was sent
    srcuser CHAR(8),        # sender (source user and host)
    srchost CHAR(20),
    dstuser CHAR(8),        # recipient (destination user and host)
    dsthost CHAR(20),
    size    BIGINT,         # message size in bytes
    INDEX   (t)
);
```

And its contents look like this:

```
+---------------------+---------+---------+---------+---------+---------+
| t                   | srcuser | srchost | dstuser | dsthost | size    |
+---------------------+---------+---------+---------+---------+---------+
| 2001-05-11 10:15:08 | barb    | saturn  | tricia  | mars    |   58274 |
| 2001-05-12 12:48:13 | tricia  | mars    | gene    | venus   |  194925 |
| 2001-05-12 15:02:49 | phil    | mars    | phil    | saturn  |    1048 |
| 2001-05-13 13:59:18 | barb    | saturn  | tricia  | venus   |     271 |
| 2001-05-14 09:31:37 | gene    | venus   | barb    | mars    |    2291 |
| 2001-05-14 11:52:17 | phil    | mars    | tricia  | saturn  |    5781 |
| 2001-05-14 14:42:21 | barb    | venus   | barb    | venus   |   98151 |
| 2001-05-14 17:03:01 | tricia  | saturn  | phil    | venus   | 2394482 |
| 2001-05-15 07:17:48 | gene    | mars    | gene    | saturn  |    3824 |
| 2001-05-15 08:50:57 | phil    | venus   | phil    | venus   |     978 |
| 2001-05-15 10:25:52 | gene    | mars    | tricia  | saturn  |  998532 |
| 2001-05-15 17:35:31 | gene    | saturn  | gene    | mars    |    3856 |
| 2001-05-16 09:00:28 | gene    | venus   | barb    | mars    |     613 |
| 2001-05-16 23:04:19 | phil    | venus   | barb    | venus   |   10294 |
| 2001-05-17 12:49:23 | phil    | mars    | tricia  | saturn  |     873 |
| 2001-05-19 22:21:51 | gene    | saturn  | gene    | venus   |   23992 |
+---------------------+---------+---------+---------+---------+---------+
```

To create the mail table and load its contents, change location into the *tables* directory of the recipes distribution and run this command:

```
% mysql cookbook < mail.sql
```

This chapter also uses other tables from time to time. Some of these were used in previous chapters, while others are new. For any that you need to create, do so the same way as for the mail table, using scripts in the *tables* directory. In addition, the text for many of the scripts and programs used in the chapter may be found in the *select* directory. You can use the files there to try out the examples more easily.

Many of the queries shown here can be tried out with *mysql*, which you can read about in Chapter 1. Some of the examples issue queries from within the context of a programming language. See Chapter 2 for background on programming techniques.

3.1 Specifying Which Columns to Display

Problem

You want to display some or all of the columns from a table.

Solution

Use * as a shortcut that selects all columns. Or name the columns you want to see explicitly.

Discussion

To indicate what kind of information you want to see from a table, name a column or a list of columns and the table to use. The easiest way to select output columns is to use the * specifier, which is a shortcut for naming all the columns in a table:

```
mysql> SELECT * FROM mail;
+---------------------+---------+---------+---------+---------+---------+
| t                   | srcuser | srchost | dstuser | dsthost | size    |
+---------------------+---------+---------+---------+---------+---------+
| 2001-05-11 10:15:08 | barb    | saturn  | tricia  | mars    |   58274 |
| 2001-05-12 12:48:13 | tricia  | mars    | gene    | venus   |  194925 |
| 2001-05-12 15:02:49 | phil    | mars    | phil    | saturn  |    1048 |
| 2001-05-13 13:59:18 | barb    | saturn  | tricia  | venus   |     271 |
...
```

Alternatively, you can list the columns explicitly:

```
mysql> SELECT t, srcuser, srchost, dstuser, dsthost, size  FROM mail;
+---------------------+---------+---------+---------+---------+---------+
| t                   | srcuser | srchost | dstuser | dsthost | size    |
+---------------------+---------+---------+---------+---------+---------+
| 2001-05-11 10:15:08 | barb    | saturn  | tricia  | mars    |   58274 |
| 2001-05-12 12:48:13 | tricia  | mars    | gene    | venus   |  194925 |
| 2001-05-12 15:02:49 | phil    | mars    | phil    | saturn  |    1048 |
| 2001-05-13 13:59:18 | barb    | saturn  | tricia  | venus   |     271 |
...
```

It's certainly easier to use * than to write out a list of column names. However, with *, there is no guarantee about the order in which columns will be returned. (The server returns them in the order they are listed in the table definition, but this may change if you change the definition. See Chapter 8.) Thus, one advantage of naming the columns explicitly is that you can place them in whatever order you want. Suppose you want hostnames to appear before usernames, rather than after. To accomplish this, name the columns as follows:

```
mysql> SELECT t, srchost, srcuser, dsthost, dstuser, size  FROM mail;
+---------------------+---------+---------+---------+---------+---------+
| t                   | srchost | srcuser | dsthost | dstuser | size    |
+---------------------+---------+---------+---------+---------+---------+
```

```
| 2001-05-11 10:15:08 | saturn | barb   | mars   | tricia |  58274 |
| 2001-05-12 12:48:13 | mars   | tricia | venus  | gene   | 194925 |
| 2001-05-12 15:02:49 | mars   | phil   | saturn | phil   |   1048 |
| 2001-05-13 13:59:18 | saturn | barb   | venus  | tricia |    271 |
...
```

Another advantage of naming the columns compared to using * is that you can name just those columns you want to see and omit those in which you have no interest:

```
mysql> SELECT size FROM mail;
+---------+
| size    |
+---------+
|   58274 |
|  194925 |
|    1048 |
|     271 |
...
mysql> SELECT t, srcuser, srchost, size FROM mail;
+---------------------+---------+---------+---------+
| t                   | srcuser | srchost | size    |
+---------------------+---------+---------+---------+
| 2001-05-11 10:15:08 | barb    | saturn  |   58274 |
| 2001-05-12 12:48:13 | tricia  | mars    |  194925 |
| 2001-05-12 15:02:49 | phil    | mars    |    1048 |
| 2001-05-13 13:59:18 | barb    | saturn  |     271 |
...
```

3.2   Avoiding Output Column Order Problems When Writing Programs

Problem

You're issuing a SELECT * query from within a program, and the columns don't come back in the order you expect.

Solution

When you use * to select columns, all bets are off; you can't assume anything about the order in which they'll be returned. Either name the columns explicitly in the order you want, or retrieve them into a data structure that makes their order irrelevant.

Discussion

The examples in the previous section illustrate the differences between using * versus a list of names to specify output columns when issuing SELECT statements from within the *mysql* program. The difference between approaches also may be significant when issuing queries through an API from within your own programs, depending on how you fetch result set rows. If you select output columns using *, the server returns them using the order in which they are listed in the table definition—an order that may change if the table structure is modified. If you fetch rows into an array, this non-determinacy of output column order makes it impossible to know which column each array element corresponds to. By naming output columns explicitly, you can fetch rows into an array with confidence that the columns will appear in the array in the same order that you named them in the query.

On the other hand, your API may allow you to fetch rows into a structure containing elements that are accessed by name. (For example, in Perl you can use a hash; in PHP you can use an associative array or an object.) If you do this, you can issue a SELECT * query and then access structure members by referring to the column names in any order you want. In this case, there is effectively no difference between selecting columns with * or by naming them explicitly: If you can access values by name within your program, their order within result set rows is irrelevant. This fact makes it tempting to take the easy way out by using SELECT * for all your queries, even if you're not actually going to use every column. Nevertheless, it's more efficient to name specifically only the columns you want so that the server doesn't send you information you're just going to ignore. (An example that explains in more detail why you may want to avoid retrieving certain columns is given in Recipe 9.8, in the section "Selecting All Except Certain Columns.")

3.3   Giving Names to Output Columns

Problem

You don't like the names of the columns in your query result.

Solution

Supply names of your own choosing using column aliases.

Discussion

Whenever you retrieve a result set, MySQL gives every output column a name. (That's how the *mysql* program gets the names that you see displayed as the initial row of column headers in result set output.) MySQL assigns default names to output columns, but if the defaults are not suitable, you can use column aliases to specify your own names.

This section explains aliases and shows how to use them to assign column names in queries. If you're writing a program that needs to retrieve information about column names, see Recipe 9.2.

If an output column in a result set comes directly from a table, MySQL uses the table column name for the result set column name. For example, the following statement selects three table columns, the names of which become the corresponding output column names:

```
mysql> SELECT t, srcuser, size FROM mail;
+---------------------+---------+---------+
| t                   | srcuser | size    |
+---------------------+---------+---------+
| 2001-05-11 10:15:08 | barb    |   58274 |
| 2001-05-12 12:48:13 | tricia  |  194925 |
| 2001-05-12 15:02:49 | phil    |    1048 |
| 2001-05-13 13:59:18 | barb    |     271 |
...
```

If you generate a column by evaluating an expression, the expression itself is the column name. This can produce rather long and unwieldy names in result sets, as illustrated by the following query that uses an expression to reformat the t column of the mail table:

```
mysql> SELECT
    -> CONCAT(MONTHNAME(t),' ',DAYOFMONTH(t),', ',YEAR(t)),
    -> srcuser, size FROM mail;
+----------------------------------------------------+---------+---------+
| CONCAT(MONTHNAME(t),' ',DAYOFMONTH(t),', ',YEAR(t)) | srcuser | size    |
+----------------------------------------------------+---------+---------+
| May 11, 2001                                       | barb    |   58274 |
| May 12, 2001                                       | tricia  |  194925 |
| May 12, 2001                                       | phil    |    1048 |
| May 13, 2001                                       | barb    |     271 |
...
```

The preceding example uses a query that is specifically contrived to illustrate how awful-looking column names can be. The reason it's contrived is that you probably wouldn't really write the query that way—the same result can be produced more easily using MySQL's DATE_FORMAT() function. But even with DATE_FORMAT(), the column header is still ugly:

```
mysql> SELECT
    -> DATE_FORMAT(t,'%M %e, %Y'),
    -> srcuser, size FROM mail;
+---------------------------+---------+---------+
| DATE_FORMAT(t,'%M %e, %Y') | srcuser | size    |
+---------------------------+---------+---------+
| May 11, 2001              | barb    |   58274 |
| May 12, 2001              | tricia  |  194925 |
| May 12, 2001              | phil    |    1048 |
| May 13, 2001              | barb    |     271 |
...
```

To give a result set column a name of your own choosing, use AS *name* to specify a column alias. The following query retrieves the same result as the previous one, but renames the first column to date_sent:

```
mysql> SELECT
    -> DATE_FORMAT(t,'%M %e, %Y') AS date_sent,
    -> srcuser, size FROM mail;
+--------------+---------+---------+
| date_sent    | srcuser | size    |
+--------------+---------+---------+
| May 11, 2001 | barb    |   58274 |
| May 12, 2001 | tricia  |  194925 |
| May 12, 2001 | phil    |    1048 |
| May 13, 2001 | barb    |     271 |
...
```

You can see that the alias makes the column name more concise, easier to read, and more meaningful. If you want to use a descriptive phrase, an alias can consist of several words. (Aliases can be fairly arbitrary, although they are subject to a few restrictions such as that they must be quoted if they are SQL keywords, contain spaces or other special characters, or are entirely numeric.) The following query retrieves the same data values as the preceding one but uses phrases to name the output columns:

```
mysql> SELECT
    -> DATE_FORMAT(t,'%M %e, %Y') AS 'Date of message',
    -> srcuser AS 'Message sender', size AS 'Number of bytes' FROM mail;
+-----------------+----------------+-----------------+
| Date of message | Message sender | Number of bytes |
+-----------------+----------------+-----------------+
| May 11, 2001    | barb           |           58274 |
| May 12, 2001    | tricia         |          194925 |
| May 12, 2001    | phil           |            1048 |
| May 13, 2001    | barb           |             271 |
...
```

Aliases can be applied to any result set column, not just those that come from tables:

```
mysql> SELECT '1+1+1' AS 'The expression', 1+1+1 AS 'The result';
+----------------+------------+
| The expression | The result |
+----------------+------------+
| 1+1+1          |          3 |
+----------------+------------+
```

Here, the value of the first column is '1+1+1' (quoted so that it is treated as a string), and the value of the second column is 1+1+1 (without quotes so that MySQL treats it as an expression and evaluates it). The aliases are descriptive phrases that help to make clear the relationship between the two column values.

If you try using a single-word alias and MySQL complains about it, the alias probably is a reserved word. Quoting it should make it legal:

```
mysql> SELECT 1 AS INTEGER;
You have an error in your SQL syntax near 'INTEGER' at line 1
mysql> SELECT 1 AS 'INTEGER';
+---------+
| INTEGER |
+---------+
|       1 |
+---------+
```

3.4 Using Column Aliases to Make Programs Easier to Write

Problem

You're trying to refer to a column by name from within a program, but the column is calculated from an expression. Consequently, it's difficult to use.

Solution

Use an alias to give the column a simpler name.

Discussion

If you're writing a program that fetches rows into an array and accesses them by numeric column indexes, the presence or absence of column aliases makes no difference, because aliases don't change the positions of columns within the result set. However, aliases make a big difference if you're accessing output columns by name, because aliases change those names. You can exploit this fact to give your program easier names to work with. For example, if your query displays reformatted message time values from the mail table using the expression DATE_FORMAT(t,'%M %e, %Y'), that expression is also the name you'd have to use when referring to the output column. That's not very convenient. If you use AS date_sent to give the column an alias, you can refer to it a lot more easily using the name date_sent. Here's an example that shows how a Perl DBI script might process such values:

```
$sth = $dbh->prepare (
            "SELECT srcuser,
            DATE_FORMAT(t,'%M %e, %Y') AS date_sent
            FROM mail");
$sth->execute ();
while (my $ref = $sth->fetchrow_hashref ())
{
    printf "user: %s, date sent: %s\n", $ref->{srcuser}, $ref->{date_sent};
}
```

In Java, you'd do something like this:

```
Statement s = conn.createStatement ();
s.executeQuery ("SELECT srcuser,"
                + " DATE_FORMAT(t,'%M %e, %Y') AS date_sent"
                + " FROM mail");
ResultSet rs = s.getResultSet ();
while (rs.next ())  // loop through rows of result set
{
    String name = rs.getString ("srcuser");
    String dateSent = rs.getString ("date_sent");
    System.out.println ("user: " + name
                        + ", date sent: " + dateSent);
}
rs.close ();
s.close ();
```

In PHP, retrieve result set rows using `mysql_fetch_array()` or `mysql_fetch_object()` to fetch rows into a data structure that contains named elements. With Python, use a cursor class that causes rows to be returned as dictionaries containing key/value pairs where the keys are the column names. (See Recipe 2.4.)

3.5 Combining Columns to Construct Composite Values

Problem

You want to display values that are constructed from multiple table columns.

Solution

One way to do this is to use `CONCAT()`. You might also want to give the column a nicer name by using an alias.

Discussion

Column values may be combined to produce composite output values. For example, this expression concatenates srcuser and srchost values into email address format:

```
CONCAT(srcuser,'@',srchost)
```

Such expressions tend to produce ugly column names, which is yet another reason why column aliases are useful. The following query uses the aliases sender and recipient to name output columns that are constructed by combining usernames and hostnames into email addresses:

```
mysql> SELECT
    -> DATE_FORMAT(t,'%M %e, %Y') AS date_sent,
    -> CONCAT(srcuser,'@',srchost) AS sender,
    -> CONCAT(dstuser,'@',dsthost) AS recipient,
```

```
    -> size FROM mail;
+--------------+---------------+---------------+---------+
| date_sent    | sender        | recipient     | size    |
+--------------+---------------+---------------+---------+
| May 11, 2001 | barb@saturn   | tricia@mars   |   58274 |
| May 12, 2001 | tricia@mars   | gene@venus    |  194925 |
| May 12, 2001 | phil@mars     | phil@saturn   |    1048 |
| May 13, 2001 | barb@saturn   | tricia@venus  |     271 |
...
```

3.6   Specifying Which Rows to Select

Problem

You don't want to see all the rows from a table, just some of them.

Solution

Add a WHERE clause to the query that indicates to the server which rows to return.

Discussion

Unless you qualify or restrict a SELECT query in some way, it retrieves every row in your table, which may be a lot more information than you really want to see. To be more precise about the rows to select, provide a WHERE clause that specifies one or more conditions that rows must match.

Conditions can perform tests for equality, inequality, or relative ordering. For some column types such as strings, you can use pattern matches. The following queries select columns from rows containing srchost values that are exactly equal to the string 'venus', that are lexically less than the string 'pluto', or that begin with the letter 's':

```
mysql> SELECT t, srcuser, srchost  FROM mail WHERE srchost = 'venus';
+---------------------+---------+---------+
| t                   | srcuser | srchost |
+---------------------+---------+---------+
| 2001-05-14 09:31:37 | gene    | venus   |
| 2001-05-14 14:42:21 | barb    | venus   |
| 2001-05-15 08:50:57 | phil    | venus   |
| 2001-05-16 09:00:28 | gene    | venus   |
| 2001-05-16 23:04:19 | phil    | venus   |
+---------------------+---------+---------+
mysql> SELECT t, srcuser, srchost FROM mail WHERE srchost < 'pluto';
+---------------------+---------+---------+
| t                   | srcuser | srchost |
+---------------------+---------+---------+
| 2001-05-12 12:48:13 | tricia  | mars    |
| 2001-05-12 15:02:49 | phil    | mars    |
| 2001-05-14 11:52:17 | phil    | mars    |
```

```
| 2001-05-15 07:17:48 | gene    | mars    |
| 2001-05-15 10:25:52 | gene    | mars    |
| 2001-05-17 12:49:23 | phil    | mars    |
+---------------------+---------+---------+
mysql> SELECT t, srcuser, srchost FROM mail WHERE srchost LIKE 's%';
+---------------------+---------+---------+
| t                   | srcuser | srchost |
+---------------------+---------+---------+
| 2001-05-11 10:15:08 | barb    | saturn  |
| 2001-05-13 13:59:18 | barb    | saturn  |
| 2001-05-14 17:03:01 | tricia  | saturn  |
| 2001-05-15 17:35:31 | gene    | saturn  |
| 2001-05-19 22:21:51 | gene    | saturn  |
+---------------------+---------+---------+
```

WHERE clauses can test multiple conditions. The following statement looks for rows where the srcuser column has any of three different values. (It asks the question, "When did gene, barb, or phil send mail?"):

```
mysql> SELECT t, srcuser, dstuser FROM mail
    -> WHERE srcuser = 'gene' OR srcuser = 'barb' OR srcuser = 'phil';
+---------------------+---------+---------+
| t                   | srcuser | dstuser |
+---------------------+---------+---------+
| 2001-05-11 10:15:08 | barb    | tricia  |
| 2001-05-12 15:02:49 | phil    | phil    |
| 2001-05-13 13:59:18 | barb    | tricia  |
| 2001-05-14 09:31:37 | gene    | barb    |
...
```

Queries such as the preceding one that test a given column to see if it has any of several different values often can be written more easily by using the IN( ) operator. IN( ) is true if the column is equal to any value in its argument list:

```
mysql> SELECT t, srcuser, dstuser FROM mail
    -> WHERE srcuser IN ('gene','barb','phil');
+---------------------+---------+---------+
| t                   | srcuser | dstuser |
+---------------------+---------+---------+
| 2001-05-11 10:15:08 | barb    | tricia  |
| 2001-05-12 15:02:49 | phil    | phil    |
| 2001-05-13 13:59:18 | barb    | tricia  |
| 2001-05-14 09:31:37 | gene    | barb    |
...
```

Different conditions can test different columns. This query finds messages sent by barb to tricia:

```
mysql> SELECT * FROM mail WHERE srcuser = 'barb' AND dstuser = 'tricia';
+---------------------+---------+---------+---------+---------+-------+
| t                   | srcuser | srchost | dstuser | dsthost | size  |
+---------------------+---------+---------+---------+---------+-------+
| 2001-05-11 10:15:08 | barb    | saturn  | tricia  | mars    | 58274 |
| 2001-05-13 13:59:18 | barb    | saturn  | tricia  | venus   |   271 |
+---------------------+---------+---------+---------+---------+-------+
```

Comparisons need only be legal syntactically; they need not make any sense semantically. The comparison in the following query doesn't have a particularly obvious meaning, but MySQL will happily execute it:[*]

```
SELECT * FROM mail WHERE srcuser + dsthost < size
```

Are Queries That Return No Rows Failed Queries?

If you issue a SELECT statement and get no rows back, has the query failed? It depends. If the lack of a result set is due to a problem such as that the statement is syntactically invalid or refers to nonexisting tables or columns, the query did indeed fail, because it could not even be executed. In this case, some sort of error condition should occur and you should investigate why your program is attempting to issue a malformed statement.

If the query executes without error but returns nothing, it simply means that the query's WHERE clause matched no rows:

```
mysql> SELECT * FROM mail WHERE srcuser = 'no-such-user';
Empty set (0.01 sec)
```

This is *not* a failed query. It ran successfully and produced a result; the result just happens to be empty because no rows have a srcuser value of no-such-user.

Columns need not be compared to literal values. You can test a column against other columns. Suppose you have a cd table lying around that contains year, artist, and title columns:[†]

```
mysql> SELECT year, artist, title FROM cd;
+------+-----------------+----------------------+
| year | artist          | title                |
+------+-----------------+----------------------+
| 1990 | Iona            | Iona                 |
| 1992 | Charlie Peacock | Lie Down in the Grass |
| 1993 | Iona            | Beyond These Shores  |
| 1987 | The 77s         | The 77s              |
| 1990 | Michael Gettel  | Return               |
| 1989 | Richard Souther | Cross Currents       |
| 1996 | Charlie Peacock | strangelanguage      |
| 1982 | Undercover      | Undercover           |
...
```

If so, you can find all your eponymous CDs (those with artist and title the same) by performing a comparison of one column within the table to another:

---

[*] If you try issuing the query to see what it returns, how do you account for the result?

[†] It's not unlikely you'll have such a table if you've been reading other database books. Many of these have you go through the exercise of creating a database to keep track of your CD collection, a scenario that seems to rank second in popularity only to parts-and-suppliers examples.

```
mysql> SELECT year, artist, title FROM cd WHERE artist = title;
+------+-----------+-----------+
| year | artist    | title     |
+------+-----------+-----------+
| 1990 | Iona      | Iona      |
| 1987 | The 77s   | The 77s   |
| 1982 | Undercover | Undercover |
+------+-----------+-----------+
```

A special case of within-table column comparison occurs when you want to compare a column to itself rather than to a different column. Suppose you collect stamps and list your collection in a `stamp` table that contains columns for each stamp's ID number and the year it was issued. If you know that a particular stamp has an ID number 42 and want to use the value in its year column to find the other stamps in your collection that were issued in the same year, you'd do so by using year-to-year comparison—in effect, comparing the year column to itself:

```
mysql> SELECT stamp.* FROM stamp, stamp AS stamp2
    -> WHERE stamp.year = stamp2.year AND stamp2.id = 42 AND stamp.id != 42;
+-----+------+------------------------+
| id  | year | description            |
+-----+------+------------------------+
|  97 | 1987 | 1-cent transition stamp |
| 161 | 1987 | aviation stamp         |
+-----+------+------------------------+
```

This kind of query involves a self-join, table aliases, and column references that are qualified using the table name. But that's more than I want to go into here. Those topics are covered in Chapter 12.

3.7   WHERE Clauses and Column Aliases

Problem

You want to refer to a column alias in a WHERE clause.

Solution

Sorry, you cannot.

Discussion

You cannot refer to column aliases in a WHERE clause. Thus, the following query is illegal:

```
mysql> SELECT t, srcuser, dstuser, size/1024 AS kilobytes
    -> FROM mail WHERE kilobytes > 500;
ERROR 1054 at line 1: Unknown column 'kilobytes' in 'where clause'
```

The error occurs because aliases name *output* columns, whereas a WHERE clause operates on *input* columns to determine which rows to select for output. To make the query legal, replace the alias in the WHERE clause with the column or expression that the alias represents:

```
mysql> SELECT t, srcuser, dstuser, size/1024 AS kilobytes
    -> FROM mail WHERE size/1024 > 500;
+---------------------+---------+---------+-----------+
| t                   | srcuser | dstuser | kilobytes |
+---------------------+---------+---------+-----------+
| 2001-05-14 17:03:01 | tricia  | phil    |   2338.36 |
| 2001-05-15 10:25:52 | gene    | tricia  |    975.13 |
+---------------------+---------+---------+-----------+
```

3.8   Displaying Comparisons to Find Out How Something Works

Problem

You're curious about how a comparison in a WHERE clause works. Or perhaps about why it doesn't seem to be working.

Solution

Display the result of the comparison to get more information about it. This is a useful diagnostic or debugging technique.

Discussion

Normally you put comparison operations in the WHERE clause of a query and use them to determine which records to display:

```
mysql> SELECT * FROM mail WHERE srcuser < 'c' AND size > 5000;
+---------------------+---------+---------+---------+---------+-------+
| t                   | srcuser | srchost | dstuser | dsthost | size  |
+---------------------+---------+---------+---------+---------+-------+
| 2001-05-11 10:15:08 | barb    | saturn  | tricia  | mars    | 58274 |
| 2001-05-14 14:42:21 | barb    | venus   | barb    | venus   | 98151 |
+---------------------+---------+---------+---------+---------+-------+
```

But sometimes it's desirable to see the result of the comparison itself (for example, if you're not sure that the comparison is working the way you expect it to). To do this, just put the comparison expression in the output column list, perhaps including the values that you're comparing as well:

```
mysql> SELECT srcuser, srcuser < 'c', size, size > 5000 FROM mail;
+---------+---------------+--------+-------------+
| srcuser | srcuser < 'c' | size   | size > 5000 |
+---------+---------------+--------+-------------+
| barb    |             1 |  58274 |           1 |
| tricia  |             0 | 194925 |           1 |
| phil    |             0 |   1048 |           0 |
| barb    |             1 |    271 |           0 |
...
```

This technique of displaying comparison results is particularly useful for writing queries that check how a test works without using a table:

```
mysql> SELECT 'a' = 'A';
+-----------+
| 'a' = 'A' |
+-----------+
|         1 |
+-----------+
```

This query result tells you that string comparisons are not by default case sensitive, which is a useful thing to know.

3.9 Reversing or Negating Query Conditions

Problem

You know how to write a query to answer a given question; now you want to ask the opposite question.

Solution

Reverse the conditions in the WHERE clause by using negation operators.

Discussion

The WHERE conditions in a query can be negated to ask the opposite questions. The following query determines when users sent mail to themselves:

```
mysql> SELECT * FROM mail WHERE srcuser = dstuser;
+---------------------+---------+---------+---------+---------+-------+
| t                   | srcuser | srchost | dstuser | dsthost | size  |
+---------------------+---------+---------+---------+---------+-------+
| 2001-05-12 15:02:49 | phil    | mars    | phil    | saturn  |  1048 |
| 2001-05-14 14:42:21 | barb    | venus   | barb    | venus   | 98151 |
| 2001-05-15 07:17:48 | gene    | mars    | gene    | saturn  |  3824 |
| 2001-05-15 08:50:57 | phil    | venus   | phil    | venus   |   978 |
| 2001-05-15 17:35:31 | gene    | saturn  | gene    | mars    |  3856 |
| 2001-05-19 22:21:51 | gene    | saturn  | gene    | venus   | 23992 |
+---------------------+---------+---------+---------+---------+-------+
```

To reverse this query, to find records where users sent mail to someone *other* than themselves, change the comparison operator from = (equal to) to != (not equal to):

```
mysql> SELECT * FROM mail WHERE srcuser != dstuser;
+---------------------+---------+---------+---------+---------+--------+
| t                   | srcuser | srchost | dstuser | dsthost | size   |
+---------------------+---------+---------+---------+---------+--------+
| 2001-05-11 10:15:08 | barb    | saturn  | tricia  | mars    |  58274 |
| 2001-05-12 12:48:13 | tricia  | mars    | gene    | venus   | 194925 |
| 2001-05-13 13:59:18 | barb    | saturn  | tricia  | venus   |    271 |
| 2001-05-14 09:31:37 | gene    | venus   | barb    | mars    |   2291 |
...
```

A more complex query using two conditions might ask when people sent mail to themselves on the same machine:

```
mysql> SELECT * FROM mail WHERE srcuser = dstuser AND srchost = dsthost;
+---------------------+---------+---------+---------+---------+-------+
| t                   | srcuser | srchost | dstuser | dsthost | size  |
+---------------------+---------+---------+---------+---------+-------+
| 2001-05-14 14:42:21 | barb    | venus   | barb    | venus   | 98151 |
| 2001-05-15 08:50:57 | phil    | venus   | phil    | venus   |   978 |
+---------------------+---------+---------+---------+---------+-------+
```

Reversing the conditions for this query involves not only changing the = operators to !=, but changing the AND to OR:

```
mysql> SELECT * FROM mail WHERE srcuser != dstuser OR srchost != dsthost;
+---------------------+---------+---------+---------+---------+---------+
| t                   | srcuser | srchost | dstuser | dsthost | size    |
+---------------------+---------+---------+---------+---------+---------+
| 2001-05-11 10:15:08 | barb    | saturn  | tricia  | mars    |   58274 |
| 2001-05-12 12:48:13 | tricia  | mars    | gene    | venus   |  194925 |
| 2001-05-12 15:02:49 | phil    | mars    | phil    | saturn  |    1048 |
| 2001-05-13 13:59:18 | barb    | saturn  | tricia  | venus   |     271 |
...
```

You may find it easier just to put the entire original expression in parentheses and negate the whole thing with NOT:

```
mysql> SELECT * FROM mail WHERE NOT (srcuser = dstuser AND srchost = dsthost);
+---------------------+---------+---------+---------+---------+---------+
| t                   | srcuser | srchost | dstuser | dsthost | size    |
+---------------------+---------+---------+---------+---------+---------+
| 2001-05-11 10:15:08 | barb    | saturn  | tricia  | mars    |   58274 |
| 2001-05-12 12:48:13 | tricia  | mars    | gene    | venus   |  194925 |
| 2001-05-12 15:02:49 | phil    | mars    | phil    | saturn  |    1048 |
| 2001-05-13 13:59:18 | barb    | saturn  | tricia  | venus   |     271 |
...
```

See Also

If a column involved in a condition may contain NULL values, reversing the condition is a little trickier. See Recipe 3.12 for details.

3.10   Removing Duplicate Rows

Problem

Output from a query contains duplicate records. You want to eliminate them.

Solution

Use DISTINCT.

Discussion

Some queries produce results containing duplicate records. For example, to see who sent mail, you could query the mail table like this:

```
mysql> SELECT srcuser FROM mail;
+---------+
| srcuser |
+---------+
| barb    |
| tricia  |
| phil    |
| barb    |
| gene    |
| phil    |
| barb    |
| tricia  |
| gene    |
| phil    |
| gene    |
| gene    |
| gene    |
| phil    |
| phil    |
| gene    |
+---------+
```

But that result is heavily redundant. Adding DISTINCT to the query removes the duplicate records, producing a set of unique values:

```
mysql> SELECT DISTINCT srcuser FROM mail;
+---------+
| srcuser |
+---------+
| barb    |
| tricia  |
| phil    |
| gene    |
+---------+
```

DISTINCT works with multiple-column output, too. The following query shows which dates are represented in the `mail` table:

```
mysql> SELECT DISTINCT YEAR(t), MONTH(t), DAYOFMONTH(t) FROM mail;
+---------+----------+---------------+
| YEAR(t) | MONTH(t) | DAYOFMONTH(t) |
+---------+----------+---------------+
|    2001 |        5 |            11 |
|    2001 |        5 |            12 |
|    2001 |        5 |            13 |
|    2001 |        5 |            14 |
|    2001 |        5 |            15 |
|    2001 |        5 |            16 |
|    2001 |        5 |            17 |
|    2001 |        5 |            19 |
+---------+----------+---------------+
```

To count the number of unique values, do this:

```
mysql> SELECT COUNT(DISTINCT srcuser) FROM mail;
+-------------------------+
| COUNT(DISTINCT srcuser) |
+-------------------------+
|                       4 |
+-------------------------+
```

COUNT(DISTINCT) requires MySQL 3.23.2 or higher.

See Also

DISTINCT is revisited in Chapter 7. Duplicate removal is discussed in more detail in Chapter 14.

3.11   Working with NULL Values

Problem

You're trying to compare column values to NULL, but it isn't working.

Solution

You have to use the proper comparison operators: IS NULL, IS NOT NULL, or <=>.

Discussion

Conditions involving NULL are special. You cannot use = NULL or != NULL to look for NULL values in columns. Such comparisons always fail because it's impossible to tell whether or not they are true. Even NULL = NULL fails. (Why? Because you can't determine whether one unknown value is the same as another unknown value.)

To look for columns that are or are not NULL, use IS NULL or IS NOT NULL. Suppose a table taxpayer contains taxpayer names and ID numbers, where a NULL ID indicates that the value is unknown:

```
mysql> SELECT * FROM taxpayer;
+---------+--------+
| name    | id     |
+---------+--------+
| bernina | 198-48 |
| bertha  | NULL   |
| ben     | NULL   |
| bill    | 475-83 |
+---------+--------+
```

You can see that = and != do not work with NULL values as follows:

```
mysql> SELECT * FROM taxpayer WHERE id = NULL;
Empty set (0.00 sec)
mysql> SELECT * FROM taxpayer WHERE id != NULL;
Empty set (0.01 sec)
```

To find records where the id column is or is not NULL, the queries should be written like this:

```
mysql> SELECT * FROM taxpayer WHERE id IS NULL;
+--------+------+
| name   | id   |
+--------+------+
| bertha | NULL |
| ben    | NULL |
+--------+------+
mysql> SELECT * FROM taxpayer WHERE id IS NOT NULL;
+---------+--------+
| name    | id     |
+---------+--------+
| bernina | 198-48 |
| bill    | 475-83 |
+---------+--------+
```

As of MySQL 3.23, you can also use <=> to compare values, which (unlike the = operator) is true even for two NULL values:

```
mysql> SELECT NULL = NULL, NULL <=> NULL;
+-------------+---------------+
| NULL = NULL | NULL <=> NULL |
+-------------+---------------+
|        NULL |             1 |
+-------------+---------------+
```

See Also

NULL values also behave specially with respect to sorting and summary operations. See Recipe 6.5 and Recipe 7.8.

3.12   Negating a Condition on a Column That Contains NULL Values

Problem

You're trying to negate a condition that involves NULL, but it's not working.

Solution

NULL is special in negations, just like it is otherwise. Perhaps even more so.

Discussion

Recipe 3.9 pointed out that you can reverse query conditions, either by changing comparison operators and Boolean operators, or by using NOT. These techniques may not work if a column can contain NULL. Recall that the taxpayer table from Recipe 3.11 looks like this:

```
+---------+--------+
| name    | id     |
+---------+--------+
| bernina | 198-48 |
| bertha  | NULL   |
| ben     | NULL   |
| bill    | 475-83 |
+---------+--------+
```

Now suppose you have a query that finds records with taxpayer ID values that are lexically less than 200-00:

```
mysql> SELECT * FROM taxpayer WHERE id < '200-00';
+---------+--------+
| name    | id     |
+---------+--------+
| bernina | 198-48 |
+---------+--------+
```

Reversing this condition by using >= rather than < may not give you the results you want. It depends on what information you want to obtain. If you want to select only records with non-NULL ID values, >= is indeed the proper test:

```
mysql> SELECT * FROM taxpayer WHERE id >= '200-00';
+------+--------+
| name | id     |
+------+--------+
| bill | 475-83 |
+------+--------+
```

But if you want all the records not selected by the original query, simply reversing the operator will not work. NULL values fail comparisons both with < and with >=, so you must add an additional clause specifically for them:

```
mysql> SELECT * FROM taxpayer WHERE id >= '200-00' OR id IS NULL;
+--------+--------+
| name   | id     |
+--------+--------+
| bertha | NULL   |
| ben    | NULL   |
| bill   | 475-83 |
+--------+--------+
```

3.13 Writing Comparisons Involving NULL in Programs

Problem

You're writing a program that issues a query, but it fails for NULL values.

Solution

Try writing the comparison selectively for NULL and non-NULL values.

Discussion

The need to use different comparison operators for NULL values than for non-NULL values leads to a subtle danger when constructing query strings within programs. If you have a value stored in a variable that might represent a NULL value, you must account for that if you use the value in comparisons. For example, in Perl, undef represents a NULL value, so to construct a statement that finds records in the taxpayer table matching some arbitrary value in an $id variable, you cannot do this:

```
$sth = $dbh->prepare ("SELECT * FROM taxpayer WHERE id = ?");
$sth->execute ($id);
```

The statement fails when $id is undef, because the resulting query becomes:

```
SELECT * FROM taxpayer WHERE id = NULL
```

That statement returns no records—a comparison of = NULL always fails. To take into account the possibility that $id may be undef, construct the query using the appropriate comparison operator like this:

```
$operator = (defined ($id) ? "=" : "IS");
$sth = $dbh->prepare ("SELECT * FROM taxpayer WHERE id $operator ?");
$sth->execute ($id);
```

This results in queries as follows for $id values of undef (NULL) or 43 (not NULL):

```
SELECT * FROM taxpayer WHERE id IS NULL
SELECT * FROM taxpayer WHERE id = 43
```

For inequality tests, set $operator like this instead:

```
$operator = (defined ($id) ? "!=" : "IS NOT");
```

3.14 Mapping NULL Values to Other Values for Display

Problem

A query's output includes NULL values, but you'd rather see something more meaningful, like "Unknown."

Solution

Convert NULL values selectively to another value when displaying them. You can also use this technique to catch divide-by-zero errors.

Discussion

Sometimes it's useful to display NULL values using some other distinctive value that has more meaning in the context of your application. If NULL id values in the taxpayer table mean "unknown," you can display that label by using IF() to map them onto the string Unknown:

```
mysql> SELECT name, IF(id IS NULL,'Unknown', id) AS 'id' FROM taxpayer;
+---------+---------+
| name    | id      |
+---------+---------+
| bernina | 198-48  |
| bertha  | Unknown |
| ben     | Unknown |
| bill    | 475-83  |
+---------+---------+
```

Actually, this technique works for any kind of value, but it's especially useful with NULL values because they tend to be given a variety of meanings: unknown, missing, not yet determined, out of range, and so forth.

The query can be written more concisely using IFNULL(), which tests its first argument and returns it if it's not NULL, or returns its second argument otherwise:

```
mysql> SELECT name, IFNULL(id,'Unknown') AS 'id' FROM taxpayer;
+---------+---------+
| name    | id      |
+---------+---------+
| bernina | 198-48  |
| bertha  | Unknown |
| ben     | Unknown |
| bill    | 475-83  |
+---------+---------+
```

In other words, these two tests are equivalent:

```
IF(expr1 IS NOT NULL,expr1,expr2)
IFNULL(expr1,expr2)
```

From a readability standpoint, IF() often is easier to understand than IFNULL(). From a computational perspective, IFNULL() is more efficient because *expr1* never need be evaluated twice, as sometimes happens with IF().

IF() and IFNULL() are especially useful for catching divide-by-zero operations and mapping them onto something else. For example, batting averages for baseball players are calculated as the ratio of hits to at-bats. But if a player has no at-bats, the ratio is undefined:

```
mysql> SET @hits = 0, @atbats = 0;
mysql> SELECT @hits, @atbats, @hits/@atbats AS 'batting average';
+-------+---------+-----------------+
| @hits | @atbats | batting average |
+-------+---------+-----------------+
|     0 |       0 |            NULL |
+-------+---------+-----------------+
```

To handle that case by displaying zero, do this:

```
mysql> SET @hits = 0, @atbats = 0;
mysql> SELECT @hits, @atbats, IFNULL(@hits/@atbats,0) AS 'batting average';
+-------+---------+-----------------+
| @hits | @atbats | batting average |
+-------+---------+-----------------+
|     0 |       0 |               0 |
+-------+---------+-----------------+
```

Earned run average calculations for a pitcher with no innings pitched can be treated the same way. Other common uses for this idiom are as follows:

```
IFNULL(expr,'Missing')
IFNULL(expr,'N/A')
IFNULL(expr,'Unknown')
```

3.15 Sorting a Result Set

Problem

Your query results aren't sorted the way you want.

Solution

MySQL can't read your mind. Add an ORDER BY clause to tell it exactly how you want things sorted.

Discussion

When you select rows, the MySQL server is free to return them in any order, unless you instruct it otherwise by saying how to sort the result. There are lots of ways to use sorting techniques. Chapter 6 explores this topic further. Briefly, you sort a result set by adding an ORDER BY clause that names the column or columns you want to sort by:

```
mysql> SELECT * FROM mail WHERE size > 100000 ORDER BY size;
+---------------------+---------+---------+---------+---------+---------+
| t                   | srcuser | srchost | dstuser | dsthost | size    |
+---------------------+---------+---------+---------+---------+---------+
| 2001-05-12 12:48:13 | tricia  | mars    | gene    | venus   |  194925 |
| 2001-05-15 10:25:52 | gene    | mars    | tricia  | saturn  |  998532 |
| 2001-05-14 17:03:01 | tricia  | saturn  | phil    | venus   | 2394482 |
+---------------------+---------+---------+---------+---------+---------+
mysql> SELECT * FROM mail WHERE dstuser = 'tricia'
    -> ORDER BY srchost, srcuser;
+---------------------+---------+---------+---------+---------+--------+
| t                   | srcuser | srchost | dstuser | dsthost | size   |
+---------------------+---------+---------+---------+---------+--------+
| 2001-05-15 10:25:52 | gene    | mars    | tricia  | saturn  | 998532 |
| 2001-05-14 11:52:17 | phil    | mars    | tricia  | saturn  |   5781 |
| 2001-05-17 12:49:23 | phil    | mars    | tricia  | saturn  |    873 |
| 2001-05-11 10:15:08 | barb    | saturn  | tricia  | mars    |  58274 |
| 2001-05-13 13:59:18 | barb    | saturn  | tricia  | venus   |    271 |
+---------------------+---------+---------+---------+---------+--------+
```

To sort a column in reverse (descending) order, add the keyword DESC after its name in the ORDER BY clause:

```
mysql> SELECT * FROM mail WHERE size > 50000 ORDER BY size DESC;
+---------------------+---------+---------+---------+---------+---------+
| t                   | srcuser | srchost | dstuser | dsthost | size    |
+---------------------+---------+---------+---------+---------+---------+
| 2001-05-14 17:03:01 | tricia  | saturn  | phil    | venus   | 2394482 |
| 2001-05-15 10:25:52 | gene    | mars    | tricia  | saturn  |  998532 |
| 2001-05-12 12:48:13 | tricia  | mars    | gene    | venus   |  194925 |
| 2001-05-14 14:42:21 | barb    | venus   | barb    | venus   |   98151 |
| 2001-05-11 10:15:08 | barb    | saturn  | tricia  | mars    |   58274 |
+---------------------+---------+---------+---------+---------+---------+
```

3.16   Selecting Records from the Beginning or End of a Result Set

Problem

You want to see only certain rows from a result set, like the first one or the last five.

Solution

Use a LIMIT clause, perhaps in conjunction with an ORDER BY clause.

Discussion

MySQL supports a LIMIT clause that tells the server to return only part of a result set. LIMIT is a MySQL-specific extension to SQL that is extremely valuable when your result set contains more rows than you want to see at a time. It allows you to retrieve just the first part of a result set or an arbitrary section of the set. Typically, LIMIT is used for the following kinds of problems:

- Answering questions about first or last, largest or smallest, newest or oldest, least or more expensive, and so forth.

- Splitting a result set into sections so that you can process it one piece at a time. This technique is common in web applications for displaying a large search result across several pages. Showing the result in sections allows display of smaller pages that are easier to understand.

The following examples use the profile table that was introduced in Chapter 2. Its contents look like this:

```
mysql> SELECT * FROM profile;
+----+---------+------------+-------+----------------------+------+
| id | name    | birth      | color | foods                | cats |
+----+---------+------------+-------+----------------------+------+
|  1 | Fred    | 1970-04-13 | black | lutefisk,fadge,pizza |    0 |
|  2 | Mort    | 1969-09-30 | white | burrito,curry,eggroll |   3 |
|  3 | Brit    | 1957-12-01 | red   | burrito,curry,pizza  |    1 |
|  4 | Carl    | 1973-11-02 | red   | eggroll,pizza        |    4 |
|  5 | Sean    | 1963-07-04 | blue  | burrito,curry        |    5 |
|  6 | Alan    | 1965-02-14 | red   | curry,fadge          |    1 |
|  7 | Mara    | 1968-09-17 | green | lutefisk,fadge       |    1 |
|  8 | Shepard | 1975-09-02 | black | curry,pizza          |    2 |
|  9 | Dick    | 1952-08-20 | green | lutefisk,fadge       |    0 |
| 10 | Tony    | 1960-05-01 | white | burrito,pizza        |    0 |
+----+---------+------------+-------+----------------------+------+
```

To select the first *n* records of a query result, add LIMIT *n* to the end of your SELECT statement:

```
mysql> SELECT * FROM profile LIMIT 1;
+----+------+------------+-------+----------------------+------+
| id | name | birth      | color | foods                | cats |
+----+------+------------+-------+----------------------+------+
|  1 | Fred | 1970-04-13 | black | lutefisk,fadge,pizza |    0 |
+----+------+------------+-------+----------------------+------+
mysql> SELECT * FROM profile LIMIT 5;
+----+------+------------+-------+----------------------+------+
| id | name | birth      | color | foods                | cats |
+----+------+------------+-------+----------------------+------+
|  1 | Fred | 1970-04-13 | black | lutefisk,fadge,pizza |    0 |
|  2 | Mort | 1969-09-30 | white | burrito,curry,eggroll |   3 |
|  3 | Brit | 1957-12-01 | red   | burrito,curry,pizza  |    1 |
|  4 | Carl | 1973-11-02 | red   | eggroll,pizza        |    4 |
|  5 | Sean | 1963-07-04 | blue  | burrito,curry        |    5 |
+----+------+------------+-------+----------------------+------+
```

However, because the rows in these query results aren't sorted into any particular order, they may not be very meaningful. A more common technique is to use ORDER BY to sort the result set. Then you can use LIMIT to find smallest and largest values. For example, to find the row with the minimum (earliest) birth date, sort by the birth column, then add LIMIT 1 to retrieve the first row:

```
mysql> SELECT * FROM profile ORDER BY birth LIMIT 1;
+----+------+------------+-------+----------------+------+
| id | name | birth      | color | foods          | cats |
+----+------+------------+-------+----------------+------+
|  9 | Dick | 1952-08-20 | green | lutefisk,fadge |    0 |
+----+------+------------+-------+----------------+------+
```

This works because MySQL processes the ORDER BY clause to sort the rows first, then applies LIMIT. To find the row with the most recent birth date, the query is similar, except that you sort in descending order:

```
mysql> SELECT * FROM profile ORDER BY birth DESC LIMIT 1;
+----+---------+------------+-------+-------------+------+
| id | name    | birth      | color | foods       | cats |
+----+---------+------------+-------+-------------+------+
|  8 | Shepard | 1975-09-02 | black | curry,pizza |    2 |
+----+---------+------------+-------+-------------+------+
```

You can obtain the same information by running these queries without LIMIT and ignoring everything but the first row. The advantage of using LIMIT is that the server returns just the first record and the extra rows don't travel over the network at all. This is much more efficient than retrieving an entire result set, only to discard all but one row.

The sort column or columns can be whatever you like. To find the row for the person with the most cats, sort by the cats column:

```
mysql> SELECT * FROM profile ORDER BY cats DESC LIMIT 1;
+----+------+------------+-------+----------------+------+
| id | name | birth      | color | foods          | cats |
+----+------+------------+-------+----------------+------+
|  5 | Sean | 1963-07-04 | blue  | burrito,curry  |    5 |
+----+------+------------+-------+----------------+------+
```

However, be aware that using LIMIT n to select the "n smallest" or "n largest" values may not yield quite the results you expect. See Recipe 3.18 for some discussion on framing LIMIT queries appropriately.

To find the earliest birthday within the calendar year, sort by the month and day of the birth values:

```
mysql> SELECT name, DATE_FORMAT(birth,'%m-%e') AS birthday
    -> FROM profile ORDER BY birthday LIMIT 1;
+------+----------+
| name | birthday |
+------+----------+
| Alan | 02-14    |
+------+----------+
```

Note that LIMIT *n* really means "return at most *n* rows." If you specify LIMIT 10 and the result set has only 3 rows, the server returns 3 rows.

See Also

You can use LIMIT in combination with RAND() to make random selections from a set of items. See Chapter 13.

As of MySQL 3.22.7, you can use LIMIT to restrict the effect of a DELETE statement to a subset of the rows that would otherwise be deleted. As of MySQL 3.23.3, the same is true for UPDATE. This can be useful in conjunction with a WHERE clause. For example, if a table contains five instances of a record, you can select them in a DELETE statement with an appropriate WHERE clause, then remove the duplicates by adding LIMIT 4 to the end of the statement. This leaves only one copy of the record. For more information about uses of LIMIT in duplicate record removal, see Chapter 14.

3.17 Pulling a Section from the Middle of a Result Set

Problem

You don't want the first or last rows of a result set. Instead, you want to pull a section of rows out of the middle of the set, such as rows 21 through 40.

Solution

That's still a job for LIMIT. But you need to tell it the starting position within the result set in addition to the number of rows you want.

Discussion

LIMIT *n* tells the server to return the first *n* rows of a result set. LIMIT also has a two-argument form that allows you to pick out any arbitrary section of rows from a result. The arguments indicate how many rows to skip and how many to return. This means that you can use LIMIT to do such things as skip two rows and return the next, thus answering questions such as "what is the *third*-smallest or *third*-largest value?," something that's more difficult with MIN() or MAX():

```
mysql> SELECT * FROM profile ORDER BY birth LIMIT 2,1;
+----+------+------------+-------+---------------+------+
| id | name | birth      | color | foods         | cats |
+----+------+------------+-------+---------------+------+
| 10 | Tony | 1960-05-01 | white | burrito,pizza |    0 |
+----+------+------------+-------+---------------+------+
```

```
mysql> SELECT * FROM profile ORDER BY birth DESC LIMIT 2,1;
+----+------+------------+-------+----------------------+------+
| id | name | birth      | color | foods                | cats |
+----+------+------------+-------+----------------------+------+
|  1 | Fred | 1970-04-13 | black | lutefisk,fadge,pizza |    0 |
+----+------+------------+-------+----------------------+------+
```

The two-argument form of LIMIT also makes it possible to partition a result set into smaller sections. For example, to retrieve 20 rows at a time from a result, issue the same SELECT statement repeatedly, but vary the LIMIT clauses like so:

```
SELECT ... FROM ... ORDER BY ... LIMIT 0, 20;    retrieve first 20 rows
SELECT ... FROM ... ORDER BY ... LIMIT 20, 20;   skip 20 rows, retrieve next 20
SELECT ... FROM ... ORDER BY ... LIMIT 40, 20;   skip 40 rows, retrieve next 20
etc.
```

Web developers often use LIMIT this way to split a large search result into smaller, more manageable pieces so that it can be presented over several pages. We'll discuss this technique further in Recipe 18.10.

If you want to know how large a result set is so that you can determine how many sections there are, you can issue a COUNT() query first. Use a WHERE clause that is the same as for the queries you'll use to retrieve the rows. For example, if you want to display profile table records in name order four at a time, you can find out how many there are with the following query:

```
mysql> SELECT COUNT(*) FROM profile;
+----------+
| COUNT(*) |
+----------+
|       10 |
+----------+
```

That tells you you'll have three sets of rows (although the last one will have fewer than four records), which you can retrieve as follows:

```
SELECT * FROM profile ORDER BY name LIMIT 0, 4;
SELECT * FROM profile ORDER BY name LIMIT 4, 4;
SELECT * FROM profile ORDER BY name LIMIT 8, 4;
```

Beginning with MySQL 4.0, you can fetch a part of a result set, but also find out how big the result would have been without the LIMIT clause. For example, to fetch the first four records from the profile table and then obtain the size of the full result, run these queries:

```
SELECT SQL_CALC_FOUND_ROWS * FROM profile ORDER BY name LIMIT 4;
SELECT FOUND_ROWS();
```

The keyword SQL_CALC_FOUND_ROWS in the first query tells MySQL to calculate the size of the entire result set even though the query requests that only part of it be returned. The row count is available by calling FOUND_ROWS(). If that function returns a value greater than four, there are other records yet to be retrieved.

3.18 Choosing Appropriate LIMIT Values

Problem

LIMIT doesn't seem to do what you want it to.

Solution

Be sure you understand what question you're asking. It may be that LIMIT is exposing some interesting subtleties in your data that you have not considered or are not aware of.

Discussion

LIMIT *n* is useful in conjunction with ORDER BY for selecting smallest or largest values from a result set. But does that actually give you the rows with the *n* smallest or largest values? Not necessarily! It does if your rows contain unique values, but not if there are duplicates. You may find it necessary to run a preliminary query first to help you choose the proper LIMIT value.

To see why this is, consider the following dataset, which shows the American League pitchers who won 15 or more games during the 2001 baseball season:

```
mysql> SELECT name, wins FROM al_winner
    -> ORDER BY wins DESC, name;
+----------------+------+
| name           | wins |
+----------------+------+
| Mulder, Mark   |   21 |
| Clemens, Roger |   20 |
| Moyer, Jamie   |   20 |
| Garcia, Freddy |   18 |
| Hudson, Tim    |   18 |
| Abbott, Paul   |   17 |
| Mays, Joe      |   17 |
| Mussina, Mike  |   17 |
| Sabathia, C.C. |   17 |
| Zito, Barry    |   17 |
| Buehrle, Mark  |   16 |
| Milton, Eric   |   15 |
| Pettitte, Andy |   15 |
| Radke, Brad    |   15 |
| Sele, Aaron    |   15 |
+----------------+------+
```

If you want to know who won the most games, adding LIMIT 1 to the preceding query will give you the correct answer, because the maximum value is 21 and there is only one pitcher with that value (Mark Mulder). But what if you want the four highest game winners? The proper queries depend on what you mean by that, which can have various interpretations:

- If you just want the first four rows, sort the records and add LIMIT 4:

```
mysql> SELECT name, wins FROM al_winner
    -> ORDER BY wins DESC, name
    -> LIMIT 4;
+----------------+------+
| name           | wins |
+----------------+------+
| Mulder, Mark   |   21 |
| Clemens, Roger |   20 |
| Moyer, Jamie   |   20 |
| Garcia, Freddy |   18 |
+----------------+------+
```

That may not suit your purposes because LIMIT imposes a cutoff that occurs in the middle of a set of pitchers with the same number of wins (Tim Hudson also won 18 games).

- To avoid making a cutoff in the middle of a set of rows with the same value, select rows with values greater than or equal to the value in the fourth row. Find out what that value is with LIMIT, then use it in the WHERE clause of a second query to select rows:

```
mysql> SELECT wins FROM al_winner
    -> ORDER BY wins DESC, name
    -> LIMIT 3, 1;
+------+
| wins |
+------+
|   18 |
+------+
mysql> SELECT name, wins FROM al_winner
    -> WHERE wins >= 18
    -> ORDER BY wins DESC, name;
+----------------+------+
| name           | wins |
+----------------+------+
| Mulder, Mark   |   21 |
| Clemens, Roger |   20 |
| Moyer, Jamie   |   20 |
| Garcia, Freddy |   18 |
| Hudson, Tim    |   18 |
+----------------+------+
```

- If you want to know all the pitchers with the four largest wins values, another approach is needed. Determine the fourth-largest value with DISTINCT and LIMIT, then use it to select rows:

```
mysql> SELECT DISTINCT wins FROM al_winner
    -> ORDER BY wins DESC, name
    -> LIMIT 3, 1;
```

```
+------+
| wins |
+------+
|   17 |
+------+
mysql> SELECT name, wins FROM al_winner
    -> WHERE wins >= 17
    -> ORDER BY wins DESC, name;
+----------------+------+
| name           | wins |
+----------------+------+
| Mulder, Mark   |   21 |
| Clemens, Roger |   20 |
| Moyer, Jamie   |   20 |
| Garcia, Freddy |   18 |
| Hudson, Tim    |   18 |
| Abbott, Paul   |   17 |
| Mays, Joe      |   17 |
| Mussina, Mike  |   17 |
| Sabathia, C.C. |   17 |
| Zito, Barry    |   17 |
+----------------+------+
```

For this dataset, each method yields a different result. The moral is that the way you use LIMIT may require some thought about what you really want to know.

3.19 Calculating LIMIT Values from Expressions

Problem

You want to use expressions to specify the arguments for LIMIT.

Solution

Sadly, you cannot. You can use only literal integers—unless you issue the query from within a program, in which case you can evaluate the expressions yourself and stick the resulting values into the query string.

Discussion

Arguments to LIMIT must be literal integers, not expressions. Statements such as the following are illegal:

```
SELECT * FROM profile LIMIT 5+5;
SELECT * FROM profile LIMIT @skip_count, @show_count;
```

The same "no expressions allowed" principle applies if you're using an expression to calculate a LIMIT value in a program that constructs a query string. You must evaluate the expression first, then place the resulting value in the query. For example, if you produce a query string in Perl (or PHP) as follows, an error will result when you attempt to execute the query:

```
$str = "SELECT * FROM profile LIMIT $x + $y";
```

To avoid the problem, evaluate the expression first:

```
$z = $x + $y;
$str = "SELECT * FROM profile LIMIT $z";
```

Or do this (but don't omit the parentheses or the expression won't evaluate properly):

```
$str = "SELECT * FROM profile LIMIT " . ($x + $y);
```

If you're constructing a two-argument LIMIT clause, evaluate both expressions before placing them into the query string.

3.20 What to Do When LIMIT Requires the "Wrong" Sort Order

Problem

LIMIT usually works best in conjunction with an ORDER BY clause that sorts rows. But sometimes the sort order is the opposite of what you want for the final result.

Solution

Rewrite the query, or write a program that retrieves the rows and sorts them into the order you want.

Discussion

If you want the last four records of a result set, you can obtain them easily by sorting the set in reverse order and using LIMIT 4. For example, the following query returns the names and birth dates for the four people in the profile table who were born most recently:

```
mysql> SELECT name, birth FROM profile ORDER BY birth DESC LIMIT 4;
+---------+------------+
| name    | birth      |
+---------+------------+
| Shepard | 1975-09-02 |
| Carl    | 1973-11-02 |
| Fred    | 1970-04-13 |
| Mort    | 1969-09-30 |
+---------+------------+
```

But that requires sorting the birth values in descending order to place them at the head of the result set. What if you want them in ascending order instead? One way to solve this problem is to use two queries. First, use COUNT() to find out how many rows are in the table:

```
mysql> SELECT COUNT(*) FROM profile;
+----------+
| COUNT(*) |
+----------+
|       10 |
+----------+
```

Then, sort the values in ascending order and use the two-argument form of LIMIT to skip all but the last four records:

```
mysql> SELECT name, birth FROM profile ORDER BY birth LIMIT 6, 4;
+---------+------------+
| name    | birth      |
+---------+------------+
| Mort    | 1969-09-30 |
| Fred    | 1970-04-13 |
| Carl    | 1973-11-02 |
| Shepard | 1975-09-02 |
+---------+------------+
```

Single-query solutions to this problem may be available if you're issuing queries from within a program and can manipulate the query result. For example, if you fetch the values into a data structure, you can reverse the order of the values in the structure. Here is some Perl code that demonstrates this approach:

```perl
my $stmt = "SELECT name, birth FROM profile ORDER BY birth DESC LIMIT 4";
# fetch values into a data structure
my $ref = $dbh->selectall_arrayref ($stmt);
# reverse the order of the items in the structure
my @val = reverse (@{$ref});
# use $val[$i] to get a reference to row $i, then use
# $val[$i]->[0] and $val[$i]->[1] to access column values
```

Alternatively, you can simply iterate through the structure in reverse order:

```perl
my $stmt = "SELECT name, birth FROM profile ORDER BY birth DESC LIMIT 4";
# fetch values into a data structure
my $ref = $dbh->selectall_arrayref ($stmt);
# iterate through the structure in reverse order
my $row_count = @{$ref};
for (my $i = $row_count - 1; $i >= 0; $i--)
{
    # use $ref->[$i]->[0] and $ref->[$i]->[1] here...
}
```

3.21 Selecting a Result Set into an Existing Table

Problem

You want to run a SELECT query but save the results into another table rather than displaying them.

Solution

If the other table exists, use INSERT INTO ... SELECT, described here. If the table doesn't exist, skip ahead to Recipe 3.22.

Discussion

The MySQL server normally returns the result of a SELECT statement to the client that issued the statement. For example, when you run a query from within *mysql*, the server returns the result to *mysql*, which in turn displays it to you on the screen. It's also possible to send the results of a SELECT statement directly into another table. Copying records from one table to another is useful in a number of ways:

- If you're developing an algorithm that modifies a table, it's safer to work with a copy of a table so that you need not worry about the consequences of mistakes. Also, if the original table is large, creating a partial copy can speed the development process because queries run against it will take less time.

- For data-loading operations that work with information that might be malformed, you can load new records into a temporary table, perform some preliminary checks, and correct the records as necessary. When you're satisfied the new records are okay, copy them from the temporary table into your main table.

- Some applications maintain a large repository table and a smaller working table into which records are inserted on a regular basis, copying the working table records to the repository periodically and clearing the working table.

- If you're performing a number of similar summary operations on a large table, it may be more efficient to select summary information once into a second table and use that for further analysis, rather than running expensive summary operations repeatedly on the original table.

This section shows how to use INSERT ... SELECT to retrieve a result set for insertion into an existing table. The next section discusses CREATE TABLE ... SELECT, a statement available as of MySQL 3.23 that allows you to create a table on the fly directly from a query result. The table names src_tbl and dst_tbl in the examples refer to the source table from which rows are selected and the destination table into which they are stored.

If the destination table already exists, use INSERT ... SELECT to copy the result set into it. For example, if dst_tbl contains an integer column i and a string column s, the following statement copies rows from src_tbl into dst_tbl, assigning column val to i and column name to s:

```
INSERT INTO dst_tbl (i, s) SELECT val, name FROM src_tbl;
```

The number of columns to be inserted must match the number of selected columns, and the correspondence between sets of columns is established by position rather than name. In the special case that you want to copy all columns from one table to another, you can shorten the statement to this form:

```
INSERT INTO dst_tbl SELECT * FROM src_tbl;
```

To copy only certain rows, add a WHERE clause that selects the rows you want:

```
INSERT INTO dst_tbl SELECT * FROM src_tbl WHERE val > 100 AND name LIKE 'A%';
```

It's not necessary to copy column values without modification from the source table into the destination table. The SELECT statement can produce values from expressions, too. For example, the following query counts the number of times each name occurs in src_tbl and stores both the counts and the names in dst_tbl:

```
INSERT INTO dst_tbl (i, s) SELECT COUNT(*), name FROM src_tbl GROUP BY name;
```

 When you use INSERT ... SELECT, you cannot use the same table both as a source and a destination.

3.22 Creating a Destination Table on the Fly from a Result Set

Problem

You want to run a SELECT query and save the result set into another table, but that table doesn't exist yet.

Solution

Create the destination table first, or create it directly from the result of the SELECT.

Discussion

If the destination table does not exist, you can create it first with a CREATE TABLE statement, then copy rows into it with INSERT ... SELECT as described in Recipe 3.21. This technique works for any version of MySQL.

In MySQL 3.23 and up, a second option is to use CREATE TABLE ... SELECT, which creates the destination table directly from the result of a SELECT. For example, to create dst_tbl and copy the entire contents of src_tbl into it, do this:

```
CREATE TABLE dst_tbl SELECT * FROM src_tbl;
```

MySQL creates the columns in dst_tbl based on the name, number, and type of the columns in src_tbl. Add an appropriate WHERE clause, should you wish to copy only certain rows. If you want to create an empty table, use a WHERE clause that is always false:

```
CREATE TABLE dst_tbl SELECT * FROM src_tbl WHERE 0;
```

To copy only some of the columns, name the ones you want in the SELECT part of the statement. For example, if src_tbl contains columns a, b, c, and d, you can copy just b and d like this:

```
CREATE TABLE dst_tbl SELECT b, d FROM src_tbl;
```

To create columns in a different order than that in which they appear in the source table, just name them in the desired order. If the source table contains columns a, b, and c, but you want them to appear in the destination table in the order c, a, and b, do this:

```
CREATE TABLE dst_tbl SELECT c, a, b FROM src_tbl;
```

To create additional columns in the destination table besides those selected from the source table, provide appropriate column definitions in the CREATE TABLE part of the statement. The following statement creates id as an AUTO_INCREMENT column in dst_tbl, and adds columns a, b, and c from src_tbl:

```
CREATE TABLE dst_tbl
(
    id INT NOT NULL AUTO_INCREMENT,
    PRIMARY KEY (id)
)
SELECT a, b, c FROM src_tbl;
```

The resulting table contains four columns in the order id, a, b, c. Defined columns are assigned their default values. (This means that id, being an AUTO_INCREMENT column, will be assigned successive sequence numbers starting from one. See Recipe 11.1.)

If you derive a column's values from an expression, it's prudent to provide an alias to give the column a name. Suppose src_tbl contains invoice information listing items in each invoice. Then the following statement generates a summary of each invoice named in the table, along with the total cost of its items. The second column includes an alias because the default name for an expression is the expression itself, which is difficult to work with:

```
CREATE TABLE dst_tbl
SELECT inv_no, SUM(unit_cost*quantity) AS total_cost
FROM src_tbl
GROUP BY inv_no;
```

In fact, prior to MySQL 3.23.6, the alias is required, not just advisable; column naming rules are stricter and an expression is not a legal name for a column in a table.

CREATE TABLE ... SELECT is extremely convenient, but does have some limitations. These stem primarily from the fact that the information available from a result set is not as extensive as what you can specify in a CREATE TABLE statement. If you derive a table column from an expression, for example, MySQL has no idea whether or not the column should be indexed or what its default value is. If it's important to include this information in the destination table, use the following techniques:

- If you want indexes in the destination table, you can specify them explicitly. For example, if src_tbl has a PRIMARY KEY on the id column, and a multiple-column index on state and city, you can specify them for dst_tbl as well:

```
CREATE TABLE dst_tbl (PRIMARY KEY (id), INDEX(state,city))
SELECT * FROM src_tbl;
```

- Column attributes such as AUTO_INCREMENT and a column's default value are not copied to the destination table. To preserve these attributes, create the table, then use ALTER TABLE to apply the appropriate modifications to the column definition. For example, if src_tbl has an id column that is not only a PRIMARY KEY but an AUTO_INCREMENT column, copy the table, then modify it:

```
CREATE TABLE dst_tbl (PRIMARY KEY (id)) SELECT * FROM src_tbl;
ALTER TABLE dst_tbl MODIFY id INT UNSIGNED NOT NULL AUTO_INCREMENT;
```

- If you want to make the destination table an exact copy of the source table, use the cloning technique described in Recipe 3.25.

3.23 Moving Records Between Tables Safely

Problem

You're moving records by copying them from one table to another and then deleting them from the original table. But some records seem to be getting lost.

Solution

Be careful to delete exactly the same set of records from the source table that you copied to the destination table.

Discussion

Applications that copy rows from one table to another can do so with a single operation, such as INSERT ... SELECT to retrieve the relevant rows from the source table and add them to the destination table. If an application needs to *move* (rather than copy) rows, the procedure is a little more complicated: After copying the rows to the destination table, you must remove them from the source table. Conceptually, this is nothing more than INSERT ... SELECT followed by DELETE. In practice, the operation may require more care, because it's necessary to select exactly the same set of rows in the source table for both the INSERT and DELETE statements. If other clients insert new rows into the source table after you issue the INSERT and before you issue the DELETE, this can be tricky.

To illustrate, suppose you have an application that uses a working log table worklog into which records are entered on a continual basis, and a long-term repository log table repolog. Periodically, you move worklog records into repolog to keep the size of the working log small, and so that clients can issue possibly long-running log analysis queries on the repository without blocking processes that create new records in the working log.[*]

How do you properly move records from worklog to repolog in this situation, given that worklog is subject to ongoing insert activity? The obvious (but incorrect) way is to issue an INSERT ... SELECT statement to copy all the worklog records into repolog, followed by a DELETE to remove them from worklog:

```
INSERT INTO repolog SELECT * FROM worklog;
DELETE FROM worklog;
```

This is a perfectly workable strategy when you're certain nobody else will insert any records into worklog during the time between the two statements. But if other clients insert new records in that period, they'll be deleted without ever having been copied, and you'll lose records. If the tables hold logs of web page requests, that may not be such a big deal, but if they're logs of financial transactions, you could have a serious problem.

What can you do to keep from losing records? Two possibilities are to issue both statements within a transaction, or to lock both tables while you're using them. These techniques are covered in Chapter 15. However, either one might block other clients longer than you'd prefer, because you tie up the tables for the duration of both queries. An alternative strategy is to move only those records that are older than some cutoff point. For example, if the log records have a column t containing a timestamp, you can limit the scope of the selected records to all those created before today. Then it won't matter whether new records are added to worklog between the copy and delete operations. Be sure to specify the cutoff properly, though. Here's a method that fails under some circumstances:

```
INSERT INTO repolog SELECT * FROM worklog WHERE t < CURDATE();
DELETE FROM worklog WHERE t < CURDATE();
```

This won't work if you happen to issue the INSERT statement at one second before midnight and the SELECT statement one second later. The value of CURDATE() will differ for the two statements, and the DELETE operation may remove too many records.

---

[*] If you use a MyISAM log table that you only insert into and never delete from or modify, you can run queries on the table without preventing other clients from inserting new log records at the end of the table.

If you're going to use a cutoff, make sure it has a fixed value, not one that may change between statements. For example, a SQL variable can be used to save the value of CURDATE() in a form that won't change as time passes:

```
SET @cutoff = CURDATE();
INSERT INTO repolog SELECT * FROM worklog WHERE t < @cutoff;
DELETE FROM worklog WHERE t < @cutoff;
```

This ensures that both statements use the same cutoff value so that the DELETE operation doesn't remove records that it shouldn't.

3.24 Creating Temporary Tables

Problem

You need a table only for a short time, then you want it to disappear automatically.

Solution

Create a TEMPORARY table and let MySQL take care of clobbering it.

Discussion

Some operations require a table that exists only temporarily and that should disappear when it's no longer needed. You can of course issue a DROP TABLE statement explicitly to remove a table when you're done with it. Another option, available in MySQL 3.23.2 and up, is to use CREATE TEMPORARY TABLE. This statement is just like CREATE TABLE except that it creates a transient table that disappears when your connection to the server closes, if you haven't already removed it yourself. This is extremely useful behavior because you need not remember to remove the table. MySQL drops it for you automatically.

Temporary tables are connection-specific, so several clients each can create a temporary table having the same name without interfering with each other. This makes it easier to write applications that use transient tables, because you need not ensure that the tables have unique names for each client. (See Recipe 3.26 for further discussion of this issue.)

Another property of temporary tables is that they can be created with the same name as a permanent table. In this case, the temporary table "hides" the permanent table for the duration of its existence, which can be useful for making a copy of a table that you can modify without affecting the original by mistake. The DELETE statement in the following set of queries removes records from a temporary mail table, leaving the original permanent one unaffected:

```
mysql> CREATE TEMPORARY TABLE mail SELECT * FROM mail;
mysql> SELECT COUNT(*) FROM mail;
```

```
+----------+
| COUNT(*) |
+----------+
|       16 |
+----------+
mysql> DELETE FROM mail;
mysql> SELECT COUNT(*) FROM mail;
+----------+
| COUNT(*) |
+----------+
|        0 |
+----------+
mysql> DROP TABLE mail;
mysql> SELECT COUNT(*) FROM mail;
+----------+
| COUNT(*) |
+----------+
|       16 |
+----------+
```

Although temporary tables created with CREATE TEMPORARY TABLE have the preceding benefits, keep the following caveats in mind:

- If you want to reuse the temporary table within a given session, you'll still need to drop it explicitly before recreating it. It's only the *last* use within a session that you need no explicit DROP TABLE for. (If you've already created a temporary table with a given name, attempting to create a second one with that name results in an error.)

- Some APIs support persistent connections in a web environment. Use of these prevents temporary tables from being dropped as you expect when your script ends, because the web server keeps the connection open for reuse by other scripts. (The server may close the connection eventually, but you have no control over when that happens.) This means it can be prudent to issue the following statement prior to creating a temporary table, just in case it's still hanging around from the previous execution of the script:

    ```
    DROP TABLE IF EXISTS tbl_name
    ```

- If you modify a temporary table that "hides" a permanent table with the same name, be sure to test for errors resulting from dropped connections. If a client program automatically reconnects after a dropped connection, you'll be modifying the *original* table after the reconnect.

3.25   Cloning a Table Exactly

Problem

You need an exact copy of a table, and CREATE TABLE ... SELECT doesn't suit your purposes because the copy must include the same indexes, default values, and so forth.

Solution

Use SHOW CREATE TABLE to get a CREATE TABLE statement that specifies the source table's structure, indexes and all. Then modify the statement to change the table name to that of the clone table and execute the statement. If you need the table contents copied as well, issue an INSERT INTO ... SELECT statement, too.

Discussion

Because CREATE TABLE ... SELECT does not copy indexes or the full set of column attributes, it doesn't necessarily create a destination table as an exact copy of the source table. Because of that, you might find it more useful to issue a SHOW CREATE TABLE query for the source table. This statement is available as of MySQL 3.23.20; it returns a row containing the table name and a CREATE TABLE statement that corresponds to the table's structure—including its indexes (keys), column attributes, and table type:

```
mysql> SHOW CREATE TABLE mail\G
*************************** 1. row ***************************
       Table: mail
Create Table: CREATE TABLE `mail` (
  `t` datetime default NULL,
  `srcuser` char(8) default NULL,
  `srchost` char(20) default NULL,
  `dstuser` char(8) default NULL,
  `dsthost` char(20) default NULL,
  `size` bigint(20) default NULL,
  KEY `t` (`t`)
) TYPE=MyISAM
```

By issuing a SHOW CREATE TABLE statement from within a program and performing a string replacement to change the table name, you obtain a statement that can be executed to create a new table with the same structure as the original. The following Python function takes three arguments (a connection object, and the names of the source and destination tables). It retrieves the CREATE TABLE statement for the source table, modifies it to name the destination table, and returns the result:

```python
# Generate a CREATE TABLE statement to create dst_tbl with the same
# structure as the existing table src_tbl.  Return None if an error
# occurs.  Requires the re module.

def gen_clone_query (conn, src_tbl, dst_tbl):
    try:
        cursor = conn.cursor ()
        cursor.execute ("SHOW CREATE TABLE " + src_tbl)
        row = cursor.fetchone ()
        cursor.close ()
        if row == None:
            query = None
        else:
```

```
                    # Replace src_tbl with dst_tbl in the CREATE TABLE statement
                    query = re.sub ("CREATE TABLE .*`" + src_tbl + "`",
                                    "CREATE TABLE `" + dst_tbl + "`",
                                    row[1])
        except:
            query = None
        return query
```

You can execute the resulting statement as is to create the new table if you like:

```
query = gen_clone_query (conn, old_tbl, new_tbl)
cursor = conn.cursor ()
cursor.execute (query)
cursor.close ()
```

Or you can get more creative. For example, to create a temporary table rather than a permanent one, change CREATE to CREATE TEMPORARY before executing the statement:

```
query = gen_clone_query (conn, old_tbl, new_tbl)
query = re.sub ("CREATE ", "CREATE TEMPORARY ", query)
cursor = conn.cursor ()
cursor.execute (query)
cursor.close ()
```

Executing the statement returned by gen_clone_query( ) creates an empty copy of the source table. To copy the contents as well, do something like this after creating the copy:

```
cursor = conn.cursor ()
cursor.execute ("INSERT INTO " + new_tbl + " SELECT * FROM " + old_tbl)
cursor.close ()
```

> Prior to MySQL 3.23.50, there are a few attributes that you can spec-
> ify in a CREATE TABLE statement that SHOW CREATE TABLE does not dis-
> play. If your source table was created with any of these attributes, the
> cloning technique shown here will create a destination table that does
> not have quite the same structure.

3.26   Generating Unique Table Names

Problem

You need to create a table with a name that is guaranteed not to exist already.

Solution

If you can create a TEMPORARY table, it doesn't matter if the name exists already. Otherwise, try to generate a value that is unique to your client program and incorporate it into the table name.

Discussion

MySQL is a multiple-client database server, so if a given script that creates a transient table might be invoked by several clients simultaneously, you must take care to keep multiple invocations of the script from fighting over the same table name. If the script creates tables using CREATE TEMPORARY TABLE, there is no problem because different clients can create temporary tables having the same name without clashing.

If you can't use CREATE TEMPORARY TABLE because the server version is older than 3.23.2, you should make sure that each invocation of the script creates a uniquely named table. To do this, incorporate into the name some value that is guaranteed to be unique per invocation. A timestamp won't work, because it's easily possible for two instances of a script to be invoked within the same second. A random number may be somewhat better. For example, in Java, you can use the java.util.Random() class to create a table name like this:

```
import java.util.Random;
import java.lang.Math;

Random rand = new Random ();
int n = rand.nextInt ();          // generate random number
n = Math.abs (n);                 // take absolute value
String tblName = "tmp_tbl_" + n;
```

Unfortunately, random numbers only reduce the possibility of name clashes, they do not eliminate it. Process ID (PID) values are a better source of unique values. PIDs are reused over time, but never for two processes at the same time, so a given PID is guaranteed to be unique among the set of currently executing processes. You can use this fact to create unique table names as follows:

Perl:

```
my $tbl_name = "tmp_tbl_$$";
```

PHP:

```
$tbl_name = "tmp_tbl_" . posix_getpid ();
```

Python:

```
import os
tbl_name = "tmp_tbl_%d" % os.getpid ()
```

Note that even if you create a table name using a value like a PID that is guaranteed to be unique to a given script invocation, there may still be a chance that the table will exist. This can happen if a previous invocation of the script with the same PID created a table with the same name, but crashed before removing the table. On the other hand, any such table cannot still be in use because it will have been created by a process that is no longer running. Under these circumstances, it's safe to remove the table if it does exist by issuing the following statement:

```
DROP TABLE IF EXISTS tbl_name
```

Then you can go ahead and create the new table.

CHAPTER 4
Working with Strings

4.0   Introduction

Like most data types, strings can be compared for equality or inequality or relative ordering. However, strings have some additional properties to consider:

- Strings can be case sensitive (or not), which can affect the outcome of string operations.
- You can compare entire strings, or just parts of them by extracting substrings.
- You can apply pattern-matching operations to look for strings that have a certain structure.

This chapter discusses several useful string operations you can perform, including how to account for whether or not strings are case sensitive.

The following table, metal, is used in several sections of this chapter:

```
mysql> SELECT * FROM metal;
+----------+
| name     |
+----------+
| copper   |
| gold     |
| iron     |
| lead     |
| mercury  |
| platinum |
| silver   |
| tin      |
+----------+
```

The table is very simple, containing only a single string column:

```
CREATE TABLE metal
(
    name      VARCHAR(20)
);
```

You can create the table using the *metal.sql* script in the *tables* directory of the recipes distribution.

Types of Strings

MySQL can operate on regular strings or binary strings. "Binary" in this context has little to do with the presence of non-ASCII values, so it's useful right at the outset to make a distinction:

- Binary *data* may contain bytes that lie outside the usual range of printable ASCII characters.
- A binary *string* in MySQL is one that MySQL treats as case sensitive in comparisons. For binary strings, the characters A and a are considered different. For nonbinary strings, they're considered the same.

A binary column type is one that contains binary strings. Some of MySQL's column types are binary (case sensitive) and others are not, as illustrated here:

Column type	Binary/case sensitive
CHAR, VARCHAR	No
CHAR BINARY, VARCHAR BINARY	Yes
TEXT	No
BLOB	Yes
ENUM, SET	No

4.1   Writing Strings That Include Quotes or Special Characters

Problem

You want to write a quoted string, but it contains quote characters or other special characters, and MySQL rejects it.

Solution

Learn the syntax rules that govern the interpretation of strings in queries.

Discussion

To write a string in a SQL statement, surround it with quote characters:

```
mysql> SELECT 'hello, world';
+--------------+
| hello, world |
```

```
+--------------+
| hello, world |
+--------------+
```

But sometimes you need to write a string that includes a quote character, and if you just put the quote into the string as is, a syntax error results:

```
mysql> SELECT 'I'm asleep';
ERROR 1064 at line 1: You have an error in your SQL syntax near 'asleep''
at line 1
```

You can deal with this several ways:

- MySQL, unlike some SQL engines, allows you to quote strings with either single quotes or double quotes, so you can enclose a string containing single quotes within double quotes:

```
mysql> SELECT "I'm asleep";
+------------+
| I'm asleep |
+------------+
| I'm asleep |
+------------+
```

  This works in reverse, too; a string containing double quotes can be enclosed within single quotes:

```
mysql> SELECT 'He said, "Boo!"';
+-----------------+
| He said, "Boo!" |
+-----------------+
| He said, "Boo!" |
+-----------------+
```

- To include a quote character within a string that is quoted by the same kind of quote, either double the quote or precede it with a backslash. When MySQL reads the query string, it will strip off the extra quote or the backslash:

```
mysql> SELECT 'I''m asleep', 'I\'m wide awake';
+------------+---------------+
| I'm asleep | I'm wide awake |
+------------+---------------+
| I'm asleep | I'm wide awake |
+------------+---------------+
1 row in set (0.00 sec)
mysql> SELECT "He said, ""Boo!""", "And I said, \"Yikes!\"";
+-----------------+----------------------+
| He said, "Boo!" | And I said, "Yikes!" |
+-----------------+----------------------+
| He said, "Boo!" | And I said, "Yikes!" |
+-----------------+----------------------+
```

A backslash turns off the special meaning of the following character. (It causes a temporary escape from normal string processing rules, so sequences such as \' and \" are called escape sequences.) This means that backslash itself is special, so to write a literal backslash within a string, you must double it:

```
mysql> SELECT 'Install MySQL in C:\\mysql on Windows';
+-------------------------------------+
| Install MySQL in C:\mysql on Windows |
+-------------------------------------+
| Install MySQL in C:\mysql on Windows |
+-------------------------------------+
```

Other escape sequences recognized by MySQL are \b (backspace), \n (newline, also called linefeed), \r (carriage return), \t (tab), and \0 (ASCII NUL).

See Also

Use of escape sequences for writing string values is best limited to text values. Values such as images that contain arbitrary data also must have any special characters escaped if you want to include them in a query string, but trying to enter an image value by typing it in is too painful even to think about. You should construct such queries from within a program where you can use the placeholder mechanism provided by the language's MySQL API. See Recipe 2.6.

4.2   Preserving Trailing Spaces in String Columns

Problem

MySQL strips trailing spaces from strings, but you want to preserve them.

Solution

Use a different column type.

Discussion

If you store a string that contains trailing spaces into the database, you may find that they're gone when you retrieve the value. This is the normal MySQL behavior for CHAR and VARCHAR columns; the server returns values from both types of columns without trailing spaces. If you want to preserve trailing spaces, use one of the TEXT or BLOB column types. (The TEXT types are not case sensitive, the BLOB types are.) The following example illustrates the difference in behavior for VARCHAR and TEXT columns:

```
mysql> CREATE TABLE t (c VARCHAR(255));
mysql> INSERT INTO t (c) VALUES('abc        ');
mysql> SELECT c, LENGTH(c) FROM t;
+------+-----------+
| c    | LENGTH(c) |
+------+-----------+
| abc  |         3 |
+------+-----------+
```

```
mysql> DROP TABLE t;
mysql> CREATE TABLE t (c TEXT);
mysql> INSERT INTO t (c) VALUES('abc      ');
mysql> SELECT c, LENGTH(c) FROM t;
+-----------+-----------+
| c         | LENGTH(c) |
+-----------+-----------+
| abc       |        10 |
+-----------+-----------+
```

There are plans to introduce a VARCHAR type that retains trailing spaces in a future version of MySQL.

4.3 Testing String Equality or Relative Ordering

Problem

You want to know whether strings are equal or unequal, or which one appears first in lexical order.

Solution

Use a comparison operator.

Discussion

Strings are subject to the usual equality and inequality comparisons:

```
mysql> SELECT name, name = 'lead', name != 'lead' FROM metal;
+----------+---------------+----------------+
| name     | name = 'lead' | name != 'lead' |
+----------+---------------+----------------+
| copper   |             0 |              1 |
| gold     |             0 |              1 |
| iron     |             0 |              1 |
| lead     |             1 |              0 |
| mercury  |             0 |              1 |
| platinum |             0 |              1 |
| silver   |             0 |              1 |
| tin      |             0 |              1 |
+----------+---------------+----------------+
```

You can also use relational operators such as <, <=, >=, and > to test strings for lexical ordering:

```
mysql> SELECT name, name < 'lead', name > 'lead' FROM metal;
+----------+---------------+---------------+
| name     | name < 'lead' | name > 'lead' |
+----------+---------------+---------------+
| copper   |             1 |             0 |
| gold     |             1 |             0 |
```

```
| iron     |            1 |            0 |
| lead     |            0 |            0 |
| mercury  |            0 |            1 |
| platinum |            0 |            1 |
| silver   |            0 |            1 |
| tin      |            0 |            1 |
+----------+--------------+--------------+
```

To find out whether a string lies within a given range of values (inclusive), you can combine two comparisons:

```
mysql> SELECT name, 'iron' <= name AND name <= 'platinum' FROM metal;
+----------+---------------------------------------+
| name     | 'iron' <= name AND name <= 'platinum' |
+----------+---------------------------------------+
| copper   |                                     0 |
| gold     |                                     0 |
| iron     |                                     1 |
| lead     |                                     1 |
| mercury  |                                     1 |
| platinum |                                     1 |
| silver   |                                     0 |
| tin      |                                     0 |
+----------+---------------------------------------+
```

You can also use the BETWEEN operator for inclusive-range testing. The following query is equivalent to the one just shown:

```
SELECT name, name BETWEEN 'iron' AND 'platinum' FROM metal;
```

See Also

The outcome of a string comparison may be affected by whether or not the operands are binary strings, as discussed in Recipe 4.9.

4.4   Decomposing or Combining Strings

Problem

You want to break apart a string to extract a substring or combine strings to form a larger string.

Solution

To obtain a piece of a string, use a substring-extraction function. To combine strings, use CONCAT().

Discussion

Parts of strings can be extracted and displayed. For example, LEFT(), MID(), and RIGHT() extract substrings from the left, middle, or right part of a string:

```
mysql> SELECT name, LEFT(name,2), MID(name,3,1), RIGHT(name,3) FROM metal;
+----------+--------------+---------------+---------------+
| name     | LEFT(name,2) | MID(name,3,1) | RIGHT(name,3) |
+----------+--------------+---------------+---------------+
| copper   | co           | p             | per           |
| gold     | go           | l             | old           |
| iron     | ir           | o             | ron           |
| lead     | le           | a             | ead           |
| mercury  | me           | r             | ury           |
| platinum | pl           | a             | num           |
| silver   | si           | l             | ver           |
| tin      | ti           | n             | tin           |
+----------+--------------+---------------+---------------+
```

For LEFT() and RIGHT(), the second argument indicates how many characters to return from the left or right end of the string. For MID(), the second argument is the starting position of the substring you want (beginning from 1) and the third argument indicates how many characters to return.

The SUBSTRING() function takes a string and a starting position, returning everything to the right of the position.*

```
mysql> SELECT name, SUBSTRING(name,4), MID(name,4) FROM metal;
+----------+-------------------+-------------+
| name     | SUBSTRING(name,4) | MID(name,4) |
+----------+-------------------+-------------+
| copper   | per               | per         |
| gold     | d                 | d           |
| iron     | n                 | n           |
| lead     | d                 | d           |
| mercury  | cury              | cury        |
| platinum | tinum             | tinum       |
| silver   | ver               | ver         |
| tin      |                   |             |
+----------+-------------------+-------------+
```

To return everything to the right or left of a given character, use SUBSTRING_INDEX(*str*,*c*,*n*). It searches into a string *str* for the *n*-th occurrence of the character *c* and returns everything to its left. If *n* is negative, the search for *c* starts from the right and returns everything to the right of the character:

```
mysql> SELECT name,
    -> SUBSTRING_INDEX(name,'r',2),
    -> SUBSTRING_INDEX(name,'i',-1)
    -> FROM metal;
```

---

* MID() acts the same way if you omit its third argument, because MID() is actually a synonym for SUBSTRING().

```
+----------+------------------------------+------------------------------+
| name     | SUBSTRING_INDEX(name,'r',2)  | SUBSTRING_INDEX(name,'i',-1) |
+----------+------------------------------+------------------------------+
| copper   | copper                       | copper                       |
| gold     | gold                         | gold                         |
| iron     | iron                         | ron                          |
| lead     | lead                         | lead                         |
| mercury  | mercu                        | mercury                      |
| platinum | platinum                     | num                          |
| silver   | silver                       | lver                         |
| tin      | tin                          | n                            |
+----------+------------------------------+------------------------------+
```

Note that if there is no *n*-th occurrence of the character, SUBSTRING_INDEX() returns the entire string. SUBSTRING_INDEX() is case sensitive.

Substrings can be used for purposes other than display, such as to perform comparisons. The following query finds metal names having a first letter that lies in the last half of the alphabet:

```
mysql> SELECT name from metal WHERE LEFT(name,1) >= 'n';
+----------+
| name     |
+----------+
| platinum |
| silver   |
| tin      |
+----------+
```

To combine strings rather than pull them apart, use the CONCAT() function. It concatenates all its arguments and returns the result:

```
mysql> SELECT CONCAT('Hello, ',USER(),', welcome to MySQL!') AS greeting;
+-----------------------------------------+
| greeting                                |
+-----------------------------------------+
| Hello, paul@localhost, welcome to MySQL! |
+-----------------------------------------+
mysql> SELECT CONCAT(name,' ends in "d": ',IF(RIGHT(name,1)='d','YES','NO'))
    -> AS 'ends in "d"?'
    -> FROM metal;
+-------------------------+
| ends in "d"?            |
+-------------------------+
| copper ends in "d": NO  |
| gold ends in "d": YES   |
| iron ends in "d": NO    |
| lead ends in "d": YES   |
| mercury ends in "d": NO |
| platinum ends in "d": NO |
| silver ends in "d": NO  |
| tin ends in "d": NO     |
+-------------------------+
```

Concatenation can be useful for modifying column values "in place." For example, the following UPDATE statement adds a string to the end of each name value in the metal table:

```
mysql> UPDATE metal SET name = CONCAT(name,'ide');
mysql> SELECT name FROM metal;
+-------------+
| name        |
+-------------+
| copperide   |
| goldide     |
| ironide     |
| leadide     |
| mercuryide  |
| platinumide |
| silveride   |
| tinide      |
+-------------+
```

To undo the operation, strip off the last three characters (the LENGTH( ) function returns the length of a string):

```
mysql> UPDATE metal SET name = LEFT(name,LENGTH(name)-3);
mysql> SELECT name FROM metal;
+----------+
| name     |
+----------+
| copper   |
| gold     |
| iron     |
| lead     |
| mercury  |
| platinum |
| silver   |
| tin      |
+----------+
```

The concept of modifying a column in place can be applied to ENUM or SET values as well, which usually can be treated as string values even though they are stored internally as numbers. For example, to concatenate a SET element to an existing SET column, use CONCAT( ) to add the new value to the existing value, preceded by a comma. But remember to account for the possibility that the existing value might be NULL or the empty string. In that case, set the column value equal to the new element, without the leading comma:

```
UPDATE tbl_name
SET set_col = IF(set_col IS NULL OR set_col = '',val,CONCAT(set_col,',',val));
```

4.5 Checking Whether a String Contains a Substring

Problem

You want to know whether a given string occurs within another string.

Solution

Use LOCATE().

Discussion

The LOCATE() function takes two arguments representing the substring that you're looking for and the string in which to look for it. The return value is the position at which the substring occurs, or 0 if it's not present. An optional third argument may be given to indicate the position within the string at which to start looking.

```
mysql> SELECT name, LOCATE('in',name), LOCATE('in',name,3) FROM metal;
+----------+-------------------+---------------------+
| name     | LOCATE('in',name) | LOCATE('in',name,3) |
+----------+-------------------+---------------------+
| copper   |                 0 |                   0 |
| gold     |                 0 |                   0 |
| iron     |                 0 |                   0 |
| lead     |                 0 |                   0 |
| mercury  |                 0 |                   0 |
| platinum |                 5 |                   5 |
| silver   |                 0 |                   0 |
| tin      |                 2 |                   0 |
+----------+-------------------+---------------------+
```

LOCATE() is not case sensitive as of MySQL 4.0.0, and is case sensitive before that.

4.6 Pattern Matching with SQL Patterns

Problem

You want to perform a pattern match rather than a literal comparison.

Solution

Use the LIKE operator and a SQL pattern, described in this section. Or use a regular expression pattern match, described in Recipe 4.7.

Discussion

Patterns are strings that contain special characters. These are known as metacharacters because they stand for something other than themselves. MySQL provides two kinds of pattern matching. One is based on SQL patterns and the other on regular expressions. SQL patterns are more standard among different database systems, but regular expressions are more powerful. The two kinds of pattern match uses different operators and different sets of metacharacters. This section describes SQL patterns; Recipe 4.7 describes regular expressions.

SQL pattern matching uses the LIKE and NOT LIKE operators rather than = and != to perform matching against a pattern string. Patterns may contain two special metacharacters: _ matches any single character, and % matches any sequence of characters, including the empty string. You can use these characters to create patterns that match a wide variety of values:

- Strings that begin with a particular substring:

    ```
    mysql> SELECT name FROM metal WHERE name LIKE 'co%';
    +--------+
    | name   |
    +--------+
    | copper |
    +--------+
    ```

- Strings that end with a particular substring:

    ```
    mysql> SELECT name FROM metal WHERE name LIKE '%er';
    +--------+
    | name   |
    +--------+
    | copper |
    | silver |
    +--------+
    ```

- Strings that contain a particular substring anywhere:

    ```
    mysql> SELECT name FROM metal WHERE name LIKE '%er%';
    +---------+
    | name    |
    +---------+
    | copper  |
    | mercury |
    | silver  |
    +---------+
    ```

- Strings that contain a substring at a specific position (the pattern matches only if pp occurs at the third position of the name column):

    ```
    mysql> SELECT name FROM metal where name LIKE '__pp%';
    +--------+
    | name   |
    +--------+
    | copper |
    +--------+
    ```

A SQL pattern matches successfully only if it matches the entire comparison value. Thus, of the following two pattern matches, only the second succeeds:

```
'abc' LIKE 'b'
'abc' LIKE '%b%'
```

To reverse the sense of a pattern match, use NOT LIKE. The following query finds strings that contain no i characters:

```
mysql> SELECT name FROM metal WHERE name NOT LIKE '%i%';
+---------+
| name    |
+---------+
| copper  |
| gold    |
| lead    |
| mercury |
+---------+
```

SQL patterns do not match NULL values. This is true both for LIKE and NOT LIKE:

```
mysql> SELECT NULL LIKE '%', NULL NOT LIKE '%';
+---------------+-------------------+
| NULL LIKE '%' | NULL NOT LIKE '%' |
+---------------+-------------------+
|          NULL |              NULL |
+---------------+-------------------+
```

In some cases, pattern matches are equivalent to substring comparisons. For example, using patterns to find strings at one end or the other of a string is like using LEFT() or RIGHT():

Pattern match	Substring comparison
str LIKE 'abc%'	LEFT(str,3) = 'abc'
str LIKE '%abc'	RIGHT(str,3) = 'abc'

If you're matching against a column that is indexed and you have a choice of using a pattern or an equivalent LEFT() expression, you'll likely find that the pattern match is faster. MySQL can use the index to narrow the search for a pattern that begins with a literal string; with LEFT(), it cannot.

4.7   Pattern Matching with Regular Expressions

Problem

You want to perform a pattern match rather than a literal comparison.

Using Patterns with Non-String Values

Unlike some other databases, MySQL allows pattern matches to be applied to numeric or date values, which can sometimes be useful. The following table shows some ways to test a DATE value d using function calls that extract date parts and using the equivalent pattern matches. The pairs of expressions are true for dates occurring in the year 1976, in the month of April, or on the first day of the month:

Function value test	Pattern match test
YEAR(d) = 1976	d LIKE '1976-%'
MONTH(d) = 4	d LIKE '%-04-%'
DAYOFMONTH(d) = 1	d LIKE '%-01'

Solution

Use the REGEXP operator and a regular expression pattern, described in this section. Or use a SQL pattern, described in Recipe 4.6.

Discussion

SQL patterns (see Recipe 4.6) are likely to be implemented by other database systems, so they're reasonably portable beyond MySQL. On the other hand, they're somewhat limited. For example, you can easily write a SQL pattern %abc% to find strings that contain abc, but you cannot write a single SQL pattern to identify strings that contain any of the characters a, b, or c. Nor can you match string content based on character types such as letters or digits. For such operations, MySQL supports another type of pattern matching operation based on regular expressions and the REGEXP operator (or NOT REGEXP to reverse the sense of the match).[*] REGEXP matching uses a different set of pattern elements than % and _ (neither of which is special in regular expressions):

Pattern	What the pattern matches
^	Beginning of string
$	End of string
.	Any single character
[...]	Any character listed between the square brackets
[^ ...]	Any character not listed between the square brackets
p1|p2|p3	Alternation; matches any of the patterns p1, p2, or p3

---

[*] RLIKE is a synonym for REGEXP. This is for mSQL (miniSQL) compatibility and may make it easier to port queries from mSQL to MySQL.

Pattern	What the pattern matches
*	Zero or more instances of preceding element
+	One or more instances of preceding element
{n}	n instances of preceding element
{m,n}	m through n instances of preceding element

You may already be familiar with these regular expression pattern characters, because many of them are the same as those used by *vi*, *grep*, *sed*, and other Unix utilities that support regular expressions. Most of them are used also in the regular expressions understood by Perl, PHP, and Python. (For example, Chapter 10 discuss pattern matching in Perl scripts.) For Java, the Jakarta ORO or Regexp class libraries provide matching capabilities that use these characters as well.

The previous section on SQL patterns showed how to match substrings at the beginning or end of a string, or at an arbitrary or specific position within a string. You can do the same things with regular expressions:

- Strings that begin with a particular substring:

```
mysql> SELECT name FROM metal WHERE name REGEXP '^co';
+--------+
| name   |
+--------+
| copper |
+--------+
```

- Strings that end with a particular substring:

```
mysql> SELECT name FROM metal WHERE name REGEXP 'er$';
+--------+
| name   |
+--------+
| copper |
| silver |
+--------+
```

- Strings that contain a particular substring at any position:

```
mysql> SELECT name FROM metal WHERE name REGEXP 'er';
+---------+
| name    |
+---------+
| copper  |
| mercury |
| silver  |
+---------+
```

- Strings that contain a particular substring at a specific position:

```
mysql> SELECT name FROM metal WHERE name REGEXP '^..pp';
+--------+
| name   |
+--------+
| copper |
+--------+
```

In addition, regular expressions have other capabilities and can perform kinds of matches that SQL patterns cannot. For example, regular expressions can contain character classes, which match any character in the class:

- To write a character class, list the characters you want the class to match inside square brackets. Thus, the pattern [abc] matches either a, b, or c.
- Classes may indicate ranges of characters by using a dash between the beginning and end of the range. [a-z] matches any letter, [0-9] matches digits, and [a-z0-9] matches letters or digits.
- To negate a character class ("match any character but these"), begin the list with a ^ character. For example, [^0-9] matches anything but digits.

MySQL's regular expression capabilities also support POSIX character classes. These match specific character sets, as described in the following table.

POSIX class	What the class matches
[:alnum:]	Alphabetic and numeric characters
[:alpha:]	Alphabetic characters
[:blank:]	Whitespace (space or tab characters)
[:cntrl:]	Control characters
[:digit:]	Digits
[:graph:]	Graphic (non-blank) characters
[:lower:]	Lowercase alphabetic characters
[:print:]	Graphic or space characters
[:punct:]	Punctuation characters
[:space:]	Space, tab, newline, carriage return
[:upper:]	Uppercase alphabetic characters
[:xdigit:]	Hexadecimal digits (0-9, a-f, A-F)

POSIX classes are intended for use within character classes, so you use them within square brackets. The following expression matches values that contain any hexadecimal digit character:

```
mysql> SELECT name, name REGEXP '[[:xdigit:]]' FROM metal;
+----------+---------------------------+
| name     | name REGEXP '[[:xdigit:]]' |
+----------+---------------------------+
| copper   |                         1 |
| gold     |                         1 |
| iron     |                         0 |
| lead     |                         1 |
| mercury  |                         1 |
| platinum |                         1 |
| silver   |                         1 |
| tin      |                         0 |
+----------+---------------------------+
```

Regular expressions can contain alternations. The syntax looks like this:

```
alternative1|alternative2|...
```

An alternation is similar to a character class in the sense that it matches if any of the alternatives match. But unlike a character class, the alternatives are not limited to single characters—they can be strings or even patterns. For example, the following alternation matches strings that begin with a vowel or end with er:

```
mysql> SELECT name FROM metal WHERE name REGEXP '^[aeiou]|er$';
+--------+
| name   |
+--------+
| copper |
| iron   |
| silver |
+--------+
```

Parentheses may be used to group alternations. For example, if you want to match strings that consist entirely of digits or entirely of letters, you might try this pattern, using an alternation:

```
mysql> SELECT 'Om' REGEXP '^[[:digit:]]+|[[:alpha:]]+$';
+------------------------------------------+
| 'Om' REGEXP '^[[:digit:]]+|[[:alpha:]]+$' |
+------------------------------------------+
|                                        1 |
+------------------------------------------+
```

But as the query result shows, the pattern doesn't work. That's because the ^ groups with the first alternative, and the $ groups with the second alternative. So the pattern actually matches strings that begin with one or more digits, or strings that end with one or more letters. However, if you group the alternatives within parentheses, the ^ and $ will apply to both of them and the pattern will act as you expect:

```
mysql> SELECT 'Om' REGEXP '^([[:digit:]]+|[[:alpha:]]+)$';
+---------------------------------------------+
| 'Om' REGEXP '^([[:digit:]]+|[[:alpha:]]+)$' |
+---------------------------------------------+
|                                           0 |
+---------------------------------------------+
```

Unlike SQL pattern matches, which are successful only if the pattern matches the entire comparison value, regular expressions are successful if the pattern matches anywhere within the value. The following two pattern matches are equivalent in the sense that each one succeeds only for strings that contain a b character, but the first is more efficient because the pattern is simpler:

```
'abc' REGEXP 'b'
'abc' REGEXP '^.*b.*$'
```

Regular expressions do not match `NULL` values. This is true both for `REGEXP` and for `NOT REGEXP`:

```
mysql> SELECT NULL REGEXP '.*', NULL NOT REGEXP '.*';
+-----------------+---------------------+
| NULL REGEXP '.*' | NULL NOT REGEXP '.*' |
+-----------------+---------------------+
|            NULL |                NULL |
+-----------------+---------------------+
```

The fact that a regular expression matches a string if the pattern is found anywhere in the string means you must take care not to inadvertently specify a pattern that matches the empty string. If you do, it will match any non-`NULL` value at all. For example, the pattern a* matches any number of a characters, even none. If your goal is to match only strings containing nonempty sequences of a characters, use a+ instead. The + requires one or more instances of the preceding pattern element for a match.

As with SQL pattern matches performed using `LIKE`, regular expression matches performed with `REGEXP` sometimes are equivalent to substring comparisons. The ^ and $ metacharacters serve much the same purpose as `LEFT( )` or `RIGHT( )`, at least if you're looking for literal strings:

Pattern match	Substring comparison
`str REGEXP '^abc'`	`LEFT(str,3) = 'abc'`
`str REGEXP 'abc$'`	`RIGHT(str,3) = 'abc'`

For non-literal strings, it's typically not possible to construct an equivalent substring comparison. For example, to match strings that begin with any nonempty sequence of digits, you can use this pattern match:

```
str REGEXP '^[0-9]+'
```

That is something that `LEFT( )` cannot do (and neither can `LIKE`, for that matter).

4.8   Matching Pattern Metacharacters Literally

Problem

You want to perform a pattern match for a literal instance of a character that's special in patterns.

Solution

Escape the special character with a backslash. Or maybe two.

Discussion

Pattern matching is based on the use of metacharacters that have a special meaning and thus stand for something other than themselves. This means that to match a literal instance of a metacharacter, you must turn off its special meaning somehow. Do this by using a backslash character (\). Assume that a table `metachar` contains the following rows:

```
mysql> SELECT c FROM metachar;
+------+
| c    |
+------+
| %    |
| _    |
| .    |
| ^    |
| $    |
| \    |
+------+
```

A pattern consisting only of either SQL metacharacter matches all the values in the table, not just the metacharacter itself:

```
mysql> SELECT c, c LIKE '%', c LIKE '_' FROM metachar;
+------+------------+------------+
| c    | c LIKE '%' | c LIKE '_' |
+------+------------+------------+
| %    |          1 |          1 |
| _    |          1 |          1 |
| .    |          1 |          1 |
| ^    |          1 |          1 |
| $    |          1 |          1 |
| \    |          1 |          1 |
+------+------------+------------+
```

To match a literal instance of a SQL pattern metacharacter, precede it with a backslash:

```
mysql> SELECT c, c LIKE '\%', c LIKE '\_' FROM metachar;
+------+-------------+-------------+
| c    | c LIKE '\%' | c LIKE '\_' |
+------+-------------+-------------+
| %    |           1 |           0 |
| _    |           0 |           1 |
| .    |           0 |           0 |
| ^    |           0 |           0 |
| $    |           0 |           0 |
| \    |           0 |           0 |
+------+-------------+-------------+
```

The principle is somewhat similar for matching regular expression metacharacters. For example, each of the following regular expressions matches every row in the table:

```
mysql> SELECT c, c REGEXP '.', c REGEXP '^', c REGEXP '$' FROM metachar;
+------+--------------+--------------+--------------+
| c    | c REGEXP '.' | c REGEXP '^' | c REGEXP '$' |
+------+--------------+--------------+--------------+
| %    |            1 |            1 |            1 |
| _    |            1 |            1 |            1 |
| .    |            1 |            1 |            1 |
| ^    |            1 |            1 |            1 |
| $    |            1 |            1 |            1 |
| \    |            1 |            1 |            1 |
+------+--------------+--------------+--------------+
```

To match the metacharacters literally, just add a backslash, right? Well, try it:

```
mysql> SELECT c, c REGEXP '\.', c REGEXP '\^', c REGEXP '\$' FROM metachar;
+------+---------------+---------------+---------------+
| c    | c REGEXP '\.' | c REGEXP '\^' | c REGEXP '\$' |
+------+---------------+---------------+---------------+
| %    |             1 |             1 |             1 |
| _    |             1 |             1 |             1 |
| .    |             1 |             1 |             1 |
| ^    |             1 |             1 |             1 |
| $    |             1 |             1 |             1 |
| \    |             1 |             1 |             1 |
+------+---------------+---------------+---------------+
```

It didn't work, because regular expressions are processed a bit differently than SQL patterns. With REGEXP, you need a double backslash to match a metacharacter literally:

```
mysql> SELECT c, c REGEXP '\\.', c REGEXP '\\^', c REGEXP '\\$' FROM metachar;
+------+----------------+----------------+----------------+
| c    | c REGEXP '\\.' | c REGEXP '\\^' | c REGEXP '\\$' |
+------+----------------+----------------+----------------+
| %    |              0 |              0 |              0 |
| _    |              0 |              0 |              0 |
| .    |              1 |              0 |              0 |
| ^    |              0 |              1 |              0 |
| $    |              0 |              0 |              1 |
| \    |              0 |              0 |              0 |
+------+----------------+----------------+----------------+
```

Because backslash suppresses the special meaning of metacharacters, backslash itself is special. To match a backslash literally, use double backslashes in SQL patterns or quadruple backslashes in regular expressions:

```
mysql> SELECT c, c LIKE '\\', c REGEXP '\\\\' FROM metachar;
+------+-------------+-----------------+
| c    | c LIKE '\\' | c REGEXP '\\\\' |
+------+-------------+-----------------+
| %    |           0 |               0 |
| _    |           0 |               0 |
| .    |           0 |               0 |
| ^    |           0 |               0 |
```

```
| $      |           0 |               0 |
| \      |           1 |               1 |
+------+------------+----------------+
```

It's even worse trying to figure out how many backslashes to use when you're issuing a query from within a program. It's more than likely that backslashes are also special to your programming language, in which case you'll need to double each one.

Within a character class, use these marks to include literal instances of the following class constructor characters:

- To include a literal] character, list it first.
- To include a literal - character, list it first or last.
- To include a literal ^ character, list it somewhere other than as the first character.
- To include a literal \ character, double it.

4.9 Controlling Case Sensitivity in String Comparisons

Problem

A string comparison is case sensitive when you don't want it to be, or vice versa.

Solution

Alter the case sensitivity of the strings.

Discussion

The examples in previous sections were performed without regard to lettercase. But sometimes you need to make sure a string operation is case sensitive that would not otherwise be, or vice versa. This section describes how to do that for ordinary comparisons. Recipe 4.10 covers case sensitivity in pattern-matching operations.

String comparisons in MySQL are not case sensitive by default:

```
mysql> SELECT name, name = 'lead', name = 'LEAD' FROM metal;
+----------+---------------+---------------+
| name     | name = 'lead' | name = 'LEAD' |
+----------+---------------+---------------+
| copper   |             0 |             0 |
| gold     |             0 |             0 |
| iron     |             0 |             0 |
| lead     |             1 |             1 |
| mercury  |             0 |             0 |
| platinum |             0 |             0 |
| silver   |             0 |             0 |
| tin      |             0 |             0 |
+----------+---------------+---------------+
```

The lack of case sensitivity also applies to relative ordering comparisons:

```
mysql> SELECT name, name < 'lead', name < 'LEAD' FROM metal;
+----------+---------------+---------------+
| name     | name < 'lead' | name < 'LEAD' |
+----------+---------------+---------------+
| copper   |             1 |             1 |
| gold     |             1 |             1 |
| iron     |             1 |             1 |
| lead     |             0 |             0 |
| mercury  |             0 |             0 |
| platinum |             0 |             0 |
| silver   |             0 |             0 |
| tin      |             0 |             0 |
+----------+---------------+---------------+
```

If you're familiar with the ASCII collating order, you know that lowercase letters have higher ASCII codes than uppercase letters, so the results in the second comparison column of the preceding query may surprise you. Those results reflect that string ordering is done by default without regard for lettercase, so A and a both are considered lexically less than B.

String comparisons are case sensitive only if at least one of the operands is a binary string. To control case sensitivity in string comparisons, use the following techniques:

- To make a string comparison case sensitive that normally would not be, cast (convert) one of the strings to binary form by using the BINARY keyword. It doesn't matter which of the strings you make binary. As long as one of them is, the comparison will be case sensitive:

```
mysql> SELECT name, name = BINARY 'lead', BINARY name = 'LEAD' FROM metal;
+----------+----------------------+----------------------+
| name     | name = BINARY 'lead' | BINARY name = 'LEAD' |
+----------+----------------------+----------------------+
| copper   |                    0 |                    0 |
| gold     |                    0 |                    0 |
| iron     |                    0 |                    0 |
| lead     |                    1 |                    0 |
| mercury  |                    0 |                    0 |
| platinum |                    0 |                    0 |
| silver   |                    0 |                    0 |
| tin      |                    0 |                    0 |
+----------+----------------------+----------------------+
```

  BINARY is available as a cast operator as of MySQL 3.23.

- To make a string comparison not case sensitive that normally would be, convert both strings to the same lettercase using UPPER( ) or LOWER( ):

```
mysql> SELECT UPPER('A'), UPPER('b'), UPPER('A') < UPPER('b');
+------------+------------+-------------------------+
| UPPER('A') | UPPER('b') | UPPER('A') < UPPER('b') |
+------------+------------+-------------------------+
| A          | B          |                       1 |
+------------+------------+-------------------------+
```

```
mysql> SELECT LOWER('A'), LOWER('b'), LOWER('A') < LOWER('b');
+------------+------------+--------------------------+
| LOWER('A') | LOWER('b') | LOWER('A') < LOWER('b')  |
+------------+------------+--------------------------+
| a          | b          |                        1 |
+------------+------------+--------------------------+
```

The same principles can be applied to string comparison functions. For example, STRCMP( ) takes two string arguments and returns –1, 0, or 1, depending on whether the first string is lexically less than, equal to, or greater than the second. Up through MySQL 4.0.0, STRCMP( ) is case sensitive; it always treats its arguments as binary strings, regardless of their actual type:

```
mysql> SELECT STRCMP('Abc','abc'), STRCMP('abc','abc'), STRCMP('abc','Abc');
+---------------------+---------------------+---------------------+
| STRCMP('Abc','abc') | STRCMP('abc','abc') | STRCMP('abc','Abc') |
+---------------------+---------------------+---------------------+
|                  -1 |                   0 |                   1 |
+---------------------+---------------------+---------------------+
```

However, as of MySQL 4.0.1, STRCMP( ) is not case sensitive:

```
mysql> SELECT STRCMP('Abc','abc'), STRCMP('abc','abc'), STRCMP('abc','Abc');
+---------------------+---------------------+---------------------+
| STRCMP('Abc','abc') | STRCMP('abc','abc') | STRCMP('abc','Abc') |
+---------------------+---------------------+---------------------+
|                   0 |                   0 |                   0 |
+---------------------+---------------------+---------------------+
```

To preserve the pre-4.0.1 behavior, make one of the arguments a binary string:

```
mysql> SELECT STRCMP(BINARY 'Abc','abc'), STRCMP(BINARY 'abc','Abc');
+----------------------------+----------------------------+
| STRCMP(BINARY 'Abc','abc') | STRCMP(BINARY 'abc','Abc') |
+----------------------------+----------------------------+
|                         -1 |                          1 |
+----------------------------+----------------------------+
```

By the way, take special note of the fact that zero and nonzero return values from STRCMP( ) indicate equality and inequality. This differs from the = comparison operator, which returns zero and nonzero for inequality and equality.

To avoid surprises in string comparisons, know the general rules that determine whether or not a string is binary:

- Any literal string, string expression, or string column can be made binary by preceding it with the BINARY keyword. If BINARY is not present, the following rules apply.
- A string expression is binary if any of its constituent strings is binary, otherwise not. For example, the result returned by this CONCAT( ) expression is binary because its second argument is binary:

  ```
  CONCAT('This is a ',BINARY 'binary',' string')
  ```

- A string column is case sensitive or not depending on the column's type. The CHAR and VARCHAR types are not case sensitive by default, but may be declared as BINARY to make them case sensitive. ENUM, SET, and TEXT columns are not case sensitive. BLOB columns are case sensitive. (See the table in Recipe 4.0.)

In summary, comparisons are case sensitive if they involve a binary literal string or string expression, or a CHAR BINARY, VARCHAR BINARY, or BLOB column. Comparisons are not case sensitive if they involve only non-binary literal strings or string expressions, or CHAR, VARCHAR, ENUM, SET, or TEXT columns.

ENUM and SET columns are not case sensitive. Furthermore, because they are stored internally as numbers, you cannot declare them case sensitive in the table definition by adding the BINARY keyword. However, you can still use the BINARY keyword before ENUM or SET values in comparisons to produce a case sensitive operation.

Case Sensitivity and String Comparison Speed

In general, case-sensitive comparisons involving binary strings are slightly faster than non–case-sensitive comparisons, because MySQL need not take lettercase into account during the comparison.

If you find that you've declared a column using a type that is not suitable for the kind of comparisons for which you typically use it, use ALTER TABLE to change the type. Suppose you have a table in which you store news articles:

```
CREATE TABLE news
(
    id      INT UNSIGNED NOT NULL AUTO_INCREMENT,
    article BLOB NOT NULL,
    PRIMARY KEY (id)
);
```

Here the article column is declared as a BLOB, which is a case-sensitive type. Should you wish to convert the column so that it is not case sensitive, you can change the type from BLOB to TEXT using either of these ALTER TABLE statements:

```
ALTER TABLE news MODIFY article TEXT NOT NULL;
ALTER TABLE news CHANGE article article TEXT NOT NULL;
```

Prior to MySQL 3.22.16, ALTER TABLE ... MODIFY is unavailable, in which case you can use only ALTER TABLE ... CHANGE. See Chapter 8 for more information.

4.10 Controlling Case Sensitivity in Pattern Matching

Problem

A pattern match is case sensitive when you don't want it to be, or vice versa.

Solution

Alter the case sensitivity of the strings.

Discussion

By default, LIKE is not case sensitive:

```
mysql> SELECT name, name LIKE '%i%', name LIKE '%I%' FROM metal;
+----------+-----------------+-----------------+
| name     | name LIKE '%i%' | name LIKE '%I%' |
+----------+-----------------+-----------------+
| copper   |               0 |               0 |
| gold     |               0 |               0 |
| iron     |               1 |               1 |
| lead     |               0 |               0 |
| mercury  |               0 |               0 |
| platinum |               1 |               1 |
| silver   |               1 |               1 |
| tin      |               1 |               1 |
+----------+-----------------+-----------------+
```

Currently, REGEXP is not case sensitive, either.

```
mysql> SELECT name, name REGEXP 'i', name REGEXP 'I' FROM metal;
+----------+-----------------+-----------------+
| name     | name REGEXP 'i' | name REGEXP 'I' |
+----------+-----------------+-----------------+
| copper   |               0 |               0 |
| gold     |               0 |               0 |
| iron     |               1 |               1 |
| lead     |               0 |               0 |
| mercury  |               0 |               0 |
| platinum |               1 |               1 |
| silver   |               1 |               1 |
| tin      |               1 |               1 |
+----------+-----------------+-----------------+
```

However, prior to MySQL 3.23.4, REGEXP operations *are* case sensitive:

```
mysql> SELECT name, name REGEXP 'i', name REGEXP 'I' FROM metal;
+----------+-----------------+-----------------+
| name     | name REGEXP 'i' | name REGEXP 'I' |
+----------+-----------------+-----------------+
| copper   |               0 |               0 |
| gold     |               0 |               0 |
| iron     |               1 |               0 |
| lead     |               0 |               0 |
| mercury  |               0 |               0 |
| platinum |               1 |               0 |
| silver   |               1 |               0 |
| tin      |               1 |               0 |
+----------+-----------------+-----------------+
```

Note that the (current) behavior of REGEXP not being case sensitive can lead to some unintuitive results:

```
mysql> SELECT 'a' REGEXP '[[:lower:]]', 'a' REGEXP '[[:upper:]]';
+-------------------------+-------------------------+
| 'a' REGEXP '[[:lower:]]' | 'a' REGEXP '[[:upper:]]' |
+-------------------------+-------------------------+
|                       1 |                       1 |
+-------------------------+-------------------------+
```

Both expressions are true because [:lower:] and [:upper:] are equivalent when case sensitivity doesn't matter.

If a pattern match uses different case-sensitive behavior than what you want, control it the same way as for string comparisons:

- To make a pattern match case sensitive, use a binary string for either operand (for example, by using the BINARY keyword). The following query shows how the non-binary column name normally is not case sensitive:

  ```
  mysql> SELECT name, name LIKE '%i%%', name REGEXP 'i' FROM metal;
  +----------+-----------------+-----------------+
  | name     | name LIKE '%i%%' | name REGEXP 'i' |
  +----------+-----------------+-----------------+
  | copper   |               0 |               0 |
  | gold     |               0 |               0 |
  | iron     |               1 |               1 |
  | lead     |               0 |               0 |
  | mercury  |               0 |               0 |
  | platinum |               1 |               1 |
  | silver   |               1 |               1 |
  | tin      |               1 |               1 |
  +----------+-----------------+-----------------+
  ```

  And this query shows how to force name values to be case sensitive using BINARY:

  ```
  mysql> SELECT name, BINARY name LIKE '%I%', BINARY name REGEXP 'I' FROM metal;
  +----------+-----------------------+-----------------------+
  | name     | BINARY name LIKE '%I%' | BINARY name REGEXP 'I' |
  +----------+-----------------------+-----------------------+
  ```

```
| copper   |                    0 |                    0 |
| gold     |                    0 |                    0 |
| iron     |                    0 |                    0 |
| lead     |                    0 |                    0 |
| mercury  |                    0 |                    0 |
| platinum |                    0 |                    0 |
| silver   |                    0 |                    0 |
| tin      |                    0 |                    0 |
+----------+----------------------+----------------------+
```

Using BINARY also has the effect of causing `[:lower:]` and `[:upper:]` in regular expressions to act as you would expect. The second expression in the following query yields a result that really is true only for uppercase letters:

```
mysql> SELECT 'a' REGEXP '[[:upper:]]', BINARY 'a' REGEXP '[[:upper:]]';
+-------------------------+--------------------------------+
| 'a' REGEXP '[[:upper:]]' | BINARY 'a' REGEXP '[[:upper:]]' |
+-------------------------+--------------------------------+
|                       1 |                              0 |
+-------------------------+--------------------------------+
```

• A pattern match against a binary column is case sensitive. To make the match not case sensitive, make both operands the same lettercase. To see how this works, modify the metal table to add a binname column that is like the name column except that it is VARCHAR BINARY rather than VARCHAR:

```
mysql> ALTER TABLE metal ADD binname VARCHAR(20) BINARY;
mysql> UPDATE metal SET binname = name;
```

The first of the following queries shows how the binary column binname normally is case sensitive in pattern matches, and the second shows how to force it not to be, using UPPER():

```
mysql> SELECT binname, binname LIKE '%I%', binname REGEXP 'I'
    -> FROM metal;
+----------+--------------------+--------------------+
| binname  | binname LIKE '%I%' | binname REGEXP 'I' |
+----------+--------------------+--------------------+
| copper   |                  0 |                  0 |
| gold     |                  0 |                  0 |
| iron     |                  0 |                  0 |
| lead     |                  0 |                  0 |
| mercury  |                  0 |                  0 |
| platinum |                  0 |                  0 |
| silver   |                  0 |                  0 |
| tin      |                  0 |                  0 |
+----------+--------------------+--------------------+
mysql> SELECT binname, UPPER(binname) LIKE '%I%', UPPER(binname) REGEXP 'I'
    -> FROM metal;
+----------+---------------------------+---------------------------+
| binname  | UPPER(binname) LIKE '%I%' | UPPER(binname) REGEXP 'I' |
+----------+---------------------------+---------------------------+
| copper   |                         0 |                         0 |
| gold     |                         0 |                         0 |
| iron     |                         1 |                         1 |
```

```
| lead     |                          0 |                          0 |
| mercury  |                          0 |                          0 |
| platinum |                          1 |                          1 |
| silver   |                          1 |                          1 |
| tin      |                          1 |                          1 |
+----------+----------------------------+----------------------------+
```

4.11   Using FULLTEXT Searches

Problem

You want to search through a lot of text.

Solution

Use a FULLTEXT index.

Discussion

You can use pattern matches to look through any number of rows, but as the amount of text goes up, the match operation can become quite slow. It's also common to look for the same text in several string columns, which with pattern matching tends to result in unwieldy queries:

```
SELECT * from tbl_name
WHERE col1 LIKE 'pat' OR col2 LIKE 'pat' OR col3 LIKE 'pat' ...
```

A useful alternative (available as of MySQL 3.23.23) is to use FULLTEXT searching, which is designed for looking through large amounts of text, and can search multiple columns simultaneously. To use this capability, add a FULLTEXT index to your table, then use the MATCH operator to look for strings in the indexed column or columns. FULLTEXT indexing can be used with MyISAM tables, for columns of type CHAR, VARCHAR, or TEXT.

FULLTEXT searching is best illustrated with a reasonably good-sized body of text. If you don't have a sample dataset, several repositories of freely available electronic text are available on the Internet. For the examples here, the one I've chosen is the complete text of the King James Version of the Bible (KJV), which is relatively large and has the advantage of being nicely structured by book, chapter, and verse. Because of its size, this dataset is not included with the recipes distribution, but is available separately as the mcb-kjv distribution at the MySQL Cookbook web site.[*] (See

---

[*] The mcb-kjv distribution is derived from the KJV text available at the Unbound Bible site at Biola University (*http://unbound.biola.edu*), but has been modified somewhat to make it easier to use for the recipes in this book. The mcb-kjv distribution includes notes that describe how it differs from the Biola distribution.

Appendix A.) The distribution includes a file *kjv.txt* that contains the verse records. Some sample records look like this:

```
O   Genesis 1    1    1    In the beginning God created the heaven and the earth.
O   Exodus  2    20   13   Thou shalt not kill.
N   Luke    42   17   32   Remember Lot's wife.
```

Each record contains the following fields:

- Book section. This is either O or N, signifying the Old or New Testament.
- Book name and corresponding book number, from 1 to 66.
- Chapter and verse numbers.
- Text of the verse.

To import the records into MySQL, create a table named kjv that looks like this:

```
CREATE TABLE kjv
(
    bsect    ENUM('O','N') NOT NULL,      # book section (testament)
    bname    VARCHAR(20) NOT NULL,        # book name
    bnum     TINYINT UNSIGNED NOT NULL,   # book number
    cnum     TINYINT UNSIGNED NOT NULL,   # chapter number
    vnum     TINYINT UNSIGNED NOT NULL,   # verse number
    vtext    TEXT NOT NULL                # text of verse
) TYPE = MyISAM;
```

Then load the *kjv.txt* file into the table using this statement:

```
mysql> LOAD DATA LOCAL INFILE 'kjv.txt' INTO TABLE kjv;
```

You'll notice that the kjv table contains columns for both book names (Genesis, Exodus, ...) and book numbers (1, 2, ...). The names and numbers have a fixed correspondence, and one can be derived from the other—a redundancy that means the table is not in normal form. It's possible to eliminate the redundancy by storing just the book numbers (which take less space than the names), and then producing the names when necessary in query results by joining the numbers to a small mapping table that associates each book number with the corresponding name. But I want to avoid using joins at this point. Thus, the table includes book names so that search results can be interpreted more easily, and numbers so that the results can be sorted easily into book order.

After populating the table, prepare it for use in FULLTEXT searching by adding a FULLTEXT index. This can be done using an ALTER TABLE statement:*

```
mysql> ALTER TABLE kjv ADD FULLTEXT (vtext);
```

---

* It's possible to include the index definition in the initial CREATE TABLE statement, but it's generally faster to create a non-indexed table and then add the index with ALTER TABLE after populating the table than to load a large dataset into an indexed table.

To perform a search using the index, use MATCH() to name the indexed column and AGAINST() to specify what text to look for. For example, to answer the question "How often does the name Mizraim occur?" (you've often wondered about that, right?), search the vtext column using this query:

```
mysql> SELECT COUNT(*) from kjv WHERE MATCH(vtext) AGAINST('Mizraim');
+----------+
| COUNT(*) |
+----------+
|        4 |
+----------+
```

To find out what those verses are, select the columns you want to see (the example here uses \G so that the results better fit the page):

```
mysql> SELECT bname, cnum, vnum, vtext
    -> FROM kjv WHERE MATCH(vtext) AGAINST('Mizraim')\G
*************************** 1. row ***************************
bname: Genesis
 cnum: 10
 vnum: 6
vtext: And the sons of Ham; Cush, and Mizraim, and Phut, and Canaan.
*************************** 2. row ***************************
bname: Genesis
 cnum: 10
 vnum: 13
vtext: And Mizraim begat Ludim, and Anamim, and Lehabim, and Naphtuhim,
*************************** 3. row ***************************
bname: 1 Chronicles
 cnum: 1
 vnum: 8
vtext: The sons of Ham; Cush, and Mizraim, Put, and Canaan.
*************************** 4. row ***************************
bname: 1 Chronicles
 cnum: 1
 vnum: 11
vtext: And Mizraim begat Ludim, and Anamim, and Lehabim, and Naphtuhim,
```

The results come out in book, chapter, and verse number order in this particular instance, but that's actually just coincidence. By default, FULLTEXT searches compute a relevance ranking and use it for sorting. To make sure a search result is sorted the way you want, add an explicit ORDER BY clause:

```
SELECT bname, cnum, vnum, vtext
FROM kjv WHERE MATCH(vtext) AGAINST('search string')
ORDER BY bnum, cnum, vnum;
```

You can include additional criteria to narrow the search further. The following queries perform progressively more specific searches to find out how often the name Abraham occurs in the entire KJV, the New Testament, the book of Hebrews, and Chapter 11 of Hebrews:

```
mysql> SELECT COUNT(*) from kjv WHERE MATCH(vtext) AGAINST('Abraham');
+----------+
| COUNT(*) |
+----------+
|      216 |
+----------+
mysql> SELECT COUNT(*) from kjv
    -> WHERE MATCH(vtext) AGAINST('Abraham')
    -> AND bsect = 'N';
+----------+
| COUNT(*) |
+----------+
|       66 |
+----------+
mysql> SELECT COUNT(*) from kjv
    -> WHERE MATCH(vtext) AGAINST('Abraham')
    -> AND bname = 'Hebrews';
+----------+
| COUNT(*) |
+----------+
|       10 |
+----------+
mysql> SELECT COUNT(*) from kjv
    -> WHERE MATCH(vtext) AGAINST('Abraham')
    -> AND bname = 'Hebrews' AND cnum = 11;
+----------+
| COUNT(*) |
+----------+
|        2 |
+----------+
```

If you expect to use search criteria that include other non-FULLTEXT columns frequently, you can increase the performance of such queries by adding regular indexes to those columns. For example, to index the book, chapter, and verse number columns, do this:

```
mysql> ALTER TABLE kjv ADD INDEX (bnum), ADD INDEX (cnum), ADD INDEX (vnum);
```

Search strings in FULLTEXT queries can include more than just a single word, and you might suppose that adding additional words would make a search more specific. But in fact that widens it, because a FULLTEXT search returns records that contain any of the words. In effect, the query performs an OR search for any of the words. This is illustrated by the following queries, which identify successively larger numbers of verses as additional search words are added:

```
mysql> SELECT COUNT(*) from kjv
    -> WHERE MATCH(vtext) AGAINST('Abraham');
+----------+
| COUNT(*) |
+----------+
|      216 |
+----------+
```

```
mysql> SELECT COUNT(*) from kjv
    -> WHERE MATCH(vtext) AGAINST('Abraham Sarah');
+----------+
| COUNT(*) |
+----------+
|      230 |
+----------+
mysql> SELECT COUNT(*) from kjv
    -> WHERE MATCH(vtext) AGAINST('Abraham Sarah Ishmael Isaac');
+----------+
| COUNT(*) |
+----------+
|      317 |
+----------+
```

To perform a search where each word in the search string must be present, see Recipe 4.13.

If you want to use a FULLTEXT search that looks though multiple columns simultaneously, name them all when you construct the index:

```
ALTER TABLE tbl_name ADD FULLTEXT (col1, col2, col3);
```

To issue a search query that uses this index, name those same columns in the MATCH() list:

```
SELECT ... FROM tbl_name
WHERE MATCH(col1, col2, col3) AGAINST('search string');
```

See Also

FULLTEXT indexes provide a quick-and-easy way to set up a simple search engine. One way to use this capability is to provide a web-based interface to the indexed text. The MySQL Cookbook site includes a basic web-based KJV search page that demonstrates this.

4.12   Using a FULLTEXT Search with Short Words

Problem

FULLTEXT searches for short words return no records.

Solution

Change the indexing engine's minimum word length parameter.

Discussion

In a text like the KJV, certain words have special significance, such as "God" and "sin." However, if you perform FULLTEXT searches on the kjv table for those words using a MySQL 3.23 server, you'll observe a curious phenomenon—both words appear to be missing from the text entirely:

```
mysql> SELECT COUNT(*) FROM kjv WHERE MATCH(vtext) AGAINST('God');
+----------+
| COUNT(*) |
+----------+
|        0 |
+----------+
mysql> SELECT COUNT(*) FROM kjv WHERE MATCH(vtext) AGAINST('sin');
+----------+
| COUNT(*) |
+----------+
|        0 |
+----------+
```

One property of the indexing engine is that it ignores words that are "too common" (that is, words that occur in more than half the records). This eliminates words such as "the" or "and" from the index, but that's not what is going on here. You can verify that by counting the total number of records, and by using SQL pattern matches to count the number of records containing each word:*

```
mysql> SELECT COUNT(*) AS 'total verses',
    -> COUNT(IF(vtext LIKE '%God%',1,NULL)) AS 'verses containing "God"',
    -> COUNT(IF(vtext LIKE '%sin%',1,NULL)) AS 'verses containing "sin"'
    -> FROM kjv;
+--------------+-------------------------+-------------------------+
| total verses | verses containing "God" | verses containing "sin" |
+--------------+-------------------------+-------------------------+
|        31102 |                    4118 |                    1292 |
+--------------+-------------------------+-------------------------+
```

Neither word is present in more than half the verses, so sheer frequency of occurrence doesn't account for the failure of a FULLTEXT search to find them. What's really happening is that by default, the indexing engine doesn't include words less than four characters long. On a MySQL 3.23 server, there's nothing you can do about that (at least, nothing short of messing around with the MySQL source code and recompiling). As of MySQL 4.0, the minimum word length is a configurable parameter, which you can change by setting the ft_min_word_len server variable. For example, to tell the indexing engine to include words containing three or more characters, add a set-variable line to the [mysqld] group of the */etc/my.cnf* file (or whatever option file you put server settings in):

```
[mysqld]
set-variable = ft_min_word_len=3
```

---

* The use of COUNT() to produce multiple counts from the same set of values is described in Recipe 7.1.

After making this change and restarting the server, rebuild the FULLTEXT index to take advantage of the new setting:

```
mysql> ALTER TABLE kjv DROP INDEX vtext;
mysql> ALTER TABLE kjv ADD FULLTEXT (vtext);
```

Then try out the new index to verify that it includes shorter words:

```
mysql> SELECT COUNT(*) FROM kjv WHERE MATCH(vtext) AGAINST('God');
+----------+
| COUNT(*) |
+----------+
|     3878 |
+----------+
mysql> SELECT COUNT(*) FROM kjv WHERE MATCH(vtext) AGAINST('sin');
+----------+
| COUNT(*) |
+----------+
|      389 |
+----------+
```

That's better!

But why do the MATCH() queries find 3878 and 389 records, whereas the earlier LIKE queries find 4118 and 1292 records? That's because the LIKE patterns match substrings and the FULLTEXT search performed by MATCH() matches whole words.

4.13 Requiring or Excluding FULLTEXT Search Words

Problem

You want to specifically require or disallow words in a FULLTEXT search.

Solution

Use a Boolean mode search.

Discussion

Normally, FULLTEXT searches return records that contain any of the words in the search string, even if some of them are missing. For example, the following query finds records that contain either of the names David or Goliath:

```
mysql> SELECT COUNT(*) FROM kjv
    -> WHERE MATCH(vtext) AGAINST('David Goliath');
+----------+
| COUNT(*) |
+----------+
|      934 |
+----------+
```

This behavior is undesirable if you want only records that contain both words. One way to do this is to rewrite the query to look for each word separately and join the conditions with AND:

```
mysql> SELECT COUNT(*) FROM kjv
    -> WHERE MATCH(vtext) AGAINST('David')
    -> AND MATCH(vtext) AGAINST('Goliath');
+----------+
| COUNT(*) |
+----------+
|        2 |
+----------+
```

As of MySQL 4.0.1, another way to require multiple words is with a Boolean mode search. To do this, precede each word in the search string with a + character and add IN BOOLEAN MODE after the string:

```
mysql> SELECT COUNT(*) FROM kjv
    -> WHERE MATCH(vtext) AGAINST('+David +Goliath' IN BOOLEAN MODE)
+----------+
| COUNT(*) |
+----------+
|        2 |
+----------+
```

Boolean mode searches also allow you to exclude words. Just precede any disallowed word with a - character. The following queries select kjv records containing the name David but not Goliath, or vice versa:

```
mysql> SELECT COUNT(*) FROM kjv
    -> WHERE MATCH(vtext) AGAINST('+David -Goliath' IN BOOLEAN MODE)
+----------+
| COUNT(*) |
+----------+
|      928 |
+----------+
mysql> SELECT COUNT(*) FROM kjv
    -> WHERE MATCH(vtext) AGAINST('-David +Goliath' IN BOOLEAN MODE)
+----------+
| COUNT(*) |
+----------+
|        4 |
+----------+
```

Another useful special character in Boolean searches is *; when appended to a search word, it acts as a wildcard operator. The following query finds records containing not only whirl, but also words such as whirls, whirleth, and whirlwind:

```
mysql> SELECT COUNT(*) FROM kjv
    -> WHERE MATCH(vtext) AGAINST('whirl*' IN BOOLEAN MODE);
+----------+
| COUNT(*) |
+----------+
|       28 |
+----------+
```

4.14 Performing Phrase Searches with a FULLTEXT Index

Problem

You want to perform a FULLTEXT search for a phrase, that is, for words that occur adjacent to each other and in a specific order.

Solution

Use the FULLTEXT phrase search capability, or combine a non-phrase FULLTEXT search with regular pattern matching.

Discussion

To find records that contain a particular phrase, you can't use a simple FULLTEXT search:

```
mysql> SELECT COUNT(*) FROM kjv
    -> WHERE MATCH(vtext) AGAINST('still small voice');
+----------+
| COUNT(*) |
+----------+
|      548 |
+----------+
```

The query returns a result, but it's not the result you're looking for. A FULLTEXT search computes a relevance ranking based on the presence of each word individually, no matter where it occurs within the vtext column, and the ranking will be non-zero as long as any of the words are present. Consequently, this kind of query tends to find too many records.

As of MySQL 4.0.2, FULLTEXT searching supports phrase searching in Boolean mode. To use it, just place the phrase within double quotes.

```
mysql> SELECT COUNT(*) FROM kjv
    -> WHERE MATCH(vtext) AGAINST('"still small voice"' IN BOOLEAN MODE);
+----------+
| COUNT(*) |
+----------+
|        1 |
+----------+
```

Prior to 4.0.2, a workaround is necessary. You could use an IN BOOLEAN MODE search to require each word to be present, but that doesn't really solve the problem, because the words can still occur in any order:

```
mysql> SELECT COUNT(*) FROM kjv
    -> WHERE MATCH(vtext)
    -> AGAINST('+still +small +voice' IN BOOLEAN MODE);
```

```
+----------+
| COUNT(*) |
+----------+
|        3 |
+----------+
```

If you use a SQL pattern match instead, it returns the correct result:

```
mysql> SELECT COUNT(*) FROM kjv
    -> WHERE vtext LIKE '%still small voice%';
+----------+
| COUNT(*) |
+----------+
|        1 |
+----------+
```

However, using a SQL pattern match is likely to be slower than a FULLTEXT search. So it seems you have the unpleasant choice of using a method that is faster but doesn't produce the desired results, or one that works properly but is slower. Fortunately, those aren't your only options. You can combine both methods in the same query:

```
mysql> SELECT COUNT(*) FROM kjv
    -> WHERE MATCH(vtext) AGAINST('still small voice')
    -> AND vtext LIKE '%still small voice%';
+----------+
| COUNT(*) |
+----------+
|        1 |
+----------+
```

What this gains you is the best of both types of matching:

- Using the MATCH() expression, MySQL can perform a FULLTEXT search to produce a set of candidate rows that contain words in the phrase. This narrows the search considerably.

- Using the SQL pattern test, MySQL can search the candidate rows to produce only those records that have all the words arranged in the proper order.

This technique will fail if all the words are less than the indexing engine's minimum word length or occur in more than half the records. In that case, the FULLTEXT search returns no records at all. You can find the records using a SQL pattern match.

## CHAPTER 5

Working with Dates and Times

5.0   Introduction

MySQL has several data types for representing dates and times, and several functions for operating on them. MySQL stores dates and times in specific formats. It's important to understand them to avoid surprises in how MySQL interprets input data. MySQL also has reformatting functions for producing date and time output in formats other than the default. This chapter covers the following aspects of working with temporal values in MySQL:

Displaying dates and times.   MySQL displays temporal values using specific formats by default, but you can produce other formats by calling the appropriate function.

Determining the current date or time.   MySQL provides functions that return the date and time, which is useful for applications that need to know these values or need to calculate other temporal values in relation to them.

Decomposing dates or times into component values.   This section explains how to split date and time values when you need only a piece, such as the month part or the hour part.

Synthesizing dates and times from component values.   The complement of splitting apart temporal values is to create them from subparts. This section shows how.

Converting between dates or times and basic units.   Some date calculations are more easily performed using the number of days or seconds represented by a date or time value than by using the value itself. MySQL makes it possible to perform several kinds of conversions between date and time values and more basic units such as days or seconds. These conversions often are useful for interval calculations (such as time elapsed between two times).

Date and time arithmetic. It's possible in MySQL to add temporal intervals to date or time values to produce other dates or times, and to calculate the interval between dates or times. Time arithmetic is easier than date arithmetic. Times involve hours, minutes, and seconds—units that always have a fixed duration. Date arithmetic can be trickier because units such as months and years vary in length.

Applications for date and time arithmetic. Using the techniques from the earlier sections, this one shows how to perform age calculation, relative date computation, date shifting, and leap year calculation.

Selecting records based on temporal constraints. The calculations discussed in the preceding sections to produce output values can also be used in WHERE clauses to specify how to select records using temporal conditions.

Using TIMESTAMP values. The TIMESTAMP column type has some special properties that make it convenient for automatically recording record creation and modification times. This section describes how TIMESTAMP columns behave and how to use them. It also discusses how to display TIMESTAMP values in more readable formats.

This chapter covers many of MySQL's functions for operating on date and time values, but there are yet others. To familiarize yourself with the full set, consult the MySQL Reference Manual. The variety of functions available to you means that it's often possible to perform a given temporal calculation more than one way. I sometimes illustrate alternative methods for achieving a given result, but many of the problems addressed in this chapter can be solved in other ways than are shown here. I invite you to experiment to find other solutions. You may find a method that's more efficient or that you find more readable.

Scripts that implement the recipes discussed in this chapter can be found in the *dates* directory of the recipes source distribution. The scripts that create the tables used here are located in the *tables* directory.

MySQL's Date and Time Formats

MySQL provides DATE and TIME column types for representing date and time values separately, and a DATETIME type for combined date-and-time values. These values have the following formats:

- DATE values are handled as strings in *CCYY-MM-DD* format, where *CC*, *YY*, *MM*, and *DD* represent the century, year within century, month, and day parts of the date.

- TIME values are represented as strings in *hh:mm:ss* format, where *hh*, *mm*, and *ss* are the hours, minutes, and seconds parts of the time. TIME values often can be thought of as time-of-day values, but MySQL actually treats them as elapsed time. Thus, they may be greater than 23:59:59 or even negative. (The actual range is -838:59:59 to 838:59:59.)

- DATETIME values are represented as combined date-and-time strings in *CCYY-MM-DD hh:mm:ss* format.

- TIMESTAMP values also include date and time parts, but are represented as strings in *CCYYMMDDhhmmss* format. This column type also has special properties that are discussed further in Recipe 5.31. More examples in this chapter use DATETIME values than TIMESTAMP values (which are less readable), but in most respects, you can treat the two column types the same way.

Many of the examples in this chapter draw on the following tables, which contain columns representing TIME, DATE, DATETIME, and TIMESTAMP values. (The time_val table has two columns for use in time interval calculation examples.)

```
mysql> SELECT t1, t2 FROM time_val;
+----------+----------+
| t1       | t2       |
+----------+----------+
| 15:00:00 | 15:00:00 |
| 05:01:30 | 02:30:20 |
| 12:30:20 | 17:30:45 |
+----------+----------+
mysql> SELECT d FROM date_val;
+------------+
| d          |
+------------+
| 1864-02-28 |
| 1900-01-15 |
| 1987-03-05 |
| 1999-12-31 |
| 2000-06-04 |
+------------+
mysql> SELECT dt FROM datetime_val;
+---------------------+
| dt                  |
+---------------------+
| 1970-01-01 00:00:00 |
| 1987-03-05 12:30:15 |
| 1999-12-31 09:00:00 |
| 2000-06-04 15:45:30 |
+---------------------+
mysql> SELECT ts FROM timestamp_val;
+----------------+
| ts             |
+----------------+
| 19700101000000 |
| 19870305123015 |
| 19991231090000 |
| 20000604154530 |
+----------------+
```

5.1   Changing MySQL's Date Format

Problem

You want to change the format that MySQL uses for representing date values.

Solution

You can't. However, you can rewrite input values into the proper format when storing dates, and you can rewrite them into fairly arbitrary format for display by using the DATE_FORMAT() function.

Discussion

The *CCYY-MM-DD* format that MySQL uses for DATE values follows the ISO 8601 standard for representing dates. This format has the useful property that because the year, month, and day parts have a fixed length and appear left to right in date strings, dates sort naturally into the proper temporal order.* However, ISO format is not used by all database systems, which can cause problems if you want to move data between different systems. Moreover, people commonly like to represent dates in other formats such as *MM/DD/YY* or *DD-MM-CCYY*. This too can be a source of trouble, due to mismatches between human expectations of what dates should look like and the way MySQL actually represents them.

A frequent question from people who are new to MySQL is, "How do I tell MySQL to store dates in a specific format such as *MM/DD/CCYY*?" Sorry, you can't. MySQL always stores dates in ISO format, a fact that has implications both for data entry and for result set display:

- For data entry purposes, to store values that are not in ISO format, you normally must rewrite them first. (If you don't want to rewrite your dates, you'll need to store them as strings, for example, in a CHAR column. But then you can't operate on them as dates.) In some cases, if your values are close to ISO format, rewriting may not be necessary. For example, the string values 87-1-7 and 1987-1-7 and the numbers 870107 and 19870107 all are interpreted by MySQL as the date 1987-01-07 when loaded into a DATE column. The topic of date rewriting for data entry is covered in Chapter 10.

- For display purposes, you can present dates in non-ISO format by rewriting them. MySQL's DATE_FORMAT() function can be helpful here. It provides a lot of flexibility for producing whatever format you want (see Recipes 5.2 and 5.4). You can also use functions such as YEAR() to extract parts of dates (see Recipe 5.5).

---

* Chapters 6 and 7 discuss ordering and grouping techniques for date-based values.

Additional discussion may be found in Chapter 10, which includes a short script that dumps table contents with the date columns reformatted.

5.2   Telling MySQL How to Display Dates or Times

Problem

You want to display dates or times in a format other than what MySQL uses by default.

Solution

Use the DATE_FORMAT( ) or TIME_FORMAT( ) functions to rewrite them.

Discussion

As already noted, MySQL displays dates in ISO format unless you tell it otherwise. To rewrite date values into other formats, use the DATE_FORMAT( ) function, which takes two arguments: a DATE, DATETIME, or TIMESTAMP value, and a string describing how to display the value. Within the formatting string, you indicate what to display using special sequences of the form %c, where c specifies which part of the date to display. For example, %Y, %M, and %d signify the four-digit year, the month name, and the two-digit day of the month. The following query shows the values in the date_val table, both as MySQL displays them by default and as reformatted with DATE_FORMAT( ):

```
mysql> SELECT d, DATE_FORMAT(d,'%M %d, %Y') FROM date_val;
+------------+----------------------------+
| d          | DATE_FORMAT(d,'%M %d, %Y') |
+------------+----------------------------+
| 1864-02-28 | February 28, 1864          |
| 1900-01-15 | January 15, 1900           |
| 1987-03-05 | March 05, 1987             |
| 1999-12-31 | December 31, 1999          |
| 2000-06-04 | June 04, 2000              |
+------------+----------------------------+
```

Clearly, DATE_FORMAT( ) tends to produce rather long column headings, so it's often useful to provide an alias to make a heading more concise or meaningful:

```
mysql> SELECT d, DATE_FORMAT(d,'%M %d, %Y') AS date FROM date_val;
+------------+-------------------+
| d          | date              |
+------------+-------------------+
| 1864-02-28 | February 28, 1864 |
| 1900-01-15 | January 15, 1900  |
```

```
| 1987-03-05 | March 05, 1987   |
| 1999-12-31 | December 31, 1999 |
| 2000-06-04 | June 04, 2000    |
+------------+-------------------+
```

The MySQL Reference Manual provides a complete list of format sequences. Some of the more common ones are shown in the following table:

Sequence	Meaning
%Y	Four-digit year
%y	Two-digit year
%M	Complete month name
%b	Month name, initial three letters
%m	Two-digit month of year (01..12)
%c	Month of year (1..12)
%d	Two-digit day of month (01..31)
%e	Day of month (1..31)
%r	12-hour time with AM or PM suffix
%T	24-hour time
%H	Two-digit hour
%i	Two-digit minute
%s	Two-digit second
%%	Literal %

The time-related format sequences shown in the table are useful only when you pass DATE_FORMAT() a value that has both date and time parts (a DATETIME or TIMESTAMP). The following query demonstrates how to display DATETIME values from the datetime_val table using formats that include the time of day:

```
mysql> SELECT dt,
    -> DATE_FORMAT(dt,'%c/%e/%y %r') AS format1,
    -> DATE_FORMAT(dt,'%M %e, %Y %T') AS format2
    -> FROM datetime_val;
+---------------------+----------------------+---------------------------+
| dt                  | format1              | format2                   |
+---------------------+----------------------+---------------------------+
| 1970-01-01 00:00:00 | 1/1/70 12:00:00 AM   | January 1, 1970 00:00:00  |
| 1987-03-05 12:30:15 | 3/5/87 12:30:15 PM   | March 5, 1987 12:30:15    |
| 1999-12-31 09:00:00 | 12/31/99 09:00:00 AM | December 31, 1999 09:00:00 |
| 2000-06-04 15:45:30 | 6/4/00 03:45:30 PM   | June 4, 2000 15:45:30     |
+---------------------+----------------------+---------------------------+
```

TIME_FORMAT() is similar to DATE_FORMAT(), but understands only time-related specifiers in the format string. TIME_FORMAT() works with TIME, DATETIME, or TIMESTAMP values.

```
mysql> SELECT dt,
    -> TIME_FORMAT(dt, '%r') AS '12-hour time',
```

```
        -> TIME_FORMAT(dt, '%T') AS '24-hour time'
        -> FROM datetime_val;
+---------------------+--------------+--------------+
| dt                  | 12-hour time | 24-hour time |
+---------------------+--------------+--------------+
| 1970-01-01 00:00:00 | 12:00:00 AM  | 00:00:00     |
| 1987-03-05 12:30:15 | 12:30:15 PM  | 12:30:15     |
| 1999-12-31 09:00:00 | 09:00:00 AM  | 09:00:00     |
| 2000-06-04 15:45:30 | 03:45:30 PM  | 15:45:30     |
+---------------------+--------------+--------------+
```

5.3   Determining the Current Date or Time

Problem

What's the date? What time is it?

Solution

Use the NOW( ), CURDATE( ), or CURTIME( ) functions.

Discussion

Some applications need to know the current date or time, such as those that produce a datestamped or timestamped status display. This kind of information is also
useful for date calculations that are performed in relation to the current date, such as
finding the first (or last) day of the month, or determining the date for Wednesday of
next week.

The current date and time are available through three functions. NOW( ) returns both the
current date and time. CURDATE( ) and CURTIME( ) return the date and time separately:

```
mysql> SELECT NOW(), CURDATE(), CURTIME();
+---------------------+------------+-----------+
| NOW()               | CURDATE()  | CURTIME() |
+---------------------+------------+-----------+
| 2002-07-15 10:59:30 | 2002-07-15 | 10:59:30  |
+---------------------+------------+-----------+
```

CURRENT_TIMESTAMP and SYSDATE( ) are synonyms for NOW( ). CURRENT_DATE and
CURRENT_TIME are synonyms for CURDATE( ) and CURTIME( ).

If you want to obtain subparts of these values (such as the current day of the month
or current hour of the day), read the next few sections.

NOW() Is Not a Valid Column Default Value

Functions such as NOW( ) and CURDATE( ) are commonly (but mistakenly) used in CREATE TABLE statements as default values:

```
mysql> CREATE TABLE testtbl (dt DATETIME DEFAULT NOW());
You have an error in your SQL syntax near 'NOW())' at line 1
```

The intent here is that values of the dt column should be initialized automatically to the date and time at which records are created. But it won't work; default values in MySQL must be constants. If you want a column set to the current date and time at record creation, use a TIMESTAMP, which MySQL will initialize automatically, or use a DATETIME and set the initial value yourself when you create records.

The restriction on non-constant default values will be lifted in the future, during the development of MySQL 4.1.

5.4 Decomposing Dates and Times Using Formatting Functions

Problem

You want to obtain just a part of a date or a time.

Solution

Use a formatting function such as DATE_FORMAT( ) or TIME_FORMAT( ) with a format string that includes a specifier for the part of the value you want to obtain.

Discussion

MySQL provides several options for decomposing dates or times to obtain their component values. The DATE_FORMAT( ) and TIME_FORMAT( ) functions provide one way to extract individual parts of temporal values:

```
mysql> SELECT dt,
    -> DATE_FORMAT(dt,'%Y') AS year,
    -> DATE_FORMAT(dt,'%d') AS day,
    -> TIME_FORMAT(dt,'%H') AS hour,
    -> TIME_FORMAT(dt,'%s') AS second
    -> FROM datetime_val;
+---------------------+------+------+------+--------+
| dt                  | year | day  | hour | second |
+---------------------+------+------+------+--------+
| 1970-01-01 00:00:00 | 1970 | 01   | 00   | 00     |
| 1987-03-05 12:30:15 | 1987 | 05   | 12   | 15     |
```

```
| 1999-12-31 09:00:00 | 1999 | 31   | 09   | 00   |
| 2000-06-04 15:45:30 | 2000 | 04   | 15   | 30   |
+---------------------+------+------+------+------+
```

Formatting functions allow you to extract more than one part of a value. For example, to extract the entire date or time from DATETIME values, do this:

```
mysql> SELECT dt,
    -> DATE_FORMAT(dt,'%Y-%m-%d') AS 'date part',
    -> TIME_FORMAT(dt,'%T') AS 'time part'
    -> FROM datetime_val;
+---------------------+------------+-----------+
| dt                  | date part  | time part |
+---------------------+------------+-----------+
| 1970-01-01 00:00:00 | 1970-01-01 | 00:00:00  |
| 1987-03-05 12:30:15 | 1987-03-05 | 12:30:15  |
| 1999-12-31 09:00:00 | 1999-12-31 | 09:00:00  |
| 2000-06-04 15:45:30 | 2000-06-04 | 15:45:30  |
+---------------------+------------+-----------+
```

One advantage of using formatting functions is that you can display the extracted values in a different form than that in which they're present in the original values. If you want to present a date differently than in *CCYY-MM-DD* format or present a time without the seconds part, that's easy to do:

```
mysql> SELECT ts,
    -> DATE_FORMAT(ts,'%M %e, %Y') AS 'descriptive date',
    -> TIME_FORMAT(ts,'%H:%i') AS 'hours/minutes'
    -> FROM timestamp_val;
+----------------+-------------------+---------------+
| ts             | descriptive date  | hours/minutes |
+----------------+-------------------+---------------+
| 19700101000000 | January 1, 1970   | 00:00         |
| 19870305123015 | March 5, 1987     | 12:30         |
| 19991231090000 | December 31, 1999 | 09:00         |
| 20000604154530 | June 4, 2000      | 15:45         |
+----------------+-------------------+---------------+
```

See Also

Recipe 5.5 discusses other functions that may be used to extract single components from dates or times. Recipe 5.6 shows how to use substring functions for component extraction.

5.5   Decomposing Dates or Times Using Component-Extraction Functions

Problem

You want to obtain just a part of a date or a time.

Solution

Invoke a function specifically intended for extracting part of a temporal value, such as MONTH( ) or MINUTE( ). For obtaining single components of temporal values, these functions are faster than using DATE_FORMAT( ) for the equivalent operation.

Discussion

MySQL includes many functions for extracting date or time parts from temporal values. Some of these are shown in the following list; consult the MySQL Reference Manual for a complete list. The date-related functions work with DATE, DATETIME, or TIMESTAMP values. The time-related functions work with TIME, DATETIME, or TIMESTAMP values.

Function	Return Value
YEAR( )	Year of date
MONTH( )	Month number (1..12)
MONTHNAME( )	Month name (January..December)
DAYOFMONTH( )	Day of month (1..31)
DAYNAME( )	Day of week (Sunday..Saturday)
DAYOFWEEK( )	Day of week (1..7 for Sunday..Saturday)
WEEKDAY( )	Day of week (0..6 for Monday..Sunday)
DAYOFYEAR( )	Day of year (1..366)
HOUR( )	Hour of time (0..23)
MINUTE( )	Minute of time (0..59)
SECOND( )	Second of time (0..59)

Here's an example:

```
mysql> SELECT dt,
    -> YEAR(dt), DAYOFMONTH(dt),
    -> HOUR(dt), SECOND(dt)
    -> FROM datetime_val;
+---------------------+----------+----------------+----------+------------+
| dt                  | YEAR(dt) | DAYOFMONTH(dt) | HOUR(dt) | SECOND(dt) |
+---------------------+----------+----------------+----------+------------+
| 1970-01-01 00:00:00 |     1970 |              1 |        0 |          0 |
| 1987-03-05 12:30:15 |     1987 |              5 |       12 |         15 |
| 1999-12-31 09:00:00 |     1999 |             31 |        9 |          0 |
| 2000-06-04 15:45:30 |     2000 |              4 |       15 |         30 |
+---------------------+----------+----------------+----------+------------+
```

Functions such as YEAR( ) or DAYOFMONTH( ) extract values that have an obvious correspondence to a substring of date values. Some date extraction functions provide access to values that have no such correspondence. One is the day-of-year value:

```
mysql> SELECT d, DAYOFYEAR(d) FROM date_val;
+------------+--------------+
| d          | DAYOFYEAR(d) |
+------------+--------------+
| 1864-02-28 |           59 |
| 1900-01-15 |           15 |
| 1987-03-05 |           64 |
| 1999-12-31 |          365 |
| 2000-06-04 |          156 |
+------------+--------------+
```

Another is the day of the week, which can be obtained either by name or by number:

- DAYNAME() returns the complete day name. There is no function for returning the three-character name abbreviation, but you can get it easily by passing the full name to LEFT():

```
mysql> SELECT d, DAYNAME(d), LEFT(DAYNAME(d),3) FROM date_val;
+------------+------------+--------------------+
| d          | DAYNAME(d) | LEFT(DAYNAME(d),3) |
+------------+------------+--------------------+
| 1864-02-28 | Sunday     | Sun                |
| 1900-01-15 | Monday     | Mon                |
| 1987-03-05 | Thursday   | Thu                |
| 1999-12-31 | Friday     | Fri                |
| 2000-06-04 | Sunday     | Sun                |
+------------+------------+--------------------+
```

- To get the day of the week as a number, use DAYOFWEEK() or WEEKDAY()—but pay attention to the range of values each function returns. DAYOFWEEK() returns values from 1 to 7, corresponding to Sunday through Saturday. WEEKDAY() returns values from 0 to 6, corresponding to Monday through Sunday.

```
mysql> SELECT d, DAYNAME(d), DAYOFWEEK(d), WEEKDAY(d) FROM date_val;
+------------+------------+--------------+------------+
| d          | DAYNAME(d) | DAYOFWEEK(d) | WEEKDAY(d) |
+------------+------------+--------------+------------+
| 1864-02-28 | Sunday     |            1 |          6 |
| 1900-01-15 | Monday     |            2 |          0 |
| 1987-03-05 | Thursday   |            5 |          3 |
| 1999-12-31 | Friday     |            6 |          4 |
| 2000-06-04 | Sunday     |            1 |          6 |
+------------+------------+--------------+------------+
```

Another way to obtain individual parts of temporal values is to use the EXTRACT() function:

```
mysql> SELECT dt,
    -> EXTRACT(DAY FROM dt),
    -> EXTRACT(HOUR FROM dt)
    -> FROM datetime_val;
+---------------------+----------------------+-----------------------+
| dt                  | EXTRACT(DAY FROM dt) | EXTRACT(HOUR FROM dt) |
+---------------------+----------------------+-----------------------+
| 1970-01-01 00:00:00 |                   1 |                     0 |
```

```
| 1987-03-05 12:30:15 |          5 |         12 |
| 1999-12-31 09:00:00 |         31 |          9 |
| 2000-06-04 15:45:30 |          4 |         15 |
+---------------------+------------+------------+
```

The keyword indicating what to extract should be a unit specifier such as YEAR, MONTH, DAY, HOUR, MINUTE, or SECOND. The EXTRACT() function is available as of MySQL 3.23.0.

Obtaining the Current Year, Month, Day, Hour, Minute, or Second

The extraction functions shown in this section can be applied to CURDATE() or NOW() to obtain the current year, month, day, or day of week:

```
mysql> SELECT CURDATE(), YEAR(CURDATE()) AS year,
    -> MONTH(CURDATE()) AS month, MONTHNAME(CURDATE()) AS monthname,
    -> DAYOFMONTH(CURDATE()) AS day, DAYNAME(CURDATE()) AS dayname;
+------------+------+-------+-----------+------+---------+
| CURDATE()  | year | month | monthname | day  | dayname |
+------------+------+-------+-----------+------+---------+
| 2002-07-15 | 2002 |     7 | July      |   15 | Monday  |
+------------+------+-------+-----------+------+---------+
```

Similarly, you can obtain the current hour, minute, and second by passing CURTIME() or NOW() to a time-component function:

```
mysql> SELECT NOW(), HOUR(NOW()) AS hour,
    -> MINUTE(NOW()) AS minute, SECOND(NOW()) AS second;
+---------------------+------+--------+--------+
| NOW()               | hour | minute | second |
+---------------------+------+--------+--------+
| 2002-07-15 11:21:12 |   11 |     21 |     12 |
+---------------------+------+--------+--------+
```

See Also

The functions discussed in this recipe provide single components of temporal values. If you want to produce a value consisting of multiple components from a given value, it may be more convenient to use DATE_FORMAT(). See Recipe 5.4.

5.6 Decomposing Dates or Times Using String Functions

Problem

You want to obtain just a part of a date or a time.

Solution

Treat a temporal value as a string and use a function such as `LEFT()` or `MID()` to extract substrings corresponding to the desired part of the value.

Discussion

Recipes 5.4 and 5.5 discuss how to extract components of temporal values using `DATE_FORMAT()` or functions such as `YEAR()` and `MONTH()`. If you pass a date or time value to a string function, MySQL treats it as a string, which means you can extract substrings. Thus, yet another way to extract pieces of temporal values is to use string functions such as `LEFT()` or `MID()`.

```
mysql> SELECT dt,
    -> LEFT(dt,4) AS year,
    -> MID(dt,9,2) AS day,
    -> RIGHT(dt,2) AS second
    -> FROM datetime_val;
+---------------------+------+------+--------+
| dt                  | year | day  | second |
+---------------------+------+------+--------+
| 1970-01-01 00:00:00 | 1970 | 01   | 00     |
| 1987-03-05 12:30:15 | 1987 | 05   | 15     |
| 1999-12-31 09:00:00 | 1999 | 31   | 00     |
| 2000-06-04 15:45:30 | 2000 | 04   | 30     |
+---------------------+------+------+--------+
```

You can pull out the entire date or time part from `DATETIME` values using string-extraction functions such as `LEFT()` or `RIGHT()`:

```
mysql> SELECT dt,
    -> LEFT(dt,10) AS date,
    -> RIGHT(dt,8) AS time
    -> FROM datetime_val;
+---------------------+------------+----------+
| dt                  | date       | time     |
+---------------------+------------+----------+
| 1970-01-01 00:00:00 | 1970-01-01 | 00:00:00 |
| 1987-03-05 12:30:15 | 1987-03-05 | 12:30:15 |
| 1999-12-31 09:00:00 | 1999-12-31 | 09:00:00 |
| 2000-06-04 15:45:30 | 2000-06-04 | 15:45:30 |
+---------------------+------------+----------+
```

The same technique also works for `TIMESTAMP` values. However, because these contain no delimiter characters, the indexes for `LEFT()` and `RIGHT()` are a little different, as are the formats of the output values:

```
mysql> SELECT ts,
    -> LEFT(ts,8) AS date,
    -> RIGHT(ts,6) AS time
    -> FROM timestamp_val;
```

```
+----------------+----------+--------+
| ts             | date     | time   |
+----------------+----------+--------+
| 19700101000000 | 19700101 | 000000 |
| 19870305123015 | 19870305 | 123015 |
| 19991231090000 | 19991231 | 090000 |
| 20000604154530 | 20000604 | 154530 |
+----------------+----------+--------+
```

Decomposition of temporal values with string functions is subject to a couple of constraints that component extraction and reformatting functions are not bound by:

- To use a substring function such as LEFT(), MID(), or RIGHT(), you must have fixed-length strings. MySQL might interpret the value 1987-1-1 as 1987-01-01 if you insert it into a DATE column, but using RIGHT('1987-1-1',2) to extract the day part will not work. If the values have variable-length substrings, you may be able to use SUBSTRING_INDEX() instead. Alternatively, if your values are close to ISO format, you can standardize them using the techniques described in Recipe 5.18.

- String functions cannot be used to obtain values that don't correspond to substrings of a date value, such as the day of the week or the day of the year.

5.7   Synthesizing Dates or Times Using Formatting Functions

Problem

You want to produce a new date from a given date by replacing parts of its values.

Solution

Use DATE_FORMAT() or TIME_FORMAT() to combine parts of the existing value with parts you want to replace.

Discussion

The complement of splitting apart a date or time value is synthesizing one from its constituent parts. Techniques for date and time synthesis include using formatting functions (discussed here) and string concatenation (discussed in Recipe 5.8).

Date synthesis often is performed by beginning with a given date, then keeping parts that you want to use and replacing the rest. For example, to find the first day of the month in which a date falls, use DATE_FORMAT() to extract the year and month parts from the date and combine them with a day value of 01:

```
mysql> SELECT d, DATE_FORMAT(d,'%Y-%m-01') FROM date_val;
+------------+---------------------------+
| d          | DATE_FORMAT(d,'%Y-%m-01') |
+------------+---------------------------+
```

```
| 1864-02-28 | 1864-02-01              |
| 1900-01-15 | 1900-01-01              |
| 1987-03-05 | 1987-03-01              |
| 1999-12-31 | 1999-12-01              |
| 2000-06-04 | 2000-06-01              |
+------------+------------------------+
```

TIME_FORMAT( ) can be used in a similar way:

```
mysql> SELECT t1, TIME_FORMAT(t1,'%H:%i:00') FROM time_val;
+----------+---------------------------+
| t1       | TIME_FORMAT(t1,'%H:%i:00') |
+----------+---------------------------+
| 15:00:00 | 15:00:00                  |
| 05:01:30 | 05:01:00                  |
| 12:30:20 | 12:30:00                  |
+----------+---------------------------+
```

5.8   Synthesizing Dates or Times Using Component-Extraction Functions

Problem

You have the parts of a date or time and want to combine them to produce a date or time value.

Solution

Put the parts together using CONCAT( ).

Discussion

Another way to construct temporal values is to use date-part extraction functions in conjunction with CONCAT( ). However, this method often is messier than the DATE_FORMAT( ) technique discussed in Recipe 5.7—and it sometimes yields slightly different results:

```
mysql> SELECT d,
    -> CONCAT(YEAR(d),'-',MONTH(d),'-01')
    -> FROM date_val;
+------------+------------------------------------+
| d          | CONCAT(YEAR(d),'-',MONTH(d),'-01') |
+------------+------------------------------------+
| 1864-02-28 | 1864-2-01                          |
| 1900-01-15 | 1900-1-01                          |
| 1987-03-05 | 1987-3-01                          |
| 1999-12-31 | 1999-12-01                         |
| 2000-06-04 | 2000-6-01                          |
+------------+------------------------------------+
```

Note that the month values in some of these dates have only a single digit. To ensure that the month has two digits—as required for ISO format—use LPAD() to add a leading zero as necessary:

```
mysql> SELECT d,
    -> CONCAT(YEAR(d),'-',LPAD(MONTH(d),2,'0'),'-01')
    -> FROM date_val;
+------------+------------------------------------------------+
| d          | CONCAT(YEAR(d),'-',LPAD(MONTH(d),2,'0'),'-01') |
+------------+------------------------------------------------+
| 1864-02-28 | 1864-02-01                                     |
| 1900-01-15 | 1900-01-01                                     |
| 1987-03-05 | 1987-03-01                                     |
| 1999-12-31 | 1999-12-01                                     |
| 2000-06-04 | 2000-06-01                                     |
+------------+------------------------------------------------+
```

Another way to solve this problem is given in Recipe 5.18.

TIME values can be produced from hours, minutes, and seconds values using methods analogous to those for creating DATE values. For example, to change a TIME value so that its seconds part is 00, extract the hour and minute parts, then recombine them using TIME_FORMAT() or CONCAT():

```
mysql> SELECT t1,
    -> TIME_FORMAT(t1,'%H:%i:00') AS method1,
    -> CONCAT(LPAD(HOUR(t1),2,'0'),':',LPAD(MINUTE(t1),2,'0'),':00') AS method2
    -> FROM time_val;
+----------+----------+----------+
| t1       | method1  | method2  |
+----------+----------+----------+
| 15:00:00 | 15:00:00 | 15:00:00 |
| 05:01:30 | 05:01:00 | 05:01:00 |
| 12:30:20 | 12:30:00 | 12:30:00 |
+----------+----------+----------+
```

5.9 Combining a Date and a Time into a Date-and-Time Value

Problem

You want to produce a combined date-and-time value from separate date and time values.

Solution

Concatenate them with a space in between.

Discussion

Combining a date value and a time value to produce a date-and-time value is just a matter of concatenating them with a space in between:

```
mysql> SET @d = '2002-02-28';
mysql> SET @t = '13:10:05';
mysql> SELECT @d, @t, CONCAT(@d,' ',@t);
+------------+----------+---------------------+
| @d         | @t       | CONCAT(@d,' ',@t)   |
+------------+----------+---------------------+
| 2002-02-28 | 13:10:05 | 2002-02-28 13:10:05 |
+------------+----------+---------------------+
```

5.10   Converting Between Times and Seconds

Problem

You have a time value but you want a value in seconds, or vice versa.

Solution

TIME values are specialized representations of a simpler unit—seconds—and you can convert back and forth from one to the other using TIME_TO_SEC() and SEC_TO_TIME().

Discussion

TIME_TO_SEC() converts a TIME value to the equivalent number of seconds, and SEC_TO_TIME() does the opposite. The following query demonstrates a simple conversion in both directions:

```
mysql> SELECT t1,
    -> TIME_TO_SEC(t1) AS 'TIME to seconds',
    -> SEC_TO_TIME(TIME_TO_SEC(t1)) AS 'TIME to seconds to TIME'
    -> FROM time_val;
+----------+-----------------+-------------------------+
| t1       | TIME to seconds | TIME to seconds to TIME |
+----------+-----------------+-------------------------+
| 15:00:00 |           54000 | 15:00:00                |
| 05:01:30 |           18090 | 05:01:30                |
| 12:30:20 |           45020 | 12:30:20                |
+----------+-----------------+-------------------------+
```

To express time values as minutes, hours, or days, perform the appropriate divisions:

```
mysql> SELECT t1,
    -> TIME_TO_SEC(t1) AS 'seconds',
    -> TIME_TO_SEC(t1)/60 AS 'minutes',
    -> TIME_TO_SEC(t1)/(60*60) AS 'hours',
    -> TIME_TO_SEC(t1)/(24*60*60) AS 'days'
    -> FROM time_val;
```

```
+----------+---------+---------+-------+------+
| t1       | seconds | minutes | hours | days |
+----------+---------+---------+-------+------+
| 15:00:00 |   54000 |  900.00 | 15.00 | 0.62 |
| 05:01:30 |   18090 |  301.50 |  5.03 | 0.21 |
| 12:30:20 |   45020 |  750.33 | 12.51 | 0.52 |
+----------+---------+---------+-------+------+
```

Use FLOOR( ) if you prefer integer values to floating-point values:

```
mysql> SELECT t1,
    -> TIME_TO_SEC(t1) AS 'seconds',
    -> FLOOR(TIME_TO_SEC(t1)/60) AS 'minutes',
    -> FLOOR(TIME_TO_SEC(t1)/(60*60)) AS 'hours',
    -> FLOOR(TIME_TO_SEC(t1)/(24*60*60)) AS 'days'
    -> FROM time_val;
+----------+---------+---------+-------+------+
| t1       | seconds | minutes | hours | days |
+----------+---------+---------+-------+------+
| 15:00:00 |   54000 |     900 |    15 |    0 |
| 05:01:30 |   18090 |     301 |     5 |    0 |
| 12:30:20 |   45020 |     750 |    12 |    0 |
+----------+---------+---------+-------+------+
```

If you pass TIME_TO_SEC( ) a date-and-time value, it extracts the time part and discards the date. This provides yet another means of extracting times from DATETIME and TIMESTAMP values (in addition to those already discussed earlier in the chapter):

```
mysql> SELECT dt,
    -> TIME_TO_SEC(dt) AS 'time part in seconds',
    -> SEC_TO_TIME(TIME_TO_SEC(dt)) AS 'time part as TIME'
    -> FROM datetime_val;
+---------------------+----------------------+-------------------+
| dt                  | time part in seconds | time part as TIME |
+---------------------+----------------------+-------------------+
| 1970-01-01 00:00:00 |                    0 | 00:00:00          |
| 1987-03-05 12:30:15 |                45015 | 12:30:15          |
| 1999-12-31 09:00:00 |                32400 | 09:00:00          |
| 2000-06-04 15:45:30 |                56730 | 15:45:30          |
+---------------------+----------------------+-------------------+
mysql> SELECT ts,
    -> TIME_TO_SEC(ts) AS 'time part in seconds',
    -> SEC_TO_TIME(TIME_TO_SEC(ts)) AS 'time part as TIME'
    -> FROM timestamp_val;
+----------------+----------------------+-------------------+
| ts             | time part in seconds | time part as TIME |
+----------------+----------------------+-------------------+
| 19700101000000 |                    0 | 00:00:00          |
| 19870305123015 |                45015 | 12:30:15          |
| 19991231090000 |                32400 | 09:00:00          |
| 20000604154530 |                56730 | 15:45:30          |
+----------------+----------------------+-------------------+
```

5.11 Converting Between Dates and Days

Problem

You have a date but want a value in days, or vice versa.

Solution

DATE values can be converted to and from days with TO_DAYS() and FROM_DAYS(). Date-and-time values also can be converted to days if you're willing to suffer loss of the time part.

Discussion

TO_DAYS() converts a date to the corresponding number of days, and FROM_DAYS() does the opposite:

```
mysql> SELECT d,
    -> TO_DAYS(d) AS 'DATE to days',
    -> FROM_DAYS(TO_DAYS(d)) AS 'DATE to days to DATE'
    -> FROM date_val;
+------------+--------------+----------------------+
| d          | DATE to days | DATE to days to DATE |
+------------+--------------+----------------------+
| 1864-02-28 |       680870 | 1864-02-28           |
| 1900-01-15 |       693975 | 1900-01-15           |
| 1987-03-05 |       725800 | 1987-03-05           |
| 1999-12-31 |       730484 | 1999-12-31           |
| 2000-06-04 |       730640 | 2000-06-04           |
+------------+--------------+----------------------+
```

When using TO_DAYS(), it's probably best to stick to the advice of the MySQL Reference Manual and avoid DATE values that occur before the beginning of the Gregorian calendar (1582). Changes in the lengths of calendar years and months prior to that date make it difficult to speak meaningfully of what the value of "day 0" might be. This differs from TIME_TO_SEC(), where the correspondence between a TIME value and the resulting seconds value is obvious and has a meaningful reference point of 0 seconds.

If you pass TO_DAYS() a date-and-time value, it extracts the date part and discards the time. This provides another means of extracting dates from DATETIME and TIMESTAMP values:

```
mysql> SELECT dt,
    -> TO_DAYS(dt) AS 'date part in days',
    -> FROM_DAYS(TO_DAYS(dt)) AS 'date part as DATE'
    -> FROM datetime_val;
```

```
+---------------------+-------------------+------------------+
| dt                  | date part in days | date part as DATE |
+---------------------+-------------------+------------------+
| 1970-01-01 00:00:00 |            719528 | 1970-01-01       |
| 1987-03-05 12:30:15 |            725800 | 1987-03-05       |
| 1999-12-31 09:00:00 |            730484 | 1999-12-31       |
| 2000-06-04 15:45:30 |            730640 | 2000-06-04       |
+---------------------+-------------------+------------------+
mysql> SELECT ts,
    -> TO_DAYS(ts) AS 'date part in days',
    -> FROM_DAYS(TO_DAYS(ts)) AS 'date part as DATE'
    -> FROM timestamp_val;
+----------------+-------------------+------------------+
| ts             | date part in days | date part as DATE |
+----------------+-------------------+------------------+
| 19700101000000 |            719528 | 1970-01-01       |
| 19870305123015 |            725800 | 1987-03-05       |
| 19991231090000 |            730484 | 1999-12-31       |
| 20000604154530 |            730640 | 2000-06-04       |
+----------------+-------------------+------------------+
```

5.12 Converting Between Date-and-Time Values and Seconds

Problem

You have a date-and-time value but want a value in seconds, or vice versa.

Solution

The UNIX_TIMESTAMP() and FROM_UNIXTIME() functions convert DATETIME or TIMESTAMP values in the range from 1970 through approximately 2037 to and from the number of seconds elapsed since the beginning of 1970. The conversion to seconds offers higher precision for date-and-time values than a conversion to days, at the cost of a more limited range of values for which the conversion may be performed.

Discussion

When working with date-and-time values, you can use TO_DAYS() and FROM_DAYS() to convert date values to days and back to dates, as shown in the previous section. For values that occur no earlier than 1970-01-01 00:00:00 GMT and no later than approximately 2037, it's possible to achieve higher precision by converting to and from seconds.* UNIX_TIMESTAMP() converts date-and-time values in this range to the

---

* It's difficult to give a precise upper bound on the range of values because it varies somewhat between systems.

number of seconds elapsed since the beginning of 1970, and FROM_UNIXTIME() does the opposite:

```
mysql> SELECT dt,
    -> UNIX_TIMESTAMP(dt) AS seconds,
    -> FROM_UNIXTIME(UNIX_TIMESTAMP(dt)) AS timestamp
    -> FROM datetime_val;
+---------------------+-----------+---------------------+
| dt                  | seconds   | timestamp           |
+---------------------+-----------+---------------------+
| 1970-01-01 00:00:00 |     21600 | 1970-01-01 00:00:00 |
| 1987-03-05 12:30:15 | 541967415 | 1987-03-05 12:30:15 |
| 1999-12-31 09:00:00 | 946652400 | 1999-12-31 09:00:00 |
| 2000-06-04 15:45:30 | 960151530 | 2000-06-04 15:45:30 |
+---------------------+-----------+---------------------+
```

The relationship between the "UNIX" in the function names and the fact that the applicable range of values begins with 1970 is that 1970-01-01 00:00:00 GMT marks the "Unix epoch." The epoch is time zero, or the reference point for measuring time in Unix systems.* That being so, you may find it curious that the preceding example shows a UNIX_TIMESTAMP() value of 21600 for the first value in the datetime_val table. What's going on? Why isn't it 0? The apparent discrepancy is due to the fact that the MySQL server converts values to its own time zone when displaying them. My server is in the U.S. Central Time zone, which is six hours (that is, 21600 seconds) west of GMT.

UNIX_TIMESTAMP() can convert DATE values to seconds, too. It treats such values as having an implicit time-of-day part of 00:00:00:

```
mysql> SELECT CURDATE(), FROM_UNIXTIME(UNIX_TIMESTAMP(CURDATE()));
+------------+------------------------------------------+
| CURDATE()  | FROM_UNIXTIME(UNIX_TIMESTAMP(CURDATE())) |
+------------+------------------------------------------+
| 2002-07-15 | 2002-07-15 00:00:00                      |
+------------+------------------------------------------+
```

5.13   Adding a Temporal Interval to a Time

Problem

You want to add a given number of seconds to a time, or to add two time values.

Solution

Use TIME_TO_SEC() as necessary to make sure all values are represented in seconds, then add them. The result will be in seconds; use SEC_TO_TIME() if you want to convert back to a time value.

---

* 1970-01-01 00:00:00 GMT also happens to be the epoch as Java measures time.

Discussion

The primary tools for performing time arithmetic are TIME_TO_SEC() and SEC_TO_TIME(), which convert between TIME values and seconds. To add an interval value in seconds to a TIME value, convert the TIME to seconds so that both values are represented in the same units, add the values together, and convert the result back to a TIME. For example, two hours is 7200 seconds (2*60*60), so the following query adds two hours to each t1 value in the time_val table:

```
mysql> SELECT t1,
    -> SEC_TO_TIME(TIME_TO_SEC(t1) + 7200) AS 't1 plus 2 hours'
    -> FROM time_val;
+----------+-----------------+
| t1       | t1 plus 2 hours |
+----------+-----------------+
| 15:00:00 | 17:00:00        |
| 05:01:30 | 07:01:30        |
| 12:30:20 | 14:30:20        |
+----------+-----------------+
```

If the interval itself is expressed as a TIME, it too should be converted to seconds before adding the values together. The following example calculates the sum of the two TIME values in the time_val table:

```
mysql> SELECT t1, t2,
    -> SEC_TO_TIME(TIME_TO_SEC(t1) + TIME_TO_SEC(t2)) AS 't1 + t2'
    -> FROM time_val;
+----------+----------+----------+
| t1       | t2       | t1 + t2  |
+----------+----------+----------+
| 15:00:00 | 15:00:00 | 30:00:00 |
| 05:01:30 | 02:30:20 | 07:31:50 |
| 12:30:20 | 17:30:45 | 30:01:05 |
+----------+----------+----------+
```

It's important to recognize that MySQL TIME values really represent elapsed time, not time of day, so they don't reset to 0 after reaching 24 hours. You can see this in the first and third output rows from the previous query. To produce time-of-day values, enforce a 24-hour wraparound using a modulo operation before converting the seconds value back to a TIME value. The number of seconds in a day is 24*60*60, or 86400, so to convert any seconds value s to lie within a 24-hour range, use the MOD() function or the % modulo operator like this:

```
MOD(s,86400)
s % 86400
```

The two expressions are equivalent. Applying the first of them to the time calculations from the preceding example produces the following result:

```
mysql> SELECT t1, t2,
    -> SEC_TO_TIME(MOD(TIME_TO_SEC(t1) + TIME_TO_SEC(t2), 86400)) AS 't1 + t2'
    -> FROM time_val;
```

```
+----------+----------+----------+
| t1       | t2       | t1 + t2  |
+----------+----------+----------+
| 15:00:00 | 15:00:00 | 06:00:00 |
| 05:01:30 | 02:30:20 | 07:31:50 |
| 12:30:20 | 17:30:45 | 06:01:05 |
+----------+----------+----------+
```

 The allowable range of TIME values is -838:59:59 to 838:59:59 (that is
-3020399 to 3020399 seconds). When you add times together, you
can easily produce a result that lies outside this range. If you try to
store such a value into a TIME column, MySQL clips it to the nearest
endpoint of the range.

5.14 Calculating Intervals Between Times

Problem

You want to know the amount of time elapsed between two times.

Solution

Convert the times to seconds with TIME_TO_SEC( ) and take the difference. For a difference represented as a time, convert the result back the other way using SEC_TO_
TIME( ).

Discussion

Calculating intervals between times is similar to adding times together, except that
you compute a difference rather than a sum. For example, to calculate intervals in
seconds between pairs of t1 and t2 values, convert the values in the time_val table to
seconds using TIME_TO_SEC( ), then take the difference. To express the resulting difference as a TIME value, pass it to SEC_TO_TIME( ). The following query shows intervals both ways:

```
mysql> SELECT t1, t2,
    -> TIME_TO_SEC(t2) - TIME_TO_SEC(t1) AS 'interval in seconds',
    -> SEC_TO_TIME(TIME_TO_SEC(t2) - TIME_TO_SEC(t1)) AS 'interval as TIME'
    -> FROM time_val;
+----------+----------+---------------------+------------------+
| t1       | t2       | interval in seconds | interval as TIME |
+----------+----------+---------------------+------------------+
| 15:00:00 | 15:00:00 |                   0 | 00:00:00         |
| 05:01:30 | 02:30:20 |               -9070 | -02:31:10        |
| 12:30:20 | 17:30:45 |               18025 | 05:00:25         |
+----------+----------+---------------------+------------------+
```

Note that intervals may be negative, as is the case when t1 occurs later than t2.

5.15 Breaking Down Time Intervals into Components

Problem

You have a time interval represented as a time, but you want the interval in terms of its components.

Solution

Decompose the interval with the HOUR( ), MINUTE( ), and SECOND( ) functions. If the calculation is complex in SQL and you're using the interval within a program, it may be easier to use your programming language to perform the equivalent math.

Discussion

To express a time interval in terms of its constituent hours, minutes, and seconds values, calculate time interval subparts in SQL using the HOUR( ), MINUTE( ), and SECOND( ) functions. (Don't forget that if your intervals may be negative, you need to take that into account.) For example, to determine the components of the intervals between the t1 and t2 columns in the time_val table, the following SQL statement does the trick:

```
mysql> SELECT t1, t2,
    -> SEC_TO_TIME(TIME_TO_SEC(t2) - TIME_TO_SEC(t1)) AS 'interval as TIME',
    -> IF(SEC_TO_TIME(TIME_TO_SEC(t2) >= TIME_TO_SEC(t1)),'+','-') AS sign,
    -> HOUR(SEC_TO_TIME(TIME_TO_SEC(t2) - TIME_TO_SEC(t1))) AS hour,
    -> MINUTE(SEC_TO_TIME(TIME_TO_SEC(t2) - TIME_TO_SEC(t1))) AS minute,
    -> SECOND(SEC_TO_TIME(TIME_TO_SEC(t2) - TIME_TO_SEC(t1))) AS second
    -> FROM time_val;
+----------+----------+------------------+------+------+--------+--------+
| t1       | t2       | interval as TIME | sign | hour | minute | second |
+----------+----------+------------------+------+------+--------+--------+
| 15:00:00 | 15:00:00 | 00:00:00         | +    |    0 |      0 |      0 |
| 05:01:30 | 02:30:20 | -02:31:10        | -    |    2 |     31 |     10 |
| 12:30:20 | 17:30:45 | 05:00:25         | +    |    5 |      0 |     25 |
+----------+----------+------------------+------+------+--------+--------+
```

But that's fairly messy, and attempting to do the same thing using division and modulo operations is even messier. If you happen to be issuing an interval-calculation query from within a program, it's possible to avoid most of the clutter. Use SQL to compute just the intervals in seconds, then use your API language to break down each interval into its components. The formulas should account for negative values and produce integer values for each component. Here's an example function time_components( ) written in Python that takes an interval value in seconds and returns a four-element tuple containing the sign of the value, followed by the hour, minute, and second parts:

```
def time_components (time_in_secs):
    if time_in_secs < 0:
        sign = "-"
        time_in_secs = -time_in_secs
    else:
        sign = ""
    hours = int (time_in_secs / 3600)
    minutes = int ((time_in_secs / 60)) % 60
    seconds = time_in_secs % 60
    return (sign, hours, minutes, seconds)
```

You might use time_components( ) within a program like this:

```
query = "SELECT t1, t2, TIME_TO_SEC(t2) - TIME_TO_SEC(t1) FROM time_val"
cursor = conn.cursor ()
cursor.execute (query)
for (t1, t2, interval) in cursor.fetchall ():
    (sign, hours, minutes, seconds) = time_components (interval)
    print "t1 = %s, t2 = %s, interval = %s%d h, %d m, %d s" \
                % (t1, t2, sign, hours, minutes, seconds)
cursor.close ()
```

The program produces the following output:

```
t1 = 15:00:00, t2 = 15:00:00, interval = 0 h, 0 m, 0 s
t1 = 05:01:30, t2 = 02:30:20, interval = -2 h, 31 m, 10 s
t1 = 12:30:20, t2 = 17:30:45, interval = 5 h, 0 m, 25 s
```

The preceding example illustrates a more general principle that's often useful when issuing queries from a program: it may be easier to deal with a calculation that is complex to express in SQL by using a simpler query and postprocessing the results using your API language.

5.16   Adding a Temporal Interval to a Date

Problem

You want to add time to a date or date-and-time value.

Solution

Use DATE_ADD( ) and DATE_SUB( ), functions intended specifically for date arithmetic. You can also use TO_DAYS( ) and FROM_DAYS( ), or UNIX_TIMESTAMP( ) and FROM_ UNIXTIME( ).

Discussion

Date arithmetic is less straightforward than time arithmetic due to the varying length of months and years, so MySQL provides special functions DATE_ADD() and DATE_SUB() for adding or subtracting intervals to or from dates.* Each function takes a date value d and an interval, expressed using the following syntax:

```
DATE_ADD(d,INTERVAL val unit)
DATE_SUB(d,INTERVAL val unit)
```

Here, *unit* is the interval unit and *val* is an expression indicating the number of units. Some of the common unit specifiers are YEAR, MONTH, DAY, HOUR, MINUTE, and SECOND. (Check the MySQL Reference Manual for the full list.) Note that all these units are specified in singular form, not plural.

Using DATE_ADD() or DATE_SUB(), you can perform date arithmetic operations such as the following:

- Determine the date three days from today:

```
mysql> SELECT CURDATE(), DATE_ADD(CURDATE(),INTERVAL 3 DAY);
+------------+------------------------------------+
| CURDATE() | DATE_ADD(CURDATE(),INTERVAL 3 DAY) |
+------------+------------------------------------+
| 2002-07-15 | 2002-07-18                         |
+------------+------------------------------------+
```

- Find the date a week ago (the query here uses 7 DAY to represent an interval of a week because there is no WEEK interval unit):

```
mysql> SELECT CURDATE(), DATE_SUB(CURDATE(),INTERVAL 7 DAY);
+------------+------------------------------------+
| CURDATE() | DATE_SUB(CURDATE(),INTERVAL 7 DAY) |
+------------+------------------------------------+
| 2002-07-15 | 2002-07-08                         |
+------------+------------------------------------+
```

- For questions where you need to know both the date and the time, begin with a DATETIME or TIMESTAMP value. To answer the question, "what time will it be in 60 hours?," do this:

```
mysql> SELECT NOW(), DATE_ADD(NOW(),INTERVAL 60 HOUR);
+---------------------+----------------------------------+
| NOW()               | DATE_ADD(NOW(),INTERVAL 60 HOUR) |
+---------------------+----------------------------------+
| 2002-07-15 11:31:17 | 2002-07-17 23:31:17              |
+---------------------+----------------------------------+
```

---

* DATE_ADD() and DATE_SUB() were introduced in MySQL 3.22.4, as were their synonyms, ADDDATE() and SUBDATE().

- Some interval specifiers comprise both date and time parts. The following adds 14 and a half hours to the current date and time:

```
mysql> SELECT NOW(), DATE_ADD(NOW(),INTERVAL '14:30' HOUR_MINUTE);
+---------------------+------------------------------------------------+
| NOW()               | DATE_ADD(NOW(),INTERVAL '14:30' HOUR_MINUTE)   |
+---------------------+------------------------------------------------+
| 2002-07-15 11:31:24 | 2002-07-16 02:01:24                             |
+---------------------+------------------------------------------------+
```

Similarly, adding 3 days and 4 hours produces this result:

```
mysql> SELECT NOW(), DATE_ADD(NOW(),INTERVAL '3 4' DAY_HOUR);
+---------------------+------------------------------------------+
| NOW()               | DATE_ADD(NOW(),INTERVAL '3 4' DAY_HOUR)  |
+---------------------+------------------------------------------+
| 2002-07-15 11:31:30 | 2002-07-18 15:31:30                       |
+---------------------+------------------------------------------+
```

DATE_ADD( ) and DATE_SUB( ) are interchangeable because one is the same as the other with the sign of the interval value flipped. For example, these two calls are equivalent for any date value d:

```
DATE_ADD(d,INTERVAL -3 MONTH)
DATE_SUB(d,INTERVAL 3 MONTH)
```

As of MySQL 3.23.4, you can also use the + and - operators to perform date interval addition and subtraction:

```
mysql> SELECT CURDATE(), CURDATE() + INTERVAL 1 YEAR;
+------------+-----------------------------+
| CURDATE()  | CURDATE() + INTERVAL 1 YEAR |
+------------+-----------------------------+
| 2002-07-15 | 2003-07-15                  |
+------------+-----------------------------+
mysql> SELECT NOW(), NOW() - INTERVAL 24 HOUR;
+---------------------+--------------------------+
| NOW()               | NOW() - INTERVAL 24 HOUR |
+---------------------+--------------------------+
| 2002-07-15 11:31:48 | 2002-07-14 11:31:48      |
+---------------------+--------------------------+
```

Another way to add intervals to date or date-and-time values is by using functions that convert to and from basic units. For example, to shift a date forward or backward a week (seven days), use TO_DAYS( ) and FROM_DAYS( ):

```
mysql> SET @d = '2002-01-01';
mysql> SELECT @d AS date,
    -> FROM_DAYS(TO_DAYS(@d) + 7) AS 'date + 1 week',
    -> FROM_DAYS(TO_DAYS(@d) - 7) AS 'date - 1 week';
+------------+---------------+---------------+
| date       | date + 1 week | date - 1 week |
+------------+---------------+---------------+
| 2002-01-01 | 2002-01-08    | 2001-12-25    |
+------------+---------------+---------------+
```

TO_DAYS() also can convert DATETIME or TIMESTAMP values to days, if you don't mind having it chop off the time part:

```
mysql> SET @dt = '2002-01-01 12:30:45';
mysql> SELECT @dt AS datetime,
    -> FROM_DAYS(TO_DAYS(@dt) + 7) AS 'datetime + 1 week',
    -> FROM_DAYS(TO_DAYS(@dt) - 7) AS 'datetime - 1 week';
+---------------------+-------------------+-------------------+
| datetime            | datetime + 1 week | datetime - 1 week |
+---------------------+-------------------+-------------------+
| 2002-01-01 12:30:45 | 2002-01-08        | 2001-12-25        |
+---------------------+-------------------+-------------------+
```

To preserve accuracy with DATETIME or TIMESTAMP values, use UNIX_TIMESTAMP() and FROM_UNIXTIME() instead. The following query shifts a DATETIME value forward and backward by an hour (3600 seconds):

```
mysql> SET @dt = '2002-01-01 09:00:00';
mysql> SELECT @dt AS datetime,
    -> FROM_UNIXTIME(UNIX_TIMESTAMP(@dt) + 3600) AS 'datetime + 1 hour',
    -> FROM_UNIXTIME(UNIX_TIMESTAMP(@dt) - 3600) AS 'datetime - 1 hour';
+---------------------+---------------------+---------------------+
| datetime            | datetime + 1 hour   | datetime - 1 hour   |
+---------------------+---------------------+---------------------+
| 2002-01-01 09:00:00 | 2002-01-01 10:00:00 | 2002-01-01 08:00:00 |
+---------------------+---------------------+---------------------+
```

The last technique requires that both your initial value and the resulting value like in the allowable range for TIMESTAMP values (1970 to sometime in the year 2037).

5.17   Calculating Intervals Between Dates

Problem

You want to know how long it is between dates.

Solution

Convert both dates to basic units and take the difference between the resulting values.

Discussion

The general procedure for calculating an interval between dates is to convert both dates to a common unit in relation to a given reference point, then take the difference. The range of values you're working with determines which conversions are available. DATE, DATETIME, or TIMESTAMP values dating back to 1970-01-01 00:00:00 GMT—the date of the Unix epoch—can be converted to seconds elapsed since the epoch. If both dates lie within that range, you can calculate intervals to an accuracy of one second. Older dates from the beginning of the Gregorian calendar (1582) on can be converted to day values and used to compute intervals in days. Dates that begin earlier than either of these reference points present more of a problem. In such cases, you may find that your programming language offers computations that are not available or are difficult to perform in SQL. If so, consider processing date values directly from within your API language. (For example, the *Date::Calc* and *Date::Manip* modules are available from the CPAN for use within Perl scripts.)

To calculate an interval in days between date or date-and-time values, convert them to days using TO_DAYS( ), then take the difference:

```
mysql> SELECT TO_DAYS('1884-01-01') - TO_DAYS('1883-06-05') AS days;
+------+
| days |
+------+
|  210 |
+------+
```

For an interval in weeks, do the same thing and divide the result by seven:

```
mysql> SELECT (TO_DAYS('1884-01-01') - TO_DAYS('1883-06-05')) / 7 AS weeks;
+-------+
| weeks |
+-------+
| 30.00 |
+-------+
```

You cannot convert days to months or years by simple division, because those units vary in length. Calculations to yield date intervals expressed in those units are covered in Recipe 5.19.

Do You Want an Interval or a Span?

Taking a difference between dates gives you the interval from one date to the next. If you want to know the range covered by the two dates, you must add a unit. For example, it's three days from 2002-01-01 to 2002-01-04, but together they span a range of four days. If you're not getting the results you expect from an interval calculation, consider whether you need to use an "off-by-one" correction.

For values occurring from the beginning of 1970 on, you can determine intervals to a resolution in seconds using the UNIX_TIMESTAMP( ) function. For example, the number of seconds between dates that lie two weeks apart can be computed like this:

```
mysql> SET @dt1 = '1984-01-01 09:00:00';
mysql> SET @dt2 = '1984-01-15 09:00:00';
mysql> SELECT UNIX_TIMESTAMP(@dt2) - UNIX_TIMESTAMP(@dt1) AS seconds;
```

```
+---------+
| seconds |
+---------+
| 1209600 |
+---------+
```

To convert the interval in seconds to other units, perform the appropriate arithmetic operation. Seconds are easily converted to minutes, hours, days, or weeks:

```
mysql> SET @interval = UNIX_TIMESTAMP(@dt2) - UNIX_TIMESTAMP(@dt1);
mysql> SELECT @interval AS seconds,
    -> @interval / 60 AS minutes,
    -> @interval / (60 * 60) AS hours,
    -> @interval / (24 * 60 * 60) AS days,
    -> @interval / (7 * 24 * 60 * 60) AS weeks;
+---------+---------+-------+------+-------+
| seconds | minutes | hours | days | weeks |
+---------+---------+-------+------+-------+
| 1209600 |   20160 |   336 |   14 |     2 |
+---------+---------+-------+------+-------+
```

For values that occur prior outside the range from 1970 to 2037, you can use an interval calculation method that is more general (but messier):

- Take the difference in days between the date parts of the values and multiply by 24*60*60 to convert to seconds.

- Offset the result by the difference in seconds between the time parts of the values.

Here's an example, using two date-and-time values that lie a week apart:

```
mysql> SET @dt1 = '1800-02-14 07:30:00';
mysql> SET @dt2 = '1800-02-21 07:30:00';
mysql> SET @interval =
    -> ((TO_DAYS(@dt2) - TO_DAYS(@dt1)) * 24*60*60)
    -> + TIME_TO_SEC(@dt2) - TIME_TO_SEC(@dt1);
mysql> SELECT @interval AS seconds;
+---------+
| seconds |
+---------+
|  604800 |
+---------+
```

To convert the interval to a TIME value, pass it to SEC_TO_TIME():

```
mysql> SELECT SEC_TO_TIME(@interval) AS TIME;
+-----------+
| TIME      |
+-----------+
| 168:00:00 |
+-----------+
```

To convert the interval from seconds to other units, perform the appropriate division:

```
mysql> SELECT @interval AS seconds,
    -> @interval / 60 AS minutes,
    -> @interval / (60 * 60) AS hours,
```

```
    -> @interval / (24 * 60 * 60) AS days,
    -> @interval / (7 * 24 * 60 * 60) AS weeks;
+---------+---------+-------+------+-------+
| seconds | minutes | hours | days | weeks |
+---------+---------+-------+------+-------+
|  604800 |   10080 |   168 |    7 |     1 |
+---------+---------+-------+------+-------+
```

I cheated here by choosing an interval that produces nice integer values for all the division operations. In general, you'll have a fractional part, in which case you may find it helpful to use FLOOR(*expr*) to chop off the fractional part and produce an integer.

5.18   Canonizing Not-Quite-ISO Date Strings

Problem

A date is in a format that's close to but not exactly ISO format.

Solution

Canonize the date by passing it to a function that always returns an ISO-format date result.

Discussion

Earlier in the chapter (Recipe 5.8), we ran into the problem that synthesizing dates with CONCAT() may produce values that are not quite in ISO format. For example, the following query produces first-of-month values in which the month part may have only a single digit:

```
mysql> SELECT d, CONCAT(YEAR(d),'-',MONTH(d),'-01') FROM date_val;
+------------+----------------------------------+
| d          | CONCAT(YEAR(d),'-',MONTH(d),'-01') |
+------------+----------------------------------+
| 1864-02-28 | 1864-2-01                        |
| 1900-01-15 | 1900-1-01                        |
| 1987-03-05 | 1987-3-01                        |
| 1999-12-31 | 1999-12-01                       |
| 2000-06-04 | 2000-6-01                        |
+------------+----------------------------------+
```

In that section, a technique using LPAD() was shown for making sure the month values have two digits.

```
mysql> SELECT d, CONCAT(YEAR(d),'-',LPAD(MONTH(d),2,'0'),'-01') FROM date_val;
+------------+------------------------------------------------+
| d          | CONCAT(YEAR(d),'-',LPAD(MONTH(d),2,'0'),'-01') |
+------------+------------------------------------------------+
| 1864-02-28 | 1864-02-01                                     |
| 1900-01-15 | 1900-01-01                                     |
```

```
| 1987-03-05 | 1987-03-01                                          |
| 1999-12-31 | 1999-12-01                                          |
| 2000-06-04 | 2000-06-01                                          |
+------------+-----------------------------------------------------+
```

Another way to standardize a close-to-ISO date is to use it in an expression that produces an ISO date result. For a date d, any of the following expressions will do:

```
DATE_ADD(d,INTERVAL 0 DAY)
d + INTERVAL 0 DAY
FROM_DAYS(TO_DAYS(d))
```

For example, the non-ISO results from the CONCAT() operation can be converted into ISO format three different ways as follows:

```
mysql> SELECT d,
    -> CONCAT(YEAR(d),'-',MONTH(d),'-01') AS 'non-ISO',
    -> DATE_ADD(CONCAT(YEAR(d),'-',MONTH(d),'-01'),INTERVAL 0 DAY) AS method1,
    -> CONCAT(YEAR(d),'-',MONTH(d),'-01') + INTERVAL 0 DAY AS method2,
    -> FROM_DAYS(TO_DAYS(CONCAT(YEAR(d),'-',MONTH(d),'-01'))) AS method3
    -> FROM date_val;
+------------+------------+------------+------------+------------+
| d          | non-ISO    | method1    | method2    | method3    |
+------------+------------+------------+------------+------------+
| 1864-02-28 | 1864-2-01  | 1864-02-01 | 1864-02-01 | 1864-02-01 |
| 1900-01-15 | 1900-1-01  | 1900-01-01 | 1900-01-01 | 1900-01-01 |
| 1987-03-05 | 1987-3-01  | 1987-03-01 | 1987-03-01 | 1987-03-01 |
| 1999-12-31 | 1999-12-01 | 1999-12-01 | 1999-12-01 | 1999-12-01 |
| 2000-06-04 | 2000-6-01  | 2000-06-01 | 2000-06-01 | 2000-06-01 |
+------------+------------+------------+------------+------------+
```

5.19 Calculating Ages

Problem

You want to know how old someone is.

Solution

This is a problem of computing the interval between dates, but with a twist. For an age in years, it's necessary to account for the relative placement of the start and end dates within the calendar year. For an age in months, it's also necessary to account for the placement of the months and the days within the month.

Discussion

Age determination is a type of date interval calculation, but one that cannot be done by computing a difference in days and dividing by 365. That doesn't work because leap years throw off the calculation. (The interval from 1995-03-01 to 1996-02-29 spans 365 days, but is not a year in age terms.) Using 365.25 is slightly more accurate, but still not correct for all dates. Instead, it's necessary to determine the difference between dates in years and then adjust for the relative location of the dates within the calendar year. (Suppose Gretchen Smith was born on April 14, 1942. To compute how old Gretchen is now, we must account for where the current date falls within the calendar year: she's one age up through April 13 of the year, and one year older from April 14 through the end of the year.) This section shows how to perform this kind of calculation to determine ages in units of years or months.

Determining Ages in Years

In general, given a birth date birth, an age in years on a target date d can be computed by the following logic:

```
if (d occurs earlier in the year than birth)
    age = YEAR(d) - YEAR(birth) - 1
if (d occurs on or later in the year than birth)
    age = YEAR(d) - YEAR(birth)
```

For both cases, the difference-in-years part of the calculation is the same. What distinguishes them is the relative ordering of the dates within the calendar year. However, this ordering cannot be determined with DAYOFYEAR(), because that only works if both dates fall during years with the same number of days. For dates in different years, different calendar days may have the same DAYOFYEAR() value, as the following query illustrates:

```
mysql> SELECT DAYOFYEAR('1995-03-01'), DAYOFYEAR('1996-02-29');
+-------------------------+-------------------------+
| DAYOFYEAR('1995-03-01') | DAYOFYEAR('1996-02-29') |
+-------------------------+-------------------------+
|                      60 |                      60 |
+-------------------------+-------------------------+
```

The fact that ISO date strings compare naturally in the proper order comes to our rescue here—or more precisely, the fact that the rightmost five characters that represent the month and day also compare properly:

```
mysql> SELECT RIGHT('1995-03-01',5), RIGHT('1996-02-29',5);
+-----------------------+-----------------------+
| RIGHT('1995-03-01',5) | RIGHT('1996-02-29',5) |
+-----------------------+-----------------------+
| 03-01                 | 02-29                 |
+-----------------------+-----------------------+
mysql> SELECT IF('02-29' < '03-01','02-29','03-01') AS earliest;
+----------+
| earliest |
+----------+
| 02-29    |
+----------+
```

This means that we can perform the "earlier-in-year" test for two dates, d1 and d2, like this:

```
RIGHT(d2,5) < RIGHT(d1,5)
```

The expression evaluates to 1 or 0, depending on the result of the test, so the result of the < comparison can be used to perform an age-in-years calculation:

```
YEAR(d2) - YEAR(d1) - (RIGHT(d2,5) < RIGHT(d1,5))
```

To make it more obvious what the comparison result evaluates to, wrap it in an IF() function that explicitly returns 1 or 0:

```
YEAR(d2) - YEAR(d1) - IF(RIGHT(d2,5) < RIGHT(d1,5),1,0)
```

The following query demonstrates how this formula works to calculate an age as of the beginning 1975 for someone born on 1965-03-01. It shows the unadjusted age difference in years, the adjustment value, and the final age:

```
mysql> SET @birth = '1965-03-01';
mysql> SET @target = '1975-01-01';
mysql> SELECT @birth, @target,
    -> YEAR(@target) - YEAR(@birth) AS 'difference',
    -> IF(RIGHT(@target,5) < RIGHT(@birth,5),1,0) AS 'adjustment',
    -> YEAR(@target) - YEAR(@birth)
    -> - IF(RIGHT(@target,5) < RIGHT(@birth,5),1,0)
    -> AS 'age';
+------------+------------+------------+------------+------+
| @birth     | @target    | difference | adjustment | age  |
+------------+------------+------------+------------+------+
| 1965-03-01 | 1975-01-01 |         10 |          1 |    9 |
+------------+------------+------------+------------+------+
```

Let's try the age-in-years formula with a sibling table that lists the birth dates of Gretchen Smith and her brothers Wilbur and Franz:

```
+----------+------------+
| name     | birth      |
+----------+------------+
| Gretchen | 1942-04-14 |
| Wilbur   | 1946-11-28 |
| Franz    | 1953-03-05 |
+----------+------------+
```

The formula produces answers for questions such as the following:

- How old are the Smith children today?

  ```
  mysql> SELECT name, birth, CURDATE() AS today,
      -> YEAR(CURDATE()) - YEAR(birth)
      -> - IF(RIGHT(CURDATE(),5) < RIGHT(birth,5),1,0)
      -> AS 'age in years'
      -> FROM sibling;
  ```

```
+----------+------------+------------+---------------+
| name     | birth      | today      | age in years  |
+----------+------------+------------+---------------+
| Gretchen | 1942-04-14 | 2002-07-15 |            60 |
| Wilbur   | 1946-11-28 | 2002-07-15 |            55 |
| Franz    | 1953-03-05 | 2002-07-15 |            49 |
+----------+------------+------------+---------------+
```

- How old were Gretchen and Wilbur when Franz was born?

```
mysql> SELECT name, birth, '1953-03-05' AS 'Franz'' birthday',
    -> YEAR('1953-03-05') - YEAR(birth)
    -> - IF(RIGHT('1953-03-05',5) < RIGHT(birth,5),1,0)
    -> AS 'age in years'
    -> FROM sibling WHERE name != 'Franz';
+----------+------------+------------------+---------------+
| name     | birth      | Franz' birthday  | age in years  |
+----------+------------+------------------+---------------+
| Gretchen | 1942-04-14 | 1953-03-05       |            10 |
| Wilbur   | 1946-11-28 | 1953-03-05       |             6 |
+----------+------------+------------------+---------------+
```

When performing calculations of this nature, be sure to remember that, for comparisons on the MM-DD part of date strings to yield correct results, you must use ISO values like 1987-07-01 and not close-to-ISO values like 1987-7-1. For example, the following comparison produces a result that is correct in lexical terms but incorrect in temporal terms:

```
mysql> SELECT RIGHT('1987-7-1',5) < RIGHT('1987-10-01',5);
+---------------------------------------------+
| RIGHT('1987-7-1',5) < RIGHT('1987-10-01',5) |
+---------------------------------------------+
|                                           0 |
+---------------------------------------------+
```

The absence of leading zeros in the month and day parts of the first date makes the substring-based comparison fail.

Determining Ages in Months

The formula for calculating ages in months is similar to that for ages in years, except that we multiply the years difference by 12, add the months difference, and adjust for the relative day-in-month values of the two dates. In this case, we need to use the month and day part of each date separately, so we may as well extract them directly using MONTH() and DAYOFMONTH() rather than performing a comparison on the MM-DD part of the date strings. The current ages of the Smith children in months thus can be calculated like this:

```
mysql> SELECT name, birth, CURDATE() AS today,
    -> (YEAR(CURDATE()) - YEAR(birth)) * 12
    -> + (MONTH(CURDATE()) - MONTH(birth))
    -> - IF(DAYOFMONTH(CURDATE()) < DAYOFMONTH(birth),1,0)
```

```
   -> AS 'age in months'
   -> FROM sibling;
+----------+------------+------------+---------------+
| name     | birth      | today      | age in months |
+----------+------------+------------+---------------+
| Gretchen | 1942-04-14 | 2002-07-15 |           723 |
| Wilbur   | 1946-11-28 | 2002-07-15 |           667 |
| Franz    | 1953-03-05 | 2002-07-15 |           592 |
+----------+------------+------------+---------------+
```

5.20   Shifting Dates by a Known Amount

Problem

You want to shift a given date by a given amount to compute the resulting date.

Solution

Use DATE_ADD() or DATE_SUB().

Discussion

If you have a reference date and want to calculate another date from it that differs by
a known interval, the problem generally can be solved by basic date arithmetic using
DATE_ADD() and DATE_SUB(). Some examples of this kind of question include finding
anniversary dates, determining expiration dates, or finding records that satisfy "this
date in history" queries. This section illustrates a couple of applications for date
shifting.

Calculating Anniversary Dates

Suppose you're getting married on August 6, 2003, and you don't want to wait a year
for your first anniversary to show your devotion to your sweetheart. Instead, you
want to get her special gifts on your 1 week, 1 month, 3 month, and 6 month anni-
versaries. To calculate those dates, shift your anniversary date forward by the desired
intervals, as follows:

```
mysql> SET @d = '2003-08-06';
mysql> SELECT @d AS 'start date',
    -> DATE_ADD(@d,INTERVAL 7 DAY) AS '1 week',
    -> DATE_ADD(@d,INTERVAL 1 MONTH) AS '1 month',
    -> DATE_ADD(@d,INTERVAL 3 MONTH) AS '3 months',
    -> DATE_ADD(@d,INTERVAL 6 MONTH) AS '6 months';
+------------+------------+------------+------------+------------+
| start date | 1 week     | 1 month    | 3 months   | 6 months   |
+------------+------------+------------+------------+------------+
| 2003-08-06 | 2003-08-13 | 2003-09-06 | 2003-11-06 | 2004-02-06 |
+------------+------------+------------+------------+------------+
```

If you're interested only in part of an anniversary date, you may be able to dispense with date arithmetic altogether. For example, if you graduated from school on June 4, 2000, and you want to know the years on which your 10th, 20th, and 40th class reunions will be, it's unnecessary to use DATE_ADD(). Just extract the year part of the reference date and use normal arithmetic to add 10, 20, and 40 to it:

```
mysql> SET @y = YEAR('2000-06-04');
mysql> SELECT @y + 10, @y + 20, @y + 40;
+---------+---------+---------+
| @y + 10 | @y + 20 | @y + 40 |
+---------+---------+---------+
|    2010 |    2020 |    2040 |
+---------+---------+---------+
```

Time Zone Adjustments

A MySQL server returns dates using the time zone of the host on which the server runs. If you're running a client program in a different time zone, you can adjust values to client local time with DATE_ADD(). To convert times for a server that is two hours ahead of the client, subtract two hours:

```
mysql> SELECT dt AS 'server time',
    -> DATE_ADD(dt,INTERVAL -2 HOUR) AS 'client time'
    -> FROM datetime_val;
+---------------------+---------------------+
| server time         | client time         |
+---------------------+---------------------+
| 1970-01-01 00:00:00 | 1969-12-31 22:00:00 |
| 1987-03-05 12:30:15 | 1987-03-05 10:30:15 |
| 1999-12-31 09:00:00 | 1999-12-31 07:00:00 |
| 2000-06-04 15:45:30 | 2000-06-04 13:45:30 |
+---------------------+---------------------+
```

Note that the server has no idea what time zone the client is in, so you are responsible for determining the amount of shift between the client and the server time zones. Within a script, you may be able to do this by getting the current local time and comparing it to the server's idea of its local time. In Perl, the localtime() function comes in handy for this:

```
my ($sec, $min, $hour, $day, $mon, $year) = localtime (time ());
my $now = sprintf ("%04d-%02d-%02d %02d:%02d:%02d",
                    $year + 1900, $mon + 1, $day, $hour, $min, $sec);
my ($server_now, $adjustment) = $dbh->selectrow_array (
        "SELECT NOW(), UNIX_TIMESTAMP(?) - UNIX_TIMESTAMP(NOW())",
        undef, $now);
print "client now: $now\n";
print "server now: $server_now\n";
print "adjustment (secs): $adjustment\n";
```

5.21 Finding First and Last Days of Months

Problem

Given a date, you want to determine the date for the first or last day of the month in which the date occurs, or the first or last day for the month *n* months away.

Solution

You can do this by date shifting.

Discussion

Sometimes you have a reference date and want to reach a target date that doesn't have a fixed relationship to the reference date. For example, to find the last day of the month, the amount that you shift the current date depends on what day of the month it is now and the length of the current month.

To find the first day of the month for a given date, shift the date back by one fewer days than its DAYOFMONTH( ) value:

```
mysql> SELECT d, DATE_SUB(d,INTERVAL DAYOFMONTH(d)-1 DAY) AS '1st of month'
    -> FROM date_val;
+------------+--------------+
| d          | 1st of month |
+------------+--------------+
| 1864-02-28 | 1864-02-01   |
| 1900-01-15 | 1900-01-01   |
| 1987-03-05 | 1987-03-01   |
| 1999-12-31 | 1999-12-01   |
| 2000-06-04 | 2000-06-01   |
+------------+--------------+
```

In the general case, to find the first of the month for any month *n* months away from a given date, calculate the first of the month for the date, then shift the result by *n* months:

```
DATE_ADD(DATE_SUB(d,INTERVAL DAYOFMONTH(d)-1 DAY),INTERVAL n MONTH)
```

For example, to find the first day of the previous and following months relative to a given date, *n* would be −1 and 1:

```
mysql> SELECT d,
    -> DATE_ADD(DATE_SUB(d,INTERVAL DAYOFMONTH(d)-1 DAY),INTERVAL -1 MONTH)
    -> AS '1st of previous month',
    -> DATE_ADD(DATE_SUB(d,INTERVAL DAYOFMONTH(d)-1 DAY),INTERVAL 1 MONTH)
    -> AS '1st of following month'
    -> FROM date_val;
```

```
+-----------+---------------------+-----------------------+
| d         | 1st of previous month | 1st of following month |
+-----------+---------------------+-----------------------+
| 1864-02-28 | 1864-01-01         | 1864-03-01            |
| 1900-01-15 | 1899-12-01         | 1900-02-01            |
| 1987-03-05 | 1987-02-01         | 1987-04-01            |
| 1999-12-31 | 1999-11-01         | 2000-01-01            |
| 2000-06-04 | 2000-05-01         | 2000-07-01            |
+-----------+---------------------+-----------------------+
```

Finding the last day of the month for a given reference date is more difficult, because months vary in length. However, the last day of the month is always the day before the first of the next month, and we know how to calculate the latter. Thus, for the general case, the last day of the month *n* months from a date can be determined using the following procedure:

1. Find the first day of the month

2. Shift the result by *n*+1 months

3. Shift back a day

The SQL expression to perform these operations look like this:

```
DATE_SUB(
    DATE_ADD(DATE_SUB(d,INTERVAL DAYOFMONTH(d)-1 DAY),INTERVAL n+1 MONTH),
    INTERVAL 1 DAY)
```

For example, to calculate the last day of the month for the previous, current, and following months relative to a given date, *n* would be −1, 0, and 1, and the expressions look like this:

```
mysql> SELECT d,
    -> DATE_SUB(
    -> DATE_ADD(DATE_SUB(d,INTERVAL DAYOFMONTH(d)-1 DAY),INTERVAL 0 MONTH),
    -> INTERVAL 1 DAY)
    -> AS 'last, prev. month',
    -> DATE_SUB(
    -> DATE_ADD(DATE_SUB(d,INTERVAL DAYOFMONTH(d)-1 DAY),INTERVAL 1 MONTH),
    -> INTERVAL 1 DAY)
    -> AS 'last, this month',
    -> DATE_SUB(
    -> DATE_ADD(DATE_SUB(d,INTERVAL DAYOFMONTH(d)-1 DAY),INTERVAL 2 MONTH),
    -> INTERVAL 1 DAY)
    -> AS 'last, following month'
    -> FROM date_val;
+-----------+-------------------+------------------+-----------------------+
| d         | last, prev. month | last, this month | last, following month |
+-----------+-------------------+------------------+-----------------------+
| 1864-02-28 | 1864-01-31       | 1864-02-29       | 1864-03-31            |
| 1900-01-15 | 1899-12-31       | 1900-01-31       | 1900-02-28            |
| 1987-03-05 | 1987-02-28       | 1987-03-31       | 1987-04-30            |
| 1999-12-31 | 1999-11-30       | 1999-12-31       | 2000-01-31            |
| 2000-06-04 | 2000-05-31       | 2000-06-30       | 2000-07-31            |
+-----------+-------------------+------------------+-----------------------+
```

The last day of the previous month is a special case for which the general expression can be simplified quite a bit:

```
mysql> SELECT d,
    -> DATE_SUB(d,INTERVAL DAYOFMONTH(d) DAY)
    -> AS 'last of previous month'
    -> FROM date_val;
+------------+------------------------+
| d          | last of previous month |
+------------+------------------------+
| 1864-02-28 | 1864-01-31             |
| 1900-01-15 | 1899-12-31             |
| 1987-03-05 | 1987-02-28             |
| 1999-12-31 | 1999-11-30             |
| 2000-06-04 | 2000-05-31             |
+------------+------------------------+
```

The key feature of the general last-of-month expression is that it begins by finding the first-of-month value for the starting date. That gives you a useful point of reference, because you can always shift it forward or backward by month units to obtain another first-of-month value, which can in turn be shifted back a day to find a last-of-month value. If you determine last-of-month values by finding the last-of-month value for the starting date and then shifting that, you won't always get the correct result, because not all months have the same number of days. For example, an incorrect method for determining the last day of a given month is to find the last day of the previous month and add a month:

```
mysql> SELECT d,
    -> DATE_ADD(DATE_SUB(d,INTERVAL DAYOFMONTH(d) DAY),INTERVAL 1 MONTH)
    -> AS 'last of month'
    -> FROM date_val;
+------------+---------------+
| d          | last of month |
+------------+---------------+
| 1864-02-28 | 1864-02-29    |
| 1900-01-15 | 1900-01-31    |
| 1987-03-05 | 1987-03-28    |
| 1999-12-31 | 1999-12-30    |
| 2000-06-04 | 2000-06-30    |
+------------+---------------+
```

This fails because the day-of-month part of the resulting date may not be correct. In the rows for 1987-03-05 and 1999-12-31, the last day of the month has been calculated incorrectly. This will be true with the preceding formula for any month in which the month preceding the reference date has fewer days than the target month.

5.22   Finding the Length of a Month

Problem

You want to know how many days there are in a month.

Solution

Determine the date of its last day, then extract the day-of-month component from the result.

Discussion

To determine the number of days for the month in which a given date occurs, calculate the date for the last day of the month as shown in the previous section, then extract the DAYOFMONTH( ) value from the result:

```
mysql> SELECT d,
    -> DAYOFMONTH(DATE_SUB(
    -> DATE_ADD(DATE_SUB(d,INTERVAL DAYOFMONTH(d)-1 DAY),INTERVAL 1 MONTH),
    -> INTERVAL 1 DAY))
    -> AS 'days in month'
    -> FROM date_val;
+------------+---------------+
| d          | days in month |
+------------+---------------+
| 1864-02-28 |            29 |
| 1900-01-15 |            31 |
| 1987-03-05 |            31 |
| 1999-12-31 |            31 |
| 2000-06-04 |            30 |
+------------+---------------+
```

See Also

Recipe 5.27 later in this chapter discusses another way to calculate month lengths. Chapter 10 discusses leap year calculations in the context of date validation.

5.23 Calculating One Date from Another by Substring Replacement

Problem

Given a date, you want to produce another date from it, and you know the two dates share some components in common.

Solution

Treat a date or time value as a string and perform direct replacement on parts of the string.

Discussion

In some cases, you can use substring replacement to calculate dates without performing any date arithmetic. For example, you can use string operations to produce the first-of-month value for a given date by replacing the day component with 01. You can do this either with DATE_FORMAT( ) or with CONCAT( ):

```
mysql> SELECT d,
    -> DATE_FORMAT(d,'%Y-%m-01') AS method1,
    -> CONCAT(YEAR(d),'-',LPAD(MONTH(d),2,'0'),'-01') AS method2
    -> FROM date_val;
+------------+------------+------------+
| d          | method1    | method2    |
+------------+------------+------------+
| 1864-02-28 | 1864-02-01 | 1864-02-01 |
| 1900-01-15 | 1900-01-01 | 1900-01-01 |
| 1987-03-05 | 1987-03-01 | 1987-03-01 |
| 1999-12-31 | 1999-12-01 | 1999-12-01 |
| 2000-06-04 | 2000-06-01 | 2000-06-01 |
+------------+------------+------------+
```

The string replacement technique can also be used to produce dates with a specific position within the calendar year. For New Year's Day (January 1), replace the month and day with 01:

```
mysql> SELECT d,
    -> DATE_FORMAT(d,'%Y-01-01') AS method1,
    -> CONCAT(YEAR(d),'-01-01') AS method2
    -> FROM date_val;
+------------+------------+------------+
| d          | method1    | method2    |
+------------+------------+------------+
| 1864-02-28 | 1864-01-01 | 1864-01-01 |
| 1900-01-15 | 1900-01-01 | 1900-01-01 |
| 1987-03-05 | 1987-01-01 | 1987-01-01 |
| 1999-12-31 | 1999-01-01 | 1999-01-01 |
| 2000-06-04 | 2000-01-01 | 2000-01-01 |
+------------+------------+------------+
```

For Christmas, replace the month and day with 12 and 25:

```
mysql> SELECT d,
    -> DATE_FORMAT(d,'%Y-12-25') AS method1,
    -> CONCAT(YEAR(d),'-12-25') AS method2
    -> FROM date_val;
+------------+------------+------------+
| d          | method1    | method2    |
+------------+------------+------------+
| 1864-02-28 | 1864-12-25 | 1864-12-25 |
| 1900-01-15 | 1900-12-25 | 1900-12-25 |
| 1987-03-05 | 1987-12-25 | 1987-12-25 |
| 1999-12-31 | 1999-12-25 | 1999-12-25 |
| 2000-06-04 | 2000-12-25 | 2000-12-25 |
+------------+------------+------------+
```

To perform the same operation for Christmas in other years, combine string replacement with date shifting. The following query shows two ways to determine the date for Christmas two years hence. The first method finds Christmas for this year, then shifts it two years forward. The second shifts the current date forward two years, then finds Christmas in the resulting year:

```
mysql> SELECT CURDATE(),
    -> DATE_ADD(DATE_FORMAT(CURDATE(),'%Y-12-25'),INTERVAL 2 YEAR)
    -> AS method1,
    -> DATE_FORMAT(DATE_ADD(CURDATE(),INTERVAL 2 YEAR),'%Y-12-25')
    -> AS method2;
+------------+------------+------------+
| CURDATE()  | method1    | method2    |
+------------+------------+------------+
| 2002-07-15 | 2004-12-25 | 2004-12-25 |
+------------+------------+------------+
```

5.24 Finding the Day of the Week for a Date

Problem

You want to know the day of the week a date falls on.

Solution

Use the DAYNAME() function.

Discussion

To determine the name of the day of the week for a given date, use DAYNAME():

```
mysql> SELECT CURDATE(), DAYNAME(CURDATE());
+------------+--------------------+
| CURDATE()  | DAYNAME(CURDATE()) |
+------------+--------------------+
| 2002-07-15 | Monday             |
+------------+--------------------+
```

DAYNAME() is often useful in conjunction with other date-related techniques. For example, to find out the day of the week for the first of the month, use the first-of-month expression from earlier in the chapter as the argument to DAYNAME():

```
mysql> SET @d = CURDATE();
mysql> SET @first = DATE_SUB(@d,INTERVAL DAYOFMONTH(@d)-1 DAY);
mysql> SELECT @d AS 'starting date',
    -> @first AS '1st of month date',
    -> DAYNAME(@first) AS '1st of month day';
```

```
+---------------+--------------------+------------------+
| starting date | 1st of month date  | 1st of month day |
+---------------+--------------------+------------------+
| 2002-07-15    | 2002-07-01         | Monday           |
+---------------+--------------------+------------------+
```

5.25   Finding Dates for Days of the Current Week

Problem

You want to compute the date for some other day of the current week.

Solution

Figure out the number of days between the starting day and the desired day, and shift the date by that many days.

Discussion

This section and the next describe how to convert one date to another when the target date is specified in terms of days of the week. To solve such problems, you need to know day-of-week values. For example, if you want to know what date it is on Tuesday of this week, the calculation depends on what day of the week it is today. If today is Monday, you add a day to CURDATE(), but if today is Wednesday, you subtract a day.

MySQL provides two functions that are useful here. DAYOFWEEK() treats Sunday as the first day of the week and returns 1 through 7 for Sunday through Saturday. WEEKDAY() treats Monday as the first day of the week and returns 0 through 6 for Monday through Sunday. (The examples shown here use DAYOFWEEK().) Another kind of day-of-week operation involves determining the name of the day. DAYNAME() can be used for that.

Calculations that determine one day of the week from another depend on the day you start from as well as the day you want to reach. I find it easiest to shift the reference date first to a known point relative to the beginning of the week, then shift forward:

- Shift the reference date back by its DAYOFWEEK() value, which always produces the date for the Saturday preceding the week.

- Add one day to the result to reach the Sunday date, two days to reach the Monday date, and so forth.

In SQL, these operations can be expressed as follows for a date d, where *n* is 1 through 7 to produce the dates for Sunday through Saturday:

```
DATE_ADD(DATE_SUB(d,INTERVAL DAYOFWEEK(d) DAY),INTERVAL n DAY)
```

That expression splits the "shift back to Saturday" and "shift forward" phases into separate operations, but because the intervals for both DATE_SUB() and DATE_ADD() are both in days, the expression can be simplified into a single DATE_ADD() call:

```
DATE_ADD(d,INTERVAL n-DAYOFWEEK(d) DAY)
```

If we apply this formula to our date_val table, using an *n* of 1 for Sunday and 7 for Saturday to find the first and last days of the week, we get this result:

```
mysql> SELECT d, DAYNAME(d) AS day,
    -> DATE_ADD(d,INTERVAL 1-DAYOFWEEK(d) DAY) AS Sunday,
    -> DATE_ADD(d,INTERVAL 7-DAYOFWEEK(d) DAY) AS Saturday
    -> FROM date_val;
+------------+----------+------------+------------+
| d          | day      | Sunday     | Saturday   |
+------------+----------+------------+------------+
| 1864-02-28 | Sunday   | 1864-02-28 | 1864-03-05 |
| 1900-01-15 | Monday   | 1900-01-14 | 1900-01-20 |
| 1987-03-05 | Thursday | 1987-03-01 | 1987-03-07 |
| 1999-12-31 | Friday   | 1999-12-26 | 2000-01-01 |
| 2000-06-04 | Sunday   | 2000-06-04 | 2000-06-10 |
+------------+----------+------------+------------+
```

5.26 Finding Dates for Weekdays of Other Weeks

Problem

You want to compute the date for some weekday of some other week.

Solution

Figure out the date for that weekday in the current week, then shift the result into the desired week.

Discussion

Calculating the date for a day of the week in some other week is a problem that breaks down into a day-within-week shift (using the formula given in the previous section) plus a week shift. These operations can be done in either order because the amount of shift within the week is the same whether or not you shift the reference date into a different week first. For example, to calculate Wednesday of a week by the preceding formula, *n* is 4. To compute the date for Wednesday two weeks ago, you can perform the day-within-week shift first, like this:

```
mysql> SET @target =
    -> DATE_SUB(DATE_ADD(CURDATE(),INTERVAL 4-DAYOFWEEK(CURDATE()) DAY),
    -> INTERVAL 14 DAY);
mysql> SELECT CURDATE(), @target, DAYNAME(@target);
```

```
+------------+------------+-------------------+
| CURDATE()  | @target    | DAYNAME(@target)  |
+------------+------------+-------------------+
| 2002-07-15 | 2002-07-03 | Wednesday         |
+------------+------------+-------------------+
```

Or you can perform the week shift first:

```
mysql> SET @target =
    -> DATE_ADD(DATE_SUB(CURDATE(),INTERVAL 14 DAY),
    -> INTERVAL 4-DAYOFWEEK(CURDATE()) DAY);
mysql> SELECT CURDATE(), @target, DAYNAME(@target);
+------------+------------+-------------------+
| CURDATE()  | @target    | DAYNAME(@target)  |
+------------+------------+-------------------+
| 2002-07-15 | 2002-07-03 | Wednesday         |
+------------+------------+-------------------+
```

Some applications need to determine dates such as the *n*-th instance of particular weekdays. For example, if you administer a payroll where paydays are the 2nd and 4th Thursdays of each month, you'd need to know what those dates are. One way to do this for any given month is to begin with the first-of-month date and shift it forward. It's easy enough to shift the date to the Thursday in that week; the trick is to figure out how many weeks forward to shift the result to reach the 2nd and 4th Thursdays. If the first of the month occurs on any day from Sunday through Thursday, you shift forward one week to reach the 2nd Thursday. If the first of the month occurs on Friday or later, you shift forward by two weeks. The 4th Thursday is of course two weeks after that.

The following Perl code implements this logic to find all paydays in the year 2002. It runs a loop that constructs the first-of-month date for the months of the year. For each month, it issues a query that determines the dates of the 2nd and 4th Thursdays:

```
my $year = 2002;
print "MM/CCYY   2nd Thursday   4th Thursday\n";
foreach my $month (1..12)
{
    my $first = sprintf ("%04d-%02d-01", $year, $month);
    my ($thu2, $thu4) = $dbh->selectrow_array (qq{
                SELECT
                    DATE_ADD(
                        DATE_ADD(?,INTERVAL 5-DAYOFWEEK(?) DAY),
                        INTERVAL IF(DAYOFWEEK(?) <= 5, 7, 14) DAY),
                    DATE_ADD(
                        DATE_ADD(?,INTERVAL 5-DAYOFWEEK(?) DAY),
                        INTERVAL IF(DAYOFWEEK(?) <= 5, 21, 28) DAY)
            }, undef, $first, $first, $first, $first, $first, $first);
    printf "%02d/%04d   %s     %s\n", $month, $year, $thu2, $thu4;
}
```

The output from the program looks like this:

```
MM/CCYY   2nd Thursday   4th Thursday
01/2002   2002-01-10     2002-01-24
```

02/2002	2002-02-14	2002-02-28
03/2002	2002-03-14	2002-03-28
04/2002	2002-04-11	2002-04-25
05/2002	2002-05-09	2002-05-23
06/2002	2002-06-13	2002-06-27
07/2002	2002-07-11	2002-07-25
08/2002	2002-08-08	2002-08-22
09/2002	2002-09-12	2002-09-26
10/2002	2002-10-10	2002-10-24
11/2002	2002-11-14	2002-11-28
12/2002	2002-12-12	2002-12-26

5.27 Performing Leap Year Calculations

Problem

You need to perform a date calculation that must account for leap years. For example, the length of a month or a year depends on knowing whether or not the date falls in a leap year.

Solution

Know how to test whether or not a year is a leap year and factor the result into your calculation.

Discussion

Date calculations are complicated by the fact that months don't all have the same number of days, and an additional headache is that February has an extra day during leap years. This section shows how to determine whether or not any given date falls within a leap year, and how to take leap years into account when determining the length of a year or month.

Determining Whether a Date Occurs in a Leap Year

To determine whether or not a date d falls within a leap year, obtain the year component using YEAR( ) and test the result. The common rule-of-thumb test for leap years is "divisible by four," which you can test using the % modulo operator like this:

```
YEAR(d) % 4 = 0
```

However, that test is not technically correct. (For example, the year 1900 is divisible by four, but is *not* a leap year.) For a year to qualify as a leap year, it must satisfy both of the following constraints:

- The year must be divisible by four.
- The year cannot be divisible by 100, unless it is also divisible by 400.

The meaning of the second constraint is that turn-of-century years are not leap years, except every fourth century. In SQL, you can express these conditions as follows:

```
(YEAR(d) % 4 = 0) AND ((YEAR(d) % 100 != 0) OR (YEAR(d) % 400 = 0))
```

Running our date_val table through both the rule-of-thumb leap-year test and the complete test produces the following results:

```
mysql> SELECT
    -> d,
    -> YEAR(d) % 4 = 0
    -> AS "rule-of-thumb test",
    -> (YEAR(d) % 4 = 0) AND ((YEAR(d) % 100 != 0) OR (YEAR(d) % 400 = 0))
    -> AS "complete test"
    -> FROM date_val;
+------------+--------------------+---------------+
| d          | rule-of-thumb test | complete test |
+------------+--------------------+---------------+
| 1864-02-28 |                  1 |             1 |
| 1900-01-15 |                  1 |             0 |
| 1987-03-05 |                  0 |             0 |
| 1999-12-31 |                  0 |             0 |
| 2000-06-04 |                  1 |             1 |
+------------+--------------------+---------------+
```

As you can see, the two tests don't always produce the same result. In particular, the rule-of-thumb test fails for the year 1900; the complete test result is correct because it accounts for the turn-of-century constraint.

 Because the complete leap-year test needs to check the century, it requires four-digit year values. Two-digit years are ambiguous with respect to the century, making it impossible to assess the turn-of-century constraint.

If you're working with date values within a program, you can perform leap-year tests with your API language rather than at the SQL level. Pull off the first four digits of the date string to get the year, then test it. If the language performs automatic string-to-number conversion of the year value, this is easy. Otherwise, you must convert the year value to numeric form before testing it.

In Perl and PHP, the leap-year test syntax is as follows:

```
$year = substr ($date, 0, 4);
$is_leap = ($year % 4 == 0) && ($year % 100 != 0 || $year % 400 == 0);
```

The syntax for Python is similar, although a type conversion operation is necessary:

```
year = int (date[0:4])
is_leap = (year % 4 == 0) and (year % 100 != 0 or year % 400 == 0)
```

Type conversion is necessary for Java as well:

```
int year = Integer.valueOf (date.substring (0, 4)).intValue ();
boolean is_leap = (year % 4 == 0) && (year % 100 != 0 || year % 400 == 0);
```

Using Leap Year Tests for Year-Length Calculations

Years are usually 365 days long, but leap years have an extra day. To determine the length of a year in which a date falls, you can use one of the leap year tests just shown to figure out whether to add a day:

```
$year = substr ($date, 0, 4);
$is_leap = ($year % 4 == 0) && ($year % 100 != 0 || $year % 400 == 0);
$days_in_year = ($is_leap ? 366 : 365);
```

Another way to compute a year's length is to compute the date of the last day of the year and pass it to DAYOFYEAR( ):

```
mysql> SET @d = '2003-04-13';
mysql> SELECT DAYOFYEAR(DATE_FORMAT(@d,'%Y-12-31'));
+---------------------------------------+
| DAYOFYEAR(DATE_FORMAT(@d,'%Y-12-31')) |
+---------------------------------------+
|                                   365 |
+---------------------------------------+
mysql> SET @d = '2004-04-13';
mysql> SELECT DAYOFYEAR(DATE_FORMAT(@d,'%Y-12-31'));
+---------------------------------------+
| DAYOFYEAR(DATE_FORMAT(@d,'%Y-12-31')) |
+---------------------------------------+
|                                   366 |
+---------------------------------------+
```

Using Leap Year Tests for Month-Length Calculations

Earlier in Recipe 5.22, we discussed how to determine the number of days in a month using date shifting to find the last day of the month. Leap-year testing provides an alternate way to accomplish the same objective. All months except February have a fixed length, so by examining the month part of a date, you can tell how long it is. You can also tell how long a given February is if you know whether or not it occurs within a leap year.

A days-in-month expression can be written in SQL like this:

```
mysql> SELECT d,
    -> ELT(MONTH(d),
    -> 31,
    -> IF((YEAR(d)%4 = 0) AND ((YEAR(d)%100 != 0) OR (YEAR(d)%400 = 0)),29,28),
    -> 31,30,31,30,31,31,30,31,30,31)
    -> AS 'days in month'
    -> FROM date_val;
+------------+---------------+
| d          | days in month |
+------------+---------------+
| 1864-02-28 | 29            |
| 1900-01-15 | 31            |
```

```
| 1987-03-05 | 31             |
| 1999-12-31 | 31             |
| 2000-06-04 | 30             |
+------------+---------------+
```

The ELT() function evaluates its first argument to determine its value *n*, then returns the *n-th* value from the following arguments. This is straightforward except for February, where ELT() must return 29 or 28 depending on whether or not the year is a leap year.

Within an API language, you can write a function that, given an ISO-format date argument, returns the number of days in the month during which the date occurs. Here's a Perl version:

```perl
sub days_in_month
{
my $date = shift;
my $year = substr ($date, 0, 4);
my $month = substr ($date, 5, 2);    # month, 1-based
my @days_in_month = (31, 28, 31, 30, 31, 30, 31, 31, 30, 31, 30, 31);
my $days = $days_in_month[$month-1];
my $is_leap = ($year % 4 == 0) && ($year % 100 != 0 || $year % 400 == 0);

    $days++ if $month == 2 && $is_leap; # add a day for Feb of leap years
    return ($days);
}
```

5.28   Treating Dates or Times as Numbers

Problem

You want to treat a temporal string as a number.

Solution

Perform a string-to-number conversion.

Discussion

In many cases, it is possible in MySQL to treat date and time values as numbers. This can sometimes be useful if you want to perform an arithmetic operation on the value. To force conversion of a temporal value to numeric form, add zero or use it in a numeric context:

```
mysql> SELECT t1,
    -> t1+0 AS 't1 as number',
    -> FLOOR(t1) AS 't1 as number',
```

```
      -> FLOOR(t1/10000) AS 'hour part'
      -> FROM time_val;
+----------+--------------+--------------+-----------+
| t1       | t1 as number | t1 as number | hour part |
+----------+--------------+--------------+-----------+
| 15:00:00 |       150000 |       150000 |        15 |
| 05:01:30 |        50130 |        50130 |         5 |
| 12:30:20 |       123020 |       123020 |        12 |
+----------+--------------+--------------+-----------+
```

The same kind of conversion can be performed for date or date-and-time values:

```
mysql> SELECT d, d+0 FROM date_val;
+------------+----------+
| d          | d+0      |
+------------+----------+
| 1864-02-28 | 18640228 |
| 1900-01-15 | 19000115 |
| 1987-03-05 | 19870305 |
| 1999-12-31 | 19991231 |
| 2000-06-04 | 20000604 |
+------------+----------+
mysql> SELECT dt, dt+0 FROM datetime_val;
+---------------------+----------------+
| dt                  | dt+0           |
+---------------------+----------------+
| 1970-01-01 00:00:00 | 19700101000000 |
| 1987-03-05 12:30:15 | 19870305123015 |
| 1999-12-31 09:00:00 | 19991231090000 |
| 2000-06-04 15:45:30 | 20000604154530 |
+---------------------+----------------+
```

A value produced by adding zero is not the same as that produced by conversion into basic units like seconds or days. The result is essentially what you get by removing all the delimiters from the string representation of the original value. Also, conversion to numeric form works only for values that MySQL interprets temporally. If you try converting a literal string to a number by adding zero, you'll just get the first component:

```
mysql> SELECT '1999-01-01'+0, '1999-01-01 12:30:45'+0, '12:30:45'+0;
+---------------+-------------------------+--------------+
| '1999-01-01'+0 | '1999-01-01 12:30:45'+0 | '12:30:45'+0 |
+---------------+-------------------------+--------------+
|          1999 |                    1999 |           12 |
+---------------+-------------------------+--------------+
```

This same thing happens with functions such as DATE_FORMAT() and TIME_FORMAT(), or if you pull out parts of DATETIME or TIMESTAMP values with LEFT() or RIGHT(). In +0 context, the results of these functions are treated as strings, not temporal types.

5.29 Forcing MySQL to Treat Strings as Temporal Values

Problem

You want a string to be interpreted temporally.

Solution

Use the string in a temporal context to give MySQL a hint about how to treat it.

Discussion

If you need to make MySQL treat a string as a date or time, use it in an expression that provides a temporal context without changing the value. For example, you can't add zero to a literal TIME string to cause a time-to-number conversion, but if you use TIME_TO_SEC() and SEC_TO_TIME(), you can:

```
mysql> SELECT SEC_TO_TIME(TIME_TO_SEC('12:30:45'))+0;
+----------------------------------------+
| SEC_TO_TIME(TIME_TO_SEC('12:30:45'))+0 |
+----------------------------------------+
|                                 123045 |
+----------------------------------------+
```

The conversion to and from seconds leaves the value unchanged but results in a context where MySQL treats the result as a TIME value. For date values, the procedure is similar, but uses TO_DAYS() and FROM_DAYS():

```
mysql> SELECT '1999-01-01'+0, FROM_DAYS(TO_DAYS('1999-01-01'))+0;
+---------------+------------------------------------+
| '1999-01-01'+0 | FROM_DAYS(TO_DAYS('1999-01-01'))+0 |
+---------------+------------------------------------+
|          1999 |                           19990101 |
+---------------+------------------------------------+
```

For DATETIME- or TIMESTAMP-formatted strings, you can use DATE_ADD() to introduce a temporal context:

```
mysql> SELECT
    -> DATE_ADD('1999-01-01 12:30:45',INTERVAL 0 DAY)+0 AS 'numeric datetime',
    -> DATE_ADD('19990101123045',INTERVAL 0 DAY)+0 AS 'numeric timestamp';
+------------------+-------------------+
| numeric datetime | numeric timestamp |
+------------------+-------------------+
|    19990101123045 |    19990101123045 |
+------------------+-------------------+
```

5.30 Selecting Records Based on Their Temporal Characteristics

Problem

You want to select records based on temporal constraints.

Solution

Use a date or time condition in the WHERE clause. This may be based on direct comparison of column values with known values. Or it may be necessary to apply a function to column values to convert them to a more appropriate form for testing, such as using MONTH( ) to test the month part of a date.

Discussion

Most of the preceding date-based techniques were illustrated by example queries that produce date or time values as output. You can use the same techniques in WHERE clauses to place date-based restrictions on the records selected by a query. For example, you can select records occurring before or after a given date, within a date range, or that match particular month or day values.

Comparing Dates to One Another

The following queries find records from the date_val table that occur either before 1900 or during the 1900s:

```
mysql> SELECT d FROM date_val where d < '1900-01-01';
+------------+
| d          |
+------------+
| 1864-02-28 |
+------------+
mysql> SELECT d FROM date_val where d BETWEEN '1900-01-01' AND '1999-12-31';
+------------+
| d          |
+------------+
| 1900-01-15 |
| 1987-03-05 |
| 1999-12-31 |
+------------+
```

If your version of MySQL is older then 3.23.9, one problem to watch out for is that BETWEEN sometimes doesn't work correctly with literal date strings if they are not in ISO format. For example, this may fail:

```
SELECT d FROM date_val WHERE d BETWEEN '1960-3-1' AND '1960-3-15';
```

If that happens, try rewriting the dates in ISO format for better results:

```
SELECT d FROM date_val WHERE d BETWEEN '1960-03-01' AND '1960-03-15';
```

You can also rewrite the expression using two explicit comparisons:

```
SELECT d FROM date_val WHERE d >= '1960-03-01' AND d <= '1960-03-15';
```

When you don't know the exact date you want for a WHERE clause, you can often calculate it using an expression. For example, to perform an "on this day in history" query to search for records in a table history to find events occurring exactly 50 years ago, do this:

```
SELECT * FROM history WHERE d = DATE_SUB(CURDATE(),INTERVAL 50 YEAR);
```

You see this kind of thing in newspapers that run columns showing what the news events were in times past. (In essence, the query compiles those events that have reached their *n*-th anniversary.) If you want to retrieve events that occurred "on this day" for any year rather than "on this date" for a specific year, the query is a bit different. In that case, you need to find records that match the current calendar day, ignoring the year. That topic is discussed in "Comparing Dates to Calendar Days" later in this section.

Calculated dates are useful for range testing as well. For example, to find dates that occur within the last six years, use DATE_SUB( ) to calculate the cutoff date:

```
mysql> SELECT d FROM date_val WHERE d >= DATE_SUB(CURDATE(),INTERVAL 6 YEAR);
+------------+
| d          |
+------------+
| 1999-12-31 |
| 2000-06-04 |
+------------+
```

Note that the expression in the WHERE clause isolates the date column d on one side of the comparison operator. This is usually a good idea; if the column is indexed, placing it alone on one side of a comparison allows MySQL to process the query more efficiently. To illustrate, the preceding WHERE clause can be written in a way that's logically equivalent, but much less efficient for MySQL to execute:

```
... WHERE DATE_ADD(d,INTERVAL 6 MONTH) >= CURDATE();
```

Here, the d column is used within an expression. That means *every* row must be retrieved so that the expression can be evaluated and tested, which makes any index on the column useless.

Sometimes it's not so obvious how to rewrite a comparison to isolate a date column on one side. For example, the following WHERE clause uses only part of the date column in the comparisons:

```
... WHERE YEAR(d) >= 1987 AND YEAR(d) <= 1991;
```

To rewrite the first comparison, eliminate the YEAR() call and replace its righthand side with a complete date:

```
... WHERE d >= '1987-01-01' AND YEAR(d) <= 1991;
```

Rewriting the second comparison is a little trickier. You can eliminate the YEAR() call on the lefthand side, just as with the first expression, but you can't just add -01-01 to the year on the righthand side. That would produce the following result, which is incorrect:

```
... WHERE d >= '1987-01-01' AND d <= '1991-01-01';
```

That fails because dates from 1991-01-02 to 1991-12-31 fail the test, but should pass. To rewrite the second comparison correctly, either of the following will do:

```
... WHERE d >= '1987-01-01' AND d <= '1991-12-31';
... WHERE d >= '1987-01-01' AND d < '1992-01-01';
```

Another use for calculated dates occurs frequently in applications that create records that have a limited lifetime. Such applications must be able to determine which records to delete when performing an expiration operation. You can approach this problem a couple of ways:

- Store a date in each record indicating when it was created. (Do this by making the column a TIMESTAMP or by setting it to NOW(); see Recipe 5.33 for details.) To perform an expiration operation later, determine which records have a creation date that is too old by comparing that date to the current date. For example, the query to expire records that were created more than *n* days ago might look like this:

  ```
  DELETE FROM tbl_name WHERE create_date < DATE_SUB(NOW(),INTERVAL n DAY);
  ```

- Store an explicit expiration date in each record by calculating the expiration date with DATE_ADD() when the record is created. For a record that should expire in *n* days, you can do that like this:

  ```
  INSERT INTO tbl_name (expire_date,...)
  VALUES(DATE_ADD(NOW(),INTERVAL n DAY),...);
  ```

  To perform the expiration operation in this case, compare the expiration dates to the current date to see which ones have been reached:

  ```
  DELETE FROM tbl_name WHERE expire_date < NOW()
  ```

Comparing Times to One Another

Comparisons involving times are similar to those involving dates. For example, to find times that occurred from 9 AM to 2 PM, use an expression like one of the following:

```
... WHERE t1 BETWEEN '09:00:00' AND '14:00:00';
... WHERE HOUR(t1) BETWEEN 9 AND 14;
```

For an indexed TIME column, the first method would be more efficient. The second method has the property that it works not only for TIME columns, but for DATETIME and TIMESTAMP columns as well.

Comparing Dates to Calendar Days

To answer questions about particular days of the year, use calendar day testing. The following examples illustrate how to do this in the context of looking for birthdays:

- Who has a birthday today? This requires matching a particular calendar day, so you extract the month and day but ignore the year when performing comparisons:

  ```
  ... WHERE MONTH(d) = MONTH(CURDATE()) AND DAYOFMONTH(d) = DAYOFMONTH(CURDATE());
  ```

  This kind of query commonly is applied to biographical data to find lists of actors, politicians, musicians, etc., who were born on a particular day of the year.

  It's tempting to use DAYOFYEAR() to solve "on this day" problems, because it results in simpler queries. But DAYOFYEAR() doesn't work properly for leap years. The presence of February 29 throws off the values for days from March through December.

- Who has a birthday this month? In this case, it's necessary to check only the month:

  ```
  ... WHERE MONTH(d) = MONTH(CURDATE());
  ```

- Who has a birthday next month? The trick here is that you can't just add one to the current month to get the month number that qualifying dates must match. That gives you 13 for dates in December. To make sure you get 1 (January), use either of the following techniques:

  ```
  ... WHERE MONTH(d) = MONTH(DATE_ADD(CURDATE(),INTERVAL 1 MONTH));
  ... WHERE MONTH(d) = MOD(MONTH(CURDATE()),12)+1;
  ```

5.31   Using TIMESTAMP Values

Problem

You want a record's creation time or last modification time to be automatically recorded.

Solution

The TIMESTAMP column type can be used for this. However, it has properties that sometimes surprise people, so read this section to make sure you know what you'll be getting. Then read the next few sections for some applications of TIMESTAMP columns.

Discussion

MySQL supports a TIMESTAMP column type that in many ways can be treated the same way as the DATETIME type. However, the TIMESTAMP type has some special properties:

- The first TIMESTAMP column in a table is special at record-creation time: its default value is the current date and time. This means you need not specify its value at all in an INSERT statement if you want the column set to the record's creation time; MySQL will initialize it automatically. This also occurs if you set the column to NULL when creating the record.

- The first TIMESTAMP is also special whenever any columns in a row are changed from their current values. MySQL automatically updates its value to the date and time at which the change was made. Note that the update happens only if you actually *change* a column value. Setting a column to its current value doesn't update the TIMESTAMP.

- Other TIMESTAMP columns in a table are not special in the same way as the first one. Their default value is zero, not the current date and time. Also, their value does not change automatically when you modify other columns; to update them, you must change them yourself.

- A TIMESTAMP column can be set to the current date and time at any time by setting it to NULL. This is true for any TIMESTAMP column, not just the first one.

The TIMESTAMP properties that relate to record creation and modification make this column type particularly suited for certain kinds of problems, such as automatically recording the times at which table rows are inserted or updated. On the other hand, there are other properties that can be somewhat limiting:

- TIMESTAMP values are represented in *CCYYMMDDhhmmss* format, which isn't especially intuitive or easy to read, and often needs reformatting for display.

- The range for TIMESTAMP values starts at the beginning of the year 1970 and extends to about 2037. If you need a larger range, you need to use DATETIME values.

The following sections show how to take advantage of the TIMESTAMP type's special properties.

5.32   Recording a Row's Last Modification Time

Problem

You want to automatically record the time when a record was last updated.

Solution

Include a TIMESTAMP column in your table.

Discussion

To create a table where each row contains a value that indicates when the record was most recently updated, include a TIMESTAMP column. The column will be set to the current date and time when you create a new row, and updated whenever you update the value of another column in the row. Suppose you create a table tsdemo1 with a TIMESTAMP column that looks like this:

```
CREATE TABLE tsdemo1
(
    t   TIMESTAMP,
    val INT
);
```

Insert a couple of records into the table and then select its contents. (Issue the INSERT queries a few seconds apart so that you can see how the timestamps differ.) The first INSERT statement shows that you can set t to the current date and time by setting it explicitly to NULL; the second shows that you set t by omitting it from the INSERT statement entirely:

```
mysql> INSERT INTO tsdemo1 (t,val) VALUES(NULL,5);
mysql> INSERT INTO tsdemo1 (val) VALUES(10);
mysql> SELECT * FROM tsdemo1;
+----------------+------+
| t              | val  |
+----------------+------+
| 20020715115825 |    5 |
| 20020715115831 |   10 |
+----------------+------+
```

Now issue a query that changes one record's val column and check its effect on the table's contents:

```
mysql> UPDATE tsdemo1 SET val = 6 WHERE val = 5;
mysql> SELECT * FROM tsdemo1;
+----------------+------+
| t              | val  |
+----------------+------+
| 20020715115915 |    6 |
| 20020715115831 |   10 |
+----------------+------+
```

The result shows that the TIMESTAMP has been updated only for the modified record.

If you modify multiple records, the TIMESTAMP values in all of them will be updated:

```
mysql> UPDATE tsdemo1 SET val = val + 1;
mysql> SELECT * FROM tsdemo1;
+----------------+------+
| t              | val  |
+----------------+------+
| 20020715115926 |    7 |
| 20020715115926 |   11 |
+----------------+------+
```

Issuing an UPDATE statement that doesn't actually change the values in the val column doesn't update the TIMESTAMP values. To see this, set every record's val column to its current value, then review the contents of the table:

```
mysql> UPDATE tsdemo1 SET val = val + 0;
mysql> SELECT * FROM tsdemo1;
+----------------+------+
| t              | val  |
+----------------+------+
| 20020715115926 |    7 |
| 20020715115926 |   11 |
+----------------+------+
```

An alternative to using a TIMESTAMP is to use a DATETIME column and set it to NOW( ) explicitly when you create a record and whenever you update a record. However, in this case, all applications that use the table must implement the same strategy, which fails if even one application neglects to do so.

5.33 Recording a Row's Creation Time

Problem

You want to record the time when a record was created, which TIMESTAMP will do, but you want that time not to change when the record is changed, and a TIMESTAMP cannot hold its value.

Solution

Actually, it can; you just need to include a second TIMESTAMP column, which has different properties than the first.

Discussion

If you want a column to be set initially to the time at which a record is created, but remain constant thereafter, a single TIMESTAMP is not the solution, because it will be updated whenever other columns in the record are updated. Instead, use two TIMESTAMP columns and take advantage of the fact that the second one won't have the same special properties of the first. Both columns can be set to the current date and time when the record is created. Thereafter, whenever you modify other columns in the record, the first TIMESTAMP column will be updated automatically to reflect the time of the change, but the second remains set to the record creation time. You can see how this works using the following table:

```
CREATE TABLE tsdemo2
(
    t_update    TIMESTAMP,  # record last-modification time
    t_create    TIMESTAMP,  # record creation time
```

```
    val INT
);
```

Create the table, then insert into it as follows a record for which both TIMESTAMP columns are set to NULL, to initialize them to the current date and time:

```
mysql> INSERT INTO tsdemo2 (t_update,t_create,val) VALUES(NULL,NULL,5);
mysql> SELECT * FROM tsdemo2;
+----------------+----------------+------+
| t_update       | t_create       | val  |
+----------------+----------------+------+
| 20020715120003 | 20020715120003 |    5 |
+----------------+----------------+------+
```

After inserting the record, change the val column, then verify that the update modifies the t_update column and leaves the t_create column set to the record-creation time:

```
mysql> UPDATE tsdemo2 SET val = val + 1;
mysql> SELECT * FROM tsdemo2;
+----------------+----------------+------+
| t_update       | t_create       | val  |
+----------------+----------------+------+
| 20020715120012 | 20020715120003 |    6 |
+----------------+----------------+------+
```

As with the tsdemo1 table, updates to tsdemo2 records that don't actually modify a column cause no change to TIMESTAMP values:

```
mysql> UPDATE tsdemo2 SET val = val + 0;
mysql> SELECT * FROM tsdemo2;
+----------------+----------------+------+
| t_update       | t_create       | val  |
+----------------+----------------+------+
| 20020715120012 | 20020715120003 |    6 |
+----------------+----------------+------+
```

An alternative strategy is to use DATETIME columns for t_create and t_update. When creating a record, set them both to NOW() explicitly. When modifying a record, update t_update to NOW() and leave t_create alone.

5.34 Performing Calculations with TIMESTAMP Values

Problem

You want to calculate intervals between TIMESTAMP values, search for records based on a TIMESTAMP column, and so forth.

Solution

TIMESTAMP values are susceptible to the same kinds of date calculations as DATETIME values, such as comparison, shifting, and component extraction.

Discussion

The following queries show some of the possible operations you can perform on TIMESTAMP values, using the tsdemo2 table from Recipe 5.33:

- Records that have not been modified since they were created:

```
SELECT * FROM tsdemo2 WHERE t_create = t_update;
```

- Records modified within the last 12 hours:

```
SELECT * FROM tsdemo2 WHERE t_update >= DATE_SUB(NOW(),INTERVAL 12 HOUR);
```

- The difference between the creation and modification times (here expressed both in seconds and in hours):

```
SELECT t_create, t_update,
UNIX_TIMESTAMP(t_update) - UNIX_TIMESTAMP(t_create) AS 'seconds',
(UNIX_TIMESTAMP(t_update) - UNIX_TIMESTAMP(t_create))/(60 * 60) AS 'hours'
FROM tsdemo2;
```

- Records created from 1 PM to 4 PM:

```
SELECT * FROM tsdemo2
WHERE HOUR(t_create) BETWEEN 13 AND 16;
```

Or:

```
SELECT * FROM tsdemo2
WHERE DATE_FORMAT(t_create,'%H%i%s') BETWEEN '130000' AND '160000';
```

Or even by using TIME_TO_SEC( ) to strip off the date part of the t_create values:

```
SELECT * FROM tsdemo2
WHERE TIME_TO_SEC(t_create)
BETWEEN TIME_TO_SEC('13:00:00') AND TIME_TO_SEC('16:00:00');
```

5.35   Displaying TIMESTAMP Values in Readable Form

Problem

You don't like the way that MySQL displays TIMESTAMP values.

Solution

Reformat them with the DATE_FORMAT( ) function.

Discussion

TIMESTAMP columns have certain desirable properties, but one that sometimes isn't so desirable is the display format (*CCYYMMDDhhmmss*). As a long unbroken string of digits, this is inconsistent with DATETIME format (*CCYY-MM-DD hh:mm:ss*) and is also more difficult to read. To rewrite TIMESTAMP values into DATETIME format, use the DATE_FORMAT( ) function. The following example uses the tsdemo2 table from Recipe 5.33:

```
mysql> SELECT t_create, DATE_FORMAT(t_create,'%Y-%m-%d %T') FROM tsdemo2;
+----------------+-------------------------------------+
| t_create       | DATE_FORMAT(t_create,'%Y-%m-%d %T')  |
+----------------+-------------------------------------+
| 20020715120003 | 2002-07-15 12:00:03                 |
+----------------+-------------------------------------+
```

You can go in the other direction, too (to display DATETIME values in TIMESTAMP format), though this is much less common. One way is to use DATE_FORMAT( ); another that's simpler is to add zero:

```
mysql> SELECT dt,
    -> DATE_FORMAT(dt,'%Y%m%d%H%i%s'),
    -> dt+0
    -> FROM datetime_val;
+---------------------+------------------------------+----------------+
| dt                  | DATE_FORMAT(dt,'%Y%m%d%H%i%s') | dt+0         |
+---------------------+------------------------------+----------------+
| 1970-01-01 00:00:00 | 19700101000000               | 19700101000000 |
| 1987-03-05 12:30:15 | 19870305123015               | 19870305123015 |
| 1999-12-31 09:00:00 | 19991231090000               | 19991231090000 |
| 2000-06-04 15:45:30 | 20000604154530               | 20000604154530 |
+---------------------+------------------------------+----------------+
```

See Recipe 5.2 for more information about rewriting temporal values in whatever format you like.

CHAPTER 6
Sorting Query Results

6.0   Introduction

This chapter covers sorting, an operation that is extremely important for controlling how MySQL displays results from SELECT statements. Sorting is performed by adding an ORDER BY clause to a query. Without such a clause, MySQL is free to return rows in any order, so sorting helps bring order to disorder and make query results easier to examine and understand. (Sorting also is performed implicitly when you use a GROUP BY clause, as discussed in Recipe 7.13.)

One of the tables used for quite a few examples in this chapter is driver_log, a table that contains columns for recording daily mileage logs for a set of truck drivers:

```
mysql> SELECT * FROM driver_log;
+--------+-------+------------+-------+
| rec_id | name  | trav_date  | miles |
+--------+-------+------------+-------+
|      1 | Ben   | 2001-11-30 |   152 |
|      2 | Suzi  | 2001-11-29 |   391 |
|      3 | Henry | 2001-11-29 |   300 |
|      4 | Henry | 2001-11-27 |    96 |
|      5 | Ben   | 2001-11-29 |   131 |
|      6 | Henry | 2001-11-26 |   115 |
|      7 | Suzi  | 2001-12-02 |   502 |
|      8 | Henry | 2001-12-01 |   197 |
|      9 | Ben   | 2001-12-02 |    79 |
|     10 | Henry | 2001-11-30 |   203 |
+--------+-------+------------+-------+
```

Many other examples use the mail table (first seen in earlier chapters):

```
mysql> SELECT * FROM mail;
+---------------------+---------+---------+---------+---------+--------+
| t                   | srcuser | srchost | dstuser | dsthost | size   |
+---------------------+---------+---------+---------+---------+--------+
| 2001-05-11 10:15:08 | barb    | saturn  | tricia  | mars    |  58274 |
| 2001-05-12 12:48:13 | tricia  | mars    | gene    | venus   | 194925 |
| 2001-05-12 15:02:49 | phil    | mars    | phil    | saturn  |   1048 |
```

```
| 2001-05-13 13:59:18 | barb   | saturn | tricia | venus  |     271 |
| 2001-05-14 09:31:37 | gene   | venus  | barb   | mars   |    2291 |
| 2001-05-14 11:52:17 | phil   | mars   | tricia | saturn |    5781 |
| 2001-05-14 14:42:21 | barb   | venus  | barb   | venus  |   98151 |
| 2001-05-14 17:03:01 | tricia | saturn | phil   | venus  | 2394482 |
| 2001-05-15 07:17:48 | gene   | mars   | gene   | saturn |    3824 |
| 2001-05-15 08:50:57 | phil   | venus  | phil   | venus  |     978 |
| 2001-05-15 10:25:52 | gene   | mars   | tricia | saturn |  998532 |
| 2001-05-15 17:35:31 | gene   | saturn | gene   | mars   |    3856 |
| 2001-05-16 09:00:28 | gene   | venus  | barb   | mars   |     613 |
| 2001-05-16 23:04:19 | phil   | venus  | barb   | venus  |   10294 |
| 2001-05-17 12:49:23 | phil   | mars   | tricia | saturn |     873 |
| 2001-05-19 22:21:51 | gene   | saturn | gene   | venus  |   23992 |
+---------------------+--------+--------+--------+--------+---------+
```

Other tables are used occasionally as well. You can create most of them with the scripts found in the *tables* directory of the recipes distribution. The *baseball1* directory contains instructions for creating the tables used in the examples relating to the *baseball1.com* baseball database.

6.1 Using ORDER BY to Sort Query Results

Problem

Output from a query doesn't come out in the order you want.

Solution

Add an ORDER BY clause to the query.

Discussion

The contents of the driver_log and mail tables shown in the chapter introduction are disorganized and difficult to make any sense of. The exception is that the values in the id and t columns are in order, but that's just coincidental. Rows do tend to be returned from a table in the order they were originally inserted, but only until the table is subjected to delete and update operations. Rows inserted after that are likely to be returned in the middle of the result set somewhere. Many MySQL users notice this disturbance in row retrieval order, which leads them to ask, "How can I store rows in my table so they come out in a particular order when I retrieve them?" The answer to this question is that it's the wrong question. Storing rows is the server's job and you should let the server do it. (Besides, even if you could specify storage order, how would that help you if you wanted to see results sorted in different orders at different times?)

When you select records, they're pulled out of the database and returned in whatever order the server happens to use. This may change, even for queries that don't sort rows, depending on which index the server happens to use when it executes a query, because the index can affect the retrieval order. Even if your rows appear to come out in the proper order naturally, a relational database makes no guarantee about the order in which it returns rows—unless you tell it how. To arrange the rows from a query result into a specific order, sort them by adding an ORDER BY clause to your SELECT statement. Without ORDER BY, you may find that the retrieval order changes when you modify the contents of your table. With an ORDER BY clause, MySQL will always sort rows the way you indicate.

ORDER BY has the following general characteristics:

- You can sort using a single column of values or multiple columns
- You can sort any column in either ascending order (the default) or descending order
- You can refer to sort columns by name, by their position within the output column list, or by using an alias

This section shows some basic sorting techniques, and the following sections illustrate how to perform more complex sorts. Paradoxically, you can even use ORDER BY to disorder a result set, which is useful for randomizing the rows, or (in conjunction with LIMIT) for picking a row at random from a result set. Those uses for ORDER BY are described in Chapter 13.

Naming the Sort Columns and Specifying Sorting Direction

The following set of examples demonstrates how to sort on a single column or multiple columns and how to sort in ascending or descending order. The examples select the rows in the driver_log table but sort them in different orders so that you can compare the effect of the different ORDER BY clauses.

This query produces a single-column sort using the driver name:

```
mysql> SELECT * FROM driver_log ORDER BY name;
+--------+-------+------------+-------+
| rec_id | name  | trav_date  | miles |
+--------+-------+------------+-------+
|      1 | Ben   | 2001-11-30 |   152 |
|      5 | Ben   | 2001-11-29 |   131 |
|      9 | Ben   | 2001-12-02 |    79 |
|      3 | Henry | 2001-11-29 |   300 |
|      4 | Henry | 2001-11-27 |    96 |
|      6 | Henry | 2001-11-26 |   115 |
|      8 | Henry | 2001-12-01 |   197 |
|     10 | Henry | 2001-11-30 |   203 |
|      2 | Suzi  | 2001-11-29 |   391 |
|      7 | Suzi  | 2001-12-02 |   502 |
+--------+-------+------------+-------+
```

The default sort direction is ascending. You can make the direction for an ascending sort explicit by adding ASC after the sorted column's name:

```
SELECT * FROM driver_log ORDER BY name ASC;
```

The opposite (or reverse) of ascending order is descending order, specified by adding DESC after the sorted column's name:

```
mysql> SELECT * FROM driver_log ORDER BY name DESC;
+--------+-------+------------+-------+
| rec_id | name  | trav_date  | miles |
+--------+-------+------------+-------+
|      2 | Suzi  | 2001-11-29 |   391 |
|      7 | Suzi  | 2001-12-02 |   502 |
|      3 | Henry | 2001-11-29 |   300 |
|      4 | Henry | 2001-11-27 |    96 |
|      6 | Henry | 2001-11-26 |   115 |
|      8 | Henry | 2001-12-01 |   197 |
|     10 | Henry | 2001-11-30 |   203 |
|      1 | Ben   | 2001-11-30 |   152 |
|      5 | Ben   | 2001-11-29 |   131 |
|      9 | Ben   | 2001-12-02 |    79 |
+--------+-------+------------+-------+
```

If you closely examine the output from the queries just shown, you'll notice that although the rows are sorted by name, the rows for any given name aren't in any special order (The trav_date values aren't in date order for Henry or Ben, for example.) That's because MySQL doesn't sort something unless you tell it to:

- The overall order of rows returned by a query is indeterminate unless you specify an ORDER BY clause.

- In the same way, within a group of rows that sort together based on the values in a given column, the order of values in other columns also is indeterminate unless you name them in the ORDER BY clause.

To more fully control output order, specify a multiple-column sort by listing each column to use for sorting, separated by commas. The following query sorts in ascending order by name and by trav_date within the rows for each name:

```
mysql> SELECT * FROM driver_log ORDER BY name, trav_date;
+--------+-------+------------+-------+
| rec_id | name  | trav_date  | miles |
+--------+-------+------------+-------+
|      5 | Ben   | 2001-11-29 |   131 |
|      1 | Ben   | 2001-11-30 |   152 |
|      9 | Ben   | 2001-12-02 |    79 |
|      6 | Henry | 2001-11-26 |   115 |
|      4 | Henry | 2001-11-27 |    96 |
|      3 | Henry | 2001-11-29 |   300 |
|     10 | Henry | 2001-11-30 |   203 |
```

```
|      8 | Henry | 2001-12-01 |    197 |
|      2 | Suzi  | 2001-11-29 |    391 |
|      7 | Suzi  | 2001-12-02 |    502 |
+--------+-------+------------+--------+
```

Multiple-column sorts can be descending as well, but DESC must be specified after each column name to perform a fully descending sort:

```
mysql> SELECT * FROM driver_log ORDER BY name DESC, trav_date DESC;
+--------+-------+------------+--------+
| rec_id | name  | trav_date  | miles  |
+--------+-------+------------+--------+
|      7 | Suzi  | 2001-12-02 |    502 |
|      2 | Suzi  | 2001-11-29 |    391 |
|      8 | Henry | 2001-12-01 |    197 |
|     10 | Henry | 2001-11-30 |    203 |
|      3 | Henry | 2001-11-29 |    300 |
|      4 | Henry | 2001-11-27 |     96 |
|      6 | Henry | 2001-11-26 |    115 |
|      9 | Ben   | 2001-12-02 |     79 |
|      1 | Ben   | 2001-11-30 |    152 |
|      5 | Ben   | 2001-11-29 |    131 |
+--------+-------+------------+--------+
```

Multiple-column ORDER BY clauses can perform mixed-order sorting where some columns are sorted in ascending order and others in descending order. The following query sorts by name in descending order, then by trav_date in ascending order for each name:

```
mysql> SELECT * FROM driver_log ORDER BY name DESC, trav_date;
+--------+-------+------------+--------+
| rec_id | name  | trav_date  | miles  |
+--------+-------+------------+--------+
|      2 | Suzi  | 2001-11-29 |    391 |
|      7 | Suzi  | 2001-12-02 |    502 |
|      6 | Henry | 2001-11-26 |    115 |
|      4 | Henry | 2001-11-27 |     96 |
|      3 | Henry | 2001-11-29 |    300 |
|     10 | Henry | 2001-11-30 |    203 |
|      8 | Henry | 2001-12-01 |    197 |
|      5 | Ben   | 2001-11-29 |    131 |
|      1 | Ben   | 2001-11-30 |    152 |
|      9 | Ben   | 2001-12-02 |     79 |
+--------+-------+------------+--------+
```

More Ways to Refer to Sort Columns

The ORDER BY clauses in the queries shown thus far refer to the sorted columns by name. You can also name the columns by their positions within the output column list or by using aliases. Positions within the output list begin with 1. The following query sorts results by the third output column, miles:

```
mysql> SELECT name, trav_date, miles FROM driver_log ORDER BY 3;
+-------+------------+-------+
| name  | trav_date  | miles |
+-------+------------+-------+
| Ben   | 2001-12-02 |    79 |
| Henry | 2001-11-27 |    96 |
| Henry | 2001-11-26 |   115 |
| Ben   | 2001-11-29 |   131 |
| Ben   | 2001-11-30 |   152 |
| Henry | 2001-12-01 |   197 |
| Henry | 2001-11-30 |   203 |
| Henry | 2001-11-29 |   300 |
| Suzi  | 2001-11-29 |   391 |
| Suzi  | 2001-12-02 |   502 |
+-------+------------+-------+
```

If an output column has an alias, you can refer to the alias in the ORDER BY clause:

```
mysql> SELECT name, trav_date, miles AS distance FROM driver_log
    -> ORDER BY distance;
+-------+------------+----------+
| name  | trav_date  | distance |
+-------+------------+----------+
| Ben   | 2001-12-02 |       79 |
| Henry | 2001-11-27 |       96 |
| Henry | 2001-11-26 |      115 |
| Ben   | 2001-11-29 |      131 |
| Ben   | 2001-11-30 |      152 |
| Henry | 2001-12-01 |      197 |
| Henry | 2001-11-30 |      203 |
| Henry | 2001-11-29 |      300 |
| Suzi  | 2001-11-29 |      391 |
| Suzi  | 2001-12-02 |      502 |
+-------+------------+----------+
```

Aliases have an advantage over positionally specified columns in ORDER BY clause. If you use positions for sorting, but then revise the query to change the output column list, you may need to revise the position numbers in the ORDER BY clause as well. If you use aliases, this is unnecessary. (But note that some database engines do not support use of aliases in ORDER BY clauses, so this feature is not portable.)

Columns specified by positions or by aliases can be sorted in either ascending or descending order, just like named columns:

```
mysql> SELECT name, trav_date, miles FROM driver_log ORDER BY 3 DESC;
+-------+------------+-------+
| name  | trav_date  | miles |
+-------+------------+-------+
| Suzi  | 2001-12-02 |   502 |
| Suzi  | 2001-11-29 |   391 |
| Henry | 2001-11-29 |   300 |
| Henry | 2001-11-30 |   203 |
| Henry | 2001-12-01 |   197 |
| Ben   | 2001-11-30 |   152 |
| Ben   | 2001-11-29 |   131 |
| Henry | 2001-11-26 |   115 |
| Henry | 2001-11-27 |    96 |
| Ben   | 2001-12-02 |    79 |
+-------+------------+-------+
```

6.2   Sorting Subsets of a Table

Problem

You don't want to sort an entire table, just part of it.

Solution

Add a WHERE clause that selects only the records you want to see.

Discussion

ORDER BY doesn't care how many rows there are; it sorts whatever rows the query returns. If you don't want to sort an entire table, add a WHERE clause to indicate which rows to select. For example, to sort the records for just one of the drivers, do something like this:

```
mysql> SELECT trav_date, miles FROM driver_log WHERE name = 'Henry'
    -> ORDER BY trav_date;
```

```
+------------+-------+
| trav_date  | miles |
+------------+-------+
| 2001-11-26 |   115 |
| 2001-11-27 |    96 |
| 2001-11-29 |   300 |
| 2001-11-30 |   203 |
| 2001-12-01 |   197 |
+------------+-------+
```

Columns named in the ORDER BY clause need not be the same as those in the WHERE clause, as the preceding query demonstrates. The ORDER BY columns need not even be the ones you display, but that's covered later (Recipe 6.4).

6.3   Sorting Expression Results

Problem

You want to sort a query result based on values calculated from a column, rather than using the values actually stored in the column.

Solution

Put the expression that calculates the values in the ORDER BY clause. For older versions of MySQL that don't support ORDER BY expressions, use a workaround.

Discussion

One of the columns in the mail table shows how large each mail message is, in bytes:

```
mysql> SELECT * FROM mail;
+---------------------+---------+---------+---------+---------+---------+
| t                   | srcuser | srchost | dstuser | dsthost | size    |
+---------------------+---------+---------+---------+---------+---------+
| 2001-05-11 10:15:08 | barb    | saturn  | tricia  | mars    |   58274 |
| 2001-05-12 12:48:13 | tricia  | mars    | gene    | venus   |  194925 |
| 2001-05-12 15:02:49 | phil    | mars    | phil    | saturn  |    1048 |
| 2001-05-13 13:59:18 | barb    | saturn  | tricia  | venus   |     271 |
...
```

Suppose you want to retrieve records for "big" mail messages (defined as those larger than 50,000 bytes), but you want them to be displayed and sorted by sizes in terms of kilobytes, not bytes. In this case, the values to sort are calculated by an expression. You can use ORDER BY to sort expression results, although the way you write the query may depend on your version of MySQL.

Prior to MySQL 3.23.2, expressions in ORDER BY clauses are not allowed. To work around this problem, specify the expression in the output column list and either refer to it by position or give it an alias and refer to the alias:*

```
mysql> SELECT t, srcuser, FLOOR((size+1023)/1024)
    -> FROM mail WHERE size > 50000
    -> ORDER BY 3;
+---------------------+---------+-------------------------+
| t                   | srcuser | FLOOR((size+1023)/1024) |
+---------------------+---------+-------------------------+
| 2001-05-11 10:15:08 | barb    |                      57 |
| 2001-05-14 14:42:21 | barb    |                      96 |
| 2001-05-12 12:48:13 | tricia  |                     191 |
| 2001-05-15 10:25:52 | gene    |                     976 |
| 2001-05-14 17:03:01 | tricia  |                    2339 |
+---------------------+---------+-------------------------+
mysql> SELECT t, srcuser, FLOOR((size+1023)/1024) AS kilobytes
    -> FROM mail WHERE size > 50000
    -> ORDER BY kilobytes;
+---------------------+---------+-----------+
| t                   | srcuser | kilobytes |
+---------------------+---------+-----------+
| 2001-05-11 10:15:08 | barb    |        57 |
| 2001-05-14 14:42:21 | barb    |        96 |
| 2001-05-12 12:48:13 | tricia  |       191 |
| 2001-05-15 10:25:52 | gene    |       976 |
| 2001-05-14 17:03:01 | tricia  |      2339 |
+---------------------+---------+-----------+
```

These techniques work for MySQL 3.23.2 and up, too, but you also have the additional option of putting the expression directly in the ORDER BY clause:

```
mysql> SELECT t, srcuser, FLOOR((size+1023)/1024)
    -> FROM mail WHERE size > 50000
    -> ORDER BY FLOOR((size+1023)/1024);
+---------------------+---------+-------------------------+
| t                   | srcuser | FLOOR((size+1023)/1024) |
+---------------------+---------+-------------------------+
| 2001-05-11 10:15:08 | barb    |                      57 |
| 2001-05-14 14:42:21 | barb    |                      96 |
| 2001-05-12 12:48:13 | tricia  |                     191 |
| 2001-05-15 10:25:52 | gene    |                     976 |
| 2001-05-14 17:03:01 | tricia  |                    2339 |
+---------------------+---------+-------------------------+
```

* Wondering about the +1023 in the FLOOR( ) expression? That's there so that size values group to the nearest upper boundary of the 1024-byte categories. Without it, the values group by lower boundaries (for example, a 2047-byte message would be reported as having a size of 1 kilobyte rather than 2). This technique is discussed in more detail in Recipe 7.12.

However, even if you can put the expression in the ORDER BY clause, there are at least two reasons you might still want to use an alias:

- It's easier to write the ORDER BY clause using the alias than by repeating the (rather cumbersome) expression.
- The alias may be useful for display purposes, to provide a more meaningful column label.

The same restriction on expressions in ORDER BY clauses applies to GROUP BY (which we'll get to in Chapter 7), and the same workarounds apply as well. If your version of MySQL is older than 3.23.2, be sure to remember these workarounds. Many of the queries in the rest of this book use expressions in ORDER BY or GROUP BY clauses; to use them with an older MySQL server, you'll need to rewrite them using the techniques just described.

6.4 Displaying One Set of Values While Sorting by Another

Problem

You want to sort a result set using values that you're not selecting.

Solution

That's not a problem. You can use columns in the ORDER BY clause that don't appear in the column output list.

Discussion

ORDER BY is not limited to sorting only those columns named in the column output list. It can sort using values that are "hidden" (that is, not displayed in the query output). This technique is commonly used when you have values that can be represented different ways and you want to display one type of value but sort by another. For example, you may want to display mail message sizes not in terms of bytes, but as strings such as 103K for 103 kilobytes. You can convert a byte count to that kind of value using this expression:

```
CONCAT(FLOOR((size+1023)/1024),'K')
```

However, such values are strings, so they sort lexically, not numerically. If you use them for sorting, a value such as 96K sorts after 2339K, even though it represents a smaller number:

```
mysql> SELECT t, srcuser,
    -> CONCAT(FLOOR((size+1023)/1024),'K') AS size_in_K
    -> FROM mail WHERE size > 50000
    -> ORDER BY size_in_K;
+---------------------+---------+-----------+
| t                   | srcuser | size_in_K |
+---------------------+---------+-----------+
| 2001-05-12 12:48:13 | tricia  | 191K      |
| 2001-05-14 17:03:01 | tricia  | 2339K     |
| 2001-05-11 10:15:08 | barb    | 57K       |
| 2001-05-14 14:42:21 | barb    | 96K       |
| 2001-05-15 10:25:52 | gene    | 976K      |
+---------------------+---------+-----------+
```

To achieve the desired output order, display the string, but use the actual numeric size for sorting:

```
mysql> SELECT t, srcuser,
    -> CONCAT(FLOOR((size+1023)/1024),'K') AS size_in_K
    -> FROM mail WHERE size > 50000
    -> ORDER BY size;
+---------------------+---------+-----------+
| t                   | srcuser | size_in_K |
+---------------------+---------+-----------+
| 2001-05-11 10:15:08 | barb    | 57K       |
| 2001-05-14 14:42:21 | barb    | 96K       |
| 2001-05-12 12:48:13 | tricia  | 191K      |
| 2001-05-15 10:25:52 | gene    | 976K      |
| 2001-05-14 17:03:01 | tricia  | 2339K     |
+---------------------+---------+-----------+
```

Displaying values as strings but sorting them as numbers also can bail you out of some otherwise difficult situations. Members of sports teams typically are assigned a jersey number, which normally you might think should be stored using a numeric column. Not so fast! Some players like to have a jersey number of zero (0), and some like double-zero (00). If a team happens to have players with both numbers, you cannot represent them using a numeric column, because both values will be treated as the same number. The way out of the problem is to store jersey numbers as strings:

```
CREATE TABLE roster
(
    name         CHAR(30),      # player name
    jersey_num   CHAR(3)        # jersey number
);
```

Then the jersey numbers will display the same way you enter them, and 0 and 00 will be treated as distinct values. Unfortunately, although representing numbers as strings solves the problem of distinguishing 0 and 00, it introduces a different problem. Suppose a team comprises the following players:

```
mysql> SELECT name, jersey_num FROM roster;
+-----------+------------+
| name      | jersey_num |
+-----------+------------+
| Lynne     | 29         |
| Ella      | 0          |
| Elizabeth | 100        |
| Nancy     | 00         |
| Jean      | 8          |
| Sherry    | 47         |
+-----------+------------+
```

The problem occurs when you try to sort the team members by jersey number. If those numbers are stored as strings, they'll sort lexically, and lexical order often differs from numeric order. That's certainly true for the team in question:

```
mysql> SELECT name, jersey_num FROM roster ORDER BY jersey_num;
+-----------+------------+
| name      | jersey_num |
+-----------+------------+
| Ella      | 0          |
| Nancy     | 00         |
| Elizabeth | 100        |
| Lynne     | 29         |
| Sherry    | 47         |
| Jean      | 8          |
+-----------+------------+
```

The values 100 and 8 are out of place. But that's easily solved. Display the string values, but use the numeric values for sorting. To accomplish this, add zero to the jersey_num values to force a string-to-number conversion:

```
mysql> SELECT name, jersey_num FROM roster ORDER BY jersey_num+0;
+-----------+------------+
| name      | jersey_num |
+-----------+------------+
| Ella      | 0          |
| Nancy     | 00         |
| Jean      | 8          |
| Lynne     | 29         |
| Sherry    | 47         |
| Elizabeth | 100        |
+-----------+------------+
```

The technique of displaying one value but sorting by another is also useful when you want to display composite values that are formed from multiple columns but that don't sort the way you want. For example, the mail table lists message senders using separate srcuser and srchost values. If you want to display message senders from the mail table as email addresses in srcuser@srchost format with the username first, you can construct those values using the following expression:

```
CONCAT(srcuser,'@',srchost)
```

However, those values are no good for sorting if you want to treat the hostname as more significant than the username. Instead, sort the results using the underlying column values rather than the displayed composite values:

```
mysql> SELECT t, CONCAT(srcuser,'@',srchost) AS sender, size
    -> FROM mail WHERE size > 50000
    -> ORDER BY srchost, srcuser;
+---------------------+---------------+---------+
| t                   | sender        | size    |
+---------------------+---------------+---------+
| 2001-05-15 10:25:52 | gene@mars     |  998532 |
| 2001-05-12 12:48:13 | tricia@mars   |  194925 |
| 2001-05-11 10:15:08 | barb@saturn   |   58274 |
| 2001-05-14 17:03:01 | tricia@saturn | 2394482 |
| 2001-05-14 14:42:21 | barb@venus    |   98151 |
+---------------------+---------------+---------+
```

The same idea commonly is applied to sorting people's names. Suppose you have a table names that contains last and first names. To display records sorted by last name first, the query is straightforward when the columns are displayed separately:

```
mysql> SELECT last_name, first_name FROM name
    -> ORDER BY last_name, first_name;
+-----------+------------+
| last_name | first_name |
+-----------+------------+
| Blue      | Vida       |
| Brown     | Kevin      |
| Gray      | Pete       |
| White     | Devon      |
| White     | Rondell    |
+-----------+------------+
```

If instead you want to display each name as a single string composed of the first name, a space, and the last name, you can begin the query like this:

```
SELECT CONCAT(first_name,' ',last_name) AS full_name FROM name ...
```

But then how do you sort the names so they come out in the last name order? The answer is to display the composite names, but refer to the constituent values in the ORDER BY clause:

```
mysql> SELECT CONCAT(first_name,' ',last_name) AS full_name
    -> FROM name
    -> ORDER BY last_name, first_name;
```

```
+---------------+
| full_name     |
+---------------+
| Vida Blue     |
| Kevin Brown   |
| Pete Gray     |
| Devon White   |
| Rondell White |
+---------------+
```

If you want to write queries that sort on non-displayed values, you'll have problems if the sort columns are expressions and you're using an older version of MySQL. This is because expressions aren't allowed in ORDER BY clauses until MySQL 3.23.2 (as discussed in Recipe 6.3).

The solution is to "unhide" the expression—add it as an extra output column, and then refer to it by position or by using an alias. For example, to write a query that lists names from the names table with the longest names first, you might do this in MySQL 3.23.2 and up:

```
mysql> SELECT CONCAT(first_name,' ',last_name) AS name
    -> FROM names
    -> ORDER BY LENGTH(CONCAT(first_name,' ',last_name)) DESC;
+---------------+
| name          |
+---------------+
| Rondell White |
| Kevin Brown   |
| Devon White   |
| Vida Blue     |
| Pete Gray     |
+---------------+
```

To rewrite this query for older versions of MySQL, put the expression in the output column list and use an alias to sort it:

```
mysql> SELECT CONCAT(first_name,' ',last_name) AS name,
    -> LENGTH(CONCAT(first_name,' ',last_name)) AS len
    -> FROM names
    -> ORDER BY len DESC;
+---------------+------+
| name          | len  |
+---------------+------+
| Rondell White |   13 |
| Kevin Brown   |   11 |
| Devon White   |   11 |
| Vida Blue     |    9 |
| Pete Gray     |    9 |
+---------------+------+
```

Or else refer to the additional output column by position:

```
mysql> SELECT CONCAT(first_name,' ',last_name) AS name,
    -> LENGTH(CONCAT(first_name,' ',last_name)) AS len
    -> FROM names
    -> ORDER BY 2 DESC;
```

```
+---------------+------+
| name          | len  |
+---------------+------+
| Rondell White |   13 |
| Kevin Brown   |   11 |
| Devon White   |   11 |
| Vida Blue     |    9 |
| Pete Gray     |    9 |
+---------------+------+
```

Whichever workaround you use, the output will of course contain a column that's there only for sorting purposes and that you really aren't interested in displaying. If you're running the query from the *mysql* program, that's unfortunate, but there's nothing you can do about the additional output. In your own programs, the extra output column is no problem. It'll be returned in the result set, but you can ignore it. Here's a Python example that demonstrates this. It runs the query, displays the names, and discards the name lengths:

```
cursor = conn.cursor (MySQLdb.cursors.DictCursor)
cursor.execute ("""
        SELECT CONCAT(first_name,' ',last_name) AS full_name,
        LENGTH(CONCAT(first_name,' ',last_name)) AS len
        FROM name
        ORDER BY len DESC
                """)
for row in cursor.fetchall ():
    print row["full_name"]  # print name, ignore length
cursor.close ()
```

6.5   Sorting and NULL Values

Problem

You want to sort a column that may contain NULL values.

Solution

The placement of NULL values in a sorted list has changed over time and depends on your version of MySQL. If NULL values don't come out in the desired position within the sort order, trick them into appearing where you want.

Discussion

When a sorted column contains NULL values, MySQL puts them all together in the sort order. It may seem a bit odd that NULL values are grouped this way, given that (as the following query shows) they are not considered equal in comparisons:

```
mysql> SELECT NULL = NULL;
+-------------+
| NULL = NULL |
+-------------+
|        NULL |
+-------------+
```

On the other hand, NULL values conceptually do seem more similar to each other than to non-NULL values, and there's no good way to distinguish one NULL from another, anyway. However, although NULL values group together, they may be placed at the beginning or end of the sort order, depending on your version of MySQL. Prior to MySQL 4.0.2, NULL values sort to the beginning of the order (or at the end, if you specify DESC). From 4.0.2 on, MySQL sorts NULL values according to the ANSI SQL specification, and thus always places them first in the sort order, regardless of whether or not you specify DESC.

Despite these differences, if you want NULL values at one end or the other of the sort order, you can force them to be placed where you want no matter which version of MySQL you're using. Suppose you have a table t with the following contents:

```
mysql> SELECT val FROM t;
+------+
| val  |
+------+
|    3 |
|  100 |
| NULL |
| NULL |
|    9 |
+------+
```

Normally, sorting puts the NULL values at the beginning:

```
mysql> SELECT val FROM t ORDER BY val;
+------+
| val  |
+------+
| NULL |
| NULL |
|    3 |
|    9 |
|  100 |
+------+
```

To put them at the end instead, introduce an extra ORDER BY column that maps NULL values to a higher value than non-NULL values:

```
mysql> SELECT val FROM t ORDER BY IF(val IS NULL,1,0), val;
+------+
| val  |
+------+
|    3 |
|    9 |
|  100 |
```

```
| NULL |
| NULL |
+------+
```

That works for DESC sorts as well:

```
mysql> SELECT val FROM t ORDER BY IF(val IS NULL,1,0), val DESC;
+------+
| val  |
+------+
|  100 |
|    9 |
|    3 |
| NULL |
| NULL |
+------+
```

If you find MySQL putting NULL values at the end of the sort order and you want them at the beginning, use the same technique, but reverse the second and third arguments of the IF() function to map NULL values to a lower value than non-NULL values:

```
IF(val IS NULL,0,1)
```

6.6   Controlling Case Sensitivity of String Sorts

Problem

String sorts are case sensitive when you don't want them to be, or vice versa.

Solution

Alter the case sensitivity of the sorted values.

Discussion

Chapter 4 discusses the fact that binary strings are case sensitive in comparisons, whereas non-binary strings are not. This property carries over into string sorting as well: ORDER BY produces lexical sorts that are case sensitive for binary strings and not case sensitive for non-binary strings. The following table textblob_val contains a TEXT column tstr and a BLOB column bstr that serve to demonstrate this:

```
mysql> SELECT * FROM textblob_val;
+------+------+
| tstr | bstr |
+------+------+
| aaa  | aaa  |
| AAA  | AAA  |
| bbb  | bbb  |
| BBB  | BBB  |
+------+------+
```

Both columns contain the same values. But they produce different sort results, because TEXT columns are not case sensitive and BLOB columns are:

```
mysql> SELECT tstr FROM textblob_val ORDER BY tstr;
+------+
| tstr |
+------+
| aaa  |
| AAA  |
| bbb  |
| BBB  |
+------+
mysql> SELECT bstr FROM textblob_val ORDER BY bstr;
+------+
| bstr |
+------+
| AAA  |
| BBB  |
| aaa  |
| bbb  |
+------+
```

To control case sensitivity in ORDER BY clauses, use the techniques discussed in Chapter 4 for affecting string comparisons. To perform a case-sensitive sort for strings that are not case sensitive (such as those in the tstr column) cast the sort column to binary-string form using the BINARY keyword:

```
mysql> SELECT tstr FROM textblob_val ORDER BY BINARY tstr;
+------+
| tstr |
+------+
| AAA  |
| BBB  |
| aaa  |
| bbb  |
+------+
```

Another possibility is to convert the output column to binary and sort that:

```
mysql> SELECT BINARY tstr FROM textblob_val ORDER BY 1;
+-------------+
| BINARY tstr |
+-------------+
| AAA         |
| BBB         |
| aaa         |
| bbb         |
+-------------+
```

You can also use the CAST( ) function that is available as of MySQL 4.0.2:

```
mysql> SELECT tstr FROM textblob_val ORDER BY CAST(tstr AS BINARY);
+------+
| tstr |
+------+
| AAA  |
```

```
| BBB |
| aaa |
| bbb |
+------+
```

The complementary operation is to sort binary strings in non–case-sensitive fashion. To do this, convert the values to uppercase or lowercase with UPPER( ) or LOWER( ):

```
mysql> SELECT bstr FROM textblob_val ORDER BY UPPER(bstr);
+------+
| bstr |
+------+
| aaa  |
| AAA  |
| bbb  |
| BBB  |
+------+
```

Alternatively, you can convert the output column and sort that—but doing so affects the displayed values, possibly in an undesirable way:

```
mysql> SELECT UPPER(bstr) FROM textblob_val ORDER BY 1;
+-------------+
| UPPER(bstr) |
+-------------+
| AAA         |
| AAA         |
| BBB         |
| BBB         |
+-------------+
```

6.7   Date-Based Sorting

Problem

You want to sort in temporal order.

Solution

Sort using a date or time column type, ignoring parts of the values that are irrelevant if necessary.

Discussion

Many types of information include date or time information and it's very often necessary to sort results in temporal order. MySQL knows how to sort temporal column types, so there's no special trick to ordering values in DATE, DATETIME, TIME, or TIMESTAMP columns. Begin with a table that contains values for each of those types:

```
mysql> SELECT * FROM temporal_val;
+------------+---------------------+----------+----------------+
| d          | dt                  | t        | ts             |
+------------+---------------------+----------+----------------+
| 1970-01-01 | 1884-01-01 12:00:00 | 13:00:00 | 19800101020000 |
| 1999-01-01 | 1860-01-01 12:00:00 | 19:00:00 | 20210101030000 |
| 1981-01-01 | 1871-01-01 12:00:00 | 03:00:00 | 19750101040000 |
| 1964-01-01 | 1899-01-01 12:00:00 | 01:00:00 | 19850101050000 |
+------------+---------------------+----------+----------------+
```

Using an ORDER BY clause with any of these columns sorts the values into the appropriate order:

```
mysql> SELECT * FROM temporal_val ORDER BY d;
+------------+---------------------+----------+----------------+
| d          | dt                  | t        | ts             |
+------------+---------------------+----------+----------------+
| 1964-01-01 | 1899-01-01 12:00:00 | 01:00:00 | 19850101050000 |
| 1970-01-01 | 1884-01-01 12:00:00 | 13:00:00 | 19800101020000 |
| 1981-01-01 | 1871-01-01 12:00:00 | 03:00:00 | 19750101040000 |
| 1999-01-01 | 1860-01-01 12:00:00 | 19:00:00 | 20210101030000 |
+------------+---------------------+----------+----------------+
mysql> SELECT * FROM temporal_val ORDER BY dt;
+------------+---------------------+----------+----------------+
| d          | dt                  | t        | ts             |
+------------+---------------------+----------+----------------+
| 1999-01-01 | 1860-01-01 12:00:00 | 19:00:00 | 20210101030000 |
| 1981-01-01 | 1871-01-01 12:00:00 | 03:00:00 | 19750101040000 |
| 1970-01-01 | 1884-01-01 12:00:00 | 13:00:00 | 19800101020000 |
| 1964-01-01 | 1899-01-01 12:00:00 | 01:00:00 | 19850101050000 |
+------------+---------------------+----------+----------------+
mysql> SELECT * FROM temporal_val ORDER BY t;
+------------+---------------------+----------+----------------+
| d          | dt                  | t        | ts             |
+------------+---------------------+----------+----------------+
| 1964-01-01 | 1899-01-01 12:00:00 | 01:00:00 | 19850101050000 |
| 1981-01-01 | 1871-01-01 12:00:00 | 03:00:00 | 19750101040000 |
| 1970-01-01 | 1884-01-01 12:00:00 | 13:00:00 | 19800101020000 |
| 1999-01-01 | 1860-01-01 12:00:00 | 19:00:00 | 20210101030000 |
+------------+---------------------+----------+----------------+
mysql> SELECT * FROM temporal_val ORDER BY ts;
+------------+---------------------+----------+----------------+
| d          | dt                  | t        | ts             |
+------------+---------------------+----------+----------------+
| 1981-01-01 | 1871-01-01 12:00:00 | 03:00:00 | 19750101040000 |
| 1970-01-01 | 1884-01-01 12:00:00 | 13:00:00 | 19800101020000 |
| 1964-01-01 | 1899-01-01 12:00:00 | 01:00:00 | 19850101050000 |
| 1999-01-01 | 1860-01-01 12:00:00 | 19:00:00 | 20210101030000 |
+------------+---------------------+----------+----------------+
```

Sometimes a temporal sort uses only part of a date or time column. In that case, you can bust out the part or parts you need and use them to order the results. Some examples of this are given in the next few sections.

6.8   Sorting by Calendar Day

Problem

You want to sort by day of the calendar year.

Solution

Sort using the month and day of a date, ignoring the year.

Discussion

Sorting in calendar order differs from sorting by date. You ignore the year part of the dates and sort using only the month and day to order records in terms of where they fall during the calendar year. Suppose you have an event table that looks like this when values are ordered by actual date of occurrence:

```
mysql> SELECT date, description FROM event ORDER BY date;
+------------+-----------------------------------+
| date       | description                       |
+------------+-----------------------------------+
| 1215-06-15 | Signing of the Magna Carta        |
| 1732-02-22 | George Washington's birthday      |
| 1776-07-14 | Bastille Day                      |
| 1789-07-04 | US Independence Day               |
| 1809-02-12 | Abraham Lincoln's birthday        |
| 1919-06-28 | Signing of the Treaty of Versailles |
| 1944-06-06 | D-Day at Normandy Beaches         |
| 1957-10-04 | Sputnik launch date               |
| 1958-01-31 | Explorer 1 launch date            |
| 1989-11-09 | Opening of the Berlin Wall        |
+------------+-----------------------------------+
```

To put these items in calendar order, sort them by month, then by day within month:

```
mysql> SELECT date, description FROM event
    -> ORDER BY MONTH(date), DAYOFMONTH(date);
+------------+-----------------------------------+
| date       | description                       |
+------------+-----------------------------------+
| 1958-01-31 | Explorer 1 launch date            |
| 1809-02-12 | Abraham Lincoln's birthday        |
| 1732-02-22 | George Washington's birthday      |
| 1944-06-06 | D-Day at Normandy Beaches         |
| 1215-06-15 | Signing of the Magna Carta        |
| 1919-06-28 | Signing of the Treaty of Versailles |
| 1789-07-04 | US Independence Day               |
| 1776-07-14 | Bastille Day                      |
| 1957-10-04 | Sputnik launch date               |
| 1989-11-09 | Opening of the Berlin Wall        |
+------------+-----------------------------------+
```

MySQL also has a DAYOFYEAR( ) function that you might think would be useful for calendar day sorting:

```
mysql> SELECT date, description FROM event ORDER BY DAYOFYEAR(date);
+------------+------------------------------------+
| date       | description                        |
+------------+------------------------------------+
| 1958-01-31 | Explorer 1 launch date             |
| 1809-02-12 | Abraham Lincoln's birthday         |
| 1732-02-22 | George Washington's birthday       |
| 1944-06-06 | D-Day at Normandy Beaches          |
| 1215-06-15 | Signing of the Magna Carta         |
| 1919-06-28 | Signing of the Treaty of Versailles |
| 1789-07-04 | US Independence Day                |
| 1776-07-14 | Bastille Day                       |
| 1957-10-04 | Sputnik launch date                |
| 1989-11-09 | Opening of the Berlin Wall         |
+------------+------------------------------------+
```

That appears to work, but only because the table doesn't have records in it that expose a problem with the use of DAYOFYEAR( ): It can generate the same value for different calendar days. For example, February 29 of leap years and March 1 of non-leap years appear to be the same day:

```
mysql> SELECT DAYOFYEAR('1996-02-29'), DAYOFYEAR('1997-03-01');
+-------------------------+-------------------------+
| DAYOFYEAR('1996-02-29') | DAYOFYEAR('1997-03-01') |
+-------------------------+-------------------------+
|                      60 |                      60 |
+-------------------------+-------------------------+
```

This property means that DAYOFYEAR( ) won't necessarily produce correct results for calendar sorting. It can group dates together that actually occur on different calendar days.

If a table represents dates using separate year, month, and day columns, calendar sorting requires no date-part extraction. Just sort the relevant columns directly. For example, the master ballplayer table from the *baseball1.com* database distribution represents names and birth dates as follows:

```
mysql> SELECT lastname, firstname, birthyear, birthmonth, birthday
    -> FROM master;
+-------------+-----------+-----------+------------+----------+
| lastname    | firstname | birthyear | birthmonth | birthday |
+-------------+-----------+-----------+------------+----------+
| AARON       | HANK      |      1934 |          2 |        5 |
| AARON       | TOMMIE    |      1939 |          8 |        5 |
| AASE        | DON       |      1954 |          9 |        8 |
| ABAD        | ANDY      |      1972 |          8 |       25 |
| ABADIE      | JOHN      |      1854 |         11 |        4 |
| ABBATICCHIO | ED        |      1877 |          4 |       15 |
| ABBEY       | BERT      |      1869 |         11 |       29 |
| ABBEY       | CHARLIE   |      1866 |         10 |       14 |
...
```

To sort those records in calendar order, use the `birthmonth` and `birthday` columns. Of course, that will leave records unsorted within any given day, so you may also want to add additional sort columns. The following query selects players with known birthdays, sorts them by calendar order, and by name for each calendar day:

```
mysql> SELECT lastname, firstname, birthyear, birthmonth, birthday
    -> FROM master
    -> WHERE birthmonth IS NOT NULL AND birthday IS NOT NULL
    -> ORDER BY birthmonth, birthday, lastname, firstname;
+-----------------+--------------+-----------+------------+----------+
| lastname        | firstname    | birthyear | birthmonth | birthday |
+-----------------+--------------+-----------+------------+----------+
| ALLEN           | ETHAN        |      1904 |          1 |        1 |
| BEIRNE          | KEVIN        |      1974 |          1 |        1 |
| BELL            | RUDY         |      1881 |          1 |        1 |
| BERTHRONG       | HARRY        |      1844 |          1 |        1 |
| BETHEA          | BILL         |      1942 |          1 |        1 |
| BISHOP          | CHARLIE      |      1924 |          1 |        1 |
| BOBB            | RANDY        |      1948 |          1 |        1 |
| BRUCKMILLER     | ANDY         |      1882 |          1 |        1 |
...
```

For large datasets, sorting using separate date part columns can be much faster than sorts based on extracting pieces of DATE values. There's no overhead for part extraction, but more important, you can index the date part columns separately—something not possible with a DATE column.

6.9   Sorting by Day of Week

Problem

You want to sort in day-of-week order.

Solution

Use DAYOFWEEK() to convert a date column to its numeric day of week value.

Discussion

Day-of-week sorting is similar to calendar day sorting, except that you use different functions to get at the relevant ordering values.

You can get the day of the week using DAYNAME(), but that produces strings that sort lexically rather than in day-of-week order (Sunday, Monday, Tuesday, etc.). Here the technique of displaying one value but sorting by another is useful (Recipe 6.4).

Display day names using DAYNAME(), but sort in day-of-week order using DAYOFWEEK(), which returns numeric values from 1 to 7 for Sunday through Saturday:

```
mysql> SELECT DAYNAME(date) AS day, date, description
    -> FROM event
    -> ORDER BY DAYOFWEEK(date);
+----------+------------+------------------------------------+
| day      | date       | description                        |
+----------+------------+------------------------------------+
| Sunday   | 1776-07-14 | Bastille Day                       |
| Sunday   | 1809-02-12 | Abraham Lincoln's birthday         |
| Monday   | 1215-06-15 | Signing of the Magna Carta         |
| Tuesday  | 1944-06-06 | D-Day at Normandy Beaches          |
| Thursday | 1989-11-09 | Opening of the Berlin Wall         |
| Friday   | 1957-10-04 | Sputnik launch date                |
| Friday   | 1958-01-31 | Explorer 1 launch date             |
| Friday   | 1732-02-22 | George Washington's birthday       |
| Saturday | 1789-07-04 | US Independence Day                |
| Saturday | 1919-06-28 | Signing of the Treaty of Versailles |
+----------+------------+------------------------------------+
```

If you want to sort in day-of-week order, but treat Monday as the first day of the week and Sunday as the last, you can use a the MOD() function to map Monday to 0, Tuesday to 1, ..., Sunday to 6:

```
mysql> SELECT DAYNAME(date), date, description
    -> FROM event
    -> ORDER BY MOD(DAYOFWEEK(date) + 5, 7);
+---------------+------------+------------------------------------+
| DAYNAME(date) | date       | description                        |
+---------------+------------+------------------------------------+
| Monday        | 1215-06-15 | Signing of the Magna Carta         |
| Tuesday       | 1944-06-06 | D-Day at Normandy Beaches          |
| Thursday      | 1989-11-09 | Opening of the Berlin Wall         |
| Friday        | 1957-10-04 | Sputnik launch date                |
| Friday        | 1958-01-31 | Explorer 1 launch date             |
| Friday        | 1732-02-22 | George Washington's birthday       |
| Saturday      | 1789-07-04 | US Independence Day                |
| Saturday      | 1919-06-28 | Signing of the Treaty of Versailles |
| Sunday        | 1776-07-14 | Bastille Day                       |
| Sunday        | 1809-02-12 | Abraham Lincoln's birthday         |
+---------------+------------+------------------------------------+
```

The following table shows the DAYOFWEEK() expressions to use for putting any day of the week first in the sort order:

Day to list first	DAYOFWEEK() expression
Sunday	DAYOFWEEK(date)
Monday	MOD(DAYOFWEEK(date) + 5, 7)
Tuesday	MOD(DAYOFWEEK(date) + 4, 7)

Day to list first	DAYOFWEEK() expression
Wednesday	MOD(DAYOFWEEK(date) + 3, 7)
Thursday	MOD(DAYOFWEEK(date) + 2, 7)
Friday	MOD(DAYOFWEEK(date) + 1, 7)
Saturday	MOD(DAYOFWEEK(date) + 0, 7)

Another function that you can use for day-of-week sorting is WEEKDAY(), although it returns a different set of values (0 for Monday through 6 for Sunday).

6.10   Sorting by Time of Day

Problem

You want to sort in time-of-day order.

Solution

Pull out the hour, minute, and second from the column that contains the time, and use them for sorting.

Discussion

Time-of-day sorting can be done different ways, depending on your column type. If the values are stored in a TIME column, just sort them directly. To put DATETIME or TIMESTAMP values in time-of-day order, extract the time parts and sort them. For example, the mail table contains DATETIME values, which can be sorted by time of day like this:

```
mysql> SELECT * FROM mail ORDER BY HOUR(t), MINUTE(t), SECOND(t);
+---------------------+---------+---------+---------+---------+--------+
| t                   | srcuser | srchost | dstuser | dsthost | size   |
+---------------------+---------+---------+---------+---------+--------+
| 2001-05-15 07:17:48 | gene    | mars    | gene    | saturn  |   3824 |
| 2001-05-15 08:50:57 | phil    | venus   | phil    | venus   |    978 |
| 2001-05-16 09:00:28 | gene    | venus   | barb    | mars    |    613 |
| 2001-05-14 09:31:37 | gene    | venus   | barb    | mars    |   2291 |
| 2001-05-11 10:15:08 | barb    | saturn  | tricia  | mars    |  58274 |
| 2001-05-15 10:25:52 | gene    | mars    | tricia  | saturn  | 998532 |
| 2001-05-14 11:52:17 | phil    | mars    | tricia  | saturn  |   5781 |
| 2001-05-12 12:48:13 | tricia  | mars    | gene    | venus   | 194925 |
...
```

You can also use TIME_TO_SEC( ), which strips off the date part and returns the time part as the corresponding number of seconds:

```
mysql> SELECT * FROM mail ORDER BY TIME_TO_SEC(t);
+---------------------+---------+---------+---------+---------+---------+
| t                   | srcuser | srchost | dstuser | dsthost | size    |
+---------------------+---------+---------+---------+---------+---------+
| 2001-05-15 07:17:48 | gene    | mars    | gene    | saturn  |    3824 |
| 2001-05-15 08:50:57 | phil    | venus   | phil    | venus   |     978 |
| 2001-05-16 09:00:28 | gene    | venus   | barb    | mars    |     613 |
| 2001-05-14 09:31:37 | gene    | venus   | barb    | mars    |    2291 |
| 2001-05-11 10:15:08 | barb    | saturn  | tricia  | mars    |   58274 |
| 2001-05-15 10:25:52 | gene    | mars    | tricia  | saturn  |  998532 |
| 2001-05-14 11:52:17 | phil    | mars    | tricia  | saturn  |    5781 |
| 2001-05-12 12:48:13 | tricia  | mars    | gene    | venus   |  194925 |
...
```

6.11   Sorting Using Substrings of Column Values

Problem

You want to sort a set of values using one or more substrings of each value.

Solution

Extract the hunks you want and sort them separately.

Discussion

This is an application of sorting by expression value (Recipe 6.3). If you want to sort records using just a particular portion of a column's values, extract the substring you need and use it in the ORDER BY clause. This is easiest if the substrings are at a fixed position and length within the column. For substrings of variable position or length, you may still be able to use them for sorting if there is some reliable way to identify them. The next several recipes show how to use substring-extraction to produce specialized sort orders.

6.12   Sorting by Fixed-Length Substrings

Problem

You want to sort using parts of a column that occur at a given position within the column.

Solution

Pull out the parts you need with LEFT( ), MID( ), or RIGHT( ) and sort them.

Discussion

Suppose you have a housewares table that acts as a catalog for houseware furnishings, and that items are identified by 11-character ID values consisting of three subparts: a three-character category abbreviation (such as DIN for "dining room" or KIT for "kitchen"), a five-digit serial number, and a two-character country code indicating where the part is manufactured:

```
mysql> SELECT * FROM housewares;
+------------+------------------+
| id         | description      |
+------------+------------------+
| DIN40672US | dining table     |
| KIT00372UK | garbage disposal |
| KIT01729JP | microwave oven   |
| BED00038SG | bedside lamp     |
| BTH00485US | shower stall     |
| BTH00415JP | lavatory         |
+------------+------------------+
```

This is not necessarily a good way to store complex ID values, and later we'll consider how to represent them using separate columns (Recipe 11.13). But for now, assume that the values must be stored as just shown.

If you want to sort records from this table based on the id values, you'd just use the entire column value:

```
mysql> SELECT * FROM housewares ORDER BY id;
+------------+------------------+
| id         | description      |
+------------+------------------+
| BED00038SG | bedside lamp     |
| BTH00415JP | lavatory         |
| BTH00485US | shower stall     |
| DIN40672US | dining table     |
| KIT00372UK | garbage disposal |
| KIT01729JP | microwave oven   |
+------------+------------------+
```

But you might also have a need to sort on any of the three subparts (for example, to sort by country of manufacture). For that kind of operation, it's helpful to use functions that pull out pieces of a column, such as LEFT( ), MID( ), and RIGHT( ). These functions can be used to break apart the id values into their three components:

```
mysql> SELECT id,
    -> LEFT(id,3) AS category,
    -> MID(id,4,5) AS serial,
    -> RIGHT(id,2) AS country
    -> FROM housewares;
```

```
+------------+----------+--------+---------+
| id         | category | serial | country |
+------------+----------+--------+---------+
| DIN40672US | DIN      | 40672  | US      |
| KIT00372UK | KIT      | 00372  | UK      |
| KIT01729JP | KIT      | 01729  | JP      |
| BED00038SG | BED      | 00038  | SG      |
| BTH00485US | BTH      | 00485  | US      |
| BTH00415JP | BTH      | 00415  | JP      |
+------------+----------+--------+---------+
```

Any of those fixed-length substrings of the id values can be used for sorting, either alone or in combination. To sort by product category, extract the category value and use it in the ORDER BY clause:

```
mysql> SELECT * FROM housewares ORDER BY LEFT(id,3);
+------------+------------------+
| id         | description      |
+------------+------------------+
| BED00038SG | bedside lamp     |
| BTH00485US | shower stall     |
| BTH00415JP | lavatory         |
| DIN40672US | dining table     |
| KIT00372UK | garbage disposal |
| KIT01729JP | microwave oven   |
+------------+------------------+
```

To sort rows by product serial number, use MID( ) to extract the middle five characters from the id values, beginning with the fourth:

```
mysql> SELECT * FROM housewares ORDER BY MID(id,4,5);
+------------+------------------+
| id         | description      |
+------------+------------------+
| BED00038SG | bedside lamp     |
| KIT00372UK | garbage disposal |
| BTH00415JP | lavatory         |
| BTH00485US | shower stall     |
| KIT01729JP | microwave oven   |
| DIN40672US | dining table     |
+------------+------------------+
```

This appears to be a numeric sort, but it's actually a string sort, because MID( ) returns strings. It just so happens that the lexical and numeric sort order are the same in this case due to the fact that the "numbers" have leading zeros to make them all the same length.

To sort by country code, use the rightmost two characters of the id values:

```
mysql> SELECT * FROM housewares ORDER BY RIGHT(id,2);
+------------+------------------+
| id         | description      |
+------------+------------------+
| KIT01729JP | microwave oven   |
| BTH00415JP | lavatory         |
| BED00038SG | bedside lamp     |
```

```
| KIT00372UK | garbage disposal |
| DIN40672US | dining table     |
| BTH00485US | shower stall     |
+------------+------------------+
```

You can also sort using combinations of substrings. For example, to sort by country code and serial number, the query looks like this:

```
mysql> SELECT * FROM housewares ORDER BY RIGHT(id,2), MID(id,4,5);
+------------+------------------+
| id         | description      |
+------------+------------------+
| BTH00415JP | lavatory         |
| KIT01729JP | microwave oven   |
| BED00038SG | bedside lamp     |
| KIT00372UK | garbage disposal |
| BTH00485US | shower stall     |
| DIN40672US | dining table     |
+------------+------------------+
```

6.13 Sorting by Variable-Length Substrings

Problem

You want to sort using parts of a column that do *not* occur at a given position within the column.

Solution

Figure out some way to identify the parts you need so you can extract them; otherwise, you're out of luck.

Discussion

If the substrings that you want to use for sorting vary in length, you need a reliable means of extracting just the part of the column values that you want. To see how this works, create a housewares2 table that is like the housewares table used in the previous section, except that it has no leading zeros in the serial number part of the id values:

```
mysql> SELECT * FROM housewares2;
+------------+------------------+
| id         | description      |
+------------+------------------+
| DIN40672US | dining table     |
| KIT372UK   | garbage disposal |
| KIT1729JP  | microwave oven   |
| BED38SG    | bedside lamp     |
| BTH485US   | shower stall     |
| BTH415JP   | lavatory         |
+------------+------------------+
```

The category and country parts of the id values can be extracted and sorted using LEFT() and RIGHT(), just as for the housewares table. But now the numeric segments of the values have different lengths and cannot be extracted and sorted using a simple MID() call. Instead, use SUBSTRING() to skip over the first three characters and return the remainder beginning with the fourth character (the first digit):

```
mysql> SELECT id, SUBSTRING(id,4) FROM housewares2;
+------------+-----------------+
| id         | SUBSTRING(id,4) |
+------------+-----------------+
| DIN40672US | 40672US         |
| KIT372UK   | 372UK           |
| KIT1729JP  | 1729JP          |
| BED38SG    | 38SG            |
| BTH485US   | 485US           |
| BTH415JP   | 415JP           |
+------------+-----------------+
```

Then take everything but the rightmost two columns. One way to do this is as follows:

```
mysql> SELECT id, LEFT(SUBSTRING(id,4),LENGTH(SUBSTRING(id,4)-2))
    -> FROM housewares2;
+------------+-----------------------------------------------+
| id         | LEFT(SUBSTRING(id,4),LENGTH(SUBSTRING(id,4)-2)) |
+------------+-----------------------------------------------+
| DIN40672US | 40672                                         |
| KIT372UK   | 372                                           |
| KIT1729JP  | 1729                                          |
| BED38SG    | 38                                            |
| BTH485US   | 485                                           |
| BTH415JP   | 415                                           |
+------------+-----------------------------------------------+
```

But that's more complex than necessary. The SUBSTRING() function takes an optional third argument specifying a desired result length, and we know that the length of the middle part is equal to the length of the string minus five (three for the characters at the beginning and two for the characters at the end). The following query demonstrates how to get the numeric middle part by beginning with the ID, then stripping off the rightmost suffix:

```
mysql> SELECT id, SUBSTRING(id,4), SUBSTRING(id,4,LENGTH(id)-5)
    -> FROM housewares2;
+------------+-----------------+------------------------------+
| id         | SUBSTRING(id,4) | SUBSTRING(id,4,LENGTH(id)-5) |
+------------+-----------------+------------------------------+
| DIN40672US | 40672US         | 40672                        |
| KIT372UK   | 372UK           | 372                          |
| KIT1729JP  | 1729JP          | 1729                         |
| BED38SG    | 38SG            | 38                           |
| BTH485US   | 485US           | 485                          |
| BTH415JP   | 415JP           | 415                          |
+------------+-----------------+------------------------------+
```

Unfortunately, although the final expression correctly extracts the numeric part from the IDs, the resulting values are strings. Consequently, they sort lexically rather than numerically:

```
mysql> SELECT * FROM housewares2
    -> ORDER BY SUBSTRING(id,4,LENGTH(id)-5);
+-----------+-----------------+
| id        | description     |
+-----------+-----------------+
| KIT1729JP | microwave oven  |
| KIT372UK  | garbage disposal|
| BED38SG   | bedside lamp    |
| DIN40672US| dining table    |
| BTH415JP  | lavatory        |
| BTH485US  | shower stall    |
+-----------+-----------------+
```

How to deal with that? One way is to add zero, which tells MySQL to perform a string-to-number conversion that results in a numeric sort of the serial number values:

```
mysql> SELECT * FROM housewares2
    -> ORDER BY SUBSTRING(id,4,LENGTH(id)-5)+0;
+-----------+-----------------+
| id        | description     |
+-----------+-----------------+
| BED38SG   | bedside lamp    |
| KIT372UK  | garbage disposal|
| BTH415JP  | lavatory        |
| BTH485US  | shower stall    |
| KIT1729JP | microwave oven  |
| DIN40672US| dining table    |
+-----------+-----------------+
```

But in this particular case, a simpler solution is possible. It's not necessary to calculate the length of the numeric part of the string, because the string-to-number conversion operation will strip off trailing non-numeric suffixes and provide the values needed to sort on the variable-length serial number portion of the id values. That means the third argument to SUBSTRING() actually isn't needed:

```
mysql> SELECT * FROM housewares2
    -> ORDER BY SUBSTRING(id,4)+0;
+-----------+-----------------+
| id        | description     |
+-----------+-----------------+
| BED38SG   | bedside lamp    |
| KIT372UK  | garbage disposal|
| BTH415JP  | lavatory        |
| BTH485US  | shower stall    |
| KIT1729JP | microwave oven  |
| DIN40672US| dining table    |
+-----------+-----------------+
```

In the preceding example, the ability to extract variable-length substrings was based on the different kinds of characters in the middle of the ID values, compared to the characters on the ends (that is, digits versus non-digits). In other cases, you may be able to use delimiter characters to pull apart column values. For the next examples, assume a housewares3 table with id values that look like this:

```
mysql> SELECT * FROM housewares3;
+---------------+-----------------+
| id            | description     |
+---------------+-----------------+
| 13-478-92-2   | dining table    |
| 873-48-649-63 | garbage disposal|
| 8-4-2-1       | microwave oven  |
| 97-681-37-66  | bedside lamp    |
| 27-48-534-2   | shower stall    |
| 5764-56-89-72 | lavatory        |
+---------------+-----------------+
```

To extract segments from these values, use SUBSTRING_INDEX(str,c,n). It searches into a string str for the n-th occurrence of a given character c and returns everything to the left of that character. For example, the following call returns 13-478:

```
SUBSTRING_INDEX('13-478-92-2','-',2)
```

If n is negative, the search for c proceeds from the right and returns the rightmost string. This call returns 478-92-2:

```
SUBSTRING_INDEX('13-478-92-2','-',-3)
```

By combining SUBSTRING_INDEX( ) calls with positive and negative indexes, it's possible to extract successive pieces from each id value. One way is to extract the first n segments of the value, then pull off the rightmost one. By varying n from 1 to 4, we get the successive segments from left to right:

```
SUBSTRING_INDEX(SUBSTRING_INDEX(id,'-',1),'-',-1)
SUBSTRING_INDEX(SUBSTRING_INDEX(id,'-',2),'-',-1)
SUBSTRING_INDEX(SUBSTRING_INDEX(id,'-',3),'-',-1)
SUBSTRING_INDEX(SUBSTRING_INDEX(id,'-',4),'-',-1)
```

The first of those expressions can be optimized, because the inner SUBSTRING_INDEX( ) call returns a single-segment string and is sufficient by itself to return the leftmost id segment:

```
SUBSTRING_INDEX(id,'-',1)
```

Another way to obtain substrings is to extract the rightmost n segments of the value, then pull off the first one. Here we vary n from −4 to −1:

```
SUBSTRING_INDEX(SUBSTRING_INDEX(id,'-',-4),'-',1)
SUBSTRING_INDEX(SUBSTRING_INDEX(id,'-',-3),'-',1)
SUBSTRING_INDEX(SUBSTRING_INDEX(id,'-',-2),'-',1)
SUBSTRING_INDEX(SUBSTRING_INDEX(id,'-',-1),'-',1)
```

Again, an optimization is possible. For the fourth expression, the inner SUBSTRING_INDEX( ) call is sufficient to return the final substring:

```
SUBSTRING_INDEX(id,'-',-1)
```

These expressions can be difficult to read and understand, and you probably should try experimenting with a few of them to see how they work. Here is an example that shows how to get the second and fourth segments from the id values:

```
mysql> SELECT
    -> id,
    -> SUBSTRING_INDEX(SUBSTRING_INDEX(id,'-',2),'-',-1) AS segment2,
    -> SUBSTRING_INDEX(SUBSTRING_INDEX(id,'-',4),'-',-1) AS segment4
    -> FROM housewares3;
+---------------+----------+----------+
| id            | segment2 | segment4 |
+---------------+----------+----------+
| 13-478-92-2   | 478      | 2        |
| 873-48-649-63 | 48       | 63       |
| 8-4-2-1       | 4        | 1        |
| 97-681-37-66  | 681      | 66       |
| 27-48-534-2   | 48       | 2        |
| 5764-56-89-72 | 56       | 72       |
+---------------+----------+----------+
```

To use the substrings for sorting, use the appropriate expressions in the ORDER BY clause. (Remember to force a string-to-number conversion by adding zero if you want the sort to be numeric rather than lexical.) The following two queries order the results based on the second id segment. The first sorts lexically, the second numerically:

```
mysql> SELECT * FROM housewares3
    -> ORDER BY SUBSTRING_INDEX(SUBSTRING_INDEX(id,'-',2),'-',-1);
+---------------+------------------+
| id            | description      |
+---------------+------------------+
| 8-4-2-1       | microwave oven   |
| 13-478-92-2   | dining table     |
| 873-48-649-63 | garbage disposal |
| 27-48-534-2   | shower stall     |
| 5764-56-89-72 | lavatory         |
| 97-681-37-66  | bedside lamp     |
+---------------+------------------+
mysql> SELECT * FROM housewares3
    -> ORDER BY SUBSTRING_INDEX(SUBSTRING_INDEX(id,'-',2),'-',-1)+0;
+---------------+------------------+
| id            | description      |
+---------------+------------------+
| 8-4-2-1       | microwave oven   |
| 873-48-649-63 | garbage disposal |
| 27-48-534-2   | shower stall     |
| 5764-56-89-72 | lavatory         |
| 13-478-92-2   | dining table     |
| 97-681-37-66  | bedside lamp     |
+---------------+------------------+
```

The substring-extraction expressions here are messy, but at least the column values to which we're applying them have a consistent number of segments. To sort values that have varying numbers of segments, the job can be more difficult. The next section shows an example illustrating why that is.

6.14   Sorting Hostnames in Domain Order

Problem

You want to sort hostnames in domain order, with the rightmost parts of the names more significant than the leftmost parts.

Solution

Break apart the names and sort the pieces from right to left.

Discussion

Hostnames are strings and therefore their natural sort order is lexical. However, it's often desirable to sort hostnames in domain order, where the rightmost segments of the hostname values are more significant than the leftmost segments. Suppose you have a table hostname that contains the following names:

```
mysql> SELECT name FROM hostname ORDER BY name;
+--------------------+
| name               |
+--------------------+
| cvs.php.net        |
| dbi.perl.org       |
| jakarta.apache.org |
| lists.mysql.com    |
| mysql.com          |
| www.kitebird.com   |
+--------------------+
```

The preceding query demonstrates the natural lexical sort order of the name values. That differs from domain order, as shown by the following table:

Lexical order	Domain order
cvs.php.net	www.kitebird.com
dbi.perl.org	mysql.com
jakarta.apache.org	lists.mysql.com
lists.mysql.com	cvs.php.net
mysql.com	jakarta.apache.org
www.kitebird.com	dbi.perl.org

Producing domain-ordered output is a substring-sorting problem, where it's necessary to extract each segment of the names so they can be sorted in right-to-left fashion. There is also an additional complication if your values contain different numbers of segments, as our example hostnames do. (Most of them have three segments, but mysql.com has only two.)

To extract the pieces of the hostnames, begin by using SUBSTRING_INDEX() in a manner similar to that described previously in Recipe 6.13. The hostname values have a maximum of three segments, from which the pieces can be extracted left to right like this:

```
SUBSTRING_INDEX(SUBSTRING_INDEX(name,'.',-3),'.',1)
SUBSTRING_INDEX(SUBSTRING_INDEX(name,'.',-2),'.',1)
SUBSTRING_INDEX(name,'.',-1)
```

These expressions work properly as long as all the hostnames have three components. But if a name has fewer than three, we don't get the correct result, as the following query demonstrates:

```
mysql> SELECT name,
    -> SUBSTRING_INDEX(SUBSTRING_INDEX(name,'.',-3),'.',1) AS leftmost,
    -> SUBSTRING_INDEX(SUBSTRING_INDEX(name,'.',-2),'.',1) AS middle,
    -> SUBSTRING_INDEX(name,'.',-1) AS rightmost
    -> FROM hostname;
+--------------------+----------+----------+-----------+
| name               | leftmost | middle   | rightmost |
+--------------------+----------+----------+-----------+
| cvs.php.net        | cvs      | php      | net       |
| dbi.perl.org       | dbi      | perl     | org       |
| lists.mysql.com    | lists    | mysql    | com       |
| mysql.com          | mysql    | mysql    | com       |
| jakarta.apache.org | jakarta  | apache   | org       |
| www.kitebird.com   | www      | kitebird | com       |
+--------------------+----------+----------+-----------+
```

Notice the output for the mysql.com row; it has mysql for the value of the leftmost column, where it should have an empty string. The segment-extraction expressions work by pulling off the rightmost n segments, then returning the leftmost segment of the result. The source of the problem for mysql.com is that if there aren't n segments, the expression simply returns the leftmost segment of however many there are. To fix this problem, prepend a sufficient number of periods to the hostname values to guarantee that they have the requisite number of segments:

```
mysql> SELECT name,
    -> SUBSTRING_INDEX(SUBSTRING_INDEX(CONCAT('..',name),'.',-3),'.',1)
    -> AS leftmost,
    -> SUBSTRING_INDEX(SUBSTRING_INDEX(CONCAT('.',name),'.',-2),'.',1)
    -> AS middle,
    -> SUBSTRING_INDEX(name,'.',-1) AS rightmost
    -> FROM hostname;
```

```
+---------------------+----------+----------+-----------+
| name                | leftmost | middle   | rightmost |
+---------------------+----------+----------+-----------+
| cvs.php.net         | cvs      | php      | net       |
| dbi.perl.org        | dbi      | perl     | org       |
| lists.mysql.com     | lists    | mysql    | com       |
| mysql.com           |          | mysql    | com       |
| jakarta.apache.org  | jakarta  | apache   | org       |
| www.kitebird.com    | www      | kitebird | com       |
+---------------------+----------+----------+-----------+
```

That's pretty ugly. But these expressions do serve to extract the substrings that are
needed for sorting hostname values correctly in right-to-left fashion:

```
mysql> SELECT name FROM hostname
    -> ORDER BY
    -> SUBSTRING_INDEX(name,'.',-1),
    -> SUBSTRING_INDEX(SUBSTRING_INDEX(CONCAT('.',name),'.',-2),'.',1),
    -> SUBSTRING_INDEX(SUBSTRING_INDEX(CONCAT('..',name),'.',-3),'.',1);
+---------------------+
| name                |
+---------------------+
| www.kitebird.com    |
| mysql.com           |
| lists.mysql.com     |
| cvs.php.net         |
| jakarta.apache.org  |
| dbi.perl.org        |
+---------------------+
```

If you had hostnames with a maximum of four segments rather than three, you'd
need to add to the ORDER BY clause another SUBSTRING_INDEX() expression that
prepends three dots to the hostname values.

6.15 Sorting Dotted-Quad IP Values in Numeric Order

Problem

You want to sort strings that represent IP numbers in numeric order.

Solution

Break apart the strings and sort the pieces numerically. Or just use INET_ATON().

Discussion

If a table contains IP numbers represented as strings in dotted-quad notation (for
example, 111.122.133.144), they'll sort lexically rather than numerically. To produce

a numeric ordering instead, you can sort them as four-part values with each part sorted numerically. To accomplish this, use a technique similar to that for sorting hostnames, but with the following differences:

- Dotted quads always have four segments, so there's no need to prepend dots to the value before extracting substrings.

- Dotted quads sort left to right, so the order in which substrings are used in the ORDER BY clause is opposite to that used for hostname sorting.

- The segments of dotted-quad values are numbers, so add zero to each substring to tell MySQL to using a numeric sort rather than a lexical one.

Suppose you have a hostip table with a string-valued ip column containing IP numbers:

```
mysql> SELECT ip FROM hostip ORDER BY ip;
+-----------------+
| ip              |
+-----------------+
| 127.0.0.1       |
| 192.168.0.10    |
| 192.168.0.2     |
| 192.168.1.10    |
| 192.168.1.2     |
| 21.0.0.1        |
| 255.255.255.255 |
+-----------------+
```

The preceding query produces output sorted in lexical order. To sort the ip values numerically, you can extract each segment and add zero to convert it to a number using an ORDER BY clause like this:

```
mysql> SELECT ip FROM hostip
    -> ORDER BY
    -> SUBSTRING_INDEX(ip,'.',1)+0,
    -> SUBSTRING_INDEX(SUBSTRING_INDEX(ip,'.',-3),'.',1)+0,
    -> SUBSTRING_INDEX(SUBSTRING_INDEX(ip,'.',-2),'.',1)+0,
    -> SUBSTRING_INDEX(ip,'.',-1)+0;
+-----------------+
| ip              |
+-----------------+
| 21.0.0.1        |
| 127.0.0.1       |
| 192.168.0.2     |
| 192.168.0.10    |
| 192.168.1.2     |
| 192.168.1.10    |
| 255.255.255.255 |
+-----------------+
```

A simpler solution is possible if you have MySQL 3.23.15 or higher. Then you can sort the IP values using the INET_ATON() function, which converts a network address directly to its underlying numeric form:

```
mysql> SELECT ip FROM hostip ORDER BY INET_ATON(ip);
+-----------------+
| ip              |
+-----------------+
| 21.0.0.1        |
| 127.0.0.1       |
| 192.168.0.2     |
| 192.168.0.10    |
| 192.168.1.2     |
| 192.168.1.10    |
| 255.255.255.255 |
+-----------------+
```

If you're tempted to sort by simply adding zero to the ip value and using ORDER BY on the result, consider the values that kind of string-to-number conversion actually will produce:

```
mysql> SELECT ip, ip+0 FROM hostip;
+-----------------+---------+
| ip              | ip+0    |
+-----------------+---------+
| 127.0.0.1       |     127 |
| 192.168.0.2     | 192.168 |
| 192.168.0.10    | 192.168 |
| 192.168.1.2     | 192.168 |
| 192.168.1.10    | 192.168 |
| 255.255.255.255 | 255.255 |
| 21.0.0.1        |      21 |
+-----------------+---------+
```

The conversion retains only as much of each value as can be interpreted as a valid number. The remainder would be unavailable for sorting purposes, each though it's necessary to produce a correct ordering.

6.16   Floating Specific Values to the Head or Tail of the Sort Order

Problem

You want a column to sort the way it normally does, except for a few values that you want at a specific spot.

Solution

Add another sort column to the ORDER BY clause that places those few values where you want them. The remaining sort columns will have their usual effect for the other values.

Discussion

If you want to sort a result set normally *except* that you want particular values first, create an additional sort column that is 0 for those values and 1 for everything else. We used this technique earlier to float NULL values to the high end of the sort order (see Recipe 6.5), but it works for other types of information as well. Suppose you want to sort mail table messages in sender/recipient order, with the exception that you want to put messages for phil first. You can do that like this:

```
mysql> SELECT t, srcuser, dstuser, size
    -> FROM mail
    -> ORDER BY IF(srcuser='phil',0,1), srcuser, dstuser;
+---------------------+---------+---------+---------+
| t                   | srcuser | dstuser | size    |
+---------------------+---------+---------+---------+
| 2001-05-16 23:04:19 | phil    | barb    |   10294 |
| 2001-05-12 15:02:49 | phil    | phil    |    1048 |
| 2001-05-15 08:50:57 | phil    | phil    |     978 |
| 2001-05-14 11:52:17 | phil    | tricia  |    5781 |
| 2001-05-17 12:49:23 | phil    | tricia  |     873 |
| 2001-05-14 14:42:21 | barb    | barb    |   98151 |
| 2001-05-11 10:15:08 | barb    | tricia  |   58274 |
| 2001-05-13 13:59:18 | barb    | tricia  |     271 |
| 2001-05-14 09:31:37 | gene    | barb    |    2291 |
| 2001-05-16 09:00:28 | gene    | barb    |     613 |
| 2001-05-15 07:17:48 | gene    | gene    |    3824 |
| 2001-05-15 17:35:31 | gene    | gene    |    3856 |
| 2001-05-19 22:21:51 | gene    | gene    |   23992 |
| 2001-05-15 10:25:52 | gene    | tricia  |  998532 |
| 2001-05-12 12:48:13 | tricia  | gene    |  194925 |
| 2001-05-14 17:03:01 | tricia  | phil    | 2394482 |
+---------------------+---------+---------+---------+
```

The value of the extra sort column is 0 for rows where the srcuser value is phil, and 1 for all other rows. By making that the most significant sort column, records for messages sent by phil float to the top of the output. (To sink them to the bottom instead, either sort the column in reverse order using DESC, or reverse the order of the second and third arguments of the IF() function.)

You can also use this technique for particular conditions, not just specific values. To put first those records where people sent messages to themselves, do this:

```
mysql> SELECT t, srcuser, dstuser, size
    -> FROM mail
    -> ORDER BY IF(srcuser=dstuser,0,1), srcuser, dstuser;
```

```
+---------------------+---------+---------+---------+
| t                   | srcuser | dstuser | size    |
+---------------------+---------+---------+---------+
| 2001-05-14 14:42:21 | barb    | barb    |   98151 |
| 2001-05-15 07:17:48 | gene    | gene    |    3824 |
| 2001-05-15 17:35:31 | gene    | gene    |    3856 |
| 2001-05-19 22:21:51 | gene    | gene    |   23992 |
| 2001-05-12 15:02:49 | phil    | phil    |    1048 |
| 2001-05-15 08:50:57 | phil    | phil    |     978 |
| 2001-05-11 10:15:08 | barb    | tricia  |   58274 |
| 2001-05-13 13:59:18 | barb    | tricia  |     271 |
| 2001-05-14 09:31:37 | gene    | barb    |    2291 |
| 2001-05-16 09:00:28 | gene    | barb    |     613 |
| 2001-05-15 10:25:52 | gene    | tricia  |  998532 |
| 2001-05-16 23:04:19 | phil    | barb    |   10294 |
| 2001-05-14 11:52:17 | phil    | tricia  |    5781 |
| 2001-05-17 12:49:23 | phil    | tricia  |     873 |
| 2001-05-12 12:48:13 | tricia  | gene    |  194925 |
| 2001-05-14 17:03:01 | tricia  | phil    | 2394482 |
+---------------------+---------+---------+---------+
```

If you have a pretty good idea about the contents of your table, you can sometimes eliminate the extra sort column. For example, srcuser is never NULL in the mail table, so the previous query can be rewritten as follows to use one less column in the ORDER BY clause (assuming that NULL values sort ahead of all non-NULL values):

```
mysql> SELECT t, srcuser, dstuser, size
    -> FROM mail
    -> ORDER BY IF(srcuser=dstuser,NULL,srcuser), dstuser;
+---------------------+---------+---------+---------+
| t                   | srcuser | dstuser | size    |
+---------------------+---------+---------+---------+
| 2001-05-14 14:42:21 | barb    | barb    |   98151 |
| 2001-05-15 07:17:48 | gene    | gene    |    3824 |
| 2001-05-15 17:35:31 | gene    | gene    |    3856 |
| 2001-05-19 22:21:51 | gene    | gene    |   23992 |
| 2001-05-12 15:02:49 | phil    | phil    |    1048 |
| 2001-05-15 08:50:57 | phil    | phil    |     978 |
| 2001-05-11 10:15:08 | barb    | tricia  |   58274 |
| 2001-05-13 13:59:18 | barb    | tricia  |     271 |
| 2001-05-14 09:31:37 | gene    | barb    |    2291 |
| 2001-05-16 09:00:28 | gene    | barb    |     613 |
| 2001-05-15 10:25:52 | gene    | tricia  |  998532 |
| 2001-05-16 23:04:19 | phil    | barb    |   10294 |
| 2001-05-14 11:52:17 | phil    | tricia  |    5781 |
| 2001-05-17 12:49:23 | phil    | tricia  |     873 |
| 2001-05-12 12:48:13 | tricia  | gene    |  194925 |
| 2001-05-14 17:03:01 | tricia  | phil    | 2394482 |
+---------------------+---------+---------+---------+
```

6.17 Sorting in User-Defined Orders

Problem

You want to define the sort order for all values in a column.

Solution

Use FIELD() to map column values onto a sequence that places the values in the desired order.

Discussion

The previous section showed how to make a specific group of rows go to the head of the sort order. If you want to impose a specific order on *all* values in a column, use the FIELD() function to map them to a list of numeric values and use the numbers for sorting. FIELD() compares its first argument to the following arguments and returns a number indicating which one of them it matches. The following FIELD() call compares *value* to *str1*, *str2*, *str3*, and *str4*, and returns 1, 2, 3, or 4, depending on which one of them *value* is equal to:

    FIELD(value,str1,str2,str3,str4)

The number of comparison values need not be four; FIELD() takes a variable-length argument list. If *value* is NULL or none of the values match, FIELD() returns 0.

FIELD() can be used to sort an arbitrary set of values into any order you please. For example, to display driver_log records for Henry, Suzi, and Ben, in that order, do this:

```
mysql> SELECT * FROM driver_log
    -> ORDER BY FIELD(name,'Henry','Suzi','Ben');
+--------+-------+------------+-------+
| rec_id | name  | trav_date  | miles |
+--------+-------+------------+-------+
|      3 | Henry | 2001-11-29 |   300 |
|      4 | Henry | 2001-11-27 |    96 |
|      6 | Henry | 2001-11-26 |   115 |
|      8 | Henry | 2001-12-01 |   197 |
|     10 | Henry | 2001-11-30 |   203 |
|      2 | Suzi  | 2001-11-29 |   391 |
|      7 | Suzi  | 2001-12-02 |   502 |
|      1 | Ben   | 2001-11-30 |   152 |
|      5 | Ben   | 2001-11-29 |   131 |
|      9 | Ben   | 2001-12-02 |    79 |
+--------+-------+------------+-------+
```

You can use `FIELD()` with column substrings, too. To sort items from the housewares table by country of manufacture using the order US, UK, JP, SG, do this:

```
mysql> SELECT id, description FROM housewares
    -> ORDER BY FIELD(RIGHT(id,2),'US','UK','JP','SG');
+------------+-----------------+
| id         | description     |
+------------+-----------------+
| DIN40672US | dining table    |
| BTH00485US | shower stall    |
| KIT00372UK | garbage disposal |
| KIT01729JP | microwave oven  |
| BTH00415JP | lavatory        |
| BED00038SG | bedside lamp    |
+------------+-----------------+
```

More generally, `FIELD()` can be used to sort any kind of category-based values into specific orders when the categories don't sort naturally into any useful sequence.

6.18   Sorting ENUM Values

Problem

ENUM values don't sort like other string columns.

Solution

Learn how they work, and exploit those properties to your own advantage.

Discussion

ENUM is considered a string column type, but ENUM values have the special property that they are stored numerically with values ordered the same way they are listed in the table definition. These numeric values affect how enumerations are sorted, which can be very useful. Suppose you have a table named weekday containing an enumeration column day that has weekday names as its members:

```
CREATE TABLE weekday
(
    day ENUM('Sunday','Monday','Tuesday','Wednesday',
             'Thursday','Friday','Saturday')
);
```

Internally, MySQL defines the enumeration values Sunday through Saturday to have numeric values from 1 to 7. To see this for yourself, create the table using the definition just shown, then insert into it a record for each day of the week. However, to make the insertion order differ from sorted order (so you can see the effect of sorting), add the days in random order:

```
mysql> INSERT INTO weekday (day) VALUES('Monday'),('Friday'),
    -> ('Tuesday'), ('Sunday'), ('Thursday'), ('Saturday'), ('Wednesday');
```

Then select the values, both as strings and as the internal numeric value (the latter are obtained by using +0 to effect a string-to-number conversion):

```
mysql> SELECT day, day+0 FROM weekday;
+-----------+-------+
| day       | day+0 |
+-----------+-------+
| Monday    |     2 |
| Friday    |     6 |
| Tuesday   |     3 |
| Sunday    |     1 |
| Thursday  |     5 |
| Saturday  |     7 |
| Wednesday |     4 |
+-----------+-------+
```

Notice that because the query includes no ORDER BY clause, the records are returned in unsorted order. If you add an ORDER BY day clause, it becomes apparent that MySQL uses the internal numeric values for sorting:

```
mysql> SELECT day, day+0 FROM weekday ORDER BY day;
+-----------+-------+
| day       | day+0 |
+-----------+-------+
| Sunday    |     1 |
| Monday    |     2 |
| Tuesday   |     3 |
| Wednesday |     4 |
| Thursday  |     5 |
| Friday    |     6 |
| Saturday  |     7 |
+-----------+-------+
```

What about occasions when you do want to sort ENUM values in lexical order? Force them to be treated as strings for sorting using the CONCAT() function. CONCAT() normally takes multiple arguments and concatenates them into a single string. But it can be used with just a single argument, which is useful when all you want is its behavior of producing a string result:

```
mysql> SELECT day, day+0 FROM weekday ORDER BY CONCAT(day);
+-----------+-------+
| day       | day+0 |
+-----------+-------+
| Friday    |     6 |
| Monday    |     2 |
```

```
| Saturday  |    7 |
| Sunday    |    1 |
| Thursday  |    5 |
| Tuesday   |    3 |
| Wednesday |    4 |
+-----------+------+
```

If you always (or nearly always) sort a non-enumeration column in a specific non-lexical order, consider changing the column type to ENUM, with its values listed in the desired sort order. To see how this works, create a color table containing a string column and populate it with some sample rows:

```
mysql> CREATE TABLE color (name CHAR(10));
mysql> INSERT INTO color (name) VALUES ('blue'),('green'),
    -> ('indigo'),('orange'),('red'),('violet'),('yellow');
```

Sorting by the name column at this point produces lexical order because the column contains CHAR values:

```
mysql> SELECT name FROM color ORDER BY name;
+--------+
| name   |
+--------+
| blue   |
| green  |
| indigo |
| orange |
| red    |
| violet |
| yellow |
+--------+
```

Now suppose you want to sort the column by the order in which colors occur in the rainbow. (This order is given by the name "Roy G. Biv," where successive letters of that name indicate the first letter of the corresponding color name.) One way to produce a rainbow sort is to use FIELD():

```
mysql> SELECT name FROM color
    -> ORDER BY
    -> FIELD(name,'red','orange','yellow','green','blue','indigo','violet');
+--------+
| name   |
+--------+
| red    |
| orange |
| yellow |
| green  |
| blue   |
| indigo |
| violet |
+--------+
```

To accomplish the same end without FIELD( ), use ALTER TABLE to convert the name column to an ENUM that lists the colors in the desired sort order:

```
mysql> ALTER TABLE color
    -> MODIFY name
    -> ENUM('red','orange','yellow','green','blue','indigo','violet');
```

After converting the table, sorting on the name column produces rainbow sorting naturally with no special treatment:

```
mysql> SELECT name FROM color ORDER BY name;
+--------+
| name   |
+--------+
| red    |
| orange |
| yellow |
| green  |
| blue   |
| indigo |
| violet |
+--------+
```

Generating Summaries

7.0 Introduction

Database systems are useful for storing and retrieving records, but they also can boil down information to summarize your data in more concise form. Summaries are useful when you want the overall picture rather than the details. They're also typically more readily understood than a long list of records. Summary techniques allow you to answer questions such as "How many?" or "What is the total?" or "What is the range of values?" If you're running a business, you may want to know how many customers you have in each state, or how much sales volume you're generating each month. You could determine the per-state count by producing a list of customer records and counting them yourself, but that makes no sense when MySQL can count them for you. Similarly, to determine sales volume by month, a list of raw order information records is not especially useful if you have to add up the order amounts yourself. Let MySQL do it.

The examples just mentioned illustrate two common summary types. The first (the number of customer records per state) is a counting summary. The content of each record is important only for purposes of placing it into the proper group or category for counting. Such summaries are essentially histograms, where you sort items into a set of bins and count the number of items in each bin. The second example (sales volume per month) is an instance of a summary that's based on the contents of records—sales totals are computed from sales values in individual order records.

Yet another kind of summary produces neither counts nor sums, but simply a list of unique values. This is useful if you don't care how many instances of each value are present, but only *which* values are present. If you want to know the states in which you have customers, you want a list of the distinct state names contained in the records, not a list consisting of the state value from every record. Sometimes it's even useful to apply one summary technique to the result of another summary. For example, to determine how many states your customers live in, generate a list of unique customer states, then count them.

The type of summaries you can perform may depend on the kind of data you're working with. A counting summary can be generated from any kind of values, whether they be numbers, strings, or dates. For summaries that involve sums or averages, only numeric values can be used. You can count instances of customer state names to produce a demographic analysis of your customer base, but you cannot add or average state names—that doesn't make sense.

Summary operations in MySQL involve the following SQL constructs:

- To compute a summary value from a set of individual values, use one of the functions known as aggregate functions. These are so called because they operate on aggregates (groups) of values. Aggregate functions include COUNT( ), which counts records or values in a query result; MIN( ) and MAX( ), which find smallest and largest values; and SUM( ) and AVG( ), which produce sums and means of values. These functions can be used to compute a value for the entire result set, or with a GROUP BY clause to group the rows into subsets and obtain an aggregate value for each one.

- To obtain a list of unique values, use SELECT DISTINCT rather than SELECT.

- To count how may distinct values there are, use COUNT(DISTINCT) rather than COUNT( ).

The recipes in this chapter first illustrate basic summary techniques, then show how to perform more complex summary operations. You'll find additional examples of summary methods in later chapters, particularly those that cover joins and statistical operations. (See Chapters 12 and 13.)

The primary tables used for examples here are the driver_log and mail tables. These were also used heavily in Chapter 6, so they should look familiar. A third table used recurrently throughout the chapter is states, which has rows containing a few pieces of information for each of the United States:

```
mysql> SELECT * FROM states ORDER BY name;
+----------------+--------+------------+----------+
| name           | abbrev | statehood  | pop      |
+----------------+--------+------------+----------+
| Alabama        | AL     | 1819-12-14 |  4040587 |
| Alaska         | AK     | 1959-01-03 |   550043 |
| Arizona        | AZ     | 1912-02-14 |  3665228 |
| Arkansas       | AR     | 1836-06-15 |  2350725 |
| California     | CA     | 1850-09-09 | 29760021 |
| Colorado       | CO     | 1876-08-01 |  3294394 |
| Connecticut    | CT     | 1788-01-09 |  3287116 |
...
```

The name and abbrev columns list the full state name and the corresponding abbreviation. The statehood column indicates the day on which the state entered the Union. pop is the state population as of April, 1990, as reported by the U.S. Census Bureau.

Other tables are used occasionally as well. You can create most of them with the scripts found in the *tables* directory of the recipes distribution. The tables containing data from the *baseball1.com* baseball database can be created using the instructions in the *baseball1* directory, and the kjv table is described in Recipe 4.11.

7.1 Summarizing with COUNT( )

Problem

You want to count the number of rows in a table, the number of rows that match certain conditions, or the number of times that particular values occur.

Solution

Use the COUNT( ) function.

Discussion

To count the number of rows in an entire table or that match particular conditions, use the COUNT( ) function. For example, to display the contents of the records in a table, you could use a SELECT * query, but to count them instead, use SELECT COUNT(*). Without a WHERE clause, the query counts all the records in the table, such as in the following query, which shows how many rows the driver_log table contains:

```
mysql> SELECT COUNT(*) FROM driver_log;
+----------+
| COUNT(*) |
+----------+
|       10 |
+----------+
```

If you don't know how many U.S. states there are, this query tells you:

```
mysql> SELECT COUNT(*) FROM states;
+----------+
| COUNT(*) |
+----------+
|       50 |
+----------+
```

COUNT(*) with no WHERE clause is very quick for ISAM or MyISAM tables. For BDB or InnoDB tables, you may want to avoid it; the query requires a full table scan for those table types, which can be slow for large tables. If an approximate row count is all you require and you have MySQL 3.23 or later, a workaround that avoids a full scan is to use SHOW TABLE STATUS and examine the Rows value in the output. Were states an InnoDB table, the query output might look like this:

```
mysql> SHOW TABLE STATUS FROM cookbook LIKE 'states'\G
*************************** 1. row ***************************
           Name: states
           Type: InnoDB
     Row_format: Dynamic
```

```
             Rows: 50
   Avg_row_length: 327
      Data_length: 16384
  Max_data_length: NULL
     Index_length: 0
        Data_free: 0
   Auto_increment: NULL
      Create_time: NULL
      Update_time: NULL
       Check_time: NULL
    Create_options:
          Comment: InnoDB free: 479232 kB
```

To count only the number of rows that match certain conditions, add an appropriate WHERE clause to the query. The conditions can be arbitrary, making COUNT() useful for answering many kinds of questions:

- How many times did drivers travel more than 200 miles in a day?

  ```
  mysql> SELECT COUNT(*) FROM driver_log WHERE miles > 200;
  +----------+
  | COUNT(*) |
  +----------+
  |        4 |
  +----------+
  ```

- How many days did Suzi drive?

  ```
  mysql> SELECT COUNT(*) FROM driver_log WHERE name = 'Suzi';
  +----------+
  | COUNT(*) |
  +----------+
  |        2 |
  +----------+
  ```

- How many states did the United States consist of at the beginning of the 20th century?

  ```
  mysql> SELECT COUNT(*) FROM states WHERE statehood < '1900-01-01';
  +----------+
  | COUNT(*) |
  +----------+
  |       45 |
  +----------+
  ```

- How many of those states joined the Union in the 19th century?

  ```
  mysql> SELECT COUNT(*) FROM states
      -> WHERE statehood BETWEEN '1800-01-01' AND '1899-12-31';
  +----------+
  | COUNT(*) |
  +----------+
  |       29 |
  +----------+
  ```

The COUNT() function actually has two forms. The form we've been using, COUNT(*), counts rows. The other form, COUNT(expr), takes a column name or expression argument and counts the number of non-NULL values. The following query shows how to produce both a row count for a table and a count of the number of non-NULL values in one of its columns:

```
SELECT COUNT(*), COUNT(mycol) FROM mytbl;
```

The fact that COUNT(*expr*) doesn't count NULL values is useful when producing multiple counts from the same set of values. To count the number of Saturday and Sunday trips in the driver_log table with a single query, do this:

```
mysql> SELECT
    -> COUNT(IF(DAYOFWEEK(trav_date)=7,1,NULL)) AS 'Saturday trips',
    -> COUNT(IF(DAYOFWEEK(trav_date)=1,1,NULL)) AS 'Sunday trips'
    -> FROM driver_log;
+----------------+--------------+
| Saturday trips | Sunday trips |
+----------------+--------------+
|              1 |            2 |
+----------------+--------------+
```

Or to count weekend versus weekday trips, do this:

```
mysql> SELECT
    -> COUNT(IF(DAYOFWEEK(trav_date) IN (1,7),1,NULL)) AS 'weekend trips',
    -> COUNT(IF(DAYOFWEEK(trav_date) IN (1,7),NULL,1)) AS 'weekday trips'
    -> FROM driver_log;
+---------------+---------------+
| weekend trips | weekday trips |
+---------------+---------------+
|             3 |             7 |
+---------------+---------------+
```

The IF() expressions determine, for each column value, whether or not it should be counted. If so, the expression evaluates to 1 and COUNT() counts it. If not, the expression evaluates to NULL and COUNT() ignores it. The effect is to count the number of values that satisfy the condition given as the first argument to IF().

See Also

The difference between COUNT(*) and COUNT(*expr*) is discussed further in "Summaries and NULL Values."

7.2   Summarizing with MIN() and MAX()

Problem

You need to determine the smallest or largest of a set of values.

Solution

Use MIN() to find the smallest value, MAX() to find the largest.

Discussion

Finding smallest or largest values is somewhat akin to sorting, except that instead of producing an entire set of sorted values, you select only a single value at one end or the other of the sorted range. This kind of operation applies to questions about smallest, largest, oldest, newest, most expensive, least expensive, and so forth. One way to find such values is to use the MIN() and MAX() functions. (Another way to address these questions is to use LIMIT; see the discussions in Recipes 3.16 and 3.18.)

Because MIN() and MAX() determine the extreme values in a set, they're useful for characterizing ranges:

- What date range is represented by the rows in the mail table? What are the smallest and largest messages sent?

```
mysql> SELECT
    -> MIN(t) AS earliest, MAX(t) AS latest,
    -> MIN(size) AS smallest, MAX(size) AS largest
    -> FROM mail;
+---------------------+---------------------+----------+---------+
| earliest            | latest              | smallest | largest |
+---------------------+---------------------+----------+---------+
| 2001-05-11 10:15:08 | 2001-05-19 22:21:51 |      271 | 2394482 |
+---------------------+---------------------+----------+---------+
```

- What are the shortest and longest trips in the driver_log table?

```
mysql> SELECT MIN(miles) AS shortest, MAX(miles) AS longest
    -> FROM driver_log;
+----------+---------+
| shortest | longest |
+----------+---------+
|       79 |     502 |
+----------+---------+
```

- What are the lowest and highest U.S. state populations?

```
mysql> SELECT MIN(pop) AS 'fewest people', MAX(pop) AS 'most people'
    -> FROM states;
+---------------+-------------+
| fewest people | most people |
+---------------+-------------+
|        453588 |    29760021 |
+---------------+-------------+
```

- What are the first and last state names, lexically speaking?

```
mysql> SELECT MIN(name), MAX(name) FROM states;
+-----------+-----------+
| MIN(name) | MAX(name) |
+-----------+-----------+
| Alabama   | Wyoming   |
+-----------+-----------+
```

`MIN()` and `MAX()` need not be applied directly to column values. They also work with expressions or values that are derived from column values. For example, to find the lengths of the shortest and longest state names, do this:

```
mysql> SELECT MIN(LENGTH(name)) AS shortest, MAX(LENGTH(name)) AS longest
    -> FROM states;
+----------+---------+
| shortest | longest |
+----------+---------+
|        4 |      14 |
+----------+---------+
```

7.3   Summarizing with SUM() and AVG()

Problem

You need to add up a set of numbers or find their average.

Solution

Use the `SUM()` or `AVG()` functions.

Discussion

`SUM()` and `AVG()` produce the total and average (mean) of a set of values:

- What is the total amount of mail traffic and the average size of each message?

```
mysql> SELECT SUM(size) AS 'total traffic',
    -> AVG(size) AS 'average message size'
    -> FROM mail;
+---------------+----------------------+
| total traffic | average message size |
+---------------+----------------------+
|       3798185 |          237386.5625 |
+---------------+----------------------+
```

- How many miles did the drivers in the `driver_log` table travel? What was the average miles traveled per day?

```
mysql> SELECT SUM(miles) AS 'total miles',
    -> AVG(miles) AS 'average miles/day'
    -> FROM driver_log;
+-------------+-------------------+
| total miles | average miles/day |
+-------------+-------------------+
|        2166 |          216.6000 |
+-------------+-------------------+
```

- What is the total population of the United States?

```
mysql> SELECT SUM(pop) FROM states;
+-----------+
| SUM(pop)  |
+-----------+
| 248102973 |
+-----------+
```

(The value represents the population reported for April, 1990. The figure shown here differs from the U.S. population reported by the U.S. Census Bureau, because the states table doesn't contain a count for Washington, D.C.)

SUM() and AVG() are strictly numeric functions, so they can't be used with strings or temporal values. On the other hand, sometimes you can convert non-numeric values to useful numeric forms. Suppose a table stores TIME values that represent elapsed time:

```
mysql> SELECT t1 FROM time_val;
+----------+
| t1       |
+----------+
| 15:00:00 |
| 05:01:30 |
| 12:30:20 |
+----------+
```

To compute the total elapsed time, use TIME_TO_SEC() to convert the values to seconds before summing them. The result also will be in seconds; pass it to SEC_TO_TIME() should you wish the sum to be in TIME format:

```
mysql> SELECT SUM(TIME_TO_SEC(t1)) AS 'total seconds',
    -> SEC_TO_TIME(SUM(TIME_TO_SEC(t1))) AS 'total time'
    -> FROM time_val;
+---------------+------------+
| total seconds | total time |
+---------------+------------+
|        117110 | 32:31:50   |
+---------------+------------+
```

See Also

The SUM() and AVG() functions are especially useful in applications that compute statistics. They're explored further in Chapter 13, along with STD(), a related function that calculates standard deviations.

7.4   Using DISTINCT to Eliminate Duplicates

Problem

You want to know which values are present in a set of values, without listing duplicate values a bunch of times. Or you want to know how many distinct values there are.

Solution

Use DISTINCT to select unique values, or COUNT(DISTINCT) to count them.

Discussion

A summary operation that doesn't use aggregate functions is to determine which values or rows are contained in a dataset by eliminating duplicates. Do this with DISTINCT (or DISTINCTROW, which is synonymous). DISTINCT is useful for boiling down a query result, and often is combined with ORDER BY to place the values in more meaningful order. For example, if you want to know the names of the drivers listed in the driver_log table, use the following query:

```
mysql> SELECT DISTINCT name FROM driver_log ORDER BY name;
+-------+
| name  |
+-------+
| Ben   |
| Henry |
| Suzi  |
+-------+
```

A query without DISTINCT produces the same names, but is not nearly as easy to understand:

```
mysql> SELECT name FROM driver_log;
+-------+
| name  |
+-------+
| Ben   |
| Suzi  |
| Henry |
| Henry |
| Ben   |
| Henry |
| Suzi  |
| Henry |
| Ben   |
| Henry |
+-------+
```

If you want to know how many different drivers there are, use COUNT(DISTINCT):

```
mysql> SELECT COUNT(DISTINCT name) FROM driver_log;
+----------------------+
| COUNT(DISTINCT name) |
+----------------------+
|                    3 |
+----------------------+
```

COUNT(DISTINCT) ignores NULL values. If you also want to count NULL as one of the values in the set if it's present, do this:

```
COUNT(DISTINCT val) + IF(COUNT(IF(val IS NULL,1,NULL))=0,0,1)
```

The same effect can be achieved using either of the following expressions:

```
COUNT(DISTINCT val) + IF(SUM(ISNULL(val))=0,0,1)
COUNT(DISTINCT val) + (SUM(ISNULL(val))!=0)
```

COUNT(DISTINCT) is available as of MySQL 3.23.2. Prior to that, you have to use some kind of workaround based on counting the number of rows in a SELECT DISTINCT query. One way to do this is to select the distinct values into another table, then use COUNT(*) to count the number of rows in that table.

DISTINCT queries often are useful in conjunction with aggregate functions to obtain a more complete characterization of your data. For example, applying COUNT(*) to a customer table indicates how many customers you have, using DISTINCT on the state values in the table tells you which states you have customers in, and COUNT(DISTINCT) on the state values tells you how many states your customer base represents.

When used with multiple columns, DISTINCT shows the different combinations of values in the columns and COUNT(DISTINCT) counts the number of combinations. The following queries show the different sender/recipient pairs in the mail table, and how many such pairs there are:

```
mysql> SELECT DISTINCT srcuser, dstuser FROM mail
    -> ORDER BY srcuser, dstuser;
+---------+---------+
| srcuser | dstuser |
+---------+---------+
| barb    | barb    |
| barb    | tricia  |
| gene    | barb    |
| gene    | gene    |
| gene    | tricia  |
| phil    | barb    |
| phil    | phil    |
| phil    | tricia  |
| tricia  | gene    |
| tricia  | phil    |
+---------+---------+
mysql> SELECT COUNT(DISTINCT srcuser, dstuser) FROM mail;
+---------------------------------+
| COUNT(DISTINCT srcuser, dstuser) |
+---------------------------------+
|                              10 |
+---------------------------------+
```

DISTINCT works with expressions, too, not just column values. To determine the number of hours of the day during which messages in the mail were sent, count the distinct HOUR() values:

```
mysql> SELECT COUNT(DISTINCT HOUR(t)) FROM mail;
+-------------------------+
| COUNT(DISTINCT HOUR(t)) |
+-------------------------+
|                      12 |
+-------------------------+
```

To find out which hours those were, list them:

```
mysql> SELECT DISTINCT HOUR(t) FROM mail ORDER BY 1;
+---------+
| HOUR(t) |
+---------+
|       7 |
|       8 |
|       9 |
|      10 |
|      11 |
|      12 |
|      13 |
|      14 |
|      15 |
|      17 |
|      22 |
|      23 |
+---------+
```

Note that this query doesn't tell you how many messages were sent each hour. That's covered in Recipe 7.15.

7.5 Finding Values Associated with Minimum and Maximum Values

Problem

You want to know the values for other columns in the row containing the minimum or maximum value.

Solution

Use two queries and a SQL variable. Or use the "MAX-CONCAT trick." Or use a join.

Discussion

MIN( ) and MAX( ) find the endpoints of a range of values, but sometimes when finding a minimum or maximum value, you're also interested in other values from the row in which the value occurs. For example, you can find the largest state population like this:

```
mysql> SELECT MAX(pop) FROM states;
+----------+
| MAX(pop) |
+----------+
| 29760021 |
+----------+
```

But that doesn't show you which state has this population. The obvious way to try to get that information is like this:

```
mysql> SELECT name, MAX(pop) FROM states WHERE pop = MAX(pop);
ERROR 1111 at line 1: Invalid use of group function
```

Probably everyone attempts something like that sooner or later, but it doesn't work, because aggregate functions like MIN() and MAX() cannot be used in WHERE clauses. The intent of the statement is to determine which record has the maximum population value, then display the associated state name. The problem is that while you and I know perfectly well what we'd mean by writing such a thing, it makes no sense at all to MySQL. The query fails because MySQL uses the WHERE clause to determine which records to select, but it knows the value of an aggregate function only *after* selecting the records from which the function's value is determined! So, in a sense, the statement is self-contradictory. You could solve this problem using a subselect, except that MySQL won't have those until Version 4.1. Meanwhile, you can use a two-stage approach involving one query that selects the maximum size into a SQL variable, and another that refers to the variable in its WHERE clause:

```
mysql> SELECT @max := MAX(pop) FROM states;
mysql> SELECT @max AS 'highest population', name FROM states WHERE pop = @max;
+--------------------+------------+
| highest population | name       |
+--------------------+------------+
| 29760021           | California |
+--------------------+------------+
```

This technique also works even if the minimum or maximum value itself isn't actually contained in the row, but is only derived from it. If you want to know the length of the shortest verse in the King James Version, that's easy to find:

```
mysql> SELECT MIN(LENGTH(vtext)) FROM kjv;
+--------------------+
| MIN(LENGTH(vtext)) |
+--------------------+
|                 11 |
+--------------------+
```

If you want to ask "What verse is that?," do this instead:

```
mysql> SELECT @min := MIN(LENGTH(vtext)) FROM kjv;
mysql> SELECT bname, cnum, vnum, vtext FROM kjv WHERE LENGTH(vtext) = @min;
+-------+------+------+-------------+
| bname | cnum | vnum | vtext       |
+-------+------+------+-------------+
| John  |   11 |   35 | Jesus wept. |
+-------+------+------+-------------+
```

Another technique you can use for finding values associated with minima or maxima is found in the MySQL Reference Manual, where it's called the "MAX-CONCAT trick." It's pretty gruesome, but can be useful if your version of MySQL precedes the introduction of SQL variables. The technique involves appending a column to the summary column using CONCAT(), finding the maximum of the resulting values using MAX(), and extracting the non-summarized part of the value from the result. For example, to find the name of the state with the largest population, you can select the maximum combined value of the pop and name columns, then extract the name part from it. It's easiest to see how this works by proceeding in stages. First, determine the maximum population value to find out how wide it is:

```
mysql> SELECT MAX(pop) FROM states;
+----------+
| MAX(pop) |
+----------+
| 29760021 |
+----------+
```

That's eight characters. It's important to know this, because each column within the combined population-plus-name values should occur at a fixed position so that the state name can be extracted reliably later. (By padding the pop column to a length of eight, the name values will all begin at the ninth character.)

However, we must be careful how we pad the populations. The values produced by CONCAT() are strings, so the population-plus-name values will be treated as such by MAX() for sorting purposes. If we left justify the pop values by padding them on the right with RPAD(), we'll get combined values like the following:

```
mysql> SELECT CONCAT(RPAD(pop,8,' '),name) FROM states;
+------------------------------+
| CONCAT(RPAD(pop,8,' '),name) |
+------------------------------+
| 4040587 Alabama              |
| 550043  Alaska               |
| 3665228 Arizona              |
| 2350725 Arkansas             |
...
```

Those values will sort lexically. That's okay for finding the largest of a set of string values with MAX(). But pop values are numbers, so we want the values in numeric order. To make the lexical ordering correspond to the numeric ordering, we must right justify the population values by padding on the left with LPAD():

```
mysql> SELECT CONCAT(LPAD(pop,8,' '),name) FROM states;
+------------------------------+
| CONCAT(LPAD(pop,8,' '),name) |
+------------------------------+
|  4040587Alabama              |
|   550043Alaska               |
|  3665228Arizona              |
|  2350725Arkansas             |
...
```

Next, use the CONCAT() expression with MAX() to find the value with the largest population part:

```
mysql> SELECT MAX(CONCAT(LPAD(pop,8,' '),name)) FROM states;
+-----------------------------------+
| MAX(CONCAT(LPAD(pop,8,' '),name)) |
+-----------------------------------+
| 29760021California                |
+-----------------------------------+
```

To obtain the final result (the state name associated with the maximum population), extract from the maximum combined value the substring that begins with the ninth character:

```
mysql> SELECT SUBSTRING(MAX(CONCAT(LPAD(pop,8,' '),name)),9) FROM states;
+------------------------------------------------+
| SUBSTRING(MAX(CONCAT(LPAD(pop,8,' '),name)),9) |
+------------------------------------------------+
| California                                      |
+------------------------------------------------+
```

Clearly, using a SQL variable to hold an intermediate result is much easier. In this case, it's also more efficient because it avoids the overhead for concatenating column values for sorting and decomposing the result for display.

Yet another way to select other columns from rows containing a minimum or maximum value is to use a join. Select the value into another table, then join it to the original table to select the row that matches the value. To find the record for the state with the highest population, use a join like this:

```
mysql> CREATE TEMPORARY TABLE t
    -> SELECT MAX(pop) as maxpop FROM states;
mysql> SELECT states.* FROM states, t WHERE states.pop = t.maxpop;
+------------+--------+------------+----------+
| name       | abbrev | statehood  | pop      |
+------------+--------+------------+----------+
| California | CA     | 1850-09-09 | 29760021 |
+------------+--------+------------+----------+
```

See Also

For more information about joins, see Chapter 12.

7.6 Controlling String Case Sensitivity for MIN() and MAX()

Problem

MIN() and MAX() select strings in case sensitive fashion when you don't want them to, or vice versa.

Solution

Alter the case sensitivity of the strings.

Discussion

When applied to string values, MIN() and MAX() produce results determined according to lexical sorting rules. One factor in string sorting is case sensitivity, so MIN() and MAX() are affected by that as well. In Chapter 6, we used a textblob_val table containing two columns of apparently identical values:

```
mysql> SELECT tstr, bstr FROM textblob_val;
+------+------+
| tstr | bstr |
+------+------+
| aaa  | aaa  |
| AAA  | AAA  |
| bbb  | bbb  |
| BBB  | BBB  |
+------+------+
```

However, although the values look the same, they don't behave the same. bstr is a BLOB column and is case sensitive. tstr, a TEXT column, is not. As a result, MIN() and MAX() will not necessarily produce the same results for the two columns:

```
mysql> SELECT MIN(tstr), MIN(bstr) FROM textblob_val;
+-----------+-----------+
| MIN(tstr) | MIN(bstr) |
+-----------+-----------+
| aaa       | AAA       |
+-----------+-----------+
```

To make tstr case sensitive, use BINARY:

```
mysql> SELECT MIN(BINARY tstr) FROM textblob_val;
+------------------+
| MIN(BINARY tstr) |
+------------------+
| AAA              |
+------------------+
```

To make bstr not case sensitive, you can convert the values to a given lettercase:

```
mysql> SELECT MIN(LOWER(bstr)) FROM textblob_val;
+------------------+
| MIN(LOWER(bstr)) |
+------------------+
| aaa              |
+------------------+
```

Unfortunately, doing so also changes the displayed value. If that's an issue, use this technique instead (and note that it may yield a somewhat different result):

```
mysql> SELECT @min := MIN(LOWER(bstr)) FROM textblob_val;
mysql> SELECT bstr FROM textblob_val WHERE LOWER(bstr) = @min;
```

```
+------+
| bstr |
+------+
| aaa  |
| AAA  |
+------+
```

7.7   Dividing a Summary into Subgroups

Problem

You want to calculate a summary for each subgroup of a set of rows, not an overall summary value.

Solution

Use a GROUP BY clause to arrange rows into groups.

Discussion

The summary queries shown so far calculate summary values over all rows in the result set. For example, the following query determines the number of daily driving records in the driver_log table, and thus the total number of days that drivers were on the road:

```
mysql> SELECT COUNT(*) FROM driver_log;
+----------+
| COUNT(*) |
+----------+
|       10 |
+----------+
```

But sometimes it's desirable to break a set of rows into subgroups and summarize each group. This is done by using aggregate functions in conjunction with a GROUP BY clause. To determine the number of days driven by each driver, group the rows by driver name, count how many rows there are for each name, and display the names with the counts:

```
mysql> SELECT name, COUNT(name) FROM driver_log GROUP BY name;
+-------+-------------+
| name  | COUNT(name) |
+-------+-------------+
| Ben   |           3 |
| Henry |           5 |
| Suzi  |           2 |
+-------+-------------+
```

That query summarizes the same column used for grouping (name), but that's not always necessary. Suppose you want a quick characterization of the driver_log table, showing for each person listed in it the total number of miles driven and the average number of miles per day. In this case, you still use the name column to place the rows in groups, but the summary functions operate on the miles values:

```
mysql> SELECT name,
    -> SUM(miles) AS 'total miles',
    -> AVG(miles) AS 'miles per day'
    -> FROM driver_log GROUP BY name;
+-------+-------------+---------------+
| name  | total miles | miles per day |
+-------+-------------+---------------+
| Ben   |         362 |      120.6667 |
| Henry |         911 |      182.2000 |
| Suzi  |         893 |      446.5000 |
+-------+-------------+---------------+
```

Use as many grouping columns as necessary to achieve as fine-grained a summary as you require. The following query produces a coarse summary showing how many messages were sent by each message sender listed in the mail table:

```
mysql> SELECT srcuser, COUNT(*) FROM mail
    -> GROUP BY srcuser;
+---------+----------+
| srcuser | COUNT(*) |
+---------+----------+
| barb    |        3 |
| gene    |        6 |
| phil    |        5 |
| tricia  |        2 |
+---------+----------+
```

To be more specific and find out how many messages each sender sent from each host, use two grouping columns. This produces a result with nested groups (groups within groups):

```
mysql> SELECT srcuser, srchost, COUNT(*) FROM mail
    -> GROUP BY srcuser, srchost;
+---------+---------+----------+
| srcuser | srchost | COUNT(*) |
+---------+---------+----------+
| barb    | saturn  |        2 |
| barb    | venus   |        1 |
| gene    | mars    |        2 |
| gene    | saturn  |        2 |
| gene    | venus   |        2 |
| phil    | mars    |        3 |
| phil    | venus   |        2 |
| tricia  | mars    |        1 |
| tricia  | saturn  |        1 |
+---------+---------+----------+
```

The preceding examples in this section have used COUNT(), SUM() and AVG() for per-group summaries. You can use MIN() or MAX(), too. With a GROUP BY clause, they will tell you the smallest or largest value per group. The following query groups mail table rows by message sender, displaying for each one the size of the largest message sent and the date of the most recent message:

```
mysql> SELECT srcuser, MAX(size), MAX(t) FROM mail GROUP BY srcuser;
+---------+-----------+---------------------+
| srcuser | MAX(size) | MAX(t)              |
+---------+-----------+---------------------+
| barb    |     98151 | 2001-05-14 14:42:21 |
| gene    |    998532 | 2001-05-19 22:21:51 |
| phil    |     10294 | 2001-05-17 12:49:23 |
| tricia  |   2394482 | 2001-05-14 17:03:01 |
+---------+-----------+---------------------+
```

You can group by multiple columns and display a maximum for each combination of values in those columns. This query finds the size of the largest message sent between each pair of sender and recipient values listed in the mail table:

```
mysql> SELECT srcuser, dstuser, MAX(size) FROM mail GROUP BY srcuser, dstuser;
+---------+---------+-----------+
| srcuser | dstuser | MAX(size) |
+---------+---------+-----------+
| barb    | barb    |     98151 |
| barb    | tricia  |     58274 |
| gene    | barb    |      2291 |
| gene    | gene    |     23992 |
| gene    | tricia  |    998532 |
| phil    | barb    |     10294 |
| phil    | phil    |      1048 |
| phil    | tricia  |      5781 |
| tricia  | gene    |    194925 |
| tricia  | phil    |   2394482 |
+---------+---------+-----------+
```

When using aggregate functions to produce per-group summary values, watch out for the following trap. Suppose you want to know the longest trip per driver in the driver_log table. That's produced by this query:

```
mysql> SELECT name, MAX(miles) AS 'longest trip'
    -> FROM driver_log GROUP BY name;
+-------+--------------+
| name  | longest trip |
+-------+--------------+
| Ben   |          152 |
| Henry |          300 |
| Suzi  |          502 |
+-------+--------------+
```

But what if you also want to show the date on which each driver's longest trip occurred? Can you just add trav_date to the output column list? Sorry, that won't work:

```
mysql> SELECT name, trav_date, MAX(miles) AS 'longest trip'
    -> FROM driver_log GROUP BY name;
+-------+------------+--------------+
| name  | trav_date  | longest trip |
+-------+------------+--------------+
| Ben   | 2001-11-30 |          152 |
| Henry | 2001-11-29 |          300 |
| Suzi  | 2001-11-29 |          502 |
+-------+------------+--------------+
```

The query does produce a result, but if you compare it to the full table (shown below), you'll see that although the dates for Ben and Henry are correct, the date for Suzi is not:

```
+--------+-------+------------+-------+
| rec_id | name  | trav_date  | miles |
+--------+-------+------------+-------+
|      1 | Ben   | 2001-11-30 |   152 |   ← Ben's longest trip
|      2 | Suzi  | 2001-11-29 |   391 |
|      3 | Henry | 2001-11-29 |   300 |   ← Henry's longest trip
|      4 | Henry | 2001-11-27 |    96 |
|      5 | Ben   | 2001-11-29 |   131 |
|      6 | Henry | 2001-11-26 |   115 |
|      7 | Suzi  | 2001-12-02 |   502 |   ← Suzi's longest trip
|      8 | Henry | 2001-12-01 |   197 |
|      9 | Ben   | 2001-12-02 |    79 |
|     10 | Henry | 2001-11-30 |   203 |
+--------+-------+------------+-------+
```

So what's going on? Why does the summary query produce incorrect results? This happens because when you include a GROUP BY clause in a query, the only values you can select are the grouped columns or the summary values calculated from them. If you display additional columns, they're not tied to the grouped columns and the values displayed for them are indeterminate. (For the query just shown, it appears that MySQL may simply be picking the first date for each driver, whether or not it matches the driver's maximum mileage value.)

The general solution to the problem of displaying contents of rows associated with minimum or maximum group values involves a join. The technique is described in Chapter 12. If you don't want to read ahead, or you don't want to use another table, consider using the MAX-CONCAT trick described earlier. It produces the correct result, although the query is fairly ugly:

```
mysql> SELECT name,
    -> SUBSTRING(MAX(CONCAT(LPAD(miles,3,' '), trav_date)),4) AS date,
    -> LEFT(MAX(CONCAT(LPAD(miles,3,' '), trav_date)),3) AS 'longest trip'
    -> FROM driver_log GROUP BY name;
+-------+------------+--------------+
| name  | date       | longest trip |
+-------+------------+--------------+
| Ben   | 2001-11-30 | 152          |
| Henry | 2001-11-29 | 300          |
| Suzi  | 2001-12-02 | 502          |
+-------+------------+--------------+
```

7.8   Summaries and NULL Values

Problem

You're summarizing a set of values that may include NULL values and you need to know how to interpret the results.

Solution

Understand how aggregate functions handle NULL values.

Discussion

Most aggregate functions ignore NULL values. Suppose you have a table expt that records experimental results for subjects who are to be given four tests each and that lists the test score as NULL for those tests that have not yet been administered:

```
mysql> SELECT subject, test, score FROM expt ORDER BY subject, test;
+---------+------+-------+
| subject | test | score |
+---------+------+-------+
| Jane    | A    |    47 |
| Jane    | B    |    50 |
| Jane    | C    |  NULL |
| Jane    | D    |  NULL |
| Marvin  | A    |    52 |
| Marvin  | B    |    45 |
| Marvin  | C    |    53 |
| Marvin  | D    |  NULL |
+---------+------+-------+
```

By using a GROUP BY clause to arrange the rows by subject name, the number of tests taken by each subject, as well as the total, average, lowest, and highest score can be calculated like this,

```
mysql> SELECT subject,
    -> COUNT(score) AS n,
    -> SUM(score) AS total,
    -> AVG(score) AS average,
    -> MIN(score) AS lowest,
    -> MAX(score) AS highest
    -> FROM expt GROUP BY subject;
+---------+---+-------+---------+--------+---------+
| subject | n | total | average | lowest | highest |
+---------+---+-------+---------+--------+---------+
| Jane    | 2 |    97 | 48.5000 |     47 |      50 |
| Marvin  | 3 |   150 | 50.0000 |     45 |      53 |
+---------+---+-------+---------+--------+---------+
```

You can see from results in the column labeled n (number of tests) that the query counts only five values. Why? Because the values in that column correspond to the number of non-NULL test scores for each subject. The other summary columns display results that are calculated only from the non-NULL scores as well.

It makes a lot of sense for aggregate functions to ignore NULL values. If they followed the usual SQL arithmetic rules, adding NULL to any other value would produce a NULL result. That would make aggregate functions really difficult to use because you'd have to filter out NULL values yourself every time you performed a summary to avoid getting a NULL result. Ugh. By ignoring NULL values, aggregate functions become a lot more convenient.

However, be aware that even though aggregate functions may ignore NULL values, some of them can still produce NULL as a result. This happens if there's nothing to summarize. The following query is the same as the previous one, with one small difference. It selects only NULL test scores, so there's nothing for the aggregate functions to operate on:

```
mysql> SELECT subject,
    -> COUNT(score) AS n,
    -> SUM(score) AS total,
    -> AVG(score) AS average,
    -> MIN(score) AS lowest,
    -> MAX(score) AS highest
    -> FROM expt WHERE score IS NULL GROUP BY subject;
+---------+---+-------+---------+--------+---------+
| subject | n | total | average | lowest | highest |
+---------+---+-------+---------+--------+---------+
| Jane    | 0 |     0 |    NULL |   NULL |    NULL |
| Marvin  | 0 |     0 |    NULL |   NULL |    NULL |
+---------+---+-------+---------+--------+---------+
```

Even under these circumstances, the summary functions still return the most sensible value. The number of scores and total score per subject each are zero and are reported that way. AVG(), on the other hand, returns NULL. An average is a ratio, calculated as a sum of values divided by the number of values. When there aren't any values to summarize, the ratio is 0/0, which is undefined. NULL is therefore the most reasonable result for AVG() to return. Similarly, MIN() and MAX() have nothing to work with, so they return NULL. If you don't want these functions to produce NULL in the query output, use IFNULL() to map their results appropriately:

```
mysql> SELECT subject,
    -> COUNT(score) AS n,
    -> SUM(score) AS total,
    -> IFNULL(AVG(score),0) AS average,
    -> IFNULL(MIN(score),'Unknown') AS lowest,
    -> IFNULL(MAX(score),'Unknown') AS highest
    -> FROM expt WHERE score IS NULL GROUP BY subject;
+---------+---+-------+---------+---------+---------+
| subject | n | total | average | lowest  | highest |
+---------+---+-------+---------+---------+---------+
| Jane    | 0 |     0 |       0 | Unknown | Unknown |
| Marvin  | 0 |     0 |       0 | Unknown | Unknown |
+---------+---+-------+---------+---------+---------+
```

COUNT() is somewhat different with regard to NULL values than the other aggregate functions. Like other aggregate functions, COUNT(*expr*) counts only non-NULL values, but COUNT(*) counts rows, regardless of their content. You can see the difference between the forms of COUNT() like this:

```
mysql> SELECT COUNT(*), COUNT(score) FROM expt;
+----------+--------------+
| COUNT(*) | COUNT(score) |
+----------+--------------+
|        8 |            5 |
+----------+--------------+
```

This tells us that there are eight rows in the expt table but that only five of them have the score value filled in. The different forms of COUNT() can be very useful for counting missing values; just take the difference:

```
mysql> SELECT COUNT(*) - COUNT(score) AS missing FROM expt;
+---------+
| missing |
+---------+
|       3 |
+---------+
```

Missing and non-missing counts can be determined for subgroups as well. The following query does so for each subject. This provides a quick way to assess the extent to which the experiment has been completed:

```
mysql> SELECT subject,
    -> COUNT(*) AS total,
    -> COUNT(score) AS 'non-missing',
    -> COUNT(*) - COUNT(score) AS missing
    -> FROM expt GROUP BY subject;
```

```
+---------+-------+-------------+---------+
| subject | total | non-missing | missing |
+---------+-------+-------------+---------+
| Jane    |    4  |          2  |      2  |
| Marvin  |    4  |          3  |      1  |
+---------+-------+-------------+---------+
```

7.9 Selecting Only Groups with Certain Characteristics

Problem

You want to calculate group summaries, but display the results only for those groups that match certain criteria.

Solution

Use a HAVING clause.

Discussion

You're familiar with the use of WHERE to specify conditions that individual records must satisfy to be selected by a query. It's natural, therefore, to use WHERE to write conditions that involve summary values. The only trouble is that it doesn't work. If you want to identify drivers in the driver_log table who drove more than three days, you'd probably first think to write the query like this:

```
mysql> SELECT COUNT(*), name
    -> FROM driver_log
    -> WHERE COUNT(*) > 3
    -> GROUP BY name;
ERROR 1111 at line 1: Invalid use of group function
```

The problem here is that WHERE specifies the initial constraints that determine which rows to select, but the value of COUNT( ) can be determined only after the rows have been selected. The solution is to put the COUNT( ) expression in a HAVING clause instead. HAVING is analogous to WHERE, but it applies to group characteristics rather than to single records. That is, HAVING operates on the already-selected-and-grouped set of rows, applying additional constraints based on aggregate function results that aren't known during the initial selection process. The preceding query therefore should be written like this:

```
mysql> SELECT COUNT(*), name
    -> FROM driver_log
    -> GROUP BY name
    -> HAVING COUNT(*) > 3;
```

```
+----------+-------+
| COUNT(*) | name  |
+----------+-------+
|        5 | Henry |
+----------+-------+
```

When you use HAVING, you can still include a WHERE clause—but only to select rows, not to test summary values.

HAVING can refer to aliases, so the previous query can be rewritten like this:

```
mysql> SELECT COUNT(*) AS count, name
    -> FROM driver_log
    -> GROUP BY name
    -> HAVING count > 3;
+-------+-------+
| count | name  |
+-------+-------+
|     5 | Henry |
+-------+-------+
```

7.10 Determining Whether Values are Unique

Problem

You want to know whether table values are unique.

Solution

Use HAVING in conjunction with COUNT( ).

Discussion

You can use HAVING to find unique values in situations to which DISTINCT does not apply. DISTINCT eliminates duplicates, but doesn't show which values actually were duplicated in the original data. HAVING can tell you which values were unique or non-unique.

The following queries show the days on which only one driver was active, and the days on which more than one driver was active. They're based on using HAVING and COUNT( ) to determine which trav_date values are unique or non-unique:

```
mysql> SELECT trav_date, COUNT(trav_date)
    -> FROM driver_log
    -> GROUP BY trav_date
    -> HAVING COUNT(trav_date) = 1;
+------------+------------------+
| trav_date  | COUNT(trav_date) |
+------------+------------------+
```

```
| 2001-11-26 |                   1 |
| 2001-11-27 |                   1 |
| 2001-12-01 |                   1 |
+------------+-------------------+
mysql> SELECT trav_date, COUNT(trav_date)
    -> FROM driver_log
    -> GROUP BY trav_date
    -> HAVING COUNT(trav_date) > 1;
+------------+-------------------+
| trav_date  | COUNT(trav_date)  |
+------------+-------------------+
| 2001-11-29 |                 3 |
| 2001-11-30 |                 2 |
| 2001-12-02 |                 2 |
+------------+-------------------+
```

This technique works for combinations of values, too. For example, to find message sender/recipient pairs between whom only one message was sent, look for combinations that occur only once in the mail table:

```
mysql> SELECT srcuser, dstuser
    -> FROM mail
    -> GROUP BY srcuser, dstuser
    -> HAVING COUNT(*) = 1;
+---------+---------+
| srcuser | dstuser |
+---------+---------+
| barb    | barb    |
| gene    | tricia  |
| phil    | barb    |
| tricia  | gene    |
| tricia  | phil    |
+---------+---------+
```

Note that this query doesn't print the count. The first two examples did so, to show that the counts were being used properly, but you can use a count in a HAVING clause without including it in the output column list.

7.11   Grouping by Expression Results

Problem

You want to group rows into subgroups based on values calculated from an expression.

Solution

Put the expression in the GROUP BY clause. For older versions of MySQL that don't support GROUP BY expressions, use a workaround.

Discussion

GROUP BY shares the property with ORDER BY that as of MySQL 3.23.2 it can refer to expressions. This means you can use calculations as the basis for grouping. For example, to find the distribution of the length of state names, group by LENGTH(name):

```
mysql> SELECT LENGTH(name), COUNT(*)
    -> FROM states GROUP BY LENGTH(name);
+--------------+----------+
| LENGTH(name) | COUNT(*) |
+--------------+----------+
|            4 |        3 |
|            5 |        3 |
|            6 |        5 |
|            7 |        8 |
|            8 |       12 |
|            9 |        4 |
|           10 |        4 |
|           11 |        2 |
|           12 |        4 |
|           13 |        3 |
|           14 |        2 |
+--------------+----------+
```

Prior to MySQL 3.23.2, you cannot use expressions in GROUP BY clauses, so the preceding query would fail. In Recipe 6.3, workarounds for this problem were given with regard to ORDER BY, and the same methods apply to GROUP BY. One workaround is to give the expression an alias in the output column list and refer to the alias in the GROUP BY clause:

```
mysql> SELECT LENGTH(name) AS len, COUNT(*)
    -> FROM states GROUP BY len;
+------+----------+
| len  | COUNT(*) |
+------+----------+
|    4 |        3 |
|    5 |        3 |
|    6 |        5 |
|    7 |        8 |
|    8 |       12 |
|    9 |        4 |
|   10 |        4 |
|   11 |        2 |
|   12 |        4 |
|   13 |        3 |
|   14 |        2 |
+------+----------+
```

Another is to write the GROUP BY clause to refer to the output column position:

```
mysql> SELECT LENGTH(name), COUNT(*)
    -> FROM states GROUP BY 1;
```

```
+--------------+----------+
| LENGTH(name) | COUNT(*) |
+--------------+----------+
|            4 |        3 |
|            5 |        3 |
|            6 |        5 |
|            7 |        8 |
|            8 |       12 |
|            9 |        4 |
|           10 |        4 |
|           11 |        2 |
|           12 |        4 |
|           13 |        3 |
|           14 |        2 |
+--------------+----------+
```

Of course, these alternative ways of writing the query work in MySQL 3.23.2 and up as well—and you may find them more readable.

You can group by multiple expressions if you like. To find days of the year on which more than one state joined the Union, group by statehood month and day, then use HAVING and COUNT( ) to find the non-unique combinations:

```
mysql> SELECT MONTHNAME(statehood), DAYOFMONTH(statehood), COUNT(*)
    -> FROM states GROUP BY 1, 2 HAVING COUNT(*) > 1;
+----------------------+-----------------------+----------+
| MONTHNAME(statehood) | DAYOFMONTH(statehood) | COUNT(*) |
+----------------------+-----------------------+----------+
| February             |                    14 |        2 |
| June                 |                     1 |        2 |
| March                |                     1 |        2 |
| May                  |                    29 |        2 |
| November             |                     2 |        2 |
+----------------------+-----------------------+----------+
```

7.12   Categorizing Non-Categorical Data

Problem

You need to perform a summary on a set of values that are mostly unique and do not categorize well.

Solution

Use an expression to group the values into categories.

Discussion

One important application for grouping by expression results is to provide categories for values that are not particularly categorical. This is useful because GROUP BY works best for columns with repetitive values. For example, you might attempt to perform a population analysis by grouping records in the states table using values in the pop column. As it happens, that would not work very well, due to the high number of distinct values in the column. In fact, they're *all* distinct, as the following query shows:

```
mysql> SELECT COUNT(pop), COUNT(DISTINCT pop) FROM states;
+------------+---------------------+
| COUNT(pop) | COUNT(DISTINCT pop) |
+------------+---------------------+
|         50 |                  50 |
+------------+---------------------+
```

In situations like this, where values do not group nicely into a small number of sets, you can use a transformation that forces them into categories. First, determine the population range:

```
mysql> SELECT MIN(pop), MAX(pop) FROM states;
+----------+----------+
| MIN(pop) | MAX(pop) |
+----------+----------+
|   453588 | 29760021 |
+----------+----------+
```

We can see from that result that if we divide the pop values by five million, they'll group into six categories—a reasonable number. (The category ranges will be 1 to 5,000,000; 5,000,001 to 10,000,000; and so forth.) To put each population value in the proper category, divide by five million and use the integer result:

```
mysql> SELECT FLOOR(pop/5000000) AS 'population (millions)',
    -> COUNT(*) AS 'number of states'
    -> FROM states GROUP BY 1;
+-----------------------+------------------+
| population (millions) | number of states |
+-----------------------+------------------+
|                     0 |               35 |
|                     1 |                8 |
|                     2 |                4 |
|                     3 |                2 |
|                     5 |                1 |
+-----------------------+------------------+
```

Hm. That's not quite right. The expression groups the population values into a small number of categories, all right, but doesn't report the category values properly. Let's try multiplying the FLOOR( ) results by five:

```
mysql> SELECT FLOOR(pop/5000000)*5 AS 'population (millions)',
    -> COUNT(*) AS 'number of states'
    -> FROM states GROUP BY 1;
+-----------------------+------------------+
| population (millions) | number of states |
+-----------------------+------------------+
|                     0 |               35 |
|                     5 |                8 |
```

```
|                    10 |                4 |
|                    15 |                2 |
|                    25 |                1 |
+----------------------+------------------+
```

Hey, that still isn't correct! The maximum state population was 29,760,021, which should go into a category for 30 million, not one for 25 million. The problem is that the category-producing expression groups values toward the lower bound of each category. To group values toward the upper bound instead, use the following little trick. For categories of size n, you can place a value x into the proper category using the following expression:

```
FLOOR((x+(n-1))/n)
```

So the final form of our query looks like this:

```
mysql> SELECT FLOOR((pop+4999999)/5000000)*5 AS 'population (millions)',
    -> COUNT(*) AS 'number of states'
    -> FROM states GROUP BY 1;
+----------------------+------------------+
| population (millions) | number of states |
+----------------------+------------------+
|                     5 |               35 |
|                    10 |                8 |
|                    15 |                4 |
|                    20 |                2 |
|                    30 |                1 |
+----------------------+------------------+
```

The result shows clearly that the majority of U.S. states have a population of five million or less.

This technique works for all kinds of numeric values. For example, you can group mail table records into categories of 100,000 bytes as follows:

```
mysql> SELECT FLOOR((size+99999)/100000) AS 'size (100KB)',
    -> COUNT(*) AS 'number of messages'
    -> FROM mail GROUP BY 1;
+--------------+--------------------+
| size (100KB) | number of messages |
+--------------+--------------------+
|            1 |                 13 |
|            2 |                  1 |
|           10 |                  1 |
|           24 |                  1 |
+--------------+--------------------+
```

In some instances, it may be more appropriate to categorize groups on a logarithmic scale. For example, the state population values can be treated that way as follows:

```
mysql> SELECT FLOOR(LOG10(pop)) AS 'log10(population)',
    -> COUNT(*) AS 'number of states'
    -> FROM states GROUP BY 1;
```

```
+------------------+------------------+
| log10(population) | number of states |
+------------------+------------------+
|                5 |                7 |
|                6 |               36 |
|                7 |                7 |
+------------------+------------------+
```

How Repetitive Is a Set of Values?

To assess how much repetition is present in a set of values, use the ratio of COUNT(DISTINCT) and COUNT(). If all values are unique, both counts will be the same and the ratio will be 1. This is the case for the t values in the mail table and the pop values in the states table:

```
mysql> SELECT COUNT(DISTINCT t) / COUNT(t) FROM mail;
+-----------------------------+
| COUNT(DISTINCT t) / COUNT(t) |
+-----------------------------+
|                        1.00 |
+-----------------------------+
mysql> SELECT COUNT(DISTINCT pop) / COUNT(pop) FROM states;
+---------------------------------+
| COUNT(DISTINCT pop) / COUNT(pop) |
+---------------------------------+
|                            1.00 |
+---------------------------------+
```

For a more repetitive set of values, COUNT(DISTINCT) will be less than COUNT() and the ratio will be smaller:

```
mysql> SELECT COUNT(DISTINCT name) / COUNT(name) FROM driver_log;
+-----------------------------------+
| COUNT(DISTINCT name) / COUNT(name) |
+-----------------------------------+
|                              0.30 |
+-----------------------------------+
```

What's the practical use for this ratio? A result close to zero indicates a high degree of repetition, which means the values will group into a small number of categories naturally. A result of 1 or close to it indicates many unique values, with the consequence that GROUP BY won't be very efficient for grouping the values into categories. (That is, there will be a lot of categories, relative to the number of values.) This tells you that to generate a summary, you'll probably find it necessary to impose an artificial categorization on the values, using the techniques described in this section.

7.13   Controlling Summary Display Order

Problem

You want to sort the result of a summary query.

Solution

Use an ORDER BY clause—if GROUP BY doesn't produce the desired sort order.

Discussion

In MySQL, GROUP BY not only groups, it sorts. Thus there is often no need for an ORDER BY clause in a summary query. But you can still use ORDER BY if you want a sort order other than the one that GROUP BY produces by default. For example, to determine the number of days driven and total miles for each person in the driver_log table, run this query:

```
mysql> SELECT name, COUNT(*) AS days, SUM(miles) AS mileage
    -> FROM driver_log GROUP BY name;
+-------+------+-------------+
| name  | days | total miles |
+-------+------+-------------+
| Ben   |    3 |         362 |
| Henry |    5 |         911 |
| Suzi  |    2 |         893 |
+-------+------+-------------+
```

But that sorts by the names. If you want to sort drivers according to who drove the most days or miles, add the appropriate ORDER BY clause:

```
mysql> SELECT name, COUNT(*) AS days, SUM(miles) AS mileage
    -> FROM driver_log GROUP BY name
    -> ORDER BY days DESC;
+-------+------+---------+
| name  | days | mileage |
+-------+------+---------+
| Henry |    5 |     911 |
| Ben   |    3 |     362 |
| Suzi  |    2 |     893 |
+-------+------+---------+
mysql> SELECT name, COUNT(*) AS days, SUM(miles) AS mileage
    -> FROM driver_log GROUP BY name
    -> ORDER BY mileage DESC;
+-------+------+---------+
| name  | days | mileage |
+-------+------+---------+
| Henry |    5 |     911 |
| Suzi  |    2 |     893 |
| Ben   |    3 |     362 |
+-------+------+---------+
```

It's necessary to use an alias (or a column position number) in the ORDER BY clause to refer to the summary values. This is true even for MySQL 3.23.2 and up, which normally allows expressions in an ORDER BY clause; those expressions must refer to individual values, not values computed from a set.

Sometimes you can reorder a summary without an ORDER BY clause by choosing an appropriate GROUP BY expression. For example, if you count how many states joined the Union on each day of the week, grouped by day name, the results will be sorted in lexical order:

```
mysql> SELECT DAYNAME(statehood), COUNT(*) FROM states
    -> GROUP BY DAYNAME(statehood);
+--------------------+----------+
| DAYNAME(statehood) | COUNT(*) |
+--------------------+----------+
| Friday             |        8 |
| Monday             |        9 |
| Saturday           |       11 |
| Thursday           |        5 |
| Tuesday            |        6 |
| Wednesday          |       11 |
+--------------------+----------+
```

From this you can see that no state entered the Union on a Sunday, but that becomes apparent only after you stare at the query result for a while. The output would be more easily understood were it sorted into day-of-week order. It's possible to do that by adding an explicit ORDER BY to sort on the numeric day-of-week value, but another way to achieve the same result without ORDER BY is to group by DAYOFWEEK() rather than by DAYNAME():

```
mysql> SELECT DAYNAME(statehood), COUNT(*)
    -> FROM states GROUP BY DAYOFWEEK(statehood);
+--------------------+----------+
| DAYNAME(statehood) | COUNT(*) |
+--------------------+----------+
| Monday             |        9 |
| Tuesday            |        6 |
| Wednesday          |       11 |
| Thursday           |        5 |
| Friday             |        8 |
| Saturday           |       11 |
+--------------------+----------+
```

 GROUP BY may not sort output rows in other database systems. To write queries for MySQL that are less likely to need revision when used with other databases, you may find it beneficial to add an explicit ORDER BY clause in all cases.

7.14   Finding Smallest or Largest Summary Values

Problem

You want to compute per-group summary values, but display only the smallest or largest of them.

Solution

Add a LIMIT clause to the query.

Discussion

MIN( ) and MAX( ) find the values at the endpoints of a range of values, but if you want to know the extremes of a set of summary values, those functions won't work. The arguments to MIN( ) and MAX( ) cannot be other aggregate functions. For example, you can easily find per-driver mileage totals:

```
mysql> SELECT name, SUM(miles)
    -> FROM driver_log
    -> GROUP BY name;
+-------+------------+
| name  | SUM(miles) |
+-------+------------+
| Ben   |        362 |
| Henry |        911 |
| Suzi  |        893 |
+-------+------------+
```

But to select only the record for the driver with the most miles, this doesn't work:

```
mysql> SELECT name, SUM(miles)
    -> FROM driver_log
    -> GROUP BY name
    -> HAVING SUM(miles) = MAX(SUM(name));
ERROR 1111 at line 1: Invalid use of group function
```

Instead, order the rows with the largest SUM( ) values first and use LIMIT to select the first record:

```
mysql> SELECT name, SUM(miles) AS 'total miles'
    -> FROM driver_log
    -> GROUP BY name
    -> ORDER BY 'total miles' DESC LIMIT 1;
+-------+-------------+
| name  | total miles |
+-------+-------------+
| Henry |         911 |
+-------+-------------+
```

An alias is used in the ORDER BY clause because ORDER BY cannot refer directly to aggregate functions, as discussed earlier in Recipe 7.13.

Note that if there is more than one row with the given summary value, this type of query won't tell you that. For example, you might attempt to ascertain the most common initial letter for state names like this:

```
mysql> SELECT LEFT(name,1) AS letter, COUNT(*) AS count FROM states
    -> GROUP BY letter ORDER BY count DESC LIMIT 1;
+--------+-------+
| letter | count |
+--------+-------+
| M      |     8 |
+--------+-------+
```

But eight state names also begin with N. If you need to know all most-frequent values when there may be more than one of them, a two-query approach will be more useful:

```
mysql> SELECT LEFT(name,1) AS letter, @max:=COUNT(*) AS count FROM states
    -> GROUP BY letter ORDER BY count DESC LIMIT 1;
mysql> SELECT LEFT(name,1) AS letter, COUNT(*) AS count FROM states
    -> GROUP BY letter HAVING count = @max;
+--------+-------+
| letter | count |
+--------+-------+
| M      |     8 |
| N      |     8 |
+--------+-------+
```

7.15   Date-Based Summaries

Problem

You want to produce a summary based on date or time values.

Solution

Use GROUP BY to categorize temporal values into bins of the appropriate duration. Often this will involve using expressions to extract the significant parts of dates or times.

Discussion

To put records in time order, you use an ORDER BY clause to sort a column that has a temporal type. If instead you want to summarize records based on groupings into time intervals, you need to determine how to categorize each record into the proper interval and use GROUP BY to group them accordingly.

Sometimes you can use temporal values directly if they group naturally into the desired categories. This is quite likely if a table represents date or time parts using separate columns. For example, the *baseball1.com* master ballplayer table represents birth dates using separate year, month, and day columns. To see how many ballplayers were born on each day of the year, perform a calendar date summary that uses the month and day values but ignores the year:

```
mysql> SELECT birthmonth, birthday, COUNT(*)
    -> FROM master
    -> WHERE birthmonth IS NOT NULL AND birthday IS NOT NULL
    -> GROUP BY birthmonth, birthday;
+------------+----------+----------+
| birthmonth | birthday | COUNT(*) |
+------------+----------+----------+
|          1 |        1 |       47 |
|          1 |        2 |       40 |
|          1 |        3 |       50 |
|          1 |        4 |       38 |
...
|         12 |       28 |       33 |
|         12 |       29 |       32 |
|         12 |       30 |       32 |
|         12 |       31 |       27 |
+------------+----------+----------+
```

A less fine-grained summary can be obtained by using only the month values:

```
mysql> SELECT birthmonth, COUNT(*)
    -> FROM master
    -> WHERE birthmonth IS NOT NULL
    -> GROUP BY birthmonth;
+------------+----------+
| birthmonth | COUNT(*) |
+------------+----------+
|          1 |     1311 |
|          2 |     1144 |
|          3 |     1243 |
|          4 |     1179 |
|          5 |     1118 |
|          6 |     1105 |
|          7 |     1244 |
|          8 |     1438 |
|          9 |     1314 |
|         10 |     1438 |
|         11 |     1314 |
|         12 |     1269 |
+------------+----------+
```

Sometimes temporal values can be used directly, even when not represented as separate columns. To determine how many drivers were on the road and how many miles were driven each day, group the records in the driver_log table by date:

```
mysql> SELECT trav_date,
    -> COUNT(*) AS 'number of drivers', SUM(miles) As 'miles logged'
    -> FROM driver_log GROUP BY trav_date;
```

```
+------------+-------------------+--------------+
| trav_date  | number of drivers | miles logged |
+------------+-------------------+--------------+
| 2001-11-26 |                 1 |          115 |
| 2001-11-27 |                 1 |           96 |
| 2001-11-29 |                 3 |          822 |
| 2001-11-30 |                 2 |          355 |
| 2001-12-01 |                 1 |          197 |
| 2001-12-02 |                 2 |          581 |
+------------+-------------------+--------------+
```

However, this summary will grow lengthier as you add more records to the table. At some point, the number of distinct dates likely will become so large that the summary fails to be useful, and you'd probably decide to change the category size from daily to weekly or monthly.

When a temporal column contains so many distinct values that it fails to categorize well, it's typical for a summary to group records using expressions that map the relevant parts of the date or time values onto a smaller set of categories. For example, to produce a time-of-day summary for records in the mail table, do this:[*]

```
mysql> SELECT HOUR(t) AS hour,
    -> COUNT(*) AS 'number of messages',
    -> SUM(size) AS 'number of bytes sent'
    -> FROM mail
    -> GROUP BY hour;
+------+--------------------+----------------------+
| hour | number of messages | number of bytes sent |
+------+--------------------+----------------------+
|    7 |                  1 |                 3824 |
|    8 |                  1 |                  978 |
|    9 |                  2 |                 2904 |
|   10 |                  2 |              1056806 |
|   11 |                  1 |                 5781 |
|   12 |                  2 |               195798 |
|   13 |                  1 |                  271 |
|   14 |                  1 |                98151 |
|   15 |                  1 |                 1048 |
|   17 |                  2 |              2398338 |
|   22 |                  1 |                23992 |
|   23 |                  1 |                10294 |
+------+--------------------+----------------------+
```

To produce a day-of-week summary instead, use the DAYOFWEEK( ) function:

```
mysql> SELECT DAYOFWEEK(t) AS weekday,
    -> COUNT(*) AS 'number of messages',
    -> SUM(size) AS 'number of bytes sent'
    -> FROM mail
    -> GROUP BY weekday;
```

---

[*] Note that the result includes an entry only for hours of the day actually represented in the data. To generate a summary with an entry for every hour, use a join to fill in the "missing" values. See Recipe 12.9.

```
+---------+--------------------+----------------------+
| weekday | number of messages | number of bytes sent |
+---------+--------------------+----------------------+
|       1 |                  1 |                  271 |
|       2 |                  4 |              2500705 |
|       3 |                  4 |              1007190 |
|       4 |                  2 |                10907 |
|       5 |                  1 |                  873 |
|       6 |                  1 |                58274 |
|       7 |                  3 |               219965 |
+---------+--------------------+----------------------+
```

To make the output more meaningful, you might want to use DAYNAME() to display weekday names instead. However, because day names sort lexically (for example, "Tuesday" sorts after "Friday"), use DAYNAME() only for display purposes. Continue to group on the numeric day values so that output rows sort that way:

```
mysql> SELECT DAYNAME(t) AS weekday,
    -> COUNT(*) AS 'number of messages',
    -> SUM(size) AS 'number of bytes sent'
    -> FROM mail
    -> GROUP BY DAYOFWEEK(t);
+-----------+--------------------+----------------------+
| weekday   | number of messages | number of bytes sent |
+-----------+--------------------+----------------------+
| Sunday    |                  1 |                  271 |
| Monday    |                  4 |              2500705 |
| Tuesday   |                  4 |              1007190 |
| Wednesday |                  2 |                10907 |
| Thursday  |                  1 |                  873 |
| Friday    |                  1 |                58274 |
| Saturday  |                  3 |               219965 |
+-----------+--------------------+----------------------+
```

A similar technique can be used for summarizing month-of-year categories that are sorted by numeric value but displayed by month name.

Uses for temporal categorizations are plentiful:

- DATETIME or TIMESTAMP columns have the potential to contain many unique values. To produce daily summaries, strip off the time of day part to collapse all values occurring within a given day to the same value. Any of the following GROUP BY clauses will do this, though the last one is likely to be slowest:

  ```
  GROUP BY FROM_DAYS(TO_DAYS(col_name))
  GROUP BY YEAR(col_name), MONTH(col_name), DAYOFMONTH(col_name)
  GROUP BY DATE_FORMAT(col_name,'%Y-%m-%e')
  ```

- To produce monthly or quarterly sales reports, group by MONTH(col_name) or QUARTER(col_name) to place dates into the correct part of the year.

- To summarize web server activity, put your server's logs into MySQL and run queries that collapse the records into different time categories. Chapter 18 discusses how to do this for Apache.

7.16 Working with Per-Group and Overall Summary Values Simultaneously

Problem

You want to produce a report that requires different levels of summary detail. Or you want to compare per-group summary values to an overall summary value.

Solution

Use two queries that retrieve different levels of summary information. Or use a programming language to do some of the work so that you can use a single query.

Discussion

Sometimes a report involves different levels of summary information. For example, the following report displays the total number of miles per driver from the driver_log table, along with each driver's miles as a percentage of the total miles in the entire table:

```
+-------+--------------+------------------------+
| name  | miles/driver | percent of total miles |
+-------+--------------+------------------------+
| Ben   |          362 |        16.712834718375 |
| Henry |          911 |        42.059095106187 |
| Suzi  |          893 |        41.228070175439 |
+-------+--------------+------------------------+
```

The percentages represent the ratio of each driver's miles to the total miles for all drivers. To perform the percentage calculation, you need a per-group summary to get each driver's miles and also an overall summary to get the total miles. Generating the report in SQL involves a couple of queries, because you can't calculate a per-group summary and an overall summary in a single query.* First, run a query to get the overall mileage total:

```
mysql> SELECT @total := SUM(miles) AS 'total miles' FROM driver_log;
+-------------+
| total miles |
+-------------+
|        2166 |
+-------------+
```

---

* Well... that's not strictly true. With a subselect, you could generate the summary with a single query. But MySQL won't have subselects until Version 4.1.

Then calculate the per-group values and use the overall total to compute the percentages:

```
mysql> SELECT name,
    -> SUM(miles) AS 'miles/driver',
    -> (SUM(miles)*100)/@total AS 'percent of total miles'
    -> FROM driver_log GROUP BY name;
+-------+--------------+------------------------+
| name  | miles/driver | percent of total miles |
+-------+--------------+------------------------+
| Ben   |          362 |        16.712834718375 |
| Henry |          911 |        42.059095106187 |
| Suzi  |          893 |        41.228070175439 |
+-------+--------------+------------------------+
```

A different form of multiple-query solution that doesn't involve a variable is to retrieve the overall summary into another table, then join that with the original table:

```
mysql> CREATE TEMPORARY TABLE t
    -> SELECT SUM(miles) AS total FROM driver_log;
mysql> SELECT driver_log.name,
    -> SUM(driver_log.miles) AS 'miles/driver',
    -> (SUM(driver_log.miles)*100)/t.total AS 'percent of total miles'
    -> FROM driver_log, t GROUP BY driver_log.name;
+-------+--------------+------------------------+
| name  | miles/driver | percent of total miles |
+-------+--------------+------------------------+
| Ben   |          362 |                  16.71 |
| Henry |          911 |                  42.06 |
| Suzi  |          893 |                  41.23 |
+-------+--------------+------------------------+
```

If you're generating the report from within a program, you can do some of the summary math using your programming language and eliminate one of the queries. Here's an example in Python:

```python
# issue query to calculate per-driver totals
cursor = conn.cursor ()
cursor.execute ("SELECT name, SUM(miles) FROM driver_log GROUP BY name")
rows = cursor.fetchall ()
cursor.close ()

# iterate once through result to calculate overall total miles
total = 0
for (name, miles) in rows:
    total = total + miles

# iterate again to print report
print "name       miles/driver  percent of total miles"
for (name, miles) in rows:
    print "%-8s        %5d               %f" \
            % (name, miles, (100*miles)/total)
```

Another type of problem that uses different levels of summary information occurs when you want to compare per-group summary values with the corresponding overall summary value. Suppose you want to determine which drivers had a lower average miles per day than the group average. Using only SQL, this task can't be performed with a single query, but you can easily do it with two. First, calculate the overall average and save it in a variable:

```
mysql> SELECT @overall_avg := AVG(miles) FROM driver_log;
+----------------------------+
| @overall_avg := AVG(miles) |
+----------------------------+
|                   216.6000 |
+----------------------------+
```

Then compare each driver's average to the saved value using a HAVING clause:

```
mysql> SELECT name, AVG(miles) AS driver_avg FROM driver_log
    -> GROUP BY name
    -> HAVING driver_avg < @overall_avg;
+-------+------------+
| name  | driver_avg |
+-------+------------+
| Ben   |   120.6667 |
| Henry |   182.2000 |
+-------+------------+
```

Just as when producing a report that uses different levels of summary information, you can solve this problem without using two queries if you're writing a program by using your programming language to do some of the work:

1. Issue a query to retrieve the per-group summary information.

2. Iterate through the result set once to calculate the overall summary value.

3. Iterate through the result set again, comparing each per-group summary value to the overall value and displaying only those records for which the comparison succeeds.

7.17 Generating a Report That Includes a Summary and a List

Problem

You want to write a query that displays a summary, together with the list of records associated with each summary value.

Solution

Recognize that this is a variant on working with different levels of summary information, and solve the problem using the same techniques.

Discussion

Suppose you want to produce a report that looks like this:

```
Name: Ben; days on road: 3; miles driven: 362
  date: 2001-11-29, trip length: 131
  date: 2001-11-30, trip length: 152
  date: 2001-12-02, trip length: 79
Name: Henry; days on road: 5; miles driven: 911
  date: 2001-11-26, trip length: 115
  date: 2001-11-27, trip length: 96
  date: 2001-11-29, trip length: 300
  date: 2001-11-30, trip length: 203
  date: 2001-12-01, trip length: 197
Name: Suzi; days on road: 2; miles driven: 893
  date: 2001-11-29, trip length: 391
  date: 2001-12-02, trip length: 502
```

The report shows, for each driver in the `driver_log` table, the following information:

- A summary line showing the driver name, the number of days on the road, and the number of miles driven.
- A list of the dates and mileages for the individual trips from which the summary values are calculated.

This scenario is a variation on the "different levels of summary information" problem discussed in the previous recipe. It may not seem like it at first, because one of the types of information is a list rather than a summary. But that's really just a "level zero" summary. This kind of problem appears in many other forms:

- You have a database that lists contributions to candidates in your political party. The party chair requests a printout that shows, for each candidate, the number of contributions and total amount contributed, as well as a list of contributor names and addresses.
- You want to make a handout for a company presentation that summarizes total sales per sales region, with a list under each region showing the sales for each state in the region.

In each case, the solutions are like those discussed in the previous recipe:

- Run separate queries to get the information for each level of detail that you require. (Just as a single query won't produce per-group summary values and an overall summary value at the same time, neither will one query produce per-group summary values and a list of each group's individual records.)
- Fetch the rows that make up the lists and perform the summary calculations yourself to eliminate the summary query.

Let's use each approach to produce the driver report shown at the beginning of this section. The following implementation (in Python) generates the report using one query to summarize the days and miles per driver, and another to fetch the individual trip records for each driver:

```
# select total miles per driver and construct a dictionary that
# maps each driver name to days on the road and miles driven
name_map = { }
cursor = conn.cursor ()
cursor.execute ("""
                SELECT name, COUNT(name), SUM(miles)
                FROM driver_log GROUP BY name
            """)
for (name, days, miles) in cursor.fetchall ():
    name_map[name] = (days, miles)

# select trips for each driver and print the report, displaying the
# summary entry for each driver prior to the list of trips
cursor.execute ("""
                SELECT name, trav_date, miles
                FROM driver_log ORDER BY name, trav_date
            """)
cur_name = ""
for (name, trav_date, miles) in cursor.fetchall ():
    if cur_name != name:   # new driver; print driver's summary info
        print "Name: %s; days on road: %d; miles driven: %d" \
                % (name, name_map[name][0], name_map[name][1])
        cur_name = name
    print "  date: %s, trip length: %d" % (trav_date, miles)
cursor.close ()
```

By performing summary calculations in the program, you can reduce the number of queries required. If you iterate through the trip list and calculate the per-driver day counts and mileage totals yourself, a single query suffices:

```
# get list of trips for the drivers
cursor = conn.cursor ()
cursor.execute ("""
                SELECT name, trav_date, miles FROM driver_log
                ORDER BY name, trav_date
            """)
rows = cursor.fetchall ()
cursor.close ()

# iterate through rows once to construct a dictionary that
# maps each driver name to days on the road and miles driven
# (the dictionary entries are lists rather than tuples because
# we need mutable values that can be modified in the loop)
name_map = { }
for (name, trav_date, miles) in rows:
    if not name_map.has_key (name): # initialize entry if nonexistent
        name_map[name] = [0, 0]
    name_map[name][0] = name_map[name][0] + 1      # count days
    name_map[name][1] = name_map[name][1] + miles  # sum miles

# iterate through rows again to print the report, displaying the
```

```
# summary entry for each driver prior to the list of trips
cur_name = ""
for (name, trav_date, miles) in rows:
    if cur_name != name:     # new driver; print driver's summary info
        print "Name: %s; days on road: %d; miles driven: %d" \
                        % (name, name_map[name][0], name_map[name][1])
        cur_name = name
    print "    date: %s, trip length: %d" % (trav_date, miles)
```

Should you require more levels of summary information, this type of problem gets more difficult. For example, you might want the report showing driver summaries and trip logs to be preceded by a line that shows the total miles for all drivers:

```
Total miles driven by all drivers combined: 2166

Name: Ben; days on road: 3; miles driven: 362
   date: 2001-11-29, trip length: 131
   date: 2001-11-30, trip length: 152
   date: 2001-12-02, trip length: 79
Name: Henry; days on road: 5; miles driven: 911
   date: 2001-11-26, trip length: 115
   date: 2001-11-27, trip length: 96
   date: 2001-11-29, trip length: 300
   date: 2001-11-30, trip length: 203
   date: 2001-12-01, trip length: 197
Name: Suzi; days on road: 2; miles driven: 893
   date: 2001-11-29, trip length: 391
   date: 2001-12-02, trip length: 502
```

In this case, you need either another query to produce the total mileage, or another calculation in your program that computes the overall total.

CHAPTER 8

Modifying Tables with ALTER TABLE

8.0   Introduction

You'll probably find it necessary on occasion to redesign some of your tables. A change in an application's specification may require that you record information not accounted for in the original definition of a table used by that application. Or you may find that an AUTO_INCREMENT column is running out of room to generate new sequence numbers and you need to change the column to use a larger integer type. MySQL offers many possibilities for modifying a table's structure. This chapter describes how to make the following types of changes:

Dropping, adding, or repositioning a column.   Columns that have become unnecessary or that you discover to be redundant may be removed to simplify a table and to save space. Or you may move columns from one table to another as part of a normalization procedure. Columns may be added when you need to record additional types of information.

Changing a column definition or name.   If a column as originally created does not serve your purposes, you may be able to correct the problem by redefining it. For example, you can convert a string column that is case sensitive to one that is not, or vice versa. Or you may have an AUTO_INCREMENT column that is a TINYINT and has room only for 127 sequence values. By changing the column to be unsigned or to use a larger integer type, you can extend the range of the sequence. Renaming a column can be useful if after an upgrade to a more recent version of MySQL you find that a column name is now a reserved word. Or maybe you just want to rename a column like num to something more descriptive like test_score to make the column's purpose more explicit.

Changing a table's type.   The various table types in MySQL have differing characteristics. If a table's type is less suitable for your applications than another type, you can convert it.

Renaming a table.   Like renaming a column, this can be done if you come up with a better name. Or you can rename for other purposes such as rotating the names of a set of tables used for logging.

Modifying a table's index structure. Dropping an index that is rarely used can improve performance of inserts and updates of table rows, because that index then need not be updated. Adding an index to a column that you reference frequently in queries can be useful for improving SELECT performance. Indexing can also be used to remove duplicate values from a table.

Most of these operations are handled by ALTER TABLE, one of MySQL's most powerful but least appreciated statements. By that I mean you can do a lot with ALTER TABLE, but many MySQL users do not fully exploit its capabilities. Perhaps this is because the ALTER TABLE statement has so many options that its syntax is somewhat daunting. I hope that this chapter will demystify the statement and make its utility more apparent.

Before you begin reading the rest of this chapter, create the following table for use in working through the examples:

```
CREATE TABLE mytbl
(
    i   INT,
    c   CHAR(1)
);
```

As you make each of the modifications shown in the following sections, you can see the resulting changes in this table's structure, either by issuing a SHOW COLUMNS FROM mytbl statement or a SHOW CREATE TABLE mytbl statement. For example, after you create mytbl, SHOW COLUMNS should display the following information:

```
mysql> SHOW COLUMNS FROM mytbl;
+-------+---------+------+-----+---------+-------+
| Field | Type    | Null | Key | Default | Extra |
+-------+---------+------+-----+---------+-------+
| i     | int(11) | YES  |     | NULL    |       |
| c     | char(1) | YES  |     | NULL    |       |
+-------+---------+------+-----+---------+-------+
```

Observe that MySQL automatically assigns default values and determines whether the columns can contain NULL values, even though the CREATE TABLE statement does not explicitly specify these attributes. The significance of this is discussed in Recipe 8.3.

8.1 Dropping, Adding, or Repositioning a Column

Problem

You want to get rid of a table column, add a new column, or move a column around within a table.

Solution

Use the DROP or ADD clauses of ALTER TABLE to remove or add a column. To move a column, drop it and then put it back where you want it.

Discussion

To remove a column from a table, use DROP followed by the column name. This statement drops the i column, leaving only the c column in mytbl:

```
ALTER TABLE mytbl DROP i;
```

DROP will not work if the column is the only one left in the table. (To verify this, try to drop the c column from mytbl after dropping the i column; an error will occur.)

To add a column, use ADD and specify the column definition. The following statement restores the i column to mytbl:

```
ALTER TABLE mytbl ADD i INT;
```

After issuing this statement, mytbl will contain the same two columns that it had when you first created the table, but will not have quite the same structure. That's because new columns are added to the end of the table by default. So even though i originally was the first column in mytbl, now it is the last one:

```
mysql> SHOW COLUMNS FROM mytbl;
+-------+---------+------+-----+---------+-------+
| Field | Type    | Null | Key | Default | Extra |
+-------+---------+------+-----+---------+-------+
| c     | char(1) | YES  |     | NULL    |       |
| i     | int(11) | YES  |     | NULL    |       |
+-------+---------+------+-----+---------+-------+
```

To indicate that you want a column at a specific position within the table, either use FIRST to make it the first column, or AFTER col_name to indicate that the new column should be placed after col_name. Try the following ALTER TABLE statements, using SHOW COLUMNS after each one to see what effect each one has:

```
ALTER TABLE mytbl DROP i;
ALTER TABLE mytbl ADD i INT FIRST;
ALTER TABLE mytbl DROP i;
ALTER TABLE mytbl ADD i INT AFTER c;
```

The FIRST and AFTER specifiers work only with the ADD clause. This means that if you want to reposition an existing column within a table, you first must DROP it and then ADD it at the new position.

8.2   Changing a Column Definition or Name

Problem

You want to change how a column is defined.

Solution

Use MODIFY or CHANGE. MODIFY is simpler, but cannot change the column name. CHANGE is more confusing to use, but can change both the name and the definition.

Discussion

To change a column's definition, use MODIFY or CHANGE.[*] Of the two, MODIFY has the simpler syntax: name the column, then specify its new definition. For example, to change column c from CHAR(1) to CHAR(10), do this:

```
ALTER TABLE mytbl MODIFY c CHAR(10);
```

With CHANGE, the syntax is a bit different. After the CHANGE keyword, you name the column you want to change, then specify the new definition, which *includes* the new name. The second column name is required, because CHANGE also allows you to rename the column, not just change its definition. For example, to change i from INT to BIGINT and rename it to j at the same time, the statement looks like this:

```
ALTER TABLE mytbl CHANGE i j BIGINT;
```

If you now use CHANGE to convert j from BIGINT back to INT without changing the column name, the statement may look a bit odd:

```
ALTER TABLE mytbl CHANGE j j INT;
```

At first glance, the statement seems incorrect—the column name appears to be given one too many times. However, it's correct as written. The fact that the CHANGE syntax requires two column names (even if they're both the same) is simply something you have to get used to. This is especially important to remember if your version of MySQL is old enough that you can't use MODIFY. Any ALTER TABLE statement that uses MODIFY *col_name* can be replaced by one that uses CHANGE *col_name col_name*. That is, the following two statements are equivalent:

```
ALTER TABLE tbl_name MODIFY col_name ... ;
ALTER TABLE tbl_name CHANGE col_name col_name ... ;
```

It would be nice to have a form of the ALTER TABLE statement that renamed a column without the need to repeat the definition, especially for working with ENUM and SET

---

[*] MODIFY requires MySQL 3.22.16 or later.

columns that have many member values. Unfortunately, there is no such statement, which makes these column types somewhat difficult to work with when using ALTER TABLE. Suppose you add to mytbl an ENUM column e that has several members:

```
ALTER TABLE mytbl ADD e
    ENUM('hardware','software','books','office supplies',
                'telecommunications','furniture','utilities',
                'shipping','tax');
```

If you want to rename the column from e to e2, you use CHANGE to indicate the new name. But you must also repeat the column definition as well:

```
ALTER TABLE mytbl CHANGE e e2
    ENUM('hardware','software','books','office supplies',
                'telecommunications','furniture','utilities',
                'shipping','tax');
```

Ugh. That's too much typing. Manually entering the proper ALTER TABLE statement for this kind of operation is quite a lot of work, not to mention error-prone. One way to avoid retyping the definition is to capture the current definition in a file and edit the file to produce the proper ALTER TABLE statement:

- Run *mysqldump* to get the CREATE TABLE statement that contains the column definition:

  ```
  % mysqldump --no-data cookbook mytbl > test.txt
  ```

  The resulting file, *test.txt*, should contain this statement:

  ```
  CREATE TABLE mytbl (
    c char(10) default NULL,
    j bigint(20) NOT NULL default '100',
    e enum('hardware','software','books','office supplies','telecommunications',
  'furniture','utilities','shipping','tax') default NULL
  ) TYPE=MyISAM;
  ```

  The *--no-data* option tells *mysqldump* not to dump the data from the table; it's used here because only the table creation statement is needed.

- Edit the *test.txt* file to remove everything but the definition for the e column:

  ```
  e enum('hardware','software','books','office supplies','telecommunications',
  'furniture','utilities','shipping','tax') default NULL
  ```

- Modify the definition to produce an ALTER TABLE statement with a semicolon at the end:

  ```
  ALTER TABLE mytbl CHANGE e e2
    enum('hardware','software','books','office supplies','telecommunications',
  'furniture','utilities','shipping','tax') default NULL;
  ```

- Write *test.txt* back out to save it, then get out of the editor and feed *test.txt* as a batch file to *mysql*:

  ```
  % mysql cookbook < test.txt
  ```

For simple columns, this procedure is more work than just typing the ALTER TABLE statement manually, of course. But for ENUM and SET columns with long and ungainly definitions, using an editor to create a *mysql* batch file from *mysqldump* output makes a lot of sense. You can also use this technique to make it easier to reorder the items in an ENUM or SET column, or to add or delete members from the column definition. For another approach to column manipulation, see Recipe 9.8, which develops a utility script that makes it trivial to add member values. The script examines the table structure and uses that information to figure out the proper ALTER TABLE statement for modifying an ENUM or SET column.

8.3 The Effect of ALTER TABLE on Null and Default Value Attributes

Problem

You changed a column definition, but MySQL modified the column's NULL value and default value attributes when you didn't tell it to.

Solution

Those attributes are part of the column definition. If you don't specify them explicitly, MySQL chooses their values for you. So just be more specific about how you want the column defined.

Discussion

When you MODIFY or CHANGE a column, you can also specify whether or not the column can contain NULL values, and what its default value is. In fact, if you don't do this, MySQL automatically assigns values for these attributes, with the result that the column may end up defined not quite the way you intend. To see this, try the following sequence of commands. First, modify j so that it cannot contain NULL values and to have a default value of 100, then see what SHOW COLUMNS tells you:[*]

```
mysql> ALTER TABLE mytbl MODIFY j INT NOT NULL DEFAULT 100;
mysql> SHOW COLUMNS FROM mytbl LIKE 'j';
+-------+---------+------+-----+---------+-------+
| Field | Type    | Null | Key | Default | Extra |
+-------+---------+------+-----+---------+-------+
| j     | int(11) |      |     | 100     |       |
+-------+---------+------+-----+---------+-------+
```

---

[*] The LIKE 'str' clause for SHOW COLUMNS causes the statement to show information only for columns having names that match the string. The string can contain SQL pattern characters if you want it to match several column names. See Recipe 9.5.

So far, so good. Now if you were to decide to change j from INT to BIGINT, you might try the following statement:

```
mysql> ALTER TABLE mytbl MODIFY j BIGINT;
```

However, that also undoes the NULL and DEFAULT specifications of the previous ALTER TABLE statement:

```
mysql> SHOW COLUMNS FROM mytbl LIKE 'j';
+-------+------------+------+-----+---------+-------+
| Field | Type       | Null | Key | Default | Extra |
+-------+------------+------+-----+---------+-------+
| j     | bigint(20) | YES  |     | NULL    |       |
+-------+------------+------+-----+---------+-------+
```

To avoid this, the MODIFY statement should specify the null and default value attributes explicitly:

```
mysql> ALTER TABLE mytbl MODIFY j BIGINT NOT NULL DEFAULT 100;
mysql> SHOW COLUMNS FROM mytbl LIKE 'j';
+-------+------------+------+-----+---------+-------+
| Field | Type       | Null | Key | Default | Extra |
+-------+------------+------+-----+---------+-------+
| j     | bigint(20) |      |     | 100     |       |
+-------+------------+------+-----+---------+-------+
```

The implication of this exercise is that if a column is defined such that its null and default value attributes are not what MySQL would assign automatically, you must specify them explicitly in your ALTER TABLE statement if you don't want them to change when you modify some other aspect of the column definition.

This fact is important for some of the recipes shown in Chapter 9, such as one program that converts a table to use VARCHAR rather than CHAR columns, and another that adds new elements to ENUM or SET columns. In each case, the programs take care to avoid unintended column changes by including NULL and DEFAULT specifiers in the ALTER TABLE statements that they generate.

8.4   Changing a Column's Default Value

Problem

You want to leave a column definition alone except for the default value.

Solution

Use SET DEFAULT to specify the default value explicitly, or DROP DEFAULT to remove the current default and allow MySQL to assign the "default default."

Discussion

A column's default value is part of its definition, but can be modified separately from other aspects of the definition. To change a default value, use `ALTER col_name SET DEFAULT`:

```
ALTER TABLE mytbl ALTER j SET DEFAULT 1000;
```

Default values must be constants. For example, you cannot set the default for a date-valued column to `NOW( )`, although that would be very useful.

To drop a default value, use `ALTER col_name DROP DEFAULT`:

```
ALTER TABLE mytbl ALTER j DROP DEFAULT;
```

In this case, the column's default value reverts to the standard default for the column type. For columns that can contain `NULL` values, this will be `NULL`. Otherwise, the general defaults are 0, the empty string, or the "zero" date or time for numeric, string, or date or time columns, respectively. (The exceptions are for `AUTO_INCREMENT`, `ENUM`, and `TIMESTAMP` columns, for which the defaults are the next sequence number, the first enumeration member, and the current date and time.)

8.5   Changing a Table Type

Problem

A table has one type, and now you realize that another table type has properties that are more desirable for the way you use the table.

Solution

Use `ALTER TABLE` to change its type with a `TYPE` clause.

Discussion

MySQL supports several tables types, each of which have differing characteristics. Sometimes it's necessary or desirable to convert a table from one type to another. Some situations where a change of table type can be useful are as follows:

- Table conversions sometimes are done to gain access to features that are supported by one table type but not another. For example, ISAM tables do not allow `NULL` values in indexed columns. Also, `AUTO_INCREMENT` behavior in ISAM tables is such that sequence values may be non-monotonic under certain conditions. (See Chapter 11, for information about this.) You can convert an ISAM table to the MyISAM type, which does not suffer from these problems. Or you might find that you need to perform transactions on a table created using a type that doesn't provide transactional capabilities. To handle this problem, you can alter the table to a type such as InnoDB or BDB that does support transactions.

- The oldest table type supported by MySQL is ISAM, but ISAM tables are deprecated and at some point no longer will be supported. If you have ISAM tables, you should convert them at some point to another table type. Otherwise, after ISAM support is dropped, you'll be unable to upgrade to new releases of MySQL.

Changing a table type is easy; use ALTER TABLE with a TYPE specifier. For example, to convert a table to the MyISAM type, use this statement:

```
ALTER TABLE tbl_name TYPE = MYISAM;
```

To find out the current type of a table, use the SHOW TABLE STATUS statement (introduced in MySQL 3.23.0) or SHOW CREATE TABLE (introduced in MySQL 3.23.20):

```
mysql> SHOW TABLE STATUS LIKE 'mytbl'\G
*************************** 1. row ***************************
           Name: mytbl
           Type: MyISAM
     Row_format: Fixed
           Rows: 0
 Avg_row_length: 0
    Data_length: 0
Max_data_length: 85899345919
   Index_length: 1024
      Data_free: 0
 Auto_increment: NULL
    Create_time: 2002-07-15 21:28:34
    Update_time: 2002-07-15 21:28:34
     Check_time: NULL
 Create_options:
        Comment:
mysql> SHOW CREATE TABLE mytbl\G
*************************** 1. row ***************************
       Table: mytbl
Create Table: CREATE TABLE `mytbl` (
  `c` char(10) default NULL,
  `j` bigint(20) default NULL,
  `e2` enum('hardware','software','books','office supplies',
'telecommunications','furniture','utilities','shipping','tax') default NULL
) TYPE=MyISAM
```

Alternatively, use the *mysqldump* command-line utility:

```
% mysqldump --no-data cookbook mytbl
CREATE TABLE mytbl (
  c char(10) default NULL,
  j bigint(20) default NULL,
  e2 enum('hardware','software','books','office supplies',
'telecommunications','furniture','utilities','shipping','tax') default NULL
) TYPE=MyISAM;
```

8.6   Renaming a Table

Problem

A table needs to be renamed.

Solution

You can use ALTER TABLE or RENAME TABLE for this.

Discussion

To rename a table, use the RENAME option of the ALTER TABLE statement:

```
ALTER TABLE old_name RENAME TO new_name;
```

As of Version 3.23.23, MySQL includes an explicit RENAME TABLE statement:

```
RENAME TABLE old_name TO new_name;
```

RENAME TABLE allows you to rename multiple tables, which allows you to do things such as swap the names of two tables in a single statement:

```
RENAME TABLE name1 TO temp_name, name2 TO name1, tmp_name to name2;
```

You can achieve the same result with ALTER TABLE, except that you need three separate statements. Because of that, the tables become available to other clients in the brief intervals between statements, which may be undesirable. Using a single RENAME TABLE statement avoids this problem.

RENAME TABLE is also useful for rotating tables. To do this without having an interval in which the log table is unavailable to clients, create an empty version under a temporary name, then rotate the files using a single RENAME TABLE statement. For example, if you want to keep monthly log tables, named using the year and month, you might do something like this:

```
CREATE TABLE log_temp (...);
RENAME TABLE log TO log_2001_05, log_temp TO log;
```

To rotate log tables to keep a set of daily tables covering the last week, you could run the following statements daily:

```
CREATE TABLE log_temp (...);
DROP TABLE IF exists log_7;
RENAME TABLE log_6 TO log_7,
    log_5 TO log_6,
    log_4 TO log_5,
    log_3 TO log_4,
    log_2 TO log_3,
    log_1 TO log_2,
    log TO log_1,
    log_tmp TO log;
```

8.7 Adding or Dropping Indexes

Problem

Table lookups are slow. Or INSERTS and UPDATES are slow.

Solution

ALTER TABLE can not only drop or add columns, it can drop or add indexes on those columns. These operations often are useful for improving the performance of a database. Typically, indexing a column that you query frequently helps SELECT statements run faster because the index allows MySQL to avoid full table scans. Dropping indexes can sometimes be useful as well. Whenever a row is modified, MySQL must update any indexes that include the modified columns. If you don't actually use a particular index very much, it's possible that your table is overindexed and that dropping the index will speed up performance of table updates.

Discussion

For the discussion in this section, it's useful to begin again with a new copy of the mytbl example table. Use DROP TABLE and CREATE TABLE to remove the existing version and recreate it in its original form:

```
DROP TABLE mytbl;
CREATE TABLE mytbl
(
    i   INT,
    c   CHAR(1)
);
```

In earlier sections of this chapter, SHOW COLUMNS was used to see the effect of table modifications. For index-changing operations, use SHOW INDEX rather than SHOW COLUMNS. Currently, the table has no indexes, because none were specified in the CREATE TABLE statement:

```
mysql> SHOW INDEX FROM mytbl;
Empty set (0.00 sec)
```

Adding Indexes

There are four types of statements for adding indexes to a table:

```
ALTER TABLE tbl_name ADD PRIMARY KEY (column_list);
ALTER TABLE tbl_name ADD UNIQUE index_name (column_list);
ALTER TABLE tbl_name ADD INDEX index_name (column_list);
ALTER TABLE tbl_name ADD FULLTEXT index_name (column_list);
```

The first statement adds a PRIMARY KEY, which means that indexed values must be unique and cannot be NULL. The second creates an index for which values must be unique (with the exception of NULL values, which may appear multiple times). The third adds an ordinary index in which any value may appear more than once. The fourth creates a special FULLTEXT index that is used for text-searching purposes. FULLTEXT searches are discussed in more detail in Recipe 4.11.

For those statements that include *index_name* in the syntax, the index name is optional. If you don't specify a name, MySQL assigns one automatically. *column_list* indicates which columns to index; it should be a list of one or more column names separated by commas. As simple examples, the first of the following statements creates a single-column index on c, and the second creates a multiple-column index that includes both c and i:

```
ALTER TABLE mytbl ADD INDEX (c);
ALTER TABLE mytbl ADD INDEX (c,i);
```

In many cases, indexed columns must be declared NOT NULL. For example, if you create mytbl as an ISAM table type, the preceding ADD INDEX statements will fail because ISAM tables do not allow NULL in any kind of index. And no matter what the table type, columns in a PRIMARY KEY cannot contain NULL values. If you try to add an index and MySQL issues a NULL-related complaint, use ALTER TABLE to change the relevant column or columns to NOT NULL and then try adding the index again. For example, if you try to make column i a PRIMARY KEY as follows, an error results:

```
mysql> ALTER TABLE mytbl ADD PRIMARY KEY (i);
ERROR 1171 at line 5: All parts of a PRIMARY KEY must be NOT NULL;
If you need NULL in a key, use UNIQUE instead
```

To deal with this, redefine i to be NOT NULL, then try again:

```
mysql> ALTER TABLE mytbl MODIFY i INT NOT NULL;
mysql> ALTER TABLE mytbl ADD PRIMARY KEY (i);
```

Alternatively, as the error message indicates, you can create a UNIQUE index rather than a PRIMARY KEY should you wish to allow NULL values in the index.

Dropping Indexes

To drop an index, use one of the following statements:

```
ALTER TABLE tbl_name DROP PRIMARY KEY;
ALTER TABLE tbl_name DROP INDEX index_name;
```

Dropping a PRIMARY KEY is easiest, because you need not know the index name:

```
ALTER TABLE mytbl DROP PRIMARY KEY;
```

To drop an index that is not a PRIMARY KEY, you must specify the index name. If you don't know the name, use SHOW INDEX. Vertical-format output (specified by \G) often is useful with this statement, to avoid long line wraparound:

```
mysql> SHOW INDEX FROM mytbl\G
*************************** 1. row ***************************
```

```
              Table: mytbl
        Non_unique: 1
          Key_name: c
      Seq_in_index: 1
       Column_name: c
         Collation: A
       Cardinality: NULL
          Sub_part: NULL
            Packed: NULL
           Comment:
*************************** 2. row ***************************
              Table: mytbl
        Non_unique: 1
          Key_name: c_2
      Seq_in_index: 1
       Column_name: c
         Collation: A
       Cardinality: NULL
          Sub_part: NULL
            Packed: NULL
           Comment:
*************************** 3. row ***************************
              Table: mytbl
        Non_unique: 1
          Key_name: c_2
      Seq_in_index: 2
       Column_name: i
         Collation: A
       Cardinality: NULL
          Sub_part: NULL
            Packed: NULL
           Comment:
```

The Key_name and Seq_in_index values show the index names and the positions of columns within an index. Those values indicate in the preceding output that mytbl has a single-column index named c and a multiple-column index named c_2. (These are the names that MySQL chose for the first two indexes created earlier.) The statement to drop the indexes looks like this:

```
ALTER TABLE mytbl DROP INDEX c, DROP INDEX c_2;
```

This statement illustrates that you can perform multiple actions with a single ALTER TABLE statement, if you separate the actions by commas.

See Also

An alternative to ALTER TABLE for modifying indexes is to use the CREATE INDEX and DROP INDEX statements. Internally, MySQL maps these onto ALTER TABLE statements, so there's nothing you can do with them that you can't do with ALTER TABLE. See the MySQL Reference Manual for more information.

8.8   Eliminating Duplicates by Adding an Index

Problem

A table has duplicates and you'd like to get rid of them.

Solution

One way to do this is to create a unique index on the column or columns containing duplicates.

Discussion

If MySQL discovers duplicate key values when you try to create a PRIMARY KEY or a UNIQUE index, it aborts the ALTER TABLE operation. To ignore the duplicates and proceed anyway, use ALTER IGNORE TABLE rather than ALTER TABLE. The IGNORE keyword tells MySQL to retain the first row containing a duplicated key value and discard the others. This is, in fact, a useful way to eliminate duplicates in a column or set of columns: just create a unique-valued index and let MySQL throw away the duplicates. (If you need to identify which key values are duplicated, though, that's not a suitable technique. See Recipe 14.3 for information on duplicate identification.)

To see how IGNORE works to eliminate duplicates, use mytbl, which now has no indexes if you've issued the index-modification statements shown earlier. First, insert some duplicate values into the table:

```
mysql> INSERT INTO mytbl (i,c) VALUES(1,'a'),(1,'a'),(1,NULL),(1,NULL),
    -> (2,'a'),(2,'a'),(2,'b'),(2,'b');
mysql> SELECT * FROM mytbl;
+---+------+
| i | c    |
+---+------+
| 1 | a    |
| 1 | a    |
| 1 | NULL |
| 1 | NULL |
| 2 | a    |
| 2 | a    |
| 2 | b    |
| 2 | b    |
+---+------+
```

Now suppose you want to create a unique-valued index comprising the i and c columns. A PRIMARY KEY cannot be used here, because c contains NULL values. You can create a UNIQUE index, but if you try to do so without using IGNORE, you'll get an error:

```
mysql> ALTER TABLE mytbl ADD UNIQUE (i,c);
ERROR 1062 at line 1: Duplicate entry '1-a' for key 1
```

Add IGNORE to the statement, then use SELECT to have a look at the table contents to see how the duplicates have been removed:

```
mysql> ALTER IGNORE TABLE mytbl ADD UNIQUE (i,c);
mysql> SELECT * FROM mytbl;
+---+------+
| i | c    |
+---+------+
| 1 | NULL |
| 1 | NULL |
| 1 | a    |
| 2 | a    |
| 2 | b    |
+---+------+
```

The output shows that duplicate records have been eliminated—except those that contain NULL in the key values. That's because UNIQUE indexes allow multiple NULL values. For another technique that removes even duplicates that contain NULLs, see Recipe 14.6.

8.9   Using ALTER TABLE to Normalize a Table

Problem

You have a table that's not in normal form.

Solution

ALTER TABLE can help you normalize it.

Discussion

The preceding sections describe how to use ALTER TABLE in fairly general terms. This section shows a more concrete application of the statement by demonstrating how ALTER TABLE can help you redesign tables that you discover to contain unnecessarily redundant data and therefore to be in non-normal form.

Suppose you have a client_billing table for recording billable items that is defined as follows:

```
CREATE TABLE client_billing
(
    id          INT UNSIGNED NOT NULL,   # client ID number
    name        CHAR(20) NOT NULL,       # client name
    address     CHAR(20) NOT NULL,       # client adddress
    date        DATE NOT NULL,           # billable item date
    minutes     INT NOT NULL,            # number of billable minutes
    description CHAR(60) NOT NULL         # what was done
);
```

When you have just one row of information per client, the table looks perfectly fine:

```
+----+------+---------------+------------+---------+-----------------+
| id | name | address       | date       | minutes | description     |
+----+------+---------------+------------+---------+-----------------+
| 21 | John | 46 North Ave. | 2001-07-15 |      48 | consult by phone|
| 43 | Toby | 123 Elm St.   | 2001-07-13 |      12 | office visit    |
+----+------+---------------+------------+---------+-----------------+
```

But when you add more records and have multiple rows per client, it becomes apparent that some of the information is redundant. In particular, names and addresses are stored in every record, even though you really need that information only once for any given client:

```
+----+------+---------------+------------+---------+-----------------+
| id | name | address       | date       | minutes | description     |
+----+------+---------------+------------+---------+-----------------+
| 21 | John | 46 North Ave. | 2001-07-15 |      48 | consult by phone|
| 21 | John | 46 North Ave. | 2001-07-19 |     120 | court appearance|
| 43 | Toby | 123 Elm St.   | 2001-07-13 |      12 | office visit    |
| 43 | Toby | 123 Elm St.   | 2001-07-14 |      60 | draft proposal  |
| 43 | Toby | 123 Elm St.   | 2001-07-16 |     180 | present proposal|
+----+------+---------------+------------+---------+-----------------+
```

The way to fix the problem is to split the information into two tables and associate the records in them using the id values:

- One table (client_info) holds the information that is unique to each client, one row per client: the ID, name, and address.
- The other table (bill_item) holds information about each billable item: date, number of minutes, and the description of what was done. Each row also should include the client ID number so that the item can be associated with the proper client_info table record.

In other words, the client information from the client_billing table can be separated as follows into the client_info and bill_item tables:

client_info table:

```
+----+------+---------------+
| id | name | address       |
+----+------+---------------+
| 21 | John | 46 North Ave. |
| 43 | Toby | 123 Elm St.   |
+----+------+---------------+
```

bill_item table:

```
+----+------------+---------+-----------------+
| id | date       | minutes | description     |
+----+------------+---------+-----------------+
| 21 | 2001-07-15 |      48 | consult by phone|
| 21 | 2001-07-19 |     120 | court appearance|
| 43 | 2001-07-13 |      12 | office visit    |
```

```
| 43 | 2001-07-14 |    60 | draft proposal   |
| 43 | 2001-07-16 |   180 | present proposal |
+----+------------+-------+------------------+
```

To accomplish this redesign, first create the client_info and bill_item tables using the following statements, where each table's columns are defined the same way as the corresponding columns from the original client_billing table:

```
CREATE TABLE client_info
(
    id        INT UNSIGNED NOT NULL,  # client ID number
    name      CHAR(20) NOT NULL,      # client name
    address   CHAR(20) NOT NULL       # client adddress
);
CREATE TABLE bill_item
(
    id          INT UNSIGNED NOT NULL,  # client ID number
    date        DATE NOT NULL,          # billable item date
    minutes     INT NOT NULL,           # number of billable minutes
    description CHAR(60) NOT NULL        # what was done
);
```

Next, use INSERT INTO ... SELECT to copy the appropriate columns from the client_billing table into the two new tables. For the client_info table, the client information can be copied like this:

```
INSERT INTO client_info (id,name,address)
SELECT id,name,address FROM client_billing;
```

Copying information to the bill_item table is similar:

```
INSERT INTO bill_item (id,date,minutes,description)
SELECT id,date,minutes,description FROM client_billing;
```

Records in the two new tables are associated based on id values, so it's a good idea to index that column in each table to allow them to be related efficiently. However, that's not simply a matter of issuing an ALTER TABLE *tbl_name* ADD INDEX (id) statement for each table. For one thing, the client_info table at this point has multiple records per client that should be collapsed down to a single record for each client. That means we should create a PRIMARY KEY or UNIQUE index on the id column, using the IGNORE keyword to tell MySQL to discard duplicate records. In addition, queries on the bill_item table are likely often to be date-based, so we can include the date column in the index. ALTER TABLE statements to create these indexes look like this:

```
ALTER IGNORE TABLE client_info ADD PRIMARY KEY (id);
ALTER TABLE bill_item ADD INDEX (id, date);
```

After performing the procedure just described, the client_billing table no longer is needed and can be removed:

```
DROP TABLE client_billing;
```

With billing records stored in multiple tables, queries to retrieve information become somewhat more complex, but relating tables is what relational databases are good at, after all. For example, to show the client name and address from the client_info table along with a sum of the billable minutes listed per client in the bill_item table, the query looks like this:

```
mysql> SELECT client_info.id, client_info.name, client_info.address,
    -> SUM(bill_item.minutes) AS 'total minutes'
    -> FROM client_info, bill_item
    -> WHERE client_info.id = bill_item.id
    -> GROUP BY client_info.id;
+----+------+---------------+---------------+
| id | name | address       | total minutes |
+----+------+---------------+---------------+
| 21 | John | 46 North Ave. |           168 |
| 43 | Toby | 123 Elm St.   |           252 |
+----+------+---------------+---------------+
```

Multiple-table queries are discussed further in Chapter 12.

The preceding example illustrates how to normalize a table for which data values are repeated *across* rows. Another kind of non-normal form occurs when you have multiple columns *within* rows that record the same kind of information. For example, if you're running a study that involves administering two tests to subjects and recording the date and score for each test, you might use a table that has the following structure:

```
CREATE TABLE test_subject
(
    id      INT UNSIGNED NOT NULL AUTO_INCREMENT,
    name    CHAR(20) NOT NULL,   # subject name
    date1   DATE,                # date and score of first test
    result1 INT,
    date2   DATE,                # score of second test
    result2 INT,
    PRIMARY KEY (id)
);
```

Information in the table looks like this:

```
+----+--------+------------+---------+------------+---------+
| id | name   | date1      | result1 | date2      | result2 |
+----+--------+------------+---------+------------+---------+
|  1 | Fred   | 2001-07-13 |      78 | 2001-07-14 |      85 |
|  2 | Barry  | 2001-07-12 |      79 | 2001-07-14 |      82 |
|  3 | Portia | 2001-07-16 |      82 | 2001-07-18 |      95 |
+----+--------+------------+---------+------------+---------+
```

When the information is contained in a table of this form, if you want to do something such as computing each subject's average score, you can do so with the following query:

```
SELECT id, name, (result1 + result2) / 2 FROM test_subject;
```

If you decide you need to add a third test, and a fourth, you can add columns to the table easily:

```
ALTER TABLE test_subject
ADD date3 DATE, ADD result3 INT,
ADD date4 DATE, ADD result4 INT;
```

But the query to compute average scores becomes more complex:

```
SELECT id, name, (result1 + result2 + result3 + result4) / 4
FROM test_subject;
```

In fact, if scores can be NULL to signify that a subject hasn't taken a test yet, the query is much messier than that, because you must add only the non-NULL values to avoid getting a NULL sum. This ballooning complexity is a clue that the table design could be improved. The problem is that the structure of the table is dependent on the number of tests you plan to give. If you change that number, you must change the table. A way around this problem is to use two tables, structured so that they need not be changed if you decide to administer additional tests:

- The first table records information unique to each subject.
- The second table records test results, one row per test. Each row can be associated with the proper subject using the subject ID number.

This is very similar to the approach used in the preceding example, where we used two tables to hold client billing information. However, instead of creating two new tables and then removing the original table, we'll use a different procedure that preserves the original table, albeit in modified form:

- Create a table test_result to hold test dates and scores, as well as the subject ID number. To allow scores to be ordered, we can also add a test number column. (The date might serve for ordering, unless it's possible for subjects to take multiple tests on the same day. An explicit test number does not have that problem.)
- Copy the subject ID, date, and score information from test_subject to test_result.
- Remove the date and score columns from test_subject, leaving only subject IDs and names.

Begin by creating a table to hold test results:

```
CREATE TABLE test_result
(
    id          INT UNSIGNED NOT NULL,
    test_num    INT NOT NULL,
    date        DATE,
    result      INT
);
```

Copy the test information from `test_subject` to `test_result`. It's necessary to do this separately for each test, because each result is copied from a different set of columns:

```
INSERT INTO test_result (id,test_num,date,result)
SELECT id,1,date1,result1 FROM test_subject WHERE result1 IS NOT NULL;

INSERT INTO test_result (id,test_num,date,result)
SELECT id,2,date2,result2 FROM test_subject WHERE result2 IS NOT NULL;
```

Each `INSERT INTO ... SELECT` statement specifies the `test_num` value "manually," because the appropriate value is not present in the `test_subject` table and cannot be derived directly from its contents. The `WHERE` clause serves to copy only rows with non-`NULL` test results. This handles the possibility that your `test_subject` records might be incomplete, such that a `NULL` score indicates a subject hasn't taken a given test. (If the `test_subject` table has no such missing test results, the `WHERE` clauses are unnecessary and can be omitted.)

The `test_result` table is populated now and can be indexed. Note that although the `id` column is a unique-valued column in the `test_subject` table, it cannot be so in `test_result` because there will be multiple rows per subject. However, it's still possible to create a unique index by using both `id` and `test_num`, assuming each test is given to each subject only once:

```
ALTER TABLE test_result ADD PRIMARY KEY (id, test_num);
```

The test result columns in `test_subject` are now unneeded and can be removed:

```
ALTER TABLE test_subject DROP date1, DROP result1, DROP date2, DROP result2;
```

The advantage of using a two-table layout like this is that queries to perform operations such as score-averaging become independent of the number of tests administered:

```
SELECT id, AVG(result) FROM test_result GROUP BY id;
```

To show subject names, too, join the `test_result` table to the `test_subject` table:

```
SELECT test_result.id, test_subject.name, AVG(test_result.result)
FROM test_subject, test_result
WHERE test_subject.id = test_result.id
GROUP BY test_result.id;
```

You also can easily identify subjects who have not completed all the tests. For example, if you've presented a total of four tests, you can find subjects who don't have four scores in the `test_result` table like this:

```
SELECT test_subject.id, test_subject.name, COUNT(test_result.result) AS count
FROM test_subject LEFT JOIN test_result ON test_subject.id = test_result.id
GROUP BY test_subject.id
HAVING count < 4;
```

This query uses `LEFT JOIN` to make sure that a count for every subject is generated, even those to whom no tests have yet been administered. (A regular join will fail to identify a subject who has a record in the `test_subject` table but no records yet in the `test_result` table, because it will find no match between the tables.) `LEFT JOIN` is discussed in Chapter 12.

## CHAPTER 9

Obtaining and Using Metadata

9.0   Introduction

Most of the queries used so far have been written to work with the data stored in the database. That is, after all, what the database is designed to hold. But sometimes you need more than just data values. You need information that characterizes or describes those values—that is, the query metadata. Metadata information is used most often in relation to processing result sets, but also is available for other aspects of your interaction with MySQL. This chapter describes how to obtain and use the following types of metadata:

Information about the result of queries. When you delete or update a set of rows, you can determine the number of rows that were changed. For a SELECT query, you can find out the number of columns in the result set, as well as information about each column in the result set, such as the column name and its display width. Such information often is essential for processing the results. For example, if you're formatting a tabular display, you can determine how wide to make each column and whether to justify values to the left or right.

Information about tables and databases. Information pertaining to the structure of tables and databases is useful for applications that need to enumerate a list of tables in a database or databases hosted on a server (for example, to present a display allowing the user to select one of the available choices). You can also use this information to determine whether tables or databases exist. Another use for table metadata is to determine the legal values for ENUM or SET columns.

Information about the MySQL server. Some APIs provide information about the database server or about the status of your current connection with the server. Knowing the server version can be useful for determining whether it supports a given feature, which helps you build adaptive applications. Information about the connection includes such items as the current user and the current database.

Some APIs try to provide a database-independent interface for types of metadata that tend to be available across a variety of database engines (such as the names of the columns in a result set). But in general, metadata information is closely tied to the structure of the database system, so it tends to be somewhat database-dependent. This means that if you port an application that uses recipes in this chapter to other databases, it may need some modification. For example, lists of tables and databases in MySQL are available by issuing SHOW statements. However, SHOW is a MySQL-specific extension to SQL, so even if you're using an API like DBI, DB-API, or JDBC that gives you a database-independent way of issuing queries, the SQL itself is database-specific and will need to be changed to work with other engines.

The scripts containing the code for the examples shown here are in the *metadata* directory of the recipes distribution. (Some of them use utility functions located in the *lib* directory.) To create any tables that you need for trying the examples, look in the *tables* directory.

In several cases, recipes developed here construct queries using a database, table, or column name that is stored in a variable. For simplicity, generally such names are inserted as is into the query string. For example:

```
$query = "SHOW COLUMNS FROM $tbl_name";
```

This works properly in the majority of cases, but there are some possible complications you should know about, and may wish to take into account when adapting these recipes for your own use. As of MySQL 3.23.6, names are allowed to contain almost any character, such as spaces. If you anticipate a need to deal with such names, surround the name with backticks:

```
$query = "SHOW COLUMNS FROM `$tbl_name`";
```

If the server is running in ANSI mode, name quoting should be done with double quotes instead:

```
$query = "SHOW COLUMNS FROM \"$tbl_name\"";
```

To deal with these issues on a general basis, you can query the server to see if it is Version 3.23.6 or later (see Recipe 9.13), and you can also use SHOW VARIABLES to see if it is running in ANSI mode. The recipes here do not perform all these checks, because doing so would obscure their main point.

9.1 Obtaining the Number of Rows Affected by a Query

Problem

You want to know how many rows were changed by a query.

Solution

Some APIs provide the count as the return value of the function that issues the query. Others have a separate function that you call after issuing the query.

Discussion

For queries that affect rows (UPDATE, DELETE, INSERT, REPLACE), each API provides a way to determine the number of rows involved. For MySQL, "affected by" normally means "changed by," so rows that are not changed by a query are not counted, even if they match the conditions specified in the query. For example, the following UPDATE statement would result in an "affected by" value of zero because it does not change any columns from their current values, no matter how many rows the WHERE clause matches:

```
UPDATE limbs SET arms = 0 WHERE arms = 0;
```

Perl

In DBI scripts, the affected-rows count is returned by do( ) or by execute( ), depending on how you execute the query:

```
# execute $query using do()
my $count = $dbh->do ($query);
# report 0 rows if an error occurred
printf "%d rows were affected\n", (defined ($count) ? $count : 0);

# execute query using prepare() plus execute()
my $sth = $dbh->prepare ($query);
my $count = $sth->execute ();
printf "%d rows were affected\n", (defined ($count) ? $count : 0);
```

When you use DBI, you have the option of asking MySQL to return the "matched by" value rather than the "affected by" value. To do this, specify mysql_client_found_rows=1 in the options part of the data source name argument of the connect( ) call when you connect to the MySQL server. Here's an example:

```
my $dsn =
    "DBI:mysql:cookbook:localhost;mysql_client_found_rows=1";
my $dbh = DBI->connect ($dsn, "cbuser", "cbpass",
                        { PrintError => 0, RaiseError => 1 });
```

mysql_client_found_rows changes the row-reporting behavior for the duration of the connection.

PHP

In PHP, invoke the mysql_affected_rows( ) function to find out how many rows a query changed:

```
$result_id = mysql_query ($query, $conn_id);
# report 0 rows if the query failed
$count = ($result_id ? mysql_affected_rows ($conn_id) : 0);
print ("$count rows were affected\n");
```

The argument to mysql_affected_rows( ) is a connection identifier. If you omit the argument, the current connection is used.

Python

Python's DB-API makes the row count available as the value of the query cursor's rowcount attribute:

```
cursor = conn.cursor ()
cursor.execute (query)
print "%d rows were affected" % cursor.rowcount
```

Java

The Java JDBC interface provides row counts two different ways, depending on the method you invoke to execute the query. If you use executeUpdate(), it returns the row count directly:

```
Statement s = conn.createStatement ();
int count = s.executeUpdate (query);
s.close ();
System.out.println (count + " rows were affected");
```

If you use execute(), that method returns true or false to indicate whether or not the statement produces a result set. For statements such as UPDATE or DELETE that return no result set, the row count is available by calling the getUpdateCount() method:

```
Statement s = conn.createStatement ();
if (!s.execute (query))
{
    // there is no result set, print the row count
    System.out.println (s.getUpdateCount () + " rows were affected");
}
s.close ();
```

For statements that modify rows, the MySQL Connector/J JDBC driver provides a rows-matched value for the row count, rather than a rows-affected value.

9.2   Obtaining Result Set Metadata

Problem

You know how to retrieve the rows of a result set, but you want to know things *about* the result, such as the column names and data types, or the number of rows and columns there are.

Solution

Use the appropriate capabilities provided by your API.

Discussion

For queries that generate a result set, you can get a number of kinds of metadata. This section discusses the information provided by each API, using programs that show how to display the result set metadata available after issuing a sample query (SELECT name, foods FROM profile). The section also discusses some applications for this information. One of the simplest uses is illustrated by several of the example programs: When you retrieve a row of values from a result set and you want to process them in a loop, the column count stored in the metadata serves as the upper bound on the loop iterator.

Perl

Using the DBI interface, you can obtain result sets two ways. These differ in the scope of result set metadata available to your scripts:

Process the query using a statement handle. In this case, you invoke prepare() to get the statement handle, then call its execute() method to generate the result set, then fetch the rows in a loop. With this approach, access to the metadata is available while the result set is active—that is, after the call to execute() and until the end of the result set is reached. When the row-fetching method finds that there are no more rows, it invokes finish() implicitly, which causes the metadata to become unavailable. (That also happens if you explicitly call finish() yourself.) Thus, normally it's best to access the metadata immediately after calling execute(), making a copy of any values that you'll need to use beyond the end of the fetch loop.

Process the query using a database handle method that returns the result set in a single operation. With this method, any metadata generated while processing the query will have been disposed of by the time the method returns, although you can still determine the number of rows and columns from the size of the result set.

When you use the statement handle approach to process a query, DBI makes result set metadata available after you invoke the handle's execute() method. This information is available primarily in the form of references to arrays. There is a separate array for each type of metadata, and each array has one element per column in the result set. Array references are accessed as attributes of the statement handle. For example, $sth->{NAME} points to the column name array. Individual column names are available as elements of this array:

```
$name = $sth->{NAMES}->[$i];
```

Or you can access the entire array like this:

```
@names = @{$sth->{NAMES}};
```

The following table lists the attribute names through which you access array-based metadata and the meaning of values in each array. Names that begin with uppercase are standard DBI attributes and should be available for most database engines. Attribute names that begin with `mysql_` are MySQL-specific and non-portable; the kinds of information they provide may be available in other databases, but under different attribute names.

Attribute name	Array element meaning
NAME	Column name
NAME_lc	Column name, lowercased
NAME_uc	Column name, uppercased
NULLABLE	1 if column values can be NULL, empty string if not
PRECISION	Column width
SCALE	Number of decimal places (for numeric columns)
TYPE	Numeric column type (DBI value)
mysql_is_blob	True if column has a BLOB (or TEXT) type
mysql_is_key	True if column is part of a non-unique key
mysql_is_num	True if column has a numeric type
mysql_is_pri_key	True if column is part of a primary key
mysql_max_length	Actual maximum length of column values in result set
mysql_table	Name of table the column is part of
mysql_type	Numeric column type (internal MySQL value)
mysql_type_name	Column type name

The exception to array-based metadata is that the number of columns in a result set is available as a scalar value:

```
$num_cols = $sth->{NUM_OF_FIELDS};
```

Here's some example code that shows how to execute a query and display the result set metadata:

```
my $query = "SELECT name, foods FROM profile";
printf "Query: %s\n", $query;
my $sth = $dbh->prepare ($query);
$sth->execute();
# metadata information becomes available at this point ...
printf "NUM_OF_FIELDS: %d\n", $sth->{NUM_OF_FIELDS};
print "Note: query has no result set\n" if $sth->{NUM_OF_FIELDS} == 0;
for my $i (0 .. $sth->{NUM_OF_FIELDS}-1)
{
    printf "--- Column %d (%s) ---\n", $i, $sth->{NAME}->[$i];
    printf "NAME_lc:         %s\n", $sth->{NAME_lc}->[$i];
    printf "NAME_uc:         %s\n", $sth->{NAME_uc}->[$i];
    printf "NULLABLE:        %s\n", $sth->{NULLABLE}->[$i];
    printf "PRECISION:       %s\n", $sth->{PRECISION}->[$i];
    printf "SCALE:           %s\n", $sth->{SCALE}->[$i];
    printf "TYPE:            %s\n", $sth->{TYPE}->[$i];
    printf "mysql_is_blob:   %s\n", $sth->{mysql_is_blob}->[$i];
```

```
        printf "mysql_is_key:      %s\n", $sth->{mysql_is_key}->[$i];
        printf "mysql_is_num:      %s\n", $sth->{mysql_is_num}->[$i];
        printf "mysql_is_pri_key: %s\n", $sth->{mysql_is_pri_key}->[$i];
        printf "mysql_max_length: %s\n", $sth->{mysql_max_length}->[$i];
        printf "mysql_table:       %s\n", $sth->{mysql_table}->[$i];
        printf "mysql_type:        %s\n", $sth->{mysql_type}->[$i];
        printf "mysql_type_name:  %s\n", $sth->{mysql_type_name}->[$i];
    }
    $sth->finish ();    # release result set, since we didn't fetch its rows
```

If you use the preceding code to execute the query SELECT name, foods FROM profile, the output looks like this:

```
Query: SELECT name, foods FROM profile
NUM_OF_FIELDS: 2
--- Column 0 (name) ---
NAME_lc:          name
NAME_uc:          NAME
NULLABLE:
PRECISION:        20
SCALE:            0
TYPE:             1
mysql_is_blob:
mysql_is_key:
mysql_is_num:     0
mysql_is_pri_key:
mysql_max_length: 7
mysql_table:      profile
mysql_type:       254
mysql_type_name:  char
--- Column 1 (foods) ---
NAME_lc:          foods
NAME_uc:          FOODS
NULLABLE:         1
PRECISION:        42
SCALE:            0
TYPE:             1
mysql_is_blob:
mysql_is_key:
mysql_is_num:     0
mysql_is_pri_key:
mysql_max_length: 21
mysql_table:      profile
mysql_type:       254
mysql_type_name:  char
```

To get a row count from a result set generated by calling execute( ), you must fetch the rows and count them yourself. (The use of $sth->rows( ) to get a count for SELECT statements is specifically deprecated in the DBI documentation.)

You can also obtain a result set by calling one of the DBI methods that uses a database handle rather than a statement handle, such as selectall_arrayref( ) or selectall_hashref( ). For these methods, no access to column metadata is provided.

That information already will have been disposed of by the time the method returns, and is unavailable to your scripts. However, you can still derive column and row counts by examining the result set itself. The way you do this depends on the kind of data structure a method produces. These structures and the way you use them to obtain result set row and column counts are discussed in Recipe 2.4.

PHP

In PHP, metadata information is available after a successful call to mysql_query() and remains accessible up to the point at which you call mysql_free_result(). To access the metadata, pass the result set identifier returned by mysql_query() to the function that returns the information you want. To get a row or column count for a result set, invoke mysql_num_rows() or mysql_num_fields(). Metadata information for a given column in a result set is packaged up in a single object. You get the object by passing the result set identifier and a column index to mysql_fetch_field(), then access the various metadata attributes as members of that object. These members are summarized in the following table:

Member name	Member meaning
blob	1 if column has a BLOB (or TEXT) type, 0 otherwise
max_length	Actual maximum length of column values in result set
multiple_key	1 if column is part of a non-unique key, 0 otherwise
name	Column name
not_null	1 if column values cannot be NULL, 0 otherwise
numeric	1 if column has a numeric type, 0 otherwise
primary_key	1 if column is part of a primary key, 0 otherwise
table	Name of table the column is part of
type	Column type name
unique_key	1 if column is part of a unique key, 0 otherwise
unsigned	1 if column has the UNSIGNED attribute, 0 otherwise
zerofill	1 if column has the ZEROFILL attribute, 0 otherwise

The following code shows how to access and display result set metadata:

```
$query = "SELECT name, foods FROM profile";
print ("Query: $query\n");
$result_id = mysql_query ($query, $conn_id);
if (!$result_id)
    die ("Query failed\n");
# metadata information becomes available at this point ...
# @ is used below because mysql_num_rows() and mysql_num_fields() print
# a message if there is no result set (under PHP 4, at least)
$nrows = @mysql_num_rows ($result_id);
print ("Number of rows: $nrows\n");
```

```
$ncols = @mysql_num_fields ($result_id);
print ("Number of columns: $ncols\n");
if ($ncols == 0)
    print ("Note: query has no result set\n");
for ($i = 0; $i < $ncols; $i++)
{
    $col_info = mysql_fetch_field ($result_id, $i);
    printf ("--- Column %d (%s) ---\n", $i, $col_info->name);
    printf ("blob:         %s\n", $col_info->blob);
    printf ("max_length:   %s\n", $col_info->max_length);
    printf ("multiple_key: %s\n", $col_info->multiple_key);
    printf ("not_null:     %s\n", $col_info->not_null);
    printf ("numeric:      %s\n", $col_info->numeric);
    printf ("primary_key:  %s\n", $col_info->primary_key);
    printf ("table:        %s\n", $col_info->table);
    printf ("type:         %s\n", $col_info->type);
    printf ("unique_key:   %s\n", $col_info->unique_key);
    printf ("unsigned:     %s\n", $col_info->unsigned);
    printf ("zerofill:     %s\n", $col_info->zerofill);
}
if ($ncols > 0)      # dispose of result set, if there is one
    mysql_free_result ($result_id);
```

The output from the program looks like this:

```
Query: SELECT name, foods FROM profile
Number of rows: 10
Number of columns: 2
--- Column 0 (name) ---
blob:         0
max_length:   7
multiple_key: 0
not_null:     1
numeric:      0
primary_key:  0
table:        profile
type:         string
unique_key:   0
unsigned:     0
zerofill:     0
--- Column 1 (foods) ---
blob:         0
max_length:   21
multiple_key: 0
not_null:     0
numeric:      0
primary_key:  0
table:        profile
type:         string
unique_key:   0
unsigned:     0
zerofill:     0
```

Python

Python's DB-API is more limited than the other APIs in providing result set metadata. The row and column counts are available, but the information about individual columns is not as extensive.

To get the row count for a result set, access the cursor's rowcount attribute. The column count is not available directly, but after calling fetchone() or fetchall(), you can determine the count as the length of any result set row tuple. It's also possible to determine the column count without fetching any rows by using cursor.description. This is a tuple containing one element per column in the result set, so its length tells you how many columns are in the set. (However, be aware that if the query generates no result set, such as for an UPDATE statement, the value of description is None.) Each element of the description tuple is another tuple that represents the metadata for the corresponding column of the result. There are seven metadata values per column; the following code shows how to access them and what they mean:

```python
query = "SELECT name, foods FROM profile"
print "Query: ", query
cursor = conn.cursor ()
cursor.execute (query)
# metadata information becomes available at this point ...
print "Number of rows:", cursor.rowcount
if cursor.description == None:  # no result set
    ncols = 0
else:
    ncols = len (cursor.description)
print "Number of columns:", ncols
if ncols == 0:
    print "Note: query has no result set"
for i in range (ncols):
    col_info = cursor.description[i]
    # print name, then other information
    print "--- Column %d (%s) ---" % (i, col_info[0])
    print "Type:          ", col_info[1]
    print "Display size: ", col_info[2]
    print "Internal size:", col_info[3]
    print "Precision:    ", col_info[4]
    print "Scale:        ", col_info[5]
    print "Nullable:     ", col_info[6]
cursor.close
```

The output from the program looks like this:

```
Query:  SELECT name, foods FROM profile
Number of rows: 10L
Number of columns: 2
--- Column 0 (name) ---
Type:        254
Display size:  7
Internal size: 20
Precision:    20
```

```
Scale:        0
Nullable:     0
--- Column 1 (foods) ---
Type:         254
Display size: 21
Internal size: 42
Precision:    42
Scale:        0
Nullable:     1
```

Java

JDBC makes result set metadata available through a ResultSetMetaData object, which you obtain by calling the getMetaData() method of your ResultSet object. The metadata object provides access to several kinds of information. Its getColumnCount() method returns the number of columns in the result set. Other types of metadata, illustrated by the following code, provide information about individual columns and take a column index as their argument. Note that for JDBC, column indexes begin at 1, not 0, which differs from DBI, PHP, and DB-API.

```java
String query = "SELECT name, foods FROM profile";
System.out.println ("Query: " + query);
Statement s = conn.createStatement ();
s.executeQuery (query);
ResultSet rs = s.getResultSet ();
ResultSetMetaData md = rs.getMetaData ();
// metadata information becomes available at this point ...
int ncols = md.getColumnCount ();
System.out.println ("Number of columns: " + ncols);
if (ncols == 0)
    System.out.println ("Note: query has no result set");
for (int i = 1; i <= ncols; i++)     // column index values are 1-based
{
    System.out.println ("--- Column " + i
                    + " (" + md.getColumnName (i) + ") ---");
    System.out.println ("getColumnDisplaySize: " + md.getColumnDisplaySize (i));
    System.out.println ("getColumnLabel:      " + md.getColumnLabel (i));
    System.out.println ("getColumnType:       " + md.getColumnType (i));
    System.out.println ("getColumnTypeName:   " + md.getColumnTypeName (i));
    System.out.println ("getPrecision:        " + md.getPrecision (i));
    System.out.println ("getScale:            " + md.getScale (i));
    System.out.println ("getTableName:        " + md.getTableName (i));
    System.out.println ("isAutoIncrement:     " + md.isAutoIncrement (i));
    System.out.println ("isNullable:          " + md.isNullable (i));
    System.out.println ("isCaseSensitive:     " + md.isCaseSensitive (i));
    System.out.println ("isSigned:            " + md.isSigned (i));
}
rs.close ();
s.close ();
```

The output from the program looks like this:

```
Query: SELECT name, foods FROM profile
Number of columns: 2
--- Column 1 (name) ---
getColumnDisplaySize: 20
getColumnLabel:       name
getColumnType:        1
getColumnTypeName:    CHAR
getPrecision:         0
getScale:             0
getTableName:         profile
isAutoIncrement:      false
isNullable:           0
isCaseSensitive:      true
isSigned:             false
--- Column 2 (foods) ---
getColumnDisplaySize: 42
getColumnLabel:       foods
getColumnType:        1
getColumnTypeName:    CHAR
getPrecision:         0
getScale:             0
getTableName:         profile
isAutoIncrement:      false
isNullable:           1
isCaseSensitive:      true
isSigned:             false
```

As with DBI, the row count is not available directly; you must fetch the rows and count them.

There actually are several other JDBC result set metadata calls than the ones shown in the preceding example, but many of them provide no useful information for MySQL. If you want to try them out, get a JDBC reference to see what the calls are and modify the program to see what, if anything, they return.

9.3 Determining Presence or Absence of a Result Set

Problem

You just executed a query obtained from an external source, so you're not sure whether it returned a result set.

Solution

Check the column count in the metadata. If the count is zero, there is no result set.

Discussion

If you write an application that accepts query strings from an external source such as a file or a user entering text at the keyboard, you may not necessarily know whether or not any given query returns a result set. That's an important distinction, because queries that return a result set are processed differently than those that do not. One way to tell the difference is to check the metadata value that indicates the column count after executing the query. Assuming that no error occurred, a column count of zero indicates that the query was an INSERT, UPDATE, or other statement that returns no result set. A nonzero value indicates the presence of a result set and you can go ahead and fetch the rows. This technique works to distinguish SELECT from non-SELECT queries, even for SELECT queries that return an empty result set. (An empty result is different than no result. The former returns no rows, but the column count is still correct; the latter has no columns at all.)

Some APIs provide other ways to distinguish query types than checking the column count. In JDBC, you can issue arbitrary queries using the execute( ) method, which directly indicates whether there is a result set by returning true or false. In Python, the value of cursor.description is None for statements that produce no result set.

9.4   Formatting Query Results for Display

Problem

You want to produce a nicely formatted result set display.

Solution

Let the result set metadata help you. It can give you important information about the structure and content of the results.

Discussion

Metadata information is valuable for formatting query results, because it tells you several important things about the columns (such as the names and display widths), even if you don't know what the query was. For example, you can write a general-purpose function that displays a result set in tabular format with no knowledge about what the query might have been. The following Java code shows one way to do this. It takes a result set object and uses it to get the metadata for the result. Then it uses both objects in tandem to retrieve and format the values in the result. The output is similar to that produced by *mysql*: a row of column headers followed by the rows of the result, with columns nicely boxed and lined up vertically. Here's a sample of what the function displays, given the result set generated by the query SELECT id, name, birth FROM profile:

```
+----------+--------------------+----------+
|id        |name                |birth     |
+----------+--------------------+----------+
|1         |Fred                |1970-04-13|
|2         |Mort                |1969-09-30|
|3         |Brit                |1957-12-01|
|4         |Carl                |1973-11-02|
|5         |Sean                |1963-07-04|
|6         |Alan                |1965-02-14|
|7         |Mara                |1968-09-17|
|8         |Shepard             |1975-09-02|
|9         |Dick                |1952-08-20|
|10        |Tony                |1960-05-01|
|11        |Juan                |NULL      |
+----------+--------------------+----------+
11 rows selected
```

The primary problem an application like this must solve is to determine the proper display width of each column. The getColumnDisplaySize() method returns the column width, but we actually need to take into account other pieces of information:

- The length of the column name has to be considered (it might be longer than the column width).

- We'll print the word "NULL" for NULL values, so if the column can contain NULL values, the display width must be at least four.

The following Java function, displayResultSet(), formats a result set, taking the preceding factors into account. It also counts rows as it fetches them to determine the row count, because JDBC doesn't make that value available directly from the metadata.

```java
public static void displayResultSet (ResultSet rs) throws SQLException
{
    ResultSetMetaData md = rs.getMetaData ();
    int ncols = md.getColumnCount ();
    int nrows = 0;
    int[] width = new int[ncols + 1];         // array to store column widths
    StringBuffer b = new StringBuffer ();     // buffer to hold bar line

    // calculate column widths
    for (int i = 1; i <= ncols; i++)
    {
        // some drivers return -1 for getColumnDisplaySize();
        // if so, we'll override that with the column name length
        width[i] = md.getColumnDisplaySize (i);
        if (width[i] < md.getColumnName (i).length ())
            width[i] = md.getColumnName (i).length ();
```

```
    // isNullable() returns 1/0, not true/false
    if (width[i] < 4 && md.isNullable (i) != 0)
        width[i] = 4;
}

// construct +---+---... line
b.append ("+");
for (int i = 1; i <= ncols; i++)
{
    for (int j = 0; j < width[i]; j++)
        b.append ("-");
    b.append ("+");
}

// print bar line, column headers, bar line
System.out.println (b.toString ());
System.out.print ("|");
for (int i = 1; i <= ncols; i++)
{
    System.out.print (md.getColumnName (i));
    for (int j = md.getColumnName (i).length (); j < width[i]; j++)
        System.out.print (" ");
    System.out.print ("|");
}
System.out.println ();
System.out.println (b.toString ());

// print contents of result set
while (rs.next ())
{
    ++nrows;
    System.out.print ("|");
    for (int i = 1; i <= ncols; i++)
    {
        String s = rs.getString (i);
        if (rs.wasNull ())
            s = "NULL";
        System.out.print (s);
        for (int j = s.length (); j < width[i]; j++)
            System.out.print (" ");
        System.out.print ("|");
    }
    System.out.println ();
}
// print bar line, and row count
System.out.println (b.toString ());
if (nrows == 1)
    System.out.println ("1 row selected");
else
    System.out.println (nrows + " rows selected");
}
```

If you want to be more elaborate, you can also test whether a column contains
numeric values, and format it right-justified if so. In DBI and PHP scripts, this is easy
to check, because you can access the mysql_is_num or numeric metadata attributes

provided by those APIs. In DB-API and JDBC, it's not so easy. There is no "column is numeric" metadata value available, so you'd have to look at the column type indicator to see if it's one of the several possible numeric types.

Another shortcoming of the displayResultSet() function is that it prints columns using the width of the column as specified in the table definition, not the maximum width of the values actually present in the result set. The latter value is often smaller. You can see this in the sample output that precedes the listing for displayResultSet(). The id and name columns are 10 and 20 characters wide, even though the widest values are only two and seven characters long, respectively. In DBI, PHP, and DB-API, you can get the maximum width of the values present in the result set. To determine these widths in JDBC, you must iterate through the result set and check the column value lengths yourself. This requires a JDBC 2.0 driver that provides scrollable result sets. Assuming that to be true, the column-width calculation code in the displayResultSet() function could be modified as follows:

```
// calculate column widths
for (int i = 1; i <= ncols; i++)
{
    width[i] = md.getColumnName (i).length ();
    // isNullable() returns 1/0, not true/false
    if (width[i] < 4 && md.isNullable (i) != 0)
        width[i] = 4;
}
// scroll through result set and adjust display widths as necessary
while (rs.next ())
{
    for (int i = 1; i <= ncols; i++)
    {
        byte[] bytes = rs.getBytes (i);
        if (!rs.wasNull ())
        {
            int len = bytes.length;
            if (width[i] < len)
                width[i] = len;
        }
    }
}
rs.beforeFirst ();  // rewind result set before displaying it
```

With that change, the result is a more compact query output display:

```
+--+-------+----------+
|id|name   |birth     |
+--+-------+----------+
|1 |Fred   |1970-04-13|
|2 |Mort   |1969-09-30|
|3 |Brit   |1957-12-01|
|4 |Carl   |1973-11-02|
|5 |Sean   |1963-07-04|
|6 |Alan   |1965-02-14|
|7 |Mara   |1968-09-17|
|8 |Shepard|1975-09-02|
```

```
|9 |Dick  |1952-08-20|
|10|Tony  |1960-05-01|
|11|Juan  |NULL      |
+--+-------+----------+
11 rows selected
```

9.5   Getting Table Structure Information

Problem

You want to find out how a table is defined.

Solution

Thre are several ways to do this, ranging from statements that return this information directly, to using metadata from a query on the table.

Discussion

Information about the structure of tables allows you to answer questions such as
"What columns does a table contain and what are their types?" or "What are the
legal values for an ENUM or SET column?" In MySQL, there are several ways to find out
about a table's structure:

- Use a SHOW COLUMNS statement.
- Use a SELECT query that selects columns from the table, then examine the query
  metadata for information about each column.
- Use the *mysqldump* command-line program or the SHOW CREATE TABLE statement
  to obtain a CREATE TABLE statement that displays the table's structure.

The following sections discuss how you can ask MySQL for table information using
each of these methods. To try out the examples, create the following item table that
lists item IDs, names, and the colors in which each item is available:

```
CREATE TABLE item
(
    id      INT UNSIGNED NOT NULL AUTO_INCREMENT,
    name    CHAR(20),
    colors  SET('chartreuse','mauve','lime green','puce') DEFAULT 'puce',
    PRIMARY KEY (id)
);
```

Using SHOW COLUMNS to Get Table Structure

The SHOW COLUMNS statement produces one row of output for each column in the table,
with each row providing various pieces of information about the corresponding

column.* I suggest that you try the SHOW COLUMNS statement with several of your own tables to get a feel for the kind of output it produces for various column types. The following example demonstrates the output that SHOW COLUMNS produces for the item table. (Note the use of \G as the statement terminator to generate "vertical" output; SHOW COLUMNS output lines often are so long that they wrap around and become difficult to read.)

```
mysql> SHOW COLUMNS FROM item\G
*************************** 1. row ***************************
 Field: id
  Type: int(10) unsigned
  Null:
   Key: PRI
Default: NULL
 Extra: auto_increment
*************************** 2. row ***************************
 Field: name
  Type: char(20)
  Null: YES
   Key:
Default: NULL
 Extra:
*************************** 3. row ***************************
 Field: colors
  Type: set('chartreuse','mauve','lime green','puce')
  Null: YES
   Key:
Default: puce
 Extra:
```

The information displayed by the statement is as follows:

Field
    Indicates the column's name

Type
    Shows the column type

Null
    YES if the column can contain NULL values, blank otherwise

Key
    Provides information about whether or not the column is indexed

Default
    Indicates the default value

Extra
    Lists miscellaneous information

The format of SHOW COLUMNS changes occasionally, but the values just described should always be available. Your version of MySQL may display additional information.

---

* SHOW COLUMNS FROM tbl_name is equivalent to SHOW FIELDS FROM tbl_name or DESCRIBE tbl_name.

SHOW COLUMNS output is easy to use from within programs. The important thing to know is that SHOW is like SELECT in that it returns a result set, so you process a SHOW query by issuing the statement and performing a row-retrieval fetch loop. Here's a PHP function that illustrates this process. It takes a table name argument, then uses SHOW COLUMNS to obtain a list of the table's column names:

```php
function get_column_names_with_show ($conn_id, $tbl_name)
{
    $query = "SHOW COLUMNS FROM $tbl_name";
    if (!($result_id = mysql_query ($query, $conn_id)))
        return (FALSE);
    $names = array ();                  # create empty array
    # first value in each output row is the column name
    while (list ($name) = mysql_fetch_row ($result_id))
        $names[] = $name;               # append name to array
    mysql_free_result ($result_id);
    return ($names);
}
```

The array returned by the function contains column names in the same order the columns appear in the table. Notice that get_column_names_with_show() takes no argument for specifying a database name. It's not necessary, because MySQL understands fully qualified table references of the form *db_name.tbl_name*. To access a table in a database other than the current one, just pass a $tbl_name argument that includes the database name:

```php
$names = get_column_names_with_show ($conn_id, "some_db.some_tbl");
```

The equivalent function in Python looks like this:

```python
def get_column_names_with_show (conn, tbl_name):
    names = [ ]
    cursor = conn.cursor ()
    cursor.execute ("SHOW COLUMNS FROM " + tbl_name)
    rows = cursor.fetchall ()
    cursor.close ()
    for row in rows:
        names.append (row[0])
    return (names)
```

In DBI, this operation is trivial, because selectcol_arrayref() returns the first column of the query result directly:

```perl
sub get_column_names_with_show
{
my ($dbh, $tbl_name) = @_;

    my $ref = $dbh->selectcol_arrayref ("SHOW COLUMNS FROM $tbl_name");
    return (defined ($ref) ? @{$ref} : ());
}
```

Interpreting the Default Value Displayed by SHOW COLUMNS

When you run SHOW COLUMNS from the *mysql* program, it displays the word "NULL" as the Default indicator for columns that may contain NULL values. However, if you issue a SHOW COLUMNS statement from within your own programs, don't look for the string "NULL." Look for the special value your API uses to represent NULL values, such as undef for DBI or None for DB-API.

If you want information only about a single column, use a LIKE clause that matches the column name:

```
mysql> SHOW COLUMNS FROM item LIKE 'colors'\G
*************************** 1. row ***************************
   Field: colors
    Type: set('chartreuse','mauve','lime green','puce')
    Null: YES
     Key:
 Default: puce
   Extra:
```

Observe that quotes surround the column name following the LIKE keyword. Quotes are required because the name isn't really a column name, it a SQL pattern string. The string is interpreted the same way as for the LIKE operator in the WHERE clause of a SELECT statement. (For information about pattern matching, see Recipe 4.6.) SHOW COLUMNS displays information for any columns having names that match the pattern; if you specify a literal column name, the string matches only that name and SHOW COLUMNS displays information only for that column. However, a trap awaits the unwary here. If your column name contains SQL pattern characters (% or _) and you want to match them literally, you must escape them with a backslash in the pattern string to avoid matching other names as well. The % character isn't used very often in column names, but _ is quite common, so it's possible that you'll run into this problem. Suppose you have a table that contains the results of carbon dioxide measurements in a column named co_2, and trigonometric cosine and cotangent calculations in columns named cos1, cos2, cot1, and cot2. If you want to get information only for the co_2 column, you can't use this query:

```
SHOW COLUMNS FROM tbl_name LIKE 'co_2';
```

The _ character means "match any character" in pattern strings, so the query would return rows for co_2, cos2, and cot2. To match only the co_2 column, write the SHOW command like this:

```
SHOW COLUMNS FROM tbl_name LIKE 'co\_2';
```

Within a program, you can use your API language's pattern matching capabilities to escape SQL pattern characters before putting the column name into a SHOW query. For example, in Perl, PHP, and Python, you can use the following expressions:

Perl:

```
$name =~ s/([%_])/\\$1/g;
```

PHP:

```
$name = ereg_replace ("([%_])", "\\\\1", $name);
```

For Python, import the re module, then do this:

```
name = re.sub (r'([%_])', r'\\\1', name)
```

If these expressions appear to have too many backslashes, remember that the API language processor itself interprets backslashes and strips off a level before performing the pattern match. To get a literal backslash into the result, it must be doubled in the pattern. PHP has another level on top of that because it strips a set and the pattern processor strips a set.

For Java, you'll need to select a regular expression class library. The following example uses the ORO library available at *jakarta.apache.org*, which includes classes that emulate Perl5 regular expressions:

```
import org.apache.oro.text.perl.*;

Perl5Util util = new Perl5Util ();
name = util.substitute ("s/([_%])/\\\\$1/g", name);
```

The need to escape % and _ characters to match a LIKE value literally also applies to other forms of the SHOW statement that allow a name pattern in the LIKE clause, such as SHOW TABLES, SHOW DATABASES, and SHOW VARIABLES.

Using Result Set Metadata to Get Table Structure

Another way to obtain table column information is to use the metadata generated when you issue a SELECT statement. (See Recipe 9.2.) Metadata information is available for any arbitrary query, and therefore can be obtained specifically for the columns of a given table. For example, the result set for SELECT * FROM *tbl_name* will contain metadata for each column in *tbl_name*. However, if you're interested *only* in the metadata, not in the data contained in the table, you'll naturally want to minimize the size of the result set so as to generate as little network traffic as possible. It's easy to guarantee that the result will be empty by adding a WHERE clause that is always false:

```
SELECT * FROM tbl_name WHERE 1 = 0
```

Although this query selects no rows, it's perfectly legal and MySQL goes ahead and generates the metadata, from which you can extract whatever information you want. For example, earlier in this section we wrote a PHP function get_column_names_with_show( ) that gets a list of the column names by issuing a SHOW COLUMNS statement. The function can be reimplemented as follows to get the column names from the query metadata instead by running a SELECT query and calling mysql_fetch_field():

```
function get_column_names_with_meta ($conn_id, $tbl_name)
{
    $query = "SELECT * FROM $tbl_name WHERE 1 = 0";
    if (!($result_id = mysql_query ($query, $conn_id)))
        return (FALSE);
    $names = array();               # create empty array
    for ($i = 0; $i < mysql_num_fields ($result_id); $i++)
    {
        if ($field = mysql_fetch_field ($result_id, $i))
            $names[] = $field->name;    # append name to array
    }
    mysql_free_result ($result_id);
    return ($names);
}
```

The equivalent function in Perl is simpler. DBI organizes metadata into arrays, so we just need to access the $sth->{NAME} reference to the column name array. The only trick is that it's necessary to make a copy of the array before calling finish(), because finish() destroys the metadata and renders the NAME array unavailable:

```
sub get_column_names_with_meta
{
my ($dbh, $tbl_name) = @_;
my ($sth, @names);

    $sth = $dbh->prepare ("SELECT * FROM $tbl_name WHERE 1=0");
    $sth->execute ();
    @names = @{$sth->{NAME}};   # make a copy; finish() destroys meta info
    $sth->finish ();            # release result set
    return (@names);
}
```

You can easily convert these functions that get column names into more general versions that allow you to specify which kind of metadata information you want. Name each function get_column_info() and add a parameter for the information type. In PHP, the function looks like this:

```
function get_column_info ($conn_id, $tbl_name, $info_type)
{
    $query = "SELECT * FROM $tbl_name WHERE 1 = 0";
    if (!($result_id = mysql_query ($query, $conn_id)))
        return (FALSE);
    $info = array();                        # create empty array
    for ($i = 0; $i < mysql_num_fields ($result_id); $i++)
    {
        if ($field = mysql_fetch_field ($result_id, $i))
            $info[] = $field->$info_type;   # append info to array
    }
    mysql_free_result ($result_id);
    return ($info);
}
```

To use the function, call it as follows:

```
$names = get_column_info ($conn_id, "item", "name");
$types = get_column_info ($conn_id, "item", "type");
$numeric = get_column_info ($conn_id, "item", "numeric");
```

The Perl version looks like this:

```
sub get_column_info
{
my ($dbh, $tbl_name, $info_type) = @_;
my ($sth, @info);

    $sth = $dbh->prepare ("SELECT * FROM $tbl_name WHERE 1=0");
    $sth->execute ();
    @info = @{$sth->{$info_type}};  # make a copy; finish() destroys meta info
    $sth->finish ();                # release result set
    return (@info);
}
```

And is invoked like this:

```
my @names = get_column_info ($dbh, "item", "NAME");
my @types = get_column_info ($dbh, "item", "mysql_type_name");
my @numeric = get_column_info ($dbh, "item", "mysql_is_num");
```

One caution to observe with get_column_info( ) is that you can't use it to determine display widths for a table's columns. (That is, it is not useful for the mysql_max_length values in Perl or the max_length values in PHP.) When you use column metadata obtained from a SELECT statement, the column display widths reflect the widths of the values *actually present in the result*. When the query is SELECT ... WHERE 1=0, the result set is empty and the display widths are all zero!

Portability of SELECT ... WHERE 1=0

The SELECT ... WHERE 1=0 query is reasonably portable across database systems, but won't necessarily work with all possible engines. If you want to use this query with database systems other than MySQL to obtain table information, be sure to test it first to make sure it works.

Using CREATE TABLE to Get Table Structure

A third way to obtain table structure information from MySQL is to use *mysqldump --no-data* from the command line to generate a CREATE TABLE statement that shows the structure of the table. The following command shows an example. The *--no-data* option tells *mysqldump* not to dump the data from the table, *--all* tells it to print all the CREATE TABLE options, and *--quote-names* causes names to be quoted in case they contain special characters.* You can omit *--all* or *--quote-names* if you don't need their effect.

```
% mysqldump --no-data --all --quote-names cookbook item
# MySQL dump 8.16
#
# Host: localhost      Database: cookbook
#--------------------------------------------------------
# Server version         3.23.46-log

#
# Table structure for table 'item'
#

CREATE TABLE `item` (
  `id` int(10) unsigned NOT NULL auto_increment,
  `name` char(20) default NULL,
  `colors` set('chartreuse','mauve','lime green','puce') default 'puce',
  PRIMARY KEY (`id`)
) TYPE=MyISAM;
```

If you have MySQL 3.23.20 or later, you can get the same information using the SHOW CREATE TABLE statement:

```
mysql> SHOW CREATE TABLE item;
+-------+--------------+
| Table | Create Table |
+-------+--------------+
| item  | CREATE TABLE `item` (
  `id` int(10) unsigned NOT NULL auto_increment,
  `name` char(20) default NULL,
  `colors` set('chartreuse','mauve','lime green','puce') default 'puce',
  PRIMARY KEY (`id`)
) TYPE=MyISAM |
+-------+--------------+
```

---

* The *--all* option was introduced in MySQL 3.22.23 and *--quote-names* was introduced in 3.23.6.

This format is highly informative and easy to read because it shows column information in a format similar to the one you use to create the table in the first place. It also shows the index structure clearly, which the other methods do not. However, you'll probably find this method for checking table structure more useful for visual examination than for use within programs. The information isn't provided in regular row-and-column format, so it's more difficult to parse. Also, the format is somewhat subject to change whenever the CREATE TABLE statement is enhanced, which happens from time to time as MySQL's capabilities are extended.

That's not to say there are no programmatic applications for SHOW CREATE TABLE output. It's useful, for example, for making an exact copy of a table, including all its indexes. The technique is described in Recipe 3.25, which discusses table cloning.

9.6   Getting ENUM and SET Column Information

Problem

You want to know what the legal members of an ENUM or SET column are.

Solution

Use SHOW COLUMNS to get the column definition and extract the member list from it.

Discussion

It's often useful to know the list of legal values for an ENUM or SET column. Suppose you want to present a web form containing a pop-up menu that has options corresponding to each legal value of an ENUM column, such as the sizes in which a garment can be ordered, or the available shipping methods for delivering a package. You could hardwire the choices into the script that generates the form, but if you alter the column later (for example, to add a new enumeration value), you introduce a discrepancy between the column and the script that uses it. If instead you look up the legal values using the table metadata, the script always produces a pop-up that contains the proper set of values. A similar approach can be used with SET columns.

To find out what values an ENUM or SET column can have, issue a SHOW COLUMNS statement for the column and look at the Type value in the result. For example, the colors column of the item table has a Type value that looks like this:

```
set('chartreuse','mauve','lime green','puce')
```

ENUM columns are similar, except that they say enum rather than set. For either column type, the allowable values can be extracted by stripping off the initial word and the parentheses, splitting at the commas, and removing the surrounding quotes from the individual values. Let's write a function get_enumorset_info( ) to break out these values from the column type definition.* While we're at it, we can have the function return the column's type, its default value, and whether or not values can be NULL. Then the function can be used by scripts that may need more than just the list of values. Here is a version in Python. It takes arguments representing a database connection, a table name, and a column name, and returns a dictionary with entries corresponding to the various aspects of the column definition:

```python
def get_enumorset_info (conn, tbl_name, col_name):
    # create dictionary to hold column information
    info = { }
    try:
        cursor = conn.cursor ()
        # escape SQL pattern characters in column name to match it literally
        col_name = re.sub (r'([%_])', r'\\\1', col_name)
        # this is *not* a use of placeholders
        cursor.execute ("SHOW COLUMNS FROM %s LIKE '%s'" \
                        % (tbl_name, col_name))
        row = cursor.fetchone ()
        cursor.close
        if row == None:
            return None
    except:
        return None

    info["name"] = row[0]
    # get column type string; make sure it begins with ENUM or SET
    s = row[1]
    match = re.match ("(enum|set)\((.*)\)$", s)
    if not match:
        return None
    info["type"] = match.group (1)      # column type

    # get values by splitting list at commas, then applying a
    # quote stripping function to each one
    s = re.split (",", match.group (2))
    f = lambda x: re.sub ("^'(.*)'$", "\\1", x)
    info["values"] = map (f, s)

    # determine whether or not column can contain NULL values
    info["nullable"] = (row[2] == "YES")

    # get default value (None represents NULL)
    info["default"] = row[4]
    return info
```

The following example shows one way to access and display each element of the dictionary value returned by get_enumorset_info():

```python
info = get_enumorset_info (conn, tbl_name, col_name)
print "Information for " + tbl_name + "." + col_name + ":"
if info == None:
```

---

* Feel free to come up with a less horrible function name.

```
        print "No information available (not an ENUM or SET column?)"
    else:
        print "Name: " + info["name"]
        print "Type: " + info["type"]
        print "Legal values: " + string.join (info["values"], ",")
        if info["nullable"]:
            print "Nullable"
        else:
            print "Not nullable"
        if info["default"] == None:
            print "Default value: NULL"
        else:
            print "Default value: " + info["default"]
```

That code produces the following output for the item table colors column:

```
Information for item.colors:
Type: set
Legal values: chartreuse,mauve,lime green,puce
Nullable
Default value: puce
```

Equivalent functions for other APIs are similar. They'll come in handy in the context of generating list elements in web forms. (See Recipes 18.2 and 18.3.)

9.7   Database-Independent Methods of Obtaining Table Information

Problem

You want a way to get table information that doesn't use MySQL-specific queries like SHOW COLUMNS.

Solution

This isn't possible for all APIs. One exception is JDBC, which provides a standard interface to table metadata.

Discussion

The preceding methods for obtaining table information used specific SHOW or SELECT queries and showed how to process them using each API. These techniques are MySQL-specific. JDBC provides a way to access this information through a standard interface that makes no reference to particular queries, so you can use it portably with database engines other than MySQL. With this interface, you use your connection object to obtain a database metadata object, then invoke the getColumns() method of that object to retrieve column information. getColumns() returns a result set containing one row per column name, so you must run a fetch loop to retrieve information about successive columns. Elements of result set rows that are relevant for MySQL are:

Index	Meaning
3	Table name
4	Column name
6	Column type name
7	Column size (for numeric columns, this is the precision)
8	Number of decimal places, for numeric columns
18	Whether or not column values can be NULL

Here's an example that shows how to use getColumns() to print a list of column names and types:

```
DatabaseMetaData md = conn.getMetaData ();
ResultSet rs = md.getColumns (dbName, "", tblName, "%");
int i = 0;
while (rs.next ())
{
    i++;
    System.out.println ("--- Column " + i + " ---");
    System.out.println ("Name: " + rs.getString (4));
    System.out.println ("Type: " + rs.getString (6));
}
rs.close ();
```

If the value of the tblName variable is "item", the output looks like this:

```
--- Column 1 ---
Name: id
Type: int
--- Column 2 ---
Name: name
Type: char
--- Column 3 ---
Name: colors
Type: enum
```

The four arguments to getColumns() are the names of the catalog, schema, and table, followed by a SQL pattern that column names must match to be selected. For MySQL, these arguments have the following meanings:

- The catalog name is the database name. To use the current database, pass an empty string.

- MySQL has no concept of schema, so the schema name argument is irrelevant and can be the empty string.

- The table name argument is a string naming the table.

- The column name pattern is analogous to using the LIKE clause in a SHOW COLUMNS statement. The example shown above uses "%", which matches all column names. You can pass a specific column name to get information for a single column. (Remember to escape any % and _ characters with a backslash if you want to match them literally.)

9.8   Applying Table Structure Information

Problem

It's all well and good to be able to obtain table structure information, but what can you use it for?

Solution

Lots of things: displaying lists of table columns, creating web form elements, producing ALTER TABLE statements for modifying ENUM or SET columns, and more.

Discussion

This section describes some applications for the table structure information that MySQL provides.

Displaying Column Lists

Probably the simplest use of table information is to present a list of the table's columns. This is common in web-based or GUI applications that allow users to construct queries interactively by selecting a table column from a list and entering a value against which to compare column values. The various versions of the get_column_names_with_show() or get_column_names_with_meta() functions shown earlier in the chapter can serve as the basis for such list displays.

Interactive Record Editing

Knowledge of a table's structure can be very useful for interactive record-editing applications. Suppose you have an application that retrieves a record from the database, displays a form containing the record's content so a user can edit it, and then updates the record in the database after the user modifies the form and submits it. You can use table structure information for validating column values. For example, if a column is an ENUM, you can find out the valid enumeration values and check the value submitted by the user against them to determine whether or not it's legal. If the column is an integer type, you check the submitted value to make sure that it consists entirely of digits, possibly preceded by a sign character. If the column contains dates, look for a legal date format.

But what if the user leaves a field empty? If the field corresponds to, say, a CHAR column in the table, do you set the column value to NULL or to the empty string? This too is a question that can be answered by checking the table's structure. Determine whether or not the column can contain NULL values. If it can, set the column to NULL; otherwise, set it to the empty string.

Mapping Column Types onto Web Page Elements

Some column types such as ENUM and SET correspond naturally to elements of web forms:

- An ENUM has a fixed set of values from which you choose a single value. This is analogous to a group of radio buttons, a pop-up menu, or a single-pick scrolling list.

- A SET column is similar, except that you can select multiple values; this corresponds to a group of checkboxes or a multiple-pick scrolling list.

If you access the information for these types of columns using SHOW COLUMNS, you can easily determine the legal values for a column and map them onto the appropriate form element automatically. This allows you to present users with a list of applicable values from which selections can be made easily without any typing. Earlier in this chapter we saw how to get ENUM and SET column metadata. The methods developed there are used in Chapter 18, which discusses form generation in more detail.

Adding Elements to ENUM or SET Column Definitions

It's really a pain to add a new element to an ENUM or SET column definition when you use ALTER TABLE, because you have to list not only the new element, but all the existing elements as well. One approach for doing this using *mysqldump* and an editor is described in Recipe 8.2. Another way to accomplish this task is to write your own program that does most of the work for you by using column metadata. Let's develop a Python script *add_element.py* that generates the appropriate ALTER TABLE statement automatically when given a table name, an ENUM or SET column name, and the new element value. Suppose you want to add "hot pink" to the colors column of the item table. The current structure of the column looks like this:

```
mysql> SHOW COLUMNS FROM item LIKE 'colors'\G
*************************** 1. row ***************************
  Field: colors
   Type: set('chartreuse','mauve','lime green','puce')
   Null: YES
    Key:
Default: puce
  Extra:
```

add_element.py will use that information to figure out the correct ALTER TABLE statement and write it out:

```
% ./add_element.py item colors "hot pink"
ALTER TABLE item
    MODIFY colors
    set('chartreuse','mauve','lime green','puce','hot pink')
    NULL DEFAULT 'puce';
```

By having *add_element.py* produce the statement as its output, you have the choice of shoving it into *mysql* for immediate execution or saving the output into a file:

```
% ./add_element.py item colors "hot pink" | mysql cookbook
% ./add_element.py item colors "hot pink" > stmt.sql
```

You might choose the latter course if you want the new element somewhere other than at the end of the list of values, which is where *add_element.py* will put it. In this case, edit *stmt.sql* to place the element where you want it, then execute the statement:

```
% vi stmt.sql
% mysql cookbook < stmt.sql
```

The first part of the *add_element.py* script imports the requisite modules and checks the command-line arguments. This is fairly straightforward:

```
#! /usr/bin/python
# add_element.py - show ALTER TABLE statement for ENUM or SET column
# (assumes cookbook database)

import sys
sys.path.insert (0, "/usr/local/apache/lib/python")
import re
import MySQLdb
import Cookbook

if len (sys.argv) != 4:
    print "Usage: add_element.py tbl_name col_name new_element"
    sys.exit (1)
tbl_name = sys.argv[1]
col_name = sys.argv[2]
elt_val = sys.argv[3]
```

After connecting to the MySQL server (code not shown), we need to run a SHOW COLUMNS query to retrieve information about the designated column. The following code does this, checking to make sure that the column really exists in the table:

```
cursor = conn.cursor ()
# escape SQL pattern characters in column name to match it literally
esc_col_name = re.sub (r'([%_])', r'\\\1', col_name)
# this is *not* a use of placeholders
cursor.execute ("SHOW COLUMNS FROM %s LIKE '%s'" % (tbl_name, esc_col_name))
info = cursor.fetchone ()
cursor.close
if info == None:
    print "Could not retrieve information for table %s, column %s" \
                                        % (tbl_name, col_name)
    sys.exit (1)
```

At this point, if the SHOW COLUMNS statement succeeded, the information produced by it is available as a tuple stored in the info variable. We'll need to use several elements from this tuple. The most important is the column type value, which provides the enum(...) or set(...) string containing the column's current definition. We can use this to verify that the column really is an ENUM or SET, then add the new element

---

to the string just before the closing parenthesis. For the colors column, we want to change this:

```
set('chartreuse','mauve','lime green','puce')
```

To this:

```
set('chartreuse','mauve','lime green','puce','hot pink')
```

It's also necessary to check whether column values can be NULL and what the default value is so that the program can add the appropriate information to the ALTER TABLE statement. The code that does all this is as follows:

```
# get column type string; make sure it begins with ENUM or SET
type = info[1]
if not re.match ('(enum|set)', type):
    print "table %s, column %s is not an ENUM or SET" % (tbl_name, col_name)
    sys.exit(1)
# add quotes, insert comma and new element just before closing paren
elt_val = conn.literal (elt_val)
type = re.sub ('\)$', ',' + elt_val + ')', type)

# determine whether column can contain NULL values
if info[2] == "YES":
    nullable = "NULL"
else:
    nullable = "NOT NULL";

# construct DEFAULT clause (add surrounding quotes unless
# value is NULL)
default = "DEFAULT " + conn.literal (info[4])

print "ALTER TABLE %s\n\tMODIFY %s\n\t%s\n\t%s %s;" \
            % (tbl_name, col_name, type, nullable, default)
```

That's it. You now have a working ENUM- or SET-altering program. Still, *add_element.py* is fairly basic and could be improved in various ways:

- Make sure that the element value you're adding to the column isn't already there.

- Allow *add_element.py* to take more than one argument after the column name and add all of them to the column definition at the same time.

- Add an option to indicate that the named element should be deleted rather than added.

- Add an option that tells the script to execute the ALTER TABLE statement immediately rather than displaying it.

- If you have a version of MySQL older than 3.22.16, it won't understand the MODIFY *col_name* syntax used by *add_element.py*. You may want to edit the script to use CHANGE *col_name* syntax instead. The following two statements are equivalent:

```
ALTER TABLE tbl_name MODIFY col_name col_definition;
ALTER TABLE tbl_name CHANGE col_name col_name col_definition;
```

  add_element.py uses MODIFY because it's less confusing than CHANGE.

Retrieving Dates in Non-ISO Format

MySQL stores dates in ISO 8601 format (*CCYY-MM-DD*), but it's often desirable or necessary to rewrite date values, such as when you need to transfer table data into another program that expects dates in another format. You can write a script that retrieves and prints table rows, using column metadata to detect DATE, DATETIME, and TIMESTAMP columns, and reformat them with DATE_FORMAT() into whatever date format you want. (For an example, see Recipe 10.33, which describes a short script named *iso_to_us.pl* that uses this technique to rewrite ISO dates into U.S. format.)

Converting Character Columns Between Fixed-Length and Variable-Length Types

CHAR columns have a fixed length, whereas VARCHAR columns are variable length. In general, tables that use CHAR columns can be processed more quickly but take up more space than tables that use VARCHAR columns. To make it easier to convert tables to use CHAR or VARCHAR columns, you can use the information provided by SHOW COLUMNS to generate an ALTER TABLE statement that performs the requisite column conversions. Here is a Python function alter_to_char() that creates a statement for changing all the VARCHAR columns to CHAR:

```python
def alter_to_char (conn, tbl_name):
    cursor = conn.cursor ()
    cursor.execute ("SHOW COLUMNS FROM " + tbl_name)
    rows = cursor.fetchall ()
    cursor.close ()
    str = ""
    for info in rows:
        col_name = info[0]
        type = info[1]
        if re.match ('varchar', type):        # it's a VARCHAR column
            type = re.sub ("var", "", type) # convert to CHAR
            # determine whether column can contain NULL values
            if info[2] == "YES":
                nullable = "NULL"
            else:
                nullable = "NOT NULL";
            # construct DEFAULT clause (add surrounding quotes unless
            # value is NULL)
            default = "DEFAULT " + conn.literal (info[4])
            # add MODIFY clause to string
            if str != "":
                str = str + ",\n\t"
            str = str + \
                    "MODIFY %s %s %s %s" % (col_name, type, nullable, default)
    cursor.close ()
    if str == "":
        return None
    return "ALTER TABLE " + tbl_name + "\n\t" + str
```

Suppose you have a table that looks like this:

```
CREATE TABLE chartbl
(
    c1  VARCHAR(10),
    c2  VARCHAR(10) BINARY,
    c3  VARCHAR(10) NOT NULL DEFAULT 'abc\'def'
);
```

If you pass the name of that table to the alter_to_varchar() function, the statement that it returns looks like this:

```
ALTER TABLE chartbl
    MODIFY c1 char(10) NULL DEFAULT NULL,
    MODIFY c2 char(10) binary NULL DEFAULT NULL,
    MODIFY c3 char(10) NOT NULL DEFAULT 'abc\'def'
```

A function to convert columns in the other direction (from CHAR to VARCHAR) would be similar. Here is an example, this time in Perl:

```perl
sub alter_to_varchar
{
my ($dbh, $tbl_name) = @_;
my ($sth, $str);

    $sth = $dbh->prepare ("SHOW COLUMNS FROM $tbl_name");
    $sth->execute ();
    while (my @row = $sth->fetchrow_array ())
    {
        if ($row[1] =~ /^char/)      # it's a CHAR column
        {
            $row[1] = "var" . $row[1];
            $str .= ",\n\t" if $str;
            $str .= "MODIFY $row[0] $row[1]";
            $str .= ($row[2] eq "YES" ? "" : " NOT") . " NULL";
            $str .= " DEFAULT " . $dbh->quote ($row[4]);
        }
    }
    $str = "ALTER TABLE $tbl_name\n\t$str" if $str;
    return ($str);
}
```

For completeness, the function generates an ALTER TABLE statement that explicitly converts all CHAR columns to VARCHAR. In practice, it's necessary to convert only one such column. MySQL notices the change of a column from fixed-length to variable-length format, and automatically converts any other fixed-length columns that have a variable-length equivalent.

Selecting All Except Certain Columns

Sometimes you want to retrieve "almost all" the columns from a table. Suppose you have an image table that contains a BLOB column named data used for storing images that might be very large, and other columns that characterize the BLOB column, such as its ID, a description, and so forth. It's easy to write a SELECT * query that retrieves all the columns, but if all you need is the descriptive information about the images and not the images themselves, it's inefficient to drag the BLOB values over the connection along with the other columns. Instead, you want to select everything in the record *except* the data column.

Unfortunately, there is no way to say directly in SQL, "select all columns except this one." You must explicitly name all the columns except data. On the other hand, it's easy to construct that kind of query by using table structure information. Extract the list of column names, delete the one to be excluded, then construct a SELECT query from those columns that remain. The following example shows how to do this in PHP, using the get_column_names_with_show() function developed earlier in the chapter to obtain the column names from a table:

```php
$names = get_column_names_with_show ($conn_id, $tbl_name);
$query = "";
# construct list of columns to select: all but "data"
reset ($names);
while (list ($index, $name) = each ($names))
{
    if ($name == "data")
        continue;
    if ($query != "")    # put commas between column names
        $query .= ",";
    $query .= $name;
}
$query = "SELECT $query FROM $tbl_name";
```

The equivalent Perl code for constructing the query is a bit shorter (and correspondingly more cryptic):

```perl
my @names = get_column_names_with_show ($dbh, $tbl_name);
my $query = "SELECT "
            . join (",", grep (!/^data$/, @names))
            . " FROM $tbl_name";
```

Whichever language you use, the result is a query that you can use to select all columns but data. It will be more efficient than SELECT * because it won't pull the BLOB values over the network. Of course, this process does involve an extra round trip to the server to execute the statement that retrieves the column names, so you should consider the context in which you plan to use the SELECT query. If you're just going to retrieve a single record, it might be more efficient simply to select the entire row than to incur the overhead of the extra round trip. But if you're selecting many rows, the reduction in network traffic achieved by skipping the BLOB columns will be worth the overhead of the additional query for getting table structure.

9.9   Listing Tables and Databases

Problem

You want a list of tables in a database or a list of databases hosted by the MySQL server.

Solution

Use SHOW TABLES or SHOW DATABASES.

Discussion

To obtain a list of tables in the current database, use this query:

```
SHOW TABLES;
```

However, if no database has been selected, the query will fail. To avoid this problem, you should either make sure there is a current database or name a database explicitly:

```
SHOW TABLES FROM db_name;
```

Another form of SHOW returns a list of databases hosted by the server:

```
SHOW DATABASES;
```

Be Careful with SHOW Statements

Be careful how you interpret the results from SHOW TABLES and SHOW DATABASES. The result from SHOW TABLES will be empty if you don't have permission to access the table. The result from SHOW DATABASES may be empty as well. If the server was started with the *--safe-show-database* or *--skip-show-database* option, you may not be able to get much information with the SHOW DATABASES statement.

If you're looking for a database-independent way to get table or database lists and you're using Perl or Java, try the following methods.

In Perl, DBI provides a tables() function that returns a list of tables. It works for the current database only:

```
my @tables = $dbh->tables ();
```

In Java, you can use JDBC methods designed to return lists of tables or databases. For each method, invoke your connection object's getMetaData() method and use the resulting DatabaseMetaData object to retrieve the information you want. Here's how to list the tables in a given database:

```
// get list of tables in database named by dbName; if
// dbName is the empty string, the current database is used
DatabaseMetaData md = conn.getMetaData ();
ResultSet rs = md.getTables (dbName, "", "%", null);
while (rs.next ())
    System.out.println (rs.getString (3));  // column 3 = table name
rs.close ();
```

A similar procedure produces a list of databases:

```
// get list of databases
DatabaseMetaData md = conn.getMetaData ();
ResultSet rs = md.getCatalogs ();
while (rs.next ())
    System.out.println (rs.getString (1));  // column 1 = database name
rs.close ();
```

9.10   Testing Whether a Table Exists

Problem

You want to know whether a table exists.

Solution

Use SHOW TABLES to see if the table is listed.

Discussion

You can use the SHOW TABLES statement to test whether a specific table exists by adding a LIKE clause that matches the name of the table:

```
SHOW TABLES LIKE 'tbl_name';
SHOW TABLES FROM db_name LIKE 'tbl_name';
```

If you get a row back, the table exists. If not, it doesn't. Here's a Perl function that performs an existence test for a table:

```
sub table_exists
{
my ($dbh, $tbl_name) = @_;
my $db_clause = "";

    ($db_clause, $tbl_name) = (" FROM $1", $2) if $tbl_name =~ /(.*)\.(.*)/;
    $tbl_name =~ s/([%_])/\\$1/g;   # escape any special characters
    return ($dbh->selectrow_array ("SHOW TABLES $db_clause LIKE '$tbl_name'"));
}
```

The function checks the table name argument to see if it's in *db_name.tbl_name* form. If so, it strips off the database name and uses it to add a FROM clause to the statement. Otherwise, the test is against the current database. Note that the function returns false if the table exists but you have no privileges for accessing it.

There are other ways to check whether or not a table exists besides SHOW TABLES. Either of the following SELECT statements will execute successfully if the table exists, and fail if it does not:

```
SELECT * FROM tbl_name WHERE 1=0;
SELECT COUNT(*) FROM tbl_name;
```

To use these statements within a program, first set your API's error trapping not to terminate your program on an error. Then attempt to execute the statement and test whether it succeed or fails.

 The SELECT * statement is preferable to SELECT COUNT(*) for some table types such as BDB or InnoDB, which require a full table scan to evaluate COUNT(*). For ISAM and MyISAM tables, the COUNT(*) statement is optimized to use the record count stored in the table.

9.11   Testing Whether a Database Exists

Problem

You want to know whether a database exists.

Solution

Use SHOW DATABASES to see if the table is listed.

Discussion

SHOW DATABASES can be used to determine whether a database exists if you add a LIKE clause that matches the database name:

```
SHOW DATABASES LIKE 'db_name';
```

The following Perl function shows how to do this:

```perl
sub database_exists
{
my ($dbh, $db_name) = @_;

    $db_name =~ s/([%_])/\\$1/g;    # escape any special characters
    return ($dbh->selectrow_array ("SHOW DATABASES LIKE '$db_name'"));
}
```

The function returns false if the database exists but the server was started with the
--skip-show-database option and you don't have MySQL root user privileges.

9.12   Getting Server Metadata

Problem

You want to the MySQL server to tell you about itself.

Solution

Several SELECT and SHOW statements return information about the server.

Discussion

MySQL offers several SQL statements that provide you with information about the
server itself and about your current client connection. A few that you may find useful are listed here. To obtain the information provided by any of them, issue the
query, then process the result set to retrieve the query output. Both SHOW statements
allow a LIKE '*pattern*' clause for limiting the results only to those rows matching the
pattern.

Statement	Information produced by statement
SELECT VERSION()	Server version string
SELECT DATABASE()	Current database name (empty if none)
SELECT USER()	Current username
SHOW STATUS	Server status indicators
SHOW VARIABLES	Server configuration variables

These queries are all MySQL-specific. If you're working in Java, JDBC provides several database-independent methods for obtaining server metadata, some of which
provide the same information as some of the preceding statements. Use your connection object to obtain the database metadata, then invoke the appropriate methods to
get the information in which you're interested. You should consult a JDBC reference
for a complete list, but here are a few representative examples:

```
DatabaseMetaData md = conn.getMetaData ();
// can also get this with SELECT VERSION()
System.out.println ("Product version: " + md.getDatabaseProductVersion ());
// this is similar to SELECT USER() but doesn't include the hostname
System.out.println ("Username: " + md.getUserName ());
```

9.13 Writing Applications That Adapt to the MySQL Server Version

Problem

You want to use a given feature that is only available as of a particular version of MySQL.

Solution

Ask the server for its version number. If the server is too old, maybe you can fall back to a workaround for the missing feature, if one exists.

Discussion

If you're writing an application that can perform certain functions only if the MySQL server supports the necessary underlying operations, the server version number allows you to determine whether those operations are available (or whether you need to perform some sort of workaround, assuming there is one).

To get the server version, issue a SELECT VERSION( ) statement. The result is a string that looks something like 3.23.27-gamma. In other words, it returns a string consisting of major, minor, and "teeny" version numbers, and possibly some suffix. The version string can be used as is for presentation purposes if you want to produce a status display for the user. However, for comparisons, it's simpler to work with a number—in particular, a 5-digit number in *Mmmtt* format, where *M*, *mm*, *tt* are the major, minor, and teeny version numbers. The conversion can be performed by splitting the string at the periods, stripping off from the third piece the suffix that begins with the first non-numeric character, and then joining the pieces.*

Here's a DBI function that takes a database handle argument and returns a two-element list containing both the string and numeric forms of the server version. The code assumes that the minor and teeny version parts are less than 100 and thus no more than two digits each. That should be a valid assumption, because the source code for MySQL itself uses the same format.

```
sub get_server_version
{
my $dbh = shift;
my ($ver_str, $ver_num);
my ($major, $minor, $teeny);
```

---

* My first attempt at the conversion algorithm was to break the version string at periods, then to strip the suffix from the third piece beginning with the - character. That algorithm failed with the release of MySQL 3.23.29a-gamma. (Stripping -gamma from 29a-gamma leaves 29a, which is not a number.)

```
    # fetch result into scalar string
    $ver_str = $dbh->selectrow_array ("SELECT VERSION()");
    return undef unless defined ($ver_str);
    ($major, $minor, $teeny) = split (/\./, $ver_str);
    $teeny =~ s/\D*$//; # strip any non-numeric suffix if present
    $ver_num = $major*10000 + $minor*100 + $teeny;
    return ($ver_str, $ver_num);
}
```

To get both forms of the version information at once, call the function like this:

```
my ($ver_str, $ver_num) = get_server_version ($dbh);
```

To get just one of the values, call it as follows:

```
my $ver_str = (get_server_version ($dbh))[0];   # string form
my $ver_num = (get_server_version ($dbh))[1];   # numeric form
```

The following examples demonstrate how to use the numeric version value to check whether the server supports certain features:

```
my $ver_num = (get_server_version ($dbh))[1];
printf "GET_LOCK()/RELEASE_LOCK(): %s\n",   ($ver_num >= 32127 ? "yes" : "no");
printf "Functional GRANT statement: %s\n", ($ver_num >= 32211 ? "yes" : "no");
printf "Temporary tables: %s\n",           ($ver_num >= 32302 ? "yes" : "no");
printf "Quoted identifiers: %s\n",         ($ver_num >= 32306 ? "yes" : "no");
printf "UNION statement: %s\n",            ($ver_num >= 40000 ? "yes" : "no");
printf "Subselects: %s\n",                 ($ver_num >= 40100 ? "yes" : "no");
```

9.14   Determining the Current Database

Problem

Has any database been selected as the current database? What is its name?

Solution

Use the DATABASE() function.

Discussion

SELECT DATABASE() returns the name of the current database, or the empty string if no database has been selected. This Python code uses the statement to present a status display containing information about the current connection:

```
cursor = conn.cursor ()
cursor.execute ("SELECT DATABASE()")
row = cursor.fetchone ()
cursor.close
if row == None or len (row) == 0 or row[0] == "":
    db = "(no database selected)"
```

```
else:
    db = row[0]
print "Current database:", db
```

9.15 Determining the Current MySQL User

Problem

What is the name of the client user and from what host was the connection made?

Solution

Use the USER( ) function.

Discussion

SELECT USER( ) returns a string in the form *user@host*, indicating the name of the current user and the host from which the user connected.* To select just the name or host parts, use these queries:

```
SELECT SUBSTRING_INDEX(USER(),'@',1);
SELECT SUBSTRING_INDEX(USER(),'@',-1);
```

You can use this information in various ways. For example, to have a Perl application greet the user, you could do something like this:

```
my ($user, $host) = $dbh->selectrow_array (q{
            SELECT SUBSTRING_INDEX(USER(),'@',1),
                   SUBSTRING_INDEX(USER(),'@',-1)
        });
print "Hello, $user!  Good to see you.\n";
print "I see you're connecting from $host.\n" unless $host eq "";
```

Alternatively, you could simply retrieve the entire USER( ) value and break it apart by using a pattern-match operation:

```
my ($user, $host) = ($dbh->selectrow_array (
                    "SELECT USER()") =~ /([^@]+)@?(.*)/);
```

Or by splitting it:

```
my ($user, $host) = split (/@/, $dbh->selectrow_array ("SELECT USER()"));
```

Another application for USER( ) values is to maintain a log of who's using an application. A simple log table might look like this (the values 16 and 60 reflect the lengths of the user and host columns in the MySQL grant tables):

```
CREATE TABLE app_log
(
```

---

* Prior to MySQL 3.22.1, the value of USER( ) does not include the *@host* part.

```
    t       TIMESTAMP,
    user    CHAR(16),
    host    CHAR(60)
);
```

To insert new records into the app_log table, use the following statement. The
TIMESTAMP column gets set automatically to the current date and time; there's no need
to specify a value for it.

```
INSERT INTO app_log
    SET user = SUBSTRING_INDEX(USER(),'@',1),
        host = SUBSTRING_INDEX(USER(),'@',-1);
```

The table stores the user and host values separately because it's more efficient to run
summary queries against those values when you don't have to break them apart. For
example, if you check periodically how many distinct hosts you're getting connections from, it's better to split the USER() value once when you create the record than
to split the value each time you issue a SELECT to generate the summary. Also, you
can index the host column if you store host values separately, which you can't do if
you store combined *user@host* values.

9.16   Monitoring the MySQL Server

Problem

You want to find out how the server was configured or monitor its state.

Solution

SHOW VARIABLES and SHOW STATUS are useful for this.

Discussion

The SHOW VARIABLES and SHOW STATUS statements provide server configuration and performance information:

```
mysql> SHOW VARIABLES;
+---------------------------------+------------------+
| Variable_name                   | Value            |
+---------------------------------+------------------+
| back_log                        | 50               |
| basedir                         | /usr/local/mysql/ |
| bdb_cache_size                  | 8388600          |
| bdb_log_buffer_size             | 0                |
| bdb_home                        |                  |
...
```

```
mysql> SHOW STATUS;
+-------------------------+----------+
| Variable_name           | Value    |
+-------------------------+----------+
| Aborted_clients         | 319      |
| Aborted_connects        | 22       |
| Bytes_received          | 32085033 |
| Bytes_sent              | 26379272 |
| Connections             | 65684    |
...
```

This information can be useful for writing administrative applications. For example, you might write a long-running program that probes the server periodically to monitor its activity. A simple application of this type might ask the server to report the number of connections it's received and its uptime, to determine a running display of average connection activity. The queries to obtain this information are:

```
SHOW STATUS LIKE 'Connections';
SHOW STATUS LIKE 'Uptime';
```

If you want to avoid having to reconnect each time you issue the queries, you can ask the server for its client timeout period and probe it at intervals shorter than that value. You can get the timeout value (in seconds) with this query:

```
SHOW VARIABLES LIKE 'wait_timeout';
```

The default value is 28800 (8 hours), but it may be different on your system.

The "MySQL Uncertainty Principle"

Heisenberg's uncertainty principle for measurement of quantum phenomena has a MySQL analog. If you monitor MySQL's status to see how it changes over time, you may notice a curious effect for some of the indicators: Each time you take a measurement, you change the value you're measuring! For example, you can determine the number of queries the server has received by using the following statement:

```
SHOW STATUS LIKE 'Questions'
```

However, that statement is itself a query, so each time you issue it, you cause the Questions value to change. In effect, your performance assessment instrument contaminates its own measurements, something you may want to take into account.

9.17 Determining Which Table Types the Server Supports

Problem

You want to know whether you can create a table using a given table type.

Solution

Ask the server which table types it supports.

Discussion

SHOW VARIABLES can tell you whether or not certain table types are available. For example, you can test the have_bdb, have_innodb, and have_gemini variables to see if the server supports transaction-safe tables. The following PHP code demonstrates how to check for a value of YES for the have_bdb variable, using a two-stage approach. First, make sure that the variable exists by testing for a nonempty result set. (The variable will not be present at all if your version of MySQL predates the inclusion of support for the table type.) Then, fetch the variable's value to see if it's YES:

```
$avail = FALSE;
# escape the variable name properly
$var_name = ereg_replace ("([%_])", "\\\\1", "have_bdb");
if ($result_id = mysql_query ("SHOW VARIABLES LIKE '$var_name'", $conn_id))
{
    if ($row = mysql_fetch_row ($result_id))
        $avail = ($row[1] == "YES" ? TRUE : FALSE);
    mysql_free_result ($result_id);
}
```

After this code executes, $avail will be TRUE or FALSE to indicate whether the server supports BDB tables. To check for a different table type, modify the code to test the appropriate server variable name.

A more general approach is to write a function that checks for all known handlers and returns a list of the ones that are supported. You cannot ask the server for a list of types directly, but if you know what the possible types are, you can determine which of them are supported using the following rules:

- Prior to MySQL 3.23, only the ISAM type is available.
- As of MySQL 3.23, MyISAM is always available. Other table handlers may also be available. For the ISAM, BDB, and Gemini types, check the have_isam, have_bdb, and have_gemini server variables (look for a value of YES). InnoDB table availability is indicated by have_innodb. However, that variable was at one time called have_innobase; for completeness, check them both.

These rules are implemented by the Perl function get_table_handlers() shown below. It returns a list containing the words drawn from the list bdb, gemini, innodb, isam, and myisam, corresponding to those table types that are found to be supported:

```
sub get_table_handlers
{
my $dbh = shift;
my @types;
my %typemap =
(
```

```
    "have_bdb"       => "bdb",
    "have_gemini"    => "gemini",
    "have_innodb"    => "innodb",
    "have_innobase" => "innodb",     # obsolete form of have_innodb
    "have_isam"      => "isam"
);

    # get server version number
    my $ver_num = (get_server_version ($dbh))[1];   # numeric form

    if ($ver_num < 32300)        # only ISAM available prior to 3.23.xx
    {
        @types = ("isam");
    }
    else
    {
        @types = ("myisam");    # MyISAM always available as of 3.23.xx

        # Issue SHOW VARIABLES query to get the 'have_' server variables
        # that indicate presence of table handlers.  (There are some 'have_'
        # variables that don't pertain to table types, but it's still more
        # efficient to issue a single query than a query for each variable.)

        my $sth = $dbh->prepare ("SHOW VARIABLES LIKE 'have\\_%'");
        $sth->execute ();
        while (my ($var, $val) = $sth->fetchrow_array ())
        {
            push (@types, $typemap{$var})
                if exists ($typemap{$var}) && $val eq "YES";
        }
    }
    return (sort (@types));
}
```

## CHAPTER 10

Importing and Exporting Data

10.0 Introduction

Suppose you have a file named *somedata.csv* that contains 12 columns of data in comma-separated values (CSV) format. From this file you want to extract only columns 2, 11, 5, and 9, and use them to create database records in a MySQL table that contains name, birth, height, and weight columns. You need to make sure that the height and weight are positive integers, and convert the birth dates from *MM/DD/YY* format to *CCYY-MM-DD* format. How can you do this?

In one sense, that problem is very specialized. But in another, it's not at all atypical, because data transfer problems with specific requirements occur frequently when transferring data into MySQL. It would be nice if datafiles were always nicely formatted and ready to load into MySQL with no preparation, but that is frequently not so. As a result, it's often necessary to preprocess information to put it into a format that MySQL finds acceptable. The reverse also is true; data exported from MySQL may need massaging to be useful for other programs.

Some data transfer operations are so difficult that they require a great deal of hand checking and reformatting, but in most cases, you can do at least part of the job automatically. Virtually all transfer problems involve at least some elements of a common set of conversion issues. This chapter discusses what these issues are, how to deal with them by taking advantage of the existing tools at your disposal, and how to write your own tools when necessary. The idea is not to cover all possible import and export situations (an impossible task), but to show some representative techniques and utilities, You can use them as is, or adapt them for problems that they don't handle. (There are also commercial conversion tools that may assist you, but my purpose here is to help you do things yourself.)

The first recipes in the chapter cover MySQL's native facilities for importing data (the LOAD DATA statement and the *mysqlimport* command-line program), and for exporting data (the SELECT ... INTO OUTFILE statement and the *mysqldump* program). For operations that don't require any data validation or reformatting, these facilities often are sufficient.

For situations where MySQL's native import and export capabilities do not suffice, the chapter moves on to cover techniques for using external supporting utilities and for writing your own. To some extent, you can avoid writing your own tools by using existing programs. For example, *cut* can extract columns from a file, and *sed* and *tr* can be used as postprocessors to convert query output into other formats. But you'll probably eventually reach the point where you decide to write your own programs. When you do, there are two broad sets of issues to consider:

- How to manipulate the structure of datafiles. When a file is in a format that isn't suitable for import, you'll need to convert it to a different format. This many involve issues such as changing the column delimiters or line-ending sequences, or removing or rearranging columns in the file.

- How to manipulate the content of datafiles. If you don't know whether the values contained in a file are legal, you may want to preprocess it to check or reformat them. Numeric values may need to be verified as lying within a specific range, dates may need to be converted to or from ISO format, and so forth.

Source code for the program fragments and scripts discussed in this chapter is located in the *transfer* directory of the recipes distribution, with the exception that some of the utility functions are contained in library files located in the *lib* directory. The code for some of the shorter utilities is shown in full. For the longer ones, the chapter generally discusses only how they work and how to use them, but you have access to the source if you wish to investigate in more detail how they're written.

The problems addressed in this chapter involve a lot of text processing and pattern matching. These are particular strengths of Perl, so the program fragments and utilities shown here are written mainly in Perl. PHP and Python provide pattern-matching capabilities, too, so they can of course do many of the same things. If you want to adapt the techniques described here for Java, you'll need to get a library that provides classes for regular expression–based pattern matching. See Appendix A for suggestions.

General Import and Export Issues

Incompatible datafile formats and differing rules for interpreting various kinds of values lead to many headaches when transferring data between programs. Nevertheless, certain issues recur frequently. By being aware of them, you'll be able to identify more easily just what you need to do to solve particular import or export problems.

In its most basic form, an input stream is just a set of bytes with no particular meaning. Successful import into MySQL requires being able to recognize which bytes represent structural information, and which represent the data values framed by that structure. Because such recognition is key to decomposing the input into appropriate units, the most fundamental import issues are these:

- What is the record separator? Knowing this allows the input stream to be partitioned into records.

- What is the field delimiter? Knowing this allows each record to be partitioned into field values. Recovering the original data values also may include stripping off quotes from around the values or recognizing escape sequences within them.

The ability to break apart the input into records and fields is important for extracting the data values from it. However, the values still might not be in a form that can be used directly, and you may need to consider other issues:

- Do the order and number of columns match the structure of the database table? Mismatches require columns to be rearranged or skipped.

- Do data values need to be validated or reformatted? If the values are in a format that matches MySQL's expectations, no further processing is necessary. Otherwise, they need to be checked and possibly rewritten.

- How should NULL or empty values be handled? Are they allowed? Can NULL values even be detected? (Some systems export NULL values as empty strings, making it impossible to distinguish one from the other.)

For export from MySQL, the issues are somewhat the reverse. You probably can assume that values stored in the database are valid, but they may require reformatting, and it's necessary to add column and record delimiters to form an output stream that has a structure another program can recognize.

The chapter deals with these issues primarily within the context of performing bulk transfers of entire files, but many of the techniques discussed here can be applied in other situations as well. Consider a web-based application that presents a form for a user to fill in, then processes its contents to create a new record in the database. That is a data import situation. Web APIs generally make form contents available as a set of already-parsed discrete values, so the application may not need to deal with record and column delimiters, On the other hand, validation issues remain paramount. You really have no idea what kind of values a user is sending your script, so it's important to check them.

File Formats

Datafiles come in many formats, two of which are used frequently in this chapter:

- Tab-delimited format. This is one of the simplest file structures; lines contain values separated by tab characters. A short tab-delimited file might look like this, where the whitespace between column values represents single tab characters:

```
a       b       c
a,b,c   d e     f
```

- Comma-separated values (CSV) format. Files written in CSV format vary somewhat, because there is apparently no actual standard describing the format. However, the general idea is that lines consist of values separated by commas, and values containing internal commas are surrounded by quotes to prevent the commas from being interpreted as value delimiters. It's also common for values containing spaces to be quoted as well. Here is an example, where each line contains three values:

```
a,b,c
"a,b,c","d e",f
```

It's trickier to process CSV files than tab-delimited files, because characters like quotes and commas have a dual meaning: they may represent file structure or be part of data values.

Another important datafile characteristic is the line-ending sequence. The most common sequences are carriage returns, linefeeds, and carriage return/linefeed pairs, sometimes referred to here by the abbreviations CR, LF, and CRLF.

Datafiles often begin with a row of column labels. In fact, a CSV file that begins with a row of names is what FileMaker Pro refers to as merge format. For some import operations, the row of labels is an annoyance because you must discard it to avoid having the labels be loaded into your table as a data record. But in other cases, the labels are quite useful:

- For import into existing tables, the labels can be used to match up datafile columns with the table columns if they are not necessarily in the same order.

- The labels can be used for column names when creating a new table automatically or semi-automatically from a datafile. For example, Recipe 10.36 later in the chapter discusses a utility that examines a datafile and guesses the CREATE TABLE statement that should be used to create a table from the file. If a label row is present, the utility uses them for column names. Otherwise, it's necessary to make up generic names like c1, c2, and so forth, which isn't very descriptive.

Tab-Delimited, Linefeed-Terminated Format

Although datafiles may be written in many formats, it's unlikely that you'll want to include machinery for reading several different formats within each file-processing utility that you write. I don't want to, either, so for that reason, many of the utilities described in this chapter assume for simplicity that their input is in tab-delimited, linefeed-terminated format. (This is also the default format for MySQL's LOAD DATA statement.) By making this assumption, it becomes easier to write programs that read files.

On the other hand, *something* has to be able to read data in other formats. To handle that problem, we'll develop a *cvt_file.pl* script that can read or write several types of files. (See Recipe 10.18.) The script is based on the Perl *Text::CSV_XS* module, which despite its name can be used for more than just CSV data. *cvt_file.pl* can convert between many file types, making it possible for other programs that require tab-delimited lines to be used with files not originally written in that format.

Notes on Invoking Shell Commands

This chapter shows a number of programs that you invoke from the command line using a shell like *bash* or *tcsh* under Unix or *CMD.EXE* ("the DOS prompt") under Windows. Many of the example commands for these programs use quotes around option values, and sometimes an option value is itself a quote character. Quoting conventions vary from one shell to another, but rules that seem to work with most of them (including *CMD.EXE* under Windows) are as follows:

- For an argument that contains spaces, surround it with double quotes to prevent the shell from interpreting it as multiple separate arguments. The shell will strip off the quotes, then pass the argument to the command intact.

- To include a double quote character in the argument itself, precede it with a backslash.

Some shell commands are so long that they're shown as you would enter them using several lines, with a backslash character as the line-continuation character:

```
% prog_name \
    argument1 \
    argument2 ...
```

That works for Unix, but not for Windows, where you'll need to omit the continuation characters and type the entire command on one line:

```
C:\> prog_name argument1 argument2 ...
```

10.1 Importing Data with LOAD DATA and mysqlimport

Problem

You want to load a datafile into a table using MySQL's built in import capabilities.

Solution

Use the LOAD DATA statement or the *mysqlimport* command-line program.

Discussion

MySQL provides a LOAD DATA statement that acts as a bulk data loader. Here's an example statement that reads a file *mytbl.txt* from your current directory and loads it into the table mytbl in the current database:

```
mysql> LOAD DATA LOCAL INFILE 'mytbl.txt' INTO TABLE mytbl;
```

MySQL also includes a utility program named *mysqlimport* that acts as a wrapper around LOAD DATA so that you can load input files directly from the command line.

The *mysqlimport* command that is equivalent to the preceding LOAD DATA statement looks like this, assuming that mytbl is in the cookbook database:[*]

```
% mysqlimport --local cookbook mytbl.txt
```

The following list describes LOAD DATA's general characteristics and capabilities; *mysqlimport* shares most of these behaviors. There are some differences that we'll note as we go along, but for the most part you can read "LOAD DATA" as "LOAD DATA or *mysqlimport*." LOAD DATA provides options to address many of the import issues mentioned in the chapter introduction, such as the line-ending sequence for recognizing how to break input into records, the column value delimiter that allows records to be broken into separate values, the quoting character that may surround column values, quoting and escaping issues within values, and NULL value representation:

- By default, LOAD DATA expects the datafile to contain the same number of columns as the table into which you're loading data, and the datafile columns must be present in the same order as in the table. If the file doesn't contain a value for every column or the values aren't in the proper order, you can specify which columns are present and the order in which they appear. If the datafile contains fewer columns than the table, MySQL assigns default values to columns for which no values are present in the datafile.

- LOAD DATA assumes that data values are separated by tab characters and that lines end with linefeeds (newlines). You can specify the data format explicitly if a file doesn't conform to these conventions.

- You can indicate that data values may have quotes around them that should be stripped, and you can specify what the quote character is.

- Several special escape sequences are recognized and converted during input processing. The default escape character is backslash (\), but you can change it if you like. The \N sequence is taken to represent a NULL value. The \b, \n, \r, \t, \\, and \0 sequences are interpreted as backspace, linefeed, carriage return, tab, backslash, and ASCII NUL characters. (NUL is a zero-valued byte, which is different than the SQL NULL value.)

- LOAD DATA provides diagnostic information, but it's a summary that doesn't give you specific information about which input lines may have caused problems. There is work in progress for MySQL 4 on providing improved feedback. In the meantime, see Recipe 10.37, which describes a LOAD DATA diagnostic utility.

The next few sections describe how to import datafiles into MySQL tables using LOAD DATA or *mysqlimport*. They assume your files contain legal data values that are acceptable to MySQL. Why make this assumption? Because although LOAD DATA has several options that control how it reads the datafile, they're concerned only with the structure of the file. LOAD DATA won't validate or reformat data values for you. It's neces-

---

[*] For *mysqlimport*, as with other MySQL programs, you may need to specify connection parameter options such as --*user* or --*host*. If so, they should precede the database name argument.

sary to perform such operations either by preprocessing the datafile before loading it, or by issuing SQL statements after loading it. If you need to check or reformat an input file first to make sure it's legal, several sections later in the chapter show how to do that.

10.2   Specifying the Datafile Location

Problem

You're not sure how to tell LOAD DATA where to look for your datafile, particularly if it's located in another directory.

Solution

It's a matter of knowing the rules that determine where MySQL looks for the file.

Discussion

When you issue a LOAD DATA statement, the MySQL server normally assumes the datafile is located on the server host. However, you may not be able to load data that way:

- If you access the MySQL server from a remote client host and have no means of transferring your file to the server host (such as a login account there), you won't be able to put the file on the server.

- Even if you have a login account on the server host, your MySQL account must be enabled with the FILE privilege, and the file to be loaded must be either world readable or located in the data directory for the current database. Most MySQL users do not have the FILE privilege (because it allows you to do dangerous things), and you may not want to make the file world readable (for security reasons) or be able to put it in the database directory.

Fortunately, if you have MySQL 3.22.15 or later, you can load local files that are located on the client host by using LOAD DATA LOCAL rather than LOAD DATA. The only permission you need to import a local file is the ability to read the file yourself.*

If the LOCAL keyword is not present, MySQL looks for the datafile on the server host using the following rules:

- An absolute pathname fully specifies the location of the file, beginning from the root of the filesystem. MySQL reads the file from the given location.

---

* As of MySQL 3.23.49, use of the LOCAL keyword may be disabled by default. You may be able to turn it on using the *--local-infile* option for *mysql*. If that doesn't work, your server has been configured not to allow LOAD DATA LOCAL at all.

- A relative pathname is interpreted two ways, depending on whether it has a single component or multiple components. For a single-component filename like *mytbl.txt*, MySQL looks for the file in the database directory for the current database. For a multiple-component filename like *xyz/mytbl.txt*, MySQL looks for the file beginning in the MySQL data directory. (It expects to find *mytbl.txt* in a directory named *xyz*.)

Database directories are located directly under the data directory, so these two statements are equivalent if the current database is cookbook:

```
mysql> LOAD DATA INFILE 'mytbl.txt' INTO TABLE mytbl;
mysql> LOAD DATA INFILE 'cookbook/mytbl.txt' INTO TABLE mytbl;
```

If the LOCAL keyword is specified, MySQL looks for the file on the client host, and interprets the pathname the same way your command interpreter does:

- An absolute pathname fully specifies the location of the file, beginning from the root of the filesystem.
- A relative pathname is interpreted relative to your current directory.

If your file is located on the client host, but you forget to indicate that it's local, you'll get an error.

```
mysql> LOAD DATA 'mytbl.txt' INTO TABLE mytbl;
ERROR 1045: Access denied for user: 'cbuser@localhost' (Using password: YES)
```

That Access denied message can be confusing, given that if you're able to connect to the server and issue the LOAD DATA statement, it would seem that you've already gained access to MySQL. What the error message means is that the MySQL tried to open *mytbl.txt* on the server host and could not access it.

mysqlimport uses the same rules for finding files as LOAD DATA. By default, it assumes the datafile is located on the server host. To use a local file, specify the *--local* (or *-L*) option on the command line.

LOAD DATA assumes the table is located in the current database unless you specify the database name explicitly. *mysqlimport* always requires a database argument:

```
% mysqlimport --local cookbook mytbl.txt
```

If you want to use LOAD DATA to load a file into a database other than the current one, you can qualify the table name with the database name. The following statement does this, indicating that the mytbl table is located in the other_db database:

```
mysql> LOAD DATA LOCAL 'mytbl.txt' INTO TABLE other_db.mytbl;
```

LOAD DATA assumes no relationship between the name of the datafile and the name of the table into which you're loading the file's contents. *mysqlimport* assumes a fixed relationship between the datafile name and the table name. Specifically, it uses the last component of the filename to determine the table name. For example, *mysqlimport* would interpret *mytbl.txt*, *mytbl.dat*, */tmp/mytbl.txt*, */u/paul/data/mytbl.csv*, and *D:\projects\mytbl.txt* all as files containing data for the mytbl table.

10.3   Specifying the Datafile Format

Problem

You have a datafile that's not in LOAD DATA's default format.

Solution

Use FIELDS and LINES clauses to tell LOAD DATA how to interpret the file.

Discussion

By default, LOAD DATA assumes that datafiles contain lines that are terminated by line-feeds (newlines) and that data values within a line are separated by tabs. The following statement does not specify anything about the format of the datafile, so MySQL assumes the default format:

```
mysql> LOAD DATA LOCAL INFILE 'mytbl.txt' INTO TABLE mytbl;
```

To specify a file format explicitly, use a FIELDS clause to describe the characteristics of fields within a line, and a LINES clause to specify the line-ending sequence. The following LOAD DATA statement specifies that the datafile contains values separated by colons and lines terminated by carriage returns:

```
mysql> LOAD DATA LOCAL INFILE 'mytbl.txt' INTO TABLE mytbl
    -> FIELDS TERMINATED BY ':'
    -> LINES TERMINATED BY '\r';
```

Each clause follows the table name. If both are present, the FIELDS clause must precede the LINES clause. The line and field termination indicators can contain multiple characters. For example, \r\n indicates that lines are terminated by carriage return/linefeed pairs.

If you use *mysqlimport*, command-line options provide the format specifiers. *mysqlimport* commands that correspond to the preceding two LOAD DATA statements look like this:

```
% mysqlimport --local cookbook mytbl.txt
% mysqlimport --local --fields-terminated-by=":" --lines-terminated-by="\r" \
    cookbook mytbl.txt
```

The order in which you specify the options doesn't matter for *mysqlimport*, except that they should all precede the database name.

Specifying Binary Format Option Characters

As of MySQL 3.22.10, you can use hex notation to specify arbitrary format characters for FIELDS and LINES clauses. Suppose a datafile has lines with Ctrl-A between fields and Ctrl-B at the end of lines. The ASCII values for Ctrl-A and Ctrl-B are 1 and 2, so you represent them as 0x01 and 0x02:

```
FIELDS TERMINATED BY 0x01 LINES TERMINATED BY 0x02
```

mysqlimport understands hex constants for format specifiers as of MySQL 3.23.30. You may find this capability helpful if you don't like remembering how to type escape sequences on the command line or when it's necessary to use quotes around them. Tab is 0x09, linefeed is 0x0a, and carriage return is 0x0d. Here's an example that indicates that the datafile contains tab-delimited lines terminated by CRLF pairs:

```
% mysqlimport --local --lines-terminated-by=0x0d0a \
    --fields-terminated-by=0x09 cookbook mytbl.txt
```

10.4 Dealing with Quotes and Special Characters

Problem

Your datafile contains quoted values or escaped characters.

Solution

Tell LOAD DATA to be aware of them so that it doesn't load the values into the database uninterpreted.

Discussion

The FIELDS clause can specify other format options besides TERMINATED BY. By default, LOAD DATA assumes that values are unquoted, and interprets the backslash (\) as an escape character for special characters. To indicate the value quoting character explicitly, use ENCLOSED BY; MySQL will strip that character from the ends of data values during input processing. To change the default escape character, use ESCAPED BY.

The three subclauses of the FIELDS clause (ENCLOSED BY, ESCAPED BY, and TERMINATED BY) may be present in any order if you specify more than one of them. For example, these FIELDS clauses are equivalent:

```
FIELDS TERMINATED BY ',' ENCLOSED BY '"'
FIELDS ENCLOSED BY '"' TERMINATED BY ','
```

The TERMINATED BY sequence can consist of multiple characters. If data values are separated within input lines by something like *@*, you'd indicate that like this:

```
FIELDS TERMINATED BY '*@*'
```

To disable escape processing entirely, specify an empty escape sequence:

```
FIELDS ESCAPED BY ''
```

When you specify ENCLOSED BY to indicate that quote characters should be stripped from data values, it's possible to include the quote character literally within data values by doubling it or by preceding it with the escape character. For example, if the quote and escape characters are " and \, the input value "a""b\"c" will be interpreted as a"b"c.

For *mysqlimport*, the corresponding command-line options for specifying quote and escape values are *--fields-enclosed-by* and *--fields-escaped-by*. (When using *mysqlimport* options that include quotes or backslashes or other characters that are special to your command interpreter, remember that you may need to quote or escape the quote or escape characters!)

10.5 Importing CSV Files

Problem

You need to load a file that is in CSV format.

Solution

Just add the appropriate format-specifier clauses to your LOAD DATA statement.

Discussion

Datafiles in CSV format contain values that are delimited by commas rather than tabs and that may be quoted with double quote characters. For example, a CSV file *mytbl.txt* containing lines that end with carriage return/linefeed pairs can be loaded into mytbl as follows using LOAD DATA:

```
mysql> LOAD DATA LOCAL INFILE 'mytbl.txt' INTO TABLE mytbl
    -> FIELDS TERMINATED BY ',' ENCLOSED BY '"'
    -> LINES TERMINATED BY '\r\n';
```

Or like this using *mysqlimport*:

```
% mysqlimport --local --lines-terminated-by="\r\n" \
    --fields-terminated-by="," --fields-enclosed-by="\"" \
    cookbook mytbl.txt
```

10.6 Reading Files from Different Operating Systems

Problem

Different operating systems use different line-ending sequences.

Solution

That's why LOAD DATA has a LINES TERMINATED BY clause.

Discussion

The line-ending sequence used in a datafile typically is determined by the system on which the file originates, not the system on which you import it. Keep this in mind when loading a file that is obtained from a different system.

Unix files normally have lines terminated by linefeeds, which you can indicate in a LOAD DATA statement like this:

```
LINES TERMINATED BY '\n'
```

However, because \n happens to be the default line terminator for LOAD DATA, you don't need to specify a LINES TERMINATED BY clause in this case unless you want to indicate explicitly what the line ending sequence is.

Files created under Mac OS or Windows usually have lines ending in carriage returns or carriage return/linefeed pairs. To handle these different kinds of line endings, use the appropriate LINES TERMINATED BY clause:

```
LINES TERMINATED BY '\r'
LINES TERMINATED BY '\r\n'
```

For example, to load a Windows file that contains tab-delimited fields and lines ending with CRLF pairs, use this LOAD DATA statement:

```
mysql> LOAD DATA LOCAL INFILE 'mytbl.txt' INTO TABLE mytbl
    -> LINES TERMINATED BY '\r\n';
```

The corresponding *mysqlimport* command is:

```
% mysqlimport --local --lines-terminated-by="\r\n" cookbook mytbl.txt
```

10.7   Handling Duplicate Index Values

Problem

Your input contains records that duplicate the values of unique keys in existing table records.

Solution

Tell LOAD DATA to ignore the new records, or to replace the old ones.

Discussion

By default, an error occurs if you attempt to load a record that duplicates an existing record in the column or columns that form a PRIMARY KEY or UNIQUE index. To control this behavior, specify IGNORE or REPLACE after the filename to tell MySQL to either ignore duplicate records or to replace old records with the new ones.

Suppose you periodically receive meteorological data about current weather conditions from various monitoring stations, and that you store measurements of various types from these stations in a table that looks like this:

```
CREATE TABLE weatherdata
(
    station INT UNSIGNED NOT NULL,
    type    ENUM('precip','temp','cloudiness','humidity','barometer') NOT NULL,
    value   FLOAT,
    UNIQUE (station, type)
);
```

To make sure that you have only one record for each station for each type of measurement, the table includes a unique key on the combination of station ID and measurement type. The table is intended to hold only current conditions, so when new measurements for a given station are loaded into the table, they should kick out the station's previous measurements. To accomplish this, use the REPLACE keyword:

```
mysql> LOAD DATA LOCAL INFILE 'data.txt' REPLACE INTO TABLE weatherdata;
```

10.8   Getting LOAD DATA to Cough Up More Information

Problem

LOAD DATA doesn't tell you much about problems in the datafile.

Solution

There is no solution. Well, maybe there is.

Discussion

When a LOAD DATA statement finishes, it returns a line of information that tells you how many errors or data conversion problems occurred. Suppose you load a file into a table and see the following message when LOAD DATA finishes.

```
Records: 134  Deleted: 0  Skipped: 2  Warnings: 13
```

These values provide some general information about the import operation:

- Records indicates the number of records found in the file.

- Deleted and Skipped are related to treatment of input records that duplicate existing table records on unique index values. Deleted indicates how many records were deleted from the table and replaced by input records, and Skipped indicates how many input records were ignored in favor of existing records.

- Warnings is something of a catch-all that indicates the number of problems found while loading data values into columns. Either a value stores into a column properly, or it doesn't. In the latter case, the value ends up in MySQL as something different and MySQL counts it as a warning. (Storing a string abc into a numeric column results in a stored value of 0, for example.)

What do these values tell you? The Records value normally should match the number of lines in the input file. If it is different than the file's line count, that's a sign that MySQL is interpreting the file as having a format that differs from the format it actually has. In this case, you're likely also to see a high Warnings value, which indicates that many values had to be converted because they didn't match the expected data type. (The solution to this problem often is to specify the proper FIELDS and LINES clauses.) Otherwise, the values may not tell you a lot. You can't tell from these numbers which input records had problems or which columns were bad. There is some work being done for MySQL 4 to make additional warning information available. In the meantime, see Recipe 10.37 for a script that examines your datafile and attempts to pinpoint troublesome data values.

10.9 Don't Assume LOAD DATA Knows More than It Does

Problem

You think LOAD DATA is smarter than it really is.

Solution

Don't assume that LOAD DATA knows anything at all about the format of your datafile. And make sure you yourself know what its format is. If the file has been transferred from one machine to another, its contents may have been changed in subtle ways of which you're not aware.

Discussion

Many LOAD DATA frustrations occur because people expect MySQL to know things that it cannot possibly know. LOAD DATA makes certain assumptions about the structure of input files, represented as the default settings for the line and field terminators, and for the quote and escape character settings. If your input doesn't match those assumptions, you need to tell MySQL about it.

When in doubt, check the contents of your datafile using a hex dump program or other utility that displays a visible representation of whitespace characters like tab, carriage return, and linefeed. Under Unix, the *od* program can display file contents in a variety of formats. If you don't have *od* or some comparable utility, the *transfer* directory of the recipes distribution contains hex dumpers written in Perl and Python (*hexdump.pl* and *hexdump.py*), as well as a couple of programs that display printable representations of all characters of a file (*see.pl* and *see.py*). You may find them useful for examining files to see what they really contain. In some cases, you may be surprised to discover that a file's contents are different than you think. This is in fact quite likely if the file has been transferred from one machine to another:

- An FTP transfer between machines running different operating systems typically translates line endings to those that are appropriate for the destination machine if the transfer is performed in text mode rather than in binary (image) mode. Suppose you have tab-delimited linefeed-terminated records in a datafile that load into MySQL on a Unix system just fine using the default LOAD DATA settings. If you copy the file to a Windows machine with FTP using a text transfer mode, the linefeeds probably will be converted to carriage return/linefeed pairs. On that machine, the file will not load properly with the same LOAD DATA statement, because its contents will have been changed. Does MySQL have any way of knowing that? No. So it's up to you to tell it, by adding a LINES TERMINATED BY '\r\n' clause to the statement. Transfers between any two systems with dissimilar default line endings can cause these changes. For example, a Macintosh file containing carriage returns may contain linefeeds after transfer to a Unix system. You should either account for such changes with a LINES TERMINATED BY clause that reflects the modified line-ending sequence, or transfer the file in binary mode so that its contents do not change.

- Datafiles pasted into email messages often do not survive intact. Mail software may wrap (break) long lines or convert line-ending sequences. If you must transfer a datafile by email, it's best sent as an attachment.

10.10 Skipping Datafile Lines

Problem

You want LOAD DATA to skip over the first line or lines of your datafile before starting to load records.

Solution

Tell LOAD DATA how many lines to ignore.

Discussion

To skip over the first *n* lines of a datafile, add an IGNORE *n* LINES clause to the LOAD DATA statement. For example, if a tab-delimited file begins with a line consisting of column headers, you can skip it like this:

```
mysql> LOAD DATA LOCAL INFILE 'mytbl.txt' INTO TABLE mytbl IGNORE 1 LINES;
```

As of MySQL 4.0.2, *mysqlimport* supports an *--ignore-lines=n* option that has the same effect.

IGNORE is often useful with files generated by external sources. For example, File-Maker Pro can export data in what it calls merge format, which is essentially CSV format with an initial line of column labels. The following statement would be appropriate for skipping the labels in a merge file created by FileMaker Pro under Mac OS that has carriage return line endings:

```
mysql> LOAD DATA LOCAL INFILE 'mytbl.txt' INTO TABLE mytbl
    -> FIELDS TERMINATED BY ',' ENCLOSED BY '"'
    -> LINES TERMINATED BY '\r'
    -> IGNORE 1 LINES;
```

Note that importing a FileMaker Pro file often is not actually this easy. For example, if it contains dates, they may not be in a format that MySQL likes. You'll need to preprocess your file first or postprocess it after loading it. (See Recipe 10.40.)

10.11 Specifying Input Column Order

Problem

The columns in your datafile aren't in the same order as the columns in the table into which you're loading the file.

Solution

Tell LOAD DATA how to match up the table and the file by indicating which table columns correspond to the datafile columns.

Discussion

LOAD DATA assumes the columns in the datafile have the same order as the columns in the table. If that's not true, you can specify a list to indicate which table columns the datafile columns should be loaded into. Suppose your table has columns a, b, and c, but successive columns in the datafile correspond to columns b, c, and a. You can load the file like this:

```
mysql> LOAD DATA LOCAL INFILE 'mytbl.txt' INTO TABLE mytbl (b, c, a);
```

The equivalent *mysqlimport* statement uses the *--columns* option to specify the column list:

```
% mysqlimport --local --columns=b,c,a cookbook mytbl.txt
```

The *--columns* option for *mysqlimport* was introduced in MySQL 3.23.17. If you have an older version, you must either use LOAD DATA directly or preprocess your datafile to rearrange the file's columns into the order in which they occur in the table. (See Recipe 10.19 for a utility that can do this.)

10.12 Skipping Datafile Columns

Problem

Your datafile contains columns that should be ignored rather than loaded into the table.

Solution

That's not a problem if the columns are at the ends of the input lines. Otherwise, you'll need to preprocess the datafile before loading it.

Discussion

Extra columns that occur at the end of input lines are easy to handle. If a line contains more columns than are in the table, LOAD DATA just ignores them (though it may indicate a nonzero warning count).

Skipping columns in the middle of lines is a bit more involved. Suppose you want to load information from a Unix password file */etc/passwd*, which contains lines in the following format:

```
account:password:UID:GID:GECOS:directory:shell
```

Suppose also that you don't want to bother loading the password column. A table to hold the information in the other columns looks like this:

```
CREATE TABLE passwd
(
```

```
    account    CHAR(8),      # login name
    uid        INT,          # user ID
    gid        INT,          # group ID
    gecos      CHAR(60),     # name, phone, office, etc.
    directory  CHAR(60),     # home directory
    shell      CHAR(60)      # command interpreter
);
```

To load the file, we need to specify that the column delimiter is a colon, which is easily handled with a FIELDS clause:

```
FIELDS TERMINATED BY ':'
```

However, we must also tell LOAD DATA to skip the second field that contains the password. That's a problem, because LOAD DATA always wants to load successive columns from the datafile. You can tell it which table column each datafile column corresponds to, but you can't tell it to skip columns in the file. To deal with this difficulty, we can preprocess the input file into a temporary file that doesn't contain the password value, then load the temporary file. Under Unix, you can use the *cut* utility to extract the columns that you want, like this:

```
% cut -d":" -f0,3- /etc/passwd > passwd.txt
```

The *-d* option specifies a field delimiter of : and the *-f* option indicates that you want to cut column one and all columns from the third to the end of the line. The effect is to cut all but the second column. (Run *man cut* for more information about the *cut* command.) Then use LOAD DATA to import the resulting *passwd.txt* file into the passwd table like this:

```
mysql> LOAD DATA LOCAL INFILE 'passwd.txt' INTO TABLE passwd
    -> FIELDS TERMINATED BY ':';
```

The corresponding *mysqlimport* command is:

```
% mysqlimport --local --fields-terminated-by=":" cookbook passwd.txt
```

See Also

cut always displays output columns in the same order they occur in the file, no matter what order you use when you list them with the *-f* option. (For example, *cut -f1,2,3* and *cut -f3,2,1* produce the same output.) Recipe 10.19 discusses a utility that can pull out and display columns in any order.

10.13 Exporting Query Results from MySQL

Problem

You want to export the result of a query from MySQL into a file or another program.

Solution

Use the SELECT ... INTO OUTFILE statement or redirect the output of the *mysql* program.

Discussion

MySQL provides a SELECT ... INTO OUTFILE statement that exports a query result directly into a file on the server host. Another way to export a query, if you want to capture the result on the client host instead, is to redirect the output of the *mysql* program. These methods have different strengths and weaknesses, so you should get to know them both and apply whichever one best suits a given situation.

Exporting with the SELECT ... INTO OUTFILE Statement

The syntax for this statement combines a regular SELECT with INTO OUTFILE *filename* at the end. The default output format is the same as for LOAD DATA, so the following statement exports the passwd table into */tmp/passwd.txt* as a tab-delimited, linefeed-terminated file:

```
mysql> SELECT * FROM passwd INTO OUTFILE '/tmp/passwd.txt';
```

You can change the output format using options similar to those used with LOAD DATA that indicate how to quote and delimit columns and records. To export the passwd table in CSV format with CRLF-terminated lines, use this statement:

```
mysql> SELECT * FROM passwd INTO OUTFILE '/tmp/passwd.txt'
    -> FIELDS TERMINATED BY ',' ENCLOSED BY '"'
    -> LINES TERMINATED BY '\r\n';
```

SELECT ... INTO OUTFILE has the following properties:

- The output file is created directly by the MySQL server, so the filename should indicate where you want the file to be written on the server host. There is no LOCAL version of the statement analogous to the LOCAL version of LOAD DATA.

- You must have the MySQL FILE privilege to execute the SELECT ... INTO statement.

- The output file must not already exist. This prevents MySQL from clobbering files that may be important.

- You should have a login account on the server host or some way to retrieve the file from that host. Otherwise, SELECT ... INTO OUTFILE likely will be of no value to you.

- Under Unix, the file is created world readable and is owned by the MySQL server. This means that although you'll be able to read the file, you may not be able to delete it.

Using the mysql Client to Export Data

Because SELECT ... INTO OUTFILE writes the datafile on the server host, you cannot use it unless your MySQL account has the FILE privilege. To export data into a local file, you must use some other strategy. If all you require is tab-delimited output, you can do a "poor-man's export" by executing a SELECT statement with the *mysql* program and redirecting the output to a file. That way you can write query results into a file on your local host without the FILE privilege. Here's an example that exports the login name and command interpreter columns from the passwd table created earlier in this chapter:

```
% mysql -e "SELECT account, shell FROM passwd" -N cookbook > shells.txt
```

The *-e* option specifies the query to execute, and *-N* tells MySQL not to write the row of column names that normally precedes query output. The latter option was added in MySQL 3.22.20; if your version is older than that, you can achieve the same end by telling *mysql* to be "really silent" with the *-ss* option instead:

```
% mysql -e "SELECT account, shell FROM passwd" -ss cookbook > shells.txt
```

Note that NULL values are written as the string "NULL". Some sort of postprocessing may be necessary to convert them, depending on what you want to do with the output file.

It's possible to produce output in formats other than tab-delimited by sending the query result into a post-processing filter that converts tabs to something else. For example, to use hash marks as delimiters, convert all tabs to # characters (*TAB* indicates where you type a tab character in the command):

```
% mysql -N -e "your query here" db_name | sed -e "s/TAB/#/g" > output_file
```

You can also use *tr* for this purpose, though the syntax may vary for different implementations of this utility. The command looks like this for Mac OS X or RedHat Linux:

```
% mysql -N -e "your query here" db_name | tr "\t" "#" > output_file
```

The *mysql* commands just shown use *-N* or *-ss* to suppress column labels from appearing in the output. Under some circumstances, it may be useful to include the labels. (For example, they may be useful when importing the file later.) If so, omit the label-suppression option from the command. In this respect, exporting query results with *mysql* is more flexible than SELECT ... INTO OUTFILE because the latter cannot produce output that includes column labels.

See Also

Another way to export query results to a file on the client host is by using the *mysql_to_text.pl* utility described in Recipe 10.17. That program has options that allow you to specify the output format explicitly. To export a query result as an Excel spreadsheet or for use with FileMaker Pro, see Recipes 10.39 and 10.40.

10.14 Exporting Tables as Raw Data

Problem

You want to export an entire table to a file.

Solution

Use the *mysqldump* program with the *--tab* option.

Discussion

The *mysqldump* program is used to copy or back up tables and databases. It can write table output either as a raw datafile, or as a set of INSERT statements that recreate the records in the table. The former capability is described here, the latter in Recipes 10.15 and 10.16.

To dump a table as a datafile, you must specify a *--tab* option that indicates the directory where you want the MySQL server to write the file. (The directory must already exist; the server won't create it.) For example, to dump the states table from the cookbook database to a file in the */tmp* directory, use a command like this:

```
% mysqldump --no-create-info --tab=/tmp cookbook states
```

mysqldump creates a datafile using the table name plus a *.txt* suffix, so this command will write a file named */tmp/states.txt*. This form of *mysqldump* is in some respects the command-line equivalent of SELECT ... INTO OUTFILE. For example, it writes out a table as a datafile on the server host, and you must have the FILE privilege to use it. See Recipe 10.13 for a list of general properties of SELECT ... INTO OUTFILE.

If you omit the *--no-create-info* option, *mysqldump* also will create a file */tmp/states.sql* that contains the CREATE TABLE statement for the table. (The latter file will be owned by you, unlike the datafile, which is owned by the server.)

You can name multiple tables after the database name, in which case *mysqldump* writes output files for each of them. If you don't name any tables, *mysqldump* writes output for every table in the database.

mysqldump creates datafiles in tab-delimited, linefeed-terminated format by default. To control the output format, use the *--fields-enclosed-by*, *--fields-terminated-by*, and *--lines-terminated-by* options (that is, the same options that *mysqlimport* understands as format specifiers). For example, to write the states table in CSV format with CRLF line endings, use this command:

```
% mysqldump --no-create-info --tab=/tmp \
    --fields-enclosed-by="\"" --fields-terminated-by="," \
    --lines-terminated-by="\r\n" cookbook states
```

A datafile exported this way can be imported using LOAD DATA or *mysqlimport*. Be sure to use matching format specifiers when importing if you didn't dump the table using the default format.

10.15 Exporting Table Contents or Definitions in SQL Format

Problem

You want to export tables or databases as SQL statements to make them easier to import later.

Solution

Use the *mysqldump* program without the *--tab* option.

Discussion

As discussed in Recipe 10.14, *mysqldump* causes the MySQL server to write tables as raw datafiles on the server host when it's invoked with the *--tab* option. If you omit the *--tab*, the server formats the table records as the INSERT statements and returns them to *mysqldump*. You can also generate the CREATE TABLE statement for each table. This provides a convenient form of output that you can capture in a file and use later to recreate a table or tables. It's common to use such dump files as backups or for copying tables to another MySQL server. This section discusses how to save dump output in a file; shows how to send it directly to another server over the network.

To export a table in SQL format to a file, use a command like this:

```
% mysqldump cookbook states > dump.txt
```

That creates an output file *dump.txt* that contains both the CREATE TABLE statement and a set of INSERT statements:

```
# MySQL dump 8.16
#
# Host: localhost    Database: cookbook
#--------------------------------------------------------
# Server version    3.23.46-log
```

```
#
# Table structure for table 'states'
#

CREATE TABLE states (
  name varchar(30) NOT NULL default '',
  abbrev char(2) NOT NULL default '',
  statehood date default NULL,
  pop bigint(20) default NULL,
  PRIMARY KEY  (abbrev)
) TYPE=MyISAM;

#
# Dumping data for table 'states'
#

INSERT INTO states VALUES ('Alaska','AK','1959-01-03',550043);
INSERT INTO states VALUES ('Alabama','AL','1819-12-14',4040587);
INSERT INTO states VALUES ('Arkansas','AR','1836-06-15',2350725);
INSERT INTO states VALUES ('Arizona','AZ','1912-02-14',3665228);
INSERT INTO states VALUES ('California','CA','1850-09-09',29760021);
INSERT INTO states VALUES ('Colorado','CO','1876-08-01',3294394);
...
```

To dump multiple tables, name them all following the database name argument. To dump an entire database, don't name any tables after the database. If you want to dump all tables in all databases, invoke *mysqldump* like this:

```
% mysqldump --all-databases > dump.txt
```

In this case, the output file also will include CREATE DATABASE and USE *db_name* statements at appropriate places so that when you read in the file later, each table will be created in the proper database. The *--all-databases* option is available as of MySQL 3.23.12.

Other options are available to control the output format:

--no-create-info

Suppress the CREATE TABLE statements. Use this option when you want to dump table contents only.

--no-data

Suppress the INSERT statements. Use this option when you want to dump table definitions only.

--add-drop-table

Precede each CREATE TABLE statement with a DROP TABLE statement. This is useful for generating a file that you can use later to recreate tables from scratch.

--no-create-db

Suppress the CREATE DATABASE statements that the *--all-databases* option normally produces.

Suppose now that you've used *mysqldump* to create a SQL-format dump file. How do you import it the file back into MySQL? One common mistake at this point is to use *mysqlimport*. After all, it's logical to assume that if *mysqldump* exports tables, *mysqlimport* must import them. Right? Sorry, no. That might be logical, but it's not always correct. It's true that if you use the *--tab* option with *mysqldump*, you can import the resulting datafiles with *mysqlimport*. But if you dump a SQL-format file, *mysqlimport* won't process it properly. Use the *mysql* program instead. The way you do this depends on what's in the dump file. If you dumped multiple databases using *--all-databases*, the file will contain the appropriate USE *db_name* statements to select the databases to which each table belongs, and you need no database argument on the command line:

```
% mysql < dump.txt
```

If you dumped tables from a single database, you'll need to tell *mysql* which database to import them into:

```
% mysql db_name < dump.txt
```

Note that with this second import command, it's possible to load the tables into a different database than the one from which they came originally. You can use this fact, for example, to create copies of a table or tables in a test database to use for trying out some data manipulating statements that you're debugging, without worrying about affecting the original tables.

10.16 Copying Tables or Databases to Another Server

Problem

You want to copy tables or databases from one MySQL server to another.

Solution

Use *mysqldump* and *mysql* together, connected by a pipe.

Discussion

SQL-format output from *mysqldump* can be used to copy tables or databases from one server to another. Suppose you want to copy the states table from the cookbook database on the local host to the cb database on the host *other-host.com*. One way to do this is to dump the output into a file (as described in Recipe 10.15):

```
% mysqldump cookbook states > dump.txt
```

Then copy *dump.txt* to *other-host.com* and run the following command there to import the table into that server's cb database:

```
% mysql cb < dump.txt
```

Another way to accomplish this without using an intermediary file is to send the output of *mysqldump* directly over the network to the remote MySQL server. If you can connect to both servers from the host where the cookbook database resides, use this command:

```
% mysqldump cookbook states | mysql -h other-host.com cb
```

The *mysqldump* half of the command connects to the local server and writes the dump output to the pipe. The *mysql* half of the command connects to the remote MySQL server on *other-host.com*. It reads the pipe for input and sends each statement to the *other-host.com* server.

If you cannot connect directly to the remote server using *mysql* from your local host, send the dump output into a pipe that uses *ssh* to invoke *mysql* remotely on *other-host.com*:

```
% mysqldump cookbook states | ssh other-host.com mysql cb
```

ssh connects to *other-host.com* and launches *mysql* there. Then it reads the *mysqldump* output from the pipe and passes it to the remote *mysql* process. Using *ssh* can be useful when you want to send a dump over the network to a machine that has the MySQL port blocked by a firewall but that allows connections on the SSH port.

If you don't have access to *ssh*, you may be able to use *rsh* instead. However, *rsh* is insecure, so *ssh* is much preferred.

To copy multiple tables over the network, name them all following the database argument of the *mysqldump* command. To copy an entire database, don't specify any table names after the database name. *mysqldump* will dump all the tables contained in the database.

If you're thinking about invoking *mysqldump* with the *--all-databases* option to send all your databases to another server, consider that the output will include the tables in the mysql database that contains the grant tables. If the remote server has a different user population, you probably don't want to replace that server's grant tables!

10.17 Writing Your Own Export Programs

Problem

MySQL's built-in export capabilities don't suffice.

Solution

Write your own utilities.

Discussion

When existing software doesn't do what you want, you can write your own programs to export data. This section shows how to write a Perl script, *mysql_to_text.pl*, that executes an arbitrary query and exports it in the format you specify. It writes output to the client host and can include a row of column labels (neither of which SELECT ... INTO OUTFILE can do). It produces multiple output formats more easily than by using *mysql* with a postprocessor, and it writes to the client host, unlike *mysqldump*, which can write only SQL-format output to the client.

mysql_to_text.pl is based on the *Text::CSV_XS* module, which you'll need to obtain if it's not installed on your system. Once it's installed, you can read the documentation like so:

```
% perldoc Text::CSV_XS
```

This module is convenient because all you have to do is provide an array of column values, and it will package them up into a properly formatted output line. This makes it relatively trivial to convert query output to CSV format. But the real benefit of using the *Text::CSV_XS* module is that it's configurable; you can tell it what kind of delimiter and quote characters to use. This means that although the module produces CSV format by default, you can configure it to write a variety of output formats. For example, if you set the delimiter to tab and the quote character to undef, *Text::CSV_XS* generates tab-delimited output. We'll take advantage of that flexibility in this section for writing *mysql_to_text.pl*, and later in to write a file-processing utility that converts files from one format to another.

mysql_to_text.pl accepts several command-line options. Some of these are for specifying MySQL connection parameters (such as *--user*, *--password*, and *--host*). You're already familiar with these, because they're used by the standard MySQL clients like *mysql*. The script also can obtain connection parameters from an option file, if you specify a [client] group in the file. The other options that *mysql_to_text.pl* accepts are as follows:

--execute=query, -e query
    Execute *query* and export its output.

--table=tbl_name, -t tbl_name
    Export the contents of the named table. This is equivalent to using *--execute* to specify a *query* value of SELECT * FROM *tbl_name*.

--labels
> Write an initial row of column labels.

--delim=str
> Set the column delimiter sequence to *str*. The option value may consist of one or more characters. The default is to use tabs.

--quote=c
> Set the column value quote character to *c*. The default is to not quote anything.

--eol=str
> Set the end-of-line sequence to *str*. The option value may consist of one or more characters. The default is to use linefeeds.

The defaults for the *--delim*, *--quote*, and *--eol* options correspond to those used by `LOAD DATA` and `SELECT ... INTO OUTFILE`.

The final argument on the command line should be the database name, unless it's implicit in the query. For example, these two commands are equivalent; each exports the `passwd` table in colon-delimited format into a file named *tmp*:

```
% mysql_to_text.pl --delim=":" --table=passwd cookbook > tmp
% mysql_to_text.pl --delim=":" --table=cookbook.passwd > tmp
```

To generate CSV output with CRLF line terminators instead, use a command like this:

```
% mysql_to_text.pl --delim="," --quote="\"" --eol="\r\n" \
    --table=cookbook.passwd > tmp
```

That's a general description of how you use *mysql_to_text.pl*. Now let's discuss how it works. The initial part of the *mysql_to_text.pl* script declares a few variables, then processes the command-line arguments, using option-processing techniques developed in Recipe 2.10. (As it happens, most of the code in the script actually is devoted to processing the command-line arguments and getting set up to run the query!)

```
#! /usr/bin/perl -w
# mysql_to_text.pl - export MySQL query output in user-specified text format

# Usage: mysql_to_text.pl [ options ] [db_name] > text_file

use strict;
use DBI;
use Text::CSV_XS;
use Getopt::Long;
$Getopt::Long::ignorecase = 0; # options are case sensitive
$Getopt::Long::bundling = 1;   # allow short options to be bundled

my $prog = "mysql_to_text.pl";

# ... construct usage message variable $usage (not shown) ...

# Variables for command line options - all undefined initially
# except for output structure, which is set to be tab-delimited,
```

```
# linefeed-terminated.
my $help;
my ($host_name, $password, $port_num, $socket_name, $user_name, $db_name);
my ($query, $tbl_name);
my $labels;
my $delim = "\t";
my $quote;
my $eol = "\n";

GetOptions (
    # =i means an integer argument is required after the option
    # =s means a string argument is required after the option
    # :s means a string argument is optional after the option
    "help"          => \$help,        # print help message
    "host|h=s"      => \$host_name,   # server host
    "password|p:s"  => \$password,    # password
    "port|P=i"      => \$port_num,    # port number
    "socket|S=s"    => \$socket_name, # socket name
    "user|u=s"      => \$user_name,   # username
    "execute|e=s"   => \$query,       # query to execute
    "table|t=s"     => \$tbl_name,    # table to export
    "labels|l"      => \$labels,      # generate row of column labels
    "delim=s"       => \$delim,       # column delimiter
    "quote=s"       => \$quote,       # column quoting character
    "eol=s"         => \$eol          # end-of-line (record) delimiter
) or die "$usage\n";

die  "$usage\n" if defined $help;

$db_name = shift (@ARGV) if @ARGV;

# One of --execute or --table must be specified, but not both
die "You must specify a query or a table name\n\n$usage\n"
    if !defined ($query) && !defined ($tbl_name);
die "You cannot specify both a query and a table name\n\n$usage\n"
    if defined ($query) && defined ($tbl_name);

# If table name was given, convert it to a query that selects entire table
$query = "SELECT * FROM $tbl_name" if defined ($tbl_name);

# convert defined/undefined state into true/false
$labels = defined ($labels);

# interpret special chars in the file structure options
$quote = interpret_option ($quote);
$delim = interpret_option ($delim);
$eol = interpret_option ($eol);
```

The interpret_option( ) function processes escape and hex sequences for the --*delim*, --*quote*, and --*eol* options. \n, \r, \t, and \0 are interpreted as linefeed, carriage return, tab, and the ASCII NUL character. Hex values may be given in the form 0x*nn* (for example, 0x0d indicates a carriage return). The function is not shown here; you can examine the script source to see how it works.

After processing the command-line options, the script constructs the data source name (DSN) and connects to the server:

```
my $dsn = "DBI:mysql:";
$dsn .= ";database=$db_name" if $db_name;
$dsn .= ";host=$host_name" if $host_name;
$dsn .= ";port=$port_num" if $port_num;
$dsn .= ";mysql_socket=$socket_name" if $socket_name;
# read [client] group parameters from standard option files
$dsn .= ";mysql_read_default_group=client";

my $dbh = DBI->connect ($dsn, $user_name, $password,
                        {PrintError => 0, RaiseError => 1});
```

The database name comes from the command line. Connection parameters can come from the command line or an option file. Use of MySQL option files is covered in Recipe 2.10.

After establishing a connection to MySQL, the script is ready to execute the query and produce some output. This is where the *Text::CSV_XS* module comes into play. First, we create a CSV object by calling new( ), which takes an optional hash of options that control how the object handles data lines. Then the script prepares and executes the query, prints a row of column labels (if the user specified the *--labels* option), and writes the rows of the result set:

```
my $csv = Text::CSV_XS->new ({
                        sep_char => $delim,
                        quote_char => $quote,
                        escape_char => $quote,
                        eol => $eol,
                        binary => 1
                });

my $sth = $dbh->prepare ($query);
$sth->execute ();
if ($labels)                            # write row of column labels
{
    $csv->combine (@{$sth->{NAME}}) or die "cannot process column labels\n";
    print $csv->string ();
}

my $count = 0;
while (my @val = $sth->fetchrow_array ())
{
    ++$count;
    $csv->combine (@val) or die "cannot process column values, row $count\n";
    print $csv->string ();
}
```

The sep_char and quote_char options in the name( ) call set the column delimiter sequence and quoting character. The escape_char option is set to the same value as quote_char so that instances of the quote character occurring within data values will be doubled in the output. The eol option indicates the line-termination sequence.

Normally, *Text::CSV_XS* leaves it to you to print the terminator for output lines. By passing a non-undef eol value to new( ), the module adds that value to every output line automatically. The binary option is useful for processing data values that contain binary characters.

The column labels are available in $sth->{NAME} after invoking execute( ). Each line of output is produced using combine( ) and string( ). The combine( ) method takes an array of values and converts them to a properly formatted string. string( ) returns the string so we can print it.

10.18 Converting Datafiles from One Format to Another

Problem

You want to convert a file to a different format to make it easier to work with, or so that another program can understand it.

Solution

Use the *cvt_file.pl* converter script described here.

Discussion

The *mysql_to_text.pl* script discussed in Recipe 10.17 uses MySQL as a data source and produces output in the format you specify via the *--delim*, *--quote*, and *--eol* options. This section describes *cvt_file.pl*, a utility that provides similar formatting options, but for both input and output. It reads data from a file rather than from MySQL, and converts it from one format to another. For example, to read a tab-delimited file *data.txt*, convert it to colon-delimited format, and write the result to *tmp*, you would invoke *cvt_file.pl* like this:

```
% cvt_file.pl --idelim="\t" --odelim=":" data.txt > tmp
```

The *cvt_file.pl* script has separate options for input and output. Thus, whereas *mysql_to_text.pl* has just a *--delim* for specifying the column delimiter, *cvt_file.pl* has separate *--idelim* and *--odelim* options to set the input and output line column delimiters. But as a shortcut, *--delim* is also supported; it sets the delimiter for both input and output. The full set of options that *cvt_file.pl* understands is as follows:

--idelim=str, --odelim=str, --delim=str
　　Set the column delimiter sequence for input, output, or both. The option value may consist of one or more characters.

--iquote=c, --oquote=c, --quote=c
　　Set the column quote character for input, output, or both.

--ieol=str, --oeol=str, --eol=str

> Set the end-of-line sequence for input, output, or both. The option value may consist of one or more characters.

--iformat=format, --oformat=format, --format=format,

> Specify an input format, an output format, or both. This option is shorthand for setting the quote and delimiter values. For example, *--iformat*=csv sets the input quote and delimiter characters to double quote and comma. *--iformat*=tab sets them to "no quotes" and tab.

--ilabels, --olabels, --labels

> Expect an initial line of column labels for input, write an initial line of labels for output, or both. If you request labels for the output but do not read labels from the input, *cvt_file.pl* uses column labels of c1, c2, and so forth.

cvt_file.pl assumes the same default file format as LOAD DATA and SELECT INTO ... OUTFILE, that is, tab-delimited lines terminated by linefeeds.

cvt_file.pl can be found in the *transfer* directory of the recipes distribution. If you expect to use it regularly, you should install it in some directory that's listed in your search path so that you can invoke it from anywhere. Much of the source for the script is similar to *mysql_to_text.pl*, so rather than showing the code and discussing how it works, I'll just give some examples illustrating how to use it:

- Read a file in CSV format with CRLF line termination, write tab-delimited output with linefeed termination:

  ```
  % cvt_file.pl --iformat=csv --ieol="\r\n" --oformat=tab --oeol="\n" \
      data.txt > tmp
  ```

- Read and write CSV format, converting CRLF line terminators to carriage returns:

  ```
  % cvt_file.pl --format=csv --ieol="\r\n" --oeol="\r" data.txt > tmp
  ```

- Produce a tab-delimited file from the colon-delimited */etc/passwd* file:

  ```
  % cvt_file.pl --idelim=":" /etc/passwd > tmp
  ```

- Convert tab-delimited query output from mysql into CSV format:

  ```
  % mysql -e "SELECT * FROM profile" cookbook \
      | cvt_file.pl --oformat=csv > profile.csv
  ```

10.19 Extracting and Rearranging Datafile Columns

Problem

You want to pull out columns from a datafile or rearrange them into a different order.

Solution

Use a utility that can produce columns from a file on demand.

Discussion

cvt_file.pl serves as a tool that converts entire files from one format to another. Another common datafile operation is to manipulate its columns. This is necessary, for example, when importing a file into a program that doesn't understand how to extract or rearrange input columns for itself. Perhaps you want to omit columns from the middle of a file so you can use it with LOAD DATA, which cannot skip over columns in the middle of data lines. Or perhaps you have a version of *mysqlimport* older than 3.23.17, which doesn't support the *--columns* option that allows you to indicate the order in which table columns appear in the file. To work around these problems, you can rearrange the datafile instead.

Recall that this chapter began with a description of a scenario involving a 12-column CSV file *somedata.csv* from which only columns 2, 11, 5, and 9 were needed. You can convert the file to tab-delimited format like this:

```
% cvt_file.pl --iformat=csv somedata.csv > somedata.txt
```

But then what? If you just want to knock out a short script to extract those specific four columns, that's fairly easy: write a loop that reads input lines and writes only the columns you want in the proper order. Assuming input in tab-delimited, line-feed-terminated format, a simple Perl program to pull out the four columns can be written like this:

```perl
#! /usr/bin/perl -w
# yank_4col.pl - 4-column extraction example

# Extracts column 2, 11, 5, and 9 from 12-column input, in that order.
# Assumes tab-delimited, linefeed-terminated input lines.

use strict;

while (<>)
{
    chomp;
    my @in = split (/\t/, $_);          # split at tabs
    # extract columns 2, 11, 5, and 9
    print join ("\t", $in[1], $in[10], $in[4], $in[8]) . "\n";
}

exit (0);
```

Run the script as follows to read the file containing 12 data columns and write output that contains only the four columns in the desired order:

```
% yank_4col.pl somedata.txt > tmp
```

But *yank_4col.pl* is a special purpose script, useful only within a highly limited context. With just a little more work, it's possible to write a more general utility *yank_col.pl* that allows any set of columns to be extracted. With such a tool, you'd specify the column list on the command line like this:

```
% yank_col.pl --columns=2,11,5,9 somedata.txt > tmp
```

Because the script doesn't use a hardcoded column list, it can be used to pull out an arbitrary set of columns in any order. Columns can be specified as a comma-separated list of column numbers or column ranges. (For example, *--columns=1,4-7,10* means columns 1, 4, 5, 6, 7, and 10.) *yank_col.pl* looks like this:

```perl
#! /usr/bin/perl -w
# yank_col.pl - extract columns from input

# Example: yank_col.pl --columns=2,11,5,9 filename

# Assumes tab-delimited, linefeed-terminated input lines.

use strict;
use Getopt::Long;
$Getopt::Long::ignorecase = 0; # options are case sensitive

my $prog = "yank_col.pl";
my $usage = <<EOF;
Usage: $prog [options] [data_file]

Options:
--help
    Print this message
--columns=column-list
    Specify columns to extract, as a comma-separated list of column positions
EOF

my $help;
my $columns;

GetOptions (
    "help"      => \$help,          # print help message
    "columns=s" => \$columns        # specify column list
) or die "$usage\n";

die  "$usage\n" if defined $help;

my @col_list = split (/,/, $columns) if defined ($columns);
@col_list or die "$usage\n";        # nonempty column list is required

# make sure column specifiers are positive integers, and convert from
# 1-based to 0-based values

my @tmp;
for (my $i = 0; $i < @col_list; $i++)
{
    if ($col_list[$i] =~ /^\d+$/)                # single column number
```

```
    {
        die "Column specifier $col_list[$i] is not a positive integer\n"
            unless $col_list[$i] > 0;
        push (@tmp, $col_list[$i] - 1);
    }
    elsif ($col_list[$i] =~ /^(\d+)-(\d+)$/)     # column range m-n
    {
        my ($begin, $end) = ($1, $2);
        die "$col_list[$i] is not a valid column specifier\n"
            unless $begin > 0 && $end > 0 && $begin <= $end;
        while ($begin <= $end)
        {
            push (@tmp, $begin - 1);
            ++$begin;
        }
    }
    else
    {
        die "$col_list[$i] is not a valid column specifier\n";
    }
}
@col_list = @tmp;

while (<>)                          # read input
{
    chomp;
    my @val = split (/\t/, $_, 10000);  # split, preserving all fields
    # extract desired columns, mapping undef to empty string (can
    # occur if an index exceeds number of columns present in line)
    @val = map { defined ($_) ? $_ : "" } @val[@col_list];
    print join ("\t", @val) . "\n";
}

exit (0);
```

The input processing loop converts each line to an array of values, then pulls out from the array the values corresponding to the requested columns. To avoid looping though the array, it uses Perl's notation that allows a list of subscripts to be specified all at once to request multiple array elements. For example, if @col_list contains the values 2, 6, and 3, these two expressions are equivalent:

```
($val[2] , $val[6], $val[3])
@val[@col_list]
```

What if you want to extract columns from a file that's not in tab-delimited format, or produce output in another format? In that case, combine *yank_col.pl* with *cvt_file.pl*. Suppose you want to pull out all but the password column from the colon-delimited */etc/passwd* file and write the result in CSV format. Use *cvt_file.pl* both to preprocess */etc/passwd* into tab-delimited format for *yank_col.pl* and to post-process the extracted columns into CSV format:

```
% cvt_file.pl --idelim=":" /etc/passwd \
    | yank_col.pl --columns=1,3-7 \
    | cvt_file.pl --oformat=csv > passwd.csv
```

If you don't want to type all of that as one long command, use temporary files for the intermediate steps:

```
% cvt_file.pl --idelim=":" /etc/passwd > tmp1
% yank_col.pl --columns=1,3-7 tmp1 > tmp2
% cvt_file.pl --oformat=csv tmp2 > passwd.csv
% rm tmp1 tmp2
```

Forcing split( ) to Return Every Field

The Perl split( ) function is extremely useful, but normally it doesn't return trailing empty fields. This means that if you write out only as many fields as split( ) returns, output lines may not have the same number of fields as input lines. To avoid this problem, pass a third argument to indicate the maximum number of fields to return. This forces split( ) to return as many fields as are actually present on the line, or the number requested, whichever is smaller. If the value of the third argument is large enough, the practical effect is to cause all fields to be returned, empty or not. Scripts shown in this chapter use a field count value of 10,000:

```
# split line at tabs, preserving all fields
my @val = split (/\t/, $_, 10000);
```

In the (unlikely?) event that an input line has more fields than that, it will be truncated. If you think that will be a problem, you can bump up the number even higher.

10.20 Validating and Transforming Data

Problem

You need to make sure the data values contained in a file are legal.

Solution

Check them, possibly rewriting them into a more suitable format.

Discussion

Earlier recipes in this chapter show how to work with the structural characteristics of files, by reading lines and busting them up into separate columns. It's important to be able to do that, but sometimes you need to work with the data content of a file, not just its structure:

- It's often a good idea to validate data values to make sure they're legal for the column types into which you're storing them. For example, you can make sure that values intended for INT, DATE, and ENUM columns are integers, dates in *CCYY-MM-DD* format, and legal enumeration values.

- Data values may need reformatting. Rewriting dates from one format to another is especially common. For example, if you're importing a FileMaker Pro file into MySQL, you'll likely need to convert dates from *MM-DD-YY* format to ISO format. If you're going in the other direction, from MySQL to FileMaker Pro, you'll need to perform the inverse date transformation, as well as split DATETIME and TIMESTAMP columns into separate date and time columns.

- It may be necessary to recognize special values in the file. It's common to represent NULL with a value that does not otherwise occur in the file, such as -1, Unknown, or N/A. If you don't want those values to be imported literally, you'll need to recognize and handle them specially.

This section begins a set of recipes that describe validation and reformatting techniques that are useful in these kinds of situations. Techniques covered here for checking values include direct comparison, pattern matching, and validation against information in a database. It's not unusual for certain validation operations to come up over and over, in which case you'll probably find it useful to to construct a library of functions. Packaging validation operations as library routines makes it easier to write utilities based on them, and the utilities make it easier to perform command-line operations on entire files so you can avoid editing them yourself.

Writing an Input-Processing Loop

Many of the validation recipes shown in the new few sections are typical of those that you perform within the context of a program that reads a file and checks individual column values. The general form of such a file-processing utility can be written like this:

```perl
#! /usr/bin/perl -w
# loop.pl - Typical input-processing loop

# Assumes tab-delimited, linefeed-terminated input lines.

use strict;

while (<>)                              # read each line
{
    chomp;
    # split line at tabs, preserving all fields
    my @val = split (/\t/, $_, 10000);
    for my $i (0 .. @val - 1)   # iterate through columns in line
    {
        # ... test $val[$i] here ...
    }
}

exit (0);
```

The while() loop reads each input line and breaks it into fields. Inside the loop, each line is broken into fields. Then the inner for() loop iterates through the fields in the line, allowing each one to be processed in sequence. If you're not applying a given test uniformly to all the fields, you'd replace the for() loop with separate column-specific tests.

This loop assumes tab-delimited, linefeed-terminated input, an assumption that is shared by most of the utilities discussed throughout the rest of this chapter. To use these programs with datafiles in other formats, you may be able to convert them into tab-delimited format using the *cvt_file.pl* script discussed in Recipe 10.18.

Putting Common Tests in Libraries

For a test that you perform often, it may be useful to package it as a library function. This makes the operation easy to perform, and also gives it a name that's likely to make the meaning of the operation clearer than the comparison code itself. For example, the following test performs a pattern match to check that $val consists entirely of digits (optionally preceded by a plus sign), then makes sure the value is greater than zero:

```
$valid = ($val =~ /^\+?\d+$/ && $val > 0);
```

In other words, the test looks for strings that represent positive integers. To make the test easier to use and its intent clearer, you might put it into a function that is used like this:

```
$valid = is_positive_integer ($val);
```

The function itself can be defined as follows:

```
sub is_positive_integer
{
my $s = shift;

    return ($s =~ /^\+?\d+$/ && $s > 0);
}
```

Then put the function definition into a library file so that multiple scripts can use it easily. The *Cookbook_Utils.pm* module file in the *lib* directory of the recipes distribution is an example of a library file that contains a number of validation functions. Take a look through it to see which functions may be useful to you in your own programs (or as a model for writing your own library files). To gain access to this module from within a script, include a use statement like this:

```
use Cookbook_Utils;
```

You must of course install the module file in a directory where Perl will find it. For details on library installation, see Recipe 2.3.

A significant benefit of putting a collection of utility routines into a library file is that you can use it for all kinds of programs. It's rare for a data manipulation problem to be completely unique. If you can pick and choose at least a few validation routines from a library, it's possible to reduce the amount of code you need to write, even for highly specialized programs.

10.21 Validation by Direct Comparison

Problem

You need to make sure a value is equal to or not equal to some specific value, or that it lies within a given range of values.

Solution

Perform a direct comparison.

Discussion

The simplest kind of validation is to perform comparisons against specific literal values:

```
# require a nonempty value
$valid = ($val ne "");
# require a specific nonempty value
$valid = ($val eq "abc");
# require one of several values
$valid = ($val eq "abc" || $val eq "def" || $val eq "xyz");
# require value in particular range (1 to 10)
$valid = ($val >= 1 && $val <= 10);
```

Most of those tests perform string comparisons. The last is a numeric comparison; however, a numeric comparison often is preceded by preliminary tests to verify first that the value doesn't contain non-numeric characters. Pattern testing, discussed in the next section, is one such way to do that.

String comparisons are case sensitive by default. To make a comparison case insensitive, convert both operands to the same lettercase:

```
# require a specific nonempty value in case-insensitive fashion
$valid = (lc ($val) eq lc ("AbC"));
```

10.22 Validation by Pattern Matching

Problem

You need to compare a value to a set of values that is difficult to specify literally without writing a really ugly expression.

Solution

Use pattern matching.

Discussion

Pattern matching is a powerful tool for validation because it allows you to test entire classes of values with a single expression. You can also use pattern tests to break up matched values into subparts for further individual testing, or in substitution operations to rewrite matched values. For example, you might break up a matched date into pieces so that you can verify that the month is in the range from 1 to 12 and the day is within the number of days in the month. Or you might use a substitution to reorder *MM-DD-YY* or *DD-MM-YY* values into *YY-MM-DD* format.

The next few sections describe how to use patterns to test for several types of values, but first let's take a quick tour of some general pattern-matching principles. The following discussion focuses on Perl's regular expression capabilities. Pattern matching in PHP and Python is similar, though you should consult the relevant documentation for any differences. For Java, the ORO pattern matching class library offers Perl-style pattern matching; Appendix A indicates where you can get it.

In Perl, the pattern constructor is /*pat*/:

```
$it_matched = ($val =~ /pat/);    # pattern match
```

Put an i after the /*pat*/ constructor to make the pattern match case insensitive:

```
$it_matched = ($val =~ /pat/i);   # case-insensitive match
```

To use a character other than slash, begin the constructor with m. This can be useful if the pattern itself contains slashes:

```
$it_matched = ($val =~ m|pat|);   # alternate constructor character
```

To look for a non-match, replace the =~ operator with the !~ operator:

```
$no_match = ($val !~ /pat/);      # negated pattern match
```

To perform a substitution in $val based on a pattern match, use s/*pat*/*replacement*/. If *pat* occurs within $val, it's replaced by *replacement*. To perform a case-insensitive match, put an i after the last slash. To perform a global substitution that replaces all instances of *pat* rather than just the first one, add a g after the last slash:

```
$val =~ s/pat/replacement/;    # substitution
$val =~ s/pat/replacement/i;   # case-insensitive substitution
$val =~ s/pat/replacement/g;   # global substitution
$val =~ s/pat/replacement/ig;  # case-insensitive and global
```

Here's a list of some of the special pattern elements available in Perl regular expressions:

Pattern	What the pattern matches
^	Beginning of string
$	End of string
.	Any character
\s, \S	Whitespace or non-whitespace character
\d, \D	Digit or non-digit character
\w, \W	Word (alphanumeric or underscore) or non-word character
[...]	Any character listed between the square brackets
[^ ...]	Any character not listed between the square brackets
p1|p2|p3	Alternation; matches any of the patterns p1, p2, or p3
*	Zero or more instances of preceding element
+	One or more instances of preceding element
{n}	n instances of preceding element
{m,n}	m through n instances of preceding element

Many of these pattern elements are the same as those available for MySQL's REGEXP regular expression operator. (See Recipe 4.7.)

To match a literal instance of a character that is special within patterns, such as *, ^, or $, precede it with a backslash. Similarly, to include a character within a character class construction that is special in character classes ([,], or -), precede it with a backslash. To include a literal ^ in a character class, list it somewhere other than as the first character between the brackets.

Many of the validation patterns shown in the following sections are of the /^pat$/ form. Beginning and ending a pattern with ^ and $ has the effect of requiring pat to match the entire string that you're testing. This is common in data validation contexts, because it's generally desirable to know that a pattern matches an entire input value, not just part of it. (If you want to be sure that a value represents an integer, for example, it doesn't do you any good to know only that it contains an integer somewhere.) This is not a hard-and-fast rule, however, and sometimes it's useful to perform a more relaxed test by omitting the ^ and $ characters as appropriate. For example, if you want to strip leading and trailing whitespace from a value, use one pattern anchored only to the beginning of the string, and another anchored only to the end:

```
$val =~ s/^\s+//;      # trim leading whitespace
$val =~ s/\s+$//;      # trim trailing whitespace
```

That's such a common operation, in fact, that it's a good candidate for being placed into a utility function. The *Cookbook_Utils.pm* file contains a function trim_whitespace() that performs both substitutions and returns the result:

```
$val = trim_whitespace ($val);
```

To remember subsections of a string that is matched by a pattern, use parentheses around the relevant parts of the pattern. After a successful match, you can refer to the matched substrings using the variables $1, $2, and so forth:

```
if ("abcdef" =~ /^(ab)(.*)$/)
{
    $first_part = $1;   # this will be ab
    $the_rest = $2;     # this will be cdef
}
```

To indicate that an element within a pattern is optional, follow it by a ? character. To match values consisting of a sequence of digits, optionally beginning with a minus sign, and optionally ending with a period, use this pattern:

```
/^-?\d+\.?$/
```

You can also use parentheses to group alternations within a pattern. The following pattern matches time values in *hh:mm* format, optionally followed by AM or PM:

```
/^\d{1,2}:\d{2}\s*(AM|PM)?$/i
```

The use of parentheses in that pattern also has the side-effect of remembering the optional part in $1. To suppress that side-effect, use (?:*pat*) instead:

```
/^\d{1,2}:\d{2}\s*(?:AM|PM)?$/i
```

That's sufficient background in Perl pattern matching to allow construction of useful validation tests for several types of data values. The following sections provide patterns that can be used to test for broad content types, numbers, temporal values, and email addresses or URLs.

The *transfer* directory of the recipes distribution contains a *test_pat.pl* script that reads input values, matches them against several patterns, and reports which patterns each value matches. The script is easily extensible, so you can use it as a test harness to try out your own patterns.

10.23 Using Patterns to Match Broad Content Types

Problem

You want to classify values into broad categories.

Solution

Use a pattern that is similarly broad.

Discussion

If you need to know only whether values are empty, nonempty, or consist only of certain types of characters, patterns such as the following may suffice:

Pattern	Type of value the pattern matches
/^$/	Empty value
/./	Nonempty value
/^\s*$/	Whitespace, possibly empty
/^\s+$/	Nonempty whitespace
/\S/	Nonempty, and not just whitespace
/^\d+$/	Digits only, nonempty
/^[a-z]+$/i	Alphabetic characters only (case insensitive), nonempty
/^\w+$/	Alphanumeric or underscore characters only, nonempty

10.24 Using Patterns to Match Numeric Values

Problem

You need to make sure a string looks like a number.

Solution

Use a pattern that matches the type of number you're looking for.

Discussion

Patterns can be used to classify values into several types of numbers:

Pattern	Type of value the pattern matches
/^\d+$/	Unsigned integer
/^-?\d+$/	Negative or unsigned integer
/^[-+]?\d+$/	Signed or unsigned integer
/^[-+]?(\d+(\.\d*)?|\.\d+)$/	Floating-point number

The pattern /^\d+$/ matches unsigned integers by requiring a nonempty value that consists only of digits from the beginning to the end of the value. If you care only that a value begins with an integer, you can match an initial numeric part and extract it. To do this, match just the initial part of the string (omit the $ that requires the pattern to match to the end of the string) and place parentheses around the \d+ part. Then refer to the matched number as $1 after a successful match:

```
if ($val =~ /^(\d+)/)
{
    $val = $1;  # reset value to matched subpart
}
```

You could also add zero to the value, which causes Perl to perform an implicit string-to-number conversion that discards the non-numeric suffix:

```
if ($val =~ /^\d+/)
{
    $val += 0;
}
```

However, if you run Perl with the *-w* option (which I recommend), this form of conversion generates warnings for values that actually have a non-numeric part. It will also convert string values like 0013 to the number 13, which may be unacceptable in some contexts.

Some kinds of numeric values have a special format or other unusual constraints. Here are a few examples, and how to deal with them:

Zip Codes

Zip and Zip+4 Codes are postal codes used for mail delivery in the United States. They have values like 12345 or 12345-6789 (that is, five digits, possibly followed by a dash and four more digits). To match one form or the other, or both forms, use the following patterns:

Pattern	Type of value the pattern matches
/^\d{5}$/	Zip Code, five digits only
/^\d{5}-\d{4}$/	Zip+4 Code
/^\d{5}(-\d{4})?$/	Zip or Zip+4 Code

Credit card numbers

Credit card numbers typically consist of digits, but it's common for values to be written with spaces, dashes, or other characters between groups of digits. For example, the following numbers would be considered equivalent:

```
0123456789012345
0123 4567 8901 2345
0123-4567-8901-2345
```

To match such values, use this pattern:

```
/^[- \d]+/
```

(Note that Perl allows the \d digit specifier within character classes.) However, that pattern doesn't identify values of the wrong length, and it may be useful to remove extraneous characters. If you require credit card values to contain 16 digits, use a substitution to remove all non-digits, then check the length of the result:

```
$val =~ s/\D//g;
$valid = (length ($val) == 16);
```

Innings pitched

In baseball, one statistic recorded for pitchers is the number of innings pitched, measured in thirds of innings (corresponding to the number of outs recorded.) These values are numeric, but must satisfy a specific additional constraint: A fractional part is allowed, but if present, must consist of a single digit 0, 1, or 2. That is, legal values are of the form 0, .1, .2, 1, 1.1, 1.2, 2, and so forth. To match an unsigned integer (optionally followed by a decimal point and perhaps a fractional digit of 0, 1, or 2), or a fractional digit with no leading integer, use this pattern:

```
/^(\d+(\.[012]?)?|\.[012])$/
```

The alternatives in the pattern are grouped within parentheses because otherwise the ^ anchors only the first of them to the beginning of the string and the $ anchors only the second to the end.

10.25 Using Patterns to Match Dates or Times

Problem

You need to make sure a string looks like a date or time.

Solution

Use a pattern that matches the type of temporal value you expect. Be sure to consider issues such as how strict to be about delimiters between subparts and the lengths of the subparts.

Discussion

Dates are a validation headache because they come in so many formats. Pattern tests are extremely useful for weeding out illegal values, but often insufficient for full verification: a date might have a number where you expect a month, but if the number is 13, the date isn't valid. This section introduces some patterns that match a few common date formats. Recipe 10.30 revisits this topic in more detail and discusses how to combine pattern tests with content verification.

To require values to be dates in ISO (*CCYY-MM-DD*) format, use this pattern:

```
/^\d{4}-\d{2}-\d{2}$/
```

The pattern requires - as the delimiter between date parts. To allow either - or / as the delimiter, use a character class between the numeric parts (the slashes are escaped with a backslash to prevent them from being interpreted as the end of the pattern constructor):

```
/^\d{4}[-\/]\d{2}[-\/]\d{2}$/
```

Or you can use a different delimiter around the pattern and avoid the backslashes:

```
m|^\d{4}[-/]\d{2}[-/]\d{2}$|
```

To allow any non-digit delimiter (which corresponds to how MySQL operates when it interprets strings as dates), use this pattern:

```
/^\d{4}\D\d{2}\D\d{2}$/
```

If you don't require the full number of digits in each part (to allow leading zeros in values like 03 to be missing, for example), just look for three nonempty digit sequences:

```
/^\d+\D\d+\D\d+$/
```

Of course, that pattern is so general that it will also match other values such as U.S. Social Security numbers (which have the format 012-34-5678). To constrain the sub-part lengths by requiring two to four digits in the year part and one or two digits in the month and day parts, use this pattern:

```
/^\d{2,4}?\D\d{1,2}\D\d{1,2}$/
```

For dates in other formats such as *MM-DD-YY* or *DD-MM-YY*, similar patterns apply, but the subparts are arranged in a different order. This pattern matches both of those formats:

```
/^\d{2}-\d{2}-\d{2}$/
```

If you need to check the values of individual date parts, use parentheses in the pattern and extract the substrings after a successful match. If you're expecting dates to be in ISO format, for example, do something like this:

```
if ($val =~ /^(\d{2,4})\D(\d{1,2})\D(\d{1,2})$/)
{
    ($year, $month, $day) = ($1, $2, $3);
}
```

The library file *lib/Cookbook_Utils.pm* in the recipes distribution contains several of these pattern tests, packaged as function calls. If the date doesn't match the pattern, they return undef. Otherwise, they return a reference to an array containing the broken-out values for the year, month, and day. This can be useful for performing further checking on the components of the date. For example, is_iso_date() looks for dates that match ISO format. It's defined as follows:

```
sub is_iso_date
{
my $s = shift;
```

```
    return undef unless $s =~ /^(\d{2,4})\D(\d{1,2})\D(\d{1,2})$/;
    return [ $1, $2, $3 ];  # return year, month, day
}
```

To use the function, do something like this:

```
my $ref = is_iso_date ($val);
if (defined ($ref))
{
    # $val matched ISO format pattern;
    # check its subparts using $ref->[0] through $ref->[2]
}
else
{
    # $val didn't match ISO format pattern
}
```

You'll often find additional processing necessary with dates, because although date-matching patterns help to weed out values that are syntactically malformed, they don't assess whether the individual components contain legal values. To do that, some range checking is necessary. That topic is covered later in Recipe 10.30.

If you're willing to skip subpart testing and just want to rewrite the pieces, you can use a substitution. For example, to rewrite values assumed to be in *MM-DD-YY* format into *YY-MM-DD* format, do this:

```
$val =~ s/^(\d+)\D(\d+)\D(\d+)$/$3-$1-$2/;
```

Time values are somewhat more orderly than dates, usually being written with hours first and seconds last, with two digits per part:

```
/^\d{2}:\d{2}:\d{2}$/
```

To be more lenient, you can allow the hours part to have a single digit, or the seconds part to be missing:

```
/^\d{1,2}:\d{2}(:\d{2})?$/
```

You can mark parts of the time with parentheses if you want to range-check the individual parts, or perhaps to reformat the value to include a seconds part of 00 if it happens to be missing. However, this requires some care with the parentheses and the ? characters in the pattern if the seconds part is optional. You want to allow the entire :\d{2} at the end of the pattern to be optional, but not to save the : character in $3 if the third time section is present. To accomplish that, use (?:*pat*), an alternative grouping notation that doesn't save the matched substring. Within that notation, use parentheses around the digits to save them. Then $3 will be undef if the seconds part is not present, but will contain the seconds digits otherwise:

```
if ($val =~ /^(\d{1,2}):(\d{2})(?::(\d{2}))?$/)
{
    my ($hour, $min, $sec) = ($1, $2, $3);
    $sec = "00" if !defined ($sec); # seconds missing; use 00
    $val = "$hour:$min:$sec";
}
```

To rewrite times in 12-hour format with AM and PM suffixes into 24-hour format, you can do something like this:

```
if ($val =~ /^(\d{1,2}):(\d{2})(?::(\d{2}))?\s*(AM|PM)?$/i)
{
    my ($hour, $min, $sec) = ($1, $2, $3);
    # supply missing seconds
    $sec = "00" unless defined ($sec);
    # convert 0 .. 11 -> 12 .. 23 for PM times
    $hour += 12 if defined ($4) && uc ($4) eq "PM";
    $val = "$hour:$min:$sec";
}
```

The time parts are placed into $1, $2, and $3, with $3 set to undef if the seconds part is missing. The suffix goes into $4 if it's present. If the suffix is AM or missing (undef), the value is interpreted as an AM time. If the suffix is PM, the value is interpreted as a PM time.

See Also

This section is just the beginning of what you can do when processing dates for data transfer purposes. Date and time testing and conversion can be highly idiosyncratic, and the sheer number of issues to consider is mind-boggling:

- What is the basic date format? Dates come in several common styles, such as ISO (*CCYY-MM-DD*), U.S. (*MM-DD-YY*), and British (*DD-MM-YY*) formats. And these are just some of the more standard formats. Many more are possible. For example, a datafile may contain dates written as June 17, 1959 or as 17 Jun '59.

- Are trailing times allowed on dates, or perhaps required? When times are expected, is the full time required, or just the hour and minute?

- Do you allow values like now or today?

- Are date parts required to be delimited by a certain character, such as - or /, or are other delimiters allowed?

- Are date parts required to have a specific number of digits? Or are leading zeros on month and year values allowed to be missing?

- Are months written numerically, or are they represented as month names like January or Jan?

- Are two-digit year values allowed? Should they be converted to have four digits? If so, what is the conversion rule? (What is the transition point within the range 00 to 99 at which values change from one century to another?)

- Should date parts be checked to ensure their validity? Patterns can recognize strings that look like dates or times, but while they're extremely useful for detecting malformed values, they may not be sufficient. A value like 1947-15-99 may match a pattern but isn't a legal date. Pattern testing is thus most useful in conjunction with range checks on the individual parts of the date.

The prevalence of these issues in data transfer problems means that you'll probably end up writing some of your own validators on occasion to handle very specific date formats. Later sections of this chapter can provide additional assistance. For example, Recipe 10.29 covers conversion of two-digit year values to four-digit form, and Recipe 10.30 discusses how to perform validity checking on components of date or time values.

10.26 Using Patterns to Match Email Addresses and URLs

Problem

You want to determine whether or not a value looks like an email address or a URL.

Solution

Use a pattern, tuned to the level of strictness you want to enforce.

Discussion

The immediately preceding sections use patterns to identify classes of values such as numbers and dates, which are fairly typical applications for regular expressions. But pattern matching has such widespread applicability that it's impossible to list all the ways you can use it for data validation. To give some idea of a few other types of values that pattern matching can be used for, this section shows a few tests for email addresses and URLs.

To check values that are expected to be email addresses, the pattern should require at least an @ character with nonempty strings on either side:

```
/.@./
```

That's a pretty minimal test. It's difficult to come up with a fully general pattern that covers all the legal values and rejects all the illegal ones, but it's easy to write a pattern that's at least a little more restrictive.[*] For example, in addition to being nonempty, the username and the domain name should consist entirely of characters other than @ characters or spaces:

```
/^[^@ ]+@[^@ ]+$/
```

You may also wish to require that the domain name part contain at least two parts separated by a dot:

```
/^[^@ ]+@[^@ .]+\.[^@ .]+/
```

---

[*] To see how hard it can be to perform pattern matching for email addresses, check Appendix E in Jeffrey Friedl's *Mastering Regular Expressions* (O'Reilly).

To look for URL values that begin with a protocol specifier of `http://`, `ftp://`, or `mailto:`, use an alternation that matches any of them at the beginning of the string. These values contain slashes, so it's easier to use a different character around the pattern to avoid having to escape the slashes with backslashes:

```
m#^(http://|ftp://|mailto:)#i
```

The alternatives in the pattern are grouped within parentheses because otherwise the ^ will anchor only the first of them to the beginning of the string. The i modifier follows the pattern because protocol specifiers in URLs are not case sensitive. The pattern is otherwise fairly unrestrictive, because it allows anything to follow the protocol specifier. I leave it to you to add further restrictions as necessary.

10.27 Validation Using Table Metadata

Problem

You need to check input values against the legal members of an ENUM or SET column.

Solution

Get the column definition, extract the list of members from it, and check data values against the list.

Discussion

Some forms of validation involve checking input values against information stored in a database. This includes values to be stored in an ENUM or SET column, which can be checked against the valid members stored in the column definition. Database-backed validation also applies when you have values that must match those listed in a lookup table to be considered legal. For example, input records that contain customer IDs can be required to match a record in a customers table, or state abbreviations in addresses can be verified against a table that lists each state. This section describes ENUM- and SET-based validation, and Recipe 10.28 discusses how to use lookup tables.

One way to check input values that correspond to the legal values of ENUM or SET columns is to get the list of legal column values into an array using the information returned by SHOW COLUMNS, then perform an array membership test. For example, the favorite-color column color from the profile table is an ENUM that is defined as follows:

```
mysql> SHOW COLUMNS FROM profile LIKE 'color'\G
*************************** 1. row ***************************
  Field: color
   Type: enum('blue','red','green','brown','black','white')
   Null: YES
    Key:
Default: NULL
  Extra:
```

If you extract the list of enumeration members from the Type value and store them in an array @members, you can perform the membership test like this:

```
$valid = grep (/^$val$/i, @members);
```

The pattern constructor begins and ends with ^ and $ to require $val to match an entire enumeration member (rather than just a substring). It also is followed by an i to specify a case-insensitive comparison, because ENUM columns are not case sensitive.

In Recipe 9.6, we wrote a function get_enumorset_info( ) that returns ENUM or SET column metadata. This includes the list of members, so it's easy to use that function to write another utility routine, check_enum_value( ), that gets the legal enumeration values and performs the membership test. The routine takes four arguments: a database handle, the table name and column name for the ENUM column, and the value to check. It returns true or false to indicate whether or not the value is legal:

```
sub check_enum_value
{
my ($dbh, $tbl_name, $col_name, $val) = @_;

    my $valid = 0;
    my $info = get_enumorset_info ($dbh, $tbl_name, $col_name);
    if ($info && $info->{type} eq "enum")
    {
        # use case-insensitive comparison; ENUM
        # columns are not case sensitive
        $valid = grep (/^$val$/i, @{$info->{values}});
    }
    return ($valid);
}
```

For single-value testing, such as to validate a value submitted in a web form, that kind of test works well. However, if you're going to be testing a lot of values (like an entire column in a datafile), it's better to read the enumeration values into memory once, then use them repeatedly to check each of the data values. Furthermore, it's a lot more efficient to perform hash lookups than array lookups (in Perl at least). To do so, retrieve the legal enumeration values and store them as keys of a hash. Then test each input value by checking whether or not it exists as a hash key. It's a little more work to construct the hash, which is why check_enum_value( ) doesn't do so. But for bulk validation, the improved lookup speed more than makes up for the hash construction overhead.[*]

Begin by getting the metadata for the column, then convert the list of legal enumeration members to a hash:

```
my $ref = get_enumorset_info ($dbh, $tbl_name, $col_name);
my %members;
foreach my $member (@{$ref->{values}})
```

---

[*] If you want to check for yourself the relative efficiency of array membership tests versus hash lookups, try the *lookup_time.pl* script in the *transfer* directory of the recipes distribution.

```
    {
        # convert hash key to consistent case; ENUM isn't case sensitive
        $members{lc ($member)} = 1;
    }
```

The loop makes each enumeration member exist as the key of a hash element. The hash key is what's important here; the value associated with it is irrelevant. (The example shown sets the value to 1, but you could use undef, 0, or any other value.) Note that the code converts the hash keys to lowercase before storing them. This is done because hash key lookups in Perl are case sensitive. That's fine if the values that you're checking also are case sensitive, but ENUM columns are not. By converting the enumeration values to a given lettercase before storing them in the hash, then converting the values you want to check similarly, you perform in effect a case insensitive key existence test:

```
    $valid = exists ($members{lc ($val)});
```

The preceding example converts enumeration values and input values to lowercase. You could just as well use uppercase—as long as you do so for all values consistently.

Note that the existence test may fail if the input value is the empty string. You'll have to decide how to handle that case on a column-by-column basis. For example, if the column allows NULL values, you might interpret the empty string as equivalent to NULL and thus as being a legal value.

The validation procedure for SET values is similar to that for ENUM values, except that an input value might consist of any number of SET members, separated by commas. For the value to be legal, each element in it must be legal. In addition, because "any number of members" includes "none," the empty string is a legal value for any SET column.

For one-shot testing of individual input values, you can use a utility routine check_set_value() that is similar to check_enum_value():

```
sub check_set_value
{
my ($dbh, $tbl_name, $col_name, $val) = @_;

    my $valid = 0;
    my $info = get_enumorset_info ($dbh, $tbl_name, $col_name);
    if ($info && $info->{type} eq "set")
    {
        #return 1 if $val eq "";         # empty string is legal element
        # use case-insensitive comparison; SET
        # columns are not case sensitive
        $valid = 1;             # assume valid until we find out otherwise
        foreach my $v (split (/,/, $val))
        {
            if (!grep (/^$v$/i, @{$info->{values}}))
            {
                $valid = 0; # value contains an invalid element
```

```
                last;
            }
        }
    }
    return ($valid);
}
```

For bulk testing, construct a hash from the legal SET members. The procedure is the same as for producing a hash from ENUM elements:

```
my $ref = get_enumorset_info ($dbh, $tbl_name, $col_name);
my %members;
foreach my $member (@{$ref->{values}})
{
    # convert hash key to consistent case; SET isn't case sensitive
    $members{lc ($member)} = 1;
}
```

To validate a given input value against the SET member hash, convert it to the same lettercase as the hash keys, split it at commas to get a list of the individual elements of the value, then check each one. If any of the elements are invalid, the entire value is invalid:

```
$valid = 1;         # assume valid until we find out otherwise
foreach my $elt (split (/,/, lc ($val)))
{
    if (!exists ($members{$elt}))
    {
        $valid = 0; # value contains an invalid element
        last;
    }
}
```

After the loop terminates, $valid is true if the value is legal for the SET column, and false otherwise. Empty strings are always legal SET values, but this code doesn't perform any special-case test for an empty string. No such test is necessary, because in that case the split() operation returns an empty list, the loop never executes, and $valid remains true.

10.28 Validation Using a Lookup Table

Problem

You need to check values to make sure they're listed in a lookup table.

Solution

Issue queries to see if the values are in the table. But the way you do this depends on the number of input values and on the size of the table.

Discussion

To validate input values against the contents of a lookup table, you can use techniques somewhat similar to those shown in Recipe 10.27 on checking ENUM and SET columns. However, whereas ENUM and SET columns are limited to a maximum of 65,536 and 64 member values respectively, a lookup table can have an essentially unlimited number of values. You may not want to read them all into memory.

Validation of input values against the contents of a lookup table can be done several ways, as illustrated in the following discussion. The tests shown in the examples perform comparisons against values exactly as they are stored in the lookup table. To perform case-insensitive comparisons, remember to convert all values to a consistent lettercase.

Issue Individual Queries

For one-shot operations, you can test a value by checking whether it's listed in the lookup table. The following query returns true (nonzero) a value that is present and false otherwise:

```
$valid = $dbh->selectrow_array (
            "SELECT COUNT(*) FROM $tbl_name WHERE val = ?",
            undef, $val);
```

This kind of test may be suitable for purposes such as checking a value submitted in a web form, but is inefficient for validating large datasets. It has no memory for the results of previous tests for values that have been seen before; consequently, you'll end up issuing a query for every single input value.

Construct a Hash from the Entire Lookup Table

If you're going to perform bulk validation of a large set of values, it's more efficient to pull the lookup values into memory, save them in a data structure, and check each input value against the contents of that structure. Using an in-memory lookup avoids the overhead of running a query for each value.

First, run a query to retrieve all the lookup table values and construct a hash from them:

```
my %members;     # hash for lookup values
my $sth = $dbh->prepare ("SELECT val FROM $tbl_name");
$sth->execute ();
while (my ($val) = $sth->fetchrow_array ())
{
    $members{$val} = 1;
}
```

Then check each value by performing a hash key existence test:

```
$valid = exists ($members{$val});
```

This reduces the database traffic to a single query. However, for a large lookup table, that may still be a lot of traffic, and you may not want to hold the entire table in memory.

Performing Lookups with Other Languages

The example shown here for bulk testing of lookup values uses a Perl hash to determine whether or not a given value is present in a set of values:

```
$valid = exists ($members{$val});
```

Similar data structures exist for other languages. In PHP, you can use an associative array and perform a key lookup like this:

```
$valid = isset ($members[$val]);
```

In Python, use a dictionary and check input values using the has_key() method:

```
valid = members.has_key (val)
```

For lookups in Java, use a HashMap and test values with the containsKey() method:

```
valid = members.containsKey (val);
```

The *transfer* directory of the recipes distribution contains some sample code for lookup operations in each of these languages.

Use a Hash as a Cache of Already-Seen Lookup Values

Another lookup technique is to mix use of individual queries with a hash that stores lookup value existence information. This approach can be useful if you have a very large lookup table. Begin with an empty hash:

```
my %members;    # hash for lookup values
```

Then, for each value to be tested, check whether or not it's present in the hash. If not, issue a query to see if the value is present in the lookup table, and record the result of the query in the hash. The validity of the input value is determined by the value associated with the key, not by the existence of the key:

```
if (!exists ($members{$val}))   # haven't seen this value yet
{
    my $count = $dbh->selectrow_array (
                "SELECT COUNT(*) FROM $tbl_name WHERE val = ?",
                undef, $val);
    # store true/false to indicate whether value was found
    $members{$val} = ($count > 0);
}
$valid = $members{$val};
```

For this method, the hash acts as a cache, so that you run a lookup query for any given value only once, no matter how many times it occurs in the input. For datasets that have a reasonable number of repeated values, this approach avoids issuing a separate query for every single value, while requiring an entry in the hash only for each unique value. It thus stands between the other two approaches in terms of the tradeoff between database traffic and program memory requirements for the hash.

Note that the hash is used in a somewhat different manner for this method than for the previous method. Previously, the existence of the input value as a key in the hash determined the validity of the value, and the value associated with the hash key was irrelevant. For the hash-as-cache method, the meaning of key existence in the hash changes from "it's valid" to "it's been tested before." For each key, the value associated with it indicates whether the input value is present in the lookup table. (If you store as keys only those values that are found to be in the lookup table, you'll issue a query for each instance of an invalid value in the input dataset, which is inefficient.)

10.29 Converting Two-Digit Year Values to Four-Digit Form

Problem

You need to convert years in date values from two digits to four digits.

Solution

Let MySQL do this for you. If MySQL's conversion rules aren't appropriate, perform the operation yourself.

Discussion

Two-digit year values are a problem because the century is not explicit in the data values. If you know the range of years spanned by your input, you can add the century without ambiguity. Otherwise, you can only guess. For example, the date 2/10/69 probably would be interpreted by most people in the U.S. as as October 2, 1969. But if it represents Mahatma Gandhi's birth date, the year actually is 1869.

One way to convert years to four digits is to let MySQL do it. If you store a date containing a two-digit year, MySQL automatically converts it to four-digit form. MySQL uses a transition point of 1970; it interprets values from 00 to 69 as the years 2000 to 2069, and values from 70 to 99 as the years 1970 to 1999. These rules are appropriate for year values in the range from 1970 to 2069. If your values lie outside this range, you should add the proper century yourself before storing them into MySQL.

To use a different transition point, convert years to four-digit form yourself. A general purpose routine to convert two-digit years to four digits and to allow an arbitrary transition point can be written like this:

```
sub yy_to_ccyy
{
my ($year, $transition_point) = @_;

    $transition_point = 70 unless defined ($transition_point);
    $year += ($year >= $transition_point ? 1900 : 2000) if $year < 100;
    return ($year);
}
```

The function uses MySQL's transition point (70) by default. An optional second argument may be given to provide a different transition point. yy_to_ccyy() also makes sure the year actually needs converting (is less than 100) before modifying it. That way you can pass year values that do or don't include the century without checking first. Some sample invocations using the default transition point have the following results:

```
$val = yy_to_ccyy (60);        # returns 2060
$val = yy_to_ccyy (1960);      # returns 1960 (no conversion done)
```

But suppose you want to convert year values as follows, using a transition point of 50:

```
00 .. 49 -> 2000 .. 2049
50 .. 99 -> 1950 .. 1999
```

To do this, pass an explicit transition point argument to yy_to_ccyy():

```
$val = yy_to_ccyy (60, 50);    # returns 1960
$val = yy_to_ccyy (1960, 50);  # returns 1960 (no conversion done)
```

The yy_to_ccyy() function is one of those included in the *Cookbook_Utils.pm* library file.

10.30 Performing Validity Checking on Date or Time Subparts

Problem

A string passes a pattern test as a date or time, but you want to perform further checking to make sure that it's legal.

Solution

Break up the value into subparts and perform the appropriate range checking on each part.

Discussion

Pattern matching may not be sufficient for checking dates or times. For example, a value like 1947-15-19 may match a date pattern, but if you insert the value into a DATE column, MySQL will convert it to 0000-00-00. If you want to find out that the value is bad before putting it into your database, combine pattern matching with range checking.

To make sure that a date is legal, break out the year, month, and day values, then check that they're within the proper ranges. Years should be less than 9999 (MySQL represents dates to an upper limit of 9999-12-31), month values should be in the range from 1 to 12, and days should be in the range from 1 to the number of days in the month. That latter part is the trickiest; it's month-dependent, and for February, it's also year-dependent because it changes for leap years.

Suppose you're checking input dates in ISO format. Earlier, in Recipe 10.25, we used an is_iso_date() function from the *Cookbook_Utils.pm* library file to perform a pattern match on a date string and break it into component values:

```
my $ref = is_iso_date ($val);
if (defined ($ref))
{
    # $val matched ISO format pattern;
    # check its subparts using $ref->[0] through $ref->[2]
}
else
{
    # $val didn't match ISO format pattern
}
```

is_iso_date() returns undef if the value doesn't satisfy a pattern that matches ISO date format. Otherwise, it returns a reference to an array containing the year, month, and day values.[*] To perform additional checking on the date parts, pass them to is_valid_date(), another library function:

```
$valid = is_valid_date ($ref->[0], $ref->[1], $ref->[2]);
```

Or, more concisely:

```
$valid = is_valid_date (@{$ref});
```

is_valid_date() checks the parts of a date like this:

```
sub is_valid_date
{
my ($year, $month, $day) = @_;

    # year must be non-negative, month and day must be positive
    return (0) if $year < 0 || $month < 1 || $day < 1;
```

---

[*] The *Cookbook_Utils.pm* file also contains is_mmddyy_date() and is_ddmmyy_date() routines that match dates in U.S. or British format and return undef or a reference to an array of date parts. (The parts are always in year, month, day order, not the order in which the parts appear in the date string.)

```
    # check maximum limits on individual parts
    return (0) if $year > 9999;
    return (0) if $month > 12;
    return (0) if $day > days_in_month ($year, $month);
    return (1);
}
```

is_valid_date() requires separate year, month, and day values, not a date string. This forces you to break apart candidate values into components before invoking it, but makes it applicable in more contexts. For example, you can use it to check dates like 12 February 2003 by mapping the month to its numeric value before calling is_valid_date(). Were is_valid_date() to take a string argument assumed to be in a given date format, it would be much less general.

is_valid_date() uses a subsidiary function days_in_month() to determine how many days there are in the month represented by the date. days_in_month() requires both the year and the month as arguments, because if the month is 2 (February), the number of days depends on whether the year is a leap year. This means you *must* pass a four-digit year value. Two-digit years are ambiguous with respect to the century, and proper leap-year testing is impossible, as discussed in Recipe 5.27. The days_in_month() and is_leap_year() functions are based on techniques taken straight from there:

```
sub is_leap_year
{
my $year = shift;

    return (($year % 4 == 0) && ((($year % 100) != 0) || ($year % 400) == 0));
}

sub days_in_month
{
my ($year, $month) = @_;
my @day_tbl = (31, 28, 31, 30, 31, 30, 31, 31, 30, 31, 30, 31);
my $days = $day_tbl[$month-1];

    # add a day for Feb of leap years
    $days++ if $month == 2 && is_leap_year ($year);
    return ($days);
}
```

To perform validity checking on time values, a similar procedure can be used, although the ranges for the subparts are different: 0 to 24 for the hour, and 0 to 59 for the minute and second. Here is a function is_24hr_time() that checks for values in 24-hour format:

```
sub is_24hr_time
{
my $s = shift;

    return undef unless $s =~ /^(\d{1,2})\D(\d{2})\D(\d{2})$/;
    return [ $1, $2, $3 ];  # return hour, minute, second
}
```

The following is_ampm_time() function looks for times in 12-hour format with an optional AM or PM suffix, converting PM times to 24-hour values:

```
sub is_ampm_time
{
my $s = shift;

    return undef unless $s =~ /^(\d{1,2})\D(\d{2})\D(\d{2})(?:\s*(AM|PM))?$/i;
    my ($hour, $min, $sec) = ($1, $2, $3);
    $hour += 12 if defined ($4) && uc ($4) eq "PM";
    return [ $hour, $min, $sec ];   # return hour, minute, second
}
```

Both functions return undef for values that don't match the pattern. Otherwise, they return a reference to a three-element array containing the hour, minute, and second values.

10.31 Writing Date-Processing Utilities

Problem

There's a given date-processing operation that you need to perform frequently, so you want to write a utility that does it for you.

Solution

The utilities in this section provide some examples showing how to do that.

Discussion

Due to the idiosyncratic nature of dates, you'll probably find it necessary to write date converters from time to time. This section shows some sample converters that serve various purposes:

- *isoize_date.pl* reads a file looking for dates in U.S. format (MM-DD-YY) and converts them to ISO format.

- *cvt_date.pl* converts dates to and from any of ISO, US, or British formats. It is more general than *isoize_date.pl*, but requires that you tell it what kind of input to expect and what kind of output to produce.

- *monddccyy_to_iso.pl* looks for dates like Feb. 6, 1788 and converts them to ISO format. It illustrates how to map dates with non-numeric parts to a format that MySQL will understand.

All three scripts are located in the *transfer* directory of the recipes distribution. They assume datafiles are in tab-delimited, linefeed-terminated format. (Use *cvt_file.pl* to work with files in a different format.)

Our first date-processing utility, *isoize_date.pl*, looks for dates in U.S. format and rewrites them into ISO format. You'll recognize that it's modeled after the general input-processing loop shown in Recipe 10.20, with some extra stuff thrown in to perform a specific type of conversion:

```perl
#! /usr/bin/perl -w
# isoize_date.pl - Read input data, look for values that match
# a date pattern, convert them to ISO format. Also converts
# 2-digit years to 4-digit years, using a transition point of 70.

# By default, this looks for dates in MM-DD-[CC]YY format.

# Assumes tab-delimited, linefeed-terminated input lines.

# Does not check whether dates actually are valid (for example,
# won't complain about 13-49-1928).

use strict;

# transition point at which 2-digit years are assumed to be 19XX
# (below they are treated as 20XX)
my $transition = 70;

while (<>)
{
    chomp;
    my @val = split (/\t/, $_, 10000);  # split, preserving all fields
    for my $i (0 .. @val - 1)
    {
        my $val = $val[$i];
        # look for strings in MM-DD-[CC]YY format
        next unless $val =~ /^(\d{1,2})\D(\d{1,2})\D(\d{2,4})$/;

        my ($month, $day, $year) = ($1, $2, $3);
        # to interpret dates as DD-MM-[CC]YY instead, replace preceding
        # line with the following one:
        #my ($day, $month, $year) = ($1, $2, $3);

        # convert 2-digit years to 4 digits, then update value in array
        $year += ($year >= $transition ? 1900 : 2000) if $year < 100;
        $val[$i] = sprintf ("%04d-%02d-%02d", $year, $month, $day);
    }
    print join ("\t", @val) . "\n";
}

exit (0);
```

If you feed *isoize_date.pl* an input file that looks like this:

```
Fred    04-13-70
Mort    09-30-69
Brit    12-01-57
Carl    11-02-73
Sean    07-04-63
```

```
Alan     02-14-65
Mara     09-17-68
Shepard  09-02-75
Dick     08-20-52
Tony     05-01-60
```

It produces the following output:

```
Fred     1970-04-13
Mort     2069-09-30
Brit     2057-12-01
Carl     1973-11-02
Sean     2063-07-04
Alan     2065-02-14
Mara     2068-09-17
Shepard  1975-09-02
Dick     2052-08-20
Tony     2060-05-01
```

isoize_date.pl serves a specific purpose: It converts only from U.S. to ISO format. It does not perform validity checking on date subparts or allow the transition point for adding the century to be specified. A more general tool would be more useful. The next script, *cvt_date.pl*, extends the capabilities of *isoize_date.pl*; it recognizes input dates in ISO, US, or British formats and converts any of them to any other. It also can convert two-digit years to four digits, allows you to specify the conversion transition point, and can warn about bad dates. As such, it can be used to preprocess input for loading into MySQL, or for postprocessing data exported from MySQL for use by other programs.

cvt_date.pl understands the following options:

--iformat=format, --oformat=format, --format=format,
> Set the date format for input, output, or both. The default *format* value is iso; *cvt_date.pl* also recognizes any string beginning with us or br as indicating U.S. or British date format.

--add-century
> Convert two-digit years to four digits.

--columns=column_list
> Convert dates only in the named columns. By default, *cvt_date.pl* looks for dates in all columns. If this option is given, *column_list* should be a list of one or more column positions separated by commas. Positions begin at 1.

--transition=n
> Specify the transition point for two-digit to four-digit year conversions. The default transition point is 70. This option turns on *--add-century*.

--warn
> Warn about bad dates. (Note that this option can produce spurious warnings if the dates have two-digit years and you don't specify *--add-century*, because leap year testing won't always be accurate in that case.)

I won't show the code for *cvt_date.pl* here (most of it is taken up with processing command-line options), but you can examine the source for yourself if you like. As an example of how *cvt_date.pl* works, suppose you have a file *newdata.txt* with the following contents:

```
name1   01/01/99    38
name2   12/31/00    40
name3   02/28/01    42
name4   01/02/03    44
```

Running the file through *cvt_date.pl* with options indicating that the dates are in U.S. format and that the century should be added produces this result:

```
% cvt_date.pl --iformat=us --add-century newdata.txt
name1   1999-01-01  38
name2   2000-12-31  40
name3   2001-02-28  42
name4   2003-01-02  44
```

To produce dates in British format instead with no year conversion, do this:

```
% cvt_date.pl --iformat=us --oformat=br newdata.txt
name1   01-01-99    38
name2   31-12-00    40
name3   28-02-01    42
name4   02-01-03    44
```

cvt_date.pl has no knowledge of the meaning of each data column, of course. If you have a non-date column with values that match the pattern, it will rewrite that column, too. To deal with that, specify a *--columns* option to limit the columns that *cvt_date.pl* attempts to convert.

isoize_date.pl and *cvt_date.pl* both operate on dates written in all-numeric formats. But dates in datafiles often are written differently, in which case it may be necessary to write a special purpose script to process them. Suppose an input file contains dates in the following format (these represent the dates on which U.S. states were admitted to the Union):

```
Delaware        Dec. 7, 1787
Pennsylvania    Dec 12, 1787
New Jersey      Dec. 18, 1787
Georgia         Jan. 2, 1788
Connecticut     Jan. 9, 1788
Massachusetts   Feb. 6, 1788
Maryland        Apr. 28, 1788
South Carolina  May 23, 1788
New Hampshire   Jun. 21, 1788
Virginia        Jun 25, 1788
...
```

The dates consist of a three-character month abbreviation (possibly followed by a period), the numeric day of the month, a comma, and the numeric year. To import this file into MySQL, you'd need to convert the dates to ISO format, resulting in a file that looks like this:

```
Delaware          1787-12-07
Pennsylvania      1787-12-12
New Jersey        1787-12-18
Georgia           1788-01-02
Connecticut       1788-01-09
Massachusetts     1788-02-06
Maryland          1788-04-28
South Carolina    1788-05-23
New Hampshire     1788-06-21
Virginia          1788-06-25
...
```

That's a somewhat specialized kind of transformation, though this general type of problem (converting a specific date format) is hardly uncommon. To perform the conversion, identify the dates as those values matching an appropriate pattern, map month names to the corresponding numeric values, and reformat the result. The following script, *monddccyy_to_iso.pl*, illustrates how to do this:

```perl
#! /usr/bin/perl -w
# monddccyy_to_iso.pl - convert dates from mon[.] dd, ccyy to ISO format

# Assumes tab-delimited, linefeed-terminated input

use strict;

my %map =          # map 3-char month abbreviations to numeric month
(
    "jan" => 1, "feb" => 2, "mar" => 3, "apr" => 4, "may" => 5, "jun" => 6,
    "jul" => 7, "aug" => 8, "sep" => 9, "oct" => 10, "nov" => 11, "dec" => 12
);

while (<>)
{
    chomp;
    my @val = split (/\t/, $_, 10000);      # split, preserving all fields
    for my $i (0 .. @val - 1)
    {
        # reformat the value if it matches the pattern, otherwise assume
        # it's not a date in the required format and leave it alone
        if ($val[$i] =~ /^([^.]+)\.? (\d+), (\d+)$/)
        {
            # use lowercase month name
            my ($month, $day, $year) = (lc ($1), $2, $3);
            if (exists ($map{$month}))
            {
                $val[$i] = sprintf ("%04d-%02d-%02d",
                                    $year, $map{$month}, $day);
            }
            else
```

```
            {
                # warn, but don't reformat
                warn "$val[$i]: bad date?\n";
            }
        }
    }
    print join ("\t", @val) . "\n";
}

exit (0);
```

The script only does reformatting, it doesn't validate the dates. To do that, modify the script to use the *Cookbook_Utils.pm* module by adding this statement after the use strict line:

```
use Cookbook_Utils;
```

That gives the script access to the module's is_valid_date() routine. To use it, change the reformatting section of the script to look like this:

```
if (exists ($map{$month})
        && is_valid_date ($year, $map{$month}, $day))
{
    $val[$i] = sprintf ("%04d-%02d-%02d",
                        $year, $map{$month}, $day);
}
else
{
    # warn, but don't reformat
    warn "$val[$i]: bad date?\n";
}
```

10.32 Using Dates with Missing Components

Problem

The dates in your data are incomplete, that is, they have missing subparts.

Solution

MySQL can represent them as ISO dates using zero for the missing parts.

Discussion

Some applications use dates that are not complete. For example, you may need to work with input values such as Mar/2001 that contain only a month and year. As of MySQL 3.23, it's possible to represent such values as ISO-format dates that have zero in the "missing" parts. (The value Mar/2001 can be stored as 2001-03-00.) To convert month/year values to ISO format for import into MySQL, set up a hash to map month names to their numeric values:

```
my %map =           # map 3-char month abbreviations to numeric month
(
    "jan" => 1, "feb" => 2, "mar" => 3, "apr" => 4, "may" => 5, "jun" => 6,
    "jul" => 7, "aug" => 8, "sep" => 9, "oct" => 10, "nov" => 11, "dec" => 12
);
```

Then convert each input value like this:

```
if ($val =~ /^([a-z]{3})\/(\d{4})$/i)
{
    my ($m, $y) = (lc ($1), $2); # use lowercase month name
    $val = sprintf ("%04d-%02d-00", $y, $map{$m})
}
```

After storing the resulting values into MySQL, you can retrieve them for display in the original month/year format by issuing a SELECT statement that rewrites the dates using a DATE_FORMAT() expression:

```
DATE_FORMAT(date_val,'%b/%Y')
```

10.33 Performing Date Conversion Using SQL

Problem

You want to convert dates using SQL statements.

Solution

For export, use the DATE_FORMAT() function to rewrite the values. For import, read the values into a string column and convert them to true DATE values.

Discussion

Suppose you want to export data from MySQL into an application that doesn't understand ISO-format dates. One way to do this is to export the data into a file, leaving the dates in ISO format. Then run the file through some kind of utility like *cvt_date.pl* that rewrites the dates into the required format.

Another approach is to export the dates directly in the required format by rewriting them with DATE_FORMAT(). Suppose you need to export data from a table, but with the dates written in U.S. (*MM-DD-CCYY*) format. The following script can accomplish this. It takes the names of a database and table as its arguments, then dumps the table in tab-delimited format with the dates in any DATE, DATETIME, or TIMESTAMP columns reformatted. The script does this by examining the table metadata to get the column types, then constructing a SELECT statement that uses DATE_FORMAT() to rewrite the dates. Other columns in the table are written without change:

```perl
#! /usr/bin/perl -w
# iso_to_us.pl - Export a table with dates rewritten from ISO format
# (CCYY-MM-DD) to U.S. format (MM-DD-CCYY).  This is done by generating a
# SELECT statement that selects all the columns of the table, but uses
# DATE_FORMAT() to rewrite the dates.

# Writes each row as a tab-delimited, linefeed-terminated line.

use strict;
use DBI;

# ... process command-line options (not shown) ...

@ARGV == 2 or die "Usage: $0 [options] db_name tbl_name\n";
my $db_name = shift (@ARGV);
my $tbl_name = shift (@ARGV);

# ... connect to database (not shown) ...

# Read table metadata from MySQL to get colum names and types.  Use the
# types to detect DATE, DATETIME, and TIMESTAMP columns so their contents
# can be rewritten with DATE_FORMAT().

my @col;

my $sth = $dbh->prepare ("SHOW COLUMNS FROM $tbl_name");
$sth->execute ();
while (my @row = $sth->fetchrow_array ())
{
    if ($row[1] =~ /^datetime|timestamp/)
    {
        $row[0] = "DATE_FORMAT($row[0], '%m-%d-%Y %T') AS $row[0]";
    }
    elsif ($row[1] =~ /^date/)
    {
        $row[0] = "DATE_FORMAT($row[0], '%m-%d-%Y') AS $row[0]";
    }
    push (@col, $row[0]);
}
my $query = "SELECT\n\t" . join (",\n\t", @col) . "\nFROM $tbl_name";

# Execute SELECT statement and dump out the result

$sth = $dbh->prepare ($query);
$sth->execute ();
while (my @val = $sth->fetchrow_array ())
{
    # convert NULL (undef) values to empty strings
    @val = map { defined ($_) ? $_ : "" } @val;
    print join ("\t", @val) . "\n";
}
```

```
$dbh->disconnect ();

exit (0);
```

To see how this script works, suppose you have the following table:

```
CREATE TABLE datetbl
(
    i   INT,
    c   CHAR(10),
    d   DATE,
    dt  DATETIME,
    ts  TIMESTAMP
);
```

The SELECT statement that the script constructs to export the contents of datetbl looks like this:

```
SELECT
    i,
    c,
    DATE_FORMAT(d, '%m-%d-%Y') AS d,
    DATE_FORMAT(dt, '%m-%d-%Y %T') AS dt,
    DATE_FORMAT(ts, '%m-%d-%Y %T') AS ts
FROM datetbl
```

Thus, if datetbl contains the following rows:

```
3    abc    2001-12-31    2001-12-31 12:05:03    20011231120503
4    xyz    2002-01-31    2002-01-31 12:05:03    20020131120503
```

The script generates output that looks like this:

```
3    abc    12-31-2001    12-31-2001 12:05:03    12-31-2001 12:05:03
4    xyz    01-31-2002    01-31-2002 12:05:03    01-31-2002 12:05:03
```

Going in the other direction (to import non-ISO dates into MySQL), normally you convert the dates to ISO format first. Otherwise, you must import them as character strings, which reduces their usefulness in temporal contexts. However, in some cases, you can import non-ISO dates as strings, then convert them to ISO-format DATE values afterward using SQL statements. Recipe 10.34 shows an example of this technique.

See Also

A variation on the technique of rewriting dates at export time is used in Recipe 10.40, which discusses a *mysql_to_filemaker.pl* script that exports MySQL tables for use with FileMaker Pro. The script uses DATE_FORMAT( ) to rewrite dates in the MM-DD-CCYY format expected by FileMaker Pro. It also uses DATE_FORMAT( ) to split date-and-time values into separate date and time columns, because FileMaker Pro has no analog for MySQL's DATETIME or TIMESTAMP column types.

10.34 Using Temporary Tables
for Data Transformation

Problem

You want to preprocess input data for MySQL, but you don't have access to external utilities for doing so.

Solution

Load the data into a temporary table, reformat it using SQL statements, then copy the records into the final destination table.

Discussion

To work with information that must be checked or transformed before it's ready to be added to a table, it's sometimes helpful to load a datafile into a temporary table first for validation purposes. (It's generally easier to work with a dataset that is isolated into its own table rather than combined with other records.) After you have made sure that the temporary table's contents are satisfactory, copy its rows to the main table and then drop it. (Note that the use of "temporary" in this context doesn't necessarily imply that you must use the keyword TEMPORARY when creating the table.* If you process the table in multiple phases over the course of several server connections, you'll need to create a non-TEMPORARY table, then drop it explicitly when you're done with it.)

The following example illustrates how to use a temporary table to solve a common problem: loading data into a table when the values do not have the format required by the table structure. Suppose you have a table main that contains three columns, name, date, and value, where date is a DATE column requiring values in ISO format (*CCYY-MM-DD*). Suppose also that you're given a datafile *newdata.txt* to be imported into the table, but the contents look like this:

```
name1    01/01/99    38
name2    12/31/00    40
name3    02/28/01    42
name4    01/02/03    44
```

Here the dates are in *MM/DD/YY* format and must be converted to ISO format to be stored as DATE values in MySQL. One way to do this would be to run the file through the *cvt_date.pl* script shown earlier in the chapter:

```
% cvt_date.pl --iformat=us --add-century newdata.txt >tmp
```

* CREATE TEMPORARY TABLE is discussed in Recipe 3.24.

Then you can load the *tmp* file into the main table. But this task also can be accomplished entirely in MySQL with no external utilities by importing the data into a temporary table and using SQL to perform the reformatting operations. Here's how:

1. Create an empty table in which to load the test data. The following statements create the table tmp as an empty copy of main and add a cdate column to hold the dates from the datafile as character strings:

```
mysql> CREATE TABLE tmp SELECT * FROM main WHERE 1 < 0;
mysql> ALTER TABLE tmp ADD cdate CHAR(8);
```

2. Load the datafile into the temporary table, storing the date values in the cdate column rather than in date:

```
mysql> LOAD DATA LOCAL INFILE 'newdata.txt' INTO TABLE tmp (name,cdate,value);
```

3. Transform the cdate values from *MM/DD/YY* format to *YY-MM-DD* format and store the results in the date column:

```
mysql> UPDATE tmp
    -> SET date = CONCAT(RIGHT(cdate,2),'-',LEFT(cdate,2),'-',MID(cdate,4,2));
```

MySQL will convert the two-digit years to four-digit years automatically, so the original *MM/DD/YY* values in the cdate column end up in the date column as ISO values in *CCYY-MM-DD* format. The following query shows what the original cdate values and the transformed date values look like after the UPDATE statement has been performed:

```
mysql> SELECT cdate, date FROM tmp;
+----------+------------+
| cdate    | date       |
+----------+------------+
| 01/01/99 | 1999-01-01 |
| 12/31/00 | 2000-12-31 |
| 02/28/01 | 2001-02-28 |
| 01/02/03 | 2003-01-02 |
+----------+------------+
```

4. Finally, copy the records from tmp to main (using the transformed date values rather than the original cdate values) and drop the temporary table:

```
mysql> INSERT INTO main (name, date, value)
    -> SELECT name, date, value FROM tmp;
mysql> DROP TABLE tmp;
```

This procedure assumes that MySQL's automatic conversion of two-digit years to four digits produces the correct century values. This means that the year part of the values must correspond to years in the range from 1970 to 2069. If that's not true, you'd need to convert the year values some other way. (See Recipe 10.29.)

The procedure also assumes that the cdate values are always exactly eight characters so that LEFT(), MID(), and RIGHT() can be used to extract the pieces. If this assumption is invalid, you'd have to modify the conversion procedure. One possibility would be to use SUBSTRING_INDEX() to break apart the strings at the / delimiters:

```
mysql> UPDATE tmp
    -> SET date =
```

```
    -> CONCAT(SUBSTRING_INDEX(cdate,'/',-1),'-',
    -> SUBSTRING_INDEX(cdate,'/',1),'-',
    -> SUBSTRING_INDEX(SUBSTRING_INDEX(cdate,'/',2),'/',-1));
```

Another application for post-import processing is name splitting. If you import values consisting of a first name, a space, and a last name into a column full_name, you can reformat the column into separate first_name and last_name columns with these statements:

```
UPDATE tbl_name SET first_name = SUBSTRING_INDEX(full_name,' ',1);
UPDATE tbl_name SET last_name = SUBSTRING_INDEX(full_name,' ',-1);
```

However, this task can easily become more difficult if any of the names have middle initials, or trailing words like Jr. or Sr. If that's the case, you're probably better off preprocessing the names prior to import, using a pattern matching utility that's smarter about breaking full names into components.

10.35 Dealing with NULL Values

Problem

You're not sure how to represent NULL values in a datafile.

Solution

Try to use a value not otherwise present, so that you can distinguish NULL from all other legitimate non-NULL values.

Discussion

There's no particular standard for representing NULL values in datafiles, which makes them a bit of a problem for import and export operations. Some of the difficulty arises from the fact that NULL indicates the *lack* of a value, and something that's not there is not easy to represent literally in a datafile. Using an empty column value is the most obvious thing to do, but that's ambiguous for string-valued columns because there is no way to distinguish a NULL represented that way from a true empty string. Empty values can be a problem for other column types as well. For example, if you load an empty value with LOAD DATA into a numeric column, it gets stored as 0 rather than as NULL, and thus becomes indistinguishable from a true 0 in the input.

The usual strategy for dealing with this problem is to represent NULL using a value that doesn't otherwise occur in the data. This is how LOAD DATA and *mysqlimport* handle the issue, with \N as the value that is understood by convention to mean NULL. Based on that fact, it's sometimes helpful to convert empty fields in a datafile to \N so that LOAD DATA will interpret them as NULL. It's easy to write a script that does this:

```
#! /usr/bin/perl -w
# empty_to_null.pl - Convert empty input fields to \N.
```

```
# \N is the MySQL LOAD DATA convention for NULL.  Running a file
# through this script and loading the result causes NULL to be loaded
# rather than empty strings.

# Assumes tab-delimited, linefeed-terminated input lines.

use strict;

while (<>)
{
    chomp;
    my @val = split (/\t/, $_, 10000);  # split, preserving all fields
    # map empty fields to \N, write as tab-delimited output line
    print join ("\t", map { /^$/ ? "\\N" : $_ } @val) . "\n";
}

exit (0);
```

You might use the script like this:

```
% empty_to_null.pl mytbl.txt > mytbl.txt2
% mysqlimport --local cookbook mytbl.txt2
```

Loading a file that has been run through the *empty_to_null.pl* script often can produce better results for columns that allow NULL values. This is shown by the following table, which compares the values that result when you use LOAD DATA or *mysqlimport* to load either an empty string or \N (NULL) into various column types when those columns allow NULL values:

Column type	Result of loading empty string	Result of loading \N
CHAR	Empty string	NULL
INT	0	NULL
DATE	0000-00-00	NULL

But what happens if you load \N rather than an empty string into columns that are defined as NOT NULL? As it happens, it doesn't make any difference either way, as shown in the next table:

Column type	Result of loading empty string	Result of loading \N
CHAR	Empty string	Empty string
INT	0	0
DATE	0000-00-00	0000-00-00

This means that it's not worth it to write a smarter version of *empty_to_null.pl* that looks at the structure of the table you want to load the data into and converts empty strings to \N only for columns that allow NULL values.

On the other hand, one reason that it *is* worth writing a smarter script is that you might want to interpret values other than empty values as signifying NULL, and you might have different conventions in different columns. Consider the following data-file, *has_nulls.txt*:

```
str1     13
str2     0
Unknown 15
Unknown 0
```

The first column contains strings, and Unknown signifies NULL. The second column contains integers, and 0 signifies NULL. What to do? To handle that kind of file, the *transfer* directory of the recipes distribution contains a *to_null.pl* script. It provides options allowing you to specify both which columns to look in and what value to look for:

--columns=column_list

Convert values only in the named columns. By default, *to_null.pl* looks in all columns. If this option is given, `column_list` should be a list of one or more column positions separated by commas. Positions begin at 1.

--null=value

Interpret `value` as the NULL value indicator and convert instances of it to \N. The default is to convert empty values, like *empty_to_null.pl*.

--case-insensitive, -i

Perform a case-insensitive comparison when looking for the NULL value indicator.

Because the *has_nulls.txt* datafile has two different NULL value indicators, it's necessary to process it using two invocations of *to_null.pl*:

```
% to_null.pl --columns=1 --null=Unknown has_nulls.txt \
    | to_null.pl --columns=2 --null=0 > tmp
```

The resulting file, *tmp*, looks like this:

```
str1    13
str2    \N
\N      15
\N      \N
```

Sometimes you don't need to preprocess your input file if you can postprocess it after importing it. For example, if a datafile contains a numeric column that uses -1 to represent NULL values, you can easily convert all -1 values after loading the file using a simple UPDATE statement:

```
UPDATE tbl_name SET col_name = NULL WHERE col_name = -1;
```

The preceding discussion pertains to interpreting NULL values for import into MySQL. It's also necessary to think about NULL values when transferring data the other way—from MySQL into other programs. Here are some examples:

- SELECT INTO ... OUTFILE writes NULL values as \N. Will another program understand that convention? If not, you'll need to convert \N to something the program will understand.

- You can use *mysql* in batch mode as an easy way to produce tab-delimited output (see Recipe 10.13), but one problem with doing so is that NULL values appear in the output as instances of the word "NULL." If that word occurs nowhere else in the output, you may be able to postprocess it to convert instances of the word to something more appropriate. A script similar to *empty_to_null.pl* would be easy to write, or you could use a one-line *sed* command:

  ```
  % sed -e "s/NULL/\\N/g" data.txt > tmp
  ```

  If the word "NULL" does appear where it represents something other than a NULL value, then it's ambiguous and you should probably use a different method of exporting your data.

10.36 Guessing Table Structure from a Datafile

Problem

Someone gives you a datafile and says, "Here, put this into MySQL for me." But no table yet exists to hold the data.

Solution

Write the CREATE TABLE statement yourself. Or use a utility that guesses the table structure by examining the contents of the datafile.

Discussion

Sometimes you need to import data into MySQL for which no table has yet been set up. You can create the table yourself, based on any knowledge you might have about the contents of the file. Or you may be able to avoid some of the work by using *guess_table.pl*, a utility located in the *transfer* directory of the recipes distribution. *guess_table.pl* reads the datafile to see what kind of information it contains, then attempts to produce an appropriate CREATE TABLE statement that matches the contents of the file. This script is necessarily imperfect, because column contents sometimes are ambiguous. (For example, a column containing a small number of distinct strings might be a CHAR column or an ENUM.) Still, it's often easier to tweak the statement that *guess_table.pl* produces than to write the entire statement from scratch. This utility also has a diagnostic function, though that's not its primary purpose. For example, you might believe a column contains only numbers, but if *guess_table.pl* indicates that it should be created using a CHAR type, that tells you the column contains at least one non-numeric value.

guess_table.pl assumes that its input is in tab-delimited, linefeed-terminated format. It also assumes valid input, because any attempt to guess column types based on possibly flawed data is doomed to failure. This means, for example, that if a date column is to be recognized as such, it should be in ISO format. Otherwise, *guess_table.pl* may characterize it as a CHAR column. If a datafile doesn't satisfy these assumptions, you may be able to reformat it first using the *cvt_file.pl* and *cvt_date.pl* utilities described in Recipes 10.18 and 10.31.

guess_table.pl understands the following options:

--labels
Interpret the first input line as a row of column labels and use them for table column names. If this option is omitted, *guess_table.pl* uses default column names of c1, c2, and so forth. Note that if the file contains a row of labels and you neglect to specify this option, the labels will be treated as data values by *guess_table.pl*. The likely result is that the script will mischaracterize any numeric column as a CHAR column, due to the presence of a non-numeric value in the column.

--lower, --upper
Force column names in the CREATE TABLE statement to be lowercase or uppercase.

--quote-names
Quote table and column names in the CREATE TABLE statement with ` characters (for example, `mytbl`). This can be useful if a name is a reserved word. The resulting statement requires MySQL 3.23.6, because quoted names are not understood by earlier versions.

--report
Generate a report rather than a CREATE TABLE statement. The script displays the information that it gathered about each column.

--tbl_name=tbl_name
Specify the table name to use in the CREATE TABLE statement. The default name is t.

Here's an example of how *guess_table.pl* works, using the *managers.csv* file from the CSV version of the *baseball1.com* baseball database distribution. This file contains records for team managers. It begins with a row of column labels, followed by rows containing data values:

```
LahmanID,Year,Team,Lg,DIV,G,W,L,Pct,Std,Half,Order,PlyrMgr,PostWins,PostLosses
cravebi01,1871,TRO,NA,,25,12,12,0.5,6,0,2,,,
deaneha01,1871,KEK,NA,,5,2,3,0.4,8,0,2,,,
hastisc01,1871,ROK,NA,,25,4,21,0.16,9,0,0,,,
paborch01,1871,CLE,NA,,29,10,19,0.345,7,0,0,,,
wrighha01,1871,BOS,NA,,31,20,10,0.667,3,0,0,,,
youngni99,1871,OLY,NA,,32,15,15,0.5,5,0,0,,,
clappjo01,1872,MAN,NA,,24,5,19,0.208,8,0,0,,,
clintji01,1872,ECK,NA,,11,0,11,0,9,0,1,,,
fergubo01,1872,BRA,NA,,37,9,28,0.243,6,0,0,,,
...
```

The first row indicates the column labels, and the following rows contain data records, one per line. *guess_table.pl* requires input in tab-delimited, linefeed-terminated format, so to work with the *managers.csv* file, first convert it using *cvt_file.pl*, writing the result to a temporary file, *managers.txt*:

```
% cvt_file.pl --iformat=csv --ieol="\r\n" managers.csv > managers.txt
```

Then run the temporary file through *guess_table.pl* (the command shown here uses
--lower because I prefer lowercase column names):

```
% guess_table.pl --table=managers --labels --lower managers.txt > managers.sql
```

The CREATE TABLE statement that *guess_table.pl* writes to *managers.sql* looks like this:

```
CREATE TABLE managers
(
    lahmanid CHAR(9) NOT NULL,
    year INT UNSIGNED NOT NULL,
    team CHAR(3) NOT NULL,
    lg CHAR(2) NOT NULL,
    div CHAR(1) NULL,
    g INT UNSIGNED NOT NULL,
    w INT UNSIGNED NOT NULL,
    l INT UNSIGNED NOT NULL,
    pct FLOAT NOT NULL,
    std INT UNSIGNED NOT NULL,
    half INT UNSIGNED NOT NULL,
    order INT UNSIGNED NOT NULL,
    plyrmgr CHAR(1) NULL,
    postwins INT UNSIGNED NULL,
    postlosses INT UNSIGNED NULL
);
```

guess_table.pl produces that statement based on deductions such as the following:

- If a column contains only integer values, it's assumed to be an INT. If none of the
  values are negative, the column is likely to be UNSIGNED as well.

- If a column contains no empty values, *guess_table.pl* assumes that it's probably
  NOT NULL.

- Columns that cannot be classified as numbers or dates are taken to be CHAR columns, with a length equal to the longest value present in the column.

You might want to edit the CREATE TABLE statement that *guess_table.pl* produces, to
make modifications such as increasing the size of character fields, changing CHAR to
VARCHAR, or adding indexes. Another reason to edit the statement is that if a column
has a name that is a reserved word in MySQL, you can change it to a different name.
For example, the managers table definition created by *guess_table.pl* contains a column named order, which is a reserved keyword. The column represents the order of
the manager during the season (in case a team had more than one manager), so a reasonable alternative name is mgrorder. After editing the statement in the *managers.sql*
file to make that change, execute it to create the table:

```
% mysql cookbook < managers.sql
```

Then you can load the datafile into the table (skipping the initial row of labels):

```
mysql> LOAD DATA LOCAL INFILE 'managers.txt' INTO TABLE managers
    -> IGNORE 1 LINES;
```

(When you do this, you'll notice that LOAD DATA reports some warnings. These are investigated further in Recipe 10.37.)

The *baseball1.com* database also is available in Access format. The Access database contains explicit information about the structure of the managers table, and this information is available to utilities like DBTools and MySQLFront that can use it to create the MySQL table for you. (See Recipe 10.38 for information about these programs.) This affords us the opportunity to see how well *guess_table.pl* guesses the table structure using only the datafile, compared to programs that have more information available to them.

One problem with utilities like DBTools or MySQLFront is that if an Access table column has a name that is a reserved word, you cannot import it into MySQL without changing the Access table to use a different column name. This is the case for the Order column in the managers table. With *guess_table.pl*, that wasn't a problem, because you can just edit the CREATE TABLE statement that it produces to change the name to something legal.* However, to deal with the Order column in the managers table for purposes of DBTools or MySQLFront, you should change the Access database itself to rename the column (for example, to MgrOrder.)

The managers table structure produced by DBTools looks like this:

```
CREATE TABLE managers (
  LahmanID char(9) NOT NULL default '',
  Year int(11) default NULL,
  Team char(3) default NULL,
  Lg char(2) default NULL,
  Div char(2) default NULL,
  G int(11) default NULL,
  W int(11) default NULL,
  L int(11) default NULL,
  Pct double default NULL,
  Std int(11) default NULL,
  Half int(11) default NULL,
  MgrOrder int(11) default NULL,
  PlyrMgr char(1) default NULL,
  PostWins int(11) default NULL,
  PostLosses int(11) default NULL,
  KEY LahmanID (LahmanID)
);
```

MySQLFront creates the table like this:

```
CREATE TABLE managers (
  LahmanID longtext,
  Year int(11) default NULL,
  Team longtext,
  Lg longtext,
```

---

* Another approach is to use the *--quote-names* option when you run *guess_table.pl*. That allows you to create the table without changing the column name, although then you must put the name within backticks whether you refer to it.

```
    Div longtext,
    G int(11) default NULL,
    W int(11) default NULL,
    L int(11) default NULL,
    Pct float default NULL,
    Std int(11) default NULL,
    Half int(11) default NULL,
    MgrOrder int(11) default NULL,
    PlyrMgr longtext,
    PostWins int(11) default NULL,
    PostLosses int(11) default NULL
);
```

Of the three programs, DBTools does the best job of determining the structure of the MySQL table. It uses the index information present in the Access file to write the KEY definition, and to create string columns with the proper lengths. MySQLFront doesn't produce the key definition and it defines strings as LONGTEXT columns—even the PlyrMgr column, which never contains a value longer than one character. The quality of the output produced by *guess_table.pl* appears to be somewhere in between. It doesn't write the key definition, but neither does it write every string column as the longest possible type. (On the other hand, the column lengths are somewhat conservative.) All in all, that's not bad, considering that *guess_table.pl* doesn't have available to it all the information contained in the original Access file. And you can use it on a cross-platform basis.

These results indicate that if you're using Windows and your records are stored in an Access file, you're probably best off letting DBTools create your MySQL tables for you. In other situations (such as when you're running under Unix or your datafile comes from a source other than Access), *guess_table.pl* can be beneficial.

10.37 A LOAD DATA Diagnostic Utility

Problem

LOAD DATA or *mysqlimport* indicates a nonzero warning count when you load a datafile into MySQL, but you have no idea which rows or columns were problematic.

Solution

Run the file through a utility that diagnoses which data values caused the warnings.

Discussion

As a bulk loader, LOAD DATA is very efficient; it can run many times faster than a set of INSERT statements that adds the same rows. However, LOAD DATA also is not very informative. It returns only a message that indicates the number of records processed, and a few other status counts. For example, in the previous section, we generated a datafile *managers.txt* to use with *guess_table.pl* for guessing the structure of the *baseball1.com* managers table. If you create that table using the resulting CREATE TABLE statement and then load the datafile into it, you will observe the following result:

```
mysql> LOAD DATA LOCAL INFILE 'managers.txt' INTO TABLE managers
    -> IGNORE 1 LINES;
Query OK, 2841 rows affected (0.06 sec)
Records: 2841  Deleted: 0  Skipped: 0  Warnings: 5082
```

Evidently, there were a quite a few problems with the file. Unfortunately, the message produced by LOAD DATA doesn't tell you anything about which rows and columns caused them. The *mysqlimport* program is similarly terse, because its message is the same as the one returned by LOAD DATA.

We'll revisit this example at the end of the section, but first consider LOAD DATA's output style. On the one hand, the minimal-report approach is the right one to take. If warning information were to be returned to the client, it potentially could include a diagnostic message for each input row, or even for each column! This might be overwhelming and certainly would entirely defeat the high-efficiency nature of LOAD DATA. On the other hand, more information about the source of errors could be useful for fixing the file to eliminate the warnings.

It's on the MySQL development "to do" list to allow LOAD DATA errors to be logged to another table so that you can get extended diagnostic information. In the meantime, you can use the *load_diag.pl* utility included in the *transfer* directory of the recipes distribution. *load_diag.pl* is useful for "pre-flighting" a datafile to get an idea of how well the file will load into the table you intend it for, and to pinpoint problems so that you can clean up the file before loading it into MySQL "for real."

load_diag.pl also can help you identify patterns of problems for situations in which it may be beneficial to write a preprocessing filter. Suppose you periodically receive files containing data to be loaded into a given MySQL table. The more frequently this occurs, the more highly motivated you'll be to automate as much of the data transfer process as possible. This may involve writing a filter to convert data values from the format in which you receive them to a format more appropriate for MySQL. Running the datafiles through *load_diag.pl* can help you assess which columns tend to be problematic and thereby assist you in determining where to concentrate your efforts in creating a transformation program for rewriting the files so they will load cleanly into MySQL.

To run *load_diag.pl*, specify the name of the database and table you intend to load the datafile into, as well as the name of the file itself:

```
% load_diag.pl db_name tbl_name file_name
```

load_diag.pl won't actually load anything into the table named on the command line, but it needs to know what the table is so that it can create a temporary table that has the same column structure to use for testing.

Initially, *load_diag.pl* loads the entire datafile into the temporary table to see if there are any warnings. If not, there's nothing else to do, so *load_diag.pl* drops the temporary table and exits. Otherwise, it loads each line of the datafile into the table individually to determine which lines caused problems, using the following procedure:

- It writes the line to a temporary file and issues a LOAD DATA statement to load the file into the table. If the warning count is zero, the line is assumed to be okay.

- If the warning count for the line is nonzero, *load_diag.pl* examines each of its columns in turn by using a series of single-column LOAD DATA statements to find out which ones generate warnings.

- If a column-specific warning occurs and the data value is empty, *load_diag.pl* determines whether the warning goes away by loading a NULL value instead. It does this because if a datafile contains empty values, you can often get better results by loading NULL than by loading empty strings. (For example, if you load an empty string into an INT column, MySQL converts the value to 0 and issues a warning.) If a datafile turns out to have a significant reduction in warnings when loading NULL rather than empty strings, you may find it useful to run the file through *to_null.pl* before loading it.

- It's also possible for warnings to occur if a line contains fewer or more columns than the number of columns in the table, so *load_diag.pl* checks that, too.

load_diag.pl prints diagnostic information about its findings while testing each input line, then prints a summary report after the entire file has been processed. The report indicates the number of lines in the file, how many warnings the initial full-file load caused, and the number of lines that had too few or too many columns. The report also includes a list that shows for each column how many values were missing, the number of warnings that occurred, how many of those warnings occurred for empty values, and the number of empty-value warnings that went away by loading NULL instead.

As you might guess, all this activity means that *load_diag.pl* isn't nearly as efficient as LOAD DATA. In fact, it has the potential to exercise your server rather heavily! But its goal is to provide maximal information, not minimal execution time. (Note too that if your MySQL server has logging enabled, using *load_diag.pl* with large datafiles can cause the logs to grow quickly.)

To see how *load_diag.pl* works, assume you have a simple table named diag_test that contains string, date, and number columns:

```
CREATE TABLE diag_test
(
    str     CHAR(10),
    date    DATE,
    num     INT
);
```

Assume you also have a datafile named *diag_sample.dat* that you plan to load into the table:

```
str1    01-20-2001    97
str2    02-28-2002
        03-01-2002    64    extra junk
```

To see if the file will have any problems loading, check it like this:

```
% load_diag.pl cookbook diag_test diag_sample.dat
line 1: 1 warning
  column 2 (date): bad value = (01-20-2001)
line 2: 2 warnings
  too few columns
  column 2 (date): bad value = (02-28-2002)
  column 3 (num): missing from input line
  column 3 (num): bad value = () (inserting NULL worked better)
line 3: 1 warning
  excess number of columns

Number of lines in file: 3
Warnings found when loading entire file: 4
Lines containing too few column values: 1
Lines containing excess column values: 1

Warnings per column:
```

Column	Times missing	Total warnings	Warnings for empty columns	Improved with NULL
str	0	0	0	0
date	0	2	0	0
num	1	1	1	1

It appears that the dates don't load very well. That's not surprising, because they appear to be in U.S. format and should be rewritten in ISO format. Converting empty fields to \N may also be beneficial, and you can get rid of the extra column value in line 3. Using some of the utilities developed earlier in this chapter, perform all those transformations, writing the result to a temporary file:

```
% yank_col.pl --columns=1-3 diag_sample.dat \
    | cvt_date.pl --iformat=us --oformat=iso \
    | to_null.pl > tmp
```

The *tmp* file produced by that command looks like this:

```
str1    2001-01-20    97
str2    2002-02-28    \N
\N      2002-03-01    64
```

Using *load_diag.pl* to check the new file produces the following result:

```
% load_diag.pl cookbook diag_test tmp
File loaded with no warnings, no per-record tests performed
```

This indicates that if you load *tmp* into the diag_test table, you should get good results, and indeed that is true:

```
mysql> LOAD DATA LOCAL INFILE 'tmp' INTO TABLE diag_test;
Records: 3  Deleted: 0  Skipped: 0  Warnings: 0
```

Clearly, that's a lot of messing around just to make a three-line file load into MySQL better. But the point of the example is to illustrate that the feedback *load_diag.pl* provides can help you figure out what's wrong with a datafile so that you can clean it up.

In addition to the required arguments that name the database, table, and datafile, *load_diag.pl* understands several options:

--columns=name1,name2,name3,...
> By default, *load_diag.pl* assumes the datafile contains columns that correspond in number and order to the columns in the table. If that is not true, use this option to specify the names of the columns that are present in the file, and in what order.

--labels
> This option indicates that the datafile contains an initial row of labels that should be skipped. (Loading labels into a table typically results in spurious warnings.)

--skip-full-load
> Skip the initial test that loads the entire datafile.

--tmp-table=tbl_name
> Specify the name to use for the temporary table. The default is _load_diag_*n*, where *n* is *load_diag.pl*'s process ID.

If necessary, you can also specify standard connection parameter options like *--user* or *--host*. Any options must precede the database name argument.

Use of *load_diag.pl* is subject to the following constraints and limitations:

- The input must be in tab-delimited, linefeed-terminated format.
- Record loading is performed with the LOCAL option of the LOAD DATA statement. LOCAL capability requires MySQL 3.22.15 or higher (and, as of 3.23.49, requires that your MySQL distribution not have been built with that capability disabled).
- When *load_diag.pl* creates the temporary table, it omits any indexes that are present in the original table. This results in faster record loading time (particularly for the initial test that loads the entire datafile). On the other hand, not using indexes means that *load_diag.pl* won't find warnings that result from duplicate key values on unique indexes.

Returning to the example with which this section began, what about all those warnings that resulted from loading the *managers.txt* file into the managers table?

load_diag.pl identifies them all as being due to missing or empty columns at the end of some of the lines:

```
% load_diag.pl --labels cookbook managers managers.txt
line 2: 2 warnings
  column 14 (postwins): bad value = () (inserting NULL worked better)
  column 15 (postlosses): bad value = () (inserting NULL worked better)
line 3: 2 warnings
  column 14 (postwins): bad value = () (inserting NULL worked better)
  column 15 (postlosses): bad value = () (inserting NULL worked better)
...
line 2839: 2 warnings
  column 14 (postwins): bad value = () (inserting NULL worked better)
  column 15 (postlosses): bad value = () (inserting NULL worked better)
line 2842: 2 warnings
  column 14 (postwins): bad value = () (inserting NULL worked better)
  column 15 (postlosses): bad value = () (inserting NULL worked better)

Number of lines in file: 2842
Warnings found when loading entire file: 5082
Lines containing too few column values: 416
Lines containing excess column values: 0

Warnings per column:
```

Column	Times missing	Total warnings	Warnings for empty columns	Improved with NULL
lahmanid	0	0	0	0
year	0	0	0	0
team	0	0	0	0
lg	0	0	0	0
div	0	0	0	0
g	0	0	0	0
w	0	0	0	0
l	0	0	0	0
pct	0	0	0	0
std	0	0	0	0
half	0	0	0	0
mgrorder	0	0	0	0
plyrmgr	16	0	0	0
postwins	416	2533	2533	2533
postlosses	416	2533	2533	2533

From this result, we can determine that 416 lines were missing the postwins and postlosses columns (and 16 of those were missing the plyrmgr column as well). The remaining errors were due to lines for which the postwins and postlosses columns were present but empty. The entire-file warning count of 5082 can be accounted for as the the number of plyrmgr values that were missing, plus the total warnings from the postwins and postlosses columns (16+2533+2533 = 5082).

The Total warnings value for the plyrmgr column is zero because it's a CHAR column, and thus loading empty values into it is legal. The Total warnings value for postwins and postlosses is nonzero because they are INT columns and loading empty values into them result in a conversion-to-zero operations. All of these problems are of the sort that can be made to go away by converting empty or missing values to \N. Run the file through *yank_col.pl* to force each line to have 15 columns, and run the result through *to_null.pl* to convert empty values to \N:

```
% yank_col.pl --columns=1-15 managers.txt | to_null.pl > tmp
```

Then see what *load_diag.pl* has to say about the resulting file:

```
% load_diag.pl --labels cookbook managers tmp
File loaded with no warnings, no per-record tests performed
```

If you load *tmp* into the managers table, no problems should occur:

```
mysql> LOAD DATA LOCAL INFILE 'tmp' INTO TABLE managers IGNORE 1 LINES;
Query OK, 2841 rows affected (0.13 sec)
Records: 2841  Deleted: 0  Skipped: 0  Warnings: 0
```

10.38 Exchanging Data Between MySQL and Microsoft Access

Problem

You want to exchange information between MySQL and Access.

Solution

To use information stored in MySQL, connect to the MySQL server directly from Access. To transfer information from Access to MySQL, use a utility that can perform the transfer directly, or else export tables from Access into files and import the files into MySQL.

Discussion

MySQL and Access both understand ODBC, so you can connect to MySQL directly from Access. By making an ODBC connection, Access becomes a frontend through which you use MySQL databases. The *mysql.com* MyODBC area contains a lot of useful information:

>   *http://www.mysql.com/products/myodbc/*

An excellent description of the procedures for setting up ODBC and for connecting from Access to MySQL over ODBC may be found in W.J. Gilmore's article at the DevShed web site:

>   *http://www.devshed.com/Server_Side/MySQL/ODBC/*

If your tables currently are in Access and you want to move them into MySQL, you'll need to create tables in MySQL to hold the information and then import the Access data into those tables. A couple of good free tools that can make this easier are DBTools and MySQLFront. They can examine the structure of tables in an Access database, create the corresponding MySQL tables for you, and copy the data directly into MySQL.

You can also choose to export Access tables to files and then import the files into MySQL. (This may be necessary, for example, if your MySQL server is on a different machine and doesn't allow connections from your Windows box.) If you elect to go this route, some of the issues you'll need to consider are the file format to use, date format conversion, and how to create the MySQL tables for the data if the tables don't already exist. Several of the scripts described earlier in the chapter (such as *cvt_file.pl*, *cvt_date.pl*, and *guess_table.pl*) can provide assistance in dealing with these issues. The procedure for importing an Access table into MySQL might go something like this:

1. Export the table from Access in some text format, perhaps including the column labels. Should you need to transform the file with other utilities that assume tab-delimited, linefeed-terminated input, it will be most useful to export in that format.

2. If the table contains dates and you did not export them in ISO format, it will be necessary to convert them for MySQL. *cvt_date.pl* can be used for this.

3. If the MySQL table into which you want to import the Access data does not exist, create it. The *guess_table.pl* utility might be helpful at this point for generating a CREATE TABLE statement.

4. Import the datafile into MySQL with LOAD DATA or *mysqlimport*.

10.39 Exchanging Data Between MySQL and Microsoft Excel

Problem

You want to exchange information between MySQL and Excel.

Solution

Use utilities such as DBTools or MySQLFront. Or use Perl modules that read and write Excel spreadsheet files to construct your own data transfer utilities.

Discussion

One way to transfer Excel files into MySQL is to use the DBTools or MySQLFront utilities that were discussed in Recipe 10.38 for working with Access files. Both programs know how to read Excel files as well. But both are Windows-specific; for a more cross-platform solution that works for both Unix and Windows, you can read and write Excel spreadsheets from within Perl scripts by installing a few modules:

- *Spreadsheet::ParseExcel::Simple* provides an easy-to-use interface for reading Excel spreadsheets.

- *Spreadsheet::WriteExcel::Simple* allows you to create files in Excel spreadsheet format.

These modules are available from the Perl CPAN. (They're actually frontends to other modules, which you'll also need to install as prerequisites.) After installing the modules, use these commands to read their documentation:

```
% perldoc Spreadsheet::ParseExcel::Simple
% perldoc Spreadsheet::WriteExcel::Simple
```

These modules make it relatively easy to write a couple of short scripts (shown below) for converting spreadsheets to and from tab-delimited file format. Combined with techniques for importing and exporting data into and out of MySQL, these scripts can help you move spreadsheet contents to MySQL tables and vice versa. Use them as is, or adapt them to suit your own purposes.

The following script, *from_excel.pl*, reads an Excel spreadsheet and converts it to tab-delimited format:

```
#! /usr/bin/perl -w
# from_excel.pl - read Excel spreadsheet, write tab-delimited,
# linefeed-terminated output to the standard output.

use strict;
use Spreadsheet::ParseExcel::Simple;

@ARGV or die "Usage: $0 excel-file\n";

my $xls = Spreadsheet::ParseExcel::Simple->read ($ARGV[0]);
foreach my $sheet ($xls->sheets ())
{
    while ($sheet->has_data ())
    {
        my @data = $sheet->next_row ();
        print join ("\t", @data) . "\n";
    }
}

exit (0);
```

The *to_excel.pl* script performs the converse operation of reading a tab-delimited file and writing it in Excel format:

```perl
#! /usr/bin/perl -w
# to_excel.pl - read tab-delimited, linefeed-terminated input, write
# Excel-format output to the standard output.

use strict;
use Spreadsheet::WriteExcel::Simple;

my $ss = Spreadsheet::WriteExcel::Simple->new ();

while (<>)                                   # read each row of input
{
    chomp;
    my @data = split (/\t/, $_, 10000); # split, preserving all fields
    $ss->write_row (\@data);            # write row to the spreadsheet
}

print $ss->data (); # write the spreadsheet

exit (0);
```

to_excel.pl assumes input in tab-delimited, linefeed-terminated format. Use it in conjunction with *cvt_file.pl* to work with files that are not in that format.

Another Excel-related Perl module, *Spreadsheet::WriteExcel::FromDB*, reads data from a table using a DBI connection and writes it in Excel format. Here's a short script that exports a MySQL table as an Excel spreadsheet:

```perl
#! /usr/bin/perl -w
# mysql_to_excel.pl - given a database and table name,
# dump the table to the standard output in Excel format.

use strict;
use DBI;
use Spreadsheet::ParseExcel::Simple;
use Spreadsheet::WriteExcel::FromDB;

# ... process command-line options (not shown) ...

@ARGV == 2 or die "Usage: $0 [options] db_name tbl_name\n";
my $db_name = shift (@ARGV);
my $tbl_name = shift (@ARGV);

# ... connect to database (not shown) ...

my $ss = Spreadsheet::WriteExcel::FromDB->read ($dbh, $tbl_name);
print $ss->as_xls ();

exit (0);
```

Each of the three utilities writes to its standard output, which you can redirect to capture the results in a file:

```
% from_excel.pl data.xls > data.txt
% to_excel.pl data.txt > data.xls
% mysql_to_excel.pl cookbook profile > profile.xls
```

10.40 Exchanging Data Between MySQL and FileMaker Pro

Problem

You want to exchange information between MySQL and FileMaker Pro.

Solution

Under Windows, you can make an ODBC connection from FileMaker Pro to the MySQL server. Alternatively, you can export tables into files from MySQL and import them into FileMaker Pro, or vice versa. But watch out for conversion issues like incompatible date column types.

Discussion

If you can connect from FileMaker Pro to your MySQL server over an ODBC connection, you can access MySQL tables that way. The procedure is similar to that for connecting to MySQL from Access. (See Recipe 10.38.)

Another option is to export data from one program into files and then import them into the other program. The *transfer* directory of the recipes distribution contains a *mysql_to_filemaker.pl* utility that exports a MySQL table to a file that you can import into FileMaker Pro. This script is designed to handle the following FileMaker Pro–specific issues:

- FileMaker Pro's default date format is *MM-DD-CCYY*. The script rewrites dates the contents of any columns in the MySQL table that contain dates so that they match FileMaker Pro's date format.

- FileMaker Pro has date and time column types, but not a combined date-and-time type. *mysql_to_filemaker.pl* exports DATETIME and TIMESTAMP columns as separate DATE and TIME values. (For example, a table column named c is exported as two columns named c_date and c_time.)

- Any internal carriage returns or linefeeds in column values are mapped to Ctrl-K, which FileMaker Pro uses to represent line separators within data values.

To process date values, *mysql_to_filemaker.pl* uses a technique similar to that shown earlier in Recipe 10.33 for constructing a SELECT statement that exports table data with the dates rewritten. That is, it reads the table metadata to detect date-based columns and exports them using calls to DATE_FORMAT() that rewrite the column values into FileMaker Pro format.

mysql_to_filemaker.pl writes output in what FileMaker Pro calls merge format, which is essentially CSV format with an initial row of column labels. Merge files are useful with FileMaker Pro for a couple of reasons:

- When creating a new table from a datafile in merge format, FileMaker Pro automatically uses the labels for the column names. This makes it easy to carry along the MySQL table column names into the FileMaker Pro database.

- When importing a merge file into an existing table, having a row of column labels makes it easier to match up datafile columns with table columns.

mysql_to_filemaker.pl requires database name and table name arguments on the command line. For example, to export the contents of the mail table to a merge file *mail.mer*, you'd invoke the script like this:

```
% mysql_to_filemaker.pl cookbook mail > mail.mer
```

The mail table has a column t that contains DATETIME values. If you examine *mail.mer*, you'll see that *mysql_to_filemaker.pl* exports t as two separate columns, t_date and t_time, with the order of the date parts rearranged from ISO to MM-DD-CCYY format:

```
t_date,t_time,srcuser,srchost,dstuser,dsthost,size
05-11-2001,10:15:08,barb,saturn,tricia,mars,58274
05-12-2001,12:48:13,tricia,mars,gene,venus,194925
05-12-2001,15:02:49,phil,mars,phil,saturn,1048
05-13-2001,13:59:18,barb,saturn,tricia,venus,271
05-14-2001,09:31:37,gene,venus,barb,mars,2291
...
```

mysql_to_filemaker.pl also understands the usual options for specifying connection parameters (such as *--user* or *--host*). Any options must precede the database name argument.

After you create the merge file, you can tell FileMaker Pro to open it directly (which will create a new table) or to import it into an existing database.

To go the other direction and import a FileMaker Pro database into MySQL, use the following procedure:

1. Export the database in some text format. If you want the file to include a row of column labels, export the database in merge format. You may then want to run the file through *cvt_file.pl* to produce tab-delimited linefeed-terminated lines. This will be useful if you need to transform the file with other utilities which assume that format.

2. If the database contains dates, it may be necessary to convert them for MySQL, depending on what format FileMaker Pro uses for exporting them. FileMaker Pro will use its default MM-DD-CCYY format if you select "don't format output"

during the export procedure. If you select "display using current layout," dates will be exported using the format in which FileMaker Pro displays them. You may be able to use *cvt_date.pl* to rewrite the dates into ISO format.

3. If the MySQL table into which you want to import the FileMaker Pro data does not exist, create it. The *guess_table.pl* utility might be helpful at this point for generating a CREATE TABLE statement.

4. Import the datafile into MySQL with LOAD DATA or *mysqlimport*.

10.41 Exporting Query Results as XML

Problem

You want to export the result of a query as an XML document.

Solution

mysql can do that, or you can write your own exporter.

Discussion

To produce XML-format output from a query result, you can use *mysql* if you have MySQL 4.0 or later. See Recipe 1.24.

You can also write your own XML-export program. One way to do this is to issue the query and then write it out, adding all the XML markup yourself. But it's easier to install a few Perl modules and let them do the work:

- *XML::Generator::DBI* issues a query over a DBI connection and passes the result to a suitable output writer.

- *XML::Handler::YAWriter* provides one such writer.

The following script, *mysql_to_xml.pl*, is somewhat similar to *mysql_to_text.pl* (Recipe 10.17), but doesn't take options for such things as the quote or delimiter characters. The options that it does understand are:

--execute=query, -e query
    Execute *query* and export its output.

--table=tbl_name, -t tbl_name
    Export the contents of the named table. This is equivalent to using *--execute* to specify a *query* value of SELECT * FROM tbl_name.

If necessary, you can also specify standard connection parameter options like *--user* or *--host*. The final argument on the command line should be the database name, unless it's implicit in the query.

Suppose you want to export the contents of an experimental-data table expt that looks like this:

```
mysql> SELECT * FROM expt;
+---------+------+-------+
| subject | test | score |
+---------+------+-------+
| Jane    | A    |    47 |
| Jane    | B    |    50 |
| Jane    | C    |  NULL |
| Jane    | D    |  NULL |
| Marvin  | A    |    52 |
| Marvin  | B    |    45 |
| Marvin  | C    |    53 |
| Marvin  | D    |  NULL |
+---------+------+-------+
```

To do that, you can invoke *mysql_to_xml.pl* using either of the following commands:

```
% mysql_to_xml.pl --execute="SELECT * FROM expt" cookbook > expt.xml
% mysql_to_xml.pl --table=cookbook.expt > expt.xml
```

The resulting XML document, *expt.xml*, looks like this:

```
<?xml version="1.0" encoding="UTF-8"?>
<rowset>
 <select query="SELECT * FROM expt">
  <row>
   <subject>Jane</subject>
   <test>A</test>
   <score>47</score>
  </row>
  <row>
   <subject>Jane</subject>
   <test>B</test>
   <score>50</score>
  </row>
  <row>
   <subject>Jane</subject>
   <test>C</test>
  </row>
  <row>
   <subject>Jane</subject>
   <test>D</test>
  </row>
  <row>
   <subject>Marvin</subject>
   <test>A</test>
   <score>52</score>
  </row>
  <row>
   <subject>Marvin</subject>
   <test>B</test>
   <score>45</score>
  </row>
```

```
    <row>
     <subject>Marvin</subject>
     <test>C</test>
     <score>53</score>
    </row>
    <row>
     <subject>Marvin</subject>
     <test>D</test>
    </row>
   </select>
  </rowset>
```

Each row is written as a <row> element. Within a row, column names and values are used as element names and values, one element per column. Note that NULL values are omitted from the output.

The script does this with very little code after it processes the command-line arguments and connects to the MySQL server (not shown). The XML-related parts of *mysql_to_xml.pl* are the use statements that pull in the necessary modules and that code that sets up and uses the XML objects. Given a database handle $dbh and a query string $query, there's not a lot to this process. The code instructs the writer object to send its results to the standard output, then connects that object to DBI and issues the query:

```perl
#! /usr/bin/perl -w
# mysql_to_xml.pl - given a database and table name,
# dump the table to the standard output in XML format.

use strict;
use DBI;
use XML::Generator::DBI;
use XML::Handler::YAWriter;

# ... process command-line options (not shown) ...

# ... connect to database (not shown) ...

# create output writer; "-" means "standard output"
my $out = XML::Handler::YAWriter->new (AsFile => "-");
# set up connection between DBI and output writer
my $gen = XML::Generator::DBI->new (
                        dbh => $dbh,            # database handle
                        Handler => $out,        # output writer
                        RootElement => "rowset" # document root element
                    );
# issue query and write XML
$gen->execute ($query);

$dbh->disconnect ();

exit (0);
```

10.42 Importing XML into MySQL

Problem

You want to import an XML document into a MySQL table.

Solution

Set up an XML parser to read the document. Then use the records in the document to construct and execute INSERT statements.

Discussion

Importing an XML document depends on being able to parse the document and extract record contents from it. The way you do this will depend on how the document is written. For example, one format might represent column names and values as attributes of `<column>` elements:

```
<?xml version="1.0" encoding="UTF-8"?>
<rowset>
  <row>
   <column name="subject" value="Jane" />
   <column name="test" value="A" />
   <column name="score" value="47" />
  </row>
  <row>
   <column name="subject" value="Jane" />
   <column name="test" value="B />
   <column name="score" value="50" />
  </row>
...
</rowset>
```

Another format is to use column names as element names and column values as the contents of those elements:

```
<?xml version="1.0" encoding="UTF-8"?>
<rowset>
  <row>
   <subject>Jane</subject>
   <test>A</test>
   <score>47</score>
  </row>
  <row>
   <subject>Jane</subject>
   <test>B</test>
   <score>50</score>
  </row>
...
</rowset>
```

Due to the various structuring possibilities, it's necessary to make some assumptions about the format you expect the XML document to have. For the example here, I'll assume the second format just shown. One way to process this kind of document is to use the *XML::XPath* module, which allows you to refer to elements within the document using path expressions. For example, the path //row selects all the <row> elements under the document root, and the path * selects all children of a given element. We can use these paths with *XML::XPath* to obtain first a list of all the <row> elements, and then for each row a list of all its columns.

The following script, *xml_to_mysql.pl*, takes three arguments:

```
% xml_to_mysql.pl db_name tbl_name xml_file
```

The filename argument indicates which document to import, and the database and table name arguments indicate which table to import it into.

xml_to_mysql.pl processes the command-line arguments and connects to MySQL (not shown), then processes the document:

```perl
#! /usr/bin/perl -w
# xml_to_mysql.pl - read XML file into MySQL

use strict;
use DBI;
use XML::XPath;

# ... process command-line options (not shown) ...

# ... connect to database (not shown) ...

# Open file for reading
my $xp = XML::XPath->new (filename => $file_name);
my $row_list = $xp->find ("//row");        # find set of <row> elements
print "Number of records: " . $row_list->size () . "\n";
foreach my $row ($row_list->get_nodelist ())        # loop through rows
{
    my @name;    # array for column names
    my @val;     # array for column values
    my $col_list = $row->find ("*");                # children (columns) of row
    foreach my $col ($col_list->get_nodelist ())    # loop through columns
    {
        # save column name and value
        push (@name, $col->getName ());
        push (@val, $col->string_value ());
    }
    # construct INSERT statement, then execute it
    my $stmt = "INSERT INTO $tbl_name ("
                . join (",", @name)
                . ") VALUES ("
                . join (",", ("?") x scalar (@val))
                . ")";
    $dbh->do ($stmt, undef, @val);
}
```

```
$dbh->disconnect ();

exit (0);
```

The script creates an XML::XPath object, which opens and parses the document. Then the object is queried for the set of <row> elements, using the path //row. The size of this set indicates how many records the document contains.

To process each row, the script uses the path * to ask for all the children of the row object. Each child corresponds to a column within the row; using * as the path for get_nodelist() this way is convenient because we need not know in advance which columns to expect. *xml_to_mysql.pl* obtains the name and value from each column and saves them in the @name and @value arrays. After all the columns have been processed, the arrays are used to construct an INSERT statement that names those columns that were found to be present in the row and that includes a placeholder for each data value. (Recipe 2.6 discusses placeholder list construction.) Then the script issues the statement, passing the column values to do() to bind them to the placeholders.

In the previous section, we used *mysql_to_xml.pl* to export the contents of the expt table as an XML document. *xml_to_mysql.pl* can be used to perform the converse operation of importing the document back into MySQL:

```
% xml_to_mysql.pl cookbook expt expt.xml
```

As it processes the document, the script generates and executes the following set of statements:

```
INSERT INTO expt (subject,test,score) VALUES ('Jane','A','47')
INSERT INTO expt (subject,test,score) VALUES ('Jane','B','50')
INSERT INTO expt (subject,test) VALUES ('Jane','C')
INSERT INTO expt (subject,test) VALUES ('Jane','D')
INSERT INTO expt (subject,test,score) VALUES ('Marvin','A','52')
INSERT INTO expt (subject,test,score) VALUES ('Marvin','B','45')
INSERT INTO expt (subject,test,score) VALUES ('Marvin','C','53')
INSERT INTO expt (subject,test) VALUES ('Marvin','D')
```

Note that these statements do not all insert the same number of columns. Statements with "missing" columns correspond to rows with NULL values.

10.43 Epilog

Recall the scenario with which this chapter began:

Suppose you have a file named *somedata.csv* that contains 12 columns of data in comma-separated values (CSV) format. From this file you want to extract only columns 2, 11, 5, and 9, and use them to create database records in a MySQL table that contains name, birth, height, and weight columns. You need to make sure that the height and weight are positive integers, and convert the birth dates from *MM/DD/YY* format to *CCYY-MM-DD* format. How can you do this?

So ... how *would* you do that, based on the techniques discussed in this chapter?

Much of the work can be done using the utility programs developed here. You can convert the file to tab-delimited format with *cvt_file.pl*, extract the columns in the desired order with *yank_col.pl*, and rewrite the date column to ISO format with *cvt_date.pl*:

```
% cvt_file.pl --iformat=csv somedata.csv \
    | yank_col.pl --columns=2,11,5,9 \
    | cvt_date.pl --columns=2 --iformat=us --add-century > tmp
```

The resulting file, *tmp*, will have four columns representing the name, birth, height, and weight values, in that order. It needs only to have its height and weight columns checked to make sure they contain positive integers. Using the is_positive_integer() library function from the *Cookbook_Utils.pm* module file, that task can be achieved using a short special-purpose script that isn't much more than an input loop:

```
#! /usr/bin/perl -w
# validate_htwt.pl - height/weight validation example

# Assumes tab-delimited, linefeed-terminated input lines.

# Input columns and the actions to perform on them are as follows:
# 1: name; echo as given
# 2: birth; echo as given
# 3: height; validate as positive integer
# 4: weight; validate as positive integer

use strict;
use lib qw(/usr/local/apache/lib/perl);
use Cookbook_Utils;

while (<>)
{
    chomp;
    my ($name, $birth, $height, $weight) = split (/\t/, $_, 4);
    warn "line $.:height $height is not a positive integer\n"
                            if !is_positive_integer ($height);
    warn "line $.:weight $weight is not a positive integer\n"
                            if !is_positive_integer ($weight);
}

exit (0);
```

The *validate_htwt.pl* script doesn't produce any output (except for warning messages), because it doesn't need to reformat any of the input values. Assuming that *tmp* passes validation with no errors, it can be loaded into MySQL with a simple LOAD DATA statement:

```
mysql> LOAD DATA LOCAL INFILE 'tmp' INTO TABLE tbl_name;
```

## CHAPTER 11

Generating and Using Sequences

11.0 Introduction

A sequence is a set of integers 1, 2, 3, ... that are generated in order on demand. Sequences are frequently used in databases because many applications require each row in a table to contain a unique value, and sequences provide an easy way to generate them. This chapter describes how to use sequences in MySQL. It covers the following topics:

Using AUTO_INCREMENT columns to create sequences. The AUTO_INCREMENT column is MySQL's mechanism for generating a sequence over a set of rows. Each time you create a row in a table that contains an AUTO_INCREMENT column, MySQL automatically generates the next value in the sequence as the column's value. This value serves as a unique identifier, making sequences an easy way to create items such as customer ID numbers, shipping package waybill numbers, invoice or purchase order numbers, bug report IDs, ticket numbers, or product serial numbers.

Retrieving sequence values. For many applications, it's not enough just to create sequence values. It's also necessary to determine the sequence value for a just-inserted record. A web application may need to redisplay to a user the contents of a record created from the contents of a form just submitted by the user. Or the value may need to be retrieved so it can be stored as part of other records in a related table.

Resequencing techniques. This section describes how to renumber a sequence that has holes in it due to record deletions—and also discusses reasons to avoid resequencing. Other topics include starting sequences at values other than 1 and adding a sequence column to a table that doesn't have one.

Using an AUTO_INCREMENT column to create multiple sequences. In many cases, the AUTO_INCREMENT column in a table is independent of other columns and its values increment throughout the table in a single monotonic sequence. However, if you create a multiple-column index that contains an AUTO_INCREMENT column, you can use it to generate multiple sequences. For example, if you run a bulletin board that categorizes messages into topics, you can number messages sequentially within each topic by tying an AUTO_INCREMENT column to a topic indicator column.

Managing multiple simultaneous AUTO_INCREMENT values. Special care is necessary when you need to keep track of multiple sequence values. This can occur when you issue a set of statements that affect a single table, or when creating records in multiple tables that each have an AUTO_INCREMENT column. This section describes what to do in these cases.

Using single-row sequence generators. Sequences also can be used as counters. For example, if you serve banner ads on your web site, you might increment a counter for each impression (that is, for each time you serve an ad). The counts for a given ad form a sequence, but because the count itself is the only value of interest, there is no need to generate a new row to record each impression. MySQL provides a solution for this problem, too, using a mechanism that allows a sequence to be easily generated within a single table row over time. To store multiple counters in the table, add a column that identifies the counter uniquely. For example, you can have an arbitrary number of ad impression counters in a table. Each row in the table identifies a specific banner ad, and the counter in each row increments independently of the others. The same mechanism also allows creation of sequences that increase by values other than one, by non-uniform values, or even by negative increments.

Numbering query output rows sequentially. This section suggests ways to generate display-only sequences for the purpose of numbering the rows of output from a query.

Sequence Generators and Portability

The engines for most database systems provide sequence generation capabilities, though the implementations tend to be engine-dependent. That's true for MySQL as well, so the material in this section is almost completely MySQL-specific, even at the SQL level. In other words, the SQL for generating sequences is itself non-portable, even if you use an API like DBI or JDBC that provides an abstraction layer. Abstract interfaces may help you process SQL statements portably, but they don't make non-portable SQL portable.

11.1 Using AUTO_INCREMENT To Set Up a Sequence Column

Problem

You want to include a sequence column in a table.

Solution

Use an AUTO_INCREMENT column.

Discussion

This section provides the basic background on how AUTO_INCREMENT columns work, beginning with a short example that demonstrates the sequence-generation mechanism. The illustration centers around a bug-collection scenario: your son (eight-year-old Junior) is assigned the task of collecting insects for a class project at school. For each insect, Junior is to record its name ("ant," "bee," and so forth), and its date and location of collection. You have long expounded the benefits of MySQL for record-keeping to Junior since his early days, so upon your arrival home from work that day, he immediately announces the necessity of completing this project and then, looking you straight in the eye, declares that it's clearly a task for which MySQL is well-suited. Who are you to argue? So the two of you get to work. Junior already collected some specimens after school while waiting for you to come home and has recorded the following information in his notebook:

Name	Date	Origin
millipede	2001-09-10	driveway
housefly	2001-09-10	kitchen
grasshopper	2001-09-10	front yard
stink bug	2001-09-10	front yard
cabbage butterfly	2001-09-10	garden
ant	2001-09-10	back yard
ant	2001-09-10	back yard
millbug	2001-09-10	under rock

Looking over Junior's notes, you're pleased to see that even at his tender age he has learned to write dates in ISO format. However, you also notice that he's collected a millipede and a millbug, neither of which actually are insects. You decide to let this pass for the moment; Junior forgot to bring home the written instructions for the project, so at this point it's unclear whether or not these specimens are acceptable.

As you consider how to create a table to store this information, it's apparent that you need at least name, date, and origin columns corresponding to the types of information Junior is required to record:

```
CREATE TABLE insect
(
    name    VARCHAR(30) NOT NULL,    # type of insect
    date    DATE NOT NULL,           # date collected
    origin  VARCHAR(30) NOT NULL     # where collected
);
```

However, those columns may not be enough to make the table easy to use. Note that the records collected thus far are not unique—both ants were collected at the same time and place. If you put the information into an insect table that has the preceding structure, neither ant record can be referred to individually, because there's nothing to distinguish them from one another. Unique IDs would be helpful to make the records distinct and to provide values that make each record easy to refer to. An AUTO_INCREMENT column is good for this purpose, so a better insect table has a structure like this:

```
CREATE TABLE insect
(
    id      INT UNSIGNED NOT NULL AUTO_INCREMENT,
    PRIMARY KEY (id),
    name    VARCHAR(30) NOT NULL,   # type of insect
    date    DATE NOT NULL,          # date collected
    origin  VARCHAR(30) NOT NULL    # where collected
);
```

Go ahead and create the insect table using this second definition. Later, in Recipe 11.3, we'll discuss the specifics of why the id column is declared the way it is.

11.2   Generating Sequence Values

Problem

Now that you have an AUTO_INCREMENT column, you want to use it to generate a new sequence value.

Solution

Insert NULL into the column, or just omit it from your INSERT statement. Either way, MySQL will create a new sequence number for you.

Discussion

One of the useful properties of an AUTO_INCREMENT column is that you don't have to assign its values yourself—MySQL does so for you. There are two ways to generate new AUTO_INCREMENT values, demonstrated here using the id column of the insect table. First, you can explicitly set the id column to NULL.* The following statement inserts the first four of Junior's specimens into the insect table this way:

```
mysql> INSERT INTO insect (id,name,date,origin) VALUES
    -> (NULL,'housefly','2001-09-10','kitchen'),
    -> (NULL,'millipede','2001-09-10','driveway'),
    -> (NULL,'grasshopper','2001-09-10','front yard'),
    -> (NULL,'stink bug','2001-09-10','front yard');
```

---

* Setting an AUTO_INCREMENT column to zero currently has the same effect as setting it to NULL. But that is not guaranteed to be true in the future, so it's better to use NULL.

Second, you can omit the id column from the INSERT statement entirely. In MySQL, you can create new records without explicitly specifying values for every column. MySQL assigns default values to the missing columns automatically, and the default for an AUTO_INCREMENT column happens to be the next sequence number. Thus, you can insert records into the insect table without naming the id column at all. This statement adds Junior's other four specimens to the insect table that way:

```
mysql> INSERT INTO insect (name,date,origin) VALUES
    -> ('cabbage butterfly','2001-09-10','garden'),
    -> ('ant','2001-09-10','back yard'),
    -> ('ant','2001-09-10','back yard'),
    -> ('millbug','2001-09-10','under rock');
```

Whichever method you use, MySQL determines the next sequence number for each record and assigns it to the id column, as you can verify for yourself:

```
mysql> SELECT * FROM insect ORDER BY id;
+----+------------------+------------+------------+
| id | name             | date       | origin     |
+----+------------------+------------+------------+
|  1 | housefly         | 2001-09-10 | kitchen    |
|  2 | millipede        | 2001-09-10 | driveway   |
|  3 | grasshopper      | 2001-09-10 | front yard |
|  4 | stink bug        | 2001-09-10 | front yard |
|  5 | cabbage butterfly| 2001-09-10 | garden     |
|  6 | ant              | 2001-09-10 | back yard  |
|  7 | ant              | 2001-09-10 | back yard  |
|  8 | millbug          | 2001-09-10 | under rock |
+----+------------------+------------+------------+
```

As Junior collects more specimens, you can add more records to the table and they'll be assigned the next values in the sequence (9, 10, ...).

The concept underlying AUTO_INCREMENT columns is simple enough in principle: each time you create a new row, MySQL generates the next number in the sequence and assigns it to the row. But there are certain subtleties to know about, as well as differences in how AUTO_INCREMENT sequences are handled for different table types. By being aware of these issues, you can use sequences more effectively and avoid surprises. For example, if you explicitly set the id column to a non-NULL value, one of two things happens:

- If the value is already present in the table, an error occurs:

  ```
  mysql> INSERT INTO insect (id,name,date,origin) VALUES
      -> (3,'cricket','2001-09-11','basement');
  ERROR 1062 at line 1: Duplicate entry '3' for key 1
  ```

  This happens because when you create an AUTO_INCREMENT column, you must declare it to be either a PRIMARY KEY or a UNIQUE index. As a result, it cannot contain duplicate values.

- If the value is not present in the table, MySQL inserts the record using that value. In addition, if it's larger than the current sequence counter, the table's counter is reset to the new value plus one. The insect table at this point has sequence values 1 through 8. If you insert a new row with the id column set to 20, that becomes the new maximum value. Subsequent inserts that automatically generate id values will begin at 21. The values 9 through 19 become unused, resulting in a gap in the sequence.

Now let's look in more detail at how to define AUTO_INCREMENT columns and how they behave.

11.3   Choosing the Type for a Sequence Column

Problem

You want to know more about how to define a sequence column.

Solution

Use the guidelines given here.

Discussion

You should follow certain guidelines when creating an AUTO_INCREMENT column. As an illustration, consider how the id column in the insect table was declared:

```
id INT UNSIGNED NOT NULL AUTO_INCREMENT,
PRIMARY KEY (id)
```

The AUTO_INCREMENT keyword informs MySQL that it should generate successive sequence numbers for the column's values, but the other information is important, too:

- INT is the column's basic type. You need not necessarily use INT, but the column must be one of the integer types: TINYINT, SMALLINT, MEDIUMINT, INT, or BIGINT. It's important to remember that AUTO_INCREMENT is a column attribute that should be applied *only* to integer types. Older versions of MySQL will allow you to create an AUTO_INCREMENT column using non-integer types such as CHAR, but bad things will happen if you do that. (Even if the initial sequence numbers appear to be generated normally, sooner or later the column will fail. A typical error is "duplicate key" after inserting a few records, even when you know the column should be able to hold more numbers.) Save yourself some trouble—always use an integer type for AUTO_INCREMENT columns.

- The column is declared as UNSIGNED. There's no need to allow negative values, because AUTO_INCREMENT sequences consist only of positive integers (normally beginning at 1). Furthermore, *not* declaring the column to be UNSIGNED cuts the range of your sequence in half. For example, TINYINT has a range of –128 to 127.

Sequences include only positive values, so the range of a `TINYINT` sequence would be 1 to 127. The range of an unsigned `TINYINT` column is 0 to 255, which increases the upper end of the sequence to 255. The maximum sequence value is determined by the specific integer type used, so you should choose a type that is big enough to hold the largest value you'll need. The maximum unsigned value of each integer type is shown in the following table, which you can use to select an appropriate type.

Column type	Maximum unsigned value
TINYINT	255
SMALLINT	65,535
MEDIUMINT	16,777,215
INT	4,294,967,295
BIGINT	18,446,744,073,709,551,615

Sometimes people omit `UNSIGNED` so that they can create records that contain negative numbers in the sequence column. (Using -1 to signify "has no ID" would be an instance of this.) MySQL makes no guarantees about how negative numbers will be treated, so you're playing with fire if you try to use them in an `AUTO_INCREMENT` column. For example, if you resequence the column, you'll find that all your negative values get turned into regular (positive) sequence numbers.

- `AUTO_INCREMENT` columns cannot contain `NULL` values, so id is declared as `NOT NULL`. (It's true that you can specify `NULL` as the column value when you insert a new record, but for an `AUTO_INCREMENT` column that really means "generate the next sequence value.") Current versions of MySQL automatically define `AUTO_INCREMENT` columns as `NOT NULL` if you forget to. However, it's best to indicate `NOT NULL` in the `CREATE TABLE` statement explicitly if there is a possibility that you might use it with an older version of MySQL sometime.

- The column is declared as a `PRIMARY KEY` to ensure that its values are unique. Tables can have only one `PRIMARY KEY`, so if the table already has some other `PRIMARY KEY` column, you can declare an `AUTO_INCREMENT` column to have a `UNIQUE` index instead:

```
id INT UNSIGNED NOT NULL AUTO_INCREMENT,
UNIQUE (id)
```

If the `AUTO_INCREMENT` column is the only column in the `PRIMARY KEY` or `UNIQUE` index, you can declare it as such in the column definition rather than in a separate clause. For example, these definitions are equivalent:

```
id INT UNSIGNED NOT NULL AUTO_INCREMENT,
PRIMARY KEY (id)

id INT UNSIGNED NOT NULL AUTO_INCREMENT PRIMARY KEY
```

As are these:

```
id INT UNSIGNED NOT NULL AUTO_INCREMENT UNIQUE

id INT UNSIGNED NOT NULL AUTO_INCREMENT,
UNIQUE (id)
```

Using a separate clause to specify the index helps to emphasize that it's not, strictly speaking, part of the column definition. (If you read through Chapter 8, you'll notice that modifying a column's indexes is discussed separately from changing the definition of the column itself.)

When creating a table that contains an AUTO_INCREMENT column, it's also important to consider the table type (MyISAM, InnoDB, and so forth). The type affects behaviors such as reuse of values that are deleted from the top of the sequence, and whether or not you can set the initial sequence value. In general, MyISAM is the best type for tables that contain AUTO_INCREMENT columns, because it offers the most features for sequence management. This will become apparent as you continue through the chapter.

11.4 The Effect of Record Deletions on Sequence Generation

Problem

You want to know what happens to a sequence when you delete records from a table that contains an AUTO_INCREMENT column.

Solution

It depends on which records you delete and on the table type.

Discussion

We have thus far considered how sequence values in an AUTO_INCREMENT column are generated for circumstances where records are only added to a table. But it's unrealistic to assume that records will never be deleted. What happens to the sequence then?

Refer again to Junior's bug-collection project, for which you currently have an insect table that looks like this:

```
mysql> SELECT * FROM insect ORDER BY id;
+----+--------------------+------------+------------+
| id | name               | date       | origin     |
+----+--------------------+------------+------------+
|  1 | housefly           | 2001-09-10 | kitchen    |
|  2 | millipede          | 2001-09-10 | driveway   |
```

```
| 3 | grasshopper       | 2001-09-10 | front yard |
| 4 | stink bug         | 2001-09-10 | front yard |
| 5 | cabbage butterfly | 2001-09-10 | garden     |
| 6 | ant               | 2001-09-10 | back yard  |
| 7 | ant               | 2001-09-10 | back yard  |
| 8 | millbug           | 2001-09-10 | under rock |
+----+-------------------+------------+------------+
```

That's about to change, because after Junior remembers to bring home the written instructions for the project, you read through them and discover two things that bear on the insect table's contents:

- Specimens should include only insects, not other insect-like creatures such as millipedes and millbugs.

- The purpose of the project is to collect as many *different* specimens as possible, not just *as many* specimens as possible. This means that only one ant record is allowed.

These instructions require that a few rows be removed from the insect table—specifically those with id values 2 (millipede), 8 (millbug), and 7 (duplicate ant). Thus, despite Junior's evident disappointment at the reduction in the size of his collection, you instruct him to remove those records by issuing a DELETE statement:

```
mysql> DELETE FROM insect WHERE id IN (2,8,7);
```

This statement illustrates one reason why it's useful to have unique ID values—they allow you to specify any record unambiguously. The ant records are identical except for the id value. Without that column in the insect table, it would be more difficult to delete just one of them.

After the unsuitable records have been removed, the resulting table contents become:

```
mysql> SELECT * FROM insect ORDER BY id;
+----+-------------------+------------+------------+
| id | name              | date       | origin     |
+----+-------------------+------------+------------+
| 1  | housefly          | 2001-09-10 | kitchen    |
| 3  | grasshopper       | 2001-09-10 | front yard |
| 4  | stink bug         | 2001-09-10 | front yard |
| 5  | cabbage butterfly | 2001-09-10 | garden     |
| 6  | ant               | 2001-09-10 | back yard  |
+----+-------------------+------------+------------+
```

The sequence in the id column now has a hole (row 2 is missing) and the values 7 and 8 at the top of the sequence are no longer present. How do these deletions affect future insert operations? What sequence number will the next new row get?

Removing row 2 created a gap in the middle of the sequence. This has no effect on subsequent inserts, because MySQL makes no attempt to fill in holes in a sequence.

On the other hand, deleting records 7 and 8 removes values at the top of the sequence, and the effect of this depends on the table type:

- With ISAM and BDB tables, the next sequence number always is the smallest positive integer not currently present in the column. If you delete rows containing values at the top of the sequence, those values will be reused. (Thus, after deleting records with values 7 and 8, the next inserted record will be assigned the value 7.)
- For MyISAM or InnoDB tables, values are not reused. The next sequence number is the smallest positive integer that has not previously been used. (For a sequence that stands at 8, the next record gets a value of 9 even if you delete records 7 and 8 first.) If you require strictly monotonic sequences, you should use one of these table types.

ISAM tables are the only table type available until MySQL 3.23, so prior to that version, reuse of values deleted from the top of a sequence is the only behavior you can get. MyISAM tables are available as of MySQL 3.23 (at which point, MyISAM also became the default table type). BDB and InnoDB tables are available as of MySQL 3.23.17 and 3.23.29, respectively.

If you're using a table with a type that differs in value-reuse behavior from the behavior you require, use ALTER TABLE to change the table to a more appropriate type. For example, if you want to change an ISAM table to be a MyISAM table (to prevent sequence values from being reused after records are deleted), do this:

```
ALTER TABLE tbl_name TYPE = MYISAM;
```

If you don't know what type a table is, use SHOW TABLE STATUS to find out:

```
mysql> SHOW TABLE STATUS LIKE 'insect'\G;
*************************** 1. row ***************************
           Name: insect
           Type: MyISAM
     Row_format: Dynamic
           Rows: 7
 Avg_row_length: 30
    Data_length: 216
Max_data_length: 4294967295
   Index_length: 2048
      Data_free: 0
 Auto_increment: 8
    Create_time: 2002-01-25 16:55:32
    Update_time: 2002-01-25 16:55:32
     Check_time: NULL
 Create_options:
        Comment:
```

The output shown here indicates that insect is a MyISAM table. (You can also use SHOW CREATE TABLE.)

In this chapter, you can assume that if a table is created with no explicit table type, it's a MyISAM table.

A special case of record deletion occurs when you clear out a table entirely using a DELETE with no WHERE clause:

```
DELETE FROM tbl_name;
```

In this case, the sequence counter may be reset to 1, even for table types for which values normally are not reused (MyISAM and InnoDB). For those types, if you wish to delete all the records while maintaining the current sequence value, tell MySQL to perform a record-at-a-time delete by including a WHERE clause that specifies some trivially true condition:

```
DELETE FROM tbl_name WHERE 1 > 0;
```

11.5   Retrieving Sequence Values

Problem

After creating a record that includes a new sequence number, you want to find out what that number is.

Solution

In a SQL statement, you can use the LAST_INSERT_ID() function. If you're writing a program, your MySQL API may provide a way to get the value directly without using LAST_INSERT_ID().

Discussion

Many applications need to determine the AUTO_INCREMENT value of a newly created record. For example, if you get ambitious and write a web-based frontend for entering records into Junior's insect table, you might have the application display each new record nicely formatted in a new page immediately after you hit the Submit button. To do this, you'll need to know the new id value so you can retrieve the proper record. Another common situation in which the AUTO_INCREMENT value is needed occurs when you're using multiple tables: after inserting a record in a master table, typically, you'll need its ID so that you can create records in other related tables that refer to the master record. (Recipe 11.15 shows how to relate multiple tables using sequence numbers.)

When you generate a new AUTO_INCREMENT value, you can get the value from the server by issuing a query that invokes the LAST_INSERT_ID() function. In addition, many MySQL APIs provide a client-side mechanism for making the value available without issuing another query. This section discusses both methods and provides a comparison of their differences.

Using LAST_INSERT_ID() to Obtain AUTO_INCREMENT Values

The obvious (but incorrect) way to determine a new record's AUTO_INCREMENT value is based on the fact that when MySQL generates the value, it becomes the largest sequence number in the column. Thus, you might try using the MAX() function to retrieve it:

```
SELECT MAX(id) FROM insect;
```

This is unreliable because it doesn't take into account the multithreaded nature of the MySQL server. The SELECT query does indeed return the maximum id value from the table—but it may not be the value that *you* generated. Suppose you insert a record that generates an id value of 9. If another client inserts a record before you issue the SELECT query, MAX(id) will return 10, not 9. Methods for solving this problem include grouping the INSERT and SELECT statements as a transaction or locking the table, but MySQL provides a LAST_INSERT_ID() function as a simpler way to obtain the proper value. It returns the most recent AUTO_INCREMENT value that you generated during the time you've been connected to the server. For example, you can insert a record into the insect table, then retrieve its id value like this:

```
mysql> INSERT INTO insect (name,date,origin)
    -> VALUES('cricket','2001-09-11','basement');
mysql> SELECT LAST_INSERT_ID();
+------------------+
| last_insert_id() |
+------------------+
|                9 |
+------------------+
```

Or you can use the new value to retrieve the entire record, without even knowing what the id is:

```
mysql> INSERT INTO insect (name,date,origin)
    -> VALUES('moth','2001-09-14','windowsill');
mysql> SELECT * FROM insect WHERE id = LAST_INSERT_ID();
+----+------+------------+------------+
| id | name | date       | origin     |
+----+------+------------+------------+
| 10 | moth | 2001-09-14 | windowsill |
+----+------+------------+------------+
```

Using API-Specific Methods to Obtain AUTO_INCREMENT Values

LAST_INSERT_ID() is a SQL function, so you can use it from within any client that understands how to issue SQL statements. On the other hand, you do have to issue a separate query to get its value. If you're writing your own programs, you may have another choice. Many MySQL interfaces include an API-specific extension that returns the AUTO_INCREMENT value without issuing another query. In particular, each of our four APIs have this capability.

Perl

Use the mysql_insertid attribute to obtain the AUTO_INCREMENT value generated by a query. This attribute is accessed through either a database handle or a statement handle, depending on how you issue the query. The following example references it through the database handle:

```
$dbh->do ("INSERT INTO insect (name,date,origin)
          VALUES('moth','2001-09-14','windowsill')");
my $seq = $dbh->{mysql_insertid};
```

If you're using prepare() and execute(), access mysql_insertid as a statement handle attribute:

```
my $sth = $dbh->prepare ("INSERT INTO insect (name,date,origin)
                         VALUES('moth','2001-09-14','windowsill')");
$sth->execute ();
my $seq = $sth->{mysql_insertid};
```

> If you find that the value of the mysql_insertid attribute is always zero, you probably have an old version of DBD::mysql that doesn't support it. Try using the insertid attribute instead. (In this case, insertid is available only as a database handle attribute.)

PHP

After issuing a query that generates an AUTO_INCREMENT value, retrieve the value by calling mysql_insert_id():

```
mysql_query ("INSERT INTO insect (name,date,origin)
            VALUES('moth','2001-09-14','windowsill')", $conn_id);
$seq = mysql_insert_id ($conn_id);
```

The argument should be a connection identifier. If no argument is given, mysql_insert_id() uses the most recently opened connection.

Python

The MySQLdb driver for DB-API provides an insert_id() cursor method for getting sequence values. Use it with the cursor object through which you execute a query that generates an AUTO_INCREMENT value:

```
cursor = conn.cursor ()
cursor.execute ("""
        INSERT INTO insect (name,date,origin)
        VALUES('moth','2001-09-14','windowsill')
    """)
seq = cursor.insert_id ()
```

Java

The MySQL Connector/J JDBC driver provides a getLastInsertID() method for obtaining AUTO_INCREMENT values. It can be used with either Statement or PreparedStatement objects. This example uses a Statement:

```
Statement s = conn.createStatement ();
s.executeUpdate (
        "INSERT INTO insect (name,date,origin)"
        + " VALUES('moth','2001-09-14','windowsill')");
long seq = ((com.mysql.jdbc.Statement) s).getLastInsertID ();
s.close ();
```

Note that because getLastInsertID() is driver-specific, you access it by casting the Statement object to the com.mysql.jdbc.Statement type. If you're using a PreparedStatement object, cast it to the com.mysql.jdbc.PreparedStatement type instead:

```
PreparedStatement s = conn.prepareStatement (
        "INSERT INTO insect (name,date,origin)"
        + " VALUES('moth','2001-09-14','windowsill')");
s.executeUpdate ();
long seq = ((com.mysql.jdbc.PreparedStatement) s).getLastInsertID ();
s.close ();
```

Server-Side and Client-Side Sequence Value Retrieval Compared

As mentioned earlier, the value of LAST_INSERT_ID( ) is maintained on a connection-specific basis on the server side of the MySQL connection. By contrast, the API-specific methods for accessing AUTO_INCREMENT values directly are implemented on the client side. Server-side and client-side sequence value retrieval methods have some similarities, but also some differences.

All methods, both server-side and client-side, have in common the property that you must access the AUTO_INCREMENT value using the same MySQL connection that was used to generate the value in the first place. If you generate an AUTO_INCREMENT value, then disconnect from the server and reconnect before attempting to access the value, you'll get zero. On the other hand, the persistence of AUTO_INCREMENT values can be much longer on the server side of the connection:

- After you issue a query that generates an AUTO_INCREMENT value, the value remains available through LAST_INSERT_ID( ) even if you issue other statements, as long as none of those statements generate an AUTO_INCREMENT value.

- The sequence value available on the client side typically is set for *every* query, not just those that generate AUTO_INCREMENT values. If you issue an INSERT statement that generates a new value, then issue some other query before accessing the client-side sequence value, it probably will have been set to zero. The precise behavior varies among APIs, but if you use the following general guideline, you should be safe: if a query generates a sequence value that you won't be using immediately, save the value in a variable that you can refer to later. Otherwise, you may find that the sequence value has been wiped out when you do try to access it.

11.6 Determining Whether to Resequence a Column

Problem

You have gaps in a sequence column and you're wondering whether you should try to resequence it.

Solution

Don't bother. Or at least don't do so without a good reason, of which there are very few.

Discussion

If you insert records into a table that has an AUTO_INCREMENT column and never delete any of them, values in the column form an unbroken sequence. But if you delete records, the sequence begins to have holes in it. For example, Junior's insect table currently looks something like this, with gaps in the sequence (assuming that you've inserted the cricket and moth records shown in the preceding section on retrieving sequence values):

```
mysql> SELECT * FROM insect ORDER BY id;
+----+------------------+------------+------------+
| id | name             | date       | origin     |
+----+------------------+------------+------------+
|  1 | housefly         | 2001-09-10 | kitchen    |
|  3 | grasshopper      | 2001-09-10 | front yard |
|  4 | stink bug        | 2001-09-10 | front yard |
|  5 | cabbage butterfly| 2001-09-10 | garden     |
|  6 | ant              | 2001-09-10 | back yard  |
|  9 | cricket          | 2001-09-11 | basement   |
| 10 | moth             | 2001-09-14 | windowsill |
+----+------------------+------------+------------+
```

MySQL won't attempt to eliminate these gaps by filling in the unused values when you insert new records. People who don't like this behavior tend to resequence AUTO_INCREMENT columns periodically to eliminate the holes. The next few sections show how to do that. It's also possible to add a sequence column to a table that doesn't currently have one, force deleted values at the top of a sequence to be reused, and to specify an initial sequence value when creating or resequencing a table.

Reasons to Avoid Resequencing

Before deciding to resequence an AUTO_INCREMENT column, consider whether you really want or need to do so. It's unnecessary in most cases. In fact, renumbering a sequence sometimes can cause you real problems. For example, you should *not* resequence a column containing values that are referenced by another table. Renumbering the values destroys their correspondence to values in the other table, making it impossible to properly relate records in the two tables to each other.

Reasons that people have for resequencing include the following:

Aesthetics. Sometimes the desire to renumber a column is for aesthetic reasons. People seem to prefer unbroken sequences to sequences with holes in them. If this is why you want to resequence, there's probably not much I can say to convince you otherwise. Nevertheless, it's not a particularly good reason.

Performance. The impetus for resequencing may stem from the notion that doing so "compacts" a sequence column by removing gaps and allows MySQL to run queries more quickly. This is not true. MySQL doesn't care whether or not there are holes, and there is no performance gain to be had by renumbering an AUTO_ INCREMENT column. In fact, resequencing affects performance negatively in the sense that the table remains locked while MySQL performs the operation— which may take a non-trivial amount of time for a large table. Other clients can read from the table while this is happening, but clients that are trying to insert new rows must wait until the operation is complete.

Running out of numbers. The upper limit of a sequence column is determined by the column's data type. If an AUTO_INCREMENT sequence is approaching the upper limit of its column type, renumbering packs the sequence and frees up more values at the top. This may be a legitimate reason to resequence a column, but it is still unnecessary in many cases to do so. You may be able to expand the column's range to increase its upper limit, without changing the values stored in the column.

11.7   Extending the Range of a Sequence Column

Problem

You want to avoid resequencing a column, but you're running out of room for new sequence numbers.

Solution

See if you can make the column UNSIGNED or change the column to use a larger integer type.

Discussion

Resequencing an AUTO_INCREMENT column changes the contents of potentially every row in the table. It's often possible to avoid this by extending the range of the column, which changes the table's structure rather than its contents:

- If the column type is signed, make it UNSIGNED and you'll double the range of available values. Suppose you have an id column that currently is defined like this:

  ```
  id MEDIUMINT NOT NULL AUTO_INCREMENT
  ```

  The upper range of a signed MEDIUMINT column is 8,388,607. This can be increased to 16,777,215 by making the column UNSIGNED with ALTER TABLE:

  ```
  ALTER TABLE tbl_name MODIFY id MEDIUMINT UNSIGNED NOT NULL AUTO_INCREMENT;
  ```

- If your column is already UNSIGNED and it is not already the largest integer type (BIGINT), converting it to a larger type increases its range. You can use ALTER

TABLE for this, too. For example, the id column in the previous example can be converted from MEDIUMINT to BIGINT like so:

```
ALTER TABLE tbl_name MODIFY id BIGINT UNSIGNED NOT NULL AUTO_INCREMENT;
```

Recipe 11.3 includes a table that shows the ranges for each integer type, which you may find helpful in assessing which type to use.

11.8   Renumbering an Existing Sequence

Problem

You're determined to resequence a column, despite my advice not to.

Solution

Drop the column from the table. Then put it back. MySQL will renumber the values in the column in unbroken sequence.

Discussion

If you determine that resequencing an AUTO_INCREMENT column is unavoidable, the way to do it is to drop the column from the table, then add it again. The following example shows how to renumber the id values in the insect table using this technique:

```
mysql> ALTER TABLE insect DROP id;
mysql> ALTER TABLE insect
    -> ADD id INT UNSIGNED NOT NULL AUTO_INCREMENT FIRST,
    -> ADD PRIMARY KEY (id);
```

The first ALTER TABLE statement gets rid of the id column (and as a result also drops the PRIMARY KEY, because the column to which it refers is no longer present.) The second statement restores the column to the table and establishes it as the PRIMARY KEY. (The FIRST keyword places the column first in the table, which is where it was originally. Normally, ADD puts columns at the end of the table.) When you add an AUTO_INCREMENT column to a table, MySQL automatically numbers all the rows consecutively, so the resulting contents of the insect table look like this:

```
mysql> SELECT * FROM insect ORDER BY id;
+----+------------------+------------+------------+
| id | name             | date       | origin     |
+----+------------------+------------+------------+
|  1 | housefly         | 2001-09-10 | kitchen    |
|  2 | grasshopper      | 2001-09-10 | front yard |
|  3 | stink bug        | 2001-09-10 | front yard |
|  4 | cabbage butterfly | 2001-09-10 | garden     |
|  5 | ant              | 2001-09-10 | back yard  |
|  6 | cricket          | 2001-09-11 | basement   |
|  7 | moth             | 2001-09-14 | windowsill |
+----+------------------+------------+------------+
```

One problem with resequencing a column using separate ALTER TABLE statements is that the table will be without that column for the interval between the two operations. This may cause difficulties for other clients that try to access the table during that time. To prevent this from happening, perform both operations with a single ALTER TABLE statement:

```
mysql> ALTER TABLE insect
    -> DROP id,
    -> ADD id INT UNSIGNED NOT NULL AUTO_INCREMENT FIRST,
    -> AUTO_INCREMENT = 1;
```

MySQL permits multiple actions to be done with ALTER TABLE (something not true for all database systems). However, notice that this multiple-action statement is not simply a concatenation of the two single-action ALTER TABLE statements. It differs in two ways:

- It's unnecessary to reestablish the PRIMARY KEY, because MySQL doesn't drop it unless the indexed column is missing after all the actions specified in the ALTER TABLE statement have been performed.

- The AUTO_INCREMENT clause ensures that MySQL begins the sequence with the value 1. This is actually necessary only prior to MySQL 3.23.39, due to a bug in which MySQL fails to reset the sequence counter when dropping and adding a column in a single ALTER TABLE statement. (For example, if you had a table containing values 8, 12, and 14, the new sequence would be numbered 15, 16, and 17 without the AUTO_INCREMENT clause.)

11.9   Reusing Values at the Top of a Sequence

Problem

You've deleted rows at the top end of your sequence. Can you avoid resequencing the column, but still reuse the values that have been deleted?

Solution

Yes, use ALTER TABLE to reset the sequence counter. MySQL will generate new sequence numbers beginning with the value that is one larger than the current maximum in the table.

Discussion

If you have removed records only from the top of the sequence, those that remain will still be in order with no gaps. (For example if you have records numbered 1 to 100 and you remove records 91 to 100, the remaining records are still in unbroken sequence from 1 to 90.) In this special case, it's unnecessary to renumber the column. Instead, just tell MySQL to resume the sequence beginning with the value one larger that the highest existing sequence number. For ISAM or BDB tables, that's the default behavior anyway, so the deleted values will be reused with no additional action on your part. For MyISAM or InnoDB tables, issue the following statement:

```
ALTER TABLE tbl_name AUTO_INCREMENT = 1
```

This causes MySQL to reset the sequence counter down as far as it can for creating new records in the future.

You can use ALTER TABLE to reset the sequence counter if a sequence column contains gaps in the middle, but doing so still will reuse only values deleted from the top of the sequence. It will not eliminate the gaps. Suppose you have a table with sequence values from 1 to 10 and then delete the records for values 3, 4, 5, 9, and 10. The maximum remaining value is 8, so if you use ALTER TABLE to reset the sequence counter, the next record will be given a value of 9, not 3. To resequence a table and eliminate the gaps as well, see Recipe 11.8.

11.10 Ensuring That Rows Are Renumbered in a Particular Order

Problem

You resequenced a column, but MySQL didn't number the rows the way you want.

Solution

Select the rows into another table, using an ORDER BY clause to place them in the order you want, and let MySQL number them as it performs the operation. Then the rows will be numbered according to the sort order.

Discussion

When you resequence an AUTO_INCREMENT column, MySQL is free to pick the rows from the table in any order, so it won't necessarily renumber them in the order that you expect. This doesn't matter at all if your only requirement is that each row have a unique identifier. But you may have an application for which it's important that the rows be assigned sequence numbers in a particular order. For example, you may want the sequence to correspond to the order in which rows were created, as indicated by a TIMESTAMP column. To assign numbers in a particular order, use this procedure:

1. Create an empty clone of the table.
2. Copy rows from the original into the clone using INSERT INTO ... SELECT. Copy all columns except the sequence column, using an ORDER BY clause to specify the order in which rows are copied (and thus assigned sequence numbers).

3. Drop the original table and rename the clone to have the original table's name.

4. If the table is large and has multiple indexes, it will be more efficient to create the new table initially with no indexes except the one on the AUTO_INCREMENT column. Then copy the original table into the new table and add the remaining indexes afterward.

An alternate procedure:

1. Create a new table that contains all the columns of the original table except the AUTO_INCREMENT column.

2. Use INSERT INTO ... SELECT to copy the non-AUTO_INCREMENT columns from the original table into the new table.

3. Delete the rows from the original table, and reset the sequence counter to 1 if necessary.

4. Copy rows from the new table back to the original table, using an ORDER BY clause to sort rows into the order in which you want sequence numbers assigned.

For information on creating a clone table, see Recipe 3.25. If you're using one of these procedures from within a program that doesn't necessarily have any prior knowledge about the structure of the table, use the table metadata to get a list of column names and to determine which column has the AUTO_INCREMENT attribute. (See Recipe 9.5.)

11.11 Starting a Sequence at a Particular Value

Problem

Sequences start at 1, but you want to use a different starting value.

Solution

Add an AUTO_INCREMENT clause to your CREATE TABLE statement when you create the table. If the table has already been created, use an ALTER TABLE statement to set the starting value.

Discussion

By default, AUTO_INCREMENT sequences start at one:

```
mysql> CREATE TABLE t
    -> (id INT UNSIGNED NOT NULL AUTO_INCREMENT, PRIMARY KEY (id));
mysql> INSERT INTO t (id) VALUES(NULL);
mysql> INSERT INTO t (id) VALUES(NULL);
mysql> INSERT INTO t (id) VALUES(NULL);
mysql> SELECT id FROM t ORDER BY id;
```

```
+----+
| id |
+----+
|  1 |
|  2 |
|  3 |
+----+
```

For MyISAM tables, you can begin the sequence at a specific initial value *n* by including an AUTO_INCREMENT = *n* clause at the end of the CREATE TABLE statement:

```
mysql> CREATE TABLE t
    -> (id INT UNSIGNED NOT NULL AUTO_INCREMENT, PRIMARY KEY (id))
    -> AUTO_INCREMENT = 100;
mysql> INSERT INTO t (id) VALUES(NULL);
mysql> INSERT INTO t (id) VALUES(NULL);
mysql> INSERT INTO t (id) VALUES(NULL);
mysql> SELECT id FROM t ORDER BY id;
+-----+
| id  |
+-----+
| 100 |
| 101 |
| 102 |
+-----+
```

Alternatively, you can create the table and then set the initial sequence value with ALTER TABLE:

```
mysql> CREATE TABLE t
    -> (id INT UNSIGNED NOT NULL AUTO_INCREMENT, PRIMARY KEY (id));
mysql> ALTER TABLE t AUTO_INCREMENT = 100;
mysql> INSERT INTO t (id) VALUES(NULL);
mysql> INSERT INTO t (id) VALUES(NULL);
mysql> INSERT INTO t (id) VALUES(NULL);
mysql> SELECT id FROM t ORDER BY id;
+-----+
| id  |
+-----+
| 100 |
| 101 |
| 102 |
+-----+
```

To start a sequence at *n* for table types other than MyISAM, you must use a hack: insert a "fake" record with sequence value *n*-1, then delete it after inserting one or more "real" records. The following example illustrates how to start a sequence at 100 for an InnoDB table:

```
mysql> CREATE TABLE t
    -> (id INT UNSIGNED NOT NULL AUTO_INCREMENT, PRIMARY KEY (id))
    -> TYPE = InnoDB;
mysql> INSERT INTO t (id) VALUES(99);
mysql> INSERT INTO t (id) VALUES(NULL);
mysql> INSERT INTO t (id) VALUES(NULL);
```

```
mysql> INSERT INTO t (id) VALUES(NULL);
mysql> DELETE FROM t WHERE id = 99;
mysql> SELECT * FROM t ORDER BY id;
+-----+
| id  |
+-----+
| 100 |
| 101 |
| 102 |
+-----+
```

Remember that if you clear out the contents of a table with a DELETE statement that has no WHERE clause, the sequence may be reset to begin with 1, even for types that normally do not reuse sequence values. (See Recipe 11.4.) In this case, you should reinitialize the sequence value explicitly after clearing the table if you don't want it to begin with 1.

11.12 Sequencing an Unsequenced Table

Problem

You forgot to include an AUTO_INCREMENT column when you created a table. Is it too late?

Solution

No, just add one using ALTER TABLE. MySQL will create the column and number the rows automatically.

Discussion

To add a sequence to a table that doesn't currently contain one, use ALTER TABLE to create an AUTO_INCREMENT column. Suppose you have a table t that contains name and age columns, but no sequence column:

```
+----------+------+
| name     | age  |
+----------+------+
| boris    |   47 |
| clarence |   62 |
| abner    |   53 |
+----------+------+
```

You can add a sequence column named id to the table as follows:

```
mysql> ALTER TABLE t
    -> ADD id INT NOT NULL AUTO_INCREMENT,
    -> ADD PRIMARY KEY (id);
mysql> SELECT * FROM t ORDER BY id;
```

```
+----------+------+----+
| name     | age  | id |
+----------+------+----+
| boris    |  47  |  1 |
| clarence |  62  |  2 |
| abner    |  53  |  3 |
+----------+------+----+
```

MySQL numbers the rows for you automatically. It's not necessary to assign the values yourself. Very handy.

By default, ALTER TABLE adds new columns to the end of the table. To place a column at a specific position, use FIRST or AFTER at the end of the ADD clause. The following ALTER TABLE statements are similar to the one just shown, but would place the id column first in the table or after the name column, respectively:

```
ALTER TABLE t
ADD id INT NOT NULL AUTO_INCREMENT FIRST,
ADD PRIMARY KEY (id);

ALTER TABLE t
ADD id INT NOT NULL AUTO_INCREMENT AFTER name,
ADD PRIMARY KEY (id);
```

For MyISAM tables, you can specify the initial value for a new sequence column by including an AUTO_INCREMENT = *n* clause in the ALTER TABLE statement:

```
mysql> ALTER TABLE t
    -> ADD id INT NOT NULL AUTO_INCREMENT FIRST,
    -> ADD PRIMARY KEY (id),
    -> AUTO_INCREMENT = 100;
mysql> SELECT * FROM t ORDER BY id;
+-----+----------+------+
| id  | name     | age  |
+-----+----------+------+
| 100 | boris    |  47  |
| 101 | clarence |  62  |
| 102 | abner    |  53  |
+-----+----------+------+
```

11.13 Using an AUTO_INCREMENT Column
to Create Multiple Sequences

Problem

You need to have sequencing behavior that is more complex than a single sequence of values. You need to tie different sequences to the values in other columns of the table.

Solution

Link the AUTO_INCREMENT column to those other columns, making them all part of the same index.

Discussion

When an AUTO_INCREMENT column is the only column in a PRIMARY KEY or UNIQUE index, it generates a single sequence 1, 2, 3, ... in which successive values increase by one each time you add a record, regardless of the contents of the rest of the record. As of MySQL 3.23.5, it's possible for MyISAM tables to create an index that combines an AUTO_INCREMENT column with other columns to generate multiple sequences within a single table.

Here's how it works: let's say that Junior develops such a passion for bug collecting that he decides to keep it up even after the school project has been completed—except that when freed from the constraints of the teacher's instructions, he's perfectly content to include insect-like bugs such as millipedes, and even to collect multiple instances of any given creature. Junior happily goes outside and collects more specimens over the next few days:

Name	Date	Origin
ant	2001-10-07	kitchen
millipede	2001-10-07	basement
beetle	2001-10-07	basement
ant	2001-10-07	front yard
ant	2001-10-07	front yard
honeybee	2001-10-08	back yard
cricket	2001-10-08	garage
beetle	2001-10-08	front yard
termite	2001-10-09	kitchen woodwork
cricket	2001-10-11	basement
termite	2001-10-11	bathroom woodwork
honeybee	2001-10-11	garden
cricket	2001-10-11	garden
ant	2001-10-11	garden

After recording this information, he's ready to enter it into the database, but wants to number each kind of bug separately (ant 1, ant 2, ..., beetle 1, beetle 2, ..., cricket 1, cricket 2, and so forth). To that end, you look over the data (noting with some alarm Junior's discovery of termites in the house and making a mental note to call the exterminator), then design a bug table for Junior that looks like this:

```
CREATE TABLE bug
(
    id      INT UNSIGNED NOT NULL AUTO_INCREMENT,
    name    VARCHAR(30) NOT NULL,   # type of bug
```

```
       PRIMARY KEY (name, id),
       date    DATE NOT NULL,           # date collected
       origin  VARCHAR(30) NOT NULL     # where collected
);
```

This is very similar to the insect table, but has one significant difference: The PRIMARY KEY comprises two columns, not one. As a result, the id column will behave somewhat differently than for the insect table. If the new set of specimens is entered into the bug table in the order in which Junior wrote them down, here's what the resulting table looks like:

```
mysql> SELECT * FROM bug;
+----+-----------+------------+-------------------+
| id | name      | date       | origin            |
+----+-----------+------------+-------------------+
|  1 | ant       | 2001-10-07 | kitchen           |
|  1 | millipede | 2001-10-07 | basement          |
|  1 | beetle    | 2001-10-07 | basement          |
|  2 | ant       | 2001-10-07 | front yard        |
|  3 | ant       | 2001-10-07 | front yard        |
|  1 | honeybee  | 2001-10-08 | back yard         |
|  1 | cricket   | 2001-10-08 | garage            |
|  2 | beetle    | 2001-10-08 | front yard        |
|  1 | termite   | 2001-10-09 | kitchen woodwork  |
|  2 | cricket   | 2001-10-10 | basement          |
|  2 | termite   | 2001-10-11 | bathroom woodwork |
|  2 | honeybee  | 2001-10-11 | garden            |
|  3 | cricket   | 2001-10-11 | garden            |
|  4 | ant       | 2001-10-11 | garden            |
+----+-----------+------------+-------------------+
```

Looking at the table that way, it appears that the id values are being assigned at random—but they're not. Sort the table by name and id and it'll be more clear how MySQL assigns the values. Specifically, MySQL creates a separate id sequence for each distinct name value:

```
mysql> SELECT * FROM bug ORDER BY name, id;
+----+-----------+------------+-------------------+
| id | name      | date       | origin            |
+----+-----------+------------+-------------------+
|  1 | ant       | 2001-10-07 | kitchen           |
|  2 | ant       | 2001-10-07 | front yard        |
|  3 | ant       | 2001-10-07 | front yard        |
|  4 | ant       | 2001-10-11 | garden            |
|  1 | beetle    | 2001-10-07 | basement          |
|  2 | beetle    | 2001-10-08 | front yard        |
|  1 | cricket   | 2001-10-08 | garage            |
|  2 | cricket   | 2001-10-10 | basement          |
|  3 | cricket   | 2001-10-11 | garden            |
|  1 | honeybee  | 2001-10-08 | back yard         |
|  2 | honeybee  | 2001-10-11 | garden            |
|  1 | millipede | 2001-10-07 | basement          |
|  1 | termite   | 2001-10-09 | kitchen woodwork  |
|  2 | termite   | 2001-10-11 | bathroom woodwork |
+----+-----------+------------+-------------------+
```

When you create a multiple-column AUTO_INCREMENT index, note the following points:

- The order in which the CREATE TABLE statement defines the indexed columns does not matter. What *is* significant is the order in which the index definition names the columns. The AUTO_INCREMENT column must be named last, or the multiple-sequence mechanism will not work.

- A PRIMARY KEY cannot contain NULL values, but a UNIQUE index can. If any of the non-AUTO_INCREMENT columns might contain NULL values, you should create a UNIQUE index rather than a PRIMARY KEY.

For the bug table, the AUTO_INCREMENT index has two columns. The same technique can be extended to more than two columns, but the basic concept is the same: for an *n*-column index where the last one is an AUTO_INCREMENT column, MySQL generates an independent sequence for each unique combination of values in the non-AUTO_INCREMENT columns. Suppose you're recording subject information for a research project in which you have control and experimental conditions that you administer to male and female subjects. To assign a separate set of sequence numbers for each sex in each of the two conditions, create a three-column AUTO_INCREMENT index:

```
CREATE TABLE subj_list
(
    name        CHAR(40),    # subject name
    condition   ENUM('control','experimental') NOT NULL,
    sex         ENUM('M','F') NOT NULL,
    id          INT UNSIGNED NOT NULL AUTO_INCREMENT,
    PRIMARY KEY (condition, sex, id)
);
```

MySQL's mechanism for multiple-column sequences can be easier to use than logically equivalent single-column values. Recall that in Recipe 6.12, we used a housewares table that contained rows with three-part product ID values composed of a three-character category abbreviation, a five-digit serial number, and a two-character code indicating country of manufacture:

```
+------------+------------------+
| id         | description      |
+------------+------------------+
| DIN40672US | dining table     |
| KIT00372UK | garbage disposal |
| KIT01729JP | microwave oven   |
| BED00038SG | bedside lamp     |
| BTH00485US | shower stall     |
| BTH00415JP | lavatory         |
+------------+------------------+
```

The table was used in that chapter to demonstrate how to break apart the id values into their constituent parts and sort them separately, using LEFT(), MID(), and RIGHT(). This led to some fairly ugly ORDER BY clauses, and an issue that I didn't even bring up in that chapter was the question of just how the serial numbers in the middle of the values are to be generated.

Sometimes you can replace this kind of multiple-part column with separate columns that are tied together as an AUTO_INCREMENT index. For example, another way to manage houseware id values like this is to represent them using category, serial, and country columns and tie them together in a PRIMARY KEY with the serial number as an AUTO_INCREMENT column. This would cause serial numbers to increment independently for each combination of category and country. To create the table from scratch, you'd write the CREATE TABLE statement like this:

```
CREATE TABLE housewares
(
    category    VARCHAR(3) NOT NULL,
    serial      INT UNSIGNED NOT NULL AUTO_INCREMENT,
    country     VARCHAR(2) NOT NULL,
    description VARCHAR(255),
    PRIMARY KEY (category, country, serial)
);
```

Alternatively, assuming you have the original housewares table already created in the form used in the earlier chapter, you can convert it to the new structure "in place" as follows:

```
mysql> ALTER TABLE housewares
    -> ADD category VARCHAR(3) NOT NULL FIRST,
    -> ADD serial INT UNSIGNED NOT NULL AUTO_INCREMENT AFTER category,
    -> ADD country VARCHAR(2) NOT NULL AFTER serial,
    -> ADD PRIMARY KEY (category, country, serial);
mysql> UPDATE housewares SET category = LEFT(id,3);
mysql> UPDATE housewares SET serial = MID(id,4,5);
mysql> UPDATE housewares SET country = RIGHT(id,2);
mysql> ALTER TABLE housewares DROP id;
mysql> SELECT * FROM housewares;
+----------+--------+---------+------------------+
| category | serial | country | description      |
+----------+--------+---------+------------------+
| DIN      |  40672 | US      | dining table     |
| KIT      |    372 | UK      | garbage disposal |
| KIT      |   1729 | JP      | microwave oven   |
| BED      |     38 | SG      | bedside lamp     |
| BTH      |    485 | US      | shower stall     |
| BTH      |    415 | JP      | lavatory         |
+----------+--------+---------+------------------+
```

With the id values split into their separate parts, sorting operations become easier to specify because you can refer to individual columns directly rather than by pulling out substrings of the original id column. You can also make sorting more efficient by adding additional indexes for the serial and country columns. But a problem remains: How to display each product ID as a single string rather than as three separate values? That can be done with CONCAT():

```
mysql> SELECT category, serial, country,
    -> CONCAT(category,LPAD(serial,5,'0'),country) AS id
    -> FROM housewares ORDER BY category, country, serial;
```

```
+----------+--------+---------+------------+
| category | serial | country | id         |
+----------+--------+---------+------------+
| BED      |     38 | SG      | BED00038SG |
| BTH      |    415 | JP      | BTH00415JP |
| BTH      |    485 | US      | BTH00485US |
| DIN      |  40672 | US      | DIN40672US |
| KIT      |   1729 | JP      | KIT01729JP |
| KIT      |    372 | UK      | KIT00372UK |
+----------+--------+---------+------------+
```

You can even eliminate the need for LPAD() by declaring serial to be a zero-filled column for which values are displayed using five digits:

```
mysql> ALTER TABLE housewares
    -> MODIFY serial INT(5) UNSIGNED ZEROFILL NOT NULL AUTO_INCREMENT;
```

Then MySQL will supply the leading zeros automatically and the CONCAT() expression becomes simpler:

```
mysql> SELECT category, serial, country,
    -> CONCAT(category,serial,country) AS id
    -> FROM housewares ORDER BY category, country, serial;
+----------+--------+---------+------------+
| category | serial | country | id         |
+----------+--------+---------+------------+
| BED      | 00038  | SG      | BED00038SG |
| BTH      | 00415  | JP      | BTH00415JP |
| BTH      | 00485  | US      | BTH00485US |
| DIN      | 40672  | US      | DIN40672US |
| KIT      | 01729  | JP      | KIT01729JP |
| KIT      | 00372  | UK      | KIT00372UK |
+----------+--------+---------+------------+
```

This example illustrates an important principle: You might think about values one way (id values as single strings), but that doesn't mean you must necessarily represent them in the database that way. If an alternate representation (separate columns) is more efficient or easier to work with, it may well be worth using—even if you must reformat the underlying columns for display purposes to give them the appearance people expect.

11.14 Managing Multiple Simultaneous AUTO_INCREMENT Values

Problem

You're working with two or more tables that contain AUTO_INCREMENT columns, and you're having a hard time keeping track of the sequence values generated for each table.

Solution

Save the values in SQL variables for later. If you're using queries from within a program, save the sequence values in program variables; or you may be able to issue the queries using separate connection or statement objects to keep them from getting mixed up.

Discussion

As described in Recipe 11.5, the LAST_INSERT_ID() server-side sequence value indicator function is set each time a query generates an AUTO_INCREMENT value, whereas client-side sequence indicators may be reset for every query. What if you issue a statement that generates an AUTO_INCREMENT value, but don't want to refer to that value until after issuing a second statement that also generates an AUTO_INCREMENT value? In this case, the original value no longer will be accessible, either through LAST_INSERT_ID() or as a client-side value. To retain access to it, you should save the value first before issuing the second statement. There are several ways to do this:

- At the SQL level, you can save the value in a SQL variable after issuing a query that generates an AUTO_INCREMENT value:

```
INSERT INTO tbl_name (id,...) VALUES(NULL,...);
SET @saved_id = LAST_INSERT_ID();
```

  Then you can issue other statements without regard to their effect on LAST_INSERT_ID(). To use the original AUTO_INCREMENT value in a subsequent query, refer to the @saved_id variable.

- At the API level, you can save the AUTO_INCREMENT value in an API language variable. This can be done either by saving the value returned from LAST_INSERT_ID() or from any API-specific extension that might be available.

- A third technique can be used from within APIs that allow you to maintain separate client-side AUTO_INCREMENT values. For example, in Python, when you use a cursor object to execute a query, the AUTO_INCREMENT value generated by the query is available by calling the cursor's insert_id() method. If you issue other queries using the same cursor, that value will be lost. However, if you use a different cursor object to execute additional queries, the original cursor's insert_id value will be unaffected:

```
cursor1 = conn.cursor ()
cursor2 = conn.cursor ()
gen_seq_val (cursor1)      # issue query that generates a sequence number
gen_seq_val (cursor2)      # issue another, using a different cursor
seq1 = cursor1.insert_id ()
seq2 = cursor2.insert_id ()
print "seq1:", seq1, "seq2:", seq2  # these values will be different
cursor1.close ()
cursor2.close ()
```

In Perl, you can achieve the same effect by means of two statement handles; the `mysql_insertid` attribute for each is unaffected by query activity on the other. In Java, use separate `Statement` or `PreparedStatement` objects.

The third technique doesn't work with PHP, because there is no client-side object or structure that maintains `AUTO_INCREMENT` values on a query-specific basis. The client-side `AUTO_INCREMENT` value is returned by `mysql_insert_id()`, which is tied to the connection, not to a statement. Yes, I know what you're thinking: a workaround would be to open a second connection to the server and issue the first and second queries over the different connections. You're right, that would work—but it's not worth the effort. The overhead of opening another connection is much higher than simply saving the `mysql_insert_id()` value in a PHP variable before issuing another query. Furthermore, opening a second connection isn't as straightforward as it might seem. If you issue a second `mysql_connect()` or `mysql_pconnect()` call with the same connection parameters as the original call, PHP returns the same connection identifier as the one it returned originally! You'd have to connect to the server as a different user to get a truly independent connection identifier. (At the risk of muddying the waters, I should point out that as of PHP 4.2.0, `mysql_connect()` supports the option of explicitly forcing a new connection to be opened. You can use this feature to maintain separate client-side `AUTO_INCREMENT` values.)

11.15 Using AUTO_INCREMENT Values to Relate Tables

Problem

You're using sequence values from one table as keys in second table so that you can relate records in the two tables properly. But the associations aren't being set up properly.

Solution

You're probably not inserting records in the proper order, or you're losing track of the sequence values. Change the insertion order, or save the sequence values so that you can refer to them when you need them.

Discussion

Be careful with `AUTO_INCREMENT` values that are used to generate ID values in a master table if you also store those values in detail table records to link the detail records to the proper master table record. This kind of situation is quite common. Suppose you have an `invoice` table listing invoice information for customer orders, and an `inv_item` table listing the individual items associated with each invoice. Here, `invoice` is the master table and inv_item is the detail table. To uniquely identify each order, the invoice table could contain an AUTO_INCREMENT column inv_id. You'd also store the appropriate invoice number in each inv_item table record so you can tell which invoice it goes with. The tables might look something like this:

```
CREATE TABLE invoice
(
    inv_id  INT UNSIGNED NOT NULL AUTO_INCREMENT,
    PRIMARY KEY (inv_id),
    date    DATE NOT NULL
    # ... other columns could go here
    # ... (customer ID, shipping address, etc.)
);
CREATE TABLE inv_item
(
    inv_id       INT UNSIGNED NOT NULL,  # invoice ID (from invoice table)
    INDEX (inv_id),
    qty          INT,                     # quantity
    description VARCHAR(40)               # description
);
```

For these kinds of table relationships, it's typical to insert a record into the master table first (to generate the AUTO_INCREMENT value that identifies the record), then insert the detail records and refer to LAST_INSERT_ID( ) to obtain the master record ID. For example, if a customer buys a hammer, three boxes of nails, and (in anticipation of finger-bashing with the hammer) a dozen bandages, the records pertaining to the order can be inserted into the two tables like so:

```
INSERT INTO invoice (inv_id,date)
    VALUES(NULL,CURDATE());
INSERT INTO inv_item (inv_id,qty,description)
    VALUES(LAST_INSERT_ID(),1,'hammer');
INSERT INTO inv_item (inv_id,qty,description)
    VALUES(LAST_INSERT_ID(),3,'nails, box');
INSERT INTO inv_item (inv_id,qty,description)
    VALUES(LAST_INSERT_ID(),12,'bandage');
```

The first INSERT adds a record to the invoice master table and generates a new AUTO_INCREMENT value for its inv_id column. The following INSERT statements each add a record to the inv_item detail table, using LAST_INSERT_ID( ) to get the invoice number. This associates the detail records with the proper master record.

What if you need to process multiple invoices? There's a right way and a wrong way to enter the information. The right way is to insert all the information for the first invoice, then proceed to the next. The wrong way is to add all the master records into the invoice table, then add all the detail records to the inv_item table. If you do that, *all* the detail records in the inv_item table will contain the AUTO_INCREMENT value from the most recently entered invoice record. Thus, all will appear to be part of the same invoice, and records in the two tables won't have the proper associations.

If the detail table contains its own AUTO_INCREMENT column, you must be even more careful about how you add records to the tables. Suppose you want to number the rows in the inv_item table sequentially for each order. The way to do that is to create a multiple-column AUTO_INCREMENT index that generates a separate sequence for the items in each invoice. (Recipe 11.13 discusses this type of index.) Create the inv_item table as follows, using a PRIMARY KEY that combines the inv_id column with an AUTO_INCREMENT column, seq:

```
CREATE TABLE inv_item
(
    inv_id      INT UNSIGNED NOT NULL,  # invoice ID (from invoice table)
    seq         INT UNSIGNED NOT NULL AUTO_INCREMENT,
    PRIMARY KEY (inv_id, seq),
    qty         INT,             # quantity
    description VARCHAR(40)      # description
);
```

The inv_id column allows each inv_item row to be associated with the proper invoice table record, just as with the original table structure. In addition, the index causes the seq values for the items in each invoice to be numbered sequentially starting at 1. However, now that both tables contain an AUTO_INCREMENT column, you cannot enter information for an invoice the same way as before. To see why it doesn't work, try it:

```
INSERT INTO invoice (inv_id,date)
    VALUES(NULL,CURDATE());
INSERT INTO inv_item (inv_id,qty,description)
    VALUES(LAST_INSERT_ID(),1,'hammer');
INSERT INTO inv_item (inv_id,qty,description)
    VALUES(LAST_INSERT_ID(),3,'nails, box');
INSERT INTO inv_item (inv_id,qty,description)
    VALUES(LAST_INSERT_ID(),12,'bandage');
```

These queries are the same as before, but now behave somewhat differently due to the change in the inv_item table structure. The INSERT into the invoice table works properly. So does the first INSERT into the inv_item table; LAST_INSERT_ID() returns the inv_id value from the master record in the invoice table. However, this INSERT also generates its own AUTO_INCREMENT value (for the seq column), which changes the value of LAST_INSERT_ID() and causes the master record inv_id value to be "lost." The result is that subsequent inserts into the inv_item store the preceding record's seq value into the inv_id column. This causes the second and following records to have incorrect inv_id values.

These are several ways to avoid this difficulty. One involves using a different INSERT syntax to add the detail records; others save the master record AUTO_INCREMENT value in a variable for later use:

Insert multiple detail records at a time. One solution to the problem is to add detail records using MySQL's INSERT syntax that allows multiple rows to be inserted with a single statement. That way you can apply the LAST_INSERT_ID() value from the master record to all the detail records:

```
INSERT INTO invoice (inv_id,date)
    VALUES(NULL,CURDATE());
INSERT INTO inv_item (inv_id,qty,description) VALUES
    (LAST_INSERT_ID(),1,'hammer'),
    (LAST_INSERT_ID(),3,'nails, box'),
    (LAST_INSERT_ID(),12,'bandage');
```

Use a SQL variable. Another method is to save the master record AUTO_INCREMENT value in a SQL variable for use when inserting the detail records:

```
INSERT INTO invoice (inv_id,date)
    VALUES(NULL,CURDATE());
SET @inv_id = LAST_INSERT_ID();
INSERT INTO inv_item (inv_id,qty,description)
    VALUES(@inv_id,1,'hammer');
INSERT INTO inv_item (inv_id,qty,description)
    VALUES(@inv_id,3,'nails, box');
INSERT INTO inv_item (inv_id,qty,description)
    VALUES(@inv_id,12,'bandage');
```

Use an API variable. A third method is similar to the second, but applies only from within an API. Insert the master record, then save the AUTO_INCREMENT value into an API variable for use when inserting detail records. For example, in Perl, you can access the AUTO_INCREMENT using the mysql_insertid attribute, so the invoice-entry procedure looks something like this:

```
$dbh->do ("INSERT INTO invoice (inv_id,date) VALUES(NULL,CURDATE())");
$inv_id = $dbh->{mysql_insertid};
$sth = $dbh->prepare ("INSERT INTO inv_item (inv_id,qty,description)
                    VALUES(?,?,?)");
$sth->execute ($inv_id, 1, "hammer");
$sth->execute ($inv_id, 3, "nails, box");
$sth->execute ($inv_id, 12, "bandage");
```

11.16 Using Single-Row Sequence Generators

Problem

You're interested only in counting events, so there's no point in creating a record for each count.

Solution

Use a different sequence-generation mechanism that uses just one row.

Discussion

AUTO_INCREMENT columns are useful for generating sequences across a set of individual records. But for some applications, you're interested only in a count of the number of times an event occurs, and there's no value in creating a separate record for each event. Instances include web page or banner ad hit counters, a count of items sold, or the number of votes in a poll. For such applications, you need only a single record to hold the count as it changes over time. MySQL provides a mechanism for this that allows counts to be treated like AUTO_INCREMENT values so that you can not only increment the count, but retrieve the updated value easily.

To count a single type of event, you can use a trivial table with a single row and column. For example, if you're selling copies of a book named "Red Horse Hill," you can create and initialize a table to record sales for it like this:

```
CREATE TABLE red_horse_hill (copies INT UNSIGNED);
INSERT INTO red_horse_hill (copies) VALUES(0);
```

However, if you're selling multiple book titles, that method won't work so well. You certainly don't want to create a separate single-row table to count sales for each book. Instead, you can count them all within a single table if you include a column that provides a unique identifier for each book. The following table, booksales, does this using a title column for the book title in addition to a copies column that records the number of copies sold:

```
CREATE TABLE booksales
(
    title   VARCHAR(60) NOT NULL,   # book title
    copies  INT UNSIGNED NOT NULL,  # number of copies sold
    PRIMARY KEY (title)
);
```

Initialize the table by adding a row for each book:

```
mysql> INSERT INTO booksales (title) VALUES
    -> ('Red Horse Hill'),
    -> ('Sparkplug of the Hornets'),
    -> ('Bulldozer'),
    -> ('The Long Trains Roll'),
    -> ('Who Rides in the Dark?');
mysql> SELECT * FROM booksales;
+--------------------------+--------+
| title                    | copies |
+--------------------------+--------+
| The Long Trains Roll     |      0 |
| Bulldozer                |      0 |
| Sparkplug of the Hornets |      0 |
| Red Horse Hill           |      0 |
| Who Rides in the Dark?   |      0 |
+--------------------------+--------+
```

That sets up the table. Now, how do you use it? One way is to increment the copies column for a given book by issuing a simple UPDATE statement that names the book:

```
UPDATE booksales SET copies = copies+1 WHERE title = 'Bulldozer';
```

To retrieve the count (so that you can display a message to the customer such as "you just purchased copy *n* of this book," for example), issue a SELECT query for the same book title:

```
SELECT copies FROM booksales WHERE title = 'Bulldozer';
```

Unfortunately, this method doesn't really work properly. Suppose that during the time between the UPDATE and SELECT statements some other person buys a copy of the book (and thus increments the copies value). Then the SELECT statement won't actually produce the value *you* incremented the sales count to, but rather its most recent value. In other words, other clients can affect the value before you have time to retrieve it. This is similar to the problem discussed earlier that can occur if you try to retrieve the most recent AUTO_INCREMENT value from a column by invoking MAX(*col_name*) rather than LAST_INSERT_ID( ).

There are ways around this (such as by grouping the two statements as a transaction or by locking the table), but MySQL provides a different solution based on LAST_INSERT_ID( ). If you call LAST_INSERT_ID( ) with an expression argument, MySQL treats it like an AUTO_INCREMENT value.* To use this feature for incrementing counters in the booksales table, modify the UPDATE statement slightly:

```
UPDATE booksales SET copies = LAST_INSERT_ID(copies+1)
WHERE title = 'Bulldozer';
```

Then you can invoke LAST_INSERT_ID( ) with no argument to retrieve the value:

```
SELECT LAST_INSERT_ID();
```

By updating the copies column this way, you can always get back the value that you set it to, even if some other client has updated it in the meantime. If you're issuing the UPDATE statement from within an API that provides a mechanism for fetching the most recent AUTO_INCREMENT value directly, you need not even issue the SELECT query. For example, in Python, you can update a count and get the new value using the insert_id( ) method:

```
cursor = conn.cursor ()
cursor.execute ("""
        UPDATE booksales SET copies = LAST_INSERT_ID(copies+1)
        WHERE title = 'Bulldozer'
    """)
count = cursor.insert_id ()
```

In Java, the operation looks like this:

```
Statement s = conn.createStatement ();
s.executeUpdate (
    "UPDATE booksales SET copies = LAST_INSERT_ID(copies+1)"
    + " WHERE title = 'Bulldozer'");
long count = ((com.mysql.jdbc.Statement) s).getLastInsertID ();
s.close ();
```

---

* The LAST_INSERT_ID(*expr*) mechanism is available as of MySQL 3.22.9.

The use of `LAST_INSERT_ID()` for sequence generation has certain other properties that differ from true `AUTO_INCREMENT` sequences:

- `AUTO_INCREMENT` values increment by one each time, whereas counter values generated by `LAST_INSERT_ID(expr)` can be incremented by whatever value you want. For example, to produce the sequence 10, 20, 30, ..., increment the count by 10 each time. You need not even increment the counter by the same value each time. If you sell a dozen copies of a book rather than a single copy, update its sales count as follows:

  ```
  UPDATE booksales SET copies = LAST_INSERT_ID(copies+12)
  WHERE title = 'Bulldozer';
  ```

- You can start the sequence at any integer, including negative values. It's also possible to produce decreasing sequences by using a negative increment. (For a column that is used to generate a sequence that includes negative values, you would omit `UNSIGNED` from the column definition, of course.)

- To reset a counter, simply set it to the desired value. Suppose you want to report to book buyers the sales for the current month, rather than the total sales (for example, to display messages like "you're the nth buyer this month"). To clear the counters to zero at the beginning of each month, run this query:

  ```
  UPDATE booksales SET copies = 0;
  ```

- One property that's not so desirable is that the value generated by `LAST_INSERT_ID(expr)` is not available uniformly via client-side retrieval methods under all circumstances. You can get it after `UPDATE` or `INSERT` queries, but not for `SET` statements. If you generate a value as follows (in Perl), the client-side value returned by `mysql_insertid` will be 0, not 48:

  ```
  $dbh->do ("SET \@x = LAST_INSERT_ID(48)");
  $seq = $dbh->{mysql_insertid};
  ```

  To get the value in this case, ask the server for it:

  ```
  $seq = $dbh->selectrow_array ("SELECT LAST_INSERT_ID()");
  ```

The single-row sequence-generation mechanism is revisited in Recipe 18.12, where it serves as the basis for implementing web page hit counters.

11.17 Generating Repeating Sequences

Problem

You need to create a sequence that contains cycles.

Solution

Generate a sequence and produce the cyclic elements using division and the modulo operator.

Discussion

Some sequence-generation problems require values that go through cycles. Suppose you're manufacturing items like pharmaceutical products or automobile parts, and you must be able to track them by lot number if manufacturing problems are discovered later that require items sold within a particular lot to be recalled. Suppose also that you pack and distribute items 12 units to a box and 6 boxes to a case. In this situation, item identifiers are three-part values: The unit number (with a value from 1 to 12), the box number (with a value from 1 to 6), and a lot number (with a value from 1 to whatever the highest case number happens to be currently).

This item-tracking problem appears to require that you maintain three counters, so you might think about generating the next identifier value using an algorithm like this:

```
retrieve most recently used case, box, and unit numbers
unit = unit + 1      # increment unit number
if (unit > 12)       # need to start a new box?
{
    unit = 1         # go to first unit of next box
    box = box + 1
}
if (box > 6)         # need to start a new case?
{
    box = 1          # go to first box of next case
    case = case + 1
}
store new case, box, and unit numbers
```

You could indeed implement an algorithm that way. On the other hand, it's also possible simply to assign each item a sequence number identifier and derive the corresponding case, box, and unit numbers from it. The identifier can come from an AUTO_INCREMENT column or a single-row sequence generator. The formulas for determining the case, box, and unit numbers for any item from its sequence number look like this:

```
unit = ((seq - 1) % 12) + 1
box = (int ((seq - 1) / 12) % 6) + 1
case = int ((seq - 1)/(6 * 12)) + 1
```

The table shown below illustrates the relationship between some sample sequence numbers and the corresponding case, box, and unit numbers:

seq	case	box	unit
1	1	1	1
12	1	1	12
13	1	2	1
72	1	6	12
73	2	1	1
144	2	6	12

11.18 Numbering Query Output Rows Sequentially

Problem

You want to number query output rows.

Solution

If you're writing your own program, just add the row number yourself.

Discussion

A type of sequence that has nothing to do with the contents of your database is to number output rows from a query. When working within an API, you can number the rows by maintaining a counter and displaying its current value with each row's contents. Here is an example in Python, using the insects table. It simply displays a numbered list of the distinct values in the origin column of the table:

```
cursor = conn.cursor ()
cursor.execute ("SELECT DISTINCT origin FROM insect")
count = 1
while 1:
    row = cursor.fetchone ()
    if row == None:
        break
    print count, row[0]
    count = count + 1
cursor.close ()
```

See Also

The *mysql* program provides no explicit row-numbering facilities, although you can use a SQL variable to include an extra row number column in a query's output. Another way to produce results that may be suitable for your purposes is to filter *mysql* output through another program that adds row numbers. These techniques are described in Recipe 1.26.

## CHAPTER 12

Using Multiple Tables

12.0 Introduction

For the most part, recipes in earlier chapters have used single tables. But for any application of even moderate complexity, it's likely that you'll need to use multiple tables. Some queries simply cannot be answered using a single table, and the real power of a relational database comes into play when you start to relate the information in tables to each other. There are several reasons to use multiple tables:

- To combine records from tables to obtain more comprehensive information than can be obtained from individual tables alone
- To hold intermediate results for a multiple-stage operation
- To insert, delete, or update records in one table based on information in another

When you use multiple tables, they may come from the same database or from different databases. On occasion, you may even need to use tables that come from databases hosted by different MySQL servers. For the first two cases, you'll need to know how to refer to columns from the different tables, which may involve using table aliases or qualifying table names with a database name. In the third case, you'll need to open a connection to each server and relate the information from them yourself.

12.1 Combining Rows in One Table with Rows in Another

Problem

You want to write a query that uses information from more than one table.

Solution

Use a join—that is, a query that refers to multiple tables and that tells MySQL how to match up information from them.

Discussion

The essential idea behind a join is that it combines rows in one table with rows in one or more other tables. A full join between tables produces all possible combinations of rows. For example, joining a 100-row table to a 200-row table produces a result containing 100×200, or 20,000 rows. With larger tables, or joins between more than two tables, a result set can easily become immense—possibly causing the MySQL server to run out of temporary table space. Because of that, and because you rarely want all the combinations anyway, a join normally includes a WHERE clause that narrows the focus of the query. This section introduces basic join syntax, and later sections show how joins help you answer specific types of questions.

Suppose that you're a very unimaginative dresser, and you have trouble picking out your wardrobe each day. So you decide to let MySQL help you. First, enter your shirts into one table and your ties into another:

```
mysql> CREATE TABLE shirt (item CHAR(20));
mysql> INSERT INTO shirt (item)
    -> VALUES('Pinstripe'),('Tie-Dye'),('Black');
mysql> CREATE TABLE tie (item CHAR(20));
mysql> INSERT INTO tie (item)
    -> VALUES('Fleur de lis'),('Paisley'),('Polka Dot');
```

You can list what's in each table by using separate single-table queries:

```
mysql> SELECT item FROM shirt;
+-----------+
| item      |
+-----------+
| Pinstripe |
| Tie-Dye   |
| Black     |
+-----------+
mysql> SELECT item FROM tie;
+--------------+
| item         |
+--------------+
| Fleur de lis |
| Paisley      |
| Polka Dot    |
+--------------+
```

But you can also ask MySQL to show you various combinations of wardrobe items by writing a query that performs a join. A join names two or more tables after the FROM keyword. In the output column list, you can name columns from any or all of the joined tables, or use expressions that are based on those columns. The simplest join involves two tables and selects all columns from each. With no WHERE clause, the join generates output for all combinations of rows. Thus, to find all possible combinations of shirts and ties, use the following query to produce a full join between the two tables:

```
mysql> SELECT * FROM shirt, tie;
```

```
+-----------+---------------+
| item      | item          |
+-----------+---------------+
| Pinstripe | Fleur de lis  |
| Tie-Dye   | Fleur de lis  |
| Black     | Fleur de lis  |
| Pinstripe | Paisley       |
| Tie-Dye   | Paisley       |
| Black     | Paisley       |
| Pinstripe | Polka Dot     |
| Tie-Dye   | Polka Dot     |
| Black     | Polka Dot     |
+-----------+---------------+
```

You can see that each item from the shirt table is paired with every item from the tie table. To use the list to guide you in your wardrobe selections, print it out and tape it up on the wall. Each day, wear the items displayed in the first unused row and cross the row off the list.

The output column list in the previous query is specified as *. For a single-table query, an output list of * means "every column from the named table." Analogously, for a join it means "every column from every named table," so the query returns the columns from both shirt and tie. Other ways to specify output columns are to use *tbl_name.** to select all columns from a particular table, or *tbl_name.col_name* to specify a single column from the table. Thus, all the following queries are equivalent:

```
SELECT * FROM shirt, tie;
SELECT shirt.*, tie.* FROM shirt, tie;
SELECT shirt.*, tie.item FROM shirt, tie;
SELECT shirt.item, tie.* FROM shirt, tie;
SELECT shirt.item, tie.item FROM shirt, tie;
```

The *tbl_name.col_name* notation that qualifies a column name with a table name is always allowable, but can be shortened to just *col_name* if the name appears in only one of the joined tables. In that case, MySQL can determine without ambiguity which table the column comes from and no table name qualifier is necessary. We can't do that for a join between shirt and tie; they both have a column with the same name (item), so the following query is ambiguous:

```
mysql> SELECT item, item FROM shirt, tie;
ERROR 1052 at line 1: Column: 'item' in field list is ambiguous
```

If the columns had distinct names such as s_item and t_item, the query could be written unambiguously without table qualifiers:

```
SELECT s_item, p_item FROM shirt, tie;
```

To make the meaning of a query clearer to human readers, it's often useful to qualify column names even when that's not strictly necessary as far as MySQL is concerned. I tend to use qualified names in join query examples for that reason.

Without a WHERE clause to restrict the output, a join produces an output row for every possible combination of input rows. For large tables, this is usually a bad idea, so it's typical to provide some kind of condition on the output rows. For example, if you're tired of having your office mates tease you about your polka dot tie, select only the *other* stylish combinations that are possible using your wardrobe items:

```
mysql> SELECT shirt.item, tie.item FROM shirt, tie
    -> WHERE tie.item != 'Polka Dot';
+-----------+--------------+
| item      | item         |
+-----------+--------------+
| Pinstripe | Fleur de lis |
| Tie-Dye   | Fleur de lis |
| Black     | Fleur de lis |
| Pinstripe | Paisley      |
| Tie-Dye   | Paisley      |
| Black     | Paisley      |
+-----------+--------------+
```

You can also limit the output other ways. To select wardrobe combinations at random, run the following query each morning to pick a single row from the full join:[*]

```
mysql> SELECT shirt.item, tie.item FROM shirt, tie
    -> ORDER BY RAND() LIMIT 1;
+---------+--------------+
| item    | item         |
+---------+--------------+
| Tie-Dye | Fleur de lis |
+---------+--------------+
```

It's possible to perform joins between more than two tables. Suppose you set up a pants table:

```
mysql> SELECT * FROM pants;
+----------+
| item     |
+----------+
| Plaid    |
| Striped  |
| Corduroy |
+----------+
```

Then you can select combinations of shirts, ties, and pants:

```
mysql> SELECT shirt.item, tie.item, pants.item FROM shirt, tie, pants;
+-----------+--------------+----------+
| item      | item         | item     |
+-----------+--------------+----------+
| Pinstripe | Fleur de lis | Plaid    |
| Tie-Dye   | Fleur de lis | Plaid    |
| Black     | Fleur de lis | Plaid    |
| Pinstripe | Paisley      | Plaid    |
| Tie-Dye   | Paisley      | Plaid    |
| Black     | Paisley      | Plaid    |
| Pinstripe | Polka Dot    | Plaid    |
```

---

* ORDER BY RAND( ) is discussed further in Chapter 13.

```
| Tie-Dye   | Polka Dot    | Plaid    |
| Black     | Polka Dot    | Plaid    |
| Pinstripe | Fleur de lis | Striped  |
| Tie-Dye   | Fleur de lis | Striped  |
| Black     | Fleur de lis | Striped  |
| Pinstripe | Paisley      | Striped  |
| Tie-Dye   | Paisley      | Striped  |
| Black     | Paisley      | Striped  |
| Pinstripe | Polka Dot    | Striped  |
| Tie-Dye   | Polka Dot    | Striped  |
| Black     | Polka Dot    | Striped  |
| Pinstripe | Fleur de lis | Corduroy |
| Tie-Dye   | Fleur de lis | Corduroy |
| Black     | Fleur de lis | Corduroy |
| Pinstripe | Paisley      | Corduroy |
| Tie-Dye   | Paisley      | Corduroy |
| Black     | Paisley      | Corduroy |
| Pinstripe | Polka Dot    | Corduroy |
| Tie-Dye   | Polka Dot    | Corduroy |
| Black     | Polka Dot    | Corduroy |
+-----------+--------------+----------+
```

Clearly, as you join more tables, the number of row combinations grows quickly, even when each individual table has few rows.

If you don't want to write out complete table names in the output column list, give each table a short alias and refer to table columns using the aliases:

```
SELECT s.item, t.item, p.item
FROM shirt AS s, tie AS t, pants AS p;
```

Aliases don't save much typing for the preceding statement, but for complicated queries that select many columns, aliases can make life much simpler. In addition, aliases are not only convenient but necessary for some types of queries, as will become evident when we get to the topic of self-joins (Recipe 12.11).

12.2 Performing a Join Between Tables in Different Databases

Problem

You want to use tables in a join, but they're not located in the same database.

Solution

Use database name qualifiers to tell MySQL where to find the tables.

Discussion

Sometimes it's necessary to perform a join on two tables that live in different databases. To do this, qualify table and column names sufficiently so that MySQL knows what you're referring to. We've been using the shirt and tie tables under the implicit understanding that both are in the cookbook database, which means that we can simply refer to the tables without specifying any database name. For example, the following query retrieves the combinations of items from the two tables:

```
mysql> SELECT shirt.item, tie.item FROM shirt, tie;
+-----------+--------------+
| item      | item         |
+-----------+--------------+
| Pinstripe | Fleur de lis |
| Tie-Dye   | Fleur de lis |
| Black     | Fleur de lis |
| Pinstripe | Paisley      |
| Tie-Dye   | Paisley      |
| Black     | Paisley      |
| Pinstripe | Polka Dot    |
| Tie-Dye   | Polka Dot    |
| Black     | Polka Dot    |
+-----------+--------------+
```

But suppose instead that shirt is in the db1 database and tie is in the db2 database. To indicate this, qualify each table name with a prefix that specifies which database it's part of. The fully qualified form of the join looks like this:

```
SELECT db1.shirt.item, db2.tie.item FROM db1.shirt, db2.tie;
```

If there is no current database, or it is neither db1 nor db2, it's necessary to use this fully qualified form. However, if the current database is db1 or db2, you can dispense with some of the qualifiers. For example, if the current database is db1, you can omit the db1 qualifiers:

```
SELECT shirt.item, db2.tie.item FROM shirt, db2.tie;
```

Conversely, if the current database is db2, no db2 qualifiers are necessary:

```
SELECT db1.shirt.item, tie.item FROM db1.shirt, tie;
```

12.3 Referring to Join Output Column Names in Programs

Problem

You need to process the result of a join query from within a program, but the column names in the result set aren't unique.

Solution

Use column aliases to assign unique names to each column, or refer to the columns by position.

Discussion

Joins often retrieve columns from similar tables, and it's not unusual for columns selected from different tables to have the same names. Consider again the three-way join between the shirt, tie, and pants tables that was used in Recipe 12.1:

```
mysql> SELECT shirt.item, tie.item, pants.item FROM shirt, tie, pants;
+-----------+--------------+----------+
| item      | item         | item     |
+-----------+--------------+----------+
| Pinstripe | Fleur de lis | Plaid    |
| Tie-Dye   | Fleur de lis | Plaid    |
| Black     | Fleur de lis | Plaid    |
| Pinstripe | Paisley      | Plaid    |
...
```

The query uses the table names to qualify each instance of item in the output column list to clarify which table each item comes from. But the column names in the output are not distinct, because MySQL doesn't include table names in the column headings. If you're processing the result of the join from within a program and fetching rows into a data structure that references column values by name, non-unique column names can cause some values to become inaccessible. The following Perl script fragment illustrates the difficulty:

```
$stmt = qq{
    SELECT shirt.item, tie.item, pants.item
    FROM shirt, tie, pants
};
$sth = $dbh->prepare ($stmt);
$sth->execute ();
# Determine the number of columns in result set rows two ways:
# - Check the NUM_OF_FIELDS statement handle attribute
# - Fetch a row into a hash and see how many keys the hash contains
$count1 = $sth->{NUM_OF_FIELDS};
$ref = $sth->fetchrow_hashref ();
$count2 = keys (%{$ref});
print "The statement is: $stmt\n";
print "According to NUM_OF_FIELDS, the result set has $count1 columns\n";
print "The column names are: " . join (",", sort (@{$sth->{NAME}})) . "\n";
print "According to the row hash size, the result set has $count2 columns\n";
print "The column names are: " . join (",", sort (keys (%{$ref}))) . "\n";
```

The script issues the wardrobe-selection query, then determines the number of columns in the result, first by checking the NUM_OF_FIELDS attribute, then by fetching a row into a hash and counting the number of hash keys. Executing this script results in the following output:

```
According to NUM_OF_FIELDS, the result set has 3 columns
The column names are: item,item,item
According to the row hash size, the result set has 1 columns
The column names are: item
```

There is a problem here—the column counts don't match. The second count is 1 because the non-unique column names cause multiple column values to be mapped onto the same hash element. As a result of these hash key collisions, some of the values are lost. To solve this problem, make the column names unique by supplying aliases. For example, the query can be rewritten from:

```
SELECT shirt.item, tie.item, pants.item
FROM shirt, tie, pants
```

to:

```
SELECT shirt.item AS shirt, tie.item AS tie, pants.item AS pants
FROM shirt, tie, pants
```

If you make that change and rerun the script, its output becomes:

```
According to NUM_OF_FIELDS, the result set has 3 columns
The column names are: pants,shirt,tie
According to the row hash size, the result set has 3 columns
The column names are: pants,shirt,tie
```

Now the column counts are the same; no values are lost when fetching into a hash.

Another way to address the problem that doesn't require renaming the columns is to fetch the row into something other than a hash. For example, you can fetch the row into an array and refer to the shirt, tie, and pants items as the first through third elements of the array:

```
while (my @val = $sth->fetchrow_array ())
{
    print "shirt: $val[0], tie: $val[1], pants: $val[2]\n";
}
```

The name-clash problem may have different solutions in other languages. For example, the problem doesn't occur in quite the same way in Python scripts. If you retrieve a row using a dictionary (Python's closest analog to a Perl hash), the MySQLdb module notices clashing column names and places them in the dictionary using a key consisting of the column name with the table name prepended. Thus, for the following query, the dictionary keys would be item, tie.item, and pants.item:

```
SELECT shirt.item, tie.item, pants.item
FROM shirt, tie, pants
```

That means column values won't get lost, but it's still necessary to be aware of non-unique names. If you try to refer to column values using just the column names, you won't get the results you expect for those names that are reported with a leading table name. If you use aliases to make each column name unique, the dictionary entries will have the names that you assign.

12.4 Finding Rows in One Table That Match Rows in Another

Problem

You want to use rows in one table to locate rows in another table.

Solution

Use a join with an appropriate WHERE clause to match up records from different tables.

Discussion

The records in the shirt, tie, and pants tables from Recipe 12.1 have no special relationship to each other, so no combination of rows is more meaningful than any other. That's okay, because the purpose of the examples that use those tables is to illustrate how to perform a join, not why you'd do so.

The "why" is that joins allow you to combine information from multiple tables when each table contains only part of the information in which you're interested. Output rows from a join are more complete than rows from either table by itself. This kind of operation often is based on matching rows in one table to rows in another, which requires that each table have one or more columns of common information that can be used to link them together logically.

To illustrate, suppose you're starting an art collection, using the following two tables to record your acquisitions. artist lists those painters whose works you want to collect, and painting lists each painting that you've purchased:

```
CREATE TABLE artist
(
    a_id    INT UNSIGNED NOT NULL AUTO_INCREMENT,   # artist ID
    name    VARCHAR(30) NOT NULL,                    # artist name
    PRIMARY KEY (a_id),
    UNIQUE (name)
);

CREATE TABLE painting
(
    a_id    INT UNSIGNED NOT NULL,                   # artist ID
    p_id    INT UNSIGNED NOT NULL AUTO_INCREMENT,    # painting ID
    title   VARCHAR(100) NOT NULL,                   # title of painting
    state   VARCHAR(2) NOT NULL,                     # state where purchased
    price   INT UNSIGNED,                            # purchase price (dollars)
    INDEX (a_id),
    PRIMARY KEY (p_id)
);
```

You've just begun the collection, so the tables contain only the following records:

```
mysql> SELECT * FROM artist ORDER BY a_id;
+------+----------+
| a_id | name     |
+------+----------+
|    1 | Da Vinci |
|    2 | Monet    |
|    3 | Van Gogh |
|    4 | Picasso  |
|    5 | Renoir   |
+------+----------+
mysql> SELECT * FROM painting ORDER BY a_id, p_id;
+------+------+-------------------+-------+-------+
| a_id | p_id | title             | state | price |
+------+------+-------------------+-------+-------+
|    1 |    1 | The Last Supper   | IN    |    34 |
|    1 |    2 | The Mona Lisa     | MI    |    87 |
|    3 |    3 | Starry Night      | KY    |    48 |
|    3 |    4 | The Potato Eaters | KY    |    67 |
|    3 |    5 | The Rocks         | IA    |    33 |
|    5 |    6 | Les Deux Soeurs   | NE    |    64 |
+------+------+-------------------+-------+-------+
```

The low values in the price column of the painting table betray the fact that your collection actually contains only cheap facsimiles, not the originals. Well, that's all right—who can afford the originals?

Each table contains partial information about your collection. For example, the artist table doesn't tell you which paintings each artist produced, and the painting table lists artist IDs but not their names. To answer certain kinds of questions, you must combine the two tables, and do so in a way that matches up records properly. The "matching up" part is a matter of writing an appropriate WHERE clause. In Recipe 12.1, I mentioned that performing a full join generally is a bad idea because of the amount of output produced. Another reason not to perform a full join is that the result may be meaningless. The following full join between the artist and painting tables makes this clear. It includes no WHERE clause, and thus produces output that conveys no useful information:

```
mysql> SELECT * FROM artist, painting;
+------+----------+------+------+-----------------+-------+-------+
| a_id | name     | a_id | p_id | title           | state | price |
+------+----------+------+------+-----------------+-------+-------+
|    1 | Da Vinci |    1 |    1 | The Last Supper | IN    |    34 |
|    2 | Monet    |    1 |    1 | The Last Supper | IN    |    34 |
|    3 | Van Gogh |    1 |    1 | The Last Supper | IN    |    34 |
|    4 | Picasso  |    1 |    1 | The Last Supper | IN    |    34 |
|    5 | Renoir   |    1 |    1 | The Last Supper | IN    |    34 |
|    1 | Da Vinci |    1 |    2 | The Mona Lisa   | MI    |    87 |
|    2 | Monet    |    1 |    2 | The Mona Lisa   | MI    |    87 |
|    3 | Van Gogh |    1 |    2 | The Mona Lisa   | MI    |    87 |
|    4 | Picasso  |    1 |    2 | The Mona Lisa   | MI    |    87 |
|    5 | Renoir   |    1 |    2 | The Mona Lisa   | MI    |    87 |
```

```
    |    1 | Da Vinci |    3 |    3 | Starry Night      | KY    |    48 |
    |    2 | Monet    |    3 |    3 | Starry Night      | KY    |    48 |
    |    3 | Van Gogh |    3 |    3 | Starry Night      | KY    |    48 |
    |    4 | Picasso  |    3 |    3 | Starry Night      | KY    |    48 |
    |    5 | Renoir   |    3 |    3 | Starry Night      | KY    |    48 |
    |    1 | Da Vinci |    3 |    4 | The Potato Eaters | KY    |    67 |
    |    2 | Monet    |    3 |    4 | The Potato Eaters | KY    |    67 |
    |    3 | Van Gogh |    3 |    4 | The Potato Eaters | KY    |    67 |
    |    4 | Picasso  |    3 |    4 | The Potato Eaters | KY    |    67 |
    |    5 | Renoir   |    3 |    4 | The Potato Eaters | KY    |    67 |
    |    1 | Da Vinci |    3 |    5 | The Rocks         | IA    |    33 |
    |    2 | Monet    |    3 |    5 | The Rocks         | IA    |    33 |
    |    3 | Van Gogh |    3 |    5 | The Rocks         | IA    |    33 |
    |    4 | Picasso  |    3 |    5 | The Rocks         | IA    |    33 |
    |    5 | Renoir   |    3 |    5 | The Rocks         | IA    |    33 |
    |    1 | Da Vinci |    5 |    6 | Les Deux Soeurs   | NE    |    64 |
    |    2 | Monet    |    5 |    6 | Les Deux Soeurs   | NE    |    64 |
    |    3 | Van Gogh |    5 |    6 | Les Deux Soeurs   | NE    |    64 |
    |    4 | Picasso  |    5 |    6 | Les Deux Soeurs   | NE    |    64 |
    |    5 | Renoir   |    5 |    6 | Les Deux Soeurs   | NE    |    64 |
    +------+----------+------+------+-------------------+-------+-------+
```

Clearly, you're not maintaining these tables to match up each artist with each painting, which is what the preceding query does. An unrestricted join in this case produces nothing more than a lot of output with no value, so a WHERE clause is essential to give the query meaning. For example, to produce a list of paintings together with the artist names, you can associate records from the two tables using a simple WHERE clause that matches up values in the artist ID column that is common to both tables and that serves as the link between them:

```
mysql> SELECT * FROM artist, painting
    -> WHERE artist.a_id = painting.a_id;
+------+----------+------+------+-------------------+-------+-------+
| a_id | name     | a_id | p_id | title             | state | price |
+------+----------+------+------+-------------------+-------+-------+
|    1 | Da Vinci |    1 |    1 | The Last Supper   | IN    |    34 |
|    1 | Da Vinci |    1 |    2 | The Mona Lisa     | MI    |    87 |
|    3 | Van Gogh |    3 |    3 | Starry Night      | KY    |    48 |
|    3 | Van Gogh |    3 |    4 | The Potato Eaters | KY    |    67 |
|    3 | Van Gogh |    3 |    5 | The Rocks         | IA    |    33 |
|    5 | Renoir   |    5 |    6 | Les Deux Soeurs   | NE    |    64 |
+------+----------+------+------+-------------------+-------+-------+
```

The column names in the WHERE clause include table qualifiers to make it clear which a_id values to compare. The output indicates who painted each painting, and, conversely, which paintings by each artist are in your collection. However, the output is perhaps overly verbose. (It includes two identical a_id columns, for example; one comes from the artist table, the other from the painting table.) You may want to see the a_id values only once. Or you may not want to see any ID columns at all. To exclude them, provide a column output list that names specifically only those columns in which you're interested:

```
mysql> SELECT artist.name, painting.title, painting.state, painting.price
    -> FROM artist, painting
    -> WHERE artist.a_id = painting.a_id;
+----------+------------------+-------+-------+
| name     | title            | state | price |
+----------+------------------+-------+-------+
| Da Vinci | The Last Supper  | IN    |    34 |
| Da Vinci | The Mona Lisa    | MI    |    87 |
| Van Gogh | Starry Night     | KY    |    48 |
| Van Gogh | The Potato Eaters| KY    |    67 |
| Van Gogh | The Rocks        | IA    |    33 |
| Renoir   | Les Deux Soeurs  | NE    |    64 |
+----------+------------------+-------+-------+
```

By adding other conditions to the WHERE clause, you can use row-matching queries to answer more specific questions, such as the following:

- Which paintings did Van Gogh paint? To answer this question, identify the record from the artist table that corresponds to the artist name, use its a_id value to find matching records in the painting table, and select the title from those records:

```
mysql> SELECT painting.title
    -> FROM artist, painting
    -> WHERE artist.name = 'Van Gogh' AND artist.a_id = painting.a_id;
+-------------------+
| title             |
+-------------------+
| Starry Night      |
| The Potato Eaters |
| The Rocks         |
+-------------------+
```

- Who painted "The Mona Lisa"? To find out, go in the other direction, using information in the painting table to find information in the artist table:

```
mysql> SELECT artist.name
    -> FROM artist, painting
    -> WHERE painting.title = 'The Mona Lisa' AND painting.a_id = artist.a_id;
+----------+
| name     |
+----------+
| Da Vinci |
+----------+
```

- Which artists' paintings did you purchase in Kentucky or Indiana? This is somewhat similar to the last query, but tests a different column in the painting table to find the initial set of records to be joined with the artist table:

```
mysql> SELECT DISTINCT artist.name
    -> FROM artist, painting
    -> WHERE painting.state IN ('KY','IN') AND artist.a_id = painting.a_id;
```

```
+----------+
| name     |
+----------+
| Da Vinci |
| Van Gogh |
+----------+
```

The query also uses DISTINCT to display each artist name just once. Try it without DISTINCT and you'll see that Van Gogh is listed twice—that's because you obtained two Van Goghs in Kentucky.

- Joins can also be used with aggregate functions to produce summaries. For example, to find out how many paintings you have per artist, use this query:

```
mysql> SELECT artist.name, COUNT(*) AS 'number of paintings'
    -> FROM artist, painting
    -> WHERE artist.a_id = painting.a_id
    -> GROUP BY artist.name;
+----------+---------------------+
| name     | number of paintings |
+----------+---------------------+
| Da Vinci |                   2 |
| Renoir   |                   1 |
| Van Gogh |                   3 |
+----------+---------------------+
```

A more elaborate query might also show how much you paid for each artist's paintings, in total and on average:

```
mysql> SELECT artist.name,
    -> COUNT(*) AS 'number of paintings',
    -> SUM(painting.price) AS 'total price',
    -> AVG(painting.price) AS 'average price'
    -> FROM artist, painting WHERE artist.a_id = painting.a_id
    -> GROUP BY artist.name;
+----------+---------------------+-------------+---------------+
| name     | number of paintings | total price | average price |
+----------+---------------------+-------------+---------------+
| Da Vinci |                   2 |         121 |       60.5000 |
| Renoir   |                   1 |          64 |       64.0000 |
| Van Gogh |                   3 |         148 |       49.3333 |
+----------+---------------------+-------------+---------------+
```

Note that the summary queries produce output only for those artists in the artist table for whom you actually have acquired paintings. (For example, Monet is listed in the artist table but is not present in the summary because you don't have any of his paintings yet.) If you want the summary to include all artists, even if you have none of their paintings yet, you must use a different kind of join—specifically, a LEFT JOIN. See Recipes 12.5 and 12.8.

12.5   Finding Rows with No Match in Another Table

Problem

You want to find rows in one table that have no match in another. Or you want to produce a list on the basis of a join between tables, but you want the list to include an entry even when there are no matches in the second table.

Solution

Use a LEFT JOIN. As of MySQL 3.23.25, you can also use a RIGHT JOIN.

Discussion

The preceding sections focused on finding matches between two tables. But the answers to some questions require determining which records do *not* have a match (or, stated another way, which records have values that are missing from the other table). For example, you might want to know which artists in the artist table you don't yet have any paintings by. The same kind of question occurs in other contexts, such as:

- You're working in sales. You have a list of potential customers, and another list of people who have placed orders. To focus your efforts on people who are not yet actual customers, you want to find people in the first list that are not in the second.

- You have one list of baseball players, another list of players who have hit home runs, and you want to know which players in the first list have *not* hit a home run. The answer is determined by finding those players in the first list who are not in the second.

For these types of questions, you need to use a LEFT JOIN.

To see why, let's determine which artists in the artist table are missing from the painting table. At present, the tables are small, so it's easy to examine them visually and determine that you have no paintings by Monet and Picasso (there are no painting records with an a_id value of 2 or 4):

```
mysql> SELECT * FROM artist ORDER BY a_id;
+------+----------+
| a_id | name     |
+------+----------+
|    1 | Da Vinci |
|    2 | Monet    |
|    3 | Van Gogh |
|    4 | Picasso  |
|    5 | Renoir   |
+------+----------+
mysql> SELECT * FROM painting ORDER BY a_id, p_id;
+------+------+-------------------+-------+-------+
| a_id | p_id | title             | state | price |
+------+------+-------------------+-------+-------+
|    1 |    1 | The Last Supper   | IN    |    34 |
|    1 |    2 | The Mona Lisa     | MI    |    87 |
|    3 |    3 | Starry Night      | KY    |    48 |
|    3 |    4 | The Potato Eaters | KY    |    67 |
|    3 |    5 | The Rocks         | IA    |    33 |
|    5 |    6 | Les Deux Soeurs   | NE    |    64 |
+------+------+-------------------+-------+-------+
```

But as you acquire more paintings and the tables get larger, it won't be so easy to eyeball them and answer the question by inspection. Can you answer the question using SQL? Sure, although first attempts at solving the problem generally look something like the following query, using a WHERE clause that looks for mismatches between the two tables:

```
mysql> SELECT * FROM artist, painting WHERE artist.a_id != painting.a_id;
+------+----------+------+------+-------------------+-------+-------+
| a_id | name     | a_id | p_id | title             | state | price |
+------+----------+------+------+-------------------+-------+-------+
|    2 | Monet    |    1 |    1 | The Last Supper   | IN    |    34 |
|    3 | Van Gogh |    1 |    1 | The Last Supper   | IN    |    34 |
|    4 | Picasso  |    1 |    1 | The Last Supper   | IN    |    34 |
|    5 | Renoir   |    1 |    1 | The Last Supper   | IN    |    34 |
|    2 | Monet    |    1 |    2 | The Mona Lisa     | MI    |    87 |
|    3 | Van Gogh |    1 |    2 | The Mona Lisa     | MI    |    87 |
|    4 | Picasso  |    1 |    2 | The Mona Lisa     | MI    |    87 |
|    5 | Renoir   |    1 |    2 | The Mona Lisa     | MI    |    87 |
|    1 | Da Vinci |    3 |    3 | Starry Night      | KY    |    48 |
|    2 | Monet    |    3 |    3 | Starry Night      | KY    |    48 |
|    4 | Picasso  |    3 |    3 | Starry Night      | KY    |    48 |
|    5 | Renoir   |    3 |    3 | Starry Night      | KY    |    48 |
|    1 | Da Vinci |    3 |    4 | The Potato Eaters | KY    |    67 |
|    2 | Monet    |    3 |    4 | The Potato Eaters | KY    |    67 |
|    4 | Picasso  |    3 |    4 | The Potato Eaters | KY    |    67 |
|    5 | Renoir   |    3 |    4 | The Potato Eaters | KY    |    67 |
```

```
|    1 | Da Vinci |    3 |    5 | The Rocks          | IA    |    33 |
|    2 | Monet    |    3 |    5 | The Rocks          | IA    |    33 |
|    4 | Picasso  |    3 |    5 | The Rocks          | IA    |    33 |
|    5 | Renoir   |    3 |    5 | The Rocks          | IA    |    33 |
|    1 | Da Vinci |    5 |    6 | Les Deux Soeurs    | NE    |    64 |
|    2 | Monet    |    5 |    6 | Les Deux Soeurs    | NE    |    64 |
|    3 | Van Gogh |    5 |    6 | Les Deux Soeurs    | NE    |    64 |
|    4 | Picasso  |    5 |    6 | Les Deux Soeurs    | NE    |    64 |
+------+----------+------+------+--------------------+-------+-------+
```

That's obviously not the correct result! The query produces a list of all combinations of values from the two rows where the values aren't the same, but what you really want is a list of values in artist that aren't present *at all* in painting. The trouble here is that a regular join can only produce combinations from values that are present in the tables. It can't tell you anything about values that are missing.

When faced with the problem of finding values in one table that have no match in (or that are missing from) another table, you should get in the habit of thinking, "aha, that's a LEFT JOIN problem." A LEFT JOIN is similar to a regular join in that it attempts to match rows in the first (left) table with the rows in the second (right) table. But in addition, if a left table row has no match in the right table, a LEFT JOIN still produces a row—one in which all the columns from the right table are set to NULL. This means you can find values that are missing from the right table by looking for NULL. It's easier to observe how this happens by working in stages. First, run a regular join to find matching rows:

```
mysql> SELECT * FROM artist, painting
    -> WHERE artist.a_id = painting.a_id;
+------+----------+------+------+--------------------+-------+-------+
| a_id | name     | a_id | p_id | title              | state | price |
+------+----------+------+------+--------------------+-------+-------+
|    1 | Da Vinci |    1 |    1 | The Last Supper    | IN    |    34 |
|    1 | Da Vinci |    1 |    2 | The Mona Lisa      | MI    |    87 |
|    3 | Van Gogh |    3 |    3 | Starry Night       | KY    |    48 |
|    3 | Van Gogh |    3 |    4 | The Potato Eaters  | KY    |    67 |
|    3 | Van Gogh |    3 |    5 | The Rocks          | IA    |    33 |
|    5 | Renoir   |    5 |    6 | Les Deux Soeurs    | NE    |    64 |
+------+----------+------+------+--------------------+-------+-------+
```

In this output, the first a_id column comes from the artist table and the second one comes from the painting table.

Now compare that result with the output you get from a LEFT JOIN. A LEFT JOIN is written in somewhat similar fashion, but you separate the table names by LEFT JOIN rather than by a comma, and specify which columns to compare using an ON clause rather than a WHERE clause:

```
mysql> SELECT * FROM artist LEFT JOIN painting
    -> ON artist.a_id = painting.a_id;
+------+----------+------+------+--------------------+-------+-------+
| a_id | name     | a_id | p_id | title              | state | price |
+------+----------+------+------+--------------------+-------+-------+
```

```
|    1 | Da Vinci  |    1 |    1 | The Last Supper    | IN   |    34 |
|    1 | Da Vinci  |    1 |    2 | The Mona Lisa      | MI   |    87 |
|    2 | Monet     | NULL | NULL | NULL               | NULL | NULL  |
|    3 | Van Gogh  |    3 |    3 | Starry Night       | KY   |    48 |
|    3 | Van Gogh  |    3 |    4 | The Potato Eaters  | KY   |    67 |
|    3 | Van Gogh  |    3 |    5 | The Rocks          | IA   |    33 |
|    4 | Picasso   | NULL | NULL | NULL               | NULL | NULL  |
|    5 | Renoir    |    5 |    6 | Les Deux Soeurs    | NE   |    64 |
+------+-----------+------+------+--------------------+------+-------+
```

The output is similar to that from the regular join, except that the LEFT JOIN also produces an output row for artist rows that have no painting table match. For those output rows, all the columns from painting are set to NULL.

Next, to restrict the output only to the non-matched artist rows, add a WHERE clause that looks for NULL values in the painting column that is named in the ON clause:

```
mysql> SELECT * FROM artist LEFT JOIN painting
    -> ON artist.a_id = painting.a_id
    -> WHERE painting.a_id IS NULL;
+------+---------+------+------+-------+-------+
| a_id | name    | a_id | p_id | title | price |
+------+---------+------+------+-------+-------+
|    2 | Monet   | NULL | NULL | NULL  | NULL  |
|    4 | Picasso | NULL | NULL | NULL  | NULL  |
+------+---------+------+------+-------+-------+
```

Finally, to show only the artist table values that are missing from the painting table, shorten the output column list to include only columns from the artist table:

```
mysql> SELECT artist.* FROM artist LEFT JOIN painting
    -> ON artist.a_id = painting.a_id
    -> WHERE painting.a_id IS NULL;
+------+---------+
| a_id | name    |
+------+---------+
|    2 | Monet   |
|    4 | Picasso |
+------+---------+
```

The preceding LEFT JOIN lists those left-table values that are not present in the right table. A similar kind of operation can be used to report each left-table value along with an indicator whether or not it's present in the right table. To do this, perform a LEFT JOIN to count the number of times each left-table value occurs in the right table. A count of zero indicates the value is not present. The following query lists each artist from the artist table, and whether or not you have any paintings by the artist:

```
mysql> SELECT artist.name,
    -> IF(COUNT(painting.a_id)>0,'yes','no') AS 'in collection'
    -> FROM artist LEFT JOIN painting ON artist.a_id = painting.a_id
    -> GROUP BY artist.name;
+---------+---------------+
| name    | in collection |
+---------+---------------+
```

```
| Da Vinci  | yes            |
| Monet     | no             |
| Picasso   | no             |
| Renoir    | yes            |
| Van Gogh  | yes            |
+-----------+----------------+
```

As of MySQL 3.23.25, you can also use `RIGHT JOIN`, which is like `LEFT JOIN` but reverses the roles of the right and left tables. In other words, `RIGHT JOIN` forces the matching process to produce a row from each table in the right table, even in the absence of a corresponding row in the left table. This means you would rewrite the preceding `LEFT JOIN` as follows to convert it to a `RIGHT JOIN` that produces the same results:

```
mysql> SELECT artist.name,
    -> IF(COUNT(painting.a_id)>0,'yes','no') AS 'in collection'
    -> FROM painting RIGHT JOIN artist ON painting.a_id = artist.a_id
    -> GROUP BY artist.name;
+-----------+----------------+
| name      | in collection  |
+-----------+----------------+
| Da Vinci  | yes            |
| Monet     | no             |
| Picasso   | no             |
| Renoir    | yes            |
| Van Gogh  | yes            |
+-----------+----------------+
```

Elsewhere in this book, I'll generally refer in discussion only to `LEFT JOIN` for brevity, but the discussions apply to `RIGHT JOIN` as well if you reverse the roles of the tables.

Other Ways to Write LEFT JOIN and RIGHT JOIN Queries

When the names of the columns to be matched are the same in both tables, an alternative to `ON` can be used for writing `LEFT JOIN` and `RIGHT JOIN` queries. This syntax substitutes `USING` for `ON`. For example, the following two queries are equivalent:

```
SELECT t1.n, t2.n FROM t1 LEFT JOIN t2 ON t1.n = t2.n;
SELECT t1.n, t2.n FROM t1 LEFT JOIN t2 USING (n);
```

As are these:

```
SELECT t1.n, t2.n FROM t1 RIGHT JOIN t2 ON t1.n = t2.n;
SELECT t1.n, t2.n FROM t1 RIGHT JOIN t2 USING (n);
```

In the special case that you want to base the comparison on all columns that appear in both tables, you can use `NATURAL LEFT JOIN` or `NATURAL RIGHT JOIN`:

```
SELECT t1.n, t2.n FROM t1 NATURAL LEFT JOIN t2;
SELECT t1.n, t2.n FROM t1 NATURAL RIGHT JOIN t2;
```

See Also

As shown in this section, LEFT JOIN is useful for finding values with no match in another table, or for showing whether each value is matched. LEFT JOIN may also be used for producing a summary that includes all items in a list, even those for which there's nothing to summarize. This is very common for characterizing the relationship between a master table and a detail table. For example, a LEFT JOIN can produce "total sales per customer" reports that list all customers, even those who haven't bought anything during the summary period. (See Recipe 12.8.)

Another application of LEFT JOIN is for performing consistency checking when you receive two datafiles that are supposed to be related, and you want to determine whether they really are. (That is, you want to check the integrity of the relationship.) Import each file into a MySQL table, then run a couple of LEFT JOIN statements to determine whether there are unattached records in one table or the other—that is, records that have no match in the other table. (If there are any such records and you want to delete them, see Recipe 12.21.)

12.6   Finding Rows Containing Per-Group Minimum or Maximum Values

Problem

You want to find which record within each group of rows in a table contains the maximum or minimum value for a given column. For example, you want to determine the most expensive painting in your collection for each artist.

Solution

Create a temporary table to hold the per-group maximum or minimum, then join the temporary table with the original one to pull out the matching record for each group.

Discussion

Many questions involve finding largest or smallest values in a particular table column, but it's also common to want to know what the other values are in the row that contains the value. For example, you can use MAX(pop) to find the largest state population recorded in the states table, but you might also want to know which state has that population. As shown in Recipe 7.5, one way to solve this problem is to use a SQL variable. The technique works like this:

```
mysql> SELECT @max := MAX(pop) FROM states;
mysql> SELECT * FROM states WHERE pop = @max;
```

```
+------------+--------+------------+----------+
| name       | abbrev | statehood  | pop      |
+------------+--------+------------+----------+
| California | CA     | 1850-09-09 | 29760021 |
+------------+--------+------------+----------+
```

Another way to answer the question is to use a join. First, select the maximum population value into a temporary table:

```
mysql> CREATE TABLE tmp SELECT MAX(pop) as maxpop FROM states;
```

Then join the temporary table to the original one to find the record matching the selected population:

```
mysql> SELECT states.* FROM states, tmp WHERE states.pop = tmp.maxpop;
+------------+--------+------------+----------+
| name       | abbrev | statehood  | pop      |
+------------+--------+------------+----------+
| California | CA     | 1850-09-09 | 29760021 |
+------------+--------+------------+----------+
```

By applying these techniques to the artist and painting tables, you can answer questions like "What is the most expensive painting in the collection, and who painted it?" To use a SQL variable, store the highest price in it, then use the variable to identify the record containing the price so you can retrieve other columns from it:

```
mysql> SELECT @max_price := MAX(price) FROM painting;
mysql> SELECT artist.name, painting.title, painting.price
    -> FROM artist, painting
    -> WHERE painting.price = @max_price
    -> AND painting.a_id = artist.a_id;
+----------+---------------+-------+
| name     | title         | price |
+----------+---------------+-------+
| Da Vinci | The Mona Lisa |    87 |
+----------+---------------+-------+
```

The same thing can be done by creating a temporary table to hold the maximum price, and then joining it with the other tables:

```
mysql> CREATE TABLE tmp SELECT MAX(price) AS max_price FROM painting;
mysql> SELECT artist.name, painting.title, painting.price
    -> FROM artist, painting, tmp
    -> WHERE painting.price = tmp.max_price
    -> AND painting.a_id = artist.a_id;
+----------+---------------+-------+
| name     | title         | price |
+----------+---------------+-------+
| Da Vinci | The Mona Lisa |    87 |
+----------+---------------+-------+
```

On the face of it, using a temporary table and a join is just a more complicated way of answering the question. Does this technique have any practical value? Yes, it does, because it leads to a more general technique for answering more difficult questions. The previous queries show information only for the most expensive single painting in the entire painting table. What if your question is, "What is the most expensive painting per artist?" You can't use a SQL variable to answer that question, because the answer requires finding one price per artist, and a variable can hold only a single value at a time. But the technique of using a temporary table works well, because the table can hold multiple values and a join can find matches for them all at once. To answer the question, select each artist ID and the corresponding maximum painting price into a temporary table. The table will contain not just the maximum painting price, but the maximum within each group, where "group" is defined as "paintings by a given artist." Then use the artist IDs and prices stored in the tmp table to match records in the painting table, and join the result with artist to get the artist names:

```
mysql> CREATE TABLE tmp
    -> SELECT a_id, MAX(price) AS max_price FROM painting GROUP BY a_id;
mysql> SELECT artist.name, painting.title, painting.price
    -> FROM artist, painting, tmp
    -> WHERE painting.a_id = tmp.a_id
    -> AND painting.price = tmp.max_price
    -> AND painting.a_id = artist.a_id;
+----------+------------------+-------+
| name     | title            | price |
+----------+------------------+-------+
| Da Vinci | The Mona Lisa    |    87 |
| Van Gogh | The Potato Eaters|    67 |
| Renoir   | Les Deux Soeurs  |    64 |
+----------+------------------+-------+
```

The same technique works for other kinds of values, such as temporal values. Consider the driver_log table that lists drivers and trips that they've taken:

```
mysql> SELECT name, trav_date, miles
    -> FROM driver_log
    -> ORDER BY name, trav_date;
+-------+------------+-------+
| name  | trav_date  | miles |
+-------+------------+-------+
| Ben   | 2001-11-29 |   131 |
| Ben   | 2001-11-30 |   152 |
| Ben   | 2001-12-02 |    79 |
| Henry | 2001-11-26 |   115 |
| Henry | 2001-11-27 |    96 |
| Henry | 2001-11-29 |   300 |
| Henry | 2001-11-30 |   203 |
| Henry | 2001-12-01 |   197 |
| Suzi  | 2001-11-29 |   391 |
| Suzi  | 2001-12-02 |   502 |
+-------+------------+-------+
```

One type of maximum-per-group problem for this table is, "show the most recent trip for each driver." It can be solved like this:

```
mysql> CREATE TABLE tmp
    -> SELECT name, MAX(trav_date) AS trav_date
    -> FROM driver_log GROUP BY name;
```

```
mysql> SELECT driver_log.name, driver_log.trav_date, driver_log.miles
    -> FROM driver_log, tmp
    -> WHERE driver_log.name = tmp.name
    -> AND driver_log.trav_date = tmp.trav_date
    -> ORDER BY driver_log.name;
+-------+------------+-------+
| name  | trav_date  | miles |
+-------+------------+-------+
| Ben   | 2001-12-02 |    79 |
| Henry | 2001-12-01 |   197 |
| Suzi  | 2001-12-02 |   502 |
+-------+------------+-------+
```

See Also

The technique illustrated in this section shows how to answer maximum-per-group questions by selecting summary information into a temporary table and joining that table to the original one. This technique has many applications. One such application is calculation of team standings, where the standings for each group of teams are determined by comparing each team in the group to the team with the best record. Recipe 12.7 discusses how to do this.

12.7   Computing Team Standings

Problem

You want to compute team standings from their win-loss records, including the games-behind (GB) values.

Solution

Determine which team is in first place, then join that result to the original records.

Discussion

Standings for sports teams that compete against each other typically are ranked according to who has the best win-loss record, and the teams not in first place are assigned a "games-behind" value indicating how many games out of first place they are. This section shows how to calculate those values. The first example uses a table containing a single set of team records, to illustrate the logic of the calculations. The second example uses a table containing several sets of records; in this case, it's necessary to use a join to perform the calculations independently for each group of teams.

Consider the following table, standings1, which contains a single set of baseball team records (they represent the final standings for the Northern League in the year 1902):

```
mysql> SELECT team, wins, losses FROM standings1
    -> ORDER BY wins-losses DESC;
+--------------+-------+---------+
| team         | wins  | losses  |
+--------------+-------+---------+
| Winnipeg     |    37 |      20 |
| Crookston    |    31 |      25 |
| Fargo        |    30 |      26 |
| Grand Forks  |    28 |      26 |
| Devils Lake  |    19 |      31 |
| Cavalier     |    15 |      32 |
+--------------+-------+---------+
```

The records are sorted by the win-loss differential, which is how to place teams in order from first place to last place. But displays of team standings typically include each team's winning percentage and a figure indicating how many games behind the leader all the other teams are. So let's add that information to the output. Calculating the percentage is easy. It's the ratio of wins to total games played and can be determined using this expression:

```
wins / (wins + losses)
```

If you want to perform standings calculations under conditions when a team may not have played any games yet, that expression evaluates to NULL because it involves a division by zero. For simplicity, I'll assume a nonzero number of games, but if you want to handle this condition by mapping NULL to zero, generalize the expression as follows:

```
IFNULL(wins / (wins + losses),0)
```

or as:

```
wins / IF(wins=0,1,wins + losses)
```

Determining the games-behind value is a little trickier. It's based on the relationship of the win-loss records for two teams, calculated as the average of two values:

- The number of games the second place team must win to have the same number of wins as the first place team
- The number of games the first place team must lose to have the same number of losses as the second place team

For example, suppose two teams A and B have the following win-loss records:

```
+------+------+---------+
| team | wins | losses  |
+------+------+---------+
| A    |   17 |      11 |
| B    |   14 |      12 |
+------+------+---------+
```

Here, team B has to win three more games and team A has to lose one more game for the teams to be even. The average of three and one is two, thus B is two games behind A. Mathematically, the games-behind calculation for the two teams can be expressed like this:

```
((winsA - winsB) + (lossesB - lossesA)) / 2
```

With a little rearrangement of terms, the expression becomes:

```
((winsA - lossesA) - (winsB - lossesB)) / 2
```

The second expression is equivalent to the first, but it has each factor written as a single team's win-loss differential, rather than as a comparison between teams. That makes it easier to work with, because each factor can be determined independently from a single team record. The first factor represents the first place team's win-loss differential, so if we calculate that value first, all the other team GB values can be determined in relation to it.

The first place team is the one with the largest win-loss differential. To find that value and save it in a variable, use this query:

```
mysql> SELECT @wl_diff := MAX(wins-losses) FROM standings1;
+------------------------------+
| @wl_diff := MAX(wins-losses) |
+------------------------------+
|                           17 |
+------------------------------+
```

Then use the differential as follows to produce team standings that include winning percentage and GB values:

```
mysql> SELECT team, wins AS W, losses AS L,
    -> wins/(wins+losses) AS PCT,
    -> (@wl_diff - (wins-losses)) / 2 AS GB
    -> FROM standings1
    -> ORDER BY wins-losses DESC, PCT DESC;
+-------------+------+------+------+------+
| team        | W    | L    | PCT  | GB   |
+-------------+------+------+------+------+
| Winnipeg    |   37 |   20 | 0.65 |    0 |
| Crookston   |   31 |   25 | 0.55 |  5.5 |
| Fargo       |   30 |   26 | 0.54 |  6.5 |
| Grand Forks |   28 |   26 | 0.52 |  7.5 |
| Devils Lake |   19 |   31 | 0.38 | 14.5 |
| Cavalier    |   15 |   32 | 0.32 |   17 |
+-------------+------+------+------+------+
```

There are a couple of minor formatting issues that can be addressed at this point. Percentages in standings generally are displayed to three decimals, and the GB value for the first place team is displayed as - rather than as 0. To display three decimals, TRUNCATE(*expr*,3) can be used. To display the GB value for the first place team

appropriately, put the expression that calculates the GB column within a call to IF()
that maps 0 to a dash:

```
mysql> SELECT team, wins AS W, losses AS L,
    -> TRUNCATE(wins/(wins+losses),3) AS PCT,
    -> IF((@wl_diff - (wins-losses)) = 0,'-',(@wl_diff - (wins-losses))/2) AS GB
    -> FROM standings1
    -> ORDER BY wins-losses DESC, PCT DESC;
+-------------+------+------+-------+------+
| team        | W    | L    | PCT   | GB   |
+-------------+------+------+-------+------+
| Winnipeg    | 37   | 20   | 0.649 | -    |
| Crookston   | 31   | 25   | 0.553 | 5.5  |
| Fargo       | 30   | 26   | 0.535 | 6.5  |
| Grand Forks | 28   | 26   | 0.518 | 7.5  |
| Devils Lake | 19   | 31   | 0.380 | 14.5 |
| Cavalier    | 15   | 32   | 0.319 | 17   |
+-------------+------+------+-------+------+
```

These queries order the teams by win-loss differential, using winning percentage as a
tie-breaker in case there are teams with the same differential value. It would be simpler just to sort by percentage, of course, but then you wouldn't always get the correct ordering. It's a curious fact that a team with a lower winning percentage can
actually be higher in the standings than a team with a higher percentage. (This generally occurs early in the season, when teams may have played highly disparate numbers of games, relatively speaking.) Consider the case where two teams A and B have
the following records:

```
+------+------+--------+
| team | wins | losses |
+------+------+--------+
| A    | 4    | 1      |
| B    | 2    | 0      |
+------+------+--------+
```

Applying the GB and percentage calculations to these team records yields the following result, where the first place team actually has a lower winning percentage than
the second place team:

```
+------+------+------+-------+------+
| team | W    | L    | PCT   | GB   |
+------+------+------+-------+------+
| A    | 4    | 1    | 0.800 | -    |
| B    | 2    | 0    | 1.000 | 0.5  |
+------+------+------+-------+------+
```

The standings calculations shown thus far can be done without a join. They involve
only a single set of team records, so the first place team's win-loss differential can be
stored in a variable. A more complex situation occurs when a dataset includes several sets of team records. For example, the 1997 Northern League had two divisions
(Eastern and Western). In addition, separate standings were maintained for the first
and second halves of the season, because season-half winners in each division played
each other for the right to compete in the league championship. The following table,

standings2, shows what these records look like, ordered by season half, division, and win-loss differential:

```
mysql> SELECT half, div, team, wins, losses FROM standings2
    -> ORDER BY half, div, wins-losses DESC;
+------+---------+-----------------+------+--------+
| half | div     | team            | wins | losses |
+------+---------+-----------------+------+--------+
|    1 | Eastern | St. Paul        |   24 |     18 |
|    1 | Eastern | Thunder Bay     |   18 |     24 |
|    1 | Eastern | Duluth-Superior |   17 |     24 |
|    1 | Eastern | Madison         |   15 |     27 |
|    1 | Western | Winnipeg        |   29 |     12 |
|    1 | Western | Sioux City      |   28 |     14 |
|    1 | Western | Fargo-Moorhead  |   21 |     21 |
|    1 | Western | Sioux Falls     |   15 |     27 |
|    2 | Eastern | Duluth-Superior |   22 |     20 |
|    2 | Eastern | St. Paul        |   21 |     21 |
|    2 | Eastern | Madison         |   19 |     23 |
|    2 | Eastern | Thunder Bay     |   18 |     24 |
|    2 | Western | Fargo-Moorhead  |   26 |     16 |
|    2 | Western | Winnipeg        |   24 |     18 |
|    2 | Western | Sioux City      |   22 |     20 |
|    2 | Western | Sioux Falls     |   16 |     26 |
+------+---------+-----------------+------+--------+
```

Generating the standings for these records requires computing the GB values separately for each of the four combinations of season half and division. Begin by calculating the win-loss differential for the first place team in each group and saving the values into a separate firstplace table:

```
mysql> CREATE TABLE firstplace
    -> SELECT half, div, MAX(wins-losses) AS wl_diff
    -> FROM standings2
    -> GROUP BY half, div;
```

Then join the firstplace table to the original standings, associating each team record with the proper win-loss differential to compute its GB value:

```
mysql> SELECT wl.half, wl.div, wl.team, wl.wins AS W, wl.losses AS L,
    -> TRUNCATE(wl.wins/(wl.wins+wl.losses),3) AS PCT,
    -> IF((fp.wl_diff - (wl.wins-wl.losses)) = 0,
    -> '-', (fp.wl_diff - (wl.wins-wl.losses)) / 2) AS GB
    -> FROM standings2 AS wl, firstplace AS fp
    -> WHERE wl.half = fp.half AND wl.div = fp.div
    -> ORDER BY wl.half, wl.div, wl.wins-wl.losses DESC, PCT DESC;
+------+---------+-----------------+------+------+-------+------+
| half | div     | team            | W    | L    | PCT   | GB   |
+------+---------+-----------------+------+------+-------+------+
|    1 | Eastern | St. Paul        |   24 |   18 | 0.571 | -    |
|    1 | Eastern | Thunder Bay     |   18 |   24 | 0.428 | 6.00 |
|    1 | Eastern | Duluth-Superior |   17 |   24 | 0.414 | 6.50 |
|    1 | Eastern | Madison         |   15 |   27 | 0.357 | 9.00 |
|    1 | Western | Winnipeg        |   29 |   12 | 0.707 | -    |
|    1 | Western | Sioux City      |   28 |   14 | 0.666 | 1.50 |
```

```
|  1 | Western | Fargo-Moorhead  | 21 | 21 | 0.500 | 8.50  |
|  1 | Western | Sioux Falls     | 15 | 27 | 0.357 | 14.50 |
|  2 | Eastern | Duluth-Superior | 22 | 20 | 0.523 | -     |
|  2 | Eastern | St. Paul        | 21 | 21 | 0.500 | 1.00  |
|  2 | Eastern | Madison         | 19 | 23 | 0.452 | 3.00  |
|  2 | Eastern | Thunder Bay     | 18 | 24 | 0.428 | 4.00  |
|  2 | Western | Fargo-Moorhead  | 26 | 16 | 0.619 | -     |
|  2 | Western | Winnipeg        | 24 | 18 | 0.571 | 2.00  |
|  2 | Western | Sioux City      | 22 | 20 | 0.523 | 4.00  |
|  2 | Western | Sioux Falls     | 16 | 26 | 0.380 | 10.00 |
+----+---------+-----------------+----+----+-------+-------+
```

That output is somewhat difficult to read, however. To make it easier to understand, you'd likely execute the query from within a program and reformat its results
to display each set of team records separately. Here's some Perl code that does that
by beginning a new output group each time it encounters a new group of standings.
The code assumes that the join query has just been executed and that its results are
available through the statement handle $sth:

```perl
my ($cur_half, $cur_div) = ("", "");
while (my ($half, $div, $team, $wins, $losses, $pct, $gb)
          = $sth->fetchrow_array ())
{
    if ($cur_half ne $half || $cur_div ne $div) # new group of standings?
    {
        # print standings header and remember new half/division values
        print "\n$div Division, season half $half\n";
        printf "%-20s  %3s  %3s  %5s  %s\n", "Team", "W", "L", "PCT", "GB";
        $cur_half = $half;
        $cur_div = $div;
    }
    printf "%-20s  %3d  %3d  %5s  %s\n", $team, $wins, $losses, $pct, $gb;
}
```

The reformatted output looks like this:

```
Eastern Division, season half 1
Team                  W    L   PCT  GB
St. Paul             24   18  0.57  -
Thunder Bay          18   24  0.43  6.00
Duluth-Superior      17   24  0.41  6.50
Madison              15   27  0.36  9.00

Western Division, season half 1
Team                  W    L   PCT  GB
Winnipeg             29   12  0.71  -
Sioux City           28   14  0.67  1.50
Fargo-Moorhead       21   21  0.50  8.50
Sioux Falls          15   27  0.36  14.50

Eastern Division, season half 2
Team                  W    L   PCT  GB
Duluth-Superior      22   20  0.52  -
St. Paul             21   21  0.50  1.00
Madison              19   23  0.45  3.00
```

```
Thunder Bay           18   24  0.43  4.00

Western Division, season half 2
Team                   W    L   PCT  GB
Fargo-Moorhead        26   16  0.62  -
Winnipeg              24   18  0.57  2.00
Sioux City           22   20  0.52  4.00
Sioux Falls          16   26  0.38  10.00
```

The code just shown that produces plain text output comes from the script *calc_standings.pl* in the *joins* directory of the recipes distribution. That directory also contains a PHP script, *calc_standings.php*, that takes the alternative approach of producing output in the form of HTML tables, which you might prefer for generating standings in a web environment.

12.8   Producing Master-Detail Lists and Summaries

Problem

Two related tables have a master-detail relationship and you want to produce a list that shows each master record with its detail records, or a list that summarizes the detail records for each master record.

Solution

The solution to this problem involves a join, but the type of join depends on the question you want answered. To produce a list containing only master records for which some detail record exists, use a regular join based on the primary key in the master table. To produce a list that includes entries for all master records, even those that have no detail records, use a LEFT JOIN.

Discussion

It's often useful to produce a list from two related tables. For tables that have a master-detail or parent-child relationship, a given record in one table might be matched by several records in the other. This section shows some questions of this type that you can ask (and answer), using the artist and painting tables from earlier in the chapter.

One form of master-detail question for these tables is, "Which artist painted each painting?" This is a simple join that matches each painting record to its corresponding artist record based on the artist ID values:

```
mysql> SELECT artist.name, painting.title
    -> FROM artist, painting WHERE artist.a_id = painting.a_id
    -> ORDER BY 1, 2;
+-----------+-------------------+
| name      | title             |
```

```
+----------+-------------------+
| Da Vinci | The Last Supper   |
| Da Vinci | The Mona Lisa     |
| Renoir   | Les Deux Soeurs   |
| Van Gogh | Starry Night      |
| Van Gogh | The Potato Eaters |
| Van Gogh | The Rocks         |
+----------+-------------------+
```

That type of join suffices, as long as you want to list only master records that have detail records. However, another form of master-detail question you can ask is, "Which paintings did each artist paint?" That question is similar, but not quite identical. It will have a different answer if there are artists listed in the artist table that are not represented in the painting table, and the question requires a different query to produce the proper answer. In that case, the join output should include records in one table that have no match in the other. That's a form of "find the non-matching records" problem (Recipe 12.5), so to list each artist record, whether or not there are any painting records for it, use a LEFT JOIN:

```
mysql> SELECT artist.name, painting.title
    -> FROM artist LEFT JOIN painting ON artist.a_id = painting.a_id
    -> ORDER BY 1, 2;
+----------+-------------------+
| name     | title             |
+----------+-------------------+
| Da Vinci | The Last Supper   |
| Da Vinci | The Mona Lisa     |
| Monet    | NULL              |
| Picasso  | NULL              |
| Renoir   | Les Deux Soeurs   |
| Van Gogh | Starry Night      |
| Van Gogh | The Potato Eaters |
| Van Gogh | The Rocks         |
+----------+-------------------+
```

The rows in the result that have NULL in the title column correspond to artists that are listed in the artist table for whom you have no paintings.

The same principles apply when producing summaries using master and detail tables. For example, to summarize your art collection by number of paintings per painter, you might ask, "how many paintings are there per artist in the painting table?" To find the answer based on artist ID, you can count up the paintings easily with this query:

```
mysql> SELECT a_id, COUNT(a_id) AS count FROM painting GROUP BY a_id;
+------+-------+
| a_id | count |
+------+-------+
|    1 |     2 |
|    3 |     3 |
|    5 |     1 |
+------+-------+
```

Of course, that output is essentially meaningless unless you have all the artist ID numbers memorized. To display the artists by name rather than ID, join the painting table to the artist table:

```
mysql> SELECT artist.name AS painter, COUNT(painting.a_id) AS count
    -> FROM artist, painting
    -> WHERE artist.a_id = painting.a_id
    -> GROUP BY artist.name;
+----------+-------+
| painter  | count |
+----------+-------+
| Da Vinci |     2 |
| Renoir   |     1 |
| Van Gogh |     3 |
+----------+-------+
```

On the other hand, you might ask, "How many paintings did each artist paint?" This is the same question as the previous one (and the same query answers it), as long as every artist in the artist table has at least one corresponding painting table record. But if you have artists in the artist table that are not yet represented by any paintings in your collection, they will not appear in the query output. To produce a count-per-artist summary that includes even artists with no paintings in the painting table, use a LEFT JOIN:

```
mysql> SELECT artist.name AS painter, COUNT(painting.a_id) AS count
    -> FROM artist LEFT JOIN painting ON artist.a_id = painting.a_id
    -> GROUP BY artist.name;
+----------+-------+
| painter  | count |
+----------+-------+
| Da Vinci |     2 |
| Monet    |     0 |
| Picasso  |     0 |
| Renoir   |     1 |
| Van Gogh |     3 |
+----------+-------+
```

Beware of a subtle error that is easy to make when writing that kind of query. Suppose you write it slightly differently, like so:

```
mysql> SELECT artist.name AS painter, COUNT(*) AS count
    -> FROM artist LEFT JOIN painting ON artist.a_id = painting.a_id
    -> GROUP BY artist.name;
+----------+-------+
| painter  | count |
+----------+-------+
| Da Vinci |     2 |
| Monet    |     1 |
| Picasso  |     1 |
| Renoir   |     1 |
| Van Gogh |     3 |
+----------+-------+
```

Now every artist appears to have at least one painting. Why the difference? The cause of the problem is that the query uses COUNT(*) rather than COUNT(painting.a_id). The way LEFT JOIN works for unmatched rows in the left table is that it generates a row with all the columns from the right table set to NULL. In the example, the right table is painting. The query that uses COUNT(painting.a_id) works correctly, because COUNT(*expr*) doesn't count NULL values. The query that uses COUNT(*) works incorrectly because it counts all values, even for rows corresponding to missing artists.

LEFT JOIN is suitable for other types of summaries as well. To produce additional columns showing the total and average values of the paintings for each artist in the artist table, use this query:

```
mysql> SELECT artist.name AS painter,
    -> COUNT(painting.a_id) AS 'number of paintings',
    -> SUM(painting.price) AS 'total price',
    -> AVG(painting.price) AS 'average price'
    -> FROM artist LEFT JOIN painting ON artist.a_id = painting.a_id
    -> GROUP BY artist.name;
```

painter	number of paintings	total price	average price
Da Vinci	2	121	60.5000
Monet	0	0	NULL
Picasso	0	0	NULL
Renoir	1	64	64.0000
Van Gogh	3	148	49.3333

Note that COUNT( ) and SUM( ) are zero for artists that are not represented, but AVG( ) is NULL. That's because AVG( ) is computed as the sum over the count; if the count is zero, the value is undefined. To display an average value of zero in that case, modify the query to test the value of AVG( ) with IFNULL( ):

```
mysql> SELECT artist.name AS painter,
    -> COUNT(painting.a_id) AS 'number of paintings',
    -> SUM(painting.price) AS 'total price',
    -> IFNULL(AVG(painting.price),0) AS 'average price'
    -> FROM artist LEFT JOIN painting ON artist.a_id = painting.a_id
    -> GROUP BY artist.name;
```

painter	number of paintings	total price	average price
Da Vinci	2	121	60.5000
Monet	0	0	0
Picasso	0	0	0
Renoir	1	64	64.0000
Van Gogh	3	148	49.3333

12.9 Using a Join to Fill in Holes in a List

Problem

You want to produce a summary for each of several categories, but some of the categories are not represented in the data to be summarized. Consequently, the summary has missing categories.

Solution

Create a reference table that lists each category and produce the summary based on a LEFT JOIN between the list and the table containing your data. Then every category in the reference table will appear in the result, even "empty" ones.

Discussion

When you run a summary query, normally it produces entries only for the values that are actually present in the data. Let's say you want to produce a time-of-day summary for the records in the mail table, which looks like this:

```
mysql> SELECT * FROM mail;
+---------------------+---------+---------+---------+---------+--------+
| t                   | srcuser | srchost | dstuser | dsthost | size   |
+---------------------+---------+---------+---------+---------+--------+
| 2001-05-11 10:15:08 | barb    | saturn  | tricia  | mars    |  58274 |
| 2001-05-12 12:48:13 | tricia  | mars    | gene    | venus   | 194925 |
| 2001-05-12 15:02:49 | phil    | mars    | phil    | saturn  |   1048 |
| 2001-05-13 13:59:18 | barb    | saturn  | tricia  | venus   |    271 |
| 2001-05-14 09:31:37 | gene    | venus   | barb    | mars    |   2291 |
| 2001-05-14 11:52:17 | phil    | mars    | tricia  | saturn  |   5781 |
...
```

To determine how many messages were sent for each hour of the day, use the following query:

```
mysql> SELECT HOUR(t) AS hour, COUNT(HOUR(t)) AS count
    -> FROM mail GROUP BY hour;
+------+-------+
| hour | count |
+------+-------+
|    7 |     1 |
|    8 |     1 |
|    9 |     2 |
|   10 |     2 |
|   11 |     1 |
|   12 |     2 |
|   13 |     1 |
```

```
|    14 |     1 |
|    15 |     1 |
|    17 |     2 |
|    22 |     1 |
|    23 |     1 |
+------+-------+
```

However, this summary is incomplete in the sense that it includes entries only for those hours of the day represented in the mail table. To produce a summary that includes all hours of the day, even those during which no messages were sent, create a reference table that lists each hour:

```
mysql> CREATE TABLE ref (h INT);
mysql> INSERT INTO ref (h)
    -> VALUES(0),(1),(2),(3),(4),(5),(6),(7),(8),(9),(10),(11),
    -> (12),(13),(14),(15),(16),(17),(18),(19),(20),(21),(22),(23);
```

Then join the reference table to the mail table using a LEFT JOIN:

```
mysql> SELECT ref.h AS hour, COUNT(HOUR(mail.t)) AS count
    -> FROM ref LEFT JOIN mail ON ref.h = HOUR(mail.t)
    -> GROUP BY hour;
+------+-------+
| hour | count |
+------+-------+
|    0 |     0 |
|    1 |     0 |
|    2 |     0 |
|    3 |     0 |
|    4 |     0 |
|    5 |     0 |
|    6 |     0 |
|    7 |     1 |
|    8 |     1 |
|    9 |     2 |
|   10 |     2 |
|   11 |     1 |
|   12 |     2 |
|   13 |     1 |
|   14 |     1 |
|   15 |     1 |
|   16 |     0 |
|   17 |     2 |
|   18 |     0 |
|   19 |     0 |
|   20 |     0 |
|   21 |     0 |
|   22 |     1 |
|   23 |     1 |
+------+-------+
```

Now the summary includes an entry for every hour of the day. The LEFT JOIN forces the output to include a row for every record in the reference table, regardless of the contents of the mail table.

The example just shown uses the reference table with a LEFT JOIN to fill in holes in the category list. By rewriting the query slightly, you can also use the reference table to find holes in the dataset—that is, to determine which categories are not present in the data to be summarized. The following query shows those hours of the day during which no messages were sent by using a HAVING clause that selects only summary rows with a zero count:

```
mysql> SELECT ref.h AS hour, COUNT(HOUR(mail.t)) AS count
    -> FROM ref LEFT JOIN mail ON ref.h = HOUR(mail.t)
    -> GROUP BY hour
    -> HAVING count = 0;
+------+-------+
| hour | count |
+------+-------+
|    0 |     0 |
|    1 |     0 |
|    2 |     0 |
|    3 |     0 |
|    4 |     0 |
|    5 |     0 |
|    6 |     0 |
|   16 |     0 |
|   18 |     0 |
|   19 |     0 |
|   20 |     0 |
|   21 |     0 |
+------+-------+
```

In this case, it's possible to write a simpler query, based on the fact that each hour value appears in the reference table only once. This means that no GROUP BY is necessary; just look for reference rows that don't match any mail table rows:

```
mysql> SELECT ref.h AS hour
    -> FROM ref LEFT JOIN mail ON ref.h = HOUR(mail.t)
    -> WHERE mail.t IS NULL;
+------+
| hour |
+------+
|    0 |
|    1 |
|    2 |
|    3 |
|    4 |
|    5 |
|    6 |
|   16 |
|   18 |
|   19 |
|   20 |
|   21 |
+------+
```

This query also has the advantage of not producing a count column (which is extraneous anyway, because the counts are always zero).

Reference tables that contain a list of categories are quite useful for summary queries, but creating such tables manually can be a mind-numbing and error-prone exercise. If a category list has a lot of entries, you might find it preferable to write a script that uses the endpoints of the range of category values to generate the reference table for you. In essence, this type of script acts as an iterator that generates a record for each value in the range. The following Perl script, *make_date_list.pl*, shows an example of this approach. It creates a reference table containing a row for every date in a particular date range:

```perl
#! /usr/bin/perl -w
# make_date_list.pl - create a table with an entry for every date in a
# given date range.  The table can be used in a LEFT JOIN with a data table
# when producing a summary, to make sure that every date appears in the
# summary, whether or not the data table actually contains any values for
# a given day.

# Usage: make_date_list.pl tbl_name col_name min_date max_date

# This script assumes that you're using the cookbook database.

use strict;
use lib qw(/usr/local/apache/lib/perl);
use Cookbook;

# Check number of arguments, perform minimal tests for ISO-format dates

@ARGV == 4
    or die "Usage: make_date_list.pl tbl_name col_name min_date max_date\n";
my ($tbl_name, $col_name, $min_date, $max_date) = (@ARGV);
$min_date =~ /^\d+\D\d+\D\d+$/
    or die "Minimum date $min_date is not in ISO format\n";
$max_date =~ /^\d+\D\d+\D\d+$/
    or die "Maximum date $max_date is not in ISO format\n";

my $dbh = Cookbook::connect ();

# Determine the number of days spanned by the date range.

my $days = $dbh->selectrow_array (qq{ SELECT TO_DAYS(?) - TO_DAYS(?) + 1 },
                                  undef, $max_date, $min_date);

print "Minimum date: $min_date\n";
print "Maximum date: $max_date\n";
print "Number of days spanned by range: $days\n";
die "Date range is too small\n" if $days < 1;
```

```
# Drop table if it exists, then recreate it

$dbh->do ("DROP TABLE IF EXISTS $tbl_name");
$dbh->do (qq{
        CREATE TABLE $tbl_name
        ($col_name DATE NOT NULL, PRIMARY KEY ($col_name))
    });

# Populate table with each date in the date range

my $sth = $dbh->prepare (qq{
        INSERT INTO $tbl_name ($col_name) VALUES(DATE_ADD(?,INTERVAL ? DAY))
    });
for (my $i = 0; $i < $days; $i++)
{
    $sth->execute ($min_date, $i);
}

$dbh->disconnect ();
exit (0);
```

Tables generated by *make_date_list.pl* can be used for per-day summaries, or to find days not represented in the table. A date-based reference table can be used for calendar-day summaries, too. For example, you could use it to summarize the *baseball1.com* master table to find out how many ballplayers in the table were born each day of the year, or to find days of the year for which there are no birthdays. When creating a calendar day reference table, be sure to use a leap year so that the table contains an entry for February 29. The year 2004 is one such year, so a suitable reference table can be created like this:

```
% make_date_list.pl ref d 2004-01-01 2004-12-31
```

The master table stores birth dates in three columns named birthday, birthmonth, birthyear. After creating the reference table, use the following query to summarize birthdays in the master table for each calendar day:

```
SELECT
MONTH(ref.d) AS month, DAYOFMONTH(ref.d) AS day,
COUNT(master.lahmanid) AS count
FROM ref LEFT JOIN master
    ON MONTH(ref.d) = master.birthmonth
    AND DAYOFMONTH(ref.d) = master.birthday
GROUP BY month, day;
```

To see if there are any days on which no birthdays occur, use this query instead:

```
SELECT MONTH(ref.d) AS month, DAYOFMONTH(ref.d) AS day
FROM ref LEFT JOIN master
    ON MONTH(ref.d) = master.birthmonth
    AND DAYOFMONTH(ref.d) = master.birthday
WHERE master.birthmonth IS NULL and master.birthday IS NULL;
```

12.10 Enumerating a Many-to-Many Relationship

Problem

You want to display a relationship between tables when records in either table may be matched by multiple records in the other table.

Solution

This is a many-to-many relationship. It requires a third table for associating your two primary tables, and a three-way join to list the correspondences between them.

Discussion

The artist and painting tables used in earlier sections are related in a one-to-many relationship: A given artist may have produced many paintings, but each painting was created by only one artist. One-to-many relationships are relatively simple and the two tables in the relationship can be related by means of a key that is common to both tables.

Even simpler is the one-to-one relationship, which often is used for performing lookups that map one set of values to another. For example, the states table contains name and abbrev columns that list full state names and their corresponding abbreviations:

```
mysql> SELECT name, abbrev FROM states;
+----------------+--------+
| name           | abbrev |
+----------------+--------+
| Alabama        | AL     |
| Alaska         | AK     |
| Arizona        | AZ     |
| Arkansas       | AR     |
...
```

This is a one-to-one relationship. It can be used to map state name abbreviations in the painting table, which contains a state column indicating the state in which each painting was purchased. With no mapping, painting entries can be displayed like this:

```
mysql> SELECT title, state FROM painting ORDER BY state;
+-------------------+-------+
| title             | state |
+-------------------+-------+
| The Rocks         | IA    |
| The Last Supper   | IN    |
| Starry Night      | KY    |
| The Potato Eaters | KY    |
| The Mona Lisa     | MI    |
| Les Deux Soeurs   | NE    |
+-------------------+-------+
```

If you want to see the full state names rather than abbreviations, it's possible to use the one-to-one relationship that exists between the two that is enumerated in the states table. Join that table to the painting table as follows, using the abbreviation values that are common to the two tables:

```
mysql> SELECT painting.title, states.name AS state
    -> FROM painting, states
    -> WHERE painting.state = states.abbrev
    -> ORDER BY state;
+-------------------+----------+
| title             | state    |
+-------------------+----------+
| The Last Supper   | Indiana  |
| The Rocks         | Iowa     |
| Starry Night      | Kentucky |
| The Potato Eaters | Kentucky |
| The Mona Lisa     | Michigan |
| Les Deux Soeurs   | Nebraska |
+-------------------+----------+
```

A more complex relationship between tables is the many-to-many relationship, which occurs when a record in one table may have many matches in the other, and vice versa. To illustrate such a relationship, this is the point at which database books typically devolve into the "parts and suppliers" problem. (A given part may be available through several suppliers; how can you produce a list showing which parts are available from which suppliers?) However, having seen that example far too many times, I prefer to use a different illustration. So, even though conceptually it's really the same idea, let's use the following scenario: You and a bunch of your friends are avid enthusiasts of euchre, a four-handed card game played with two teams of partners. Each year, you all get together, pair off, and run a friendly tournament. Naturally, to avoid controversy about the results of each tournament, you record the pairings and outcomes in a database. One way to store the results would be with a table that is set up as follows, where for each tournament year, you record the team names, win-loss records, players, and player cities of residence:

```
mysql> SELECT * FROM euchre ORDER BY year, wins DESC, player;
+----------+------+------+--------+----------+-------------+
| team     | year | wins | losses | player   | player_city |
+----------+------+------+--------+----------+-------------+
| Kings    | 2001 |   10 |      2 | Ben      | Cork        |
| Kings    | 2001 |   10 |      2 | Billy    | York        |
| Crowns   | 2001 |    7 |      5 | Melvin   | Dublin      |
| Crowns   | 2001 |    7 |      5 | Tony     | Derry       |
| Stars    | 2001 |    4 |      8 | Franklin | Bath        |
| Stars    | 2001 |    4 |      8 | Wallace  | Cardiff     |
| Sceptres | 2001 |    3 |      9 | Maurice  | Leeds       |
| Sceptres | 2001 |    3 |      9 | Nigel    | London      |
| Crowns   | 2002 |    9 |      3 | Ben      | Cork        |
| Crowns   | 2002 |    9 |      3 | Tony     | Derry       |
| Kings    | 2002 |    8 |      4 | Franklin | Bath        |
| Kings    | 2002 |    8 |      4 | Nigel    | London      |
```

```
| Stars    | 2002 |    5 |     7 | Maurice  | Leeds       |
| Stars    | 2002 |    5 |     7 | Melvin   | Dublin      |
| Sceptres | 2002 |    2 |    10 | Billy    | York        |
| Sceptres | 2002 |    2 |    10 | Wallace  | Cardiff     |
+----------+------+------+--------+---------+-------------+
```

As shown by the table, each team has multiple players, and each player has participated in multiple teams. The table captures the nature of this many-to-many relationship, but it's also in non-normal form, because each row unnecessarily stores quite a bit of repetitive information. (Information for each team is recorded multiple times, as is information about each player.) A better way to represent this many-to-many relationship is as follows:

- Store each team name, year, and record once, in a table named euchre_team.

- Store each player name and city of residence once, in a table named euchre_player.

- Create a third table, euchre_link, that stores team-player associations and serves as a link, or bridge, between the two primary tables. To minimize the information stored in this table, assign unique IDs to each team and player within their respective tables, and store only those IDs in the euchre_link table.

The resulting team and player tables look like this:

```
mysql> SELECT * FROM euchre_team;
+----+----------+------+------+--------+
| id | name     | year | wins | losses |
+----+----------+------+------+--------+
|  1 | Kings    | 2001 |   10 |      2 |
|  2 | Crowns   | 2001 |    7 |      5 |
|  3 | Stars    | 2001 |    4 |      8 |
|  4 | Sceptres | 2001 |    3 |      9 |
|  5 | Kings    | 2002 |    8 |      4 |
|  6 | Crowns   | 2002 |    9 |      3 |
|  7 | Stars    | 2002 |    5 |      7 |
|  8 | Sceptres | 2002 |    2 |     10 |
+----+----------+------+------+--------+
mysql> SELECT * FROM euchre_player;
+----+----------+---------+
| id | name     | city    |
+----+----------+---------+
|  1 | Ben      | Cork    |
|  2 | Billy    | York    |
|  3 | Tony     | Derry   |
|  4 | Melvin   | Dublin  |
|  5 | Franklin | Bath    |
|  6 | Wallace  | Cardiff |
|  7 | Nigel    | London  |
|  8 | Maurice  | Leeds   |
+----+----------+---------+
```

The euchre_link table associates teams and players as follows:

```
mysql> SELECT * FROM euchre_link;
+---------+-----------+
| team_id | player_id |
+---------+-----------+
|       1 |         1 |
|       1 |         2 |
|       2 |         3 |
|       2 |         4 |
|       3 |         5 |
|       3 |         6 |
|       4 |         7 |
|       4 |         8 |
|       5 |         5 |
|       5 |         7 |
|       6 |         1 |
|       6 |         3 |
|       7 |         4 |
|       7 |         8 |
|       8 |         2 |
|       8 |         6 |
+---------+-----------+
```

To answer questions about the teams or players using these tables, you need to per-form a three-way join, using the link table to relate the two primary tables to each other. Here are some examples:

- List all the pairings that show the teams and who played on them. This query enumerates all the correspondences between the euchre_team and euchre_player tables and reproduces the information that was originally in the non-normal euchre table:

```
mysql> SELECT t.name, t.year, t.wins, t.losses, p.name, p.city
    -> FROM euchre_team AS t, euchre_link AS l, euchre_player AS p
    -> WHERE t.id = l.team_id AND p.id = l.player_id
    -> ORDER BY t.year, t.wins DESC, p.name;
+----------+------+------+--------+----------+---------+
| name     | year | wins | losses | name     | city    |
+----------+------+------+--------+----------+---------+
| Kings    | 2001 |   10 |      2 | Ben      | Cork    |
| Kings    | 2001 |   10 |      2 | Billy    | York    |
| Crowns   | 2001 |    7 |      5 | Melvin   | Dublin  |
| Crowns   | 2001 |    7 |      5 | Tony     | Derry   |
| Stars    | 2001 |    4 |      8 | Franklin | Bath    |
| Stars    | 2001 |    4 |      8 | Wallace  | Cardiff |
| Sceptres | 2001 |    3 |      9 | Maurice  | Leeds   |
| Sceptres | 2001 |    3 |      9 | Nigel    | London  |
| Crowns   | 2002 |    9 |      3 | Ben      | Cork    |
| Crowns   | 2002 |    9 |      3 | Tony     | Derry   |
| Kings    | 2002 |    8 |      4 | Franklin | Bath    |
| Kings    | 2002 |    8 |      4 | Nigel    | London  |
| Stars    | 2002 |    5 |      7 | Maurice  | Leeds   |
```

```
| Stars    | 2002 |   5 |      7 | Melvin  | Dublin  |
| Sceptres | 2002 |   2 |     10 | Billy   | York    |
| Sceptres | 2002 |   2 |     10 | Wallace | Cardiff |
+----------+------+------+--------+---------+---------+
```

- List the members for a particular team (the 2001 Crowns):

```
mysql> SELECT p.name, p.city
    -> FROM euchre_team AS t, euchre_link AS l, euchre_player AS p
    -> WHERE t.id = l.team_id AND p.id = l.player_id
    -> AND t.name = 'Crowns' AND t.year = 2001;
+--------+--------+
| name   | city   |
+--------+--------+
| Tony   | Derry  |
| Melvin | Dublin |
+--------+--------+
```

- List the teams that a given player (Billy) has been a member of:

```
mysql> SELECT t.name, t.year, t.wins, t.losses
    -> FROM euchre_team AS t, euchre_link AS l, euchre_player AS p
    -> WHERE t.id = l.team_id AND p.id = l.player_id
    -> AND p.name = 'Billy';
+----------+------+------+--------+
| name     | year | wins | losses |
+----------+------+------+--------+
| Kings    | 2001 |   10 |      2 |
| Sceptres | 2002 |    2 |     10 |
+----------+------+------+--------+
```

Note that although questions about many-to-many relationships involve a three-way join, a three-way join in itself does not necessarily imply a many-to-many relationship. Earlier in this section, we joined the states table to the painting table to map state abbreviations to full names:

```
mysql> SELECT painting.title, states.name AS state
    -> FROM painting, states
    -> WHERE painting.state = states.abbrev
    -> ORDER BY state;
+-------------------+----------+
| title             | state    |
+-------------------+----------+
| The Last Supper   | Indiana  |
| The Rocks         | Iowa     |
| Starry Night      | Kentucky |
| The Potato Eaters | Kentucky |
| The Mona Lisa     | Michigan |
| Les Deux Soeurs   | Nebraska |
+-------------------+----------+
```

To display the artist who painted each painting, modify the query slightly by joining the results with the artist table:

```
mysql> SELECT artist.name, painting.title, states.name AS state
    -> FROM artist, painting, states
    -> WHERE artist.a_id = painting.a_id AND painting.state = states.abbrev;
```

```
+----------+-------------------+----------+
| name     | title             | state    |
+----------+-------------------+----------+
| Da Vinci | The Last Supper   | Indiana  |
| Da Vinci | The Mona Lisa     | Michigan |
| Van Gogh | Starry Night      | Kentucky |
| Van Gogh | The Potato Eaters | Kentucky |
| Van Gogh | The Rocks         | Iowa     |
| Renoir   | Les Deux Soeurs   | Nebraska |
+----------+-------------------+----------+
```

The query now involves a three-way join, but the nature of the relationship between artists and paintings remains the same. It's still one-to-many, not many-to-many.

12.11 Comparing a Table to Itself

Problem

You want to compare records in a table to other records in the same table. For example, you want to find all paintings in your collection by the artist who painted "The Potato Eaters." Or you want to know which states listed in the states table joined the Union in the same year as New York. Or you want to know which of the people listed in the profile table have some favorite food in common.

Solution

Problems that require comparing a table to itself involve an operation known as a self-join. It's much like other joins, except that you must always use table aliases so that you can refer to the same table different ways within the query.

Discussion

A special case of joining one table to another occurs when both tables are the same. This is called a self-join. Although many people find the idea confusing or strange to think about at first, it's perfectly legal. Be assured that you'll get used to the concept, and more than likely will find yourself using self-joins quite often because they are so important.

A tip-off that you need a self-join is when you want to know which pairs of elements in a table satisfy some condition. For example, suppose your favorite painting is "The Potato Eaters" and you want to identify all the items in your collection that were done by the artist who painted it. You can do so as follows:

1. Identify the row in the painting table that contains the title "The Potato Eaters," so that you can refer to its a_id value.

2. Use the a_id value to match other rows in the table that have the same a_id value.

3. Display the titles from those matching rows.

The artist ID and painting titles that we begin with look like this:

```
mysql> SELECT a_id, title FROM painting ORDER BY a_id;
+------+------------------+
| a_id | title            |
+------+------------------+
|    1 | The Last Supper  |
|    1 | The Mona Lisa    |
|    3 | Starry Night     |
|    3 | The Potato Eaters|
|    3 | The Rocks        |
|    5 | Les Deux Soeurs  |
+------+------------------+
```

A two-step method for picking out the right titles without a join is to look up the artist's ID with one query, then use the ID in a second query that selects records that match it:

```
mysql> SELECT @id := a_id FROM painting WHERE title = 'The Potato Eaters';
+-------------+
| @id := a_id |
+-------------+
|           3 |
+-------------+
mysql> SELECT title FROM painting WHERE a_id = @id;
+-------------------+
| title             |
+-------------------+
| Starry Night      |
| The Potato Eaters |
| The Rocks         |
+-------------------+
```

Another solution—one that requires only a single query—is to use a self-join. The trick to this lies in figuring out the proper notation to use. The way many people first try to write a query that joins a table to itself looks something like this:

```
mysql> SELECT title FROM painting, painting
    -> WHERE title = 'The Potato Eaters' AND a_id = a_id;
ERROR 1066 at line 1: Not unique table/alias: 'painting'
```

The problem with that query is that the column references are ambiguous. MySQL can't tell which instance of the painting table any given column name refers to. The solution is to give at least one instance of the table an alias so that you can distinguish column references by using different table qualifiers. The following query shows how to do this, using the aliases p1 and p2 to refer to the painting table different ways:

```
mysql> SELECT p2.title
    -> FROM painting AS p1, painting AS p2
```

```
    -> WHERE p1.title = 'The Potato Eaters'
    -> AND p1.a_id = p2.a_id;
+-------------------+
| title             |
+-------------------+
| Starry Night      |
| The Potato Eaters |
| The Rocks         |
+-------------------+
```

The query output illustrates something typical of self-joins: when you begin with a reference value in one table instance ("The Potato Eaters") to find matching records in a second table instance (paintings by the same artist), the output includes the reference value. That makes sense—after all, the reference matches itself. If you want to find only *other* paintings by the same artist, explicitly exclude the reference value from the output:

```
mysql> SELECT p2.title
    -> FROM painting AS p1, painting AS p2
    -> WHERE p1.title = 'The Potato Eaters' AND p2.title != 'The Potato Eaters'
    -> AND p1.a_id = p2.a_id;
+--------------+
| title        |
+--------------+
| Starry Night |
| The Rocks    |
+--------------+
```

A more general way to exclude the reference value without naming it literally is to specify that you don't want output rows to have the same title as the reference, whatever that title happens to be:

```
mysql> SELECT p2.title
    -> FROM painting AS p1, painting AS p2
    -> WHERE p1.title = 'The Potato Eaters' AND p1.title != p2.title
    -> AND p1.a_id = p2.a_id;
+--------------+
| title        |
+--------------+
| Starry Night |
| The Rocks    |
+--------------+
```

The preceding queries use comparisons of ID values to match records in the two table instances, but any kind of value can be used. For example, to use the states table to answer the question "Which states joined the Union in the same year as New York?," perform a temporal pairwise comparison based on the year part of the dates in the table's statehood column:

```
mysql> SELECT s2.name, s2.statehood
    -> FROM states AS s1, states AS s2
    -> WHERE s1.name = 'New York'
    -> AND YEAR(s1.statehood) = YEAR(s2.statehood)
    -> ORDER BY s2.name;
```

```
+----------------+------------+
| name           | statehood  |
+----------------+------------+
| Connecticut    | 1788-01-09 |
| Georgia        | 1788-01-02 |
| Maryland       | 1788-04-28 |
| Massachusetts  | 1788-02-06 |
| New Hampshire  | 1788-06-21 |
| New York       | 1788-07-26 |
| South Carolina | 1788-05-23 |
| Virginia       | 1788-06-25 |
+----------------+------------+
```

Here again, the reference value (New York) appears in the output. If you want to prevent that, add an expression to the WHERE clause that explicitly excludes the reference:

```
mysql> SELECT s2.name, s2.statehood
    -> FROM states AS s1, states AS s2
    -> WHERE s1.name = 'New York' AND s1.name != s2.name
    -> AND YEAR(s1.statehood) = YEAR(s2.statehood)
    -> ORDER BY s2.name;
+----------------+------------+
| name           | statehood  |
+----------------+------------+
| Connecticut    | 1788-01-09 |
| Georgia        | 1788-01-02 |
| Maryland       | 1788-04-28 |
| Massachusetts  | 1788-02-06 |
| New Hampshire  | 1788-06-21 |
| South Carolina | 1788-05-23 |
| Virginia       | 1788-06-25 |
+----------------+------------+
```

Like the problem of finding other paintings by the painter of "The Potato Eaters," the statehood problem could have been solved by using a SQL variable and two queries. That will always be true when you're seeking matches for one particular row in your table. Other problems require finding matches between several pairs of rows, in which case the two-query method will not work. Suppose you want to determine which pairs of people listed in the profile table have favorite foods in common. In this case, the output potentially can include any pair of people in the table. There is no fixed reference value, so you cannot store the reference in a variable.

A self-join is perfect for this problem, although there is the question of how to identify which foods values share common elements. The foods column contains SET values, each of which may indicate multiple foods, so an exact comparison will not work:

- The comparison is true only if both foods values name an identical set of foods; this is unsuitable if you require only a common element.

- Two empty values will compare as equal, even though they have no foods in common.

To identify SET values that share common elements, use the fact that MySQL represents them as bit fields and perform the comparison using the & (bitwise AND) operator to look for pairs that have a non-zero intersection:

```
mysql> SELECT t1.name, t2.name, t1.foods, t2.foods
    -> FROM profile AS t1, profile AS t2
    -> WHERE t1.id != t2.id AND (t1.foods & t2.foods) != 0
    -> ORDER BY t1.name, t2.name;
+------+------+---------------------+---------------------+
| name | name | foods               | foods               |
+------+------+---------------------+---------------------+
| Alan | Brit | curry,fadge         | burrito,curry,pizza |
| Alan | Fred | curry,fadge         | lutefisk,fadge,pizza |
| Alan | Mara | curry,fadge         | lutefisk,fadge      |
| Alan | Sean | curry,fadge         | burrito,curry       |
| Brit | Alan | burrito,curry,pizza | curry,fadge         |
| Brit | Carl | burrito,curry,pizza | eggroll,pizza       |
| Brit | Fred | burrito,curry,pizza | lutefisk,fadge,pizza |
| Brit | Sean | burrito,curry,pizza | burrito,curry       |
| Carl | Brit | eggroll,pizza       | burrito,curry,pizza |
| Carl | Fred | eggroll,pizza       | lutefisk,fadge,pizza |
| Fred | Alan | lutefisk,fadge,pizza | curry,fadge         |
| Fred | Brit | lutefisk,fadge,pizza | burrito,curry,pizza |
| Fred | Carl | lutefisk,fadge,pizza | eggroll,pizza       |
| Fred | Mara | lutefisk,fadge,pizza | lutefisk,fadge      |
| Mara | Alan | lutefisk,fadge      | curry,fadge         |
| Mara | Fred | lutefisk,fadge      | lutefisk,fadge,pizza |
| Sean | Alan | burrito,curry       | curry,fadge         |
| Sean | Brit | burrito,curry       | burrito,curry,pizza |
+------+------+---------------------+---------------------+
```

Some self-join problems are of the "Which values have no match?" variety. An instance of this is the question, "Which message senders in the mail table didn't send any messages to themselves?" First, check who sent mail to who:

```
mysql> SELECT DISTINCT srcuser, dstuser FROM mail
    -> ORDER BY srcuser, dstuser;
+---------+---------+
| srcuser | dstuser |
+---------+---------+
| barb    | barb    |
| barb    | tricia  |
| gene    | barb    |
| gene    | gene    |
| gene    | tricia  |
| phil    | barb    |
| phil    | phil    |
| phil    | tricia  |
| tricia  | gene    |
| tricia  | phil    |
+---------+---------+
```

Of those pairs, several are for people that did send mail to themselves:

```
mysql> SELECT DISTINCT srcuser, dstuser FROM mail
    -> WHERE srcuser = dstuser;
+---------+---------+
| srcuser | dstuser |
+---------+---------+
| phil    | phil    |
| barb    | barb    |
| gene    | gene    |
+---------+---------+
```

Finding people who didn't send mail to themselves is a "non-match" problem, which is the type of problem that typically involves a LEFT JOIN. In this case, the solution requires a LEFT JOIN of the mail table to itself:

```
mysql> SELECT DISTINCT m1.srcuser
    -> FROM mail AS m1 LEFT JOIN mail AS m2
    -> ON m1.srcuser = m2.srcuser AND m2.srcuser = m2.dstuser
    -> WHERE m2.dstuser IS NULL;
+---------+
| srcuser |
+---------+
| tricia  |
+---------+
```

For each record in the mail table, the query selects matches where the sender and recipient are the same. For records having no such match, the LEFT JOIN forces the output to contain a row anyway, with all the m2 columns set to NULL. These rows identify the senders who sent no messages to themselves.

Using a LEFT JOIN to join a table to itself also provides another way to answer maximum-per-group questions of the sort discussed in Recipe 12.6, but without using a secondary temporary table. Recall that in that recipe we found the most expensive painting per artist as follows using a temporary table:

```
mysql> CREATE TABLE tmp
    -> SELECT a_id, MAX(price) AS max_price FROM painting GROUP BY a_id;
mysql> SELECT artist.name, painting.title, painting.price
    -> FROM artist, painting, tmp
    -> WHERE painting.a_id = tmp.a_id
    -> AND painting.price = tmp.max_price
    -> AND painting.a_id = artist.a_id;
+----------+-------------------+-------+
| name     | title             | price |
+----------+-------------------+-------+
| Da Vinci | The Mona Lisa     |    87 |
| Van Gogh | The Potato Eaters |    67 |
| Renoir   | Les Deux Soeurs   |    64 |
+----------+-------------------+-------+
```

Another way to identify the paintings and then pull out values from each of those rows is with a LEFT JOIN. The following query identifies the paintings:

```
mysql> SELECT p1.a_id, p1.title, p1.price
    -> FROM painting p1
    -> LEFT JOIN painting p2
    -> ON p1.a_id = p2.a_id AND p1.price < p2.price
    -> WHERE p2.a_id IS NULL;
+------+-------------------+-------+
| a_id | title             | price |
+------+-------------------+-------+
|    1 | The Mona Lisa     |    87 |
|    3 | The Potato Eaters |    67 |
|    5 | Les Deux Soeurs   |    64 |
+------+-------------------+-------+
```

To display the artist names, join the result with the artist table:

```
mysql> SELECT artist.name, p1.title, p1.price
    -> FROM (painting p1
    -> LEFT JOIN painting p2
    -> ON p1.a_id = p2.a_id AND p1.price < p2.price), artist
    -> WHERE p2.a_id IS NULL AND p1.a_id = artist.a_id;
+----------+-------------------+-------+
| name     | title             | price |
+----------+-------------------+-------+
| Da Vinci | The Mona Lisa     |    87 |
| Van Gogh | The Potato Eaters |    67 |
| Renoir   | Les Deux Soeurs   |    64 |
+----------+-------------------+-------+
```

Note that a given "compare a table to itself" problem does not necessarily require a self-join, even if it's possible to solve it that way. The mail table serves to illustrate this. One way to determine which senders sent themselves a message is to use a self-join:

```
mysql> SELECT DISTINCT m1.srcuser, m2.dstuser
    -> FROM mail AS m1, mail AS m2
    -> WHERE m1.srcuser = m2.srcuser AND m2.dstuser = m1.srcuser;
+---------+---------+
| srcuser | dstuser |
+---------+---------+
| phil    | phil    |
| barb    | barb    |
| gene    | gene    |
+---------+---------+
```

But that's silly. The query doesn't need to compare records to each other. It needs only to compare different columns within each row, so a non-join query is sufficient, and simpler to write:

```
mysql> SELECT DISTINCT srcuser, dstuser FROM mail
    -> WHERE srcuser = dstuser;
```

```
+---------+---------+
| srcuser | dstuser |
+---------+---------+
| phil    | phil    |
| barb    | barb    |
| gene    | gene    |
+---------+---------+
```

12.12 Calculating Differences Between Successive Rows

Problem

You have a table containing successive cumulative values in its rows and you want to compute the differences between pairs of successive rows.

Solution

Use a self-join that matches up pairs of adjacent rows and calculates the differences between members of each pair.

Discussion

Self-joins are useful when you have a set of absolute (or cumulative) values that you want to convert to relative values representing the differences between successive pairs of rows. For example, if you take an automobile trip and write down the total miles traveled at each stopping point, you can compute the difference between successive points to determine the distance from one stop to the next. Here is such a table that shows the stops for a trip from San Antonio, Texas to Madison, Wisconsin. Each row shows the total miles driven as of each stop:

```
mysql> SELECT seq, city, miles FROM trip_log ORDER BY seq;
+-----+-----------------+-------+
| seq | city            | miles |
+-----+-----------------+-------+
|   1 | San Antonio, TX |     0 |
|   2 | Dallas, TX      |   263 |
|   3 | Benton, AR      |   566 |
|   4 | Memphis, TN     |   745 |
|   5 | Portageville, MO|   878 |
|   6 | Champaign, IL   |  1164 |
|   7 | Madison, WI     |  1412 |
+-----+-----------------+-------+
```

A self-join can convert these cumulative values to successive differences that represent the distances from each city to the next. The following query shows how to use the sequence numbers in the records to match up pairs of successive rows and compute the differences between each pair of mileage values:

```
mysql> SELECT t1.seq AS seq1,  t2.seq AS seq2,
    -> t1.city AS city1, t2.city AS city2,
    -> t1.miles AS miles1, t2.miles AS miles2,
    -> t2.miles-t1.miles AS dist
    -> FROM trip_log AS t1, trip_log AS t2
    -> WHERE t1.seq+1 = t2.seq
    -> ORDER BY t1.seq;
+------+------+------------------+------------------+--------+--------+------+
| seq1 | seq2 | city1            | city2            | miles1 | miles2 | dist |
+------+------+------------------+------------------+--------+--------+------+
|    1 |    2 | San Antonio, TX  | Dallas, TX       |      0 |    263 |  263 |
|    2 |    3 | Dallas, TX       | Benton, AR       |    263 |    566 |  303 |
|    3 |    4 | Benton, AR       | Memphis, TN      |    566 |    745 |  179 |
|    4 |    5 | Memphis, TN      | Portageville, MO |    745 |    878 |  133 |
|    5 |    6 | Portageville, MO | Champaign, IL    |    878 |   1164 |  286 |
|    6 |    7 | Champaign, IL    | Madison, WI      |   1164 |   1412 |  248 |
+------+------+------------------+------------------+--------+--------+------+
```

The presence of the seq column in the trip_log table is important for calculating successive difference values. It's needed for establishing which row precedes another and matching each row *n* with row *n+1*. The implication is that a table should include a sequence column that has no gaps if you want to perform relative-difference calculations from absolute or cumulative values. If the table contains a sequence column but there are gaps, renumber it. If the table contains no such column, add one. Recipe 11.8 and Recipe 11.12 describe how to perform these operations.

A somewhat more complex situation occurs when you compute successive differences for more than one column and use the results in a calculation. The following table, player_stats, shows some cumulative numbers for a baseball player at the end of each month of his season. ab indicates the total at-bats and h the total hits the player has had as of a given date. (The first record indicates the starting point of the player's season, which is why the ab and h values are zero.)

```
mysql> SELECT id, date, ab, h, TRUNCATE(IFNULL(h/ab,0),3) AS ba
    -> FROM player_stats ORDER BY id;
+----+------------+-----+----+-------+
| id | date       | ab  | h  | ba    |
+----+------------+-----+----+-------+
|  1 | 2001-04-30 |   0 |  0 | 0.000 |
|  2 | 2001-05-31 |  38 | 13 | 0.342 |
|  3 | 2001-06-30 | 109 | 31 | 0.284 |
|  4 | 2001-07-31 | 196 | 49 | 0.250 |
|  5 | 2001-08-31 | 304 | 98 | 0.322 |
+----+------------+-----+----+-------+
```

The last column of the query result also shows the player's batting average as of each date. This column is not stored in the table, but is easily computed as the ratio of hits to at-bats. The result provides a general idea of how the player's hitting performance changed over the course of the season, but it doesn't give a very informative picture of how the player did during each individual month. To determine that, it's necessary to calculate relative differences between pairs of rows. This is easily done with a self-join that matches each row *n* with row *n+1*, to calculate differences between pairs of at-bats and hits values. These differences allow batting average during each month to be computed:

```
mysql> SELECT
    -> t1.id AS id1, t2.id AS id2,
    -> t2.date,
    -> t1.ab AS ab1, t2.ab AS ab2,
    -> t1.h AS h1, t2.h AS h2,
    -> t2.ab-t1.ab AS abdiff,
    -> t2.h-t1.h AS hdiff,
    -> TRUNCATE(IFNULL((t2.h-t1.h)/(t2.ab-t1.ab),0),3) AS ba
    -> FROM player_stats AS t1, player_stats AS t2
    -> WHERE t1.id+1 = t2.id
    -> ORDER BY t1.id;
+-----+-----+------------+-----+-----+----+----+--------+-------+-------+
| id1 | id2 | date       | ab1 | ab2 | h1 | h2 | abdiff | hdiff | ba    |
+-----+-----+------------+-----+-----+----+----+--------+-------+-------+
|   1 |   2 | 2001-05-31 |   0 |  38 |  0 | 13 |     38 |    13 | 0.342 |
|   2 |   3 | 2001-06-30 |  38 | 109 | 13 | 31 |     71 |    18 | 0.253 |
|   3 |   4 | 2001-07-31 | 109 | 196 | 31 | 49 |     87 |    18 | 0.206 |
|   4 |   5 | 2001-08-31 | 196 | 304 | 49 | 98 |    108 |    49 | 0.453 |
+-----+-----+------------+-----+-----+----+----+--------+-------+-------+
```

These results show much more clearly than the original table does that the player started off well, but had a slump in the middle of the season, particularly in July. They also indicate just how strong his performance was in August.

12.13 Finding Cumulative Sums and Running Averages

Problem

You have a set of observations measured over time and want to compute the cumulative sum of the observations at each measurement point. Or you want to compute a running average at each point.

Solution

Use a self-join to produce the sets of successive observations at each measurement point, then apply aggregate functions to each set of values to compute its sum or average.

Discussion

Recipe 12.12 illustrates how a self-join can produce relative values from absolute values. A self-join can do the opposite as well, producing cumulative values at each successive stage of a set of observations. The following table shows a set of rainfall measurements taken over a series of days. The values in each row show the observation date and the amount of precipitation in inches:

```
mysql> SELECT date, precip FROM rainfall ORDER BY date;
+------------+--------+
| date       | precip |
+------------+--------+
| 2002-06-01 |   1.50 |
| 2002-06-02 |   0.00 |
| 2002-06-03 |   0.50 |
| 2002-06-04 |   0.00 |
| 2002-06-05 |   1.00 |
+------------+--------+
```

To calculate cumulative rainfall for a given day, sum that day's precipitation value with the values for all the previous days. For example, the cumulative rainfall as of 2002-06-03 is determined like this:

```
mysql> SELECT SUM(precip) FROM rainfall WHERE date <= '2002-06-03';
+-------------+
| SUM(precip) |
+-------------+
|        2.00 |
+-------------+
```

If you want the cumulative figures for all days that are represented in the table, it would be tedious to compute the value for each of them separately. A self-join can do this for all days with a single query. Use one instance of the rainfall table as a reference, and determine for the date in each row the sum of the precip values in all rows occurring up through that date in another instance of the table. The following query shows the daily and cumulative precipitation for each day:

```
mysql> SELECT t1.date, t1.precip AS 'daily precip',
    -> SUM(t2.precip) AS 'cum. precip'
    -> FROM rainfall AS t1, rainfall AS t2
    -> WHERE t1.date >= t2.date
    -> GROUP BY t1.date;
+------------+--------------+-------------+
| date       | daily precip | cum. precip |
+------------+--------------+-------------+
| 2002-06-01 |         1.50 |        1.50 |
| 2002-06-02 |         0.00 |        1.50 |
| 2002-06-03 |         0.50 |        2.00 |
| 2002-06-04 |         0.00 |        2.00 |
| 2002-06-05 |         1.00 |        3.00 |
+------------+--------------+-------------+
```

The self-join can be extended to display the number of days elapsed at each date, as well as the running averages for amount of precipitation each day:

```
mysql> SELECT t1.date, t1.precip AS 'daily precip',
    -> SUM(t2.precip) AS 'cum. precip',
    -> COUNT(t2.precip) AS days,
    -> AVG(t2.precip) AS 'avg. precip'
    -> FROM rainfall AS t1, rainfall AS t2
    -> WHERE t1.date >= t2.date
    -> GROUP BY t1.date;
+------------+--------------+-------------+------+-------------+
| date       | daily precip | cum. precip | days | avg. precip |
+------------+--------------+-------------+------+-------------+
| 2002-06-01 |         1.50 |        1.50 |    1 |    1.500000 |
| 2002-06-02 |         0.00 |        1.50 |    2 |    0.750000 |
| 2002-06-03 |         0.50 |        2.00 |    3 |    0.666667 |
| 2002-06-04 |         0.00 |        2.00 |    4 |    0.500000 |
| 2002-06-05 |         1.00 |        3.00 |    5 |    0.600000 |
+------------+--------------+-------------+------+-------------+
```

In the preceding query, the number of days elapsed and the precipitation running averages can be computed easily using COUNT( ) and AVG( ) because there are no missing days in the table. If missing days are allowed, the calculation becomes more complicated, because the number of days elapsed for each calculation no longer will be the same as the number of records. You can see this by deleting the records for the days that had no precipitation to produce a couple of "holes" in the table:

```
mysql> DELETE FROM rainfall WHERE precip = 0;
mysql> SELECT date, precip FROM rainfall ORDER BY date;
+------------+--------+
| date       | precip |
+------------+--------+
| 2002-06-01 |   1.50 |
| 2002-06-03 |   0.50 |
| 2002-06-05 |   1.00 |
+------------+--------+
```

Deleting those records doesn't change the cumulative sum or running average for the dates that remain, but does change how they must be calculated. If you try the self-join again, it yields incorrect results for the days-elapsed and average precipitation columns:

```
mysql> SELECT t1.date, t1.precip AS 'daily precip',
    -> SUM(t2.precip) AS 'cum. precip',
    -> COUNT(t2.precip) AS days,
    -> AVG(t2.precip) AS 'avg. precip'
    -> FROM rainfall AS t1, rainfall AS t2
    -> WHERE t1.date >= t2.date
    -> GROUP BY t1.date;
```

```
+------------+--------------+-------------+------+-------------+
| date       | daily precip | cum. precip | days | avg. precip |
+------------+--------------+-------------+------+-------------+
| 2002-06-01 |         1.50 |        1.50 |    1 |    1.500000 |
| 2002-06-03 |         0.50 |        2.00 |    2 |    1.000000 |
| 2002-06-05 |         1.00 |        3.00 |    3 |    1.000000 |
+------------+--------------+-------------+------+-------------+
```

To fix the problem, it's necessary to determine the number of days elapsed a different way. Take the minimum and maximum date involved in each sum and calculate a days-elapsed value from them using the following expression:

```
TO_DAYS(MAX(t2.date)) - TO_DAYS(MIN(t2.date)) + 1
```

That value must be used for the days-elapsed column and for computing the running averages. The resulting query is as follows:

```
mysql> SELECT t1.date, t1.precip AS 'daily precip',
    -> SUM(t2.precip) AS 'cum. precip',
    -> TO_DAYS(MAX(t2.date)) - TO_DAYS(MIN(t2.date)) + 1 AS days,
    -> SUM(t2.precip) / (TO_DAYS(MAX(t2.date)) - TO_DAYS(MIN(t2.date)) + 1)
    -> AS 'avg. precip'
    -> FROM rainfall AS t1, rainfall AS t2
    -> WHERE t1.date >= t2.date
    -> GROUP BY t1.date;
+------------+--------------+-------------+------+-------------+
| date       | daily precip | cum. precip | days | avg. precip |
+------------+--------------+-------------+------+-------------+
| 2002-06-01 |         1.50 |        1.50 |    1 |      1.5000 |
| 2002-06-03 |         0.50 |        2.00 |    3 |      0.6667 |
| 2002-06-05 |         1.00 |        3.00 |    5 |      0.6000 |
+------------+--------------+-------------+------+-------------+
```

As this example illustrates, calculation of cumulative values from relative values requires only a column that allows rows to be placed into the proper order. (For the rainfall table, that's the date column.) Values in the column need not be sequential, or even numeric. This differs from calculations that produce difference values from cumulative values (Recipe 12.12), which require that a table have a column that contains an unbroken sequence.

The running averages in the rainfall examples are based on dividing cumulative precipitation sums by number of days elapsed as of each day. When the table has no gaps, the number of days is the same as the number of values summed, making it easy to find successive averages. When records are missing, the calculations become more complex. What this demonstrates is that it's necessary to consider the nature of your data and calculate averages appropriately. The next example is conceptually similar to the previous ones in that it calculates cumulative sums and running averages, but it performs the computations yet another way.

The following table shows a marathon runner's performance at each stage of a 26-kilometer run. The values in each row show the length of each stage in kilometers and how long the runner took to complete the stage. In other words, the values pertain to intervals within the marathon and thus are relative to the whole:

```
mysql> SELECT stage, km, t FROM marathon ORDER BY stage;
+-------+----+----------+
| stage | km | t        |
+-------+----+----------+
|     1 |  5 | 00:15:00 |
|     2 |  7 | 00:19:30 |
|     3 |  9 | 00:29:20 |
|     4 |  5 | 00:17:50 |
+-------+----+----------+
```

To calculate cumulative distance in kilometers at each stage, use a self-join that looks like this:

```
mysql> SELECT t1.stage, t1.km, SUM(t2.km) AS 'cum. km'
    -> FROM marathon AS t1, marathon AS t2
    -> WHERE t1.stage >= t2.stage
    -> GROUP BY t1.stage;
+-------+----+---------+
| stage | km | cum. km |
+-------+----+---------+
|     1 |  5 |       5 |
|     2 |  7 |      12 |
|     3 |  9 |      21 |
|     4 |  5 |      26 |
+-------+----+---------+
```

Cumulative distances are easy to compute because they can be summed directly. The calculation for accumulating time values is a little more involved. It's necessary to convert times to seconds, sum the resulting values, and convert the sum back to a time value. To compute the runner's average speed at the end of each stage, take the ratio of cumulative distance over cumulative time. Putting all this together yields the following query:

```
mysql> SELECT t1.stage, t1.km, t1.t,
    -> SUM(t2.km) AS 'cum. km',
    -> SEC_TO_TIME(SUM(TIME_TO_SEC(t2.t))) AS 'cum. t',
    -> SUM(t2.km)/(SUM(TIME_TO_SEC(t2.t))/(60*60)) AS 'avg. km/hour'
    -> FROM marathon AS t1, marathon AS t2
    -> WHERE t1.stage >= t2.stage
    -> GROUP BY t1.stage;
+-------+----+----------+---------+----------+--------------+
| stage | km | t        | cum. km | cum. t   | avg. km/hour |
+-------+----+----------+---------+----------+--------------+
|     1 |  5 | 00:15:00 |       5 | 00:15:00 |      20.0000 |
|     2 |  7 | 00:19:30 |      12 | 00:34:30 |      20.8696 |
|     3 |  9 | 00:29:20 |      21 | 01:03:50 |      19.7389 |
|     4 |  5 | 00:17:50 |      26 | 01:21:40 |      19.1020 |
+-------+----+----------+---------+----------+--------------+
```

We can see from this that the runner's average pace increased a little during the second stage of the race, but then (presumably as a result of fatigue) decreased thereafter.

12.14 Using a Join to Control Query Output Order

Problem

You want to sort a query's output using a characteristic of the output that cannot be specified using ORDER BY. For example, you want to sort a set of rows by subgroups, putting first those groups with the most rows and last those groups with the fewest rows. But "number of rows in each group" is not a property of individual rows, so you can't sort by it.

Solution

Derive the ordering information and store it in another table. Then join the original table to the derived table, using the derived table to control the sort order.

Discussion

Most of the time when you sort a query result, you use an ORDER BY (or GROUP BY) clause to name the column or columns to use for sorting. But sometimes the values you want to sort by aren't present in the rows to be sorted. This is the case, for example, if you want to use group characteristics to order the rows. The following example uses the records in the driver_log table to illustrate this. The table looks like this:

```
mysql> SELECT * FROM driver_log ORDER BY id;
+--------+-------+------------+-------+
| rec_id | name  | trav_date  | miles |
+--------+-------+------------+-------+
|      1 | Ben   | 2001-11-30 |   152 |
|      2 | Suzi  | 2001-11-29 |   391 |
|      3 | Henry | 2001-11-29 |   300 |
|      4 | Henry | 2001-11-27 |    96 |
|      5 | Ben   | 2001-11-29 |   131 |
|      6 | Henry | 2001-11-26 |   115 |
|      7 | Suzi  | 2001-12-02 |   502 |
|      8 | Henry | 2001-12-01 |   197 |
|      9 | Ben   | 2001-12-02 |    79 |
|     10 | Henry | 2001-11-30 |   203 |
+--------+-------+------------+-------+
```

The preceding query sorts the records using the ID column, which is present in the rows. But what if you want to display a list and sort it on the basis of a summary value not present in the rows? That's a little trickier. Suppose you want to show each driver's records by date, but place those drivers who drive the most miles first. You can't do this with a summary query, because then you wouldn't get back the individual driver records. But you can't do it without a summary query, either, because the summary values are required for sorting. The way out of the dilemma is to create another table containing the summary values, then join it to the original table. That way you can produce the individual records, and also sort them by the summary values.

To summarize the driver totals into another table, do this:

```
mysql> CREATE TABLE tmp
    -> SELECT name, SUM(miles) AS driver_miles FROM driver_log GROUP BY name;
```

That produces the values we need to put the names in the proper order:

```
mysql> SELECT * FROM tmp ORDER BY driver_miles DESC;
+-------+--------------+
| name  | driver_miles |
+-------+--------------+
| Henry |          911 |
| Suzi  |          893 |
| Ben   |          362 |
+-------+--------------+
```

Then use the name values to join the summary table to the driver_log table, and use the driver_miles values to sort the result. The query below shows the mileage totals in the result. That's only to make it clearer how the values are being sorted, it's not actually necessary to display them. They're needed only for the ORDER BY clause.

```
mysql> SELECT tmp.driver_miles, driver_log.*
    -> FROM driver_log, tmp
    -> WHERE driver_log.name = tmp.name
    -> ORDER BY tmp.driver_miles DESC, driver_log.trav_date;
+--------------+--------+-------+------------+-------+
| driver_miles | rec_id | name  | trav_date  | miles |
+--------------+--------+-------+------------+-------+
|          911 |      6 | Henry | 2001-11-26 |   115 |
|          911 |      4 | Henry | 2001-11-27 |    96 |
|          911 |      3 | Henry | 2001-11-29 |   300 |
|          911 |     10 | Henry | 2001-11-30 |   203 |
|          911 |      8 | Henry | 2001-12-01 |   197 |
|          893 |      2 | Suzi  | 2001-11-29 |   391 |
|          893 |      7 | Suzi  | 2001-12-02 |   502 |
|          362 |      5 | Ben   | 2001-11-29 |   131 |
|          362 |      1 | Ben   | 2001-11-30 |   152 |
|          362 |      9 | Ben   | 2001-12-02 |    79 |
+--------------+--------+-------+------------+-------+
```

12.15 Converting Subselects to Join Operations

Problem

You want to use a query that involves a subselect, but MySQL will not support subselects until Version 4.1.

Solution

In many cases, you can rewrite a subselect as a join. Or you can write a program that simulates the subselect. Or you can even make *mysql* generate SQL statements that simulate it.

Discussion

Assume you have two tables, t1 and t2 that have the following contents:

```
mysql> SELECT col1 FROM t1;
+------+
| col1 |
+------+
| a    |
| b    |
| c    |
+------+
mysql> SELECT col2 FROM t2;
+------+
| col2 |
+------+
| b    |
| c    |
| d    |
+------+
```

Now suppose that you want to find values in t1 that are also present in t2, or values in t1 that are not present in t2. These kinds of questions sometimes are answered using subselect queries that nest one SELECT inside another, but MySQL won't have subselects until Version 4.1. This section shows how to work around that problem.

The following query shows an IN( ) subselect that produces the rows in table t1 having col1 values that match col2 values in table t2:

```
SELECT col1 FROM t1 WHERE col1 IN (SELECT col2 FROM t2);
```

That's essentially just a "find matching rows" query, and it can be rewritten as a simple join like this:

```
mysql> SELECT t1.col1 FROM t1, t2 WHERE t1.col1 = t2.col2;
+------+
| col1 |
+------+
| b    |
| c    |
+------+
```

The converse question (rows in t1 that have no match in t2) can be answered using a NOT IN( ) subselect:

```
SELECT col1 FROM t1 WHERE col1 NOT IN (SELECT col2 FROM t2);
```

That's a "find non-matching rows" query. Sometimes these can be rewritten as a LEFT JOIN, a type of join discussed in Recipe 12.5. For the case at hand, the NOT IN( ) subselect is equivalent to the following LEFT JOIN:

```
mysql> SELECT t1.col1 FROM t1 LEFT JOIN t2 ON t1.col1 = t2.col2
    -> WHERE t2.col2 IS NULL;
+------+
| col1 |
+------+
| a    |
+------+
```

Within a program, you can simulate a subselect by working with the results of two queries. Suppose you want to simulate the IN( ) subselect that finds matching values in the two tables:

```
SELECT * FROM t1 WHERE col1 IN (SELECT col2 FROM t2);
```

If you expect that the inner SELECT will return a reasonably small number of col2 values, one way to achieve the same result as the subselect is to retrieve those values and generate an IN( ) clause that looks for them in col1. For example, the query SELECT col2 FROM t2 will produce the values b, c, and d. Using this result, you can select matching col1 values by generating a query that looks like this:

```
SELECT col1 FROM t1 WHERE col1 IN ('b','c','d')
```

That can be done as follows (shown here using Python):

```
cursor = conn.cursor ()
cursor.execute ("SELECT col2 FROM t2")
if cursor.rowcount > 0:      # do nothing if there are no values
    val = []                 # list to hold data values
    s = ""                   # string to hold placeholders
    # construct %s,%s,%s, ... string containing placeholders
    for (col2,) in cursor.fetchall ():  # pull col2 value from each row
        if s != "":
            s = s + ","      # separate placeholders by commas
        s = s + "%s"         # add placeholder
        val.append (col2)    # add value to list of values
    stmt = "SELECT col1 FROM t1 WHERE col1 IN (" + s + ")"
    cursor.execute (stmt, val)
    for (col1,) in cursor.fetchall ():  # pull col1 values from final result
        print col1
cursor.close ()
```

If you expect lots of col2 values, you may want to generate individual SELECT queries for each of them instead:

```
SELECT col1 FROM t1 WHERE col1 = 'b'
SELECT col1 FROM t1 WHERE col1 = 'c'
SELECT col1 FROM t1 WHERE col1 = 'd'
```

This can be done within a program as follows:

```
cursor = conn.cursor ()
cursor2 = conn.cursor ()
```

```
cursor.execute ("SELECT col2 FROM t2")
for (col2,) in cursor.fetchall ():  # pull col2 value from each row
    stmt = "SELECT col1 FROM t1 WHERE col1 = %s"
    cursor2.execute ("SELECT col1 FROM t1 WHERE col1 = %s", (col2,))
    for (col1,) in cursor2.fetchall (): # pull col1 values from final result
        print col1
cursor.close ()
cursor2.close ()
```

If you have so many col2 values that you don't want to construct a single huge IN( ) clause, but don't want to issue zillions of individual SELECT statements, either, another option is to combine the approaches. Break the set of col2 values into smaller groups and use each group to construct an IN( ) clause. This gives you a set of shorter queries that each look for several values:

```
SELECT col1 FROM t1 WHERE col1 IN (first group of col2 values)
SELECT col1 FROM t1 WHERE col1 IN (second group of col2 values)
SELECT col1 FROM t1 WHERE col1 IN (second group of col2 values)
...
```

This approach can be implemented as follows:

```
grp_size = 1000              # number of IDs to select at once
cursor = conn.cursor ()
cursor.execute ("SELECT col2 FROM t2")
if cursor.rowcount > 0:      # do nothing if there are no values
    col2 = []                # list to hold data values
    for (val,) in cursor.fetchall ():   # pull col2 value from each row
        col2.append (val)
    nvals = len (col2)
    i = 0
    while i < nvals:
        if nvals < i + grp_size:
            j = nvals
        else:
            j = i + grp_size
        group = col2[i : j]
        s = ""                    # string to hold placeholders
        val_list = []
        # construct %s,%s,%s, ... string containing placeholders
        for val in group:
            if s != "":
                s = s + ","        # separate placeholders by commas
            s = s + "%s"           # add placeholder
            val_list.append (val)  # add value to list of values
        stmt = "SELECT col1 FROM t1 WHERE col1 IN (" + s + ")"
        print stmt
        cursor.execute (stmt, val_list)
        for (col1,) in cursor.fetchall (): # pull col1 values from result
            print col1
        i = i + grp_size          # go to next group of values
cursor.close ()
```

Simulating a NOT IN( ) subselect from within a program is a bit trickier than simulating an IN( ) subselect. The subselect looks like this:

```
SELECT col1 FROM t1 WHERE col1 NOT IN (SELECT col2 FROM t2);
```

The technique shown here works best for smaller numbers of col1 and col2 values, because you must hold at least the values returned by the inner SELECT in memory, so that you can compare them to the value returned by the outer SELECT. The example shown here holds both sets in memory. First, retrieve the col1 and col2 values:

```
cursor = conn.cursor ()
cursor.execute ("SELECT col1 FROM t1")
col1 = []
for (val, ) in cursor.fetchall ():
    col1.append (val)
cursor.execute ("SELECT col2 FROM t2")
col2 = []
for (val, ) in cursor.fetchall ():
    col2.append (val)
cursor.close ()
```

Then check each col1 value to see whether or not it's present in the set of col2 values. If not, it satisfies the NOT IN( ) constraint of the subselect:

```
for val1 in col1:
    present = 0
    for val2 in col2:
        if val1 == val2:
            present = 1
            break
    if not present:
        print val1
```

The code shown here performs a lookup in the col2 values by looping through the array that holds them. You may be able to perform this operation more efficiently by using an associative data structure. For example, in Perl or Python, you could put the col2 values in a hash or dictionary. Recipe 10.28 shows an example that uses that approach.

Yet another way to simulate subselects, at least those of the IN( ) variety, is to generate the necessary SQL from within one instance of *mysql* and feed it to another instance to be executed. Consider the result from this query:

```
mysql> SELECT CONCAT('SELECT col1 FROM t1 WHERE col1 = \'', col2, '\';')
    -> FROM t2;
+-----------------------------------------------------------+
| CONCAT('SELECT col1 FROM t1 WHERE col1 = \'', col2, '\';') |
+-----------------------------------------------------------+
| SELECT col1 FROM t1 WHERE col1 = 'b';                     |
| SELECT col1 FROM t1 WHERE col1 = 'c';                     |
| SELECT col1 FROM t1 WHERE col1 = 'd';                     |
+-----------------------------------------------------------+
```

The query retrieves the col2 values from t2 and uses them to produce a set of SELECT statements that find matching col1 values in t1. If you issue that query in batch mode and suppress the column heading, *mysql* produces only the text of the SQL statements, not all the other fluff. You can feed that output into another instance of *mysql* to execute the queries. The result is the same as the subselect. Here's one way to carry out this procedure, assuming that you have the SELECT statement containing the CONCAT( ) expression stored in a file named *make_select.sql*:

```
% mysql -N cookbook < make_select.sql > tmp
```

Here *mysql* includes the -N option to suppress column headers so that they won't get written to the output file, *tmp*. The contents of *tmp* will look like this:

```
SELECT col1 FROM t1 WHERE col1 = 'b';
SELECT col1 FROM t1 WHERE col1 = 'c';
SELECT col1 FROM t1 WHERE col1 = 'd';
```

To execute the queries in that file and generate the output for the simulated subselect, use this command:

```
% mysql -N cookbook < tmp
b
c
```

This second instance of *mysql* also includes the -N option, because otherwise the output will include a header row for each of the SELECT statements that it executes. (Try omitting -N and see what happens.)

One significant limitation of using *mysql* to generate SQL statements is that it doesn't work well if your col2 values contain quotes or other special characters. In that case, the queries that this method generates would be malformed.[*]

12.16 Selecting Records in Parallel from Multiple Tables

Problem

You want to select rows one after the other from several tables, or several sets of rows from a single table—all as a single result set.

Solution

Use a UNION operation to combine multiple result sets into one.

---

[*] As we go to press, a QUOTE( ) function has been added to MySQL 4.0.3 that allows special characters to be escaped so that they are suitable for use in SQL statements.

Discussion

A join is useful for combining columns from different tables side by side. It's not so useful when you want a result set that includes a set of rows from several tables one after the other, or different sets of rows from the same table. These are instances of the type of operation for which a UNION is useful. A UNION allows you to run several SELECT statements and concatenate their results "vertically." You receive the output in a single result set, rather than running multiple queries and receiving multiple result sets.

UNION is available as of MySQL 4.0. This section illustrates how to use it, then describes some workarounds if you have an older version of MySQL.

Suppose you have two tables that list prospective and actual customers, a third that lists vendors from whom you purchase supplies, and you want to create a single mailing list by merging names and addresses from all three tables. UNION provides a way to do this. Assume the three tables have the following contents:

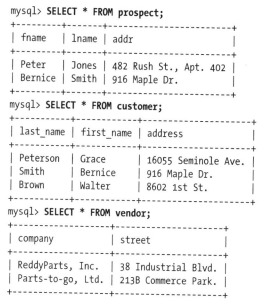

```
mysql> SELECT * FROM prospect;
+---------+-------+----------------------+
| fname   | lname | addr                 |
+---------+-------+----------------------+
| Peter   | Jones | 482 Rush St., Apt. 402 |
| Bernice | Smith | 916 Maple Dr.        |
+---------+-------+----------------------+
mysql> SELECT * FROM customer;
+-----------+------------+---------------------+
| last_name | first_name | address             |
+-----------+------------+---------------------+
| Peterson  | Grace      | 16055 Seminole Ave. |
| Smith     | Bernice    | 916 Maple Dr.       |
| Brown     | Walter     | 8602 1st St.        |
+-----------+------------+---------------------+
mysql> SELECT * FROM vendor;
+-----------------+---------------------+
| company         | street              |
+-----------------+---------------------+
| ReddyParts, Inc.| 38 Industrial Blvd. |
| Parts-to-go, Ltd.| 213B Commerce Park. |
+-----------------+---------------------+
```

The tables have columns that are similar but not identical. prospect and customer use different names for the first name and last name columns, and the vendor table includes only a single name column. None of that matters for UNION; all you need do is make sure to select the same number of columns from each table, and in the same order. The following query illustrates how to select names and addresses from the three tables all at once:

```
mysql> SELECT fname, lname, addr FROM prospect
    -> UNION
    -> SELECT first_name, last_name, address FROM customer
    -> UNION
    -> SELECT company, '', street FROM vendor;
```

```
+-------------------+----------+-----------------------+
| fname             | lname    | addr                  |
+-------------------+----------+-----------------------+
| Peter             | Jones    | 482 Rush St., Apt. 402 |
| Bernice           | Smith    | 916 Maple Dr.         |
| Grace             | Peterson | 16055 Seminole Ave.   |
| Walter            | Brown    | 8602 1st St.          |
| ReddyParts, Inc.  |          | 38 Industrial Blvd.   |
| Parts-to-go, Ltd. |          | 213B Commerce Park.   |
+-------------------+----------+-----------------------+
```

The names and types in the result set are taken from the names and types of the columns retrieved by the first SELECT statement. Notice that, by default, a UNION eliminates duplicates; Bernice Smith appears in both the prospect and customer tables, but only once in the final result. If you want to select all records, including duplicates, follow the first UNION keyword with ALL:

```
mysql> SELECT fname, lname, addr FROM prospect
    -> UNION ALL
    -> SELECT first_name, last_name, address FROM customer
    -> UNION
    -> SELECT company, '', street FROM vendor;
+-------------------+----------+-----------------------+
| fname             | lname    | addr                  |
+-------------------+----------+-----------------------+
| Peter             | Jones    | 482 Rush St., Apt. 402 |
| Bernice           | Smith    | 916 Maple Dr.         |
| Grace             | Peterson | 16055 Seminole Ave.   |
| Bernice           | Smith    | 916 Maple Dr.         |
| Walter            | Brown    | 8602 1st St.          |
| ReddyParts, Inc.  |          | 38 Industrial Blvd.   |
| Parts-to-go, Ltd. |          | 213B Commerce Park.   |
+-------------------+----------+-----------------------+
```

Because it's necessary to select the same number of columns from each table, the SELECT for the vendor table (which has just one name column) retrieves a dummy (empty) last name column. Another way to select the same number of columns is to combine the first and last name columns from the prospect and customer tables into a single column:

```
mysql> SELECT CONCAT(lname,', ',fname) AS name, addr FROM prospect
    -> UNION
    -> SELECT CONCAT(last_name,', ',first_name), address FROM customer
    -> UNION
    -> SELECT company, street FROM vendor;
+-------------------+-----------------------+
| name              | addr                  |
+-------------------+-----------------------+
| Jones, Peter      | 482 Rush St., Apt. 402 |
| Smith, Bernice    | 916 Maple Dr.         |
| Peterson, Grace   | 16055 Seminole Ave.   |
| Brown, Walter     | 8602 1st St.          |
| ReddyParts, Inc.  | 38 Industrial Blvd.   |
| Parts-to-go, Ltd. | 213B Commerce Park.   |
+-------------------+-----------------------+
```

To sort the result set as a whole, add an ORDER BY clause after the final SELECT statement. Any columns specified by name in the ORDER BY should refer to the column names used in the first SELECT, because those are the names used for the result set. For example, to sort by name, do this:

```
mysql> SELECT CONCAT(lname,', ',fname) AS name, addr FROM prospect
    -> UNION
    -> SELECT CONCAT(last_name,', ',first_name), address FROM customer
    -> UNION
    -> SELECT company, street FROM vendor
    -> ORDER BY name;
+------------------+-----------------------+
| name             | addr                  |
+------------------+-----------------------+
| Brown, Walter    | 8602 1st St.          |
| Jones, Peter     | 482 Rush St., Apt. 402 |
| Parts-to-go, Ltd. | 213B Commerce Park.  |
| Peterson, Grace  | 16055 Seminole Ave.   |
| ReddyParts, Inc. | 38 Industrial Blvd.   |
| Smith, Bernice   | 916 Maple Dr.         |
+------------------+-----------------------+
```

It's possible in MySQL to sort the results of individual SELECT statements within the UNION. To do this, enclose a given SELECT (including its ORDER BY clause) within parentheses:

```
mysql> (SELECT CONCAT(lname,', ',fname) AS name, addr
    -> FROM prospect ORDER BY 1)
    -> UNION
    -> (SELECT CONCAT(last_name,', ',first_name), address
    -> FROM customer ORDER BY 1)
    -> UNION
    -> (SELECT company, street FROM vendor ORDER BY 1);
+------------------+-----------------------+
| name             | addr                  |
+------------------+-----------------------+
| Jones, Peter     | 482 Rush St., Apt. 402 |
| Smith, Bernice   | 916 Maple Dr.         |
| Brown, Walter    | 8602 1st St.          |
| Peterson, Grace  | 16055 Seminole Ave.   |
| Parts-to-go, Ltd. | 213B Commerce Park.  |
| ReddyParts, Inc. | 38 Industrial Blvd.   |
+------------------+-----------------------+
```

Similar syntax can be used for LIMIT as well. That is, you can limit the result set as a whole with a trailing LIMIT clause, or for individual SELECT statements by enclosing them within parentheses. In some cases, it may even be useful to combine ORDER BY and LIMIT. Suppose you want to select a lucky prizewinner for some kind of promotional giveaway. To select a single winner at random from the combined results of the three tables, do this:

```
mysql> SELECT CONCAT(lname,', ',fname) AS name, addr FROM prospect
    -> UNION
```

```
    -> SELECT CONCAT(last_name,', ',first_name), address FROM customer
    -> UNION
    -> SELECT company, street FROM vendor
    -> ORDER BY RAND() LIMIT 1;
+-----------------+----------------------+
| name            | addr                 |
+-----------------+----------------------+
| Peterson, Grace | 16055 Seminole Ave.  |
+-----------------+----------------------+
```

To select a single winner from each table and combine the results, do this instead:

```
mysql> (SELECT CONCAT(lname,', ',fname) AS name, addr
    -> FROM prospect ORDER BY RAND() LIMIT 1)
    -> UNION
    -> (SELECT CONCAT(last_name,', ',first_name), address
    -> FROM customer ORDER BY RAND() LIMIT 1)
    -> UNION
    -> (SELECT company, street
    -> FROM vendor ORDER BY RAND() LIMIT 1);
+-------------------+----------------------+
| name              | addr                 |
+-------------------+----------------------+
| Smith, Bernice    | 916 Maple Dr.        |
| ReddyParts, Inc.  | 38 Industrial Blvd.  |
+-------------------+----------------------+
```

If that result surprises you ("Why didn't it pick three rows?"), remember that Bernice is listed in two tables and that UNION eliminates duplicates. If the first and second SELECT statements each happen to pick Bernice, one instance will be eliminated and the final result will have only two rows. (If there are no duplicates among the three tables, the query will always return three rows.) You could of course assure three records in all cases by using UNION ALL, or by running the SELECT statements individually.

If you don't have MySQL 4.0, you can't use UNION. But you can achieve a similar result by creating a temporary table, storing the result of multiple SELECT queries into that table, and then selecting its contents. With MySQL 3.23, you can use CREATE TABLE ... SELECT for the first SELECT, then successively retrieve the other result sets into it:

```
mysql> CREATE TABLE tmp SELECT CONCAT(lname,', ',fname) AS name, addr
    -> FROM prospect;
mysql> INSERT INTO tmp (name, addr)
    -> SELECT CONCAT(last_name,', ',first_name), address
    -> FROM customer;
mysql> INSERT INTO tmp (name, addr)
    -> SELECT company, street FROM vendor;
```

If your version of MySQL is older than 3.23, create the table first, then select each result set into it:

```
mysql> CREATE TABLE tmp (name CHAR(40), addr CHAR(40));
mysql> INSERT INTO tmp (name, addr)
    -> SELECT CONCAT(lname,', ',fname), addr
    -> FROM prospect;
```

```
mysql> INSERT INTO tmp (name, addr)
    -> SELECT CONCAT(last_name,', ',first_name), address
    -> FROM customer;
mysql> INSERT INTO tmp (name, addr)
    -> SELECT company, street FROM vendor;
```

After selecting the individual results into the temporary table, select its contents:

```
mysql> SELECT * FROM tmp;
+-------------------+-----------------------+
| name              | addr                  |
+-------------------+-----------------------+
| Jones, Peter      | 482 Rush St., Apt. 402 |
| Smith, Bernice    | 916 Maple Dr.         |
| Peterson, Grace   | 16055 Seminole Ave.   |
| Smith, Bernice    | 916 Maple Dr.         |
| Brown, Walter     | 8602 1st St.          |
| ReddyParts, Inc.  | 38 Industrial Blvd.   |
| Parts-to-go, Ltd. | 213B Commerce Park.   |
+-------------------+-----------------------+
```

Note that the result is more like UNION ALL than UNION, because duplicates are not suppressed. To achieve the effect of UNION, create the table with a unique index on the name and addr columns:

```
mysql> CREATE TABLE tmp (name CHAR(40), addr CHAR(40), UNIQUE (name, addr));
mysql> INSERT INTO ...
...
mysql> SELECT * FROM tmp;
+-------------------+-----------------------+
| name              | addr                  |
+-------------------+-----------------------+
| Brown, Walter     | 8602 1st St.          |
| Jones, Peter      | 482 Rush St., Apt. 402 |
| Parts-to-go, Ltd. | 213B Commerce Park.   |
| Peterson, Grace   | 16055 Seminole Ave.   |
| ReddyParts, Inc.  | 38 Industrial Blvd.   |
| Smith, Bernice    | 916 Maple Dr.         |
+-------------------+-----------------------+
```

If you create the table without a unique index, you can remove duplicates at retrieval time by using DISTINCT, though that is less efficient.

12.17 Inserting Records in One Table That Include Values from Another

Problem

You need to insert a record into a table that requires an ID value. But you know only the name associated with the ID, not the ID itself.

Solution

Assuming that you have a lookup table that associates names and IDs, create the record using INSERT INTO ... SELECT, where the SELECT performs a name lookup to obtain the corresponding ID value.

Discussion

We've used lookup tables often in this chapter in join queries, typically to map ID values or codes onto more descriptive names or labels. But lookup tables are useful for more than just SELECT statements. They can help you create new records as well. To illustrate, we'll use the artist and painting tables containing information about your art collection. Suppose you travel to Minnesota, where you find a bargain on a $51 reproduction of "Les jongleurs" by Renoir. Renoir is already listed in the artist table, so no new record is needed there. But you do need a record in the painting table. To create it, you need to store the artist ID, the title, the state where you bought it, and the price. You already know all of those except the artist ID, but it's tedious to look up the ID from the artist table yourself. Because Renoir is already listed there, why not let MySQL look up the ID for you? To do this, use INSERT ... SELECT to add the new record. Specify all the literal values that you know in the SELECT output column list, and use a WHERE clause to look up the artist ID from the name:

```
mysql> INSERT INTO painting (a_id, title, state, price)
    -> SELECT a_id, 'Les jongleurs', 'MN', 51
    -> FROM artist WHERE name = 'Renoir';
```

Naturally, you wouldn't want to write out the full text of such a query by hand each time you get a new painting. But it would be easy to write a short script that, given the artist name, painting title, origin, and price, would generate and issue the query for you. You could also write the code to make sure that if the artist is not already listed in the artist table, you generate a new ID value for the artist first. Just issue a statement like this prior to creating the new painting record:

```
INSERT IGNORE INTO artist (name) VALUES('artist name');
```

12.18 Updating One Table Based on Values in Another

Problem

You need to update existing records in one table based on the contents of records in another table, but MySQL doesn't yet allow join syntax in the WHERE clause of UPDATE statements. So you have no way to associate the two tables.

Solution

Create a new table that is populated from the result of a join between the original table and the table containing the new information. Then replace the original table with the new one. Or write a program that selects information from the related table and issues the queries necessary to update the original table. Or use *mysql* to generate and execute the queries.

Discussion

Sometimes when updating records in one table, it's necessary to refer to records in another table. Recall that the states table used in several earlier recipes contains rows that look like this:

```
mysql> SELECT * FROM states;
+----------------+--------+------------+----------+
| name           | abbrev | statehood  | pop      |
+----------------+--------+------------+----------+
| Alaska         | AK     | 1959-01-03 |   550043 |
| Alabama        | AL     | 1819-12-14 |  4040587 |
| Arkansas       | AR     | 1836-06-15 |  2350725 |
| Arizona        | AZ     | 1912-02-14 |  3665228 |
...
```

Now suppose that you want to add some new columns to this table, using information from another table, city, that contains information about each state's capital city and largest (most populous) city:

```
mysql> SELECT * FROM city;
+----------------+----------------+----------------+
| state          | capital        | largest        |
+----------------+----------------+----------------+
| Alabama        | Montgomery     | Birmingham     |
| Alaska         | Juneau         | Anchorage      |
| Arizona        | Phoenix        | Phoenix        |
| Arkansas       | Little Rock    | Little Rock    |
...
```

It would be easy enough to add new columns named capital and largest to the states table structure using an ALTER TABLE statement. But then how would you modify the rows to fill in the new columns with the appropriate values? The most convenient way to do this would be to run an UPDATE query that uses join syntax in the WHERE clause:

```
UPDATE states,city
SET states.capital = city.capital, states.largest = city.largest
WHERE states.name = city.state;
```

That doesn't work, because MySQL does not yet support this syntax. Another solution would be to use a subselect in the WHERE clause, but subselects are not scheduled for inclusion until MySQL 4.1. What are the alternatives? Clearly, you don't want to update each row by hand. That's unacceptably tedious—and silly, too, given that the new information is already stored in the city table. The states and city tables contain a common key (state names), so let's use that information to relate the two tables and perform the update. There are a few techniques you can use to achieve the same result as a multiple-table update:

- Create a new table that is like the original states table, but includes the additional columns to be added from the related table, city. Populate the new table using the result of a join between the states and city tables, then replace the original states table with the new one.

- Write a program that uses the information from the city table to generate and execute UPDATE statements that update the states table one state at a time.

- Use *mysql* to generate the UPDATE statements.

Performing a Related-Table Update Using Table Replacement

The table-replacement approach works as follows. To extend the states table with the capital and largest columns from the city table, create a tmp table that is like the states table but adds capital and largest columns:

```
CREATE TABLE tmp
(
    name        VARCHAR(30) NOT NULL,   # state name
    abbrev      CHAR(2) NOT NULL,       # 2-char abbreviation
    statehood   DATE,                   # date of entry into the Union
    pop         BIGINT,                 # population as of 4/1990
    capital     VARCHAR(30),            # capital city
    largest     VARCHAR(30),            # most populous city
    PRIMARY KEY (abbrev)
);
```

Then populate tmp using the result of a join between states and city that matches up rows in the two tables using state names:

```
INSERT INTO tmp (name, abbrev, statehood, pop, capital, largest)
SELECT
    states.name, states.abbrev, states.statehood, states.pop,
    city.capital, city.largest
FROM
    states LEFT JOIN city ON states.name = city.state;
```

The query uses a LEFT JOIN for a reason. Suppose the city table is incomplete and doesn't contain a row for every state. In that case, a regular join will fail to produce an output row for any states that are missing from the city table, and the resulting tmp table will be missing records for those states, even though they are present in the states table. Not good! The LEFT JOIN ensures that the SELECT produces output for every row in the states table, whether or not it's matched by a city table row. Any state that is missing in the city table would end up with NULL values in the tmp table for the capital and largest columns, but that's appropriate when you don't know the city names—and generating an incomplete row certainly is preferable to losing the row entirely.

The resulting tmp table is like the original one, but has two new columns, capital and largest. You can examine it to see this. After verifying that you're satisfied with the tmp table, use it to replace the original states table:

```
DROP TABLE states;
ALTER TABLE tmp RENAME TO states;
```

If you want to make sure there is no time, however brief, during which the states table is unavailable, perform the replacement like this instead:

```
RENAME TABLE states TO states_old, tmp TO states;
DROP TABLE states_old;
```

Performing a Related-Table Update by Writing a Program

The table-replacement technique is efficient because it lets the server do all the work. On the other hand, it is most appropriate when you're updating all or most of the rows in the table. If you're updating just a few rows, it may be less work to update the table "in place" for just those rows that need it. Also, table replacement requires more than twice the space of the original states table while you're carrying out the update procedure. If you have a huge table to update, you may not want to use all that space.

A second technique for updating a table based on a related table is to read the information from the related table and use it to generate UPDATE statements. For example, to update states with the information stored in the city table, read the city names and use them to create and issue a series of queries like this:

```
UPDATE states SET capital = 'Montgomery', largest = 'Birmingham'
WHERE name = 'Alabama';
UPDATE states SET capital = 'Juneau', largest = 'Anchorage'
WHERE name = 'Alaska';
UPDATE states SET capital = 'Phoenix', largest = 'Phoenix'
WHERE name = 'Arizona';
UPDATE states SET capital = 'Little Rock', largest = 'Little Rock'
WHERE name = 'Arkansas';
...
```

To carry out this procedure, first alter the states table so that it includes the new columns:*

```
ALTER TABLE states ADD capital VARCHAR(30), ADD largest VARCHAR(30);
```

---

* If you've already modified states using the table-replacement procedure, first restore the table to its original structure by dropping the capital and largest columns:
```
ALTER TABLE states DROP capital, DROP largest;
```

Next, write a program that reads the city table and uses its contents to produce UPDATE statements that modify the states table. Here is an example script, *update_cities.pl*, that does so:

```perl
#! /usr/bin/perl -w
# update_cities.pl - update states table capital and largest city columns,
# using contents of city table.  This assumes that the states table has
# been modified to include columns named capital and largest.

use strict;
use lib qw(/usr/local/apache/lib/perl);
use Cookbook;

my $dbh = Cookbook::connect ();

my $sth = $dbh->prepare ("SELECT state, capital, largest FROM city");
$sth->execute ();
while (my ($state, $capital, $largest) = $sth->fetchrow_array ())
{
    $dbh->do ("UPDATE states SET capital = ?, largest = ? WHERE name = ?",
              undef, $capital, $largest, $state);
}

$dbh->disconnect ();

exit (0);
```

The script has all the table and column names built in to it, which makes it very special purpose. You could generalize this procedure by writing a function that accepts parameters indicating the table names, the columns to use for matching records in the two tables, and the columns to use for updating the rows. The *update_related.pl* script in the *joins* directory of the recipes distribution shows one way to do this.

Performing a Related-Table Update Using mysql

If your data values don't require any special handling for internal quotes or other special characters, you can use *mysql* to generate and process the UPDATE statements. This is similar to the technique shown in Recipe 12.17 for using *mysql* to simulate a subselect.

Put the following statement in a file, *update_cities.sql*:

```sql
SELECT CONCAT('UPDATE states SET capital = \'',capital,
    '\', largest = \'',largest,'\' WHERE name = \'',state,'\';')
FROM city;
```

The query reads the rows of the city table and uses them to generate statements that update states. Execute the query and save the result in *tmp*:

```
% mysql -N cookbook < update_cities.sql > tmp
```

tmp will contain statements that look like the queries generated by the *update_cities.pl* script. Assuming that you're added the capital and largest columns to the states table, you can execute these statements as follows to update the table:

```
% mysql cookbook < tmp
```

12.19 Using a Join to Create a Lookup Table from Descriptive Labels

Problem

A table stores long descriptive labels in an identifier column. You want to convert this column to short ID values and use the labels to create a lookup table that maps IDs to labels.

Solution

Use one of the related-table update techniques described in Recipe 12.18.

Discussion

It's a common strategy to store ID numbers or codes rather than descriptive strings in a table to save space. It also improves performance, because it's quicker to index and retrieve numbers than strings. (For queries in which you need to produce the names, join the ID values with an ID-to-name lookup table.) When you're creating a new table, you can keep this strategy in mind and design the table from the outset to be used with a lookup table. But you may also have an existing table that stores descriptive strings and that could benefit from a conversion to use ID values. This section discusses how to create the lookup table that maps each label to its ID, and how to convert the labels to IDs in the original table. The technique combines ALTER TABLE with a related-table update.

Suppose you collect coins, and you've begun to keep track of them in your database using the following table:

```
CREATE TABLE coin
(
    id      INT UNSIGNED NOT NULL AUTO_INCREMENT,
    date    CHAR(5) NOT NULL,   # 4 digits + mint letter
    denom   CHAR(20) NOT NULL,  # denomination (e.g., Lincoln cent)
    PRIMARY KEY (id)
);
```

Each coin is assigned an ID automatically as an AUTO_INCREMENT value, and you also record each coin's date of issue and denomination. The records that you've entered into the table thus far are as follows:

```
mysql> SELECT * FROM coin;
+----+-------+---------------------+
| id | date  | denom               |
+----+-------+---------------------+
|  1 | 1944s | Lincoln cent        |
|  2 | 1977  | Roosevelt dime      |
|  3 | 1955d | Lincoln cent        |
|  4 | 1938  | Jefferson nickel    |
|  5 | 1964  | Kennedy half dollar |
|  6 | 1959  | Lincoln cent        |
|  7 | 1945  | Jefferson nickel    |
|  8 | 1905  | Buffalo nickel      |
|  9 | 1924  | Mercury head dime   |
| 10 | 2001  | Roosevelt dime      |
| 11 | 1937  | Mercury head dime   |
| 12 | 1977  | Kennedy half dollar |
+----+-------+---------------------+
```

The table holds the information in which you're interested, but you notice that it's a waste of space to write out the denomination names in every record, and that the problem will become worse as you enter additional records into the table. It would be more space-efficient to store coded denomination IDs in the coin table rather than the names, then look up the names when necessary from a denom table that lists each denomination name and its ID code. (The benefit of this may not be evident with such a small table, but when your collection grows to include 10,000 coins, the space savings from storing numbers rather than strings will become more significant.)

The procedure for setting up the lookup table and converting the coin table to use it is as follows:

1. Create the denom lookup table to hold the ID-to-name mapping.

2. Populate the denom table using the denomination names currently in the coin table.

3. Replace the denomination names in the coin table with the corresponding ID values.

The denom table needs to record each denomination name and its associated ID, so it can be created using the following structure:

```
CREATE TABLE denom
(
    denom_id    INT UNSIGNED NOT NULL AUTO_INCREMENT,
    name        CHAR(20) NOT NULL,
    PRIMARY KEY (denom_id)
);
```

To populate the table, insert into it the set of denomination names that are present in the coin table. Use SELECT DISTINCT for this, because each name should be inserted just once:

```
INSERT INTO denom (name) SELECT DISTINCT denom FROM coin;
```

The INSERT statement adds only the denomination name to the denom table; denom_id is an AUTO_INCREMENT column, so MySQL will assign sequence numbers to it automatically. The resulting table looks like this:

```
+----------+--------------------+
| denom_id | name               |
+----------+--------------------+
|        1 | Lincoln cent       |
|        2 | Roosevelt dime     |
|        3 | Jefferson nickel   |
|        4 | Kennedy half dollar|
|        5 | Buffalo nickel     |
|        6 | Mercury head dime  |
+----------+--------------------+
```

With MySQL 3.23 and up, you can create and populate the denom table using a single CREATE TABLE ... SELECT statement:

```
CREATE TABLE denom
(
    denom_id    INT UNSIGNED NOT NULL AUTO_INCREMENT,
    PRIMARY KEY (denom_id)
)
SELECT DISTINCT denom AS name FROM coin;
```

After setting up the denom table, the next step is to convert the denomination names in the coin table to their associated IDs:

- Create a tmp table that is like coin but has a denom_id column rather than a denom column.

- Populate tmp from the result of a join between the coin and denom tables.

- Use the tmp table to replace the original coin table.

To create the tmp table, use a CREATE TABLE statement that is like the one used originally to create coin, but substitute a denom_id column for the denom column:

```
CREATE TABLE tmp
(
    id          INT UNSIGNED NOT NULL AUTO_INCREMENT,
    date        CHAR(5) NOT NULL,   # 4 digits + mint letter
    denom_id    INT UNSIGNED NOT NULL,  # denomination ID
    PRIMARY KEY (id)
);
```

Then populate tmp using a join between coin and denom:

```
INSERT INTO tmp (id, date, denom_id)
SELECT coin.id, coin.date, denom.denom_id
```

```
FROM coin, denom
WHERE coin.denom = denom.name;
```

Finally, replace the original coin table with the tmp table:

```
DROP TABLE coin;
ALTER TABLE tmp RENAME TO coin;
```

With MySQL 3.23 and up, you can create and populate the tmp table using a single statement:

```
CREATE TABLE tmp
(
    PRIMARY KEY (id)
)
SELECT coin.id, coin.date, denom.denom_id
FROM coin, denom
WHERE coin.denom = denom.name;
```

Then replace coin with tmp, as before.

Another method for converting the coin table after creating the denom table is to modify coin in place without using a tmp table:

1. Add a denom_id column to the coin table with ALTER TABLE.
2. Fill in the denom_id value in each row with the ID corresponding to its denom name.
3. Drop the denom column.

To carry out this procedure, add a column to coin to hold the denomination ID values:

```
ALTER TABLE coin ADD denom_id INT UNSIGNED NOT NULL;
```

Then fill in the denom_id column with the proper values using the denomination name-to-ID mapping in the denom table. One way to do that is to write a script to update the ID values in the coin table one denomination at a time. Here is a short script that does so:

```
#! /usr/bin/perl -w
# update_denom.pl - For each denomination in the denom table,
# update the coin table records having that denomination with the
# proper denomination ID.

use strict;
use lib qw(/usr/local/apache/lib/perl);
use Cookbook;

my $dbh = Cookbook::connect ();

my $sth = $dbh->prepare ("SELECT denom_id, name FROM denom");
$sth->execute ();
while (my ($denom_id, $name) = $sth->fetchrow_array ())
{
    # For coin table records with the given denomination name,
    # add the corresponding denom_id value from denom table
```

```
        $dbh->do ("UPDATE coin SET denom_id = ? WHERE denom = ?",
                undef, $denom_id, $name);
}

$dbh->disconnect ();
exit (0);
```

The script retrieves each denomination ID/name pair from the denom table and constructs an appropriate UPDATE statement to modify all coin table rows containing the denomination name by setting their denom_id values to the corresponding ID. When the script finishes, all rows in the coin table will have the denom_id column updated properly. At that point, the denom column is no longer necessary and you can jettison it:

```
ALTER TABLE coin DROP denom;
```

Whichever method you use to convert the coin table, the resulting contents look like this:

```
mysql> SELECT * FROM coin;
+----+-------+----------+
| id | date  | denom_id |
+----+-------+----------+
|  1 | 1944s |        1 |
|  2 | 1977  |        2 |
|  3 | 1955d |        1 |
|  4 | 1938  |        3 |
|  5 | 1964  |        4 |
|  6 | 1959  |        1 |
|  7 | 1945  |        3 |
|  8 | 1905  |        5 |
|  9 | 1924  |        6 |
| 10 | 2001  |        2 |
| 11 | 1937  |        6 |
| 12 | 1977  |        4 |
+----+-------+----------+
```

When you need to display coin records with denomination names rather than IDs in a query result, perform a join using denom as a lookup table:

```
mysql> SELECT coin.id, coin.date, denom.name
    -> FROM coin, denom
    -> WHERE coin.denom_id = denom.denom_id;
+----+-------+--------------------+
| id | date  | name               |
+----+-------+--------------------+
|  1 | 1944s | Lincoln cent       |
|  2 | 1977  | Roosevelt dime     |
|  3 | 1955d | Lincoln cent       |
|  4 | 1938  | Jefferson nickel   |
|  5 | 1964  | Kennedy half dollar |
|  6 | 1959  | Lincoln cent       |
|  7 | 1945  | Jefferson nickel   |
|  8 | 1905  | Buffalo nickel     |
|  9 | 1924  | Mercury head dime  |
```

```
| 10 | 2001  | Roosevelt dime      |
| 11 | 1937  | Mercury head dime   |
| 12 | 1977  | Kennedy half dollar |
+----+-------+---------------------+
```

That result looks like the contents of the original coin table, even though the table no longer stores a long descriptive string in each row.

What about entering new items into the coin table? Using the original coin table, you'd enter the denomination name into each record. But with the denominations converted to ID values, that won't work. Instead, use an INSERT INTO ... SELECT statement to look up the denomination ID based on the name. For example, to enter a 1962 Roosevelt dime, use this statement:

```
INSERT INTO coin (date, denom_id)
SELECT 1962, denom_id FROM denom WHERE name = 'Roosevelt dime';
```

This technique is described further in Recipe 12.17.

12.20 Deleting Related Rows in Multiple Tables

Problem

You want to delete related records from multiple tables. This is common, for example, when you have tables that are related in master-detail or parent-child fashion; deleting a parent record typically requires all the associated child records to be deleted as well.

Solution

You have several options. MySQL 4.0 supports cascaded delete with a multiple-table DELETE syntax; you can replace the table with new versions that contain only the records *not* to be deleted; you can write a program to construct appropriate DELETE statements for each table, or you may be able to use *mysql* to do so.

Discussion

Applications that use related tables need to operate on both tables at once for many operations. Suppose you use MySQL to record information about the contents of software distributions that you maintain. The master (or parent) table lists each distribution's name, version number, and release date. The detail (or child) table lists information about the files in the distributions, thus serving as the manifest for each distribution's contents. To allow the parent and child records to be associated, each parent record has a unique ID number, and that number is stored in the child records. The tables might be defined something like this:

```
CREATE TABLE swdist_head
(
```

```
    dist_id     INT UNSIGNED NOT NULL AUTO_INCREMENT,    # distribution ID
    name        VARCHAR(40),                             # distribution name
    ver_num     NUMERIC(5,2),                            # version number
    rel_date    DATE NOT NULL,                           # release date
    PRIMARY KEY (dist_id)
);
CREATE TABLE swdist_item
(
    dist_id     INT UNSIGNED NOT NULL,    # parent distribution ID
    dist_file   VARCHAR(255) NOT NULL     # name of file in distribution
);
```

For the examples here, assume the tables contain the following records:

```
mysql> SELECT * FROM swdist_head ORDER BY name, ver_num;
+---------+------------+---------+------------+
| dist_id | name       | ver_num | rel_date   |
+---------+------------+---------+------------+
|       1 | DB Gadgets |    1.59 | 1996-03-25 |
|       3 | DB Gadgets |    1.60 | 1998-12-26 |
|       4 | DB Gadgets |    1.61 | 1998-12-28 |
|       2 | NetGizmo   |    3.02 | 1998-11-10 |
|       5 | NetGizmo   |    4.00 | 2001-08-04 |
+---------+------------+---------+------------+
mysql> SELECT * FROM swdist_item ORDER BY dist_id, dist_file;
+---------+----------------+
| dist_id | dist_file      |
+---------+----------------+
|       1 | db-gadgets.sh  |
|       1 | README         |
|       2 | NetGizmo.exe   |
|       2 | README.txt     |
|       3 | db-gadgets.sh  |
|       3 | README         |
|       3 | README.linux   |
|       4 | db-gadgets.sh  |
|       4 | README         |
|       4 | README.linux   |
|       4 | README.solaris |
|       5 | NetGizmo.exe   |
|       5 | README.txt     |
+---------+----------------+
```

The tables describe the distributions for three versions of DB Gadgets and two versions of NetGizmo. But the tables are difficult to make sense of individually, so to display information for a given distribution, you'd use a join to select rows from both tables. For example, the following query shows the information stored for DB Gadgets 1.60:

```
mysql> SELECT swdist_head.dist_id, swdist_head.name,
    -> swdist_head.ver_num, swdist_head.rel_date, swdist_item.dist_file
    -> FROM swdist_head, swdist_item
    -> WHERE swdist_head.name = 'DB Gadgets' AND swdist_head.ver_num = 1.60
    -> AND swdist_head.dist_id = swdist_item.dist_id;
```

```
+---------+------------+---------+------------+---------------+
| dist_id | name       | ver_num | rel_date   | dist_file     |
+---------+------------+---------+------------+---------------+
|       3 | DB Gadgets |    1.60 | 1998-12-26 | README        |
|       3 | DB Gadgets |    1.60 | 1998-12-26 | README.linux  |
|       3 | DB Gadgets |    1.60 | 1998-12-26 | db-gadgets.sh |
+---------+------------+---------+------------+---------------+
```

Similarly, to delete a distribution, you'd need to access both tables. DB Gadgets 1.60 has an ID of 3, so one way to get rid of it would be to issue DELETE statements for each of the tables manually:

```
mysql> DELETE FROM swdist_head WHERE dist_id = 3;
mysql> DELETE FROM swdist_item WHERE dist_id = 3;
```

That's quick and easy, but problems can occur if you forget to issue DELETE statements for both tables (which is easier to do than you might think). In that case, your tables become inconsistent, with parent records that have no children, or children that are referenced by no parent. Also, manual deletion doesn't work well in situations where you have a large number of distributions to remove, or when you don't know in advance which ones to delete. Suppose you decide to purge all the old records, keeping only those for the most recent version of each distribution. (For example, the tables contain information for DB Gadgets distributions 1.59, 1.60, and 1.61, so you'd remove records for Versions 1.59 and 1.60.) For this kind of operation, you'd likely determine which distributions to remove based on some query that figures out the IDs of those that are not the most recent. But then what do you do? The query might produce many IDs; you probably wouldn't want to delete each distribution manually. And you don't have to. There are several options for deleting records from multiple tables:

- Use the multiple-table DELETE syntax that is available as of MySQL 4.0.0. This way you can write a query that takes care of identifying and removing records from both tables at once. You need not remember to issue multiple DELETE statements each time you remove records from related tables.

- Approach the problem in reverse: select the records that are not to be deleted into new tables, then use those tables to replace the original ones. The effect is the same as deleting the unwanted records.

- Use a program that determines the IDs of the distributions to be removed and generates the appropriate DELETE statements for you. The program might be one you write yourself, or an existing program such as *mysql*.

The remainder of this section examines each of these options in turn, showing how to use them to solve the problem of deleting old distributions. Because each example removes records from the swdist_head and swdist_item tables, you'll need to create and populate them anew before trying each method, so that you begin at the same starting point each time. You can do this using the *swdist_create.sql* script in the *joins* directory of the recipes distribution. Scripts that demonstrate each multiple-table delete method shown in the examples may be found in that directory as well.

Using Foreign Keys to Enforce Referential Integrity

One feature a database may offer for helping you maintain consistency between tables is the ability to define foreign key relationships. This means you can specify explicitly in the table definition that a primary key in a parent table (such as the dist_id column of the swdist_head table) is a parent to a key in another table (the dist_id column in the swdist_item table). By defining the ID column in the child table as a foreign key to the ID column in the parent, the database can enforce certain constraints against illegal operations. For example, it can prevent you from creating a child record with an ID that is not present in the parent, or from deleting parent records without also deleting the corresponding child records first. A foreign key implementation may also offer cascaded delete: if you delete a parent record, the database engine cascades the effect of the delete to any child tables and automatically deletes the child records for you. The InnoDB table type in MySQL offers support for foreign keys as of Version 3.23.44, and for cascaded delete as of 3.23.50. In addition, there are plans to implement foreign key support for all the table types in MySQL 4.1.

Performing a Cascaded Delete with a Multiple-Table DELETE Statement

As of MySQL 4.0.0, DELETE supports a syntax that allows you to identify records to be removed from multiple tables and clobber them all with a single statement. To use this for deleting software distributions from the swdist_head and swdist_item tables, determine the IDs of the relevent distributions and then apply the list to those tables.

First, determine which version of each distribution is the most recent and select the names and version numbers into a separate table. The following query selects each distribution name and the highest version number for each one:

```
mysql> CREATE TABLE tmp
    -> SELECT name, MAX(ver_num) AS newest
    -> FROM swdist_head
    -> GROUP BY name;
```

The resulting table looks like this:

```
mysql> SELECT * FROM tmp;
+------------+--------+
| name       | newest |
+------------+--------+
| DB Gadgets |   1.61 |
| NetGizmo   |   4.00 |
+------------+--------+
```

Next, determine the ID numbers of the distributions that are older than those listed in the tmp table:

```
mysql> CREATE TABLE tmp2
    -> SELECT swdist_head.dist_id, swdist_head.name, swdist_head.ver_num
    -> FROM swdist_head, tmp
    -> WHERE swdist_head.name = tmp.name AND swdist_head.ver_num < tmp.newest;
```

Note that you actually need select only the dist_id column into tmp2. The example selects the name and version number as well so that you can look at tmp2 and see more easily that the IDs it chooses are indeed those for the older distributions that are to be deleted:

```
mysql> SELECT * FROM tmp2;
+---------+------------+---------+
| dist_id | name       | ver_num |
+---------+------------+---------+
|       1 | DB Gadgets |    1.59 |
|       3 | DB Gadgets |    1.60 |
|       2 | NetGizmo   |    3.02 |
+---------+------------+---------+
```

The table does not contain the IDs for DB Gadgets 1.61 or NetGizmo 4.00, which are the most recent distributions.

Now apply the ID list in tmp2 to the distribution tables using a multiple-table DELETE. The general form of this statement is:

```
DELETE tbl_list1 FROM tbl_list2 WHERE conditions;
```

tbl_list1 names the tables from which to delete records. tbl_list2 names the tables used in the WHERE clause, which specifies the conditions that identify the records to delete. Each table list can name one or more tables, separated by commas. For the situation at hand, the tables to delete from are swdist_head and swdist_item. The tables used to identify the deleted records are those tables and the tmp2 table:

```
mysql> DELETE swdist_head, swdist_item
    -> FROM tmp2, swdist_head, swdist_item
    -> WHERE tmp2.dist_id = swdist_head.dist_id
    -> AND tmp2.dist_id = swdist_item.dist_id;
```

The resulting tables look like this:

```
mysql> SELECT * FROM swdist_head;
+---------+------------+---------+------------+
| dist_id | name       | ver_num | rel_date   |
+---------+------------+---------+------------+
|       4 | DB Gadgets |    1.61 | 1998-12-28 |
|       5 | NetGizmo   |    4.00 | 2001-08-04 |
+---------+------------+---------+------------+
mysql> SELECT * FROM swdist_item;
+---------+-----------+
| dist_id | dist_file |
+---------+-----------+
|       4 | README    |
```

```
      |        4 |  README.linux   |
      |        4 |  README.solaris |
      |        4 |  db-gadgets.sh  |
      |        5 |  README.txt     |
      |        5 |  NetGizmo.exe   |
      +----------+-----------------+
```

For the tables that we're using, the DELETE statement just shown works as expected. But be aware that it will fail for tables containing parent records that should be deleted but for which there are no corresponding child records. The WHERE clause will find no match for the parent record in the client table, and thus not select the parent record for deletion. To make sure that the query selects and deletes the parent record even in the absence of matching child records, use a LEFT JOIN:

```
mysql> DELETE swdist_head, swdist_item
    -> FROM tmp2 LEFT JOIN swdist_head ON tmp2.dist_id = swdist_head.dist_id
    -> LEFT JOIN swdist_item ON swdist_head.dist_id = swdist_item.dist_id;
```

LEFT JOIN is discussed in Recipe 12.5.

Performing a Multiple-Table Delete Using Table Replacement

Another way to delete related rows from multiple tables is to select only the records that should *not* be deleted into new tables, then replace the original tables with the new ones. This is especially useful when you want to delete more records than you want to keep.

Begin by creating two tables tmp_head and tmp_item that have the same structure as the swdist_head and swdist_item tables:

```
CREATE TABLE tmp_head
(
    dist_id    INT UNSIGNED NOT NULL AUTO_INCREMENT,   # distribution ID
    name       VARCHAR(40),                            # distribution name
    ver_num    NUMERIC(5,2),                           # version number
    rel_date   DATE NOT NULL,                          # release date
    PRIMARY KEY (dist_id)
);
CREATE TABLE tmp_item
(
    dist_id    INT UNSIGNED NOT NULL,  # parent distribution ID
    dist_file  VARCHAR(255) NOT NULL   # name of file in distribution
);
```

Then determine the IDs of the distributions you want to keep (that is, the most recent version of each distribution). The IDs are found as follows, using queries similar to those just described in the multiple-table delete section:

```
mysql> CREATE TABLE tmp
    -> SELECT name, MAX(ver_num) AS newest
    -> FROM swdist_head
```

```
    -> GROUP BY name;
mysql> CREATE TABLE tmp2
    -> SELECT swdist_head.dist_id
    -> FROM swdist_head, tmp
    -> WHERE swdist_head.name = tmp.name AND swdist_head.ver_num = tmp.newest;
```

Next, select into the new tables the records that should be retained:

```
mysql> INSERT INTO tmp_head
    -> SELECT swdist_head.*
    -> FROM swdist_head, tmp2
    -> WHERE swdist_head.dist_id = tmp2.dist_id;
mysql> INSERT INTO tmp_item
    -> SELECT swdist_item.*
    -> FROM swdist_item, tmp2
    -> WHERE swdist_item.dist_id = tmp2.dist_id;
```

Finally, replace the original tables with the new ones:

```
mysql> DROP TABLE swdist_head;
mysql> ALTER TABLE tmp_head RENAME TO swdist_head;
mysql> DROP TABLE swdist_item;
mysql> ALTER TABLE tmp_item RENAME TO swdist_item;
```

Performing a Multiple-Table Delete by Writing a Program

The preceding two methods for deleting related rows from multiple tables are SQL-only techniques. Another approach is to write a program that generates the DELETE statements for you. The program should determine the key values (the distribution IDs) for the records to delete, then process the keys to turn them into appropriate DELETE statements. Identifying the IDs can be done the same way as shown for the previous methods, but you have some latitude in how you want to use them to delete records:

- Handle each ID individually. Construct DELETE statements that remove records from the tables one ID at a time.

- Handle the IDs as a group. Construct an IN( ) clause that names all the IDs, and use it with each table to delete all the matching IDs at once.

- If the ID list is huge, break it into smaller groups to construct shorter IN( ) clauses.

- You can also solve the problem by reversing the perspective. Select the IDs for the distributions you want to retain and use them to construct a NOT IN( ) clause that deletes all the other distributions. This will usually be less efficient, because MySQL will not use an index for NOT IN( ) operations.

I'll show how to implement each method using Perl.

For each of the first three methods, begin by generating a list of the distribution IDs for the records to be deleted:

```
# Identify the newest version for each distribution name

$dbh->do ("CREATE TABLE tmp
```

```
                    SELECT name, MAX(ver_num) AS newest
                    FROM swdist_head
                    GROUP BY name");
```

```
    # Identify the IDs for versions that are older than those.
```

```
    my $ref = $dbh->selectcol_arrayref (
                    "SELECT swdist_head.dist_id
                    FROM swdist_head, tmp
                    WHERE swdist_head.name = tmp.name
                    AND swdist_head.ver_num < tmp.newest");
```

```
    # selectcol_arrayref() returns a reference to a list.  Convert the reference
    # to a list, which will be empty if $ref is undef or points to an empty list.
```

```
    my @val = ($ref ? @{$ref} : ());
```

At this point, @val contains the list of IDs for the records to remove. To process them individually, run the following loop:

```
    # Use the ID list to delete records, one ID at a time
```

```
    foreach my $val (@val)
    {
        $dbh->do ("DELETE FROM swdist_head WHERE dist_id = ?", undef, $val);
        $dbh->do ("DELETE FROM swdist_item WHERE dist_id = ?", undef, $val);
    }
```

The loop will generate statements that look like this:

```
    DELETE FROM swdist_head WHERE dist_id = '1'
    DELETE FROM swdist_item WHERE dist_id = '1'
    DELETE FROM swdist_head WHERE dist_id = '3'
    DELETE FROM swdist_item WHERE dist_id = '3'
    DELETE FROM swdist_head WHERE dist_id = '2'
    DELETE FROM swdist_item WHERE dist_id = '2'
```

A drawback of this approach is that for large tables, the ID list may be quite large and you'll generate lots of DELETE statements. To be more efficient, combine the IDs into a single IN( ) clause that names them all at once. Generate the ID list the same way as for the first method, then process the list like this:[*]

```
    # Use the ID list to delete records for all IDs at once.  If the list
    # is empty, don't bother; there's nothing to delete.
```

```
    if (@val)
    {
        # generate list of comma-separated "?" placeholders, one per value
        my $where = "WHERE dist_id IN (" . join (",", ("?") x @val) . ")";
        $dbh->do ("DELETE FROM swdist_head $where", undef, @val);
        $dbh->do ("DELETE FROM swdist_item $where", undef, @val);
```

---

[*] In Perl, you can't bind an array to a placeholder, but you can construct the query string to contain the proper number of ? characters (see Recipe 2.6). Then pass the array to be bound to the statement, and each element will be bound to the corresponding placeholder.

```
}
```

This method generates only one DELETE statement per table:

```
DELETE FROM swdist_head WHERE dist_id IN ('1','3','2')
DELETE FROM swdist_item WHERE dist_id IN ('1','3','2')
```

If the list of IDs is *extremely* large, you may be in danger of producing DELETE statements that exceed the maximum query length (a megabyte by default). In this case, you can break the ID list into smaller groups and use each one to construct a shorter IN( ) clause:

```
# Use the ID list to delete records, using parts of the list at a time.

my $grp_size = 1000;     # number of IDs to delete at once

for (my $i = 0; $i < @val; $i += $grp_size)
{
    my $j = (@val < $i + $grp_size ? @val : $i + $grp_size);
    my @group = @val[$i .. $j-1];
    # generate list of comma-separated "?" placeholders, one per value
    my $where = "WHERE dist_id IN (" . join (",", ("?") x @group) . ")";
    $dbh->do ("DELETE FROM swdist_head $where", undef, @group);
    $dbh->do ("DELETE FROM swdist_item $where", undef, @group);
}
```

Each of the preceding programming methods finds the IDs of the records to remove and then deletes them. You can also achieve the same objective using reverse logic: select the IDs for the records you want to keep, then delete everything else. This approach can be useful if you expect to retain fewer records than you'll delete. To implement it, determine the newest version for each distribution and find the associated IDs. Then use the ID list to construct a NOT IN( ) clause:

```
# Identify the newest version for each distribution name

$dbh->do ("CREATE TABLE tmp
            SELECT name, MAX(ver_num) AS newest
            FROM swdist_head
            GROUP BY name");

# Identify the IDs for those versions.

my $ref = $dbh->selectcol_arrayref (
            "SELECT swdist_head.dist_id
            FROM swdist_head, tmp
            WHERE swdist_head.name = tmp.name
            AND swdist_head.ver_num = tmp.newest");

# selectcol_arrayref() returns a reference to a list.  Convert the reference
# to a list, which will be empty if $ref is undef or points to an empty list.

my @val = ($ref ? @{$ref} : ());

# Use the ID list to delete records for all *other* IDs at once.
# The WHERE clause is empty if the list is empty (in that case,
```

```
                            # no records are to be kept, so they all can be deleted).

    my $where = "";
    if (@val)
    {
        # generate list of comma-separated "?" placeholders, one per value
        $where = "WHERE dist_id NOT IN (" . join (",", ("?") x @val) . ")";
    }
    $dbh->do ("DELETE FROM swdist_head $where", undef, @val);
    $dbh->do ("DELETE FROM swdist_item $where", undef, @val);
```

Note that with this reverse-logic approach, you *must* use the entire ID list in a single
NOT IN( ) clause. If you try breaking the list into smaller groups and using NOT IN( )
with each of those, you'll empty your tables completely when you don't intend to.

Performing a Multiple-Table Delete Using mysql

If the keys that indicate which records to delete do not include quotes or other special characters, you can generate DELETE statements using *mysql*. For the software distribution tables, the keys (dist_id values) are integers, so they're susceptible to this
approach. Generate the ID list using the same queries as those described in the multiple-table DELETE section, then use the list to create the DELETE statements:

```
    CREATE TABLE tmp
    SELECT name, MAX(ver_num) AS newest
    FROM swdist_head
    GROUP BY name;

    CREATE TABLE tmp2
    SELECT swdist_head.dist_id
    FROM swdist_head, tmp
    WHERE swdist_head.name = tmp.name AND swdist_head.ver_num < tmp.newest;

    SELECT CONCAT('DELETE FROM swdist_head WHERE dist_id=',dist_id,';') FROM tmp2;
    SELECT CONCAT('DELETE FROM swdist_item WHERE dist_id=',dist_id,';') FROM tmp2;
```

If you have those statements in a file *swdist_mysql_delete.sql*, execute the file as follows to produce the set of DELETE statements:

```
    % mysql -N cookbook < swdist_mysql_delete.sql > tmp
```

The file *tmp* will look like this:

```
    DELETE FROM swdist_head WHERE dist_id=1;
    DELETE FROM swdist_head WHERE dist_id=3;
    DELETE FROM swdist_head WHERE dist_id=2;
    DELETE FROM swdist_item WHERE dist_id=1;
    DELETE FROM swdist_item WHERE dist_id=3;
    DELETE FROM swdist_item WHERE dist_id=2;
```

Then execute the contents of *tmp* as follows:

```
    % mysql cookbook < tmp
```

12.21 Identifying and Removing Unattached Records

Problem

You have tables that are related (for example, they have a master-detail relationship). But you suspect that some of the records are unattached and can be removed.

Solution

Use a LEFT JOIN to identify unmatched values and delete them by adapting the techniques shown in Recipe 12.20. Or use a table-replacement procedure that selects the matched records into a new table and replaces the original table with it.

Discussion

The previous section shows how to delete related records from multiple tables at once, using the relationship that exists between the tables. Sometimes the opposite problem presents itself, where you want to delete records based on the *lack* of relationship. Problems of this kind typically occur when you have tables that are supposed to match up, but some of the records are unattached—that is, they are unmatched by any corresponding record in the other table.

This can occur by accident, such as when you delete a parent record but forget to delete the associated child records, or vice versa. It can also occur as an anticipated consequence of a deliberate action. Suppose an online discussion board uses a parent table that lists discussion topics and a child table that records the articles posted for each topic. If you purge the child table of old article records, that may result in any given topic record in the parent table no longer having any children. If so, the lack of recent postings for the topic indicates that it is probably dead and that the parent record in the topic table can be deleted, too. In such a situation, you delete a set of child records with the explicit recognition that the operation may strand parent records and cause them to become eligible for being deleted as well.

However you arrive at the point where related tables have unmatched records, restoring the tables to a consistent state is a matter of identifying the unattached records and then deleting them:

- To identify the unattached records, use a LEFT JOIN, because this is a "find unmatched records" problem. (See Recipe 12.5 for information about LEFT JOIN.)
- To delete the records that have the unmatched IDs, use techniques similar to those shown in Recipe 12.20, for removing records from multiple related tables.

The examples here use the `swdist_head` and `swdist_item` software distribution tables that were used in Recipe 12.20. Create the tables in their initial state using the *swdist_create.sql* script in the *joins* directory of the recipes distribution. They'll look like this:

```
mysql> SELECT * FROM swdist_head;
+---------+------------+---------+------------+
| dist_id | name       | ver_num | rel_date   |
+---------+------------+---------+------------+
|       1 | DB Gadgets |    1.59 | 1996-03-25 |
|       2 | NetGizmo   |    3.02 | 1998-11-10 |
|       3 | DB Gadgets |    1.60 | 1998-12-26 |
|       4 | DB Gadgets |    1.61 | 1998-12-28 |
|       5 | NetGizmo   |    4.00 | 2001-08-04 |
+---------+------------+---------+------------+
mysql> SELECT * FROM swdist_item;
+---------+----------------+
| dist_id | dist_file      |
+---------+----------------+
|       1 | README         |
|       1 | db-gadgets.sh  |
|       3 | README         |
|       3 | README.linux   |
|       3 | db-gadgets.sh  |
|       4 | README         |
|       4 | README.linux   |
|       4 | README.solaris |
|       4 | db-gadgets.sh  |
|       2 | README.txt     |
|       2 | NetGizmo.exe   |
|       5 | README.txt     |
|       5 | NetGizmo.exe   |
+---------+----------------+
```

The records in the tables are fully matched at this point: For every `dist_id` value in the parent table, there is at least one child record, and each child record has a parent. To "damage" the integrity of this relationship for purposes of illustration, remove a few records from each table:

```
mysql> DELETE FROM swdist_head WHERE dist_id IN (1,4);
mysql> DELETE FROM swdist_item WHERE dist_id IN (2,5);
```

The result is that there are unattached records in both tables:

```
mysql> SELECT * FROM swdist_head;
+---------+------------+---------+------------+
| dist_id | name       | ver_num | rel_date   |
+---------+------------+---------+------------+
|       2 | NetGizmo   |    3.02 | 1998-11-10 |
|       3 | DB Gadgets |    1.60 | 1998-12-26 |
|       5 | NetGizmo   |    4.00 | 2001-08-04 |
+---------+------------+---------+------------+
```

```
mysql> SELECT * FROM swdist_item;
+---------+---------------+
| dist_id | dist_file     |
+---------+---------------+
|       1 | README        |
|       1 | db-gadgets.sh |
|       3 | README        |
|       3 | README.linux  |
|       3 | db-gadgets.sh |
|       4 | README        |
|       4 | README.linux  |
|       4 | README.solaris|
|       4 | db-gadgets.sh |
+---------+---------------+
```

A little inspection reveals that only distribution 3 has records in both tables. Distributions 2 and 5 in the swdist_head table are unmatched by any records in the swdist_item table. Conversely, distributions 1 and 4 in the swdist_item table are unmatched by any records in the swdist_head table.

The problem now is to identify the unattached records (by some means other than visual inspection), and then remove them. Identification is a matter of using a LEFT JOIN. For example, to find childless parent records in the swdist_head table, use the following query:

```
mysql> SELECT swdist_head.dist_id AS 'unmatched swdist_head IDs'
    -> FROM swdist_head LEFT JOIN swdist_item
    -> ON swdist_head.dist_id = swdist_item.dist_id
    -> WHERE swdist_item.dist_id IS NULL;
+---------------------------+
| unmatched swdist_head IDs |
+---------------------------+
|                         2 |
|                         5 |
+---------------------------+
```

Conversely, to find the IDs for orphaned children in the swdist_item table that have no parent, reverse the roles of the two tables:

```
mysql> SELECT swdist_item.dist_id AS 'unmatched swdist_item IDs'
    -> FROM swdist_item LEFT JOIN swdist_head
    -> ON swdist_item.dist_id = swdist_head.dist_id
    -> WHERE swdist_head.dist_id IS NULL;
+---------------------------+
| unmatched swdist_item IDs |
+---------------------------+
|                         1 |
|                         1 |
|                         4 |
|                         4 |
|                         4 |
|                         4 |
+---------------------------+
```

Note that in this case, an ID will appear more than once in the list if there are multiple children for a missing parent. Depending on how you choose to delete the unmatched records, you may want to use DISTINCT to select each unmatched child ID only once:

```
mysql> SELECT DISTINCT swdist_item.dist_id AS 'unmatched swdist_item IDs'
    -> FROM swdist_item LEFT JOIN swdist_head
    -> ON swdist_item.dist_id = swdist_head.dist_id
    -> WHERE swdist_head.dist_id IS NULL;
+--------------------------+
| unmatched swdist_item IDs |
+--------------------------+
|                        1 |
|                        4 |
+--------------------------+
```

After you identify the unattached records, the question becomes how to get rid of them. You can use either of the following techniques, which you'll recognize as similar to those discussed in Recipe 12.20:

- Use the IDs in a multiple-table DELETE statement. You'll be removing records from just one table at a time, but the syntax for this form of DELETE is still useful because it allows you to identify the records to remove by means of a join between the related tables.

- Run a program that selects the unmatched IDs and uses them to generate DELETE statements.

To use a multiple-table DELETE statement for removing unmatched records, just take the SELECT statement that you use to identify those records and replace the stuff leading up to the FROM keyword with DELETE *tbl_name*. For example, the SELECT that identifies childless parents looks like this:

```
SELECT swdist_head.dist_id AS 'unmatched swdist_head IDs'
FROM swdist_head LEFT JOIN swdist_item
    ON swdist_head.dist_id = swdist_item.dist_id
WHERE swdist_item.dist_id IS NULL;
```

The corresponding DELETE looks like this:

```
DELETE swdist_head
FROM swdist_head LEFT JOIN swdist_item
    ON swdist_head.dist_id = swdist_item.dist_id
WHERE swdist_item.dist_id IS NULL;
```

Conversely, the query to identify parentless children is as follows:

```
SELECT swdist_item.dist_id AS 'unmatched swdist_item IDs'
FROM swdist_item LEFT JOIN swdist_head
    ON swdist_item.dist_id = swdist_head.dist_id
WHERE swdist_head.dist_id IS NULL;
```

And the corresponding DELETE statement removes them:

```
DELETE swdist_item
FROM swdist_item LEFT JOIN swdist_head
    ON swdist_item.dist_id = swdist_head.dist_id
WHERE swdist_head.dist_id IS NULL;
```

To remove unmatched records by writing a program, select the ID list and turn it into a set of DELETE statements. Here's a Perl program that does so, first for the parent table and then for the child table:

```
#! /usr/bin/perl -w
use strict;
use lib qw(/usr/local/apache/lib/perl);
use Cookbook;

my $dbh = Cookbook::connect ();

# Identify the IDs of childless parent records

my $ref = $dbh->selectcol_arrayref (
            "SELECT swdist_head.dist_id
            FROM swdist_head LEFT JOIN swdist_item
                ON swdist_head.dist_id = swdist_item.dist_id
            WHERE swdist_item.dist_id IS NULL");

# selectcol_arrayref() returns a reference to a list.  Convert the reference
# to a list, which will be empty if $ref is undef or points to an empty list.

my @val = ($ref ? @{$ref} : ());

# Use the ID list to delete records for all IDs at once.  If the list
# is empty, don't bother; there's nothing to delete.

if (@val)
{
    # generate list of comma-separated "?" placeholders, one per value
    my $where = "WHERE dist_id IN (" . join (",", ("?") x @val) . ")";
    $dbh->do ("DELETE FROM swdist_head $where", undef, @val);
}

# Repeat the procedure for the child table.  Use SELECT DISTINCT so that
# each ID is selected only once.

$ref = $dbh->selectcol_arrayref (
            "SELECT DISTINCT swdist_item.dist_id
            FROM swdist_item LEFT JOIN swdist_head
                ON swdist_item.dist_id = swdist_head.dist_id
            WHERE swdist_head.dist_id IS NULL");

@val = ($ref ? @{$ref} : ());
```

```
if (@val)
{
    # generate list of comma-separated "?" placeholders, one per value
    my $where = "WHERE dist_id IN (" . join (",", ("?") x @val) . ")";
    $dbh->do ("DELETE FROM swdist_item $where", undef, @val);
}

$dbh->disconnect ();

exit (0);
```

The program uses IN( ) to delete all the affected records in a given table at once. See Recipe 12.20 for other related approaches.

You can also use *mysql* to generate the DELETE statements; a script that shows how to do this can be found in the *joins* directory of the recipes distribution.

A different type of solution to the problem is to use a table-replacement procedure. This method comes at the problem in reverse. Instead of finding and removing unmatched records, find and keep matched records. For example, you can use a join to select matched records into a new table. Then replace the original table with it. Unattached records don't get carried along by the join, and so in effect are removed when the new table replaces the original one.

The table replacement procedure works as follows. For the swdist_head table, create a new table with the same structure:

```
CREATE TABLE tmp
(
    dist_id    INT UNSIGNED NOT NULL AUTO_INCREMENT,   # distribution ID
    name       VARCHAR(40),                            # distribution name
    ver_num    NUMERIC(5,2),                           # version number
    rel_date   DATE NOT NULL,                          # release date
    PRIMARY KEY (dist_id)
);
```

Then select into the tmp table those swdist_head records that have a match in the swdist_item table:

```
INSERT IGNORE INTO tmp
SELECT swdist_head.*
FROM swdist_head, swdist_item
WHERE swdist_head.dist_id = swdist_item.dist_id;
```

Note that the query uses INSERT IGNORE; a parent record may be matched by multiple child records, but we want only one instance of its ID. (The symptom of failing to use IGNORE is that the query will fail with a "duplicate key" error.)

Finish by replacing the original table with the new one:

```
DROP TABLE swdist_head;
ALTER TABLE tmp RENAME TO swdist_head;
```

The procedure for replacing the child table with a table containing only matched child records is similar, except that IGNORE is not needed—each child that is matched will be matched by only one parent:

```
CREATE TABLE tmp
(
    dist_id    INT UNSIGNED NOT NULL,   # parent distribution ID
    dist_file  VARCHAR(255) NOT NULL    # name of file in distribution
);

INSERT INTO tmp
SELECT swdist_item.*
FROM swdist_head, swdist_item
WHERE swdist_head.dist_id = swdist_item.dist_id;

DROP TABLE swdist_item;
ALTER TABLE tmp RENAME TO swdist_item;
```

12.22 Using Different MySQL Servers Simultaneously

Problem

You want to run a query that uses tables in databases that are hosted by different MySQL servers.

Solution

There is no SQL-only solution to this problem. One workaround is to open separate connections to each server and relate the information from the two tables yourself. Another is to copy one of the tables from one server to the other so that you can work with both tables using a single server.

Discussion

Throughout this chapter, I've been making the implicit assumption that all the tables involved in a multiple-table operation are managed by a single MySQL server. If this assumption is invalid, the tables become more difficult to work with. A connection to a MySQL server is specific to that server. You can't write a SQL statement that refers to tables hosted by another server. (I've seen claims that this can be done, but they always turn out to have been made by people who haven't actually tried it.)

Here is an example that illustrates the problem, using the artist and painting tables. Suppose you want to find the names of paintings by Da Vinci. This requires determining the ID for Da Vinci in the artist table and matching it to records in the painting table. If the both tables are located within the same database, you can identify the paintings by using the following query to perform a join between the tables:

```
mysql> SELECT painting.title
    -> FROM artist, painting
    -> WHERE artist.name = 'Da Vinci' AND artist.a_id = painting.a_id;
+-----------------+
| title           |
+-----------------+
| The Last Supper |
| The Mona Lisa   |
+-----------------+
```

If the tables are in different databases, but still managed by the same MySQL server, the query need only be modified a bit to include database qualifiers. (This technique is discussed in Recipe 12.2.) For the two tables at hand, the query looks something like this:

```
mysql> SELECT db2.painting.title
    -> FROM db1.artist, db2.painting
    -> WHERE db1.artist.name = 'Da Vinci'
    -> AND db1.artist.a_id = db2.painting.a_id;
+-----------------+
| title           |
+-----------------+
| The Last Supper |
| The Mona Lisa   |
+-----------------+
```

If the artist and painting tables are managed by different servers, you cannot issue a single query to perform a join between them. You must send a query to one server to fetch the appropriate artist ID:

```
mysql> SELECT a_id FROM artist WHERE name = 'Da Vinci';
+------+
| a_id |
+------+
|    1 |
+------+
```

Then use that a_id value (1) to construct a second query that you send to the other server:

```
mysql> SELECT title FROM painting WHERE a_id = 1;
+-----------------+
| title           |
+-----------------+
| The Last Supper |
| The Mona Lisa   |
+-----------------+
```

The preceding example uses a relatively simple example, which has a correspondingly simple solution. It's simple because it retrieves only a single value from the first table, and because it displays information only from the second table. If you wanted instead to display the artist name with the painting title, and to do so for several artists, the problem becomes correspondingly more difficult. You might solve it by writing a program that simulates a join:

1. Open a separate connection to each database server.

2. Run a loop that fetches artist IDs and names from the server that manages the artist table.

3. Each time through the loop, use the current artist ID to construct a query that looks for painting table rows that match the artist ID value. Send the query to the server that manages the painting table. As you retrieve painting titles, display them along with the current artist name.

This technique allows simulation of a join between tables located on any two servers. Incidentally, it also can be used when you need to work with tables that are hosted by different types of database engines. (For example, you can simulate a join between a MySQL table and a PostgreSQL table this way.) However, it's still messy, so when faced with this kind of problem, you may wish to consider another alternative: copy one of the tables from one server to the other. Then you can work with both tables using the same server, which allows you to perform a proper join between them. See Recipe 10.16 for information on copying tables between servers.

## CHAPTER 13

Statistical Techniques

13.0 Introduction

This chapter covers several topics that relate to basic statistical techniques. For the most part, these recipes build on those described in earlier chapters, such as the summary techniques discussed in Chapter 7. The examples here thus show additional ways to apply the material from those chapters. Broadly speaking, the topics discussed in this chapter include:

- Techniques for data characterization, such as calculating descriptive statistics, generating frequency distributions, counting missing values, and calculating least-squares regressions or correlation coefficients

- Randomization methods, such as how to generate random numbers and apply them to randomization of a set of rows or to selecting individual items randomly from the rows

- Rank assignments

Statistics covers such a large and diverse array of topics that this chapter necessarily only scratches the surface, and simply illustrates a few of the potential areas in which MySQL may be applied to statistical analysis. Note that some statistical measures can be defined in different ways (for example, do you calculate standard deviation based on n degrees of freedom, or $n-1$?). For that reason, if the definition I use for a given term doesn't match the one you prefer, you'll need to adapt the queries or algorithms shown here to some extent.

You can find scripts related to the examples discussed here in the *stats* directory of the recipes distribution, and scripts for creating some of the example tables in the *tables* directory.

13.1 Calculating Descriptive Statistics

Problem

You want to characterize a dataset by computing general descriptive or summary statistics.

Solution

Many common descriptive statistics, such as mean and standard deviation, can be obtained by applying aggregate functions to your data. Others, such as median or mode, can be calculated based on counting queries.

Discussion

Suppose you have a table testscore containing observations representing subject ID, age, sex, and test score:

```
mysql> SELECT subject, age, sex, score FROM testscore ORDER BY subject;
+---------+-----+-----+-------+
| subject | age | sex | score |
+---------+-----+-----+-------+
|       1 |   5 | M   |     5 |
|       2 |   5 | M   |     4 |
|       3 |   5 | F   |     6 |
|       4 |   5 | F   |     7 |
|       5 |   6 | M   |     8 |
|       6 |   6 | M   |     9 |
|       7 |   6 | F   |     4 |
|       8 |   6 | F   |     6 |
|       9 |   7 | M   |     8 |
|      10 |   7 | M   |     6 |
|      11 |   7 | F   |     9 |
|      12 |   7 | F   |     7 |
|      13 |   8 | M   |     9 |
|      14 |   8 | M   |     6 |
|      15 |   8 | F   |     7 |
|      16 |   8 | F   |    10 |
|      17 |   9 | M   |     9 |
|      18 |   9 | M   |     7 |
|      19 |   9 | F   |    10 |
|      20 |   9 | F   |     9 |
+---------+-----+-----+-------+
```

A good first step in analyzing a set of observations is to generate some descriptive statistics that summarize their general characteristics as a whole. Common statistical values of this kind include:

- The number of observations, their sum, and their range (minimum and maximum)
- Measures of central tendency, such as mean, median, and mode
- Measures of variation, such as standard deviation or variance

Aside from the median and mode, all of these can be calculated easily by invoking aggregate functions:

```
mysql> SELECT COUNT(score) AS n,
    -> SUM(score) AS sum,
    -> MIN(score) AS minimum,
    -> MAX(score) AS maximum,
    -> AVG(score) AS mean,
    -> STD(score) AS 'std. dev.'
    -> FROM testscore;
+----+------+---------+---------+--------+-----------+
| n  | sum  | minimum | maximum | mean   | std. dev. |
+----+------+---------+---------+--------+-----------+
| 20 | 146  |       4 |      10 | 7.3000 |    1.7916 |
+----+------+---------+---------+--------+-----------+
```

The aggregate functions as used in this query count only non-NULL observations. If you use NULL to represent missing values, you may want to perform an additional characterization to assess the extent to which values are missing. (See Recipe 13.4.)

Variance is not shown in the query, and MySQL has no function for calculating it. However, variance is just the square of the standard deviation, so it's easily computed like this:

```
STD(score) * STD(score)
```

STDDEV( ) is a synonym for STD( ).

Standard deviation can be used to identify outliers—values that are uncharacteristically far from the mean. For example, to select values that lie more than three standard deviations from the mean, you can do something like this:

```
SELECT @mean := AVG(score), @std := STD(score) FROM testscore;
SELECT score FROM testscore WHERE ABS(score-@mean) > @std * 3;
```

For a set of n values, the standard deviation produced by STD( ) is based on n degrees of freedom. This is equivalent to computing the standard deviation "by hand" as follows (@ss represents the sum of squares):

```
mysql> SELECT
    -> @n := COUNT(score),
    -> @sum := SUM(score),
    -> @ss := SUM(score*score)
    -> FROM testscore;
```

```
mysql> SELECT @var := ((@n * @ss) - (@sum * @sum)) / (@n * @n);
mysql> SELECT SQRT(@var);
+------------+
| SQRT(@var) |
+------------+
|   1.791647 |
+------------+
```

To calculate a standard deviation based on *n*–1 degrees of freedom instead, do it like this:

```
mysql> SELECT
    -> @n := COUNT(score),
    -> @sum := SUM(score),
    -> @ss := SUM(score*score)
    -> FROM testscore;
mysql> SELECT @var := ((@n * @ss) - (@sum * @sum)) / (@n * (@n - 1));
mysql> SELECT SQRT(@var);
+------------+
| SQRT(@var) |
+------------+
|   1.838191 |
+------------+
```

Or, more simply, like this:

```
mysql> SELECT @n := COUNT(score) FROM testscore;
mysql> SELECT STD(score)*SQRT(@n/(@n-1)) FROM testscore;
+----------------------------+
| STD(score)*SQRT(@n/(@n-1)) |
+----------------------------+
|                   1.838191 |
+----------------------------+
```

MySQL has no built-in function for computing the mode or median of a set of values, but you can compute them yourself. The mode is the value that occurs most frequently. To determine what it is, count each value and see which one is most common:

```
mysql> SELECT score, COUNT(score) AS count
    -> FROM testscore GROUP BY score ORDER BY count DESC;
+-------+-------+
| score | count |
+-------+-------+
|     9 |     5 |
|     6 |     4 |
|     7 |     4 |
|     4 |     2 |
|     8 |     2 |
|    10 |     2 |
|     5 |     1 |
+-------+-------+
```

In this case, 9 is the modal score value.

The median of a set of ordered values can be calculated like this:[*]

- If the number of values is odd, the median is the middle value.
- If the number of values is even, the median is the average of the two middle values.

Based on that definition, use the following procedure to determine the median of a set of observations stored in the database:

- Issue a query to count the number of observations. From the count, you can determine whether the median calculation requires one or two values, and what their indexes are within the ordered set of observations.
- Issue a query that includes an ORDER BY clause to sort the observations, and a LIMIT clause to pull out the middle value or values.
- Take the average of the selected value or values.

For example, if a table t contains a score column with 37 values (an odd number), you need to select a single value, using a query like this:

```
SELECT score FROM t ORDER BY 1 LIMIT 18,1
```

If the column contains 38 values (an even number), the query becomes:

```
SELECT score FROM t ORDER BY 1 LIMIT 18,2
```

Then you can select the value or values returned by the query and compute the median from their average.

The following Perl function implements a median calculation. It takes a database handle and the names of the table and column that contain the set of observations, then generates the query that retrieves the relevant values, and returns their average:

```perl
sub median
{
my ($dbh, $tbl_name, $col_name) = @_;
my ($count, $limit);

    $count = $dbh->selectrow_array ("SELECT COUNT($col_name) FROM $tbl_name");
    return undef unless $count > 0;
    if ($count % 2 == 1)    # odd number of values; select middle value
    {
        $limit = sprintf ("LIMIT %d,1", ($count-1)/2);
    }
    else                    # even number of values; select middle two values
    {
        $limit = sprintf ("LIMIT %d,2", $count/2 - 1);
    }

    my $sth = $dbh->prepare (
                    "SELECT $col_name FROM $tbl_name ORDER BY 1 $limit");
    $sth->execute ();
```

---

[*] Note that the definition of median given here isn't fully general; it doesn't address what to do if there's duplication of the middle values in the dataset.

```
    my ($n, $sum) = (0, 0);
    while (my $ref = $sth->fetchrow_arrayref ())
    {
        ++$n;
        $sum += $ref->[0];
    }
    return ($sum / $n);
}
```

The preceding technique works for a set of values stored in the database. If you happen to have already fetched an ordered set of values into an array @val, you can compute the median like this instead:

```
if (@val == 0)          # if array is empty, median is undefined
{
    $median = undef;
}
elsif (@val % 2 == 1)   # if array size is odd, median is middle number
{
    $median = $val[(@val-1)/2];
}
else                    # array size is even; median is average
{                       # of two middle numbers
    $median = ($val[@val/2 - 1] + $val[@val/2]) / 2;
}
```

The code works for arrays that have an initial subscript of 0; for languages that used 1-based array indexes, adjust the algorithm accordingly.

13.2 Per-Group Descriptive Statistics

Problem

You want to produce descriptive statistics for each subgroup of a set of observations.

Solution

Use aggregate functions, but employ a GROUP BY clause to arrange observations into the appropriate groups.

Discussion

The preceding section shows how to compute descriptive statistics for the entire set of scores in the testscore table. To be more specific, you can use GROUP BY to divide the observations into groups and calculate statistics for each of them. For example, the subjects in the testscore table are listed by age and sex, so it's possible to calculate similar statistics by age or sex (or both) by application of appropriate GROUP BY clauses.

By age:

```
mysql> SELECT age, COUNT(score) AS n,
    -> SUM(score) AS sum,
    -> MIN(score) AS minimum,
    -> MAX(score) AS maximum,
    -> AVG(score) AS mean,
    -> STD(score) AS 'std. dev.'
    -> FROM testscore
    -> GROUP BY age;
```

age	n	sum	minimum	maximum	mean	std. dev.
5	4	22	4	7	5.5000	1.1180
6	4	27	4	9	6.7500	1.9203
7	4	30	6	9	7.5000	1.1180
8	4	32	6	10	8.0000	1.5811
9	4	35	7	10	8.7500	1.0897

By sex:

```
mysql> SELECT sex, COUNT(score) AS n,
    -> SUM(score) AS sum,
    -> MIN(score) AS minimum,
    -> MAX(score) AS maximum,
    -> AVG(score) AS mean,
    -> STD(score) AS 'std. dev.'
    -> FROM testscore
    -> GROUP BY sex;
```

sex	n	sum	minimum	maximum	mean	std. dev.
M	10	71	4	9	7.1000	1.7000
F	10	75	4	10	7.5000	1.8574

By age and sex:

```
mysql> SELECT age, sex, COUNT(score) AS n,
    -> SUM(score) AS sum,
    -> MIN(score) AS minimum,
    -> MAX(score) AS maximum,
    -> AVG(score) AS mean,
    -> STD(score) AS 'std. dev.'
    -> FROM testscore
    -> GROUP BY age, sex;
```

age	sex	n	sum	minimum	maximum	mean	std. dev.
5	M	2	9	4	5	4.5000	0.5000
5	F	2	13	6	7	6.5000	0.5000
6	M	2	17	8	9	8.5000	0.5000
6	F	2	10	4	6	5.0000	1.0000
7	M	2	14	6	8	7.0000	1.0000
7	F	2	16	7	9	8.0000	1.0000

```
|   8 | M   | 2 |   15 |     6 |     9 | 7.5000 |    1.5000 |
|   8 | F   | 2 |   17 |     7 |    10 | 8.5000 |    1.5000 |
|   9 | M   | 2 |   16 |     7 |     9 | 8.0000 |    1.0000 |
|   9 | F   | 2 |   19 |     9 |    10 | 9.5000 |    0.5000 |
+-----+-----+---+------+---------+---------+--------+-----------+
```

13.3   Generating Frequency Distributions

Problem

You want to know the frequency of occurrence for each value in a table.

Solution

Derive a frequency distribution that summarizes the contents of your dataset.

Discussion

A common application for per-group summary techniques is to generate a break-down of the number of times each value occurs. This is called a frequency distribu-tion. For the testscore table, the frequency distribution looks like this:

```
mysql> SELECT score, COUNT(score) AS occurrence
    -> FROM testscore GROUP BY score;
+-------+------------+
| score | occurrence |
+-------+------------+
|     4 |          2 |
|     5 |          1 |
|     6 |          4 |
|     7 |          4 |
|     8 |          2 |
|     9 |          5 |
|    10 |          2 |
+-------+------------+
```

If you express the results in terms of percentages rather than as counts, you produce a relative frequency distribution. To break down a set of observations and show each count as a percentage of the total, use one query to get the total number of observa-tions, and another to calculate the percentages for each group:

```
mysql> SELECT @n := COUNT(score) FROM testscore;
mysql> SELECT score, (COUNT(score)*100)/@n AS percent
    -> FROM testscore GROUP BY score;
+-------+---------+
| score | percent |
+-------+---------+
|     4 |      10 |
|     5 |       5 |
|     6 |      20 |
|     7 |      20 |
```

```
|     8 |    10 |
|     9 |    25 |
|    10 |    10 |
+-------+---------+
```

The distributions just shown summarize the number of values for individual scores. However, if the dataset contains a large number of distinct values and you want a distribution that shows only a small number of categories, you may wish to lump values into categories and produce a count for each category. "Lumping" techniques are discussed in Recipe 7.12.

One typical use of frequency distributions is to export the results for use in a graphing program. In the absence of such a program, you can use MySQL itself to generate a simple ASCII chart as a visual representation of the distribution. For example, to display an ASCII bar chart of the test score counts, convert the counts to strings of * characters:

```
mysql> SELECT score, REPEAT('*',COUNT(score)) AS occurrences
    -> FROM testscore GROUP BY score;
+-------+-------------+
| score | occurrences |
+-------+-------------+
|     4 | **          |
|     5 | *           |
|     6 | ****        |
|     7 | ****        |
|     8 | **          |
|     9 | *****       |
|    10 | **          |
+-------+-------------+
```

To chart the relative frequency distribution instead, use the percentage values:

```
mysql> SELECT @n := COUNT(score) FROM testscore;
mysql> SELECT score, REPEAT('*',(COUNT(score)*100)/@n) AS percent
    -> FROM testscore GROUP BY score;
+-------+----------------------------+
| score | percent                    |
+-------+----------------------------+
|     4 | *********                  |
|     5 | *****                      |
|     6 | *******************        |
|     7 | *******************        |
|     8 | *********                  |
|     9 | ************************   |
|    10 | *********                  |
+-------+----------------------------+
```

The ASCII chart method is fairly crude, obviously, but it's a quick way to get a picture of the distribution of observations, and it requires no other tools.

If you generate a frequency distribution for a range of categories where some of the categories are not represented in your observations, the missing categories will not appear in the output. To force each category to be displayed, use a reference table and a LEFT JOIN (a technique discussed in Recipe 12.9). For the testscore table, the possible scores range from 0 to 10, so a reference table should contain each of those values:

```
mysql> CREATE TABLE ref (score INT);
mysql> INSERT INTO ref (score)
    -> VALUES(0),(1),(2),(3),(4),(5),(6),(7),(8),(9),(10);
```

Then join the reference table to the test scores to generate the frequency distribution:

```
mysql> SELECT ref.score, COUNT(testscore.score) AS occurrences
    -> FROM ref LEFT JOIN testscore ON ref.score = testscore.score
    -> GROUP BY ref.score;
+-------+-------------+
| score | occurrences |
+-------+-------------+
|     0 |           0 |
|     1 |           0 |
|     2 |           0 |
|     3 |           0 |
|     4 |           2 |
|     5 |           1 |
|     6 |           4 |
|     7 |           4 |
|     8 |           2 |
|     9 |           5 |
|    10 |           2 |
+-------+-------------+
```

This distribution includes rows for scores 0 through 3, none of which appear in the frequency distribution shown earlier.

The same principle applies to relative frequency distributions:

```
mysql> SELECT @n := COUNT(score) FROM testscore;
mysql> SELECT ref.score, (COUNT(testscore.score)*100)/@n AS percent
    -> FROM ref LEFT JOIN testscore ON ref.score = testscore.score
    -> GROUP BY ref.score;
+-------+---------+
| score | percent |
+-------+---------+
|     0 |       0 |
|     1 |       0 |
|     2 |       0 |
|     3 |       0 |
|     4 |      10 |
|     5 |       5 |
|     6 |      20 |
|     7 |      20 |
|     8 |      10 |
|     9 |      25 |
|    10 |      10 |
+-------+---------+
```

13.4 Counting Missing Values

Problem

A set of observations is incomplete. You want to find out how much so.

Solution

Count the number of NULL values in the set.

Discussion

Values can be missing from a set of observations for any number of reasons: A test may not yet have been administered, something may have gone wrong during the test that requires invalidating the observation, and so forth. You can represent such observations in a dataset as NULL values to signify that they're missing or otherwise invalid, then use summary queries to characterize the completeness of the dataset.

If a table t contains values to be summarized along a single dimension, a simple summary will do to characterize the missing values. Suppose t looks like this:

```
mysql> SELECT subject, score FROM t ORDER BY subject;
+---------+-------+
| subject | score |
+---------+-------+
|       1 |    38 |
|       2 |  NULL |
|       3 |    47 |
|       4 |  NULL |
|       5 |    37 |
|       6 |    45 |
|       7 |    54 |
|       8 |  NULL |
|       9 |    40 |
|      10 |    49 |
+---------+-------+
```

COUNT(*) counts the total number of rows and COUNT(score) counts only the number of non-missing scores. The difference between the two is the number of missing scores, and that difference in relation to the total provides the percentage of missing scores. These calculations are expressed as follows:

```
mysql> SELECT COUNT(*) AS 'n (total)',
    -> COUNT(score) AS 'n (non-missing)',
    -> COUNT(*) - COUNT(score) AS 'n (missing)',
    -> ((COUNT(*) - COUNT(score)) * 100) / COUNT(*) AS '% missing'
    -> FROM t;
+-----------+-----------------+-------------+-----------+
| n (total) | n (non-missing) | n (missing) | % missing |
+-----------+-----------------+-------------+-----------+
|        10 |               7 |           3 |     30.00 |
+-----------+-----------------+-------------+-----------+
```

As an alternative to counting NULL values as the difference between counts, you can count them directly using SUM(ISNULL(score)). The ISNULL() function returns 1 if its argument is NULL, zero otherwise:

```
mysql> SELECT COUNT(*) AS 'n (total)',
    -> COUNT(score) AS 'n (non-missing)',
    -> SUM(ISNULL(score)) AS 'n (missing)',
    -> (SUM(ISNULL(score)) * 100) / COUNT(*) AS '% missing'
    -> FROM t;
+-----------+-----------------+-------------+-----------+
| n (total) | n (non-missing) | n (missing) | % missing |
+-----------+-----------------+-------------+-----------+
|        10 |               7 |           3 |     30.00 |
+-----------+-----------------+-------------+-----------+
```

If values are arranged in groups, occurrences of NULL values can be assessed on a per-group basis. Suppose t contains scores for subjects that are distributed among conditions for two factors A and B, each of which has two levels:

```
mysql> SELECT subject, A, B, score FROM t ORDER BY subject;
+---------+------+------+-------+
| subject | A    | B    | score |
+---------+------+------+-------+
|       1 |    1 |    1 |    18 |
|       2 |    1 |    1 |  NULL |
|       3 |    1 |    1 |    23 |
|       4 |    1 |    1 |    24 |
|       5 |    1 |    2 |    17 |
|       6 |    1 |    2 |    23 |
|       7 |    1 |    2 |    29 |
|       8 |    1 |    2 |    32 |
|       9 |    2 |    1 |    17 |
|      10 |    2 |    1 |  NULL |
|      11 |    2 |    1 |  NULL |
|      12 |    2 |    1 |    25 |
|      13 |    2 |    2 |  NULL |
|      14 |    2 |    2 |    33 |
|      15 |    2 |    2 |    34 |
|      16 |    2 |    2 |    37 |
+---------+------+------+-------+
```

In this case, the query uses a GROUP BY clause to produce a summary for each combination of conditions:

```
mysql> SELECT A, B, COUNT(*) AS 'n (total)',
    -> COUNT(score) AS 'n (non-missing)',
    -> COUNT(*) - COUNT(score) AS 'n (missing)',
    -> ((COUNT(*) - COUNT(score)) * 100) / COUNT(*) AS '% missing'
    -> FROM t
    -> GROUP BY A, B;
+------+------+-----------+-----------------+-------------+-----------+
| A    | B    | n (total) | n (non-missing) | n (missing) | % missing |
+------+------+-----------+-----------------+-------------+-----------+
|    1 |    1 |         4 |               3 |           1 |     25.00 |
|    1 |    2 |         4 |               4 |           0 |      0.00 |
```

```
| 2 | 1 |         4 |               2 |             2 |    50.00 |
| 2 | 2 |         4 |               3 |             1 |    25.00 |
+------+------+-----------+-----------------+-------------+----------+
```

13.5   Calculating Linear Regressions or Correlation Coefficients

Problem

You want to calculate the least-squares regression line for two variables, or the correlation coefficient that expresses the strength of the relationship between them.

Solution

Apply summary functions to calculate the necessary terms.

Discussion

When the data values for two variables X and Y are stored in a database, the least-squares regression for them can be calculated easily using aggregate functions. The same is true for the correlation coefficient. The two calculations are actually fairly similar, and many terms for performing the computations are common to the two procedures.

Suppose you want to calculate a least-squares regression using the age and test score values for the observations in the testscore table:

```
mysql> SELECT age, score FROM testscore;
+-----+-------+
| age | score |
+-----+-------+
|   5 |     5 |
|   5 |     4 |
|   5 |     6 |
|   5 |     7 |
|   6 |     8 |
|   6 |     9 |
|   6 |     4 |
|   6 |     6 |
|   7 |     8 |
|   7 |     6 |
|   7 |     9 |
|   7 |     7 |
|   8 |     9 |
|   8 |     6 |
|   8 |     7 |
|   8 |    10 |
|   9 |     9 |
|   9 |     7 |
```

```
|   9 |    10 |
|   9 |     9 |
+-----+-------+
```

A regression line is expressed as follows, where a and b are the intercept and slope of the line:

```
Y = bX + a
```

Letting age be X and score be Y, begin by computing the terms needed for the correlation equation. These include the number of observations, the means, sums, and sums of squares for each variable, and the sum of the products of each variable:[*]

```
mysql> SELECT
    -> @n := COUNT(score) AS N,
    -> @meanX := AVG(age) AS "X mean",
    -> @sumX := SUM(age) AS "X sum",
    -> @sumXX := SUM(age*age) "X sum of squares",
    -> @meanY := AVG(score) AS "Y mean",
    -> @sumY := SUM(score) AS "Y sum",
    -> @sumYY := SUM(score*score) "Y sum of square",
    -> @sumXY := SUM(age*score) AS "X*Y sum"
    -> FROM testscore\G
*************************** 1. row ***************************
            N: 20
       X mean: 7.0000
        X sum: 140
X sum of squares: 1020
       Y mean: 7.3000
        Y sum: 146
Y sum of square: 1130
      X*Y sum: 1053
```

From those terms, the regression slope and intercept are calculated as follows:

```
mysql> SELECT
    -> @b := (@n*@sumXY - @sumX*@sumY) / (@n*@sumXX - @sumX*@sumX)
    -> AS slope;
+-------+
| slope |
+-------+
| 0.775 |
+-------+
mysql> SELECT @a :=
    -> (@meanY - @b*@meanX)
    -> AS intercept;
+-----------+
| intercept |
+-----------+
|     1.875 |
+-----------+
```

---

[*] You can see where these terms come from by consulting any standard statistics text.

The regression equation then is:

```
mysql> SELECT CONCAT('Y = ',@b,'X + ',@a) AS 'least-squares regression';
+--------------------------+
| least-squares regression |
+--------------------------+
| Y = 0.775X + 1.875       |
+--------------------------+
```

To compute the correlation coefficient, many of the same terms are used:

```
mysql> SELECT
    -> (@n*@sumXY - @sumX*@sumY)
    -> / SQRT((@n*@sumXX - @sumX*@sumX) * (@n*@sumYY - @sumY*@sumY))
    -> AS correlation;
+------------------+
| correlation      |
+------------------+
| 0.61173620442199 |
+------------------+
```

13.6   Generating Random Numbers

Problem

You need a source of random numbers.

Solution

Invoke MySQL's RAND( ) function.

Discussion

MySQL has a RAND( ) function that can be invoked to produce random numbers between 0 and 1:

```
mysql> SELECT RAND(), RAND(), RAND();
+------------------+------------------+------------------+
| RAND( )          | RAND( )          | RAND( )          |
+------------------+------------------+------------------+
| 0.31466114177803 | 0.89354679723601 | 0.52375059157959 |
+------------------+------------------+------------------+
```

When invoked with an integer argument, RAND( ) uses that value to seed the random number generator. Each time you seed the generator with a given value, RAND( ) will produce a repeatable series of numbers:

```
mysql> SELECT RAND(1), RAND(), RAND();
+------------------+------------------+------------------+
| RAND(1)          | RAND( )          | RAND( )          |
+------------------+------------------+------------------+
| 0.18109050223705 | 0.75023211143001 | 0.20788908117254 |
+------------------+------------------+------------------+
```

```
mysql> SELECT RAND(20000000), RAND(), RAND();
+------------------+-------------------+------------------+
| RAND(20000000)   | RAND()            | RAND()           |
+------------------+-------------------+------------------+
| 0.24628307879556 | 0.020315642487552 | 0.36272900678472 |
+------------------+-------------------+------------------+
mysql> SELECT RAND(1), RAND(), RAND();
+------------------+-------------------+------------------+
| RAND(1)          | RAND()            | RAND()           |
+------------------+-------------------+------------------+
| 0.18109050223705 | 0.75023211143001  | 0.20788908117254 |
+------------------+-------------------+------------------+
mysql> SELECT RAND(20000000), RAND(), RAND();
+------------------+-------------------+------------------+
| RAND(20000000)   | RAND()            | RAND()           |
+------------------+-------------------+------------------+
| 0.24628307879556 | 0.020315642487552 | 0.36272900678472 |
+------------------+-------------------+------------------+
```

If you want to seed RAND( ) randomly, pick a seed value based on a source of entropy. Possible sources are the current timestamp or connection identifier, alone or perhaps in combination:

```
mysql> SELECT RAND(UNIX_TIMESTAMP()) AS rand1,
    -> RAND(CONNECTION_ID()) AS rand2,
    -> RAND(UNIX_TIMESTAMP()+CONNECTION_ID()) AS rand3;
+------------------+-------------------+------------------+
| rand1            | rand2             | rand3            |
+------------------+-------------------+------------------+
| 0.50452774158169 | 0.18113064782799  | 0.50456789089792 |
+------------------+-------------------+------------------+
```

However, it's probably better to use other seed value sources if you have them. For example, if your system has a *dev/random* or */dev/urandom* device, you can read the device and use it to generate a value for seeding RAND( ).

13.7   Randomizing a Set of Rows

Problem

You want to randomize a set of rows or values.

Solution

Use ORDER BY RAND( ).

Discussion

MySQL's RAND( ) function can be used to randomize the order in which a query returns its rows. Somewhat paradoxically, this randomization is achieved by adding an ORDER BY clause to the query. The technique is roughly equivalent to a spreadsheet randomization method. Suppose you have a set of values in a spreadsheet that looks like this:

```
Patrick
Penelope
Pertinax
Polly
```

To place these in random order, first add another column that contains randomly chosen numbers:

```
Patrick    .73
Penelope   .37
Pertinax   .16
Polly      .48
```

Then sort the rows according to the values of the random numbers:

```
Pertinax   .16
Penelope   .37
Polly      .48
Patrick    .73
```

At this point, the original values have been placed in random order, because the effect of sorting the random numbers is to randomize the values associated with them. To re-randomize the values, choose another set of random numbers and sort the rows again.

In MySQL, a similar effect is achieved by associating a set of random numbers with a query result and sorting the result by those numbers. For MySQL 3.23.2 and up, this is done with an ORDER BY RAND( ) clause:

```
mysql> SELECT name FROM t ORDER BY RAND();
+----------+
| name     |
+----------+
| Pertinax |
| Penelope |
| Patrick  |
| Polly    |
+----------+
mysql> SELECT name FROM t ORDER BY RAND();
+----------+
| name     |
+----------+
| Patrick  |
| Pertinax |
| Penelope |
| Polly    |
+----------+
```

How Random Is RAND()?

Does the RAND() function generate evenly distributed numbers? Check it out for your-self with the following Python script, *rand_test.py*, from the *stats* directory of the recipes distribution. It uses RAND() to generate random numbers and constructs a fre-quency distribution from them, using .1-sized categories. This provides a means of assessing how evenly distributed the values are.

```
#! /usr/bin/python
# rand_test.pl - create a frequency distribution of RAND() values.
# This provides a test of the randomness of RAND().

# Method is to draw random numbers in the range from 0 to 1.0,
# and count how many of them occur in .1-sized intervals (0 up
# to .1, .1 up to .2, ..., .9 up *through* 1.0).

import sys
sys.path.insert (0, "/usr/local/apache/lib/python")
import MySQLdb
import Cookbook

npicks = 1000        # number of times to pick a number

bucket = [0] * 10

conn = Cookbook.connect ()
cursor = conn.cursor ()

for i in range (0, npicks):
    cursor.execute ("SELECT RAND()")
    (val,) = cursor.fetchone ()
    slot = int (val * 10)
    if slot > 9:
        slot = 9        # put 1.0 in last slot
    bucket[slot] = bucket[slot] + 1

cursor.close ()
conn.close ()

# Print the resulting frequency distribution

for slot in range (0, 9):
    print "%2d  %d" % (slot+1, bucket[slot])

sys.exit (0)
```

The *stats* directory also contains equivalent scripts in other languages.

For versions of MySQL older than 3.23.2, ORDER BY clauses cannot refer to expressions, so you cannot use RAND() there (see Recipe 6.3). As a workaround, add a column of random numbers to the column output list, alias it, and refer to the alias for sorting:

```
mysql> SELECT name, name*0+RAND() AS rand_num FROM t ORDER BY rand_num;
+----------+--------------------+
| name     | rand_num           |
+----------+--------------------+
| Penelope | 0.372227413926485  |
| Patrick  | 0.431537678867148  |
| Pertinax | 0.566524063764628  |
| Polly    | 0.715938107777329  |
+----------+--------------------+
```

Note that the expression for the random number column is name*0+RAND(), not just RAND(). If you try using the latter, the pre-3.23 MySQL optimizer notices that the column contains only a function, assumes that the function returns a constant value for each row, and optimizes the corresponding ORDER BY clause out of existence. As a result, no sorting is done. The workaround is to fool the optimizer by adding extra factors to the expression that don't change its value, but make the column look like a non-constant. The query just shown illustrates one easy way to do this: Take any column name, multiply it by zero, and add the result to RAND(). Granted, it may seem a little strange to use name in a mathematical expression, because that column's values aren't numeric. That doesn't matter; MySQL sees the * multiplication operator and performs a string-to-number conversion of the name values before the multiply operation. The important thing is that the result of the multiplication is zero, which means that name*0+RAND() has the same value as RAND().

Applications for randomizing a set of rows include any scenario that uses selection without replacement (choosing each item from a set of items, until there are no more items left). Some examples of this are:

- Determining the starting order for participants in an event. List the participants in a table and select them in random order.

- Assigning starting lanes or gates to participants in a race. List the lanes in a table and select a random lane order.

- Choosing the order in which to present a set of quiz questions.

- Shuffling a deck of cards. Represent each card by a row in a table and shuffle the deck by selecting the rows in random order. Deal them one by one until the deck is exhausted.

To use the last example as an illustration, let's implement a card deck shuffling algorithm. Shuffling and dealing cards is randomization plus selection without replacement: each card is dealt once before any is dealt twice; when the deck is used up, it is reshuffled to re-randomize it for a new dealing order. Within a program, this task can be performed with MySQL using a table deck that has 52 rows, assuming a set of cards with each combination of 13 face values and 4 suits:

- Select the entire table and store it into an array.
- Each time a card is needed, take the next element from the array.
- When the array is exhausted, all the cards have been dealt. "Reshuffle" the table to generate a new card order.

Setting up the deck table is a tedious task if you insert the 52 card records by writing out all the INSERT statements manually. The deck contents can be generated more easily in combinatorial fashion within a program by generating each pairing of face value with suit. Here's some PHP code that creates a deck table with face and suit columns, then populates the table using nested loops to generate the pairings for the INSERT statements:

```
mysql_query ("
        CREATE TABLE deck
        (
            face    ENUM('A', 'K', 'Q', 'J', '10', '9', '8',
                         '7', '6', '5', '4', '3', '2') NOT NULL,
            suit    ENUM('hearts', 'diamonds', 'clubs', 'spades') NOT NULL
        )", $conn_id)
    or die ("Cannot issue CREATE TABLE statement\n");

$face_array = array ("A", "K", "Q", "J", "10", "9", "8",
                     "7", "6", "5", "4", "3", "2");
$suit_array = array ("hearts", "diamonds", "clubs", "spades");

# insert a "card" into the deck for each combination of suit and face

reset ($face_array);
while (list ($index, $face) = each ($face_array))
{
    reset ($suit_array);
    while (list ($index2, $suit) = each ($suit_array))
    {
        mysql_query ("INSERT INTO deck (face,suit) VALUES('$face','$suit')",
                     $conn_id)
            or die ("Cannot insert card into deck\n");
    }
}
```

Shuffling the cards is a matter of issuing this statement:

```
SELECT face, suit FROM deck ORDER BY RAND();
```

To do that and store the results in an array within a script, write a shuffle_deck() function that issues the query and returns the resulting values in an array (again shown in PHP):

```
function shuffle_deck ($conn_id)
{
    $query = "SELECT face, suit FROM deck ORDER BY RAND()";
```

```
$result_id = mysql_query ($query, $conn_id)
    or die ("Cannot retrieve cards from deck\n");
$card = array ();
while ($obj = mysql_fetch_object ($result_id))
    $card[] = $obj;      # add card record to end of $card array
mysql_free_result ($result_id);
return ($card);
}
```

Deal the cards by keeping a counter that ranges from 0 to 51 to indicate which card to select. When the counter reaches 52, the deck is exhausted and should be shuffled again.

13.8 Selecting Random Items from a Set of Rows

Problem

You want to pick an item or items randomly from a set of values.

Solution

Randomize the values, then pick the first one (or the first few, if you need more than one).

Discussion

When a set of items is stored in MySQL, you can choose one at random as follows:

- Select the items in the set in random order, using ORDER BY RAND( ) as described in Recipe 13.7.
- Add LIMIT 1 to the query to pick the first item.

For example, a simple simulation of tossing a die can be performed by creating a die table containing rows with values from 1 to 6 corresponding to the six faces of a die cube, then picking rows from it at random:

```
mysql> SELECT n FROM die ORDER BY RAND() LIMIT 1;
+------+
| n    |
+------+
|    6 |
+------+
mysql> SELECT n FROM die ORDER BY RAND() LIMIT 1;
+------+
| n    |
+------+
|    4 |
+------+
```

```
mysql> SELECT n FROM die ORDER BY RAND() LIMIT 1;
+------+
| n    |
+------+
|    5 |
+------+
mysql> SELECT n FROM die ORDER BY RAND() LIMIT 1;
+------+
| n    |
+------+
|    4 |
+------+
```

As you repeat this operation, you pick a random sequence of items from the set. This is a form of selection with replacement: An item is chosen from a pool of items, then returned to the pool for the next pick. Because items are replaced, it's possible to pick the same item multiple times when making successive choices this way. Other examples of selection with replacement include:

- Selecting a banner ad to display on a web page
- Picking a row for a "quote of the day" application.
- "Pick a card, any card" magic tricks that begin with a full deck of cards each time.

If you want to pick more than one item, change the LIMIT argument. For example, to draw five winning entries at random from a table named drawing that contains contest entries, use RAND() in combination with LIMIT:

```
SELECT * FROM drawing ORDER BY RAND() LIMIT 5;
```

A special case occurs when you're picking a single row from a table that you know contains a column with values in the range from 1 to n in unbroken sequence. Under these circumstances, it's possible to avoid performing an ORDER BY operation on the entire table by picking a random number in that range and selecting the matching row:

```
SET @id = FLOOR(RAND()*n)+1;
SELECT ... FROM tbl_name WHERE id = @id;
```

This will be much quicker than ORDER BY RAND() LIMIT 1 as the table size increases.

13.9 Assigning Ranks

Problem

You want to assign ranks to a set of values.

Solution

Decide on a ranking method, then put the values in the desired order and apply the method to them.

Discussion

Some kinds of statistical tests require assignment of ranks. I'll describe three ranking methods and show how each can be implemented using SQL variables. The examples assume that a table t contains the following scores, which are to be ranked with the values in descending order:

```
mysql> SELECT score FROM t ORDER BY score DESC;
+-------+
| score |
+-------+
|     5 |
|     4 |
|     4 |
|     3 |
|     2 |
|     2 |
|     2 |
|     1 |
+-------+
```

One type of ranking simply assigns each value its row number within the ordered set of values. To produce such rankings, keep track of the row number and use it for the current rank:

```
mysql> SET @rownum := 0;
mysql> SELECT @rownum := @rownum + 1 AS rank, score
    -> FROM t ORDER BY score DESC;
+------+-------+
| rank | score |
+------+-------+
|    1 |     5 |
|    2 |     4 |
|    3 |     4 |
|    4 |     3 |
|    5 |     2 |
|    6 |     2 |
|    7 |     2 |
|    8 |     1 |
+------+-------+
```

That kind of ranking doesn't take into account the possibility of ties (instances of values that are the same). A second ranking method does so by advancing the rank only when values change:

```
mysql> SET @rank = 0, @prev_val = NULL;
mysql> SELECT @rank := IF(@prev_val=score,@rank,@rank+1) AS rank,
    -> @prev_val := score AS score
    -> FROM t ORDER BY score DESC;
+------+-------+
| rank | score |
+------+-------+
|    1 |     5 |
```

```
| 2 |    4 |
| 2 |    4 |
| 3 |    3 |
| 4 |    2 |
| 4 |    2 |
| 4 |    2 |
| 5 |    1 |
+------+-------+
```

A third ranking method is something of a combination of the other two methods. It ranks values by row number, except when ties occur. In that case, the tied values each get a rank equal to the row number of the first of the values. To implement this method, keep track of the row number and the previous value, advancing the rank to the current row number when the value changes:

```
mysql> SET @rownum = 0, @rank = 0, @prev_val = NULL;
mysql> SELECT @rownum := @rownum + 1 AS row,
    -> @rank := IF(@prev_val!=score,@rownum,@rank) AS rank,
    -> @prev_val := score AS score
    -> FROM t ORDER BY score DESC;
+------+------+-------+
| row  | rank | score |
+------+------+-------+
|    1 |    1 |     5 |
|    2 |    2 |     4 |
|    3 |    2 |     4 |
|    4 |    4 |     3 |
|    5 |    5 |     2 |
|    6 |    5 |     2 |
|    7 |    5 |     2 |
|    8 |    8 |     1 |
+------+------+-------+
```

Ranks are easy to assign within a program as well. For example, the following PHP fragment ranks the scores in t using the third ranking method:

```
$result_id = mysql_query ("SELECT score FROM t ORDER BY score DESC", $conn_id)
                or die ("Cannot select scores\n");
$rownum = 0;
$rank = 0;
unset ($prev_score);
print ("Row\tRank\tScore\n");
while (list ($score) = mysql_fetch_row ($result_id))
{
    ++$rownum;
    if ($rownum == 1 || $prev_score != $score)
        $rank = $rownum;
    print ("$rownum\t$rank\t$score\n");
    $prev_score = $score;
}
mysql_free_result ($result_id);
```

The third type of ranking is commonly used outside the realm of statistical methods. Recall that in Recipe 3.18, we used a table al_winner that contains the top 15 winning pitchers in the American League for 2001:

```
mysql> SELECT name, wins FROM al_winner ORDER BY wins DESC, name;
+----------------+------+
| name           | wins |
+----------------+------+
| Mulder, Mark   |   21 |
| Clemens, Roger |   20 |
| Moyer, Jamie   |   20 |
| Garcia, Freddy |   18 |
| Hudson, Tim    |   18 |
| Abbott, Paul   |   17 |
| Mays, Joe      |   17 |
| Mussina, Mike  |   17 |
| Sabathia, C.C. |   17 |
| Zito, Barry    |   17 |
| Buehrle, Mark  |   16 |
| Milton, Eric   |   15 |
| Pettitte, Andy |   15 |
| Radke, Brad    |   15 |
| Sele, Aaron    |   15 |
+----------------+------+
```

These pitchers can be assigned ranks using the third method as follows:

```
mysql> SET @rownum = 0, @rank = 0, @prev_val = NULL;
mysql> SELECT @rownum := @rownum + 1 AS row,
    -> @rank := IF(@prev_val!=wins,@rownum,@rank) AS rank,
    -> name,
    -> @prev_val := wins AS wins
    -> FROM al_winner ORDER BY wins DESC;
+------+------+----------------+------+
| row  | rank | name           | wins |
+------+------+----------------+------+
|    1 |    1 | Mulder, Mark   |   21 |
|    2 |    2 | Clemens, Roger |   20 |
|    3 |    2 | Moyer, Jamie   |   20 |
|    4 |    4 | Garcia, Freddy |   18 |
|    5 |    4 | Hudson, Tim    |   18 |
|    6 |    6 | Abbott, Paul   |   17 |
|    7 |    6 | Mays, Joe      |   17 |
|    8 |    6 | Mussina, Mike  |   17 |
|    9 |    6 | Sabathia, C.C. |   17 |
|   10 |    6 | Zito, Barry    |   17 |
|   11 |   11 | Buehrle, Mark  |   16 |
|   12 |   12 | Milton, Eric   |   15 |
|   13 |   12 | Pettitte, Andy |   15 |
|   14 |   12 | Radke, Brad    |   15 |
|   15 |   12 | Sele, Aaron    |   15 |
+------+------+----------------+------+
```

## CHAPTER 14

Handling Duplicates

14.0 Introduction

Tables or result sets sometimes contain duplicate records. In some cases this is acceptable. For example, if you conduct a web poll that records dates and client IP numbers along with the votes, duplicate records may be allowable, because it's possible for large numbers of votes to appear to originate from the same IP number for an Internet service that routes traffic from its customers through a single proxy host. In other cases, duplicates will be unacceptable, and you'll want to take steps to avoid them. Operations related to handling of duplicate records include the following:

- Counting the number of duplicates to determine whether they occur and to what extent.

- Identifying duplicated values (or the records containing them) so you can see what they are and where they occur.

- Eliminating duplicates to ensure that each record is unique. This may involve removing rows from a table to leave only unique records. Or it may involve selecting a result set in such a way that no duplicates appear in the output. (For example, to display a list of the states in which you have customers, you probably wouldn't want a long list of state names from all customer records. A list showing each state name only once suffices and is easier to understand.)

- Preventing duplicates from being created within a table in the first place. If each record in a table is intended to represent a single entity (such as a person, an item in a catalog, or a specific observation in an experiment), the occurrence of duplicates presents significant difficulties in using it that way. Duplicates make it impossible to refer to some records in the table unambiguously, so it's best to make sure duplicates never occur.

Several tools are at your disposal for dealing with duplicate records. These can be chosen according to the objective you're trying to achieve:

- Creating a table to include a unique index will prevent duplicates from being added to the table. MySQL will use the index to enforce the requirement that each record in the table contains a unique key in the indexed column or columns.

- In conjunction with a unique index, the INSERT IGNORE and REPLACE statements allow you to handle insertion of duplicate records gracefully without generating errors. For bulk-loading operations, the same options are available in the form of the IGNORE or REPLACE modifiers for the LOAD DATA statement.

- If you need to determine whether or not a table contains duplicates, GROUP BY categorizes rows into groups, and COUNT( ) shows how many rows are in each group. These are described in Chapter 7 in the context of producing summaries, but they're useful for duplicate counting and identification as well. After all, a counting summary is essentially an operation that groups values into categories to determine how frequently each occurs.

- SELECT DISTINCT is useful for removing duplicate rows from a result set to leave only unique records. Adding a unique index to a table can remove duplicates that are present in the table. If you determine that there are n identical records in a table, you can use DELETE ... LIMIT to eliminate $n-1$ instances from that specific set of rows.

This chapter describes how each of these techniques applies to duplicate identification and removal, but before proceeding further, I should define what "duplicate" means here. When people say "duplicate record," they may mean different things. For purposes of this chapter, one record is a duplicate of another if both rows contain the same values in columns that are supposed to distinguish them. Consider the following table:

```
mysql> SELECT * FROM person;
+------+-----------+------------+----------------+------+
| id   | last_name | first_name | address        | age  |
+------+-----------+------------+----------------+------+
|    1 | Smith     | Jim        | 428 Mill Road  |   36 |
|    2 | Smith     | Joan       | 428 Mill Road  |   36 |
|    3 | Smith     | Junior     | 428 Mill Road  |   12 |
+------+-----------+------------+----------------+------+
```

None of these records are duplicates if you compare rows using all the columns, because then the records contain the id and first_name columns, each of which happen to contain only unique values. However, if you look only at the last_name or address columns, all the records contain duplicated values. Lying between these extremes, a result set consisting of the age column contains a mix of unique and duplicated values.

Scripts related to the examples shown in this chapter are located in the *dups* directory of the recipes distribution. For scripts that create the tables used here, look in the *tables* directory.

14.1 Preventing Duplicates from Occurring in a Table

Problem

You want to prevent a table from ever containing duplicates, so that you won't have to worry about eliminating them later.

Solution

Use a PRIMARY KEY or a UNIQUE index.

Discussion

To make sure that records in a table are unique, some column or combination of columns must be required to contain unique values in each row. When this requirement is satisfied, you can refer to any record in the table unambiguously using its unique identifier. To make sure a table has this characteristic, include a PRIMARY KEY or UNIQUE index in the table structure when you create the table. The following table contains no such index, so it would allow duplicate records:

```
CREATE TABLE person
(
    last_name    CHAR(20),
    first_name   CHAR(20),
    address      CHAR(40)
);
```

To prevent multiple records with the same first and last name values from being created in this table, add a PRIMARY KEY to its definition. When you do this, it's also necessary to declare the indexed columns to be NOT NULL, because a PRIMARY KEY does not allow NULL values:

```
CREATE TABLE person
(
    last_name    CHAR(20) NOT NULL,
    first_name   CHAR(20) NOT NULL,
    address      CHAR(40),
    PRIMARY KEY (last_name, first_name)
);
```

The presence of a unique index in a table normally causes an error to occur if you insert a record into the table that duplicates an existing record in the column or columns that define the index. Recipe 14.2 discusses how to handle such errors or modify MySQL's duplicate-handling behavior.

Another way to enforce uniqueness is to add a UNIQUE index rather than a PRIMARY KEY to a table. The two types of indexes are identical, with the exception that a UNIQUE index can be created on columns that allow NULL values. For the person table, it's likely that you'd require both the first and last names to be filled in. If so, you'd still declare the columns as NOT NULL, and the following table declaration would be effectively equivalent to the preceding one:

```
CREATE TABLE person
(
    last_name   CHAR(20) NOT NULL,
    first_name  CHAR(20) NOT NULL,
    address     CHAR(40),
    UNIQUE (last_name, first_name)
);
```

If a UNIQUE index does happen to allow NULL values, NULL is special because it is the one value that can occur multiple times. The rationale for this is that it is not possible to know whether one unknown value is the same as another, so multiple unknown values are allowed.

It may of course be that you'd want the person table to reflect the real world, in which people do sometimes have the same name. In this case, you cannot set up a unique index based on the name columns, because duplicate names must be allowed. Instead, each person must be assigned some sort of unique identifier, which becomes the value that distinguishes one record from another. In MySQL, a common technique for this is the AUTO_INCREMENT column:

```
CREATE TABLE person
(
    id          INT UNSIGNED NOT NULL AUTO_INCREMENT,
    last_name   CHAR(20),
    first_name  CHAR(20),
    address     CHAR(40),
    PRIMARY KEY (id)
);
```

In this case, when you create a record with an id value of NULL, MySQL assigns that column a unique ID automatically. Another possibility is to assign identifiers externally and use those IDs as unique keys. For example, citizens in a given country might have unique taxpayer ID numbers. If so, those numbers can serve as the basis for a unique index:

```
CREATE TABLE person
(
    tax_id      INT UNSIGNED NOT NULL,
    last_name   CHAR(20),
```

```
    first_name  CHAR(20),
    address     CHAR(40),
    PRIMARY KEY (tax_id)
);
```

See Also

AUTO_INCREMENT columns are discussed further in Chapter 11.

14.2 Dealing with Duplicates at Record-Creation Time

Problem

You've created a table with a unique index to prevent duplicate values in the indexed column or columns. But this results in an error if you attempt to insert a duplicate record, and you want to avoid having to deal with such errors.

Solution

One approach is to just ignore the error. Another is to use either an INSERT IGNORE or REPLACE statement, each of which modifies MySQL's duplicate-handling behavior. For bulk-loading operations, LOAD DATA has modifiers that allow you to specify how to handle duplicates.

Discussion

By default, MySQL generates an error when you insert a record that duplicates an existing unique key. For example, you'll see the following result if the person table contains a unique index on the last_name and first_name columns:

```
mysql> INSERT INTO person (last_name, first_name)
    -> VALUES('X1','Y1');
Query OK, 1 row affected (0.00 sec)
mysql> INSERT INTO person (last_name, first_name)
    -> VALUES('X1','Y1');
ERROR 1062 at line 1: Duplicate entry 'X1-Y1' for key 1
```

If you're issuing the statements from the *mysql* program interactively, you can simply say, "Okay, that didn't work," ignore the error, and continue. But if you write a program to insert the records, an error may terminate the program. One way to avoid this is to modify the program's error-handling behavior to trap the error and then ignore it. See Recipe 2.2 for information about error-handling techniques.

If you want to prevent the error from occurring in the first place, you might consider using a two-query method to solve the duplicate-record problem: issue a SELECT to see if the record is already present, followed by an INSERT if it's not. But that doesn't really work. Another client might insert the same record after the SELECT and before the INSERT, in which case the error would still occur. To make sure that doesn't happen, you could use a transaction or lock the tables, but then you're up from two statements to four. MySQL provides two single-query solutions to the problem of handling duplicate records:

- Use INSERT IGNORE rather than INSERT. If a record doesn't duplicate an existing record, MySQL inserts it as usual. If the record is a duplicate, the IGNORE keyword tells MySQL to discard it silently without generating an error:

```
mysql> INSERT IGNORE INTO person (last_name, first_name)
    -> VALUES('X2','Y2');
Query OK, 1 row affected (0.00 sec)
mysql> INSERT IGNORE INTO person (last_name, first_name)
    -> VALUES('X2','Y2');
Query OK, 0 rows affected (0.00 sec)
```

  The row count value indicates whether the record was inserted or ignored. From within a program, you can obtain this value by checking the rows-affected function provided by your API. (See Recipes 2.4 and 9.1.)

- Use REPLACE rather than INSERT. If the record is new, it's inserted just as with INSERT. If it's a duplicate, the new record replaces the old one:

```
mysql> REPLACE INTO person (last_name, first_name)
    -> VALUES('X3','Y3');
Query OK, 1 row affected (0.00 sec)
mysql> REPLACE INTO person (last_name, first_name)
    -> VALUES('X3','Y3');
Query OK, 2 rows affected (0.00 sec)
```

  The rows-affected value in the second case is 2 because the original record is deleted and the new record is inserted in its place.

INSERT IGNORE and REPLACE should be chosen according to the duplicate-handling behavior you want to effect. INSERT IGNORE keeps the first of a set of duplicated records and discards the rest. REPLACE keeps the last of a set of duplicates and kicks out any earlier ones. INSERT IGNORE is more efficient than REPLACE because it doesn't actually insert duplicates. Thus, it's most applicable when you just want to make sure a copy of a given record is present in a table. REPLACE, on the other hand, is often more appropriate for tables in which other non-key columns may need updating. Suppose you're maintaining a table named passtbl for a web application that contains email addresses and passwords and that is keyed by email address:

```
CREATE TABLE passtbl
(
    email       CHAR(60) NOT NULL,
    password    CHAR(20) BINARY NOT NULL,
    PRIMARY KEY (email)
);
```

How do you create records for new users, and change passwords for existing users? Without REPLACE, creating a new user and changing an existing user's password must be handled differently. A typical algorithm for handling record maintenance might look like this:

- Issue a SELECT to see if a record already exists with a given email value.
- If no such record exists, add a new one with INSERT.
- If the record does exist, update it with UPDATE.

All of that must be performed within a transaction or with the tables locked to prevent other users from changing the tables while you're using them. With REPLACE, you can simplify both cases to the same single-statement operation:

```
REPLACE INTO passtbl (email,password) VALUES(address,passval);
```

If no record with the given email address exists, MySQL creates a new one. If a record does exist, MySQL replaces it; in effect, this updates the password column of the record associated with the address.

INSERT IGNORE and REPLACE have the benefit of eliminating overhead that might otherwise be required for a transaction. But this benefit comes at the price of portability, because both are MySQL-specific statements. If portability is a high priority, you might prefer to stick with a transactional approach.

For bulk-load operations in which you use the LOAD DATA statement to load a set of records from a file into a table, duplicate-record handling can be controlled using the statement's IGNORE and REPLACE modifiers. These produce behavior analogous to that of the INSERT IGNORE and REPLACE statements. See Recipe 10.7 for more information.

14.3   Counting and Identifying Duplicates

Problem

You want to find out if a table contains duplicates, and to what extent they occur. Or you want to see the records that contain the duplicated values.

Solution

Use a counting summary that looks for and displays duplicated values. To see the records in which the duplicated values occur, join the summary to the original table to display the matching records.

Discussion

Suppose that your web site includes a sign-up page that allows visitors to add themselves to your mailing list to receive periodic product catalog mailings. But you forgot to include a unique index in the table when you created it, and now you suspect that some people are signed up multiple times. Perhaps they forgot they were already on the list, or perhaps people added friends to the list who were already signed up. Either way, the result of the duplicate records is that you mail out duplicate catalogs. This is an additional expense to you, and it annoys the recipients. This section discusses how to find out if duplicates are present in a table, how prevalent they are, and how to display the duplicated records. (For tables that do contain duplicates, Recipe 14.6 describes how to eliminate them.)

To determine whether or not duplicates occur in a table, use a counting summary, a topic covered in Chapter 7. Summary techniques can be applied to identifying and counting duplicates by grouping records with GROUP BY and counting the rows in each group using COUNT( ). For the examples, assume that catalog recipients are listed in a table named cat_mailing that has the following contents:

```
mysql> SELECT * FROM cat_mailing;
+-----------+-------------+--------------------------+
| last_name | first_name  | street                   |
+-----------+-------------+--------------------------+
| Isaacson  | Jim         | 515 Fordam St., Apt. 917 |
| Baxter    | Wallace     | 57 3rd Ave.              |
| McTavish  | Taylor      | 432 River Run            |
| Pinter    | Marlene     | 9 Sunset Trail           |
| BAXTER    | WALLACE     | 57 3rd Ave.              |
| Brown     | Bartholomew | 432 River Run            |
| Pinter    | Marlene     | 9 Sunset Trail           |
| Baxter    | Wallace     | 57 3rd Ave., Apt 102     |
+-----------+-------------+--------------------------+
```

Suppose you want to define "duplicate" using the last_name and first_name columns. That is, recipients with the same name are assumed to be the same person. (This is a simplification, of course.) The following queries are typical of those used to characterize the table and to assess the existence and extent of duplicate values:

- The total number of rows in the table:

```
mysql> SELECT COUNT(*) AS rows FROM cat_mailing;
+------+
| rows |
+------+
|    8 |
+------+
```

- The number of distinct names:

```
mysql> SELECT COUNT(DISTINCT last_name, first_name) AS 'distinct names'
    -> FROM cat_mailing;
+----------------+
| distinct names |
+----------------+
|              5 |
+----------------+
```

- The number of rows containing duplicated names:

```
mysql> SELECT COUNT(*) - COUNT(DISTINCT last_name, first_name)
    -> AS 'duplicate names'
    -> FROM cat_mailing;
+-----------------+
| duplicate names |
+-----------------+
|               3 |
+-----------------+
```

- The fraction of the records that contain unique or non-unique names:

```
mysql> SELECT COUNT(DISTINCT last_name, first_name) / COUNT(*)
    -> AS 'unique',
    -> 1 - (COUNT(DISTINCT last_name, first_name) / COUNT(*))
    -> AS 'non-unique'
    -> FROM cat_mailing;
+--------+------------+
| unique | non-unique |
+--------+------------+
|   0.62 |       0.38 |
+--------+------------+
```

These queries help you characterize the extent of duplicates, but don't show you which values are duplicated. To see which names are duplicated in the cat_mailing table, use a summary query that displays the non-unique values along with the counts:

```
mysql> SELECT COUNT(*) AS repetitions, last_name, first_name
    -> FROM cat_mailing
    -> GROUP BY last_name, first_name
    -> HAVING repetitions > 1;
+-------------+-----------+------------+
| repetitions | last_name | first_name |
+-------------+-----------+------------+
|           3 | Baxter    | Wallace    |
|           2 | Pinter    | Marlene    |
+-------------+-----------+------------+
```

The query includes a HAVING clause that restricts the output to include only those names that occur more than once. (If you omit the clause, the summary lists unique names as well, which is useless when you're interested only in duplicates.) In general, to identify sets of values that are duplicated, do the following:

- Determine which columns contain the values that may be duplicated.
- List those columns in the column selection list, along with COUNT(*).
- List the columns in the GROUP BY clause as well.
- Add a HAVING clause that eliminates unique values by requiring group counts to be greater than one.

Queries constructed this way have the following form:

```
SELECT COUNT(*), column_list
FROM tbl_name
GROUP BY column_list
HAVING COUNT(*) > 1
```

It's easy to generate duplicate-finding queries like that within a program, given a table name and a nonempty set of column names. For example, here is a Perl function, make_dup_count_query(), that generates the proper query for finding and counting duplicated values in the specified columns:

```
sub make_dup_count_query
{
my ($tbl_name, @col_name) = @_;

    return (
        "SELECT COUNT(*)," . join (",", @col_name)
        . "\nFROM $tbl_name"
        . "\nGROUP BY " . join (",", @col_name)
        . "\nHAVING COUNT(*) > 1"
    );
}
```

make_dup_count_query() returns the query as a string. If you invoke it like this:

```
$str = make_dup_count_query ("cat_mailing", "last_name", "first_name");
```

The resulting value of $str is:

```
SELECT COUNT(*),last_name,first_name
FROM cat_mailing
GROUP BY last_name,first_name
HAVING COUNT(*) > 1
```

What you do with the query string is up to you. You can execute it from within the script that creates it, pass it to another program, or write it to a file for execution later. The *dups* directory of the recipes distribution contains a script named *dup_count.pl* that you can use to try out the function (as well as some translations into other languages). Later in this chapter, Recipe 14.6 uses the make_dup_count_query() function to implement a duplicate-removal technique.

Summary techniques are useful for assessing the existence of duplicates, how often they occur, and displaying which values are duplicated. But a summary in itself cannot display the entire content of the records that contain the duplicate values. (For example, the summaries shown thus far display counts of duplicated names in the cat_mailing table or the names themselves, but don't show the addresses associated with those names.) To see the original records containing the duplicate names, join the summary information to the table from which it's generated. The following example shows how to do this to display the cat_mailing records that contain duplicated names. The summary is written to a temporary table, which then is joined to the cat_mailing table to produce the records that match those names:

```
mysql> CREATE TABLE tmp
    -> SELECT COUNT(*) AS count, last_name, first_name
    -> FROM cat_mailing GROUP BY last_name, first_name HAVING count > 1;
mysql> SELECT cat_mailing.*
    -> FROM tmp, cat_mailing
    -> WHERE tmp.last_name = cat_mailing.last_name
    -> AND tmp.first_name = cat_mailing.first_name
    -> ORDER BY last_name, first_name;
+-----------+------------+----------------------+
| last_name | first_name | street               |
+-----------+------------+----------------------+
| Baxter    | Wallace    | 57 3rd Ave.          |
| BAXTER    | WALLACE    | 57 3rd Ave.          |
| Baxter    | Wallace    | 57 3rd Ave., Apt 102 |
| Pinter    | Marlene    | 9 Sunset Trail       |
| Pinter    | Marlene    | 9 Sunset Trail       |
+-----------+------------+----------------------+
```

Duplicate Identification and String Case Sensitivity

Non-binary strings that differ in lettercase are considered the same for comparison purposes. To consider them as distinct, use the BINARY keyword to make them case sensitive.

14.4   Eliminating Duplicates from a Query Result

Problem

You want to select rows in a query result in such a way that it contains no duplicates.

Solution

Use SELECT DISTINCT.

Discussion

Rows in query results sometimes contain duplicate rows. This is particularly common when you select only a subset of the columns in a table, because that reduces the amount of information available that might otherwise distinguish one row from another. To obtain only the unique rows in a result, eliminate the duplicates by adding the DISTINCT keyword. That tells MySQL to return only one instance of each set of column values. For example, if you select the name columns from the cat_mailing table without using DISTINCT, several duplicates occur:

```
mysql> SELECT last_name, first_name
    -> FROM cat_mailing ORDER BY last_name, first_name;
+-----------+-------------+
| last_name | first_name  |
+-----------+-------------+
| Baxter    | Wallace     |
| BAXTER    | WALLACE     |
| Baxter    | Wallace     |
| Brown     | Bartholomew |
| Isaacson  | Jim         |
| McTavish  | Taylor      |
| Pinter    | Marlene     |
| Pinter    | Marlene     |
+-----------+-------------+
```

With DISTINCT, the duplicates are eliminated:

```
mysql> SELECT DISTINCT last_name, first_name
    -> FROM cat_mailing ORDER BY last_name;
+-----------+-------------+
| last_name | first_name  |
+-----------+-------------+
| Baxter    | Wallace     |
| Brown     | Bartholomew |
| Isaacson  | Jim         |
| McTavish  | Taylor      |
| Pinter    | Marlene     |
+-----------+-------------+
```

An alternative to DISTINCT is to add a GROUP BY clause that names the columns you're selecting. This has the effect of removing duplicates and selecting only the unique combinations of values in the specified columns:

```
mysql> SELECT last_name, first_name FROM cat_mailing
    -> GROUP BY last_name, first_name;
+-----------+-------------+
| last_name | first_name  |
+-----------+-------------+
| Baxter    | Wallace     |
| Brown     | Bartholomew |
| Isaacson  | Jim         |
| McTavish  | Taylor      |
| Pinter    | Marlene     |
+-----------+-------------+
```

See Also

SELECT DISTINCT is discussed further in Recipe 7.4.

14.5 Eliminating Duplicates from a Self-Join Result

Problem

Self-joins often produce rows that are "near" duplicates—that is, rows that contain the same values but in different orders. Because of this, SELECT DISTINCT will not eliminate the duplicates.

Solution

Select column values in a specific order within rows to make rows with duplicate sets of values identical. Then you can use SELECT DISTINCT to remove duplicates. Alternatively, retrieve rows in such a way that near-duplicates are not even selected.

Discussion

Self-joins can produce rows that are duplicates in the sense that they contain the same values, yet are not identical. Consider the following query, which uses a self-join to find all pairs of states that joined the Union in the same year:

```
mysql> SELECT YEAR(s2.statehood) AS year, s1.name, s2.name
    -> FROM states AS s1, states AS s2
    -> WHERE YEAR(s1.statehood) = YEAR(s2.statehood)
    -> AND s1.name != s2.name
    -> ORDER BY year, s1.name, s2.name;
+------+---------------+---------------+
| year | name          | name          |
+------+---------------+---------------+
| 1787 | Delaware      | New Jersey    |
| 1787 | Delaware      | Pennsylvania  |
| 1787 | New Jersey    | Delaware      |
| 1787 | New Jersey    | Pennsylvania  |
| 1787 | Pennsylvania  | Delaware      |
| 1787 | Pennsylvania  | New Jersey    |
...
| 1912 | Arizona       | New Mexico    |
| 1912 | New Mexico    | Arizona       |
| 1959 | Alaska        | Hawaii        |
| 1959 | Hawaii        | Alaska        |
+------+---------------+---------------+
```

The condition in the WHERE clause that requires state pair names not to be identical eliminates the trivially true rows showing that each state joined the Union in the same year as itself. But each remaining pair of states still appears twice. For example, there is one row that lists Delaware and New Jersey, and another that lists New Jersey and Delaware. Each such pair of rows may be considered as effective duplicates because they contain the same values. However, because the values are not listed in the same order within the rows, they are not identical and you can't get rid of the duplicates by adding DISTINCT to the query.

One way to solve this problem is to make sure that state names are always listed in a specific order within a row. This can be done by selecting the names with a pair of expressions that place the lesser value first in the output column list:

```
IF(val1<val2,val1,val2) AS lesser_value,
IF(val1<val2,val2,val1) AS greater_value
```

Applying this technique to the state-pairs query yields the following result, where the expressions display state names in lexical order within each row:

```
mysql> SELECT YEAR(s2.statehood) AS year,
    -> IF(s1.name<s2.name,s1.name,s2.name) AS state1,
    -> IF(s1.name<s2.name,s2.name,s1.name) AS state2
    -> FROM states AS s1, states AS s2
    -> WHERE YEAR(s1.statehood) = YEAR(s2.statehood)
    -> AND s1.name != s2.name
    -> ORDER BY year, state1, state2;
+------+------------+--------------+
| year | state1     | state2       |
+------+------------+--------------+
| 1787 | Delaware   | New Jersey   |
| 1787 | Delaware   | New Jersey   |
| 1787 | Delaware   | Pennsylvania |
| 1787 | Delaware   | Pennsylvania |
| 1787 | New Jersey | Pennsylvania |
| 1787 | New Jersey | Pennsylvania |
...
| 1912 | Arizona    | New Mexico   |
| 1912 | Arizona    | New Mexico   |
| 1959 | Alaska     | Hawaii       |
| 1959 | Alaska     | Hawaii       |
+------+------------+--------------+
```

Duplicate rows are still present in the output, but now duplicate pairs are identical and the extra copies can be eliminated by adding DISTINCT to the query:

```
mysql> SELECT DISTINCT YEAR(s2.statehood) AS year,
    -> IF(s1.name<s2.name,s1.name,s2.name) AS state1,
    -> IF(s1.name<s2.name,s2.name,s1.name) AS state2
    -> FROM states AS s1, states AS s2
    -> WHERE YEAR(s1.statehood) = YEAR(s2.statehood)
    -> AND s1.name != s2.name
    -> ORDER BY year, state1, state2;
+------+------------+--------------+
| year | state1     | state2       |
+------+------------+--------------+
| 1787 | Delaware   | New Jersey   |
| 1787 | Delaware   | Pennsylvania |
| 1787 | New Jersey | Pennsylvania |
...
| 1912 | Arizona    | New Mexico   |
| 1959 | Alaska     | Hawaii       |
+------+------------+--------------+
```

An alternative approach to removing non-identical duplicates relies not so much on detecting and eliminating them as on selecting rows in such a way that only one row from each pair ever appears in the query result. This makes it unnecessary to reorder values within output rows or to use DISTINCT. For the state-pairs query, selecting only those rows where the first state name is lexically less than the second automatically eliminates rows where the names appear in the other order:[*]

```
mysql> SELECT YEAR(s2.statehood) AS year, s1.name, s2.name
    -> FROM states AS s1, states AS s2
    -> WHERE YEAR(s1.statehood) = YEAR(s2.statehood)
    -> AND s1.name < s2.name
    -> ORDER BY year, s1.name, s2.name;
+------+---------------+---------------+
| year | name          | name          |
+------+---------------+---------------+
| 1787 | Delaware      | New Jersey    |
| 1787 | Delaware      | Pennsylvania  |
| 1787 | New Jersey    | Pennsylvania  |
...
| 1912 | Arizona       | New Mexico    |
| 1959 | Alaska        | Hawaii        |
+------+---------------+---------------+
```

14.6 Eliminating Duplicates from a Table

Problem

You want to remove duplicate records from a table so that it contains only unique rows.

Solution

Select the unique rows from the table into a second table that you use to replace the original one. Or add a unique index to the table using ALTER TABLE, which will remove duplicates as it builds the index. Or use DELETE ... LIMIT n to remove all but one instance of a specific set of duplicate rows.

Discussion

If you forget to create a table with a unique index to prevent the occurrence of duplicates within the table, you may discover later that it's necessary to apply some sort of duplicate-removal technique. The cat_mailing table used in earlier sections is an example of this, because it contains several instances where the same person is listed multiple times.

---

[*] The same constraint also eliminates those rows where the state names are identical.

```
mysql> SELECT * FROM cat_mailing ORDER BY last_name, first_name;
+-----------+-------------+-------------------------+
| last_name | first_name  | street                  |
+-----------+-------------+-------------------------+
| Baxter    | Wallace     | 57 3rd Ave.             |
| BAXTER    | WALLACE     | 57 3rd Ave.             |
| Baxter    | Wallace     | 57 3rd Ave., Apt 102    |
| Brown     | Bartholomew | 432 River Run           |
| Isaacson  | Jim         | 515 Fordam St., Apt. 917|
| McTavish  | Taylor      | 432 River Run           |
| Pinter    | Marlene     | 9 Sunset Trail          |
| Pinter    | Marlene     | 9 Sunset Trail          |
+-----------+-------------+-------------------------+
```

The table contains redundant entries and it would be a good idea to remove them, to eliminate duplicate mailings and reduce postage costs. To do this, you have several options:

- Select the table's unique rows into another table, then use that table to replace the original one. The result is to remove the table's duplicates. This works when "duplicate" means "the entire row is the same as another."

- Add a unique index to the table using ALTER TABLE. This operation will remove duplicate rows based on the contents of the indexed columns.

- You can remove duplicates for a specific set of duplicate rows by using DELETE ... LIMIT *n* to remove all but one of the rows.

This section discusses each of these duplicate-removal methods. When you consider which of them to choose under various circumstances, note that the applicability of a given method to a specific problem often will be determined by two factors:

- Does the method require the table to have a unique index?

- If the columns in which duplicate values occur may contain NULL, will the method remove duplicate NULL values?

Removing Duplicates Using Table Replacement

One way to eliminate duplicates from a table is to select its unique records into a new table that has the same structure. Then replace the original table with the new one. If a row is considered to duplicate another only if the entire row is the same, you can use SELECT DISTINCT to select the unique rows:

```
mysql> CREATE TABLE tmp SELECT DISTINCT * FROM cat_mailing;
mysql> SELECT * FROM tmp ORDER BY last_name, first_name;
+-----------+-------------+-------------------------+
| last_name | first_name  | street                  |
+-----------+-------------+-------------------------+
| Baxter    | Wallace     | 57 3rd Ave.             |
| Baxter    | Wallace     | 57 3rd Ave., Apt 102    |
| Brown     | Bartholomew | 432 River Run           |
+-----------+-------------+-------------------------+
```

```
| Isaacson | Jim     | 515 Fordam St., Apt. 917 |
| McTavish | Taylor  | 432 River Run            |
| Pinter   | Marlene | 9 Sunset Trail           |
+----------+---------+--------------------------+
```

This method works in the absence of an index (though it might be slow for large tables), and for tables that contain duplicate NULL values, it will remove those duplicates. Note that this method considers the rows for Wallace Baxter that have slightly different street values to be distinct.

If duplicates are defined only with respect to a subset of the columns in the table, create a new table that has a unique index first, then select rows into it using INSERT IGNORE.

```
mysql> CREATE TABLE tmp (
    -> last_name CHAR(40) NOT NULL,
    -> first_name CHAR(40) NOT NULL,
    -> street CHAR(40) NOT NULL,
    -> PRIMARY KEY (last_name, first_name));
mysql> INSERT IGNORE INTO tmp SELECT * FROM cat_mailing;
mysql> SELECT * FROM tmp ORDER BY last_name, first_name;
+-----------+-------------+--------------------------+
| last_name | first_name  | street                   |
+-----------+-------------+--------------------------+
| Baxter    | Wallace     | 57 3rd Ave.              |
| Brown     | Bartholomew | 432 River Run            |
| Isaacson  | Jim         | 515 Fordam St., Apt. 917 |
| McTavish  | Taylor      | 432 River Run            |
| Pinter    | Marlene     | 9 Sunset Trail           |
+-----------+-------------+--------------------------+
```

The index prevents records with duplicate key values from being inserted into tmp, and IGNORE tells MySQL not to stop with an error if a duplicate is found. One shortcoming of this method is that if the indexed columns can contain NULL values, you must use a UNIQUE index rather than a PRIMARY KEY, in which case the index will not remove duplicate NULL keys. (UNIQUE indexes allow multiple NULL values.)

After creating the new table tmp that contains unique rows, use it to replace the original cat_mailing table. The effective result is that cat_mailing no longer will contain duplicates:

```
mysql> DROP TABLE cat_mailing;
mysql> ALTER TABLE tmp RENAME TO cat_mailing;
```

Removing Duplicates by Adding an Index

To remove duplicates from a table "in place," add a unique index to the table with ALTER TABLE, using the IGNORE keyword to tell it to discard records with duplicate key values during the index construction process. The original cat_mailing table looks like this without an index:

```
mysql> SELECT * FROM cat_mailing ORDER BY last_name, first_name;
+-----------+-------------+--------------------------+
| last_name | first_name  | street                   |
+-----------+-------------+--------------------------+
| Baxter    | Wallace     | 57 3rd Ave.              |
| BAXTER    | WALLACE     | 57 3rd Ave.              |
| Baxter    | Wallace     | 57 3rd Ave., Apt 102     |
| Brown     | Bartholomew | 432 River Run            |
| Isaacson  | Jim         | 515 Fordam St., Apt. 917 |
| McTavish  | Taylor      | 432 River Run            |
| Pinter    | Marlene     | 9 Sunset Trail           |
| Pinter    | Marlene     | 9 Sunset Trail           |
+-----------+-------------+--------------------------+
```

Add a unique index, then see what effect doing so has on the table contents:

```
mysql> ALTER IGNORE TABLE cat_mailing
    -> ADD PRIMARY KEY (last_name, first_name);
mysql> SELECT * FROM cat_mailing ORDER BY last_name, first_name;
+-----------+-------------+--------------------------+
| last_name | first_name  | street                   |
+-----------+-------------+--------------------------+
| Baxter    | Wallace     | 57 3rd Ave.              |
| Brown     | Bartholomew | 432 River Run            |
| Isaacson  | Jim         | 515 Fordam St., Apt. 917 |
| McTavish  | Taylor      | 432 River Run            |
| Pinter    | Marlene     | 9 Sunset Trail           |
+-----------+-------------+--------------------------+
```

If the indexed columns can contain NULL, you must use a UNIQUE index rather than a PRIMARY KEY. In that case, the index will not remove duplicate NULL key values.

Removing Duplicates of a Particular Row

As of MySQL 3.22.7, you can use LIMIT to restrict the effect of a DELETE statement to a subset of the rows that it otherwise would delete. This makes the statement applicable to removing duplicate records. Suppose you have a table t with the following contents:

```
+-------+
| color |
+-------+
| blue  |
| green |
| blue  |
| blue  |
| red   |
| green |
| red   |
+-------+
```

The table lists blue three times, and green and red twice each. To remove the extra instances of each color, do this:

```
mysql> DELETE FROM t WHERE color = 'blue' LIMIT 2;
mysql> DELETE FROM t WHERE color = 'green' LIMIT 1;
mysql> DELETE FROM t WHERE color = 'red' LIMIT 1;
mysql> SELECT * FROM t;
+-------+
| color |
+-------+
| blue  |
| green |
| red   |
+-------+
```

This technique works in the absence of a unique index, and it will eliminate duplicate NULL values. It's handy if you want to remove duplicates only for a specific set of rows within a table. However, if there are many different sets of duplicates that you want to remove, this is not a procedure you'd want to carry out by hand. The process can be automated by using the techniques discussed earlier in Recipe 14.3 for determining which values are duplicated. Recall that in that recipe we wrote a make_dup_count_query() function to generate the query needed to count the number of duplicate values in a given set of columns in a table:

```
sub make_dup_count_query
{
my ($tbl_name, @col_name) = @_;

    return (
        "SELECT COUNT(*)," . join (",", @col_name)
        . "\nFROM $tbl_name"
        . "\nGROUP BY " . join (",", @col_name)
        . "\nHAVING COUNT(*) > 1"
    );
}
```

We can write another function delete_dups() that uses make_dup_count_query() to find out which values in a table are duplicated and how often. From that information, we can figure out how many duplicates to remove with DELETE ... LIMIT n, so that only unique instances remain. The delete_dups() function looks like this:

```
sub delete_dups
{
my ($dbh, $tbl_name, @col_name) = @_;

    # Construct and run a query that finds duplicated values

    my $dup_info = $dbh->selectall_arrayref (
                    make_dup_count_query ($tbl_name, @col_name)
                );
    return unless defined ($dup_info);
```

```
# For each duplicated set of values, delete all but one instance
# of the rows containing those values

foreach my $row_ref (@{$dup_info})
{
    my ($count, @col_val) = @{$row_ref};
    next unless $count > 1;
    # Construct condition string to match values, being
    # careful to match NULL with IS NULL
    my $str;
    for (my $i = 0; $i < @col_name; $i++)
    {
        $str .= " AND " if $str;
        $str .= defined ($col_val[$i])
                    ? "$col_name[$i] = " . $dbh->quote ($col_val[$i])
                    : "$col_name[$i] IS NULL";
    }
    $str = "DELETE FROM $tbl_name WHERE $str LIMIT " . ($count - 1);
    $dbh->do ($str);
}
}
```

Suppose we have an employee table that contains the following records:

```
mysql> SELECT * FROM employee;
+----------+------------+
| name     | department |
+----------+------------+
| Fred     | accounting |
| Fred     | accounting |
| Fred     | accounting |
| Fred     | accounting |
| Bob      | shipping   |
| Mary Ann | shipping   |
| Mary Ann | shipping   |
| Mary Ann | sales      |
| Mary Ann | sales      |
| Mary Ann | sales      |
| Mary Ann | sales      |
| Mary Ann | sales      |
| Mary Ann | sales      |
| Boris    | NULL       |
| Boris    | NULL       |
+----------+------------+
```

To use the delete_dups() function to eliminate duplicates on the name and department columns of the employee table, call it like this:

```
delete_dups ($dbh, "employee", "name", "department");
```

delete_dups() calls make_dup_count_query() and executes the SELECT query that it generates. For the employee table, that query produces the following results:

```
+----------+----------+------------+
| COUNT(*) | name     | department |
+----------+----------+------------+
|        2 | Boris    | NULL       |
|        4 | Fred     | accounting |
|        6 | Mary Ann | sales      |
|        2 | Mary Ann | shipping   |
+----------+----------+------------+
```

delete_dups() uses that information to generate the following DELETE statements:

```
DELETE FROM employee
WHERE name = 'Boris' AND department IS NULL LIMIT 1
DELETE FROM employee
WHERE name = 'Fred' AND department = 'accounting' LIMIT 3
DELETE FROM employee
WHERE name = 'Mary Ann' AND department = 'sales' LIMIT 5
DELETE FROM employee
WHERE name = 'Mary Ann' AND department = 'shipping' LIMIT 1
```

In general, using DELETE ... LIMIT n is likely to be slower than removing duplicates by using a second table or by adding a unique index. Those methods keep the data on the server side and let the server do all the work. DELETE ... LIMIT n involves a lot of client-server interaction because it uses a SELECT query to retrieve information about duplicates, followed by several DELETE statements to remove instances of duplicated rows.

 When you issue DELETE ... LIMIT n statements from within a program, be sure to execute them only for values of n greater than zero. That is not only sensible (why waste bandwidth issuing a query to delete nothing?), but it's also necessary to avoid a bug that affects some versions of MySQL. Logically, one would expect that a statement of the form DELETE ... LIMIT 0 would delete no records, and that's what happens for current versions of MySQL. But versions prior to 3.23.40 have a bug such that LIMIT 0 is treated as though the LIMIT clause is not present at all; the result is that DELETE deletes *all* the selected rows! (For affected versions of MySQL, this problem also occurs for UPDATE ... LIMIT 0.)

CHAPTER 15

Performing Transactions

15.0 Introduction

The MySQL server can service multiple clients at the same time because it is multi-threaded. To deal with contention among clients, the server performs any necessary locking so that two clients cannot modify the same data at once. However, as the server executes statements, it's very possible that successive queries received from a given client will be interleaved with queries from other clients. If a client issues multiple statements that are dependent on each other, the fact that other clients may be updating tables in between those statements can cause difficulties. Statement failures can be problematic, too, if a multiple-statement operation does not run to completion. Suppose you have a `flight` table containing information about airline flight schedules and you want to update the record for flight 578 by choosing a pilot from among those available. You might do so using three statements as follows:

```
SELECT @p_val := pilot_id FROM pilot WHERE available = 'yes' LIMIT 1;
UPDATE pilot SET available = 'no' WHERE pilot_id = @p_val;
UPDATE flight SET pilot_id = @p_val WHERE flight_id = 578;
```

The first statement chooses one of the available pilots, the second marks the pilot as unavailable, and the third assigns the pilot to the flight. That's straightforward enough in practice, but in principle there are a couple of significant difficulties with the process:

Concurrency issues. The MySQL server can handle multiple clients at the same time. If two clients want to schedule pilots, it's possible that both of them would run the initial SELECT query and retrieve the same pilot ID number before either of them has a chance to set the pilot's status to unavailable. If that happens, the same pilot would be scheduled for two flights at once.

Integrity issues. All three statements must execute successfully as a unit. For example, if the SELECT and the first UPDATE run successfully, but the second UPDATE fails, the pilot's status is set to unavailable without the pilot being assigned a flight. The database will be left in an inconsistent state.

To prevent concurrency and integrity problems in these types of situations, transactions are helpful. A transaction groups a set of statements and guarantees the following properties:

- No other client can update the data used in the transaction while the transaction is in progress; it's as though you have the server all to yourself. For example, other clients cannot modify the pilot or flight records while you're booking a pilot for a flight. By preventing other clients from interfering with the operations you're performing, transactions solve concurrency problems arising from the multiple-client nature of the MySQL server. In effect, transactions serialize access to a shared resource across multiple-statement operations.

- Statements in a transaction are grouped and are committed (take effect) as a unit, but only if they all succeed. If an error occurs, any actions that occurred prior to the error are rolled back, leaving the relevant tables unaffected as though none of the statements had been issued at all. This keeps the database from becoming inconsistent. For example, if an update to the flights table fails, rollback causes the change to the pilots table to be undone, leaving the pilot still available. Rollback frees you from having to figure out how to undo a partially complete operation yourself.

This chapter discusses how to determine whether or not your MySQL server supports transactions and shows the syntax for the SQL statements that begin and end transactions. It also describes how to implement transactional operations from within programs, using error detection to determine whether to commit or roll back. The final section discusses some workarounds you can use if your MySQL server doesn't support transactions.

Scripts related to the examples shown here are located in the *transactions* directory of the recipes distribution.

15.1 Verifying Transaction Support Requirements

Problem

You want to use transactions, but don't know whether your MySQL server supports them.

Solution

Check your server version to be sure it's recent enough, and determine what table types it supports. You can also try creating a table with a transactional type and see whether MySQL actually uses that type for the table definition.

Discussion

To use transactions in MySQL, you need a server that is recent enough to support transaction-safe table handlers, and your applications must use tables that have a transactional type. To check the version of your server, use the following query:

```
mysql> SELECT VERSION();
+----------------+
| VERSION()      |
+----------------+
| 4.0.4-beta-log |
+----------------+
```

Transaction support first appeared in MySQL 3.23.17 with the inclusion of the BDB (Berkeley DB) transactional table type. Since then, the InnoDB type has become available; as of MySQL 3.23.29, both types can be used. In general, I'd recommend using as recent a version of MySQL as possible. Transaction support (and MySQL itself) have improved a lot since Version 3.23.29.

Even if your server is recent enough to include transaction support, it may not actually have transactional capabilities. The handlers for the appropriate table types may not have been configured in when the server was compiled. It's also possible for handlers to be present but disabled, if the server has been started with the *--skip-bdb* or *--skip-innodb* options. To check the availability and status of the transactional table handlers, use SHOW VARIABLES:

```
mysql> SHOW VARIABLES LIKE 'have_bdb';
+---------------+-------+
| Variable_name | Value |
+---------------+-------+
| have_bdb      | YES   |
+---------------+-------+
mysql> SHOW VARIABLES LIKE 'have_innodb';
+---------------+-------+
| Variable_name | Value |
+---------------+-------+
| have_innodb   | YES   |
+---------------+-------+
```

The query output shown here indicates that BDB and InnoDB tables both can be used. If either of these queries produces no output or the Value column says something other than YES (such as NO or DISABLED), the corresponding table type cannot be used.

For programmatic methods of checking the server version and the set of table types that the server supports, see Recipes 9.13 and 9.17.

Another way to check the availability of a specific table type is to try creating a table with that type. Then issue a SHOW CREATE TABLE statement to see what type MySQL actually uses. For example, try creating t as an InnoDB table by executing the following statements:

```
mysql> CREATE TABLE t (i INT) TYPE = InnoDB;
mysql> SHOW CREATE TABLE t\G
```

```
*************************** 1. row ***************************
       Table: t
Create Table: CREATE TABLE `t` (
  `i` int(11) default NULL
) TYPE=InnoDB
```

If the InnoDB type is available, the last part of the SHOW statement will say
TYPE=InnoDB. If not, MySQL will create the table using MyISAM (the default table
type), and the last part of the statement will say TYPE=MyISAM instead. (You can also
use SHOW TABLE STATUS to check the type of a table.)

In the event that your MySQL server doesn't include the transaction-safe table handlers you want to use, you'll need to replace it with one that does. If you install
MySQL from a source distribution, the installation instructions indicate which configuration flags to use to enable the desired handlers. If you prefer binaries, be sure to
install a distribution that was built to include BDB or InnoDB handlers.

After you've verified that your server supports the appropriate transactional table
types, your applications can go ahead and use them:

- If you're writing a new application, you can create its tables to have a transactional type right from the beginning. All that's necessary to create such a table is
  to add TYPE = *tbl_type* to the end of the CREATE TABLE statement:

  ```
  CREATE TABLE t1 (i INT) TYPE = BDB;
  CREATE TABLE t2 (i INT) TYPE = INNODB;
  ```

- If you modify an existing application in such a way that it becomes necessary to
  perform transactions with existing tables that were not originally created with
  transactions in mind, you can change the tables to have a different type. For
  example, the ISAM and MyISAM types are non-transactional. Trying to use
  them for transactions will yield incorrect results because they do not support
  rollback. In this case, you can use ALTER TABLE to convert the tables to a transactional type. Suppose t is a MyISAM table. To make it an InnoDB table, do this:

  ```
  ALTER TABLE t TYPE = INNODB;
  ```

  Note that changing a table's type to support transactions may affect its behavior
  in other ways. For example, MyISAM tables provide more flexible handling of
  AUTO_INCREMENT columns than do other table types. If you rely on MyISAM-only
  sequence features, changing the table type will cause problems. See Chapter 11
  for more information.

If your server does not support transactions and you cannot replace it with one that
does, you may be able to achieve somewhat the same effect in other ways. Sometimes it's possible to lock your tables across multiple statements using LOCK and
UNLOCK. This prevents other clients from interfering, although there is no rollback if
any of the statements fail. Another alternative may be to rewrite queries so that they
don't require transactions. See Recipe 15.8 for information about both types of
workarounds.

15.2 Performing Transactions Using SQL

Problem

You need to issue a set of queries that must succeed or fail as a unit.

Solution

Manipulate MySQL's auto-commit mode to allow multiple-statement transactions, then commit or roll back the statements depending on whether they succeed or fail.

Discussion

This section describes the SQL statements that control transactional behavior in MySQL. The immediately following sections discuss how to perform transactions from within programs. Some APIs require that you implement transactions by issuing the SQL statements discussed in this section; others provide a special mechanism that allows transaction management without writing SQL directly. However, even in the latter case, the API mechanism will map program operations onto transactional SQL statements, so reading this section will give you a better understanding of what the API is doing on your behalf.

MySQL normally operates in auto-commit mode, which commits the effect of each statement as it executes. (In effect, each statement is its own transaction.) To perform a multiple-statement transaction, you must disable auto-commit mode, issue the statements that make up the transaction, and then either commit or roll back your changes. In MySQL, you can do this two ways:

- Issue a BEGIN (or BEGIN WORK) statement to suspend auto-commit mode, then issue the queries that make up the transaction. If the queries succeed, record their effect in the database and terminate the transaction by issuing a COMMIT statement:

```
mysql> CREATE TABLE t (i INT) TYPE = InnoDB;
mysql> BEGIN;
mysql> INSERT INTO t (i) VALUES(1);
mysql> INSERT INTO t (i) VALUES(2);
mysql> COMMIT;
mysql> SELECT * FROM t;
+------+
| i    |
+------+
|    1 |
|    2 |
+------+
```

If an error occurs, don't use `COMMIT`. Instead, cancel the transaction by issuing a `ROLLBACK` statement. In the following example, t remains empty after the transaction because the effects of the `INSERT` statements are rolled back:

```
mysql> CREATE TABLE t (i INT) TYPE = InnoDB;
mysql> BEGIN;
mysql> INSERT INTO t (i) VALUES(1);
mysql> INSERT INTO t (x) VALUES(2);
ERROR 1054 at line 5: Unknown column 'x' in 'field list'
mysql> ROLLBACK;
mysql> SELECT * FROM t;
Empty set (0.00 sec)
```

• Another way to group statements is to turn off auto-commit mode explicitly. Then each statement you issue becomes part of the current transaction. To end the transaction and begin the next one, issue a `COMMIT` or `ROLLBACK` statement:

```
mysql> CREATE TABLE t (i INT) TYPE = InnoDB;
mysql> SET AUTOCOMMIT = 0;
mysql> INSERT INTO t (i) VALUES(1);
mysql> INSERT INTO t (i) VALUES(2);
mysql> COMMIT;
mysql> SELECT * FROM t;
+------+
| i    |
+------+
|    1 |
|    2 |
+------+
```

To turn auto-commit mode back on, use this statement:

```
mysql> SET AUTOCOMMIT = 1;
```

Not Everything Can Be Undone

Transactions have their limits, because not all statements can be part of a transaction. For example, if you issue a `DROP DATABASE` statement, don't expect to get back the database by executing a `ROLLBACK`.

15.3 Performing Transactions from Within Programs

Problem

You're writing a program that needs to implement transactional operations.

Solution

Use the transaction abstraction provided by your language API, if it has such a thing. If it doesn't, use the API's usual query execution mechanism to issue the transactional SQL statements directly.

Discussion

When you run queries interactively from *mysql* (as in the examples shown in the previous section), you can see by inspection whether statements succeed or fail and determine on that basis whether to commit or roll back. From within a non-interactive SQL script stored in a file, that doesn't work so well. You cannot commit or roll back conditionally according to statement success or failure, because MySQL includes no IF/THEN/ELSE construct for controlling the flow of the script. (There is an IF() function, but that's not the same thing.) For this reason, it's most common to perform transactional processing from within a program, because you can use your API language to detect errors and take appropriate action. This section discusses some general background on how to do this. The next sections provide language-specific details for the Perl, PHP, Python, and Java APIs.

Every API supports transactions, even if only in the sense that you can explicitly issue transaction-related SQL statements such as BEGIN and COMMIT. However, some APIs also provide a transaction abstraction that allows you to control transactional behavior without working directly with SQL. This approach hides the details and provides better portability to other databases that support transactions but for which the underlying SQL syntax may differ. The Perl, Python, and Java MySQL interfaces provide such an abstraction. PHP does not; you must issue the SQL statements yourself.

The next few sections each implement the same example to illustrate how to perform program-based transactions. They use a table t that has the following initial contents that show how much money two people have:

```
+------+------+
| name | amt  |
+------+------+
| Eve  |   10 |
| Ida  |    0 |
+------+------+
```

The sample transaction is a simple financial transfer that uses two UPDATE statements to give six dollars of Eve's money to Ida:

```
UPDATE money SET amt = amt - 6 WHERE name = 'Eve';
UPDATE money SET amt = amt + 6 WHERE name = 'Ida';
```

The result is a table that looks like this:

```
+------+------+
| name | amt  |
+------+------+
| Eve  |    4 |
| Ida  |    6 |
+------+------+
```

It's necessary to execute both statements within a transaction to ensure that both of them take effect at once. Without a transaction, Eve's money disappears without being credited to Ida if the second statement fails. By using a transaction, the table will be left unchanged if statement failure occurs.

The example programs for each language are located in the *transactions* directory of the recipes distribution. If you compare them, you'll see that they all employ a similar framework for performing transactional processing:

- The statements of the transaction are grouped within a control structure, along with a commit operation.

- If the status of the control structure indicates that it did not execute successfully to completion, the transaction is rolled back.

That logic can be expressed as follows, where `block` represents the control structure used to group statements:

```
block:
    statement 1
    statement 2
    ...
    statement n
    commit
if the block failed:
    roll back
```

In Perl, the control structure is an `eval` block that succeeds or fails and returns an error code. Python and Java use a `try` block that executes to the end if the transaction was successful. If an error occurs, an exception is raised that triggers execution of a corresponding error-handling block to roll back the transaction. PHP does not have these constructs, but you can achieve the same effect by executing the statements of the transaction and a commit operation within a function. If the function fails, roll back.

The benefit of structuring your code as just described is that it minimizes the number of tests needed to determine whether to roll back. The alternative—checking the result of each statement within the transaction and rolling back on individual statement errors—quickly turns your code into an unreadable mess.

A subtle point to be aware of when rolling back within languages that raise exceptions is that it may be possible for the rollback itself to fail, causing another exception to be raised. If you don't want to deal with that, issue the rollback within another block that has an empty exception handler. The example programs for Perl, Python, and Java do this.

15.4   Using Transactions in Perl Programs

Problem

You want to perform a transaction in a DBI script.

Solution

Use the standard DBI transaction support mechanism.

Discussion

The DBI mechanism for performing transactions is based on explicit manipulation of
auto-commit mode. The procedure is as follows:

1. Turn on the RaiseError attribute if it's not enabled and disable PrintError if it's
   on. You want errors to raise exceptions without printing anything; leaving
   PrintError enabled can interfere with failure detection in some cases.

2. Disable the AutoCommit attribute so that a commit will be done only when you
   say so.

3. Execute the statements that make up the transaction within an eval block so
   that errors raise an exception and terminate the block. The last thing in the
   block should be a call to commit( ), which commits the transaction if all its statements completed successfully.

4. After the eval executes, check the $@ variable. If $@ contains the empty string, the
   transaction succeeded. Otherwise, the eval will have failed due to the occurrence of some error and $@ will contain an error message. Invoke rollback( ) to
   cancel the transaction. If you want to display an error message, print $@ before
   calling rollback( ).

The following code shows how to implement this procedure to perform our example
transaction. It does so in such a way that the current values of the error-handling and
auto-commit attributes are saved before and restored after executing the transaction.
That may be overkill for your own applications. For example, if you know that
RaiseError and PrintError are set properly already, you need not save or restore them.

```
# save error-handling and auto-commit attributes,
# then make sure they're set correctly.
$save_re = $dbh->{RaiseError};
$save_pe = $dbh->{PrintError};
$save_ac = $dbh->{AutoCommit};
$dbh->{RaiseError} = 1; # raise exception if an error occurs
$dbh->{PrintError} = 0; # don't print an error message
$dbh->{AutoCommit} = 0; # disable auto-commit

eval
{
    # move some money from one person to the other
    $dbh->do ("UPDATE money SET amt = amt - 6 WHERE name = 'Eve'");
    $dbh->do ("UPDATE money SET amt = amt + 6 WHERE name = 'Ida'");
    # all statements succeeded; commit transaction
    $dbh->commit ();
};

if ($@) # an error occurred
{
    print "Transaction failed, rolling back. Error was:\n$@\n";
    # roll back within eval to prevent rollback
    # failure from terminating the script
    eval { $dbh->rollback (); };
}

# restore attributes to original state
$dbh->{AutoCommit} = $save_ac;
$dbh->{PrintError} = $save_pe;
$dbh->{RaiseError} = $save_re;
```

You can see that the example goes to a lot of work just to issue a couple of statements. To make transaction processing easier, you might want to create a couple of convenience functions to handle the processing that occurs before and after the eval:

```
sub transact_init
{
my $dbh = shift;
my $attr_ref = {};  # create hash in which to save attributes

    $attr_ref->{RaiseError} = $dbh->{RaiseError};
    $attr_ref->{PrintError} = $dbh->{PrintError};
    $attr_ref->{AutoCommit} = $dbh->{AutoCommit};
    $dbh->{RaiseError} = 1; # raise exception if an error occurs
    $dbh->{PrintError} = 0; # don't print an error message
    $dbh->{AutoCommit} = 0; # disable auto-commit
    return ($attr_ref);      # return attributes to caller
}

sub transact_finish
{
my ($dbh, $attr_ref, $error) = @_;

    if ($error) # an error occurred
    {
```

```
        print "Transaction failed, rolling back. Error was:\n$error\n";
        # roll back within eval to prevent rollback
        # failure from terminating the script
        eval { $dbh->rollback (); };
    }
    # restore error-handling and auto-commit attributes
    $dbh->{AutoCommit} = $attr_ref->{AutoCommit};
    $dbh->{PrintError} = $attr_ref->{PrintError};
    $dbh->{RaiseError} = $attr_ref->{RaiseError};
}
```

By using those two functions, our example transaction can be simplified considerably:

```
$ref = transact_init ($dbh);
eval
{
    # move some money from one person to the other
    $dbh->do ("UPDATE money SET amt = amt - 6 WHERE name = 'Eve'");
    $dbh->do ("UPDATE money SET amt = amt + 6 WHERE name = 'Ida'");
    # all statements succeeded; commit transaction
    $dbh->commit ();
};
transact_finish ($dbh, $ref, $@);
```

As of DBI 1.20, an alternative to manipulating the AutoCommit attribute manually is to begin a transaction by invoking begin_work(). This method disables AutoCommit and causes it to be enabled again automatically when you invoke commit() or rollback() later.

Transactions and Older Versions of DBD::mysql

The DBI transaction mechanism requires *DBD::mysql* 1.2216 or newer. For earlier versions, setting the AutoCommit attribute has no effect, so you'll need to issue the transaction-related SQL statements yourself (BEGIN, COMMIT, ROLLBACK).

15.5 Using Transactions in PHP Programs

Problem

You want to perform a transaction in a PHP script.

Solution

Issue the SQL statements that begin and end transactions.

Discussion

PHP provides no special transaction mechanism, so it's necessary to issue the relevant SQL statements directly. This means you can either use BEGIN to start a transaction, or disable and enable the auto-commit mode yourself using SET AUTOCOMMIT. The following example uses BEGIN. The statements of the transaction are placed within a function to avoid a lot of messy error checking. To determine whether or not to roll back, it's necessary only to test the function result:

```
function do_queries ($conn_id)
{
    # move some money from one person to the other
    if (!mysql_query ("BEGIN", $conn_id))
        return (0);
    if (!mysql_query ("UPDATE money SET amt = amt - 6 WHERE name = 'Eve'", $conn_id))
        return (0);
    if (!mysql_query ("UPDATE money SET amt = amt + 6 WHERE name = 'Ida'", $conn_id))
        return (0);
    if (!mysql_query ("COMMIT", $conn_id))
        return (0);
    return (1);
}

if (!do_queries ($conn_id))
{
    print ("Transaction failed, rolling back. Error was:\n"
            . mysql_error ($conn_id) . "\n");
    mysql_query ("ROLLBACK", $conn_id);
}
```

The do_queries() function tests each method and returns failure if any of them fail. That style of testing lends itself to situations in which you may need to perform additional processing between statements or after executing the statements and before returning success. For the example shown, no other processing is necessary, so do_queries() could be reimplemented as a single long expression:

```
function do_queries ($conn_id)
{
    # move some money from one person to the other
    return
    (
        mysql_query ("BEGIN", $conn_id)
        &&
        mysql_query ("UPDATE money SET amt = amt - 6 WHERE name = 'Eve'", $conn_id)
        &&
        mysql_query ("UPDATE money SET amt = amt + 6 WHERE name = 'Ida'", $conn_id)
        &&
        mysql_query ("COMMIT", $conn_id)
    );
}
```

15.6   Using Transactions in Python Programs

Problem

You want to perform a transaction in a DB-API script.

Solution

Use the standard DB-API transaction support mechanism.

Discussion

The Python DB-API abstraction provides transaction processing control through connection object methods. Invoke begin() to begin a transaction and either commit() or rollback() to end it. The begin() and commit() calls go into a try block, and the rollback() goes into the corresponding except block to cancel the transaction if an error occurs:

```
try:
    conn.begin ()
    cursor = conn.cursor ()
    # move some money from one person to the other
    cursor.execute ("UPDATE money SET amt = amt - 6 WHERE name = 'Eve'")
    cursor.execute ("UPDATE money SET amt = amt + 6 WHERE name = 'Ida'")
    cursor.close ()
    conn.commit()
except MySQLdb.Error, e:
    print "Transaction failed, rolling back. Error was:"
    print e.args
    try:    # empty exception handler in case rollback fails
        conn.rollback ()
    except:
        pass
```

15.7   Using Transactions in Java Programs

Problem

You want to perform a transaction in a JDBC script.

Solution

Use the standard JDBC transaction support mechanism.

Discussion

To perform transactions in Java, use your Connection object to turn off auto-commit mode. Then, after issuing your queries, use the object's commit() method to commit the transaction or rollback() to cancel it. Typically, you execute the statements for the transaction in a try block, with commit() at the end of the block. To handle failures, invoke rollback() in the corresponding exception handler:

```
try
{
    conn.setAutoCommit (false);
    Statement s = conn.createStatement ();
    // move some money from one person to the other
    s.executeUpdate ("UPDATE money SET amt = amt - 6 WHERE name = 'Eve'");
    s.executeUpdate ("UPDATE money SET amt = amt + 6 WHERE name = 'Ida'");
    s.close ();
    conn.commit ();
    conn.setAutoCommit (true);
}
catch (SQLException e)
{
    System.err.println ("Transaction failed, rolling back.");
    Cookbook.printErrorMessage (e);
    // empty exception handler in case rollback fails
    try
    {
        conn.rollback ();
        conn.setAutoCommit (true);
    }
    catch (Exception e2) { }
}
```

15.8 Using Alternatives to Transactions

Problem

You need to perform transactional processing, but your MySQL server doesn't support transactions.

Solution

Some transactional operations are amenable to workarounds such as explicit table locking. In certain cases, you may not actually even need a transaction; by rewriting your queries, you can eliminate the need for a transaction entirely.

Discussion

Transactions are valuable, but sometimes they need not be or cannot be used:

- Your server may not support transactions at all. (It may be too old or not configured with the appropriate table handlers, as discussed in Recipe 15.1). In this case, you have no choice but to use some kind of workaround for transactions. One strategy that can be helpful in some situations is to use explicit table locking to prevent concurrency problems.

- Applications sometimes use transactions when they're not really necessary. You may be able to eliminate the need for a transaction by rewriting statements. This may even result in a faster application.

Grouping Statements Using Locks

If your server doesn't have transactional capabilities but you need to execute a group of queries without interference by other clients, you can do so by using LOCK TABLE and UNLOCK TABLE:[*]

- Use LOCK TABLE to obtain locks for all the tables you intend to use. (Acquire write locks for tables you need to modify, and read locks for the others.) This prevents other clients from modifying the tables while you're using them.
- Issue the queries that must be executed as a group.
- Release the locks with UNLOCK TABLE. Other clients will regain access to the tables.

Locks obtained with LOCK TABLE remain in effect until you release them and thus can apply over the course of multiple statements. This gives you the same concurrency benefits as transactions. However, there is no rollback if errors occur, so table locking is not appropriate for all applications. For example, you might try performing an operation that transfers funds from Eve to Ida like this:

```
LOCK TABLE money WRITE;
UPDATE money SET amt = amt - 6 WHERE name = 'Eve';
UPDATE money SET amt = amt + 6 WHERE name = 'Ida';
UNLOCK TABLE;
```

Unfortunately, if the second update fails, the effect of the first update is not rolled back. Despite this caveat, there are certain types of situations where table locking may be sufficient for your purposes:

- A set of statements consisting only of SELECT queries. If you want to run several SELECT statements and prevent other clients from modifying the tables while you're querying them, locking will do that. For example, if you need to run several summary queries on a set of tables, your summaries may appear to be based on different sets of data if other clients are allowed to change records in between your summary queries. This will make the summaries inconsistent. To prevent that from happening, lock the tables while you're using them.
- Locking also can be useful for a set of queries where only the *last* statement is an update. In this case, the earlier statements don't make any changes and there is nothing that needs to be rolled back should the update fail.

---

[*] LOCK TABLES and UNLOCK TABLES are synonyms for LOCK TABLE and UNLOCK TABLE.

Rewriting Queries to Avoid Transactions

Sometimes applications use transactions unnecessarily. Suppose you have a table meeting that records meeting and convention information (including the number of tickets left for each event), and that you're writing a Perl application containing a function get_ticket() that dispenses tickets. One way to implement the function is to check the ticket count, decrement it if it's positive, and return a status indicating whether a ticket was available. To prevent multiple clients from attempting to grab the last ticket at the same time, issue the queries within a transaction:[*]

```
sub get_ticket
{
my ($dbh, $meeting_id) = @_;

    my $ref = transact_init ($dbh);
    my $count = 0;
    eval
    {
        # check the current ticket count
        $count = $dbh->selectrow_array (
            "SELECT tix_left FROM meeting
             WHERE meeting_id = ?", undef, $meeting_id);
        # if there are tickets left, decrement the count
        if ($count > 0)
        {
            $dbh->do (
                "UPDATE meeting SET tix_left = tix_left-1
                 WHERE meeting_id = ?", undef, $meeting_id);
        }
        $dbh->commit ();
    };
    $count = 0 if $@;   # if an error occurred, no tix available
    transact_finish ($dbh, $ref, $@);
    return ($count > 0)
}
```

The function dispenses tickets properly, but involves a certain amount of unnecessary work. It's possible to do the same thing without using a transaction at all. Decrement the ticket count only if the count is greater than zero, then check whether the statement affected a row:

```
sub get_ticket
{
my ($dbh, $meeting_id) = @_;

    my $count = $dbh->do ("UPDATE meeting SET tix_left = tix_left-1
                WHERE meeting_id = ? AND tix_left > 0",
                undef, $meeting_id);
    return ($count > 0);
}
```

[*] The transact_init() and transact_finish() functions are discussed in Recipe 15.4.

In MySQL, the row count returned by an UPDATE statement indicates the number of rows changed. This means that if there are no tickets left for an event, the UPDATE won't change the row and the count will be zero. This makes it easy to determine whether a ticket is available using a single query rather than with the multiple queries required by the transactional approach. The lesson here is that although transactions are important and have their place, you may be able to avoid them and end up with a faster application as a result. (The single-query solution is an example of what the MySQL Reference Manual refers to as an "atomic operation." The manual discusses these as an efficient alternative to transactions.)

## CHAPTER 16

Introduction to MySQL on the Web

16.0 Introduction

The next few chapters discuss some of the ways that MySQL can help you build a better web site. In general, the principal benefit is that MySQL makes it easier to provide dynamic rather than static content. Static content exists as pages in the web server's document tree that are served exactly as is. Visitors can access only the documents that you place in the tree, and changes occur only when you add, modify, or delete those documents. By contrast, dynamic content is created on demand. Rather than opening a file and serving its contents directly to the client, the web server executes a script that generates the page and sends the resulting output. As a simple example, a script can look up the current hit counter value in the database for a given web page, update the counter, and return the new value for display in the page. Each time the script executes, it produces a different value. More complex examples are scripts that show the names of people that have a birthday today, retrieve and display items in a product catalog, or provide information about the current status of the server. And that's just for starters; web scripts have access to the power of the programming language in which they're written, so the actions that they perform to generate pages can be quite extensive. For example, web scripts are important for form processing, and a single script may be responsible for generating a form and sending it to the user, processing the contents of the form when the user submits it later, and storing the contents in a database. By communicating with users this way, web scripts bring a measure of interactivity to your web site.

This chapter covers the introductory aspects of writing scripts that use MySQL in a web environment. Some of the initial material is not particularly MySQL-specific, but it is necessary to establish the general groundwork for using your database from within the context of web programming. The topics covered here include:

- How web scripting differs from writing static HTML documents or scripts intended to be executed from the command line.

- Some of the prerequisites for running web scripts. In particular, you must have a web server installed and it must be set up to recognize your scripts as programs to be executed, rather than as static files to be served literally over the network.

- How to use each of our API languages to write a short web script that queries the MySQL server for information and displays the results in a web page.

- How to properly encode output. HTML consists of text to be displayed interspersed with special markup constructs. However, if the text contains special characters, you must encode them to avoid generating malformed web pages. Each API provides a mechanism for doing this.

The following chapters go into more detail on topics such as how to display query results in various formats (paragraphs, lists, tables, and so forth), working with images, form processing, and tracking a user across the course of several page requests as part of a single user session.

This book uses the Apache web server for Perl, PHP, and Python scripts, and the Tomcat server for Java scripts—written using JavaServer Pages (JSP) notation. Both servers are available from the Apache Group:

http://httpd.apache.org/
http://jakarta.apache.org/

Because Apache installations are fairly prevalent, I'm going to assume that it is already installed on your system and that you just need to configure it. Recipe 16.2 discusses how to configure Apache for Perl, PHP, and Python, and how to write a short web script in each language. Tomcat is less widely deployed than Apache, so some additional installation information is provided in Appendix B. Recipe 16.3 discusses JSP script writing using Tomcat. You can use different servers if you like, but you'll need to adapt the instructions given here.

The web-based example scripts in the recipes distribution may be found under the directories named for the servers used to run them. For Perl, PHP, and Python examples, look under the *apache* directory; for JSP examples, look under *tomcat*.

I will assume that you have some basic familiarity with HTML. For Tomcat, it's also helpful to know something about XML, because Tomcat's configuration files are written as XML documents, and JSP pages contain elements written using XML syntax. If you don't know any XML, see the quick summary in the sidebar "XML and XHTML in a Nutshell." In general, the web scripts in this book produce output that is valid not only as HTML, but as XHTML, the transitional format between HTML and XML. (This is another reason to become familiar with XML.) For example, XHTML requires closing tags, so paragraphs are written with a closing </p> tag following the paragraph body. The use of this output style will be obvious for scripts written using languages like PHP in which the HTML tags are included literally in the script. For interfaces that generate HTML for you, like the Perl CGI.pm module, conformance to XHTML is a matter of whether or not the module itself produces

XHTML. CGI.pm does so beginning with Version 2.69, though its XHTML conformance improves in more recent versions.

XML and XHTML in a Nutshell

XML is similar in some ways to HTML, and because more people know HTML, it's perhaps easiest to characterize XML in terms of how it differs from HTML:

- Lettercase for HTML tag and attribute names does not matter; in XML, the names are case sensitive.
- In HTML, tag attributes can be specified with a quoted or unquoted value, or sometimes with no value at all. In XML, every tag attribute must have a value, and the value must be quoted.
- Every opening tag in XML must have a corresponding closing tag. This is true even if there is no body, although in that case, a shortcut tag form can be used. For example, in HTML, you can write <br>, but XML requires a closing tag. You could write this as
</br>, but the element has no body, so a shortcut form <br/> can be used that combines the opening and closing tags. However, when writing XML that will be translated into HTML, it's safer to write the tag as <br /> with a space preceding the slash. The space helps browsers not to misinterpret the tag name as br/ and consequently ignore it as unrecognized.

XHTML is a transitional format used for the migration of the Web away from HTML and toward XML. It's less strict than XML, but more strict than HTML. For example, XHTML tag and attribute names must be lowercase and attributes must have a double-quoted value.

In HTML you might write a radio button element like this:

```
<INPUT TYPE=RADIO NAME="my button" VALUE=3 CHECKED>
```

In XHTML, the tag name must be lowercase, the attribute values must be quoted, the checked attribute must be given a value, and there must be a closing tag:

```
<input type="radio" name="my button" value="3" checked="checked"></input>
```

The element has no body in this case, so the single-tag shortcut form can be used:

```
<input type="radio" name="my button" value="3" checked="checked" />
```

Appendix C lists some references if you want additional general information about HTML, XHTML, or XML.

16.1 Basic Web Page Generation

Problem

You want to produce a web page from a script rather than by writing it manually.

Solution

Write a program that generates the page when it executes. This gives you more control over what gets sent to the client than when you write a static page, although it may also require that you provide more parts of the response. For example, it may be necessary to write the headers that precede the page body.

Discussion

HTML is a markup language (that's what the "ML" stands for) that consists of a mix of plain text to be displayed and special markup indicators or constructs that control how the plain text is displayed. Here is a very simple HTML page that specifies a title in the page header, and a body with white background containing a single paragraph:

```
<html>
<head>
<title>Web Page Title</title>
</head>
<body bgcolor="white">
<p>Web page body.</p>
</body>
</html>
```

It's possible to write a script that produces the same page, but doing so differs in some ways from writing a static page. For one thing, you're writing in two languages at once. (The script is written in your programming language, and the script itself writes HTML.) Another difference is that you may have to produce more of the response that is sent to the client. When a web server sends a static page to a client, it actually sends a set of one or more header lines first that provide additional information about the page. For example, an HTML document would be preceded by a Content-Type: header that lets the client know what kind of information to expect, and a blank line that separates any headers from the page body:

```
Content-Type: text/html

<html>
<head>
<title>Web Page Title</title>
</head>
<body bgcolor="white">
<p>Web page body.</p>
</body>
</html>
```

The web server produces header information automatically for static HTML pages. When you write a web script, you may need to provide the header information yourself. Some APIs (such as PHP) may send a content-type header automatically, but allow you to override the default type. For example, if your script sends a JPEG image to the client instead of an HTML page, you would want to have the script change the content type from text/html to image/jpeg.

Writing web scripts also differs from writing command-line scripts, both for input and for output. On the input side, the information given to a web script is provided by the web server rather than by command-line arguments or by input that you type in. This means your scripts do not obtain input using read statements. Instead, the web server puts information into the execution environment of the script, which then extracts that information from its environment and acts on it.

On the output side, command-line scripts typically produce plain text output, whereas web scripts produce HTML, images, or whatever other type of content you need to send to the client. Output produced in a web environment usually must be highly structured, to ensure that it can be understood by the receiving client program.

Any API allows you to generate output by means of print statements, but some also offer special assistance for producing web pages. This support can be either built into the API itself or provided by means of special modules:

- For Perl scripts, a popular module is CGI.pm. It provides features for generating HTML markup, form processing, and more.
- PHP scripts are written as a mix of HTML and embedded PHP code. That is, you write HTML literally into the script, then drop into "program mode" whenever you need to generate output by executing code. The code is replaced by its output in the resulting page that is sent to the client.
- Python includes cgi and urllib modules that help perform web programming tasks.
- For Java, we'll write scripts according to the JSP specification, which allows scripting directives and code to be embedded into web pages. This is similar to the way PHP works.

Other page-generating packages are available besides those used in this book—some of which can have a marked effect on the way you use a language. For example, Mason, embPerl, ePerl, and AxKit allow you to treat Perl as an embedded language, somewhat like the way that PHP works. Similarly, the *mod_snake* Apache module allows Python code to be embedded into HTML templates.

Before you can run any scripts in a web environment, your web server must be set up properly. Information about doing this for Apache and Tomcat is provided in Recipes 16.2 and 16.3, but conceptually, a web server typically runs a script in one of two ways. First, the web server can use an external program to execute the script. For example, it can invoke an instance of the Python interpreter to run a Python script. Second, if the server has been enabled with the appropriate language processing ability, it can execute the script itself. Using an external program to run scripts requires no special capability on the part of the web server, but is slower because it involves starting up a separate process, as well as some additional overhead for writing request information to the script and reading the results from it. If you embed a language processor into the web server, it can execute scripts directly, resulting in much better performance.

Like most web servers, Apache can run external scripts. It also supports the concept of extensions (modules) that become part of the Apache process itself (either by being compiled in or dynamically loaded at runtime). One common use of this feature is to embed language processors into the server to accelerate script execution. Perl, PHP, and Python scripts can be executed either way. Like command-line scripts, externally executed web scripts are written as executable files that begin with a #! line specifying the pathname of the appropriate language interpreter. Apache uses the pathname to determine which interpreter runs the script. Alternatively, you can extend Apache using modules such as *mod_perl* for Perl, *mod_php* for PHP, and *mod_python* or *mod_snake* for Python. This gives Apache the ability to directly execute scripts written in those languages.

For Java JSP scripts, the scripts are compiled into Java servlets and run inside a process known as a servlet container. This is similar to the embedded-interpreter approach in the sense that the scripts are run by a server process that manages them, rather than by starting up an external process for each script. The first time a JSP page is requested by a client, the container compiles it into a servlet in the form of executable Java byte code, then loads it and runs it. The container caches the byte code, so subsequent requests for the script run directly with no compilation phase. If you modify the script, the container notices this when the next request arrives, recompiles the script into a new servlet, and reloads it. The JSP approach provides a significant advantage over writing servlets directly, because you don't have to compile code yourself or handle servlet loading and unloading. Tomcat can handle the responsibilities of both the servlet container and of the web server that communicates with the container.

If you run multiple servers on the same host, they must listen for requests on different port numbers. In a typical configuration, Apache listens on the default HTTP port (80) and Tomcat listens on another port such as 8080. The examples here use server hostnames of *apache.snake.net* and *tomcat.snake.net* to represent URLs for scripts processed using Apache and Tomcat. These may or may not map to the same physical machine, depending on your DNS settings, so the examples use a different port (8080) for Tomcat. Typical forms for URLs that you'll see in this book are as follows:

> *http://apache.snake.net/cgi-bin/my_perl_script.pl*
> *http://apache.snake.net/cgi-bin/my_python_script.py*
> *http://apache.snake.net/mcb/my_php_script.php*
> *http://tomcat.snake.net:8080/mcb/my_jsp_script.jsp*

You'll need to change the hostname and port number appropriately for pages served by your own servers.

16.2   Using Apache to Run Web Scripts

Problem

You want to run Perl, PHP, or Python programs in a web environment.

Solution

Execute them using the Apache server.

Discussion

This section describes how to configure Apache for running Perl, PHP, and Python scripts, and illustrates how to write web-based scripts in each language.

There are typically several directories under the Apache root directory, which I'll assume here to be *usr/local/apache*. These directories include:

bin
> Contains *httpd*—that is, Apache itself—and other Apache-related executable programs

conf
> For configuration files, notably *httpd.conf*, the primary file used by Apache

htdocs
> The root of the document tree

logs
> For log files

To configure Apache for script execution, edit the *httpd.conf* file in the *conf* directory. Typically, executable scripts are identified either by location or by filename suffix. A location can be either language-neutral or language-specific.

Apache configurations often have a *cgi-bin* directory under the server root directory where you can install scripts that should run as external programs. It's configured using a ScriptAlias directive:

```
ScriptAlias /cgi-bin/ /usr/local/apache/cgi-bin/
```

The second argument is the actual location of the script directory in your filesystem, and the first is the pathname in URLs that corresponds to that directory. Thus, the directive just shown associates scripts located in */usr/local/apache/cgi-bin* with URLs that have *cgi-bin* following the hostname. For example, if you install the script *myscript.py* in the directory */usr/local/apache/cgi-bin* on the host *apache.snake.net*, you'd request it with this URL:

> *http://apache.snake.net/cgi-bin/myscript.py*

When configured this way, the *cgi-bin* directory can contain scripts written in any language. Because of this, the directory is language-neutral, so Apache needs to be able to figure out which language processor to use to execute each script that is installed there. To provide this information, the first line of the script should begin with #! followed by the pathname to the program that executes the script, and possibly some options. For example, a script that begins with the following line will be run by Perl, and the *-w* option tells Perl to warn about questionable language constructs:

```
#! /usr/bin/perl -w
```

Under Unix, you must also make the script executable (use *chmod +x*), or it won't run properly. The #! line just shown is appropriate for a system that has Perl installed as */usr/bin/perl*. If your Perl interpreter is installed somewhere else, modify the line accordingly. If you're on a Windows machine with Perl installed as *D:\Perl\ bin\perl.exe*, the #! line should look like this:

```
#! D:\Perl\bin\perl -w
```

For Windows users, another option that is simpler is to set up a filename extension association between script names that end with a *.pl* suffix and the Perl interpreter. Then the script can begin like this:

```
#! perl -w
```

A `ScriptAlias` directive sets up a directory that can be used for scripts written in any language. It's also possible to associate a directory with a specific language processor, so that any script found there is assumed to be written in a particular language. For example, to designate */usr/local/apache/cgi-perl* as a *mod_perl* directory, you might configure Apache like this:

```
<IfModule mod_perl.c>
    Alias /cgi-perl/ /usr/local/apache/cgi-perl/
    <Location /cgi-perl>
        SetHandler perl-script
        PerlHandler Apache::Registry
        PerlSendHeader on
        Options +ExecCGI
    </Location>
</IfModule>
```

In this case, Perl scripts located in the designated directory would be invoked as follows:

```
http://apache.snake.net/cgi-perl/myscript.pl
```

Using *mod_perl* is beyond the scope of this book, so I won't say any more about it. Check Appendix C for some useful *mod_perl* resources.

Directories used only for scripts generally are placed outside of your Apache document tree. As an alternative to using specific directories for scripts, you can identify scripts by filename extension, so that files with a particular suffix become associated with a specific language processor. In this case, you can place them anywhere in the document tree. This is the most common way to use PHP. For example, if you have Apache configured with PHP support built in using the *mod_php* module, you can tell it that scripts having names ending with *.php* should be interpreted as PHP scripts. To do so, add this line to *httpd.conf*:

```
AddType application/x-httpd-php .php
```

Then if you install a PHP script *myscript.php* under *htdocs* (the Apache document root directory), the URL for invoking the script becomes:

http://apache.snake.net/myscript.php

If PHP runs as an external standalone program, you'll need to tell Apache where to find it. For example, if you're running Windows and you have PHP installed as *D:\ Php\php.exe*, put the following lines in *httpd.conf* (note the use of forward slashes in the pathnames rather than backslashes):

```
ScriptAlias /php/ "D:/Php/"
AddType application/x-httpd-php .php
Action application/x-httpd-php /php/php.exe
```

For purposes of showing URLs in examples, I'm going to assume that Perl and Python scripts are in your *cgi-bin* directory, and that PHP scripts are in the *mcb* directory of your document tree, identified by the *.php* extension. This means that URLs for scripts in these languages will look like this:

http://apache.snake.net/cgi-bin/myscript.pl
http://apache.snake.net/cgi-bin/myscript.py
http://apache.snake.net/mcb/myscript.php

If you plan to use a similar setup, make sure you have a *cgi-bin* directory under your Apache root, and an *mcb* directory under your Apache document root. Then, to deploy Perl or Python web scripts, copy them to the *cgi-bin* directory. To deploy PHP scripts, copy them to the *mcb* directory.

If you request a web script and get an error page in response, have a look at the Apache error log, which can be a useful source of diagnostic information when you're trying to figure out why a script doesn't work. A common name for this log is *error_log* in the *logs* directory. If you don't find any such file, check *httpd.conf* for an ErrorLog directive to see where Apache logs its errors.

After Apache has been configured to support script execution, you can begin to write scripts that generate web pages. The remainder of this section describes how to do so for Perl, PHP, and Python. The examples for each language connect to the MySQL server, run a SHOW TABLES query, and display the results in a web page. The scripts shown here indicate any additional modules or libraries that web scripts typically need to include. (Later on, I'll generally assume that the proper modules have been referenced and show only script fragments.)

Web Security Note

Under Unix, scripts run with particular user and group IDs. Scripts that you execute from the command line run with your user and group IDs, and have the filesystem privileges associated with your account. However, scripts executed by a web server probably won't run with your user and group ID, nor will they have your user privileges. Instead, they run under the user and group ID of the account the web server has been set to run as, and with that account's privileges. (To determine what account this is, look for User and Group directives in the *httpd.conf* configuration file.) This means that if you expect web scripts to read and write files, those files must be accessible to the account used to run the web server. For example, if your server runs under the nobody account and you want a script to be able to store uploaded image files into a directory called *uploads* in the document tree, you must make that directory readable to and writable by the nobody user.

Another implication is that if other people can write scripts for your web server, those scripts too will run as nobody and they can read and write the same files as your own scripts. Solutions to this problem include using the suEXEC mechanism for Apache 1.x, or using Apache 2.x, which allows you to designate which user and group IDs to use for running a given set of scripts.

Perl

Our first web-based Perl script, *show_tables.pl*, is shown below. It produces an appropriate Content-Type: header, a blank line to separate the header from the page content, and the initial part of the page. Then it retrieves and displays a list of tables in the cookbook database. The table list is followed by the trailing HTML tags that close the page:

```
#! /usr/bin/perl -w
# show_tables.pl - Issue SHOW TABLES query, display results
# by generating HTML directly

use strict;
use lib qw(/usr/local/apache/lib/perl);
use Cookbook;

# Print header, blank line, and initial part of page

print <<EOF;
Content-Type: text/html

<html>
<head>
<title>Tables in cookbook Database</title>
</head>
<body bgcolor="white">
```

```
<p>Tables in cookbook database:</p>
EOF

# Connect to database, display table list, disconnect

my $dbh = Cookbook::connect ();
my $sth = $dbh->prepare ("SHOW TABLES");
$sth->execute ();
while (my @row = $sth->fetchrow_array ())
{
    print "$row[0]<br />\n";
}
$dbh->disconnect ();


# Print page trailer

print <<EOF;
</body>
</html>
EOF

exit (0);
```

To try out the script, install it in your *cgi-bin* directory and invoke it from your browser as follows:

> *http://apache.snake.net/cgi-bin/show_tables.pl*

show_tables.pl generates HTML by including literal tags in print statements. Another approach to web page generation is to use the CGI.pm module, which makes it easy to write web scripts without writing tags literally. CGI.pm provides an object-oriented interface and a function call interface, so you can use it to write web pages in either of two styles. Here's a script, *show_tables_oo.pl*, that uses the CGI.pm object-oriented interface to produce the same report as *show_tables.pl*:

```
#! /usr/bin/perl -w
# show_tables_oo.pl - Issue SHOW TABLES query, display results
# using the CGI.pm object-oriented interface

use strict;
use lib qw(/usr/local/apache/lib/perl);
use CGI;
use Cookbook;

# Create CGI object for accessing CGI.pm methods

my $cgi = new CGI;

# Print header, blank line, and initial part of page
```

```
print $cgi->header ();
print $cgi->start_html (-title => "Tables in cookbook Database",
                        -bgcolor => "white");

print $cgi->p ("Tables in cookbook database:");

# Connect to database, display table list, disconnect

my $dbh = Cookbook::connect ();
my $sth = $dbh->prepare ("SHOW TABLES");
$sth->execute ();
while (my @row = $sth->fetchrow_array ())
{
    print $row[0] . $cgi->br ();
}
$dbh->disconnect ();

# Print page trailer

print $cgi->end_html ();

exit (0);
```

The script includes the CGI.pm module with a use CGI statement, then creates a CGI object, $cgi, through which it invokes the various HTML-generation calls. header() generates the Content-Type: header and start_html() produces the initial page tags up through the opening <body> tag. After generating the first part of the page, *show_tables_oo.pl* retrieves and displays information from the server. Each table name is followed by a <br /> tag, produced by invoking the br() method. end_html() produces the closing </body> and </html> tags. When you install the script in your *cgi-bin* directory and invoke it from a browser, you can see that it generates the same type of page as *show_tables.pl*.

CGI.pm calls often take multiple parameters, many of which are optional. To allow you to specify just those parameters you need, CGI.pm understands *-name => value* notation in parameter lists. For example, in the start_html() call, the title parameter sets the page title and bgcolor sets the background color. The *-name => value* notation also allows parameters to be specified in any order, so these two statements are equivalent:

```
print $cgi->start_html (-title => "My Page Title", -bgcolor => "white");
print $cgi->start_html (-bgcolor => "white", -title => "My Page Title");
```

To use the CGI.pm function call interface rather than the object-oriented interface, you must write scripts a little differently. The use line that references CGI.pm imports the method names into your script's namespace so that you can invoke them directly as functions without having to create a CGI object. For example, to import the most commonly used methods, the script should include this statement:

```
use CGI qw(:standard);
```

The following script, *show_tables_fc.pl*, is the function call equivalent of the *show_tables_oo.pl* script just shown. It uses the same CGI.pm calls, but invokes them as standalone functions rather than through a $cgi object:

```perl
#! /usr/bin/perl -w
# show_tables_fc.pl - Issue SHOW TABLES query, display results
# using the CGI.pm function-call interface

use strict;
use lib qw(/usr/local/apache/lib/perl);
use CGI qw(:standard);  # import standard method names into script namespace
use Cookbook;

# Print header, blank line, and initial part of page

print header ();
print start_html (-title => "Tables in cookbook Database",
                  -bgcolor => "white");

print p ("Tables in cookbook database:");

# Connect to database, display table list, disconnect

my $dbh = Cookbook::connect ();
my $sth = $dbh->prepare ("SHOW TABLES");
$sth->execute ();
while (my @row = $sth->fetchrow_array ())
{
    print $row[0] . br ();
}
$dbh->disconnect ();

# Print page trailer

print end_html ();

exit (0);
```

Install the *show_tables_fc.pl* script in your *cgi-bin* directory and try it out to verify that it produces the same output as *show_tables_oo.pl*.

This book uses the CGI.pm function call interface for Perl-based web scripts from this point on. You can get more information about CGI.pm at the command line by using the following commands to read the installed documentation:

```
% perldoc CGI
% perldoc CGI::Carp
```

Other references for this module, both online and in print form, are listed in Appendix C.

PHP

PHP doesn't provide much in the way of tag shortcuts, which is surprising given its web orientation. On the other hand, because PHP is an embedded language, you can simply write your HTML literally in your script without using print statements. Here's a script *show_tables.php* that shifts back and forth between HTML mode and PHP mode:

```php
<?php
# show_tables.php - Issue SHOW TABLES query, display results

include "Cookbook.php";

?>

<html>
<head>
<title>Tables in cookbook Database</title>
</head>
<body bgcolor="white">

<p>Tables in cookbook database:</p>

<?php

# Connect to database, display table list, disconnect
$conn_id = cookbook_connect ();
$result_id = mysql_query ("SHOW TABLES", $conn_id);
while (list ($tbl_name) = mysql_fetch_row ($result_id))
    print ("$tbl_name<br />\n");
mysql_free_result ($result_id);
mysql_close ($conn_id);

?>

</body>
</html>
```

To try the script, put it in the *mcb* directory of your web server's document tree and invoke it as follows:

http://apache.snake.net/mcb/show_tables.php

Unlike the Perl versions of the MySQL show-tables script, the PHP script includes no code to produce the Content-Type: header, because PHP produces it automatically. (If you want to override this behavior and produce your own headers, consult the header( ) function section in the PHP manual.)

Except for the break tags, *show_tables.php* includes HTML content by writing it outside of the <?php and ?> tags so that the PHP interpreter simply writes it without interpretation. Here's a different version of the script that produces all the HTML using print statements:

```php
<?php
# show_tables_print.php - Issue SHOW TABLES query, display results
# using print() to generate all HTML

include "Cookbook.php";

print ("<html>\n");
print ("<head>\n");
print ("<title>Tables in cookbook Database</title>\n");
print ("</head>\n");
print ("<body bgcolor=\"white\">\n");
print ("<p>Tables in cookbook database:</p>\n");

# Connect to database, display table list, disconnect
$conn_id = cookbook_connect ();
$result_id = mysql_query ("SHOW TABLES", $conn_id);
while (list ($tbl_name) = mysql_fetch_row ($result_id))
    print ("$tbl_name<br />\n");
mysql_free_result ($result_id);
mysql_close ($conn_id);

print ("</body>\n");
print ("</html>\n");
?>
```

Sometimes it makes sense to use one approach, sometimes the other—and sometimes both within the same script. If a section of HTML doesn't refer to any variable or expression values, it can be clearer to write it in HTML mode. Otherwise it may be clearer to write it using print or echo statements, to avoid switching between HTML and PHP modes frequently.

Python

A standard installation of Python includes cgi and urllib modules that are useful for web programming. However, we don't actually need them yet, because the only web-related activity of our first Python web script is to generate some simple HTML. Here's a Python version of the MySQL status script:

```python
#! /usr/bin/python
# show_tables.py - Issue SHOW TABLES query, display results

import sys
sys.path.insert (0, "/usr/local/apache/lib/python")
import MySQLdb
import Cookbook

# Print header, blank line, and initial part of page

print """Content-Type: text/html
```

```
<html>
<head>
<title>Tables in cookbook Database</title>
</head>
<body bgcolor="white">

<p>Tables in cookbook database:</p>
"""

# Connect to database, display table list, disconnect

conn = Cookbook.connect ()
cursor = conn.cursor ()
cursor.execute ("SHOW TABLES")
for (tbl_name, ) in cursor.fetchall ():
    print tbl_name + "<br />"
cursor.close ()
conn.close ()

# Print page trailer
print """
</body>
</html>
"""
```

Put the script in Apache's *cgi-bin* directory and invoke it like this:

http://apache.snake.net/cgi-bin/show_tables.py

16.3   Using Tomcat to Run Web Scripts

Problem

You want to run Java-based programs in a web environment.

Solution

Write programs using JSP notation and execute them using a servlet container.

Discussion

As described in Recipe 16.2, Apache can be used to run Perl, PHP, and Python scripts. For Java, a different approach is needed, because Apache doesn't serve JSP pages. Instead, we'll use Tomcat, a server designed for processing Java in a web environment. Apache and Tomcat are very different servers, but there is a familial relationship—Tomcat is part of the Jakarta Project, which is overseen by the Apache Software Foundation.

This section provides an overview of JSP programming with Tomcat, but makes several assumptions:

- You have a some familiarity with the concepts underlying JavaServer Pages, such as what a servlet container is, what an application context is, and what the basic JSP scripting elements are.
- The Tomcat server has been installed so that you can execute JSP pages, and you know how to start and stop it.
- You are familiar with the Tomcat *webapps* directory and how a Tomcat application is structured. In particular, you understand the purpose of the *WEB-INF* directory and the *web.xml* file.
- You know what a tag library is and how to use one.

I recognize that this is a lot to assume, because the use of JSP and Tomcat in the MySQL world is not so widespread as the use of our other languages with Apache. If you're unfamiliar with JSP or need instructions for installing Tomcat, Appendix B provides the necessary background information.

Once you have Tomcat in place, you should install the following components so that you can work through the JSP examples in this book:

- The mcb sample application located in the *tomcat* directory of the recipes distribution.
- A MySQL JDBC driver. You may already have one installed for use with the scripts in earlier chapters, but Tomcat needs a copy, too.
- The JSP Standard Tag Library (JSTL), which contains tags for performing database activities, conditional testing, and iterative operations within JSP pages.

I'll discuss how to install these components, provide a brief overview of some of the JSTL tags, and then describe how to write the JSP equivalent of the MySQL show-tables script that was implemented in Recipe 16.2 using Perl, PHP, and Python.

Installing the mcb Application

Web applications for Tomcat typically are packaged as WAR (web archive) files and installed under its *webapps* directory, which is roughly analogous to Apache's *htdocs* document root directory. The recipes distribution includes a sample application named mcb that you can use for trying the JSP examples described here. Look in the distribution's *tomcat* directory, where you will find a file named *mcb.war*. Copy that file to Tomcat's *webapps* directory.

Here's an example installation procedure for Unix, assuming that the recipes distribution and Tomcat are located at */u/paul/recipes* and */usr/local/jakarta-tomcat*. The command to install *mcb.war* would look like this:

```
% cp /u/paul/recipes/tomcat/mcb.war /usr/local/jakarta-tomcat/webapps
```

For Windows, if the relevant directories are *D:\recipes* and *D:\jakarta-tomcat*, the command looks like this:

```
C:\> copy D:\recipes\tomcat\mcb.war D:\jakarta-tomcat\webapps
```

After copying the *mcb.war* file to the *webapps* directory, restart Tomcat. As distributed, Tomcat is configured by default to look for WAR files under *webapps* when it starts up and automatically unpack any that have not already been unpacked. This means that copying *mcb.war* to the *webapps* directory and restarting Tomcat should be enough to unpack the mcb application. When Tomcat finishes its startup sequence, look under *webapps* and you should see a new *mcb* directory under which are all the files contained in *mcb.war*. (If Tomcat doesn't unpack *mcb.war* automatically, see the sidebar "Unpacking a WAR File Manually.") If you like, have a look around in the *mcb* directory at this point. It should contain several files that clients can request using a browser. There should also be a *WEB-INF* subdirectory, which is used for information that is private—that is, available for use by scripts in the *mcb* directory, but not directly accessible by clients.

Next, verify that Tomcat can serve pages from the mcb application context by requesting some of them from your browser. The following URLs request in turn a static HTML page, a servlet, and a simple JSP page:

http://tomcat.snake.net:8080/mcb/test.html
http://tomcat.snake.net:8080/mcb/servlet/SimpleServlet
http://tomcat.snake.net:8080/mcb/simple.jsp

Adjust the hostname and port number in the URLs appropriately for your installation.

Unpacking a WAR File Manually

WAR files are actually ZIP-format archives that can be unpacked using *jar*, *WinZip*, or any other tool that understands ZIP files. However, when unpacking a WAR file manually, you'll need to create its top-level directory first. The following sequence of steps shows one way to do this, using the *jar* utility to unpack a WAR file named *mcb.war* that is assumed to be located in Tomcat's *webapps* directory. For Unix, change location to the *webapps* directory, then issue the following commands:

```
% mkdir mcb
% cd mcb
% jar xf ../mcb.war
```

For Windows, the commands are only slightly different:

```
C:\> mkdir mcb
C:\> cd mcb
C:\> jar xf ..\mcb.war
```

Unpacking the WAR file in the *webapps* directory creates a new application context, so you'll need to restart Tomcat before it notices the new application.

Installing the JDBC Driver

The JSP pages in the mcb application need a JDBC driver for connecting to the cookbook database. The following instructions describe how to install the MySQL Connector/J driver; the installation procedure for other drivers should be similar.

To install MySQL Connector/J for use by Tomcat applications, place a copy of it in Tomcat's directory tree. Assuming that the driver is packaged as a JAR file (as is the case for MySQL Connector/J), there are three likely places under the Tomcat root directory where you can install it, depending on how visible you want the driver to be:

- To make the driver available only to the mcb application, place it in the *mcb/WEB-INF/lib* directory under Tomcat's *webapps* directory.
- To make the driver available to all Tomcat applications but not to Tomcat itself, place it in the *lib* directory under the Tomcat root.
- To make the driver available both to applications and to Tomcat, place it in the *common/lib* directory under the Tomcat root.

I recommend installing a copy of the driver in the *common/lib* directory. That gives it the most global visibility (it will be accessible both by Tomcat and by applications), and you'll need to install it only once. If you enable the driver only for the mcb application by placing a copy in *mcb/WEB-INF/lib*, but then develop other applications that use MySQL, you'll need to either copy the driver into those applications or move it to a more global location.

Making the driver more globally accessible also is useful if you think it likely that at some point you'll elect to use JDBC-based session management or realm authentication. Those activities are handled by Tomcat itself above the application level, so Tomcat needs access to the driver to carry them out.

Here's an example installation procedure for Unix, assuming that the MySQL Connector/J driver and Tomcat are located at */src/Java/mysql-connector-java-bin.jar* and */usr/local/jakarta-tomcat*. The command to install the driver would look like this:

```
% cp /src/Java/mysql-connector-java-bin.jar /usr/local/jakarta-tomcat/common/lib
```

For Windows, if the components are installed at *D:\mysql-connector-java-bin.jar* and *D:\jakarta-tomcat*, the command looks like this:

```
C:\> copy D:\mysql-connector-java-bin.jar D:\jakarta-tomcat\common\lib
```

After installing the driver, restart Tomcat and then request the following mcb application page to verify that Tomcat can find the JDBC driver properly:

http://tomcat.snake.net:8080/mcb/jdbc_test.jsp

You may need to edit *jdbc_test.jsp* first to change the connection parameters.

Installing the JSTL Distribution

Most of the scripts that are part of the mcb sample application use JSTL, so it's necessary to install it or those scripts won't work. To install a tag library into an application context, copy the library's files into the proper locations under the application's *WEB-INF* directory. Generally, this means installing at least one JAR file and a tag library descriptor (TLD) file, and adding some tag library information to the application's *web.xml* file. JSTL actually consists of several tag sets, so there are there are several JAR files and TLD files. The following instructions describe how to install JSTL for use with the mcb application:

- Make sure that the *mcb.war* file has been unpacked to create the mcb application directory hierarchy under the Tomcat *webapps* directory. (See "Installing the mcb Application.") This is necessary because the JSTL files must be installed under the *mcb/WEB-INF* directory, which will not exist until *mcb.war* has been unpacked.

- Get the JSTL distribution from the Jakarta Project web site. Go to the Jakarta Taglibs project page, which is accessible at this URL:

  http://jakarta.apache.org/taglibs/

  Follow the Standard Taglib link to get to the JSTL information page; the latter has a Downloads section from which you can get the binary JSTL distribution.

- Unpack the JSTL distribution into some convenient location, preferably outside of the Tomcat hierarchy. The commands to do this are similar to those used to unpack Tomcat itself (see "Installing a Tomcat Distribution" in Appendix B). For example, to unpack a ZIP format distribution, use the following command, adjusting the filename as necessary:

  ```
  % jar xf jakarta-taglibs-standard.zip
  ```

- Unpacking the distribution will create a directory containing several files. Copy the JAR files (*jstl.jar*, *standard.jar*, and so forth) to the *mcb/WEB-INF/lib* directory. These files contain the class libraries that implement the JSTL tag actions. Copy the tag library descriptor files (*c.tld*, *sql.tld*, and so forth) to the *mcb/WEB-INF* directory. These files define the interface for the actions implemented by the classes in the JAR files.

- The *mcb/WEB-INF* directory contains a file named *web.xml* that is the web application deployment descriptor file (a fancy name for "configuration file"). Modify *web.xml* to add <taglib> entries for each of the JSTL TLD files. The entries will look something like this:

  ```
  <taglib>
      <taglib-uri>http://java.sun.com/jstl/core</taglib-uri>
      <taglib-location>/WEB-INF/c.tld</taglib-location>
  </taglib>
  ```

```
<taglib>
    <taglib-uri>http://java.sun.com/jstl/sql</taglib-uri>
    <taglib-location>/WEB-INF/sql.tld</taglib-location>
</taglib>
```

Each `<taglib>` entry contains a `<taglib-uri>` element that specifies the symbolic name by which mcb JSP pages will refer to the corresponding TLD file, and a `<taglib-location>` element that indicates the location of the TLD file under the mcb application directory. (You'll find that *web.xml* as distributed already contains these entries. However, you should take a look at them to make sure they match the filenames of the TLD files that you just installed in the previous step.)

- The *mcb/WEB-INF* directory also contains a file named *jstl-mcb-setup.inc*. This file is not part of JSTL itself, but it contains a JSTL `<sql:setDataSource>` tag that is used by many of the mcb JSP pages to set up a data source for connecting to the cookbook database. The file looks like this:

```
<sql:setDataSource var="conn"
    driver="com.mysql.jdbc.Driver" url="jdbc:mysql://localhost/cookbook"
    user="cbuser" password="cbpass" />
```

Edit the `driver`, `url`, `user`, and `password` tag attributes as necessary to change the connection parameters to those that you use for accessing the cookbook database. Do not change the var attribute.

- The JSTL distribution also includes WAR files containing documentation and examples (*standard-doc.war* and *standard-examples.war*). If you wish to install these, copy them into Tomcat's *webapps* directory. (You probably should install the documentation so that you can access it locally from your own server. It's useful to install the examples as well, because they provide helpful demonstrations showing how to use JSTL tags in JSP pages.)

- Restart Tomcat so that it notices the changes you've just made to the mcb application and so that it unpacks the WAR files containing the JSTL documentation and examples. If Tomcat doesn't unpack WAR files for you automatically, see the sidebar "Unpacking a WAR File Manually."

After installing JSTL, restart Tomcat and request the following mcb application page to verify that Tomcat can find the JSTL tags properly:

http://tomcat.snake.net:8080/mcb/jstl_test.jsp

Writing JSP Pages with JSTL

This section discusses the syntax for some of the JSTL tags used most frequently by mcb JSP pages. The descriptions are very brief, and many of these tags have additional attributes that allow them to be used in ways other than those shown here. For more information, consult the JSTL specification (see Appendix C).

A JSP page that uses JSTL must include a taglib directive for each tag set that the page uses. Examples in this book use the core and database tags, identified by the following taglib directives:

```
<%@ taglib uri="http://java.sun.com/jstl/sql" prefix="sql" %>
<%@ taglib uri="http://java.sun.com/jstl/core" prefix="c" %>
```

The uri values should match the symbolic values that are listed in the *web.xml* <taglib> entries (see "Installing the JSTL Distribution"). The prefix values indicate the initial string used in tag names to identify tags as part of a given tag library.

JSTL tags are written in XML format, using a special syntax for tag attributes to include expressions. Within tag attributes, text is interpreted literally unless enclosed within ${...}, in which case it is interpreted as an expression to be evaluated.

The following tags are part of the JSTL core tag set:

<c:out>

This tag evaluates its value attribute and is replaced by the result. One common use for this tag is to provide content for the output page. The following tag would produce the value 3:

```
<c:out value="${1+2}" />
```

<c:set>

This tag assigns a value to a variable. For example, to assign a string to a variable named title and then use the variable later in the <title> element of the output page, do this:

```
<c:set var="title" value="JSTL Example Page" />

<html>
<head>
<title><c:out value="${title}" /></title>
</head>
...
```

This example illustrates a principle that is generally true for JSTL tags: To specify a variable into which a value is to be stored, name it without using ${...} notation. To refer to that variable's value later, use it within ${...} so that it is interpreted as an expression to be evaluated.

<c:if>

This tag evaluates the conditional test given in its test attribute. If the test result is true, the tag body is evaluated and becomes the tag's output; if the result is false, the body is ignored:

```
<c:if test="${1 != 0}">
1 is not equal to 0
</c:if>
```

The comparison operators are ==, !=, <, >, <=, and >=. The alternative operators eq, ne, lt, gt, le, and ge make it easier to avoid using special HTML characters in expressions. Arithmetic operators are +, -, *, / (or div), and % (or mod). Logical operators are && (and), || (or), and ! (not). The special empty operator is true if a value is empty or null:

```
<c:set var="x" value="" />
<c:if test="${empty x}">
x is empty
</c:if>
<c:set var="y" value="hello" />
<c:if test="${!empty y}">
y is not empty
</c:if>
```

`<c:choose>`

This is another conditional tag, but it allows multiple conditions to be tested. Include a `<c:when>` tag for each condition that you want to test explicitly, and a `<c:otherwise>` tag if there is a "default" case:

```
<c:choose>
    <c:when test="${count == 0}">
        Please choose an item
    </c:when>
    <c:when test="${count > 1}">
        Please choose only one item
    </c:when>
    <c:otherwise>
        Thank you for choosing an item
    </c:otherwise>
</c:choose>
```

`<c:forEach>`

This tag acts as an iterator, allowing you to loop over a set of values. The following example uses a `<c:forEach>` tag to loop through a set of rows in the result set from a query (represented here by the rs variable):

```
<c:forEach var="row" items="${rs.rows}">
    id = <c:out value="${row.id}" />,
    name = <c:out value="${row.name}" />
    <br />
</c:forEach>
```

Each iteration of the loop assigns the current row to the variable row. Assuming that the query result includes columns named id and name, the column values are accessible as row.id and row.name.

The JSTL database tags are used to issue queries and access their results:

`<sql:setDataSource>`

This tag sets up connection parameters to be used when JSTL contacts the database server. For example, to specify parameters for using the MySQL Connector/J driver to access the cookbook database, the tag looks like this:

```
<sql:setDataSource var="conn"
    driver="com.mysql.jdbc.Driver" url="jdbc:mysql://localhost/cookbook"
    user="cbuser" password="cbpass" />
```

The driver, url, user, and password attributes specify the connection parameters, and the var attribute names the variable to associate with the connection.

By convention, JSP pages in this book use the variable conn, so tags occurring later in the page that require a data source can refer to the connection using the expression ${conn}.

To avoid listing connection parameters in each JSP page that uses MySQL, a `<sql:setDataSource>` tag for connecting to the cookbook database is placed in the include file *WEB-INF/jstl-mcb-setup.inc*. A JSP page can access the file as follows to set up the connection:

```
<%@ include file="/WEB-INF/jstl-mcb-setup.inc" %>
```

To change the connection parameters used by the mcb pages, just edit *jstl-mcb-setup.inc*.

`<sql:update>`

To issue a statement such as UPDATE, DELETE, or INSERT that doesn't return rows, use a `<sql:update>` tag. A dataSource tag attribute indicates the data source, the affected-rows count resulting from the statement is returned in the variable named by the var attribute, and the statement itself should be specified in the tag body:

```
<sql:update var="count" dataSource="${conn}">
    DELETE FROM profile WHERE id > 100
</sql:update>
Number of rows deleted: <c:out value="${count}" />
```

`<sql:query>`

To process queries that return a result set, use `<sql:query>`. As with `<sql:update>`, the text of the query is given in the tag body, and the dataSource attribute indicates the data source. The `<sql:query>` tag also takes a var attribute that names the variable you want to associate with the result set:

```
<sql:query var="rs" dataSource="${conn}">
    SELECT id, name FROM profile ORDER BY id
</sql:query>
```

The mcb JSP pages use rs as the name of the result set variable. Strategies for accessing the contents of a result set are outlined below.

`<sql:param>`

You can write data values literally into a query string, but JSTL also allows the use of placeholders, which is helpful for values that contain characters that are special in SQL statements. Use a ? character for each placeholder in the query string, and provide values to be bound to the placeholders using `<sql:param>` tags in the body of the query-issuing tag. The data value can be specified either in the body of the `<sql:param>` tag or in its value attribute:

```
<sql:update var="count" dataSource="${conn}">
    DELETE FROM profile WHERE id > ?
    <sql:param>100</sql:param>
</sql:update>

<sql:query var="rs" dataSource="${conn}">
    SELECT id, name FROM profile WHERE cats = ? AND color = ?
```

```
    <sql:param value="1" />
    <sql:param value="green" />
</sql:query>
```

The contents of a result set returned by `<sql:query>` are accessible several ways. Assuming that a result set is available through a variable rs, row *i* of the result can be accessed either as `rs.rows[i]` or as `rs.rowsByIndex[i]`, where row number values begin at 0. The first form produces a row with columns that can be accessed by name. The second form produces a row with columns that can be accessed by column number (beginning with 0). For example, if a result set has columns named id and name, you can access the values for row three using column names like this:

```
<c:out value="${rs.rows[2].id}" />
<c:out value="${rs.rows[2].name}" />
```

To use column numbers instead, do this:

```
<c:out value="${rs.rowsByIndex[2][0]}" />
<c:out value="${rs.rowsByIndex[2][1]}" />
```

You can also use `<c:forEach>` as an iterator to loop through the rows in a result set. Iterate through `rs.rows` if you want to access column values by name:

```
<c:forEach var="row" items="${rs.rows}">
    id = <c:out value="${row.id}" />,
    name = <c:out value="${row.name}" />
    <br />
</c:forEach>
```

Iterate through `rs.rowsByIndex` to access column values by number:

```
<c:forEach var="row" items="${rs.rowsByIndex}">
    id = <c:out value="${row[0]}" />,
    name = <c:out value="${row[1]}" />
    <br />
</c:forEach>
```

The row count is available as `rs.rowCount`:

```
Number of rows selected: <c:out value="${rs.rowCount}" />
```

Names of the columns in the result set are available using `rs.columnNames`:

```
<c:forEach var="name" items="${rs.columnNames}">
    <c:out value="${name}" />
    <br />
</c:forEach>
```

Writing a MySQL Script using JSP and JSTL

Recipe 16.2 shows how to write Perl, PHP, and Python versions of a script to display the names of the tables in the cookbook database. With the JSTL tags, we can write a JSP page that provides that information as follows:

```
<%-- show_tables.jsp - Issue SHOW TABLES query, display results --%>

<%@ taglib uri="http://java.sun.com/jstl/core" prefix="c" %>
```

```
<%@ taglib uri="http://java.sun.com/jstl/sql" prefix="sql" %>
<%@ include file="/WEB-INF/jstl-mcb-setup.inc" %>

<html>
<head>
<title>Tables in cookbook Database</title>
</head>
<body bgcolor="white">

<p>Tables in cookbook database:</p>

<sql:query var="rs" dataSource="${conn}">
    SHOW TABLES
</sql:query>

<c:forEach var="row" items="${rs.rowsByIndex}">
    <c:out value="${row[0]}" /><br />
</c:forEach>

</body>
</html>
```

The taglib directives identify which tag libraries the script needs, and the include directive pulls in the code that sets up a data source for accessing the cookbook database. The rest of the script generates the page content.

This script should be installed in the *mcb* subdirectory of your Tomcat server's *webapps* directory, and you can invoke it as follows:

http://tomcat.snake.net:8080/mcb/show_tables.jsp

Like the PHP script shown in Recipe 16.2, the JSP script does not produce any Content-Type: header explicitly. The JSP engine produces a default header with a content type of text/html automatically.

16.4   Encoding Special Characters in Web Output

Problem

Certain characters are special in HTML pages and must be encoded if you want to display them literally. Because database content often contains these characters, scripts that include query results in web pages should encode those results to prevent browsers from misinterpreting the information.

Solution

Use the methods that are provided by your API for performing HTML-encoding and URL-encoding.

Discussion

HTML is a markup language—it uses certain characters as markers that have a special meaning. To include literal instances of these characters in a page, you must encode them so that they are not interpreted as having their special meanings. For example, < should be encoded as < to keep a browser from interpreting it as the beginning of a tag. Furthermore, there are actually two kinds of encoding, depending on the context in which you use a character. One encoding is appropriate for general HTML text, another is used for text that is part of a URL in a hyperlink.

The MySQL show-tables scripts shown in Recipes 16.2 and 16.3 are simple demonstrations of how to produce web pages using programs. But with one exception, the scripts have a common failing: they take no care to properly encode special characters that occur in the information retrieved from the MySQL server. (The exception is the JSP version of the script; the <c:out> tag used there handles encoding automatically, as we'll discuss shortly.)

As it happens, I deliberately chose information to display that is unlikely to contain any special characters, so they should work properly even in the absence of any encoding. However, in the general case, it's unsafe to assume that a query result will contain no special characters and thus you must be prepared to encode it. Neglecting to do this often results in scripts that generate pages containing malformed HTML that displays incorrectly.

This section describes how to handle special characters, beginning with some general principles, and then discusses how each API implements encoding support. The API-specific examples show how to process information drawn from a database table, but they can be adapted to any content you include in a web page, no matter its source.

General Encoding Principles

One form of encoding applies to characters that are used in writing HTML constructs, another applies to text that is included in URLs. It's important to understand this distinction so that you don't encode text inappropriately. Note too that encoding text for inclusion in a web page is an entirely different issue than encoding special characters in data values for inclusion in a SQL statement. The latter issue is discussed in Recipe 2.7.

Encoding characters that are special in HTML

HTML markup uses < and > characters to begin and end tags, & to begin special entity names (such as   to signify a non-breaking space), and " to quote attribute values in tags (such as <p align="left">). Consequently, to display literal instances of these characters, you must encode them as HTML entities so that browsers or other clients understand your intent. To do this, convert <, >, &, and " to the corresponding HTML entity designators < (less than), > (greater than), & (ampersand), and " (quote).

Suppose you want to display the following string literally in a web page:

```
Paragraphs begin and end with <p> & </p> tags.
```

If you send this text to the client browser exactly as shown, the browser will misinterpret it. (The `<p>` and `</p>` tags will be taken as paragraph markers and the & may be taken as the beginning of an HTML entity designator.) To display the string the way you intend, the special characters should be encoded as the <, >, and &, entities:

```
Paragraphs begin and end with &lt;p&gt; &amp; &lt;/p&gt; tags.
```

The principle of encoding text this way is also useful within tags. For example, HTML tag attribute values usually are enclosed within double quotes, so it's important to perform HTML-encoding on attribute values. Suppose you want to include a text input box in a form, and you want to provide an initial value of Rich "Goose" Gossage to be displayed in the box. You cannot write that value literally in the tag like this:

```
<input type="text" name="player_name" value="Rich "Goose" Gossage" />
```

The problem here is that the double-quoted value attribute includes internal double quotes, which makes the `<input>` tag malformed. The proper way to write it is to encode the double quotes:

```
<input type="text" name="player_name" value="Rich &quot;Goose&quot; Gossage" />
```

When a browser receives this text, it will decode the " entities back to " characters and interpret the value attribute value properly.

Encoding characters that are special in URLs

URLs for hyperlinks that occur within HTML pages have their own syntax, and their own encoding. This encoding applies to attributes within several tags:

```
<a href="URL">
<img src="URL">
<form action="URL">
<frame src="URL">
```

Many characters have special meaning within URLs, such as :, /, ?, =, &, and ;. The following URL contains some of these characters:

http://apache.snake.net/myscript.php?id=428&name=Gandalf

Here the : and / characters segment the URL into components, the ? character indicates that parameters are present, and the & characters separates the parameters, each of which is specified as a *name=value* pair. (The ; character is not present in the URL just shown, but commonly is used instead of & to separate parameters.) If you want to include any of these characters literally within a URL, you must encode them to prevent the browser from interpreting them with their usual special meaning. Other characters such as spaces require special treatment as well. Spaces are not allowed within a URL, so if you want to reference a page named *my home page.html* on the site *apache.snake.net*, the URL in the following hyperlink won't work:

```
<a href="http://apache.snake.net/my home page.html">My Home Page</a>
```

URL-encoding for special and reserved characters is performed by converting each such character to % followed by two hexadecimal digits representing the character's ASCII code. For example, the ASCII value of the space character is 32 decimal, or 20 hexadecimal, so you'd write the preceding hyperlink like this:

```
<a href="http://apache.snake.net/my%20home%20page.html">My Home Page</a>
```

Sometimes you'll see spaces encoded as + in URLs. This too is legal.

Encoding interactions

Be sure to encode information properly for the context in which you're using it. Suppose you want to create a hyperlink to trigger a search for items matching a search term, and you want the term itself to appear as the link label that is displayed in the page. In this case, the term appears as a parameter in the URL, and also as HTML text between the <a> and </a> tags. If the search term is "cats & dogs", the unencoded hyperlink construct looks like this:

```
<a href="/cgi-bin/myscript?term=cats & dogs">cats & dogs</a>
```

That is incorrect because & is special in both contexts and the spaces are special in the URL. The link should be written like this instead:

```
<a href="/cgi-bin/myscript?term=cats%20%26%20dogs">cats &amp; dogs</a>
```

Here, & is HTML-encoded as & for the link label, and is URL-encoded as %26 for the URL, which also includes spaces encoded as %20.

Granted, it's a pain to encode text before writing it to a web page, and sometimes you know enough about a value that you can skip the encoding (see the sidebar "Do You Always Need to Encode Web Page Output?"). But encoding is the safe thing to do most of the time. Fortunately, most APIs provide functions to do the work for you. This means you need not know every character that is special in a given context. You just need to know which kind of encoding to perform, and call the appropriate function to produce the intended result.

Encoding Special Characters Using Web APIs

The following encoding examples show how to pull values out of MySQL and perform both HTML-encoding and URL-encoding on them to generate hyperlinks. Each example reads a table named phrase that contains short phrases, using its contents to

Do You Always Need to Encode Web Page Output?

If you *know* a value is legal in a particular context within a web page, you need not encode it. For example, if you obtain a value from an integer-valued column in a database table that cannot be NULL, it must necessarily be an integer. No HTML- or URL-encoding is needed to include the value in a web page, because digits are not special in HTML text or within URLs. On the other hand, suppose you solicit an integer value using a field in a web form. You might be expecting the user to provide an integer, but the user might be confused and enter an illegal value. You could handle this by displaying an error page that shows the value and explains that it's not an integer. But if the value contains special characters and you don't encode it, the page won't display the value properly, possibly confusing the user further.

construct hyperlinks that point to a (hypothetical) script that searches for instances of the phrases in some other table. The table looks like this:

```
mysql> SELECT phrase_val FROM phrase ORDER BY phrase_val;
+--------------------------+
| phrase_val               |
+--------------------------+
| are we "there" yet?      |
| cats & dogs              |
| rhinoceros               |
| the whole > sum of parts |
+--------------------------+
```

The goal here is to generate a list of hyperlinks using each phrase both as the hyperlink label (which requires HTML-encoding) and in the URL as a parameter to the search script (which requires URL-encoding). The resulting links look like this:

```
<a href="/cgi-bin/mysearch.pl?phrase=are%20we%20%22there%22%20yet%3F">
are we &quot;there&quot; yet?</a>
<a href="/cgi-bin/mysearch.pl?phrase=cats%20%26%20dogs">
cats &amp; dogs</a>
<a href="/cgi-bin/mysearch.pl?phrase=rhinoceros">
rhinoceros</a>
<a href="/cgi-bin/mysearch.pl?phrase=the%20whole%20%3E%20sum%20of%20parts">
the whole &gt; sum of parts</a>
```

The links produced by some APIs will look slightly different, because they encode spaces as + rather than as %20.

Perl

The Perl CGI.pm module provides two methods, escapeHTML( ) and escape( ), that handle HTML-encoding and URL-encoding. There are three ways to use these methods to encode a string $str:

- Invoke escapeHTML() and escape() as CGI class methods using a CGI:: prefix:

```
use CGI;
printf "%s\n%s\n", CGI::escape ($str), CGI::escapeHTML ($str);
```

- Create a CGI object and invoke escapeHTML() and escape() as object methods:

```
use CGI;
my $cgi = new CGI;
printf "%s\n%s\n", $cgi->escape ($str), $cgi->escapeHTML ($str);
```

- Import the names explicitly into your script's namespace. In this case, neither a CGI object nor the CGI:: prefix is necessary and you can invoke the methods as standalone functions. The following example imports the two method names in addition to the set of standard names:

```
use CGI qw(:standard escape escapeHTML);
printf "%s\n%s\n", escape ($str), escapeHTML ($str);
```

I prefer the last alternative because it is consistent with the CGI.pm function call interface that you use for other imported method names. Just remember to include the encoding method names in the use CGI statement for any Perl script that requires them, or you'll get "undefined subroutine" errors when the script executes.

The following code reads the contents of the phrase table and produces hyperlinks from them using escapeHTML() and escape():

```
my $query = "SELECT phrase_val FROM phrase ORDER BY phrase_val";
my $sth = $dbh->prepare ($query);
$sth->execute ();
while (my ($phrase) = $sth->fetchrow_array ())
{
    # URL-encode the phrase value for use in the URL
    # HTML-encode the phrase value for use in the link label
    my $url = "/cgi-bin/mysearch.pl?phrase=" . escape ($phrase);
    my $label = escapeHTML ($phrase);
    print a ({-href => $url}, $label) . br () . "\n";
}
```

PHP

In PHP, the htmlspecialchars() and urlencode() functions perform HTML-encoding and URL-encoding. They're used as follows:

```
$query = "SELECT phrase_val FROM phrase ORDER BY phrase_val";
$result_id = mysql_query ($query, $conn_id);
if ($result_id)
{
    while (list ($phrase) = mysql_fetch_row ($result_id))
    {
        # URL-encode the phrase value for use in the URL
        # HTML-encode the phrase value for use in the link label
        $url = "/mcb/mysearch.php?phrase=" . urlencode ($phrase);
        $label = htmlspecialchars ($phrase);
        printf ("<a href=\"%s\">%s</a><br />\n", $url, $label);
```

```
    }
    mysql_free_result ($result_id);
}
```

Python

In Python, the `cgi` and `urllib` modules contain the relevant encoding methods. `cgi.escape()` performs HTML-encoding and `urllib.quote()` does URL-encoding:

```
import cgi
import urllib

query = "SELECT phrase_val FROM phrase ORDER BY phrase_val"
cursor = conn.cursor ()
cursor.execute (query)
for (phrase,) in cursor.fetchall ():
    # URL-encode the phrase value for use in the URL
    # HTML-encode the phrase value for use in the link label
    url = "/cgi-bin/mysearch.py?phrase=" + urllib.quote (phrase)
    label = cgi.escape (phrase, 1)
    print "<a href=\"%s\">%s</a><br />" % (url, label)
cursor.close ()
```

The first argument to `cgi.escape()` is the string to be HTML-encoded. By default, this function converts <, >, and & characters to their corresponding HTML entities. To tell `cgi.escape()` also to convert double quotes to the " entity, pass a second argument of 1, as shown in the example. This is especially important if you're encoding values to be placed into a double-quoted tag attribute.

Java

The `<c:out>` JSTL tag automatically performs HTML-encoding for JSP pages. (Strictly speaking, it performs XML-encoding, but the set of characters affected is <, >, &, ", and ', which includes all those needed for HTML-encoding.) By using `<c:out>` to display text in a web page, you need not even think about converting special characters to HTML entities. If for some reason you want to suppress encoding, invoke `<c:out>` like this:

```
<c:out value="value to display" encodeXML="false" />
```

To URL-encode parameters for inclusion in a URL, use the `<c:url>` tag. Specify the URL string in the tag's value attribute, and include any parameter values and names in `<c:param>` tags in the body of the `<c:url>` tag. A parameter value can be given either in the value attribute of a `<c:param>` tag or in its body. Here's an example that shows both ways:

```
<c:url var="urlStr" value="myscript.jsp">
    <c:param name="id" value ="47" />
    <c:param name="color">sky blue</c:param>
</c:url>
```

This will URL-encode the values of the id and color parameters and add them to the end of the URL. The result is placed in an object named urlStr, which you can display as follows:

```
<c:out value="${urlStr}" />
```

The <c:url> tag does not encode special characters such as spaces in the string supplied in its value attribute. You must encode them yourself, so it's probably best just to avoid creating pages with spaces in their names, to avoid the likelihood that you'll need to refer to them.

The <c:out> and <c:url> tags can be used as follows to display entries from the phrase table:

```
<sql:query var="rs" dataSource="${conn}">
    SELECT phrase_val FROM phrase ORDER BY phrase_val
</sql:query>

<c:forEach var="row" items="${rs.rows}">
    <%-- URL-encode the phrase value for use in the URL --%>
    <%-- HTML-encode the phrase value for use in the link label --%>
    <c:url var="urlStr" value="/mcb/mysearch.jsp">
        <c:param name="phrase" value ="${row.phrase_val}" />
    </c:url>
    <a href="<c:out value="${urlStr}" />"><c:out value="${row.phrase_val}" />
    </a>
    <br />
</c:forEach>
```

## CHAPTER 17

Incorporating Query Results into Web Pages

17.0 Introduction

When you store information in your database, you can easily retrieve it for use on the Web in a variety of ways. Query results can be displayed as unstructured paragraphs or as structured elements such as lists or tables; you can display static text or create hyperlinks. Query metadata can be useful when formatting query results, too, such as when generating an HTML table that displays a result set and uses its metadata to get the column headings for the table. These tasks combine query processing with web scripting, and are primarily a matter of properly encoding any special characters in the results (like & or <) and adding the appropriate HTML tags for the types of elements you want to produce.

This chapter shows how to generate several types of web output from query results. It also covers techniques for inserting binary data into your database and for retrieving and transferring that kind of information to clients. (It's easiest and most common to work with text for creating web pages from database content, but you can also use MySQL to help service requests for binary data such as images, sounds, or PDF files.)

The recipes here build on the techniques shown in Chapter 16 for generating web pages from scripts and for encoding output for display. See that chapter if you need some background in these topics.

The scripts from which the examples in this chapter are drawn can be found in the recipes distribution under the directories named for the servers used to run them. For Perl, PHP, and Python examples, look under the *apache* directory. For Java (JSP) examples, look under *tomcat*; you should already have installed these in the process of setting up the mcb application context (Recipe 16.3). The exception to this is that some of the utility routines used here are found in library files in the *lib* directory.

Note that not all languages are represented in every section. If a particular section seems to be "missing" an example for the language you're interested in, check the recipes distribution; it may contain the implementation you want, even if it's not shown here.

17.1 Displaying Query Results as Paragraph Text

Problem

You want to display a query result as free text.

Solution

Display it with no surrounding HTML structure other than paragraph tags.

Discussion

Paragraphs are useful for displaying free text with no particular structure. In this case all you need to do is retrieve the text to be displayed, encode it to convert special characters to the corresponding HTML entities, and wrap each paragraph within <p> and </p> tags. The following examples show how to produce a paragraph for a status display that includes the current date and time, the server version, the client username, and the current database name (if any). These values are available from the following query:

```
mysql> SELECT NOW(), VERSION(), USER(), DATABASE();
+---------------------+---------------+----------------+------------+
| NOW()               | VERSION()     | USER()         | DATABASE() |
+---------------------+---------------+----------------+------------+
| 2002-05-18 11:33:12 | 4.0.2-alpha-log | paul@localhost | cookbook   |
+---------------------+---------------+----------------+------------+
```

In Perl, the CGI.pm module provides a p( ) function that adds paragraph tags around the string you pass to it. p( ) does not HTML-encode its argument, so you should take care of that by calling escapeHTML( ):

```
($now, $version, $user, $db) =
    $dbh->selectrow_array ("SELECT NOW(), VERSION(), USER(), DATABASE()");
$db = "NONE" unless defined ($db);
$para = <<EOF;
Local time on the MySQL server is $now.
The server version is $version.
The current user is $user.
The current database is $db.
EOF
print p (escapeHTML ($para));
```

In PHP, you can print the <p> and </p> tags around the encoded paragraph text:

```
$query = "SELECT NOW(), VERSION(), USER(), DATABASE()";
$result_id = mysql_query ($query, $conn_id);
if ($result_id)
{
    list ($now, $version, $user, $db) = mysql_fetch_row ($result_id);
    mysql_free_result ($result_id);
    if (!isset ($db))
```

```
        $db = "NONE";
    $para = "Local time on the MySQL server is $now."
              . " The server version is $version."
              . " The current user is $user."
              . " The current database is $db.";
    print ("<p>" . htmlspecialchars ($para) . "</p>\n");
}
```

Or, after fetching the query result, you can print the paragraph by beginning in HTML mode and switching between modes:

```
<p>
Local time on the MySQL server is
<?php print (htmlspecialchars ($now)); ?>.
The server version is
<?php print (htmlspecialchars ($version)); ?>.
The current user is
<?php print (htmlspecialchars ($user)); ?>.
The current database is
<?php print (htmlspecialchars ($db)); ?>.
</p>
```

To display a paragraph in Python, do something like this::

```
cursor = conn.cursor ()
cursor.execute ("SELECT NOW(), VERSION(), USER(), DATABASE()")
row = cursor.fetchone ()
if row is not None:
    if row[3] is None:  # check database name
        row[3] = "NONE"
    para = ("Local time on the MySQL server is %s." +
            " The server version is %s." +
            " The current user is %s." +
            " The current database is %s.") % (row)
    print "<p>" + cgi.escape (para, 1) + "</p>"
cursor.close ()
```

In JSP, the display might be produced as follows:

```
<sql:query var="rs" dataSource="${conn}">
    SELECT NOW(), VERSION(), USER(), DATABASE()
</sql:query>
<c:set var="row" value="${rs.rowsByIndex[0]}" />
<c:set var="db" value="${row[3]}" />
<c:if test="${empty db}">
    <c:set var="db" value="NONE" />
</c:if>

<p>
Local time on the server is <c:out value="${row[0]}" />.
The server version is <c:out value="${row[1]}" />.
The current user is <c:out value="${row[2]}" />.
The current database is <c:out value="${db}" />.
</p>
```

The JSP script uses `rowsByIndex` so that the result set row's columns can be accessed by numeric index.

17.2 Displaying Query Results as Lists

Problem

A query result contains a set of items that should be displayed as a structured list.

Solution

Write the list items within the proper HTML tags for the desired type of list.

Discussion

More structured than paragraphs and less structured than tables, lists provide a useful way to display a set of individual items. HTML provides several styles of lists, such as ordered lists, unordered lists, and definition lists. You may also wish to nest lists, which requires list-within-list formatting.

Lists generally consist of an opening and closing tag that surround a set of items, each of which is delimited by its own tags. List items correspond naturally to rows returned from a query, so generating an HTML list structure from within a program is a matter of encoding your query result, surrounding each row with the proper item tags, and adding the opening and closing list tags. Two approaches to list generation are common. If you want to print the tags as you process the result set, do this:

1. Print the list opening tag.
2. Fetch and print each result set row as a list item, including the item tags.
3. Print the list closing tag.

Alternatively, you can process the list in memory:

1. Store the list items in an array.
2. Pass the array to a list generation function that adds the appropriate tags, then print the result.

The examples that follow demonstrate both approaches.

Ordered Lists

An ordered list consists of items that have a particular sequence. Browsers typically display ordered lists as a set of numbered items:

```
1. First item
2. Second item
3. Third item
```

You need not specify the item numbers, because the browser will add them automatically. The HTML for an ordered list begins and ends with `<ol>` and `</ol>` opening and closing tags, and contains items surrounded by `<li>` and `</li>` tags:

```
<ol>
  <li>First item</li>
  <li>Second item</li>
  <li>Third item</li>
</ol>
```

Suppose you have an `ingredient` table that contains numbered ingredients for a cooking recipe:

```
+----+--------------------------------+
| id | item                           |
+----+--------------------------------+
|  1 | 3 cups flour                   |
|  2 | 1/2 cup raw ("unrefined") sugar |
|  3 | 3 eggs                         |
|  4 | pinch (< 1/16 teaspoon) salt   |
+----+--------------------------------+
```

The table contains an `id` column, but you need only fetch the text values in the proper order to display them as an ordered list, because a browser will add item numbers itself. The items contain the special characters " and <, so you should HTML-encode them before adding the tags that convert the items to an HTML list. The result will look like this:

```
<ol>
<li>3 cups flour</li>
<li>1/2 cup raw (&quot;unrefined&quot;) sugar</li>
<li>3 eggs</li>
<li>pinch (&lt; 1/16 teaspoon) salt</li>
</ol>
```

One way to create such list from a script is by printing the HTML as you fetch the rows of the result set. Here's how you might do so in a JSP page using the JSTL tags:

```
<sql:query var="rs" dataSource="${conn}">
    SELECT item FROM ingredient ORDER BY id
</sql:query>
<ol>
<c:forEach var="row" items="${rs.rows}">
    <li><c:out value="${row.item}" /></li>
</c:forEach>
</ol>
```

In PHP, the same operation can be performed like this:

```
$query = "SELECT item FROM ingredient ORDER BY id";
$result_id = mysql_query ($query, $conn_id);
if (!$result_id)
    die (htmlspecialchars (mysql_error ($conn_id)));
print ("<ol>\n");
while (list ($item) = mysql_fetch_row ($result_id))
```

```
        print ("<li>" . htmlspecialchars ($item) . "</li>\n");
    mysql_free_result ($result_id);
    print ("</ol>\n");
```

It's not necessary to add the newlines after the closing tags as this example does; web browsers don't care if they're present or not. I like to add them because the HTML produced by a script is easier to examine directly if it's not all on a single line, which simplifies debugging.

The preceding examples use an approach to HTML generation that interleaves record fetching and output generation. It's also possible to separate or decouple the two operations: retrieve the data first, then write the output. Queries tend to vary from list to list, but generating the list itself often is fairly stereotypical. If you put the list-generation code into a utility function, you can reuse it for different queries. The two issues the function must handle are HTML-encoding of the items (if they aren't already encoded) and adding the proper HTML tags. For example, in PHP, a function make_ordered_list() can be written as follows. It takes the list items as an array argument and returns the list as a string:

```
function make_ordered_list ($items, $encode = TRUE)
{
    if (!is_array ($items))
        return ("make_ordered_list: items argument must be an array");
    $str = "<ol>\n";
    reset ($items);
    while (list ($k, $v) = each ($items))
    {
        if ($encode)
            $v = htmlspecialchars ($v);
        $str .= "<li>$v</li>\n";
    }
    $str .= "</ol>\n";
    return ($str);
}
```

After writing the utility function, you can fetch the data and print HTML like so:

```
# fetch items for list
$query = "SELECT item FROM ingredient ORDER BY id";
$result_id = mysql_query ($query, $conn_id);
if (!$result_id)
    die (htmlspecialchars (mysql_error ($conn_id)));
$items = array ();
while (list ($item) = mysql_fetch_row ($result_id))
    $items[] = $item;
mysql_free_result ($result_id);

# generate HTML list
print (make_ordered_list ($items));
```

In Python, the utility function can be defined like this:

```
def make_ordered_list (items, encode = 1):
    if type (items) not in (types.ListType, types.TupleType):
        return ("make_ordered_list: items argument must be a list")
```

```
        list = "<ol>\n"
        for item in items:
            if item is None:      # handle possibility of NULL item
                item = ""
            # make sure item is a string, then encode if necessary
            if type (item) is not types.StringType:
                item = `item`
            if encode:
                item = cgi.escape (item, 1)
            list = list + "<li>" + item + "</li>\n"
        list = list + "</ol>\n"
        return list
```

And used as follows:

```
    # fetch items for list
    query = "SELECT item FROM ingredient ORDER BY id"
    cursor = conn.cursor ()
    cursor.execute (query)
    items = [ ]
    for (item,) in cursor.fetchall ():
        items.append (item)
    cursor.close ()

    # generate HTML list
    print make_ordered_list (items)
```

The PHP and Python versions of make_ordered_list() check their first argument to make sure it's an array. If it's not, they return an error string indicating the problem. Returning a descriptive string makes problems immediately obvious in the web page when you look at the output produced by the function. You could return some other kind of error indicator if you like, or perhaps raise an exception or terminate the script.

The second argument to make_ordered_list() indicates whether it should perform HTML-encoding of the list items. The easiest thing is to let the function handle this for you (which is why the default is true). However, if you're creating a list from items that themselves include HTML tags, you wouldn't want the function to encode the special characters in those tags. For example, if you're creating a list of hyperlinks, each list item will contain <a> tags. To prevent these from being converted to <a>, pass make_ordered_list() a second argument of FALSE (for PHP) or 0 (for Python).

If your API provides functions to generate HTML structures, you need not write them yourself, of course. That's the case for Perl CGI.pm module: generate each item by invoking its li() function to add the opening and closing item tags, save up the items in an array, and pass the array to ol() to add the opening and closing list tags:

```
    my $query = "SELECT item FROM ingredient ORDER BY id";
    my $sth = $dbh->prepare ($query);
    $sth->execute ();
    my @items = ();
```

```
while (my $ref = $sth->fetchrow_arrayref ())
{
    # handle possibility of NULL (undef) item
    my $item = (defined ($ref->[0]) ? escapeHTML ($ref->[0]) : "");
    push (@items, li ($item));
}
print ol (@items);
```

The reason for converting undef (NULL) values to the empty string is to avoid having Perl generate uninitialized-value warnings when run with the -*w* option. (The ingredient table doesn't actually contain any NULL values, but the technique is useful for dealing with tables that might.)

The previous example intertwines record fetching and HTML generation. To use a more decoupled approach that separates fetching the items from printing the HTML, first retrieve the items into an array. Then pass the array by reference to li() and the result to ol():

```
# fetch items for list
my $query = "SELECT item FROM ingredient ORDER BY id";
my $item_ref = $dbh->selectcol_arrayref ($query);

# generate HTML list, handling possibility of NULL (undef) items
$item_ref = [ map { defined ($_) ? escapeHTML ($_) : "" } @{$item_ref} ];
print ol (li ($item_ref));
```

Note two things about the li() function:

- It doesn't perform any HTML-encoding; you must do that yourself.
- It can handle a single value or an array of values. However, if you pass an array, you should pass it by reference. When you do that, li() adds <li> and </li> tags to each array element, then concatenates them and returns the resulting string. If you pass the array itself rather than a reference, li() concatenates the items first, then adds a single set of tags around the result, which is usually not what you want. This behavior is shared by several other CGI.pm functions that can operate on single or multiple values. For example, the table data td() function adds a single set of <td> and </td> tags if you pass it a scalar or list. If you pass a list reference, it add the tags to each item in the list.

Unordered Lists

An unordered list is like an ordered list except that browsers display all the items with the same marker character, such as a bullet:

- First item
- Second item
- Third item

Should You Intertwine or Decouple Record Fetching and HTML Generation?

If you want to write a script in a hurry, you can probably get it running most quickly by writing code that prints HTML from query rows as you fetch them. There are, however, certain advantages to separating data retrieval from output production. The most obvious ones are that by using a utility function to generate the HTML, you have to write the function only once, and you can share it among scripts. (And if your API provides the function, you don't have to write it even once; so much the better.) But there are other benefits as well:

- Functions that generate HTML structures can be used with data obtained from other sources, not just from a database.

- The decoupled approach takes advantage of the fact that you need not generate output directly. You can construct a page element in memory, then print it when you're ready. This is particularly useful for building pages that consist of several components, because it gives you more latitude to create the components in the order that's most convenient.

- Decoupling record fetching and output generation gives you more flexibility in the types of output you produce. If you decide to generate an unordered list rather than an ordered list, just call a different output function; the data collection phase need not change. This is true even if you decide to use a different output format (XML or WML rather than HTML, for example). In this case, you still need only a different output function; data collection remains unchanged.

- By prefetching the list items, you can make adaptive decisions about what type of list to create. Although we are not yet to the point of discussing web forms, they make heavy use of their own kinds of lists. In that context, having items in hand before generating an HTML structure from them can be useful if you want to choose the list type based on the size of the list. For example, you can display a set of radio buttons if the number of items is small, or a pop-up menu or scrolling list if the number is large.

"Unordered" refers to the fact that the marker character provides no sequence information. You can of course display the items in any order you choose. The HTML for an unordered list is the same as for an ordered list except that the opening and closing tags are <ul> and </ul> rather than <ol> and </ol>:

```
<ul>
  <li>First item</li>
  <li>Second item</li>
  <li>Third item</li>
</ul>
```

For APIs where you print the tags directly, use the same procedure as for ordered lists, but print `<ul>` and `</ul>` instead of `<ol>` and `</ol>`. Here is an example in JSP:

```
<sql:query var="rs" dataSource="${conn}">
    SELECT item FROM ingredient ORDER BY id
</sql:query>
<ul>
<c:forEach var="row" items="${rs.rows}">
    <li><c:out value="${row.item}" /></li>
</c:forEach>
</ul>
```

In Perl, create an unordered list by using the CGI.pm `ul()` function rather than `ol()`:

```
# fetch items for list
my $query = "SELECT item FROM ingredient ORDER BY id";
my $item_ref = $dbh->selectcol_arrayref ($query);

# generate HTML list, handling possibility of NULL (undef) items
$item_ref = [ map { defined ($_) ? escapeHTML ($_) : "" } @{$item_ref} ];
print ul (li ($item_ref));
```

If you're writing your own utility function for unordered lists, it's easily derived from a function that generates ordered lists. For example, it's simple to adapt the PHP and Python versions of `make_ordered_list()` to create `make_unordered_list()` functions, because they differ only in the opening and closing list tags used.

Definition Lists

A definition list consists of two-part items, each including a term and a definition. "Term" and "definition" have loose meanings, because you can display any kind of information you want. For example, the following `doremi` table associates the name of each note in a musical scale with a mnemonic phrase for remembering it, but the mnemonics aren't exactly what you'd call definitions:

```
+----+------+---------------------------+
| id | note | mnemonic                  |
+----+------+---------------------------+
|  1 | do   | A deer, a female deer     |
|  2 | re   | A drop of golden sun      |
|  3 | mi   | A name I call myself      |
|  4 | fa   | A long, long way to run   |
|  5 | so   | A needle pulling thread   |
|  6 | la   | A note to follow so       |
|  7 | ti   | I drink with jam and bread |
+----+------+---------------------------+
```

Nevertheless, the note and mnemonic columns can be displayed as a definition list:

```
do
    A deer, a female deer
re
    A drop of golden sun
mi
    A name I call myself
```

```
fa
    A long, long way to run
so
    A needle pulling thread
la
    A note to follow so
ti
    I drink with jam and bread
```

The HTML for a definition list begins and ends with <dl> and </dl> tags. Each item has a term delimited by <dt> and </dt>, and a definition delimited by <dd> and </dd>:

```
<dl>
  <dt>do</dt> <dd>A deer, a female deer</dd>
  <dt>re</dt> <dd>A drop of golden sun</dd>
  <dt>mi</dt> <dd>A name I call myself</dd>
  <dt>fa</dt> <dd>A long, long way to run</dd>
  <dt>so</dt> <dd>A needle pulling thread</dd>
  <dt>la</dt> <dd>A note to follow so</dd>
  <dt>ti</dt> <dd>I drink with jam and bread</dd>
</dl>
```

In a JSP page, you can generate the definition list like this:

```
<sql:query var="rs" dataSource="${conn}">
    SELECT note, mnemonic FROM doremi ORDER BY note
</sql:query>
<dl>
<c:forEach var="row" items="${rs.rows}">
    <dt><c:out value="${row.note}" /></dt>
    <dd><c:out value="${row.mnemonic}" /></dd>
</c:forEach>
</dl>
```

In PHP, create the list like this:

```
$query = "SELECT item FROM ingredient ORDER BY id";
$result_id = mysql_query ($query, $conn_id);
if (!$result_id)
    die (htmlspecialchars (mysql_error ($conn_id)));
print ("<dl>\n");
while (list ($note, $mnemonic) = mysql_fetch_row ($result_id))
{
    print ("<dt>" . htmlspecialchars ($note) . "</dt>\n");
    print ("<dd>" . htmlspecialchars ($mnemonic) . "</dt>\n");
}
mysql_free_result ($result_id);
print ("</dl>\n");
```

Or write a utility function that takes arrays of terms and definitions and returns the list as a string:

```
function make_definition_list ($terms, $definitions, $encode = TRUE)
{
    if (!is_array ($terms))
        return ("make_definition_list: terms argument must be an array");
    if (!is_array ($definitions))
```

```
        return ("make_definition_list: definitions argument must be an array");
    if (count ($terms) != count ($definitions))
        return ("make_definition_list: term and definition list size mismatch");
    $str = "<dl>\n";
    reset ($terms);
    reset ($definitions);
    while (list ($dtk, $dtv) = each ($terms))
    {
        list ($ddk, $ddv) = each ($definitions);
        if ($encode)
        {
            $dtv = htmlspecialchars ($dtv);
            $ddv = htmlspecialchars ($ddv);
        }
        $str .= "<dt>$dtv</dt>\n<dd>$ddv</dd>\n";
    }
    $str .= "</dl>\n";
    return ($str);
}
```

Use the `make_definition_list()` function like this:

```
# fetch items for list
$query = "SELECT note, mnemonic FROM doremi ORDER BY id";
$result_id = mysql_query ($query, $conn_id);
if (!$result_id)
    die (htmlspecialchars (mysql_error ($conn_id)));
$terms = array ();
$defs = array ();
while (list ($note, $mnemonic) = mysql_fetch_row ($result_id))
{
    $terms[] = $note;
    $defs[] = $mnemonic;
}
mysql_free_result ($result_id);

# generate HTML list
print (make_definition_list ($terms, $defs));
```

In Perl, create the terms and definitions by invoking dt() and dd(), save them in an array, and pass the array to dl():

```
my $query = "SELECT note, mnemonic FROM doremi ORDER BY id";
my $sth = $dbh->prepare ($query);
$sth->execute ();
my @items = ();
while (my ($note, $mnemonic) = $sth->fetchrow_array ())
{
    # handle possibility of NULL (undef) values
    $note = (defined ($note) ? escapeHTML ($note) : "");
    $mnemonic = (defined ($mnemonic) ? escapeHTML ($mnemonic) : "");
    push (@items, dt ($note));
    push (@items, dd ($mnemonic));
}
print dl (@items);
```

Here is a slightly more complex example. Each term is a database name, and the corresponding definition indicates how many tables are in the database. The numbers are obtained by issuing a SHOW TABLES query for each database and counting the number of rows in the result:

```
# get list of database names
my $db_ref = $dbh->selectcol_arrayref ("SHOW DATABASES");
my @items = ();
foreach my $db_name (@{$db_ref})
{
    # get list of table names in database; disable RaiseError for
    # this query, to prevent script termination in case the current
    # user has no access to the database
    $dbh->{RaiseError} = 0;
    my $tbl_ref = $dbh->selectcol_arrayref ("SHOW TABLES FROM $db_name");
    $dbh->{RaiseError} = 1;
    my $tbl_count = (defined ($tbl_ref)          # error?
                    ? @{$tbl_ref} . " tables"    # no, get table count
                    : "cannot access");          # yes, indicate problem
    push (@items, dt (escapeHTML ($db_name)));
    push (@items, dd (escapeHTML ($tbl_count)));
}
print dl (@items);
```

Note that it's necessary to take care not to die on an error when issuing SHOW TABLES statements, should the user running the script not have access to a given database.

Unmarked Lists

A type of list not normally discussed as such is a list with no markings at all. This is simply a set of items, each on a separate line. An unmarked list is very easy to produce: fetch each item and add a break tag after it. Here's an example in JSP:

```
<c:forEach var="row" items="${rs.rows}">
    <c:out value="${row.item}" /><br />
</c:forEach>
```

If you already have the items in an array, just iterate through it. For example, in Perl, if you have a set of items in an array named @items, generate the list like this:

```
foreach my $item (@items)
{
    # handle possibility of NULL (undef) values
    $item = (defined ($item) ? escapeHTML ($item) : "");
    print $item . br ();
}
```

Nested Lists

Some applications display information that is most easily understood when presented as a list of lists. The following example displays state names as a definition

---

list, grouped by the initial letter of the names. For each item in the list, the term is the initial letter, and the definition is an unordered list of the state names beginning with that letter:

```
A
    • Alabama
    • Alaska
    • Arizona
    • Arkansas
C
    • California
    • Colorado
    • Connecticut
D
    • Delaware
...
```

One way to produce such a list (in Perl) is as follows:

```perl
# get list of initial letters
my $ltr_ref = $dbh->selectcol_arrayref (
            "SELECT DISTINCT UPPER(LEFT(name,1)) AS letter
            FROM states ORDER BY letter");
my @items = ();
# get list of states for each letter
foreach my $ltr (@{$ltr_ref})
{
    my $item_ref = $dbh->selectcol_arrayref (
                "SELECT name FROM states WHERE LEFT(name,1) = ?
                ORDER BY name", undef, $ltr);
    $item_ref = [ map { escapeHTML ($_) } @{$item_ref} ];
    # convert list of states to unordered list
    my $item_list = ul (li ($item_ref));
    # for each definition list item, the initial letter is
    # the term, and the list of states is the definition
    push (@items, dt ($ltr));
    push (@items, dd ($item_list));
}
print dl (@items);
```

The preceding example uses one query to get the list of distinct letters, then another query for each letter to find the states associated with each letter. You could also retrieve all the information using a single query, then march through the result set and begin a new list item each time you reach a new letter:

```perl
my $sth = $dbh->prepare ("SELECT name FROM states ORDER BY name");
$sth->execute ();
my @items = ();
my @names = ();
my $cur_ltr = "";
while (my ($name) = $sth->fetchrow_array ())
{
    my $ltr = uc (substr ($name, 0, 1));    # initial letter of name
    if ($cur_ltr ne $ltr)                   # beginning a new letter?
```

```
    {
        if (@names)          # any stored-up names from previous letter?
        {
            # for each definition list item, the initial letter is
            # the term, and the list of states is the definition
            push (@items, dt ($cur_ltr));
            push (@items, dd (ul (li (\@names))));
        }
        @names = ();
        $cur_ltr = $ltr;
    }
    push (@names, escapeHTML ($name));
}
if (@names)                          # any remaining names from final letter?
{
    push (@items, dt ($cur_ltr));
    push (@items, dd (ul (li (\@names))));
}
print dl (@items);
```

A third approach uses a single query but separates the data-collection and HTML-generation phases:

```
# collect state names and associate each with the proper initial-letter list
my $sth = $dbh->prepare ("SELECT name FROM states ORDER BY name");
$sth->execute ();
my %ltr = ();
while (my ($name) = $sth->fetchrow_array ())
{
    my $ltr = uc (substr ($name, 0, 1));    # initial letter of name
    # initialize letter list to empty array if this
    # is first state for it, then add state to array
    $ltr{$ltr} = [] unless exists ($ltr{$ltr});
    push (@{$ltr{$ltr}}, $name);
}

# now generate the output lists
my @items = ();
foreach my $ltr (sort (keys (%ltr)))
{
    # encode list of state names for this letter, generate unordered list
    my $ul_str = ul (li ([ map { escapeHTML ($_) } @{$ltr{$ltr}} ]));
    push (@items, dt ($ltr), dd ($ul_str));
}
print dl (@items);
```

17.3   Displaying Query Results as Tables

Problem

You want to display a query result as an HTML table.

Solution

Use each row of the result as a table row. If you want an initial row of column labels, either supply your own, or use the query metadata to obtain the names of the columns in the query result.

Discussion

HTML tables are useful for presenting highly structured output. One reason they're popular for displaying the results of queries is that they consist of rows and columns, so there's a natural conceptual correspondence between HTML tables and database tables or query results. In addition, you can obtain column headers for the table by accessing the query metadata. The basic structure of an HTML table is as follows:

- The table begins and ends with <table> and </table> tags and encloses a set of rows.
- Each row begins and ends with <tr> and </tr> tags and encloses a set of cells.
- Tags for data cells are <td> and </td>. Tags for header cells are <th> and </th>. (Typically, browsers display header cells using boldface or other emphasis.)
- Tags may include attributes. For example, to put a border around each cell, add a border="1" attribute to the <table> tag. To right-justify a table cell, add an align="right" attribute to the <td> tag.

Note that you should always supply the closing tag for each table element. This is a good idea in general for any HTML element, but especially so for tables. If you omit closing tags, some browsers will supply them automatically, but others may lock up or crash.

Suppose you want to display the contents of your CD collection:

```
mysql> SELECT year, artist, title FROM cd ORDER BY artist, year;
+------+----------------+-----------------------+
| year | artist         | title                 |
+------+----------------+-----------------------+
| 1992 | Charlie Peacock | Lie Down in the Grass |
| 1996 | Charlie Peacock | strangelanguage       |
| 1990 | Iona           | Iona                  |
| 1993 | Iona           | Beyond These Shores   |
| 1990 | Michael Gettel | Return                |
| 1989 | Richard Souther | Cross Currents        |
| 1987 | The 77s        | The 77s               |
| 1982 | Undercover     | Undercover            |
+------+----------------+-----------------------+
```

To display this query result as a bordered HTML table, you need to produce output that looks something like this:

```
<table border="1">
  <tr>
    <th>Year</th>
    <th>Artist</th>
    <th>Title</th>
  </tr>
  <tr>
    <td>1992</td>
    <td>Charlie Peacock</td>
    <td>Lie Down in the Grass</td>
  </tr>
  <tr>
    <td>1996</td>
    <td>Charlie Peacock</td>
    <td>strangelanguage</td>
  </tr>
  ... other rows here ...
  <tr>
    <td>1982</td>
    <td>Undercover</td>
    <td>Undercover</td>
  </tr>
</table>
```

Converting the results of a query to an HTML table requires that you wrap each value from a given result set row in cell tags, each row in row tags, and the entire set of rows in table tags. A JSP page might produce an HTML table from the cd table query like this:

```
<table border="1">
    <tr>
        <th>Year</th>
        <th>Artist</th>
        <th>Title</th>
    </tr>
<sql:query var="rs" dataSource="${conn}">
    SELECT year, artist, title FROM cd ORDER BY artist, year
</sql:query>
<c:forEach var="row" items="${rs.rows}">
    <tr>
        <td><c:out value="${row.year}" /></td>
        <td><c:out value="${row.artist}" /></td>
        <td><c:out value="${row.title}" /></td>
    </tr>
</c:forEach>

</table>
```

In Perl scripts, the table, row, data cell, and header cell elements are produced by the CGI.pm functions table(), tr(), td(), and th(). However, the tr() function that generates a table row should be invoked as Tr() to avoid a conflict with the built-in Perl tr function that transliterates characters.* Thus, to display the contents of the cd table as an HTML table, do this:

```
my $sth = $dbh->prepare (
            "SELECT year, artist, title FROM cd ORDER BY artist, year"
        );
$sth->execute ();
my @rows = ();
push (@rows, Tr (th ("Year"), th ("Artist"), th ("Title")));
while (my ($year, $artist, $title) = $sth->fetchrow_array ())
{
    push (@rows, Tr (
                td (escapeHTML ($year)),
                td (escapeHTML ($artist)),
                td (escapeHTML ($title))
        ));
}
print table ({-border => "1"}, @rows);
```

Sometimes a table can be easier to understand if you display the rows in alternating colors, particularly if the table cells don't include borders. To do this, add a bgcolor attribute to each <th> and <td> tag, and alternate the color value for each row. An easy way to do this is by using a variable that flip-flops between two values. In the following example, the $bgcolor variable alternates between the values silver and white:

```
my $sth = $dbh->prepare (
            "SELECT year, artist, title FROM cd ORDER BY artist, year"
        );
$sth->execute ();
my $bgcolor = "silver";
my @rows = ();
push (@rows, Tr (
                th ({-bgcolor => $bgcolor}, "Year"),
                th ({-bgcolor => $bgcolor}, "Artist"),
                th ({-bgcolor => $bgcolor}, "Title")
        ));
while (my ($year, $artist, $title) = $sth->fetchrow_array ())
{
    $bgcolor = ($bgcolor eq "silver" ? "white" : "silver");
    push (@rows, Tr (
                td ({-bgcolor => $bgcolor}, escapeHTML ($year)),
                td ({-bgcolor => $bgcolor}, escapeHTML ($artist)),
                td ({-bgcolor => $bgcolor}, escapeHTML ($title))
        ));
}
print table ({-border => "1"}, @rows);
```

---

* If you use the CGI.pm object-oriented interface, there is no ambiguity. In that case, you invoke the tr() method through a CGI object and it is unnecessary to invoke it as Tr():

```
$cgi->tr ( ... );
```

The preceding table-generation examples hardwire the column headings into the code, as well as knowledge about the number of columns. With a little effort, you can write a more general function that takes a database handle and an arbitrary query, then executes the query and returns the result as an HTML table. The function can automatically get the column labels from the query metadata; to get labels that differ from the table column names, specify column aliases in the query:

```
my $tbl_str = make_table_from_query (
                $dbh,
                "SELECT
                    year AS Year, artist AS Artist, title AS Title
                FROM cd
                ORDER BY artist, year"
            );
print $tbl_str;
```

Any kind of query that returns a result set can be passed to this function. You could, for example, use it to construct an HTML table that shows all the column metadata for a database table:

```
my $tbl_str = make_table_from_query ($dbh, "SHOW COLUMNS FROM profile");
print $tbl_str;
```

What does the make_table_from_query() function look like? Here's an implementation in Perl:

```
sub make_table_from_query
{
# db handle, query string, parameters to be bound to placeholders (if any)
my ($dbh, $query, @param) = @_;

    my $sth = $dbh->prepare ($query);
    $sth->execute (@param);
    my @rows = ();
    # use column names for cells in the header row
    push (@rows, Tr (th ([ map { escapeHTML ($_) } @{$sth->{NAME}} ])));
    # fetch each data row
    while (my $row_ref = $sth->fetchrow_arrayref ())
    {
        # encode cell values, avoiding warnings for undefined
        # values and using   for empty cells
        my @val = map {
                    defined ($_) && $_ !~ /^\s*$/ ? escapeHTML ($_) : " "
                } @{$row_ref};
        my $row_str;
        for (my $i = 0; $i < @val; $i++)
        {
            # right-justify numeric columns
            if ($sth->{mysql_is_num}->[$i])
            {
                $row_str .= td ({-align => "right"}, $val[$i]);
            }
            else
```

```
                {
                    $row_str .= td ($val[$i]);
                }
            }
            push (@rows, Tr ($row_str));
        }
        return (table ({-border => "1"}, @rows));
    }
```

make_table_from_query( ) does some extra work to right-justify numeric columns so that the values line up better. It also allows you to pass values to be bound to place-holders in the query. Just specify them after the query string:

```
    my $tbl_str = make_table_from_query (
                    $dbh,
                    "SELECT
                        year AS Year, artist AS Artist, title AS Title
                    FROM cd
                    WHERE year < ?
                    ORDER BY artist, year",
                    1990
                );
    print $tbl_str;
```

The   Trick for Empty Table Cells

A display problem sometimes occurs for HTML tables that include borders around cells: when a table cell is empty or contains only whitespace, many browsers do not show a border around the cell. This makes the table look irregular. To avoid this problem, the make_table_from_query( ) function puts a non-breaking space ( ) into cells that would otherwise be empty. This causes borders for those cells to be displayed properly.

One thing to watch out for with program-generated tables is that browsers cannot render a table in a window until they've seen the entire thing. If you have a very large result set, it may take a very long time to display. Strategies for dealing with this problem include partitioning your data across multiple tables within a single page (so that the browser can display each table as it receives it), or across multiple pages. If you use multiple tables on a page, you should probably include some width attribute information in your header and data cell tags. Otherwise, each table will be sized to the actual widths of the values in its columns. If these differ across tables, your page will have a vertically ragged appearance.

See Also

To display a table in such a way that the user can click on any column heading to sort the table's contents by that column, see Recipe 18.11.

17.4 Displaying Query Results as Hyperlinks

Problem

You want to use database content to generate clickable hyperlinks.

Solution

Add the proper tags to the content to generate anchor elements.

Discussion

The examples in the preceding sections generate static text, but database content also is useful for creating hyperlinks. If you store web site URLs or email addresses in a table, you can easily convert them to active links in web pages. All you need to do is encode the information properly and add the appropriate HTML tags.

Suppose you have a table that contains company names and web sites, such as the following book_vendor table that lists book sellers and publishers:

```
mysql> SELECT * FROM book_vendor ORDER BY name;
+-----------------------+-------------------+
| name                  | website           |
+-----------------------+-------------------+
| Barnes & Noble        | www.bn.com        |
| Bookpool              | www.bookpool.com  |
| Borders               | www.borders.com   |
| Fatbrain              | www.fatbrain.com  |
| O'Reilly & Associates | www.oreilly.com   |
+-----------------------+-------------------+
```

This table has content that readily lends itself to the creation of hyperlinked text. To produce a hyperlink from a row, add the http:// protocol designator to the website value, use the result as the href attribute for an <a> anchor tag, and use the name value in the body of the tag to serve as the link label. For example, the row for Barnes & Noble can be written like this:

```
<a href="http://www.bn.com">Barnes &amp; Noble</a>
```

JSP code to produce a bullet (unordered) list of hyperlinks from the table contents looks like this:

```
<sql:query var="rs" dataSource="${conn}">
    SELECT name, website FROM book_vendor ORDER BY name
</sql:query>

<ul>
<c:forEach var="row" items="${rs.rows}">
    <li>
        <a href="http://<c:out value="${row.website}" />">
            <c:out value="${row.name}" /></a>
```

```
        </li>
    </c:forEach>
    </ul>
```

When displayed in a web page, each vendor name in the list becomes an active link that may be selected to visit the vendor's web site. In Python, the equivalent operation looks like this:

```
query = "SELECT name, website FROM book_vendor ORDER BY name"
cursor = conn.cursor ()
cursor.execute (query)
items = []
for (name, website) in cursor.fetchall ():
    items.append ("<a href=\"http://%s\">%s</a>" \
                % (urllib.quote (website), cgi.escape (name, 1)))
cursor.close ()

# print items, but don't encode them; they're already encoded
print make_unordered_list (items, 0)
```

CGI.pm-based Perl scripts produce hyperlinks by invoking the a( ) function as follows:

```
a ({-href => "url-value"}, "link label")
```

The function can be used to produce the vendor link list like this:

```
my $sth = $dbh->prepare (
                "SELECT name, website
                FROM book_vendor
                ORDER BY name");
$sth->execute ();
my @items = ();
while (my ($name, $website) = $sth->fetchrow_array ())
{
    push (@items, a ({-href => "http://$website"}, escapeHTML ($name)));
}
print ul (li (\@items));
```

Generating links using email addresses is another common web programming task. Assume that you have a table newsstaff that lists the department, name, and (if known) email address for the news anchors and reporters employed by a television station, WRRR:

```
mysql> SELECT * FROM newsstaff;
+------------------+----------------+-------------------------+
| department       | name           | email                   |
+------------------+----------------+-------------------------+
| Sports           | Mike Byerson   | mbyerson@wrrr-news.com  |
| Sports           | Becky Winthrop | bwinthrop@wrrr-news.com |
| Weather          | Bill Hagburg   | bhagburg@wrrr-news.com  |
| Local News       | Frieda Stevens | NULL                    |
| Local Government | Rex Conex      | rconex@wrrr-news.com    |
| Current Events   | Xavier Ng      | xng@wrrr-news.com       |
| Consumer News    | Trish White    | twhite@wrrr-news.com    |
+------------------+----------------+-------------------------+
```

From this you want to produce an online directory containing email links to all personnel, so that site visitors can easily send mail to any staff member. For example, a record for a sports reporter named Mike Byerson with an email address of mbyerson@wrrr-news.com will become an entry in the listing that looks like this:

```
Sports: <a href="mailto:mbyerson@wrrr-news.com">Mike Byerson</a>
```

It's easy to use the table's contents to produce such a directory. First, let's put the code to generate an email link into a helper function, because it's the kind of operation that's likely to be useful in several scripts. In Perl, the function might look like this:

```perl
sub make_email_link
{
my ($name, $addr) = @_;

    # return name as static text if address is undef or empty
    return (escapeHTML ($name)) if !defined ($addr) || $addr eq "";
    # return a hyperlink otherwise
    return (a ({-href => "mailto:$addr"}, escapeHTML ($name)));
}
```

The function is written to handle instances where the person has no email address by returning just the name as static text. To use the function, write a loop that pulls out names and addresses and displays each email link preceded by the staff member's department:

```perl
my $sth = $dbh->prepare (
            "SELECT department, name, email
            FROM newsstaff
            ORDER BY department, name");
$sth->execute ();
my @items = ();
while (my ($dept, $name, $email) = $sth->fetchrow_array ())
{
    push (@items, escapeHTML ($dept) . ": " . make_email_link ($name, $email));
}
print ul (li (\@items));
```

Equivalent email link generator functions for PHP and Python look like this:

```php
function make_email_link ($name, $addr)
{
    # return name as static text if address is unset or empty
    if (!isset ($addr) || $addr == "")
        return (htmlspecialchars ($name));
    # return a hyperlink otherwise
    return (sprintf ("<a href=\"mailto:%s\">%s</a>",
                    $addr, htmlspecialchars ($name)));
}
```

```python
def make_email_link (name, addr):
    # return name as static text if address is None or empty
    if addr is None or addr == "":
```

```
        return (cgi.escape (name, 1))
    # return a hyperlink otherwise
    return ("<a href=\"mailto:%s\">%s</a>" % (addr, cgi.escape (name, 1)))
```

For a JSP page, you can produce the newsstaff listing as follows:

```
<sql:query var="rs" dataSource="${conn}">
    SELECT department, name, email
    FROM newsstaff
    ORDER BY department, name
</sql:query>

<ul>
<c:forEach var="row" items="${rs.rows}">
    <li>
        <c:out value="${row.department}" />:
        <c:set var="name" value="${row.name}" />
        <c:set var="email" value="${row.email}" />
        <c:choose>
            <%-- null or empty value test --%>
            <c:when test="${empty email}">
                <c:out value="${name}" />
            </c:when>
            <c:otherwise>
                <a href="mailto:<c:out value="${email}" />">
                    <c:out value="${name}" /></a>
            </c:otherwise>
        </c:choose>
    </li>
</c:forEach>
</ul>
```

17.5 Creating a Navigation Index from Database Content

Problem

A list of items in a web page is long. You want to make it easier to move around in the page.

Solution

Create a navigational index containing links to different sections of the list.

Discussion

It's easy to display lists in web pages (Recipe 17.2). But if a list contains a lot of items, the page containing it may become quite long. In such cases, it's often useful to break up the list into sections and provide a navigation index, in the form of hyperlinks that allow users to reach sections of the list quickly without scrolling the page manually. For example, if you retrieve records from a table and display them grouped into sections, you can include an index that lets the user jump directly to any section. The same idea can be applied to multiple-page displays as well, by providing a navigation index in each page so that users can reach any other page easily.

This section provides two examples to illustrate these techniques, both of which are based on the kjv table that was introduced in Recipe 4.11. The examples implement two kinds of display, using the verses from the book of Esther stored in the kjv table:

- A single-page display that lists all verses in all chapters of Esther. The list is broken into 10 sections (one per chapter), with a navigation index that has links pointing to the beginning of each section.

- A multiple-page display consisting of pages that each show the verses from a single chapter of Esther, and a main page that instructs the user to choose a chapter. Each of these pages also displays a list of chapters as hyperlinks to the pages that display the corresponding chapter verses. These links allow any page to be reached easily from any other.

Creating a Single-Page Navigation Index

This example displays all verses in Esther in a single page, with verses grouped into sections by chapter. To display the page so that each section contains a navigation marker, place an `<a name>` anchor element before each chapter's verses:

```
<a name="1">Chapter 1</a>
    ... list of verses in chapter 1...
<a name="2">Chapter 2</a>
    ... list of verses in chapter 2...
<a name="3">Chapter 3</a>
    ... list of verses in chapter 3...
...
```

This generates a list that includes a set of markers named 1, 2, 3, and so forth. To construct the navigation index, build a set of hyperlinks, each of which points to one of the name markers:

```
<a href="#1">Chapter 1</a>
<a href="#2">Chapter 2</a>
<a href="#3">Chapter 3</a>
...
```

The # in each href attribute signifies that the link points to a location within the same page. For example, href="#3" points to the anchor with the name="3" attribute.

To implement this kind of navigation index, you can use a couple of approaches:

- Retrieve the verse records into memory and determine from them which entries are needed in the navigation index. Then print both the index and verse list.

- Figure out all the applicable anchors in advance and construct the index first. The list of chapter numbers can be determined by this statement:

```
SELECT DISTINCT cnum FROM kjv WHERE bname = 'Esther' ORDER BY cnum;
```

You can use the query result to build the navigation index, then fetch the verses for the chapters later to create the page sections that the index entries point to.

Here's a script, *esther1.pl*, that uses the first approach. It's an adaptation of one of the nested-list examples shown in Recipe 17.2.

```perl
#! /usr/bin/perl -w
# esther1.pl - display book of Esther in a single page, with navigation index

use strict;
use lib qw(/usr/local/apache/lib/perl);
use CGI qw(:standard escape escapeHTML);
use Cookbook;

my $title = "The Book of Esther";

my $page = header ()
            . start_html (-title => $title, -bgcolor => "white")
            . h3 ($title);

my $dbh = Cookbook::connect ();

# Retrieve verses from the book of Esther and associate each one with the
# list of verses for the chapter it belongs to.

my $sth = $dbh->prepare (
            "SELECT cnum, vnum, vtext FROM kjv
            WHERE bname = 'Esther'
            ORDER BY cnum, vnum");
$sth->execute ();
my %verses = ();
while (my ($cnum, $vnum, $vtext) = $sth->fetchrow_array ())
{
    # initialize chapter's verse list to empty array if this
    # is first verse for it, then add verse number/text to array.
    $verses{$cnum} = [] unless exists ($verses{$cnum});
    push (@{$verses{$cnum}}, p (escapeHTML ("$vnum. $vtext")));
}

# Determine all chapter numbers and use them to construct a navigation
# index.  These are links of the form <a href="#num>Chapter num</a>, where
# num is a chapter number a'#' signifies a within-page link.  No URL- or
# HTML-encoding is done here (the text that is displayed here doesn't need
# it).  Make sure to sort chapter numbers numerically (use { a <=> b }).
# Separate links by non-breaking spaces.

my $nav_index;
foreach my $cnum (sort { $a <=> $b } keys (%verses))
{
    $nav_index .= " " if $nav_index;
```

```
        $nav_index .= a ({-href => "#$cnum"}, "Chapter $cnum");
    }

    # Now display list of verses for each chapter.  Precede each section with
    # a label that shows the chapter number and a copy of the navigation index.

    foreach my $cnum (sort { $a <=> $b } keys (%verses))
    {
        # add an <a name> anchor for this section of the state display
        $page .= p (a ({-name => $cnum}, font ({-size => "+2"}, "Chapter $cnum"))
                    . br ()
                    . $nav_index);
        $page .= join ("", @{$verses{$cnum}});  # add array of verses for chapter
    }

    $dbh->disconnect ();

    $page .= end_html ();

    print $page;

    exit (0);
```

Creating a Multiple-Page Navigation Index

This example shows a Perl script, *esther2.pl*, that is capable of generating any of several pages, all based on the verses in the book of Esther stored in the kjv table. The initial page displays a list of the chapters in the book, along with instructions to select a chapter. Each chapter in the list is a hyperlink that reinvokes the script to display the list of verses in the corresponding chapter. Because the script is responsible for generating multiple pages, it must be able to determine which page to display each time it runs. To make that possible, the script examines its own URL for a chapter parameter that indicates the number of the chapter to display. If no chapter parameter is present, or its value is not an integer, the script will display its initial page.

The URL to request the initial page looks like this:

http://apache.snake.net/cgi-bin/esther2.pl

The links to individual chapter pages have the following form, where *cnum* is a chapter number:

http://apache.snake.net/cgi-bin/esther2.pl?chapter=cnum

esther2.pl uses the CGI.pm param( ) function to obtain the chapter parameter value like so:

```
my $cnum = param ("chapter");
if (!defined ($cnum) || $cnum !~ /^\d+$/)
{
    # No artist ID was present or it was malformed
```

```
}
else
{
    # A valid artist ID was present
}
```

If no chapter parameter is present in the URL, $cnum will be undef. Otherwise, $cnum is set to the parameter value, which we check to make sure that it's an integer. (That covers the case where a garbage value may have been specified by someone trying to crash the script.)

Here is the entire *esther2.pl* script:

```
#! /usr/bin/perl -w
# esther2.pl - display book of Esther over multiple pages, one page per
# chapter, with navigation index

use strict;
use lib qw(/usr/local/apache/lib/perl);
use CGI qw(:standard escape escapeHTML);
use Cookbook;

my $title = "The Book of Esther";

my $page = header () . start_html (-title => $title, -bgcolor => "white");

my ($left_panel, $right_panel);

my $dbh = Cookbook::connect ();

my $cnum = param ("chapter");
if (!defined ($cnum) || $cnum !~ /^\d+$/)
{
    # Missing or malformed chapter; display main page with a left panel
    # that lists all chapters as hyperlinks and a right panel that provides
    # instructions.
    $left_panel = get_chapter_list ($dbh, 0);
    $right_panel = p (strong ("The Book of Esther"))
                    . p ("Select a chapter from the list at left.");
}
else
{
    # Chapter number was given; display a left panel that lists chapters
    # chapters as hyperlinks (except for current chapter as bold text)
    # and a right panel that lists the current chapter's verses.
    $left_panel = get_chapter_list ($dbh, $cnum);
    $right_panel = p (strong ("The Book of Esther"))
                    . get_verses ($dbh, $cnum);
}

$dbh->disconnect ();

# Arrange the page as a one-row, three-cell table (middle cell is a spacer)
```

```
$page .= table (Tr (
                td ({-valign => "top", -width => "15%"}, $left_panel),
                td ({-valign => "top", -width => "5%"}, " "),
                td ({-valign => "top", -width => "75%"}, $right_panel)
            ));

$page .= end_html ();

print $page;

exit (0);

# --------------------------------------------------------------------

# Construct navigation index as a list of links to the pages for each chapter
# in the the book of Esther.  Labels are of the form "Chapter n"; the chapter
# numbers are incorporated into the links as chapter=num parameters

# $dbh is the database handle, $cnum is the number of the chapter for
# which information is currently being displayed.  The label in the chapter
# list corresponding to this number is displayed as static text; the others
# are displayed as hyperlinks to the other chapter pages.  Pass 0 to make
# all entries hyperlinks (no valid chapter has a number 0).

# No encoding is done because the chapter numbers are digits and don't
# need it.

sub get_chapter_list
{
my ($dbh, $cnum) = @_;

    my $nav_index;
    my $ref = $dbh->selectcol_arrayref (
                "SELECT DISTINCT cnum FROM kjv
                WHERE bname = 'Esther' ORDER BY cnum"
            );
    foreach my $cur_cnum (@{$ref})
    {
        my $link = url () . "?chapter=$cur_cnum";
        my $label = "Chapter $cur_cnum";
        $nav_index .= br () if $nav_index;          # separate entries by <br>
        # use static bold text if entry is for current artist,
        # use a hyperlink otherwise
        $nav_index .= ($cur_cnum == $cnum
                        ? strong ($label)
                        : a ({-href => $link}, $label));
    }
    return ($nav_index);
}

# Get the list of verses for a given chapter.  If there are none, the
# chapter number was invalid, but handle that case sensibly.
```

```
sub get_verses
{
my ($dbh, $cnum) = @_;

    my $ref = $dbh->selectall_arrayref (
                    "SELECT vnum, vtext FROM kjv
                    WHERE bname = 'Esther' AND cnum = ?",
                    undef, $cnum);
    my $verses = "";
    foreach my $row_ref (@{$ref})
    {
        $verses .= p (escapeHTML ("$row_ref->[0]. $row_ref->[1]"));
    }
    return ($verses eq ""           # no verses?
            ? p ("No verses in chapter $cnum were found.")
            : p ("Chapter $cnum:") . $verses);
}
```

See Also

esther2.pl examines its execution environment using the param( ) function. Web script parameter processing is discussed further in Recipe 18.5.

17.6   Storing Images or Other Binary Data

Problem

You want to store images in MySQL.

Solution

That's not difficult, provided you follow the proper precautions for encoding the image data.

Discussion

Web sites are not limited to displaying text. They can also serve various forms of binary data such as images, sounds, PDF documents, and so forth. However, images are by far the most common kind of binary data, and because image storage is a natural application for a database, a very common question is "How do I store images in MySQL?" Many people will answer this question by saying, "Don't do it!" and some of the reasons for this are discussed in the sidebar "Should You Store Images in Your Database?" Because it's important to know how to work with binary data, this section does show how to store images in MySQL. Nevertheless, in recognition that that may not always be the best thing to do, the section also shows how to store images in the filesystem.

Although the discussion here is phrased in terms of working with images, the principles apply to any kind of binary data, such as PDF files or compressed text. In fact, they apply to any kind of data at all, including text; people tend to think of images as special somehow, but they're not.

One reason image storage confuses people more often than does storing other types of information like text strings or numbers is that it's difficult to type in an image value manually. For example, you can easily use *mysql* to enter an INSERT statement to store a number like 3.48 or a string like Je voudrais une bicyclette rouge, but images contain binary data and it's not easy to refer to them by value. So you need to do something else. Your options are:

- Use the LOAD_FILE() function.
- Write a program that reads in the image file and constructs the proper INSERT query for you.

Storing Images with LOAD_FILE()

The LOAD_FILE() function takes an argument indicating a file to be read and stored in the database. For example, an image stored in */tmp/myimage.png* might be loaded into a table like this:

```
mysql> INSERT INTO mytbl (image_data) VALUES(LOAD_FILE('/tmp/myimage.png'));
```

To load images into MySQL with LOAD_FILE(), certain requirements must be satisfied:

- The image file must be located on the MySQL server host.
- The file must be readable by the server.
- You must have the FILE privilege.

These constraints mean that LOAD_FILE() is available only to some MySQL users.

Storing Images Using a Script

If LOAD_FILE() is not an option or you don't want to use it, you can write a short program to load your images. The program should either read the contents of an image file and create a record that contains the image data, or create a record that indicates where in the filesystem the image file is located. If you elect to store the image in MySQL, you include the image data in the record-creation statement the same way as any other kind of data. That is, you either use a placeholder and bind the data value to it, or else encode the data and put it directly into the query string.

The script shown in this section, *store_image.pl*, runs from the command line and stores an image file for later use. The script takes no side in the debate over whether to store images in the database or the filesystem. Instead, it demonstrates how to implement *both* approaches! Of course, this takes double the storage space, so to

Should You Store Images in Your Database?

Deciding where to store images is a matter of trade-offs. There are pros and cons whether you store images in the database or in the filesystem:

- Storing images in a database table bloats the table. With a lot of images, you're more likely to approach any limits your operating system places on table size. On the other hand, if you store images in the filesystem, directory lookups may become slow. To avoid this, you may be able to implement some kind of hierarchical storage or use a filesystem that has good lookup performance for large directories (such as the Reiser filesystem).

- Using a database localizes storage for images that are used across multiple web servers on different hosts. Images stored in the filesystem must be stored locally on the web server host. In a multiple-host situation, that means you must replicate the set of images to the filesystem of each host. If you store the images in MySQL, only one copy of the images is required; each web server can get the images from the same database server.

- When images are stored in the filesystem, they constitute in essence a foreign key. Image manipulation requires two operations: one in the database and one in the filesystem. This in turn means that if you require transactional behavior, it's more difficult to implement—not only do you have two operations, they take place in different domains. Storing images in the database is simpler because adding, updating, or removing an image requires only a single record operation. It becomes unnecessary to make sure the image table and the filesystem remain in sync.

- It can be faster to serve images over the Web from the filesystem than from the database, because the web server itself opens the file, reads it, and writes it to the client. Images stored in the database must be read and written twice. First, the MySQL server reads the image from the database and writes it to your web script. Then the script reads the image and writes it to the client.

- Images stored in the filesystem can be referred to directly in web pages by means of `<img>` tag links that point to the image files. Images stored in MySQL must be served by a script that retrieves an image and sends it to the client. However, even if images are stored in the filesystem and accessible to the web server, you might still want to serve them through a script. This would be appropriate if you need to account for the number of times you serve each image (such as for banner ad displays where you charge customers by the number of ad impressions) or if you want to select an image at request time (such as when you pick an ad at random).

- If you store images in the database, you need to use a column type such as a `BLOB`. This is a variable length type, so the table itself will have variable-length rows. Operations on fixed-length rows are often quicker, so you may gain some table lookup speed by storing images in the filesystem and using fix-length types for the columns in the image table.

adapt this script for your own use, you'll want to retain only the parts that are appropriate for whichever storage method you want to implement. The necessary modifications are discussed at the end of this section.

The *store_image.pl* script uses an image table that includes columns for the image ID, name, and MIME type, and a column in which to store the image data:

```
CREATE TABLE image
(
    id      INT UNSIGNED NOT NULL AUTO_INCREMENT,   # image ID number
    name    VARCHAR(30) NOT NULL,                   # image name
    type    VARCHAR(20) NOT NULL,                   # image MIME type
    data    MEDIUMBLOB NOT NULL,                    # image data
    PRIMARY KEY (id),                               # id and name are unique
    UNIQUE (name)
);
```

The name column indicates the name of the image file in the directory where images are stored in the filesystem. The data column is a MEDIUMBLOB, which is good for images smaller than 16 MB. If you need larger images, use a LONGBLOB column.

It is possible to use the name column to store full pathnames to images in the database, but if you put them all under the same directory, you can store names that are relative to that directory and name values will take less space. *store_image.pl* does this, but of course it needs to know the pathname of the image storage directory. That's what the $image_dir variable is for. You should check this variable's value and modify it as necessary before running the script. The default value reflects where I like to store images, but you'll need to change it according to your own preferences. Make sure to create the directory if it doesn't exist before you run the script. You'll also need to check and possibly change the image directory pathname in the *display_image.pl* script discussed later in this chapter.

store_image.pl looks like this:

```
#! /usr/bin/perl -w
# store_image.pl - read an image file, store in that image table and
# in the filesystem.  (Normally, you'd store images only in one
# place or another; this script demonstrates how to do both.)

use strict;
use lib qw(/usr/local/apache/lib/perl);
use Fcntl;       # for O_RDONLY, O_WRONLY, O_CREAT
use FileHandle;
use Cookbook;

# Default image storage directory and pathname separator
# (CHANGE THESE AS NECESSARY)
my $image_dir = "/usr/local/apache/htdocs/mcb/images";
my $path_sep = "/";

# Reset directory and pathname separator for Windows/DOS
if ($^O =~ /^MSWin/i || $^O =~ /^dos/)
```

```
{
    $image_dir = "D:\\apache\\htdocs\\mcb\\images";
    $path_sep = "\\";
}

-d $image_dir or die "$0: image directory ($image_dir)\ndoes not exist\n";

# Print help message if script was not invoked properly

(@ARGV == 2 || @ARGV == 3) or die <<EOF;
Usage: $0 image_file mime_type [image_name]

image_file = name of the image file to store
mime_time = the image MIME type (e.g., image/jpeg or image/png)
image_name = alternate name to give the image

image_name is optional; if not specified, the default is the
image file basename.
EOF

my $file_name = shift (@ARGV);  # image filename
my $mime_type = shift (@ARGV);  # image MIME type
my $image_name = shift (@ARGV); # image name (optional)

# if image name was not specified, use filename basename
# (allow either / or \ as separator)
($image_name = $file_name) =~ s|.*[/\\]|| unless defined $image_name;

my $fh = new FileHandle;
my ($size, $data);

sysopen ($fh, $file_name, O_RDONLY)
    or die "Cannot read $file_name: $!\n";
binmode ($fh);       # helpful for binary data
$size = (stat ($fh))[7];
sysread ($fh, $data, $size) == $size
    or die "Failed to read entire file $file_name: $!\n";
$fh->close ();

# Save image file in filesystem under $image_dir.  (Overwrite file
# if an old version exists.)

my $image_path = $image_dir . $path_sep . $image_name;

sysopen ($fh, $image_path, O_WRONLY|O_CREAT)
    or die "Cannot open $image_path: $!\n";
binmode ($fh);       # helpful for binary data
syswrite ($fh, $data, $size) == $size
    or die "Failed to write entire image file $image_path: $!\n";
$fh->close ();

# Save image in database table.  (Use REPLACE to kick out any old image
# with same name.)
```

```
my $dbh = Cookbook::connect ();
$dbh->do ("REPLACE INTO image (name,type,data) VALUES(?,?,?)",
          undef,
          $image_name, $mime_type, $data);
$dbh->disconnect ();

exit (0);
```

If you invoke the script with no arguments, it displays a short help message. Otherwise, it requires two arguments that specify the name of the image file and the MIME type of the image. By default, the file's basename (final component) is also used as the name of the image stored in the database and in the image directory. To use a different name, provide it using an optional third argument.

The script is fairly straightforward. It performs the following actions:

1. Check that the proper number of arguments was given and initialize some variables from them.

2. Make sure the image directory exists. If it does not, the script cannot continue.

3. Open and read the contents of the image file.

4. Store the image as a file in the image directory.

5. Store a record containing identifying information and the image data in the image table.

store_image.pl uses REPLACE rather than INSERT so that you can replace an old image with a new version having the same name simply by loading the new one. The query specifies no id column value; id is an AUTO_INCREMENT column, so MySQL assigns it a unique sequence number automatically. (Note that if you replace an image by loading a new one with the same name as an existing image, the REPLACE statement will generate a new id value. If you want to keep the old value, you should issue a SELECT first to see if the name already exists, then modify the REPLACE to specify the existing id value if a record was found, and NULL otherwise.)

The REPLACE statement that stores the image information into MySQL is relatively mundane:

```
$dbh->do ("REPLACE INTO image (name,type,data) VALUES(?,?,?)",
          undef,
          $image_name, $mime_type, $data);
```

If you examine the statement looking for some special indicator of how to handle binary data, you'll be disappointed, because the $data variable that contains the image isn't treated as special in any way. The query refers to all column values uniformly using ? placeholder characters and the values are passed at the end of the do() call. Another way to accomplish the same result is to perform escape processing on the column values explicitly and then insert them directly into the query string:

```
$image_name = $dbh->quote ($image_name);
$mime_type = $dbh->quote ($mime_type);
```

```
$data = $dbh->quote ($data);
$dbh->do ("REPLACE INTO image (name,type,data)
          VALUES($image_name,$mime_type,$data)");
```

Many people make image-handling a lot more troublesome than it really is. If you properly handle image data in a query by using placeholders or by encoding it, you'll have no problems. If you don't, you'll get errors. Simple as that. This is *no* different than how you should handle other kinds of data, even text. After all, if you insert into a query a piece of text that contains quotes or other special characters without escaping them, the query will blow up in your face. So the need for placeholders or encoding is not some special thing that's necessary only for images—it's necessary for all data. Say it with me: "I will always use placeholders or encode my column values. Always. Always, always, *always*." (Having said that, I feel obliged to point out that if you know enough about a given value—for example, if you're absolutely certain that it's an integer—there are times you can get away with breaking this rule. Nevertheless, it's never wrong to follow it.)

To try out the script, change location into the *apache/images* directory of the recipes distribution. This directory contains the *store_image.pl* script, and some sample images are in its *flags* subdirectory (they're pictures of national flags for several countries). To load one of these images, run the script like this under Unix:

```
% ./store_image.pl flags/iceland.jpg image/jpeg
```

Or like this under Windows:

```
C:\> store_image.pl flags\iceland.jpg image/jpeg
```

store_image.pl takes care of image storage, and the next section discusses how to retrieve images to serve them over the Web. What about deleting images? I'll leave it to you to write a utility to remove images that you no longer want. If you are storing images in the filesystem, remember to delete both the database record *and* the image file that the record points to.

store_image.pl stores each image both in the database and in the filesystem for illustrative purposes, but of course that makes it inefficient. Earlier, I mentioned that if you use this script as a basis for your own applications, you should modify it to store images only in one place—either in the database or in the filesystem—not in both places. The modifications are as follows:

- To adapt the script to store images only in MySQL, don't define an image directory and delete the code that checks for that directory's existence and that writes image files there.
- To adapt the script for storage only in the filesystem, drop the data column from the image table, and modify the REPLACE statement so it doesn't refer to that column.

These modifications also apply to the *display_image.pl* image processing script shown in Recipe 17.7.

See Also

Recipe 17.7 shows how to retrieve images for display over the Web. Recipe 18.8 discusses how to upload images from a web page for storage into MySQL.

17.7   Retrieving Images or Other Binary Data

Problem

Okay, you can store images or other binary data values in your database, using the techniques discussed in Recipe 17.6. How do you get them back out?

Solution

You need nothing more than a SELECT statement. Of course, what you *do* with the information after you retrieve it might be a little more involved.

Discussion

As described in Recipe 17.6, it's difficult to issue a statement manually that stores a literal image value. However, there is no problem at all entering a query that retrieves an image:

```
mysql> SELECT * FROM image WHERE id = 1;
```

But binary information tends not to display well on ASCII devices, so you probably don't want to do this interactively from the *mysql* program unless you want your terminal window to turn into a horrible mess of gibberish (and possibly even to lock up). It's more common to use the information for display in a web page. Or you might send it to the client for downloading, though that is more common for non-image binary data such as PDF files. Downloading is discussed in Recipe 17.9.

Displaying an image in a web page is done by including an <img> tag in that page that tells the client's web browser where to get the image. If you've stored images as files in a directory that the web server has access to, you can refer to an image directly. For example, if the image file *iceland.jpg* is located in the directory */mcb/images* under the server's document root, you can reference it like this:

```
<img src="/mcb/images/iceland.jpg" />
```

If you use this approach, make sure that each image filename has an extension (such as *.gif* or *.png*) that allows the web server to determine what kind of Content-Type: header to send in the response.

If the images are stored in a database table instead, or in a directory that is not accessible to the web server, the <img> tag can refer to a script that knows how to fetch images and send them to clients. To do this, the script should respond by sending a

Content-Type: header that indicates the image format, a Content-Length: header that indicates the number of bytes of image data, a blank line, and finally the image itself as the body of the response.

The following script, *display_image.pl*, demonstrates how to serve images over the Web. It requires a name parameter that indicates which image to display, and allows an optional location parameter that specifies whether to retrieve the image from the image table or from the filesystem. The default is to retrieve image data from the image table. For example, the following URLs display an image from the database and from the filesystem, respectively:

> *http://apache.snake.net/cgi-bin/display_image.pl?name=iceland.jpg*
> *http://apache.snake.net/cgi-bin/display_image.pl?name=iceland.jpg;location=fs*

The script looks like this:

```perl
#! /usr/bin/perl -w
# display_image.pl - display image over the Web

use strict;
use lib qw(/usr/local/apache/lib/perl);
use CGI qw(:standard escapeHTML);
use FileHandle;
use Cookbook;

# Default image storage directory and pathname separator
# (CHANGE THESE AS NECESSARY)
my $image_dir = "/usr/local/apache/htdocs/mcb/images";
my $path_sep = "/";

# Reset directory and pathname separator for Windows/DOS
if ($^O =~ /^MSWin/i || $^O =~ /^dos/)
{
    $image_dir = "D:\\apache\\htdocs\\mcb\\images";
    $path_sep = "\\";
}

my $name = param ("name");
my $location = param ("location");

# make sure image name was specified
defined ($name) or error ("image name is missing");
# use default of "db" if the location is not specified or is not "db" or "fs"
(defined ($location) && $location eq "fs") or $location = "db";

my $dbh = Cookbook::connect ();

my ($type, $data);

# If location is "db", get image data and MIME type from image table.
# If location is "fs", get MIME type from image table and read the image
# data from the filesystem.
```

```
if ($location eq "db")
{
    ($type, $data) = $dbh->selectrow_array (
                        "SELECT type, data FROM image WHERE name = ?",
                        undef,
                        $name)
                or error ("Cannot find image with name $name");
}
else
{
    $type = $dbh->selectrow_array (
                        "SELECT type FROM image WHERE name = ?",
                        undef,
                        $name)
                or error ("Cannot find image with name $name");
    my $fh = new FileHandle;
    my $image_path = $image_dir . $path_sep . $name;
    open ($fh, $image_path)
        or error ("Cannot read $image_path: $!");
    binmode ($fh);        # helpful for binary data
    my $size = (stat ($fh))[7];
    read ($fh, $data, $size) == $size
        or error ("Failed to read entire file $image_path: $!");
    $fh->close ();
}

$dbh->disconnect ();

# Send image to client, preceded by Content-Type: and Content-Length:
# headers.

print header (-type => $type, -Content_Length => length ($data));
print $data;

exit (0);

# ----------------------------------------------------------------------

sub error
{
my ($msg) = shift;

    print header (), start_html ("Error"), p (escapeHTML ($msg)), end_html ();
    exit (0);
}
```

17.8   Serving Banner Ads

Problem

You want to display banner ads by choosing images on the fly from a set of images.

Solution

Use a script that selects a random row from an image table and sends the image to the client.

Discussion

The *display_image.pl* script just shown assumes that the URL contains a parameter that names the image to be sent to the client. Another application might determine which image to display for itself. One popular image-related use for web programming is to serve banner advertisements for display in web pages. A simple way to do this is by means of a script that picks an image at random each time it is invoked. The following Python script, *banner.py*, shows how to do this, where the "ads" are the flag images in the image table:

```
#! /usr/bin/python
# banner.py - server randomly chosen banner ad from image table
# (sends no response if no image can be found)

import sys
sys.path.insert (0, "/usr/local/apache/lib/python")
import MySQLdb
import Cookbook

conn = Cookbook.connect ()

try:
    query = "SELECT type, data FROM image ORDER BY RAND() LIMIT 1"
    cursor = conn.cursor ()
    cursor.execute (query)
    row = cursor.fetchone ()
    cursor.close ()
    if row is not None:
        (type, data) = row
        # Send image to client, preceded by Content-Type: and
        # Content-Length: headers.  The Expires:, Cache-Control:, and
        # Pragma: headers help keep browsers from caching the image
        # and reusing it for sucessive requests for this script.
        print "Content-Type: %s" % type
        print "Content-Length: %s" % len (data)
        print "Expires: Sat, 01 Jan 2000 00:00:00 GMT"
        print "Cache-Control: no-cache"
        print "Pragma: no-cache"
        print ""
        print data
except MySQLdb.Error, e:
    pass

conn.close ()
```

banner.py sends a few headers in addition to the usual Content-Type: and Content-Length: headers. The extra headers help keep browsers from caching the image.

Expires: specifies a date in the past to tell the browser that the image is out of date. The Cache-Control: and Pragma: headers tell the browser not to cache the image. The script sends both headers because some browsers understand one, and some the other.

Why suppress caching? Because if you don't, the browser will send a request for *banner.py* only the first time it sees it in a link. On subsequent requests for the script, the brower will reuse the image, which rather defeats the intent of having each such link resolve to a randomly chosen image.

Install the *banner.py* script in your *cgi-bin* directory. Then, to place a banner in a web page, use an <img> tag that invokes the script. For example, if the script is installed as */cgi-bin/banner.py*, the following page references it to include an image below the introductory paragraph:

```
<!-- bannertest1.html - page with single link to banner-ad script -->
<html>
<head>
<title>Banner Ad Test Page 1</title>
</head>
<body bgcolor="white">

<p>You should see an image below this paragraph.</p>

<img src="/cgi-bin/banner.py" />

</body>
</html>
```

If you request this page, it should display an image, and you should see a succession of randomly chosen images each time you reload the page. (I am assuming here that you have loaded several images into the image table by now using the *load_image.pl* script discussed in Recipe 17.6. Otherwise you may not see any images at all!) If you modify *banner.py* not to send the cache-related headers, you likely will see the same image each time you reload the page.

The cache-control headers suppress caching for links to *bannery.py* that occur over the course of successive page requests. Another complication occurs if multiple links to the script occur within the *same* page. The following page illustrates what happens:

```
<!-- bannertest2.html - page with multiple links to banner-ad script -->
<html>
<head>
<title>Banner Ad Test Page 2</title>
</head>
<body bgcolor="white">

<p>You should see two images below this paragraph,
and they probably will be the same.</p>

<img src="/cgi-bin/banner.py" />
<img src="/cgi-bin/banner.py" />
```

```
<p>You should see two images below this paragraph,
and they probably will be different.</p>

<img src="/cgi-bin/banner.py?image1" />
<img src="/cgi-bin/banner.py?image2" />

</body>
</html>
```

The first two links to *banner.py* are identical. What you'll probably find when you request this page is that your browser will notice that fact, send only a single request to the web server, and use the image that is returned where both links appear in the page. As a result, the first two images displayed in the page will be identical. The second two links to *banner.py* show how to solve this problem. The links include some extra fluff at the end of the URLs that make them look different. *banner.py* doesn't use that information at all, but making the links look different fools the browser into sending two image requests. The result is that the second two images will differ from each other—unless *banner.py* happens to randomly select the same image both times, of course.

See Also

If you run a version of MySQL older than 3.23.2, the ORDER BY RAND( ) clause used in the image-selection query will fail. See Recipe 13.7 for a workaround.

17.9 Serving Query Results for Download

Problem

You want to send database information to a browser for downloading rather than for display.

Solution

Unfortunately, there's no good way to force a download. A browser will process information sent to it according to the Content-Type: header value, and if it has a handler for that value, it will treat the information accordingly. However, you may be able to trick the browser by using a "generic" content type for which it's unlikely to have a handler.

Discussion

Earlier sections of this chapter discuss how to incorporate the results of database queries into web pages, to display them as paragraphs, lists, tables, or images. But what if you want to produce a query result that the user can download to a file instead? It's not difficult to generate the response itself: send a Content-Type: header preceding the information, such as text/plain for plain text, image/jpeg for a JPEG image, or application/pdf or application/msexcel for a PDF or Excel document. Then send a blank line and the content of the query result. The problem is that there's no way to force the browser to download the information. If it knows what to do with the response based on the content type, it will try to handle the information as it sees fit. If it knows how to display text or images, it will. If it thinks it's supposed to give a PDF or Excel document to a PDF viewer or to Excel, it will. Most browsers allow the user to select a download explicitly (for example, by right-clicking or control-clicking on a link), but that's a client-side mechanism. You have no access to it on the server end.

About the only thing you can do is try to fool the browser by faking the content type. The most generic type is application/octet-stream. Most users are unlikely to have any content handler specified for it, so if you send a response using that type, it's likely to trigger a download by the browser. The disadvantage of this, of course, is that the response contains a false indicator about the type of information it contains. You can try to alleviate this problem by suggesting a default filename for the browser to use when it saves the file. If the filename has a suffix indicative of the file type, such as *.txt*, *.jpg*, *.pdf*, or *.xls*, that may help the client (or the operating system on the client host) determine how to process the file. To suggest a name, include a Content-Disposition: header in the response that looks like this:

```
Content-disposition: attachment; filename="suggested_name"
```

The following PHP script, *download.php*, demonstrates one way to produce downloadable content. When first invoked, it presents a page containing a link that can be selected to initiate the download. The link points back to *download.php* but includes a download parameter. When you select the link, it reinvokes the script, which sees the parameter and responds by issuing a query, retrieving a result set, and sending it to the browser for downloading. The Content-Type: and Content-Disposition: headers in the response are set by invoking the header() function. (This must be done before the script produces any other output, or header() will have no effect.)

```php
<?php
# download.php - retrieve result set and send it to user as a download
# rather than for display in a web page

include "Cookbook.php";
include "Cookbook_Webutils.php";

$title = "Result Set Downloading Example";

# If no download parameter is present, display instruction page

if (!get_param_val ("download"))
{
  # construct self-referential URL that includes download parameter
  $url = get_self_path () . "?download=1";
?>
```

```
<html>
<head>
<title><?php print ($title); ?></title>
</head>
<body bgcolor="white">

<p>
Select the following link to commence downloading:
<a href="<?php print ($url); ?>">download</a>
</p>

</body>
</html>

<?php
    exit ();
}   # end of "if"

# The download parameter was present; retrieve a result set and send
# it to the client as a tab-delimited, newline-terminated document.
# Use a content type of application/octet-stream in an attempt to
# trigger a download response by the browser, and suggest a default
# filename of "result.txt".

$conn_id = cookbook_connect ();

$query = "SELECT * FROM profile";
if (!($result_id = mysql_query ($query, $conn_id)))
    die ("Cannot execute query\n");

header ("Content-Type: application/octet-stream");
header ("Content-Disposition: attachment; filename=\"result.txt\"");

while ($row = mysql_fetch_row ($result_id))
    print (join ("\t", $row) . "\n");
mysql_free_result ($result_id);

mysql_close ($conn_id);

?>
```

download.php uses a couple of functions we haven't covered yet. get_self_path()
returns the script's own pathname. This is used to construct a URL that points back
to the script and that includes a download parameter. get_param_val() is used to
determine whether that parameter is present. These functions are included in the
Cookbook_Webutils.php file and are discussed further in Recipes 18.1 and 18.5.

Another possibility for producing downloadable content is to generate the query
result, write it to a file on the server side, compress it, and send the result to the
browser. The browser will likely run some kind of uncompress utility to recover the
original file.

## CHAPTER 18

Processing Web Input with MySQL

18.0 Introduction

The previous chapter describes how to retrieve information from MySQL and display it in web pages using various types of HTML constructs such as tables or hyperlinks. That's a use of MySQL to send information in one direction (from web server to user), but web-based database programming can also serve to collect information sent in the other direction from user to web server, such as the contents of a submitted form. If you're processing a survey form, you might store the information for later use. If the form contains search keywords, you'd use them as the basis for a query that searches the database for information the user wants to see.

MySQL comes into these activities in a fairly obvious way, as the repository for storing information or as the source from which search results are drawn. But before you can process input from a form, you have to create the form and send it to the user. MySQL can help with this, too, because it's often possible to use information stored in your database to generate form elements such as radio buttons, checkboxes, pop-up menus, or scrolling lists:

- You can select a set of items from a table that lists countries, states, or provinces and convert them into a pop-up menu for use in a form that collects address information.

- You can use the list of legal values for an ENUM column that contains allowable salutations (Mr., Mrs., and so forth) to generate a set of radio buttons.

- You can use lists of available colors, sizes, or styles stored in an inventory database to construct fields for a clothing ordering form.

- If you have an application that allows the user to pick a database or table, you can run a SHOW DATABASES or SHOW TABLES query and use the resulting names to create a list element.

By using database content to generate form elements, you lessen the amount of table-specific knowledge your programs must have and allow them to determine what they need automatically. A script that uses a database to figure out for itself how to generate form elements adaptively handles changes to the database. To add a new country, create a new row in the table that stores the list of countries. To add a new salutation, change the definition of the ENUM column. In each case, you change the set of items in a form element by updating the database, not by modifying the script; the script adapts to the change automatically, without additional programming.

The first part of this chapter covers the following topics relating to web input processing:

Generating forms and form elements. One way to use database content for form construction is by selecting a list of items from a table and using them to create the options in a list element. But metadata can be used as well. There is a natural correspondence between ENUM columns and single-pick form elements like radio button sets or pop-up menus. In both cases, only one from a set of possible values may be chosen. There is a similar correspondence between SET columns and multiple-pick elements like checkbox groups; any or all of the possible values may be chosen. To construct metadata-based form elements, obtain the column description from the table information returned by SHOW COLUMNS, extract the set of possible values, and use them for the items in the form element.

Initializing forms using database contents. In addition to using the database to create structural elements of forms, you can also use it to initialize form field values. For example, to allow a user to modify an existing record, retrieve it from the database and load it into an editing form's fields before sending the form to the user.

Processing input gathered over the Web. This includes input not only from form fields, but also the contents of uploaded files, or parameters that are present in URLs. Regardless of where the information comes from, you'll face a common set of issues in dealing with it: extracting and decoding the information, performing constraint or validity checking on it, and re-encoding the information for query construction to avoid generating malformed queries or storing information inaccurately.

The second part of the chapter illustrates a few ways to apply the techniques developed in the first part. These include applications that show how to use MySQL to present a web-based search interface, create paged displays that contain next-page and previous-page links, implement per-page hit counting and logging, and perform general Apache logging to a database.

For the Perl, PHP, and Python example scripts discussed in this chapter, look under the *apache* directory of the recipes distribution. For JSP, the scripts are under the *tomcat* directory; you should already have installed these in the process of setting up the mcb application context (Recipe 16.3). Library routines used by the example scripts are located in files found under the *lib* directory. Scripts to create the tables used here are located in the *tables* directory.

Note that although the scripts in this chapter are intended to be invoked from your browser after they have been installed, many of them (JSP pages excepted) can also be invoked from the command line if you wish to see the raw HTML they produce.

To provide a concrete context for discussion, many of the form-processing examples in this chapter are based on the following scenario: in the lucrative field of "construct-a-cow" business endeavors, you run an operation that manufactures build-to-order ceramic bovine figurines, and you want to design an online ordering application that lets customers make selections for several aspects of the product. For each order, it's necessary to collect several types of information:

Cow color. The particular list of colors available at any particular time changes occasionally, so for flexibility, the values can be stored in a database table. To change the set of colors that customers can choose from, just update the table.

Cow size. There is a fixed set of sizes that doesn't change often (small, medium, large), so the values can be represented as elements of an ENUM column.

The all-important cow accessory items. These include a bell, horns, a sporty-looking tail ribbon, and a nose ring. Accessories can be represented in a SET column, because a customer may wish to select more than one of them. In addition, you know from past experience that most customers order horns and a cow bell, so it's reasonable to use those for the column's default value.

Customer name and address (street, city, state). The possible state names are already stored in the states table, so they can be used as the basis for the corresponding form element.

Given the preceding discussion, a cow_order table might be designed like this:

```
CREATE TABLE cow_order
(
    id          INT UNSIGNED NOT NULL AUTO_INCREMENT,
    # cow color, figurine size, and accessory items
    color       CHAR(20),
    size        ENUM('small','medium','large') DEFAULT 'medium',
    accessories SET('cow bell','horns','nose ring','tail ribbon')
                DEFAULT 'cow bell,horns',
    # customer name, street, city, and state (abbreviation)
    cust_name   CHAR(40),
    cust_street CHAR(40),
    cust_city   CHAR(40),
    cust_state  CHAR(2),
    PRIMARY KEY (id)
);
```

The id column provides a unique identifier for each record. It's a good idea to have such a value, and in fact will be necessary when we get to Recipe 18.4, which shows how to use web forms to edit existing records. For that type of activity, you must be able to tell which record to update, which is difficult without a unique record identifier.

The list of available colors is maintained in a separate table, cow_color:

```
CREATE TABLE cow_color
(
    color   CHAR(20)
);
```

For purposes of illustration, assume that the color table looks like this:

```
+---------------+
| color         |
+---------------+
| Black         |
| Black & White |
| Brown         |
| Cream         |
| Red           |
| Red & White   |
| See-Through   |
+---------------+
```

An application can use these tables to generate list elements in an order entry form, making it unnecessary for the application to have a lot of specialized built-in knowledge about the available options. The next several sections describe how to do this, and how to process the input that you obtain when a user submits a form.

18.1 Creating Forms in Scripts

Problem

You want to write a script that gathers input from a user.

Solution

Create a fill-in form from within your script and send it to the user. The script can arrange to have itself invoked again to process the form's contents when the user submits it.

Discussion

Web forms are a convenient way to allow your visitors to submit information, for example, to provide search keywords, a completed survey result, or a response to a questionnaire. Forms are also beneficial for you as a developer because they provide a structured way to associate data values with names by which to refer to them.

A form begins and ends with <form> and </form> tags. Between those tags, you can place other HTML constructs, including special elements that become input fields in the page that the browser displays. The <form> tag that begins a form should include two attributes, action and method. The action attribute tells the browser what to do with the form when the user submits it. This will be the URL of the script that should be invoked to process the form's contents. The `method` attribute indicates to the browser what kind of HTTP request it should use to submit the form. The value will be either `GET` or `POST`, depending on the type of request you want the form submission to generate. The difference between these two request methods is discussed in Recipe 18.5; for now, we'll always use `POST`.

Most of the form-based web scripts shown in this chapter share some common behaviors:

- When first invoked, the script generates a form and sends it to the user to be filled in.

- The `action` attribute of the form points back to the same script, so that when the user completes the form and submits it, the script gets invoked again to process the form's contents.

- The script determines whether it's being invoked by a user for the first time or whether it should process a submitted form by checking its execution environment to see what input parameters are present. For the initial invocation, the environment will contain none of the parameters named in the form.

This approach isn't the only one you can adopt, of course. One alternative is to place a form in a static HTML page and have it point to the script that processes the form. Another is to have one script generate the form and a second script process it.

If a form-creating script wants to have itself invoked again when the user submits the form, it should determine its own pathname within the web server tree and use that value for the `action` attribute of the opening `<form>` tag. For example, if a script is installed as *cgi-bin/myscript* in your web tree, the tag can be written like this:

```
<form action="/cgi-bin/myscript" method="POST">
```

Each API provides a way for a script to obtain its own pathname, so you don't have to hardwire the name into the script. That gives you greater latitude to install the script where you want.

In Perl scripts, the CGI.pm module provides three methods that are useful for creating `<form>` elements and constructing the `action` attribute. `start_form()` and `end_form()` generate the opening and closing form tags, and `url()` returns the script's own path. Using these methods, a script can generate a form like this:

```
print start_form (-action => url (), -method => "POST");
# ... generate form elements here ...
print end_form ();
```

Actually, it's unnecessary to provide a `method` argument; if you omit it, `start_form()` supplies a default request method of `POST`.

In PHP, a simple way to get a script's pathname is to use the $PHP_SELF global variable:

```
print ("<form action=\"$PHP_SELF\" method=\"POST\">\n");
# ... generate form elements here ...
print ("</form>\n");
```

However, that won't work under some configurations of PHP, such as when the register_globals setting is disabled.* Another way to get the script path is to access the "PHP_SELF" member of the $HTTP_SERVER_VARS array or (as of PHP 4.1) the $_SERVER array. Unfortunately, checking several different sources of information is a lot of fooling around just to get the script pathname in a way that works reliably for different versions and configurations of PHP, so a utility routine to get the path is useful. The following function, get_self_path(), shows how to use $_SERVER if it's available and fall back to $HTTP_SERVER_VARS or $PHP_SELF otherwise. The function thus prefers the most recently introduced language features, but still works for scripts running under older versions of PHP:

```
function get_self_path ()
{
global $HTTP_SERVER_VARS, $PHP_SELF;

    if (isset ($_SERVER["PHP_SELF"]))
        $val = $_SERVER["PHP_SELF"];
    else if (isset ($HTTP_SERVER_VARS["PHP_SELF"]))
        $val = $HTTP_SERVER_VARS["PHP_SELF"];
    else
        $val = $PHP_SELF;
    return ($val);
}
```

$HTTP_SERVER_VARS and $PHP_SELF are global variables, but must be declared as such explicitly using the global keyword if used in a non-global scope (such as within a function). $_SERVER is a "superglobal" array and is accessible in any scope without being declared as global.

The get_self_path() function is part of the *Cookbook_Webutils.php* library file located in the *lib* directory of the recipes distribution. If you install that file in a directory that PHP searches when looking for include files, a script can obtain its own pathname and use it to generate a form as follows:

```
include "Cookbook_Webutils.php";

$self_path = get_self_path ();
print ("<form action=\"$self_path\" method=\"POST\">\n");
# ... generate form elements here ...
print ("</form>\n");
```

Python scripts can get the script pathname by importing the os module and accessing the SCRIPT_NAME member of the os.environ object:

```
import os

print "<form action=\"" + os.environ["SCRIPT_NAME"] + "\" method=\"POST\">"
# ... generate form elements here ...
print "</form>"
```

* register_globals is discussed further in Recipe 18.5.

In JSP pages, the request path is available through the implicit request object that the JSP processor makes available. Use that object's getRequestURI() method as follows:

```
<form action="<%= request.getRequestURI () %>" method="POST">
<%-- ... generate form elements here ... --%>
</form>
```

See Also

The examples in this section all have an empty body between the opening and closing form tags. For a form to be useful, you'll need to create body elements that correspond to the types of information that you want to obtain from users. It's possible to hard-wire these elements into a script, but Recipes 18.2 and 18.3 describe how MySQL can help you create the elements on the fly based on information stored in your database.

18.2 Creating Single-Pick Form Elements from Database Content

Problem

A form needs to present a field that offers the user a set of options but allows only one of them to be selected.

Solution

Use a single-pick list element. These include radio button sets, pop-up menus, and scrolling lists.

Discussion

Single-pick form elements allow you to present multiple choices from which a single option can be selected. Our example involves several sets of single-pick choices:

- The list of colors in the cow_color table. These can be obtained with the following query:

```
mysql> SELECT color FROM cow_color ORDER BY color;
+---------------+
| color         |
+---------------+
| Black         |
| Black & White |
| Brown         |
| Cream         |
| Red           |
| Red & White   |
| See-Through   |
+---------------+
```

Note that some of the colors contain a & character, which is special in HTML. This means they will need HTML-encoding when placed into list elements. (Actually, we'll perform encoding for all the list elements in the form, but these values illustrate why it's a good idea to get in that habit.)

- The list of legal figurine sizes in the size column of the cow_order table. The column is represented as an ENUM, so the possible values and the default value can be obtained using SHOW COLUMNS:

```
mysql> SHOW COLUMNS FROM cow_order LIKE 'size'\G
*************************** 1. row ***************************
  Field: size
   Type: enum('small','medium','large')
   Null: YES
    Key:
Default: medium
  Extra:
```

- The list of state names and abbreviations. These are available from the states table:

```
mysql> SELECT abbrev, name FROM states ORDER BY name;
+--------+-------------+
| abbrev | name        |
+--------+-------------+
| AL     | Alabama     |
| AK     | Alaska      |
| AZ     | Arizona     |
| AR     | Arkansas    |
| CA     | California  |
| CO     | Colorado    |
| CT     | Connecticut |
...
```

The number of choices varies for each of these lists. As shown, there are 3 sizes, 7 colors, and 50 states. The size values are best represented as a set of radio buttons or a pop-up menu; a scrolling list is unnecessary because the number of choices is small. The set of colors can reasonably be displayed using any of the single-pick element types; it's small enough that a set of radio buttons wouldn't take a lot of space, but large enough that you may want to allow scrolling—particularly if you make additional colors available. The list of states is likely to have more items than you'd want to present as a set of radio buttons, so it's most suitable for presentation as a pop-up menu or scrolling list.

I will discuss the HTML syntax for these types of elements, then show how to generate them from within scripts.

Radio buttons. A group of radio buttons consists of <input> elements of type radio, all with the same name attribute. Each element also includes a value attribute. A label to display can be given after the <input> tag. To mark an item as the default initial selection, add a checked attribute. The following radio button group displays the possible cow figurine sizes, using checked to mark medium as the initially selected value:

```
<input type="radio" name="size" value="small" />small
<input type="radio" name="size" value="medium" checked="checked" />medium
<input type="radio" name="size" value="large" />large
```

Pop-up menus. A pop-up menu is a list enclosed within <select> and </select> tags, with each item in the menu enclosed within <option> and </option> tags. Each <option> element has a value attribute, and its body provides a label to be displayed. To indicate a default selection, add a selected attribute to the appropriate <option> item. If no item is so marked, the first item becomes the default, as is the case for the following pop-up menu:

```
<select name="color">
<option value="Black">Black</option>
<option value="Black &amp; White">Black &amp; White</option>
<option value="Brown">Brown</option>
<option value="Cream">Cream</option>
<option value="Red">Red</option>
<option value="Red &amp; White">Red &amp; White</option>
<option value="See-Through">See-Through</option>
</select>
```

Scrolling lists. A scrolling list is displayed as a set of items in a box. The list may contain more items than are visible in the box, in which case the browser displays a scrollbar that the user can use to bring the other items into view. The HTML syntax for scrolling lists is similar to that for pop-up menus, except that the opening <select> tag includes a size attribute indicating how many rows of the list should be visible in the box. By default, a scrolling list is a single-pick element; Recipe 18.3 discusses how to allow multiple picks.

The following single-pick scrolling list includes an item for each U.S. state, of which six will be visible at a time:

```
</select>
<select name="state" size="6">
<option value="AL">Alabama</option>
<option value="AK">Alaska</option>
<option value="AZ">Arizona</option>
<option value="AR">Arkansas</option>
<option value="CA">California</option>
...
<option value="WV">West Virginia</option>
<option value="WI">Wisconsin</option>
<option value="WY">Wyoming</option>
</select>
```

These list elements all have several things in common:

- A name for the element. When the user submits the form, the browser associates this name with whatever value the user selected.

- A set of values, one for each item in the list. These determine the values that are available for selection.

- An optional default value that determines which item in the list is selected initially when the browser displays the list.
- A set of labels, one for each item. These determine what the user sees when the form is displayed, but are discarded when the form is submitted.

To produce a list element for a form using database content, issue a query to select the appropriate values and labels, encode any special characters they contain, and add the HTML tags that are appropriate for the kind of list you want to display. Should you wish to indicate a default selection, add a checked or selected attribute to the proper item in the list.

Let's consider how to produce form elements for the color and state lists first, both of which are produced by fetching a set of rows from a table.

In JSP, you can display a set of radio buttons for the colors using JSTL tags as follows. The color names are used as both the values and the labels, so you print them twice:

```
<sql:query var="rs" dataSource="${conn}">
    SELECT color FROM cow_color ORDER BY color
</sql:query>

<c:forEach var="row" items="${rs.rows}">
    <input type="radio" name="color"
        value="<c:out value="${row.color}" />"
    /><c:out value="${row.color}" /><br />
</c:forEach>
```

<c:out> performs HTML entity encoding, so the & character that is present in some of the color values will be converted to & automatically and will not cause display problems in the resulting web page.

To display a pop-up menu instead, the query is the same, but you change the row-fetching loop:

```
<sql:query var="rs" dataSource="${conn}">
    SELECT color FROM cow_color ORDER BY color
</sql:query>

<select name="color">
<c:forEach var="row" items="${rs.rows}">
    <option value="<c:out value="${row.color}" />">
        <c:out value="${row.color}" /></option>
</c:forEach>
</select>
```

The pop-up menu can be changed easily to a scrolling list; just add a size attribute to the opening <select> tag. For example, to make three colors visible at a time, generate the list like this:

```
<sql:query var="rs" dataSource="${conn}">
    SELECT color FROM cow_color ORDER BY color
</sql:query>
```

```
<select name="color" size="3">
<c:forEach var="row" items="${rs.rows}">
    <option value="<c:out value="${row.color}" />">
    <c:out value="${row.color}" /></option>
</c:forEach>
</select>
```

Generating a list element for the set of states is similar, except that the labels are not the same as the values. To make the labels more meaningful to customers, display the full state names. But the value that is returned when the form is submitted should be an abbreviation, because that is what gets stored in the cow_order table. To produce a list that way, select both the abbreviations and the full names, then insert them into the proper parts of each list item. For example, to create a pop-up menu, do this:

```
<sql:query var="rs" dataSource="${conn}">
    SELECT abbrev, name FROM states ORDER BY name
</sql:query>
```

```
<select name="state">
<c:forEach var="row" items="${rs.rows}">
    <option value="<c:out value="${row.abbrev}" />">
    <c:out value="${row.name}" /></option>
</c:forEach>
</select>
```

These JSP examples use an approach that prints each list item individually. List element generation in CGI.pm-based Perl scripts proceeds on a different basis: extract the information from the database first, then pass it all to a function that returns a string representing the form element. The functions that generate single-pick elements are radio_group(), popup_menu(), and scrolling_list(). These have several arguments in common:

name
    Indicates what you want to call the element.

values
    Specifies the values for the items in the list. This should be a reference to an array.

default
    Indicates the initially selected item in the element. This argument is optional. For a radio button set, CGI.pm automatically selects the first button by default if this argument is missing. To defeat that behavior, provide a default value that is not present in the values list. (This value cannot be undef or the empty string.)

labels
    Provides the labels to associate with each value. This argument is optional; if it's missing, CGI.pm uses the values as the labels. Otherwise, the labels argument should be a reference to a hash that associates each value with its corresponding label. For example, to produce a list element for cow colors, the values and labels are the same, so no labels argument is necessary. However, to produce a state list, labels will be a reference to a hash that maps each state abbreviation to its full name.

Some of the functions take additional arguments. For radio_group(), you can supply a linebreak argument to specify that the buttons should be displayed vertically rather than horizontally. scrolling_list() takes a size argument indicating how many items should be visible at a time. (The CGI.pm documentation describes additional arguments that are not used here at all. For example, there are arguments for laying out radio buttons in tabular form, but I'm not going to be that fancy.)

To construct a form element using the colors in the cow_color table, we need to retrieve them into an array:

```
my $color_ref = $dbh->selectcol_arrayref (
                    "SELECT color FROM cow_color ORDER BY color");
```

selectcol_arrayref() returns an array reference, which could if necessary be coerced to an array like this:

```
my @colors = @{$color_ref};
```

But the values argument for the CGI.pm functions that create list elements should be a reference anyway, so we'll just use $color_ref as is. To create a group of radio buttons, a pop-up menu, or a single-pick scrolling list, invoke the functions as follows:

```
print radio_group (-name => "color",
                   -values => $color_ref,
                   -linebreak => 1);       # display buttons vertically

print popup_menu (-name => "color",
                  -values => $color_ref);

print scrolling_list (-name => "color",
                      -values => $color_ref,
                      -size => 3);          # display 3 items at a time
```

The values and the labels for the color list are the same, so no labels argument need be given; CGI.pm will use the values as labels by default. Note that we haven't HTML-encoded the colors here, even though some of them contain a & character. CGI.pm functions for generating form elements automatically perform HTML-encoding, unlike its functions for creating non-form elements.

To produce a list of states for which the values are abbreviations and the labels are full names, we do need a labels argument. It should be a reference to a hash that maps each value to the corresponding label. Construct the value list and label hash as follows:

```
my @state_values;
my %state_labels;
my $sth = $dbh->prepare ("SELECT abbrev, name FROM states ORDER BY name");
$sth->execute ();
while (my ($abbrev, $name) = $sth->fetchrow_array ())
{
    push (@state_values, $abbrev);  # save each value in an array
    $state_labels{$abbrev} = $name; # map each value to its label
}
```

Pass the resulting list and hash by reference to popup_menu() or scrolling_list(), depending on which kind of list element you want to produce:

```
print popup_menu (-name => "state",
                     -values => \@state_values,
                     -labels => \%state_labels);

print scrolling_list (-name => "state",
                     -values => \@state_values,
                     -labels => \%state_labels,
                     -size => 6);              # display 6 items at a time
```

If you're using an API that doesn't provide a ready-made set of functions for producing form elements the way CGI.pm does, you may elect either to print HTML as you fetch list items from MySQL, or write utility routines that generate the form elements for you. The following discussion considers how to implement both approaches, using PHP and Python.

In PHP, the list of values from the cow_color table can be presented in a pop-up as follows using a fetch-and-print loop like this:

```
$query = "SELECT color FROM cow_color ORDER BY color";
$result_id = mysql_query ($query, $conn_id);
print ("<select name=\"color\">\n");
while (list ($color) = mysql_fetch_row ($result_id))
{
    $color = htmlspecialchars ($color);
    print ("<option value=\"$color\">$color</option>\n");
}
mysql_free_result ($result_id);
print ("</select>\n");
```

Python code to do the same is similar:

```
query = "SELECT color FROM cow_color ORDER BY color"
cursor = conn.cursor ()
cursor.execute (query)
print "<select name=\"color\">"
for (color, ) in cursor.fetchall ():
    color = cgi.escape (color, 1)
    print "<option value=\"%s\">%s</option>" % (color, color)
cursor.close ()
print "</select>"
```

The state list requires different values and labels, so the code is slightly more complex. In PHP, it looks like this:

```
$query = "SELECT abbrev, name FROM states ORDER BY name";
$result_id = mysql_query ($query, $conn_id);
print ("<select name=\"state\">\n");
while (list ($abbrev, $name) = mysql_fetch_row ($result_id))
{
    $abbrev = htmlspecialchars ($abbrev);
    $name = htmlspecialchars ($name);
    print ("<option value=\"$abbrev\">$name</option>\n");
}
```

```
mysql_free_result ($result_id);
print ("</select>\n");
```

And in Python, like this:

```
query = "SELECT abbrev, name FROM states ORDER BY name"
cursor = conn.cursor ()
cursor.execute (query)
print "<select name=\"state\">"
for (abbrev, name) in cursor.fetchall ():
    abbrev = cgi.escape (abbrev, 1)
    name = cgi.escape (name, 1)
    print "<option value=\"%s\">%s</option>" % (abbrev, name)
cursor.close ()
print "</select>"
```

Radio buttons and scrolling lists can be produced in similar fashion. But rather than doing so, let's try a different approach and construct a set of functions that generate form elements, given the proper information. The functions return a string representing the appropriate kind of form element, and are invoked with the following arguments:

```
make_radio_group (name, values, labels, default, vertical)
make_popup_menu (name, values, labels, default)
make_scrolling_list (name, values, labels, default, size, multiple)
```

These functions have several arguments in common:

name
> Indicates the name of the form element.

values
> An array or list of values for the items in the element.

labels
> Another array that provides the corresponding element label to display for each value. The two arrays must be the same size. (If you want to use the values as the labels, just pass the same array to the function twice.)

default
> Indicates the initial value of the form element. This should be a scalar value, except for make_scrolling_list(). We'll write that function to handle either single-pick or multiple-pick lists (and use it for the latter purpose in Recipe 18.3), so its default value is allowed to be either a scalar or an array. If there is no default, pass a value that isn't contained in the values array; typically, an empty string will do.

Some of the functions also have additional arguments that apply only to particular element types:

- vertical applies to radio button groups. If true, it indicates that the items should be stacked vertically rather than horizontally.

- The size and multiple arguments apply to scrolling lists. size indicates how many items in the list are visible, and multiple should be true if the list allows multiple selections.

The implementation of some of these list-generating functions is discussed here, but you can find the code for all of them in the *lib* directory of the recipes distribution. All of them act like CGI.pm for form element functions in the sense that they automatically perform HTML-encoding on argument values that are incorporated into the list.

In PHP, the make_radio_group() function for creating a set of radio buttons can be written like this:

```php
function make_radio_group ($name, $values, $labels, $default, $vertical)
{
    if (!is_array ($values))
        return ("make_radio_group: values argument must be an array");
    if (!is_array ($labels))
        return ("make_radio_group: labels argument must be an array");
    if (count ($values) != count ($labels))
        return ("make_radio_group: value and label list size mismatch");
    $str = "";
    for ($i = 0; $i < count ($values); $i++)
    {
        # select the item if it corresponds to the default value
        $checked = ($values[$i] == $default ? " checked=\"checked\"" : "");
        $str .= sprintf (
                "<input type=\"radio\" name=\"%s\" value=\"%s\"%s />%s",
                htmlspecialchars ($name),
                htmlspecialchars ($values[$i]),
                $checked,
                htmlspecialchars ($labels[$i]));
        if ($vertical)
            $str .= "<br />";    # display items vertically
        $str .= "\n";
    }
    return ($str);
}
```

The function performs some preliminary argument checking, then constructs the form element as a string, which it returns. To use the function to present cow colors, invoke it after fetching the items from the cow_color table as follows:

```php
$values = array ();
$query = "SELECT color FROM cow_color ORDER BY color";
$result_id = mysql_query ($query, $conn_id);
if ($result_id)
{
    while (list ($color) = mysql_fetch_row ($result_id))
        $values[] = $color;
    mysql_free_result ($result_id);
}

print (make_radio_group ("color", $values, $values, "", TRUE));
```

The $values array is passed to the function twice because it's used for both the values and the labels.

If you want to present a pop-up menu, use the following function instead:

```
function make_popup_menu ($name, $values, $labels, $default)
{
    if (!is_array ($values))
        return ("make_popup_menu: values argument must be an array");
    if (!is_array ($labels))
        return ("make_popup_menu: labels argument must be an array");
    if (count ($values) != count ($labels))
        return ("make_popup_menu: value and label list size mismatch");
    $str = "";
    for ($i = 0; $i < count ($values); $i++)
    {
        # select the item if it corresponds to the default value
        $checked = ($values[$i] == $default ? " selected=\"selected\"" : "");
        $str .= sprintf (
                "<option value=\"%s\"%s>%s</option>\n",
                htmlspecialchars ($values[$i]),
                $checked,
                htmlspecialchars ($labels[$i]));
    }
    $str = sprintf (
            "<select name=\"%s\">\n%s</select>\n",
            htmlspecialchars ($name),
            $str);
    return ($str);
}
```

make_popup_menu() has no $vertical parameter, but otherwise you invoke it the same way as make_radio_group():

```
print (make_popup_menu ("color", $values, $values, ""));
```

The make_scrolling_list() function is similar to make_popup_menu(), so I won't show its implementation here. To invoke it to produce a single-pick list, pass the same arguments as for make_popup_menu(), but indicate how many rows should be visible at once, and add a multiple argument of FALSE:

```
print (make_scrolling_list ("color", $values, $values, "", 3, FALSE));
```

The state list uses different values and labels. Fetch them like this:

```
$values = array ();
$labels = array ();
$query = "SELECT abbrev, name FROM states ORDER BY name";
$result_id = mysql_query ($query, $conn_id);
if ($result_id)
{
    while (list ($abbrev, $name) = mysql_fetch_row ($result_id))
    {
        $values[] = $abbrev;
        $labels[] = $name;
```

```
    }
    mysql_free_result ($result_id);
}
```

Then use the values and labels to produce the type of list you want:

```
print (make_popup_menu ("state", $values, $labels, ""));

print (make_scrolling_list ("state", $values, $labels, "", 6, FALSE));
```

Python implementations of the utility functions are similar to the PHP versions. For example, make_popup_menu( ) looks like this:

```
def make_popup_menu (name, values, labels, default):
    if type (values) not in (types.ListType, types.TupleType):
        return ("make_popup_group: values argument must be a list")
    if type (labels) not in (types.ListType, types.TupleType):
        return ("make_popup_group: labels argument must be a list")
    if len (values) != len (labels):
        return ("make_popup_group: value and label list size mismatch")
    str = ""
    for i in range (len (values)):
        value = values[i]
        label = labels[i]
        # make sure value and label are strings
        if type (value) is not types.StringType:
            value = `value`
        if type (label) is not types.StringType:
            label = `label`
        # select the item if it corresponds to the default value
        if type (default) is not types.StringType:
            default = `default`
        if value == default:
            checked = " selected=\"selected\""
        else:
            checked = ""
        str = str + \
                "<option value=\"%s\"%s>%s</option>\n" \
                    % (cgi.escape (value, 1),
                        checked,
                        cgi.escape (label, 1))

    if type (name) is not types.StringType:
        name = `name`
    str = "<select name=\"%s\">\n%s</select>\n" \
                % (cgi.escape (name, 1), str)
    return (str)
```

To present the cow colors in a form, fetch them like this:

```
values = []
query = "SELECT color FROM cow_color ORDER BY color"
cursor = conn.cursor ()
cursor.execute (query)
for (color, ) in cursor.fetchall ():
    values.append (color)
cursor.close ()
```

Then convert the list to a form element as follows:

```
print make_radio_group ("color", values, values, "", 1)

print make_popup_menu ("color", values, values, "")

print make_scrolling_list ("color", values, values, "", 3, 0)
```

To present the state list, fetch the names and abbreviations:

```
values = [ ]
labels = [ ]
query = "SELECT abbrev, name FROM states ORDER BY name"
cursor = conn.cursor ()
cursor.execute (query)
for (abbrev, name) in cursor.fetchall ():
    values.append (abbrev)
    labels.append (name)
cursor.close ()
```

Then pass them to the appropriate function:

```
print make_popup_menu ("state", values, labels, "")

print make_scrolling_list ("state", values, labels, "", 6, 0)
```

One thing the Python functions do that their PHP counterparts do not is to explicitly convert argument values that get incorporated into the list to string form. This is necessary because cgi.escape() raises an exception if you try to use it to HTML-encode a non-string value.

We have thus far considered how to fetch rows from the cow_color and states tables and convert them to form elements. Another element that needs to be part of the form for the online cow-ordering application is the field for specifying cow figurine size. The legal values for this field come from the size column in the cow_order table. That column is an ENUM, so getting the legal values for the corresponding form element is a matter of getting the column definition and parsing it apart.

Fortunately, a lot of the work involved in this task has already been done in Recipe 9.6, which develops utility routines to get ENUM or SET column metadata. In Perl, for example, invoke the get_enumorset_info() function as follows to get the size column metadata:

```
my $size_info = get_enumorset_info ($dbh, "cow_order", "size");
```

The resulting $size_info value is a reference to a hash that has several members, two of which are relevant to our purposes here:

```
$size_info->{values}
$size_info->{default}
```

The values member is a reference to a list of the legal enumeration values, and default is the column's default value. This information is in a format that can be converted directly to a form element such as a group of radio buttons or a pop-up menu as follows:

```
print radio_group (-name => "size",
                   -values => $size_info->{values},
                   -default => $size_info->{default},
                   -linebreak => 1);      # display buttons vertically

print popup_menu (-name => "size",
                  -values => $size_info->{values},
                  -default => $size_info->{default});
```

The default value is medium, so that's the value that will be selected initially when the browser displays the form.

The equivalent metadata-fetching function for PHP returns an associative array. Use it like this to generate form elements from the size column metadata:

```
$size_info = get_enumorset_info ($conn_id, "cow_order", "size");

print (make_radio_group ("size",
                         $size_info["values"],
                         $size_info["values"],
                         $size_info["default"],
                         TRUE));    # display items vertically

print (make_popup_menu ("size",
                        $size_info["values"],
                        $size_info["values"],
                        $size_info["default"]));
```

The Python version of the function returns a dictionary, which is used similarly:

```
size_info = get_enumorset_info (conn, "cow_order", "size")

print make_radio_group ("size",
                        size_info["values"],
                        size_info["values"],
                        size_info["default"],
                        1)

print make_popup_menu ("size",
                       size_info["values"],
                       size_info["values"],
                       size_info["default"])
```

When you use ENUM values like this to create list elements, the values are displayed in the order they are listed in the column definition. The size column definition lists the values in the proper display order (small, medium, large), but for columns for which you want a different order, sort the values appropriately.

To demonstrate how to process column metadata to generate form elements in JSP pages, I'm going to use a function embedded into the page. A better approach would be to write a custom action in a tag library that maps onto a class that returns the information, but custom tag writing is beyond the scope of this book. The examples take the following approach instead:

- Use the JSTL tags to execute a SHOW COLUMNS query to get the ENUM column definition, then move the definition into page context.
- Write a function that extracts the definition from page context, parses it into an array of individual enumeration values, and moves the array back into page context.
- Access the array using a JSTL iterator that displays each of its values as a list item. For each value, compare it to the column's default value and mark it as the initially selected item if it's the same.

The function that extracts legal values from an ENUM or SET column definition is named getEnumOrSetValues( ). Place it into a JSP page like this:[*]

```
<%@ page import="java.util.*" %>
<%@ page import="org.apache.oro.text.perl.*" %>

<%!
// declare a class method for busting up ENUM/SET values.
// typeDefAttr - the name of the page context attribute that contains
// the columm type definition
// valListAttr - the name of the page context attribute to stuff the
// column value list into

void getEnumOrSetValues (PageContext ctx,
                         String typeDefAttr,
                         String valListAttr)
{
    Perl5Util util = new Perl5Util ();
    String typeDef = ctx.getAttribute (typeDefAttr).toString ();
    // strip off leading "enum(" and trailing ")", leaving
    // comma-separated list of quoted values
    String qValStr = util.substitute ("s/^(enum|set)\\((.*)\\)$/$2/", typeDef);
    List quotedVal = new ArrayList ();
    List unquotedVal = new ArrayList ();
    // split string at commas to produce list of quoted values
    util.split (quotedVal, "/,/", qValStr);
    for (int i = 0; i < quotedVal.size (); i++)
    {
        // strip quotes from each value
        String s = quotedVal.get (i).toString ();
        s = util.substitute ("s/^'(.*)'$/$1/g", s);
        unquotedVal.add (s);
    }
    ctx.setAttribute (valListAttr, unquotedVal);
}

%>
```

[*] The getEnumOrSetValues( ) function requires the Jakarta ORO regular expression library, which can be obtained at the Jakarta site, *http://jakarta.apache.org*. Copy its JAR file to Tomcat's *common/lib* directory and restart Tomcat to make the library available to your JSP pages.

The function takes three arguments:

- The page context object.
- The name of the page attribute that contains the column definition. This is the function "input."
- The name of the page attribute into which to place the resulting array of legal column values. This is the function "output."

To generate a list element from the size column, begin by fetching the column metadata: extract the column value list into a JSTL variable named values and the default value into a variable named default as follows:

```
<sql:query var="rs" dataSource="${conn}">
    SHOW COLUMNS FROM cow_order LIKE 'size'
</sql:query>
<c:set var="typeDef" scope="page" value="${rs.rowsByIndex[0][1]}" />
<% getEnumOrSetValues (pageContext, "typeDef", "values"); %>
<c:set var="default" scope="page" value="${rs.rowsByIndex[0][4]}" />
```

Then use the value list and default value to construct a form element. For example, produce a set of radio buttons like this:

```
<c:forEach var="val" items="${values}">
    <input type="radio" name="size"
        value="<c:out value="${val}" />"
        <c:if test="${val == default}">checked="checked"</c:if>
    /><c:out value="${val}" /><br />
</c:forEach>
```

Or a pop-up menu like this:

```
<select name="size">
<c:forEach var="val" items="${values}">
    <option
        value="<c:out value="${val}" />"
        <c:if test="${val == default}">selected="selected"</c:if>
    >
    <c:out value="${val}" /></option>
</c:forEach>
</select>
```

The list-generating methods discussed here are not tied to any particular database table, so they can be used to create form elements for all kinds of data, not just those shown for the cow-ordering scenario. For example, to allow a user to pick a table name in a database administration application, you can generate a scrolling list containing an item for each table in the database. A CGI.pm-based script might do so like this:

```
my $table_ref = $dbh->selectcol_arrayref ("SHOW TABLES");
print scrolling_list (-name => "table",
                      -values => $table_ref,
                      -size => 10);              # display 10 items at a time
```

Query results need not necessarily even be related to database tables. For example, if you want to present a list with an entry for each of the last seven days from within a JSP page, you can calculate the dates using this query:

```
<sql:query var="rs" dataSource="${conn}">
    SELECT
        DATE_SUB(CURDATE(),INTERVAL 5 DAY),
        DATE_SUB(CURDATE(),INTERVAL 4 DAY),
        DATE_SUB(CURDATE(),INTERVAL 3 DAY),
        DATE_SUB(CURDATE(),INTERVAL 2 DAY),
        DATE_SUB(CURDATE(),INTERVAL 1 DAY),
        CURDATE()
</sql:query>
```

Then use the dates to generate a list element:

```
<c:set var="dateList" value="${rs.rowsByIndex[0]}" />
<c:forEach var="date" items="${dateList}">
    <input type="radio" name="date"
        value="<c:out value="${date}" />"
    /><c:out value="${date}" /><br />
</c:forEach>
```

(Of course, if your API makes it reasonably easy to perform date calculations, it likely will be more efficient to generate the list of dates on the client side without sending a query to the MySQL server.)

18.3 Creating Multiple-Pick Form Elements from Database Content

Problem

A form needs to present a field that offers the user a set of options and allows any number of them to be selected.

Solution

Use a multiple-pick list element, such as a set of checkboxes or a scrolling list.

Discussion

Multiple-pick form elements allow you to present multiple choices, any number of which can be selected, or possibly even none of them. For our example scenario in which customers order cow figurines online, the multiple-pick element is represented by the set of accessory items that are available. The accessory column in the cow_order table is represented as a SET, so the allowable and default values can be obtained from the following query:

```
mysql> SHOW COLUMNS FROM cow_order LIKE 'accessories'\G
*************************** 1. row ***************************
  Field: accessories
   Type: set('cow bell','horns','nose ring','tail ribbon')
   Null: YES
    Key:
Default: cow bell,horns
  Extra:
```

This set of items can reasonably be represented as either a set of checkboxes or as a multiple-pick scrolling list. In both cases, the cow bell and horns items should be selected initially, because each is present in the column's default value. I will discuss the HTML syntax for these elements, then show how to generate them from within scripts. (The material in this section relies heavily on Recipe 18.2, which discusses radio buttons, pop-up menus, and single-pick scrolling lists. I assume you've already read that section.)

Checkboxes. A group of checkboxes is similar to a group of radio buttons in that it consists of `<input>` elements that all have the same name attribute. However, the type attribute is checkbox rather than radio, and you can specify checked for as many items in the group as you want to be selected by default. If no items are marked as checked, none are selected initially. The following checkbox set shows the cow accessory items with the first two items selected by default:

```
<input type="checkbox" name="accessories" value="cow bell"
    checked="checked" />cow bell
```

```
<input type="checkbox" name="accessories" value="horns"
    checked="checked" />horns
<input type="checkbox" name="accessories" value="nose ring" />nose ring
<input type="checkbox" name="accessories" value="tail ribbon" />tail ribbon
```

Scrolling list. A multiple-pick scrolling list is constructed in much the same manner as its single-pick counterpart. The differences are that you include a multiple attribute in the opening <select> tag, and the default value behavior is different. For a single-pick list, you can add selected to at most one item, and the first item is selected by default in the absence of an explicit selected attribute. With a multiple-pick list, you can add a selected attribute to as many of the items as you like, and no items are selected by default in the absence of selected attributes.

If the set of cow accessories is represented as a multiple-pick scrolling list with cow bell and horns selected initially, it looks like this:

```
<select name="accessories" size="3" multiple="multiple">
<option value="cow bell" selected="selected">cow bell</option>
<option value="horns" selected="selected">horns</option>
<option value="nose ring">nose ring</option>
<option value="tail ribbon">tail ribbon</option>
</select>
```

In CGI.pm-based Perl scripts, you create checkbox sets or scrolling lists by invoking checkbox_group() or scrolling_list(). These functions take name, values, labels, and default arguments, just like their single-pick cousins. But because multiple items can be selected initially, CGI.pm allows the default argument to be specified as either a scalar value or a reference to an array of values. (It also accepts the argument name defaults as a synonym for default.)

To get the list of legal values for a SET column, we can do the same thing as in Recipe 18.2 for ENUM columns—that is, call a utility routine that returns the column metadata:

```
my $acc_info = get_enumorset_info ($dbh, "cow_order", "accessories");
```

However, the default value for a SET column is not in a form that is directly usable for form element generation. MySQL represents SET default values as a comma-separated list of items. (For example, the default for the accessories column is cow bell,horns.) That doesn't match the list-of-values format that the CGI.pm functions expect, so it's necessary to split the default value at the commas to obtain an array. The following expression shows how to do so, taking into account the possibility that the default value might be undef (NULL):

```
my @acc_def = (defined ($acc_info->{default})
                ? split (/,/, $acc_info->{default})
                : () );
```

After splitting the default value, pass the resulting array by reference to whichever of the list-generating functions you want to use:

```
print checkbox_group (-name => "accessories",
                      -values => $acc_info->{values},
                      -default => \@acc_def,
                      -linebreak => 1);        # display buttons vertically

print scrolling_list (-name => "accessories",
                      -values => $acc_info->{values},
                      -default => \@acc_def,
                      -size => 3,              # display 3 items at a time
                      -multiple => 1);         # create multiple-pick list
```

When you use SET values like this to create list elements, the values are displayed in the order they are listed in the column definition. That may not correspond to the order in which you want them to appear; if not, sort the values appropriately.

For PHP and Python, we can create utility functions to generate multiple-pick items. They'll have the following invocation syntax:

```
make_checkbox_group (name, values, labels, default, vertical)
make_scrolling_list (name, values, labels, default, size, multiple)
```

The name, values, and labels arguments to these functions are similar to those of the PHP and Python single-pick utility routines described in Recipe 18.2. make_checkbox_group() takes a vertical argument that indicates that the items should be stacked vertically rather than horizontally if it's true. make_scrolling_list() has already been described in Recipe 18.2 for producing single-pick lists; to use it here, the multiple argument should be true to produce a multiple-pick list. For both functions, the default argument can be an array of multiple values if several items should be selected initially.

make_checkbox_group() looks like this (shown here in Python; the PHP version is similar):

```
def make_checkbox_group (name, values, labels, default, vertical):
    if type (values) not in (types.ListType, types.TupleType):
        return ("make_checkbox_group: values argument must be a list")
    if type (labels) not in (types.ListType, types.TupleType):
        return ("make_checkbox_group: labels argument must be a list")
    if len (values) != len (labels):
        return ("make_checkbox_group: value and label list size mismatch")
    if type (default) not in (types.ListType, types.TupleType):
        default = [ default ]        # convert scalar to list
    str = ""
    for i in range (len (values)):
        value = values[i]
        label = labels[i]
        # make sure value and label are strings
        if type (value) is not types.StringType:
            value = `value`
        if type (label) is not types.StringType:
```

```
                label = `label`
        # select the item if it corresponds to one of the default values
        checked = ""
        for d in default:
            if type (d) is not types.StringType:
                d = `d`
            if value == d:
                checked = " checked=\"checked\""
                break
        if type (name) is not types.StringType:
            name = `name`
        str = str + \
                "<input type=\"checkbox\" name=\"%s\" value=\"%s\"%s />%s" \
                    % (cgi.escape (name, 1),
                        cgi.escape (value, 1),
                        checked,
                        cgi.escape (label, 1))
        if vertical:
            str = str + "<br />"    # display items vertically
        str = str + "\n"
    return (str)
```

To fetch the cow accessory information and present it using checkboxes, do this:

```
import re              # needed for re.split()

acc_info = get_enumorset_info (conn, "cow_order", "accessories")
if acc_info["default"] == None:
    acc_def = ""
else:
    acc_def = re.split (",", acc_info["default"])

print make_checkbox_group ("accessories",
                            acc_info["values"],
                            acc_info["values"],
                            acc_def,
                            1)          # display items vertically
```

To display a scrolling list instead, invoke make_scrolling_list():

```
print make_scrolling_list ("accessories",
                            acc_info["values"],
                            acc_info["values"],
                            acc_def,
                            3,          # display 3 items at a time
                            1)          # create multiple-pick list
```

In PHP, fetch the accessory information, then present checkboxes or a scrolling list as follows:

```
$acc_info = get_enumorset_info ($conn_id, "cow_order", "accessories");
$acc_def = explode (",", $acc_info["default"]);

print (make_checkbox_group ("accessories[]",
                            $acc_info["values"],
                            $acc_info["values"],
```

```
                    $acc_def,
                    TRUE));    # display items vertically

print (make_scrolling_list ("accessories[]",
                    $acc_info["values"],
                    $acc_info["values"],
                    $acc_def,
                    3,          # display 3 items at a time
                    TRUE));     # create multiple-pick list
```

Note that the field name in the PHP examples is specified as accessories[] rather than as accessories. In PHP, you must add [] to the name if you want to allow a field to have multiple values. If you omit the [], the user will be able to select multiple items while filling in the form, but PHP will return only one of them to your script. This issue will come up again when we discuss how to process the contents of submitted forms in Recipe 18.5.

In JSP pages, the getEnumOrSetValues() function used earlier to get the value list for the size column (an ENUM) can also be used for the accessory column (a SET). The column definition and default value are in the second and fifth column of the SHOW COLUMNS query that returns information about the accessory column. Run the query, parse the type definition into a list of values named values, and put the default value in defList like this:

```
<sql:query var="rs" dataSource="${conn}">
    SHOW COLUMNS FROM cow_order LIKE 'accessories'
</sql:query>
<c:set var="typeDef" scope="page" value="${rs.rowsByIndex[0][1]}" />
<% getEnumOrSetValues (pageContext, "typeDef", "values"); %>
<c:set var="defList" scope="page" value="${rs.rowsByIndex[0][4]}" />
```

For a SET column, the defList value might contain multiple values, separated by commas. It needs no special treatment; the JSTL <c:forEach> tag knows how to iterate over such a string, so the default values for a checkbox set can be initialized as follows:

```
<c:forEach var="val" items="${values}">
    <input type="checkbox" name="accessories"
        value="<c:out value="${val}" />"
        <c:forEach var="default" items="${defList}">
            <c:if test="${val == default}">checked="checked"</c:if>
        </c:forEach>
    /><c:out value="${val}" /><br />
</c:forEach>
```

For a multiple-pick scrolling list, do this:

```
<select name="accessories" size="3" multiple="multiple">
<c:forEach var="val" items="${values}">
    <option
        value="<c:out value="${val}" />"
        <c:forEach var="default" items="${defList}">
            <c:if test="${val == default}">selected="selected"</c:if>
```

```
        </c:forEach>
    >
    <c:out value="${val}" /></option>
  </c:forEach>
</select>
```

18.4 Loading a Database Record into a Form

Problem

You want to display a form but initialize it using the contents of a database record. This allows you to present a record-editing form.

Solution

Generate the form as you usually would, but instead of using the usual defaults, set the form elements to the values of columns in the database record.

Discussion

The form field generation examples shown in earlier sections have either supplied no default value or have used the default value as specified in an ENUM or SET column definition as the field default. That's most appropriate for presenting a "blank" form that you expect the user to fill in. However, for applications that present a web-based interface for record editing, it's more likely that you'd want to fill in the form using the content of an existing record for the initial values. This section discusses how to do that.

The examples shown here illustrate how to generate an editing form for records from the cow_order table. Normally, you would allow the user to specify which record to edit. For simplicity, assume the use of the record that has an id value of 1, with the following contents:

```
mysql> SELECT * FROM cow_order WHERE id = 1\G
*************************** 1. row ***************************
         id: 1
      color: Black & White
       size: large
accessories: cow bell,nose ring
  cust_name: Farmer Brown
cust_street: 123 Elm St.
  cust_city: Katy
 cust_state: TX
```

To generate a form with contents that correspond to a database record, use the column values for the element defaults as follows:

- For <input> elements such as radio buttons or checkboxes, add a checked attribute to each list item that matches the column value.

- For `<select>` elements such as pop-up menus or scrolling lists, add a `selected` attribute to each list item that matches the column value.

- For text fields represented as `<input>` elements of type `text`, set the value attribute to the corresponding column value. For example, a 60-character field for cust_name can be presented initialized to Farmer Brown like this:

  ```
  <input type="text" name="cust_name" value="Farmer Brown" size="60" />
  ```

  To present a `<textarea>` element instead, set the body to the column value. To create a field 40 columns wide and 3 rows high, write it like this:

  ```
  <textarea name="cust_name" cols="40" rows="3">
  Farmer Brown
  </textarea>
  ```

- In a record-editing situation, it's a good idea to include a unique value in the form so that you can tell which record the form contents represent when the user submits it. A hidden field is one way to do this. Its value is not displayed to the user, but the browser returns it with the rest of the field values. Our sample record has an `id` column with a value of 1, so the hidden field looks like this:

  ```
  <input type="hidden" name="id" value="1" />
  ```

The following examples show how to produce a form with `id` represented as a hidden field, `color` as a pop-up menu, `size` as a set of radio buttons, and `accessories` as a set of checkboxes. The customer information values are represented as text input boxes, except that `cust_state` is a single-pick scrolling list. You could make other choices, of course, such as to present the sizes as a pop-up menu rather than as radio buttons.

The scripts for the examples in this section are named *edit_cow.pl*, *edit_cow.jsp*, and so forth.

The following procedure outlines how to load the sample `cow_table` record into an editing form for a CGI.pm-based script:

1. Retrieve the column values for the record that you want to load into the form:

   ```
   my $id = 1;          # select record number 1
   my ($color, $size, $accessories,
       $cust_name, $cust_street, $cust_city, $cust_state) =
               $dbh->selectrow_array (
                   "SELECT
                       color, size, accessories,
                       cust_name, cust_street, cust_city, cust_state
                   FROM cow_order WHERE id = ?",
                   undef, $id);
   ```

2. Begin the form:

   ```
   print start_form (-action => url ());
   ```

3. Generate the hidden field containing the `id` value that uniquely identifies the cow_order record:

   ```
   print hidden (-name => "id", -value => $id, -override => 1);
   ```

The override argument forces CGI.pm to use the value specified in the value argument as the hidden field value. This is because CGI.pm normally tries to use values present in the script execution environment to initialize form fields, even if you provide values in the field-generating calls. (CGI.pm does this to make it easier to redisplay a form with the values the user just submitted. For example, if you find that a form has been filled in incorrectly, you can redisplay it and ask the user to correct any problems. To make sure that a form element contains the value you specify, it's necessary to override this behavior.)

4. Create the fields that describe the cow figurine specifications. These fields are generated the same way as described in Recipes 18.2 and 18.3, except that the default values come from the contents of record 1. The code here presents color as a pop-up menu, size as a set of radio buttons, and accessories as a set of checkboxes. Note that it splits the accessories value at commas to produce an array of values, because the column value might name several accessory items:

```
my $color_ref = $dbh->selectcol_arrayref (
                    "SELECT color FROM cow_color ORDER BY color");

print br (), "Cow color:", br ();
print popup_menu (-name => "color",
                    -values => $color_ref,
                    -default => $color,
                    -override => 1);

my $size_info = get_enumorset_info ($dbh, "cow_order", "size");

print br (), "Cow figurine size:", br ();
print radio_group (-name => "size",
                    -values => $size_info->{values},
                    -default => $size,
                    -override => 1,
                    -linebreak => 1);

my $acc_info = get_enumorset_info ($dbh, "cow_order", "accessories");
my @acc_val = (defined ($accessories)
                    ? split (/,/, $accessories)
                    : () );

print br (), "Cow accessory items:", br ();
print checkbox_group (-name => "accessories",
                    -values => $acc_info->{values},
                    -default => \@acc_val,
                    -override => 1,
                    -linebreak => 1);
```

5. Create the customer information fields. These are represented as text input fields, except the state, which is shown here as a single-pick scrolling list:

```
print br (), "Customer name:", br ();
print textfield (-name => "cust_name",
                    -value => $cust_name,
                    -override => 1,
                    -size => 60);
```

```
print br (), "Customer street address:", br ();
print textfield (-name => "cust_street",
                         -value => $cust_street,
                         -override => 1,
                         -size => 60);

print br (), "Customer city:", br ();
print textfield (-name => "cust_city",
                         -value => $cust_city,
                         -override => 1,
                         -size => 60);

my @state_values;
my %state_labels;
my $sth = $dbh->prepare ("SELECT abbrev, name FROM states ORDER BY name");
$sth->execute ();
while (my ($abbrev, $name) = $sth->fetchrow_array ())
{
    push (@state_values, $abbrev);  # save each value in an array
    $state_labels{$abbrev} = $name; # map each value to its label
}

print br (), "Customer state:", br ();
print scrolling_list (-name => "cust_state",
                         -values => \@state_values,
                         -labels => \%state_labels,
                         -default => $cust_state,
                         -override => 1,
                         -size => 6);              # display 6 items at a time
```

6. Create a form submission button and terminate the form:

```
print br (),
            submit (-name => "choice", -value => "Submit Form"),
            end_form ();
```

The same general procedure applies to other APIs. For example, in a JSP page, you can fetch the record to be edited and extract its contents into scalar variables like this:

```
<c:set var="id" value="1" />
<sql:query var="rs" dataSource="${conn}">
    SELECT
        id, color, size, accessories,
        cust_name, cust_street, cust_city, cust_state
    FROM cow_order WHERE id = ?
    <sql:param value="${id}" />
</sql:query>

<c:set var="row" value="${rs.rows[0]}" />
<c:set var="id" value="${row.id}" />
<c:set var="color" value="${row.color}" />
<c:set var="size" value="${row.size}" />
```

```
<c:set var="accessories" value="${row.accessories}" />
<c:set var="cust_name" value="${row.cust_name}" />
<c:set var="cust_street" value="${row.cust_street}" />
<c:set var="cust_city" value="${row.cust_city}" />
<c:set var="cust_state" value="${row.cust_state}" />
```

Then use the values to initialize the various form elements, such as:

- The hidden field for the ID value:

```
<input type="hidden" name="id" value="<c:out value="${id}" />" />
```

- The color pop-up menu:

```
<sql:query var="rs" dataSource="${conn}">
    SELECT color FROM cow_color ORDER BY color
</sql:query>
<br />Cow color:<br />
<select name="color">
<c:forEach var="row" items="${rs.rows}">
    <option
        value="<c:out value="${row.color}" />"
        <c:if test="${row.color == color}">selected="selected"</c:if>
    ><c:out value="${row.color}" /></option>
</c:forEach>
</select>
```

- The cust_name text field:

```
<br />Customer name:<br />
<input type="text" name="cust_name"
    value="<c:out value="${cust_name}" />"
    size="60" />
```

For PHP or Python, create the form using the utility functions developed in Recipes 18.2 and 18.3. See the *cow_edit.php* and *cow_edit.py* scripts for details.

18.5 Collecting Web Input

Problem .

You want to extract the input parameters that were submitted as part of a form or specified at the end of a URL.

Solution

Each API provides a means of accessing the names and values of the input parameters in the execution environment of a web script.

Discussion

Earlier sections of this chapter discuss how to retrieve information from MySQL and use it to generate various forms of output, such as static text, hyperlinks, or form elements. In this section, we'll discuss the opposite problem—how to collect input from the Web. Applications for such input are many. For example, you can use the techniques shown in this section to extract the contents of a form submitted by a user. You might interpret the information as search keywords, then run a query against a product catalog and show the matching items to a customer. In this case, you use the Web to collect information from which you can determine the client's interests. From that you construct an appropriate search query and display the results. If a form represents a survey, a mailing list sign-up sheet, or a poll, you might just store the values, using the data to create a new database record (or perhaps to update an existing record).

A script that receives input over the Web and uses it to interact with MySQL generally processes the information in a series of stages:

1. Extract the input from the execution environment. When a request arrives that contains input parameters, the web server places the input into the environment of the script that handles the request, and the script queries its environment to obtain the parameters. It may be necessary to decode special characters in the parameters to recover the actual values submitted by the client, if the extraction mechanism provided by your API doesn't do it for you. (For example, you may need to convert %20 to space.)

2. Validate the input to make sure it's legal. You cannot trust users to send legal values, so it's a good idea to check input parameters to make sure they look reasonable. For example, if you expect a user to enter a number into a field, you should check the value to be sure it's really numeric. If a form contains a pop-up menu that was constructed using the allowable values of an ENUM column, you might expect the value that you actually get back to be one of these values. But there's no way to be sure except to check. If you don't, you run the risk of entering garbage into your database.

3. Construct a query based on the input. Typically, input parameters are used to add a record to a database, or to to retrieve information from the database for display to the client. Either way, you use the input to construct a query and send it to the MySQL server. Query construction based on user input should be done with care, using proper escaping to avoid creating malformed or dangerous SQL statements.

The rest of this section explores the first of these three stages of input processing. Recipes 18.6 and 18.7 cover the second and third stages. The first stage (pulling input from the execution environment) has little to do with MySQL, but is covered here because it's necessarily the means by which you obtain the information used in the later processing stages.

Input obtained over the Web can be received in several ways, two of which are most common:

- As part of a GET request, in which case input parameters are appended to the end of the URL. For example, the following URL invokes a PHP script *price_quote. php* and specifies item and quantity parameters with values D-0214 and 60:

    http://apache.snake.net/mcb/price_quote.php?item=D-0214&quantity=60

    Such requests commonly are received when a user selects a hyperlink or submits a form that specifies method="GET" in the <form> tag. A parameter list in a URL begins with ? and consists of *name=value* pairs separated by ; or & characters. (It's also possible to place information in the middle of a URL, but this book doesn't cover that.)

- As part of a POST request, such as a form submission that specifies method="POST" in the <form> tag. The contents of a form for a POST request are sent as input parameters in the body of the request, rather than at the end of the URL.

You may also have occasion to process other types of input, such as uploaded files. Those are sent using POST requests, but as part of a special kind of form that is discussed in Recipe 18.8.

When you gather input for a web script, you may need to be concerned with how the input was sent. (Some APIs distinguish between input sent via GET and POST, others do not.) However, once you have pulled out the information that was sent, the request method doesn't matter. The validation and query construction stages do not need to know whether parameters were sent using GET or POST.

The recipes distribution includes some scripts in the *apache/params* directory (*tomcat/mcb* for JSP) that process input parameters. Each script allows you to submit GET or POST requests, and shows how to extract and display the parameter values thus submitted. Examine these scripts to see how the parameter extraction methods for the various APIs are used. Utility routines invoked by the scripts can be found in the library modules in the *lib* directory of the distribution.

Web Input Extraction Conventions

To obtain input parameters passed to a script, you should familiarize yourself with your API's conventions so that you know what it does for you, and what you must do yourself. For example, you should know the answers to these questions:

- How do you determine which parameters are available?
- How do you pull a parameter value from the environment?
- Are values thus obtained the actual values submitted by the client, or do you need to decode them further?
- How are multiple-valued parameters handled (for example, if several items in a checkbox group are selected)?

- For parameters submitted in a URL, which separator character does the API expect between parameters? This may be & for some APIs and ; for others. ; is preferable as a parameter separator because it's not special in HTML like & is, but many browsers or other user agents separate parameters using &. If you construct a URL within a script that includes parameters at the end, be sure to use a parameter separator character that the receiving script will understand.

Perl

The Perl CGI.pm module makes input parameters available to scripts through the param( ) function. param( ) provides access to input submitted via either GET or POST, which simplifies your task as the script writer. If a form containing id and name parameters was submitted via POST, you can process it the same way as if the parameters were submitted at the end of the URL via GET. You don't need to perform any decoding, either; param( ) handles that as well.

To obtain a list of names of all available parameters, call param( ) with no arguments:

```
@names = param ();
```

To obtain the value of a specific parameter, pass its name to param( ).

```
$id = param ("id");
@options = param ("options");
```

In scalar context, param( ) returns the parameter value if it is single-valued, the first value if it is multiple-values, or undef if the parameter is not available. In array context, param( ) returns a list containing all the parameter's values, or an empty list if the parameter is not available.

A parameter with a given name might not be available if the form field with the same name was left blank, or if there isn't any field with that name. Note too that a parameter value may be defined but empty. For good measure, you may want to check both possibilities. For example, to check for an age parameter and assign a default value of unknown if the parameter is missing or empty, you can do this:

```
$age = param ("age");
$age = "unknown" if !defined ($age) || $age eq "";
```

CGI.pm understands both ; and & as URL parameter separator characters.

PHP

Input parameters can be available to PHP in several ways, depending on your version of PHP and on your configuration settings:

- If the register_globals setting is on, parameters are assigned to global variables of the same name. In this case, the value of a field named id will be available as the variable $id, regardless of whether the request was sent via GET or POST.

- If the `track_vars` configuration setting is on, parameters are available in the `$HTTP_GET_VARS` and `$HTTP_POST_VARS` arrays. For example, if a form contains a field named `id`, the value will be available as `$HTTP_GET_VARS["id"]` or `$HTTP_POST_VARS["id"]`, depending on whether the form was submitted via GET or POST. `$HTTP_GET_VARS` and `$HTTP_POST_VARS` must be declared using the `global` keyword to make them accessible in a non-global script, such as within a function.

- As of PHP 4.1, parameters are available in the `$_GET` and `$_POST` arrays. These are analogous to `$HTTP_GET_VARS` and `$HTTP_POST_VARS` except that they are "super-global" arrays that are automatically available in any scope. (For example, it is unnecessary to declare `$_GET` and `$_POST` with `global` inside functions.) The `$_GET` and `$_POST` arrays are now the preferred means of getting at input parameters.

The `track_vars` and `register_globals` settings can be compiled in or configured in the PHP *php.ini* file. As of PHP 4.0.3, `track_vars` is always on, and I suspect that most installations of earlier versions enable this setting as well. For this reason, I'll assume your version of PHP has `track_vars` enabled.

`register_globals` makes it convenient to access input parameters through global variables, but the PHP developers recommend that it be disabled for security reasons. Why is that? Well, suppose you write a script that requires the user to supply a password, which is represented by the $password variable. You might check the password in a script like this:

```
if (check_password ($password))
    $password_is_ok = 1;
```

The intent here is that if the password matches, the script sets $password_is_ok to 1. Otherwise $password_is_ok is left unset (which compares false in Boolean expressions). But suppose `register_variables` is enabled and someone invokes your script as follows:

http://your.host.com/chkpass.php?password_is_ok=1

In this case, PHP sees that the `password_is_ok` parameter is set to 1, and sets the $password_is_ok variable to 1. The result is that when your script executes, $password_is_ok is 1 no matter what password was given, or even if *no* password was given! The problem with `register_globals` is that it allows outside users to supply default values for global variables in your scripts. One solution is to disable `register_globals`, in which case you'll need to check the global arrays ($_GET, $_POST) for input parameter values. If you don't want to do that, you should take care not to assume that PHP variables have no value initially. Unless you're expecting a global variable to be set from an input parameter, it's best to initialize it explicitly to a known value. The password-checking code should be written like this to make sure that $password_is_ok is assigned a value whatever the result of the test:

```
$password_is_ok = 0;
if (check_password ($password))
    $password_is_ok = 1;
```

The PHP scripts in this book do not rely on register_globals. Instead, they obtain input through the global parameter arrays.

Another complicating factor when retrieving input parameters in PHP is that they may need some decoding, depending on the value of the magic_quotes_gpc configuration setting. If magic quotes are enabled, any quote, backslash, and NUL characters in input parameter values will be escaped with backslashes. I guess this is supposed to save you a step by allowing you to extract values and use them directly in query strings. However, that's only useful if you plan to use web input in a query with no preprocessing or validity checking, which is dangerous. You should check your input first, in which case it's necessary to strip out the slashes anyway. That means having magic quotes turned on isn't really very useful.

Given the various sources through which input parameters may be available, and the fact that they may or may not contain extra backslashes, extracting input in PHP scripts can be an interesting problem. If you have control of your server and can set the values of the various configuration settings, you can of course write your scripts based on those settings. But if you do not control your server or are writing scripts that need to run on several machines, you may not know in advance what the settings are. Fortunately, with a bit of effort it's possible to write reasonably general purpose parameter extraction code that works correctly with very few assumptions about your PHP operating environment. The following utility function, get_param_val(), takes a parameter name as its argument and returns the corresponding parameter value. If the parameter is not available, the function returns an unset value.

```
function get_param_val ($name)
{
global $HTTP_GET_VARS, $HTTP_POST_VARS;

    unset ($val);
    if (isset ($_GET[$name]))
        $val = $_GET[$name];
    else if (isset ($_POST[$name]))
        $val = $_POST[$name];
    else if (isset ($HTTP_GET_VARS[$name]))
        $val = $HTTP_GET_VARS[$name];
    else if (isset ($HTTP_POST_VARS[$name]))
        $val = $HTTP_POST_VARS[$name];
    if (isset ($val) && get_magic_quotes_gpc ())
        $val = strip_slash_helper ($val);
    return (@$val);
}
```

To use this function to obtain the value of a single-valued parameter named id, call it like this:

```
$id = get_param_val ("id");
```

You can test $id to determine whether the id parameter was present in the input:

```
if (isset ($id))
    ... id parameter is present ...
```

```
else
    ... id parameter is not present ...
```

For a form field that may have multiple values (such as a checkbox group or a multiple-pick scrolling list), you should represent it in the form using a name that ends in [ ]. For example, a list element constructed from the SET column accessories in the cow_order table has one item for each allowable set value. To make sure PHP treats the element value as an array, don't name the field accessories, name it accessories[ ]. (See Recipe 18.3 for an example.) When the form is submitted, PHP places the array of values in a parameter named without the [ ], so to access it, do this:

```
$accessories = get_param_val ("accessories");
```

The $accessories variable will be an array. (This will be true whether the parameter has multiple values, a single value, or even no values. The determining factor is not whether the parameter actually *has* multiple values, but whether you name the corresponding field in the form using [ ] notation.)

The get_param_val() function checks the $_GET, $_POST, $HTTP_GET_VARS, and $HTTP_POST_VARS arrays for parameter values. Thus, it works correctly for PHP 3 and PHP 4, whether the request was made by GET or POST, and whether or not register_globals is turned on. The only thing that the function assumes is that track_vars is enabled.

get_param_val() also works correctly regardless of whether magic quoting is enabled. It uses a helper function strip_slash_helper() that performs backslash stripping from parameter values if necessary:

```
function strip_slash_helper ($val)
{
    if (!is_array ($val))
        $val = stripslashes ($val);
    else
    {
        reset ($val);
        while (list ($k, $v) = each ($val))
            $val[$k] = strip_slash_helper ($v);
    }
    return ($val);
}
```

strip_slash_helper() checks whether a value is a scalar or an array and processes it accordingly. The reason it uses a recursive algorithm for array values is that in PHP 4 it's possible to create nested arrays from input parameters.

To make it easy to obtain a list of all parameter names, write another utility function:

```
function get_param_names ()
{
global $HTTP_GET_VARS, $HTTP_POST_VARS;

    # construct an associative array in which each element has a
    # parameter name as both key and value.  (Using an associative
    # array eliminates duplicates.)
```

```
    $keys = array ();
    if (isset ($_GET))
    {
        reset ($_GET);
        while (list ($k, $v) = each ($_GET))
            $keys[$k] = $k;
    }
    else if (isset ($HTTP_GET_VARS))
    {
        reset ($HTTP_GET_VARS);
        while (list ($k, $v) = each ($HTTP_GET_VARS))
            $keys[$k] = $k;
    }
    if (isset ($_POST))
    {
        reset ($_POST);
        while (list ($k, $v) = each ($_POST))
            $keys[$k] = $k;
    }
    else if (isset ($HTTP_POST_VARS))
    {
        reset ($HTTP_POST_VARS);
        while (list ($k, $v) = each ($HTTP_POST_VARS))
            $keys[$k] = $k;
    }
    return ($keys);
}
```

get_param_names() returns a list of parameter names present in the HTTP variable arrays, with duplicate names removed if there is overlap between the arrays. The return value is an associative array with both the keys and values set to the parameter names. This way you can use either the keys or the values as the list of names. The following example prints the names, using the values:

```
$param_names = get_param_names ();
while (list ($k, $v) = each ($param_names))
    print (htmlspecialchars ($v) . "<br />\n");
```

For PHP 3 scripts, the parameters in URLs should be separated by & characters. That's also the default for PHP 4, although you can change it using the arg_separator configuration setting in the PHP initialization file.

Python

The Python cgi module provides access to the input parameters that are present in the script environment. Import that module, then create a FieldStorage object using a method of the same name:

```
import cgi

param = cgi.FieldStorage ()
```

The `FieldStorage` method returns information for parameters submitted via either GET or POST requests, so you need not know which method was used to send the request. The `FieldStorage` object contains an element for each parameter present in the environment. You can get a list of available parameter names like this:

```
names = param.keys ()
```

If a given parameter, name, is single-valued, the value associated with it will be a scalar that you can access as follows:

```
val = param[name].value
```

If the parameter is multiple-valued, `param[name]` will be a list of `MiniFieldStorage` objects that have name and value attributes. Each of these has the same name (it will be equal to name) and one of the parameter's values. To create a list containing all the values for such a parameter, do this:

```
val = []
for item in param[name]:
    val.append (item.value)
```

You can distinguish single-valued from multiple-valued parameters by checking the type. The following code shows how to get the parameter names and loop through each parameter to print its name and value, printing multiple-valued parameters as a comma-separated list:[*]

```
param = cgi.FieldStorage ()
param_names = param.keys ()
param_names.sort ()
print "<p>Parameter names:", param_names, "</p>"
items = []
for name in param_names:
    if type (param[name]) is not types.ListType:    # it's a scalar
        ptype = "scalar"
        val = param[name].value
    else:                                            # it's a list
        ptype = "list"
        val = []
        for item in param[name]:          # iterate through MiniFieldStorage
            val.append (item.value)       # items to get item values
        val = string.join (val, ",")      # convert to string for printing
    items.append ("type=" + ptype + ", name=" + name + ", value=" + val)
print make_unordered_list (items)
```

Python will raise an exception if you try to access a parameter that is not present in the `FieldStorage` object. To avoid this, use has_key() to find out if the parameter exists:

```
if param.has_key (name):
    print "parameter " + name + " exists"
else:
    print "parameter " + name + " does not exist"
```

---

[*] This code requires that you import the string and types module in addition to the cgi module.

Single-valued parameters have attributes other than value. For example, a parameter representing an uploaded file has additional attributes you can use to get the file's contents. This is discussed further in Recipe 18.8.

The cgi module expects URL parameters to be separated by & characters. If you generate a hyperlink to a script based on the cgi module and the URL includes parameters, don't separate them with ; characters.

Java

Within JSP pages, the implicit request object provides access to the request parameters through the following methods:

getParameterNames()
> Returns an enumeration of String objects, one for each parameter name present in the request.

getParameterValues(String name)
> Returns an array of String objects, one for each value associated with the parameter, or null if the parameter does not exist.

getParameterValue(String name)
> Returns the first value associated with the parameter, or null if the parameter does not exist.

The following example shows one way to use these methods to display request parameters:

```
<%@ page import="java.util.*" %>

<ul>
<%
    Enumeration e = request.getParameterNames ();
    while (e.hasMoreElements ())
    {
        String name = (String) e.nextElement ();
        // use array in case parameter is multiple-valued
        String[] val = request.getParameterValues (name);
        out.println ("<li> name: " + name + "; values:");
        for (int i = 0; i < val.length; i++)
            out.println (val[i]);
        out.println ("</li>");
    }
%>
</ul>
```

Request parameters are also available within JSTL tags, using the special variables param and paramValues. param[name] returns the first value for a given parameter and thus is most suited for single-valued parameters:

```
color value:
<c:out value="${param['color']}" />
```

paramValues[name] returns an array of values for the parameter, so it's useful for parameters that may have multiple values:

```
accessory values:
<c:forEach var="val" items="${paramValues['accessories']}">
    <c:out value="${val}" />
</c:forEach>
```

You can also access a parameter using dot notation if the parameter name is legal as an object property name:

```
color value:
<c:out value="${param.color}" />
accessory values:
<c:forEach var="val" items="${paramValues.accessories}">
    <c:out value="${val}" />
</c:forEach>
```

To produce a list of parameter objects with key and value attributes, iterate over the paramValues variable:

```
<ul>
    <c:forEach var="p" items="${paramValues}">
        <li>
            name:
            <c:out value="${p.key}" />;
            values:
            <c:forEach var="val" items="${p.value}">
                <c:out value="${val}" />
            </c:forEach>
        </li>
    </c:forEach>
</ul>
```

To construct URLs that point to JSP pages and that have parameters at the end, you should separate the parameters by & characters.

18.6   Validating Web Input

Problem

After extracting the parameters supplied to a script, it's a good idea to check them to be sure they're valid.

Solution

Web input processing is one form of data import, so after you've extracted the input parameters, you can validate them using the techniques discussed in Chapter 10.

Discussion

One phase of form processing is to extract the input that comes back when the user submits the form. It's also possible to receive input in the form of parameters at the end of a URL. But no matter the input source, if you're going to store it in your database, it's a good idea to check it to be sure it's valid.

When a client sends input to you over the Web, you don't really know what they're sending. If you present a form for users to fill out, most of the time they'll probably be nice and enter the kinds of values you expect. But a malicious user can save the form to a file, modify the file to allow form options you don't intend, reload the file into a browser window, and submit the modified form. Your form-processing script won't know the difference. If you write it only to process the kinds of values that well-intentioned users will submit, the script may misbehave or crash when presented with unexpected input—or perhaps even do bad things to your database. (Recipe 18.7 discusses what kinds of bad things can happen.) For this reason, it's prudent to perform some validity checking on web input before using it to construct database queries.

Preliminary checking is a good idea even for non-malicious users. If you require a field to be filled in and the user forgets to provide a value, you'll need to remind the user to supply one. This can involve a simple "Is the parameter present?" check, or it may be more involved. Typical types of validation operations include the following:

- Checking content format, such as making sure a value looks like an integer or a date. This may involve some reformatting for acceptability to MySQL (for example, changing a date from *MM/DD/YY* to ISO format).

- Determining whether or not a value is a member of a legal set of values. Perhaps the value must be listed in the definition for an ENUM or SET column, or must be present in a lookup table.

- Filtering out extraneous characters such as spaces or dashes from telephone numbers or credit card numbers.

Some of these operations have little to do with MySQL, except in the sense that you want values to be appropriate to the types of the columns you'll store them in or perform matches against. For example, if you're going to store a value in an INT column, you can make sure it's an integer first, using a test like this (shown here using Perl):

```
$val =~ /^\d+$/
    or die "Hey! '" . escapeHTML ($val) . "' is not an integer!\n";
```

For other types of validation, MySQL is intimately involved. If a field value is to be stored into an ENUM column, you can make sure the value is one of the legal enumeration values by checking the column definition with SHOW COLUMNS.

Having described some of the kinds of web input validation you might want to carry out, I won't further discuss them here. These and other forms of validation testing are described in Chapter 10. That chapter is oriented largely toward bulk input validation, but the techniques discussed there apply to web programming as well, because processing form input or URL parameters is, in essence, performing a data import operation.

18.7   Using Web Input to Construct Queries

Problem

Input obtained over the Web cannot be trusted and should not be placed into a query without taking the proper precautions.

Solution

Sanitize data values by using placeholders or a quoting function.

Discussion

After you've extracted input parameter values and checked them to make sure they're valid, you're ready to use them to construct a query. This is actually the easy part, though it's necessary to take the proper precautions to avoid making a mistake that you'll regret. First, let's consider what can go wrong, then see how to prevent the problem.

Suppose you have a search form containing a keyword field that acts as a frontend to a simple search engine. When a user submits a keyword, you intend to use it to find matching records in a table by constructing a query like this:

```
SELECT * FROM mytbl WHERE keyword = 'keyword_val'
```

Here, *keyword_val* represents the value entered by the user. If the value is something like eggplant, the resulting query is:

```
SELECT * FROM mytbl WHERE keyword = 'eggplant'
```

The query returns all eggplant-matching records, presumably generating a small result set. But suppose the user is tricky and tries to subvert your script by entering the following value:

```
eggplant' OR 'x'='x
```

In this case, the query becomes:

```
SELECT * FROM mytbl WHERE keyword = 'eggplant' OR 'x'='x'
```

That query matches every record in the table! If the table is quite large, the input effectively becomes a form of denial-of-service attack, because it causes your system to devote resources away from legitimate requests into doing useless work. Likely results are:

- Extra load on the MySQL server
- Out-of-memory problems in your script as it tries to digest the result set received from MySQL
- Extra network bandwidth consumption as the script sends the results to the client

If your script generates a DELETE statement, the consequences of this kind of subversion can be much worse—your script might issue a query that empties a table completely, when you intended to allow it to delete only a single record at a time.

The implication is that providing a web interface to your database opens you up to certain forms of attack. However, you can prevent this kind of problem by means of a simple precaution that you should already be following: don't put data values literally into query strings. Use placeholders or an encoding function instead. For example, in Perl you can handle an input parameter like this using placeholders:

```
$keyword = param ("keyword");
$sth = $dbh->prepare ("SELECT * FROM mytbl WHERE keyword = ?");
$sth->execute ($keyword);
# ... fetch result set ...
```

Or like this using quote( ):

```
$keyword = param ("keyword");
$keyword = $dbh->quote ($keyword);
$sth = $dbh->prepare ("SELECT * FROM mytbl WHERE keyword = $keyword");
$sth->execute ();
# ... fetch result set ...
```

Either way, if the user enters the subversive value, the query becomes:

```
SELECT * FROM mytbl WHERE keyword = 'eggplant\' OR \'x\'=\'x'
```

The input is rendered harmless, and the result is that the query will match no records rather than all records—definitely a more suitable response to someone who's trying to break your script.

Placeholder and quoting techniques for PHP, Python, and Java are similar, and have been discussed in Recipes 2.6 and 2.7. For JSP pages written using the JSTL tag library, you can quote input parameter values using placeholders and the <sql:param> tag (Recipe 16.3). For example, to use the value of a form parameter named keyword in a SELECT statement, do this:

```
<sql:query var="rs" dataSource="${conn}">
    SELECT * FROM mytbl WHERE keyword = ?
    <sql:param value="${param['keyword']}" />
</sql:query>
```

Placeholders and encoding functions apply only to SQL data values. One issue not addressed by them is how to handle web input used for other kinds of query elements such as the names of databases, tables, and columns. If you intend to insert such values into a query, you must insert them literally, which means you should check them first. For example, if you construct a query such as the following, you should verify that $tbl_name contains a reasonable value:

```
SELECT * FROM $tbl_name;
```

But what does "reasonable" mean? If you don't have tables containing strange characters in their names, it may be sufficient to make sure that $tbl_name contains only alphanumeric characters or underscores. An alternative is to issue a SHOW TABLES query to make sure that the table name in question is in the database. This is more foolproof, at the cost of an additional query.

Another issue not covered by placeholder techniques involves a question of interpretation: if a form field is optional, what should you store in the database if the user leaves the field empty? Perhaps the value represents an empty string—or perhaps it should be interpreted as NULL. One way to resolve this question is to consult the column metadata. If the column can contain NULL values, then interpret an empty field as NULL. Otherwise, take an empty field to mean an empty string.

Try to Break Your Scripts

The discussion in this section has been phrased in terms of guarding against other users from attacking your scripts. But it's not a bad idea to put yourself in the place of an attacker and adopt the mindset, "How can I break this application?" That is, consider whether there is some input you can submit to it that the application won't handle, and that will cause it to generate a malformed query? If you can cause it to misbehave, so can other people, either deliberately or accidentally. Be wary of bad input, and write your applications accordingly. It's better to be prepared than to just hope.

See Also

Several later sections in this chapter illustrate how to incorporate web input into queries. Recipe 18.8 shows how to upload files and load them into MySQL. Recipe 18.9 demonstrates a simple search application using input as search keywords. Recipes 18.10 and 18.11 process parameters in URLs.

18.8 Processing File Uploads

Problem

You want to allow files to be uploaded your web server and stored in your database.

Solution

Present the user with a web form that includes a file field. Use a file field in a web form. When the user submits the form, extract the file and store it in MySQL.

Discussion

One special kind of web input is an uploaded file. A file is sent as part of a POST request, but it's handled differently than other POST parameters, because a file is represented by several pieces of information such as its contents, its MIME type, its original filename on the client, and its name in temporary storage on the web server host.

To handle file uploads, you must send a special kind of form to the user; this is true no matter what API you use to create the form. However, when the user submits the form, the operations that check for and process an uploaded file are API-specific.

To create a form that allows files to be uploaded, the opening `<form>` tag should specify the POST method and must also include an `enctype` (encoding type) attribute with a value of `multipart/form-data`:

```
<form method="POST" enctype="multipart/form-data" action="script_name">
```

If you don't specify this kind of encoding, the form will be submitted using the default encoding type (`application/x-www-form-urlencoded`) and file uploads will not work properly.

To include a file upload field in the form, use an `<input>` element of type `file`. For example, to present a 60-character file field named `upload_file`, the element looks like this:

```
<input type="file" name="upload_file" size="60" />
```

The browser displays this field as a text input box into which the user can enter the name manually. It also presents a Browse button for selecting the file via the standard file-browsing system dialog. When the user chooses a file and submits the form, the browser encodes the file contents for inclusion into the resulting POST request. At that point, the web server receives the request and invokes your script to process it. The specifics vary for particular APIs, but file uploads generally work like this:

- The file will already have been uploaded and stored in a temporary directory by the time your upload-handling script begins executing. All your script has to do is read it. The temporary file will be available to your script either as an open file descriptor or the temporary filename, or perhaps both. The size of the file can be obtained through the file descriptor. The API may also make available other information about the file, such as its MIME type. (But note that some browsers may not send a MIME value.)

- Uploaded files are deleted automatically by the web server when your script terminates. If you want a file's contents to persist beyond the end of your script's execution, you'll have to save it to a more permanent location (for example, in a database or somewhere else in the filesystem). If you save it in the filesystem, the directory where you store it must be accessible to the web server.

- The API may allow you to control the location of the temporary file directory or the maximum size of uploaded files. Changing the directory to one that is accessible only to your web server may improve security a bit against local exploits by other users with login accounts on the server host.

This section discusses how to create forms that include a file upload field. It also demonstrates how to handle uploads using a Perl script, *post_image.pl*. The script is somewhat similar to the *store_image.pl* script for loading images from the command line (Recipe 17.6). *post_image.pl* differs in that it allows you to store images over the Web by uploading them, and it stores images only in MySQL, whereas *store_image.pl* stores them in both MySQL and the filesystem.

This section also discusses how to obtain file upload information using PHP and Python. It does not repeat the entire image-posting scenario shown for Perl, but the recipes distribution contains equivalent implementations of *post_image.pl* for PHP and Python.

Perl

You can specify multipart encoding for a form several ways using the CGI.pm module. The following statements are all equivalent:

```
print start_form (-action => url (), -enctype => "multipart/form-data");
print start_form (-action => url (), -enctype => MULTIPART ());
print start_multipart_form (-action => url ());
```

The first statement specifies the encoding type literally. The second uses the CGI.pm MULTIPART() function, which is easier than trying to remember the literal encoding value. The third statement is easiest of all, because start_multipart_form() supplies the enctype parameter automatically. (Like start_form(), start_multipart_form() uses a default request method of POST, so you need not include a method argument.)

Here's a simple form that includes a text field for assigning a name to an image, a file field for selecting the image file, and a submit button:

```
print start_multipart_form (-action => url ()),
        "Image name:", br (),
        textfield (-name =>"image_name", -size => 60),
        br (), "Image file:", br (),
        filefield (-name =>"upload_file", -size => 60),
        br (), br (),
        submit (-name => "choice", -value => "Submit"),
        end_form ();
```

When the user submits an uploaded file, begin processing it by extracting the parameter value for the file field:

```
$file = param ("upload_file");
```

The value for a file upload parameter is special in CGI.pm because you can use it two ways. You can treat it as an open file handle to read the file's contents, or pass it to uploadInfo( ) to obtain a reference to a hash that provides information about the file such as its MIME type. The following listing shows how *post_image.pl* presents the form and processes a submitted form. When first invoked, *post_image.pl* generates a form with an upload field. For the initial invocation, no file will have been uploaded, so the script does nothing else. If the user submitted an image file, the script gets the image name, reads the file contents, determines its MIME type, and stores a new record in the image table. For illustrative purposes, *post_image.pl* also displays all the information that the uploadInfo( ) function makes available about the uploaded file.

```perl
#! /usr/bin/perl -w
# post_image.pl - allow user to upload image files via POST requests

use strict;
use lib qw(/usr/local/apache/lib/perl);
use CGI qw(:standard escapeHTML);
use Cookbook;

print header (), start_html (-title => "Post Image", -bgcolor => "white");

# Use multipart encoding because the form contains a file upload field

print start_multipart_form (-action => url ()),
        "Image name:", br (),
        textfield (-name =>"image_name", -size => 60),
        br (), "Image file:", br (),
        filefield (-name =>"upload_file", -size => 60),
        br (), br (),
        submit (-name => "choice", -value => "Submit"),
        end_form ();

# Get a handle to the image file and the name to assign to the image

my $image_file = param ("upload_file");
my $image_name = param ("image_name");

# Must have either no parameters (in which case that script was just
# invoked for the first time) or both parameters (in which case the form
# was filled in).  If only one was filled in, the user did not fill in the
# form completely.

my $param_count = 0;
++$param_count if defined ($image_file) && $image_file ne "";
++$param_count if defined ($image_name) && $image_name ne "";

if ($param_count == 0)          # initial invocation
{
```

```
    print p ("No file was uploaded.");
}
elsif ($param_count == 1)        # incomplete form
{
    print p ("Please fill in BOTH fields and resubmit the form.");
}
else                             # a file was uploaded
{
my ($size, $data);

    # If an image file was uploaded, print some information about it,
    # then save it in the database.

    # Get reference to hash containing information about file
    # and display the information in "key=x, value=y" format
    my $info_ref = uploadInfo ($image_file);
    print p ("Information about uploaded file:");
    foreach my $key (sort (keys (%{$info_ref})))
    {
        printf p ("key="
                    . escapeHTML ($key)
                    . ", value="
                    . escapeHTML ($info_ref->{$key}));
    }
    $size = (stat ($image_file))[7]; # get file size from file handle
    print p ("File size: " . $size);

    binmode ($image_file);  # helpful for binary data
    if (sysread ($image_file, $data, $size) != $size)
    {
        print p ("File contents could not be read.");
    }
    else
    {
        print p ("File contents were read without error.");

        # Get MIME type, use generic default if not present

        my $mime_type = $info_ref->{'Content-Type'};
        $mime_type = "application/octet-stream" unless defined ($mime_type);

        # Save image in database table.  (Use REPLACE to kick out any
        # old image with same name.)

        my $dbh = Cookbook::connect ();
        $dbh->do ("REPLACE INTO image (name,type,data) VALUES(?,?,?)",
                    undef,
                    $image_name, $mime_type, $data);
        $dbh->disconnect ();
    }
}

print end_html ();

exit (0);
```

PHP

To write an upload form in PHP, include a file field. If you wish, you may also include a hidden field preceding the file field that has a name of MAX_FILE_SIZE and a value of the largest file size you're willing to accept:

```
<form method="POST" enctype="multipart/form-data"
    action="<?php print (get_self_path ()); ?>">
<input type="hidden" name="MAX_FILE_SIZE" value="4000000" />
Image name:<br />
<input type="text" name="image_name" size="60" />
<br />
Image file:<br />
<input type="file" name="upload_file" size="60" />
<br /><br />
<input type="submit" name="choice" value="Submit" />
</form>
```

Be aware that MAX_FILE_SIZE is advisory only, because it can be subverted easily. To specify a value that cannot be exceeded, use the upload_max_filesize configuration setting in the PHP initialization file. There is also a file_uploads setting that controls whether or not file uploads are allowed at all.

When the user submits the form, file upload information may be obtained as follows:

- As of PHP 4.1, file upload information from POST requests is placed in a separate array, $_FILES, which has one entry for each uploaded file. Each entry is itself an array with four elements. For example, if a form has a file field named upload_file and the user submits a file, information about it is available in the following variables:

$_FILES["upload_file]["name"]	*original filename on client host*
$_FILES["upload_file]["tmp_name"]	*temporary filename on server host*
$_FILES["upload_file]["size"]	*file size, in bytes*
$_FILES["upload_file]["type"]	*file MIME type*

  Be careful here, because there may be an entry for an upload field even if the user submitted no file. In this case, the tmp_name value will be the empty string or the string none.

- Earlier PHP 4 releases have file upload information in a separate array, $HTTP_POST_FILES, which has entries that are structured like those in $_FILES. For a file field named upload_file, information about it is available in the following variables:

$HTTP_POST_FILES["upload_file]["name"]	*original filename on client host*
$HTTP_POST_FILES["upload_file]["tmp_name"]	*temporary filename on server host*
$HTTP_POST_FILES["upload_file]["size"]	*file size, in bytes*
$HTTP_POST_FILES["upload_file]["type"]	*file MIME type*

- Prior to PHP 4, file upload information for a field named upload_file is available in a set of four $HTTP_POST_VARS variables:

$HTTP_POST_VARS["upload_file_name"]	*original filename on client host*
$HTTP_POST_VARS["upload_file"]	*temporary filename on server host*

```
        $HTTP_POST_VARS["upload_file_size"]        file size, in bytes
        $HTTP_POST_VARS["upload_file_type"]        file MIME type
```

$_FILES is a superglobal array (global in any scope). $HTTP_POST_FILES and $HTTP_POST_VARS must be declared with the global keyword if used in a non-global scope, such as within a function.

To avoid having to fool around figuring out which array contains file upload information, it makes sense to write a utility routine that does all the work. The following function, get_upload_info( ), takes an argument corresponding to the name of a file upload field. Then it examines the $_FILES, $HTTP_POST_FILES, and $HTTP_POST_VARS arrays as necessary and returns an associative array of information about the file, or an unset value if the information is not available. For a successful call, the array element keys are "tmp_name", "name", "size", and "type" (that is, the keys are the same as those in the entries within the $_FILES or $HTTP_POST_FILES arrays.)

```
function get_upload_info ($name)
{
global $HTTP_POST_FILES, $HTTP_POST_VARS;

    unset ($unset);
    # Look for information in PHP 4.1 $_FILES array first.
    # Check the tmp_name member to make sure there is a file. (The entry
    # in $_FILES might be present even if no file was uploaded.)
    if (isset ($_FILES))
    {
        if (isset ($_FILES[$name])
                && $_FILES[$name]["tmp_name"] != ""
                && $_FILES[$name]["tmp_name"] != "none")
            return ($_FILES[$name]);
        return (@$unset);
    }
    # Look for information in PHP 4 $HTTP_POST_FILES array next.
    if (isset ($HTTP_POST_FILES))
    {
        if (isset ($HTTP_POST_FILES[$name])
                && $HTTP_POST_FILES[$name]["tmp_name"] != ""
                && $HTTP_POST_FILES[$name]["tmp_name"] != "none")
            return ($HTTP_POST_FILES[$name]);
        return (@$unset);
    }
    # Look for PHP 3 style upload variables.
    # Check the _name member, because $HTTP_POST_VARS[$name] might not
    # actually be a file field.
    if (isset ($HTTP_POST_VARS[$name])
        && isset ($HTTP_POST_VARS[$name . "_name"]))
    {
        # Map PHP 3 elements to PHP 4-style element names
        $info = array ();
        $info["name"] = $HTTP_POST_VARS[$name . "_name"];
        $info["tmp_name"] = $HTTP_POST_VARS[$name];
        $info["size"] = $HTTP_POST_VARS[$name . "_size"];
        $info["type"] = $HTTP_POST_VARS[$name . "_type"];
```

```
        return ($info);
    }
    return (@$unset);
}
```

See the *post_image.php* script for details about how to use this function to get image information and store it in MySQL.

The `upload_tmp_dir` PHP configuration setting controls where uploaded files are saved. This is */tmp* by default on many systems, but you may want to override it to reconfigure PHP to use a different directory that's owned by the web server user ID and thus more private.

Python

A simple upload form in Python can be written like this:

```
print "<form method=\"POST\" enctype=\"multipart/form-data\" action=\"%s\">" \
        % (os.environ["SCRIPT_NAME"])
print "Image name:<br />"
print "<input type=\"text\" name=\"image_name\", size=\"60\" />"
print "<br />"
print "Image file:<br />"
print "<input type=\"file\" name=\"upload_file\", size=\"60\" />"
print "<br /><br />"
print "<input type=\"submit\" name=\"choice\" value=\"Submit\" />"
print "</form>"
```

When the user submits the form, its contents can be obtained using the `FieldStorage()` method of the `cgi` module. (See Recipe 18.5.) The resulting object contains an element for each input parameter. For a file upload field, you get this information as follows:

```
form = cgi.FieldStorage ()
if form.has_key ("upload_file") and form["upload_file"].filename != "":
    image_file = form["upload_file"]
else:
    image_file = None
```

According to most of the documentation that I have read, the `file` attribute of an object that corresponds to a file field should be true if a file has been uploaded. Unfortunately, the `file` attribute seems to be true even when the user submits the form but leaves the file field blank. It may even be the case that the `type` attribute is set when no file actually was uploaded (for example, to `application/octet-stream`). In my experience, a more reliable way to determine whether a file really was uploaded is to test the `filename` attribute:

```
form = cgi.FieldStorage ()
if form.has_key ("upload_file") and form["upload_file"].filename:
    print "<p>A file was uploaded</p>"
else:
    print "<p>A file was not uploaded</p>"
```

Assuming that a file was uploaded, access the parameter's value attribute to read the file and obtain its contents:

```
data = form["upload_file"].value
```

See the *post_image.py* script for details about how to use this function to get image information and store it in MySQL.

18.9   Performing Searches and Presenting the Results

Problem

You want to implement a web-based search interface.

Solution

Present a form containing fields that allow the user to supply search parameters such as keywords. Use the keywords to construct a query, then display the results.

Discussion

A script that implements a web-based search interface provides a convenience for people who visit your web site because they don't have to know any SQL to find information in your database. Instead, visitors supply keywords that describe what they're interested in and your script figures out the appropriate queries to run on their behalf. A common paradigm for this activity involves a form containing one or more fields for entering search parameters. The user fills in the form, submits it, and receives back a new page containing the records that match the parameters.

The issues that you as the writer of the script must handle are:

- Generate the form and send it to the users.
- Interpret the submitted form and construct a query from its contents. This includes proper use of placeholders or quoting to prevent bad input from crashing your script.
- Displaying the query result. This can be simple if the result set is small, or more complex if it is large. In the latter case, you may want to present the matching records using a paged display—that is, a display consisting of multiple pages, each of which shows a subset of the entire query result. Multiple-page displays have the benefit of not overwhelming the user with huge amounts of information all at once. They are discussed in Recipe 18.10.

This section demonstrates a script that implements a minimal search interface: a form with one keyword field, from which a query is constructed that returns at most one record. The script performs a two-way search through the contents of the states table. If the user enters a state name, it looks up the corresponding abbreviation. Conversely, if the user enters an abbreviation, it looks up the name. The script, *search_state.pl*, looks like this:

```perl
#! /usr/bin/perl -w
# search_state.pl - simple "search for state" application

# Present a form with an input field and a submit button.  User enters
# a state abbreviation or a state name into the field and submits the
# form.  Script finds the abbreviation and displays the full name, or
# finds the name and displays the abbreviation.

use strict;
use lib qw(/usr/local/apache/lib/perl);
use CGI qw(:standard escapeHTML);
use Cookbook;

my $title = "State Name or Abbreviation Lookup";

print header (), start_html (-title => $title, -bgcolor => "white");

# Extract keyword parameter.  If it's present and nonempty,
# attempt to perform a lookup.

my $keyword = param ("keyword");

if (defined ($keyword) && $keyword !~ /^\s*$/)
{
    my $dbh = Cookbook::connect ();
    my $found = 0;
    my $s;

    # first try looking for keyword as a state abbreviation;
    # if that fails, try looking for it as a name
    $s = $dbh->selectrow_array ("SELECT name FROM states WHERE abbrev = ?",
                                undef, $keyword);
    if ($s)
    {
        ++$found;
        print p ("You entered the abbreviation: " . escapeHTML ($keyword));
        print p ("The corresponding state name is : " . escapeHTML ($s));
    }
    $s = $dbh->selectrow_array ("SELECT abbrev FROM states WHERE name = ?",
                                undef, $keyword);
    if ($s)
    {
        ++$found;
        print p ("You entered the state name: " . escapeHTML ($keyword));
        print p ("The corresponding abbreviation is : " . escapeHTML ($s));
    }
    if (!$found)
    {
```

```
                    print p ("You entered the keyword: " . escapeHTML ($keyword));
                    print p ("No match was found.");
              }

              $dbh->disconnect ();
        }

        print p (qq{
        Enter a state name into the form and select Search, and I will show you
        the corresponding abbreviation.
        Or enter an abbreviation and I will show you the full name.
        });

        print start_form (-action => url ());

        print "State: ";
        print textfield (-name => "keyword", -size => 20);
        print br (),
              submit (-name => "choice", -value => "Search"),
              end_form ();

        print end_html ();

        exit (0);
```

The script first checks to see if a keyword parameter is present. If so, it runs the queries that look for a match to the parameter value in the states table and displays the results. Then it presents the form so that the user can enter a new search.

When you try the script, you'll notice that the value of the keyword field carries over from one invocation to the next. That's due to CGI.pm's behavior of initializing form fields with values from the script environment. If you don't like this behavior, to defeat it and make the field come up blank each time, supply an empty value explicitly and an override parameter in the textfield() call:

```
print textfield (-name => "keyword",
                    -value => "",
                    -override => 1,
                    -size => 20);
```

Or else clear the parameter's value in the environment before generating the field:

```
param (-name => "keyword", -value => "");
print textfield (-name => "keyword", -size => 20);
```

18.10 Generating Previous-Page and Next-Page Links

Problem

A query matches so many records that displaying them all in a single web page produces an unwieldy result.

Solution

Split the query output across several pages and include links that allow the user to navigate among pages.

Discussion

If a query matches a large number of records, showing them all in a single web page can result in a display that's difficult to navigate. For such cases, it can be more convenient for the user if you split the result among multiple pages. Such a paged display avoids overwhelming the user with too much information, but is more difficult to implement than a single-page display.

A paged display typically is used in a search context to present records that match the search parameters supplied by the user. To simplify things, the examples in this section don't have any search interface. Instead, they implement a paged display that presents 10 rows at a time from the result of a fixed query:

```
SELECT name, abbrev, statehood, pop  FROM states ORDER BY name;
```

MySQL makes it easy to select just a portion of a result set: add a LIMIT clause that indicates which records you want. The two-argument form of LIMIT takes values indicating how many records to skip at the beginning of the result set, and how many to select. The query to select a section of the states table thus becomes:

```
SELECT name, abbrev, statehood, pop  FROM states ORDER BY name
LIMIT skip,select;
```

One issue, then, is to determine the proper values of *skip* and *select* for any given page. Another is to generate the links that point to other pages or the query result. One style of paged display presents only "previous page" and "next page" links. To do this, you need to know whether any records precede or follow those you're displaying in the current page. Another paging style displays a link for each available page. This allows the user to jump directly to any page, not just the previous or next page. To present this kind of navigation, you have to know how the total number of records in the result set and the number of records per page, so that you can determine how many pages there are.

Paged Displays with Previous-Page and Next-Page Links

The following script, *state_pager1.pl*, presents records from the states table in a paged display that includes navigation links only to the previous and next pages. For a given page, we can determine which links are needed as follows:

- A "previous page" link is needed if there are records in the result set preceding those shown in the current page. If the current page starts at record one, there are no such records.

- A "next page" link is needed if there are records in the result set following those shown in the current page. You can determine this by issuing a SELECT COUNT(*) query to see how many records the query matches in total. Another method is to select one more record than you need. For example, if you're displaying 10 records at a time, try to select 11 records. If you get 11, there is a next page. If you get 10 or less, there isn't. *state_pager1.pl* uses the latter approach.

To determine its current position in the result set and how many records to display, *state_pager1.pl* looks for start and per_page input parameters. When you first invoke the script, these parameters won't be present, so they're initialized to 1 and 10, respectively. Thereafter, the script generates "previous page" and "next page" links to itself that include the proper parameter values in the URLs for selecting the previous or next sections of the result set.

```perl
#! /usr/bin/perl -w
# state_pager1.pl - paged display of states, with prev-page/next-page links

use strict;
use lib qw(/usr/local/apache/lib/perl);
use CGI qw(:standard escape escapeHTML);
use Cookbook;

my $title = "Paged US State List";

my $page = header ()
            . start_html (-title => $title, -bgcolor => "white")
            . h3 ($title);

my $dbh = Cookbook::connect ();

# Collect parameters that determine where we are in the display.
# Default to beginning of result set, 10 records/page if parameters
# are missing/malformed.

my $start = param ("start");
$start = 1
    if !defined ($start) || $start !~ /^\d+$/ || $start < 1;

my $per_page = param ("per_page");
$per_page = 10
    if !defined ($per_page) || $per_page !~ /^\d+$/ || $per_page < 1;;

# If start > 1, then we'll need a live "previous page" link.
# To determine whether or not there is a next page, try to select one
# more record than we need.  If we get that many, display only the first
# $per_page records, but add a live "next page" link.

# Select the records in the current page of the result set, and
# attempt to get an extra record.  (If we get the extra one, we
# won't display it, but its presence tells us there is a next
# page.)
```

```
my $query = sprintf (
                "SELECT name, abbrev, statehood, pop
                FROM states
                ORDER BY name LIMIT %d,%d",
                $start - 1,          # number of records to skip
                $per_page + 1);      # number of records to select

my $tbl_ref = $dbh->selectall_arrayref ($query);

$dbh->disconnect ();

# Display results as HTML table
my @rows;
push (@rows, Tr (th (["Name", "Abbrevation", "Statehood", "Population"])));
for (my $i = 0; $i < $per_page && $i < @{$tbl_ref}; $i++)
{
    # get data values in row $i
    my @cells = @{$tbl_ref->[$i]};  # get data values in row $i
    # map values to HTML-encoded values, or to   if null/empty
    @cells = map {
                defined ($_) && $_ ne "" ? escapeHTML ($_) : " "
                } @cells;
    # add cells to table
    push (@rows, Tr (td (\@cells)));
}

$page .= table ({-border => 1}, @rows) . br ();

# If we're not at the beginning of the query result, present a live
# link to the previous page.  Otherwise present static text.

if ($start > 1)                # live link
{
    my $url = sprintf ("%s?start=%d;per_page=%d",
                        url (),
                        $start - $per_page,
                        $per_page);
    $page .= "[" . a ({-href => $url}, "previous page") . "] ";
}
else                           # static text
{
    $page .= "[previous page]";
}

# If we got the extra record, present a live link to the next page.
# Otherwise present static text.

if (@{$tbl_ref} > $per_page)    # live link
{
    my $url = sprintf ("%s?start=%d;per_page=%d",
                        url (),
                        $start + $per_page,
                        $per_page);
    $page .= "[" . a ({-href => $url}, "next page") . "]";
```

```
}
else                         # static text
{
    $page .= "[next page]";
}

$page .= end_html ();

print $page;

exit (0);
```

Paged Displays with Links to Each Page

The next script, *state_pager2.pl*, is much like *state_pager1.pl*, but presents a paged display that includes navigation links to each page of the query result. To do this, it's necessary to know how many row there are in all. *state_pager2.pl* determines this by running a SELECT COUNT(*) query. Because it then knows the total row count, it's unnecessary to select an extra row when fetching the section of the result to be displayed.

Omitting the parts of *state_pager2.pl* that are the same as *state_pager1.pl*, the middle part that retrieves records and generates links is implemented as follows:

```
# Determine total number of records

my $total_recs = $dbh->selectrow_array ("SELECT COUNT(*) FROM states");

# Select the records in the current page of the result set

my $query = sprintf (
                "SELECT name, abbrev, statehood, pop
                FROM states
                ORDER BY name LIMIT %d,%d",
                $start - 1,        # number of records to skip
                $per_page);        # number of records to select

my $tbl_ref = $dbh->selectall_arrayref ($query);

$dbh->disconnect ();

# Display results as HTML table
my @rows;
push (@rows, Tr (th (["Name", "Abbrevation", "Statehood", "Population"])));
for (my $i = 0; $i < @{$tbl_ref}; $i++)
{
    # get data values in row $i
    my @cells = @{$tbl_ref->[$i]};  # get data values in row $i
    # map values to HTML-encoded values, or to   if null/empty
    @cells = map {
                defined ($_) && $_ ne "" ? escapeHTML ($_) : " "
                } @cells;
```

```
    # add cells to table
    push (@rows, Tr (td (\@cells)));
}

$page .= table ({-border => 1}, @rows) . br ();

# Generate links to all pages of the result set.  All links are
# live, except the one to the current page, which is displayed as
# static text.  Link label format is "[m to n]" where m and n are
# the numbers of the first and last records displayed on the page.

for (my $first = 1; $first <= $total_recs; $first += $per_page)
{
    my $last = $first + $per_page - 1;
    $last = $total_recs if $last > $total_recs;
    my $label = "$first to $last";
    my $link;

    if ($first != $start)   # live link
    {
        my $url = sprintf ("%s?start=%d;per_page=%d",
                           url (),
                           $first,
                           $per_page);
        $link = a ({-href => $url}, $label);
    }
    else                    # static text
    {
        $link = $label;
    }
    $page .= "[$link] ";
}
```

18.11 Generating "Click to Sort" Table Headings

Problem

You want to display a query result in a web page as a table that allows the user to select which column to sort the table rows by.

Solution

Make each column heading a hyperlink that redisplays the table, sorted by the corresponding column.

Discussion

When a web script runs, it can determine what action to take by querying its environment to find out what parameters are present and what their values are. In many cases these parameters come from a user, but there's no reason a script cannot add parameters to URLs itself. This is one way a given invocation of a script can send information to the next invocation. The effect is that the script communicates with itself by means of URLs that it generates to cause specific actions. An application of this technique is for showing the result of a query such that a user can select which column of the result to use for sorting the display. This is done by making the column headers active links that redisplay the table, sorted by the selected column.

The examples here use the mail table, which looks like this:

```
mysql> SELECT * FROM mail;
+---------------------+---------+---------+---------+---------+---------+
| t                   | srcuser | srchost | dstuser | dsthost | size    |
+---------------------+---------+---------+---------+---------+---------+
| 2001-05-11 10:15:08 | barb    | saturn  | tricia  | mars    |   58274 |
| 2001-05-12 12:48:13 | tricia  | mars    | gene    | venus   |  194925 |
| 2001-05-12 15:02:49 | phil    | mars    | phil    | saturn  |    1048 |
| 2001-05-13 13:59:18 | barb    | saturn  | tricia  | venus   |     271 |
| 2001-05-14 09:31:37 | gene    | venus   | barb    | mars    |    2291 |
| 2001-05-14 11:52:17 | phil    | mars    | tricia  | saturn  |    5781 |
| 2001-05-14 14:42:21 | barb    | venus   | barb    | venus   |   98151 |
| 2001-05-14 17:03:01 | tricia  | saturn  | phil    | venus   | 2394482 |
| 2001-05-15 07:17:48 | gene    | mars    | gene    | saturn  |    3824 |
| 2001-05-15 08:50:57 | phil    | venus   | phil    | venus   |     978 |
| 2001-05-15 10:25:52 | gene    | mars    | tricia  | saturn  |  998532 |
| 2001-05-15 17:35:31 | gene    | saturn  | gene    | mars    |    3856 |
| 2001-05-16 09:00:28 | gene    | venus   | barb    | mars    |     613 |
| 2001-05-16 23:04:19 | phil    | venus   | barb    | venus   |   10294 |
| 2001-05-17 12:49:23 | phil    | mars    | tricia  | saturn  |     873 |
| 2001-05-19 22:21:51 | gene    | saturn  | gene    | venus   |   23992 |
+---------------------+---------+---------+---------+---------+---------+
```

To retrieve the table and display its contents as an HTML table, you can use the techniques discussed in Recipe 17.3. Here we'll use those same concepts but modify them to produce "click to sort" table column headings.

A "plain" HTML table would include a row of column headers consisting only of the column names:

```
<tr>
  <th>t</th>
  <th>srcuser</th>
  <th>srchost</th>
  <th>dstuser</th>
  <th>dsthost</th>
  <th>size</th>
</tr>
```

To make the headings active links that reinvoke the script to produce a display sorted by a given column name, we need to produce a header row that looks like this:

```
<tr>
  <th><a href="script_name?sort=t">t</a></th>
  <th><a href="script_name?sort=srcuser">srcuser</a></th>
  <th><a href="script_name?sort=srchost">srchost</a></th>
```

```
    <th><a href="script_name?sort=dstuser">dstuser</a></th>
    <th><a href="script_name?sort=dsthost">dsthost</a></th>
    <th><a href="script_name?sort=size">size</a></th>
</tr>
```

To generate such headings, the script needs to know the names of the columns in the table, as well as its own URL. Recipes 9.5 and 18.1 show how to obtain this information using query metadata and information in the script's environment. For example, in PHP, a script can generate the header row for the columns in a given query like this:

```
$self_path = get_self_path ();
print ("<tr>\n");
for ($i = 0; $i < mysql_num_fields ($result_id); $i++)
{
    $col_name = mysql_field_name ($result_id, $i);
    printf ("<th><a href=\"%s?sort=%s\">%s</a></th>\n",
            $self_path,
            urlencode ($col_name),
            htmlspecialchars ($col_name));
}
print ("</tr>\n");
```

The following script, *clicksort.php*, implements this kind of table display. It checks its environment for a sort parameter that indicates which column to use for sorting. The script then uses the parameter to construct a query of the following form:

```
SELECT * FROM $tbl_name ORDER BY $sort_col LIMIT 50
```

(If no sort parameter is present, the script uses ORDER BY 1 to produce a default of sorting by the first column.) The LIMIT clause is simply a precaution to prevent the script from dumping huge amounts of output if the table is large.

Here's what the script looks like:

```
<?php
# clicksort.php - display query result as HTML table with "click to sort"
# column headings

# Rows from the database table are displayed as an HTML table.
# Column headings are presented as hyperlinks that reinvoke the
# script to redisplay the table sorted by the corresponding column.
# The display is limited to 50 rows in case the table is large.

include "Cookbook.php";
include "Cookbook_Webutils.php";

$title = "Table Display with Click-To-Sort Column Headings";

?>

<html>
<head>
<title><?php print ($title); ?></title>
```

```
</head>
<body bgcolor="white">

<?php
# ----------------------------------------------------------------------

$tbl_name = "mail";     # table to display; change as desired

$conn_id = cookbook_connect ();

print ("<p>Table: " . htmlspecialchars ($tbl_name) . "</p>\n");
print ("<p>Click on a column name to sort the table by that column.</p>\n");

# Get the name of the column to sort by (optional).  If missing, use
# column one.  If present, perform simple validation on column name;
# it must consist only of alphanumeric or underscore characters.

$sort_col = get_param_val ("sort");     # column name to sort by (optional)
if (!isset ($sort_col))
    $sort_col = "1";        # just sort by first column
else if (!ereg ("^[0-9a-zA-Z_]+$", $sort_col))
    die (htmlspecialchars ("Column name $sort_col is invalid"));

# Construct query to select records from the named table, optionally sorting
# by a particular column.  Limit output to 50 rows to avoid dumping entire
# contents of large tables.

$query = "SELECT * FROM $tbl_name";
$query .= " ORDER BY $sort_col";
$query .= " LIMIT 50";

$result_id = mysql_query ($query, $conn_id);
if (!$result_id)
    die (htmlspecialchars (mysql_error ($conn_id)));

# Display query results as HTML table.  Use query metadata to get column
# names, and display names in first row of table as hyperlinks that cause
# the table to be redisplayed, sorted by the corresponding table column.

print ("<table border=\"1\">\n");
$self_path = get_self_path ();
print ("<tr>\n");
for ($i = 0; $i < mysql_num_fields ($result_id); $i++)
{
    $col_name = mysql_field_name ($result_id, $i);
    printf ("<th><a href=\"%s?sort=%s\">%s</a></th>\n",
                $self_path,
                urlencode ($col_name),
                htmlspecialchars ($col_name));
}
print ("</tr>\n");
while ($row = mysql_fetch_row ($result_id))
{
    print ("<tr>\n");
```

```
        for ($i = 0; $i < mysql_num_fields ($result_id); $i++)
        {
            # encode values, using   for empty cells
            $val = $row[$i];
            if (isset ($val) && $val != "")
                $val = htmlspecialchars ($val);
            else
                $val = " ";
            printf ("<td>%s</td>\n", $val);
        }
        print ("</tr>\n");
    }
    mysql_free_result ($result_id);
    print ("</table>\n");

    mysql_close ($conn_id);

    ?>

    </body>
    </html>
```

In Recipe 18.7, I mentioned that placeholder techniques apply only to data values, not to identifiers such as column names. Our sort parameter is a column name, so it cannot be "sanitized" using placeholders or an encoding function. Instead, the script performs a rudimentary test to verify that the name contains only alphanumeric characters and underscores. This is a simple test that works for the majority of table names, though it may fail if you have tables with unusual names. The same kind of test applies also to database, index, column, and alias names.

Another approach to validating the column name is to run a SHOW COLUMNS query to find out which columns the table actually has. If the sort column is not one of them, it is invalid. The *clicksort.php* script shown here does not do that. However, the recipes distribution contains a Perl counterpart script, *clicksort.pl*, that does perform this kind of check. Have a look at it if you want more information.

The cells in the rows following the header row contain the data values from the database table, displayed as static text. Empty cells are displayed using   so that they display with the same border as nonempty cells (see Recipe 17.3).

18.12 Web Page Access Counting

Problem

You want to count the number of times a page has been accessed. This can be used to display a hit counter in the page. The same technique can be used to record other types of information as well, such as the number of times each of a set of banner ads has been served.

Solution

Implement a hit counter, keyed to the page you want to count.

Discussion

This section discusses access counting, using hit counters for the examples. Counters that display the number of times a web page has been accessed are not such a big thing as they used to be, presumably because page authors now realize that most visitors don't really care how popular a page is. Still, the general concept has application in several contexts. For example, if you're displaying banner ads in your pages (Recipe 17.7), you may be charging vendors by the number of times you serve their ads. To do so, you need to count the number of accesses for each one. You can adapt the technique shown in this section for purposes such as these.

There are several methods for writing a page that displays a count of the number of times it has been accessed. The most basic is to maintain the count in a file. When the page is requested, you open the file, read the count, increment it and write the new count back to the file and display it in the page. This has the advantage of being easy to implement and the disadvantage that it requires a counter file for each page that includes a hit count. It also doesn't work properly if two clients access the page at the same time, unless you implement some kind of locking protocol in the file access procedure. It's possible to reduce counter file litter by keeping multiple counts in a single file, but that makes it more difficult to access particular values within the file, and it doesn't solve the simultaneous-access problem. In fact, it makes it worse, because a multiple-counter file has a higher likelihood of being accessed by multiple clients simultaneously than does a single-counter file. So you end up implementing storage and retrieval methods for processing the file contents, and locking protocols to keep multiple processes from interfering with each other. Hmm... those sound suspiciously like the problems that MySQL already takes care of! Keeping the counts in the database centralizes them into a single table, SQL provides the storage and retrieval interface, and the locking problem goes away because MySQL serializes access to the table so that clients can't interfere with each other. Furthermore, depending on how you manage the counters, you may be able to update the counter and retrieve the new sequence value using a single query.

I'll assume that you want to log hits for more than one page. To do that, create a table that has one row for each page to be counted. This means it's necessary to have a unique identifier for each page, so that counters for different pages don't get mixed up. You could assign identifiers somehow, but it's easier just to use the page's path within your web tree. Web programming languages typically make this path easy to obtain; in fact, we've already discussed how to do so in Recipe 18.1. On that basis, you can create a hitcount table as follows:

```
CREATE TABLE hitcount
(
```

```
    path    VARCHAR(255) BINARY NOT NULL,
    hits    BIGINT UNSIGNED NOT NULL,
    PRIMARY KEY (path)
);
```

This table definition involves some assumptions:

- The BINARY keyword in the path column definition makes the column values case sensitive. That's appropriate for a web platform where pathnames are case sensitive, such as most versions of Unix. For Windows or for HFS+ filesystems under Mac OS X, filenames are not case sensitive, so you'd omit BINARY from the definition.

- The path column has a maximum length of 255 characters, which limits you to page paths no longer than that. If you expect to require longer values, use a BLOB or TEXT type rather than VARCHAR. But in this case, you're still limited to indexing a maximum of the leftmost 255 characters of the column values, so you'd use a non-unique index rather than a PRIMARY KEY.

- The mechanism works for a single document tree, such as when your web server is used to serve pages for a single domain. If you institute a hit count mechanism on a host that servers multiple virtual domains, you may want to add a column for the domain name. This value is available in the SERVER_NAME value that Apache puts into your script's environment. In this case, the hitcount table index would include both the hostname and the page path.

The general logic involved in hit counter maintenance is to increment the hits column of the record for a page, then retrieve the updated counter value. One way to do that is by using the following two queries:

```
UPDATE hitcount SET hits = hits + 1 WHERE path = 'page path';
SELECT hits FROM hitcount WHERE path = 'page path';
```

Unfortunately, if you use that approach, you may often not get the correct value. If several clients request the same page simultaneously, several UPDATE statements may be issued in close temporal proximity. The following SELECT statements then wouldn't necessarily get the corresponding hits value. This can be avoided by using a transaction or by locking the hitcount table, but that slows down hit counting. MySQL provides a solution that allows each client to retrieve its own count, no matter how many updates happen at the same time:

```
UPDATE hitcount SET hits = LAST_INSERT_ID(hits+1) WHERE path = 'page path';
SELECT LAST_INSERT_ID();
```

The basis for updating the count here is LAST_INSERT_ID(expr), which was discussed in Recipe 11.16. The UPDATE statement finds the relevant record and increments its counter value. The use of LAST_INSERT_ID(hits+1) rather than just hits+1 tells MySQL to treat the value as though it were an AUTO_INCREMENT value. This allows it to be retrieved in the second query using LAST_INSERT_ID(). The LAST_INSERT_ID() function returns a connection-specific value, so you always get back the value corresponding to the UPDATE issued on the same connection. In addition, the SELECT statement doesn't need to query a table, so it's very fast. A further efficiency may be gained by eliminating the SELECT query altogether, which is possible if your API provides a means for direct retrieval of the most recent sequence number. For example, in Perl, you can update the count and get the new value with a single query like this:

```
$dbh->do (
    "UPDATE hitcount SET hits = LAST_INSERT_ID(hits+1) WHERE path = ?",
    undef, $page_path);
$hits = $dbh->{mysql_insertid};
```

However, there's still a problem here. What if the page isn't listed in the hitcount table? In that case, the UPDATE statement finds no record to modify and you get a counter value of zero. You could deal with this problem by requiring that any page that includes a hit counter must be registered in the hitcount table before the page goes online. A friendlier alternate approach is to create a counter record automatically for any page that is found not to have one. That way, page designers can put counters in pages with no advance preparation. To make the counter mechanism easier to use, put the code in a utility function that takes a page path as its argument, handles the missing-record logic internally, and returns the count. Conceptually, the function acts like this:

```
update the counter
if the update modifies a row
    retrieve the new counter value
else
    insert a record for the page with the count set to 1
```

The first time you request a count for a page, the update modifies no rows because the page won't be listed in the table yet. The function creates a new counter and returns a value of one. For each request thereafter, the update modifies the existing record for the page and the function returns successive access counts.

In Perl, a hit-counting function might look like this, where the arguments are a database handle and the page path:

```
sub get_hit_count
{
my ($dbh, $page_path) = @_;

    my $rows = $dbh->do (
        "UPDATE hitcount SET hits = LAST_INSERT_ID(hits+1) WHERE path = ?",
        undef, $page_path);
    return ($dbh->{mysql_insertid}) if $rows > 0; # counter was incremented

    # If the page path wasn't listed in the table, register it and
    # initialize the count to one.  Use IGNORE in case another client
    # tries same thing at the same time.

    $dbh->do ("INSERT IGNORE INTO hitcount (path,hits) VALUES(?,1)",
                    undef, $page_path);
    return (1);
}
```

The CGI.pm `script_name()` function returns the local part of the URL, so you use `get_hit_count()` like this:

```
my $hits = get_hit_count ($dbh, script_name ());
print p ("This page has been accessed $hits times.");
```

The counting mechanism potentially involves multiple queries, and we haven't used a transactional approach, so the algorithm still has a race condition that can occur for the first access to a page. If multiple clients simultaneously request a page that is not yet listed in the `hitcount` table, each of them may issue the `UPDATE` query, find the page missing, and as a result issue the `INSERT` query to register the page and initialize the counter. The algorithm uses `INSERT IGNORE` to suppress errors if simultaneous invocations of the script attempt to initialize the counter for the same page, but the result is that they'll all get a count of one. Is it worth trying to fix this problem by using transactions or table locking? For hit counting, I'd say no. The slight loss of accuracy doesn't warrant the additional processing overhead. For a different application, the priority may be accuracy over efficiency, in which case you would opt for transactions to avoid losing a count.

A PHP version of the hit counter looks like this:

```
function get_hit_count ($conn_id, $page_path)
{
    $query = sprintf ("UPDATE hitcount SET hits = LAST_INSERT_ID(hits+1)
                        WHERE path = %s", sql_quote ($page_path));
    if (mysql_query ($query, $conn_id) && mysql_affected_rows ($conn_id) > 0)
        return (mysql_insert_id ($conn_id));

    # If the page path wasn't listed in the table, register it and
    # initialize the count to one.  Use IGNORE in case another client
    # tries same thing at the same time.

    $query = sprintf ("INSERT IGNORE INTO hitcount (path,hits)
                        VALUES(%s,1)", sql_quote ($page_path));
    mysql_query ($query, $conn_id);
    return (1);
}
```

To use it, call the `get_self_path()` function that returns the script pathname (see Recipe 18.1):

```
$self_path = get_self_path ();
$hits = get_hit_count ($conn_id, $self_path);
print ("<p>This page has been accessed $hits times.</p>\n");
```

In Python, the function looks like this:

```
def get_hit_count (conn, page_path):
    cursor = conn.cursor ()
    cursor.execute ("""
            UPDATE hitcount SET hits = LAST_INSERT_ID(hits+1)
```

```
        WHERE path = %s
    """, (page_path,))
if cursor.rowcount > 0:      # a counter was incremented
    count = cursor.insert_id ()
    cursor.close ()
    return (count)

# If the page path isn't listed in the table, register it and
# initialize the count to one.  Use IGNORE in case another client
# tries same thing at the same time.

cursor.execute ("""
        INSERT IGNORE INTO hitcount (path,hits) VALUES(%s,1)
    """, (page_path,))
cursor.close ()
return (1)
```

And is used as follows:

```
self_path = os.environ["SCRIPT_NAME"]
count = get_hit_count (conn, self_path)
print "<p>This page has been accessed %d times.</p>" % count
```

The recipes distribution includes demonstration scripts hit counter scripts for Perl, PHP, and Python under the *apache* directory. A JSP version is under the *tomcat* directory. Install any of these in your web tree, invoke it a few times, and watch the count increase. (First you'll need to create the hitcount table, as well as the hitlog table described in Recipe 18.13. Both tables can be created from the *hits.sql* script provided in the *tables* directory.)

18.13 Web Page Access Logging

Problem

You want to know more about a page than just the number of times it's been accessed, such as the time of access and the host from which the request originated.

Solution

Maintain a hit log rather than a simple counter.

Discussion

The hitcount table records only the count for each page registered in it. If you want to record other information about page access, use a different approach. Suppose you want to track the client host and time of access for each request. In this case, you need a log for each page rather than just a count. But you can still maintain the

counts by using a multiple-column index that combines the page path and an AUTO_
INCREMENT sequence column:

```
CREATE TABLE hitlog
(
    path    VARCHAR(255) BINARY NOT NULL,
    hits    BIGINT UNSIGNED NOT NULL AUTO_INCREMENT,
    t       TIMESTAMP,
    host    VARCHAR(64),
    PRIMARY KEY (path,hits)
);
```

To insert new records, use this query:

```
INSERT INTO hitlog (path, host) VALUES(path_val,host_val);
```

For example, in a JSP page, hits can be logged like this:

```
<c:set var="host">
    <%= request.getRemoteHost () %>
</c:set>
<c:if test="${empty host}">
    <c:set var="host">
        <%= request.getRemoteAddr () %>
    </c:set>
</c:if>
<c:if test="${empty host}">
    <c:set var="host">
        UNKNOWN
    </c:set>
</c:if>

<sql:update dataSource="${conn}">
    INSERT INTO hitlog (path, host) VALUES(?,?)
    <sql:param><%= request.getRequestURI () %></sql:param>
    <sql:param value="${host}" />
</sql:update>
```

The hitlog table has the following useful properties:

- Access times are recorded automatically in the TIMESTAMP column t when you
  insert new records.

- By linking the path column to an AUTO_INCREMENT column hits, the counter values for a given page path increment automatically whenever you insert a new
  record for that path. The counters are maintained separately for each distinct
  path value. (For more information on how multiple-column sequences work, see
  Recipe 11.14.)

- There's no need to check whether the counter for a page already exists, because
  you insert a new row each time you record a hit for a page, not just for the first hit.

- If you want to determine the current counters for each page, select the record for
  each distinct path value that has the largest hits value:

```
SELECT path, MAX(hits) FROM hitlog GROUP BY path;
```

18.14 Using MySQL for Apache Logging

Problem

You don't want to use MySQL to log accesses for just a few pages, as shown in Recipe 18.13. You want to log all pages accesses, and you don't want to have to put logging actions in each page explicitly.

Solution

Tell Apache to log pages accesses to MySQL.

Discussion

The uses for MySQL in a web context aren't limited just to page generation and processing. You can use it to help you run the web server itself. For example, most Apache servers are set up to log a record of web requests to a file. But it's also possible to send log records to a program instead, from which you can write the records wherever you like—such as to a database. With log records in a database rather than a flat file, the log becomes more highly structured and you can apply SQL analysis techniques to it. Log file analysis tools may be written to provide some flexibility, but often this is a matter of deciding which summaries to display and which to suppress. It's more difficult to tell a tool to display information it wasn't built to provide. With log entries in a table, you gain additional flexibility. Want to see a particular report? Write the SQL statements that produce it. To display the report in a specific format, issue the queries from within an API and take advantage of your language's output production capabilities.

By handling log entry generation and storage using separate processes, you gain some additional flexibility. Some of the possibilities are to send logs from multiple web servers to the same MySQL server, or to send different logs generated by a given web server to different MySQL servers.

This section shows how to set up web request logging from Apache into MySQL and demonstrates some summary queries you may find useful.

Setting Up Database Logging

Apache logging is controlled by directives in the *httpd.conf* configuration file. For example, a typical logging setup uses LogFormat and CustomLog directives that look like this:

```
LogFormat "%h %l %u %t \"%r\" %>s %b" common
CustomLog /usr/local/apache/logs/access_log common
```

The `LogFormat` line defines a format for log records and gives it the nickname `common`. The `CustomLog` directive indicates that lines should be written in that format to the *access_log* file in Apache's *logs* directory. To set up logging to MySQL instead, use the following procedure:[*]

- Decide what values you want to record and set up a table that contains the appropriate columns.

- Write a program to read log lines from Apache and write them into the database.

- Set up a `LogFormat` line that defines how to write log lines in the format the program expects, and a `CustomLog` directive that tells Apache to write to the program rather than to a file.

Suppose you want to record the date and time of each request, the host that issued the request, the request method and URL pathname, the status code, the number of bytes transferred, and the user agent (typically a browser or spider name). A table that includes columns for these values can be created as follows:

```
CREATE TABLE httpdlog
(
    dt      DATETIME NOT NULL,              # request date
    host    VARCHAR(255) NOT NULL,          # client host
    method  VARCHAR(4) NOT NULL,            # request method (GET, PUT, etc.)
    url     VARCHAR(255) BINARY NOT NULL,   # URL path
    status  INT NOT NULL,                   # request status
    size    INT,                            # number of bytes transferred
    agent   VARCHAR(255)                    # user agent
);
```

Most of the string columns use `VARCHAR` and are not case sensitive. The exception, `url`, is declared as a binary string as is appropriate for a server running on a system with case-sensitive filenames. If you're using a server where URL lettercase doesn't matter, you can omit the word BINARY.

The `httpdlog` table definition shown here doesn't include any indexes. You should add some, because otherwise any summary queries you run will slow down dramatically as the table becomes large. The choice of which columns to index will be based on the types of queries you intend to run to analyze the table contents. For example, queries to analyze the distribution of client host values will benefit from an index on the `host` column.

Next, you need a program to process log lines produced by Apache and insert them into the `httpdlog` table. The following script, *httpdlog.pl*, opens a connection to the MySQL server, then loops to read input lines. It parses each line into column values and inserts the result into the database. When Apache exits, it closes the pipe to the

---

[*] If you're using logging directives such as `TransferLog` rather than `LogFormat` and `CustomLog`, you'll need to adapt the instructions in this section.

logging program. That causes *httpdlog.pl* to see end of file on its input, terminate the loop, disconnect from MySQL, and exit.

```perl
#! /usr/bin/perl -w
# httpdlog.pl - Log Apache requests to httpdlog table

use strict;
use lib qw(/usr/local/apache/lib/perl);
use Cookbook;

my $dbh = Cookbook::connect ();
my $sth = $dbh->prepare (qq{
        INSERT INTO httpdlog (dt,host,method,url,status,size,agent)
        VALUES (?,?,?,?,?,?,?)
    });

while (<>)  # loop reading input
{
    chomp;
    my ($dt, $host, $method, $url, $status, $size, $agent)
                                        = split (/\t/, $_);
    # map "-" to NULL for some columns
    $size = undef if $size eq "-";
    $agent = undef if $agent eq "-";
    $sth->execute ($dt, $host, $method, $url, $status, $size, $agent);
}

$dbh->disconnect ();
exit (0);
```

Install the *httpdlog.pl* script where you want Apache to look for it. On my system, the Apache root directory is */usr/local/apache*, so */usr/local/apache/bin* is a reasonable installation directory. The path to this directory will be needed shortly for constructing the CustomLog directive that instructs Apache to log to the script.

httpdlog.pl assumes that input lines contain httpdlog column values delimited by tabs (to make it easy to break apart input lines), so Apache must write log entries in a matching format. The LogFormat field specifiers to produce the appropriate values are as follows:

%{%Y-%m-%d %H:%M:%S}
> The date and time of the request, in MySQL's DATETIME format

%h
> The host from which the request originated

%m
> The request method (GET, POST, and so forth)

%U
> The URL path

%>s
> The status code

%b

The number of bytes transferred

%{User-Agent}i

The user agent

To define a logging format named mysql that produces these values with tabs in between, add the following LogFormat directive to your *httpd.conf* file:

```
LogFormat "%{%Y-%m-%d %H:%M:%S}t\t%h\t%m\t%U\t%>s\t%b\t%{User-Agent}i" mysql
```

Most of the pieces are in place now. We have a log table, a program that writes to it, and a mysql format for producing log entries. All that remains is to tell Apache to write the entries to the *httpdlog.pl* script. However, until you know that the output format really is correct and that the program can process log entries properly, it's premature to tell Apache to log directly to the program. To make testing and debugging a bit easier, have Apache log mysql-format entries to a file instead. That way, you can look at the file to check the output format, and you can use it as input to *httpdlog.pl* to verify that the program works correctly. To instruct Apache to log lines in mysql format to the file *test_log* in Apache's log directory, use this CustomLog directive:

```
CustomLog /usr/local/apache/logs/test_log mysql
```

Then restart Apache to enable the new logging directives. After your web server receives a few requests, take a look at the *test_log* file. Verify that the contents are as you expect, then feed the file to *httpdlog.pl*. If you're in Apache's *logs* directory and the *bin* and *logs* directories are both under the Apache root, the command looks like this:

```
% ../bin/httpdlog.pl test_log
```

After *httpdlog.pl* finishes, take a look at the httpdlog table to make sure that it looks correct. Once you're satisfied, tell Apache to send log entries directly to *httpdlog.pl* by modifying the CustomLog directive as follows:

```
CustomLog "|/usr/local/apache/bin/httpdlog.pl" mysql
```

The | character at the beginning of the pathname tells Apache that *httpdlog.pl* is a program, not a file. Restart Apache and new entries should appear in the httpdlog table as visitors request pages from your site.

Nothing you have done to this point changes any logging you may have been doing originally. For example, if you were logging to an *access_log* file before, you still are now. Thus, Apache will be sending entries both to the original log file and to MySQL. If that's what you want, fine. Apache doesn't care if you log to multiple destinations. But you'll use more disk space if you do. To disable file logging, comment out your original CustomLog directive by placing a # character in front of it, then restart Apache.

Analyzing the Log File

Now that you have Apache logging into the database, what can you do with the information? That depends on what you want to know. Here are some examples that show the kinds of questions you can use MySQL to answer easily:

- How many records are in the request log?

  ```
  SELECT COUNT(*) FROM httpdlog;
  ```

- How many different client hosts have sent requests?

  ```
  SELECT COUNT(DISTINCT host) FROM httpdlog;
  ```

- How many different pages have clients requested?

  ```
  SELECT COUNT(DISTINCT url) FROM httpdlog;
  ```

- What are the ten most popular pages?

  ```
  SELECT url, COUNT(*) AS count FROM httpdlog
  GROUP BY url ORDER BY count DESC LIMIT 10;
  ```

- How many requests have been received for those useless, wretched *favicon.ico* files that certain browsers like to check for?

  ```
  SELECT COUNT(*) FROM httpdlog WHERE url LIKE '%/favicon.ico%';
  ```

- What is the range of dates spanned by the log?

  ```
  SELECT MIN(dt), MAX(dt) FROM httpdlog;
  ```

- How many requests have been received each day?

  ```
  SELECT FROM_DAYS(TO_DAYS(dt)) AS day, COUNT(*) FROM httpdlog GROUP BY day;
  ```

  Answering this question requires stripping off the time-of-day part from the dt values so that requests received on a given date can be grouped. The query does this using TO_DAYS() and FROM_DAYS() to convert DATETIME values to DATE values. However, if you intend to run a lot of queries that use just the date part of the dt values, it would be more efficient to create the httpdlog table with separate DATE and TIME columns, change the LogFormat directive to produce the date and time as separate output values, and modify *httpdlog.pl* accordingly. Then you can operate on the request dates directly without stripping off the time, and you can index the date column for even better performance.

- What is the hour-of-the-day request histogram?

  ```
  SELECT HOUR(dt) AS hour, COUNT(*) FROM httpdlog GROUP BY hour;
  ```

- What is the average number of requests received each day?

  ```
  SELECT COUNT(*)/(TO_DAYS(MAX(dt)) - TO_DAYS(MIN(dt)) + 1) FROM httpdlog;
  ```

  The numerator is the total number of requests in the table. The denominator is the number of days spanned by the records.

- What is the longest URL recorded in the table?

  ```
  SELECT MAX(LENGTH(url)) FROM httpdlog;
  ```

If the url column is defined as VARCHAR(255) and this query produces a value of 255, it's likely that some URL values were too long to fit in the column and were truncated at the end. To avoid this, you can convert the column to BLOB or TEXT (depending on whether or not you want the values to be case sensitive). For example, if you want case-sensitive values up to 65,535 characters long, modify the url column as follows:

```
ALTER TABLE httpdlog MODIFY url BLOB NOT NULL;
```

- What is the total number of bytes served and the average bytes per request?

```
SELECT
    COUNT(size) AS requests,
    SUM(size) AS bytes,
    AVG(size) AS 'bytes/request'
FROM httpdlog;
```

The query uses COUNT(size) rather than COUNT(*) to count only those requests with a non-NULL size value. (If a client requests a page twice, the server may respond to the second request by sending a header indicating that the page hasn't changed rather than by sending content. In this case, the log entry for the request will have NULL in the size column.)

- How much traffic has there been for each kind of file (based on filename extension such as .html, .jpg, or .php)?

```
SELECT
    SUBSTRING_INDEX(SUBSTRING_INDEX(url,'?',1),'.',-1) AS extension,
    COUNT(size) AS requests,
    SUM(size) AS bytes,
    AVG(size) AS 'bytes/request'
FROM httpdlog
WHERE url LIKE '%.%'
GROUP BY extension;
```

The WHERE clause selects only url values that have a period in them, to eliminate pathnames that name files that have no extension. To extract the extension values for the output column list, the inner SUBSTRING_INDEX() call strips off any parameter string at the right end of the URL and leaves the rest. (This turns a value like /cgi-bin/script.pl?id=43 into /cgi-bin/script.pl. If the value has no parameter part, SUBSTRING_INDEX() returns the entire string.) The outer SUBSTRING_INDEX() call strips everything up to and including the rightmost period from the result, leaving only the extension.

Other Logging Issues

I've chosen a simple method for hooking Apache to MySQL, which is to write a short script that communicates with MySQL and then tell Apache to write to the script rather than to a file. This works well if you log all requests to a single file, but certainly won't be appropriate for every possible configuration that Apache is capable of. For example, if you have virtual servers defined in your *httpd.conf* file, you might have separate CustomLog directives defined for each of them. To log them all to MySQL, you can change each directive to write to *httpdlog.pl*, but then you'll have a separate logging process running for each virtual server. That brings up two issues:

- How do you associate log records with the proper virtual server? One solution is to create a separate log table for each server and modify *httpdlog.pl* to take an argument that indicates which table to use. Another is to add a virt_host column to the httpdlog table and modify *httpdlog.pl* to take a hostname argument indicating a server name to write to the virt_host column.

- Do you really want a lot of *httpdlog.pl* processes running? If you have many virtual servers, you may want to consider using a logging module that installs directly into Apache. Some of these can multiplex logging for multiple virtual hosts through a single connection to the database server, reducing resource consumption for logging activity.

Logging to a database rather than to a file allows you to bring the full power of MySQL to bear on log analysis, but it doesn't eliminate the need to think about space management. Web servers can generate a lot of activity, and log records use space regardless of whether you write them to a file or to a database. One way to save space is to expire records now and then. For example, to remove log records that are more than a year old, run the following query periodically:

```
DELETE FROM httpdlog WHERE dt < DATE_SUB(NOW(),INTERVAL 1 YEAR);
```

Another option is to archive old records into compressible tables. (This requires that you use MyISAM tables so that you can compress them with the *myisampack* utility.) For example, when the date changes from September 2001 to October 2001, you know that Apache won't generate any more records with September dates and that you can move them into another table that will remain static. Create a table named httpdlog_2001_09 that has the same structure as httpdlog (including any indexes). Then transfer September's log records from httpdlog into httpdlog_2001_09 using these queries:

```
INSERT INTO httpdlog_2001_09
    SELECT * FROM httpdlog
    WHERE dt >= '2001-09-01' AND dt < '2001-10-01';
DELETE FROM httpdlog
    WHERE dt >= '2001-09-01' AND dt < '2001-10-01';
```

Finally, run *myisampack* on httpdlog_2001_09 to compress it and make it read-only.

This strategy has the potential drawback of spreading log entries over many tables. If you want to treat the tables as a single entity so that you can run queries on your entire set of log records, create a MERGE table that includes them all. Suppose the set of tables includes the current table and tables for September 2001 through April 2002. The statement to create the MERGE table would look like this:

```
CREATE TABLE httpdlog_all
(
    dt      DATETIME NOT NULL,                  # request date
    host    VARCHAR(255) NOT NULL,              # client host
    method  VARCHAR(4) NOT NULL,                # request method (GET, PUT, etc.)
    url     VARCHAR(255) BINARY NOT NULL,       # URL path
    status  INT NOT NULL,                       # request status
    size    INT,                                # number of bytes transferred
    agent   VARCHAR(255)                        # user agent
)
TYPE = MERGE
UNION = (httpdlog, httpdlog_2001_09, httpdlog_2001_10, httpdlog_2001_11,
httpdlog_2001_12, httpdlog_2002_01, httpdlog_2002_02, httpdlog_2002_03,
httpdlog_2002_04);
```

The UNION clause should name all the tables that you want to include in the MERGE table. Note that you'll need to drop and recreate the httpdlog_all definition each time you generate a new static monthly log table. (Also, if you add an index, you'll need to add it to each of the individual tables, and recreate the MERGE table to include the index definition as well.)

Reports run against the httpdlog_all table will be based on all log entries. To produce monthly reports, just refer to the appropriate individual table.

With respect to disk space consumed by web logging activity, be aware that if you have query logging enabled for the MySQL server, each request will be written to the httpdlog table and also to the query log. Thus, you may find disk space disappearing more quickly than you expect, so it's a good idea to have some kind of log rotation or expiration set up for the MySQL server.

CHAPTER 19

Using MySQL-Based Web Session Management

19.0 Introduction

Many web applications interact with users over a series of requests and, as a result need to remember information from one request to the next. A set of related requests is called a session. Sessions are useful for activities such as performing login operations and associating a logged-in user with subsequent requests, managing a multiple-stage online ordering process, gathering input from a user in stages (possibly tailoring the questions asked to the user's earlier responses), and remembering user preferences from visit to visit. Unfortunately, HTTP is a stateless protocol, which means that web servers treat each request independently of any other—unless you take steps to ensure otherwise.

This chapter shows how to make information persist across multiple requests, which will help you develop applications for which one request retains memory of previous ones. The techniques shown here are general enough that you should be able to adapt them to a variety of state-maintaining web applications.

Session Management Issues

Some session management methods rely on information stored on the client. One way to implement client-side storage is to use cookies, which are implemented as information transmitted back and forth in special request and response headers. When a session begins, the application generates and sends the client a cookie containing the initial information to be stored. The client returns the cookie to the server with each subsequent request to identify itself and to allow the application to associate the requests as belonging to the same client session. At each stage of the session, the application uses the data in the cookie to determine the state (or status) of the client. To modify the session state, the application sends the client a new cookie containing updated information to replace the old cookie. This mechanism allows data to persist across requests while still affording the application the opportunity to update the information as necessary. Cookies are easy to use, but have some disadvantages. For example, it's possible for the client to modify cookie contents, possibly tricking the application into misbehaving. Other client-side session storage techniques suffer the same drawback.

The alternative to client-side storage is to maintain the state of a multiple-request session on the server side. With this approach, information about what the client is doing is stored somewhere on the server, such as in a file, in shared memory, or in a database. The only information maintained on the client side is a unique identifier that the server generates and sends to the client when the session begins. The client sends this value to the server with each subsequent request so that the server can associate the client with the appropriate session. Common techniques for tracking the session ID are to store it in a cookie or to encode it in request URLs. (The latter is useful for clients who have cookies disabled.) The server can get the ID as the cookie value or by extracting it from the URL.

Server-side session storage is more secure than storing information on the client, because the application maintains control over the contents of the session. The only value present on the client side is the session ID, so the client can't modify session data unless the application permits it. It's still possible for a client to tinker with the ID and send back a different one, but if IDs are unique and selected from a very large pool of possible values, it's extremely unlikely that a malicious client will be able to guess the ID of another valid session.*

Server-side methods for managing sessions commonly store session contents in persistent storage such as a file or a database. Database-backed storage has different characteristics than file-based storage, such as that you eliminate the filesystem clutter that results from having many session files, and you can use the same MySQL server to handle session traffic for multiple web servers. If this appeals to you, the techniques shown in the chapter will help you integrate MySQL-based session management into your applications. The chapter shows how to implement server-side database-backed session management for three of our API languages:†

- For Perl, the *Apache::Session* module includes most of the capabilities you need for managing sessions. It can store session information in files or in any of several databases, including MySQL, PostgreSQL, and Oracle.

- PHP includes native session support as of PHP 4. The implementation uses temporary files by default, but is sufficiently flexible that applications can supply

---

* If you are concerned about other clients stealing valid session IDs by network snooping, you should set up a secure connection, for example, by using SSL. But that is beyond the scope of this book.

† Python is not included in the chapter because I have not found a standalone Python session management module I felt was suitable for discussion here, and I didn't want to write one from scratch. If you're writing Python applications that require session support, you might want to look into a toolkit like Zope, WebWare, or Albatross.

---

their own handler routines for session storage. This makes it possible to plug in a storage module that writes information to MySQL.

- For Java-based web applications running under the Tomcat web server, Tomcat provides session support at the server level. All you need to do is modify the server configuration to use MySQL for session storage. Application programs need do nothing to take advantage of this capability, so there are no changes at the application level.

Session support for these APIs are implemented using very different approaches. For Perl, the language itself provides no session support, so a script must include a module such as *Apache::Session* explicitly if it wants to implement a session. In PHP, the session manager is built in. Scripts can use it with no special preparation, but only as long as they want to use the default storage method, which is to save session information in files. To use an alternate method (such as storing sessions in MySQL), an application must provide its own routines for the session manager to use. Still another approach is used for Java applications running under Tomcat, because Tomcat itself manages many of the details associated with session management, including where to store session data. Individual applications need not know or care where this information is stored.

Despite the differing implementations, session management typically involves a common set of tasks:

- Determining whether the client provided a session ID. If not, it's necessary to generate a unique session ID and send it to the client. Some session managers figure out how to transmit the session ID between the server and the client automatically. PHP does this, as does Tomcat for Java programs. The Perl *Apache::Session* module leaves it up to the application developer to manage ID transmission.

- Storing values into the session for use by later requests and retrieving values placed into the session by earlier requests. This involves performing whatever actions are necessary that involve session data: incrementing a counter, validating a login request, updating a shopping cart, and so forth.

- Terminating the session when it's no longer needed. Some session managers make provision for expiring sessions automatically after a certain period of inactivity. Sessions may also be ended explicitly, if the request indicates that the session should terminate (such as when the client selects a logout action). In response, the session manager destroys the session record. it might also be necessary to tell the client to release information. If the client sends the session identifier by means of a cookie, the application should instruct the client to discard the cookie. Otherwise, the client may continue to submit it after its usefulness has ended.

Another thing session managers have in common is that they impose little constraint on what applications can store in session records. Sessions usually can accommodate relatively arbitrary data, such as scalars, arrays, or objects. To make it easy to store and retrieve session data, session managers typically serialize session information (convert it to a coded scalar string value) before storing it and unserialize it after retrieval. The conversion to and from serialized strings generally is not something you must deal with when providing storage routines. It's necessary only to make sure the storage manager has a large enough repository in which to store the serialized strings. For backing store implemented using MySQL, this means you use a BLOB or TEXT column.

The rest of the chapter shows a session-based script for each API. Each script performs two tasks. It maintains a counter value that indicates how many requests have been received during the current session, and records a timestamp for each request. In this way, the scripts illustrate how to store and retrieve a scalar value (the counter) and a non-scalar value (the timestamp array). They require very little user interaction. You just reload the page to issue the next request, which results in extremely simple code.

Session-based applications often include some way for the user to log out explicitly and terminate the session. The example scripts implement a form of "logout," but it is based on an implicit mechanism: sessions are given a limit of 10 requests. As you reinvoke a script, it checks the counter to see if the limit has been reached and destroys the session data if so. The effect is that the session values will not be present on the next request, so the script starts a new session.

The example session scripts for Perl and PHP can be found under the *apache* directory of the recipes distribution, the PHP session module is located in the *lib* directory, and the JSP examples are under the *tomcat* directory. The SQL scripts for creating the session storage tables are located in the *tables* directory. As used here, the session tables are created in the cookbook database and accessed through the same MySQL account as that used elsewhere in this book. If you don't want to mix session management activities with those pertaining to the other cookbook tables, consider setting up a separate database and MySQL account to be used only for session data. This is true particularly for Tomcat, where session management takes place above the application level. You might not want the Tomcat server storing information in "your" database; if not, give the server its own database.

19.1 Using MySQL-Based Sessions in Perl Applications

Problem

You want to use session storage for Perl scripts.

Solution

The *Apache::Session* module provides a convenient way to use several different storage types, including one based on MySQL.

Discussion

Apache::Session is an easy-to-use Perl module for maintaining state information across multiple web requests. Despite the name, this module is not dependent on Apache and can be used in non-web contexts, for example, to maintain persistent state across multiple invocations of a command-line script. On the other hand, *Apache::Session* doesn't handle any of the issues associated with tracking the session ID (sending it to the client in response to the initial request and extracting it from subsequent requests). The example application shown here uses cookies to pass the session ID, on the assumption that the client has cookies enabled.

Installing Apache::Session

If you don't have *Apache::Session*, you can get it from the CPAN (visit *http://cpan. perl.org*). Installation is straightforward, although *Apache::Session* does require several other modules that you may need to get first. (When you install it, *Apache:: Session* should tell you which required modules you need if any are missing.) After you have everything installed, create a table in which to store session records. The specification for the table comes from the MySQL storage handler documentation, which you can read using this command:

```
% perldoc Apache::Session::Store::MySQL
```

The table can be placed in any database you like (we'll use cookbook), but the table name must be named sessions and have this structure:

```
CREATE TABLE sessions
(
    id          CHAR(32) NOT NULL,  # session identifier
    a_session   BLOB,               # session data
    PRIMARY KEY (id)
);
```

The id column holds session identifiers, which are 32-character MD5 values generated by *Apache::Session*. The a_session column holds session data in the form of serialized strings. *Apache::Session* uses the Storable module to serialize and unserialize session data.

The Apache::Session Interface

To use the sessions table in a script, include the MySQL-related session module:

```
use Apache::Session::MySQL;
```

Apache:Session represents session information using a hash. It uses Perl's tie mechanism to map hash operations onto the storage and retrieval methods used by the underlying storage manager. Thus, to open a session, you should declare a hash variable and pass it to tie. The other arguments to tie are the name of the session module, the session ID, and information about the database to use. There are two ways to specify the database connection. First, you can pass a reference to a hash that contains connection parameters:

```
my %session;
tie %session,
    "Apache::Session::MySQL",
    $sess_id,
    {
        DataSource => "DBI:mysql:host=localhost;database=cookbook",
        UserName => "cbuser",
        Password => "cbpass",
        LockDataSource => "DBI:mysql:host=localhost;database=cookbook",
        LockUserName => "cbuser",
        LockPassword => "cbpass"
    };
```

In this case, *Apache::Session* uses the parameters to open its own connection to MySQL, which it closes when you close or destroy the session. Second, you can pass the handle for an already open database connection (represented here by $dbh):

```
my %session;
tie %session,
    "Apache::Session::MySQL",
    $sess_id,
    {
        Handle => $dbh,
        LockHandle => $dbh
    };
```

If you pass a handle to an open connection like this, *Apache::Session* leaves it open when you close or destroy the session, on the assumption that you're using the handle for other purposes elsewhere in the script. You should close the connection yourself when you're done with it.

The $sess_id argument to tie represents the session identifier. Its value should be either undef to begin a new session, or a valid ID corresponding to an existing session record. In the latter case, the value should match that of the id column in some existing sessions table record.

After the session has been opened, you can access its contents. For example, after opening a new session, you'll want to determine what its identifier is so you can send it to the client. That value can be obtained like this:

```
$sess_id = $session{_session_id};
```

Session hash element names that begin with an underscore (such as _session_id) are reserved by *Apache::Session* for internal use. Other than that, you can use names of your own choosing for storing session values. For example, you might maintain a scalar counter value as follows, where the counter is initialized if the session is new, then incremented and retrieved for display:

```
$session{count} = 0 if !exists ($session{count});   # initialize counter
++$session{count};                                   # increment counter
print "counter value: $session{count}\n";            # print value
```

To save a non-scalar value such as an array or a hash into the session record, store a reference to it:

```
$session{my_array} = \@my_array;
$session{my_hash} = \%my_hash;
```

In this case, changes made to @my_array or %my_hash before you close the session will be reflected in the session contents. To save an independent copy of an array or hash in the session that will not change when you modify the original, create a reference to it like this:

```
$session{my_array} = [ @my_array ];
$session{my_hash} = { %my_hash };
```

To retrieve a non-scalar value, dereference the reference stored in the session:

```
@my_array = @{$session{my_array}};
%my_hash = %{$session{my_hash}};
```

To close a session when you're done with it, pass it to untie:

```
untie (%session);
```

When you close a session, *Apache::Session* saves it to the sessions table if you've made changes to it. This also makes the session values inaccessible, so don't close the session until you're done accessing it.

> *Apache::Session* notices changes to "top-level" session record values, but might not detect a change to a member of a value stored by reference (such as an array element). If this is a problem, you can force *Apache::Session* to save a session when you close it by assigning any top-level session element a value. The session ID is always present in the session hash, so it provides a convenient way to force session saving:
>
> ```
> $session{_session_id} = $session{_session_id};
> ```
>
> An open session may be terminated rather than closed. Doing so removes the corresponding record from the sessions table, so that it can be used no longer:
>
> ```
> tied (%session)->delete ();
> ```

A Sample Application

The following script, *sess_track.pl*, is a complete (if short) implementation of an application that uses a session. It uses *Apache::Session* to keep track of the number of requests in the session and the time of each request, updating and displaying the information each time it is invoked. *sess_track.pl* uses a cookie named PERLSESSID to pass the session ID. This is done with the CGI.pm cookie management interface.[*]

---

[*] For information about CGI.pm cookie support, use the following command and read the section describing the cookie() function:

```
% perldoc CGI
```

```perl
#! /usr/bin/perl -w
# sess_track.pl - session request counting/timestamping demonstration

use strict;
use lib qw(/usr/local/apache/lib/perl);
use CGI qw(:standard);
use Cookbook;
use Apache::Session::MySQL;

my $title = "Perl Session Tracker";

my $dbh = Cookbook::connect ();          # connection to MySQL
my $sess_id = cookie ("PERLSESSID");     # session ID (undef if new session)
my %session;                             # session hash
my $cookie;                              # cookie to send to client

# open the session

tie %session, "Apache::Session::MySQL", $sess_id,
        {
            Handle => $dbh,
            LockHandle => $dbh
        };
if (!defined ($sess_id))                  # this is a new session
{
    # get new session ID, initialize session data, create cookie for client
    $sess_id = $session{_session_id};
    $session{count} = 0;                  # initialize counter
    $session{timestamp} = [ ];            # initialize timestamp array
    $cookie = cookie (-name => "PERLSESSID", -value => $sess_id);
}

# increment counter and add current timestamp to timestamp array

++$session{count};
push (@{$session{timestamp}}, scalar (localtime (time ())));

# construct content of page body

my $page_body =
    p ("This session has been active for $session{count} requests.")
    . p ("The requests occurred at these times:")
    . ul (li ($session{timestamp}));

if ($session{count} < 10)   # close (and save) session
{
    untie (%session);
}
else                        # destroy session after 10 invocations
{
    tied (%session)->delete ();
    # reset cookie to tell browser to discard session cookie
```

```
    $cookie = cookie (-name => "PERLSESSID",
                      -value => $sess_id,
                      -expires => "-1d");      # "expire yesterday"
}

$dbh->disconnect ();

# generate the output page

print
    header (-cookie => $cookie) # send cookie in headers (if it's defined)
    . start_html (-title => $title, -bgcolor => "white")
    . $page_body
    . end_html ();

exit (0);
```

Try the script by installing it in your *cgi-bin* directory and requesting it from your browser. To reinvoke it, use your browser's Reload function.

sess_track.pl opens the session and increments the counter prior to generating any page output. This is necessary because the client must be sent a cookie containing the session name and identifier if the session is new. Any cookie sent must be part of the response headers, so the page body cannot be printed until after the headers are sent.

The script also generates the part of the page body that uses session data but saves it in a variable rather than writing it immediately. The reason for this is that, should the session need to be terminated, the script resets the cookie to be one that tells the browser to discard the one it has. This too must be determined prior to sending the headers or any page count.

Session Expiration

The *Apache::Session* module requires only the id and a_session columns in the sessions table, and makes no provision for timing out or expiring sessions. On the other hand, the module doesn't restrict you from adding other columns, so you could include a TIMESTAMP column in the table to record the time of each session's last update. For example, you can add a TIMESTAMP column t to the sessions table using ALTER TABLE:

```
ALTER TABLE sessions ADD t TIMESTAMP NOT NULL;
```

Then you'd be able to expire sessions by running a query periodically to sweep the table and remove old records. The following query uses an expiration time of four hours:

```
DELETE FROM sessions WHERE t < DATE_SUB(NOW(),INTERVAL 4 HOUR);
```

Be aware that deleting session records can cause a problem: tie will raise an exception if you attempt to look up a session record using a non-undef session ID for which no record exists. This means, for example, that if a client provides an ID for a session that has been expired, your script may die with an error. One way to handle this is to open the session within an eval block so that you can trap the error. If one occurs, create a new session record:

```
eval
{
    tie %session, "Apache::Session::MySQL", $sess_id,
        {
            Handle => $dbh,
            LockHandle => $dbh
        };
};
if ($@) # if an error occurred, old session is unavailable; create a new one
{
    $sess_id = undef;
    tie %session, "Apache::Session::MySQL", $sess_id,
        {
            Handle => $dbh,
            LockHandle => $dbh
        };
}
```

19.2 Using MySQL-Based Storage with the PHP Session Manager

Problem

You want to use session storage for PHP scripts.

Solution

PHP 4 includes session managment. By default, it uses temporary files for backing store, but you can configure it to use MySQL instead.

Discussion

PHP 4 includes a native session manager. This section shows how to use it and how to extend it by implementing a storage module that saves session data in MySQL.[*] If your PHP configuration has both the track_vars and register_globals configuration directives enabled, session variables will exist as global variables of the same names in your script. (track_vars is enabled automatically for PHP 4.0.3 or later; for earlier versions, you should enable it explicitly.) If register_globals is not enabled, you'll need to access session variables as elements of the $HTTP_SESSION_VARS global array or the $_SESSION superglobal array. This is less convenient than relying on

---

[*] PHP 3 provides no session support. PHP 3 users who require session support may wish to look into PHPLIB or another package that includes a session manager.

register_globals, but is also more secure. (Recipe 18.5 discusses PHP's global and superglobal arrays and the security implications of register_globals.)

The PHP 4 Session Management Interface

PHP's session management capabilities are based on a small set of functions, all of which are documented in the PHP manual. The following list describes those likely to be most useful for day-to-day session programming:

session_start ()

Opens a session and extracts any variables previously stored in it, making them available in the script's global namespace. For example, a session variable named x becomes available as $_SESSION["x"] or $HTTP_SESSION_VARS["x"]. If register_globals is enabled, x also becomes available as the global variable $x.

session_register (*var_name*)

Registers a variable in the session by setting up an association between the session record and a variable in your script. For example, to register $count, do this:

```
session_register ("count");
```

If you make any changes to the variable while the session remains open, the new value will be saved to the session record when the session is closed. Observe that variables are registered by name rather than by value or by reference:

```
session_register ($count);      # incorrect
session_register (&$count);     # incorrect
```

Several variables may be registered at once by passing an array that contains multiple names rather than by passing a single name:

```
session_register (array ("count", "timestamp"));
```

Registering a variable implicitly starts a session, which means that if a script calls session_register(), it need not call session_start() first. However, session_register() is effective only if register_globals is enabled. To avoid reliance on register_globals, you should call session_start() explicitly and get your session variables from either the $_SESSION or the $HTTP_SESSION_VARS array.

session_unregister (*var_name*)

Unregisters a session variable so that it is not saved to the session record.

session_write_close ()

Writes the session data and closes the session. Normally you need not call this function; PHP saves an open session automatically when your script ends. However, it may be useful to save and close the session explicitly if you want to modify session variables without having the changes tracked in the session data. In that case, you should call this function to close the session before making the changes.

session_destroy ()

Removes the session and any data associated with it.

```
session_name ($name)
```

The PHP session manager knows which session to use by means of the session identifier. It looks for the identifier in a global variable named $PHPSESSID; in a cookie, GET, or POST variable named PHPSESSID; or in a URL parameter of the form PHPSESSID=*value*. (If none of these are found, the session manager generates a new identifier and begins a new session.) The default identifier name is PHPSESSID, but you can change it. To make a global (site-wide) change, edit the session.name configuration directive in *php.ini*. To make the change for an individual script, call session_name($name) before starting the session, where $name represents the session name to use. To find out the current session identifier name, call session_name() with no argument.

The following example demonstrates one of the simplest uses for a session, which is to display a counter showing the number of requests received so far during the course of the session:

```
session_start ();
session_register ("count");
if (!isset ($count))
    $count = 0;
++$count;
printf ("This session has been active for %d requests.", $count);
```

session_start() opens the session and extracts its contents into the script's global namespace. (For the initial request, this has no effect because the session is empty.) session_register() registers the count session variable to cause changes to the corresponding PHP variable $count to be tracked in the session data. For the first request, no such variable will be present in the session. This is detected by the isset() test, which initializes the counter. (On subsequent requests, registering count will cause $count to have the value assigned to it during the previous request.) Next, the counter's value is incremented and printed. When the script ends, PHP implicitly invokes session_write_close(), which saves the new counter value to the session automatically.

The example uses session_register() and thus assumes that register_globals is enabled. Later on, we'll discuss how to avoid this limitation.

Specifying a User-Defined Storage Module

The PHP session management interface just described makes no reference to any kind of backing store. That is, the description specifies nothing about how session information actually gets saved. By default, PHP uses temporary files to store session data, but the session interface is extensible so that other storage modules can be defined. To override the default storage method and store session data in MySQL, you must do several things:

- Set up a table to hold session records and write the routines that implement the storage module. This is done once, prior to writing any scripts that use the new module.
- Tell PHP that you're supplying a user-defined storage manager. You can do this globally in *php.ini* (in which case you make the change once), or within individual scripts (in which case it's necessary to declare your intent in each script).
- Register the storage module routines within each script that wants to use the module.

Creating the session table

Any MySQL-based storage module needs a database table in which to store session information. Create a table named php_session that includes the following columns:

```
CREATE TABLE php_session
(
    id      CHAR(32) NOT NULL,
    data    BLOB,
    t       TIMESTAMP NOT NULL,
    PRIMARY KEY (id)
);
```

You'll recognize the structure of this table as quite similar to the sessions table used by the *Apache::Session* Perl module. The id column holds session identifiers, which are unique 32-character strings (they look suspiciously like *Apache:Session* identifiers, which is not surprising, given that PHP uses MD5 values, just like the Perl module). data holds session information. PHP serializes session data into a string before storing it, so php_session needs only a large generic string column to hold the resulting serialized value. The t column is a TIMESTAMP that MySQL updates automatically whenever a session record is updated. This column is not required, but it's useful for implementing a garbage collection policy based on each session's last update time.

A small set of queries suffices to manage the contents of the php_session table as we have defined it:

- To retrieve a session's data, issue a simple SELECT based on the session identifier:
  ```
  SELECT data FROM php_session WHERE id = 'sess_id';
  ```
- To write session data, a REPLACE serves to update an existing record (or to create a new one if no such record exists):
  ```
  REPLACE INTO php_session (id,data) VALUES('sess_id','sess_data');
  ```
  REPLACE also updates the timestamp in the record when creating or updating a record, which is important for garbage collection.

  Some storage manager implementations use a combination of INSERT and a fall-back to UPDATE if the INSERT fails because a record with the given session ID already exists (or an UPDATE with a fallback to INSERT if the UPDATE fails because a record with the ID does *not* exist). In MySQL, a dual-query approach is unnecessary; REPLACE performs the required task with a single query.

- To destroy a session, delete the corresponding record:
    ```
    DELETE FROM php_session WHERE id = 'sess_id';
    ```
- Garbage collection is performed by removing old records. The following query deletes records that have a timestamp value more than *sess_life* seconds old:
    ```
    DELETE FROM php_session
    WHERE t < DATE_SUB(NOW(),INTERVAL sess_life SECOND);
    ```

These queries form the basis of the routines that make up our MySQL-backed storage module. The primary function of the module is to open and close MySQL connections and to issue the proper queries at the appropriate times.

Writing the storage management routines

User-defined session storage modules have a specific interface, implemented as a set of handler routines that you register with PHP's session manager by calling session_set_save_handler(). The format of the function is as follows, where each argument is a handler routine name specified as a string:

```
session_set_save_handler (
    "mysql_sess_open",      # function to open a session
    "mysql_sess_close",     # function to close a session
    "mysql_sess_read",      # function to read session data
    "mysql_sess_write",     # function to write session data
    "mysql_sess_destroy",   # function to destroy a session
    "mysql_sess_gc"         # function to garbage-collect old sessions
);
```

You can name the handler routines as you like; they need not necessarily be named mysql_sess_open(), mysql_sess_close(), and so forth. They should, however, be written according to the following specifications:

mysql_sess_open ($save_path, $sess_name)

Performs whatever actions are necessary to begin a session. $save_path is the name of the location where sessions should be stored; this is useful for file storage only. $sess_name indicates the name of the session identifier (for example, PHPSESSID). For a MySQL-based storage manager, both arguments can be ignored. The function should return TRUE or FALSE to indicate whether or not the session was opened successfully.

mysql_sess_close ()

Closes the session, returning TRUE for success or FALSE for failure.

mysql_sess_read ($sess_id)

Retrieves the data associated with the session identifier and returns it as a string. If there is no such session, the function should return an empty string. If an error occurs, it should return FALSE.

`mysql_sess_write ($sess_id, $sess_data)`

Saves the data associated with the session identifier, returning TRUE for success or FALSE for failure. PHP itself takes care of serializing and unserializing the session contents, so the read and write functions need deal only with serialized strings.

`mysql_sess_destroy ($sess_id)`

Destroys the session and any data associated with it, returning TRUE for success or FALSE for failure. For MySQL-based storage, destroying a session amounts to deleting the record from the php_session table that is associated with the session ID.

`mysql_sess_gc ($gc_maxlife)`

Performs garbage collection to remove old sessions. This function is invoked on a probabilistic basis. When PHP receives a request for a page that uses sessions, it calls the garbage collector with a probability defined by the session.gc_probability configuration directive in *php.ini*. For example, if the probability value is 1 (that is, 1%), PHP calls the collector approximately once every hundred requests. If the value is 100, it calls the collector for every request—which probably would result in more processing overhead than you'd want.

The argument to gc() is the maximum session lifetime in seconds. Sessions older than that should be considered subject to removal. The function should return TRUE for success or FALSE for failure.

The handler routines are registered by calling session_set_save_handler(), which should be done in conjunction with informing PHP that you'll be using a user-defined storage module. The default storage management method is defined by the session.save_handler configuration directive. You can change the method globally by modifying the *php.ini* initialization file, or within individual scripts:

- To change the storage method globally, edit *php.ini*. The default directive setting specifies the use of file-based session storage management:

      session.save_handler = files;

  Modify this to indicate that sessions will be handled by a user-level mechanism:

      session.save_handler = user;

  If you're using PHP as an Apache module, you'll need to restart Apache after modifying *php.ini* so that PHP notices the changes.

  The problem with making a global change is that every PHP script that uses sessions will be expected to provide its own storage management routines. This may have unintended side effects for other script writers if they are unaware of the change. For example, other developers that use the web server may wish to continue using file-based sessions.

- The alternative to making a global change is to specify a different storage method by calling ini_set() on a per-script basis:

      ini_set ("session.save_handler", "user");

`ini_set()` is less intrusive than a global configuration change. The storage manager we'll develop here uses `ini_set()` so that database-backed session storage is triggered only for those scripts that request it.

To make it easy to access an alternative session storage module, it's useful to create a library file, *Cookbook_Session.php*. Then the only thing a script need do to use the library file is to include it prior to starting the session. The outline of the file looks like this:

```php
<?php
# Cookbook_Session.php - MySQL-based session storage module

include_once "Cookbook.php";

# Define the handler routines

function mysql_sess_open ($save_path, $sess_name) ...
function mysql_sess_close () ...
function mysql_sess_read ($sess_id) ...
function mysql_sess_write ($sess_id, $sess_data) ...
function mysql_sess_destroy ($sess_id) ...
function mysql_sess_gc ($gc_maxlife) ...

# Initialize connection identifier, select user-defined session
# handling and register the handler routines

$mysql_sess_conn_id = FALSE;
ini_set ("session.save_handler", "user");
session_set_save_handler (
                "mysql_sess_open",
                "mysql_sess_close",
                "mysql_sess_read",
                "mysql_sess_write",
                "mysql_sess_destroy",
                "mysql_sess_gc"
            );
?>
```

The library file includes *Cookbook.php* so that it can access the connection routine for opening a connection to the cookbook database. Then it defines the handler routines (we'll get to the details of these functions shortly). Finally, it initializes the connection identifier, tells PHP to get ready to use a user-defined session storage manager, and registers the handler functions. Thus, a PHP script that wants to store sessions in MySQL performs all the necessary setup simply by including the *Cookbook_Session.php* file:

```php
include_once "Cookbook_Session.php";
```

The interface provided by the *Cookbook_Session.php* library file exposes a global database connection identifier variable ($mysql_sess_conn_id) and a set of handler routines named `mysql_sess_open()`, `mysql_sess_close()`, and so forth. Scripts that use the library should avoid using these global names for other purposes.

Now let's see how to implement each handler routine.

Opening a session. PHP passes two arguments to this function: the save path and the session name. The save path is used for file-based storage, and we don't need to know the session name, so both arguments are irrelevant for our purposes and can be ignored. The function therefore need do nothing but open a connection to MySQL:

```
function mysql_sess_open ($save_path, $sess_name)
{
global $mysql_sess_conn_id;

    # open connection to MySQL if it's not already open
    $mysql_sess_conn_id or $mysql_sess_conn_id = cookbook_connect ();
    return (TRUE);
}
```

Closing a session. The close handler checks whether or not a connection to MySQL is open, and closes it if so:

```
function mysql_sess_close ()
{
global $mysql_sess_conn_id;

    if ($mysql_sess_conn_id)          # close connection if it's open
    {
        mysql_close ($mysql_sess_conn_id);
        $mysql_sess_conn_id = FALSE;
    }
    return (TRUE);
}
```

Reading session data. The `mysql_sess_read()` function uses the session ID to look up the data for the corresponding session record and returns it. If no such record exists, it returns the empty string:

```
function mysql_sess_read ($sess_id)
{
global $mysql_sess_conn_id;

    $sess_id = addslashes ($sess_id);
    $query = "SELECT data FROM php_session WHERE id = '$sess_id'";
    if ($res_id = mysql_query ($query, $mysql_sess_conn_id))
    {
        list ($data) = mysql_fetch_row ($res_id);
        mysql_free_result ($res_id);
        if (isset ($data))
            return ($data);
    }
    return ("");
}
```

Writing session data. mysql_sess_write() updates a session record (or creates one if there is no record for the session yet):

```
function mysql_sess_write ($sess_id, $sess_data)
{
global $mysql_sess_conn_id;

    $sess_id = addslashes ($sess_id);
    $sess_data = addslashes ($sess_data);
    $query = "REPLACE php_session (id, data) VALUES('$sess_id','$sess_data')";
    return (mysql_query ($query, $mysql_sess_conn_id));
}
```

Destroying a session. When a session is no longer needed, mysql_sess_destroy() removes the corresponding record:

```
function mysql_sess_destroy ($sess_id)
{
global $mysql_sess_conn_id;

    $sess_id = addslashes ($sess_id);
    $query = "DELETE FROM php_session WHERE id = '$sess_id'";
    return (mysql_query ($query, $mysql_sess_conn_id));
}
```

Performing garbage collection. The TIMESTAMP column t in each session record indicates when the session was last updated. mysql_sess_gc() uses this value to implement garbage collection. The argument $sess_maxlife specifies how old sessions can be (in seconds). Older sessions are considered expired and candidates for removal, which is easily done by deleting session records having a timestamp that differs from the current time by more than the allowed lifetime:

```
function mysql_sess_gc ($sess_maxlife)
{
global $mysql_sess_conn_id;

    $query = sprintf ("DELETE FROM php_session
                        WHERE t < DATE_SUB(NOW(),INTERVAL %d SECOND)",
                        $sess_maxlife);
    mysql_query ($query, $mysql_sess_conn_id);
    return (TRUE);  # ignore errors
}
```

Using the storage module

Install the *Cookbook_Session.php* file in a public library directory accessible to your scripts. (On my system, I put PHP library files in */usr/local/apache/lib/php*.) To try out the storage module, install the following example script, *sess_track.php*, in your web tree and invoke it a few times to see how the information display changes (or, rather, to see *if* it changes; under some circumstances, the script will fail, as we'll discuss shortly):

```
<?php
# sess_track.php - session request counting/timestamping demonstration
```

```
# (assumes that register_globals is enabled)

include_once "Cookbook_Session.php";
include_once "Cookbook_Webutils.php";    # needed for make_unordered_list()

$title = "PHP Session Tracker";

# Open session and register session variables

session_start ();
session_register ("count");
session_register ("timestamp");

# If the session is new, initialize the variables

if (!isset ($count))
    $count = 0;
if (!isset ($timestamp))
    $timestamp = array ();

# Increment counter, add current timestamp to timestamp array

++$count;
$timestamp[] = date ("Y-m-d H:i:s T");

if ($count >= 10)    # destroy session variables after 10 invocations
{
    session_unregister ("count");
    session_unregister ("timestamp");
}

# Produce the output page

?>
<html>
<head>
<title><?php print ($title); ?></title>
</head>
<body bgcolor="white">

<?php

printf ("<p>This session has been active for %d requests.</p>\n", $count);
print ("<p>The requests occurred at these times:</p>\n");
print make_unordered_list ($timestamp);

?>

</body>
</html>
```

The script includes the *Cookbook_Session.php* library file to enable the MySQL-based storage module, then uses the PHP session manager interface in typical fashion. First, it opens the session, registers the session variables, and initializes them if the session is new. The scalar variable $count starts out at zero, and the non-scalar variable $timestamp starts out as an empty array. Then the script increments the counter, adds the current timestamp to the end of the timestamp array, and produces an output page that displays the count and the access times.

If the session limit of 10 invocations has been reached, the script unregisters the session variables, which causes $count and $timestamp not to be saved to the session record. The effect is that the session restarts on the next request.

sess_track.php does not call session_write_close() explicitly; that is unnecessary because PHP saves the session automatically when the script terminates.

The output page is produced only after updating the session record because PHP might determine that a cookie containing the session ID needs to be sent to the client. That determination must be made before generating the page body because cookies are sent in the headers.

The problem with *sess_track.php* as written is that it works only if PHP's register_globals configuration setting is enabled. If that is so, registering session variables named count and timestamp causes their values to be made available as the PHP global variables $count and $timestamp. However, when register_globals is disabled, session_register() does nothing and *sess_track.php* will not work properly (the count will always be one, and only a single timestamp will be shown).

The issue is a significant one because the PHP developers now recommend that register_globals be turned off for security reasons. That means session_register() is essentially obsolete and that existing session-based applications that rely on it will begin to fail as more and more sites follow the recommendation to disable register_globals. To deal with this problem and write code that works regardless of the register_globals setting, we need to get session variables another way. The two possiblities are to use the $HTTP_SESSION_VARS global array or (as of PHP 4.1) the $_SESSION superglobal array. For example, a session variable named count will be available as $HTTP_SESSION_VARS["count"] or $_SESSION["count"].

It's possible to modify the *sess_track.php* script relatively easily so that it does not rely on the setting of register_globals, but still allows you to work with simple variable names to manipulate session variables:

- Don't use session_register(). Instead, copy session variables directly from a global session variable array into the $count and $timestamp variables.

- After you're done using your session variables, copy them back into the session variable array. Do this before writing the session, if you call session_write() explicitly.

This approach does require that you determine which global array to use for session variable storage, which may depend on your version of PHP. Instead of doing this each time you want to access a session variable, it's easier to write a couple of utility functions that do the work:

```
function get_session_val ($name)
{
global $HTTP_SESSION_VARS;

    unset ($val);
    if (isset ($_SESSION[$name]))
        $val = $_SESSION[$name];
    else if (isset ($HTTP_SESSION_VARS[$name]))
        $val = $HTTP_SESSION_VARS[$name];
    return (@$val);
}

function set_session_val ($name, $val)
{
global $HTTP_SESSION_VARS;

    if (PHP_VERSION >= "4.1")
        $_SESSION[$name] = $val;
    $HTTP_SESSION_VARS[$name] = $val;
}
```

These routines can be found in the *Cookbook_Webutils.php* library file, along with the routines that get other kinds of web parameter values (see Recipe 18.5). They are in *Cookbook_Webutils.php* rather than in *Cookbook_Session.php* so that you can call them even if you elect not to use the MySQL-based session storage that *Cookbook_Session.php* implements.

The following script, *sess_track2.php*, shows how avoid reliance on register_globals by making only small changes to the main logic of the script:

```
<?php
# sess_track2.php - session request counting/timestamping demonstration
# (does not rely on register_globals)

include_once "Cookbook_Session.php";
include_once "Cookbook_Webutils.php";   # needed for make_unordered_list()
                                        # get_session_val(), set_session_val()

$title = "PHP Session Tracker";

# Open session and extract session values

session_start ();
$count = get_session_val ("count");
$timestamp = get_session_val ("timestamp");
```

```
# If the session is new, initialize the variables

if (!isset ($count))
    $count = 0;
if (!isset ($timestamp))
    $timestamp = array ();

# Increment counter, add current timestamp to timestamp array

++$count;
$timestamp[] = date ("Y-m-d H:i:s T");

if ($count < 10)     # save modified values into session variable array
{
    set_session_val ("count", $count);
    set_session_val ("timestamp", $timestamp);
}
else                # destroy session variables after 10 invocations
{
    session_unregister ("count");
    session_unregister ("timestamp");
}

# Produce the output page

?>
<html>
<head>
<title><?php print ($title); ?></title>
</head>
<body bgcolor="white">

<?php

printf ("<p>This session has been active for %d requests.</p>\n", $count);
print ("<p>The requests occurred at these times:</p>\n");
print make_unordered_list ($timestamp);

?>

</body>
</html>
```

sess_track2.php is identical to *sess_track.php*, with two exceptions:

- *sess_track.php* calls session_start() to open a session, but that is not strictly required, because it uses session_register(), which implicitly opens the session for you. *sess_track2.php* does not use session_register(). Instead, it gets the variable values directly from global session variable storage. With that approach, you *must* call session_start() first to open the session explicitly.

- If the session limit of 10 requests has not yet been reached, *sess_track2.php* explicitly stores the $count and $timestamp session values back into the global session variable arrays by invoking set_session_val().

19.3 Using MySQL for Session Backing Store with Tomcat

Problem

You want to use session storage for Java-based scripts.

Solution

Tomcat handles session management for you. By default, it uses temporary files for backing store, but you can configure it to use MySQL instead by supplying the appropriate JDBC parameters in Tomcat's *server.xml* configuration file.

Discussion

The Perl and PHP session mechanisms described earlier in this chapter both require applications to indicate explicitly that they want to use MySQL-based session storage. For Perl, a script must state that it wants to use the appropriate *Apache::Session* module. For PHP 4, the session manager is built into the language, but each application that wants to use the MySQL storage module must register it.

For Java applications that run under Tomcat, a different framework applies. Tomcat itself manages sessions, and if you want to store session information in MySQL, you do so by reconfiguring Tomcat, not your applications. In other words, web-based Java programs are relieved of some of the messy session-related details that must be handled at the application level in other languages. For example, session IDs are handled by the Tomcat server rather than at the application level. Tomcat checks whether cookies are enabled, and uses URL rewriting to encode the session ID in the URL if cookies are unavailable. Application developers need not care which method is used, because the ID is available the same way regardless of how it's transmitted.

To illustrate the independence of applications from the session management method used by Tomcat, this section shows a simple JSP application that uses a session. Then it shows how to reconfigure Tomcat to store session information in MySQL rather than in the default session store—without requiring any changes at all to the application. First, though, it's necessary to describe the session interface.

The Servlet and JSP Session Interface

Tomcat uses the standard session interface described in the Java Servlet Specification. This interface can be used both by servlets and by JSP pages. Within a servlet, you gain access to the session by importing the `javax.servlet.http.HttpSession` class and invoking the `getSession()` method of your `HttpRequest` object:

```
import javax.servlet.http.*;
HttpSession session = request.getSession ();
```

In JSP pages, session support is enabled by default, so it's as though those statements have already been issued by the time the page begins executing. That is, the session is available implicitly through a session variable that's already been set up for you.

The complete session interface is defined in the HttpSession section of the Java Servlet Specification (see Appendix C). Some representative methods of session objects are listed below:

isNew ()

Returns true or false to indicate whether or not the session has just begun with the current request.

getAttribute (String attrName)

Session contents consist of attributes, which are objects that are bound to names. To access a session attribute, specify its name. The getAttribute() method returns the Object bound to the given name, or null if there is no object with that name.

setAttribute (String attrName, Object obj)

Adds the object to the session and binds it to the given name.

removeAttribute (String attrName)

Removes the attribute with the given name from the session.

invalidate ()

Invalidates the session and any data associated with it. The next request from the client will begin a new session.

A Sample JSP Session Application

The following example shows a JSP page, *sess_track.jsp*, that maintains a session request counter and a log of the request times. To illustrate the session-related operations more explicitly, this page consists primarily of embedded Java code that uses the HttpSession session interface directly:

```
<%-- sess_track.jsp - session request counting/timestamping demonstration --%>

<%@ page import="java.util.*" %>
<%
    // get session variables, initializing them if not present

    int count;
    Object obj = session.getAttribute ("count");
    if (obj == null)
        count = 0;
    else
        count = Integer.parseInt (obj.toString ());

    ArrayList timestamp = (ArrayList) session.getAttribute ("timestamp");
    if (timestamp == null)
        timestamp = new ArrayList ();
```

```
    // increment counter, add current timestamp to timestamp array

    count = count + 1;
    timestamp.add (new Date ());

    if (count < 10)      // save updated values in session object
    {
        session.setAttribute ("count", String.valueOf (count));
        session.setAttribute ("timestamp", timestamp);
    }
    else                 // restart session after 10 requests
    {
        session.removeAttribute ("count");
        session.removeAttribute ("timestamp");
    }
%>

<html>
<head>
<title>JSP Session Tracker</title>
</head>
<body bgcolor="white">

<p>This session has been active for <%= count %> requests.</p>

<p>The requests occurred at these times:</p>
<ul>
<%
    for (int i = 0; i < timestamp.size (); i++)
        out.println ("<li>" + timestamp.get (i) + "</li>");
%>
</ul>

</body>
</html>
```

Invoke *sess_track.jsp* a few times from your browser to see how the display changes.

The session.setAttribute() method used in *sess_track.jsp* places information into the session so that it can be found by later invocations of the script. But session attributes also can be shared with other scripts. To see this, make a copy of *sess_track.jsp* and invoke the copy from your browser. You'll see that it accesses the same session information as *sess_track.jsp*.

Some of the session related operations shown in *sess_track.jsp* can be done using tags from JSTL, which provides a sessionScope variable for getting at the implicit JSP session object:

```
<%-- sess_track2.jsp - session request counting/timestamping demonstration --%>

<%@ page import="java.util.*" %>
<%@ taglib uri="http://java.sun.com/jstl/core" prefix="c" %>

<c:if test="${empty sessionScope.count}">
```

```
        <c:set var="count" scope="session" value="0" />
    </c:if>
    <c:set var="count" scope="session" value="${sessionScope.count+1}" />

    <%
        ArrayList timestamp = (ArrayList) session.getAttribute ("timestamp");
        if (timestamp == null)
            timestamp = new ArrayList ();
        // add current timestamp to timestamp array, store result in session
        timestamp.add (new Date ());
        session.setAttribute ("timestamp", timestamp);
    %>

    <html>
    <head>
    <title>JSP Session Tracker 2</title>
    </head>
    <body bgcolor="white">

    <p>This session has been active for
    <c:out value="${sessionScope.count}" />
    requests.</p>

    <p>The requests occurred at these times:</p>
    <ul>
    <c:forEach var="t" items="${sessionScope.timestamp}">
        <li><c:out value="${t}" /></li>
    </c:forEach>
    </ul>

    <%-- has session limit of 10 requests been reached? --%>

    <c:if test="${sessionScope.count ge 10}">
        <c:remove var="count" scope="session" />
        <c:remove var="timestamp" scope="session" />
    </c:if>

    </body>
    </html>
```

Telling Tomcat to Save Session Records in MySQL

The Tomcat documentation pertaining to session management may be found at:

> *http://jakarta.apache.org/tomcat/tomcat-4.0-doc/config/manager.html*

Tomcat has its own default session storage mechanism (temporary files). To override the default and save sessions in MySQL via JDBC instead, use the following procedure:

1. Create a table to hold session records.
2. Make sure that Tomcat has access to the proper JDBC driver.
3. Modify Tomcat's *server.xml* configuration file to specify use of a persistent session manager for the relevant application context or contexts.

None of these steps involve modifying the sample session application in any way, which is a reflection of how Tomcat implements session support above the application level.

Create the Tomcat session table

Tomcat stores several types of information into the session table:

- The session ID. By default, these are 32-character MD5 values.
- The session data. This is a serialized string.
- Whether or not the session is valid, as a single byte.
- The maximum inactivity time allowed, as a 32-bit integer measured in seconds.
- The last access time, as a 64-bit integer.

These specifications are satisfied by the following table, which you should create before proceeding to the next section:

```
CREATE TABLE tomcat_session
(
    id              CHAR(32) NOT NULL,
    data            BLOB,
    valid_session   CHAR(1) NOT NULL,
    max_inactive    INT NOT NULL,
    last_access     BIGINT NOT NULL,
    PRIMARY KEY (id)
);
```

Place the JDBC driver where Tomcat can find It

Because Tomcat itself manages sessions, it must be able to access the JDBC driver used to store sessions in a database. It's common to store drivers in the *lib* directory of the Tomcat tree so that all applications have access to them. But for a driver to be accessible to Tomcat as well, it should go in the *common/lib* directory. (Thus, if you have the MySQL Connector/J driver installed in *lib*, move it to *common/lib*.) After a restart, Tomcat will be able to use it. For more information, see Recipe 16.3.

Modify the Tomcat Configuration File

To tell Tomcat to use the tomcat_session table, it's necessary to modify the *server.xml* file in Tomcat's *conf* directory. Do this by placing a <Manager> element in the body of the <Context> element of each application context that should use MySQL-based session storage. (If a context has no such element, create one.) For the mcb application context, the <Context> element can be created like this:

```
<Context path="/mcb" docBase="mcb" debug="0" reloadable="true">
  <Manager
    className="org.apache.catalina.session.PersistentManager"
    debug="0"
    saveOnRestart="true"
```

```
      minIdleSwap="900"
      maxIdleSwap="1200"
      maxIdleBackup="600">
      <Store
        className="org.apache.catalina.session.JDBCStore"
        driverName="com.mysql.jdbc.Driver"
        connectionURL=
          "jdbc:mysql://localhost/cookbook?user=cbuser&amp;password=cbpass"
        sessionTable="tomcat_session"
        sessionIdCol="id"
        sessionDataCol="data"
        sessionValidCol="valid_session"
        sessionMaxInactiveCol="max_inactive"
        sessionLastAccessedCol="last_access"
      />
    </Manager>
  </Context>
```

The <Manager> element attributes specify general session-related options. Within the
<Manager> element body, the <Store> element attributes provide the specifics pertain-
ing to the JDBC driver. The following discussion focuses on the attributes shown in the
example, but there are others that you can use. See the Tomcat session-manage-
ment documentation for more information.

The <Manager> attributes shown in the example have the following meanings:

className
> Indicates the Java class that implements persistent session storage. It must be
> org.apache.catalina.session.PersistentManager.

debug
> Indicates the logging detail level. A value of zero disables debug output; higher
> numbers generate more output.

saveOnRestart
> Allows application sessions to survive server restarts. Should be true if you want
> Tomcat to save current sessions when it shuts down (and reload them when it
> starts up).

maxIdleBackup
> Indicates the number of seconds before inactive sessions are eligible for being
> saved to MySQL. A value of -1 means "never."

minIdleSwap
> Indicates how many seconds a session can be idle before becoming eligible to be
> swapped (saved to MySQL and passivated out of server memory). A value of -1
> means "never."

maxIdleSwap
> Indicates how many seconds a session can be idle before it should be swapped. A
> value of -1 means "never." If this feature is enabled, the value should be greater
> than minIdleSwap and maxIdleBackup.

Within the body of the `<Manager>` element, the `<Store>` element indicates how to connect to the database server, which database and table to use for storing session records, and the names of the columns in the table:

className

> The name of a class that implements the `org.apache.catalina.Store` interface. For JDBC-based storage managers, the value of this attribute must be `org.apache.catalina.session.JDBCStore`.

driverName

> The class name for the JDBC driver. For the MySQL Connector/J driver, the attribute value should be `com.mysql.jdbc.Driver`.

connectionURL

> Indicates how to connect to the database server. The following URL connects to the MySQL server on the local host, using a username and password of `cbuser` and `cbpass`:

> ```
> jdbc:mysql://localhost/cookbook?user=cbuser&password=cbpass
> ```

> However, *server.xml* entries are written in XML, so the & character that separates the `user` and `password` connection parameters must be written as the `&amp;` entity, like so:

> ```
> jdbc:mysql://localhost/cookbook?user=cbuser&amp;password=cbpass
> ```

> When Tomcat reads the *server.xml* file, the file parser converts `&amp;` back to &, which is what gets passed to the JDBC driver.

sessionTable

> Names the table in which to store session records. For our example, this is the `tomcat_session` table described earlier.

The remaining `<Store>` attributes in the example indicate the column names in the session table. These attributes are `sessionIdCol`, `sessionDataCol`, `sessionValidCol`, `sessionMaxInactiveCol`, `sessionLastAccessedCol` which correspond in the obvious way to the columns contained in the `tomcat_session` table.

After you modify the *server.xml* file, restart Tomcat. Then invoke the *sess_track.jsp* or *sess_track2.jsp* scripts a few times to initiate a session. Each should behave the same way as before you reconfigured Tomcat. After a period of inactivity equal to the `<Manager>` element `maxIdleBackup` attribute value, you should see a session record appear in the `tomcat_session` table. If you watch the MySQL query log, you should also see sessions being saved to MySQL when you shut down Tomcat.

Changing *server.xml* is a global change, somewhat similar to changing `session.save_handler` in PHP's *php.ini* file. However, unlike PHP, where modifying the global initialization file affects other developers on the same host in such a way that they may have to change their session-based scripts, modifying Tomcat's configuration to use JDBC-based backing store for session management is completely invisible to servlets and JSP pages. Thus, you can make the change without worrying that other developers who use the same Tomcat server will accuse you of acting toward them with premeditated malice.

Session Expiration in Tomcat

Session persistence is 60 minutes by default. To provide an explicit duration for a session manager, add a `maxInactiveInterval` to the appropriate `<Manager>` element in the server's *conf/server.xml* file. To provide a duration that is specific to a particular application context, add a `<session-config>` element to the context's *WEB-INF/web.xml* file. For example, to use a value of 30 minutes, specify it like this:

```
<session-config>
  <session-timeout>30</session-timeout>
</session-config>
```

If you modify either *server.xml* or *web.xml*, restart Tomcat.

Session Tracking in Tomcat

Although your JSP pages need do nothing to have Tomcat set up sessions or to use JDBC for session storage, they may need to take a small step to make sure that sessions move from request to request properly. This is necessary if you generate pages that contain hyperlinks to other pages that participate in the same session.

Tomcat automatically generates a session identifier and tracks the session using cookies if it receives a cookie from the client that contains the session ID. If the client has cookies disabled, Tomcat tracks the session by rewriting URLs to include the session ID. You need not determine which method Tomcat is using, but you should take care to ensure proper propagation of the session ID in case it is being passed by URL rewriting. This means that if you create a page that includes a link to another page that is part of the session, you should not just list the path to the page like this:

```
To go to the next page,
<a href="nextpage.jsp">click here</a>.
```

This link doesn't contain the session ID. If Tomcat does happen to be tracking the session using URL rewriting, you'll lose the ID when the user selects the link. Instead, pass the link to `encodeURL()` to allow Tomcat to add the session ID to the URL as necessary:

```
To go to the next page,
<a href="<%= response.encodeURL ("nextpage.jsp") %>">click here</a>.
```

If Tomcat is tracking the session with cookies, `encodeURL()` returns the URL unchanged. However, if Tomcat is tracking the session by means of URL rewriting, `encodeURL()` adds the session ID to the page path automatically, so that it looks something like this:

```
mypage.jsp;jsessionid=xxxxxxxxxxxxxxxx
```

You should generate URLs using encodeURL() like this for links in any tag that takes the user to a page in the current session. This includes <a>, <form>, and <frame> tags, and possibly even <img> tags, if for some reason those tags invoke a script that generates images on a session-specific basis.

It's probably best to develop the habit of using encodeURL() as a matter of routine when writing URLs for session-based applications. Even if you think everyone who uses the application will have cookies enabled, your assumption may prove incorrect some day.

The java.net.URLEncoder.encode() method has a name similar to encodeURL(), but it's different. It performs conversion of special characters to %xx notation to make them safe for use in URLs.

Obtaining MySQL Software

Many of the table definitions and programs discussed in this book are available online so that you can avoid typing them in yourself. To run the examples, you'll also need access to MySQL, of course, as well as the appropriate MySQL-specific interfaces for the languages you wish to use. This appendix describes where to get the software you need.

Obtaining Sample Source Code and Data

The examples in this book are based on source code and sample data from three distributions. Two of these (the recipes and mcb-kjv distributions) are available at the *MySQL Cookbook* companion web site, which you can visit at this address:

> *http://www.kitebird.com/mysql-cookbook/*

The recipes distribution is the primary source of examples. It's available as a compressed *tar* file (*recipes.tar.gz*) or as a ZIP file (*recipes.zip*). Either distribution format when unpacked will create a directory named *recipes*.

The recipes distribution contains programs as shown in the book, but in many cases also includes implementations in additional languages. For example, a recipe shown in the book using Python may be available on the site in Perl, PHP, or Java as well. This may save you some translation effort should you wish to convert a program as shown in the book to a different language. I expect to update the distribution from time to time, so you may want to check back occasionally for updates. If you would like to contribute a translation for inclusion into the distribution, let me know by sending email to *mysql-cookbook@kitebird.com*.

The Kitebird site also provides access to the mcb-kjv distribution, which contains the text of the King James Version of the Bible, formatted suitably for loading into MySQL. It's used in Chapter 4, as the source of a reasonably large body of of text for examples that demonstrate FULLTEXT searches, and occasionally elsewhere in the book. This distribution is provided separately from the recipes distribution due to its size. It's available as a compressed *tar* file (*mcb-kjv.tar.gz*) or as a ZIP file (*mcb-kjv.zip*). Either distribution format when unpacked will create a directory named *mcb-kjv*.

The `mcb-kjv` distribution is derived from the KJV text available at the Unbound Bible site at Biola University (*http://unbound.biola.edu*). The distribution includes notes that describe how it differs from the one available at Biola.

Text files in the `recipes` and `mcb-kjv` distributions were created with tabstops set every four spaces. If a file doesn't seem to line up properly when you view it in your editor, try setting your tabstops similarly. For printing, you can run files through *expand -4*. For example, if you normally print a file like this:

```
% pr filename | lpr
```

Try this instead:

```
% expand -4 filename | pr | lpr
```

The third source of information used for examples in this book is the baseball database produced by The Baseball Archive. If you want to try out the examples that use this database, visit the Archive's web site at:

http://baseball1.com/

Examples in this book use Version 4.5 of the baseball database, which is available in Access 2000, Access 97, and comma-delimited text file formats. See the *baseball1* directory of the recipes distribution for instructions that describe how to load the comma-delimited format into MySQL. (See also Recipe 10.36.)

Obtaining MySQL and Related Software

If you're going to access a MySQL server run by somebody else, you need only the MySQL client software on your own machine. If you're going to run your own server, a full MySQL distribution is required.

To write your own MySQL-based programs, you'll need to communicate with the server through a language-specific API. The Perl, PHP, and Python interfaces rely on the MySQL C API client library to handle the low-level client-server protocol. For Perl and Python, you must install the C client library and header files first. PHP includes the MySQL client support files. Java JDBC drivers for MySQL implement the client-server protocol themselves, so they do not require the MySQL C client library.

You may not need to install the client software yourself—it may already have been built and installed for you by others. This is a common situation if you have an account with an Internet Service Provider (ISP) for computing services such as a web server that is already enabled to provide access to MySQL. Under such circumstances, the MySQL libraries and header files will already have been installed by the ISP staff.

MySQL

Visit the main MySQL site to obtain a distribution of MySQL:

http://www.mysql.com/

Distributions include installation instructions, and the MySQL Reference Manual also provides extensive installation information. The manual is available online at the MySQL site and in printed form from O'Reilly & Associates. If you plan to use ODBC connections, you'll also want to obtain MyODBC.

If you need to install the MySQL C client library and header files, they're available if you install MySQL from a source distribution, or if you install a non-RPM binary distribution under Unix. Under Linux, you have the option of installing MySQL using RPM files, but be aware that the client library and header files are not installed unless you install the development RPM. (There are separate RPM files for the server, the standard client programs, and the development libraries and header files.) If you don't install the development RPM, you'll join the many Linux users who've asked, "I installed MySQL, but I cannot find the libraries or header files; where are they?"

Perl Support

General Perl information is available at:

http://www.perl.org/

Perl software may be obtained from the Comprehensive Perl Archive Network (CPAN):

http://cpan.perl.org/

To write MySQL-based Perl programs, you'll need the DBI module and the MySQL-specific DBD module, *DBD::mysql*.

To install these modules under Unix, it may be easiest to let Perl itself help you. For example, to install DBI and *DBD::mysql*, run the following commands (you'll probably need to do this as root):

```
# perl -MCPAN -e shell
cpan> install DBI
cpan> install DBD::mysql
```

Under ActiveState Perl for Windows, you can use the *ppm* utility:

```
C:\> ppm
ppm> install DBI
ppm> install DBD::mysql
```

You can use the CPAN shell or *ppm* to install other Perl modules mentioned in this book as well.

PHP Support

PHP software distributions and installation instructions may be obtained at:

http://www.php.net/

PHP source distributions include the MySQL client library, so you need not obtain it separately. If you use a binary distribution, be sure it includes MySQL support.

Python Support

Python software distributions and installation instructions may be obtained at:

http://www.python.org/

MySQLdb, the DB-API driver module that provides MySQL support, is available at:

http://sourceforge.net/projects/mysql-python/

Java Support

You'll need a Java compiler to build and run Java programs. The *javac* and *jikes* compilers are two possible choices. On many systems, you'll find these installed already. Otherwise, you can get a compiler as part of the Java Software Development Kit (SDK). If no SDK is installed on your system, versions are available for Solaris, Linux, and Windows at Sun's Java site:

http://java.sun.com/js2e/

Several Java drivers are available that provide MySQL connectivity for the JDBC (Java Database Connectivity) interface. The one used in this book is MySQL Connector/J (formerly known as MM.MySQL), which is available at:

http://www.mysql.com/downloads/

Web Servers

In the web programming chapters, this book uses Apache for Perl, PHP, and Python scripts, and Tomcat for JavaServer Pages scripts. Apache and Tomcat both are available from the Apache Software Group; visit the following sites:

http://httpd.apache.org/
http://jakarta.apache.org/

The latter site also provides access to the Jakarta implementation of the JSP Standard Tag Library that is used in this book for writing JSP pages:

http://jakarta.apache.org/taglibs/

Miscellaneous Software

Chapter 10 mentions a Windows-based application, DBTools, that is useful for performing data transfers to and from MySQL. This application is available at the following site:

http://dbtools.vila.bol.com.br/

The gnu.getopt.Getopt Java class library discussed in Recipe 2.10 is available at:

http://www.urbanophile.com/arenn/hacking/download.html

The Jakarta Project site that hosts Tomcat also provides access to the ORO regular expression class library used in this book to perform pattern-matching operations:

http://jakarta.apache.org/oro/

APPENDIX B

JSP and Tomcat Primer

This appendix describes some essential concepts of JavaServer Pages (JSP) programming, which is used earlier in this book beginning with Chapter 16. The necessary background is fairly extensive, which is why the material is presented here in a separate appendix rather than breaking up the flow of that chapter. The topics discussed here are:

- A brief overview of servlet and JSP technologies
- Setting up the Tomcat server
- Tomcat's directory structure
- The layout of web applications
- Elements of JSP pages

For additional information about JSP pages, servlets, or Tomcat, see Appendix C.

Servlet and JavaServer Pages Overview

Java servlet technology is a means by which to execute Java programs efficiently in a web environment. The Java Servlet Specification defines the conventions of this environment, which may be summarized briefly as follows:

- Servlets run inside a servlet container, which itself either runs inside a web server or communicates with one. Servlet containers are also known as servlet engines.
- The servlet container receives requests from the web server and executes the appropriate servlet to process the request. The container then receives the response from the servlet and gives it to the web server, which in turn returns it to the client. A servlet container thus provides the connection between servlets and the web server under which they run. The container acts as the servlet runtime environment, with responsibilities that include determining the mapping between client requests and the servlets that handle them, as well as loading, executing, and unloading servlets as necessary.

- Servlets communicate with their container according to established conventions. Each servlet is expected to implement methods with well-known names to be called in response to various kinds of requests. For example, GET and POST requests are routed to methods named doGet() and doPost().

- Servlets that can be run by a container are arranged into logical groupings called "contexts." (Contexts might correspond, for example, to subdirectories of the document tree that is managed by the container.) Contexts also can include resources other than servlets, such as HTML pages, images, or configuration files.

- A context provides the basis for an "application," that is, a group of related servlets that work together, without interference from other unrelated servlets. Servlets within a given application context can share information with each other, but servlets in different contexts cannot. For example, a gateway or login servlet might establish a user's credentials, which then are placed into the context environment to be shared with other servlets within the same context as proof that the user has logged in properly. Should those servlets find the proper credentials not to be present in the environment when they execute, they can redirect to the gateway servlet automatically to require the user to log in. Servlets in another context cannot gain access to these credentials. Contexts thus provide a measure of security by preventing one application from invading another. They also can insulate applications from the effects of another application crashing; the container can keep the non-crashed applications running while it restarts the one that failed.

- Sharing of information between servlets may take place at several scope levels, which allows them to work together within the scope of a single request or across multiple requests.

The following listing shows what a simple servlet looks like. It's a Java program that implements a SimpleServlet class. The class has a doGet() method to be invoked by the servlet container when it receives a GET request for the servlet. It also has a doPost() method to handle the possibility that a POST request may be received instead; it's simply a wrapper that invokes doGet(). SimpleServlet produces a short HTML page that includes some static text that is the same each time the servlet runs, and two dynamic elements (the current date and client IP address) that vary over time and for each client:

```
import java.io.*;
import java.util.*;
import javax.servlet.*;
import javax.servlet.http.*;

public class SimpleServlet extends HttpServlet
{
    public void doGet (HttpServletRequest request,
                        HttpServletResponse response)
        throws IOException, ServletException
    {
        PrintWriter out = response.getWriter ();
```

```
            response.setContentType ("text/html");
            out.println ("<html>");
            out.println ("<head>");
            out.println ("<title>Simple Servlet</title>");
            out.println ("</head>");
            out.println ("<body bgcolor=\"white\">");
            out.println ("<p>Hello.</p>");
            out.println ("<p>The current date is "
                             + new Date ()
                             + ".</p>");
            out.println ("<p>Your IP address is "
                             + request.getRemoteAddr ()
                             + ".</p>");
            out.println ("</body>");
            out.println ("</html>");
        }

        public void doPost (HttpServletRequest request,
                            HttpServletResponse response)
            throws IOException, ServletException
        {
            doGet (request, response);
        }
    }
```

As you will no doubt observe, this "simple" servlet really isn't so simple! It requires a fair amount of machinery to import the requisite classes and to establish the doGet() and doPost() methods that provide the standard interface to the servlet container. Compare the servlet to the following PHP script, which does the same thing in a much more concise fashion:

```
<html>
<head>
<title>Simple PHP Page</title>
</head>
<body bgcolor="white">

<p>Hello.</p>
<p>The current date is <?php print (date ("D M d H:i:s T Y")); ?>.</p>
<p>Your IP address is <?php print ($_SERVER["REMOTE_ADDR"]); ?>.</p>

</body>
</html>
```

The contrast between the Java servlet and the PHP script illustrates one of the problems with writing servlets—the amount of repetitious overhead:

- A certain minimal set of classes must be imported into each servlet.

- The framework for setting up the servlet class and the doGet() or doPost() methods is fairly stereotypical, often varying among servlets only in the servlet class name.

- Each fragment of HTML is produced with an output statement.

The first two points can be addressed by using a prototype file that you copy when beginning a new servlet. The third point (wrapping each line of HTML within a print statement) is not so easily addressed and is possibly the single most tedious aspect of servlet writing. It also leads to another issue: a servlet's code may be easy enough to read as Java, but it's sometimes difficult to discern the structure of the HTML that the code generates. The problem is that you're really trying to write in two languages at once (i.e., you're writing Java that writes HTML), which isn't really optimal for either language.

JSP Pages—An Alternative to Servlets

One of the reasons for the invention of JavaServer Pages was to relieve the burden involved in creating web pages by means of lots of print statements. JSP uses a notational approach that is similar to PHP: HTML is written literally without being wrapped in print statements, and code to be executed is embedded in the page within special markers. The following listing shows a JSP page that is equivalent to the SimpleServlet servlet, but looks much more like the corresponding PHP script:

```
<html>
<head>
<title>Simple JSP Page</title>
</head>
<body bgcolor="white">

<p>Hello.</p>
<p>The current date is <%= new java.util.Date () %>.</p>
<p>Your IP address is <%= request.getRemoteAddr () %>.</p>

</body>
</html>
```

The JSP page is more concise than the servlet in several ways:

- The standard set of classes required to run a servlet need not be imported.
- The HTML is written more naturally, without using print statements.
- No class definition is required, nor are any doGet() or doPost() methods.
- The response and out objects need not be declared, because they're set up for you and ready to use as implicit objects. In fact, the JSP page just shown doesn't refer to out explicitly at all, because its output-producing constructs write to out automatically.
- The default content type is text/html; there's no need to specify it explicitly.
- The script includes literal Java by placing it within special markers. The page just shown uses <%= and %>, which mean "evaluate the expression and produce its result." There are other markers as well, each of which has a specific purpose. (For a brief summary, see "Elements of JSP Pages" later in this appendix.)

When a servlet container receives a request for a JSP page, it treats the page as a template containing literal text plus executable code embedded within special markers. The container produces an output page from the template to send to the client. Literal text from the template is left unmodified, the executable code is replaced by any output that it generates, and the combined result is returned to the client as the response to the request. That's the conceptual view of JSP processing, at least. What really happens when a container processes a JSP request is as follows:

- The JSP page is translated into a servlet—that is, into an equivalent Java program. Instances of template text are converted to print statements that output the text literally. Instances of code are placed into the program so that they execute with the intended effect. This is all placed within a wrapper that provides a unique class name and that includes import statements to pull in the standard set of classes necessary for the servlet to run properly in a web environment.
- The container compiles the servlet to produce an executable class file.
- The container executes the class file to generate an output page, which is returned to the client as the response to the request.
- The container also caches the executable class so that when the next request for the JSP page arrives, the container can execute the class directly and skip the translation and compilation phases. If the container notices that a JSP page has been modified the next time it is requested, it discards the cached class and recompiles the modified page into a new executable class.

Notationally, JSP pages provide a more natural way to write web pages than do servlets. Operationally, the JSP engine provides the benefits of automatic compilation after the page is installed in the document tree or modified thereafter. When you write a servlet, any changes require recompiling the servlet, unloading the old one, and loading the new one. That can lead to an emphasis on messing with the servlet itself rather than a focus on the servlet's purpose. JSP reverses the emphasis so that you think more about what the page does than about the mechanics of getting it compiled and loaded properly.

The differences between servlets and JSP pages do not imply any necessity of choosing to use only one or the other. Application contexts in a servlet container can include both, and because JSP pages are converted into servlets anyway, they can all intercommunicate.

JSP is similar enough to certain other technologies that it can provide a migration path away from them. For example, the JSP approach is much like that used in Microsoft's Active Server Pages (ASP). However, JSP is vendor and platform neutral, whereas ASP is proprietary. JSP thus provides an attractive alternative technology for anyone looking to move away from ASP.

Custom Actions and Tag Libraries

A servlet looks a lot like a Java program, because that's what it is. The JSP approach encourages a cleaner separation of HTML (presentation) and code, because you need not generate HTML from within Java print statements. On the other hand, JSP doesn't *require* separation of HTML and code, so it's still possible to end up with lots of embedded Java in a page if you're not careful.

One way to avoid inclusion of literal Java in JSP pages is to use another JSP feature known as custom actions. These take the form of special tags that look a lot like HTML tags (because they are written as XML elements). Custom actions allow tags to be defined that perform tasks on behalf of the page in which they occur. For example, a `<sql:query>` tag might communicate with a database server to issue a query. Custom actions typically come in groups, which are known as tag libraries and are designed as follows:

- The actions performed by the tags are implemented by a set of classes. These are just regular Java classes, except that they are written according to a set of interface conventions that allow the servlet container to communicate with them in a standard way. (The conventions define how tag attributes and body content are passed to tag handler classes, for example.) Typically, the set of classes is packaged into a JAR file.

- The library includes a Tag Library Descriptor (TLD) file that specifies which tags are associated with which classes. This allows the JSP processor to determine which class to invoke for each custom tag that appears in a JSP page. The TLD file also indicates how each tag behaves, such as whether it has any required attributes. This information is used at page translation time to determine whether a JSP page uses the tags in the library correctly. For example, if a tag requires a particular attribute and the tag is used in a page without it, the JSP processor can detect that problem and issue an appropriate error message.

Tag libraries make it easier to write entire pages using tag notation rather than switching between tags and Java code. The notation is JSP-like, not Java-like, but the effect of placing a custom tag in a JSP page is like making a method call. This is because a tag reference in a JSP page maps onto a method invocation in the servlet that the page is translated into.

To illustrate the difference between the embedded-Java and tag library approaches, compare two JSP scripts that set up a connection to a MySQL server and display a list of tables in the cookbook database. The first one does so using Java embedded within the page:

```
<%@ page import="java.sql.*" %>

<html>
<head>
<title>Tables in cookbook Database</title>
```

```
    </head>
    <body bgcolor="white">

    <p>Tables in cookbook database:</p>

    <%
        Connection conn = null;
        String url = "jdbc:mysql://localhost/cookbook";
        String user = "cbuser";
        String password = "cbpass";

        Class.forName ("com.mysql.jdbc.Driver").newInstance ();
        conn = DriverManager.getConnection (url, user, password);

        Statement s = conn.createStatement ();
        s.executeQuery ("SHOW TABLES");
        ResultSet rs = s.getResultSet ();
        while (rs.next ())
            out.println (rs.getString (1) + "<br />");
        rs.close ();
        s.close ();
        conn.close ();
    %>

    </body>
    </html>
```

The same thing can be done using a tag library, such as the JSP Standard Tag Library
(JSTL). JSTL consists of several tag sets grouped by function. Using its core and database tags, the preceding JSP page can be converted as follows to avoid entirely the
use of literal Java:

```
    <%@ taglib uri="http://java.sun.com/jstl/core" prefix="c" %>
    <%@ taglib uri="http://java.sun.com/jstl/sql" prefix="sql" %>

    <html>
    <head>
    <title>Tables in cookbook Database</title>
    </head>
    <body bgcolor="white">

    <p>Tables in cookbook database:</p>

    <sql:setDataSource var="conn"
        driver="com.mysql.jdbc.Driver" url="jdbc:mysql://localhost/cookbook"
        user="cbuser" password="cbpass" />

    <sql:query var="rs" dataSource="${conn}">SHOW TABLES</sql:query>
    <c:forEach var="row" items="${rs.rowsByIndex}">
        <c:out value="${row[0]}" /><br />
    </c:forEach>

    </body>
    </html>
```

The `taglib` directives identify the TLD files that the page uses and indicate that actions from the corresponding tag sets will be identified by prefixes of c and sql. (In effect, a prefix sets up a namespace for a set of tags.) The `<sql:dataSource>` tag sets up the parameters for connecting to the MySQL server, `<sql:query>` issues a query, `<c:forEach>` loops through the result, and `<c:out>` adds each table name in the result to the output page. (I'm glossing over details, of course; the JSTL tags are described further in Recipe 16.3.)

If it's likely that you'd connect to the database server the same way from most JSP pages in your application context, a further simplification can be achieved by moving the `<sql:dataSource>` tag to an include file. If you name the file *jstl-mcb-setup.inc* and place it in the application's *WEB-INF* directory,* any page within the application context can set up the connection to the MySQL server by accessing the file with an `include` directive. Modifying the preceding page to use the include file results in a script that looks like this:

```
<%@ taglib uri="http://java.sun.com/jstl/core" prefix="c" %>
<%@ taglib uri="http://java.sun.com/jstl/sql" prefix="sql" %>
<%@ include file="/WEB-INF/jstl-mcb-setup.inc" %>

<html>
<head>
<title>Tables in cookbook Database</title>
</head>
<body bgcolor="white">

<p>Tables in cookbook database:</p>

<sql:query var="rs" dataSource="${conn}">SHOW TABLES</sql:query>
<c:forEach var="row" items="${rs.rowsByIndex}">
    <c:out value="${row[0]}" /><br />
</c:forEach>

</body>
</html>
```

You're still *using* Java when you use a tag library, because tag actions map onto Java class invocations. But the notation follows XML conventions, so it's less like writing program code and more like writing HTML page elements. If your organization produces web content using a "separation of powers" workflow, custom actions allow elements of the page that are produced dynamically to be packaged in a way that is easier for designers and other non-programmers to deal with. They don't have to develop or work directly with the classes that implement tag actions; that's left to the programmers that write the classes that correspond to the tags.

---

* By convention, application contexts use their *WEB-INF* directory for private context-specific information. See the section "Web Application Structure."

Setting Up a Tomcat Server

The preceding discussion provides a brief introduction to servlets and JSP pages, but says nothing about how you actually use a server to run them. This section describes how to install Tomcat, a JSP-aware web server. Tomcat is part of the Jakarta Project, which like Apache is a development effort of the Apache Software Foundation.

As described earlier, servlets execute inside a container, which is an engine that communicates with or plugs into a web server to handle requests for pages that are produced by executing servlets. Some servlet containers can operate in standalone fashion, such that they function both as container and web server. That is how Tomcat works, so by installing it, you get a fully functioning server with servlet-processing capabilities. In fact, Tomcat is a reference implementation for both the servlet and JSP specifications, so it also acts as a JSP engine, providing JSP-to-servlet translation services. The servlet container part is named Catalina, and the JSP processor is named Jasper.

It's possible to use the container part of Tomcat in conjunction with other web servers. For example, you can set up a cooperative arrangement between Apache and Tomcat under which Apache acts as a frontend that passes servlet and JSP requests through to Tomcat and handles other requests itself. You can find information about setting up Apache and Tomcat to work together this way on the Jakarta project web site.

To run a Tomcat server, you need three things:

A Java Software Development Kit (SDK). This is required because Tomcat needs to compile Java servlets as part of its operation. You most likely already have an SDK installed if you've been compiling Java programs while reading earlier chapters. If you don't have an SDK, see Recipe 2.1 for information on obtaining and installing one.

Tomcat itself. Tomcat is available from the Jakarta Project site, *http://jakarta. apache.org*. A fair amount of Tomcat documentation is available there, too. In particular, if you're a newcomer to Tomcat, I recommend that you read the Introduction and the Application Developer's Guide.

Some knowledge of XML. Tomcat configuration files are written as XML documents, and many scripting elements within JSP pages follow XML syntax rules. If you're new to XML, the "XML and XHTML in a Nutshell" sidebar in Recipe 16.0 describes some of its characteristics in comparison to HTML.

Installing a Tomcat Distribution

Currently, Tomcat is available in 3.x and 4.x versions. This section describes Tomcat 4.x, which is what I recommend you install. If you use 3.x, be prepared for some differences. For example, the directory structures used by 3.x and 4.x servers are not quite the same.

To install Tomcat, get a binary distribution from *jakarta.apache.org*. (I assume you don't intend to build it from source, which is more difficult.) Tomcat distributions are available in several file formats, distinguished by filename extension:

.tar.gz
> Indicates a compressed *tar* file, usually used for Unix installs.

.zip
> Indicates a ZIP archive, applicable to either Unix or Windows.

.rpm (RedHat Package Manager)
> These files can be used on Linux systems.

.exe
> Signifies an executable installer, used on Windows only.

For a distribution packaged as a *tar* or ZIP file, you should place it in the directory under which you want to install Tomcat, then run the installation command in that directory to unpack the distribution there. RPM files contain internal installation location information, so you can run the installation command from anywhere. The Windows *.exe* installer prompts you to indicate where to install Tomcat, so it too can be run from any directory. The following commands are representative of those needed to install each distribution type. (Change the version numbers in the filenames to reflect the actual Tomcat distribution that you're using.)

To install Tomcat from a compressed *tar* file, unpack it like this:

```
% tar zxf jakarta-tomcat-4.0.4.tar.gz
```

If you're unpacking a Tomcat *tar* file distribution under Mac OS X, use *gnutar* rather than *tar*. Both programs are available, but *tar* has some problems with long filenames that *gnutar* does not. It may also be necessary to use a GNU-compatible version of *tar* under Solaris.

If your version of *tar* doesn't understand the *z* option, do this instead:

```
% gunzip jakarta-tomcat-4.0.4.tar.gz | tar xf -
```

If you use a ZIP archive, you can unpack it with the *jar* utility or any other program that understands ZIP format (such as the Windows *WinZip* application). For example, to use *jar*, do this:

```
% jar xf jakarta-tomcat-4.0.4.zip
```

Linux users have the option of installing from RPM files. Two RPMs must be installed. The first contains the server software, the second contains several applications. (The other distribution formats consist of a single archive file that includes the applications.) Typically you must run the RPM installation commands as root:

```
# rpm --install tomcat4-4.0.4-full.2jpp.noarch.rpm
# rpm --install tomcat4-webapps-4.0.4-full.2jpp.noarch.rpm
```

Depending on the version of Tomcat, you may also need to install other prerequisite distributions, such as the *regex*, *servletapi*, and *xerces* RPM files. If these are necessary, *rpm* will tell you when you install the Tomcat RPMs.

After installing the RPM files, edit */etc/tomcat4/conf/tomcat4.conf* to set the value of JAVA_HOME to the pathname of the directory in which your Java SDK is installed.

The Windows *.exe* distribution is directly executable. Launch it, then indicate where you want to place Tomcat when the installer prompts for a location. If you use this installer, be sure that you already have a Java SDK installed first; the installer puts some files into the SDK hierarchy, an operation that fails if the SDK isn't present. For versions of Windows that have service management (such as Windows NT, 2000, or XP), the *.exe* installer gives you the option of installing Tomcat as a service so that it starts automatically at system boot time.

Most of the installation methods create a directory and unpack Tomcat under it. The top-level directory of the resulting hierarchy is the Tomcat root directory. I'll assume here that the Tomcat root is */usr/local/jakarta-tomcat* under Unix and *D:\jakarta-tomcat* under Windows. (The actual directory name likely will have a version number at the end.) The Tomcat root contains various text files containing information that is useful in the event that you have general or platform-specific problems. It also contains a number of directories. If you want to explore these now, see the section "Tomcat's Directory Structure." Otherwise, proceed to the next section, "Starting and Stopping Tomcat," to find out how to run Tomcat.

Note that if you installed Tomcat from RPM files, you may find that the distribution is somewhat spread out, rather than installed with everything under a single directory. For example, you might find most of the components under */var/tomcat4* and the documents under */usr/doc/tomcat4*. To determine where the contents of a given RPM file were installed, use the following command:

```
% rpm -qpl rpmfile
```

(That's the lowercase letter "l," not the number "1.")

Starting and Stopping Tomcat

Tomcat can be controlled manually, and also set to run automatically when your system starts up. It's good to become familiar with the Tomcat startup and shutdown commands that apply to your platform, because you'll probably find yourself needing to stop and restart Tomcat fairly often—at least while you're setting it up initially. For example, if you modify Tomcat's configuration files or install a new application, you must restart Tomcat to get it to notice the changes.

Before running Tomcat, you'll need to set a couple of environment variables. Make sure JAVA_HOME is set to the pathname of your SDK so that Tomcat can find it, and set CATALINA_HOME to the pathname of the Tomcat root directory. (Tomcat 3.x uses TOMCAT_HOME rather than CATALINA_HOME, and you may also need to set CLASSPATH.)

To start and stop Tomcat manually under Unix, change location into the *bin* directory under the Tomcat root. You can control Tomcat with the following two shell scripts:

```
% ./startup.sh
% ./shutdown.sh
```

To run Tomcat automatically at system boot time, look for a startup script such as */etc/rc.local* or */etc/rc.d/rc.local* (the pathname depends on your operating system) and add a few lines to it:

```
export JAVA_HOME=/usr/local/java/jdk
export CATALINA_HOME=/usr/local/jakarta-tomcat
$CATALINA_HOME/bin/startup.sh &
```

These commands will run Tomcat as root, however. To run it under a different user account, change the last command to invoke Tomcat with *su* instead and specify the username:

```
su -c $CATALINA_HOME/bin/startup.sh user_name &
```

If you use *su* to specify a username, make sure that Tomcat's directory tree is accessible to that user or you will have file permission problems when Tomcat tries to access files. One way to do this is to run the following command as root in the Tomcat root directory:

```
# chown -R user_name .
```

Linux users who install Tomcat from RPM files will find that the installation creates a script *tomcat4* in the */etc/rc.d/init.d* directory that can be used manually or for automatic startup. To use the script manually, change location into that directory and use these commands:

```
% ./tomcat4 start
% ./tomcat4 stop
```

For automatic startup, you must activate the script by running the following command as root:

```
# chkconfig --add tomcat4
```

The Linux RPM installation also creates a user account with a login name of tomcat4 that is intended to be used for running Tomcat.

For Windows users, a pair of batch files is provided in the *bin* directory for controlling Tomcat manually:

```
C:\> startup.bat
C:\> shutdown.bat
```

If you elected to install Tomcat as a service for versions of Windows that have service management, such as Windows NT, 2000, or XP, you should control Tomcat using the services console. You can use this to start or stop Tomcat, or to set Tomcat to run automatically when Windows starts. (The service name is Apache Tomcat.)

To try out Tomcat, start it up using whatever instructions are applicable to your platform. Then request the default page using your browser. The URL will look something like this:

http://tomcat.snake.net:8080/

Adjust your hostname and port number appropriately. For example, Tomcat normally runs on port 8080 by default, but if you install from RPM files under Linux, Tomcat may use a port number of 8180. If your browser receives the page correctly, you should see the Tomcat logo and links to examples and documentation. It's useful at this point to follow the examples link and try out a few of the JSP pages there, to see if they compile and execute properly.

If you find that, despite setting the JAVA_HOME variable, Tomcat can't find your Java compiler, try setting your PATH environment variable to explicitly include the directory containing the compiler. Normally this is the *bin* directory under your SDK installation. You probably already have PATH set to something already. If so, you'll want to add the *bin* directory to the current PATH setting:

```
export PATH=${PATH}:/usr/local/java/jdk/bin      (sh, bash, etc.)
setenv PATH ${PATH}:/usr/local/java/jdk/bin      (csh, tcsh, etc.)
set PATH=%PATH%;D:\jdk\bin                        (Windows)
```

Tomcat's Directory Structure

For writing JSP pages, it's not strictly necessary to be familiar with the hierarchy of Tomcat's directory layout. But it certainly doesn't hurt, so change location into the Tomcat root directory and have a look around. You'll find a number of standard directories, which are described below, grouped by function. Note that your installation layout may not be exactly as described here, particularly if you're using Tomcat 3.x rather than 4.x. Even for Tomcat 4.x, some distribution formats omit a few of the directories, and the *logs* and *work* directories may not be created until you've started Tomcat for the first time.

Application directories

From the point of view of an application developer, the *webapps* directory is the most important part of Tomcat's directory hierarchy. Each application context has its own directory, which is placed within the *webapps* directory under the Tomcat root.

Tomcat processes client requests by mapping them onto locations under the *webapps* directory. For a request that begins with the name of a directory located under *webapps*, Tomcat looks for the appropriate page within that directory. For example, the following two requests would be served using the *index.html* and *test.jsp* pages in the *mcb* directory:

http://tomcat.snake.net:8080/mcb/index.html
http://tomcat.snake.net:8080/mcb/test.jsp

Requests that don't begin with the name of a *webapps* subdirectory are served out of a special subdirectory named *ROOT*, which provides the default application context.[*] For the following request, Tomcat would serve the *index.html* page from the *ROOT* directory:

http://tomcat.snake.net:8080/index.html

Applications typically are packaged as web archive (WAR) files and Tomcat by default looks for WAR files that need to be unpacked when it starts up. Thus, to install an application, you generally copy its WAR file to the *webapps* directory, restart Tomcat, and let Tomcat unpack it. The layout of individual application directories is described in the section "Web Application Structure."

The Java Servlet Specification defines a web application as follows: "A web application is a collection of servlets, html pages, classes, and other resources that make up a complete application on a web server." Essentially what this means for Tomcat is that an application is everything under a subdirectory of the *webapps* directory. Because contexts are kept separate by servlet containers like Tomcat, one practical implication of this structure is that scripts in one application directory can't mess with anything in another application directory.

Configuration and control directories

Two directories contain configuration and control files. The *bin* directory contains control scripts for Tomcat startup and shutdown, and *conf* contains Tomcat's configuration files, which are written as XML documents. Tomcat reads its configuration files only at startup time. If you modify any of them, you must restart Tomcat for your changes to take effect.

The most important configuration file is *server.xml*, which controls Tomcat's overall behavior. Another file, *web.xml*, provides application configuration defaults. This file is used in conjunction with any *web.xml* file an application may have of its own. The *tomcat-users.xml* file defines credentials for users that have access to protected server functions, such as the Manager application that allows you to control applications from your browser. (See "Restarting Applications Without Restarting Tomcat.") This file can be superceded by other user information storage mechanisms. For example, you can store Tomcat user records in MySQL instead. For instructions, look in the *tomcat* directory of the recipes distribution.

Class directories

Several Tomcat directories are used for class files and libraries. They differ in function according to whether you want to make classes visible to applications, to Tomcat, or to both:

---

[*] The *webapps/ROOT* directory is distinct from the Tomcat root directory, which is the top-level directory of the Tomcat tree.

classes

>These class files are visible to applications but not to Tomcat.

common

>This directory has two subdirectories, *classes* and *lib*, for class files and libraries that should be visible both to applications and to Tomcat.

lib

>These class libraries are visible to applications but not to Tomcat.

server

>This directory has two subdirectories, *classes* and *lib*, for class files and libraries that are visible to Tomcat but not to applications.

Tomcat 3.x uses a different class loading algorithm than Tomcat 4.x, and has a different class directory structure. In particular, Tomcat 3.x has no *common* directory.

Operational directories

If they weren't set up as part of the Tomcat installation process, Tomcat creates two additional directories that serve operational purposes when you start it for the first time. Tomcat writes log files to the *log* directory and uses a *work* directory for temporary files.

The files in the *logs* directory can be useful for diagnosing problems. For example, if Tomcat doesn't seem to start up properly, the reason usually will have been written into one of the log files.

When Tomcat translates a JSP page into a servlet and compiles it into an executable class file, it stores the resulting *.java* and *.class* files under the *work* directory. (When you first begin working with JSP pages, you may find it instructive to have a look under the *work* directory to compare your original JSP pages with the corresponding servlets that Tomcat produces.)

Restarting Applications Without Restarting Tomcat

If you modify a JSP page, Tomcat recompiles it automatically when the page is next requested. But if the page uses a JAR or class file under the application's *WEB-INF* directory and you update one of them, Tomcat normally won't notice the change until you restart it.

One way to avoid restarts for an application is to provide a `<Context>` element for the application in Tomcat's *server.xml* file that specifies a `reloadable` attribute of true. That will cause Tomcat to look for changes not only in JSP pages that are requested directly, but also for changes in classes and libraries under the *WEB-INF* directory that the pages use. For example, to write such a `<Context>` element for an application named mcb, you could add a line like this to Tomcat's *server.xml* file:

```
<Context path="/mcb" docBase="mcb" debug="0" reloadable="true" />
```

The <Context> element attributes tell Tomcat four things:

path
> Indicates the URL that maps to pages from the application context. The value is the part of the URL that follows the hostname and port number.

docBase
> Indicates where the application context directory is located, relative to the *webapps* directory in the Tomcat tree.

debug
> Sets the context debugging level. A value of zero disables debug output; higher numbers generate more output.

reloadable
> Specifies Tomcat recompilation behavior when a client requests a JSP page located in the application context. By default, Tomcat recompiles a page only after noticing a modification to the page itself. Setting reloadable to true tells Tomcat to also check any classes or libraries stored under the application's *WEB-INF* directory that the page uses.

After modifying *server.xml* to add the <Context> element, restart Tomcat to make the change take effect.

Having Tomcat check for class and library changes can be extremely useful during application development to avoid repeated restarts. However, as you might expect, automatic class checking adds a lot of processing overhead and incurs a significant performance penalty. It's better used on development systems than on production systems.

Another way to get Tomcat to recognize application changes without restarting the entire server is to use the Manager application. This allows you to reload applications on request from a browser, without the overhead caused by enabling the reloadable attribute. The Manager application is invoked using the path */manager* at the end of the URL by which you access your Tomcat server. The URL will also include the command you wish to execute. For example, the following request shows which contexts are running:

> *http://tomcat.snake.net:8080/manager/list*

To shut down and reload the mcb application without restarting Tomcat, use a URL like this:

> *http://tomcat.snake.net:8080/manager/reload?path=/mcb*

For more information on using the Manager application and what its allowable commands are, see the Manager App HOW-TO:

> *http://jakarta.apache.org/tomcat/tomcat-4.0-doc/manager-howto.html*

This document may also be available locally by following the documentation link on your Tomcat server's home page. Note particularly the part that describes how to set up a Tomcat user with the manager role, because you'll need to provide a name and password to gain access to the Manager application. By default, user records are defined in Tomcat's *tomcat-users.xml* configuration file. The *tomcat* directory of the recipes distribution contains some information on storing Tomcat user records in MySQL instead.

Web Application Structure

Each web application corresponds to a single servlet context and exists as a collection of resources. Some of these resources are visible to clients, while others are not. For example, an application's JSP pages may be available to clients, but the configuration, property, or class files that are used by the JSP pages can be hidden. The location of components within the application hierarchy determines whether or not clients can see them. This allows you to make resources public or private depending on where you put them.

Java Servlet Specification 2.3 defines the standard for web application layout. This helps application developers by providing conventions that indicate where to put what, along with rules that define which parts of the application the container will make available to clients and which parts are hidden.

Each web application corresponds to a single servlet context. In Tomcat, these are represented by directories under the *webapps* directory that serves as the "parent" of all web applications. Within an application directory, you'll find a *WEB-INF* subdirectory, and usually other files such as HTML pages, JSP pages, or image files. The files that are located in the application's top-level directory are public and may be requested by clients. The *WEB-INF* directory has special significance. Its mere presence signifies to Tomcat that its parent directory actually represents an application. *WEB-INF* is thus the only required component of a web application; it must exist, even if it's empty. If *WEB-INF* is nonempty, it typically contains application-specific configuration files, classes, and possibly other information. Three of its most common primary components are:

> *WEB-INF/web.xml*
> *WEB-INF/classes*
> *WEB-INF/lib*

web.xml is the web application deployment descriptor file. It gives the container a standard way to discover how to handle the resources that make up the application. The deployment descriptor is often used for purposes such as defining the behavior of JSP pages and servlets, setting up access control for protected information, specifying error pages to be used when problems occur, and defining where to find tag libraries.

The *classes* and *lib* directories under *WEB-INF* hold class files and libraries, and sometimes other information. Individual class files go under *classes*, using a directory structure that corresponds to the class hierarchy. (For example, a class file *MyClass.class* that implements a class named com.kitebird.jsp.MyClass would be stored in the directory *classes/com/kitebird/jsp*.) Class libraries packaged as JAR files go in the *lib* directory instead. Tomcat looks in the *classes* and *lib* directories automatically when processing requests for pages from the application. This allows your pages to use application-specific information with a minimum of fuss.

The *WEB-INF* directory is also special in that it is private. Its contents are available to the application's servlets and JSP pages but cannot be accessed directly through a browser, so you can place information there that should not be displayed to clients. For example, you can store a properties file under *WEB-INF* that contains connection parameters for a database server. Or if you have an application that allows image files to be uploaded by one page and downloaded later by another page, putting the images into a directory under *WEB-INF* makes them private. Because Tomcat will not serve the contents of *WEB-INF* directly, your JSP pages can implement an access control policy that determines who can perform image operations. (A simple policy might require clients to specify a name and password before being allowed to upload images.) The *WEB-INF* directory is also beneficial in that it gives you a known location for private files that is fixed with respect to the application's root directory, no matter what machine you deploy the application on.

Clients that attempt to circumvent the private nature of the *WEB-INF* directory by issuing requests containing names such as *Web-Inf* in the path will find that its name is interpreted in case-sensitive fashion, even on systems with filenames that are not case sensitive, such as Windows or HFS+ filesystems under Mac OS X. Note that on such systems you should take care not to create the *WEB-INF* directory with a name like *Web-Inf*, *web-inf*, and so forth. The operating system itself may not consider the name any different than *WEB-INF*, but Tomcat will. The result is that none of the resources in the directory will be available to your JSP pages. Under Windows, it may be necessary to create a *WEB-INF* directory from the DOS prompt. (Windows Explorer may not respect the lettercase you use when creating or renaming a directory, just as it does not necessarily display directory names the same way the *DIR* command does from the DOS prompt.)

The preceding discussion describes web application layout in terms of a directory hierarchy, because that's the easiest way to explain it. However, an application need not necessarily exist that way. A web application typically is packaged as a WAR file, using the standard layout for components prescribed by the servlet specification. But some containers can run an application directly from its WAR file without unpacking it. Furthermore, a container that does unpack WAR files is free to do so into any filesystem structure it wishes.

Tomcat uses the simplest approach, which is to store an application in the filesystem using a directory structure that is the same as the directory tree from which the file was originally created. You can see this correspondence by comparing the structure of a WAR file to the directory hierarchy that Tomcat creates by unpacking it. For example, the WAR file for an application someapp can be examined using the this command:

```
% jar tf someapp.war
```

The list of pathnames displayed by the command corresponds to the layout of the *someapp* directory created by Tomcat when it unpacks the file under the *webapps* directory. To verify this, recursively list the contents of the *someapp* directory using one of these commands:

```
% ls -R someapp              (Unix)
C:\> dir /s someapp          (Windows)
```

If you were to set up a context manually for an application named myapp, the steps would be something like those shown in the following procedure. (If you want to see what the resulting application hierarchy should be, have a look at the *tomcat/myapp* directory of the recipes distribution.)

• Change directory into the *webapps* subdirectory of the Tomcat directory tree.

• Create a directory in the *webapps* directory with the same name as the application (*myapp*), then change location into that directory.

• In the *myapp* directory, create a directory named *WEB-INF*. The presence of this directory signals to Tomcat that *myapp* is an application context, so it must exist. Then restart Tomcat so it notices the new application.

• Create a short test page named *page1.html* in the *myapp* directory that you can request from a browser to make sure that Tomcat is serving pages for the application. This is just a plain HTML file, to avoid complications that might arise from use of embedded Java, tag libraries, and so forth:

```
<html>
<head>
<title>Test Page</title>
</head>
<body bgcolor="white">
<p>
This is a test.
</p>
</body>
</html>
```

To request the page, use a URL like this, adjusting it appropriately for your own server hostname and port number:

http://tomcat.snake.net:8080/myapp/page1.html

- To try out a simple JSP page, make a copy of *page1.html* named *page2.jsp*. That creates a valid JSP page (even though it contains no executable code), so you should be able to request it and see output identical to that produced by *page1.html*:

    http://tomcat.snake.net:8080/myapp/page2.jsp

- Copy *page2.jsp* to *page3.jsp* and modify the latter to contain some embedded Java code by adding a couple of lines that print the current date and client IP number:

```
<html>
<head>
<title>Test Page</title>
</head>
<body bgcolor="white">
<p>
This is a test.
The current date is <%= new java.util.Date() %>.
Your IP number is <%= request.getRemoteAddr () %>.
</p>
</body>
</html>
```

The Date() method returns the current date, and getRemoteAddr() returns the client IP number from the object associated with the client request. After making the changes, request *page3.jsp* from your browser and the output should include the current date and the IP number of the host from which you requested the page.

At this point, you have a simple application context that consists of three pages (one of which contains executable code) and an empty *WEB-INF* directory. For most applications, *WEB-INF* will contain a *web.xml* file that serves as the web application deployment descriptor file to tell Tomcat how the application is configured. If you look through *web.xml* files in other applications that you install under Tomcat, you'll find that they can be rather complex, but a minimal deployment descriptor file looks like this:

```
<?xml version="1.0" encoding="ISO-8859-1"?>
<!DOCTYPE web-app
    PUBLIC "-//Sun Microsystems, Inc.//DTD Web Application 2.3//EN"
    "http://java.sun.com/dtd/web-app_2_3.dtd">

<web-app>

</web-app>
```

Adding information to the *web.xml* file is a matter of placing new elements between the <web-app> and </web-app> tags. As a simple illustration, you can add a <welcome-file-list> element to specify a list of files that Tomcat should look for when clients send a request URL that ends with *myapp* and no specific page. Whichever file Tomcat finds first becomes the default page that is sent to the client. For example, to specify that Tomcat should consider *page3.jsp* and *index.html* to be valid default pages, create a *web.xml* file in the *WEB-INF* directory that looks like this:

```
<?xml version="1.0" encoding="ISO-8859-1"?>
<!DOCTYPE web-app
     PUBLIC "-//Sun Microsystems, Inc.//DTD Web Application 2.3//EN"
     "http://java.sun.com/dtd/web-app_2_3.dtd">

<web-app>
  <welcome-file-list>
    <welcome-file>page3.jsp</welcome-file>
    <welcome-file>index.html</welcome-file>
  </welcome-file-list>
</web-app>
```

Restart Tomcat so it reads the new application configuration information, then issue a request that specifies no explicit page:

http://tomcat.snake.net:8080/myapp/

The *myapp* directory contains a page named *page3.jsp*, which is listed as one of the default pages in the *web.xml* file, so Tomcat should execute *page3.jsp* and send the result to your browser.

Elements of JSP Pages

An earlier section of this appendix described some general characteristics of JSP pages. This section discusses in more detail the kinds of constructs you can use.

JSP pages are templates that contain static parts and dynamic parts:

- Literal text in a JSP page that is not enclosed within special markers is static; it's sent to the client without change. The JSP examples in this book produce HTML pages, so the static parts of JSP scripts are written in HTML. But you can also write pages that produce other forms of output, such as plain text, XML, or WML.

- The non-static (dynamic) parts of JSP pages consist of code to be evaluated. The code is distinguished from static text by being enclosed within special markers. Some markers indicate page-processing directives or scriptlets. A directive gives the JSP engine information about how to process the page, whereas a scriptlet is a mini-program that is evaluated and replaced by whatever output it produces. Other markers take the form of tags written as XML elements; they are associated with classes that act as tag handlers to perform the desired actions.

The following sections discuss the various types of dynamic elements that JSP pages can contain.

Scripting Elements

Several sets of scripting markers allow you to embed Java code or comments in a JSP page:

`<% ... %>`

The `<%` and `%>` markers indicate a scriptlet—that is, embedded Java code. The following scriptlet invokes `print()` to write a value to the output page:

```
<% out.print (1+2); %>
```

`<%= ... %>`

These markers indicate an expression to be evaluated. The result is added to the output page, which makes it easy to display values with no explicit print statement. For example, these two constructs both display the value 3, but the second is easier to write:

```
<% out.print (1+2); %>
<%= 1+2 %>
```

`<%! ... %>`

The `<%!` and `%>` markers allow class variables and methods to be declared.

`<%-- ... --%>`

Text within these markers is treated as a comment and ignored. JSP comments disappear entirely and do not appear in the output that is returned to the client. If you're writing a JSP page that produces HTML and you want the comment to appear in the final output page, use an HTML comment instead:

```
<%-- this comment will not be part of the final output page --%>
<!-- this comment will be part of the final output page -->
```

When a JSP page is translated into a servlet, all scripting elements effectively become part of the same servlet. This means that a variable declared in one element can be used by other elements later in the page. It also means that if you declare a given variable in two elements, the resulting servlet is illegal and an error will occur.

The `<% ... %>` and `<%! ... %>` markers both can be used to declare variables, but differ in their effect. A variable declared within `<% ... %>` is an object (or instance) variable; it is initialized each time that the page is requested. A variable declared within `<%! ... %>` is a class variable, initialized only at the beginning the life of the page. Consider the following JSP page, *counter.jsp*, which declares counter1 as an object variable and counter2 as a class variable:

```
<%-- counter.jsp - demonstrate object and class variable counters --%>

<% int counter1 = 0; %>          <%-- object variable --%>
<%! int counter2 = 0; %>         <%-- class variable --%>
<% counter1 = counter1 + 1; %>
<% counter2 = counter2 + 1; %>
<p>Counter 1 is <%= counter1 %></p>
<p>Counter 2 is <%= counter2 %></p>
```

If you install the page and request it several times, the value of `counter1` will be 1 for every request. The value of `counter2` increments across successive requests (even if different clients request the page), until Tomcat is restarted.

In addition to variables that you declare yourself, JSP pages have access to a number of objects that are declared for you implicitly. These are discussed in "Implicit JSP Objects."

JSP Directives

The `<%@ and %>` markers indicate a JSP directive that provides the JSP processor with information about the kind of output the page produces, the classes or tag libraries it requires, and so forth.

`<%@ page ... %>`

page directives provide several kinds of information, which are indicated by one or more *attribute="value"* pairs following the page keyword. The following directive specifies that the page scripting language is Java and that it produces an output page with a content type of `text/html`:

```
<%@ page language="java" contentType="text/html" %>
```

This particular directive need not actually be specified at all, because java and text/html are the default values for their respective attributes.

If a JSP page produces non-HTML output, be sure to override the default content type. For example, if a page produces plain text, use this directive:

```
<%@ page contentType="text/plain" %>
```

An import attribute causes Java classes to be imported. In a regular Java program, you would do this using an import statement. In a JSP page, use a page directive instead:

```
<%@ page import="java.util.Date" %>
<p>The date is <%= new Date () %>.</p>
```

If you refer to a particular class only once, it may be more convenient to omit the directive and just refer to the class by its full name when you use it:

```
<p>The date is <%= new java.util.Date () %>.</p>
```

`<%@ include ... %>`

The include directive inserts the contents of a file into the page translation process. That is, the directive is replaced by the contents of the included file, which is then translated itself. The following directive causes inclusion of a file named *my-setup-stuff.inc* from the application's *WEB-INF* directory:

```
<%@ include file="/WEB-INF/my-setup-stuff.inc" %>
```

A leading / indicates a filename relative to the application directory (a context-relative path). No leading / means the file is relative to the location of the page containing the include directive.

Include files allow content (either static or dynamic) to be shared easily among a set of JSP pages. For example, you can use them to provide standard headers or footers for a set of JSP pages, or to execute code for common operations such as setting up a connection to a database server.

`<%@ taglib ... %>`

A `taglib` directive indicates that the page uses custom actions from a given tag library. The directive includes attributes that tell the JSP engine how to locate the TLD file for the library and also the name you'll use in the rest of the page to signify tags from the library. For example, a page that uses the core and database-access tags from JSTL might include the following `taglib` directives:

```
<%@ taglib uri="http://java.sun.com/jstl/core" prefix="c" %>
<%@ taglib uri="http://java.sun.com/jstl/sql" prefix="sql" %>
```

The uri (Uniform Resource Identifier) attribute uniquely identifies the tag library so that the JSP engine can find its TLD file. The TLD defines the behavior (the interface) of the actions so that the JSP processor can make sure the page uses the library's tags correctly. A common convention for constructing unique uri values is to use a string that includes the host from which the tag library originates. That makes the uri value look like a URL, but it's just an identifier; it doesn't mean that the JSP engine actually goes to that host to fetch the descriptor file. The rules for interpreting the uri value are described in "Using a Tag Library."

The `prefix` attribute indicates how tags from the library will be invoked. The directives just shown indicate that core and database tags will have the forms `<c:xxx>` and `<sql:xxx>`. For example, you can use the out tag from the core library as follows to display a value:

```
<c:out value="Hello, world." />
```

Or you might issue a query with the database query tag like this:

```
<sql:query var="result" dataSource="${conn}">
    SHOW TABLES
</sql:query>
```

Action Elements

Action element tags can refer to standard (predefined) JSP actions, or to custom actions in a tag library. Tag names include a prefix and a specific action:

- Tag names with a `jsp` prefix indicate predefined action elements. For example, `<jsp:forward>` forwards the current request to another page. This action is available to any page run under a standard JSP processor.

- Custom actions are implemented by tag libraries. The prefix of the tag name must match the `prefix` attribute of a `taglib` directive that appears earlier in the page, so that the JSP processor can determine which library the tag is part of. To use custom tags, the library must be installed first. See "Using a Tag Library."

Actions are written as XML elements within a JSP page, and their syntax follows normal XML rules. An element with a body is written with separate opening and closing tags:

```
<c:if test="${x == 0}">
    x is zero
</c:if>
```

If the tag has no body, the opening and closing tags can be combined:

```
<jsp:forward page="some_other_page.jsp" />
```

Using a Tag Library

Suppose that you have a tag library consisting of a JAR file *mytags.jar* and a tag library descriptor file *mytags.tld*. To make the library available to the JSP pages in a given application, both files must be installed. Typically, you'd put the JAR file in the application's *WEB-INF/lib* directory and the TLD file in the *WEB-INF* directory.

A JSP page that uses the tag library must include an appropriate `taglib` directive before using any of the actions that the library provides:

```
<%@ taglib uri="tld-location" prefix="taglib-identifier" %>
```

The `prefix` attribute tells Tomcat how you'll refer to tags from the library in the rest of the JSP page. If you use a `prefix` value of `mytags`, you can refer to tags later in the page like this:

```
<mytags:sometag attr1="attribute value 1" attr2="attribute value 2">
tag body
</mytags:sometag>
```

The `prefix` value is a name of your own choosing, but you must use it consistently throughout the page, and you cannot use the same value for two different tag libraries.

The `uri` attribute tells the JSP processor how to find the tag library's TLD file. The value can be either direct or indirect:

- You can specify the `uri` value directly as the pathname to the TLD file, which typically will be installed in the *WEB-INF* directory:

  ```
  <%@ taglib uri="/WEB-INF/mytags.tld" prefix="mytags" %>
  ```

  A leading / indicates a filename relative to the application directory (a context-relative path). No leading / means the file is relative to the location of the page containing the `taglib` directive.

  If an application uses lots of tag libraries, a common convention for keeping TLD files from cluttering up the *WEB-INF* directory is to put them in a *tld* sub-directory of the *WEB-INF* directory. In that case, the `uri` value would be written like this instead:

  ```
  <%@ taglib uri="/WEB-INF/tld/mytags.tld" prefix="mytags" %>
  ```

The disadvantage of specifying a TLD file pathname directly is that if a new version of the tag library is released and the TLD file has a different name, you'll need to modify the taglib directive in every JSP page that refers to the file.

- Another way to specify the location of the TLD file is by using the pathname to the tag library JAR file:

```
<%@ taglib uri="/WEB-INF/lib/mytags.jar" prefix="mytags" %>
```

The JSP processor can find the TLD file this way, provided a copy of it is included in the JAR file as *META-INF/taglib.tld*. However, this method suffers the same problem as specifying the TLD filename directly—if a new version of the library comes out with a different JAR file pathname, you must update taglib directives in individual JSP pages. It also doesn't work for containers that can't find TLD files in JAR files. (Older versions of Tomcat have this problem, for example.)

- A third way to specify the location of the TLD file is to do so indirectly. Assign a symbolic name to the library and add a <taglib> entry to the application's *web.xml* file that maps the symbolic name to the pathname of the TLD file. Then refer to the symbolic name in your JSP pages. Suppose you define the symbolic name for the mytags tag library as:

```
http://terrific-tags.com/mytags
```

The <taglib> entry in *web.xml* should list the symbolic name and provide the path to the corresponding TLD file. If the file is installed in the *WEB-INF* directory, write the entry like this:

```
<taglib>
    <taglib-uri>http://terrific-tags.com/mytags</taglib-uri>
    <taglib-location>/WEB-INF/mytags.tld</taglib-location>
</taglib>
```

If the file is installed in *WEB-INF/tld* instead, write the entry like this:

```
<taglib>
    <taglib-uri>http://terrific-tags.com/mytags</taglib-uri>
    <taglib-location>/WEB-INF/tld/mytags.tld</taglib-location>
</taglib>
```

Either way, you refer to the tag library in JSP pages using the symbolic name, like this:

```
<%@ taglib uri="http://terrific-tags.com/mytags" prefix="mytags" %>
```

Using a symbolic TLD name involves a level of indirection, but has a significant advantage in that it provides a more stable means by which to refer to the tag library in JSP pages. You specify the actual location of the TLD file only in *web.xml*, rather than in individual JSP pages. If a new version of the tag library comes out and the TLD file has a different name, just change the <taglib-location> value in *web.xml* and restart Tomcat to allow your JSP pages to use the new library. There's no need to change any of the JSP pages.

Implicit JSP Objects

When a servlet runs, the servlet container passes it two arguments representing the request and the response, but you must declare other objects yourself. For example, you can use the response argument to obtain an output-writing object like this:

```
PrintWriter out = response.getWriter ();
```

A convenience that JSP provides in comparison to servlet writing is a set of implicit objects—that is, standard objects that are provided as part of the JSP execution environment. You can refer to any of these objects without explicitly declaring them. Thus, in a JSP page, the out object can be treated as having already been set up and made available for use. Some of the more useful implicit objects are:

pageContext
> An object that provides the environment for the page.

request
> An object that contains information about the request received from the client, such as the parameters submitted in a form.

response
> The response being constructed for transmission to the client. You can use it to specify response headers, for example.

out
> The output object. Writing to this object through methods such as print() or println() adds text to the response page.

session
> Tomcat provides access to a session that can be used to carry information from request to request. This allows you to write applications that interact with the user in what seems to the user as a cohesive series of events. Sessions are described more fully in Chapter 19.

application
> This object provides access to information that is shared on an application-wide basis.

Levels of Scope in JSP Pages

JSP pages have access to several scope levels, which can be used to store information that varies in how widely available it is. The scope levels are:

Page scope
> Information that is available only to the current JSP page.

Request scope
> Information that is available to any of the JSP pages or servlets that are servicing the current client request. It's possible for one page to invoke another during

request processing; placing information in request scope allows such pages to communicate with each other.

Session scope

Information that is available to any page servicing a request that is part of a given session. Session scope can span multiple requests from a given client.

Application scope

Information that is available to any page that is part of the application context. Application scope can span multiple requests, sessions, or clients.

One context knows nothing about other contexts, but pages served from within the same context can share information with each other by registering attributes (objects) in one of the scopes that are higher than page scope.

To move information into or out of a given scope, use the setAttribute() or getAttribute() methods of the implicit object corresponding to that scope (pageContext, request, session, or application). For example, to place a string value tomcat.snake.net into request scope as an attribute named myhost, use the request object:

```
request.setAttribute ("myhost", "tomcat.snake.net");
```

setAttribute() stores the value as an Object. To retrieve the value later, fetch it by name using getAttribute() and then coerce it back to string form:

```
Object obj;
String host;
obj = request.getAttribute ("myhost");
host = obj.toString ();
```

When used with the pageContext object, setAttribute() and getAttribute() default to page context. Alternatively, they can be invoked with an additional parameter of PAGE_SCOPE, REQUEST_SCOPE, SESSION_SCOPE, or APPLICATION_SCOPE to specify a scope level explicitly. The following statements have the same effect as those just shown:

```
pageContext.setAttribute ("myhost", "tomcat.snake.net",
                          pageContext.REQUEST_SCOPE);
obj = pageContext.getAttribute ("myhost", pageContext.REQUEST_SCOPE);
host = obj.toString ();
```

References

This appendix lists some references that you should find helpful if you want more information about topics discussed in this book.

MySQL Resources

Michael Widenius, David Axmark and MySQL AB. *MySQL Reference Manual.* O'Reilly & Associates.

Paul DuBois. *MySQL.* New Riders.

A FAQ for MySQL is available at *http://www.bitbybit.dk/mysqlfaq/.* This site also provides a useful index of changes and updates to MySQL, which is helpful for determining whether a feature you're trying to use is present in your version.

Perl Resources

Alligator Descartes and Tim Bunce. *Programming the Perl DBI.* O'Reilly & Associates.

Lincoln D. Stein. *Official Guide to Programming with CGI.pm.* Wiley Computer Publishing.

Paul DuBois. *MySQL and Perl for the Web.* New Riders.

Geoffrey Young, Paul Lindner, and Randy Kobes. *mod_perl Developer's Cookbook.* Sams Publishing.

Additional DBI and CGI.pm documentation is available from the command line:

```
% perldoc DBI
% perldoc DBI::FAQ
% perldoc DBD::mysql
% perldoc CGI.pm
```

Or online:

http://dbi.perl.org/
http://stein.cshl.org/WWW/software/CGI/

PHP Resources

The primary PHP web site is *http://www.php.net/*, which provides access to PHP distributions and documentation. The site for PEAR, the PHP Extension and Add-on Repository, is *http://pear.php.net/*. PEAR includes a database abstraction module.

Python Resources

The primary Python web site is *http://www.python.org/*, which provides access to Python distributions and documentation.

General documentation for the DB-API database access interface is available at *http://www.python.org/topics/database/*. Documentation for MySQLdb, the MySQL-specific DB-API driver, is at *http://sourceforge.net/projects/mysql-python/*.

The Vaults of Parnassus serves as a general repository for Python source code: *http://www.vex.net/~x/parnassus/*.

David M. Beazley. *Python Essential Reference.* New Riders.

Java Resources

Sun's Java site provides access to documentation (including the specifications) for JDBC, servlets, JSP, and the JSP Standard Tag Library:

- JDBC general information: *http://java.sun.com/products/jdbc/index.html*
- JDBC documentation: *http://java.sun.com/j2se/1.3/docs/guide/jdbc/index.html*
- Java servlets: *http://java.sun.com/products/servlet/*
- JavaServer Pages: *http://java.sun.com/products/jsp/*
- JSP Standard Tag Library: *http://java.sun.com/products/jsp/jstl/*

George Reese. *Database Programming with JDBC and Java.* O'Reilly & Associates.

David Flanagan. *Java Examples in a Nutshell.* O'Reilly & Associates.

Hans Bergsten. *JavaServer Pages.* O'Reilly & Associates.

David Harms. *JSP, Servlets, and MySQL.* M & T Books.

Simon Brown, et al. *Professional JSP.* Wrox Press.

Shawn Bayern. *JSTL in Action.* Manning Publications.

Apache Resources

Wainwright, Peter. *Professional Apache.* Wrox Press.

Other Resources

Chuck Musciano and Bill Kennedy. *HTML & XHTML: The Definitive Guide.* O'Reilly & Associates.

Erik T. Ray. *Learning XML.* O'Reilly & Associates.

Jeffrey E. F. Friedl. *Mastering Regular Expressions.* O'Reilly & Associates.

Index

Symbols

& (parameter separator, URLs to JSP
   pages), 855
  (non-breaking space), 789
-> (prompt), 15
"> (prompt), 17
* (wildcard), 205, 580
   for column selection, 151
   in Boolean searches, 225
@ (warning-suppression operator), 69
@ARGV array, 134
^ (caret), 204, 208
:= (SQL variables, assignment of values), 20
{m,n} (wildcard), 205
{n} (wildcard), 205
$ (dollar sign), 204, 208
${...} (expression enclosers, JSTL tags), 758
= (equals), and SQL pattern matching, 202
=== (triple-equals) operator (PHP), 117, 128
!= (does not equal), and SQL pattern
   matching, 202
#! (pathname indicator), 43, 742, 744
<?php and ?> tags, 79
( ) (parentheses), 207
% (percent sign), 202
   time-formatting strings, 232, 233
% (format specifier, Python), 105
. (period), 204
./ (current directory path), 43
+ (wildcard), 205
? (placeholder), 102
" (double quotes), 194
' (single quotes), 194

; (semicolon), 14, 23
\ (backslash), 194, 208, 449, 453
\b (backspace), 449
\c (cancel query command), 17
\G (query terminator for vertical output), 37
\g (statement terminator), 14
\# (force auto-completion), 20
\N (NULL value sequence), 449, 513
\n (linefeed or new line), 29, 449
\P (paging toggle), 29
\r (carriage return), 449
\s (status command), 16
\t (tab), 449
\0 (ASCII NUL characters), 449
[ ] (multiple value form fields, PHP), 851
[...] (square brackets), pattern matching
   with, 204
_ (underscore), 202
   pattern matching with, 417

Numbers

0E0 (zero value, scientific notation), 88

A

absolute pathnames, 450
"access denied" message, 6
ad counters, using sequences for, 540
ADD clause, 380
   FIRST and AFTER specifiers, 380
add_element.py, 427
AFTER, 380
ages, calculating in years, 259–262
   in months, 262

We'd like to hear your suggestions for improving our indexes. Send email to *index@oreilly.com*.

aggregate functions, 336
   correlation coefficients, calculating, 686
   GROUP BY, used with, 350
   linear regressions, calculating, 686
   NULL values and, 354
   per-group descriptive statistics,
      calculation using, 679
   statistical data, calculation using, 676
   WHERE clauses and, 346
aliases, 585
   for columns in sorting operations, 295
   for expressions
      used as sorting criteria, 299
   for expressions{aliases
      expressions], 360
   for self-joins, 620
   for tables, 582
ALL keyword, 641
ALTER IGNORE TABLE statement, 391
ALTER TABLE statement, 214, 378–397
   columns
      adding, 380
      AUTO_INCREMENT type,
         adding, 561
      AUTO_INCREMENT type,
         resequencing, 557
      default values, changing, 384
      dropping, 380
      moving, 380
      renaming, 381
      type, reassigning, 381
   default value attributes and, 383
   indexes, 388–392
      adding, 388
      dropping, 389
   NULL value attributes and, 383
   sequence counter, resetting, 557
   sequence range, extension using, 555
   sequencing behavior, changing with, 548
   using table normalization, 392–397
   tables
      transaction supporting types.
         converting to, 723
   tables, renaming, 387
   TYPE clauses, 385
alternations, 204, 207
AND operator in FULLTEXT searches, 225
anniversary dates, calculating, 263
Apache, 738
   API extension modules for, 742
   CustomLog directive, 888

directory structure, 743
error log, 745
logging to MySQL, 885–892
   logfiles, analyzing, 889
   set up, 885
PHP, configuring for, 745
references, 960
suEXEC mechanism, 746
web scripts
   Perl-based, 746–749
   PHP-based, 750
   Python-based, 751
web scripts, directory location for, 744
web scripts, running on, 743–752
Apache Software Group, web sites, 928
Apache::Session module, 896, 897
   obtaining, 897
APIs (application programming
      interfaces), 48–52
   Apache, extension modules for, 742
   C API, 49
   communications protocols and, 48
   connection, database selection,
      disconnection, 53–65
      Java, using, 61–65
      Perl, using, 54–56
      PHP, using, 57–59
      Python, using, 59–61
   database server independence, designing
      for, 118
   datafile columns, extraction and
      rearranging of, 475–478
   datafile formats, converting, 473
   dependencies, 52
   duplicates, detecting
      programmatically, 708
   encoding special characters
      using, 765–769
      Java, 768
      Perl, 766
      PHP, 767
      Python, 768
   event counts, retrieval using, 574
   export programs, writing, 468–473
   HTML-encoding methods, 762
   input extraction conventions, 847–855
   MySQL drivers and, 49
   NOT IN( ) subselects, simulating in
      programs, 638
   pattern matching and SQL pattern
      characters, 417

programmatic multiple table deletes, 661
related table updates, performing
    programmatically, 648
reports, generating, 375
rollbacks and exception handling, 727
sequence values, accessing with, 551
session management, 894
SHOW COLUMNS, using to get table
    structure information, 416
software, obtaining, 926–929
sort operations, using for, 295
statement terminators, absence of, 87
subselect queries, simulating in
    programs, 636
summary calculations using, 373
table information, methods of
    getting, 424
transactions
    abstractions, mapping onto SQL, 728
    program control structures, 727
    in programs, 725–728
    support, 726
unattached records, deleting
    programmatically, 669
URL-encoding methods, 762
web script generation using, 741
web scripts, pathname acquisition, 818
application programming interfaces (see
    APIs)
application/octet-stream content type,
    forcing download with, 812
applications, customizing for MySQL
    versions, 437
arithmetic operators, JSTL, 758
AS clause, 156, 585
ASC sort order, 293
ASCII charts, 682
atomic operations as alternative to
    transactions, 736
auto-commit mode, suspending, 724
auto-completion, 19
    database and table names, 19
AUTOEXEC.BAT, PATH environment
    variable, setting, 13
AUTO_INCREMENT columns, 541–558
    adding to existing tables, 561
    creating multiple sequences
        using, 562–567
    duplicate values, impact on, 543
    extending sequence range, 555
    generating multiple sequences using, 539

hit logs, using in, 884
integer types requirement, 544
item tracking using, 576
multi-column indexes, setting up, 565
multiple sequence tables,
    managing, 567–569
NULL values and, 545
record deletions, impact on, 546
reinitializing the sequence, 544
resequencing, advisability, 554
sequence columns, setting up, 541–542
sequence values, generating in, 542–544
sequencing behavior, changing, 548
starting value, setting, 559
table types and, 546
UNSIGNED typing, 544
using values to relate tables, 569–572
AVG( ), 341
    strings, inapplicability to, 342

B

backquoting database, table, and column
    names, 114
backslash (\), 194, 208
"Bad command or invalid filename"
    error, 10
banner ads, serving from a
    database, 808–811
    caching control for cycling of ads, 810
banner.py, 809
bash, PATH environment variable,
    setting, 13
--batch option, 31
batting averages, calculating, 627
BDB tables, 386
    sequencing in, 548
BEGIN statement, 724
BETWEEN clause, 280
BINARY clause, 212
binary column types, 193
binary data, 193
    retrieving from MySQL, 806
    storing in MySQL, 799–806
        LOAD_FILE( ), using, 800
        scripts, using, 800
BINARY keyword, 307, 709
binary strings, 193
bind_param( ) (Perl), 103
bugs, MySQL's DELETE ... LIMIT
    statement, 719

C

C API, 49
    option files, support for, 142
calculated values, sorting by, 297
calculations, using mysql to evaluate, 41
calendar order, 310
cascaded deletes, 658
    LEFT JOINs, for deleting childless parent
        records, 660
case and sorting, 306
case sensitivity
    ENUM columns, 494
    hash lookups, Perl, 494
    HTML, 739
    MIN( ) and MAX( ), control of while
        using, 348
    pattern matching and, 211
    XML, 739
CAST( ), 307
Catalina, 938
cgi-bin directory, 743
    language neutrality, 744
cgi.escape( ) (Python), 768
CGI.pm
    default form initialization behavior, 869
    file upload parameter, 862
CHANGE keyword, 381
CHAR columns, conversion to VARCHAR
        types, 430
character columns, conversion from
        fixed-length to variable-length
        types, 430
checkboxes, 836
checkbox_group( ) (Perl), 837
check_enum_value( ), 493
check_set_value( ), 494
chmod command, 43
click to sort headings, query results
        tables, 874
clickable hyperlinks, generating from query
        results, 790–793
clicksort.php, 876
client library, 49
clients, 1, 439
    accounts, creating, 2
    APIs, 48–52
        capabilities, 50
    finding out who's connected, 439
    sequences, retrieving on, 549
        server-side retrieval, compared to, 553
    (see also mysql)
client-server architecture, 1

client-server protocol, 48
cmdline.java, 138
cmdline.pl, 134
    problems with, 136
cmdline.py, 137
code reuse, 73
column definitions
    files for ALTER TABLE statements, 382
    NULL and default value attributes, impact
        on, 383
column types, 193, 195
    AUTO_INCREMENT columns, integer
        types requirement, 544
    date and time, 228–289
        DATE, 229
        DATETIME, 229, 235
        functions used on, 237
        TIME, 229, 250
        TIMESTAMP, 230, 235
            first in record, 284
            records, creation and modification
                time, 283
columns
    adding to tables, 380
    aliases, 90
        as input columns in queries, 161
        column concatenation and, 157
        joins and, 583
        using in programs, 156
    BINARY type, case sensitivity, 217
    character conversion from fixed-length to
        variable-length types, 430
    combining to construct composite
        values, 157
    default values, 385
    displaying, 151
        with column name aliases, 153
        order, control of, 152
    dropping from tables, 380
    extraction, rearranging, 474
    indexes, numbering, 408
    lists, displaying using table
        information, 426
    LONGBLOB, 802
    MEDIUMBLOB, 802
    metadata, getting for, 419
    moving in tables, 380
    names, quoting in pattern strings, 417
    non-unique column names, handling in
        result sets, 583
    NULL values and empty fields,
        distinguishing, 513

renaming, 381
selection of all but a few, 431
specifying input order in data loads, 459
trailing spaces, preserving in string
    columns, 195
types
    case sensitivity of, 214
    changing, 381
    mapping to web page elements, 427
combine( ) (Perl), 473
"Command not found" error, 10
command-line options (see options)
comma-separated values file format (see CSV)
COMMIT statement, 724
communications protocols and APIs, 48
comparison operators
    for NULL values, 169
        in records, 166
    JSTL, 758
    strings, using on, 196
component extraction functions, using for
    decomposing dates and times, 236
computed summaries, 335
    (see also summaries)
CONCAT( ), 157, 199, 242, 269
    MAX-CONCAT trick, 347
    single strings, representing multiple
        column values as, 566
configuration variables, for specifying library
    file locations, 75
connect( ) (Java), implementing from library
    file, 82
connect( ) (Perl), 55–56
    arguments, 55
connect( ) (PHP MySQL_Access class), 124
connect( ) (Python), 60
connection parameters, 6
    obtaining, 132–147
        from option files, 141–147
        Java, 138–141, 146
        Perl, 134–136, 142
        PHP, 136, 144
        Python, 137–138
    option files, specifying with, 7
connection parameters, obtaining
    Python
        from option files, 145
Connect.java, 62
connect.php
    testing, 58
connect.pl, 54

connect.py, 60
content-type headers, 740
<Context> elements, 944
cookbook_connect( ) (PHP), 120
Cookbook_DB_Access class (PHP), 119, 123
cookies, 893
    PERLSESSID, 899
correlation coefficients, calculating, 686–688
COUNT(*)
    avoiding errors using, 608
COUNT( ), 337
    COUNT(*) and COUNT(expr), 338
    IF( ) and, 339
    NULL values and, 356
    speed on different table types, 337
    WHERE clauses and, 337
count( ) PHP
    column counts and, 95
COUNT(DISTINCT), 342
    NULLs, including in a count, 343
counting summaries, 335, 337
    (see also summaries)
count_rows.sh, 46
<c:out> tag (JSTL), 768
CREATE DATABASE statement, 4
CREATE INDEX statement, 390
CREATE TABLE ... SELECT statement, 184
CREATE TABLE statement, 4, 189
    AUTO_INCREMENT columns,
        including, 542
    multi-column PRIMARY KEYs, creating
        tables with, 566
    specifying transactional type, 723
    table structure, getting with, 420
CREATE TEMPORARY TABLE
    statement, 187, 191
credit card numbers, pattern for
    matching, 486
csh
    PATH environment variable, setting, 13
CSV (comma-separated values) file
    format, 446, 454
CSV (comma-separated values) format,
    converting output to, 32
cumulative sums, finding using
    self-joins, 629–633
CURDATE( ), 186, 234, 235, 271
, 768
current date or time, determining, 234
cursors
    MySQL and, 95

CURTIME( ), 234
CustomLog directives, 885, 888
cut utility, 461
cvt_date.pl, 504
cvt_file.pl, 473
    options, 473
cycles, generating, 575
Cygwin (Cygnus tools for Windows), 47

D

data
    exporting and importing (see data
        transfers)
data source name (see DSN)
data transfers, 444–538
    between MySQL and Microsoft
        Access, 526
    data content issues, 445
    databases, copying between servers, 467
    date values, converting year format from
        two-digit to four-digit, 498
    dates, exportation in new format, Perl
        script for, 508–510
    exporting files with NULL values from
        MySQL, 515
    FileMaker Pro and MySQL,
        between, 530–532
    format conversion issues, 445
    importing files with NULLs into
        MySQL, 513
    LOAD DATA (see LOAD DATA
        statement)
    Microsoft Excel and MySQL,
        between, 527–530
    mysql, redirection of output, 463
    mysqlimport, 448
    NULLs, 446
    query results, exporting from
        MySQL, 461
    recurring problems, 445
    shell command invocation, 448
    tables, copying between servers, 467
    tables, exporting to files, 464
    temporary tables, via, 511–513
    validation, 492–495
    XML, exporting query results
        as, 532–534
    (see also datafiles)
data types, case sensitivity, 214
DATABASE( ), 16
database name qualifiers, 582

database-independent architecture, 118
databases
    copying to another server, 467
    current database, determining, 438
    design guidelines, 392
    listing all on a server, 433
    multi-database table joins, 582
    selecting, 15
    SQL format, exporting in, 465
    storing images on, pros and cons, 801
    tables, listing all, 433
    testing for existence of, 435
datafiles
    columns, extracting and rearranging, 474
    formats, 446
        converting, 473
    hex dump programs, checking with, 458
    line-ending sequences, 447
    loading (see LOAD DATA statement)
    NULLs, checking representation of, 479
    NULLs, representing in, 513
    structural information, 445
    tab-delimited file format,
        linefeed-terminated, 447
    table structure, determining
        from, 516–520
    validating, 478–516
DATE column type, 229
date formats and pattern matching, 487
DATE_ADD( ), 252, 263, 279
date-and-time values
    conversion to seconds, 247
    generation from a date and time, 243
DATE_FORMAT( ), 232, 233, 241, 269, 508
    TIMESTAMP values, for
        reformatting, 288
    using for portions of dates, 235
date-related functions, 237–239
dates
    adding time to, 252–255
    anniversary dates, calculating, 263
    calculated, for setting record
        lifetimes, 282
    calculating intervals between, 255–258
        Perl, using, 256
    calculating one from another using
        substring replacement, 268
    comparison, 280
    conversion to days, 246
    date conversion utilities, writing, 502
    date values, combining with time
        values, 243

decomposing, 235–241
  component-extraction functions,
    using, 236–239
  formatting functions, using, 235
  string functions, using, 239
determining for current week days, 271
finding for weekdays of other weeks, 272
  Perl, using, 273
finding the day of the week for, 270
first and last days of month,
    determining, 265–267
intervals, calculating in years, 259–262
  in months, 262
intervals vs. spans, 256
ISO 8601 standard, 231
ISO dates, generating from non-ISO
    dates, 258
leap years, detection of, 501
numbers, treating as, 277
retrieving in non-ISO format, 430
shifting by a given amount, 263–264
sorting by, 308
SQL statement, conversion
    using, 508–510
synthesizing, 241–243
  component-extraction functions,
    using, 242
  formatting functions, using, 241
temporary tables, format conversion
    using, 511–513
time zone adjustments, 264
validity checking on subparts, 499
with missing components, conversion to
    ISO format, 507
written month to numeric month format,
    conversion from, 505
year format, conversion from two-digit to
    four-digit, 498
DATE_SUB( ), 252, 263, 281
DATETIME column type, 229, 235
  vs. TIMESTAMP for recording record
    modification time, 286
DATETIME values, grouping in managable
    categories, 371
DAYNAME( ), 238, 270, 271, 371
DAYOFMONTH( ), 237, 265, 268
DAYOFWEEK( ), 238, 271, 312, 370
DAYOFYEAR( ), 237, 276
  "on this day" problems, and, 283
  sorting issues, 311
days, conversion to dates, 246
days_in_month( ), 501

DBD::mysql module, 54
DBI module (Perl), 54, 55
  error checking, attributes for, 66
DBI:mysql:options module, 55
DBTools, 528
  datafiles, determining table structure
    using, 519
  importation, Microsoft Accesss tables to
    MySQL, 527
  web site, 929
default values
  ALTER TABLE and, 384
  columns, 385
defined( ) (Perl), 115
definition lists, web scripting query results
    as, 779
  (see also lists)
DELETE ... LIMIT, 717
  bug affecting some MySQL versions, 719
  for removal of duplicate records from
    tables, 717
DELETE statement, 657
  multiple-table syntax, 657
  rows, finding the number affected, 400
  unattached records, deleting, 668
delete_dups( ), 717
deleting related rows in multiple tables, 655
  by replacing tables, 660
  cascaded deletes, 658
  mysql, using, 664
  programmatic deletion, 661
DESC sort order, 293, 294
DictCursor cursor type (Python), 96
disconnect( ) (PHP MySQL_Access
    class), 126
display_image.pl, 807
displayResultSet( ) (Java), 411, 413
DISTINCT, 165, 342
  and expressions, 344
do( ) (Perl), 88
  placeholders, binding values to, 103
  rows affected by a query, counting, 400
doGet( ) (Java), 931
doPost( ) (Java), 931
DOS command-line environment, limitations
    of, 47
double quotes ("), 194
download.php, 812
DriverManager.getConnection( ) (Java), 63
DROP clause, 380
DROP DATABASE statement, immunity to
    ROLLBACK, 725

DROP INDEX statement, 390
DSN (data source name), 55
   MySQL, format for, 55
duplicate records, 699–719
  case sensitivity and, 709
  identifying
    joining a summary to the original
      table, 708
  identifying and counting, 705–709
  identifying specific records, 707
  methods of handling, 699
  preventing, 701
    at record-creation time, 703–705
    AUTO_INCREMENT columns for
      PRIMARY KEYs, 702
    bulk-load operations, during, 705
    INSERT IGNORE statement, 703
    REPLACE statement, 703
  queries, detecting with, 706
  queries that result in none, 709
  self-joins, eliminating from, 711–713
  specific instances, removal using
    LIMIT, 716–719
  tables, eliminating from, 713
    by adding an index, 715
    table replacement, using, 714

E

ELT( ), 277
email addresses, links to,
    generating, 791–793
email addressing, pattern matching for, 491
email damage to datafiles, 458
embedded queries
  comparisons including NULL, 169
empty_to_null.pl, 513
encapsulation, 73
  security advantages, 74
ENCLOSED BY subclause, 453
encoding of column values, 805
end_form( ) (Perl), 818
ENUM columns
  case sensitivity, 494
  column definitions, adding elements
    to, 427
  definitions, obtaining, 422
  hashes, for testing legality of data, 493
  input values, validating, 492
  member lists, obtaining, 422
  radio buttons, using for, 814
  renaming, column definition issues, 381

ENUM values, treatment as strings, 200
environment variables, 12
  for specifying library file locations, 75
  PATH, 11
  PERL5LIB, 78
  PYTHONPATH, 81
  sys.path (Python), 81
error( ) (PHP MySQL_Access class), 126
error checking, 65–73
  importance of, 87
  Java API, using, 71–73
  MySQL query log, 66
  Perl API, using, 66–68
  PHP API, using, 69
  post-connection check, 67
  Python API, using, 70
  testing of, 65
error handling, PHP MySQL_Access
    class, 126
Error.java, 71
escape( ) (Perl), 766
escape sequences, 193–195, 449
ESCAPED BY subclause, 453
escapeHTML( ) (Perl), 766
escaping of characters, parameter binding
    operations and, 102
etEnumOrSetValues( ) (Java), 840
eval blocks, 68
events, counting, 572
  client specific value, retrieving, 574
except blocks (Python), 59
execute( ) (Java), 99
execute( ) (Perl)
  placeholders, binding values to, 103
  rows affected by a query, counting, 400
--execute option, 27
executeQuery( ) (Java), 97, 106
executeUpdate( ) (Java), 97, 106
  rows affected by a query, counting, 401
exporting data (see data transfers)
expressions
  results, grouping by, 359
  results, sorting by, 297
  using aliases in sort operations, 299
EXTRACT( ), 238
  applied to CURDATE( ) or NOW( ), 239

F

fetchall( ) (Python), 96
fetchrow_array( ) (Perl), 89
fetchrow_arrayref( ) (Perl), 89
fetchrow_hashref( ) (Perl), 90

field delimiters, 446
FIELDS clause, 452
    format characters, specification in hex notation, 453
    subclauses, 453
FieldStorage( ) (Python), 852
FILE privilege, 450
file uploads, 860
    processing, 859–867
FileMaker Pro
    Ctrl-K, mapping of carriage returns, linefeeds to, 530
    merge files, 531
    merge format, 447
    MySQL, data exchange with, 530–532
filename extensions
    indication of processor type, using, 744
filename extensions in Windows, 7
files, storing queries in, 23
filesystems, storing images on, 801
finish( ) (Perl), 89
FIRST, 380
floating-point numbers, pattern for matching, 485
FLOOR( ), 245, 362
foreign keys, 658
<form> tags, 817
    file uploads, enabling, 860
format specifier, Python (%), 105
formatting functions, using to decompose dates and times, 235
formatting of result sets for display, 410–414
forms, 817–845
    database records, loading to, 841–845
        column values, using for element defaults, 841
        hidden unique value fields, inclusion of, 842
    file uploads, enabling, 860
    input
        collecting, 845–855
        POST, 847
        queries, constructing from, 857–859
        validating, 855
        via GET, 847
    lists, HTML encoding of content, 835
    malicious input, handling, 856
    multiple-pick elements, creating from database content, 836–841
    single-pick elements, creating from database content, 820–835

free_result( ) (PHP MySQL_Access class), 128
frequency distributions, 681
    charting in MySQL, 682
    forcing inclusion of categories outside the range, 682
    generating, 681–683
frequency distributions, generating uses for, 682
FROM_DAYS( ), 246, 254, 279
from_excel.pl, 528
FROM_UNIXTIME( ), 248, 255
FTP transfers, line-terminator translation, 458
full joins, 579
    results, potential size of, 579
FULLTEXT indexes, 389
FULLTEXT searches, 218–227
    AND operator, 225
    IN BOOLEAN MODE, 225
    index
        adding, 219
        minimum word length, 223
    MATCH( ), 220
    phrase searches, 226
    search words, requiring or excluding, 224
    vs. SQL pattern matching, 227
    SQL pattern matching, combining with, 227
fully qualified names for databases, 583
fully qualified table references, 15, 580
functions
    Python vs. PHP, 831

G

G (statement terminator), 415
GB (games-behind) value, 599
    joins, for calculating values, 602–605
GET requests, 847
getColumnCount( ) (Java), 408
getColumnDisplaySize( ) (Java), 411
getEnumOrSetValues( ) (Java), 833
getLastInsertID( ) (Java), 552
getMetaData( ) (Java), 408
getObject( ) (Java), 99
getopt( ) (Python), 137
Getopt class (Java), 138
GetOptions( ) (Perl)
    -p support, peculiarities of, 136
Getopt::Long module, 135

get_param_val( ) (PHP), 850, 851
getResultSet( ) (Java), 98
get_self_path( ) (PHP), 819
get_table_handlers( ) (Perl), 442
get_upload_info( ) (PHP), 865
GRANT statement, 2
GROUP BY clause
    duplicates, preventing in query results
        with, 710
    per-group descriptive statistics,
        application to, 679
GROUP BY clauses, 350, 365
    errors associated with, 352
    expressions, using with, 359
    range values, 361
    summaries for temporal values and, 368
groups, 8
guess_table.pl, 516–519

H

Harness.java, 84
harness.php, 79
harness.pl, 77
harness.py, 81
hash keys, 494
hashes
    caching of checked lookup values, using
        for, 497
    ENUM values, for testing legality of, 493
    hash key collisions, 585
    lookup tables, creation from, 496
HAVING clauses, 357
    COUNT( ), using with, 358
headers, 740
here-documents, 45
hex dump programs, datafile checking
        with, 458
history files, 40
hit counters, 878–883
    counting multiple pages, 879
    methods for writing, 879
    Perl, 881
    PHP, 882
hit logging, 883
    client and host information, tracking, 883
    Java, 884
host, default values, 2
HOUR( ), 237, 251

HTML (Hypertext Markup Language), 740
    form lists, encoding of, 835
    query results, outputting to, 770–813
    special characters, encoding for
        display, 762–764
    (see also web pages)
--html option, 33
htmlspecialchars( ) (PHP), 70, 767
httpdlog.pl, 886
hyperlinks, generating from query
        results, 790–793

I

ID values, joining to descriptive information
        in another table, 654
id values, multiple columns as single strings,
        representing, 567
IF( ), 339
IFNULL( ), 608
IGNORE clause, 456
IGNORE keyword, 391
IGNORE n LINES clause, 459
images
    database vs. filesystem storage, 801
    filename extensions for Content-Type
        headers, 806
    retrieving from MySQL, 806
    storing in MySQL, 799–806
        LOAD_FILE( ), using, 800
        scripts, using, 800
<img> tags, 806
    for script references instead of
        images, 806
import java.sql.* statement, 63
importing data (see data transfers)
In, 928
IN( ) subselects, 635
    mysql, simulating with two
        instances, 638
IN BOOLEAN MODE searches, 225
@INC array@ atINC], 77
include files, handling of PHP code, 79
indexes, 388–392
    adding to tables, 388
    AUTO_INCREMENT columns, with
        more than one, 565
    dropping from tables, 389
    joins and, 591
    multi-column, setting up, 565

ini_set( ) (PHP), 907
InnoDB tables, 386
    sequencing in, 548
input
    copy and paste as source, 27
<input> element for file uploads, 860
INSERT IGNORE statement
    duplicates, preventing with, 704
INSERT INTO ... SELECT statement, 182
INSERT INTO ... SELECT statement
    inserting records in a table that include
        values from another, 645
INSERT query
    rows, finding the number affected, 400
INSERT statement, 4
insert_id( ) (Python), 552
insertid attribute (Perl), 551
integer types
    AUTO_INCREMENT columns and, 544
    value ranges, 545
interpret_option( ) (Perl), 471
IS NOT NULL, 166
IS NULL, 166
is_24hr_time( ), 501
ISAM tables, 385
    MySQL versioning and, 548
    rollback support, lack of, 723
    sequencing in, 548
is_ampm_time( ), 502
ISNULL( ), 685
ISO 8601 standard (dates), 231
isoize_date.pl, 503
isset( ) (PHP), 116
issue_query( ) (PHP MySQL_Access
        class), 127
    parameter binding with, 130
is_valid_date( ), 500, 507
item-tracking via cyclic sequences, 576

J

Jakarta ORO library, 205
Jasper, 938
Java
    applications, 931
    Class.for.Name( ), Java implementation
        issues, 64
    client-server connectivity, 49
    column indexes, numbering, 408
    connection, database selection,
        disconnection, 61–65

connection parameters,
        obtaining, 138–141
    from option files, 146
encoding special characters using, 768
error handling, 61, 71–73
event counts, retrieval using, 574
form elements, generation from column
        metadata, 832
hit logging, 884
JSP scripts, 742
library files, 82
multi-pick list elements, creating, 840
NULL values
    explicit checking, 117
    representing in, 117
pattern matching libraries, 205
programs running in a web
        environment, 752–762
queries, 97–100
    column values, retrieving, 98
    JDBC objects, closure of, 100
    reusable, writing, 106
query results, web scripting
    definition lists, 780
    email addresses, outputting as, 793
    hyperlinks, outputting as, 790
    ordered lists, outputting as, 774
    paragraph text, displaying as, 772
    tables, displaying, 786
    unordered lists, 779
records changed by a query,
        counting, 401
references, 959
result set metadata, obtaining, 408–409
SDK (software development kit),
        installing, 62
sequence values, accessing with, 552
server information, acquisition using, 436
servlet containers (servlet engines), 930
servlets, 742, 930–933
    contexts, 931
    vs. PHP, 932
session management
    JSP session application, 916
    methods, 916
table information, methods of
        obtaining, 424
transactions, 732
web input extraction conventions, 854
web scripts in the JSP specification, 741
web scripts, request path, 820
web site, 928

Java Database Connectivity (see JDBC)
JDBC (Java Database Connectivity), 49,
    61–65
    AUTO_INCREMENT values, obtaining
        via, 552
    drivers
        installing, 755
        Tomcat servers, making available
            to, 919
    methods, exceptions thrown by, 71
    MySQL driver, lack of option
        support, 146
    null values and, 117
    placeholder support, 106
    queries, 97–100
        reusable, writing, 106
    sessions in MySQL, saving via, 918
    Tomcat servers
        drivers, directory location on, 919
        drivers, installing on, 755
        MySQL, drivers for, 753
    transactions, 732
    Version 2, scrollable result set, 101
jdbc_test.jsp, 755
joins, 348, 578–639
    filling holes in a list, 609–613
    full joins, 579
        results, potential size of, 579
    indexes and, 591
    LEFT JOINs, 591–595
    minimum or maximum values per group,
        finding, 596
    NATURAL LEFT JOINs, 595
    NATURAL RIGHT JOINs, 595
    query output order, controlling
        with, 633–634
    related table updates, using for, 647
    result sets and aliases, 583
    RIGHT JOINs, 595
    self-joins (see self-joins)
    subselects, rewriting as, 635–639
        IN( ) subselects, 635
    summaries via, 590
    between tables in different databases, 582
    team standings, calculation
        using, 602–605
    three-way joins, 614–619
        many-to-many relationships, 614–619
        one-to-many relationships, 618
    USING and, 595

using to create lookup tables from
    descriptive labels, 650–655
WHERE clauses and, 579
    using to match rows in two tables, 586
JSP (JavaServer Pages), 752–762, 930–957
    action elements, 953
    custom actions, 935
    directives, 952
    elements of, 950–957
    form elements, generation with
        metadata, 832
    hit logging, 884
    implicit objects, 956
    JDBC drivers, installation for, 755
    JSP requests, 934
    JSTL distribution, installing for, 756
    JSTL, writing with, 757–761
    levels of scope, 956
    vs. Microsoft's Active Server Pages
        (ASP), 934
    multi-pick list elements, creating, 840
    MySQL scripts, using for, 761
    MySQL scripts, writing with, 761
    placeholder and quoting techniques, 858
    pop-up menus, 824
    query results, displaying
        as definition lists, 780
        as hyperlinks, 790, 793
        as lists, 774
        as paragraphs, 772
        as tables, 786
        as unmarked lists, 782
        as unordered lists, 779
    radio buttons, displaying, 823
    request path, 820
    scripting elements, 951
    scripts, functioning of, 742
    session application example, 916
    session support, 916
    tag libraries, using, 954–955
    Tomcat servers and, 738, 752
    Tomcat session interface, 915
    vs. servlets, 933–937
    web input extraction conventions, 854
    web page generation, 741
    XML and, 738
JSTL (JSP Standard Tag Library), 753, 936
    comparison, arithmetic, and logical
        operators, 758
    core tags, 758

database tags, 759
distribution, getting and installing, 756
JAR and TLD files, directory locations for, 756
JSP, installing for, 756
JSP pages, writing with, 757–761
MySQL scripts, using for, 761
TLD files, 756

K

key values in hash tables
for checked data, 497
for validation checking, 494
keys
multiple columns, comprising, 563, 566
ksh
PATH environment variable, setting, 13

L

LAST_INSERT_ID( ), 550
client-specific count value, retrieving with, 574
connection-specific basis for value, 551
leap year calculations, 274
conditions for determining, 274
four-digit year values and, 275
month-length calculations, using for, 276
Perl, using, 277
testing a year for leap year, 274
year-length calculations using, 276
LEFT( ), 198
LEFT JOINs, 591–595
cascaded deletes and childless parent records, 660
consistency checks, using for, 596
identifying unattached records, 665
NOT IN( ) subselects, using in place of, 636
ON clauses and, 593
related table updates, using for, 647
in self-joins, 624
unattached records, finding and removing from related tables, 665–671
WHERE clauses and, 594
li( ) (Perl), 777
library files, 51
connection, error checking, 74
installation location, 75
ownership and access issues, 74
security advantages of, 74
writing, 73–84

LIKE clauses, 417
database existence, testing for with, 435
tables, testing for existence using, 434
LIKE operators, 202
LIMIT clause, 172, 175, 367, 642
appropriate values, choosing, 177–179
duplicate records, using to remove, 716–719
LIMIT values, calculating from expressions, 179
sorting of results, 180
line terminators, different operating systems, 455
linear regressions, calculating, 686–688
line-ending sequences, 447
LINES clause, 452
format characters, specification in hex notation, 453
LINES TERMINATED BY clause, 455, 458
links
using to sort query results in a web page, 874
Linux
Tomcat servers, starting and stopping, 941
lists, 773
web scripting query results as, 773–784
definition lists, 779–782
nested lists, 782–784
ordered lists, 773–778
unmarked lists, 782
unordered lists, 777
LOAD DATA statement, 448–461
CSV files, importing, 454
datafile, contents, checking, 458
datafile location, specifying, 450–452
default file format for, 447
duplicate index values, handling, 456
email damage to datafiles, 458
end of process messages, interpreting, 456
error warning
diagnostic utility for, 520–526
error warnings, 520
escaped characters, handling, 453
file format, specifying, 452
FTP transfers, data load errors caused by, 458
IGNORE n LINES clause, 459
important limitations, 457
LINES TERMINATED BY clause, 455

LOAD DATA statement (*continued*)
  LOCAL keyword, 450
    absolute and relative pathnames, 451
  NULLs, representation by, 513
  quoted values, handling, 453
  reading files from different operating
    systems, 455
  skipping datafile columns, 460
  specifying column input order, 459
  (see also data transfers)
load_diag.pl, 521–526
  limitations, 524
  logging on MySQL logging enabled
    servers, 522
  options to, 524
LOAD_FILE( ), 800
localtime( ) (Perl), 264
LOCATE( ), 201
  case sensitivity, 201
LOCK statement, 723
locking
  transactions, as alternative to, 733
logfiles
  analyzing, 889
  indexing of, 886
  purging and archiving, 891
LogFormat directives, 885
LogFormat field specifiers, 887
logging, 439
  of interactive sessions, 39
  of users, 439
  to server databases, 885–892
    logfiles, analyzing, 889
    set up, 885
LONGBLOB columns, 802
lookup tables
  caching of checked values in a hash, 497
  data storage space, saving with, 650–655
  hashes, constructing from, 496
  using for creation of new records, 645
LOWER( ), 212, 308
LPAD( ), 243
  canonizing dates to ISO standard, 258

M

Mac OS file line terminators, 455
magic_quotes_gpc setting, PHP, 850
make_checkbox_group( ) (Python), 838
make_date_list.pl, 612
make_dup_count_query( ) (Perl), 708
make_ordered_list( ) (PHP), 776

make_ordered_list( ) (Python), 776
make_popup_menu( ) (PHP), 829
make_popup_menu( ) (Python), 830
make_radio_group( ) (PHP), 828
make_scrolling_list( ) (PHP), 829
make_table_from_query( ), 788
many-to-many relationships, 614, 615
  tables, designing for, 617
map( ) (Perl), 116
master-detail lists and summaries,
    producing, 605–608
MATCH( ), 220
MAX( ), 339, 596
  case sensitivity, managing, 348
  legal arguments to, 367
  sequence values and, 550
MAX-CONCAT trick, 346, 354
mcb sample application, installation, 753
mcb/WEB-INF directory, 756
mean, calculation using aggregate
    functions, 676
median, calculating, 678–679
MEDIUMBLOB columns, 802
merge files, FileMaker Pro, 531
merge format, 447
metacharacters, 209
metadata, 398–443
  attribute names, array-based
    metadata, 402
  attributes, PHP, 405
  database dependence of, 399
  databases, listing, 433
  ENUM columns, validation of input data,
    using for, 492–495
  formatting of result sets, using
    for, 410–414
  getting table structure information
    SHOW COLUMNS statement,
      using, 414–418
  hash, conversion of legal ENUM members
    to, 493
  records, obtaining number affected by a
    query, 399
    using Java, 401
    using Perl, 400
    using PHP, 400
    using Python, 401
  result set information,
    obtaining, 401–409
    Java, using, 408–409
    Perl, using, 402–405

PHP, using, 405–406
Python, using, 407
SELECT... WHERE, getting with, 418
for servers, obtaining, 436
SET columns, validation of input data,
    using for, 492–495
table structure, getting
    using result set metadata, 418–421
table structure information, getting, 414
table structure information, using in
    SELECT queries, 431
tables
    structure information, uses for, 426
tables, listing, 433
Microsoft
  Access
    MySQL, data exchange with, 526
  Excel
    MySQL, data exchange with, 527–530
  Windows (see Windows)
MID( ), 198
MIN( ), 339
  case sensitivity, managing, 348
  legal arguments to, 367
MINUTE( ), 237, 251
missing values, counting, 684
MOD( ), 249, 313
mode, calculating, 677
MODIFY statement, 381
  explicit specification, NULLs and default
    values, 384
modularization, 73
monddccyy_to_iso.pl, 506
MONTH( ), 237
month-length calculations and leap
    years, 276
MONTHNAME( ), 237
months
  length determining, 267
months, first and last days,
    determining, 265–267
multi-column indexes, setting up, 565
multipage navigation indexes, generating
    from database content, 796–799
multiple-pick form elements, 836
  creating form database content, 836–841
  types, 836
my.cnf, 141
my.cnf file, 7

my.ini, 141
MyISAM tables, 385
  AUTO_INCREMENT columns and, 546
  initial value for new sequence columns,
    specifying, 562
  multi-column keys, 563
  rollback support, lack of, 723
  sequence features, 723
  sequencing in, 548
MyODBC, 526
my_print_defaults utility, 9
MySQL
  Apache servers, logging, 885–892
    logfiles, analyzing, 889
    set up, 885
  binary data, storing in, 799–806
    LOAD_FILE( ), using, 800
    retrieving from, 806
    scripts, using, 800
  client library, 49
  clients, 1
  column types, 195
  cursors and, 95
  date format, 231
  date year format, conversion criteria
    for, 498
  DELETE ... LIMIT bug, 719
  drivers and APIs, 49
  escape sequences, 193–195
  FileMaker Pro, data exchange
    with, 530–532
  images, storing in, 799–806
    LOAD_FILE( ), using, 800
    scripts, using, 800
  JDBC drivers, 753
  library files (see library files)
  localhost, 54
  Microsoft Access, data exchange
    with, 526
  Microsoft Excel, data exchange
    with, 527–530
  object-oriented interfaces, 118
  PHP object-oriented interfaces, 118–132
  producing interactive content on the Web,
    using for, 737
  prompts used in, 17
  query results, exporting, 461
  references, 958

MySQL (*continued*)
  scripts
    JSP and JSTL, writing with, 761
  servers, 1
    Telnet and, 50
  session information storage, using
      for, 893–923
    Perl interface, 896–902
    PHP interface, 902–914
    Tomcat server (Java), 915–923
  software, obtaining, 925–929
    source code and sample data, 925
  TIME values, 249
  user accounts, creating, 2
  versions
    customizing applications for, 437
    3.23.2 and ORDER BY clauses, 303
  web input processing, 814–892
  web site, 927
  XML documents, importing into, 535
mysql, 1–47
  auto-completion, 19
  "Bad command or invalid filename"
      error, 10
  batch mode, 23
  calculator, using as, 41
  "Command not found" error, 10
  command syntax, 16
  command-line options (see options)
  connection parameters, 6
    option files, specifying with, 7
  -e option, 463
  host, default values for, 2
  IN( ) subselects, simulating with two
      instances, 638
  logging interactive sessions, 39
  -N option, 463
  options (see options)
  PATH, 10
  queries, reading from other programs, 26
  query editor, 18
  redirection of output, 463
  related table updates, 649
  sessions
    queries reusing, 40
  shell scripts, invocation within, 42
  -ss option, 463
  starting and terminating, 5
  statement terminator (semicolon), 14
  unattached records, deletion using, 670

MySQL servers
  alternatives to transaction support, 723
  concurrency, 720
  integrity, 720
  monitoring, 440
    impact of monitoring, 441
  transactions (see transactions)
MySQL_Access class (PHP), 119, 122–132
  issue_query( )
    parameter binding with, 130
  methods, 124–132
    connect( ), 124
    disconnect( ), 126
    error( ), 126
    free_result( ), 128
    issue_query( ), 127
  prepare_query( ), 130
  sql_quote( ), 129
mysql_affected_rows( ) (PHP), 93
  rows affected by a query, counting, 400
mysqlc, line editing in Win95, 98, or Me, 19
mysql_connect( ), 58
mysqld, 1
mysql_data_seek( ) (PHP), 101
mysqldump, 26
  --all-databases option and grant table
      issues, 468
  databases, copying between servers, 467
  FILE privilege, requirement for, 464
  output format, controlling, 464
  output formatting options, 466
  piped to mysql, 467
  --tab option, 464
    without --tab option, 465
  table structure information, getting
      with, 414, 420
  tables, copying between servers, 467
  tables, exporting to files, 464
    tables, specifying, 464
mysql_errno( ), 69
mysql_error( ), 69
mysql_fetch_assoc( ) (PHP), 94
mysql_fetch_object( ) (PHP), 94
mysql_field_count( ) (PHP), 95
mysql_free_result( ) (PHP), 94
MySQLFront, 528
  datafiles, determining table structure
      using, 519
  importation of Microsoft Access tables
      into MySQL, 527

.mysql_history file, 40
mysqlimport, 448
    column input order, specifying, 460
    CSV files, importing, 455
    datafile location, specifying, 451
    dump files, inapplicability to, 467
    error warning
      diagnostic utility for, 520–526
    error warnings, 521
    escape values, specifying, 454
    file format, specifying, 452
    --ignore-lines option, 459
    --lines-terminated-by option, 455
    --local option, 451
    NULLs, representation by, 513
    quote values, specifying, 454
mysql_insert_id( ) (PHP), 552
mysql_insertid attribute (Perl), 551
mysql_pconnect( ), 58
MysqlPerl, 54
mysql_query( )
    result sets and, 93
mysql_query( ) (PHP), 93
mysql_select_db( ), 58
mysql_socket option, 56
mysql_to_excel.pl, 529
mysql_to_filemaker.pl, 530
mysql_to_text.pl, 469
    command-line options, 469
mysql_to_xml.pl, 532
mysql_uptime.bat, 46
mysql_uptime.sh, 43

N

name( ) (Perl), 472
navigation indexes, 793
    generating from database
      content, 793–799
      multipage indexes, 796–799
      single page indexes, 794–796
negation operators in queries, 163
negative integers, pattern for matching, 485
nested lists, web scripting query results
    as, 782
    (see also lists)
new( ) (Perl), 472
--no-auto-rehash, 20
None (Python), 117
non-string values, pattern matching to, 204

normalizing of tables, 392–397
NOT IN( ) subselects, 635
    programs, simulating in, 638
NOT LIKE operators, 202
NOT NULL clause and PRIMARY
    KEYs, 701
NOT REGEXP, 204
NOW( ), 234, 235
NUL, 449
NULL values
    aggregate functions and, 354
    ALTER TABLE and, 384
    AUTO_INCREMENT columns and, 545
    COUNT( ) and, 356
    COUNT(DISTINCT), inclusion by, 343
    counting for summaries, 684
    detection values or functions, 115
    embedded queries, handling in, 169
    file transfers, validating format for, 479
    Java, representation, 117
    mapping to higher values than
      non-NULLs, 305
    mapping to other values for display, 170
    mapping to zero, 600
    Perl, representing in, 115
    PHP, representing in, 116
    Python, representation in, 117
    queries and, 166–172
      inclusion in, 106–114
    representing in datafiles, 513
    sorting operations and, 304
    SQL pattern matching and, 203
    summaries and, 354
    UNIQUE indexes and, 702
numeric values, pattern matching of, 485

O

object-oriented MySQL interfaces, 118
    PHP, 118–132
    two-level architecture, 118
    vs. function-based scripts (PHP), 120
od program, 458
ODBC, 526
ON clauses, LEFT JOINs and, 593
one-to-many relationships, 614
one-to-one relationships, 614
operating systems, xxvii
    line-ending sequences, 455

option files
  C API support, 142
  connection parameters, obtaining
     from, 141–147
    Java, 146
    Perl, 142
    PHP, 144
    Python, 145
  format, 7
  groups, 8
  long form options, 8
  platform specific issues, 141
  securing, 9
  specifying connections using, 7
options
  -A (--no-auto-rehash), 20
  -B (--batch), 31
  command-line parameters, short or
     long, 134
  connection parameters
    option files, 7
  -e (--execute), 27
  -E (--vertical), 38
  -H (--html), 33
  -N (--skip-column-names, MySQL
     3.22.20), 35
  --pager, 28
  -s, 38
  short and long, 134
  --silent, 36
  \t and \T (--tee), 39
  -t (--table), 31
  -v, 38
  -X (--xml, MySQL 4.0), 34
ORDER BY clauses, 171, 292, 365
  case sensitivity, binary and non-binary
     strings, 306
  expressions and MySQL versions, 298
  (see also sorting)
ORDER BY RAND( ) clause, 689, 690
ordered lists, web scripting query results
    as, 773
  (see also lists)
output
  delimiters, selecting, 31
  format in non-interactive mode, 30
  format, setting, 31
  paging of, 28
  redirection, 29
  style, interactive vs. batch mode, 23
  verbosity of, controlling, 38
override argument (Perl), 843

P

p( ) (Perl), 771
p1|p2|p3 (matching any of listed
    patterns), 204
paged displays, 867
  links to each page of a query result, 873
  paging styles, 870
  presenting output in linked
    pages, 869–874
  previous and next page links, 870
page-generating packages, 741
PAGER, 28
paging output, 28
param( ) (Perl), 848
parameter binding operations and reserved
    characters, 102
parameters
  command-line and option file, mixing, 10
  connection, specifying, 6
parent-child relationship of keys and foreign
    keys, 658
parentheses ( ), 207
parentheses, for sorting SELECT results in
    UNIONs, 642
passwords
  securing, 9, 10
PATH environment variable, 11
  setting, 13
pattern matching, 201
  alternations, 204
  case sensitivity, controlling, 211
  case sensitivity, managing in, 215
  column names, escaping SQL pattern
    characters in, 417
  dates, 487–491
  email addresses, 491
  ENUM column input data, validation
    via, 493
  vs. FULLTEXT searches, 218
  literal metacharacters, 209
  non-string values, 204
  patterns, 485
    for numeric values, 485
  regular expressions, using, 203
  SET column input data, validation
    via, 493
  times, 487–491
  URLs, 491
  (see also SQL, pattern matching)
pattern metacharacters, matching
    literally, 209

PEAR (PHP Extension and Add-on
      Repository), 119
  archive, xxx
per-group descriptive statistics,
      calculating, 679
Perl
  @ARGV array, 134
  array-based metadata attribute
      names, 402
  attribute names for access of array-based
      metadata, 402
  attributes, enabling or disabling, 66
  calculating month lengths accounting for
      leap years, 277
  CGI.pm module, 738, 741
    input parameters, 848
    override argument to form
      initialization, 843
  checkboxes, creating, 837
  connect script, 54
  connection, database selection,
      disconnection, 54–56
    error handling, 56
  connection parameters,
      obtaining, 134–136
    from option files, 142
  data exchange between MySQL and
      Excel, using for, 527
  datafiles
    columns, extraction and rearranging
      of, 475–478
    formats, converting, 473
  date conversion
    and validity checking, 504
    SQL script, using, 508–510
    U.S. to ISO format, 503
  delimiters, selection using, 32
  do( ), 88
  duplicates, finding programmatically, 708
  encoding special characters using, 766
  error checking, 66–68
    MySQL numeric error codes,
      enabling, 66
    trace( ), 68
  finding all paydays for a given year, 273
  form creating methods, 818
  hash lookups, case sensitivity, 494
  hit counter, 881
  @INC array, 77
  input extraction conventions, 848
  library files, 76

  LOAD DATA statement, diagnostic utility
      for, 521–526
  metadata, organization in arrays, 419
  modules, 76
  MySQL and, xxii
  MySQL, dependencies, 54
  NULL values, representation, 115
  NULLs, representing in transferred data,
      script for, 513
  placeholders, implementation, 103
    quotes and, 103
  queries, 88–92
    error checking, 88
    result sets, processing, 88
    reusable, writing, 103
  query results, exporting, 469–473
  query results, web scripting
    definition lists, 781
    email addresses, outputting as, 792
    hyperlinks, outputting as, 791
    make_table_from_query( ), 788
    nested lists, 783
    ordered lists, outputting as, 776
    paragraph text, displaying as, 771
    tables, displaying, 786
    unordered lists, 779
  records changed by a query,
      counting, 400
  reference tables, using to create, 612
  references, 958
  resources, xxx
  result set metadata, obtaining, 402–405
    database handles, using, 402
    statement handles, using, 402
  scrolling lists, creating
    multiple-pick, 837
  sequence values, accessing with, 551
  servers, querying for supported table
      types, 442
  session management with
      MySQL, 896–902
    database connection parameters, 897
    session expiration, 901
    session records table, creating, 897
  SET column values, converting to
      arrays, 837
  single-pick list elements
    functions and arguments, 824
    value lists and label hashes, 825
  Spreadsheet::ParseExcel::Simple
      module, 528

Perl (*continued*)
   Spreadsheet::WriteExcel::FromDB
      module, 529
   Spreadsheet::WriteExcel::Simple
      module, 528
   Text::CSV_XS module, documentation,
      accessing, 469
   uploading files from forms, 861
   validation using a lookup table, 495
   -w option, 55
   web scripts
      Apache servers, 746–749
   web sites, 927
   XML, modules for exporting query results
      to, 532
   XML::XPath module, 536
Perl DBI
   metadata, organization in arrays, 419
   retrieval methods, 90
      RaiseError and, 92
PERL5LIB environment variable, 78
PERLSESSID cookie, 899
perror (print error) utility, 25
PHP
   checkboxes or scrolling lists,
      presentation, 839
   class constructor functions, 123
   classes, 119
   connection, database selection,
      disconnection, 57–59
   connection parameters, obtaining, 136
      from option files, 144
   dependencies for MySQL, 57
   encoding special characters using, 767
   error checking, 69
   error messages
      displaying special characters, 70
      suppressing, 69
   error_reporting( ), 69
   hit counter, 882
   include files and, 79
   input extraction conventions
      input parameters, 848
   vs. Java servlets, 932
   library files, 78
   magic_quotes_gpc, 850
   metadata attributes, 405
   multi-pick list elements, creating, 838
   MySQL and, xxii
   MySQL interface, non-portability of, 119
   mysql_connect( ), 58
   mysql_errno( ), 69

mysql_error( ), 69
mysql_pconnect( ), 58
mysql_select_db( ), 58
NULL values, representation, 116
object-oriented MySQL
      interfaces, 118–132
   vs. function-based scripts, 120
   (see also MySQL_Access class)
$php_errormsg global variable, 69
placeholder support, lack of, 105
   adding, 129
pop-up menus, creating, 829
port number option, 59
queries, 93–95
   column counts, getting, 95
query results, web scripting
   definition lists, 780
   downloading, 812
   email addresses, outputting as, 792
   ordered lists, outputting as, 774
   paragraph text, displaying as, 771
quoting, 129
radio buttons, creating, 828
ranking, programmatic assignment, 697
records changed by a query,
      counting, 400
references, 959
register_globals, security issues, 912
resources, xxx
result set metadata, obtaining, 405–406
result sets
   NULL values, determining, 128
scripts, 57
scrolling lists, creating, 829
sequence values, accessing with, 552
servers, querying for supported table
      types, 442
session management, 902–914
   closing a session, 909
   destroying a session, 910
   garbage collection, 910
   handler routines, 906
   MySQL, for backing store, 904
   opening a session, 909
   overriding default interface, 904
   reading session data, 909
   session table, creating, 905
   storage management routines,
      writing, 906
   storage method, globally
      changing, 907
   writing session data, 910

single-pick list elements, scripting
    for, 826
socket pathname option, 59
uploading files from forms, 864
    save locations, setting, 866
Version 4 session management
    interface, 903
    functions, 903
version constraints, 121
versions
    error checking, problems with
      pre-4.0.6, 69
web script pathname acquisition, 818
web scripting in, 741
web scripts
    Apache servers, 750
web site, 928
<?php and ?> tags, 79
.php extension, 57
PHP Extension and Add-on Repository
    (PEAR), 119
.php filename extension, 745
php.ini, 907
phrase searches using FULLTEXT
    indexes, 226
pipes, 26, 45
placeholders, 102, 805
    generating a list, 104
    including special characters or NULLS in
      queries, using for, 106–114
    PHP, supporting under, 129
    positions, numbering of, 103
.pm file extension, 76
PNP
    parameter binding, 130
pop-up menus, 822
POSIX character classes, 206
POST, 818
POST requests, 847
postal (Zip) codes, pattern for matching, 486
post_image.pl, 862
prepare( ) (Perl), 88
prepare_query( ) (PHP MySQL_Access class)
    , 130
previous-page, next-page links, generating for
    web output, 869–874
PRIMARY KEY, 456
PRIMARY KEY indexes, 388
PRIMARY KEYs, 701
    AUTO_INCREMENT columns and, 543
    declaring, 545

NULL values and, 565
NULLs and, 701
PrintError
    selective enabling, 67
PrintError (Perl DBI), 66
profile table, 52
    resetting, 148
programmatic deletion of multiple
    tables, 661
    large tables, handling, 662
programs, executing in shells, 43
prompts in MySQL, meaning of, 17
Python
    % (format specifier), 105
    cgi and urllib modules, 741
    connection, database selection,
      disconnection, 59–61
    connection parameters,
      obtaining, 137–138
    from option files, 145
    DB-API interface, 59
    DictCursor, 96
    encoding special characters using, 768
    error handling, 59
    event counts, retrieval using, 574
    input extraction conventions, 852
    joins on tables sharing column
      names, 585
    library files, 80
    multi-pick list elements, creating, 838
    MySQL and, xxii
    NULL values, representing in, 117
    placeholders, implementation, 105
    pop-up menus, creating, 830
    queries, 95–96
      cursor object, using, 95
      reusable, writing, 105
    query output, numbering of rows, 577
    query results, web scripting
      email addresses, outputting as, 792
      hyperlinks, outputting as, 791
      ordered lists, outputting as, 775
      paragraph text, displaying as, 772
    records changed by a query,
      counting, 401
    references, 959
    reports, generating, 375
    resources, xxx
    result set metadata, obtaining, 407
    sequence values, accessing with, 552

Python (*continued*)
    single-pick list elements, scripting
        for, 826
    subselects, simulating using, 636
    summary calculations using for, 373
    sys.path variable, 81
    uploading files from forms, 866
    web scripts
        Apache servers, 751
        pathname acquisition, 819
    web sites about, 928
PYTHONPATH environment variable, 81

Q

queries, 14
    canceling, 17
    column headings in output,
        suppression, 35
    command-line, specifying on, 26
    copy and paste, generation using, 27
    data values, placeholders, 101–106
    duplicates, eliminating from result
        set, 709
    duplicates, for detecting, 706
    editing, 18
    embedded in programs (see embedded
        queries)
    execution, checking, 87
    external, checking for result set from, 409
    files, reading from, 23
    form input, constructing from, 857–859
        encoding functions, advantages
            of, 858
        placeholders, advantages of, 858
        security risks, 857
    formatting output, 31
    \G, terminating with, 37
    generic and reusable, writing, 101–106
    HTML output, generating, 33
    issuing, 85–100
    Java processing(see under Java, JDBC)
    joins (see joins)
    legibility of output, improving, 37
    NULL values, including in, 106–114
    numbering output lines, 36
    on multiple tables (see joins)
    ORDER BY clauses, 292
    output order, controlling with
        joins, 633–634

output rows, sequential numbering
    of, 577
output, specifying, 580
paging output, 28
Perl (see under Perl)
PHP (see under PHP)
Python (see under Python)
reading from other programs, 26
redirection of output, 29
repeating, 18
result sets
    first or last rows, selecting, 172
    middle rows, selecting, 175
    saving to new tables, 183
    saving to other tables, 182
result sets, sorting, 171
results
    eliminating duplicate values, 342
    exporting from MySQL, 461
    list elements, creating from, 814
    previous-page, next-page links,
        generating for, 869–874
    serving for download, 811–813
    in web pages, 770–813
    XML, exporting as, 532–534
results, formatting for display, 410
results, retrieving, 85–100
results, sorting (see sorting operations)
reusing from earlier sessions, 40
rows, obtaining number affected by a
    query, 399
running against databases on separate
    servers, 671–673
SELECT COUNT(*), 337
SELECT (see SELECT statement)
server information, used for
    acquiring, 436
special characters, including in, 106–114
SQL variables, using in, 20
transactions, writing to avoid, 735
types of, 85, 86
WHERE clauses, 296
without results, 160
XML output, generating, 34
query terminators, 14
QUIT, 5, 6
quotes
    in strings, 193
quoting functions, 108

R

radio buttons, 821
RaiseError
    behavior, 67
    error trapping with, 68
    selective enabling, 67
RaiseError (Perl DBI), 66
RAND( ), 581, 688
    evaluating, 691
    rows, for randomizing, 689
    seeding, 689
random numbers, generating, 688
randomizing a set of rows, 689–694
rand_test.py, 691
ranks, assigning, 695–698
    advancing on value changes, 696
    by low number excepting ties, 697
    by row within the ordered set, 696
    programmatic assignment, 697
raw protocol, 48
    Java drivers, handling by, 49
ReadPropsFile.java, 146
record editing forms, 841–845
record retrieval techniques, 149–191
    conditional selection, 158
record separators, 445
records
    combining from two tables (see joins)
    creation or modification time, 283
    creation time, recording
        permanently, 286
    duplicates (see duplicate records)
    editing using table information, 426
    recording modification time, 284
    setting storage lifetime, 282
    tables, moving between, 185
    (see also rows)
redundancy in data, 393
reference tables, 609–613
    APIs, creating with, 612
referential integrity and foreign keys, 658
Regexp class library, 205
REGEXP operator, 204
register_globals directive (PHP), 902
register_globals setting (PHP), 848
regression line, 687

regular expressions, 203
    POSIX character class support, 206
    SQL pattern matching, compared to, 207
    wildcards, 204
REHASH, 20
related table updates, 645–650
    deleting unrelated records, 665–671
    using programs, 648
    using mysql, 649
    via table replacement, 647
        using joins, 647
        using LEFT JOINs, 647
related tables
    unattached records, finding and
        removing, 665
related-table updates
    lookup tables, creating with, 650
relative frequency distributions, 681
relative pathnames, 451
RENAME TABLE statement, 387
repetition, measuring in a set of values, 364
REPLACE query
    rows, finding the number affected, 400
REPLACE statement, 456
    duplicates, preventing with, 704
    for serving image files on web pages, 804
require and require_once statement, PHP, 79
resequencing, 556
    of AUTO_INCREMENT columns, 553
        advisability, 554
    ordering, control of, 558
    (see also AUTO_INCREMENT columns)
    (see also sequences)
result sets
    iteration through, 100
    movement within, 100
    presence or absence, determining, 409
    rewinding, 101
results
    sorting (see sorting operations)
ResultSetMetaData object (Java), 408
retrieving from, 806
reusing code, 73
rewinding result sets, 101
RIGHT( ), 198
RIGHT JOINs, 595
ROLLBACK statement, 725
rotating tables, 387

rowcount attribute (Python), 95
rows
    combining rows from two tables (see
        joins)
    deleting related rows in multiple
        tables, 655
        by replacing tables, 660
        cascaded deletes, 658
        mysql, using, 664
        programmatic deletion, 661
    duplicates (see duplicate records)
    ID values, joining to descriptive
        information in another table, 654
    inserting records in a table that include
        values from another, 645
    matching in separate tables, 586
    per group minimum or maximum values,
        finding, 596
    random selection from a set, 694
    randomizing, 689–694
    selecting in parallel from multiple
        tables, 639–644
    unattached records, finding and
        removing, 665
    (see also records)
.rpm (RedHat Package Manager), 939
running averages, calculation using
    self-joins, 630

S

-s option (--silent), 36
script program, 39
ScriptAlias directive, 743, 744
scrolling lists, 822
    multiple pick, 837
scrolling_list( ) (Perl), 837
SDK (Java Software Development Kit)
    Tomcat servers and, 938
search interfaces, implementing, 867–869
search_state.pl, 868
SECOND( ), 237, 251
seconds values, conversion
    to date-and-time, 247
    to time, 244
SEC_TO_TIME( ), 244, 248, 250, 279
security
    encapsulation, advantages of, 74
    library files and, 74
    option files, 9
    scripts in the document tree, risks, 74

sed
    delimiters, selection using, 32
SELECT statement
    columns, displaying
        with column name aliases, 153
SELECT ... INTO OUTFILE statement, 462
    FILE privilege, requirement for, 463
SELECT DATABASE( ), 438
SELECT DISTINCT statement, 709
SELECT statement, 5, 149–191
    calculations, using for, 41
    columns, displaying, 151
        output order, control ling, 152
    eliminating duplicate rows, 165
    identifying unattached records for
        deletion, 667
    Perl placeholders for, 103
    selection criteria, testing, 162
    uses for, 149
    WHERE clauses, 158
        aliases and input columns, 161
        finding NULL values, 166
        negation operators, 163
        NULLs, query conditions that
            miss, 168
SELECT USER( ), 439
SELECT VERSION( )
    customizing applications and, 437
SELECT... WHERE query
    metadata, getting with, 418
    portability across DBMSs, 420
selectall_arrayref( ) (Perl), 92
    for obtaining metadata, 404
    placeholders, using with, 104
selectall_hashref( ) (Perl), 92
    for obtaining metadata, 404
selectcol_arrayref( ) (Perl), 92
selectrow_array( ) (Perl), 91
    placeholders, using with, 104
selectrow_arrayref( ) (Perl), 91
selectrow_hashref( ) (Perl), 91
self-joins, 619–633
    aliases and, 620
    cumulative sums, finding, 629–633
    duplicates, eliminating from, 711–713
    excluding the reference value from
        results, 621
    LEFT JOIN self-joins, 624
    without reference values, 622
    running averages, finding, 629–633

successive rows, calculating differences
	between, 626–628
		seqence columns, need for, 627
	table aliases and, 619
	types of questions requiring, 619
semicolon (;), 14, 23
sequences, 539
	event counts, using for, 572
	extending sequence range, 555
	generating, 539–577
	lack of portability, 540
	multiple sequences in one table,
		creating, 562–567
	record deletions, impact on, 546
	repeating sequences (cycles),
		generating, 575
	resequencing, advisability, 554
	retrieving values for, 549
	reusing values at the top, 557
	server-side retrieval, 551
		compared to client-side methods, 553
	starting value, setting, 559
	using as counters, 540
servers, 1
	databases on, listing, 433
	metadata, getting, 436
		Java, using, 436
	raw protocol, 48
	table types, determining support for, 441
	user accounts, creating, 2
	(see also mysqld)
servers (MySQL)
	monitoring, 440
		impact of monitoring, 441
server-side storage, 894
session hash element names, 898
session identifiers, 897
session IDs, 894
session management
	client-side vs. server-side storage, 893
		security aspects, 894
	common tasks, 895
	Perl, using, 896
	server-side, database-backed, 894
session-based scripts, 896
sessions, 893
	logging, 39
	terminating, 6
session_set_save_handler( ) (PHP), 906, 907
sess_track.jsp, 916
sess_track.php, 910

sess_track.pl, 899
SET, 22
	calculations, using for, 42
SET column type
	renaming, column definition issues, 381
SET columns
	column definitions, adding, 427
	comparing in self-joins, 623
	definitions, obtaining, 422
	hashes, for testing legality of data, 495
	input values, validating, 492, 494
	member lists, obtaining, 422
SET values
	stings, treatment as, 200
sh
	PATH environment variable, setting, 13
	shell scripting, 42
shell scripts
	Unix, writing in, 43
	Windows, writing in, 46
shell scripts, invocation of mysql in, 42
SHOW COLUMNS queries
	ENUM columns, validation of input with
		query results, 492
	SET columns, validation of input with
		query results, 492
SHOW COLUMNS statement, 379
	default values displayed, interpreting, 417
	ENUM column information, using to
		get, 422
	SET column information, using to
		get, 422
	table structure information, getting
		APIs, using, 416
	table structure information, getting
		with, 414–418
SHOW CREATE TABLE statement, 189,
		379, 386
	checking available table types using, 722
	table structure information, getting
		with, 414
SHOW DATABASES query
	complete listing of databases, obtaining
		with, 433
	interpreting, 433
SHOW DATABASES statement
	testing for existence of a database, using
		for, 435
SHOW INDEX statement, 388
SHOW STATUS statement, 43
	MySQL servers, monitoring using, 440

SHOW TABLE STATUS statement, 337, 386
SHOW TABLES queries
    interpreting, 433
SHOW TABLES query
    complete listing of tables, obtaining
        with, 433
SHOW TABLES statement
    Java, issuing programatically using, 761
SHOW VARIABLES statement
    determining a server's supported table
        types, 442
    MySQL servers, monitoring using, 440
signed integers, pattern for matching, 485
--silent option, 39
SimpleServlet class, 931
single page navigation indexes, generating
        from database content, 794–796
single strings, representing as, 566
single-pick form elements, 820
    creating from database content, 820–835
    types, 821
single-pick list elements, 822
    functions and arguments, 824
    functions, constructing for, 827
    value lists and label hashes, 825
single-row sequence generators, 572
    item tracking using, 576
--skip-column-names (MySQL 3.22.20), 35
| (program indicator, Apache), 888
somedata.csv problem, 444
    solution, 537
sorting
    aliasing of expressions, 299
    APIs, using, 295
    ascending order, 293
    by calendar day, 310
    column aliases, using, 295
    columns, positional references for, 294
    on dates or times, 308
    by day of week, 312
        mapping first day from Sunday to
            Monday, 313
    DAYOFYEAR( ), problems using, 311
    default sort direction, 293
    descending order, 293, 294
    displaying as strings values sorted as
        numbers, 300
    expression results, using, 297

lexical vs. numerical order, 301
MIN( ), MAX( ), and case sensitivity, 349
multiple column sorts, 293
    mixed-order sorting, 294
NULL values and, 304
of result sets, 171
on single-columns, 292
string sorts and case sensitivity, 306
on table subsets, 296
by time of day, 314
on unselected values, 299–304
sorting operations, 290–334
SOURCE, 23, 24
source loops, 25
special characters
    database, table, and column names, 114
    encoding in web output, 762–769
        APIs, using, 765–769
        encoding interactions, 765
        HTML special characters, 763
        URL special characters, 764
    in strings, 193
    including in queries, 106–114
Spreadsheet::ParseExcel::Simple
        module, 528
Spreadsheet::WriteExcel::FromDB
        module, 529
Spreadsheet::WriteExcel::Simple
        module, 528
SQL
    date conversion using, 508–510
    pattern matching, 201–203
        vs. FULLTEXT searching, 227
        NULL values and, 203
        regular expressions, contrasted
            with, 202
    reformatting of data in temporary
        tables, 511–513
    statements, 86
    variables, 20
        calculation results, storing in, 42
        non MySQL database engines, and, 22
        for numbering query output lines, 36
sql_quote( ) (PHP MySQL_Access
        class), 129
ssh, using for dumps between servers, 468
standard deviation
    calculation using aggregate functions, 676
    uses, 676

start_form( ) (Perl), 818
start_multipart_form( ) (Perl), 861
startup files, 12
statement recall utility, 18
    Windows systems, 19
statement terminator, mysql, 14
statement terminators
    APIs and, 87
statements
    types of, 85, 86
state_pager1.pl, 870, 871
state_pager2.pl, 873
statistical techniques, 674–698
    aggregate functions in the calculation of
        statistical data, 676
    calculating descriptive statistics, 675–679
    correlation coefficients,
        calculating, 686–688
    counting missing values (NULLs), 684
    frequency distributions,
        generating, 681–683
        uses for, 682
    linear regressions, calculating, 686–688
    median, calculating, 678–679
    mode, calculating, 677
    per-group descriptive statistics,
        calculating, 679
    random number generation, 688
    randomizing a set of rows, 689–694
    assigning ranks, 695–698
    selecting randomly from a set of
        rows, 694
STATUS, 44
STATUS command, 16
STD( ), 676
STDDEV( ), 676
store_image.pl, 800, 802
    image storage configuration for database
        or filesystem, 805
STRCMP( ), 213
string( ) (Perl), 473
string functions
    extraction of date and time values
        using, 240
strings, 192–227
    calculating one date from another using
        substring replacement, 268
    case sensitivity
        MIN( ) and MAX( ), 349
    case sensitivity in comparisons,
        controlling, 211

case sensitivity, managing in
    comparisons, 215
combining in larger strings, 197
equality, testing for, 196
forcing interpretation as temporal
    values, 279
numbers, conversion to, 277
pattern matching (see pattern matching)
relative ordering, 196
string types, 193
substrings, extraction, 197
substrings, matching to, 201
trailing spaces, preserving, 195
strip_slash_helper( ) (PHP), 851
subselect queries, 635
    converting to join operations, 635–639
SUBSTRING( ), 198
SUBSTRING_INDEX( ), 198
SUBSTRING_INDEX( ), for breaking apart
    strings at delimiters, 512
substrings, extraction from strings, 197
suEXEC mechanism, 746
SUM( ), 341
    strings, inapplicability to, 342
summaries, 335–377
    averages, 341
    calculations, using APIs for, 373
    computed summaries, 335
    COUNT( ), 337
    counting summaries, 335
    date-based, 368–371
        distinct values, categorizing, 370
    determining whether values are
        unique, 358
    display order, controlling, 365–366
    getting distinct values without
        DISTINCT, 352
    duplicates, detecting with, 706, 708
    duplicates, eliminating from, 342
    expression results, grouping by, 359
    finding smallest or largest values, 367
        multiple sets of values, handling, 368
    finding values associated with minimum
        and maximum values, 345
        using joins, 348
        MAX-CONCAT trick, 346
        two-query approach, 346
    grouping data by ranges, 361–364
    HAVING clauses, 357
        COUNT( ), using with, 358
    joins, producing with, 590

summaries (*continued*)
    LEFT JOINs and reference tables, creating
        with, 609–613
    LIMIT clauses and, 367
    master-detail summaries,
        producing, 605–608
    MIN( ) and MAX( ), 339
    missing values, incorporating, 684
    on non-categorical data, 361–364
    NULL values and, 354
    of per-group and overall summary
        values, 372–374
    ranges, defining, 340
    repetition, measuring in value sets, 364
    reports, generating, 374–377
    selection, groups with certain
        characteristics, 357
    subgroups, dividing into, 350
    sums, 341
    techniques, 336
    time-based, 368–371
        distinct values, categorizing, 370
    types of, 335
    using temporary tables and joins, 634
sys.argv (Python), 137
sys.path variable, 81

T

Tab key, autocompletion using, 20
tab-delimited file format, 446
tab-delimited, linefeed-terminated
    format, 447
--table option, 31
table types
    evaluating tables for type, 386
tables
    adding indexes, 388
    aliasing of names, 582
    ALTER TABLE (see ALTER TABLE
        statement)
    AUTO_INCREMENT columns, dropping
        to resequence, 556
    AUTO_INCREMENT columns,
        including, 542
    click to sort headings for query
        results, 874
    columns
        adding, 380
        dropping, 380
        moving, 380

    columns, displaying, 151
    combining rows from two tables (see
        joins)
    conversion to transaction supporting
        types, 723
    copying to another server, 467
    creating, 85
    creating two tables from one, 393
        new indexes, adding, 394
    databases, listing all the tables in, 433
    deleting related rows in multiple
        tables, 655
        by replacing tables, 660
        cascaded deletes, 658
        mysql, using, 664
        programmatic deletion, 661
design
    saving data storage space, 650–651
dropping indexes, 389
duplicates, eliminating, 713
exporting as raw data, 464
fully qualified table references, 416
getting table structure information, 414
HTML, structure in, 785
information, database-independent
    methods of obtaining, 424
joining a table to itself, 619–633
joining from more than one database, 582
matching rows from 2 or more, 586
metadata, getting
    methodology, choosing, 421
moving records between, 185
with multiple sequences,
    creating, 562–567
normalizing, 392–397
redesigning, 393
related table updates (see related table
    updates)
renaming, 387
session records table creating, 897
SQL format, exporting in, 465
structure information, getting with result
    set metadata, 418–421
table names, specifying in queries, 580
table structure information
    uses for, 426
temporary tables, 597
TEMPORARY tables, creating, 187
temporary tables, using for data
    transformation, 511–513
testing for existence, 434

types, 385
types, determining server support for, 441
unique names for, generating, 190
using multiple, 578–673
web scripting query results as, 784–789
    aliasing column names, 788
    borderless empty table cells fix, 789
    display, managing, 789
    visual appearance, 787
XML, importing into MySQL, 535
tag libraries, 935
taglib directives, 758, 762
<taglib> entries, 756
TCP/IP connections to local host, 54
tcsh, PATH environment variable, setting, 13
team standings, computing, 599–605
tee files, 39
    for reuse of queries, 40
--tee option, 39
temporal values, 228–289
    addition of zero for conversion to
        numbers, 277
    current time, determining, 234
    default values, enabling, 235
    interpreting strings as, 279
TEMPORARY tables, 187, 190
temporary tables, 597
    using for data tranformation, 511–513
TERMINATED BY subclause, 453
terminator characters, 14
test harness programs, 74
test harness scripts, PHP, 79
Text::CSV_XS module, accessing
       documentation, 469
TIME column type, 229
    values, allowable ranges, 250
time intervals, decomposing, 251
    Python, using, 251
time of day, sorting by, 314
time values
    addition of, 248
    combining with date values, 243
    (see also temporal values)
time zone discrepancies in time
       conversions, 248
time_components( ) (Python), 251
TIME_FORMAT( ), 232, 233, 241
    using for portions of times, 235
time-formatting sequences, 233
time-related functions, 237–239

times
    adding temporal intervals to, 248
    calculating intervals between, 250
    comparisons, 282
    conversion to seconds, 244
    decomposing, 235–241
        component-extraction functions,
           using, 236–239
        formatting functions, using, 235
        string functions, using, 239
    numbers, treating as, 277
    synthesizing, 241–243
        component-extraction functions,
           using, 242
        formatting functions, using, 241
    time zone adjustments, 264
    validity checking on subparts, 499
    validity checking on values, 501
TIMESTAMP columns, 230, 235, 283–289
    calculations on values, 287
    vs. DATETIME for recording record
       modification time, 286
    for permanent record creation time,
       using, 286
    format of values, 284
    potential impacts of moving, 381
    recording creation or modification time of
       records, 283
    records, recording modification time, 284
    values, reformatting for display, 288
TIMESTAMP values
    cgrouping in manageable categories, 371
timestamps, safeguarding table data
       with, 186
TIME_TO_SEC( ), 244, 248, 279, 315
TINYINT, range of, 544
TLD files, 954–955
TLDs (Tag Library Descriptors), 935
TO_DAYS( ), 246, 254, 256, 279
to_excel.pl, 529
Tomcat, 938–946
    built-in session management
       capabilities, 895
    dependencies, 938
    directory structure, 942, 948
        applications, 942
        classes, 943
        configuration and control, 943
        operational directories, 944
    environment variables, 940

Tomcat (*continued*)
  installing, 938
  JDBC driver directory location, 919
  JDBC drivers and, 753
  JDBC drivers, installing, 755
  JSPs and, 752
  Manager application, 945
  mcb sample application, installation, 753
  restarting applications without restarting
    the server, 944
  servlet and JSP session interface, 915
  session management
    Java methods, 916
    MySQL, saving records in, 918
  session management with
    MySQL, 915–923
    server configuration files,
      changing, 919
    session expiration, 922
    session tables, creating, 919
    tracking, 922
  starting and stopping, 940
    Linux, 941
    Windows version, 941
  WAR (web archive) files, 753
  web scripts
    directory location, 753
  web scripts, running on, 752–762
  web site, 928
  webapps directory, 753
  WEB-INF directory, 946–947
  XML and, 738
Tomcat server, 738
to_null.pl, 515
track_vars configuration setting (PHP), 849
track_vars directive (PHP), 902
trailing spaces, preserving, 195
transactions, 720–736
  alternatives to, in nonsupporting
    environments, 733
  atomic operations as alternative to, 736
  BEGIN statement, 724
  canceling with ROLLBACK
    statement, 725
  Java programs, using in, 732
  MySQL, supporting versions, 722
  performing in programs, 725–728
  server concurrency, 720
  server integrity, 720
  SQL, performing with, 724

table type availability, checking, 722
tables, transactional types,
    specifying, 723
transaction-safe table handlers, installing
    on server, 723
verifying server support of, 721–723
  SHOW VARIABLES statement,
    checking with, 722
triple-equals operator (===), 117, 128
TRUNCATE( ), 601
try blocks (Python), 59
TYPE clauses, 385

U

unattached records
  deleting, 668
    via mysql, 670
    programmatic deletion, 669
  identifying, 665
undef (Perl), 115
undefined values, testing for in Perl, 115
UNIONs, 640
  column selection constraints, 640
  for selecting records in parallel from
    multiple tables, 639–644
  parentheses, for sorting select results, 642
  simulating with temporary tables, 643
UNIQUE indexes, 388, 456, 701
  AUTO_INCREMENT columns and, 543
  declaring, 545
  NULL values and, 565
  NULLs and, 702
Unix
  cut utility, 461
  file line terminators, 455
  JDBC drivers, installing, 755
  loading image files to MySQL, 805
  od program, 458
  path, indicating, 43
  shell scripts, writing, 43
  Unix epoch, 248
  user-specific option files, 141
  web scripts, path to language processor,
    indicating, 744
UNIX_TIMESTAMP( ), 247, 255
  intervals, determination using, 256
UNLOCK statement, 723
unmarked lists, web scripting query results
    as, 782
  (see also lists)

unordered lists, web scripting query results as, 777
  (see also lists)
unsigned integers, pattern for matching, 485
UNSIGNED typing, AUTO_INCREMENT columns, 544
UPDATE query
  rows, finding the number affected, 400
update_related.pl, 649
UPPER( ), 212, 308
url( ) (Perl), 818
urlencode( ) (PHP), 767
urllib.quote( ) (Python), 768
URLs (uniform resource locators)
  encoding of special characters, 764
  pattern matching for, 491
  web script locations, indicating via, 745
USE, 15
use DBI (Perl), 55
USER( ), 439
user accounts (MySQL)
  creating, 2
  login accounts, contrasted with, 3
user-defined storage module, setting for PHP sessions, 904
users
  finding out who's connected, 439
  logging, 439
UWIN (Unix for Windows), 47

V

validation of data, 478–516
  dates and times, checking of subparts, 499
  ENUM columns, input values for, 492
  lookup tables, using, 495–498
    Java, 497
    Perl, 495–498
    PHP, 497
  pattern matching for, 484–492
  SET columns, for, 494
  table metadata, using, 492–495
VARCHAR columns, conversions to CHAR types, 430
variable checking (Perl), 55
variable substitution, 46
variance, calculation using standard deviation, 676
--verbose option, 39
verbosity of output, setting, 38

--vertical option, 38
vertical output format, 37
virtual servers
  associating log records with, 891

W

-w option (Perl), 55
WAR (web archive) files, 753
  unpacking manually, 754
wasNull( ) (Java), 117
web application structure, 946
web forms (see forms)
web pages
  access counting, 878–883
  displaying query results in, 770–813
    as email addresses, 791–793
    as hyperlinks, 790–793
    as lists, 773–784
    as navigation indexes, 793–799
    as paragraph text, 771–773
    as tables, 784–789
    record fetching and HTML generation, 778
  hit logging, 883
  mapping column types to elements, 427
  serving query results for download, 811–813
    forcing client download, 812
web scripting
  extensions, 742
web scripts, 737
  Apache servers, running on, 743–752
  compared to HTML, 740
  directory location
    Tomcat servers, 753
  directory locations for, Apache servers, 744
  filename extension, for processor type identification, 744
  forms, 817–845
    behaviors, 818
    database records, loading to, 841–845
    with file upload fields, 860
    input, collecting, 845–855
    multiple-pick elements, creating from database content, 836–841
    queries, constructing from input, 857–859
    single-pick elements, creating from database content, 820–835
    validating input, 855

web scripts (*continued*)
    HTML and XHTML output, 738
    images, storage using, 800
    in Perl
        Apache servers, 746–749
    in PHP
        Apache servers, 750
    in Python
        Apache servers, 751
    input processing, 815
        file uploads, 859–867
        MySQL, using for, 814–892
        search interfaces,
            implementing, 867–869
    query results
        paragraph text, displaying as, 771
    server configuration for self-enabled or
        external script execution, 741
    source HTML, viewing, 816
    testing, 859
    Tomcat servers, running on, 752–762
    vs. command-line scripts, 741
    web page generation using, 739
web servers
    privileges and permissions, 746
    sharing, risks of, 74
    software, obtaining, 928
webapps directory, 753
WEB-INF directory, 946–947
WEB-INF subdirectory, 754
web.xml file, 756
WEEKDAY( ), 238, 314
WHERE clauses, 158, 296
    aggregate functions, incompatibility, 346
    COUNT( ), using with, 337
    data and comparison operators, use in
        efficient queries, 281
    excluding reference values in
        self-joins, 622
    group selection and, 357
    joins and, 579
    LEFT JOINs and, 594
    matching rows in separate tables, 586

wildcards (pattern matching), 204
Windows
    DOS command-line environment,
        limitations, 47
    executing programs in, 43
    file line terminators, 455
    filename extensions, 7
    JCBC drivers, installing, 755
    library files
        specifying location
    loading image file to MySQL, 805
    PATH environment variable, setting, 13
    shell scripting, 46
    statement recall capabilities, 19
    Tomcat server, starting and stopping, 941
    user-specific option files, 141
    web scripts, path to language processor,
        indicating, 744

X

XHTML, 738
    HTML, compared to, 739
XML
    MySQL, importing into, 535
    query results, exportation as, 532–534
    Tomcat servers and, 938
--xml option (MySQL 4.0), 34
xml_to_mysql.pl, 536
XML::XPath module, 536

Y

yank_col.pl, 476
YEAR( ), 231, 237, 274
year-length calculations and leap years, 276

Z

zero, addition to temporal string values, 277
Zip and Zip+4 postal codes, pattern for
    matching, 486

About the Author

Paul DuBois is one of the primary contributors to the MySQL Reference Manual, a renowned online manual that has supported MySQL administrators and database developers for years. He is also the author of *Using csh & tcsh* and *Software Portability with imake* by O'Reilly, as well as *MySQL* and *MySQL and Perl for the Web* by New Riders.

Colophon

Our look is the result of reader comments, our own experimentation, and feedback from distribution channels. Distinctive covers complement our distinctive approach to technical topics, breathing personality and life into potentially dry subjects.

The animal on the cover of *MySQL Cookbook* is a green anole. These common lizards can be found in the Southeastern United States, the Caribbean, and South America. Green anoles dwell in moist, shady environments, such as trees and shrubs. They subsist on small insects such as crickets, roaches, moths, grubs, and spiders.

Green anoles are slight in build, with narrow heads and long, slender tails that can be twice as long as their bodies. The special padding on their feet enables them to climb, cling, and run on any surface. They range from six to eight inches long. Though, as their name implies, green anoles are usually bright green, their color can change to match their surroundings, varying between gray-brown, brown, and green. Male anoles have pink dewlaps that they extend when courting or to protect their territory.

Linley Dolby was the production editor and proofreader for *MySQL Cookbook*. Colleen Gorman, Jeff Holcomb, Brian Sawyer, and Claire Cloutier provided quality control. John Bickelhaupt wrote the index.

Ellie Volckhausen designed the cover of this book, based on a series design by Edie Freedman. The cover image is a 19th-century engraving from the Dover Pictorial Archive. Emma Colby produced the cover layout with QuarkXPress 4.1 using Adobe's ITC Garamond font.

David Futato designed the interior layout. This book was converted to FrameMaker 5.5.6 with a format conversion tool created by Erik Ray, Jason McIntosh, Neil Walls, and Mike Sierra that uses Perl and XML technologies. The text font is Linotype Birka; the heading font is Adobe Myriad Condensed; and the code font is LucasFont's TheSans Mono Condensed. The tip and warning icons were drawn by Christopher Bing. This colophon was written by Linley Dolby.

Other Titles Available from O'Reilly

Linux

Linux in a Nutshell, 3rd Edition

*By Ellen Siever, Stephen Spainhour,
Jessica P. Hekman & Stephen Figgins
3rd Edition August 2000
800 pages, ISBN 0-596-00025-1*

Linux in a Nutshell covers the core
commands for common Linux distributions. This complete reference user,
programming, administration, and
networking commands with options also documents a
wide range of GNU tools. New material in the third edition includes common configuration tasks for the
GNOME and KDE desktops and the fvwm2 window
manager, the dpkg Debian package manager, expanded
coverage of the rpm Red Hat package manager, and
many new commands.

Running Linux, 4th Edition

*By Matt Welsh, Matthias Kalle
Dalheimer, Terry Dawson &
Lar Kaufman
4th Edition October 2002 (est.)
755 pages (est.), ISBN 0-596-00272-6*

After six years, this classic is still rec-
ommended by knowledgeable Linux
users over any other guide. Everything you need for
understanding, installing, and using the Linux operating system is explained in detail. In the new fourth edition, Running Linux delves deeper into installation,
configuring the windowing system, system administration, and networking. Several new topics about laptops,
cameras and scanners, sound and multimedia, ADSL,
the GNOME desktop, MySQL, PHP, and configuring an
NFS server are included.

The Root of All Evil

*By Illiad
1st Edition August 2001
144 pages, ISBN 0-596-00193-2*

It's back to Columbia Internet, "the
friendliest, hardest-working, and most
neurotic little Internet Service
Provider in the world," for our third installment from
the hit online comic, User Friendly. The cast: hardcore
techies, self-absorbed sales staff, well-meaning execs,
and assorted almost-humans. The background: too little
office space, warring operating systems, and eternally
clueless customers.

Practical PostgreSQL

*By Command Prompt, Inc
1st Edition January 2002
636 pages, ISBN 1-56592-846-6*

Practical PostgreSQL is a fast-paced,
business-oriented guide to installing,
config-uring, and running PostgreSQL. Readers will find all the
basics here, such as how to create databases and objects,
such as tables, within those databases. Or they can go
straight to advanced topics like inheritance, replication,
user management, and backup and recovery. The book
also introduces the PL/pgSQL procedural language.
Finally, a complete PostgreSQL command reference
makes "looking it up" easy.

Learning Red Hat Linux, 2nd Edition

*By Bill McCarty
1st Edition January 2001
368 pages, ISBN 0-59600-071-5*

This second edition of Learning Red
Hat Linux is an excellent introduction
to one of the most popular distributions of Linux in the U.S. This is the
book for first-time Linux users who want to learn how
to install and configure Red Hat Linux on their personal computer, or convert an existing system over to Linux.

Peer-to-Peer: Harnessing the Power of Disruptive Technologies

*Edited by Andy Oram
1st Edition March 2001
448 pages, ISBN 0-596-00110-X*

This book presents the goals that
drive the developers of the best-
known peer-to-peer systems, the problems they've faced, and the technical
solutions they've found. The contributors are leading
developers of well-known peer-to-peer systems, such as
Gnutella, Freenet, Jabber, Popular Power, SETI@Home,
Red Rover, Publius, Free Haven, Groove Networks, and
Reputation Technologies. Topics include metadata, performance, trust, resource allocation, reputation, security,
and gateways between systems.

O'REILLY®

To order: 800-998-9938 • order@oreilly.com • www.oreilly.com
Online editions of most O'Reilly titles are available by subscription at safari.oreilly.com
Also available at most retail and online bookstores.

How to stay in touch with O'Reilly

1. Visit our award-winning web site

http://www.oreilly.com/

★ "Top 100 Sites on the Web"—PC Magazine
★ CIO Magazine's Web Business 50 Awards

Our web site contains a library of comprehensive product information (including book excerpts and tables of contents), downloadable software, background articles, interviews with technology leaders, links to relevant sites, book cover art, and more. File us in your bookmarks or favorites!

2. Join our email mailing lists

Sign up to get email announcements of new books and conferences, special offers, and O'Reilly Network technology newsletters at:

http://www.elists.oreilly.com

It's easy to customize your free elists subscription so you'll get exactly the O'Reilly news you want.

3. Get examples from our books

To find example files for a book, go to:

http://www.oreilly.com/catalog

select the book, and follow the "Examples" link.

4. Work with us

Check out our web site for current employment opportunities:

http://jobs.oreilly.com/

5. Register your book

Register your book at:

http://register.oreilly.com

6. Contact us

O'Reilly & Associates, Inc.
1005 Gravenstein Hwy North
Sebastopol, CA 95472 USA
TEL: 707-827-7000 or 800-998-9938
     (6am to 5pm PST)
FAX: 707-829-0104

order@oreilly.com
For answers to problems regarding your order or our products. To place a book order online visit:

http://www.oreilly.com/order_new/

catalog@oreilly.com
To request a copy of our latest catalog.

booktech@oreilly.com
For book content technical questions or corrections.

corporate@oreilly.com
For educational, library, and corporate sales.

proposals@oreilly.com
To submit new book proposals to our editors and product managers.

international@oreilly.com
For information about our international distributors or translation queries. For a list of our distributors outside of North America check out:

http://international.oreilly.com/distributors.html

O'REILLY®

To order: *800-998-9938* • *order@oreilly.com* • *www.oreilly.com*
Online editions of most O'Reilly titles are available by subscription at *safari.oreilly.com*
Also available at most retail and online bookstores.